AMAZING ATHLETES
of the
TWENTIETH CENTURY

AMAZING ATHLETES
of the
TWENTIETH CENTURY

M ike M cGovern

Checkmark Books®

An imprint of Facts On File, Inc.

Amazing Athletes of the Twentieth Century

Copyright © 2001 by Mike McGovern

All rights reserved. No part of this book may be reproduced or utilized in any form or by any means, electronic or mechanical, including photocopying, recording, or by any information storage or retrieval systems, without permission in writing from the publisher. For information contact:

Checkmark Books
An imprint of Facts On File, Inc.
132 West 31st Street
New York NY 10001

Library of Congress Cataloging-in-Publication Data
McGovern, Michael.
  [Encyclopedia of twentieth-century athletes]
  Amazing athletes of the twentieth century / Michael McGovern.
    p. cm.
  Originally published: The encyclopedia of twentieth-century athletes. New York : Facts On File, c2001.
  Includes bibliographical references and index.
  ISBN 0-8160-4882-7 (pbk : alk. paper)
    1. Athletes—Biography—Encyclopedias. I. Title.
  GV697.A1 M2615 2002
  796'.092'2—dc21
  2001047412

Checkmark Books are available at special discounts when purchased in bulk quantities for businesses, associations, institutions, or sales promotions. Please call our Special Sales Department in New York at (212) 967-8800 or (800) 322-8755.

You can find Facts On File on the World Wide Web at
http://www.factsonfile.com

Text design by Joan M. Toro
Cover design by Cathy Rincon

Printed in the United States of America

VB FOF 10 9 8 7 6 5 4 3 2 1

This book is printed on acid-free paper.

Contents

Acknowledgments ix
Introduction xi

The Athletes **1**
Baseball **3**
Basketball **77**
Boxing **127**
Football **149**
Golf **205**
Hockey **235**
Olympians **263**
Tennis **301**
Motorsports **323**
Other Sports **339**

Appendix 1: Timeline 353
Appendix 2: Directories 371
Appendix 3: Halls of Fame 381
Glossary 395
Bibliography 401
Index 407

To Susan, who is, in all ways, the best person I've ever known

Acknowledgments

Sincere thanks to Bert Holtje, my agent, whose encouragement and faith in me throughout this project were much appreciated; Carol Turkington, whose friendship, guidance, and reassurance helped me realize that I wasn't the only author who considered changing careers in midstream; James Chambers at Facts On File, for his patience and understanding; Diane Staskowski, a terrific photographer; Julie Pelchar and Gwenn Miller, for their willingness to pitch in; and Chuck Gallagher, the managing editor of the *Reading Eagle/Times,* for his help and support.

My deepest appreciation goes to my kids, Sara and Ryan, for cooperating while their daddy was surrounded by books and typing away on his laptop, even though they would've preferred to do something fun, and to my wife, Susan, whose optimism and sense of humor were invaluable.

Introduction

Along with politics and religion, there are few other subjects that spark debate the way sports does. Sports fans will argue back and forth on anything and everything: Who's better, Ken Griffey, Jr., or Barry Bonds? How well would Shaquille O'Neal have fared playing against Bill Russell and Wilt Chamberlain? Was Michael Jordan the best player in the history of the NBA? Will Dan Marino's place in history be downgraded because he failed to win a Super Bowl?

The discussions are never-ending and always spirited. I hope this book, with the information provided about the outstanding athletes of the 20th century, will help settle some of those debates. I've tried to strike a balance between the statistics that helped set those athletes apart and their personal stories and experiences that helped shape their lives. But I would be naive to think that this book won't also ignite some debate about the athletes who appear—or don't appear—in these pages.

The selection process was a challenge, to say the least, given the parameters and the size of the book, and the scope of the subject. The athletes who made the cut are, in all but a few cases, members of their sport's Hall of Fame. But not all Hall of Famers in all sports are included, mainly because if they had been, you'd need help lifting the book. So the athletes chosen are the best of the best, in my judgment.

And should you find my judgment flawed, because of who's in or who's not—let the debate begin.

Mike McGovern

The Athletes

Baseball

Aaron, Hank

Born: February 5, 1934 in Mobile, Alabama

When Hank Aaron broke into professional baseball as an 18-year-old shortstop with the Indianapolis Clowns of the Negro American League, it was preposterous to think that he would break one of the most cherished records in all of baseball: Babe Ruth's career home run record. But he developed into an accomplished hitter, thanks in large part to quick, powerful wrists, as well as one of the game's most consistent swings.

In 1952, the Boston Braves signed Aaron and assigned him to their Class C team in Eau Claire, Wis., and in 1953 to their franchise in the South Atlantic ("Sally") League in Jacksonville, Fla., where he was the first black player in the league.

Aaron, a right-handed hitter, batted with a cross-handed grip (his right hand below his left on the bat). But he adopted a conventional grip by the time he reached the major leagues. He broke in with the Milwaukee Braves in 1954, taking over in left field for Bobby Thomson, who broke his ankle. He hit .280 with 13 home runs in his rookie year, which ended prematurely when he broke his ankle in September.

In 1956, Aaron started in right field for the Braves. He won the batting title (.328) and hit 26 home runs. The following year, he led the league in home runs (44), runs batted in—RBI—(132), and runs scored (118). Aaron was named the National League's Most Valuable Player. The Braves beat the New York Yankees in the World Series, in which Aaron hit safely in all seven games, batted .393, hit three home runs, and drove in seven runs.

For 20 seasons (1955–74), Aaron was a model of consistency, hitting at least 20 home runs. He hit 40 or more eight times and 30 or more 15 times. He also hit over .300 14 times, including .355 in 1959. In addition to hitting for power, Aaron's lifetime batting average was .305. Through the 1999 season, he held major league records for total bases (6,856), extra base hits (1,477), RBIs (2,287), All-Star Games (25), and home runs (755). He ranked third in hits (3,771) and is tied for third in runs scored (2,174).

Aaron was a low-key player throughout his career. He played in the shadow of Willie Mays and in cities—Milwaukee and Atlanta, where the Braves moved in 1996—not in the media limelight. But that all changed on April 8, 1974. Playing in his first home game of the season, Aaron faced Al Downing of the Los Angeles Dodgers, who served up one of the most historic pitches in baseball history. Aaron homered into the Braves bullpen in left field. It was the 715th home run of his career, one more than Babe Ruth, who had established the record 39 years earlier.

Aaron left the Braves after the 1974 season and ended his career with the expansion Milwaukee Brewers of the American League. He was a designated hitter for the Brewers and hit 22 home runs in Milwaukee, bringing his total to 755.

Hank Aaron *Reading Eagle/Times*

Aaron returned to Atlanta after his retirement to become a front office executive for the Braves. He was inducted into the Baseball Hall of Fame in 1982 on the first ballot and was named to the All-Century Team selected in 1999.

Alexander, Grover Cleveland
Born: February 16, 1887 in St. Paul, Nebraska
Died: November 4, 1950

Grover Cleveland Alexander broke into the major leagues in 1911 with the Philadelphia Phillies and had a spectacular rookie season. His record was 28–13, with 31 complete games and seven shutouts. He also led the National League in innings pitched with 367.

Alexander won 19 and 22 games in each of the next two seasons, and then became the premier pitcher in the National League, leading the league in wins for four straight years—27 wins in 1914, 31 in 1915, 33 in 1916, and 30 in 1917.

From 1915 through 1917, Alexander posted league-leading earned run averages (ERA) of 1.22, 1.55, and 1.86. He led the league in strikeouts (214, 241, 167) and

threw 36 shutouts, including a record 16 in 1916. What makes that three-year stretch even more remarkable is the small size of the Phillies home stadium, the Baker Bowl. The right-field fence was just 272 feet and it was just 300 feet to right center.

Following the 1917 season, Alexander was traded to the Cubs. In his seven seasons with the Phillies, he averaged 27 wins a year. After spending most of the 1918 season in the Army, Alexander returned not quite as dominant a pitcher. He lost the hearing in one ear due to the shelling and he also developed epilepsy.

Still, Alexander led the league in strikeouts in 1920 (173) and in ERA in 1919 (1.72) and 1920 (1.91).

Alexander had a variety of pitches—a hard fastball and a big-breaking curve—that he could throw with pinpoint control. But that control did not extend to his off-the-field activities. Upon his return from World War I, he started drinking heavily, eventually becoming an alcoholic. His lifestyle contributed to the decline in his ability.

Alexander won 22 games for the Cubs in 1923, but two years later he was committed to a sanatorium. In 1926, the Cubs suspended him and then waived him. He was picked up by the St. Louis Cardinals, who won the pennant in 1926. During the World Series, Alexander took center stage in the seventh game, even though he was still suffering from the night before. With the Cardinals leading 3–2 in the seventh game, Alexander was in the bullpen dozing. He was awakened, began warming up, and entered the game to pitch to Tony Lazzeri of the New York Yankees. Alexander struck him out on four pitches, and went on to throw two more scoreless innings, earning a save and helping the Cardinals win the Series.

Alexander's last good year came in 1927, when he went 21–10. After two more mediocre seasons, he was released in 1930.

Through the 2000 season, Alexander's 373 career wins were tied with Christy Mathewson for third all-time—behind Cy Young (511) and Walter Johnson (417)—and were the most in National League history. He lost 208 games.

Alexander ranked 10th all-time in innings pitched (5,189.2) and second in shutouts (90). He led the National League in shutouts and complete games (437). He struck out 2,198 and walked only 951, an average of fewer than two per game. He was inducted into the Baseball Hall of Fame in 1938.

Alomar, Roberto
Born: February 5, 1968 in Ponce, Puerto Rico

Roberto Alomar was the complete package—a good-hitting, slick-fielding second baseman. In 12 full seasons in the major leagues, he has never hit lower than .282. Alomar began his career with the San Diego Padres in 1988. After three solid seasons, he was traded to the Toronto Blue Jays and blossomed, especially at the plate, hitting .300 or better in four of his five seasons with the team. His best season with the Blue Jays was 1993, when he hit .326 with 17 home runs and 93 runs batted in (RBI).

Following the 1995 season, Alomar signed as a free agent with the Baltimore Orioles. In his three years with the Orioles, he hit .328, .333, and .282. During the final week of the 1996 regular season, Alomar spit in the face of umpire John Hirschbeck. Alomar was suspended for the first five games of the 1997 season, a decision that did not sit well with the umpires' union, which threatened to strike unless the suspension was immediate. But a judge barred the umpires from striking.

Alomar played a key role in the 1996 division playoff series against the Cleveland Indians. His home run in the 12th inning of the deciding game lifted Baltimore into the American League Championship Series.

Alomar signed with the Indians as a free agent and in 1999 hit .323 with 24 home runs and 120 RBI.

Through the 2000 season, Alomar had a lifetime batting average of .304 with 138 home runs and 761 RBI. An 11-time All-Star, he won eight Gold Gloves. He held American League records for most consecutive errorless games by a second baseman (104) and fewest errors by a second baseman (5).

Aparicio, Luis

Born: April 29, 1934 in Maracaibo, Venezuela

Luis Aparicio was one of the best fielding shortstops and one of the best base stealers of his time. As the story goes, Hank Greenberg, general manager of the Cleveland Indians, was deciding between two Venezuelan shortstops. Because he thought Aparicio wasn't worth a $10,000 bonus, he traded for Chico Carrasquel, who had a solid career. Aparicio went on to become a Hall of Famer.

Aparicio joined the Chicago White Sox in 1956. He hit .262, led the American League with 21 stolen bases, and was named the Rookie of the Year. Aparicio led the league in steals for the first nine seasons of his career. In 1959, he stole 56 bases, hit .257, and helped the White Sox reach the World Series. He finished second in voting for the Most Valuable Player Award to his teammate, second baseman Nellie Fox.

Aparicio was traded to the Baltimore Orioles in 1963, and in 1964 he stole a career-high 57 bases. It was the last year he led the league in steals. In 1966, he helped the Orioles win the American League pennant and sweep the Los Angeles Dodgers in the World Series.

Aparicio was traded back to the White Sox in 1968, and hit .300 for the only time in his career (.313 in 1970). After three seasons, he was traded to the Boston Red Sox, with whom he spent three seasons, retiring in 1973.

The double-play combination of Fox and Aparicio was one of the best ever. They won more fielding titles together than any other double-play combination, and no shortstop ever led the league in as many fielding categories as Aparicio. He won nine Gold Gloves and through the 1999 season held major league records for games played at shortstop (2,581), assists (8,016), and double plays (1,553).

Aparicio attributed his excellence in the field to his use of a heavier glove during infield practice, so that during the game, his regular glove felt lighter.

Aparicio spent 18 years in the major leagues and played 2,599 games. His lifetime batting average was .262, and he stole 506 bases. He was inducted into the Baseball Hall of Fame in 1984.

Appling, Luke (Lucius)

Born: April 2, 1907 in High Point, North Carolina
Died: January 3, 1991

Luke Appling was as renowned for his hypochondria as he was for his ability as a shortstop with the Chicago White Sox. Nicknamed "Old Aches and Pains," Appling always seemed to be complaining about something. His afflictions over the years included a stiff neck, fallen arches, gout, astigmatism, and a throbbing kneecap. The only legitimate injuries he ever suffered were a broken finger and a broken leg. He routinely complained to his manager, Jimmy Dykes, "Honest, Jimmy, I'm dying."

None of these conditions affected his play, although he did not achieve stardom immediately. Appling joined the White Sox in 1930, and in 1931 went 0-for-28 and committed an error every other day. But he became the regular shortstop in 1933, when he hit .322. It was the first of nine straight seasons in which he would hit .300 or better, including 1936, when he went 4-for-4 on the final day of the season to become the first shortstop to win the American League batting title (.388). He was the only shortstop in the 20th century to hit for that high an average.

In 1942, the only season Appling claimed he was healthy from start to finish, his average dropped to .262.

The following season, Appling hit .328 to win his second batting title. Appling missed all of the 1944 season and most of the 1945 season due to military service. He returned in 1946 and hit .300 or better in each of the next three seasons. His average dipped to .234 in 1950, after which he retired.

Appling, a mediocre fielder, did manage to lead the American League in assists for seven years in a row, a record at the time.

After having success as a minor league manager, he managed briefly in 1967, going 10–30 with the Kansas City Athletics and finishing last.

Appling's lifetime batting average was .310. Had it not been for the missed time due to military service, he likely would have reached 3,000 hits. He had 2,749 and hit .300 or better 16 times in 17 years. His walk to strike-out ratio was nearly 3-to-1. He was inducted into the Baseball Hall of Fame in 1964.

Ashburn, Rich

Born: March 19, 1927 in Tilden, Nebraska
Died: September 9, 1997

Rich Ashburn wasn't blessed with power, but he more than made up for it with bat control, a good eye, and blazing speed. He was also a consummate center fielder. Ashburn joined the Philadelphia Phillies in 1948 and was playing behind Harry "The Hat" Walker, who had won the 1947 National League batting title. But when Walker was injured and out of the lineup through May, Ashburn hit .346 in his absence and won the job.

He batted .333 that year, led the league with 32 stolen bases, was the only rookie named to the All-Star team, and was the Rookie of the Year.

Over the next 11 seasons, Ashburn, nicknamed "Whitey," hit .300 or better seven times, including .338 in 1955 and .350 in 1958, when he won batting titles. Ashburn led the league in hits three times (221 in 1951, 205 in 1953, 215 in 1958), walks four times (125 in 1954, 94 in 1957, 97 in 1958, 116 in 1960), and doubles twice (14 in 1950, 13 in 1958).

In 1950, Ashburn was part of the Phillies "Whiz Kids" team that won the National League pennant. In the final game of the regular season, with the score tied 1–1 in the bottom of the ninth, Ashburn threw out Brooklyn's Cal Abrams, who tried to score from second on a Duke Snider single. The Phillies won the game in the 10th on a Dick Sisler home run.

Ashburn was traded to the Chicago Cubs in 1960 and spent his final season, 1962, with the New York Mets, who were in their first year in the league. He hit .306 and was named to the All-Star team.

Through the 1999 season, Ashburn was the only outfielder to record 500 or more putouts in four different seasons and 400 or more assists in nine different seasons. He tied Max Carey for the most times leading the league in putouts and assists with nine.

After he retired, Ashburn became a broadcaster for the Philadelphia Phillies, a position he held until he died of a heart attack in Manhattan, where the Phillies were staying for a series against the New York Mets.

Ashburn's lifetime batting average was .308, and he had 2,574 hits and 571 stolen bases. He was inducted into the Baseball Hall of Fame in 1995.

Banks, Ernie

Born: January 31, 1931 in Dallas, Texas

Ernie Banks, nicknamed "Mr. Cub" and famous for his saying "Let's play two," proved that you didn't have to be a hulking specimen to hit for power. Banks measured 6-1 and weighed only 180 pounds, but the numbers he put up were impressive. His power was concentrated in his wrists and his forearms.

Banks joined the Chicago Cubs after he was spotted playing for the Kansas City Monarchs of the Negro American League in 1950. He spent two years in the Army before joining the Cubs near the end of the 1953 season. He never played in the minor leagues. In 1954, his first full season with the Cubs, he batted .275 and hit 19 home runs. The following year, he batted .295 and hit 44 home runs, a record for a shortstop.

Banks hit 43 home runs in 1956 and led the National League with 47 in 1958, when he was named Most Valuable Player. He batted .313, with a league-leading 129 runs batted in (RBI).

In 1959, Banks was named Most Valuable Player again. He batted .304 with 45 home runs and a league-leading 143 RBI.

Banks' final season as a full-time shortstop was 1960, when he led the league in home runs with 41. He also led the league in fielding three times, including a .985 fielding percentage in 1959. But a knee injury and vision problems, caused by a collision, forced him to move, first to left field, then to first base, where he played for the rest of his career.

After the move to first, Banks hit more than 30 homers only twice and never batted higher than .278. In 1970, Banks had lost his starting job, appearing in only 72 games. He retired following the 1971 season.

Through the 2000 season, Banks, who spent his entire career with the Cubs, was tied for 13th all-time with 512 home runs and ranked 19th all-time with 1,636 RBI. He was an 11-time All-Star and was inducted into the Baseball Hall of Fame in 1977.

Bell, Cool Papa (James)

Born: May 17, 1903 in Starkville, Mississippi
Died: March 7, 1991

Cool Papa Bell was a speed merchant. A prolific base stealer, he might have been the fastest player in baseball history.

Bell, a switch-hitting center fielder, never made it to the major leagues because of the color barrier, so he spent his entire career playing in the Negro League.

Bell began his career with the St. Louis Stars in 1922, when he hit .417. Although the statistics are incomplete, Bell hit .300 or better 14 times. He also played with the Pittsburgh Crawfords, the Chicago American Giants, and the Homestead Grays, as well as with the Dominican Republic and Mexico in winter ball.

Bell, who stood 6 feet tall and weighed 143 pounds, was reported to have stolen as many as 175 bases in a 200-game season. He also supposedly stole two bases on one pitch, and, in a 1948 exhibition game against the Cleveland Indians, he scored from first base on a bunt.

His speed also helped him in the outfield. He could play very shallow in center field, sometimes sneaking in to pick off runners at second.

Hall of Famer Paul Waner called Bell "the smoothest center fielder I've ever seen."

Bell, who was known as the "black Ty Cobb," retired in 1946 and became the manager of the Kansas City Stars. He also served as a scout for the St. Louis Browns in the American League. He was inducted into the Baseball Hall of Fame in 1974.

Bench, Johnny
Born: December 7, 1947 in Oklahoma City, Oklahoma

Johnny Bench is regarded as the best catcher in baseball history. He was as good at the plate as he was behind it.

Bench became a starter for the Cincinnati Reds in 1968, when he played in 154 games and hit 40 doubles, both records for a catcher. He was named National League Rookie of the Year.

Twice, Bench was named the National League's Most Valuable Player, in 1970 (.293, 45 home runs, 148 runs batted in) and 1972 (.270, 40 home runs, 125 RBI). He led the league in home runs and RBI each time. He also led the league in RBI in 1974 with 129.

Through the 2000 season, Bench was the only catcher to lead the National League in home runs and one of just four to lead in RBI.

He helped spark the Reds, known as the "Big Red Machine," to six Western Division titles, four National League pennants, and two World Series championships (1975–76).

His defense was as impressive as his hitting. Bench, blessed with a strong arm, was taught by his father to throw 254 feet, twice the distance to second base, from a crouch. His career fielding percentage was .990 and he won 10 Gold Glove Awards (1968–77) as the outstanding fielder at his position. Bench also pioneered the one-hand style of catching, keeping his throwing hand behind his back to protect it from foul tips; he was the first to wear a batting helmet while catching; and he popularized the use of an oversized mitt.

In 1978, knee problems began to slow Bench. In the last several years of his career, he played primarily at first base. He also played third base and in the outfield. He retired in 1983.

Bench hit 389 career home runs, 327 as a catcher, ranking him second all-time to Carlton Fisk. He twice hit 40 or more home runs, and he drove in 100 runs six times

in eight years (1970–77). A 12-time National League All-Star, Bench was inducted into the Baseball Hall of Fame in 1989 and was named to the All-Century Team selected in 1999.

Berra, Yogi (Lawrence)
Born: May 12, 1925 in St. Louis, Missouri

Yogi Berra became a fine defensive catcher and was one of the best-hitting catchers in baseball history. But as great as was his prowess on the field, he is just as well known for his malaprops.

As his boyhood friend Joe Garagiola, former major league player and broadcaster, put it: "[Yogi] doesn't use the wrong words. He just puts words together in ways nobody else would ever do."

A sampling: "I really didn't say everything I said"; "A nickel ain't worth a dime anymore"; "It's déjà vu all over again"; "We made too many wrong mistakes"; "Why buy good luggage if you only use it when you travel"; "Ninety percent of the game is half mental"; "Steve McQueen looks good in this movie; he must have made it before he died."

But there was much more to Berra's career than just his "Yogi-isms." He joined the Yankees during the final stages of the 1946 season and hit a home run in his first game. For the next two seasons, he was a backup catcher, but when Casey Stengel took over as manager in 1949, he made Berra the starting catcher.

At first, Berra was a defensive liability. During the 1947 World Series, the Brooklyn Dodgers ran the bases at will, forcing Berra to be replaced. But thanks to the coaching of catching great Bill Dickey, Berra improved markedly. From July 1957 to May 1959, he handled 950 chances, over a span of 148 games, without an error.

As a hitter, Berra frequently swung at bad pitches, but was often successful. He also was a productive hitter in the clutch. He could hit to all fields, and he rarely struck out, averaging only one strikeout for every 18 times at bat.

Berra hit over .300 three times, including .322 in 1950, when he also hit 28 home runs and drove in 124 runs. He exceeded 100 runs batted in (RBI) five times in his career. His season high was 125 in 1954, when he batted .307, hit 22 home runs, and won the second of his three American League Most Valuable Player Awards. Berra also was named MVP in 1951 (.294, 27 home runs, 88 RBI) and 1955 (.272, 27 home runs, 108 RBI).

Berra was a key cog in the New York Yankees' dynasty that played in 14 World Series during his 19-year career. The Yankees won five straight World Series from 1949 to 1953 and 10 overall during Berra's career. Through the 2000 season, he held a variety of World Series records: games (75), at-bats (259), hits (71), and doubles (10). He ranked third in home runs (12), second in runs (41), second in RBI (39), third in walks (32), and second in total bases (117).

Berra retired in 1964 and was named manager of the Yankees, leading them to the American League pennant. But because he lost the World Series in seven games to the St. Louis Cardinals, he was fired. He joined the New York Mets as a coach in 1965, a position he held until 1972, when he was named manager.

The Mets won the National League pennant under Berra in 1973, but lost the World Series to the Oakland Athletics in seven games. Berra was fired in 1975, the result of a dispute with management.

He coached with the Houston Astros and returned to manage the Yankees in 1984. He lasted just 16 games into the 1985 season, going 6–10, before he was fired by Yankees owner George Steinbrenner. Berra was so angry over the firing that he vowed never to set foot in Yankee Stadium as long as Steinbrenner was the owner. He kept that promise until 1999, when he and Steinbrenner made peace.

Berra had a lifetime batting average of .285, with 358 home runs, 321 doubles, 49 triples, and 1,430 RBI. He was inducted into the Baseball Hall of Fame in 1972 and was named to the All-Century Team in 1999.

Boggs, Wade
Born: June 15, 1958 in Omaha, Nebraska

Wade Boggs was one of the most consistent hitters in the game for nearly two decades. He rarely struck out, could produce in the clutch, and was at his best with two strikes.

Boggs, a left-handed hitting third baseman, joined the Boston Red Sox in 1982 and hit .349. That was the first of 10 straight seasons in which Boggs hit .300 or better and the first of seven straight seasons he had 200 or more hits, an American League record. He won five American League batting titles in a six-year stretch, beginning in 1983, when he hit .361. In 1985, he batted .368 and led the league with 240 hits; in 1986, he hit .357; in 1987, he hit .363; and in 1988, he hit .366 and led the league in doubles (45), runs (128), and walks (125).

Boggs left the Red Sox following the 1992 season and signed with the New York Yankees as a free agent. In five seasons with the Yankees, Boggs hit .300 or better four times, and in his final season, 1997, he hit .292.

Boggs, who went to high school in Tampa, Fla., signed as a free agent with the Tampa Bay Devil Rays in 1998. He hit .280 in 1998 and .301 in 1999, when he became the 23rd player in major league history to reach the 3,000-hit plateau. His 3,000th hit happened to be a home run, one of only two he hit all season. He became the first player to reach 3,000 hits with a home run.

Boggs retired in November 1999. Only Lou Gehrig, with seven, had more seasons with 200 hits and 100 walks than Boggs, who had four. Only Pete Rose, Ty Cobb, Gehrig, Willie Keeler, and Paul Waner had more 200-hit seasons than Boggs, who had seven.

Six times, Boggs led the American League in on-base percentage. He won two Gold Gloves (1994–95) and was a 12-time All-Star.

Boggs' lifetime batting average was .328. Through the 2000 season, he ranked 21st all-time in hits (3,010) and 13th all-time in doubles (578).

Bonds, Barry
Born: July 24, 1964 in Riverside, California

Barry Bonds is recognized as one of the greatest and most versatile players of his time, one who can hit for average and power, field, and steal bases. The son of former major leaguer Bobby Bonds, Barry carries himself with a swagger that many think borders on arrogance. But his confidence is backed up by performance.

He broke in with the Pittsburgh Pirates organization and was called up during the 1986 season, when he batted .223 with 16 home runs and 26 stolen bases.

Over the next three seasons, his average never exceeded .283, but in 1990 he fulfilled his considerable potential. That year, Bonds, a left-handed hitter, was named the National League's Most Valuable Player. He batted .301, with 33 home runs, 114 runs batted in (RBI), 104 runs, and 52 stolen bases. After a solid season in 1991 (.292, 25 home runs, 116 RBI), Bonds won his second Most Valuable Player Award in 1992, when he batted .311, with 34 home runs, 103 RBI, a league-leading .624 slugging percentage, and 109 runs.

Bonds helped the Pirates to the National League Championship Series for three straight years, beginning in 1990. His average during those three playoffs was .191. He joined the San Francisco Giants in 1993 and won his third Most Valuable Player Award, batting .336, with a league-leading 46 home runs, 123 RBI, and .677 slugging percentage.

Bonds continued his stellar play, hitting .312 with 37 home runs in 1994, .294 with 33 home runs in 1995, .308 with 42 home runs in 1996, .291 with 40 home runs in 1997, and .303 with 37 home runs in 1998.

In 1999, Bonds was hampered by elbow, groin, and knee injuries. He played in only 102 games and hit .262 with 34 home runs. It was the eighth straight season he hit 30 or more home runs.

Bonds is the only member of the 400-400 club: no other player has hit 400 home runs and stolen 400 bases. Only three other players—Willie Mays, Andre Dawson, and Bobby Bonds—have ever reached the 300-300 plateau.

Bonds is one of eight players in major league history to win the Most Valuable Player Award three times. Through the 1999 season, Bonds' lifetime batting average was .288. His 445 home runs ranked 22nd all-time. His .559 slugging percentage ranked 18th all-time. He was an eight-time All-Star and an eight-time Gold Glove winner.

Boudreau, Lou
Born: July 17, 1917 in Harvey, Illinois

Lou Boudreau was a good-hitting, slick-fielding shortstop who later became an innovative manager. He began his career in the Cleveland Indians organization, playing in the minor leagues while he attended the University of Illinois.

He joined the Indians in 1939 and became their regular shortstop in 1940, when he hit .295 with 101 runs batted in (RBI). Boudreau hit .300 or better four times, including .327 in 1944, when he led the American League in batting and doubles (45). Boudreau also led the league in doubles in 1941 (45) and 1947 (45).

In 1942, at age 24, Boudreau became the youngest manager in the majors. He wrote Indians owner Alva Bradley a letter, requesting to be considered as a candidate for the job. After a two-hour interview, 11 of 12 people on the Indians staff voted against him, but the one vote in his favor was cast by George Martin, the team's president. So Boudreau was named player-manager.

In Boudreau's first five seasons as manager, the Indians never contended for the pennant. In 1948, when Bill Veeck bought the team, he thought about replacing Boudreau, but the fans made it clear they wanted him to stay. Boudreau led the Indians to their first pennant since 1920. He also hit .355 with 18 home runs and 106 RBI. He was named the American League's Most Valuable Player and the Associated Press Male Athlete of the Year. Cleveland went on to win the World Series.

One of the innovations devised by Boudreau as manager was the "Williams Shift," designed to stop Ted Williams of the Boston Red Sox. It happened in July 1946. In the first game of a doubleheader, Boudreau had four doubles and a homer, making him the only American League player to get five extra-base hits in one game. Williams, though, went 4-for-5, with three home runs and eight RBI, lifting the Red Sox to an 11–10 win. In the second game, Boudreau was determined to stop Williams, so he ordered seven players to play to the right of second base. Williams grounded out once to the right side. He also walked twice and doubled, but the move established Boudreau as an innovator.

Boudreau left the Indians after the 1950 season and spent his last two seasons with the Boston Red Sox, retiring in 1952. He managed the Red Sox from 1952 to 1954 and the Kansas City Athletics from 1955 to 1957. After becoming a Chicago Cubs broadcaster in 1960, Boudreau took over as the Cubs manager. But he lasted only one season and returned to the broadcast booth, where he remained until 1989.

Boudreau led American League shortstops in fielding percentage nine times and had a career fielding percentage of .973. His lifetime batting average was .295, with 1,779 hits, including 385 doubles and 66 triples. A seven-time All-Star, Boudreau was inducted into the Baseball Hall of Fame in 1970.

Brett, George
Born: May 15, 1953 in Glen Dale, West Virginia

George Brett was one of the best third basemen in baseball history. He had the ability to hit the ball where it was pitched and he could also hit for power. The key to his development as a hitter was working with Charley Lau, the batting instructor for the Kansas City Royals. Lau changed Brett from a free-swinger to a more controlled hitter. Said Jim Frey, one of his managers with the Royals, "George Brett could get good wood on an aspirin."

Brett joined the Kansas City Royals in 1973, appearing in 13 games, and then became the regular third baseman in 1974. In 1975, he led the American League in at-bats (634), hits (195), and triples (13). In 1976, he won his first batting title (.333) and again led in at-bats (645), hits (215), and triples (14).

From 1975 through 1990, Brett hit .300 or better 11 times, his average never falling below .282. In 1980, Brett made a run at becoming the first player since Ted Williams in 1941 to hit .400. He was on target until a September thumb injury slowed him. He ended up hitting .390, which was good enough to win his second batting title and lead the Royals into the World Series, which they lost in six games to the Philadelphia Phillies.

Brett won batting titles in three different decades, his third and last coming in 1990, when he batted .329 and also led the league in doubles with 45.

Brett's .329 average in 1990 was the last time he hit above .300. The nagging injuries he suffered throughout his career began to catch up with him. He hit .255, the lowest average of his career, in 1991. He lasted two more years and retired following the 1993 season.

Brett, who was renowned as a great hitter in the clutch, was instrumental in helping the Royals reach the American League Championship Series (ALCS) six times and the World Series twice. The Royals won the Series in 1985, defeating the St. Louis Cardinals.

Brett hit .340 in the ALCS, with 35 hits, four triples, nine home runs, 22 runs scored, and 19 runs batted in (RBI). In two World Series appearances, he hit .373.

Overall, Brett's lifetime batting average was .305, and he hit 317 home runs. Through the 2000 season, he ranked 13th all-time with 3,154 hits, 14th in at-bats

(10,349), 13th in total bases (5,044), tied for 22nd in RBI (1,595) and 10th in extra base hits (1,119). Brett was named to the American League All-Star team 13 times; he won the Gold Glove in 1985; and he was inducted into the Baseball Hall of Fame in 1999.

Brock, Lou

Born: June 18, 1939 in El Dorado, Arkansas

Lou Brock was a fine hitter who wreaked havoc after he reached base. He elevated base stealing to an art form.

Brock, a left fielder, began his career with the Chicago Cubs in 1961, when he appeared in six games. He spent the next two-plus seasons with the Cubs, before being traded to the St. Louis Cardinals in one of the most one-sided deals ever made. Brock went to the Cardinals in exchange for pitchers Ernie Broglio and Bobby Shantz and outfielder Doug Clemens. Broglio, Shantz, and Clemens had nowhere near the impact for the Cubs that Brock had for the Cardinals.

He blossomed as an all-around player in St. Louis. In the 103 games Brock played with the Cards in 1964 after the trade, he hit .348 and helped lead the team to the National League pennant. The Cards trailed the Philadelphia Phillies by 6 1/2 games with 10 to play, and Brock hit .461 during the stretch to help win the pennant. In the World Series against the New York Yankees, Brock hit .300, with a home run and five runs batted in (RBI).

The Cardinals played in two more World Series. In 1967, Brock hit .414 with 12 hits, four for extra bases; three RBI; and seven stolen bases. In 1968, he hit .464 with 13 hits, six for extra bases; five RBI; and seven stolen bases. Brock's 14 stolen bases is a World Series record.

Starting in 1966, Brock led the National League in stolen bases for four straight seasons and nine of 10, including a career-high 118 at age 35 in 1974. That was an all-time single-season high at the time, breaking Maury Wills' mark of 104, and still ranks second to Rickey Henderson's 130.

A consistent .280 to .290 hitter through the first half of his career, Brock, a left-handed batter, hit .300 or better six times in seven seasons from 1970–76. He played three more years, hitting .304 in 1979, his last season.

Brock, a leadoff man for most of his career, registered more than 600 at-bats in 11 straight seasons (1964–74), getting 200 or more hits four times and 190 or more hits four times. His lifetime batting average was .293, with 3,023 hits, which ranked 20th all-time through the 2000 season. Brock was second all-time in stolen bases—to Henderson—with 938. A six-time All-Star, he was inducted into the Baseball Hall of Fame in 1985.

Brown, Three Finger (Mordecai)

Born: October 18, 1876 in Nyesville, Indiana
Died: February 14, 1948

When Mordecai Brown was seven years old, he got his hand caught in a corn chopper and lost most of his index finger. Several weeks later, he broke the third and fourth fingers on his right hand while chasing a hog. The hand never healed properly. Despite the injury, or perhaps because of it, Brown became an effective pitcher. The injury allowed him to throw what Ty Cobb called a "devastating" curveball.

Brown started his baseball career as a third baseman, but became a pitcher, joining the St. Louis Cardinals in 1903. The following year, he went to the Chicago Cubs. From 1906 through 1911, Brown won 26, 20, 39, 27, 25, and 21 games, respectively. He averaged 25 wins and nine losses.

In 1906, he led the National League in earned run average—ERA—(1.04) and shutouts (9); in 1909, he led in victories (27), complete games (32), and innings pitched (342.2); and in 1910 he led in shutouts (7).

In 1908, Brown was the first pitcher to throw four consecutive shutouts. He pitched in four World Series (1906–08, '10) and had a 5–4 record and 2.81 ERA. Brown's last 20-win season came in 1911. He went 49–41 over the last five seasons of his career. He retired in 1916.

Brown's career record was 239–129 with 1,375 strikeouts. Through the 2000 season, his 2.06 ERA ranked third all-time. He was inducted into the Baseball Hall of Fame in 1949.

Bunning, Jim

Born: October 23, 1931 in Southgate, Kentucky

Jim Bunning was the first pitcher to win at least 100 games and record 1,000 strikeouts in both the National and American Leagues. He also was the first pitcher to appear in the All-Star Game for both leagues.

Bunning joined the Detroit Tigers in 1955, and two years later he went 20–8 with a 2.69 earned run average (ERA) and 182 strikeouts. He led the league in victories and innings pitched (267.1). On July 20, 1958, Bunning threw a no-hitter against the Boston Red Sox, winning 3–0.

Bunning led the league in strikeouts in 1959 (201) and 1960 (201). He never again won 20 games in Detroit, and after falling to 12–13 in 1963, he was traded to the Philadelphia Phillies.

On June 21, 1964, Father's Day, Bunning threw a perfect game against the New York Mets at Shea Stadium. He struck out 10 and needed only 90 pitches. It was the first perfect game since Charlie Robertson of the Chicago White Sox did it on April 30, 1922. It was the first perfect game in the National League since Lee Richmond did it on June 12, 1880.

Bunning won 19 games in 1964 and went on to win 19 games in both 1965 and 1966. He twice led the league in games started (41 in 1966, 40 in 1967), shutouts twice (5 in 1966, 6 in 1966), and strikeouts once (253 in 1967).

In 1968, Bunning was traded to the Pittsburgh Pirates. He also spent part of 1969 with the Los Angeles Dodgers, before returning to the Phillies in 1970. He retired in 1971.

Bunning managed in the Phillies minor league system and later became a player agent and an investment broker. After serving several terms in the U.S. House of Representatives (R-Ky.), he was elected to his first term in the U.S. Senate in 1998.

Bunning was inducted into the Baseball Hall of Fame in 1996.

Campanella, Roy
Born: November 19, 1921 in Philadelphia, Pennsylvania
Died: June 26, 1993

Roy Campanella's career, delayed because of the color barrier in Major League Baseball and cut short by a tragic automobile accident, was nonetheless one of the greatest of any catcher in baseball history.

He began playing for a semipro team in the Philadelphia area called the Bacharach Giants, and then joined the Baltimore Elite Giants of the Negro National League. He was a three-time All-Star and one of the league's biggest stars.

He spent eight years in the Negro League and was one of the players considered by the Brooklyn Dodgers' Branch Rickey to break the color barrier. Jackie Robinson was chosen instead. Campanella joined the Dodgers organization in 1946 and made it to the major leagues as the first black catcher in 1948 at the age of 26. He was sent down to the minors early in the 1948 season, but was called up after 35 games and became a fixture. After solid seasons in 1949 and 1950, Campanella broke through with the first of his three seasons as the National League's Most Valuable Player (MVP) in 1951. He batted .325 with 33 home runs and 108 runs batted in (RBI). He won his second MVP Award in 1953, hitting .312 with 41 home runs and a league-leading 142 RBI. It was the second-most productive season ever for a catcher who played at least 130 games. Only Johnny Bench's 1970 season with the Cincinnati Reds (45 home runs, 148 RBI) was better.

Campanella's third MVP Award came in 1955. He hit .318 with 32 home runs and 107 RBI.

Besides his impressive statistics, Campanella became a fan favorite for his easygoing nature and happy-go-lucky demeanor. This was important given the racial tensions at the time.

Campanella, who was blessed with a strong arm in addition to his powerful bat, helped the Dodgers win five National League pennants and one World Series (1955) in a seven-year stretch, starting in 1949. Those Dodgers teams averaged 96 wins a year. Because a variety of injuries suffered throughout his career began to take their toll, Campanella's average dropped to .219 in 1956 and rebounded only slightly, to .242, in 1957, which turned out to be his final season.

Realizing that he couldn't play baseball forever, Campanella opened a liquor store in Harlem to help provide for his wife and five children. On January 28, 1958, he was driving to his home in Glen Cove, Long Island, when his car skidded on a patch of ice and crashed into a telephone pole. He fractured two vertebrae. He underwent a life-saving operation, but it could not restore movement. He was paralyzed from the chest down. Campanella, faced with a rigorous rehabilitation period, got through it and eventually became an instructor in the Dodgers organization. His fighting spirit was an inspiration. In May 1959, Campanella was honored at the Los Angeles Coliseum (the Dodgers had moved from Brooklyn after the 1957 season) and a record crowd of 93,103 fans attended. Confined to a wheelchair, he nevertheless became one of the game's most-loved ambassadors.

Campanella, who played in seven All-Star Games, had a lifetime batting average of .276, with 242 home runs and 856 RBI. His fielding percentage was .988. He was the second black player (after Jackie Robinson) inducted into the Baseball Hall of Fame, in 1969. His autobiography, *Lucky to Be Alive*, was made into a television movie in 1974.

Canseco, Jose
Born: July 2, 1964 in Havana, Cuba

Designated hitter Jose Canseco, boasting a rare blend of speed and power, was a 15th-round draft choice by the Oakland Athletics in 1982. In 1986, his first full season with the Athletics, Canseco was named the American League Rookie of the Year. He hit .240 with 33 home runs and 117 runs batted in (RBI). In 1987, he hit .257 with 31 home runs and 113 RBI, and in 1988, he was named the American League's Most Valuable Player, batting .307 with a league-leading 42 home runs, 124 RBI, and 40 stolen bases. He became the first player in major league history to hit 40 or more home runs and steal 40 bases in the same season. He helped the Athletics reach the World Series in 1988, 1989, and 1990. The Athletics won the world championship in 1989, sweeping the San Francisco Giants. Canseco hit .357.

In 1991, Canseco shared the home run title with 42. He also drove in 122 runs. In August 1992, Canseco was traded to the Texas Rangers, who traded him to the Boston Red Sox following the 1994 season.

A spate of injuries began to take their toll on Canseco. He spent parts of the 1990, 1992, 1993, 1995, and 1996 seasons on the disabled list.

The Red Sox traded him to Oakland in 1997. He signed with the Toronto Blue Jays as a free agent in 1998, and after one season, in which he hit 46 home runs and drove in 107 runs, Canseco signed with the Tampa Bay Devil Rays as a free agent. Canseco was on the disabled list for six weeks in July and August, due to back surgery, but he hit .279 with 34 home runs and 95 RBI.

Through the 2000 season, his 446 home runs ranked 23rd all-time, his 1,309 RBI ranked 31st, and his 1,867 strikeouts tied for fourth.

Carew, Rod
Born: October 1, 1945 in Gatun, Panama

Rod Carew was a hitting machine whom pitchers found nearly impossible to get out. He could hit the ball to all fields, he rarely went into slumps, and he was a masterful bunter.

Carew, a left-handed hitter, began his major league career as a second baseman in 1967 with the Minnesota Twins and was named American League Rookie of the Year. He hit .292 and .273 his first two years, then hit .300 or better for 15 straight seasons.

In 1969, Carew won his first batting title, hitting .332. He hit .366 the following year, but didn't have enough at-bats to qualify for the title. In 1971, he batted .307, then won the batting title four straight years and six of the next seven. He hit .318 in 1972, .350 in 1973, .364 in 1974, .359 in 1975, .388 in 1977, and .333 in 1978. His 1977 season, which also included leading the league in hits (239) and runs (128), earned him the American League Most Valuable Player Award. He also hit 14 home runs and had 100 runs batted in.

Only three players—Ty Cobb, Honus Wagner, and Tony Gwynn—won more batting titles than Carew, who is tied with Stan Musial and Rogers Hornsby with seven. Carew led the league in hits three times (203 in 1973, 218 in 1974, 239 in 1977) and in runs once (128 in 1977).

Carew was traded to the California Angels in 1979 and hit .300 or better in all except his last two seasons, when his averages dipped to .295 and .280, respectively. He got his 3,000th hit in his final season.

Carew never played in a World Series, but did appear in four American League Championship Series, two each with the Twins and the Angels.

Carew had a lifetime batting average of .328, and through the 2000 season, his 3,053 hits ranked 19th all-time. He stole 353 bases, including a record-tying seven steals of home in 1969; scored 1,424 runs; and drove in 1,015 runs. He was inducted into the Baseball Hall of Fame in 1991, his first year of eligibility.

Carlton, Steve
Born: December 22, 1944 in Miami, Florida

Steve Carlton had an overpowering fastball and a confounding curve and slider, all thrown with pinpoint control. He adopted an unorthodox training program involving martial arts, among them kung fu, and isometrics. His devotion to workouts paid off: He didn't go on the disabled list until 1985.

Carlton began his career with the St. Louis Cardinals in 1965. After his best season in St. Louis (20–9 in 1971), the left-hander was traded to the Philadelphia Phillies. In 1972, he had one of the most dominating seasons any pitcher has ever had. He went 27–10 and led the league in wins, earned run average—ERA—(1.97), games started (41), complete games (30), innings pitched (346.1), hits allowed (257), and strikeouts (310). He accomplished all this while playing for a last-place team. Carlton accounted for 45 percent of the Phillies' 59 victories and won the National League Cy Young Award.

In 1973, Carlton slumped to a 13–20 record, but he bounced back in 1974 to go 16–13 and led the league in strikeouts (240). From 1974 through 1984, Carlton never won fewer than 13 games, and he won at least 20 games four times.

He won his second Cy Young Award in 1977, going 23–10 with a 2.64 ERA. Carlton won two more Cy Young Awards—in 1980 (24–9, 2.34 ERA, league-leading 286 strikeouts) and 1982 (23–11, 3.10 ERA, league-leading 286 strikeouts).

Carlton, nicknamed "Lefty," pitched in five National League Championship Series with the Phillies and two World Series, including the 1980 World Series in which the Phillies won their only championship. He won two Series games and struck out 17 in 15 innings.

Carlton went 15–16 in 1984, but led the league in strikeouts for the fifth time, with 275. From 1985 through 1988, he pitched for the Phillies, the San Francisco Giants, the Chicago White Sox, the Cleveland Indians, and the Minnesota Twins, but won only 16 games and lost 37. He retired in 1988.

Also notable about Carlton was his disdain for the press. For the last 15 years of his career, he rarely gave interviews.

Carlton struck out 4,136, ranking him second all-time to Nolan Ryan through the 2000 season. He ranked ninth in wins (329), ninth in innings pitched (5,216.2), and 15th in shutouts (55). A 10-time All-Star, he was inducted into the Baseball Hall of Fame in 1994.

Carter, Gary
Born: April 8, 1954 in Culver City, California

Gary Carter was a catcher who was great at the plate and behind it. He turned down more than 100 football scholarships to sign with the Montreal Expos in 1974. He became the starting catcher in 1977, and in 1978 he allowed just one passed ball in 157 games.

From 1977 through 1984, Carter hit 20 or more home runs seven times, including 31 in 1977 and 29 in 1980 and 1982. In 1984, he led the National League in runs batted in (RBI) with 106.

Carter was traded to the New York Mets in 1985, when he hit 32 home runs and had 100 RBI. In 1986, Carter helped the Mets reach the World Series. He hit 24 home runs and drove in 105 runs. In the Series victory against the Boston Red Sox, he hit two home runs and drove in six runs.

Starting in 1987, Carter's numbers began to fall off. The Mets released him in 1989, and he played three more years, spending one season each with the San Francisco Giants, the Los Angeles Dodgers, and the Expos. He retired in 1992 with a lifetime batting average of .262, 324 home runs, and 1,225 RBI. He is one of only four catchers to hit 300 or more home runs, score 1,000 runs, and drive in 1,000 runs. The other three are Yogi Berra, Johnny Bench, and Carlton Fisk.

Carter, Joe
Born: March 7, 1960 in Oklahoma City, Oklahoma
Joe Carter was one of the most consistent and productive hitters of his time. He had 10 seasons of 100 or more runs batted in (RBI), including an American League–leading 121 in 1986 with the Cleveland Indians. From 1986 through 1997, Carter hit 20 or more home runs in every season, and he hit 30 or more home runs six times.

Carter played with the Chicago Cubs (1983), the Cleveland Indians (1985–89), the San Diego Padres (1990), the Toronto Blue Jays (1991–1997), the Baltimore Orioles (1998), and the San Francisco Giants (1998).

He led the Blue Jays to two World Series championships—in 1992 against the Atlanta Braves and in 1993 against the Philadelphia Phillies. Carter's three-run homer in game 6 off reliever Mitch Williams marked the first time in World Series history that a home run brought a team from behind to clinch the Series.

Carter, a five-time All-Star, retired after the 1998 season with a lifetime batting average of .259, 2,184 hits, 396 home runs, and 1,445 RBI.

Cepeda, Orlando
Born: September 17, 1937 in Ponce, Puerto Rico
Orlando Cepeda was a power-hitting first baseman who broke into the major leagues with the San Francisco Giants when he was just 20 years old.

Cepeda, the son of Puerto Rican baseball star Perucho "The Bull" Cepeda, was known as the "Baby Bull."

He was named the National League Rookie of the Year in 1958, when he batted .312, hit 25 home runs and had 96 runs batted in (RBI). After two more solid seasons when he hit 27 and 24 home runs and drove in 105 and 96 runs, respectively, Cepeda led the National League with 46 home runs in 1961.

Cepeda averaged 33 home runs and 103 RBI, and hit .300 or better in each of the next three seasons. But a knee injury in 1965 limited him to just 34 at-bats. Early in the 1966 season, he was traded to the St. Louis Cardinals. In 1967, he batted .325, hit 25 home runs, and had 111 RBI. He was named the National League Most Valuable Player and led the Cardinals to the pennant. They lost the World Series in seven games to the Boston Red Sox.

Cepeda was traded to the Atlanta Braves in 1969, and he had his last great season in 1970, batting .305, hitting 34 home runs, and driving in 111 runs. He finished his career with brief stays with the Oakland Athletics, Boston Red Sox, and Kansas City Royals. He retired in 1974.

In 17 major league seasons, Cepeda batted .297, hit 379 home runs, and had 1,365 RBI. His induction into the Hall of Fame, which occurred in 1999, was more than likely delayed by his arrest on charges of trying to pick up 160 pounds of marijuana at an airport. He was sentenced to five years, but served only 10 months at a state prison.

Charleston, Oscar
Born: October 14, 1896 in Indianapolis, Indiana
Died: October 6, 1954
Considered by many to be the greatest all-around player in the history of the Negro Leagues, Oscar Charleston could hit for power and average, run, and field. He was said to be Ty Cobb, Tris Speaker, and Babe Ruth all rolled into one.

John McGraw, the legendary manager of the New York Giants, called Charleston the greatest player he had ever seen.

Charleston began his career in 1915 with the Indianapolis ABCs. He also played for the New York Lincoln Giants, the Chicago American Giants, the St. Louis Giants, the Harrisburg Giants, the Philadelphia Hillsdales, the Homestead Grays, and the Pittsburgh Crawfords.

He was a perennial .300 hitter, with his average rarely dipping below .350. He is credited with hitting .400 or better three times, including a career-high .445 in 68 games in 1925.

Charleston was a consummate center fielder, whose great speed allowed him to play just behind second base and dare batters to hit the ball over his head. He also had a mean streak, sliding with his spikes high when the situation called for it.

Charleston served as a player-manager as early as 1922 with Harrisburg. He served as the player-manager for the great Pittsburgh Crawfords starting in 1932, when they went 99–36.

Charleston retired in 1944, missing by three years the integration of baseball. He was inducted into the Baseball Hall of Fame in 1974.

Clemens, Roger

Born: August 4, 1962 in Dayton, Ohio

Roger Clemens, nicknamed the "Rocket," has been the model of consistency throughout his career. Known for his intensity and a blazing fastball, Clemens, a right-hander, joined the Boston Red Sox in 1984. He went a combined 16–9 in his first two seasons, then he became a star. In 1986, following shoulder surgery, Clemens was 24–4 with 238 strikeouts. He led the American League in victories, winning percentage (.857), and earned run average—ERA—(2.48). He was named the American League's Most Valuable Player and was the winner of the Cy Young Award.

Clemens repeated as the Cy Young Award winner in 1987, when he was 20–9 with a 2.97 ERA. He led the league in victories, winning percentage (.690), complete games (18), and shutouts (7).

From 1988 through 1992, Clemens averaged 18 wins a year and won his third Cy Young Award in 1991, when he was 18–10 with league-leading totals in ERA (2.62), strikeouts (241), and shutouts (4). He also led the league in ERA in 1990 (1.93) and 1992 (2.41); in strikeouts in 1988 (291); and in shutouts in 1988 (8), 1990 (4), and 1992 (4).

Arm and shoulder trouble began to take their toll on Clemens starting in 1993, when he was 11–14 with a 4.46 ERA. He went 9–7 and 10–5 the next two seasons, but slumped to 10–13 in 1996, although he did lead the league in strikeouts (257).

Clemens signed with the Toronto Blue Jays as a free agent and won his fourth and fifth Cy Young Awards. In 1997, he was 21–7 and led the league in victories, ERA (2.05), complete games (9), strikeouts (292), and shutouts (3). In 1998, he was 20–6 and led the league in victories, ERA (2.65), and strikeouts (271).

In February 1999, Clemens was traded to the New York Yankees. He had a disappointing season, going 14–10 with a 4.60 ERA, which was nearly two runs higher than in 1998.

In the 1999 American League Championship Series against Boston, Clemens was beaten by his former team, but the Yankees went on to win the series. In the World Series, Clemens won his only start in a four-game sweep of the Atlanta Braves.

Clemens has twice struck out 20 batters in one game—against the Seattle Mariners in 1986 and the Detroit Tigers in 1996.

Through the 2000 season, Clemens was 260–142 with a 3.05 ERA. He struck out 200 or more 10 times. He ranked eighth all-time in strikeouts (3,504) and 16th in winning percentage (.647). A six-time All-Star, Clemens was named to the All-Century Team in 1999.

Clemente, Roberto

Born: August 18, 1934 in Carolina, Puerto Rico
Died: December 31, 1972

Roberto Clemente was a complex person. He was brooding, distrustful of the press, and often felt his accomplishments weren't given their just due. He was also altruistic and a great humanitarian, who died in a plane crash while delivering food to earthquake victims in Nicaragua.

Perhaps his many achievements were overlooked, because he played in Pittsburgh, which is not a media capital, and because he was a contemporary of Willie Mays and Hank Aaron. But there is no denying Clemente's greatness.

Clemente joined the Pirates in 1955 and was their starting right fielder for 18 seasons. During his first five seasons, he hit over .300 only once. But in 1960, he hit .314 with 16 home runs in helping the Pirates win the World Series over the New York Yankees.

Over the next seven years, Clemente, a notorious bad-ball hitter with an unorthodox batting stance, won the batting title four times—1961 (.351), 1964 (.339), 1965 (.329), and 1967 (.357). He didn't win the batting title in 1966, but he was named the National League's Most Valuable Player when he hit .317 with 29 home runs and 119 runs batted in.

In the 1971 World Series, Clemente hit .414 with 12 hits, including two doubles, a triple, and two home runs, and was named the Series Most Valuable Player in leading the Pirates to a seven-game victory after trailing 3–1 to Baltimore.

Clemente got his 3,000th hit September 30, 1972. It was also his last hit, as the plane crash that took his life occurred three months later.

The customary five-year waiting period for entrance to the Baseball Hall of Fame was waived, and Clemente was inducted in August 1973.

Clemente had a lifetime batting average of .317. He won 12 Gold Gloves, as the best fielder at his position, and made 12 All-Star Game appearances.

Cobb, Ty

Born: December 18, 1886 in Narrows, Georgia
Died: July 17, 1961

Ty Cobb was a accomplished player, one of the greatest of all time, but he was also one of the most feared and disliked players in history. He was a mean-spirited, violent player with a win-at-all-costs mentality. He thought nothing of hurling insults at opposing players from his dugout, and he wore razor-sharp spikes that he used to deliberately injure opposing players.

Much of Cobb's anger was traced to the death of his father in 1905. W.H. Cobb, who suspected his wife, Amanda, of infidelity, climbed a ladder to look into the bedroom window. Cobb's mother, believing her husband was a burglar, shot and killed him. Cobb was very close to his father and rarely saw his mother after the incident. He didn't even attend her funeral.

But in spite of his unpopular status, there is no denying his greatness. Cobb, nicknamed the "Georgia Peach," was a fine hitter who possessed remarkable bat control and was unstoppable on the basepaths.

Cobb's first year in the major leagues was 1905. He joined the Detroit Tigers in August and hit just .240, while establishing himself as a loner. He refused to room with anyone, he spoke to his teammates infrequently, and he ate his meals alone.

In his second season, Cobb, a center fielder, hit .316. He would hit at least .320 or better for the next 22 years. He also hit .400 three times, including .401 in 1922, when he lost the batting title to George Sisler, who hit .420. A left-handed hitter, he choked up on the bat and used a split grip. In addition to being able to direct the ball almost at will, he was also a master bunter.

Cobb won 12 batting titles, including nine straight, starting in 1907, and his career average of .367 remains the best in history.

Cobb led the American League in stolen bases six times (1907, '09, '11, '15–17), ranked fourth all-time with 892, and was successful on 83 percent of his attempts. Through the 2000 season, he ranked first all-time in .300 seasons (23), batting titles (12), and runs (2,246). He was second in hits (4,189), singles (3,053), and triples (295); fourth in games (3,053), doubles (724), and total bases (5,864); and fifth in runs batted in (1,937). When Cobb retired in 1928, at age 42, he held 90 all-time records. He led the Tigers to three straight World Series, starting in 1906, but none over the last 17 years of his career. The Tigers lost all three World Series appearances.

In 1921, the Tigers named Cobb player-manager, which was surprising, given his unpopularity. He had some success, leading the Tigers to a second-place finish in 1923 and two third-place finishes. Following the 1926 season, the Tigers released Cobb because of a letter he was alleged to have written that implicated him and Tris Speaker in fixing a game. But Commissioner Kenesaw Mountain Landis cleared Cobb and Speaker. Cobb finished his career with the Philadelphia Athletics, retiring in 1928. He hit .357 and .323 with the Athletics.

Cobb was in the first class inducted into the Baseball Hall of Fame in 1936. He received 98.2 percent of the vote, compared to Babe Ruth's 95.1 percent. He was also named to the All-Century Team selected in 1999.

Cochrane, Mickey (Gordon)
Born: April 6, 1903 in Bridgewater, Massachusetts
Died: June 28, 1962

Mickey Cochrane was the entire package: a fine defensive catcher, with a strong arm, who could hit for average and played with intensity and intelligence. He was obsessed with winning and had a difficult time accepting defeat.

Cochrane was an all-around athlete at Boston University, where he played baseball, football, basketball, and track. He also played semipro baseball during the summers. He used an alias, "Frank King," to maintain his eligibility.

After graduating in 1923, Cochrane played for minor league teams in Dover, Del., and Portland, Ore., before becoming the starting catcher for the Philadelphia Athletics in 1925, when he hit .331 as a rookie.

During his 13-year career, Cochrane hit .300 or better nine times and never hit lower than .270.

In 1928, Cochrane was named the American League's Most Valuable Player, even though he hit only .293. The award was given for his defense and leadership.

From 1929 through 1931, Cochrane helped the Athletics to three American League pennants and two World Series championships, hitting .331, .357, and .349, respectively.

Cochrane spent one more season with the Athletics, 1933, when he hit .322, then he was sold to the Detroit Tigers for $100,000, because the Depression caused the team to sell off its high-priced players. He became the Tigers player-manager in 1934. In his first season with the Tigers, he hit .320 and won his second Most Valuable Player Award. Detroit won the pennant in 1934 and 1935 and the World Series in 1935.

In 1936, Cochrane's intensity caused him to suffer a nervous breakdown midway through the season. He came back in 1937, but on May 25, he was hit by a pitch from New York's Bump Hadley. Cochrane's skull was fractured in three places. He lay in a coma for 10 days.

Cochrane was back as manager in 1938, but he was replaced in August. He went on to serve as a coach and general manager for the Athletics, and as a scout and vice president for the Tigers. He died in 1961 from a respiratory ailment.

Cochrane's lifetime batting average of .320 was the highest in the 20th century for catchers. Early in his career, he was unquestionably the best catcher in baseball. Later, it was a toss-up between Cochrane and Bill Dickey of the New York Yankees. Cochrane was inducted into the Baseball Hall of Fame in 1947.

Collins, Eddie

Born: May 2, 1887 in Millerton, New York
Died: March 25, 1951

Eddie Collins, nicknamed "Cocky" for his aggressive style of play, was one of the game's most consistent and productive hitters, a proficient bunter, and an expert base stealer. He wasn't blessed with a lot of power, but he was a master of getting on base and scoring runs. He also led the league in fielding eight times.

Collins, a graduate of Columbia University, didn't play his senior year in college, because he had joined the Philadelphia Athletics the previous summer. He tried to mask his professional status by playing under the name of Eddie Sullivan. It didn't work, and he was ineligible his senior year.

After spending parts of the 1906 and 1907 seasons with the Athletics, Collins joined the A's for the entire 1908 season and became their full-time second baseman a year later, when he hit .346 and stole 67 bases.

Collins hit over .300 18 times, but never won a batting title, because his best years coincided with Ty Cobb's. Cobb won the American League batting title 12 times in 13 years.

Collins led the league in stolen bases four times (1910, '19, '23–24) and was named the league's Most Valuable Player in 1914, when he hit .344 and scored a league-leading 122 runs.

The Athletics won the World Series in 1910, 1911, and 1913, with Collins hitting .429, .286, and .421, respectively. He stole 14 bases in World Series play, tying him with Lou Brock for first all-time.

After the 1914 season, Collins was sold by manager Connie Mack to the Chicago White Sox. He helped the White Sox to two World Series appearances—a victory over the New York Giants in 1917, when he hit .409, and a loss to Cincinnati in the infamous Black Sox Scandal of 1919.

Eight members of the White Sox were indicted for their efforts to throw the Series. All were banned from baseball for life. Collins was not involved with the conspiracy.

In 1925, Collins became the player-manager of the White Sox. He returned to the Athletics in 1927, primarily as a coach, and retired in 1930.

Through the 2000 season, Collins, with a lifetime batting average of .333, ranked ninth all-time in hits (3,313), 12th in runs (1,820), and seventh in stolen bases (744). His walk-to-strikeout ratio was 5–1. He was inducted into the Baseball Hall of Fame in 1939.

Collins, Jimmy

Born: January 16, 1870 in Niagara Falls, New York
Died: March 6, 1943

Jimmy Collins hit .300 or better five times during his 14-year major league career as a third baseman (1895–1908) with the Boston Braves, the Boston Red Sox, and the Philadelphia Athletics. He also was responsible for changing the way third basemen played. He played away from the base, which allowed him to cut off balls hit between him and the shortstop. He also was the first to charge bunts and field them bare-handed. Collins' lifetime batting average was .294. He had 1,997 hits and led the National League in home runs (15) in 1898. He was inducted into the Baseball Hall of Fame in 1945.

Crawford, Sam

Born: April 18, 1880 in Wahoo, Nebraska
Died: June 15, 1968

Sam Crawford was one of the best hitters in the "dead-ball era." It has been said that if Crawford had been born 20 years later, when a livelier ball was used, his home run totals might have rivaled Babe Ruth's.

Crawford was an outstanding base runner and in superb physical condition. Crawford, nicknamed "Wahoo Sam," hit .300 or better 10 times, including a career-high .378 in 1911. He was the league leader in triples six times (23 in 1902, 25 in 1903, 19 in 1910, 23 in 1913, 26 in 1914, 19 in 1915), runs batted in (RBI) three times (120 in 1910, 104 in 1914, 112 in 1915), and home runs twice (16 in 1901, 7 in 1908). He was the first player to lead both leagues in home runs. He was with Cincinnati of the National League in 1901 and with Detroit of the American League in 1908.

Crawford's best seasons came in Detroit (1905–1917), when he played center field with Ty Cobb in left. Crawford helped lead the Tigers to three consecutive American League pennants (1907–09).

Crawford retired in 1917 with a lifetime batting average of .309. Through the 2000 season, he was the all-time leader in triples with 311. He had 2,961 hits and 1,525 RBI. After being passed over numerous times, Crawford was inducted into the Baseball Hall of Fame in 1940.

Cronin, Joe

Born: October 12, 1906 in San Francisco, California
Died: September 7, 1984

Joe Cronin spent three years in the major leagues before emerging as a star. He spent two seasons with the Pittsburgh Pirates (1926–27) and joined the Washington Senators in 1928. In his third season with the Senators, Cronin hit .346 with 203 hits, 41 doubles, and 126 runs batted in (RBI). From 1930 through 1943, Cronin hit

.300 or better nine times, including .325 in 1938, when he led the league in doubles (51). He also drove in 100 or more runs eight times.

In 1933, Cronin became the player-manager of the Senators and led them to the American League pennant. After the 1934 season, when the Senators dropped to seventh, Cronin was traded to the Boston Red Sox. He managed the Red Sox through 1947 and played until 1945, when a broken leg ended his career.

Cronin's lifetime batting average was .301. He had 2,285 hits, including 515 doubles and 118 triples. He was inducted into the Baseball Hall of Fame in 1956.

Dawson, Andre

Born: July 10, 1954 in Miami, Florida

Andre Dawson was a solid, productive right fielder through his 21-year major league career. He joined the Montreal Expos in 1976 and became a full-time outfielder the following season. From 1978 through 1992, Dawson hit 20 or more home runs 13 times, including 32 in 1983, when he also led the league in hits (183), and a league-leading 49 in 1987, his first season with the Chicago Cubs. He also led the league in runs batted in (RBI) with 137 in 1987 and was named the National League's Most Valuable Player.

Dawson spent six seasons with the Cubs, joined the Boston Red Sox in 1993, and ended his career after two seasons with the Florida Marlins.

Dawson, who was plagued by knee problems throughout his career, was nevertheless a fine defensive outfielder, who won eight Gold Gloves and never made more than nine errors in a season.

Dawson's lifetime batting average was .279. Through the 2000 season, he ranked 25th all-time in home runs (436), 25th in RBI (1,591), and 19th in extra base hits (1,039).

Dean, Dizzy (Jay)

Born: January 16, 1910 in Lucas, Arkansas
Died: July 17, 1974

Dizzy Dean was one of the best pitchers of his day and one of the most colorful athletes of all time. He was glib and charismatic with a down home sense of humor. He pitched with the Army team starting in 1927 and joined the St. Louis Cardinals after he was discharged in 1930. By 1932, he was a mainstay of the Cardinals' famed "Gashouse Gang" teams. He won 18 games in 1932 and led the league in strikeouts with 191. He then strung together four consecutive seasons during which he was masterful. Dean went 20–18 in 1933, leading the league in games (48), complete games (26), and strikeouts (199). The following season, he was 30–7, and he led the league in victories, winning percentage

(.811), complete games (24), strikeouts (195), and shutouts (7). He was named the National League's Most Valuable Player and the Associated Press Male Athlete of the Year.

The Cardinals won the National League pennant and the World Series in 1934. Dean won two games, had a 1.73 earned run average (ERA), and struck out 17 in 26 innings.

Dean followed up his 30-win season by going 28–12 in 1935. He led the league in victories, games started (36), complete games (29), innings pitched (325.1), and strikeouts (190).

Dean's last great season came in 1936. He went 24–13 and led the league in games (51), complete games (28), innings pitched (315), and saves (11).

Dean was never the same after being hit on the foot by a line drive by Earl Averill in the 1937 All-Star Game. Dean returned before his broken big toe was completely healed. He altered his delivery to compensate for the injury, causing arm trouble, and from 1938 until his retirement in 1947, he won a total of only 16 games.

Dean became a broadcaster for the St. Louis Cardinals and the St. Louis Browns and also did network telecasts of the major league game of the week. He frequently used the word "ain't," which upset teachers, but his listeners rallied around him.

Dean's career record was 150–83 with an ERA of 3.02. He and his brother, Paul, hold the single-season record for victories by a brother combination (49, 1934). Dean was inducted into the Baseball Hall of Fame in 1953.

Dickey, Bill

Born: June 6, 1907 in Bastrop, Louisiana
Died: November 12, 1993

Bill Dickey, one of the most durable catchers in baseball history, was the link between New York Yankees dynasties. He was part of the Ruth-Gehrig teams and lasted beyond the Joe DiMaggio teams of the late 40s.

Dickey played for Little Rock (Ark.) College and also began playing for a semipro team near Hot Springs, Ark. He was signed by the Yankees in 1925 and joined the team in 1928, appearing in 10 games. Dickey took over as the Yankees' full-time catcher in 1929 and caught at least 100 games for the next 13 seasons.

Dickey was a terrific defensive catcher with a strong arm and the ability to handle pitchers very well, keeping them on an even keel. He led the American League in fielding percentage four times, his lifetime fielding average was .988, and in 1931, he caught 131 games without a passed ball.

Dickey never led the league in batting, home runs, or runs batted in (RBI), but his consistency set him apart. From 1929 through 1939, he hit .300 or better 10 times.

He hit at least 20 home runs and drove in at least 100 runs in four straight seasons, starting in 1936.

Dickey's productive seasons from 1936 to 1939 helped the Yankees win the World Series each year, the first time a team ever won four straight.

Dickey appeared in eight World Series and played for seven champions. His World Series average was .255 with five home runs and 24 RBI.

For the most part, Dickey was a quiet, mild-mannered player, except for one incident during the 1932 season. After a home plate collision in which Carl Reynolds crashed into Dickey, Dickey, still groggy from the impact, punched Reynolds and broke his jaw. Dickey was fined $1,000 and suspended for 30 days. At the time, it was the most severe penalty ever imposed.

Dickey served in the Navy in 1944–45 and returned to play one more season in 1946. He managed in the minor leagues for the Yankees and then became a coach under manager Casey Stengel through 1957.

Dickey's lifetime batting average was .313, with 202 home runs and 1,209 RBI. He was inducted into the Baseball Hall of Fame in 1954.

DiMaggio, Joe

Born: November 1914 in Martinez, California
Died: March 8, 1999

Joe DiMaggio was a baseball icon and an American hero, albeit a reluctant hero. DiMaggio was aloof and intensely guarded his privacy. But the charisma and mystique that he exuded and the grace and dignity with which he conducted himself made him one of the most popular players of all time. That he spent his entire career with the fabled New York Yankees only added to his appeal and his legend.

DiMaggio, who had only one year of high school, joined the San Francisco Seals of the Pacific Coast League in 1933. He hit .340, drove in a league-leading 169 runs, and hit in 61 consecutive games.

Despite a knee injury suffered in 1934, the Yankees signed him late in that season. He spent one more season in the minor leagues and joined the Yankees in 1936. His debut was delayed until May 3, because of an ankle injury, but he lived up to the high expectations. He hit .323 with 29 home runs and 126 runs batted in (RBI). He helped the Yankees to the first of four straight World Series championships, starting the season in right field, then moving to center, where he remained for the rest of his career.

DiMaggio, nicknamed the "Yankee Clipper" and "Joltin' Joe," quickly became a fan favorite. He was accorded the same status as Babe Ruth and Lou Gehrig, Yankee heroes before him.

DiMaggio lived up to the acclaim. In 1937, he led the American League in home runs with 46; in 1938, he hit .324; and in 1939, he won the American League Most Valuable Player Award with a league-leading .381 average. He won his second batting title in 1940, hitting .352.

DiMaggio made history in 1941, setting a record that may never be broken. He hit successfully in 56 consecutive games, getting 91 hits from May 15 to July 16. He won his second Most Valuable Player Award and was named the Associated Press Male Athlete of the Year.

DiMaggio spent three seasons in the Army (1943–45). He returned in 1946, hitting .290, and in 1947, he was named the Most Valuable Player, hitting .315, with 31 doubles, 10 triples, 20 home runs, and 97 RBI. It was the first time in seven seasons that DiMaggio failed to drive in at least 100 runs.

In 1948, DiMaggio rebounded with league-leading totals in home runs (39) and RBI (155). The following year, he became the first baseball player to earn $100,000. A heel injury limited him to 76 games.

DiMaggio's last great season came in 1950. He batted .301, hit 32 home runs, and drove in 122 runs. He retired following the 1951 season, when he batted just .263 and hit 12 home runs.

"When baseball is no longer fun, it's no longer a game," said DiMaggio. "And so I've just played my last game."

DiMaggio had a lifetime batting average of .325. He had 2,214 hits, 361 home runs, and 1,537 RBI. He was also a consummate center fielder, who played so effortlessly that he made even the difficult plays look routine. During his 13-year career, he led the Yankees to 10 American League pennants and nine World Series titles.

Even though DiMaggio retired, he did not leave the public eye. In January 1954, he married Marilyn Monroe, a relationship that made him even more interesting to the public. Rarely have two so famous people married: one of the greatest and most popular athletes and one of the most high-profile actresses.

DiMaggio also worked as a spring training instructor with the Yankees and a coach with the Oakland Athletics, and he was a broadcaster and a television spokesperson, endorsing products such as Mr. Coffee.

DiMaggio was immortalized in the song "Mrs. Robinson" by Simon and Garfunkel, who sang, "Where have you gone, Joe DiMaggio? A nation turns its lonely eyes to you."

Such was the impact that he had on his fans and his time.

DiMaggio was inducted into the Baseball Hall of Fame in 1955, his second year of eligibility, and named to the All-Century Team selected in 1999.

Early in 1999, DiMaggio underwent surgery for lung cancer and lapsed into a coma, from which doctors believed he would never emerge. He rallied, but died March 8.

Doby, Larry

Born: December 13, 1924 in Camden, South Carolina

Larry Doby was the first African American to play in the American League. His debut with the Cleveland Indians came in July 1947, three months after Jackie Robinson broke the color barrier with the Brooklyn Dodgers.

In 1948, Doby's first full season, he hit .301 with 24 home runs and 85 runs batted in (RBI) and helped the Indians to the World Series. From 1948 through 1956, he hit at least 20 home runs a season, including 32 in 1952 and 32 in 1954. He led the league in home runs each time. In 1952, he led the league in runs (104) and in 1954 he led in RBI (126).

Doby was traded to the Chicago White Sox in 1956. He spent two seasons with the White Sox, a season in Cleveland, and parts of the 1959 season, his last, with the Detroit Tigers and the White Sox.

In 1978, Doby became the second African American manager in the major leagues. He was named the manager of the Chicago White Sox. He went 37-50 and was replaced late in the 1978 season.

Doby, a fine defensive outfielder and a seven-time All-Star, had a lifetime batting average of .283. He hit 253 home runs and drove in 969. He was inducted into the Baseball Hall of Fame in 1998.

Drysdale, Don

Born: July 23, 1936 in Van Nuys, California
Died: July 3, 1993

Don Drysdale was one of the most intimidating pitchers of his time. He stood 6-6, threw with a sidearm motion, and didn't hesitate to brush batters back or knock them down. He led the National League in hit batsmen every year from 1958 through 1961, and he holds the career record of 154.

Drysdale, a right-hander, didn't pitch until his senior year at Van Nuys High School, but because of his potential, the Brooklyn Dodgers signed him right out of high school.

He spent two seasons with Bakersfield in the Class C California League and joined the Dodgers in 1956, when he went 5–5 with a 2.64 earned run average (ERA). Drysdale joined the starting rotation in 1957, the Dodgers' last year in Brooklyn before moving to Los Angeles. He went 17–9 with a 2.69 ERA and became a fixture for the next decade.

Drysdale led the league in games started four times (41 in 1962, 42 in 1963, 40 in 1964, 42 in 1965), strikeouts three times (242 in 1959, 246 in 1960, 232 in 1962), innings pitched twice (314.1 in 1962, 321.1 in 1964), and shutouts once (4 in 1959).

In 1962, he went 25–9 with a 2.83 ERA, led the league in victories, and won the Cy Young Award. In 1965, Drysdale helped the Dodgers to the World Series, where they defeated the Minnesota Twins by going 23–12 with a 2.77 ERA and 210 strikeouts. Following the 1965 season, Drysdale and Dodgers' left-handed ace Sandy Koufax staged a joint holdout—each wanted a three-year, $500,000 contract. At the time, only Willie Mays of the San Francisco Giants and Mickey Mantle of the New York Yankees earned more than $100,000. The impasse lasted into spring training, with Koufax signing for $130,000 and Drysdale for $105,000.

In 1968, Drysdale went 58.1 consecutive scoreless innings without allowing a run. In the process, he threw six straight shutouts and broke Carl Hubbell's National League record (46) and Walter Johnson's major league record (56).

It looked as if Drysdale's streak ended at 44 innings when he hit a batter with the bases loaded, forcing in a run. But the umpire ruled that the batter made no attempt to avoid the pitch. Drysdale got him out and the next two hitters to preserve his streak.

Drysdale suffered a torn rotator cuff in 1969, ending his career. His lifetime record was 209–166 with a 2.95 ERA. He was inducted into the Baseball Hall of Fame in 1984.

Eckersley, Dennis

Born: October 3, 1954 in Oakland, California

Dennis Eckersley, a right-handed pitcher, had two careers—the first as a starter and the second as one of the best relievers ever.

Playing for the Cleveland Indians, Boston Red Sox, and Chicago Cubs from 1975 to 1986, Eckersley was a starting pitcher. His best season was 1978 with Boston, when he was 20–8 with a 2.99 earned run average (ERA). He won 151 games as a starter, including a no-hitter while he was with Cleveland, against the California Angels in May 1977.

Eckersley suffered arm trouble in 1986, when he went 6–11, and he was traded in 1987 to the Oakland Athletics. Many thought his career as effective pitcher was over, but he was moved to the bullpen and he became a premier closer.

He led the American League in saves with 45 in 1988 and 51 in 1992, when he struck out 93 and walked 11 in 80 innings and had a 1.91 ERA. He was named the American League's Most Valuable Player and the Cy Young Award winner. From 1988 through 1993, he averaged 43 saves a year. He also helped the Athletics to the World Series in 1988–90.

In 1996, he was traded to the St. Louis Cardinals. He saved 66 games in two seasons for the Cards. He signed with the Boston Red Sox as a free agent in 1998. He went 4–1 with only one save and announced his retirement after the season.

Eckersley's career record was 197–171 with a 3.50 ERA. Through the 2000 season, he ranked second all-time in appearances (1,071) and third all-time in saves (390).

Feller, Bob
Born: November 3, 1918 in Van Meter, Iowa

One of the hardest-throwing pitchers ever, Bob Feller began his major league career before he graduated from high school. He grew up on a farm and developed strength in his arm by doing chores around the farm and by throwing into a backstop made by his father out of two-by-fours and chicken wire.

At age 16, Feller was spotted by a scout while playing for a semipro team in Dubuque, Iowa. He joined the Cleveland Indians as a non-roster player in 1936, meaning he could travel and work out with the club. His signing bonus included two autographed baseballs and a scorecard from the 1935 All-Star Game.

Feller's first appearance for the Indians came in an exhibition game against the St. Louis Cardinals' famed "Gashouse Gang," featuring Frankie Frisch, Pepper Martin, Joe Medwick, Leo Durocher, and Dizzy Dean. Feller worked three innings and struck out eight.

Feller's official major league debut came several weeks later, against the St. Louis Browns. He struck out 15. Three weeks later, Feller pitched a two-hitter against the Philadelphia Athletics, striking out 17 to tie Dizzy Dean's major league record.

Feller finished 5–3 during his rookie season, striking out 76 in 62 innings. After the season was over, he returned to Iowa to finish high school.

Arm trouble plagued Feller in 1937, but in 1938 he led the league in strikeouts with 240. Over the next three seasons, Feller led the league in strikeouts and victories. He won 76 games during those three seasons and averaged 256 strikeouts.

After the 1941 season, Feller left the Indians to join the Navy. He missed the next three seasons entirely and pitched in only nine games in 1945. As impressive as his statistics are, that nearly four-season absence cost him an even greater résumé.

In 1946, his first full season after serving in the Navy, Feller picked up where he left off. He led the league in victories (26), complete games (36), innings pitched (277.1), strikeouts (348), and shutouts (10). The following year was a virtual carbon copy with league-leading totals in victories (20), innings pitched (299), strikeouts (196), and shutouts (5).

In 1948, Feller helped the Indians to the World Series, going 19–15, with a league-leading 164 strikeouts. The Indians won the Series over the Boston Braves, but Feller was ineffective (0–2, 5.02 earned run average, seven strikeouts in 14 innings pitched).

After winning 15 and 16 games, respectively, in 1949 and 1950, Feller rebounded with the last 20-win season of his career in 1951. He went 22–8 with a league-leading .733 winning percentage.

Starting in 1952, Feller became a spot starter. He went 13–3 in 1954, but retired after the 1956 season, when he was 0–4.

Nicknamed "Rapid Robert," Feller possessed not only an overpowering fastball, but a big, sweeping curveball, the contrast of which stymied hitters throughout his career.

Feller, whose career record was 266–162, pitched three no-hitters and 12 one-hitters. Through the 2000 season, he ranked 18th all-time in strikeouts (2,581). He was inducted into the Baseball Hall of Fame in 1962.

Fingers, Rollie
Born: August 25, 1946 in Steubenville, Ohio

Rollie Fingers redefined relief pitching as the best reliever of his time. He began his career with the Oakland Athletics in 1968 as a starting pitcher. But he didn't adapt to the role, because he worried so much about each start and was ineffective. He was moved to the bullpen in 1971 and found his niche.

Fingers developed into a specialist, a closer who would enter the game to protect a lead and get the final few outs.

From 1971 through 1976, Fingers appeared in 346 games and recorded 105 saves. He was a key player in the Athletics' three straight World Series championships (1972–74). In those three Series, he was 2–2 with a 1.35 earned run average (ERA) and six saves, which was a major league record through the 2000 season.

In the 1974 Series, Fingers was named Most Valuable Player, getting one win and two saves.

In 1977, Fingers was traded to the San Diego Padres because of a contract dispute. He spent four years with the Padres, twice leading the National League in saves (35 in 1977, 37 in 1978).

In 1981, Fingers switched teams again, moving to the Milwaukee Brewers. He became the first reliever to win the Cy Young Award and the Most Valuable Player Award. He was 6–3 with a 1.04 ERA and league-leading 28 saves in a strike-shortened season.

Fingers went 5–6 with 29 saves in 1982 and missed the entire 1983 season with tendinitis. He returned in 1984, going 1–2, and retired after the 1985 season.

Fingers, whose signature handlebar mustache was his trademark, had a career record of 114–118 with a 2.90 ERA. Through the 2000 season, he ranked eighth all-time in appearances (944) and sixth in saves (341). He struck out 1,299 and walked only 492 in 1,701 innings. He was inducted into the Baseball Hall of Fame in 1992.

Fisk, Carlton

Born: December 26, 1947 in Bellows Falls, Vermont

Carlton Fisk, who played in four decades, was one of the best and most durable catchers of his time. He turned down a scholarship to the University of New Hampshire to sign with the Boston Red Sox in 1967. After spending the next several seasons mostly in the minor leagues, he became the Red Sox starting catcher in 1972, when he hit .293, with 22 home runs, 61 runs batted in (RBI), and an American League–leading nine triples. He was named to the All-Star team and was the first unanimous winner of the American League Rookie of the Year Award.

In 1975, he rebounded from injuries that kept him out of much of the 1974 season and the early part of the 1975 season to hit .331 and helped the Red Sox win the pennant. In the World Series against the Cincinnati Reds, renowned as one of the greatest series ever played, Fisk hit what ranks as one of the most dramatic home runs in World Series history in game 6. In the bottom of the 12th in a 6–6 game at Fenway Park, Fisk hit Pat Darcy's second pitch just inside the foul pole. Fisk's body language, trying to will the ball to stay fair, is one of baseball's most recognizable highlights. The Red Sox evened the Series on Fisk's home run, but squandered a 3–0 lead in game 7 and lost.

Fisk signed with the Chicago White Sox in 1980 as a free agent. Instead of wearing his familiar No. 27 in Chicago, he opted for 72 to signify the turnaround in his career. Fisk's best season with the White Sox was 1985, when he hit .238 with 37 home runs and 107 RBI. His most unexpected season came two years earlier, in 1983. He was hitting .136 and was replaced in both games of a doubleheader by his manager, Tony La Russa. Fisk was enraged and let LaRussa know it. But the benching lit a fuse under Fisk, who, over the next 71 games, hit 16 home runs, drove in 49 runs, and raised his average 100 points. He finished the season hitting .289 with 26 home runs and 86 RBI. In 1993, Fisk was released by the White Sox after he had played in just 25 games. The move was unpopular among fans and the media, but Fisk's career was over. He had a lifetime batting average of .269, with 376 home runs, 1,330 RBI, and 1,276 runs scored. He is one of only four catchers—Johnny Bench, Yogi Berra, and Gary Carter are the others—to hit 300 home runs, drive in 1,000 runs, and score 1,000 runs. He hit 350 home runs as a catcher, a record. Fisk was inducted into the Baseball Hall of Fame in 2000.

Flood, Curt

Born: January 18, 1938 in Houston, Texas
Died: January 20, 1997

Curt Flood had a solid 15-year career (1956–71), spent mostly with the St. Louis Cardinals. He hit .300 or better six times as full-time outfielder, including .335 in

1967. He was also a fine defensive center fielder, who won six Gold Gloves. He also helped the Cardinals to three World Series (1964, '67–68).

But he is best known for challenging baseball's reserve clause. Flood was traded by the Cardinals to the Philadelphia Phillies in 1970. He refused to report and filed a lawsuit, supported by the players union, claiming that the reserve clause forced players into "involuntary servitude," a violation of the 13th Amendment, which prohibited slavery. A federal judge ruled against Flood in August 1970 and the Supreme Court upheld the ruling in June 1972.

Flood was out of baseball in 1970 and retired in 1971 after spending 13 games with the Washington Senators.

Even though Flood lost his battle, the case increased public awareness and threatened legislative action that helped team owners to accept arbitration to decide grievances. The reserve clause was eventually struck down in 1975.

Ford, Whitey (Edward)

Born: October 21, 1926 in New York, New York

Whitey Ford wasn't an overpowering pitcher, but what he lacked in speed he made up for with pinpoint control, intelligence, confidence, determination, and a variety of pitches. Ford threw a fastball, curve, sinker, and slider with different deliveries to confuse hitters. But his curve was the pitch that kept hitters guessing—and frustrated. He also had an outstanding pickoff move to first base.

Ford, a left-hander, signed with the Yankees in 1947 and was sent to their Middle Atlantic League farm club. He spent three years in the minor leagues, moving up a class each year and improving his stats, as well.

Ford was called up to the Yankees near the end of the 1950 season. He lost his first decision, but then won nine straight to help the Yankees with the American League pennant. In the World Series against the Philadelphia Phillies, he won the deciding fourth game.

Ford left baseball to join the service during the Korean War, and didn't pitch again until 1953, when he went 18–6. In 1955, he led the American League in victories (18) and complete games (18). The following season, he led in winning percentage (.760) and earned run average—ERA—(2.47). He also led the league in ERA in 1958 (2.01).

Ford had his best season in 1961, going 25–4 and winning the Cy Young Award. He led the league in victories, winning percentage (.862), games started (39), and innings pitched (283).

In 1963, Ford had his last great season. He went 24–7, leading the league in wins, winning percentage (.774), games started, (37), and innings pitched (269.1).

Ford won 17 and 16 games the next two seasons, before shoulder trouble began to take its toll. He won only two games in each of the next two seasons. He retired in 1967. During his 16-year career, Ford pitched in 11 World Series. He is the all-time leader in victories (10), games (22), innings pitched (146), consecutive scoreless innings (33.2), and strikeouts (94). He ranks second in shutouts (3) and fourth in complete games (7). Overall, Ford's record was 236–106. His winning percentage of .690 is higher than any 200-game winner in the modern era, and his ERA of 2.75 is the lowest of any starting pitcher since World War II.

Ford was selected to play in six All-Star Games and was inducted into the Baseball Hall of Fame in 1974.

Fox, Nelson

Born: December 25, 1927 in St. Thomas, Pennsylvania
Died: December 1, 1975

Nellie Fox was a solid, dependable, and durable second baseman who could hit, field, and throw. After spending three years with the Philadelphia Athletics (1947–49), he joined the Chicago White Sox, for whom he was a fixture for the next 14 seasons.

Fox, known for the ever-present chaw of tobacco bulging out of his cheeks, hit .300 or better six times. Noted for his keen batting eye, Fox struck out only 216 times in over 9,000 career at-bats. He led the American League in fielding six times, at-bats five times, hits four times (192 in 1952, 201 in 1954, 196 in 1957, 187 in 1958), and triples once. His best season was 1959, when he was named the American League's Most Valuable Player. He batted .306 and led the league in fielding percentage (.988). The White Sox won the pennant that season, and Fox hit .375 in the World Series, which the Los Angeles Dodgers won in six games.

Fox was traded to the Houston Astros in 1964. He retired the following season after playing in 21 games. His lifetime batting average was .288, with 2,663 hits. He was inducted into the Baseball Hall of Fame in 1997.

Foxx, Jimmie

Born: October 22, 1907 in Sudlersville, Maryland
Died: July 21, 1967

Jimmie Foxx was known for his power and his tape-measure home runs. He broke in as a catcher with the Philadelphia Athletics in 1925, but didn't play much, because Mickey Cochrane, the best catcher in the game at the time, was on the team. Four years later, Foxx was converted to a first baseman. He hit .354 with 33 home runs and 117 runs batted in (RBI). That was the first of a dozen consecutive seasons in which he hit at least 30 home runs and drove in at least 100 runs.

In 1932, Foxx led the American League with 58 home runs—a record for right-handed hitters, shared with Hank Greenberg—and 169 RBI. He lost two home runs, which would have tied Babe Ruth's record of 60 in one season, when a game was called before it was official.

Foxx, nicknamed "Double XX," won the Triple Crown in 1933, leading the league in average (.356), home runs (48), and RBI (163). He also led the league in batting in 1938 (.349), in home runs in 1935 (36) and 1939 (35), and in RBI in 1938 (175). He was named the American League Most Valuable Player in 1932, 1933, and 1938. Foxx was best known for his power, but he also hit for average and was a fine defensive player who was capable at catcher, first base, third base, and in the outfield. He helped lead the Athletics to three straight American League pennants (1930–32). He was traded to the Boston Red Sox following the 1935 season. After five successful seasons with the Red Sox, Foxx was released and picked up by the Chicago Cubs. He retired, made a comeback, then ended his career in 1945 with the Philadelphia Phillies.

Foxx had a lifetime batting average of .325. Through the 2000 season, he ranked 16th all-time in total bases (4,956), 10th in home runs (534), sixth in RBI (1,921), tied for 11th in extra base hits (1,117), and fourth in slugging percentage (.609). He was inducted into the Baseball Hall of Fame in 1951.

Frisch, Frankie

Born: September 9, 1898 in The Bronx, New York
Died: March 12, 1973

Frankie Frisch exerted his talent, influence, and leadership capabilities on two successful teams—the New York Giants of the 1920s and the St. Louis Cardinals of the 1930s. He was an intense competitor and a winner everywhere he went.

Frisch was a four-sport athlete and a second-team All-American halfback at Fordham University. After graduating in 1919, he signed with the New York Giants, having never spent a day in the minor leagues.

In 1921, his third season with the Giants, the "Fordham Flash" hit .341 with 211 hits and a National League–leading 49 stolen bases.

That season was the first of 12 straight of hitting .300 or better, including six times of .330 or better. Frisch helped the Giants win four straight pennants, starting in 1921, and two World Series (1921–22). He hit .300, .471, .400, and .333 in 26 Series games, collecting 37 hits.

Frisch was a feisty player who wouldn't hesitate to argue with an umpire or his manager, the legendary John McGraw. After taking a verbal beating from McGraw during the 1926 season, Frisch disappeared for several days. After the season, he was traded to the St. Louis Cardinals, along with pitcher Jimmy Ring, for Rogers Hornsby. The trade was a blockbuster, because most New York fans assumed that Frisch would succeed McGraw.

The St. Louis fans, angry that Hornsby, a popular player, was traded, took a while to accept Frisch. But he led the Cardinals to pennants in 1928, 1930, 1931, and 1934. In 1931, Frisch was the first player to be named the National League's Most Valuable Player by the Baseball Writers Association of America. He hit .311 and led the league with 28 steals.

During the 1933 season, he was named player-manager, and one year later, he took the famous "Gashouse Gang" to another World Series championship.

Frisch limited his playing time starting in 1934. His final season as a player was 1937. He was fired as manager during the 1938 season.

Frisch alternated between radio announcing and managing and coaching through 1951. He managed the Pittsburgh Pirates from 1940 to 1946, coached with the Giants in 1948, and managed the Chicago Cubs in 1949 until he was fired midway through the 1951 season.

Frisch died from injuries suffered in a car accident.

Frisch's lifetime batting average was .316. He had 200 hits or more three times and 100 or more runs scored seven times. He led the league in steals three times and in fielding three times.

Frisch was a member of more championship teams than any other National Leaguer. Through the 2000 season, he ranked fourth in World Series at-bats (197) and third in hits (58). He was inducted into the Baseball Hall of Fame in 1947.

Garciaparra, Nomar
Born: July 23, 1973 in Whittier, California

Nomar Garciaparra, like Alex Rodriguez of the Seattle Mariners, provides more power than you would expect from a shortstop. His first full season in the major leagues was 1997 with the Boston Red Sox. He hit .306 with 30 home runs, 98 runs batted in (RBI), and league-leading totals in hits (209) and triples (11). He was named the American League's Rookie of the Year.

Garciaparra hit .323 in 1998 with 35 home runs and 122 RBI, and in 1999, he led the league with a .357 average, hit 27 home runs, and drove in 104 runs.

Through the 2000 season, Garciaparra held the American League record for longest hitting streak by a rookie (30 games), and he also shared the major league record for most grand slams in one game (two, May 10, 1999).

Garvey, Steve
Born: December 22, 1948 in Tampa, Florida

Steve Garvey was a good-hitting, slick-fielding first baseman who set a National League record for consecutive games played (1,207) from September 3, 1975, through July 29, 1983.

He joined the Los Angeles Dodgers in 1969, and after four seasons as a reserve, playing first and third base, Garvey became the starting first baseman in 1974. From 1973 through 1980, Garvey hit .300 or better six times.

In 1974, he batted .312, with 200 hits, 21 home runs, and 111 runs batted in (RBI) to win the National League Most Valuable Player Award. The Dodgers reached the World Series that season. They were swept by the Oakland Athletics. Garvey hit .381 with eight hits.

Garvey twice led the league in hits, getting 202 in 1978 and 200 in 1980. He also won four Gold Gloves.

In 1983, he was traded to the San Diego Padres. He spent five seasons with the Padres, retiring following the 1987 season.

Garvey played in five World Series—four with the Dodgers and one with the Padres. His overall average was .319. In five National League Championship Series appearances, he hit .356 with 32 hits, eight home runs, 21 RBI, and a .678 slugging percentage.

Gehrig, Lou
Born: June 19, 1903 in New York, New York
Died: June 2, 1941

Lou Gehrig, quiet and unassuming, played in the shadow of his New York Yankees teammate Babe Ruth. But Gehrig's achievements can't be minimized. He was a durable power hitter who was at his best with men on base.

Gehrig signed with the Yankees in 1923 and spent much of his first two seasons in the minor leagues. On June 1, 1925, Yankees manager Miller Huggins sent Gehrig in to pinch-hit for Pee Wee Wanninger. The next day, Gehrig started in place of regular first baseman Wally Pipp and remained in the lineup every game until April 30, 1939, a streak of 2,130 consecutive games, a record that stood for 56 years until it was broken by Cal Ripken, Jr., of the Baltimore Orioles.

When Gehrig removed himself from the lineup on May 2, 1939, he had no idea he had contracted a debilitating disease—amyotrophic lateral sclerosis (ALS)—that would come to be known as Lou Gehrig's disease.

The "Iron Man," as he was nicknamed, hit behind Ruth in the Yankees lineup and formed a dangerous combination and the heart of the team's Murderer's Row lineup. Gehrig was named the American League's Most Valuable Player in 1927, when he led the league in runs batted in (RBI) with 175. He led the league in RBI in 1928 (142), 1930 (174), 1931 (184), and 1934 (165), when he won the Triple Crown, also leading the league in home runs (49) and average (.363).

In 1932, Gehrig became the first player in the 20th century to hit four consecutive home runs in a game. He had 13 straight seasons of 100-plus RBI and his 184 RBI in 1931 is an American League record. His .340 lifetime average is the 14th highest in major league history.

Early in the 1939 season, Gehrig lost weight and lacked strength and energy. He asked Miller Huggins to take him out of the lineup May 2. A trip to the Mayo Clinic confirmed that Gehrig had ALS, a hardening of the spinal cord. He had only two or three years to live, a diagnosis that his wife kept from him until the end.

Gehrig's career was over, but he returned to the Yankees as captain, presenting the lineups at home plate before each game. In 1939, the Baseball Hall of Fame waived its rule that players must be retired for a year (now five years) before being eligible for the Hall. Gehrig was granted his spot in Cooperstown.

On July 4, 1939, the Yankees held Lou Gehrig Day before a packed house of nearly 62,000 fans at Yankee Stadium. Between games of a doubleheader, his teammates from the 1927 Yankees, including Ruth, came to honor him. When Gehrig stepped to the microphone to speak, he proclaimed himself "the luckiest man on the face of the earth." In addition to a moment of profound sentiment, the occasion also started the tradition of old-timers games.

Less than two years after the ceremony, Gehrig lapsed into a coma and passed away.

In 1999, Gehrig was named to the All-Century Team. He was the leading vote-getter among first basemen.

Gehringer, Charlie
Born: May 11, 1903 in Fowlerville, Michigan
Died: January 21, 1993

Charlie Gehringer spent his entire career, 19 seasons, with the Detroit Tigers, demonstrating consistent excellence at the plate and in the field as a second baseman. He played baseball and football for one year at the University of Michigan, but left after his freshman year to play baseball in the Michigan–Ontario League.

Gehringer, known for his expressionless face and quiet demeanor, appeared in five games in 1924 and eight in 1925 before joining the Tigers as their starting second baseman in 1926, when he hit .277. Over the next 14 seasons, he hit .300 or better 13 times. Six times he hit over .330.

Said his teammate Mickey Cochrane: "He says hello opening day, goodbye closing day and in between, hits .350."

Gehringer, nicknamed "Mechanical Man," led the league in runs twice (131 in 1929, 134 in 1934) and hits twice (215 in 1929, 214 in 1934). He scored 100 runs or more 12 times, drove in 100 runs or more seven times, and had 200 or more hits seven times in nine years.

In 1937, Gehringer was named the American League's Most Valuable Player. He batted .371, winning his only batting title, with 209 hits, 133 runs, and a .520 slugging percentage.

Gehringer helped the Tigers to three American League pennants and one World Series championship (1934). His World Series career batting average was .321 in 20 games. In 1941, after his average dropped to .220, Gehringer announced his retirement, but he was convinced to return as a backup in 1942, because players were so scarce due to World War II.

Gehringer served as a Navy fitness instructor for four years, then became wealthy through an auto parts business. In 1951, he was hired as general manager of the Tigers and later served as the team's vice president.

Through the 2000 season, Gehringer, whose lifetime batting average was .320, ranked 16th all-time in runs scored (1,774). He was the starting second baseman in the first All-Star Game in 1933 and was inducted into the Baseball Hall of Fame in 1949.

Gibson, Bob
Born: November 9, 1935 in Omaha, Nebraska

Bob Gibson was an intimidating, glowering, dominant right-hander who spent his entire 17-year career with the St. Louis Cardinals. He had an overpowering fastball and a sharp-breaking slider. He didn't hesitate to pitch inside to those batters who crowded the plate, always aiming for the ribs.

Gibson began his career in 1959, when he also played with the Harlem Globetrotters during the offseason. He won three games in each of his first two seasons. Midway through his third season, the Cardinals fired manager Solly Hemus and replaced him with Johnny Keane, who had managed Gibson in the minor leagues. The change proved beneficial. From 1962 through 1964, Gibson won 15, 18, and 19 games, respectively. In the 1964 World Series, Gibson won two games and struck out 31 in 27 innings.

Starting in 1965, Gibson won 20 or more games in five of the next six seasons. In 1968, he had one of the best seasons in history, winning the Cy Young Award and the Most Valuable Player Award. He went 22–9 and led the league in earned run average—ERA—(1.12), strikeouts (268), and shutouts (13).

His ERA was lowest in history for a pitcher with 300 or more innings, and his 13 shutouts were the most since Grover Cleveland Alexander threw 16 in 1916. In the 1968 World Series, Gibson won two games; struck out 35, including a record 17 in game 1, and posted a 1.67 ERA.

Gibson's World Series totals were seven wins, two losses, a 1.89 ERA, two shutouts, and 92 strikeouts in 81 innings, only two fewer than Whitey Ford's record.

In 1970, Gibson won his second Cy Young Award. He went 23–7, with a 3.12 ERA, 274 strikeouts, and three shutouts. That was his last 20-win season. Over the next five seasons, he averaged 12 wins a year, including a 3–10 mark in 1975, the year he retired.

Gibson finished with a 251–174 record and a 2.91 ERA. Through the 2000 season, he ranked 11th all-time in strikeouts (3,117) and 14th in shutouts (56). He was inducted into the Baseball Hall of Fame in his first year of eligibility and was named to the All-Century Team selected in 1999.

Gibson, Josh
Born: December 21, 1911 in Buena Vista, Georgia
Died: January 20, 1947

Josh Gibson, often called the "black Babe Ruth," was one of the most prolific home run hitters of all time. But because he was black and barred from playing in the major leagues, Gibson's exact statistics will never be known.

There was no doubt, however, that Gibson was a remarkable player. Said Roy Campanella, a Hall of Fame catcher who played for the Brooklyn Dodgers, "When I broke in with the Baltimore Elite Giants in 1957, there were already a thousand legends about him. Once you saw him play, you knew all of them were true."

The Negro League Baseball Museum in Kansas City credits Gibson with 972 home runs in his 18-year career. Gibson's plaque in the Baseball Hall of Fame in Cooperstown, N.Y., says he hit "almost 800."

It has also been said that he hit as many as 84 in one season.

Gibson began his Negro League career with the Homestead Grays and enjoyed his greatest success with the Pittsburgh Crawfords in the mid-1930s. Gibson's Pittsburgh teammates included Satchel Paige, Cool Papa Bell, Judy Johnson, and Oscar Charleston. In one four-year stretch, Gibson hit .464, .384, .440, and .457.

In addition to his power at the plate, Gibson was a catcher of considerable skill. Walter Johnson, a pitcher and a charter member of the Baseball Hall of Fame, said Gibson was a better catcher than Bill Dickey, renowned as the best of his time.

There were rumors that Gibson would be the first black player to break the color barrier, and the Pittsburgh Pirates and Washington Senators considered making him a contract offer, but neither team did. Gibson's frustration caused serious bouts of depression. It also led him to excessive drinking and drugs. While he was still active, he spent some time in sanatoriums as he battled nervous breakdowns. He died of a cerebral hemorrhage in January 1947 at age 35, just three months before Jackie Robinson broke the color barrier in Major League Baseball.

Gibson was inducted into the Baseball Hall of Fame in 1972.

Glavine, Tom
Born: March 25, 1966 in Concord, Massachusetts

Tom Glavine was a baseball star and a hockey star at Billerica High School in Massachusetts. In 1984, he was selected by the Atlanta Braves in the second round of the free agent baseball draft and in the fourth round by the Los Angeles Kings of the National Hockey League entry draft.

He chose baseball and, after three-plus seasons in the minor league, joined the Braves in 1987. His first full season with the team was 1988, when he went 7–17 with a 4.56 earned run average (ERA). But three years later, Glavine, a left-hander, was one of the best pitchers in baseball, leading the National League in victories from 1991 to 1993.

In 1991, he went 20–11 with a 2.55 ERA, 192 strikeouts, and a league-leading nine complete games. He was named the winner of the Cy Young Award. In 1992, he went 20–8 with a 2.76 ERA, 129 strikeouts, and a league-leading five shutouts. In 1993, he went 22–6 with a 3.20 ERA, 120 strikeouts, and a league-leading 36 starts.

Over the next four seasons, Glavine averaged 15 wins a year as part of an outstanding pitching staff that included Greg Maddux and John Smoltz.

In 1998, Glavine won his second Cy Young Award, going 20–6, with a 2.47 ERA and 157 strikeouts. He led the league in victories and starts (35).

Glavine helped lead the Braves to five division series (2–0, 2.48), eight National League Championship Series (4–8, 3.59), and five World Series (4–3, 5.71). In the 1995 World Series, won by the Braves over the Cleveland Indians, Glavine, who went 2–0 with a 1.29 ERA, was named the Series Most Valuable Player.

Through the 2000 season, Glavine, a seven-time All-Star, was 200–125 with a 3.39 ERA, 1,810 strikeouts, and 20 shutouts.

Gomez, Lefty (Vernon)
Born: November 26, 1908 in Rodeo, California
Died: February 17, 1989

Lefty Gomez was as renowned for his wit and sense of humor as for his pitching prowess. Nicknamed "El Goofy," Gomez was famous for his happy-go-lucky attitude, locker room pranks, and unusual on-field antics, such as the time he stepped off the mound during a 1936 World Series game to watch a plane fly overhead.

But Gomez wasn't just a jester, he was an outstanding left-handed pitcher. He stood 6-2 and never weighed more than 175 pounds, but he threw the ball with surprising velocity. He had one of the best fastballs in the game and complemented that with a slow curve that left batters shaking their heads as they returned to the dugout.

Gomez joined the New York Yankees in 1930 and went 2–5 with a 5.55 earned run average (ERA). The following year, he went 21–9 with a 2.63 ERA. In 1932, he went 24–7, with a 4.21 ERA, and in 1933, he went 16–10 and led the American League in strikeouts with 163.

Gomez registered his third 20-win season in four years in 1934, and it was a masterly season. He went 26–5 and led the league in victories, winning percentage (.839), ERA (2.33), complete games (25), innings pitched (281.2), strikeouts (158), and shutouts (6). Over the next two seasons, Gomez battled arm trouble. His record fell to 12–15 in 1935 but rebounded to 13–7 in 1936.

In 1937, Gomez returned to form to win his second pitching Triple Crown. He went 21–11, leading the league in victories, ERA (2.33), and strikeouts (194). He also threw a league-leading six shutouts.

He won a combined 30 games during the next two seasons, and then arm trouble struck again, limiting Gomez to a 3–3 record in 1940.

In 1941, Gomez appeared in only 23 games, but his .750 winning percentage, based on his 15–5 record, led the league.

Gomez spent his last season with the Yankees in 1942, going 6–4. He went to the Washington Senators in 1942 and retired after losing his only start.

Gomez helped the Yankees win five World Series and was 6–0. He also won three All-Star Games. His lifetime record was 189–102 with a 3.34 ERA, and he completed 173 of his 320 starts. He was inducted into the Baseball Hall of Fame in 1972.

Gonzalez, Juan

Born: October 16, 1969 in Vega Baja, Puerto Rico

Juan Gonzalez was one of the most productive hitters in the American League during the 1990s. An outfielder and designated hitter, his first full season with the Texas Rangers was 1991, when he batted .264, hit 27 home runs, and drove in 102 runs. In each of the next two years, he led the American League in home runs (43 in 1992, 46 in 1993) and had 109 and 118 runs batted in (RBI), respectively.

In 1996, he won the first of two American League Most Valuable Player Awards, batting .314 with 47 home runs and 114 RBI. He followed that season by hitting .296 with 42 home runs and 131 RBI, and in 1998, won his second MVP Award, batting .318 with 45 home runs and a league-leading 157 RBI.

Through the 2000 season, Gonzalez, a two-time All-Star, hit 20 or more home runs nine times and had 100 or more RBI seven times. His career batting average was .293 with 362 home runs and 1,142 RBI. His slugging percentage of .572 ranked 13th all-time.

In November 1999, Gonzalez was traded to the Detroit Tigers.

Goslin, Goose (Leon)

Born: October 16, 1900 in Salem, New Jersey
Died: May 15, 1971

Goose Goslin was a feared hitter who produced in the clutch. He swung hard, crowded the plate, and dared pitchers to try to throw the ball by him.

He became the Washington Senators' starting left fielder in 1923, his third year with the team. He hit .300 and started a streak of six straight seasons and eight of nine in which he hit .300 or better. In 1928, Goslin led the American League in batting (.379).

From 1924 through 1929, Goslin drove in at least 100 runs a season, including 1924, when he led the league with 129.

Goslin led the Senators to three pennants and one World Series championship (1924). He hit seven home runs in his three World Series.

Goslin was traded to the St. Louis Browns during the 1930 season. After three solid seasons in St. Louis, in which he hit .300 twice and .299, driving in at least 100 runs each year, Goslin was traded back to the Senators. A year later, he was dealt to the Detroit Tigers. He helped the Tigers to World Series appearances in 1934 and 1935. The Tigers lost to the St. Louis Cardinals in 1934, but beat the Chicago Cubs in 1935, Goslin getting the game-winning hit with two out in the bottom of the ninth in the sixth game. Goslin returned to Washington for the 1938 season, his last. He retired after appearing in 38 games, ending an 18-year career.

Goslin's lifetime batting average was .316. He drove in 100 or more runs 11 times—one of only nine players to reach the 100-RBI plateau 10 times. Through the 2000 season, his 1,606 RBI ranked 22nd all-time. He had 2,735 hits and 248 home runs. Goslin was inducted into the Baseball Hall of Fame in 1968.

Gossage, Goose (Richard)

Born: July 5, 1951 in Colorado Springs, Colorado

Goose Gossage was one of the most effective relief pitchers of his time. He was a hard-throwing, intimidating right-hander who stood 6-3. His size, the perpetual scowl on his face, and the trademark mustache combined to make him a force.

He broke into the major leagues in 1972 with the Chicago White Sox. He spent five seasons in Chicago and led the American League in saves in 1975 with 26.

The White Sox traded him to the Pittsburgh Pirates in 1977, when he led National League relief pitchers in wins (11), and after one season with the Pirates, he signed with the New York Yankees as a free agent.

Gossage had his greatest success with the Yankees. In his six seasons with the team, he averaged 25 saves a year, twice he led the American League in saves (27 in 1978, 33 in 1980), and his earned run average (ERA) never was higher than 2.64. He helped the Yankees win two pennants (1978, '81) and the 1978 World Series.

In 1984, Gossage signed with the San Diego Padres as a free agent. In his first three seasons as a Padre, he totaled 72 saves, but in 1987, he developed arm trouble, and his effectiveness was never the same.

From 1988 through 1994, when he retired, Gossage pitched for the Chicago Cubs, San Francisco Giants, Yankees, Texas Rangers, Oakland Athletics, and Seattle Mariners. He spent the 1990 season pitching in Japan.

Gossage's career record was 124–107 with a 3.01 ERA. Through the 2000 season, he ranked sixth all-time in appearances (1,002) and 10th in saves (310).

Greenberg, Hank

Born: January 1, 1911 in New York, New York
Died: September 4, 1986

Despite playing only nine full seasons, Hank Greenberg put up some monstrous numbers. He enrolled at New York University in 1929, but dropped out to sign a contract with the Detroit Tigers. Greenberg got one at-bat in 1930, spent three seasons in the minors, and didn't rejoin the Tigers until 1933, when he became the starting first baseman.

At 6-4, Greenberg wasn't a natural in the field, nor was he very fast. But he worked hard to improve his defense, and he worked tirelessly to improve his hitting, especially his ability to hit the curveball.

Greenberg hit .300 or better in each of his first three seasons as a starter, including .328 in 1935, when he was named the American League's Most Valuable Player and helped the Tigers win the World Series. He led the league in home runs with 36 and runs batted in (RBI) with 170.

Greenberg, who broke his wrist in the second game of the Series, broke it again in 1936, when he appeared in only 12 games.

But in 1937, Greenberg, nicknamed "Hammerin' Hank," was healthy again and so were his statistics. He hit .337, with 40 home runs and a league-leading 183 RBI, the third-highest single-season total ever.

In 1938, Greenberg batted .315 and hit 58 home runs to tie Jimmie Foxx's record for a right-handed hitter and come within two of Babe Ruth's record.

Greenberg won his second Most Valuable Player Award in 1940, when he batted .340, with league-leading total in doubles (50), home runs (41), and RBI (150).

In 1941, Greenberg was drafted into the Army Air Corps and participated in the first bombing raids on Tokyo in 1944. He returned to the Tigers during the 1945 season, playing in only 78 games. But he did hit a grand slam on the final day of the season to help Detroit clinch the pennant. The Tigers went on to win the World Series, beating the Chicago Cubs in seven games. Greenberg hit .304, with two home runs and seven RBI. His career World Series average was .318.

Greenberg's last season in Detroit was 1946, and he led the American League in home runs (44) and RBI (127). He was sold to the Pittsburgh Pirates, for whom he played one season, retiring after hitting .249. After his playing days were over, Greenberg became a vice president and farm director for the Cleveland Indians. In 1959, he joined the Chicago White Sox as vice president.

Greenberg topped 30 home runs six times and 100 RBI seven times. His lifetime batting average was .313, and his average of .92 RBI a game is second only to Lou Gehrig in the 20th century. He hit 331 home runs and drove in 1,276. He was inducted into the Baseball Hall of Fame in 1956.

Griffey, Ken, Jr.

Born: November 21, 1969 in Donora, Pennsylvania

Through the 1999 season, Ken Griffey, Jr., was widely regarded as the best player in Major League Baseball and on his way to becoming one of the best of all time. The center fielder, nicknamed "Junior," could hit for power and average, and he could run, throw, and field.

Griffey, a left-handed hitter with a picture-perfect swing, was the first pick overall by the Seattle Mariners in the 1987 free agent draft. After spending 1987 and 1988 in the minor leagues, he joined the Mariners in 1989 and spent three seasons as a teammate of his father, Ken Griffey, Sr.

Griffey hit .264 with 16 home runs and 61 runs batted in (RBI) in 1989. Over the next five seasons, he hit .300 or better five times and drove in 100 or more runs three times. In 1993, he hit 45 home runs, and in 1994 he led the American League with 40 home runs.

Griffey spent much of the 1995 season on the disabled list with a wrist injury, hitting .258 with 17 home runs and 42 RBI. But in 1996, he hit .303 with 49 home runs and 140 RBI. In 1997, Griffey had a career year, hitting .304 and leading the league in home runs (56), runs (125), slugging percentage (.646), and RBI (147). He was named the American League's Most Valuable Player.

Griffey continued his power assault in 1998, hitting a league-leading 56 home runs and driving in 146, and in 1999, hitting a league-leading 48 home runs and driving in 134.

Prior to spring training in 2000, Griffey was traded to Cincinnati. He wanted to return to his hometown—his father, Ken Griffey, Sr., was a star with the Reds in the 1970s—and he wanted to play for a team that trained in Florida, where he and his family live.

Through the 2000 season, Griffey's lifetime batting average was .296 with 438 home runs and 1,270 RBI. He shared the major league record for consecutive games with one or more home runs (8, July 20–28, 1993). A 10-time Gold Glove winner and an eight-time All-Star, Griffey was named to the All-Century Team in 1999.

Grove, Lefty (Robert)
Born: March 6, 1900 in Lonaconing, Maryland
Died: May 22, 1975

Lefty Grove was famous for his blazing fastball and his nasty temper. He threw tantrums when things didn't go well, and he would give teammates the silent treatment for days after they made an error.

He overcame wildness early in his career to develop into one of the most consistent winners in baseball history.

Grove began his major league career with the Philadelphia Athletics in 1925, but not until age 25. Starting with his rookie season, he led the American League in strikeouts for seven straight years.

In 1927, Grove began a string of seven consecutive seasons in which he won at least 20 games, and he led the league in victories four times. In 1930 and 1931, Grove won the pitching Triple Crown, leading the league in victories, earned-run average (ERA), and strikeouts. He went 28–5, with a 2.54 ERA and 209 strikeouts in 1930, and in 1931, he went 31–4, with a 2.06 ERA and 175 strikeouts. Grove was also named the AL's Most Valuable Player in 1931.

Between 1927 and 1933, Grove averaged 25 wins and only eight losses a year. From 1929 through 1931, when the A's won the American League pennant each year, Grove won 79 and lost only 15.

Because of money troubles during the Depression, Grove was traded from Philadelphia to the Boston Red Sox in 1934. Arm trouble began to take its toll on Grove's fastball, but he developed an effective curve and sinker, allowing him to remain a solid pitcher. He led the league in ERA four times over the next five years.

He retired after the 1941 season with 300 wins and 141 losses—a .680 winning percentage, which ranks first all-time for pitchers with 300 wins or more. Grove was inducted into the Baseball Hall of Fame in 1947 and was named to the All-Century Team in 1999.

Gwynn, Tony
Born: May 9, 1960 in Los Angeles, California

Tony Gwynn has been one of the most consistent and productive hitters in major league history. A student of the game who has turned hitting into a science, Gwynn has produced in the clutch and demonstrated leadership throughout his career. He carried his own videocassette recorder with him so he could study his at-bats, always intent on improving his craft.

He joined the San Diego Padres in 1982 and became the full-time right fielder in 1984. The 2000 season was his 19th with the Padres.

Nine times he hit .330 or higher and seven times he hit .350 or higher. He is one of only four players to hit .350 or better in five consecutive seasons, joining Ty Cobb (11), Rogers Hornsby (6), and Al Simmons (5).

Through the 2000 season, Gwynn, a left-handed hitter, won eight National League batting titles. Only Ty Cobb, who won 12, has won more.

Gwynn won titles in 1984 (.351), 1987 (.370), 1988 (.313), 1989 (.336), 1994 (.394), 1995 (.368), 1996 (.353), and 1997 (.372).

Gwynn also led the league in hits seven times (213 in 1984, 211 in 1986, 218 in 1987, 203 in 1989, 165 in 1994, 197 in 1995, 220 in 1997) and runs once (107 in 1986). Gwynn became the 22nd player in major league history to reach the 3,000-hit plateau, achieving the milestone August 6, 1999. Only two players—Ty Cobb and Napoleon Lajoie—reached 3,000 hits in fewer games.

Tony Gwynn *San Diego Padres*

Gwynn, one of the game's most effective ambassadors, is a rarity among athletes in that he has spent his entire career with the same team. He helped the Padres to two division titles (1996, '98), two National League Championship Series (1984, '98), and two World Series (1984, '98). His overall World Series average is .371.

Through the 2000 season, his lifetime batting average was .338, which ranked 17th all-time. He also ranked 17th in hits (3,067). Gwynn had 522 doubles, 84 triples, 133 home runs, and 1,104 runs batted in. He is a five-time Gold Glove winner and a 13-time All-Star.

Hartnett, Gabby (Charles)
Born: December 20, 1900 in Woonsocket,
Rhode Island
Died: December 20, 1972

Gaby Hartnett was signed by the Chicago Cubs while still in high school and became their regular catcher in 1924, his third season with the team. Hartnett batted .300 or better five times with the Cubs, including a three-season stretch, starting in 1935, when he hit .344, .307, and .354. He was named the National League's Most Valuable Player in 1935, when he also hit 13 home runs and drove in 91.

Hartnett took part in three of the game's most storied moments. He was the opposing catcher when Babe Ruth hit his "called shot" home run in the 1932 World Series; he was the catcher in the 1934 All-Star Game when Carl Hubbell struck out Ruth, Lou Gehrig, Jimmie Foxx, Al Simmons, and Joe Cronin in succession; and he hit the "Homer in the Gloamin'" that helped the Cubs win the 1938 pennant. His home run was hit as darkness fell at Wrigley Field, and it gave the Cubs a lead they never relinquished. Hartnett was named player-manager of the Cubs in July 1938, a position he held until 1940. He spent his final season, 1941, with the New York Giants.

Hartnett's lifetime batting average was .297. He had 1,912 hits and a .984 fielding percentage. He caught 100 or more games 12 times and led the league in putouts four times, assists six times, and fielding percentage six times. He was inducted into the Baseball Hall of Fame in 1955.

Heilmann, Harry
Born: August 3, 1894 in San Francisco, California
Died: July 9, 1951

Harry Heilmann's contemporaries included Ty Cobb, Rogers Hornsby, Tris Speaker, George Sisler, Babe Ruth, and Lou Gehrig. So it's understandable that his career is overshadowed. But Heilmann was one of the best hitters of his time.

Heilmann, an outfielder who was slow afoot, joined the Detroit Tigers in 1914, played in 67 games, but was sent down to the minor leagues and didn't return to the Tigers until 1916. Over the next five seasons, Heilmann hit .300 or better twice. In 1921, Cobb was named manager of the Tigers. He instructed Heilmann to hit from a crouch and to move his feet closer together. That season Heilmann led the American League with a .394 average and 237 hits.

From 1921 through 1930, when he joined the Cincinnati Reds, Heilmann never hit lower than .328. He won three batting titles during that span (.403 in 1923, .393 in 1925, .398 in 1927).

Heilmann, a right-handed hitter, had a short, choppy stroke and was known for hitting line drives. He had three times as many doubles (542) as home runs (183). After one season in Cincinnati, Heilmann missed the 1931 season due to arthritis. He came back in 1932, but appeared in only 15 games before retiring.

In 17 seasons, Heilmann had 100 or more runs batted in eight times and 200 or more hits four times. His lifetime batting average was .342, which tied him for ninth all-time, through the 1999 season. He was inducted into the Baseball Hall of Fame in 1952, seven months after his death from lung cancer.

Henderson, Rickey
Born: December 25, 1958 in Chicago, Illinois

Rickey Henderson has been called the most effective leadoff hitter of all time and the game's best base stealer. He also has the reputation as a malingerer and a prima donna, his arrogance annoying to fans, opponents, and even his own teammates. Henderson, a left fielder, joined the Oakland Athletics in 1979 and became a full-time player in 1980, when he hit .303 and led the American League with 100 stolen bases. That was the first of 12 seasons in which he led the league in steals, including a major league–record 130 in 1982. Henderson also led the league in steals in 1981 (56), 1983 (108), 1984 (66), 1985 (80), 1986 (87), 1988 (93), 1989 (77), 1990 (65), 1991 (58), and 1998 (66).

He also led the league in runs scored five times (89 in 1981, 146 in 1985, 130 in 1986, 113 in 1989, 119 in 1990) and averaged 100 runs a year.

Through the 2000 season, Henderson had five different stints with the Athletics (1979–84, '89–93, '94–95, '98). He also played with the New York Yankees (1985–89), the Toronto Blue Jays (1993), the San Diego Padres (1996–97), the Anaheim Angels (1997), the New York Mets (1999–2000), and the Seattle Mariners (2000).

Henderson has played in three division series, five American League Championship Series, one National League Championship Series, and three World Series, in which he batted .339.

Through the 2000 season, he held major league records for stolen bases (1,334), most times leading the league in stolen bases (12), and most times leading off a game with a home run (75). He held American League records for most years with 50 or more steals (12) and most consecutive years with 50 or more stolen bases (7, 1980–86). In 1990, Henderson, on his second tour of duty with the Athletics, batted .325 with 28 home runs, 61 runs batted in, 119 runs, and 65 stolen bases. He was named the American League's Most Valuable Player in 1990.

Henderson, whose lifetime batting average was .284 with 2,893 hits, won a Gold Glove in 1981 and through the 2000 season was a 10-time All-Star.

Hodges, Gil

Born: April 4, 1924 in Princeton, Indiana
Died: April 2, 1972

Gil Hodges was a solid hitter with power and was one of the best-fielding first basemen of his time. He joined the Brooklyn Dodgers in 1943 and two years later became their starting first baseman.

From 1949 through 1955, Hodges drove in at least 100 runs a season, including a career-high 130 in 1954, when he batted .304 and hit 42 home runs. Hodges hit 23 or more home runs in 11 consecutive seasons, beginning in 1949 and six times hit 30 or more.

Hodges played in seven World Series and three times hit .300 or better (.364 in 1953, .304 in 1956, .391 in 1959). In the 1952 Series against the New York Yankees, Hodges went 0-for-21.

Hodges left the Dodgers after the 1961 season and joined the New York Mets. He retired in 1963, appearing in only 11 games. That same season, he became the manager of the Washington Senators. After the 1967 season, he was named the manager of the New York Mets. After finishing ninth in 1968, the Mets under Hodges won the National League pennant in 1969. In the World Series against the heavily favored Baltimore Orioles, the Mets won in five games.

The Mets finished in third place in 1970 and 1971, and at spring training in 1972, Hodges suffered a fatal heart attack.

Hodges played 18 seasons and had a lifetime batting average of .273. He hit 370 home runs and drove in 1,274 runs. In 2001, he failed to get the necessary votes from the Veterans Committee for induction into the Baseball Hall of Fame.

Hornsby, Rogers

Born: April 27, 1896 in Winters, Texas
Died: January 5, 1963

When Rogers Hornsby made his major league debut in September 1915, he weighed just 135 pounds and had difficulty getting the bat around. His greatest potential at the time was as a fielder. Ironically, Hornsby came to be known as perhaps the greatest right-handed hitter ever.

After the 1915 season, Horsnby was told he wasn't big and strong enough. So that winter he worked hard and increased his weight to 160 pounds, much of it muscle. He also changed his batting stance, moving to the back of the batter's box and shifting his hands to the bottom of the bat handle. The difference was immediately noticeable. He hit .313 in his first full year with the Cardinals, playing mostly at third base and shortstop, and he hit at least .300 in three of his first four seasons. In 1920, Hornsby was moved to second base, where he was acclaimed as one of the best ever to play the position. He also began a hitting streak that has gone unsurpassed, winning six consecutive batting titles (1920–25). Three times he hit over .400, and his average during that stretch was never lower than .370. His .424 average in 1924 is the highest in modern baseball history.

Hornsby won two Triple Crowns (tops in batting average, home runs, and runs batted in), the only National Leaguer to do so. In 1922, he batted .401, hit 42 homers, drove in 152 runs, and established a National League record of 450 total bases. In 1925, he batted .403, hit 39 homers, and drove in 143 runs.

During the 1925 season, Hornsby was named manager of the Cardinals. He had to be talked into taking the job, because he feared it would take away from his performance on the field. But Hornsby, in addition to winning the Triple Crown, was also named the league's Most Valuable Player. His managerial skills were effective enough to lead a demoralized team into the first division of the National League standings.

In 1926, Hornsby led the Cardinals to the National League pennant and a victory over the New York Yankees in the World Series.

Following the 1926 season, Hornsby, who was considered aloof and a loner by his teammates and a troublemaker by management, got into a contract dispute with management. He was traded to the New York Giants for Frankie Frisch.

Hornsby spent just one season with the Giants, hitting .361 and leading the league in runs scored. He was traded to the Boston Braves in 1928, when he hit .387 and won his seventh batting title.

In 1929, Hornsby was traded again, this time to the Chicago Cubs. He won his second Most Valuable Player Award, batting .380, with 39 home runs, and 149 runs batted in. Starting with the 1930 season, Hornsby, who was named manager of the Cubs, began to limit his playing time, appearing in only 100 games. He was fired by the Cubs during the 1932 season, returned to the Cardinals in 1933, then left to manage and play for the St. Louis Browns in the American League. He retired in July 1937.

Hornsby spent the next 15 years coaching and managing in the minor leagues, eventually returning to the major leagues in 1952 to manage the Browns. He was fired by June of that year, then was hired by the Cincinnati Reds in August. He lasted with the Reds until late in the 1953 season. He ended his career as a coach and scout for the Cubs and the New York Mets.

Hornsby's .358 lifetime average is second to Ty Cobb's on the all-time list and is the highest ever in the National League. He was inducted in the Baseball Hall of Fame in 1942 and was named to the All-Century Team in 1999.

Hubbell, Carl
Born: June 22, 1903 in Carthage, Missouri
Died: November 21, 1988

Carl Hubbell was the master of the screwball, which was known in his day as the butterfly, the reverse curve, or the fadeaway. He went to spring training with the Detroit Tigers in 1926, but manager Ty Cobb would not allow him to throw the pitch, for fear it would damage his arm.

In 1928, Hubbell was sold to the New York Giants, for whom he pitched for his entire career. He threw a sidearm screwball, which faded down and away from right-handed hitters, and an overhand screwball that traveled straight, until it suddenly dropped. Those gimmick pitches, along with pinpoint control, allowed him to stymie National League hitters for 16 seasons.

During his first five seasons with the Giants, Hubbell averaged 15 wins a year. From 1933 through 1938, he averaged 23 wins a year and was a combined 115–50. He led the league in victories three times during that stretch (23 in 1933, 26 in 1936, 22 in 1937). He led the league in earned run average (ERA) in 1933 (1.66), 1934 (2.30), and 1936 (2.31). In 1937, he led the league in strikeouts (159).

Hubbell was named the National League's Most Valuable Player in 1933 and 1936.

Hubbell was responsible for three of the game's most remarkable feats: an 18-inning, 1–0 win over the St. Louis Cardinals in 1933; consecutive strikeouts of Babe Ruth, Lou Gehrig, Jimmie Foxx, Al Simmons, and Joe Cronin in the 1934 All-Star Game; and 24 straight wins in the 1936 and 1937 seasons, a major league record. He finished 1936 with 16 straight wins and opened 1937 with eight more.

The Giants won three National League pennants and one World Series championship (1933) during Hubbell's career. He was 4–2 with a 1.79 ERA and 32 strikeouts in the three Series (50.1 innings pitched).

By 1938, the arm trouble that Cobb had predicted began to affect Hubbell. He underwent elbow surgery following the 1938 season and he was never as effective. He didn't retire until 1943, but over the last five years of his career, he didn't win more than 11 games in a season.

Hubbell moved into the Giants' front office as the director of player development from 1943 through 1977. From 1978 through 1985 he was a scout. He had a career record of 253–124, with a 2.98 ERA. He had 1,677 strikeouts and only 725 walks in 3,589.1 innings. He was inducted into the Baseball Hall of Fame in 1947.

Hunter, Catfish (Jim)
Born: April 8, 1946 in Hertford, North Carolina
Died: September 9, 1999

It appeared that Catfish Hunter's career as a pitcher was over before it began. He was a star in high school and in American Legion ball, but a hunting accident—Hunter's brother shot him in the foot and he lost the little toe on his right foot—seemed to be the end.

But determined to prove people wrong, Hunter was back pitching as soon as he could stand. And while most major league teams didn't want to take a chance on him, the Kansas City Athletics signed him in June 1964.

The Athletics owner, Charles O. Finley, decided Hunter needed a nickname, so he instructed Hunter to tell the press that he had been missing one night and his parents found him down by a stream, fishing for catfish. Hunter did as he was told and the name stuck.

Hunter spent 10 seasons with the Athletics and was a major reason they won three consecutive World Series (1972–74).

In May 1968, the season the Athletics moved to Oakland, Hunter threw the American League's first regular season perfect game since 1922. He defeated the Minnesota Twins 4–0. He threw 107 pitches and struck out 11.

He had his first 20-win season in 1971, going 21–11. In 1972 and 1973, he won 21 games each season and led the league in winning percentage (.750 in 1972, .808 in 1973). In 1974, he led the league in victories (25) and earned run average—ERA—(2.49) and won the American League Cy Young Award.

Just as the 1974 World Series was about to begin, Hunter claimed Finley failed to honor his contract, because an insurance payment wasn't made. As a result, Hunter claimed the contract should be voided and he should be declared a free agent. The case went to arbitration, and the arbitrator ruled in Hunter's favor. A bidding war ensued, and he eventually signed a five-year deal with the New York Yankees for an estimated $3.75 million.

In Hunter's first season with the Yankees he went 23–14 with a 2.58 ERA. He led the league in victories, complete games (30), and innings pitched (328). He won 17 games in 1976, but arm trouble began to take its toll. He spent three more seasons with the Yankees, going a combined 23–24.

Hunter's career record was 224–166, with a 3.26 ERA and 2,012 strikeouts. He had five straight 20-win seasons (1971–75), was an eight-time All-Star, and was inducted into the Baseball Hall of Fame in 1987.

Hunter was diagnosed with Lou Gehrig's disease in September 1998. He died one year later.

Irvin, Monte

Born: February 25, 1919 in Columbia, Alabama

Monte Irvin was a star in the Negro League and the Mexican League before he joined the New York Giants in 1949. After moving to New Jersey, Irvin was an all-state athlete in baseball, basketball, and football. He was offered a football scholarship to the University of Michigan, but when he requested $100 in expenses to get to Ann Arbor, Mich., he was turned down.

He went to Lincoln University in Pennsylvania instead and began playing under an assumed name, "Jimmy Nielson," for the Newark Eagles in the Negro National League in 1937.

Irvin was considered by Brooklyn Dodgers general manager Branch Rickey to be the player to break the color barrier in the major leagues, but he entered the Army in 1942, after playing in the Mexican League. Jackie Robinson was chosen instead. Irvin returned to play for the Newark Eagles in 1946, but the team disbanded in 1948. The Dodgers claimed Irvin, but Eagles owner Effie Manley wouldn't release Irvin from his contract. He played in the Cuban Winter League until 1949, when he was offered a contract by the Giants.

Irvin spent eight years in the major leagues—seven with the Giants and his final season with the Chicago Cubs in 1956. He was a part-time player his first two seasons, but in 1951, he batted .312 with 24 home runs and a league-leading 121 runs batted in (RBI). The Giants won the National League pennant, but lost to the New York Yankees in the World Series, in which Irvin batted .458 with 11 hits in 24 at-bats.

In April 1952, Irvin broke his leg in spring training while sliding. He played in only 46 games, but hit .310. In 1953, he hit .329 with 21 home runs and 97 RBI.

During his final three seasons, Irvin never hit higher than .271. He retired after the 1956 season. He went on to work as a scout for the New York Mets and later became a public relations representative for the commissioner. He was inducted into the Baseball Hall of Fame in 1973.

Jackson, Bo (Vincent)

(also football)

Born: November 30, 1962 in Bessemer, Alabama

Bo Jackson can lay claim to the title of being one of the best athletes of all time. Unfortunately, his baseball and football careers were cut short by an injury.

Jackson was the eighth of Florence Jackson Bond's 10 children. He was named after Vince Edwards, her favorite television actor, who starred in *Ben Casey*, and picked up the nickname "Bo," which was short for boarhog, because he was a wild child.

Jackson won two state decathlon championships at McAdory High in McCalla, Ala. In football, he gained 1,173 yards, averaged 10.9 yards a carry, and scored 17 touchdowns in his senior year. In baseball, he hit 20 home runs in 25 games.

The New York Yankees selected him in the second round of the 1982 amateur draft, but Jackson chose football instead, accepting a scholarship to Auburn University, where he was an outstanding running back. He gained 4,303 yards and scored 43 touchdowns during his career with the Tigers. In 1985, his senior season, he rushed for 1,786 yards, including four games of more than 200 yards, and won the Heisman Trophy as the best college football player in the nation.

Jackson was drafted by the Tampa Bay Buccaneers in 1986, but instead he pursued his lifelong dream of becoming a major league baseball player. He signed with the Kansas City Royals, spent 53 games in the minor leagues, and got a hit in his first big-league at-bat, off Steve Carlton, on September 2, 1986.

In 1987, Jackson was again eligible for the NFL draft because he didn't sign with Tampa Bay. The Oakland Raiders selected him, knowing he would be a part-time player after the baseball season was concluded. He signed a four-year contract.

His feats in both sports were legendary. He hit a 461-foot home run off future Hall of Fame fastballer Nolan Ryan. He threw a runner out, on the fly, at home plate from the warning track in center field in Seattle. He literally scaled an outfield wall to make a catch. He ran 91 yards for a touchdown against the Seattle Seahawks, running over linebacker Brian Bosworth on *Monday Night Football*, continuing through the end zone and into the tunnel.

During a 1991 playoff game against the Cincinnati Bengals, Jackson suffered a hip injury that ended both careers. The condition that resulted from the injury, avascular necrosis, led to the cartilage and bone around the hip deteriorating.

Jackson made the All-Star Game in baseball in 1989 and the Pro Bowl in football in 1990, making him the first athlete selected to play in all-star games for two major sports. But the injury occurred just weeks before the Pro Bowl, and Jackson was unable to play.

He never played football again, and when it became clear that Jackson was a shadow of his former self, the Royals released him. He was picked up by the Chicago White Sox. He played 23 games for the White Sox, then underwent hip replacement surgery. He returned in 1993, hit 16 home runs, and batted .232. He was released by the White Sox and played his final season with the Anaheim Angels.

Jackson hit .250, had 141 home runs, and 415 runs batted in during his eight seasons of Major League Baseball. As a running back for the Raiders, he gained 2,782 yards (5.4-yard average) and scored 18 touchdowns. He is the only player in NFL history to have two touchdowns of 90 or more yards.

After his retirement, Jackson returned to Auburn and earned his degree in family and child development in December 1995. He had promised his mother, who died of cancer in 1992, that he would graduate from college.

Jackson, Joe

Born: July 16, 1889 in Pickens County,
South Carolina
Died: December 5, 1951

Ty Cobb, Babe Ruth, Tris Speaker, Nap Lajoie, and Eddie Collins, among others, all considered "Shoeless" Joe Jackson the greatest natural hitter they had ever seen. The left-handed hitter stood back in the batter's box and was a big swinger, which wasn't the norm in the early 1900s.

Jackson began his professional career with the Philadelphia Athletics, for whom he played sparingly for two seasons. In 1910, he joined the Cleveland Indians. He spent five-plus seasons with the Indians. He hit .408 in 1911, .395 in 1912, .373 in 1913, and .338 in 1914. Unfortunately for Jackson, his career coincided with Ty Cobb's, so he never won a batting title. In 1911, when Jackson hit .408, Cobb hit .420.

During the 1915 season, Jackson was traded to the Chicago White Sox, where he continued to have success, batting .340 or better in three of his four full seasons. In 1918, he was limited to just 17 games, because of his wartime work in a shipyard.

Jackson hit .351 to lead the White Sox to the 1919 World Series, where they lost to the Cincinnati Reds in what was known as the "Black Sox Scandal."

Eight members of the White Sox, Jackson included, were accused of accepting a bribe to throw the World Series. A grand jury investigation produced an indictment, but all eight were acquitted of the charges. Yet Commissioner Kenesaw Mountain Landis banned them all from baseball for life.

It has always been unclear whether Jackson was really involved, and if he was involved, whether he understood what he had gotten himself into. Judging by Jackson's performance in that World Series, it was clear he didn't do anything to cause the loss. Jackson batted .375, collected a record 12 hits, and played errorless ball in the outfield. Landis' ban was enforced after the 1920 season, in which Jackson hit .382, with 121 runs batted in and a league-leading 20 triples. He returned to his native South Carolina and ran a liquor store for the rest of his life.

Along with the lifetime ban came exclusion from the Baseball Hall of Fame, even though his numbers are good enough to warrant enshrinement. Jackson's lifetime batting average of .356 ranks third all-time, behind Cobb and Rogers Hornsby.

Jackson, Reggie

Born: May 18, 1946 in Wyncote, Pennsylvania

Reggie Jackson, one of the great clutch hitters of all time, was also a lightning rod for controversy. He was combative and cocky; he threw tantrums; and he had the reputation of a "hot dog." But there was no denying his talent and charisma.

He broke into the major leagues in 1967 with the Kansas City Athletics, who moved to Oakland the following season.

While with the Athletics, Jackson led the league in home runs twice (32 in 1973, 36 in 1975) and in runs batted in (RBI) once (117 in 1973). He was named the league's Most Valuable Player in 1973.

Jackson played with the Athletics for nine seasons and helped them to five American League Championship Series appearances, three American League pennants, and three World Series titles (1972–74). He missed the 1972 World Series with a leg injury, but was named Most Valuable Player in the 1973 World Series, driving in two runs in game 6 and homering in game 7.

He was traded to the Baltimore Orioles in 1976, spent one season there, and then signed as a free agent with the New York Yankees, where he spent five seasons. Jackson, whose outspoken personality caused numerous run-ins with his teammates and manager, Billy Martin, was the center of attention as far as the New York media were concerned. But in spite of the unrest, Jackson was one of the main reasons the Yankees reached four AL Championship Series (1977–78, '80–81), and won three AL pennants (1977–78, '81) and two World Series (1977–78).

In the 1977 World Series against the Los Angeles Dodgers, Jackson solidified his title as "Mr. October." He hit four consecutive home runs—his last at-bat in game 5 and his first three at-bats in game 6. Each home run came on the first pitch and each was off a different pitcher. Overall, he batted .450, with five home runs, eight RBI, and a 1.250 slugging percentage. He was named Most Valuable Player.

In the 1978 World Series, Jackson batted .391, with two home runs and eight RBI.

Jackson led the American League in home runs in 1980 (41), batting .300 with 111 RBI. In 1981, hampered by injuries, he played in only 94 games and hit .237 with 15 home runs.

Following the 1981 season, Jackson joined the California Angels as a free agent. In five seasons, he helped the Angels to two American League Championship Series appearances (1982, '86). He also led the league in home runs in 1981 with 39.

Jackson returned to Oakland in 1987. He retired after that season, hitting .220 with 15 home runs.

Jackson played 21 seasons and had a lifetime batting average of .262. Through the 2000 season, he ranked sixth all-time in home runs (563), 17th in RBI (1,701), 15th in extra base hits (1,075), 16th in games played (2,820), and first in strikeouts (2,597). His strikeout total is 661 ahead of the Pittsburgh Pirates' Willie Stargell, who is second.

Jackson, who appeared in 12 All-Star Games, was inducted into the Baseball Hall of Fame in 1993.

Jenkins, Ferguson
Born: December 13, 1943 in Chatham, Ontario, Canada

Ferguson Jenkins, a hard-throwing right-hander, was an all-around athlete. He played hockey, basketball, and baseball. He broke in with the Philadelphia Phillies in 1965, but was traded early in the 1966 season to the Chicago Cubs. After going 6–8 with a 3.32 earned run average (ERA) in 1966, Jenkins reeled off six straight 20-win seasons, a feat made even more impressive considering that he pitched in Wrigley Field, which is not a pitcher-friendly ballpark.

From 1967 through 1972, Jenkins averaged 21 victories a year. He led the National League in games started three times (40 in 1968, 42 in 1969, 39 in 1971), in complete games three times (20 in 1967, 24 in 1970, 30 in 1971), and in strikeouts once (273 in 1969).

Jenkins' best season with the Cubs came in 1971, when he went 24–13, with a 2.77 ERA and 263 strikeouts. He won the National League Cy Young Award.

After slipping to 14–16 in 1973, Jenkins was traded to the Texas Rangers. He went 25–12 in 1974 and led the American League in victories and complete games (29). He was named the American League's Comeback Player of the Year.

That was the last 20-win season of Jenkins' career. In 1976, he was traded to the Boston Red Sox, and after two seasons, returned to the Texas Rangers. In four seasons with the Rangers, he won 51 games. He went back to the Cubs in 1982 and retired after the 1983 season.

Jenkins' career record was 284–226, with a 3.34 ERA. Through the 2000 season, he ranked 25th all-time in victories, 10th in strikeouts (3,192), and second in home runs allowed (484). He is the only pitcher to record 3,000 strikeouts without walking 1,000.

In 1980, Jenkins was arrested at a Canadian airport and charged with drug possession. He denied the charge and alleged he was set up. Many believe the incident delayed his induction into the Baseball Hall of Fame, which came in 1991, two years after he was eligible.

Jeter, Derek
Born: June 26, 1974 in Pequannock, New Jersey

Derek Jeter has been a big reason why the New York Yankees have played and won three World Series in his four years with the club.

He joined the team as the full-time shortstop in 1996. He batted .314 with 10 home runs, 78 runs batted in (RBI), and was named the American League's Rookie of the Year. In 1998, he batted .324 with 19 home runs and 84 RBI, and in 1999, he batted .349 with 24 home runs, 102 RBI, and a league-leading 219 hits.

Jeter, one of the most popular players on the Yankees, hit .319 in three American League Championship Series and .315 in three World Series.

Through the 2000 season, Jeter, a three-time All-Star, had a lifetime batting average of .322 with 1,008 hits, 78 home runs, and 414 RBI.

Johnson, Randy
Born: September 10, 1963 in Walnut Creek, California

Randy Johnson was one of the most dominating and feared pitchers in baseball during the 1990s. A 6-10, 225-pound left-hander, he was so overpowering, especially against left-handed hitters, that many left-handers wouldn't face him.

He began his career in the Montreal Expos organization, but was traded to the Seattle Mariners in 1989. In his first three full seasons with the Mariners, he won 14, 13, and 12 games, respectively; led the American League in walks in each season; and led the league in strikeouts in 1992 (241).

Johnson began to develop more control. In 1993, he went 19–8 with a 3.24 earned run average (ERA), 99 walks, and an American League–leading 308 strikeouts. He won 13 games and led the league in strikeouts (204) in 1994, and then had a breakout season. In 1995, Johnson went 18–2 and led the league in winning percentage (.900), ERA (2.48), and strikeouts (294). He was named the American League Cy Young Award winner. Johnson was plagued by injuries in 1996 and spent most of the season on the disabled list. In 1997, he went 20–4 with a 2.33 ERA, 291 strikeouts, and a league-leading winning percentage (.833).

In July 1998, Johnson was traded to the Houston Astros because of a contract dispute and because the Astros were looking for a pitcher to help them in a pennant race. He was 9–10 with the Mariners with a 4.33 ERA, but with the Astros, he went 10–1 with a 1.28 ERA, four shutouts, and 116 strikeouts, and helped win the

National League Central. In the division series against the San Diego Padres, Johnson was 0–2.

Johnson became a free agent following the 1998 season and signed with the Arizona Diamondbacks. In 1999, he won his second Cy Young Award, going 17–9. He led the league in ERA (2.48), games started (35), complete games (12), innings pitched (271.2), and strikeouts (364), the fourth highest single-season total in major league history. He became one of three pitchers to win a Cy Young Award in each league.

Through 2000, Johnson's career record was 179-95 with a 3.20 ERA. He ranked 12th all-time in strikeouts (3,040) and 14th all-time in winning percentage (.653).

Johnson, a seven-time All-Star, held the major league single-game record for most strikeouts by a left-hander (19, twice); he held the National League record for most games with 10 strikeouts or more (10, 1999); and he pitched a no-hitter against Detroit in June 1990.

Johnson, Walter

Born: November 6, 1887 in Humboldt, Kansas
Died: December 10, 1946

Walter "Big Train" Johnson is widely regarded as the best pitcher in baseball history. He was a hard-throwing, power-pitching right-hander who achieved great success while pitching for the Washington Senators, who usually fielded weak teams. From 1910 through 1920, the Senators averaged 76 wins a year, with Johnson averaging 26 wins for the same period.

Johnson joined the Senators in 1907, without having played in the minor leagues. In 1908, he threw three shutouts in a four-day period against the New York Yankees and allowed a total of 12 hits.

After going 14–14 that season and 13–25 in 1909, Johnson began a remarkable string in 1910: He won at least 20 games for 10 consecutive seasons, including 25 wins or more in seven consecutive seasons. Johnson went 33–12 in 1912, winning 16 straight, and 36–7 in 1913 with a 1.13 earned run average (ERA) and a scoreless innings streak of 55.2. He was voted the American League Most Valuable Player in 1913.

Said Ty Cobb about what to expect when facing Johnson: "just speed, raw speed, blinding speed, too much speed."

Johnson led the American League in strikeouts a record 12 times, including eight straight (1911–19). He also led the league in ERA five times.

Johnson won 38 games by a 1–0 score, including his only no-hitter, against Boston in 1920. He lost 65 games when the Senators were shut out, including 27 by 1–0 scores.

After four relatively mediocre seasons, there were those who thought Johnson's career might be over. But

in 1924, he returned to form, going 23–7, throwing six shutouts, striking out 158, and registering a 2.72 ERA, all of which led the league. The Senators won their first pennant that season, and Johnson claimed his second Most Valuable Player Award. He lost his two World Series starts, but pitched four innings of relief in the seventh game as Washington defeated the New York Giants.

Johnson's last season was in 1927, when he went 20–7. He managed the Senators for four years, then took over as Cleveland's manager in 1933. He was fired in 1935. Johnson won 417 games in his career, second all-time to Cy Young. Through the 1999 season, he ranked seventh all-time in strikeouts (3,508), third in innings pitched (5,923.2), seventh in earned-run average (2.17), and first in shutouts (110).

In addition to his pitching records, Johnson was also a fine fielder. He had six seasons in which he didn't commit an error.

In 1936, Johnson was elected as a charter member to the Baseball Hall of Fame and was named to the All-Century Team in 1999.

Jones, Chipper (Larry)

Born: April 24, 1972 in Deland, Florida

In the latter half of the 1990s, Chipper Jones developed into one of the outstanding players in the game. He was the first pick overall by the Atlanta Braves in the 1990 free agent draft. He played in eight games with the Braves in 1993, missed the entire 1994 season due to injury, and became the Braves' starting third baseman in 1995, when he hit .265 with 23 home runs and 86 runs batted in (RBI).

Over the next five seasons, Jones hit .309 or better three times; he had 30 or more home runs four times; and he drove in 100 or more runs five times.

In 1999, Jones hit a career-high .319 with 45 home runs and 110 RBI. He was named the National League's Most Valuable Player. The 45 home runs were a National League single-season record for a switch hitter.

Jones has helped the Braves reach the postseason in each of his six seasons. He hit .310 in the division series, .324 in the National League Championship Series, and .273 in three World Series.

Through 2000, Jones, a four-time All-Star, had a .302 career batting average with 189 homes runs and 635 RBI.

Kaline, Al

Born: December 19, 1934 in Baltimore, Maryland

Al Kaline wasn't a flashy player, but his consistent excellence, at the plate and in the outfield, made him a Hall of Famer.

Kaline joined the Detroit Tigers in 1953, appeared in 30 games, and hit .250. Two years later, at age 20 and in just his second season as a full-time player, he won the American League batting title (.340), with a league-leading 200 hits. He was the youngest batting champion in major league history. Over the next eight seasons, Kaline hit .300 or better six times.

Kaline was also an outstanding outfielder, with a strong throwing arm. He won 10 Gold Gloves and led American League outfielders in fielding percentage twice (.993, 1966; 1.000, 1971).

Tigers reached the postseason just once in Kaline's career, in 1968. In the World Series against the St. Louis Cardinals, the Tigers rallied from a 3–1 deficit to win. Kaline hit .379 with 11 hits, two home runs, and eight runs batted in.

He had to labor under the weight of great expectations because of his early success. As a result, he would go through periods of depression. But his career statistics prove that he more than fulfilled his promise.

Kaline had a lifetime batting average of .297. Through the 2000 season, he ranked 22nd all-time in hits (3,007), 14th in games played (2,834), 19th in at-bats (10,116), and 20th in total bases (4,852). He hit 399 home runs, played in 16 All-Star Games, and was inducted into the Baseball Hall of Fame in 1980.

Keeler, Willie

Born: March 3, 1872 in Brooklyn, New York
Died: January 1, 1923

"Wee" Willie Keeler relied on speed and bat control to become one of the finest hitters of his time. He was a masterful bunter and perfected the "Baltimore chop," bouncing the ball into the hard infield dirt, over the heads of charging infielders. He broke into the major leagues in 1892, appearing in 41 games during his first two seasons. He became a full-time outfielder in 1894 and hit .300 or better for 13 consecutive seasons. Eight times he hit .350 or better, and twice he led the National League in hitting—.424 in 1897 and .385 in 1898. He also led the league in hits three times (239, 1897; 216, 1898; 204, 1900).

He continued to be an outstanding hitter for the first seven seasons of the 20th century, when he hit .362, .355, .338, .318, .343, .302, and .304. But in 1907, his average plummeted to .234. He became a part-time player for the last three seasons of his career, and he retired in 1910.

Keeler's lifetime batting average of .343 ranks eighth all-time. He and Lou Gehrig are tied for the most seasons—eight—with 200 or more hits and 100 or more runs scored. Keeler was inducted into the Baseball Hall of Fame in 1939.

Killebrew, Harmon

Born: June 29, 1936 in Payette, Idaho

Harmon Killebrew's nickname, "Killer," was the perfect fit. He was one of the most powerful and consistent home run hitters ever. He wasn't fast, nor was he a particularly good fielder, which explains why he was shifted from third base to first base to the outfield throughout his career. But he more than made up for those deficiencies with his home run stroke.

Killebrew broke into the major leagues in 1954 with the Washington Senators. He was painfully shy as a rookie, and he remained a soft-spoken, respectful player throughout his career.

For the first five years of his career, he was a part-time player who never appeared in more than 44 games in any one season. Finally in 1959, he moved into the starting lineup, primarily as a third baseman, and led the American League with 42 home runs. He hit 31 home runs in 1960, the team's final year in Washington before moving to Minnesota and becoming the Twins.

Killebrew hit 46 home runs in 1961 and led the league for the next three years, hitting 48, 45, and 49, respectively. He also led the league in runs batted in (RBI) with 126 in 1962.

Killebrew failed to hit 40 home runs in 1965 (25), when he was injured and missed 49 games, or in 1966 (39), but in 1967, he hit 44 to again lead the league. Injuries in 1968 limited him to 100 games and 17 home runs. He rebounded in 1969 with league-leading totals in home runs (40) and RBI (140). He was named Most Valuable Player in the American League.

In 1970, Killebrew had his last 40-home-run season, hitting 41 with 113 RBI. He led the league in RBI in 1971 (119), but his home run production dropped to 28.

Killebrew left the Twins after the 1974 season and spent the 1975 season with the Kansas City Athletics before retiring.

Killebrew appeared in one World Series, in 1965 when the Twins lost to the Los Angeles Dodgers in seven games. He hit .286 in the Series with one home run and two RBI. He also played in two American League Championship Series (1969–70), hitting .211 with two home runs and four RBI.

Through the 2000 season, his 573 home runs ranked fifth all-time, and his 1,584 RBI were 26th. No American League right-handed hitter has more home runs than Killebrew, and in major league history only Babe Ruth, Mark McGwire, and Ralph Kiner hit home runs more frequently than Killebrew, who hit one every 14.22 at-bats. Killebrew was such a dangerous hitter that he led the league in walks four times and seven times walked more than 100 times a season. He finished with 100 or more RBI in a season nine times. He was inducted into the Baseball Hall of Fame in 1984.

Kiner, Ralph

Born: October 27, 1922 in Santa Rita, New Mexico

Ralph Kiner was a home run machine. His career was relatively short—10 years—but his ability to hit home runs was uncanny. His home run percentage (number of home runs per 100 times at-bat) of 7.1 was second to Babe Ruth's 8.5.

Kiner, 6-2, 195 pounds, was solidly built, with broad shoulders and strong arms. He joined the Pittsburgh Pirates in 1946, became their starting left fielder, and led the National League in home runs with 23.

Kiner, a right-handed hitter, led the league or tied for the lead in home runs for the first seven seasons of his career, the longest consecutive streak in major league history. Ruth is second with six straight (1926–31).

Kiner hit 51 in 1947, 40 in 1948, 54 in 1949, 47 in 1950, 42 in 1951, and 37 in 1952. That's an average of 36 home runs a season.

Kiner also led the league in slugging percentage three times (.639 in 1947, .658 in 1949, .627 in 1951) and runs batted in once (127 in 1949).

During the 1953 season, Kiner was traded to the Chicago Cubs. He hit 35 homers in 1953 and 22 the following year. In 1955, he went to the Cleveland Indians. He hit 18 home runs that season, his last. Kiner was forced to retire because of chronic back problems.

Kiner was a one-dimensional player. He was a mediocre fielder and a ponderously slow base runner. But in spite of his healthy home run swing, he averaged only 75 strikeouts per season, and he walked an average of 101 times a season, leading the league three times. He also scored 100 or more runs six times, including 1951, when he led the league with 124.

Kiner's lifetime batting average was .279. He hit 369 home runs and drove in 1,115. Through the 2000 season, he worked as a broadcaster for the New York Mets. He was inducted into the Baseball Hall of Fame in 1975.

Klein, Chuck

Born: October 7, 1904 in Indianapolis, Indiana
Died: March 28, 1958

Chuck Klein had such an impressive five-year stretch during the Depression that he earned comparisons to Babe Ruth.

Klein, a left-handed hitting outfielder, joined the Philadelphia Phillies during the 1928 season, appeared in 64 games, and batted .360. That season foreshadowed the next five, when he never hit lower than .337 nor hit fewer than 28 home runs.

Starting in 1929, Klein hit .356, .386, .337, .348, and a league-leading .368. He led the league in hits twice (226 in 1932, 223 in 1933), home runs four times (43 in 1929, 31 in 1931, 38 in 1932, 28 in 1933), runs three times (158 in 1930, 121 in 1931, 152 in 1933), slugging percentage three times (.584 in 1931, .646 in 1932, .602 in 1933) doubles twice (59 in 1930, 44 in 1933), and runs batted in (RBI) twice (121 in 1931, 120 in 1933).

In 1932, Klein was named the National League Most Valuable Player, and in 1933 he won the Triple Crown, when he led the league in batting average, home runs, and RBI.

Klein also was a fine outfielder. In 1930, he recorded 44 assists, a 20th-century record that still stands.

In 1934, the Phillies, who were in financial trouble, sold Klein to the Chicago Cubs. He never came close to duplicating his statistics of 1929–33. Only once did he hit more than 21 homers in a season and only once did he bat higher than .306. Klein spent two-plus seasons in Chicago and returned to the Phillies midway through the 1936 season, when he hit four home runs in a game against the Pittsburgh Pirates. Klein is one of only 12 players to accomplish that feat.

Klein was traded to Pittsburgh during the 1939 season, but returned to the Phillies in 1940. He became a part-time player and pinch hitter with the Phillies. He retired in 1944 after appearing in four games.

Klein's lifetime batting average was .320. He had 2,076 hits, 300 home runs, and 1,202 RBI. He was inducted into the Baseball Hall of Fame in 1980.

Koufax, Sandy (Sanford)

Born: December 30, 1935

Sandy Koufax's career took a while to get started, and it ended relatively quickly, but in between, he became one of the dominant pitchers of all time.

Koufax went to the University of Cincinnati on a basketball scholarship in 1953. But after he was encouraged to join the baseball team and struck out 51 batters in 32 innings, he left college and signed with the Brooklyn Dodgers for a bonus of $14,000.

During his first spring training in 1955, Koufax, a left-hander, was so nervous and tense he couldn't pitch effectively, but he went north with the Dodgers because of a rule that mandated that any player receiving a bonus be kept on the major league team. For his first six seasons (1955–60), Koufax was 36–40, but he was plagued by wildness and walked an average of six batters per nine innings.

But during the spring of 1961, Koufax had a revelation of sorts. Thanks to advice given by catcher Norm Sherry, Koufax stopped trying to overthrow his fastball. Instead of forcing it, he threw it easier and mixed in some change-ups. The difference was immediate. He won six of his first seven starts that season and finished 18–13 with a 3.52 earned run average (ERA). He led the league with 269 strikeouts, pitched 15 complete games, and surpassed 200 innings for the first time in his career.

That season was the start of an amazing run. From 1961 through 1966, Koufax was virtually unhittable. He went 129–47; led the National League in ERA five straight years, beginning in 1962; won 25 or more games three times; and won three Cy Young Awards (1963, '65–66) as the league's best pitcher. He also led the league in shutouts three times, in strikeouts four times, and in innings pitched twice.

In 1963, Koufax was named the National League's Most Valuable Player and the Associated Press Male Athlete of the Year. He went 25–5, with 11 shutouts, 306 strikeouts, and a 1.88 ERA. He helped the Dodgers to the World Series, where they swept the New York Yankees. Koufax was 2–0 with a 1.50 ERA and a Series-record 23 strikeouts in 18 innings.

In the 1965 World Series victory against Minnesota, Koufax went 2–1 with a 0.38 ERA and 29 strikeouts in 24 innings.

Koufax won 26 games in 1965 and led the league in winning percentage (.765), ERA (2.04), complete games (27), innings pitched (335.2), and strikeouts (382). The following year, he went 27–9, leading the league in ERA (1.73), complete games (27), innings pitched (323), strikeouts (317), and shutouts (5).

And then he retired. Koufax pitched in pain for most of his last three seasons, arthritis ruining his arm. He quit rather than risk permanent damage to his arm. Because his career was so short—he won only 165 games—Koufax isn't among the all-time leaders in any major categories. But because he was so overpowering during those last six years, he was inducted into the Hall of Fame in 1972, the youngest ever to be enshrined.

Koufax averaged 10.5 strikeouts per nine innings over the last six seasons of his career, and he threw no-hitters in four consecutive seasons (1963–66), the last of which was a perfect game against the Chicago Cubs.

Koufax, whose mystique was enhanced by the manner in which he protected his privacy during and after his career, was named to the All-Century Team.

Lajoie, Napoleon

Born: September 5, 1874 in Woonsocket, Rhode Island
Died: February 7, 1959

Nap Lajoie, a graceful fielder at second base, was also one of the best hitters of his time. He began his pro career with the Philadelphia Phillies in 1896, and after two years as a first baseman, he was moved to second base, where he excelled.

He spent five seasons in all with the Phillies, hitting .320 or better in each, then went to Philadelphia Athletics of the newly established American League. Lajoie, who was earning the National League minimum of $2,400 with the Phillies, was lured to the Athletics when

he was offered $4,000 by manager Connie Mack. Lajoie gave the new league instant credibility.

In his first season with the Athletics (1901), Lajoie hit .422 and led the league in runs (145), hits (232), doubles (48), home runs (14), and runs batted in (125). In addition to being the first American Leaguer to win the Triple Crown, Lajoie led the Athletics to the pennant.

But in 1902, the Phillies obtained an injunction, prohibiting Lajoie from playing for the Athletics. American League president Ban Johnson ordered that Lajoie play for the Cleveland Indians, where he spent the next 12 1/2 seasons.

Lajoie won the batting title in 1903 (.355) and 1904 (.381). He hit .300 or better 10 times with the Indians, including eight seasons of .330 or better. In 1905, Lajoie became the Indians' player-manager. He continued both jobs until resigning as manager in 1909. It wasn't until 1914 that his average began to decline. He hit .258 in his final season with the Indians, then returned to the Athletics, for whom he played his final two years, retiring in 1916.

Lajoie had a lifetime batting average of .338, which ranked 18th all-time through the 2000 season. He ranked 12th all-time in hits (3,244) and sixth in doubles (658). Lajoie was inducted into the Baseball Hall of Fame in 1937.

Larsen, Don

Born: August 7, 1929 in Michigan City, Indiana

Don Larsen spent 14 years in the major leagues and played with 10 different teams. His career record (81–91) and his earned run average—ERA—(3.78) are mediocre at best. But he is remembered for throwing the only perfect game in World Series history.

Larsen joined the New York Yankees in 1955 and went 9–2 with a 3.06 ERA. In 1956, he went 11–5 with a 3.26 ERA as the Yankees won the American League pennant. He started the second game of the World Series against the Brooklyn Dodgers, but didn't make it out of the second inning. Larsen was the starting pitcher in game 5 with the Series tied 2–2.

Larsen retired all 27 batters he faced and went to a three-ball count only once. The closest the Dodgers came to a hit was a long fly ball to left center on which Mickey Mantle made a running, backhanded grab. Larsen got the final out on a called third strike on Dale Mitchell.

Lemon, Bob

Born: September 22, 1920 in San Bernardino, California
Died: January 11, 2000

Bob Lemon began his professional career as a shortstop, but was converted into a pitcher in 1946 by Cleveland

Indians manager Lou Boudreau. In 1948, his third season with the Indians, Lemon went 20–14 and led the league in complete games (20), innings pitched (293.2), and shutouts (10). He also threw a no-hitter against the Detroit Tigers. In the 1948 World Series, which the Indians won over the Boston Braves in six games, Lemon was 2–0 with a 1.65 earned run average (ERA).

From 1948 through 1956, Lemon won 20 or more games seven times. In 1950, he went 23–11 with a 3.84 ERA and league-leading totals in games started (37), complete games (22), innings pitched (288), and strikeouts (170). He also led the league in victories in 1954 (23) and 1955 (18).

In 1957, Lemon suffered a leg injury that for all intents and purposes ended his career. He retired in 1958 after making one appearance.

Lemon scouted for several teams and managed in the International League and the Pacific Coast League. He managed the Kansas City Athletics from 1970 through 1972. In 1977, he was named the manager of the Chicago White Sox. He was fired 74 games into the 1978 season, but hired by the New York Yankees to replace the controversial Billy Martin. Lemon's low-key personality was credited with helping the Yankees win the pennant and the World Series.

Lemon was fired in 1979 and then brought back in 1981 and 1982. His record as a manager was 430–403.

His career record on the mound was 207–128 with a 3.23 ERA. A seven-time All-Star, Lemon was inducted into the Baseball Hall of Fame in 1976.

Leonard, Buck (Walter)

Born: September 8, 1907 in Rocky Mount,
North Carolina
Died: November 27, 1997

Buck Leonard was known as the Lou Gehrig of the Negro Leagues. Along with Josh Gibson, who was known as the Babe Ruth of the Negro Leagues, they formed a powerful 1-2 combination for the Homestead Grays.

Leonard, a left-handed first baseman, joined Homestead in 1934 and spent his entire 17-year career with the team, which also featured pitcher Satchel Paige.

Although the Negro League statistics were not up to the precise standards of the National and American Leagues, according to *The Baseball Encyclopedia,* Leonard hit .300 or better 10 times and .400 or better three times. He also was a solid fielder with a strong arm and good range.

Because of the color barrier, Leonard never got a chance to play in the major leagues. He was offered a chance to join the St. Louis Browns in 1952, but refused, realizing he was past his prime at age 44. But he did face major league players in the offseason barnstorming tours.

Leonard would play in as many as three games a day. Said Roy Campanella, a Hall of Fame catcher, "He was major league all the way." After Leonard retired, he became a vice president of the Class A minor league team in Rocky Mount, N.C. He was inducted into the Baseball Hall of Fame in 1972.

Maddux, Greg

Born: April 14, 1966 in San Angelo, Texas

Greg Maddux isn't overpowering or menacing on the mound. He's just the opposite: cagey, crafty, and scientific. He frustrates batters with his pinpoint control and command of all his pitches. He works quickly, efficiently, and rarely walks a batter.

He broke into the major leagues with the Chicago Cubs in 1986. He won 18 games in 1988 and 19 in 1989. It was 1992 when he had a breakthrough season, going 20–11 with a 2.18 earned run average (ERA). He struck out 199, walked only 70 in a league-leading 268 innings pitched, and won the National League Cy Young Award.

Following the 1992 season, Maddux signed with the Atlanta Braves as a free agent. He won the Cy Young Award in each of the next three seasons, making him the only pitcher in major league history to win four Cy Young Awards consecutively.

In 1993, Maddux went 20–10, with a league-leading 2.36 ERA. He also led the league in games started (36), complete games (8), and innings pitched (267).

In 1994, he was 16–6 and led the league in victories, ERA (1.56), complete games (10), innings pitched (202), and shutouts (3).

In 1995, Maddux was 19–2 and led the league in victories, winning percentage (.905), ERA (1.63), complete games (10), innings pitched (209.2), and shutouts (3).

From 1996 through 2000, Maddux was a combined 81–38. He led the league in winning percentage in 1997, going 19–4 (.826), and in ERA in 1998 (2.22).

One of the most telling measures of Maddux's effectiveness is the comparison between his ERA and that of the rest of the league. For six years (1992–97), his ERA was between 1.3 and 2.6 runs better than the league average. No other ERA leaders, regardless of their ERAs, have been so far ahead of the league average ERA.

Maddux appeared in six National League Division Series (4–2), seven National League Championship Series (4–6, 3.58 ERA), and three World Series (2–3, 2.09 ERA).

Through the 2000 season, Maddux was 240–135 with a 2.83 ERA. He struck out 2,350, walked 733, and threw 31 shutouts. He won the Gold Glove from 1990 to 2000.

Mantle, Mickey

Born: October 20, 1931 in Spavinaw, Oklahoma
Died: August 13, 1995

Like Babe Ruth and Joe DiMaggio before him, Mickey Mantle was a member of the New York Yankees who became a baseball icon. Mantle could hit for average and power, and he could run with superior speed. He was soft-spoken and down-home, yet charismatic.

Mantle, a country boy from Oklahoma and the son of a semipro baseball player, was named after Mickey Cochrane, one of the best catchers in baseball history. He could switch hit by the time he was five, and when he joined the Yankees in 1951 at age 19, greatness was predicted.

Mantle was anointed as the successor to DiMaggio in center field, but he struggled at first, the pressure and strain taking their toll. So the Yankees sent him to the minors, where he got only one hit in his first 22 at-bats. He complained to his father that he wasn't good enough and that he'd never make it.

Said Elvin "Mutt" Mantle, "Well, Mick, if that's all the guts you have, I think you better quit."

He finished the season in the minors by hitting .410 and was called up to the Yankees near the end of the season. He started the World Series in right field. But in the second game of the Series, Mantle, chasing a fly ball, caught his spikes in a storm drain at Yankee Stadium and tore cartilage in his right knee. It would be the first of many injuries that plagued him throughout his career.

With DiMaggio retired, Mantle took over in center field in 1952, but his struggles continued, and the fans voiced their displeasure.

Finally, in 1954, Mantle began to perform as advertised. He batted .300 with 27 home runs, 102 runs batted in (RBI), and a league-leading 129 runs.

In 1955, he led the American League with 37 home runs, and in 1956, he won the Triple Crown, leading the league with a .353 average, 52 home runs, and 130 RBI. He was named the league's Most Valuable Player that year and in 1957, when he batted .365, with 34 home runs and 94 RBI.

Mantle led the league in home runs in 1958 with 42 and again in 1960 with 40. In 1961, he hit 54, but lost the home run race to his teammate, Roger Maris, who hit 61 and broke Babe Ruth's record of 60.

In 1962, Mantle won his third Most Valuable Player Award, batting .321, with 30 home runs and 89 RBI. It was his last Mantle-like season. Injuries began to take their toll. He suffered from shin splints, torn muscles, pinched nerves, and a broken foot. His legs had to be heavily taped before each game.

Mantle hit .300 for the last time in 1964, and he retired following the 1968 season. At a ceremony held at Yankee Stadium early in the 1969 season, the fans gave him a 10-minute standing ovation.

Mantle helped lead the Yankees to 12 American League pennants and seven World Series championships during his 18-year career. Through the 2000 season, his 536 career home runs ranked ninth on the all-time list. In World Series play, Mantle was the all-time leader in runs (42), home runs (18), RBI (40), and total bases (123). He was second in three other categories.

Were it not for his many injuries and his alcoholism, Mantle's numbers, impressive as they are, could have been off the charts.

Mantle, inducted into the Baseball Hall of Fame in 1974 and named to the All-Century Team in 1999, died of liver cancer in August 1995 while awaiting a transplant. He remained a hero until the end.

Said NBC sportscaster Bob Costas, who delivered the eulogy at Mantle's funeral: "He was our symbol of baseball at a time when the game meant something to us that perhaps it no longer does. Mickey Mantle had those dual qualities so seldom seen—exuding dynamism and excitement, but at the same time, touching your heart, flawed, wounded. We knew there was something poignant about Mickey Mantle before we knew what poignant meant. We didn't just root for him, we felt for him."

Marichal, Juan

Born: October 20, 1937 in Laguna Verde, Dominican Republic

Juan Marichal's delivery, which featured his left leg kicking high above his head, confused hitters. His control and variety of pitches got them out. He was one of the most accomplished pitchers of his era, but he had the misfortune of pitching at the same time as Sandy Koufax of the Los Angeles Dodgers and Bob Gibson of the St. Louis Cardinals. But even though Marichal, a right-hander, never won a Cy Young Award, he was nonetheless one of the best pitchers ever.

He joined the Giants midway through the 1960 season, going 6–2 with a 2.66 earned run average (ERA), and pitching a one-hit 1–0 shutout in his major league debut against the Philadelphia Phillies. The following season, he joined the starting rotation and was a mainstay for the Giants for the next 10 years.

In 1963, he led the National League in victories with 25 and innings pitched with 321.1. It was the first of six 20-win seasons in seven years. He won 21 games in 1964; 22, with a league-leading 10 shutouts, in 1965; 25, with a league-leading .806 winning percentage, in 1966; 26, with a league-leading 30 complete games and 325.2 innings pitched, in 1968; and 21, with a league-leading 2.10 ERA and eight shutouts, in 1969.

From 1964 through 1969, Marichal averaged 24 complete games in 35 starts. In the four years he might have won the Cy Young—1963, 1964, 1966, 1968—his record was 97–31. The combined record of the Cy Young winners (Koufax, twice; Gibson; Dean Chance) was 94–32.

Marichal won more games in the 1960s—191—than any other major league pitcher. He threw a fastball, curve, slide, and screwball, but threw them at different speeds and using different motions.

Following his 21-win season in 1969, Marichal never won 20 again. In his last two seasons with the Giants (1972–73), he was a combined 17–31. He appeared in 11 games with the Boston Red Sox in 1974 and in two games with the Dodgers in 1975 before retiring.

His lifetime record was 243–142 (.631 winning percentage) with a 2.89 ERA. He struck out 2,303 and registered 52 shutouts. In 3,509 innings, he walked only 709 batters, an average of one every 4.94 innings. He was inducted into the Baseball Hall of Fame in 1983.

Marichal's greatness, however, is tarnished by an incident involving Dodgers catcher John Roseboro. In 1965, during a brawl, Marichal hit Roseboro over the head with a bat.

Maris, Roger
Born: September 10, 1934 in Hibbing, Minnesota
Died: December 14, 1985

Roger Maris broke one of baseball's most storied records: Babe Ruth's mark of 60 home runs in a season. But the experience was anything but enjoyable for Maris, who was overwhelmed by the pressure and disliked by the fans, many of whom considered him unworthy of breaking Ruth's record.

After rejecting a football scholarship offer from the University of Oklahoma and being told by the Chicago Cubs that he would never make it in the major leagues, Maris signed with the Cleveland Indians. He made it to the Indians in 1957, was traded to the Kansas City Athletics in 1958, and was traded again to the New York Yankees in 1960. In his first season with the Yankees, Maris batted .283, hit 39 home runs, and led the American League in slugging percentage (.581) and runs batted in—RBI—(112). He was named the American League's Most Valuable Player.

In 1961, Maris and his teammate Mickey Mantle waged a season-long battle for the home run title. As the pressure increased, Maris showed its effects. He was short with sportswriters, reluctant to do interviews, and began to lose his hair in big clumps. By the middle of September, Mantle tailed off, largely because of a hip injury. He finished with 54 home runs. But Maris maintained the pace. He entered the 154th game of the season against the Baltimore Orioles with 58 home runs. He hit no. 58 and just missed no. 59, which went foul.

He finally hit no. 61 on the final day of the season off Tracy Stallard of the Boston Red Sox. His record was

achieved in 161 games. Ruth hit 60 home runs in a 154-game season.

Maris, who hit .269 with a league-leading 132 runs and 141 RBI, won his second straight American League Most Valuable Player Award and was also named Associated Press Male Athlete of the Year.

Maris hit 33 home runs and had 100 RBIs in 1962, but he never again hit more than 26 home runs in a season or had more than 86 RBI.

In 1967, Maris was traded to the St. Louis Cardinals, but he left New York a bitter man. The Yankees questioned the severity of a hand injury that Maris complained about. That injury, he claimed, was responsible for his average dipping to .233 and his home run total to 13, with only 43 RBI. As it turned out, he had played the entire season with a broken bone in his hand. The Yankees' doctors had not been able to diagnose the injury.

Maris spent the final two seasons of his career playing in two World Series. He retired following the 1968 season.

Maris, who also was an outstanding right fielder and an intelligent base runner, had a lifetime batting average of .260, with 275 home runs and 850 RBI.

Maris, who died of cancer in 1985, had his single-season home run record broken in 1998 by Mark McGwire (70) of the Cardinals and Sammy Sosa (66) of the Chicago Cubs.

Martinez, Pedro
Born: July 25, 1971 in Manoguayabo, Dominican Republic

Pedro Martinez made his major league debut with the Los Angeles Dodgers in 1992, going 10–5 with a 2.61 earned run average (ERA). He was traded to the Montreal Expos, and after four solid seasons was traded to the Boston Red Sox. In 1998, Martinez went 19–7 with a 2.89 ERA and 251 strikeouts.

In 1999, he was dominant, going 23–4 and leading the league in victories, winning percentage (.852), ERA (2.07), and strikeouts (313). He won the American League Cy Young Award and led the Red Sox to the American League Championship Series. Through the 2000 season, Martinez was 125–56 with a 2.69 ERA and 1,818 strikeouts.

In 2000, he was 18–6 with 284 strkeouts. He won the Cy Young Award unanimously.

Mathews, Eddie
Born: October 13, 1931 in Texarkana, Texas
Died: February 18, 2001

Eddie Mathews was one of the best ever to play third base. He was a powerful hitter with good speed and quickness, and a strong arm.

Mathews, the only player to play for the Braves in Boston, Milwaukee, and Atlanta, was offered $10,000 to sign with the Brooklyn Dodgers, but accepted Boston's offer of $6,000, because he thought he'd reach the major leagues faster with the Braves. He joined the Braves in 1952 as their starting third baseman. The Braves moved to Milwaukee the following year, and Mathews led the National League with 47 home runs. He hit 40 or more home runs in each of the next two seasons—40 in 1953 and 41 in 1954, when he led the league in runs batted in (RBI) with 109.

Mathews helped the Braves with the National League pennant in 1957 and 1958 and the World Series in 1957. In 1957, he hit 32 home runs, with 94 RBI, and in 1958, he hit 31 home runs with 77 RBI.

In 1959, Mathews won his second home run title, hitting 46. He also batted .306 that season with 114 RBI.

Mathews and Hank Aaron formed one of the most feared combinations at that time. Aaron hit third in the Braves lineup, Mathews fourth. The two combined for 863 home runs, making them the most prolific home run–hitting combination for one franchise. Babe Ruth and Lou Gehrig of the New York Yankees were second on that list with 859.

Mathews continued to be a solid offensive player. From 1960 to 1965, he averaged 30 home runs a season. It wasn't until 1966, when the Braves moved to Atlanta, that Mathews' home run production declined. He hit 16 home runs in 1966 and 16 in 1967, which he spent with the Houston Astros (101 games) and the Detroit Tigers (36 games). He retired during the 1968 season, in which he appeared in 31 games.

Mathews scored 95 or more runs in 10 straight seasons (1953–62) and hit 30 or more home runs in nine straight seasons (1953–61). Only Ruth has more consecutive seasons of 30-plus home runs (12). Mathews is tied with Gehrig and Mike Schmidt for second.

Mathews' lifetime batting average was .271. He hit 512 career home runs and through the 2000 season was tied with Ernie Banks of the Chicago Cubs for 13th all-time. He was inducted into the Baseball Hall of Fame in 1978.

Mathewson, Christy

Born: August 12, 1880 in Factoryville, Pennsylvania
Died: October 7, 1925

According to Grantland Rice, Christy Mathewson brought baseball "a certain indefinable lift in culture, brains and personality." Unlike the rough-and-tumble, hard-drinking players of the early 1900s, Mathewson was educated at Bucknell University, where he was the class president and a member of the glee club and the literary society. He dropped out of Bucknell in 1899 to play professional baseball, joining the New York Giants in 1900.

He was sent to the minor leagues after a 0–3 start, but returned to the Giants in 1901.

Mathewson, a right-hander, didn't rely on throwing hard, which was customary of that era, but rather on finesse and pinpoint control. He threw a curve; a fade-away curve, called a screwball today; and a dry spitter, now known as a knuckleball. He rarely walked a batter, going 68 consecutive innings in 1913 without yielding a base on balls, and usually required between 80 and 90 pitches per game.

From 1901 through 1914, Mathewson averaged 26 wins a season, won 30 or more games four times, and won at least 20 each year. He won 37 games in 1908, 34 of them complete games, a National League record for the 20th century. He also won 30, 33, and 31 from 1903 to 1905.

In the 1905 World Series against the Philadelphia Athletics, Mathewson pitched three shutouts, giving up only 14 hits and one walk in 27 innings. He struck out 18.

Mathewson, nicknamed "Big Six" after the fastest fire engine in New York, led the league in strikeouts five times and in earned run average (ERA) five times. He won the pitching Triple Crown (wins, strikeouts, ERA) in 1905 and 1908.

The Giants won the National League pennant from 1911 through 1913, with Mathewson winning 26, 23, and 25 games, respectively. He went 24–13 in 1914 and slumped to 8–14 the next season, when he was traded to Cincinnati so he could become the team's manager. Mathewson managed the Reds from 1916 until he was drafted in 1918. He pitched for the final time on Labor Day 1916.

While in the service in Europe, Mathewson's lungs were damaged by poison gas. When he returned from the war, he was a coach with the Giants for three years before being admitted to a sanatorium for tuberculosis. He was released in 1923, but was back in the sanatorium in 1925, when he died.

Mathewson ended his career with 373 wins, tied for third all-time. Through the 2000 season, he was eighth in winning percentage (.665), fifth in ERA (2.13), and third in shutouts (80). He was inducted as a charter member of the Baseball Hall of Fame in 1936 and was named to the All-Century Team in 1999.

Mattingly, Don

Born: April 20, 1961 in Evansville, Indiana

Don Mattingly spent his entire 14-year career with the New York Yankees. He was a consistent hitter and an excellent-fielding first baseman.

Mattingly, a left-handed batter, hit .300 or better six consecutive seasons, starting in 1984, when he hit .343 and led the league in batting, doubles (44), and hits

(207). In 1985, he batted .324 with 211 hits. He led the league in doubles (48) and runs batted in—RBI—(145) and was named the American League's Most Valuable Player.

Mattingly hit .352 in 1986 and led the league in slugging percentage (.573), hits (238), and doubles (53).

In 1990, Mattingly spent six weeks on the disabled list due to a back injury, his average dropping to .256. His back continued to plague him throughout the rest of his career. He hit over .300 only one more time, .304 in 1994.

Mattingly retired after the 1995 season. His lifetime batting average was .307 with 2,153 hits, 222 home runs, and 1,099 RBI. A six-time All-Star, Mattingly won nine Gold Gloves and, through the 2000 season, held the career record for highest fielding percentage for a first baseman (.996).

Mays, Willie

Born: May 6, 1931 in Westfield, Alabama

Willie Mays was one of baseball's most versatile and charismatic talents. He could hit for average and power, run, field, and throw. He also played the game with boyish enthusiasm and exuberance.

Leo Durocher, Mays' first manager with the New York Giants said: "Willie is without a doubt the most dynamic, most dramatic, most fantastic, most exciting performer in action today. He is Joe Louis, Jascha Heifetz, Sammy Davis, and Nashua rolled into one."

Nicknamed the "Say Hey Kid," Mays was 15 years old when he began playing for the Birmingham Barons in the Negro National League. After one season at in the Class B Interstate League, Mays moved up to Class AAA, playing for the Minneapolis Lakers, before the Giants called him up early in the 1951 season.

He started slowly, failing to get a hit in his first 22 at-bats, homering off Warren Spahn, and then going hitless in his next 13 at-bats. But he finished the season hitting .274 with 20 home runs and 68 runs batted in (RBI), helping the Giants win the National League pennant.

In 1952 and 1953, Mays was in the Army, but he returned in 1954 to lead the Giants to another pennant. He led the league in hitting (.345), slugging percentage (.667), and triples (13). He also hit 41 home runs, drove in 119 runs, won the National League Most Valuable Player Award, and was named the Associated Press Male Athlete of the Year.

It was in game 1 of the 1954 World Series, which the Giants won in four games over Cleveland, that Mays made the most famous catch in baseball history. The Indians had two men on, with none out in the eighth inning of a 2–2 game. Cleveland's Vic Wertz hit a long drive to the deepest part of center field at the Polo Grounds. Mays ran the ball down, caught it over his shoulder, with his back to home plate. Then, in one motion, he whirled and threw the ball back to the infield, holding the runners. Not surprisingly, the play became known as "The Catch."

As famous as "The Catch" has become, those who saw him play regularly cite many other plays made by Mays in center field that they consider just as spectacular. Using his signature basket catch (his glove held belt-high), Mays' fielding skills were unsurpassed.

Mays led the league in home runs in 1951 (51) and again in 1962 (49), 1964 (47), and 1965 (52), when he won his second Most Valuable Player Award.

Mays led the league in stolen bases from 1956 through 1959. He was the first player to hit at least 30 home runs and steal at least 30 bases in the same season in the National League. He hit 36 homers and stole 40 bases in 1956, and hit 35 homers and stole 38 bases in 1957. Mays was also the first to hit 200 home runs and steal 200 bases in a career.

When the New York Giants moved to San Francisco in 1958, Mays encountered racial prejudice. He bought a home in a formerly all-white neighborhood. But by 1962, he was a fan favorite. He led the league in home runs, hit .304, drove in 141 runs, and helped lead the Giants to the World Series.

Mays' 1965 MVP season was the last in which he hit .300. He left the Giants early in the 1972 season to play for the New York Mets. He hit just .250 in 1972, then retired after the 1973 season, after batting only .211.

Mays, who had a .302 career batting average, finished with 660 home runs, third all-time. Through the 2000 season, he ranked 10th in hits (3,283), seventh in games played (2,992), 10th in at-bats (10,881), third in total bases (6,066), sixth in runs (2,062), fourth in extra base hits (1,323), and eighth in RBI (1,903).

Mays was inducted into the Baseball Hall of Fame in 1979 and was named to the All-Century Team in 1999.

Mazeroski, Bill

Born: September 5, 1936 in Wheeling, West Virginia

Bill Mazeroski spent his entire 17-year major league career with the Pittsburgh Pirates and is best known for hitting a home run in the bottom of the ninth inning in game 7 of the 1960 World Series to beat the New York Yankees.

Mazeroski joined the Pirates in 1956 and became their regular second baseman a year later. In 1958, Mazeroski batted .275 with 19 home runs. But in 1959, in an attempt to continue to hit home runs, he tried to pull everything, and his average dropped to .241. The slump continued into the 1960 season, when George

Sisler, one of the Pirates coaches, suggested that Mazeroski stand deeper in the batter's box. The tip worked. Mazeroski raised his average from .237 on Aug. 3 to .273 as the Pirates won the pennant. Mazeroski hit .320 in the Series with two home runs and five runs batted in (RBI) in 25 at-bats. In the seventh game, the Pirates took a 9–7 lead in the eighth, the Yankees tied it in the ninth, and Mazeroski won it, hitting Ralph Terry's second pitch over the left field wall of Forbes Field.

Mazeroski was a seven-time All-Star and an eight-time Gold Glove winner. He set a National League record for double plays by a second baseman (144) in 1961 and set the major league record (150) in 1966. In March 2001, he received the necessary votes from the Veterans Committee for induction into the Baseball Hall of Fame.

McCovey, Willie

Born: January 10, 1938 in Mobile, Alabama

Willie McCovey was an intimidating presence at the plate. At 6-4, 220 pounds, the left-handed hitting first baseman was one of the most feared power hitters of his time. He joined the San Francisco Giants in July 1959, appeared in 52 games, batted .354, hit 13 home runs, and was named the National League Rookie of the Year. He spent the first part of the 1952 season at the Giants farm team in Phoenix, where he was tutored by Ted Williams, his idol. In McCovey's first game with the Giants, he went 4-for-4 with two singles and two triples off future Hall of Famer Robin Roberts.

But the Giants had a problem in that they had Orlando Cepeda, who also was to become a Hall of Famer, playing first base. So McCovey was a part-time player for the next three seasons, including 1962, when the Giants won the National League pennant and lost the World Series to the New York Yankees in seven games. McCovey came to bat in the ninth inning in the seventh game with runners on second and third, two out, and the Giants trailing 1–0. He hit a vicious line drive that second baseman Bobby Richardson caught.

In 1963, he was moved to the outfield so that the Giants could get his bat in the lineup. He batted .280 and led the league with 44 home runs.

In 1965, Cepeda was injured and McCovey played 156 games at first base. The following season, Cepeda was traded to the St. Louis Cardinals, giving McCovey the job at first base. From 1965 through 1970, he hit 30 or more home runs each season, including league-leading totals of 36 in 1968 and 45 in 1969. He also led the league in runs batted in (RBI) during those seasons, with 105 and 126, respectively.

McCovey hit 39 home runs and drove in 126 in 1970, but injuries during the next two seasons—torn

knee cartilage in 1971, a broken arm in 1972—limited him to a total of 32 home runs.

He rebounded in 1973 to hit 29 home runs, but was traded to the San Diego Padres, where he spent two-plus seasons. Midway through the 1976 season, he was traded to the Oakland Athletics. In 1977, McCovey returned to the Giants. He batted .280, hit 28 home runs, and was named the Comeback Player of the Year.

McCovey played two more years with the Giants, retiring after the 1980 season. McCovey had a lifetime batting average of .270, and his 521 home runs ties him for 11th all-time with Ted Williams. Only Lou Gehrig and Eddie Murray hit more grand slams than McCovey, who had 18. Injuries kept McCovey's numbers down. He averaged only 372 at-bats a year over his 22-year career. He was inducted into the Hall of Fame in 1986.

McGwire, Mark

Born: October 1, 1963 in Pomona, California

Mark McGwire of the St. Louis Cardinals had one of the most magical seasons in the history of baseball in 1998 when he broke one of the most storied records in all of sports—the single-season home run mark of 61, held by the late Roger Maris, who played with the New York Yankees.

McGwire, along with Sammy Sosa of the Chicago Cubs, waged a duel for the record that was as compelling as anything the game has ever seen. McGwire and Sosa reinvigorated Major League Baseball, turning the attention of the nation on their battle, and they did it with class and dignity.

Ever since McGwire broke in with the Oakland Athletics in 1986, he seemed to be a threat to make a run at the record. He hit 49 home runs in his first full season in 1987, when he was named American League Rookie of the Year.

He followed that with 32, 33, and 39 home runs over the next three seasons. In 1991, he hit 22, rebounded to hit 42 in 1992, then spent the next two seasons battling foot injuries. McGwire, who played in only 27 games in 1993 and 47 in 1994, considered retiring.

But he regained his home run stroke in 1995, hitting 39, and he followed that with a league-leading 52 in 1996. By mid-1997, Oakland realized it couldn't afford McGwire, so he was traded to the St. Louis Cardinals, having hit 34 home runs with the Athletics. He hit 24 more in St. Louis to finish with 58—the third-highest single-season total in history.

At first, McGwire considered signing with a team in Southern California so he could be closer to his only child, Matthew. But because of an amicable relationship with his former wife, McGwire was able to see Matthew frequently. That, and his love for St. Louis, one of the great baseball towns in America, led him to sign with the Cardinals. McGwire, who stands 6-5 and weighs 225 pounds, began his assault on the record book on Opening Day, when he became the first player in Cardinals history to hit an Opening Day grand slam. He went on to hit four home runs in his first four games. By the end of April he had 11 homers, and by the end of May he had 27, thanks to a stretch in which he hit 10 in nine days (May 16–25).

Sosa, who trailed McGwire 27–13 May 30, joined the race by hitting 20 home runs in June to close within 36–33. At the end of July, McGwire led 45–42, and at the end of August they were even with 55 each. McGwire became the first player in history to hit at least 50 home runs in three consecutive seasons.

The nation was captivated. Even the most casual baseball fan was eager to find out if McGwire and/or Sosa homered.

McGwire hit no. 60 on Sept. 5, and tied Maris with no. 61 Sept. 7. The record-breaker came the following night at Busch Stadium in St. Louis. Steve Trachsel of the Chicago Cubs served up no. 62.

Sosa hit his 62nd Sept. 13 and actually took the lead, 66–65, on Sept. 25. But McGwire closed in a rush, hitting five home runs Sept. 25–27. He finished with 70 home runs, four more than Sosa.

There was some controversy surrounding McGwire's record season. It was determined he used a dietary supplement that was banned by several athletic organizations, but not Major League Baseball.

In 1999, McGwire hit 65 home runs and led the National League in runs batted in with 147. From 1996 to 1999, he averaged 61 home runs a season and homered every 8.13 at-bats. His career ratio of home runs to at-bats was 10.6 through the 2000 season, which was better than Babe Ruth's 11.76.

Through the 2000 season, McGwire's lifetime batting average was .265. His 554 home runs ranked him seventh all-time and his slugging percentage of .593 ranked sixth.

Medwick, Joe

Born: November 24, 1911 in Carteret, New Jersey
Died: March 21, 1975

Joe Medwick, a rough-and-tumble outfielder, was aggressive, intense, and more than willing to mix it up—with opponents or teammates. His St. Louis Cardinals teams were referred to as the "Gashouse Gang," because of the aggressive style of play. Medwick epitomized the personality of those teams.

Medwick, nicknamed "Ducky," because he walked like a duck, joined the Cardinals in 1932, appeared in 26 games and hit .349. The next season he took over as a full-time outfielder and began a streak of 10 straight

seasons in which he hit .300 or better, including three seasons when he hit .350 or better.

A right-handed hitter, Medwick led the National League in triples (18) in 1934 and in hits (233), doubles (64), and runs batted in—RBI—(138) in 1936.

The 1934 Cardinals reached the World Series against the Detroit Tigers. In the seventh game, with St. Louis winning 11–0, Medwick slid hard into third baseman Marv Owen after hitting a triple. The fans were so enraged by what they considered an unnecessarily hard slide that they pelted Medwick with garbage and bottles when he took his spot in left field. Commissioner Kenesaw Mountain Landis ordered him removed from the game for his own protection.

In 1937, Medwick had a career year, leading the league in batting (.374), slugging percentage (.641), hits (237), doubles (56), home runs (31), runs (111), and RBI (154). He was named the league's Most Valuable Player and was the last National Leaguer to win the Triple Crown.

Medwick led the league in doubles (47) and RBI (122) for the third straight season in 1938.

In 1939, Medwick was traded to the Brooklyn Dodgers because of a salary dispute. Shortly after the trade, Medwick was beaned by Bob Bowman, a former teammate with the Cardinals. His career was nearly ended. He returned, but never again hit with the same authority.

Medwick retired in 1948 with a lifetime batting average of .324. He was inducted into the Baseball Hall of Fame in 1968.

Mize, Johnny

Born: January 7, 1913 in Demorest, Georgia
Died: June 2, 1993

Johnny Mize, nicknamed "Big Cat," was a left-handed-hitting slugger who joined the St. Louis Cardinals as a first baseman in 1936. Mize hit .300 or better in each of his first nine seasons, including .364 in 1938 and a league-leading .349 in 1939, when he also led the league in slugging percentage (.626), home runs (28), and runs batted in—RBI—(137).

He also led the league in home runs in 1940 (43), 1947 (51), and 1948 (40); in RBI in 1942 (110) and 1947 (138); in slugging percentage in 1938 (.614), 1940 (.636), and 1942 (.521); and in triples in 1937 (16).

After the 1941 season, Mize was traded to the New York Giants. He missed three years while serving in the Navy during World War II, but returned in 1946 to hit .337 with 22 home runs, although he played in only 101 games because of a broken hand. He led the National League in home runs the next two seasons, before being traded to the New York Yankees midway through the

1949 season. He spent four seasons with the Yankees, retiring in 1953.

While with the Yankees, Mize appeared in five World Series. He batted .286 with three home runs and nine RBI in 18 games. During the 1952 Series, Mize was the first player ever to hit home runs in three consecutive games.

Mize had a lifetime average of .312, with 359 home runs and 1,337 RBI. He is the only player to hit 50 or more home runs while striking out fewer than 50 times. Through the 2000 season, he ranked 17th all-time in slugging percentage (.562). He was inducted into the Baseball Hall of Fame in 1981.

Molitor, Paul

Born: August 22, 1956 in St. Paul, Minnesota

Paul Molitor, who battled injuries in the first half of his career, missing nearly 500 games in his first 10 years, got better with age.

Molitor joined the Milwaukee Brewers in 1978 and for the first nine seasons of his career was a solid hitter, batting .300 or higher three times. But starting in 1987,

Paul Molitor   *Minnesota Twins*

after Molitor got healthy, he batted .300 or better nine times over the next 11 seasons, including a career-high .353 in 1987. He led the American League in at-bats twice (666 in 1982, 665 in 1991), in hits twice (216 in 1991, 211 in 1993), in doubles once (41 in 1987), in triples once (13 in 1991), and in runs scored three times (136 in 1982, 114 in 1987, 133 in 1991).

In 1982, Molitor helped the Brewers in the American League pennant. He hit .316 with two home runs and four runs batted in (RBI) in the American League Championship Series and .355 in the Series, which the Brewers lost to the St. Louis Cardinals.

After 15 seasons with the Brewers, Molitor signed with the Toronto Blue Jays as a free agent in December 1992. He hit .332 in 1993 as the Blue Jays won the pennant and defeated the Philadelphia Phillies in the World Series. Molitor hit .391 in the League Championship Series and .500 in the World Series, with two doubles, two triples, two home runs, 10 runs, and eight RBI. He was named the World Series MVP. His career .418 Series average is first all-time.

Molitor spent two more seasons with the Blue Jays, hitting .341 in 1994 and .270 in 1995. He signed as a free agent with the Minnesota Twins in December 1995. He hit .341 in 1996, leading the league in hits with 225; .305 in 1997; and .281 in 1998, his final season.

Molitor's lifetime batting average was .306. Through the 2000 season, he ranked eighth all-time in hits (3,319), 11th in at-bats (10,835), 19th in total bases (4,854), and 15th in runs (1,782). He had 605 doubles, 114 triples, 234 home runs, and 1,307 RBI. A six-time All-Star, Molitor played all four infield positions, the outfield, and was a designated hitter.

Morgan, Joe

Born: September 19, 1943 in Bonham, Texas

Joe Morgan could do it all. He was a slick-fielding second baseman who could hit for average, power, and in the clutch.

Morgan began his career with the Houston Astros in 1963. He appeared in eight games that season and 10 the following year, before becoming the regular second baseman. He had seven solid seasons with the Astros, before being traded in 1971 to the Cincinnati Reds.

Morgan was a key member of the "Big Red Machine," which won four National League pennants and two World Series (1975–76).

During his first three seasons in Cincinnati, Morgan was a .290 hitter. In 1972, he led the league in runs (122) and walks (115).

In 1975, Morgan won the first of two consecutive Most Valuable Player Awards. Remembered for the way he always flapped his left elbow while awaiting the pitch, he batted .327 with 17 home runs, 94 runs batted in

(RBI), 67 stolen bases, and a league-leading 132 walks. He also delivered two key hits in the Reds' World Series victory over the Boston Red Sox. He won the third game with a 10th-inning single, and he also had the game-winning hit in the seventh game.

In 1976, Morgan had the best all-around season of his career. He batted .320, with 27 home runs, 111 RBI, 113 runs, and 60 stolen bases. In the World Series, he hit .333 in a sweep of the New York Yankees.

Morgan spent three more seasons in Cincinnati, before returning to Houston as a free agent. He hit .243 with the Astros in 1980, then was traded to the San Francisco Giants, where he hit .240 in 1981 and .289 in 1982. Morgan was traded to the Philadelphia Phillies in December 1982. He played 117 games at second base and hit .230, with 16 home runs, to help the Phillies win the 1983 National League pennant. They lost the World Series to the Baltimore Orioles.

The final year of Morgan's career was in 1984 with the Oakland Athletics. He hit .244 with six home runs in 116 games.

Morgan, who was one of the game's most intelligent players, had a lifetime batting average of .271. He had 2,517 hits, including 268 home runs, and drove in 1,133 runs. He ranks fourth all-time in walks (1,985) and 10th all-time in stolen bases (689). He won five Gold Glove Awards, scored 100 run eight times, and was an eight-time All-Star. He was inducted into the Baseball Hall of Fame in 1990 and, through 2000, worked as a broadcaster for ESPN and NBC.

Munson, Thurman
Born: June 7, 1947 in Akron, Ohio
Died: August 2, 1979

Thurman Munson was one of the best catchers in the American League, often contending with Carlton Fisk for that distinction. He could hit for average and power, and he was solid behind the plate.

He joined the New York Yankees in 1969, appearing in 26 games, and became the team's regular catcher in 1970, when he was named American League Rookie of the Year. He batted .302 with six home runs and 53 runs batted in (RBI). In 1971, he led the league's catchers in fielding percentage (.998), commtting only one error.

From 1973 through 1977, Munson hit .300 or better four times and had 100 or more RBI three times. In 1976, he was named the Yankees captain, the first time the team had a captain since Lou Gehrig. Munson turned in a career year, batting .302 with 17 home runs and 105 RBI. He was named the American League's Most Valuable Player. Munson led the Yankees to the World Series, where they were swept by the Cincinnati Reds, but he batted .529.

Munson helped the Yankees reach the next two World Series. In 1977, he batted .308 with 18 home runs and 100 RBI, and in 1978, he hit .297 with six home runs and 71 RBI. He hit .320 in each of the two Series, both victories over the Los Angeles Dodgers. Through the 2000 season, his .373 World Series average ranked fifth all-time. On Aug. 2, 1979, Munson died in a plane crash in Canton, Ohio, where he was practicing takeoffs and landings in a twin-engine plane.

Munson's lifetime batting average was .292, with 113 home runs and 701 RBI. He won three Gold Gloves.

Murphy, Dale
Born: March 12, 1956 in Portland, Oregon

Dale Murphy was drafted by the Atlanta Braves as a catcher and was touted to become the next Johnny Bench. But Murphy developed a mental block about throwing to second base. So the Braves moved him to first base in 1978, and he responded by hitting 23 home runs and knocking in 79 runs. In 1980, he was moved again, to center field, and he blossomed into one of the game's best players.

From 1980 through 1989, he hit 20 or more home runs nine times, 30 or more five times, and a career-high 44 in 1987.

Murphy was named the National League's Most Valuable Player in 1982 (.281, 36 home runs, league-leading 109 runs batted in—RBI) and 1983 (.302, 36 home runs, league-leading 121 RBI). He joined Ernie Banks, Mike Schmidt, Joe Morgan, and Barry Bonds as the only National League players to win consecutive MVP Awards. Said Nolan Ryan after Murphy won his first MVP Award, "I can't imagine Joe DiMaggio was a better all-around player than Dale Murphy."

Murphy led the league in home runs in 1984 (36) and 1985 (37). From 1986 through 1989, he averaged 29 home runs and 87 RBI for the Braves. In August 1990, Murphy was traded to the Philadelphia Phillies, where he stayed until 1993, when he was traded to the Colorado Rockies. He retired in May 1993.

Murphy's lifetime batting average was .265 with 398 home runs and 1,266 RBI. He was an outstanding fielder as well, winning five consecutive Gold Gloves (1982–86).

Murray, Eddie
Born: February 24, 1956 in Los Angeles, California

Eddie Murray was one of the great switch-hitters of all time, with the ability to hit for power and average. He joined the Baltimore Orioles in 1973, appearing in 160 games, mostly as a designated hitter. He batted .273 with 27 home runs and 88 runs batted in (RBI) and was named the American League Rookie of the Year.

Murray became Baltimore's regular first baseman in 1978 and remained with the Orioles through the 1988 season. During that time, he never hit less than .277, and six times he hit .300 or better. In the strike-shortened 1981 season, he led the league with 22 home runs and 78 RBI.

Murray helped the Orioles reach the World Series in 1979 and 1983. He hit .417 in the 1979 American League Championship Series (ALCS) and .154 in the World Series. In 1983, he hit .267 in the ALCS and .250 in the World Series.

Following the 1988 season, Murray was traded to the Los Angeles Dodgers, where he spent three seasons and hit a career-high .330 in 1990, with 26 home runs and 95 RBI.

He spent two seasons (1992–93) with the New York Mets and two seasons with the Cleveland Indians (1994–95). He hit .323 with the Indians in 1995, helping them win the pennant and reach the World Series, where he struggled again, hitting .105. He also played with the Anaheim Angels, retiring in 1997.

Murray, a brooding person who always seemed to have a scowl on his face, was a consistent performer throughout his career. His lifetime batting average was .290. He is the only switch-hitter in major league history to get 3,000 hits and 500 home runs. Through the 2000 season, his 3,255 hits ranked 11th all-time and first among switch-hitters. His 504 home runs ranked 16th all-time and second among switch-hitters to Mickey Mantle, who hit 536. Murray hit home runs from both sides of the plate in the same game 11 times, another major league record.

Through the 2000 season, Murray also ranked fifth in games played (3,026), fifth in at-bats (11,336), eighth in total bases (5,397), seventh in RBI (1,917), and 13th in extra base hits (1,099). He holds the major league record for games played at first base (2,413).

Murray was a three-time Gold Glove winner and a seven-time All-Star.

Musial, Stan
Born: November 21, 1920 in Donora, Pennsylvania
When Stan "The Man" Musial was 18, he signed a contract with the St. Louis Cardinals in 1938 and was sent to the low minor leagues to begin his professional career—as a left-handed pitcher. He went 6–6 in his first season and 9–2 in his second, when he also was used as a pinch hitter.

In 1940, Musial was promoted to Daytona Beach in the Florida State League, where he pitched and played the outfield. His career appeared to be over when he injured his left shoulder while playing the outfield, but the Cardinals manager, Dickie Kerr, converted Musial to a full-time outfielder. He finished the 1940 season, hitting

.311. Late in the 1941 season, Musial was promoted to the Cardinals. He hit .426 in 12 games and remained a fixture in St. Louis until his retirement in 1963.

In his first season as a starter in left field (1941), Musial hit .311. It was the first of 16 consecutive seasons in which he hit over .310.

In 1943, Musial was named the National League's Most Valuable Player, leading the league in average (.357), hits (220), doubles (48), triples (20), and slugging percentage (.562).

Musial also won batting titles in 1946 (.365), 1948 (.376), 1950 (.364), 1951 (.355), 1952 (.336), and 1957 (.351). Only Tony Gwynn and Honus Wagner won more National League batting titles (8).

In 1946, after serving one year in the Navy, Musial returned to the Cardinals, and in addition to winning the batting title, won his second Most Valuable Player Award. He hit .365, with 124 runs, 228 hits, 50 doubles, 20 triples, and a .587 slugging percentage. He also won the Most Valuable Player Award in 1948, hitting .376, with 39 home runs and 111 runs batted in (RBI).

Musial's "corkscrew" batting stance was unorthodox. He crouched low, turned his back toward the pitcher, and held his bat straight up in the air. He didn't as much swing as uncoil, and he consistently made contact, never striking out more than 50 times in any one season.

Musial retired in 1963 with a lifetime batting average of .331. Through the 2000 season, he ranked fourth all-time in hits (3,630), tied for fifth in games played (3,026), ninth in at-bats (10,972), second in total bases (6,134), tied for 19th in home runs (475), seventh in runs (1,949), second in extra base hits (1,377), and fifth in RBI (1,951). Inducted into the Baseball Hall of Fame in 1969 and named to the All-Century Team in 1999, Musial was one of the game's great goodwill ambassadors.

Newcombe, Don
Born: June 14, 1926 in Madison, New Jersey
Don Newcombe was the first African American pitcher to make a name for himself in the major leagues. After a successful career with the Newark Eagles of the Negro National League, Newcombe joined the Brooklyn Dodgers in 1949, when he went 17–9 with a .317 earned run average (ERA), 149 strikeouts, and a league-leading five shutouts. He was named the National League Rookie of the Year.

Over the next five seasons, Newcombe put together the most impressive stretch of his career. He won 19 games in 1950 and 20 in 1952, when he led the league with 164 strikeouts. In 1955, Newcombe went 20–5 with a 3.20 ERA, 143 strikeouts, and a league-leading winning percentage of .800.

In 1956, Newcombe went 27–7 with a 3.06 ERA and 139 strikeouts. He led the league in victories and winning percentage (.794) and was named the winner of the first Cy Young Award as well as National League Most Valuable Player.

Newcombe, who developed arm trouble in 1957, was traded early in the 1958 season to the Cincinnati Reds. Early in the 1960 season, the Reds traded him to the Cleveland Indians. He retired after going 6–9 with a 4.48 ERA.

Newcombe's career record was 149–90 with a 3.56 ERA and 1,129 strikeouts.

Newhouser, Hal

Born: May 20, 1921 in Detroit, Michigan
Died: November 10, 1998

Hal Newhouser joined the Detroit Tigers in 1939, when he appeared in one game. Over the next four seasons, Newhouser, a left-hander, was 34–51 and showed no signs of greatness. But then he developed another pitch, a slider, and the difference was remarkable.

In 1944, he went 29–9 with a 2.22 earned run average (ERA) and a league-leading 187 strikeouts. He was named the American League's Most Valuable Player. In 1945, he went 25–9 and led the league in victories, winning percentage (.735), ERA (1.81), games started (36), complete games (29), innings pitched (313.1), strikeouts (212), and shutouts (8). He was again named the Most Valuable Player, making him the only pitcher ever to win consecutive MVP Awards.

The Tigers reached the World Series in 1945, and Newhouser won two of his three decisions, against the Chicago Cubs, including game 7.

In 1946, Newhouser went 26–9 with 275 strikeouts and led the league in victories and ERA (1.94). He had one more 20-win season (21–12 in 1948) and won 18 and 15 games in 1949 and 1950, respectively.

Then Newhouser developed arm trouble. In his last three seasons with the Tigers, he was a combined 15–16. He was traded to the Cleveland Indians in 1954, when he was used as a reliever, going 7–2 with a 2.51 ERA for an Indians team that won the pennant. He retired in 1955 after appearing in two games.

Newhouser's career record was 207–150 with a 3.06 ERA. He struck out 1,796 and recorded 33 shutouts.

Newhouser was inducted into the Baseball Hall of Fame in 1992, and in 1997, became only the fourth player in the history of the Detroit Tigers to have his number retired.

Niekro, Phil

Born: April 1, 1939 in Blaine, Ohio

Phil Niekro was famous for his knuckleball, which he learned at age 10 when he was playing catch with his father. His father threw it as a joke, but Niekro was taken by the pitch and learned how to throw it. The Milwaukee Braves were impressed enough by his knuckler that they signed him.

After spending several years in the minor leagues, Niekro was called up to the Braves to stay in 1965, the year before they moved to Atlanta.

Niekro, a right-hander, began his career as a relief pitcher, going 11–9 and leading the National League in earned run average—ERA—(1.87) in 1967. But by 1968, he became almost exclusively a starter.

Niekro went 23–13 with a 2.57 ERA and 193 strikeouts in 1969, when the Braves won the National League West title.

After four mediocre seasons, during which he went a combined 56–54, Niekro rebounded to go 20–11 with a 2.38 ERA, 195 strikeouts, and league-leading totals in victories, complete games (18), and innings pitched (302).

Niekro developed arm trouble in 1973, and he was sent to the bullpen. He returned to the starting rotation Aug. 5, 1973, and pitched a no-hitter against the San Diego Padres. It was the first no-hitter by a Braves pitcher since Warren Spahn in 1961.

From 1975 through 1983, Niekro led the league in victories once (21 in 1979), losses four times (20 in 1977, 18 in 1978, 20 in 1979, 18 in 1980), games started four times (43 in 1977, 42 in 1978, 44 in 1979, 38 in 1980), complete games three times (20 in 1977, 22 in 1978, 23 in 1979), innings pitched three times (330 in 1977, 334 in 1978, 342 in 1979), and strikeouts once (262 in 1977).

Following the 1983 season, Niekro signed with the New York Yankees after being released by the Braves. He spent two seasons with the Yankees, winning 16 games in each. In 1986, he signed with the Cleveland Indians, and in 1987 he spent time with three teams: the Indians, the Toronto Blue Jays and the Braves. He retired after a 7–13 record in 1987.

Niekro's career record was 318–274. Through the 2000 season, he ranked 14th all-time in victories, ninth in strikeouts (3,342), fifth in losses (274), fourth in innings pitched (5,403.1), third in walks allowed (1,809), and third in home runs allowed (482). Niekro had the misfortune of playing for the Braves when they were near the bottom of the standings. From 1970 through 1983, his final year with the team, the Braves had only four .500 or better finishes. Niekro lost 49 games by shutout, the third-highest total in major league history.

He and his brother, Joe, hold the record for the most major league wins by a brother combination (539). Niekro, who won 121 games after he turned 40, was inducted into the Baseball Hall of Fame in 1997.

Ott, Mel

Born: March 2, 1909 in Gretna, Louisiana
Died: November 21, 1958

Mel Ott was signed by New York Giants manager John McGraw when he was only 16 years old and playing for a semipro team in Patterson, La. He had been a catcher, but McGraw converted him to an outfielder.

Ott joined the Giants in 1926 and spent most of his two seasons learning the game. He sat next to McGraw in the dugout and realized the importance of hustle and anticipation, both of which were important to McGraw.

Ott, nicknamed "Master Melvin," became the Giants starting right fielder in 1928. He hit .322 with 18 home runs and 77 runs batted in (RBI). Over the next 18 seasons, he hit .300 or better nine times, including a career high .349 in 1930.

Ott led the National League in RBI once (1934) and in home runs six times (1932, '34, '36–38, '42). He surpassed 100 RBI nine times and 30 home runs eight times. He was the youngest player to hit 40 home runs, hitting 42 in 1929, ironically a year in which he didn't lead the league.

Ott, a left-handed hitter, had an unusual batting style, lifting up his right leg and striding forward into the ball. He took advantage of the short right-field fence (258 feet) at the Polo Grounds, the Giants' home field, hitting 63 percent of his home runs there. Ott helped the Giants win three National League pennants and the 1933 World Series championship. In three Series appearances, he hit .295 with four home runs and 10 RBI. In 1942, the Giants followed a popular custom of the day and named Ott player-manager. He won his last home run title that year. He also led the league in runs (118) and walks (109).

Ott slipped to a .234 batting average in 1943, hit .288 and .308 the following two seasons, and by 1946 focused primarily on managing. He appeared in 31 games in 1946 and four in 1947, when he retired. The Giants replaced him as manager in 1948.

Ott then managed in the minor leagues and did some radio announcing for the Detroit Tigers. He died in an automobile crash in 1958, pulling out onto U.S. 90 in St. Louis and colliding with another car.

Through the 2000 season, Ott, who had a lifetime batting average of .304, ranked 14th all-time in total bases (5,041), 15th in home runs (511), ninth in RBI (1,861), 10th in runs (1,859), 16th in extra base hits (1,071), and seventh in walks (1,708).

Ott, who spent his entire 22-year career with the Giants, was inducted into the Baseball Hall of Fame in 1951.

Paige, Satchel (Leroy)

Born: July 7, 1906 in Mobile, Alabama
Died: June 8, 1982

Satchel Paige was considered by many to be perhaps one of the greatest pitchers in the history of baseball. Even though the color barrier kept him out of the major leagues until 1948, when he was 42, Paige dominated the Negro League through the 1930s and 1940s. Paige, who was given his nickname for carrying bags at the Mobile train station, learned to play baseball at the Industrial School for Negro Children, where he was sent at age 12 for stealing toys. After pitching for the Mobile Tigers, a semipro team, Paige was signed by the Chattanooga Black Lookouts of the Negro Southern League, and by the time he was 18, he was pitching for the Birmingham Black Barons of the Negro League. Paige threw a blazing fastball with pinpoint control. He called his fastball his "small ball." By the time it reached the batter, he likened it to a "fish egg."

Because exact records weren't kept, it's estimated that Paige pitched in approximately 2,500 games during his Negro League career, winning 2,000 and throwing some 250 shutouts and 55 no-hitters. He once started 29 games in one month, and during some year-round seasons pitched in as many as 200 games.

Paige left the Negro League in 1934 over a contract dispute with the Pittsburgh Crawfords and formed the Satchel Paige All-Stars, a team that barnstormed the United States. He billed himself as "the world's greatest pitcher—guaranteed to strike out the first nine men."

Paige's team faced the best players in the major leagues and won praise from such stars as Joe DiMaggio, Charlie Gehringer, Jimmie Foxx, Rogers Hornsby, and Hack Wilson.

In 1938, after returning to the Negro League and also pitching in the Dominican Republic and the Mexican League, Paige developed a sore arm and it seemed his career was over. But he learned how to throw a breaking ball, and he led the Kansas City Monarchs to five pennants and two Negro League World Series titles.

Paige, who cared deeply about civil rights, was disappointed when Jackie Robinson was chosen instead of him to break the major league color barrier. But in 1948, Paige was signed by the Cleveland Indians. In 21 games, mostly in relief, he was 6–1 with a 2.48 earned run average (ERA). He helped the Indians win the pennant and the World Series.

The Indians released him after a subpar season in 1949, and Paige returned to barnstorming, before joining the St. Louis Browns for three seasons (1951–53). In 1952, he was the best relief pitcher in the American League, going 12–10 with 10 saves and a 3.07 ERA, and was named to the All-Star team.

Paige made one more comeback, in 1965 at age 59 with the Kansas City Athletics. He pitched in one game and worked three scoreless innings against the Boston Red Sox.

He was hired as a coach by the Atlanta Braves in 1968 so he could get the 158 days he needed to qualify for his pension.

Paige, in addition to being such an effective pitcher, was also one of the game's great showmen and ambassadors. He filled stadiums when he pitched in the Negro League, and more than 200,000 fans attended his first three starts in Cleveland.

When the Baseball Hall of Fame created a wing for the Negro League, Paige refused to be inducted, preferring to wait for formal induction, which came in 1971.

Palmer, Jim
Born: October 15, 1945 in New York, New York

Jim Palmer was one of the dominant pitchers of his time, as well as one of the most outspoken. Palmer was famous for his verbal battles with his Baltimore Orioles manager, Earl Weaver.

Weaver challenged Palmer about his myriad—and mysterious—injuries, many of which Weaver believed were imagined, and Palmer would fire back about his manager's lack of height or pitching knowledge.

Palmer began his career in Baltimore as a reliever in 1965, but the following season, he joined the starting rotation. He went 15–10 and helped the Orioles win the American League pennant and sweep the Los Angeles Dodgers in the World Series. Palmer threw a shutout in game 2, beating Sandy Koufax.

Over the next two seasons, Palmer battled arm trouble. He pitched in just three games in 1967 and missed 1968 entirely. But he rebounded in 1969 to go 16–4 and lead the league in winning percentage (.800). He won 20 or more games in each of the next four seasons, leading the league in earned run average—ERA—(2.40) in 1973, when he went 22–9 and won the Cy Young Award.

More arm trouble in 1974 limited Palmer to seven wins, but he came back strong. He led the league in wins in 1975 (23), 1976 (22), and 1977 (20) and won the Cy Young Award in 1975 and 1976.

In 1975, Palmer went 23–11 with league-leading totals in ERA (2.09) and shutouts (10). In 1976, he went 22–13, with a 2.51 ERA, and led the league in games started (40) and innings pitched (315). It was the first of three straight seasons he led the league in innings pitched.

Palmer had his last 20-game season in 1978, going 21–12 with a 2.46 ERA. Over the next four seasons, he went a combined 48–29, including 15–5 in 1982, when he led the league in winning percentage (.750).

In 1982, when the Orioles rallied down the stretch to get back into contention for the American League East title, Palmer won 11 straight during the stretch drive, but lost to future Hall of Famer Don Sutton on the final day of the season.

After going 5–4 in 1983 and 0–3 in 1984, Palmer announced his retirement. Through the 2000 season, he ranked 29th all-time with 268 wins. He had a career ERA

of 2.86, fifth best among pitchers with 3,000 or more innings. He struck out 2,212 and threw 53 shutouts.

He helped the Orioles to five pennants and won the clinching game in four of them. He was 4–1 with a 1.96 ERA and 46 strikeouts in the American League Championship Series, and he was 4–2 with a 3.20 ERA with 44 strikeouts in the World Series.

He won more games (186) than any pitcher in the 1970s, and he joined Walter Johnson and Lefty Grove as the only American League pitchers to win 20 or more games eight times.

Palmer, who was strikingly handsome, did television commercials and also worked as a broadcaster for ABC Sports and the Baltimore Orioles. He was inducted into the Baseball Hall of Fame in 1990.

Perez, Tony
Born: May 14, 1942 in Camaguey, Cuba

Tony Perez was the backbone of the Cincinnati Reds' "Big Red Machine," in the mid-1970s. He was a productive hitter, especially in the clutch, and provided leadership for a team that won four National League pennants and two World Series.

Perez left a job at a sugarcane factory in Havana to sign a contract with the Reds organization in 1960. He spent five-plus seasons in the minors, was a part-time player with the Reds through 1966, and then in 1967 became the team's regular third baseman. Perez switched to first base in 1972, and joined Joe Morgan, Pete Rose, and Johnny Bench to form one of the most effective lineups ever. From 1967 through 1976, Perez hit .280 or better seven times, hit 25 or more home runs six times, and drove in 100 or more runs six times.

Following the 1976 season, Perez was traded to the Montreal Expos, a move Reds president Bob Howsam called the worst he had ever made. He spent three seasons with the Expos, hitting .270 or better each year and averaging 15 home runs and 80 runs batted in (RBI) a year.

Perez signed with the Boston Red Sox as a free agent in 1980 and had his last great season. He hit .275 with 25 home runs and 105 RBI. He played two more seasons with the Red Sox, one with the Philadelphia Phillies, and his final three seasons with the Reds. Over those last six seasons, he had a total of 31 home runs and never more than 43 RBI in a season.

Perez managed the Reds briefly in 1993, going 20–24, and has since worked in the front office of the Florida Marlins.

Perez, a seven-time All-Star, had a lifetime batting average of .279, with 339 home runs and 2,732 hits. Through the 2000 season, he ranked 21st all-time in games played (2,777) and 18th all-time in RBI (1,652). He was inducted into the Baseball Hall of Fame in 2000.

Perry, Gaylord

Born: September 13, 1938 in Williamston,
North Carolina

Gaylord Perry, besides being an effective right-handed pitcher throughout most of his 22-year career, was probably best known for his use of the spitball, an illegal pitch that appeared to be a fastball until it abruptly dropped. Just the possibility that Perry might throw the spitter was enough to unnerve hitters and rob them of their concentration.

Perry joined the San Francisco Giants in 1962 and had his first great season in 1966, when he went 21–8 with a 2.99 earned run average (ERA) with 201 strikeouts. Over the next three years, Perry was a combined 50–46. In 1970, he went 23–13 with a 3.20 ERA and 214 strikeouts. He led the National League in games started (41), innings pitched (329), and shutouts (5).

Following the 1971 season, Perry was traded to the Cleveland Indians. He went 24–16 with a 1.92 ERA and 234 strikeouts. He led the American League in victories and complete games (29) and won the Cy Young Award.

Perry was traded to the Texas Rangers during the 1975 season, then went to the San Diego Padres in 1978, when he went 21–6 with a 2.72 ERA and 154 strikeouts. He led the league in victories and winning percentage (.778) and became the only pitcher at the time to win the Cy Young Award in both leagues.

Perry left the Padres after the 1979 season and spent time with the Rangers, New York Yankees, Atlanta Braves, Seattle Mariners, and Kansas City Royals, retiring in 1983. After his Cy Young Award–winning season in 1978, Perry finished above .500 only one more time, going 12–11 in 1979.

Perry's career record was 314–265, with a 3.10 ERA. Through the 2000 season, he ranked 15th all-time in victories, sixth in strikeouts (3,534), and sixth in innings pitched (5,350.1). A five-time All-Star, he was inducted into the Baseball Hall of Fame in 1991.

Piazza, Mike

Born: September 4, 1968 in Norristown, Pennsylvania

Mike Piazza was a 62nd-round draft choice by the Los Angeles Dodgers in 1988. He was drafted as a favor by Dodgers manager Tommy Lasorda, who was a friend of the Piazza family. From those humble beginnings, Piazza became one of the best catchers in baseball.

Piazza spent five full seasons with the Dodgers (1993–97) and averaged 33 home runs and 105 runs batted in (RBI) a year. He also hit .318, .319, .346, .336, and .362 during those five seasons. In 1993, he hit 35 home runs, drove in 112 runs, and was named the National League Rookie of the Year.

In 1998, the Dodgers traded Piazza to the Florida Marlins, who kept him for one week before trading him to the New York Mets. In his two seasons in New York, Piazza hit .348 with 23 home runs and 76 RBI in 1998 and hit .303 with 40 home runs and 124 RBI in 1999.

Piazza helped lead the Mets into the National League Championship Series in 1999 against the Atlanta Braves, who won the series in six games. In 2000, he helped the Mets reach the World Series.

Through the 2000 season, Piazza's career batting average was .327 with 1,356 hits, 278 home runs, and 881 RBI. Piazza, an eight-time All-Star, shared the major league record with Bill Dickey for the highest single-season batting average by a catcher (.362 in 1997)

Plank, Eddie

Born: August 31, 1875 in Gettysburg, Pennsylvania
Died: February 24, 1926

Eddie Plank was one of the most successful pitchers in baseball history and also one of the most deliberate. In an era when it was customary for pitchers to work quickly, Plank was ponderously slow, his delay tactics a form of gamesmanship that frustrated hitters.

He joined the Philadelphia Athletics in 1901, at age 25, after graduating from Gettysburg College, where he was first introduced to the game. He won 17 games in his rookie season, then 20 or more games in five of the next six seasons. He led the American League in complete games in 1905 (36), winning percentage (.760) in 1906, and shutouts (8) in 1907.

Plank, a left-hander, relied on a fastball, curveball, and "crossfire," a pitch delivered sidearm that seemed to be coming from first base. He had pinpoint control with all his pitches.

After failing to win 20 games from 1908 to 1910, Plank rebounded to go 23–8 in 1911 and 26–6 in 1912. He spent two more seasons in Philadelphia, then bolted for the Federal League, where he played with the St. Louis Terriers. The league folded after one season, and Plank joined the St. Louis Browns of the American League. He played two seasons, winning a total of 21 games, and retired in 1917 after losing a 1–0 decision to Walter Johnson.

Plank averaged 20 wins a year from 1901 through 1916. He helped the Athletics to four American League pennants and two World Series championships (1911, '13). His World Series record was 2–5, but it wasn't that he didn't pitch well. His earned run average was a sparkling 1.32.

Through the 2000 season, Plank's 326 wins ranked 10th all-time. He ranked 13th in ERA (2.34) and fifth in shutouts (69). He walked just 1,072 batters in 4,503 innings. Despite his impressive statistics, Plank was not inducted into the Baseball Hall of Fame until 1946—29 years after his retirement.

Puckett, Kirby

Born: March 14, 1961 in Chicago, Illinois

Kirby Puckett, one of the most popular players in Minnesota Twins history, was a consistent hitter and charismatic presence whose passion for the game was obvious every time he took the field.

He spent his entire career with the Twins and never hit below .288. He hit .300 or better eight times. From 1986 through 1989, Puckett batted .328, .322, .356, and .359, which led the American League. He also led the league in at-bats twice (691 in 1985, 657 in 1988), in hits four times (207 in 1987, 234 in 1988, 215 in 1989, 210 in 1992), and in runs batted in (RBI) once (112 in 1994).

Puckett helped the Twins win two World Series—in 1987 over the St. Louis Cardinals and 1991 over the Atlanta Braves. He hit .308 in 14 World Series games, and he hit .311 in 10 American League Championship Series games.

Puckett, a center fielder, was also an outstanding defensive player with a strong arm. He routinely robbed opposing hitters of home runs by scaling the fence at the Metrodome.

Puckett's career was cut short in 1996, when blurred vision in his right eye was diagnosed as glaucoma. He never played again.

Kirby Puckett   *Minnesota Twins*

Puckett's lifetime batting average was .318, with 2,304 hits, 207 home runs, and 1,085 RBI.

He was inducted into the Baseball Hall of Fame in 2001.

Reese, Pee Wee (Harold)

Born: July 23, 1918 in Ekron, Kentucky
Died: August 14, 1999

Pee Wee Reese, nicknamed for his expertise in shooting a marble called a "pee wee," was an outstanding shortstop with the Brooklyn Dodgers' "Boys of Summer" teams, but he was best known for his leadership and for his welcoming of Jackie Robinson, who broke the major league color barrier in 1947.

Reese was in the Boston Red Sox organization when he was sold to the Dodgers. He joined the Dodgers in 1940 and became the regular shortstop during the season, when he hit .272. His average dipped to .229 in 1941, and he led the league with 47 errors. But he turned things around in 1942, hitting .255, leading the National League in putouts and assists and making the All-Star team.

For the next three years, Reese served in the Navy during World War II. When he returned in 1946, he was the Dodgers' undisputed leader. In 1947, when Robinson joined the team, Reese set the tone by giving Robinson a friendly hug, which helped the rest of the Dodgers accept him.

Reese led the National League in walks in 1947 (104), in runs in 1949 (132), and in stolen bases in 1952 (30). He hit over .300 only once, .309 in 1954.

Reese played in seven World Series with the Dodgers, including Brooklyn's only championship, in 1955. His World Series average was .272, and through the 1999 season, he ranked fifth all-time in hits with 46.

Reese retired after appearing in 59 games of the 1958 season, the Dodgers' first in Los Angeles. His lifetime average was .269 with 2,170 hits. An eight-time All-Star, he was inducted into the Baseball Hall of Fame in 1984. He was a coach for the Dodgers in 1959 and did baseball telecasts for CBS and NBC.

Rice, Jim

Born: March 8, 1953 in Anderson, South Carolina

Jim Rice, a powerful right-handed hitter, joined the Boston Red Sox for 24 games in 1974, and the following season became their regular left fielder. He and teammate Fred Lynn battled for Rookie of the Year and Most Valuable Player honors, but Lynn won both awards. Rice hit .309 with 22 home runs and 102 runs batted in (RBI).

From 1975 through 1986, Rice hit 20 or more home runs every season but one. He led the American League three times (39 in 1977, 46 in 1978, 39 in 1983). In 1978, he was named Most Valuable Player. In addition to the 46 home runs, he also led the league in slugging percentage (.600), at-bats (677), hits (213), triples (15), and RBI (139).

Rice also led the league in slugging percentage in 1977 (.593) and in RBI in 1983 (126). He hit .300 or better six times, and from 1975 through 1987, he never hit lower than .277.

Only in the last two years of Rice's career did his numbers tail off. He hit .264 with 15 home runs and 72 RBI in 1988 and .234 with three home runs and 28 RBI in 56 games in 1989, when he retired.

Rice's lifetime batting average was .298. He had 382 home runs, 1,451 RBI, and 2,452 hits, including 834 for extra bases. He also won four Gold Gloves.

Ripken, Cal, Jr.
Born: August 24, 1960 in Havre de Grace, Maryland
Cal Ripken is the Ironman of major league baseball. In 1995, he broke a record that once was considered untouchable—the consecutive games streak of New York Yankees first baseman Lou Gehrig, established in 1939.

The streak began in 1982, Ripken's first full season with the Orioles. He started at shortstop in the second game of a doubleheader May 29, 1982. Ripken broke Gehrig's streak Sept. 6, 1995, when he played in his 2,131st consecutive game.

The outpouring of affection from the sold-out crowd at Oriole Park at Camden Yards, the emotional victory lap that Ripken took around the stadium, and the goodwill that ensued from the celebration provided a shot in the arm for baseball.

Ripken was named Associated Press Male Athlete of the Year and *Sports Illustrated*'s Sportsman of the Year.

In addition to starting his historic streak in 1982, Ripken also was named American League Rookie of the Year. He hit .264 with 28 home runs and 93 runs batted in (RBI).

The 1982 season was the first of 10 straight seasons in which Ripken hit 20 or more home runs, a record for a shortstop. He hit 27, with 102 RBI in 1983, when he helped the Orioles to a World Series championship and was named the American League's Most Valuable Player.

He won his second Most Valuable Player Award in 1991, when he hit .323 with 114 RBI and 210 hits, including 46 doubles.

Ripken had two more 20-homer seasons—in 1993, when he hit 24, with 90 RBI and in 1996, when he hit 26, with 102 RBI.

From 1997 through the 1999 season, Ripken remained a solid performer, averaging .285, 16 home runs, and 67 RBI a year. Injuries in 1999 limited him to 86 games, but he batted .340 and hit 18 home runs.

Ripken also was an accomplished fielder. At 6-4, 215 pounds, he was not built like the prototypical shortstop, but he excelled with the glove. He won the Gold Glove in 1990 and 1991.

In 1990, he went 95 straight games without committing an error to set an American League record for shortstops. He committed only three errors that season and had a .996 fielding percentage.

From 1989 through 1996, he averaged less than 10 errors a year. In 1997, he was moved to third base. He led all American League third basemen in fielding percentage in 1998, committing just eight errors for a .979 fielding percentage.

Ripken's consecutive game streak finally ended Sept. 20, 1998, against the New York Yankees, when he asked manager Ray Miller to keep him out of the lineup. He played in 2,632 straight games, including 501 after he broke Gehrig's record. Through the 2000 season, Ripken's lifetime batting average was .278. He ranked 18th all-time in hits (3,070), 11th in games played (2,873), sixth in at-bats (11,074), 15th in total bases (4,996), and 17th in extra base hits (1,048). A 17-time All-Star, Ripken became an icon in Baltimore, having spent his entire career with the Orioles. He is actively involved in the community and has won the Roberto Clemente Award and the Lou Gehrig Award for his humanitarian endeavors.

Roberts, Robin
Born: September 30, 1926 in Springfield, Illinois
Robin Roberts was a hard-throwing right-handed pitcher for the Philadelphia Phillies who had one of the most dominant stretches any pitcher has ever had. He threw an overpowering fastball and had excellent control.

Roberts, who went to Michigan State University on a basketball scholarship, also played baseball and got the attention of the Phillies, who gave him a $25,000 signing bonus. He went 7–9 in his rookie year in 1948 and 15–15 in 1949. But over the next six seasons, he won 138 games, an average of 23 wins a season.

From 1950 to 1955, Roberts led the league in games started six times, complete games four times, innings pitched five times, strikeouts twice, and shutouts once.

In 1950, Roberts went 20–11 and helped the Phillies, known as the "Whiz Kids," to their first World Series in 35 years. Two years later, he went 28–7 with a 2.59 earned run average (ERA). He completed 30 of his 37 starts.

Roberts won 23 games in each of the next three seasons and was selected for the All-Star Game for seven straight seasons, starting in 1950.

By 1957, the wear and tear of pitching so many innings—he averaged 323 innings 1950–55—took its toll.

Robin Roberts   *Reading Eagle/Times*

Roberts dropped to 10–22. He spent four more seasons with the Phillies, who traded him to the New York Yankees after he went 1–10 in 1961. The Yankees cut Roberts during spring training, and he joined the Baltimore Orioles. He spent three-plus seasons with the Orioles and was a combined 32–36. He concluded his career with short stints with the Houston Astros and Chicago Cubs.

Roberts' career record was 286–245, with a 3.41 ERA. Through the 2000 season, he ranked 23rd all-time in victories and first in home runs allowed (505), a dubious distinction that can be attributed, in part, to his outstanding control, which allowed hitters to dig in at the plate.

That control also kept Roberts' walks to a minimum. He issued a base on balls once every 5.2 innings. His strikeout-to-walk ratio was 10.6 to one.

Roberts, who was also a durable pitcher, not being placed on the disabled list until 1961, when he was 34, was inducted into the Baseball Hall of Fame in 1976.

Robinson, Brooks
Born: May 18, 1937 in Little Rock, Arkansas

Brooks Robinson is regarded as the finest fielding third baseman in baseball history. He was not a fast runner, nor was his arm all that strong. But his reflexes and anticipation, and his quick-release, accurate throws allowed him to turn hits into outs for 23 years.

Robinson, nicknamed the "Human Vacuum Cleaner" or "Hoover," broke in with the Baltimore Orioles in 1955, but didn't become the regular third baseman until 1960, when he hit .294, with 14 home runs and 88 runs batted in (RBI). Also that season, he won the first of 16 consecutive Gold Gloves, a record for nonpitchers, and made the first of his 15 consecutive All-Star Game appearances.

In 1964, Robinson hit .317, with 28 home runs and a league-leading 118 RBI. He was named the American League's Most Valuable Player. Robinson was a mainstay for the Orioles, who won four pennants and two World Series (1966, '70) between 1966 and 1971.

Robinson's performance in the 1970 World Series against the Cincinnati Reds was particularly memorable. He hit .429 with two home runs and four RBI in five games. He also excelled at third, making several acrobatic plays to keep the Reds from scoring, and was named Most Valuable Player.

Robinson, who spent his entire career with the Orioles, was an effective clutch hitter as well as a source of leadership in the clubhouse. He retired in 1977, having hit 20 or more home runs six times.

Robinson had a lifetime batting average of .267. He led the league in putouts eight times and assists eight times. He leads all third baseman in putouts, assists, chances, and double plays. Through the 2000 season, he ranked 10th all-time in games played (2,896) and 12th in at-bats (10,654). Robinson, who enjoys icon status in Baltimore and is a member of the Orioles broadcasting team, was inducted into the Baseball Hall of Fame in 1983.

Robinson, Frank
Born: August 31, 1935 in Beaumont, Texas

Frank Robinson was a hard-nosed, hard-working player who excelled in both leagues. He broke in with the

55

Cincinnati Reds in 1956 as a right-fielder and was named the National League Rookie of the Year, hitting 38 home runs and driving in 122.

Robinson was the model of consistency during his 21-year career. From 1956 through 1971, his batting average dropped below .270 just three times. Hit .300 or better nine times, including a career-high .342 in 1962, when he hit 39 home runs, drove in 136 runs, and led the league in slugging percentage (.624), doubles (51), and runs (134). In 1961, Robinson was named the National League's Most Valuable Player. He batted .323, hit 37 home runs, drove in 124 runs, and led the league with a .611 slugging percentage.

Robinson got into trouble when he was arrested for carrying a concealed weapon, which many think led to the Reds trading him to the Baltimore Orioles following the 1965 season. Robinson had the best season of his career. He won the Triple Crown, leading the league in batting (.316), home runs (49), and runs batted in—RBI—(122). He won his second Most Valuable Player Award and is the only player ever to win the MVP Award in both leagues.

Robinson, whose distinctive batting style saw him crouch, lean forward, and crowd the plate, spent six productive seasons with Orioles, hitting .300 or better four times. He was traded to the Los Angeles Dodgers after the 1971 season. In 1972, he was dealt to the California Angels and was picked up on waivers by the Cleveland Indians in 1974. In October 1974, Robinson was named the player-manager of the Indians, making him the first black manager in Major League Baseball history.

Robinson retired as a player in 1976 and lasted 57 games into the 1977 seasons as the Indians manager before being fired. He managed the San Francisco Giants from 1981 to 1984 and the Baltimore Orioles from 1988 to 1991. His career record as a manager is 680–751.

Through the 2000 season, Robinson ranked fourth all-time in home runs (586), 14th in RBI (1,812), 11th in runs (1,829), sixth in extra base hits (1,186), 17th in games played (2,808), 21st in at-bats (10,006), and ninth in total bases (5,373). He was inducted into the Baseball Hall of Fame in 1982.

Robinson, Jackie

Born: January 31, 1919 in Cairo, Georgia
Died: October 24, 1972

Jackie Robinson broke the color barrier in Major League Baseball in 1947 and is one of the most socially significant athletes in any sport.

Robinson, who was one year old when his father left the family, moved with his mother to a poor neighborhood in Pasadena, Calif. Many boys in the neighborhood got into trouble, but Robinson chose to get involved in organized sports. After attending Pasadena Junior College, he earned a scholarship to UCLA, where he was a four-sport athlete and the first to letter in four sports—baseball, basketball, football, and track. In basketball, Robinson led the Pacific Coast Conference in scoring as a junior and senior. In football, he led the nation in 1939 in yards per carry (12) and in average punt-return yardage (20). He also won swimming championships, reached the semifinals of the national Negro League tennis tournament, and won the 1940 NCAA long jump title. He chose to leave school in 1941 before getting his degree to take a job as an assistant athletic director for the National Youth Administration.

Robinson was drafted into the Army and earned a commission as a second lieutenant. He was discharged in 1944 and joined the Kansas City Monarchs of the Negro American League in 1945. At the same time, Branch Rickey, the Brooklyn Dodgers president, was looking for a player to become the first black to appear in a Major League Baseball game since 1889. Rickey called it his "noble experiment."

In late August 1945, Rickey met with Robinson to inform him that he was the choice to make history and to warn him about what he would face.

"We're tackling something big here, Jackie," Rickey told Robinson. "If we fail, no one will try it again for 20 years. I know you're a good ballplayer. What I don't know is whether you have the guts."

Robinson asked Rickey if he was looking for "a Negro who is afraid to fight back." Rickey answered, "Robinson, I'm looking for a ballplayer with guts enough not to fight back."

Robinson, who was instructed to hold his tongue and keep his temper, said: "I'm not concerned with your liking or disliking me. All I ask is that you respect me as a human being."

Robinson spent the 1946 season playing with the Montreal Royals, the Dodgers farm team in the International League. He led the league in batting (.349), runs (113), and fielding percentage (.985 at shortstop).

On April 15, 1947, at age 28, Robinson made his major league debut with Brooklyn and was named the National League Rookie of the Year.

He was called names and racial epithets; he was brushed back by pitchers and spiked by base runners; he was subjected to death threats; and in Philadelphia, where the treatment was particularly cruel, a black cat was thrown at him. But Robinson conducted himself with grace and dignity, refusing to respond. He allowed his performance on the field to do the talking.

He batted .297, with 175 hits, 125 runs, 12 home runs, 48 runs batted in (RBI), and a league-leading 29 stolen bases. In the 1947 World Series against the New York Yankees, he batted .259 with seven hits, three RBI, and two stolen bases.

Robinson was named the National League's Most Valuable Player in 1949, when he batted a league-leading .342, with 203 hits, 16 home runs, 124 RBI, and 37 stolen bases.

The 1949 season was his first of six straight hitting .300 or better, including .328 in 1950 and .338 in 1951.

Robinson's speed and daring on bases brought a new flair and excitement to the game. Robinson, who began his career as a first baseman, became predominantly a second baseman through 1952, leading the league in fielding three times, after which he played the outfield and third base most of the time.

After hitting less than .300 in 1955 and 1956, the Dodgers traded Robinson to the New York Giants, but rather than report, he announced his retirement.

Robinson went to work as a vice president for Chock Full O' Nuts Corp. and later became one of the founders of the Freedom National Bank. He also became active in the civil rights movement as a spokesperson for the National Association for the Advancement of Colored People (NAACP).

In spite of his harrowing beginnings in the league, Robinson eventually became one of the leaders of the Brooklyn Dodgers, helping them win six pennants and one World Series in his 10 seasons.

Robinson had a lifetime batting average of .311, with 1,518 hits, 137 home runs, 734 RBI, and 197 stolen bases. His statistics would have been markedly better had he not lost the prime years of his career to the color barrier.

Said Robinson's teammate and friend Pee Wee Reese: "I don't know any other ballplayer who could have done what he did. To be able to hit with everybody yelling at him. He had to block all that out. To do what he did has got to be the most tremendous thing I've ever seen in sports."

Duke Snider, the Hall of Fame center fielder, called Robinson "the greatest competitor I've ever seen. . . ."

Robinson was a pioneer and a role model for the black ballplayers who followed him. Said Willie Mays, the Hall of Fame center fielder, "Every time I look at my pocketbook, I see Jackie Robinson."

Robinson was inducted into the Baseball Hall of Fame in 1962, his first year of eligibility. He suffered from diabetes, from which he developed heart disease and blindness in one eye. In 1972, on the 25th anniversary of his major league debut, Robinson threw out the first ball at the World Series. He died nine days later of a massive heart attack, at age 53.

Rodriguez, Alex
Born: July 27, 1975 in New York, New York

In his three full seasons with the Seattle Mariners (1997–99), Alex Rodriguez demonstrated power not usually associated with a shortstop.

He was the first pick overall in the 1993 free agent draft. After spending parts of the 1994, 1995, and 1996 seasons with the Mariners, he became the team's regular shortstop in 1997, when he hit .300, with 23 home runs and 84 runs batted in (RBI). In 1998, he hit .310 with 42 home runs and 124 RBI, and in 1999, he hit .285 with 42 home runs and 111 RBI.

In 2000, he hit .316 with 41 home runs and 132 RBI. He signed with the Texas Rangers for $252 million.

Rose, Pete
Born: April 14, 1942 in Cincinnati, Ohio

Pete Rose was an overachiever. He wasn't blessed with a lot of natural ability, but he worked so diligently and played so hard that through sheer determination, he made himself into one of the great players of all time.

Known for sprinting to first after drawing a walk and his frequent headfirst slides, Rose was nicknamed "Charlie Hustle." Rarely has a nickname been more appropriate. His intense, aggressive style was typified by a play in the 1970 All-Star Game when he barreled into Ray Fosse, the catcher for the American League at the plate to score the winning run.

Rose was named the National League Rookie of the Year in 1963 with the Cincinnati Reds. He batted .273 and scored 101 runs.

Between 1965 and 1981, Rose hit .300 or better 15 times, including batting titles in 1968 (.335), 1969 (.348), and 1973 (.338), when he led the league in hits (230) and was named Most Valuable Player.

From 1965 through 1979, Rose averaged 200 hits a season. He led the league in runs four times; in hits, seven; in doubles, five; and in on-base percentage, once.

Rose was an integral part of the Cincinnati teams known as the "Big Red Machine," which won two National League pennants and two World Series.

In 1979, Rose became a free agent and joined the Philadelphia Phillies, a team that was talented, but without a leader to rally around. Rose became that leader and in 1980 sparked the Phillies to their first World Series championship.

Rose played on seven pennant-winning teams and three world championship teams. In seven National League Championship Series, he hit .357 or better six times.

Rose left the Phillies after the 1983 season and joined the Montreal Expos. Late in the 1984 season, Rose returned to the Reds as player-manager. He retired as a player in 1986. Rose played 24 seasons and was an All-Star 17 times, at four different positions. He is the all-time leader in hits (4,256). He broke Ty Cobb's seemingly unbreakable record in 1985. Through the 2000 season, he was also first all-time in games played (3,562) and at-bats (14,053). He ranked sixth in total bases (5,732), fifth in runs scored (2,165), 18th in extra base hits (1,041), second in doubles (746), and 11th in walks (1,566). His 44-game hitting streak in 1978 is tied for second all-time.

Those are Hall of Fame numbers, but Rose isn't in the Hall of Fame, because in 1989 he was banned from baseball by commissioner A. Bartlett Giamatti, and as a result is ineligible for enshrinement.

Rose, who also served five months in prison for income tax evasion, was found to have bet on baseball, including games involving his own team.

Despite a 225-page report by investigator John Dowd, with seven volumes of additional material, Rose denied he bet on baseball. He accepted the permanent ban from baseball in exchange for baseball not reaching a formal finding that he bet on the game.

The subject of Rose's exclusion from the Hall of Fame comes up periodically, but in 1999, it reached a crescendo. After being named to the All-Century Team, Rose was interviewed after the ceremony. The questions from NBC's Jim Gray focused exclusively on his gambling. The public was outraged at Gray's line of questioning, and public sentiment, already in Rose's favor, became stronger.

In January 2000, Rose's legal team met with Major League Baseball, but no change in Rose's status was forthcoming.

Ruffing, Red (Charles)
Born: May 3, 1904 in Granville, Illinois
Died: February 17, 1986

Red Ruffing had a long, successful career, despite a mining accident in 1921. Ruffing, who left school at age 15 to work in the mines in Nokomis, Illinois, got his left foot caught between two mining cars. He lost four toes.

Ruffing, who had been a first baseman and an outfielder playing for the company team, gave up baseball for a year, but then returned as a right-handed pitcher. He signed his first pro contract in 1923, and joined the Boston Red Sox in 1924, appearing in eight games.

Ruffing's first five full seasons in the majors were unsuccessful. He went a combined 39–93 and twice led the American League in losses (25 in 1928, 22 in 1929). During the 1929 season, he lost 12 straight games.

Early in the 1930 season, Ruffing was traded to the New York Yankees. The change of scenery made all the difference. Ruffing won between 15 and 19 games in five of the next six seasons, and in 1932, he led the league in strikeouts with 190.

From 1936 through 1939, Ruffing won 20, 20, 21, and 21 games, respectively. He led the league in winning percentage in 1938 (.750) and in shutouts in 1938 (4) and 1939 (5).

Over the next three seasons, Ruffing went 44–25. After missing two full seasons and half of the 1945 season, Ruffing returned, going 7–3 in 1945 and 5–1 in 1946, when he broke his kneecap. The Yankees released him, and he spent his last season, 1948, with the Chicago White Sox, going 3–5.

Ruffing played in seven World Series with the Yankees, going 7–2 with a 2.63 earned run average (ERA). Through the 2000 season, he ranked fourth all-time in wins, third in innings pitched (85.2), fifth in complete games (7), and fifth in strikeouts (61).

His career record was 273–225, with a 3.80 (ERA). Through the 2000 season, Ruffing ranked 27th all-time in victories and 10th in walks allowed (1,541). Ruffing was also a fine hitter. His lifetime batting average was .269 with 273 runs batted in, a major league record for pitchers. He hit 36 home runs, third all-time. He was inducted into the Baseball Hall of Fame in 1967.

Ruth, Babe (George Herman)
Born: February 6, 1895 in Baltimore, Maryland
Died: August 16, 1948

Babe Ruth remains one of the most accomplished and enduring athletes in all of sports. His remarkable achievements as a pitcher and a hitter have stood the test of time. Those feats, combined with an appetite for life that included carousing and drinking (even during Prohibition) made him a legendary figure who has lost none of his appeal or allure over the years. That he is said to have saved the game, in the wake of the Black Sox Scandal in 1919, and changed the game, with his 714 career home runs, only add to the mystique.

Ruth, the product of a broken home, spent most of his childhood at St. Mary's Industrial School in Baltimore. He entered in 1902 when he was seven years old. He was supposed to remain at St. Mary's until he was 21, but his baseball talent—he was made a pitcher because of his strong arm—led the Baltimore Orioles to sign him to a contract for the 1914 season. In July 1914, Ruth was sold to the Boston Red Sox, who sent him to their minor league club in Providence, R.I. He won 22 games that summer for his two teams, and the next season, 1918, he was promoted to the major leagues.

In his first full major league season, 1915, Ruth won 18 games for the Red Sox, and over the next several seasons became the best left-handed pitcher in the game. He followed his 18-win season with 23 wins and a league-leading 1.75 earned run average (ERA) in 1916 and 24 wins in 1917. In the 1914 World Series, he pitched a 14-inning complete game, winning 2–1, and won two more World Series games in 1918, when he went 13–8 and also led Major League Baseball in home runs with 11.

During the 1916 and 1918 World Series, Ruth compiled a 3–0 record, a 0.87 ERA, and a scoreless-inning streak of 29.2 innings, a record that stood until 1961.

In 1919, Ruth won only eight games, but that was because he primarily played the outfield. His overall record as a pitcher was 94–46, including 65 wins from 1915 to 1917, and a career ERA of 2.28. But while his pitching career wound down in 1919, his reputation as a power hitter was enhanced. He hit an all-time record 29 home runs. He also led the majors in runs scored, runs batted in, extra base hits, total bases, and slugging percentage.

Prior to the 1920 season, Babe Ruth was sold by the cash-strapped Red Sox to the New York Yankees, to that point an unsuccessful team whose new owners were trying to upgrade the roster. The Yankees paid $100,000 for Ruth, double the previous high, and gave the Red Sox owners a $300,000 mortgage loan on Fenway Park.

Most of the Ruth legend was created with the Yankees. In 1920, he hit a record 54 home runs and followed that with 59 in 1921, when he became the major league leader in home runs with 137, eclipsing the record set by Roger Connor. It took Connor 18 years to reach 136 home runs. Ruth got there in just his third full season as a hitter.

By this time Ruth had captivated the New York fans, who clamored to see him. The New York sportswriters gave him nicknames such as "The Sultan of Swat," "Bambino," and, of course, "Babe."

In 1922, Ruth was suspended for six weeks because he barnstormed in the offseason. He was suspended four more times during the season for altercations with umpires, fans, and teammates. As a result, he didn't win the home run title.

But he bounced back to win the home run title in each of the next two seasons. In 1923, he hit 41 home runs, batted .393, and drove in 151 runs. He was named the American League's Most Valuable Player. In 1924, he hit .378 to win his only batting title. He also hit 46 home runs and drove in 143 runs.

With the roaring 20s at their peak, Ruth's lifestyle mirrored the times. In 1925, when he was breaking up with his first wife, the drinking got to him. He had surgery to remove an abdominal ulcer and was out of the lineup until June. He refused to obey his manager, Miller Huggins, and was suspended and fined $5,000, a huge sum in those days. He played in just 98 games that season, and, at age 32, many thought his best days were behind him.

But Ruth changed his ways and came back to win the home run title in each of the next six seasons, during which he never hit fewer than 46 home runs. In 1927, he hit an astounding 60, a record that stood until 1961, and he followed that with 54.

By 1933, Ruth's skills were beginning to erode. His average dropped to .301 and his home run total to 34. In 1934, he batted .288 and hit 22 home runs. Ruth made it clear he wanted to manage the Yankees, but there was no interest on the part of the team. Because he was no longer the player he once was, the Yankees gave him his unconditional release in February 1935. He joined the Boston Braves briefly and also served as a coach with the Brooklyn Dodgers. At the end of the 1938 season, he retired from baseball for good. His accomplishments have stood the test of time. Ruth won 12 American League home run titles, six runs batted in titles, and had four seasons of 50 or more home runs. His career batting average was .342. He also averaged 40.8 homers a season and hit a home run every 11.76 at-bats.

Twice, in 1920 and in 1927, Ruth hit more homers than any team in the league. In 1920, his 54 home runs were four more than the St. Louis Browns hit, and in 1927, his 60 home runs were four more than the Philadelphia Athletics hit.

Ruth led the Yankees to three World Series titles, including 1932, when he hit his famous "called shot" home run, pointing to the spot in the outfield where the home run would eventually land.

Ruth was stricken with throat cancer in 1946. He was honored in June 1948 at Yankee Stadium, dubbed "The House that Ruth Built," and died less than two months later. He was inducted into the Baseball Hall of Fame in 1936, and in 1999 he was named the no. 2 athlete of the century by ESPN and to Major League Baseball's All-Century Team.

Ryan, Nolan

Born: January 31, 1947 in Refugio, Texas

Nolan Ryan was a hard-throwing, durable right-hander who, even in his last season, threw a 95-mph fastball. Ryan broke in with the New York Mets in 1966 and was still "bringing it" 27 years later, when he retired in 1993 at age 46.

After joining the Mets at the end of the 1966 season, Ryan was inserted into the Mets' starting rotation the following year, but a blister problem limited his effectiveness. Ryan took to soaking his finger in pickle brine to toughen the skin.

In 1969, the year the Mets won the World Series, Ryan couldn't crack the starting rotation of the pitching-rich Mets, and manager Gil Hodges alternated him between starting and relieving. Frustrated with his inability to become a starter, Ryan asked to be traded and was traded, to the California Angels.

Ryan spent eight seasons with the Angels, developing a curve and a change-up to complement his fastball. The combination of pitches made Ryan a success. In his first season in California, he won 19 and led the

American League in strikeouts with 329. It was the first of seven times he would lead the AL in strikeouts, including a career high of 383 in 1973, when he went 21–16. Ryan had the only other 20-win season of his career in 1974, when he went 22–16.

The number of strikeouts was tempered by the number of walks—more than four a game—and his overall record of 62–61.

In 1980, Ryan was traded to the Houston Astros. He spent nine seasons with the Astros, but never won more than 16 games. He led the league in earned run average (ERA) twice (1.69 in 1981, 2.76 in 1987) and in strikeouts twice (270 in 1987, 228 in 1988). Despite the low ERA and high strikeout total in 1987, Ryan's record was 8–16. Ryan became a free agent after the 1988 season and signed with the Texas Rangers. He led the American League in strikeouts in 1989 (301) and again in 1990 (232). He never won more than 16 games with the Rangers.

Injuries began to take their toll, starting in 1991, when he finished 12–6, his last winning season. He went a combined 10–14 in 1992 and 1993, when he retired.

Ryan, who topped the 300-strikeout mark six times, is the all-time leader with 5,714—1,578 more than Steve Carlton, who is second all-time. He also leads in hits per game (6.55) and opponents batting average (.204). Ryan threw seven no-hitters—three more than second-place Sandy Koufax. The first no-hitter came in 1981, the last a decade later, when he was 44 years old. He also threw 12 one-hitters.

Through the 2000 season, Ryan was tied for 12th all-time in victories (324). He was fifth in innings pitched (5,387) and tied for seventh in shutouts (61). His winning percentage was only .526 (324–292), but that can be attributed to his playing for mediocre teams. On the negative side, Ryan is the all-time leader in walks allowed (2,795)—962 more than Carlton, who ranked second.

Ryan was inducted into the Baseball Hall of Fame in 1999 and was named to the All-Century Team the same year.

Sandberg, Ryne

Born: September 18, 1959 in Spokane, Washington

Ryne Sandberg developed into one of the best all-around players in Major League Baseball from the mid-1980s to the early 1990s. An All-American high school quarterback, Sandberg was drafted by the Philadelphia Phillies. He played in 13 games with the Phillies in 1981, and then in 1982 was a throw-in in a deal with the Chicago Cubs. In 1984, Sandberg won the National League Most Valuable Player Award. He hit .314 with 19 home runs, 101 runs batted in, and league-leading totals in runs (114) and triples (19). He also stole 32 bases and led the league in fielding percentage for second basemen (.993).

From 1985 through 1993, Sandberg hit .300 or better four times. He led the league in runs twice (104 in 1989, 116 in 1990). He hit 30 home runs in 1989 and led the league with 40 home runs in 1990.

From June 21, 1989, to May 17, 1990, Sandberg played in 123 consecutive games and fielded 582 chances without committing an error, a major league record for all infielders except first baseman. Fifteen times he put together streaks of 30 or more errorless games.

Sandberg retired in 1994, made a brief comeback in 1996, and retired following the 1997 season.

Schmidt, Mike

Born: September 27, 1949 in Dayton, Ohio

Mike Schmidt is widely regarded as the greatest third baseman ever to play the game. He could hit for average, hit for power, and field his position well enough to win 10 Gold Gloves in 18 years.

Schmidt began his career as a shortstop in the Philadelphia Phillies organization. He made his major league debut in September 1972, then played 132 games at all four infield positions in 1973. His offensive numbers were woeful—.196 batting average and 136 strikeouts in 367 at-bats.

Schmidt played winter ball in Puerto Rico during that offseason and discovered the swing that would make him an all-time great.

Schmidt, who moved to third base permanently in 1974, hit 36 home runs to lead the National League that year. He also led the league in homers in 1975 and 1976, hitting 38 each season.

In 1980, when the Phillies won the first—and only—World Series title in their history, Schmidt batted .286, led the league with 48 home runs and a .624 slugging percentage, drove in 104 runs, and was named the National League's Most Valuable Player.

In the World Series against the Kansas City Royals, Schmidt batted .381 with two home runs and seven runs batted in (RBI).

In 1981, Schmidt repeated as Most Valuable Player. He batted .316 and led the league in home runs (31) and RBI (91), despite losing 60 games to a players' strike. Schmidt won his third Most Valuable Player Award in 1986, when he batted .290, with league-leading totals in home runs (37) and RBI (119).

Schmidt's last great season came in 1987, when he batted .293, hit 35 home runs, and drove in 113 runs. Injuries began to take their toll in 1988, when he hit only .249 and 12 home runs. He retired after 42 games of the 1989 season.

In all, Schmidt led the league in home runs eight times, second only to Babe Ruth's 12 times. He hit 40 or more home runs three times and 35 or more 11 times. Only Hank Aaron and Willie Mays hit more home runs

Mike Schmidt   *Stephen Dunn/Allsport Photography*

in the National League. Through the 2000 season, Schmidt's 548 career home runs ranked eighth all-time.

Despite his statistics, Schmidt did not have it easy in Philadelphia, a city notorious for its demanding fans. His aloof nature and the ease with which the game came to him made his relationship with the fans a difficult one. It was only as he reached the twilight of his career and after he retired that they realized how great he was.

Schmidt was inducted into the Baseball Hall of Fame in 1995 and was a member of the All-Century Team selected in 1999.

Schoendienst, Red (Albert)
Born: February 2, 1923 in Germantown, Illinois
Red Schoendienst was a fine fielding, switch-hitting shortstop who had excellent bat control and bunting ability. He joined the St. Louis Cardinals in 1945. He led the National League in stolen bases (46) and played mostly in the outfield. In 1946, he moved to second base, hit .281, and helped the Cardinals win the National League pennant. He hit .300 or better in three straight years, beginning in 1952, including a career-high .342 in 1953.

Schoendienst was traded to the New York Giants early in the 1956 season. The Giants traded him to the Milwaukee Braves midway through the 1957 season. He helped the Braves reach the World Series in 1957, hitting .309 with a league-leading 200 hits. The Braves also won the pennant in 1958, but Schoendienst hit .262 and played in only 105 games because of illness and injury.

After the 1958 season, it was determined that he had tuberculosis. He spent most of the season in treatment and played in only five games. He made a solid comeback in 1960, winning back his job and hitting .257 in 68 games.

Schoendienst spent his final three seasons as a reserve infielder with the Cardinals, retiring in 1963 after appearing in only six games.

Schoendienst was named the manager of the Cardinals in 1965 and led them to two pennants (1967–68) and one World Series championship (1968). He was replaced as the St. Louis manager in 1976, joined the Oakland Athletics as a coach for two years, and returned to serve as interim manager of the Cardinals for 37 games in 1980 and 24 games in 1990.

Schoendienst's career batting average was .289. He had 2,449 hits, led second basemen in fielding seven times, and was selected to play in 10 All-Star Games. He was inducted into the Baseball Hall of Fame in 1989.

Seaver, Tom
Born: November 17, 1944 in Fresno, California
Tom Seaver was a powerful right-handed pitcher who could throw a fastball, curve, and slider with pinpoint control. He was a meticulous pitcher, keeping a book on the strengths and weaknesses of every major league hitter. He also was known for the strength in his legs that helped propel his pitches. His distinctive delivery and follow through often saw his right knee touch the ground.

Seaver was coveted by the Cleveland Indians, New York Mets, and Philadelphia Phillies. He became a New York Met in 1966, when baseball commissioner William Eckert picked his name out of a hat for New York. He was assigned to the Mets' minor league club in Jacksonville.

He was promoted to the major leagues in 1967 and went 16–13 with a 2.76 earned run average (ERA) during his rookie season. Seaver was 16–12 with a 2.20 ERA the following season, and then, in 1969, led the Mets to an improbable World Series championship over the heavily favored Baltimore Orioles.

The Mets were known as "lovable losers." They finished in ninth place in 1968, but won it all in 1969, largely due to Seaver's performance. He went 25–7, with a 2.21 ERA and a league-leading 208 strikeouts. He won the National League Cy Young Award.

Tom Seaver   *Johnathan Daniel/Allsport Photography*

In 1970, Seaver, nicknamed "Tom Terrific" and "The Franchise," led the league in strikeouts (283) and ERA (2.81), and in a game against the San Diego Padres struck out 19, including the last 10 in a row—a major league record.

Even though Seaver went 20–10 and led the league in ERA (1.76) and strikeouts (289) in 1971, he lost the Cy Young Award to Ferguson Jenkins. But he won his second Cy Young two years later, going 19–10 and leading the league in ERA (2.08), complete games (18), strikeouts (251), and opponents' batting average (.206).

Seaver won his final Cy Young Award in 1975, going 22–9 with a 2.38 ERA and a league-leading 243 strikeouts.

In 1977, a contract dispute led to his trade to Cincinnati, where he spent five-plus seasons. Seaver, who started the season with the Mets, finished with the Reds and went 21–6 with a 2.58 ERA and 196 strikeouts. It was Seaver's last 20-win season.

He returned to the Mets in 1983, spent the next two-plus seasons with the Chicago White Sox, and retired in 1986 as a member of the Boston Red Sox.

Seaver had two solid seasons with the White Sox, winning 15 and 16 games, respectively. But in 1986, he went a combined 7–13 with the White Sox and Red Sox and decided to call it quits.

Seaver pitched 20 seasons and won 20 or more games five times and topped 200 strikeouts in nine consecutive seasons (1968–76). His career ERA was 2.86. Through the 2000 season, his 311 wins tied him for 16th all-time. He ranked fourth in strikeouts (3,640), 15th in innings pitched (4,782.2), and tied for seventh in shutouts (61).

Seaver, who became a broadcaster after he retired, was inducted into the Baseball Hall of Fame in 1992.

Simmons, Al

Born: May 22, 1903 in Milwaukee, Wisconsin
Died: May 26, 1956

Al Simmons was recognized as one of the best all-around and fundamentally sound players of all time. He was blessed with a strong arm, which helped him cut down base runners who dared to try for the extra base, and an unorthodox batting stroke. Nicknamed "Bucketfoot Al," Simmons, a right-handed hitter, stood deep in the batter's box and stepped toward third base instead of toward the pitcher. The unusual stance didn't keep him from being considered the second-best right-handed hitter behind Rogers Hornsby.

Simmons' real name was Aloys Szymanski. As legend has it, when he was playing for Milwaukee in the American Association in the early 1920s, he saw a sign advertising Simmons Hardware and adopted the name.

Simmons spent two years in the minor leagues before joining the Philadelphia Athletics in 1924, when he became the starting left fielder. He spent nine seasons with the A's and hit .300 or better each season, including six times of .350 or better. He led the National League in batting in 1930 (.381) and 1931 (.390), and in runs batted in (RBI) in 1929 (157).

For three straight years, starting in 1929, the A's appeared in the World Series and Simmons drove in 450 runs during that stretch. Simmons hit .300, .364, and .333 in three Series with six home runs.

In 1932, a season in which Simmons led the American League in hits with 216, the Athletics released several of their higher-paid players, including Simmons, who were sold to the Chicago White Sox for $150,000.

After three seasons with the White Sox, in two of which he hit .330 or better, he was sold to Detroit, where he spent the 1936 season. Simmons then went to the Washington Senators, the Boston Braves, the Cincinnati Reds, the Athletics, the Boston Braves, and the Athletics. He retired in 1944.

During Simmons' 20-year major league career, he had a lifetime batting average of .334, which ranks 20th all-time. He ranks 13th in RBI (1,827), and had 307 home runs. In 19 World Series games he batted .329 with six home runs and 17 RBI.

Simmons, who became the director of a sandlot baseball program in New York City, was inducted into the Baseball Hall of Fame in 1953.

Sisler, George
Born: March 24, 1893 in Manchester, Ohio
Died: March 26, 1973

George Sisler was overshadowed by Babe Ruth and Ty Cobb, and he played in virtual anonymity with the lowly St. Louis Browns in the American League. But during his 15-year career, he put up numbers that were remarkable.

Sisler, a graduate of the University of Michigan, began his career as a left-handed pitcher. He was signed by the Pittsburgh Pirates out of college, but his college coach, Branch Rickey, voided the contract because it was signed without parental consent. Sisler signed with the Browns, who were managed by Rickey.

Sisler went a combined 5–6 in 1915–16, before being switched to first base, where he spent the rest of his career. He hit .340 or better in three of his first five seasons and .300 or better in four of his first five seasons.

In 1920, Sisler had a season that still stands out as one of the greatest ever. He hit a league-leading .407, with 257 hits, a major league record that still stands. He had 49 doubles, 18 triples, and 19 home runs.

Sisler hit .371 the following year, and then won his second batting title in 1922, hitting .420 (third-highest average ever). He led the league with 246 hits, 18 triples, 134 runs, and 51 stolen bases, and was named the league's Most Valuable Player. From 1920 to 1922, Sisler averaged .399, got 719 hits, and struck out a total of 60 times. His 41-game hitting streak in 1922 stood as the major league record until Joe DiMaggio hit in 56 straight in 1941.

Sisler missed the 1923 season because of sinusitis, a disease that caused double vision. He came back in 1924 as player-manager of the Browns and hit .300 or better in six of the next seven seasons. But he never considered himself as effective a hitter. Sisler spent three years as player-manager, but resigned because he thought it adversely affected his hitting. He hit .327 the season after he quit, but the Browns sold him to the Washington Senators, who sold him to the Boston Braves, with whom he spent his final two seasons, retiring in 1930.

Sisler worked in the printing and sporting goods industries until 1943, when he joined Rickey in Brooklyn as a scout and instructor for the Dodgers. One of his pupils was Duke Snider. Sisler left Brooklyn and followed Rickey to Pittsburgh, where he tutored Roberto Clemente.

Through the 2000 season, Sisler's career batting average of .340 ranked 14th all-time. He was inducted into the Baseball Hall of Fame in 1939.

Slaughter, Enos
Born: April 27, 1916 in Roxboro, North Carolina

Enos Slaughter, an outfielder, spent 19 years in the major leagues, starting in 1938 with the St. Louis Cardinals. From 1938 through 1953, he batted .300 or better eight times. In 1939 he led the National League in doubles (52); in 1953 he led in hits (188) and triples (17); in 1946 he led in runs batted in—RBI—(130); and in 1949 he led in triples (13). Slaughter, nicknamed "Country," was traded to the New York Yankees in 1954, and the Yankees traded him to the Kansas City Athletics midway through the 1955 season. The Athletics traded him back to the Yankees near the end of the 1956 season. He remained with the Yankees as a part-time player and pinch hitter until 1959, when he was traded to the Milwaukee Braves. He retired at the end of that season.

Slaughter's lifetime batting average was .300, with 2,383 hits. He played in five World Series, batting .291 overall with 23 hits and eight RBI. He was inducted into the Baseball Hall of Fame in 1985.

Smith, Lee

Born: December 4, 1957 in Jamestown, Louisiana

At 6-5 and 220 pounds, Lee Smith was an imposing figure on the mound. He was one of the game's premier relief pitchers, whose long and distinguished career lasted 16 seasons.

Smith broke into the majors with the Chicago Cubs in 1980, and in 1983 had a 1.65 earned run average and led the National League with 29 saves. Over the next four seasons, Smith averaged 33 saves a year.

In 1988, Smith was traded to the Boston Red Sox, who traded him to the St. Louis Cardinals in May 1990. In 1991 and 1992, Smith led the National League with 47 and 43 saves, respectively. He had 46 saves in 1993, when he was traded to the New York Yankees in August. Smith signed with the Baltimore Orioles as a free agent in 1994, when he led the American League with 33 saves.

He left Baltimore and joined the California Angels as a free agent in 1995, recording 37 saves. The Angels traded him to the Cincinnati Reds in 1996, and he signed as a free agent with the Montreal Expos in 1997. He appeared in 25 games in 1997 and announced his retirement July 15.

Through the 2000 season, Smith, a seven-time All-Star, was ranked first all-time in saves (478), 58 more than John Franco's second-place total. He also ranked fifth in appearances (1,022). He struck out 1,251 and walked 486 in 1,290 innings.

Smith, Ozzie (Osborne)

Born: December 26, 1954

If Ozzie Smith isn't the greatest defensive shortstop of all-time, he certainly is near the top of a very short list. Blessed with great range, quickness, and anticipation, Smith made a career out of turning sure hits into outs.

He broke into the major leagues with the San Diego Padres in 1978, becoming the team's regular shortstop after playing just 68 games in the minor leagues. Smith nicknamed the "Wizard of Oz," spent four seasons with the Padres. In 1982, he was traded to the St. Louis Cardinals because Cardinals manager Whitey Herzog considered Smith the team's "missing link." Smith helped lead the Cardinals to three World Series (1982, '85, '87) and one championship (1982).

Smith, never an offensive threat with the Padres, became a much better hitter with the Cardinals, eventually developing into a solid .280 hitter, with the ability to handle the bat, move the runners, and execute the hit and run. His best offensive season came in 1987, when he hit .303 with 75 runs batted in (RBI), without hitting a home run. He also was among the National League leaders in hits, doubles, and stolen bases. He finished third in voting for the Most Valuable Player Award.

Smith, who retired following the 1996 season, holds several records: National League record for games played at shortstop (2,511), major league record for most assists in a season (621 in 1980), major league record for assists in a career (8,375), and major league record for double play assists in a career (1,590).

Smith, a 14-time All-Star, led the National League in assists eight times, in games played five times, in putouts twice, and in fielding percentage eight times. He is tied with Honus Wagner for consecutive 20-steal seasons with 16. He won 13 consecutive Gold Gloves (1980–92). Only Baltimore Orioles third baseman Brooks Robinson, with 16, has won more.

Smith's career batting average was .262. He had 2,460 hits, 793 RBI, and 580 stolen bases. He was also honored for his humanitarianism and community involvement, winning the Branch Rickey Award, the Lou Gehrig Memorial Award, the Roberto Clemente Award, and the Brotherhood Award from the National Conference of Christians and Jews.

Snider, Duke (Edwin)

Born: September 19, 1926 in Los Angeles, California

Duke Snider was part of a golden age in New York City, where he, Mickey Mantle, and Willie Mays played center field for the Brooklyn Dodgers, New York Yankees, and New York Giants, respectively.

Mantle and Mays received most of the accolades, but Snider's statistics prove that, during his peak years, he deserved to be in their class.

Known as "The Duke of Flatbush" and one of the famed "Boys of Summer," Snider joined the Dodgers in 1947, and two years later became the full-time center fielder, hitting .292.

In 1950, Snider batted .321, hit 31 home runs, and led the National League in hits (199). After two more solid seasons in which he hit .277 with 29 home runs in 1951 and .303 with 21 home runs in 1952, Snider became one of just three players to hit 40 or more home runs for five consecutive years. Babe Ruth did it for seven years in a row (1926–32) and Ralph Kiner for five (1947–51).

Snider hit 42 home runs in 1953, 40 in 1954, 42 in 1955, a league-leading 43 in 1956, and 40 in 1957. He led the league in runs three times (132 in 1953, 120 in 1954, and 126 in 1956) and in runs batted in (RBI) in 1955 (136).

It's no coincidence that the Dodgers won four National League pennants and their first World Series (1955) during Snider's most productive seasons. He also produced in the postseason. Snider batted .324 in the World Series (1952–53, '55–56), including .345 in 1952, with 10 home runs and 24 RBI. Overall in six Series, Snider hit .286, with 11 home runs and 26 RBI.

In the Dodgers' 1955 World Series win over the New York Yankees, he batted .320 with four home runs, five runs scored, and seven RBI.

In addition to his ability to hit for power and average, Snider also was a fine defensive outfielder with a strong arm. But in spite of his all-around talents, the Brooklyn fans never gave Snider the credit he thought he deserved.

Snider, a left-handed pull hitter, benefited from playing in tiny Ebbets Field, where it was only 297 feet down the right-field line. But when the Dodgers moved to Los Angeles in 1958, Snider's numbers fell off because he could never become accustomed to the more spacious Los Angeles Memorial Coliseum. Injuries also began to take their toll. He hit just 15 home runs his first year in Los Angeles, only once hitting more than 20 (23 in 1959). His highest RBI total was 88 the same season.

Snider left the Dodgers to join the New York Mets in 1963. He retired after spending the 1964 season with the San Francisco Giants.

Snider's lifetime batting average was .286, and he hit 407 home runs. An eight-time All-star, Snider was inducted into the Baseball Hall of Fame in 1980.

Sosa, Sammy

Born: November 12, 1968 in San Pedro de Macoris, Dominican Republic

Through the first four years of his career, spent with the Texas Rangers and Chicago White Sox, Sammy Sosa gave no indication he was a home run hitter. But that all changed in 1993, his first full season with the Chicago Cubs, to whom he was traded in 1992.

From 1993 through 2000, Sosa, a right-handed hitting outfielder, hit 25 or more home runs each season and had 100 or more runs batted in (RBI) six times (1995–00). But no season was more memorable than 1998, when Sosa and Mark McGwire of the St. Louis Cardinals waged a season-long battle for one of the most storied records in all of sports—Roger Maris' single-season home run record of 61, set in 1961.

McGwire took a big early lead. By May 25, he had hit 25 home runs to Sosa's nine. By May 30, McGwire led 27–13. But Sosa went on a tear in June, hitting a major league–record 20 home runs and pulling to within 36–33 of McGwire.

McGwire stretched his lead to 43–36 on July 20, but Sosa tied McGwire at 46 on August 10 and went ahead 48–47 on August 19.

By this time, the nation was captivated. Even the casual baseball fan was eager to find out if McGwire and/or Sosa had hit a home run.

On August 31, they were tied at 55. McGwire hit his 61st on September 7, tying Maris' mark, and his 62nd on September 8. Sosa hit his 61st and 62nd on September 13. He went ahead of McGwire 66–65 on September 25, but McGwire hit five home runs in the last three days of the season to finish with 70. Sosa had 66.

The interest sparked by the home run duel and the class with which Sosa and McGwire carried themselves throughout revitalized baseball.

Sosa hit .308 with a league-leading 158 RBI and 134 runs in 1998, and he was named the National League's Most Valuable Player.

He followed 1998 with another successful season. He batted .288 with 63 home runs and 141 RBI in 1999. He led the league in total bases both seasons (416 in 1998, 397 in 1999).

Through the 2000 season, Sosa, a three-time All-Star, had a lifetime batting average of .267 with 1,606 hits, 386 home runs, and 941 RBI.

Spahn, Warren

Born: April 23, 1921 in Buffalo, New York

Warren Spahn is the winningest left-handed pitcher in baseball history. He threw a variety of pitches, all with pinpoint control. A slow, fluid motion, with a high leg kick and an overhand delivery made it tough for hitters to pick up the ball.

Spahn didn't win his first major league game until he was 25 years old, with the Boston Braves in 1946, but from 1947 through 1963, he averaged 20 victories a year and registered thirteen 20-win seasons. He led the National League in victories eight times (1949–50, '53, '57–61), in strikeouts four times (1949–51), and earned run average (ERA) three times (1947, '53, '61).

In 1957, Spahn won his only Cy Young Award, going 21–11, with 18 complete games and a 2.69 ERA.

The Braves moved to Milwaukee in 1953, and Spahn helped lead the Braves to National League pennants in 1957 and 1958 and the World Series championship in 1957.

In 1960, at age 39, Spahn pitched a no-hitter against the Philadelphia Phillies, striking out 15. He no-hit the San Francisco Giants the following year.

Spahn's last hurrah came in 1963, when he went 23–7 with a 2.60 ERA. But in 1964, he slumped to 6–13, and he was sold to the New York Mets and then went to the San Francisco Giants. He retired in 1965, came back in 1967 to pitch three games, and then retired for good. He served as a minor league manager and as the pitching coach for the Cleveland Indians for two seasons.

Through the 2000 season, his 363 victories ranked fifth all-time. He was 17th all-time in strikeouts (2,583), eighth in innings pitched (5,243.2), and sixth in shutouts (63). Spahn was inducted into the Baseball Hall of Fame in 1973 and was named to the All-Century Team in 1999.

Speaker, Tris

Born: April 4, 1888 in Hubbard, Texas
Died: December 8, 1958

Tris Speaker, who began playing baseball as a right-hander, broke his arm when he fell off a horse as a youngster. So he learned to play left-handed and became one of the game's great hitters and center fielders.

Speaker left school as a high school sophomore in 1906 to begin his professional career. He played a total of 38 games for the Boston Red Sox in 1907 and 1908, but the following season he became the starting center fielder. He hit .300 or better for seven seasons, including .383 in 1912, when he was named the American League's Most Valuable Player.

After nine productive seasons in Boston, Speaker was asked to take a 50 percent pay cut, which he refused to accept. So the Red Sox traded him to the Cleveland Indians. During his first season in Cleveland, Speaker, nicknamed "The Gray Eagle," led the league in hitting (.386), hits (211), slugging percentage (.502), and doubles (41).

From 1916 through 1926, Speaker failed to hit .300 only once. Eight times his average was .340 or higher, and six times it was .360 or higher. He also led the league in doubles three times while in Cleveland.

In 1919, Speaker became the player-manager of the Indians. The following season, he led them to the World Series championship.

But in 1926, Speaker retired abruptly. It was later discovered that he and Ty Cobb were implicated in trying to fix a game. They were later cleared by Commissioner Kenesaw Mountain Landis, and Speaker joined the Washington Senators in 1927, batting .327. He retired in 1928, after playing with the Philadelphia Athletics.

Through the 2000 season, Speaker's lifetime batting average of .345 ranked fifth all-time. He ranked first all-time in doubles (792), fifth in hits (3,514), 11th in total bases (5,103), ninth in runs (1,881), and ninth in extra base hits (1,132).

As an outfielder, Speaker was just as impressive. Because of his great speed and anticipation, he was able to play the shallowest center field in history. He holds the record for career assists (448). He led the American League in putouts seven times, in double plays five times, in assists three times, and in fielding percentage twice. Speaker was inducted into the Baseball Hall of Fame in 1937.

Stargell, Willie

Born: March 6, 1940 in Earlsboro, Oklahoma
Died: April 9, 2001

Willie Stargell was one of the most-feared sluggers of his time. He stood 6-3, weighed 225 pounds, and was known for his monstrous home runs.

Stargell joined the Pittsburgh Pirates in 1962 and became a full-time player by 1965, alternating between the outfield and first base. Through 1970, Stargell put up solid numbers, hitting .300 or better twice and hitting at least 25 home runs four times.

In 1971, Stargell had his best season, hitting .295 with a league-leading 48 home runs and 125 runs batted in (RBI). He helped the Pirates win the National League pennant. They won the World Series, but he hit only .208 with five hits in the Series. Over the next four seasons, Stargell never hit less than .293, and in 1973, he led the league in home runs (44) and RBI (119).

In 1979, Stargell shared the National League's Most Valuable Player Award with Keith Hernandez of the St. Louis Cardinals. He hit .281 with 32 home runs and 82 RBI in leading the Pirates to the National League pennant and the World Series championship. They came back from a 3–1 deficit to beat the Baltimore Orioles.

Stargell, nicknamed "Pops," was a most inspiring team leader, rallying the Pirates with his now-famous "We Are Family" approach. He handed out "Stargell Stars" for players who hustled or made good plays. He also led by example, hitting .455 in the National League Championship Series, with two home runs and six RBI, and .400 in the World Series with 12 hits (seven for extra bases), three home runs, and seven RBI. He was named Most Valuable Player in both series. He also was named the Associated Press Male Athlete of the Year and shared *Sports Illustrated*'s Sportsman of the Year award with Terry Bradshaw of the Pittsburgh Steelers.

Stargell, who retired in 1982, had a lifetime batting average of .282. Through the 2000 season, he ranked 19th all-time in home runs (475) and second in strikeouts (1,936). He hit two balls out of Dodger Stadium, seven out of Forbes Field (Pittsburgh), and four into the upper deck of Three Rivers Stadium. A seven-time All-Star, Stargell was inducted into the Baseball Hall of Fame in 1988, his first year of eligibility.

Sutter, Bruce

Born: January 8, 1953 in Lancaster, Pennsylvania

Bruce Sutter was one of the most effective relief pitchers in baseball during the late 1970s and early 1980s, thanks to his mastery of the split-fingered fastball. The pitch breaks sharply downward as it reaches home plate. Sutter frustrated hitters with his splitter for 12 seasons.

He spent his first four seasons with the Chicago Cubs, starting in 1976. He led the National League in saves in 1979 (37) and 1980 (28). In 1979, Sutter had an earned run average (ERA) of 2.23 with 110 strikeouts and 32 walks in 101 innings pitched. He won the National League Cy Young Award.

In 1981, he was traded to the St. Louis Cardinals. In three of his four seasons with the Cardinals, Sutter led the league in saves (25 in 1981, 36 in 1982, 45 in 1984).

In the 1982 postseason, Sutter was 1–0 with a 0.00 ERA in the National League Championship Series victory over Atlanta. In the World Series, which the Cardinals won over the Milwaukee Brewers, he was 1–0 with a 4.70 ERA.

In 1985, Sutter signed with the Atlanta Braves as a free agent. Arm trouble cost him most of the 1986 season and all of 1987. He returned in 1988, appeared in 38 games, then was forced to retired.

Sutter's career record was 68–71 with a 2.84 ERA. He struck out 861 and walked 309 in 1,040.2 innings pitched. Through the 2000 season, Sutter ranked 13th all-time with 300 saves.

Sutton, Don

Born: April 2, 1945 in Clio, Alabama

Don Sutton's 23-year major league career was a testament to consistency and excellence. He never spent a day on the disabled list, and he was an effective pitcher in three different decades.

Sutton, a right-hander, broke in with the Los Angeles Dodgers in 1966. He went 12–12 with a 2.99 earned run average (ERA) and struck out 209 that season, the most by a National League rookie since Grover Alexander in 1911.

Sutton led the league in shutouts (9) in 1972, in games started (40) in 1974, and in ERA (2.21) in 1980. From 1970 through 1980, Sutton won 15 or more games seven times. In 1976, he went 21–10, the only 20-win season of his career.

Sutton signed with the Houston Astros as a free agent in 1981, and in August 1982 was traded to the Milwaukee Brewers, who were in a pennant race with the Baltimore Orioles. Sutton defeated Baltimore's Jim Palmer on the final day of the season to clinch the pennant for the Brewers.

Sutton was traded to the Oakland Athletics in 1985. Over the next three years, he also played with the California Angels and the Dodgers in 1988, his final year.

Sutton's career record was 324–256, with a 3.26 ERA. Through the 2000 season, he ranked 12th all-time in victories, seventh in losses, fifth in strikeouts (3,574), seventh in innings pitched (5,280.1), and 10th in shutouts (58). He pitched five one-hitters, nine two-hitters, and became the first pitcher to win 300 games with only one 20-win season. He struck out 100 or more in 21 consecutive seasons.

A four-time All-Star, Sutton, the broadcaster for the Atlanta Braves, was inducted into the Baseball Hall of Fame in 1998.

Terry, Bill

Born: October 30, 1896 in Atlanta, Georgia
Died: January 9, 1989

Bill Terry was no-nonsense, businesslike, and obsessed with making money. He was also one of the best hitters of his time. He grew up in poverty, dropped out of high school at age 13, and at age 15 was unloading freight cars. He earned a spot on a semipro team as a pitcher and was signed to a contract in the Georgia State League in 1914. But he quit when he wasn't making enough money and joined Standard Oil, which had its own semipro team.

Terry was offered a chance to play for the New York Giants, but insisted on making more money than he was making with Standard Oil. Manager John McGraw considered it for three weeks before offering Terry $5,000, a generous amount at the time.

Terry, who was converted into a first baseman, appeared in three games in the 1923 season and alternated with George Kelly in 1924. In 1925, Terry became the regular first baseman and hit .319. His average dropped to .289 in 1926, but that was the last time he failed to hit over .300.

Starting in 1927 and continuing for the last 11 years of his career, Terry never hit lower than .310 (in his last season), and four times hit .350 or better.

In 1930, he led the National League in average (.401) and hits (254). He also had 39 doubles, 15 triples, 23 home runs, and 129 runs batted in (RBI.) No National Leaguer has hit .400 since.

In addition to being known for his hard line drives, Terry's demeanor was also memorable. He was strong-willed and frequently clashed with McGraw. They once went a year and a half without speaking. But when McGraw stepped down in 1932, he handpicked Terry to be his successor.

As a player-manager, Terry led the Giants to two National League pennants and a World Series victory over the Washington Senators (1933).

In Terry's final season, 1936, he appeared in only 79 games because of bad knees. He managed the Giants until 1941 and then served as the director of the team's farm system, before returning to his real estate operations and his 304-acre cotton plantation in Memphis, Tenn.

Through the 2000 season, Terry ranked 13th all-time in batting average (.341). He had 2,193 hits, 373 doubles, 112 triples, and 1,078 RBI.

Terry, who had a .555 winning percentage as a manager, was inducted into the Baseball Hall of Fame in 1954.

Thomas, Frank

Born: May 27, 1968 in Columbus, Georgia

Frank Thomas, the seventh overall pick in the 1989 free agent draft by the Chicago White Sox, became one of the most productive hitters in the American League in the 1990s.

His first full season with the White Sox, 1991, he batted .318 with 32 home runs and 109 runs batted in (RBI). From 1992 through 1998, Thomas, a right-handed hitter nicknamed "The Big Hurt," had 24 or more home runs seven times, including 40 or more three times, and 100 RBI or more seven times.

He became the first player since Babe Ruth to have more than 100 RBI and more than 100 walks in his first three full seasons.

Twice, in 1993 and 1994, Thomas, 6-5, 270 pounds, was named the American League's Most Valuable Player. In 1993, he batted .317 with 41 home runs and 128 RBI. In 1994, he batted .353 with 38 home runs, 101 RBI, and a league-leading 106 runs.

In 1997, Thomas won the American League batting title with a .347 average, making him the only player ever to hit over .300 with at least 20 home runs, 100 RBI, 100 walks, and 100 runs scored in seven straight seasons.

In 1998, Thomas' average fell to .265, although he hit 29 home runs and knocked in 109 runs. In 1999, his average improved to .305, but he hit only 15 home runs and drove in 77 runs in a season shortened by foot surgery.

Through the 2000 season, Thomas's .321 lifetime batting average was the fourth highest among active players. He had 1,679 hits, 344 home runs, and 1,183 RBI. He was selected for the All-Star Game five times.

Traynor, Pie (Harold)

Born: November 11, 1899 in Framingham, Massachusetts
Died: March 16, 1972

Pie Traynor joined the Pittsburgh Pirates in 1920 as a shortstop, but he was switched to third base because he made too many errors. By 1922, Traynor became the Pirates regular third baseman, as well as one of the best fielding third basemen of all time.

It was virtually impossible to hit a ball past Traynor because of his great range and quick reflexes. He could cut off balls to his left and snare balls to his right, going across the bag with the ability to make strong throws from awkward positions. He also could charge toward the plate to field bunts.

In addition to his talent in the field, Traynor was a fine hitter, who batted .300 or better 10 times in a 12-year stretch, beginning in 1923. From 1927 through 1930, he hit .342, .337, .356, and .366, respectively.

In 1925, when the Pirates won the National League pennant, Traynor hit .320 with 189 hits and 106 runs batted in (RBI). In the World Series, in which the Pirates defeated the Washington Senators, he hit .346.

Traynor also played in the 1927 World Series against the New York Yankees and "Murderers' Row," which included Babe Ruth and Lou Gehrig. The Yankees won the Series in four games, Traynor hitting just .200.

Traynor was named player-manager of the Pirates in 1934, when he broke his arm. He appeared in only 57 games in 1935 and didn't play at all in 1936. His final season was 1937, when he played in just five games.

He continued as manager into the 1939 season. After he was replaced, he became a scout and then a radio announcer for the Pirates.

Traynor had a lifetime batting average of .320. He had 2,416 hits and 1,273 RBI, but hit just 58 home runs, although in seven seasons he had over 100 RBI with fewer than 10 home runs. He was inducted into the Baseball Hall of Fame in 1948, and in 1969 he was named the greatest third baseman of all time as part of Major League Baseball's centennial celebration.

Waddell, Rube (George)

Born: October 13, 1876 in Bradford, Pennsylvania
Died: April 1, 1914

Rube Waddell was a left-handed pitcher and one of the game's great characters. He was known to leave the park when he heard a siren because he loved fire engines. He wrestled alligators, had a leading role in a play, and often got raises by threatening to leave baseball and join vaudeville.

In 1900, his third major league season, Waddell, pitching for the Pittsburgh Pirates, led the National League in earned run average—ERA—(2.37) and strikeouts (130). In 1902, he joined the Philadelphia Athletics and went 24–7 with a 3.01 ERA and an American League–leading 210 strikeouts. That was the first of six straight seasons in which he led the league in strikeouts (302 in 1903, 349 in 1904, 287 in 1905, 196 in 1906, 232 in 1907). He also led the league in complete games (34) in 1903 and in victories (27), winning percentage (.730), ERA (1.48), and games (46) in 1905.

From 1902 through 1905, Waddell averaged 24 victories a year. In 1908, Waddell was traded to the St. Louis Browns, for whom he played three seasons. He went a combined 33–29 and retired in 1910, appearing in just 10 games.

Waddell played in the minor leagues for three more years. In 1912, while building a levee out of sandbags to protect Hickman, N.Y., from a flood, Waddell developed a bad cold that turned into tuberculosis. He eventually entered a sanatorium in Texas and died there.

Waddell's career record was 192–144. Through the 2000 season, his 2.16 ERA ranked sixth all-time. He was inducted into the Baseball Hall of Fame in 1946.

Wagner, Honus (John Peter)

Born: February 24, 1874 in Mansfield, Pennsylvania
Died: December 8, 1955

Honus Wagner, with his long arms, barrel chest, and bowed legs, looked nothing like a shortstop. But looks can be deceiving, because Wagner was one of the best fielding shortstops in baseball history. It was said that you could get a barrel between his legs, but not a baseball.

Wagner was also one of the game's greatest hitters and one of its most versatile players. During his 21-year career, spent almost entirely with the Pittsburgh Pirates, he played every position. Legendary manager John Mc-Graw called Wagner the best player he'd ever seen.

Wagner, nicknamed the "Flying Dutchman," began his professional career with the Louisville Cardinals in 1897. When the team disbanded two years later, he joined the Pirates. For 16 straight seasons, beginning in 1897, he hit .300 or better, and he won the National League batting title eight times (1900, '03–04, '06–09, '11), second only to Cobb's record of 12.

He led the league in runs batted in four times (1901–02, '08–09) and stolen bases five times (1901–02, '04, '07–08).

Wagner was to the Pirates what Ruth was to the New York Yankees and what Ty Cobb was to the Detroit Tigers. Wagner and Cobb were mirror images of each other on the field. Each could hit, run, field, and throw. The difference between them was their temperaments. They were polar opposites.

Wagner was a gentleman, easy-going and mild-mannered. Cobb was a dirty player—unpopular, mean-spirited, and given to violent outbursts.

In the 1909 World Series, the Pirates faced the Tigers. Wagner and Cobb received much of the attention. According to the story, Cobb taunted Wagner throughout the Series, and in the second game he finally vowed to make good on his threats. When Cobb reached first, he yelled to Wagner at shortstop, "Hey Krauthead, I'm coming down on the next pitch."

Wagner didn't respond, and on the first pitch Cobb attempted to steal second in customary fashion—with his spikes held high. When Cobb got to the bag, Wagner, with the ball, was waiting. Wagner let Cobb have it with a hard tag to the face that cut his lip and loosened his teeth. Afterward, Cobb said, "Wagner is the only man in the game I can't scare."

The Pirates won the Series, and Wagner won the individual battle with Cobb, outhitting him .333 to .231 and outstealing him six bases to two.

Arthritis took its toll on Wagner, whose last season as a player was 1917. He also managed the Pirates that year.

When he retired, Wagner was the major league leader in hits, runs, RBIs, steals, and total bases. He led the National League in singles, doubles, and triples.

More than 80 years after his retirement, Wagner's numbers have stood the test of time. He ranks seventh in hits (3,418), seventh in doubles (643), third in triples (252), and ninth in stolen bases (720).

Wagner was a charter member of the Baseball Hall of Fame, entering in 1936 along with Cobb, Ruth, Christy Mathewson, and Walter Johnson, and was named to the All-Century Team in 1999.

Walsh, Ed

Born: May 14, 1881 in Plains, Pennsylvania
Died: May 26, 1959

Ed Walsh was a workhorse pitcher and a master of the spitball. His fastball was solid and his curve average, but the spitball, which he added to his repertoire in 1906, elevated him to greatness.

Walsh, a right-hander, joined the Chicago White Sox in 1904. He was 14–6 his first two years. In 1906, he went 17–13 and helped the White Sox, known as the "Hitless Wonder White Sox," into the World Series. The White Sox batted .230 as a team and hit only six home runs all season. Nevertheless, they beat the Chicago Cubs in the Series, with Walsh winning two games.

Over the next two seasons, Walsh was as effective as he was durable. He thrived on a heavy workload. In 1907, he went 24–18 and led the league in earned run average (ERA) (.160), games (56), games started (46), complete games (37), innings pitched (422.1), and saves (6).

In 1908, Walsh was even better. He went 40–15, with a 1.42 ERA and led the league in winning percentage (.727), games (66), games started (49), complete games (42), innings pitched (464), strikeouts (269), shutouts (11), and saves (6). Walsh had two more outstanding seasons. He went 27–18 in 1911, when he led the league in games (56), innings pitched (368.2), strikeouts (255), and saves (4). In 1912, he went 27–17 and led the league in games (62), games started (41), innings pitched (393), and saves (10).

In 1913, arm troubles began to take their toll. Walsh appeared in just 29 games for Chicago over the next four seasons. In 1917, he was traded to the Boston Braves, for whom he appeared in four games and then retired.

Walsh's career record was 195–126. Through the 2000 season, he ranked first all-time in career ERA (1.82) and tied for 11th all-time in shutouts (57). He was inducted into the Baseball Hall of Fame in 1946.

Waner, Paul

Born: April 16, 1903 in Harrah, Oklahoma
Died: August 29, 1965

Paul Waner, and his brother, Lloyd, produced more hits than any brother combination in the history of Major League Baseball. The Waners' 5,611 hits are comfortably ahead of the Aaron brothers—Hank and Tommie (3,987).

Paul Waner, nicknamed "Big Poison," was a left-handed hitter who had remarkable bat control. He was fast enough to beat out infield hits, and he rarely struck out. During his 20-year career, only once, in 1937, did Waner strike out more than 30 times (34).

Paul Waner joined the Pittsburgh Pirates in 1926 after playing for the San Francisco Seals of the Pacific Coast League in 1925. Originally a pitcher, Waner was switched to the outfield because of his ability to hit. In one season with the Seals, he batted .401 with 280 hits.

Waner hit .336 as a rookie and led the National League with 22 triples. In 1927, he won the batting title, hitting .380. He also led the league in hits (237), triples (17), and runs batted in (131), and was named the National League's Most Valuable Player.

Waner hit .300 or better in the first 12 seasons of his career, including six times batting .350 or higher. He reached the 200-hit mark eight times during that stretch, including a league-leading 217 in 1934, when he won his second batting title (.362). He also led the league in runs that year (122).

In 1936, Waner won his final batting title, hitting .373 with 218 hits. He spent four more seasons with the Pirates, hitting .300 only once. After his average dropped to .290 in 1940, he was released by Pittsburgh and spent the next four seasons with the Brooklyn Dodgers and Boston Braves. He was traded to the New York Yankees in 1945, appeared in one game, and then retired at age 42.

Through the 2000 season, Waner's lifetime batting average of .333 ranked 21st all-time. He ranked 14th all-time in hits (3,152). After his retirement, he wrote a booklet on hitting and worked as a hitting instructor for several major league teams. He was inducted into the Baseball Hall of Fame in 1952.

Wilhelm, Hoyt

Born: July 26, 1923 in Huntersville, North Carolina

Hoyt Wilhelm, who relied almost exclusively on the knuckleball, spent years in the minor leagues and didn't make his major league debut until 1952, when he was 28 years old. As a right-handed reliever for the New York Giants, he went 15–3 and led the National League in winning percentage (.833), earned run average—ERA—(2.43), and appearances (71). He also led the league in appearances (68) in 1953.

The Giants won the National League pennant in 1954, and in the World Series against the Cleveland Indians, Wilhelm pitched in two games and didn't give up a run. In 1957, Wilhelm was traded to the St. Louis Cardinals, who sold him to the Cleveland Indians that same season. He was picked up on waivers in 1958 by the Bal-

timore Orioles and led the American League in ERA (2.19), making him the only pitcher to lead both leagues in ERA.

In 1963, Wilhelm was traded to the Chicago White Sox. His ERA was less than 2.00 in five straight seasons, starting in 1964.

Wilhelm was traded to the California Angels in 1969 and sold to the Atlanta Braves the same season. In 1970, the Braves sold him to the Chicago Cubs. He rejoined the Braves in 1971 and finished his career with the Los Angeles Dodgers, retiring after being released five days prior to his 49th birthday.

Wilhelm's career record was 143–122 with a 2.52 ERA, 1,610 strikeouts, and 778 walks. Through the 2000 season, he ranked third all-time in appearances (1,070) and 21st in saves (227). He has more victories (124) than any reliever in major league history, and he was the first reliever inducted into the Baseball Hall of Fame (1985).

Williams, Billy

Born: June 15, 1938 in Whistler, Alabama

Billy Williams was a model of consistency throughout his career. He hit for average and power, and was a solid outfielder.

Williams, who grew up in Mobile, Ala., earned a football letter as a defensive end, and got a scholarship offer from Grambling State University. But instead of going to college and playing football, he played semipro baseball for the Mobile Black Bears. He was signed by the Chicago Cubs, joined the team in 1959, and became the team's regular left fielder in 1961, when he batted .278 with 25 home runs and 86 runs batted in (RBI). He was named the National League Rookie of the Year.

From 1961 through 1974, Williams, a left-handed hitter with a flawless swing, never hit lower than .276, and he hit .300 or better five times, including .322 in 1970, .301 in 1971, and .333 in 1972, when he led the league in batting and slugging percentage (.606). Williams, with 37 home runs and 122 RBI, finished second to Cincinnati Reds catcher Johnny Bench in both categories. Williams also finished second to Bench in voting for the Most Valuable Player Award.

In 1970, Williams led the league in hits (205) and runs (137). His home run production was as consistent as his batting average. He had 14 seasons of 20 or more, five seasons of 30 or more, and one season, 1970, when he hit a career-high 42.

Williams was also a durable player. From September 1963 through September 1970, he played in 1,117 consecutive games, a National League record that existed until 1983, when it was broken by Steve Garvey.

In 1968, Williams hit for the cycle and tied a major league record by hitting home runs in five consecutive at-bats.

Williams was traded to Oakland after the 1974 season. He spent two seasons with the Athletics, retiring after the 1976 season.

Williams' lifetime batting average was .290. He had 2,711 hits, 426 home runs, and 1,475 RBI. A six-time All-Star, Williams was inducted into the Baseball Hall of Fame in 1987.

Williams, Ted

Born: August 30, 1918 in San Diego, California

The combination of lightning-quick reflexes, impeccable timing, and remarkable eyesight helped Ted Williams become perhaps the greatest hitter in baseball history. A left-handed batter, Williams kept his hands back until the last possible moment before whipping them around. His forearms were powerful and his eyes were, according to the Navy doctors who examined him, one in a hundred thousand.

Williams went to spring training in 1938 with the Boston Red Sox, but was sent to the minor leagues for more seasoning.

In 1939, Williams became a starter in right field with Boston and had a successful rookie year, hitting .327, leading the American League in runs batted in (RBI) with 147 and finishing second in doubles and third in home runs.

Williams moved to left field in 1940, when he hit .344 and led the league with 134 runs scored. In 1941, Williams hit .406, the last player ever to reach the .400 mark. On the last day of the season, Williams' average was exactly .400. Asked by his manager, Joe Cronin, if he wanted to sit out a doubleheader against the Philadelphia Athletics to protect his average, Williams chose to

Ted Williams   *Reading Eagle/Times*

play both ends of the doubleheader. He got four hits in the first game, including a home run, and two more hits in the second game. He finished the season with a .406 average and his first batting title.

The closest Williams came to the .400 mark again was in 1957, at age 40, when he hit .388.

In 1942, Williams won the first of his two Triple Crowns. He led the league in average (.356), home runs (36), and RBI (137). He also won the Triple Crown in 1947—.343 average, 32 home runs, 114 RBI.

Williams missed all of the 1943, 1944, and 1945 seasons because he served in the Marine Corps during World War II. He also missed most of the 1952 and 1953 seasons, because of the Korean War. In all, he missed 727 games to military service, more than any other player.

But each time he returned from the service, he picked up where he had left off. In 1946, Williams hit .342 with 38 home runs and 123 RBI. He was named the American League's Most Valuable Player. He won his fourth batting title in 1948, when he hit .369, and in 1949 he won his second Most Valuable Player Award, batting .343 with a league-leading 43 home runs and 159 RBI.

After rejoining the Red Sox in late 1953, Williams won batting titles in 1957 (.388) and 1958 (.328), when he became the oldest player ever to lead the league in hitting.

Williams played two more years, retiring at the end of the 1960 season. In the last at-bat of his career, he hit a home run and received a standing ovation from the fans in Fenway Park. But Williams, who had a contentious relationship with the fans and the press throughout his career, refused to doff his cap at such an occasion.

Williams, an avid fisherman, stayed away from baseball until 1969, when he was named manager of the Washington Senators and received the Manager of the Year Award. The team moved to Texas in 1972, and Williams retired after that season. Through the 2000 season, Williams' lifetime batting average of .344 ranked sixth all-time. He had 2,654 hits, 521 home runs, 1,839 RBI, 19 All-Star Game selections, and was inducted into the Baseball Hall of Fame in 1966 and was named to the All-Century Team in 1999. The numbers could have been even better had he not lost so much time to the military.

Wills, Maury

Born: October 2, 1932 in Washington, D.C.

Maury Wills joined the Los Angeles Dodgers in 1959 and became the first player in Major League Baseball history to steal more than 100 bases in a season. He stole 104 in 1962, when he hit .299, and led the National League in at-bats (695) and triples (10). He was named the league's

Most Valuable Player and the Associated Press' Male Athlete of the Year.

Wills, a switch-hitting shortstop, led the league in steals six straight seasons, starting in 1961. Through the 2000 season, his 104 steals is the seventh highest single-season total of all time. He stole 94 in 1965, which is the 12th highest total all-time.

Wills spent eight seasons with the Dodgers, appearing in four World Series. He was traded to the Pittsburgh Pirates in 1967. In 1969, he joined the Montreal Expos, and he finished his career with the Dodgers, retiring in 1972.

In 1980, Wills was named the manager of the Seattle Mariners. He became the third African American manager in major league history. He was fired 25 games into the 1981 season. His record was 26–56.

Wills' lifetime batting average was .281, with 2,134 hits, including 177 doubles and 77 triples. Through the 2000 season, he ranked 18th all-time with 586 stolen bases.

Wilson, Hack (Lewis)

Born: April 26, 1900 in Elwood City, Pennsylvania
Died: November 23, 1948

Hack Wilson, 5-6, 190 pounds, was a barrel-chested, happy-go-lucky outfielder whose reputation for drinking and carousing was well earned.

Wilson got the nickname "Hack" because of a resemblance to George Hackenschmidt, a professional wrestler and strongman. Others claim he got the name because of his resemblance to Hack Miller, an outfielder for the Chicago Cubs who was said to be the strongest man in baseball. There were those who thought he was called Hack because of the way he played the outfield.

Wilson quit school in the sixth grade, worked at a variety of jobs, including printer's apprentice, ironworker in a locomotive factory, and shipyard laborer. He began playing for Martinsburg Blue Socks in the Blue Ridge League in 1921, and in 1923 joined the New York Giants. After three seasons in New York, Wilson was picked up by the Chicago Cubs in 1926, when he hit .321 and led the National League in home runs (21). He also led the league in home runs in 1927 (30), 1928, (31), and 1930 (56).

Wilson's 1930 season was remarkable. In addition to the 56 home runs, he also batted .356, had a .756 slugging percentage, and drove in 191 runs, a major league single-season record. His 1929 season was almost as good. He batted .345 with a .618 slugging percentage, 39 home runs, and 159 runs batted in (RBI).

Wilson was traded to the Brooklyn Dodgers in 1932. He finished his career with the Philadelphia Phillies, retiring in 1934.

Wilson's lifetime batting average was .307 over 12 seasons. He had 244 home runs and 1,062 RBI. He played in two World Series (1924, '29), hitting .319. He was inducted into the Baseball Hall of Fame in 1979.

Winfield, Dave

Born: October 3, 1951 in St. Paul, Minnesota

Dave Winfield was an all-around player who was dangerous at the plate and talented in the outfield. A graduate of the University of Minnesota, Winfield was drafted by three professional leagues—the Minnesota Vikings of the National Football League, the Utah Stars of the now-defunct American Basketball Association, and the Atlanta Hawks of the National Basketball Association.

But he signed a contract with the San Diego Padres. He joined the Padres in 1973, without ever having played in the minor leagues, and a year later, became the starting right fielder. He put up solid numbers in San Diego, twice hitting over .300, including .308 in 1979, when he hit 34 home runs and led the National League in runs batted in (RBI) with 118.

In 1980, Winfield became a free agent and joined the New York Yankees. Between 1981 and 1988, he again put up solid numbers, hitting .340 with 19 home runs and 100 RBI in 1984 and .322 with 25 home runs and 107 RBI in 1988. Winfield spent seven full seasons with the Yankees and hit 24 or more home runs in six of them.

Much of his stay in New York was overshadowed by an ongoing feud with Yankees owner George Steinbrenner, who never seemed satisfied with Winfield's production. The owner's dissatisfaction began with Winfield's performance in the 1981 World Series, which the Yankees lost to the Los Angeles Dodgers. Winfield went 1-for-22 and hit .045.

In 1989, Winfield missed the entire season with a herniated disk. He returned in 1990 and played 20 games before he was traded to the California Angels. When Steinbrenner discovered that in spite of the trade, he had to pay Winfield $7 million in cost-of-living expenses, per his contract, Steinbrenner hired a convicted felon, Howard Spira, to spread damaging information about Winfield. Baseball commissioner Fay Vincent ended up banishing Steinbrenner from baseball for a time.

Winfield was with the Angels through the 1991 season. He joined the Toronto Blue Jays as a free agent in 1992, hit .290 with 26 home runs and 108 RBI, and helped them to a World Series championship against the Atlanta Braves. Winfield spent two seasons with the Minnesota Twins and ended his career in 1995 with the Cleveland Indians.

Winfield's lifetime batting average was .283. Through the 2000 season, he ranked 16th all-time in hits (3,110), eighth in games played (2,973), eighth in at-bats (11,003), 10th in total bases (5,221), 21st in home runs (465), 12th in RBI (1,833), and 14th in extra base hits (1,093).

Winfield, an eight-time All-Star, is one of just three players in major league history—Hank Aaron and Willie Mays are the others—to collect 3,000 hits (3,110), 450 home runs (465), and 200 stolen bases (223).

In 2000, he was inducted into the Baseball Hall of Fmae.

Wynn, Early

Born: January 6, 1920 in Hartford, Alabama
Died: March 4, 1999

Early Wynn was a fierce competitor who used intimidation and intensity to unnerve hitters. A hard-throwing right-hander with a good fastball and curve, Wynn did whatever was necessary to win. He was so tough that he once got hit on the chin by a line drive, a blow that required 16 stiches and knocked out seven teeth, but wanted to stay in the game.

He decided to play baseball after breaking his leg in a high school football game. It wasn't too long before the Washington Senators offered him $100 a month to pitch in their minor league system.

Wynn was used sparingly during his first two seasons with the Senators (1939, '41), but in 1942, he became part of the starting rotation, going 10–16 with a 5.12 earned run average (ERA).

Wynn remained with the Senators through the 1948 season, going a combined 72–87. He was traded to Cleveland in 1948. He added a curveball to his fastball and knuckleball, and it increased his effectiveness. Wynn went 11–7 and 18–8 in his first two seasons with the Indians, leading the American League with a 3.20 ERA in 1950.

In 1951, Wynn went 20–13 with a 3.02 ERA and led the league in games started (34) and innings pitched (274.1). He went 23–12 in 1952 with a 2.90 ERA and, after winning 17 games in 1953, went 23–11 in 1954 with a 2.73 ERA and league-leading totals in victories, games started (36), and innings pitched (270.2).

Wynn had one more 20-win season with the Indians—20–9 in 1956. In 1957, he led the league in games started (37) and strikeouts (184).

In 1957, Wynn was traded to the Chicago White Sox. In his first season with the White Sox, he led the league in strikeouts with 179. His best season in Chicago came in 1959, when he went 22–10 with a 3.17 ERA and league-leading totals in games started (37) and innings pitched (255.2). He won the American League Cy Young Award. That was Wynn's last good season. From 1960 through 1963, his last season, which he spent with the Cleveland Indians, Wynn went a combined 29–31. The last victory of his career also was his 300th.

Wynn's career record was 300–244 with a 3.54 ERA. Through the 2000 season, he ranked 19th all-time in victories and fourth in walks allowed (1,775). He was inducted into the Baseball Hall of Fame in 1972.

Yastrzemski, Carl

Born: August 22, 1939 in Southampton, New York

Carl Yastrzemski had the unenviable task of taking over for Boston Red Sox legend Ted Williams. As a result, the Fenway Park fans never seemed to give "Yaz," as he was known, his due. But his statistics are proof of a remarkable career.

Yastrzemski got contract offers from 14 major league teams while he was enrolled at Notre Dame. The Cincinnati Reds bid the highest ($125,000), but he took less money from the Red Sox so that he could play closer to home.

He joined the Red Sox and became the starting left fielder in 1961, when he hit .266 with 11 home runs. In 1963, the left-handed hitter won his first batting title, hitting .321, also leading the league in hits (183) and doubles (40). After three more solid seasons, Yastrzemski won the Triple Crown in 1967. He hit .326 with 44 home runs and 121 runs batted in (RBI). He also led the league in slugging percentage (.622), hits (189), and runs (112).

The Red Sox won the American League pennant in 1967, and Yastrzemski helped during the stretch drive, hitting .523 over the last two weeks of the season and getting 10 hits in his last 13 at-bats. He hit .400 with three home runs in the World Series against the St. Louis Cardinals, who won in seven games.

In 1968, Yastrzemski won his third—and final—batting title, hitting .301. He hit .300 twice more during his career—.329 in 1970, .301 in 1974—but from 1971 on hit mostly in the .270 to .280 range.

In addition to his offense, Yastrzemski also was a fine defensive player with a strong arm and the ability to play the left field wall—Fenway Park's famed Green Monster. Seven times he led American League outfielders in assists.

Yastrzemski led the league in 23 offensive categories during his 23-year career, all with the Red Sox—on-base percentage five times, slugging average three times, batting three times, runs three times, doubles three times, walks twice, hits twice, home runs once, and RBI once.

Through the 2000 season, Yastrzemski, whose lifetime batting average was .285, ranked sixth all-time in hits (3,419), second in games played (3,308), third in at-bats (11,988), seventh in total bases (5,539), 22nd in home runs (452), 10th in RBI (1,844), 13th in runs (1,816), and seventh in extra base hits (1,157). He was inducted into the Baseball Hall of Fame in 1989 in his first year of eligibility.

Young, Cy (Denton)

Born: March 29, 1867 in Gilmore, Ohio
Died: November 5, 1955

Cy Young is the all-time winningest pitcher in baseball history with 511 victories. A force in two centuries, Young won 267 games in the 19th century and 244 in the 20th century.

He has 94 more wins than Walter Johnson, who ranked second all-time with 417, and 138 more than Christy Mathewson and Grover Cleveland Alexander, who were tied for third with 373.

Young stood 6-2, weighed 210 pounds, and threw a fastball and curve, both with good control. Named Denton True Young, he was nicknamed Cy, which was short for "Cyclone." As legend has it, the name came from batters who couldn't see his pitches, but could hear them whizzing by.

His first year in professional baseball was 1890 with Cleveland in the National League. He went 9–7 as a rookie, then won 20 or more games for 14 consecutive seasons and 16 times overall. He won at least 30 games five times.

Through the 2000 season, Young was also the all-time leader in losses (316), complete games (750), and innings pitched (7,356). He ranked fourth in shutouts with 76 and 11th in appearances with 906. He completed more than 90 percent of his starts. Young pitched three no-hitters, his last coming in June 1908 at age 41. He also threw the first pitch in World Series history (1903), and he threw the first perfect game of the 20th century (May 1904, vs. Philadelphia Athletics).

Young retired at age 44, not because his arm failed him, but because the rest of him wasn't in as good shape.

He was inducted into the Baseball Hall of Fame in 1937, the second year of its existence, and was named to the All-Century Team in 1999.

Yount, Robin

Born: September 16, 1955 in Danville, Illinois

Robin Yount was as versatile as he was consistent. He began his career with the Milwaukee Brewers in 1974 as a shortstop, but then was switched to center field, and he was just as effective—at the plate and in the field.

Yount was the third overall pick in the 1973 draft. He was signed right out of high school, and he joined the Brewers in 1974, when he became their starting shortstop. He was 18 years old and the youngest regular in the majors since 1906. The first six years of his career were solid, but in 1980, he began to show signs that he was destined for stardom. He batted .293 with 23 home runs, 10 triples, 87 runs batted in (RBI), and an American League–leading 49 doubles.

In 1982, he batted .331 and led the league in slugging percentage (.578), hits (210), and doubles (46). He also topped the 100-RBI mark for the first time with 114 and was named Most Valuable Player in the American League. He led the Brewers to the World Series, where he batted .414 with one home run and six RBI in a seven-game loss to the St. Louis Cardinals.

Yount hit .300 or better in five of the next seven seasons, including .318 with 21 home runs and 103 RBI. He won his second Most Valuable Player Award.

In 1985, Yount began suffering from shoulder problems and could no longer make long throws from shortstop, so he was moved to center field, where he excelled.

His fielding percentage was .990 or better in six of his nine seasons as an outfielder.

On September 9, 1992, Yount got his 3,000th hit. He and Honus Wagner are the only shortstops to reach that milestone, through the 2000 season.

Yount, who spent his entire 20-year career with the Brewers, retired following the 1993 season. He had a lifetime batting average of .285. Through the 2000 season, he ranked 15th all-time in hits (3,142), 12th in games played (2,856), first in sacrifice flies (123), and seventh in at-bats (11,008). He was inducted into the Baseball Hall of Fame in 1999, his first year of eligibility.

Basketball

Abdul-Jabbar, Kareem

Born: April 16, 1947 in New York, New York

Kareem Abdul-Jabbar was one of the game's dominant centers, but he dominated in ways that other centers—before and since—did not. Abdul-Jabbar, who stood 7-2, didn't dominate with his size and strength. He wasn't a physical player; instead, he was graceful and versatile. In addition to possessing a deft shooting touch, especially with his trademark sky hook, which was virtually unstoppable, Abdul-Jabbar was an excellent passer, defender, shot blocker, and rebounder. He was arguably the most versatile center ever.

Abdul-Jabbar was known as Lew Alcindor until he became a Muslim in 1971 and changed his name, which means "noble, powerful servant."

He drew national attention while a high school player at Power Memorial in New York City, where he had 2,067 points and 2,002 rebounds. He led his team to 53 straight wins and was a three-time All-American.

Alcindor was recruited by more than 200 colleges, but he chose to play for coach John Wooden at UCLA. He led the Bruins to three consecutive national championships (1967–69) and an 88–2 record. He was a three-time All-American, three times the most outstanding player in the Final Four, and the national player of the year in 1967 and 1969.

Alcindor averaged 26.4 points and 15.5 rebounds a game for UCLA, and he led Division I in field goal percentage in 1967 (.667) and 1969 (.635).

Said Wooden: "Kareem was the finest, truly big man ever to play basketball. He could do anything you asked of him, and do it almost to perfection."

When his college career ended, Alcindor was heavily recruited by both pro leagues—the NBA and the ABA. Alcindor's ABA rights were assigned to the New York franchise. His NBA rights were won by the Milwaukee Bucks in a coin flip. In order to avoid a bidding war, Alcindor asked for a sealed bid from each team. He accepted the Bucks' offer of more than $1 million.

Alcindor's impact was immediate. He averaged 28.8 points and 14.5 rebounds a game and was named the NBA Rookie of the Year.

In 1971, he averaged a league-leading 31.7 points and 16 rebounds a game in leading the Bucks to the NBA championship.

Abdul-Jabbar spent four more seasons with the Bucks before he was traded to the Los Angeles Lakers in June 1975. He averaged at least 20 points a game in 11 of his 14 seasons with the Lakers and led them to five titles and seven appearances in the finals in an eight-year stretch (1980–88).

Abdul-Jabbar was, by nature, a distant and aloof person who had the reputation of being unapproachable. But by the time he retired after the 1989 season, he was given an enthusiastic send-off in every NBA city.

Through the 1999–2000 season, Abdul-Jabbar ranked first all-time in points (38,387), field goals

(15,837), field goals attempted (28,307), games played (1,560), and minutes played (57,446). He was named the NBA's Most Valuable Player a record six times (1971–72, '74, '76–77, '80). He was All-NBA 10 times, NBA All-Defensive first team five times, and played in a record 19 All-Star Games.

In the postseason, Abdul-Jabbar holds the record for most games (237), most field goals (2,356), most blocked shots (476), and most personal fouls (797). He was twice named the NBA Finals' Most Valuable Player (1971, '85).

Abdul-Jabbar was named one of the NBA's 50 greatest players in 1996 and was inducted into the Naismith Memorial Basketball Hall of Fame in 1995.

Archibald, Nate (Nathaniel)
Born: September 2, 1948 in New York, New York

Nate Archibald had the unselfishness usually associated with a point guard and the ability to score himself. The combination made him a difficult player to defend.

Archibald grew up in poverty in the South Bronx. Basketball was his way of avoiding the pitfalls of inner city life, such as drugs and violence. He was cut from his high school team as a sophomore, made the team as a junior, and received All-City honors as a senior.

His grades weren't good enough to earn a college scholarship, so he attended Arizona Western Community College, then transferred to the University of Texas-El Paso (UTEP), where he averaged 22.4 points a game as a junior and 21.4 as a senior.

Despite being undersized (6-1, 160 pounds)—hence his nickname "Tiny"—Archibald was drafted in the second round by the Cincinnati Royals in the 1970 NBA draft. He became a starter in his third season, when he led the league in scoring (34 points a game) and assists (11.8) a game.

Archibald spent the 1976–77 season with the New Jersey Nets, and missed the 1977–78 season with a torn Achilles tendon. In August 1978, he was traded to the Boston Celtics, where he played with Larry Bird, Kevin McHale, and Robert Parish. He helped the team win the 1981 NBA championship.

Archibald retired after the 1984 season, which he spent with the Milwaukee Bucks. He averaged 18.8 points and 7.4 assists a game in his 14 seasons. He was All-NBA three times and played in six All-Star Games. He was inducted into the Naismith Memorial Basketball Hall of Fame in 1990 and named one of the 50 greatest players in NBA history in 1996.

Arizin, Paul
Born: April 9, 1928 in Philadelphia, Pennsylvania

Paul Arizin made a major impact on basketball, even though he got a late start. He waited until his senior year to try out for his high school team, only to be cut. So he played in a variety of recreational leagues, playing on as many as seven teams at one time.

Arizin pioneered the jump shot, and it happened by accident. Because some of his games were played on dance floors, which were slippery, Arizin began to jump while shooting to keep from slipping. Before long, all of his shots were jump shots, which he fired with a quick release.

He enrolled at Villanova University and did not plan to play basketball, preferring instead to concentrate on his chemistry major and continuing to play in city leagues. But when Villanova basketball coach Al Severance heard that Arizin was averaging as many as 30 points a game, and then found out he was going to school at Villanova, he was persuaded to join the team.

In 1950, his senior year at Villanova, he scored 85 points in a game against Philadelphia Naval Air Materials Center, an NCAA-sanctioned team, and led Division I teams in scoring, averaging 25.3 points a game. Arizin, nicknamed "Pitchin Paul," was a draft pick of the Philadelphia Warriors in 1950.

He spent 10 seasons with the Warriors, missing the 1953 and 1954 seasons because he served with the Marine Corps, and led the league in scoring twice (25.4 in 1952, 25.6 in 1956). Only in his rookie season did he fail to average at least 20 points a game.

Arizin, who led the Warriors to the 1956 NBA title, suffered from asthma, which made his accomplishments that much more impressive.

Arizin averaged 22.8 points a game for his career, which ranked him 18th all-time, through the 1999–2000 season. He was an All-NBA selection three times, an All-Star 10 times, and named one of the NBA's 50 greatest players in 1996. He was inducted into the Naismith Memorial Basketball Hall of Fame in 1977.

Barkley, Charles
Born: February 20, 1963 in Leeds, Alabama

Charles Barkley was one of the most talented, quotable, outspoken, and controversial players in the history of the NBA. There's nothing he wouldn't say, and if challenged, no one he would back down to. He once spit at a fan and hit an 8-year-old girl by mistake; he once threw a patron through a plate glass window at an Orlando bar; and he even claimed he was misquoted in his own autobiography, entitled *Outrageous*. He was the ultimate loose cannon.

But his brash nature didn't keep Barkley from having an outstanding career. He played his college ball at Auburn University, where he was known as the "Round Mound of Rebound," and averaged 14.1 points and 9.6 rebounds in three seasons. He was selected by the Philadelphia 76ers in the first round of the 1984 NBA draft.

At 6-6, 252 pounds, Barkley was a small forward and a power forward all in one. He was a ferocious and tenacious rebounder who could score.

He played seven seasons with the Sixers (1985–92) and led the league in rebounding in 1987, averaging 14.6 a game. In all but his first season, he averaged at least 20 points a game, including a career-high 28.3 in 1988.

But the Sixers never made a serious run at a title, and Barkley's frustration forced a trade. In June 1992, he was dealt to the Phoenix Suns, where he spent four seasons and reached the NBA Finals against the Chicago Bulls in 1993. The Bulls won the series in six games.

Barkley averaged 25.6 points and 12.2 rebounds a game in 1993 and was named the NBA's Most Valuable Player, edging Michael Jordan of the Bulls.

Barkley averaged 21 points or more and at least 11 rebounds in each of his four seasons with the Suns. In August 1996, he was traded to the Houston Rockets, where he joined Clyde Drexler and Hakeem Olajuwon.

The Rockets reached the Western Conference finals in 1997, losing to the Utah Jazz, but in the following two seasons, they failed to get out of the first round.

On December 8, 1999, Barkley suffered a career-ending knee injury during a game in Philadelphia. He tore the left quadriceps away from his knee cap. He missed four months, but returned to play his final game April 19. He played six minutes and scored two points against the Vancouver Grizzlies. Knee injury or not, it's likely the 2000 season would have been his last.

In 16 seasons, Barkley averaged 22.1 points and 11.7 rebounds a game. He had 23,757 points and 12,546 rebounds. Through the 1999–2000 season, he ranked 13th all-time in points.

Barkley was All-NBA five times and an NBA All-Star 11 times. In 1992 and 1996 he was selected to play on the U.S. Olympic men's basketball team, also known as the Dream Team, and he was the leading scorer in each Olympics, and in both of which the U.S. won the gold medal.

Barkley was named one of the NBA's 50 greatest players in 1996.

Barry, Rick

Born: March 28, 1944 in Elizabeth, New Jersey

Rick Barry was one of the great scorers in NBA history, but not necessarily because he was a great shooter. Although Barry could hit the jump shot, his forte was getting the ball in the basket in any way he could—on a drive, off a rebound, or because of his hustle and work ethic.

Barry played his college ball at the University of Miami, where he led the nation in scoring (34.7 points a game) and was an All-American in 1965. He was chosen by the San Francisco Warriors in the first round of the

1965 NBA draft. He spent two seasons with the Warriors, the second of which he led the NBA in scoring, averaging 35.6 points a game. He was named the NBA's Rookie of the Year.

After the 1967 season, he jumped to the Oakland Oaks of the rival American Basketball Association. He sat out the 1967–68 season because of a court fight over his move, then joined the Oaks in 1968, when he led the ABA in scoring, averaging 34 points a game.

Barry was such a potent offensive threat that teams would double- and triple-team him, the result of which was his development into one of the game's best passing forwards.

Barry spent three more seasons in the ABA, one with Washington and two with New York, before returning to the Warriors, who were known as the Golden State Warriors.

In 1975, Barry led the Warriors to the NBA championship over the heavily favored Washington Bullets in a four-game sweep. He was named Most Valuable Player in the playoffs. He averaged 28 points a game.

Barry remained with Golden State through the 1978 season and finished his career by playing two seasons with the Houston Rockets. He retired in 1980.

Barry was one of the game's all-around great players. He also had the reputation of being a most unpopular person. He was very demanding, a perfectionist, who did not tolerate mistakes made by his teammates or himself. He criticized teammates, coaches, referees, and opponents.

"I was not an easy person to get along with," said Barry. "I did not have a lot of tact."

Barry played 10 seasons in the NBA and four seasons in the ABA. He scored 18,395 points in the NBA (23.2 average) and 6,684 points in the ABA (30.5 average). In combined NBA–ABA career scoring, Barry ranked 15th all-time with 25,279 points.

Using an old-fashioned underhand technique, he led the NBA in foul shooting six times and the ABA three times. Barry is the only person to have led the NCAA, the NBA, and the ABA in scoring.

Barry was All-NBA five times and All-ABA four times. He was inducted into the Naismith Memorial Basketball Hall of Fame in 1986 and named one of the NBA's 50 greatest players in 1996.

Barry is the father of Jon, Brent, and Drew, each of whom played or continues to play in the NBA.

Baylor, Elgin

Born: September 16, 1934 in Washington, D.C.

Elgin Baylor was the first modern basketball player, in that he was creative, explosive, athletic, and acrobatic. He was able to do things that no one before him could manage. He was the first skywalker, a prelude to Julius Erving and Michael Jordan.

Baylor was an offensive machine who could shoot the jumper or drive the lane, with the ability to make the spectacular play at any time. He also was an excellent passer and an outstanding rebounder.

He began his college career at the College of Idaho on a football scholarship, but when the basketball coach noticed him playing in a pickup game, he got Baylor to switch sports. He eventually transferred to Seattle University. Baylor led the nation in rebounding during his junior year (1957), averaging 20.3 a game. As a senior, he averaged 32.5 points and 19.3 rebounds a game, and was a consensus All-American and Most Valuable Player of the Final Four.

Baylor was the first pick overall in the 1958 draft by the Minneapolis Lakers, who moved to Los Angeles after the 1960 season.

Baylor was named NBA Rookie of the Year in 1959. He averaged 24.9 points and 15 rebounds a game.

In 1960, the Lakers drafted Jerry West, and he and Baylor formed an effective 1-2 combination.

In November 1961, Baylor scored 71 points against the New York Knicks. Through the 1999–2000 season, this ranked as the seventh-highest single-game performance. He also scored 64 points against Boston in 1959.

Baylor averaged 24 or more points a game in 11 of his 14 seasons. From 1960 to 1963, he averaged 33.4, 38.1, 38.6, and 32.6, respectively. He also averaged 11 rebounds or more nine times.

As good as his numbers were, they might have been even better had Baylor not been plagued by knee injuries, starting in 1963 and lasting throughout his career. He also had the misfortune of playing in the same era as Wilt Chamberlain, which kept him from winning scoring titles, and the multitime NBA champion Boston Celtics, which kept the Lakers from winning NBA titles.

The Lakers reached the NBA Finals eight times in Baylor's career, but never won a championship. Ironically, the Lakers won the 1972 NBA championship, but Baylor retired after playing only nine games that season.

In 14 seasons, Baylor had 23,149 points (27.4 average) and 11,463 rebounds (13.5). Through the 1999–2000 season, he ranked 17th all-time in points and fourth all-time in scoring average.

In the playoffs, he scored, 1,762 points (26.7 average) and had 730 rebounds (11.1). He ranked ninth in points and fourth in scoring average.

Baylor was All-NBA 10 times and an 11-time All-Star. He was inducted into the Naismith Memorial Basketball Hall of Fame in 1976 and named one of the NBA's 50 greatest players in 1996.

Through 1999–2000, he was in his 14th season as the vice president of basketball operations for the Los Angeles Clippers.

Bellamy, Walt

Born: July 24, 1939 in New Bern, North Carolina

Walt Bellamy, a 6-11, 245-pound center, was one of the most durable and dependable players in NBA history. He played his college ball at Indiana University, where he averaged 20.6 points and 15.5 rebounds a game.

Bellamy was the starting center on the 1960 U.S. Olympic basketball team, which won the gold medal. The team was coached by the legendary Pete Newell and featured Jerry West, Oscar Robertson, and Jerry Lucas.

In 1961, Bellamy was the first pick overall by the Chicago Packers, which moved to Baltimore and became the Bullets after the 1963 season.

Bellamy, nicknamed "Bells," was the NBA Rookie of the Year in 1961–62. He averaged 31.6 points and 19 rebounds a game. He finished second in the league in scoring to Wilt Chamberlain, who averaged 50.4 points, and third in rebounding behind Chamberlain and Bill Russell.

While Bellamy continued to be a solid performer throughout his career, he never reached the heights he reached as a rookie. Through 1965, he averaged at least 22.8 points and 14.6 rebounds a game. But from the 1966–67 season until the end of his career in 1975, his scoring average was never higher than 19 points a game.

Bellamy spent time with the New York Knicks, Detroit Pistons, Atlanta Hawks, and New Orleans Jazz. In 1968–69, he played in an NBA-record 88 regular season games, because at the time of a trade that sent him from New York to Detroit, the Pistons had not played as many games as the Knicks.

Bellamy played in 1,043 of a possible 1,055 games and averaged nearly 38 minutes a game.

In 14 seasons, Bellamy had 20,941 points (20.1 average) and 14,241 rebounds (13.7). Through the 2000 season, he ranked 21st all-time in points and eighth all-time in rebounds. A four-time All-Star, Bellamy was inducted into the Naismith Memorial Basketball Hall of Fame in 1993.

Bing, Dave

Born: November 24, 1943 in Washington, D.C.

Dave Bing was a complete guard who could score off the jump shot or the drive, pass effectively, and provide outstanding leadership. That he made it to the NBA at all is a testament to his perseverance and determination.

When Bing was five years old, he was playing a game of "horsey," using two sticks that had been nailed together. He fell and one of the nails penetrated his left eye. The eye was saved by surgery, but he suffered from blurred vision. Bing overcame the difficulty and went on to have a stellar career at Syracuse University, where he averaged 24.8 points a game during his career and was an All-American as a senior in 1966.

Bing was the second overall pick in the 1966 NBA draft by the Detroit Pistons. He was named Rookie of the Year in 1967, averaging 20 points a game. In 1968, he led the league in scoring, averaging 27.1 points a game.

In a 1971 preseason game, Bing suffered what looked to be a career-ending eye injury, a partially detached retina, this time to the right eye. He lay for three days in a hospital, not able to see a thing. But doctors' expectations that he was finished playing were unfounded. He played only 45 games in the 1971–72 season, but returned in time to play all 82 games.

After nine seasons in Detroit, seven of which he averaged 22 points a game or more, Bing was traded to the Washington Bullets. He spent two seasons in Washington and his final season, 1978, with the Boston Celtics.

Bing scored 18,327 points (20.3 average) in 12 seasons. He was All-NBA twice and an All-Star seven times. He was inducted into the Naismith Memorial Basketball Hall of Fame in 1989 and was named one of the NBA's 50 greatest players in 1996.

After his retirement, Bing went into business, starting Bing Steel in Detroit. Within 10 years, it was one of the 10 largest African American–owned companies in the country. He was honored as the National Small Business Person of the Year and the National Minority Supplier of the Year.

Bird, Larry
Born: December 7, 1956 in French Lick, Indiana

Larry Bird was the epitome of a team player. He was determined, never stopped hustling, and was blessed with a will to win that was unsurpassed. He was outstanding in every phase of the game and as fundamentally sound a player as ever played. He could score off the jump shot or the drive, he could pass, and he could defend. He was known for his blind passes and his uncanny instincts. He was arguably the best forward ever to play the game.

Bird, 6-9, 220 pounds, began his college career at Indiana University in 1974, but dropped out after a month. He attended Northwood Institute (Ind.), a junior college, but lasted only a month. Then he accepted a scholarship to Indiana State University. After sitting out the 1975–76 season, according to NCAA rules, because he was a transfer student, Bird averaged 32.8 points a game as a sophomore and 30 as a junior. The Boston Celtics drafted him in the first round of the NBA draft in 1978, the year his original class graduated. Bird opted to return to Indiana State for the 1978–79 season. He averaged 28.6 points a game and led the Sycamores to the NCAA title game against Michigan State, led by Earvin "Magic" Johnson.

Michigan State defeated Indiana State, but Bird and Johnson would be linked for the rest of their careers as the Celtics, Bird's team, and the Los Angeles Lakers,

Johnson's team, were fierce rivals. It was that rivalry between Bird and Johnson that many people credit for reviving the NBA, which had declined in popularity.

Bird entered the league with a lot of people doubting his ability to play at the NBA level. He was not particularly fast, nor was he a leaper. But he proved he belonged, winning the NBA Rookie of the Year award in 1980, averaging 21.3 points and 10.4 rebounds a game.

In Bird's second season, he led the Celtics to the NBA championship in six games over the Houston Rockets. He averaged 21.2 points and 10.9 rebounds during the regular season and 21.9 points and 14 rebounds during the playoffs.

Bird was named the NBA's Most Valuable Player in 1984, averaging 24.2 points and 10.1 rebounds a game and leading the Celtics to another NBA title in seven games over the Lakers. He averaged a career-high 27.5 points and 11 rebounds a game in the postseason and was the Most Valuable Player in the NBA Finals.

Bird repeated as Most Valuable Player in 1985 and 1986. He averaged 28.7 points and 10.5 rebounds in 1985 and 25.8 points and 9.8 rebounds in 1986. The Celtics lost to the Lakers in the NBA Finals in 1985 in six games. In 1986, the Celtics won the title by beating Houston in six games. Bird was the Most Valuable Player in the 1986 NBA Finals, averaging 25.9 points and 9.3 rebounds. He also was the Associated Press Male Athlete of the Year and the *Sports Illustrated* Sportsman of the Year.

Boston made it back to the NBA Finals in 1987, but lost to the Lakers in six games.

In 1988, injuries began to take their toll on Bird. Operations on both heels caused him to see action in only six games in the 1988–89 season, and a back problem plagued him in the final two years of his career, 1991 and 1992, when he retired, just after winning a gold medal as a member of the U.S. Olympic basketball team, the original Dream Team.

Bird was revered in Boston by Celtics fans. He had risen to icon status and was nicknamed "Larry Legend" by his adoring fans.

Bird played 13 seasons with the Celtics. He had 21,791 points (24.3 average) and 8,974 rebounds (10). Through the 2000 season, he ranked 19th all-time in points and 13th all-time in scoring average.

In the postseason, Bird had 3,297 points (23.8) and 1,683 rebounds (10.3). He ranked fifth all-time in points and 15th all-time in scoring average.

Bird was All-NBA nine times and an All-Star 12 times. He led the league in free throw percentage four times and averaged less than 20 points a game in only two seasons. Bird was inducted into the Naismith Memorial Basketball Hall of Fame in 1998 and was named one of the NBA's 50 greatest players in 1996.

Bird served as a special assistant for the Celtics from 1992 through 1997, when he was named head coach of the Indiana Pacers. He served three seasons as the Pacers coach, leading them to the NBA Finals in 2000. The Pacers lost to the Lakers in six games. Bird announced his retirement as a coach one day later.

Blazejowski, Carol

Born: September 29, 1956 in Elizabeth, New Jersey

Carol Blazejowski was one of the pioneers of women's basketball. One of the all-time great shooters, "Blaze," as she was called, learned the game playing against boys in pickup games in Cranford, N.J. She began playing organized ball in her senior year in high school. She played her college ball at Montclair (N.J.) State College, where she was dominant.

Blazejowski, a 5-10 forward, led the nation in scoring with 33.5 points a game in 1977 and 38.6 points in 1978. In three varsity seasons, she scored 3,199 points and averaged a career-record 31.7 points a game. In March 1977, she scored 52 points against Queens College in Madison Square Garden, a record at the time for either sex.

Blazejowski was a three-time All-American and the recipient of the inaugural Wade Trophy, emblematic of women's basketball player of the year.

It should be noted that Blazejowski's records are unofficial, because she compiled them prior to 1982, when the NCAA officially sanctioned women's play.

Blazejowski led the U.S. team to the gold medal in the World University Games in 1979, and in 1980 she was selected to the U.S. Olympic team, but the boycott of the games held in Moscow denied her the chance to compete.

In 1980, Blazejowski played for the New Jersey Gems of the Women's Basketball League. She led the league in scoring and was named Most Valuable Player, but the league went bankrupt after one season and her career was over. After her forced retirement, she worked in promotions and marketing for sporting goods companies, and in 1990 took a job with the NBA. While working for the NBA, she helped develop the idea for the Women's National Basketball Association (WNBA), which debuted in 1997. Through the 2000 season, she was the vice president and general manager of the WNBA's New York Liberty. She was inducted into the Naismith Memorial Basketball Hall of Fame in 1994.

Bradley, Bill

Born: July 28, 1943 in Crystal City, Missouri

Bill Bradley was one of the most complete players in the game and one of the most heralded college players ever. He took up the game to overcome the stigma attached to being the son of a wealthy banker in a town that was decidedly working class. At first he struggled, because he wasn't physically gifted. So he stuffed lead in his sneakers to increase the strength in his legs. To improve his ballhandling, he put blinders on his glasses to obstruct his lower range of vision.

Bradley was an appealing combination for a college. He was a straight-A student, and developed into an outstanding basketball player through hard work. After an intense recruiting process, he attended Princeton University, where he achieved greatness like few others, before or since.

Bradley, an accomplished passer and shooter, used intelligence, wits, and guile to lead Princeton to three straight Ivy League championships and the 1965 NCAA Final Four. The Tigers, despite 58 points by Bradley, lost in the third-place game to Wichita State.

His court sense and basketball savvy were the subject of a series of articles by John McPhee in *The New Yorker* magazine. The articles were the basis of a book, *A Sense of Where You Are.*

Bradley, who averaged 38 points a game as a senior, scored 2,503 points and averaged 30.2 points a game in his three varsity seasons. His importance to the Tigers was never more obvious than in the 1964 Holiday Festival. In a game against Michigan, Bradley scored 41 points to help the Tigers to a 75–63 lead. He fouled out with less than five minutes to play, during which time Michigan outscored Princeton 17–3 and won 80–78.

Bradley was a two-time All-American (1964–65) and the consensus national player of the year (1965). In 1965, he was the first basketball player to win the Sullivan Award, as the nation's outstanding amateur athlete, and in 1964, he was a member of the U.S. Olympic team that won the gold medal in Tokyo.

The New York Knicks drafted Bradley in 1965, but he delayed his NBA career for two years to accept a Rhodes scholarship for two years of study at Oxford University.

Bradley missed basketball and played professionally in the Italian League on weekends. When he returned to the United States in 1967, he signed a contract with the Knicks for $100,000 a year, a record at the time. The deal earned him the nickname "Dollar Bill," which was hardly an affectionate term. His critics became more vocal after his rookie season, in which he averaged only 8 points a game.

But in his second season, Bradley was shifted from guard to forward, where his lack of quickness wasn't so critical. His scoring average increased to 12.4 points a game. In the 1969–70 season, Bradley's innate sense of the game, his ability to move without the ball, and his commitment to team play blossomed. He averaged 14.5 points a game and helped the Knicks record the best record in the league (60–22). They beat the Los Angeles Lakers in seven games to win the NBA championship.

The Knicks returned to the NBA Finals in 1972, but lost to the Lakers in five games. In 1973, they won their second NBA title, beating the Lakers in five games. The 1973 season was the best of Bradley's career. He averaged 16.5 points a game and made his only All-Star Game appearance.

Bradley retired after the 1977 season. He scored 9,217 points (12.4 average). In the postseason, he averaged 12.9 points a game. He was inducted into the Naismith Memorial Basketball Hall of Fame in 1982.

Bradley, a Democrat, spent three terms as a U.S. Senator from New Jersey (1978–96). After deciding not to run for reelection in 1996, he was an educator at Stanford, the University of Maryland, and Notre Dame. In 1999, he mounted a campaign for the Democratic presidential nomination, but ended his bid in early 2000, after disappointing primary showings.

Bryant, Kobe

Born: August 23, 1978 in Philadelphia, Pennsylvania
Following a spectacular high school career at Lower Merion in suburban Philadelphia, after which he was named an All-American and the consensus national player of the year, Kobe Bryant decided to skip college and make himself available for the NBA draft.

He was drafted in the first round of the 1996 NBA draft by the Charlotte Hornets, who traded his rights to the Los Angeles Lakers.

Despite the absence of college experience and numbers that weren't overwhelming as a rookie (7.6 points, 1.9 rebounds a game), it was clear that Bryant had the moves, the athletic ability, the wherewithal, and the charisma to develop into a superstar. He made his NBA debut November 3, 1996. He was the youngest player—at 18 years, 2 months, 11 days old—to appear in an NBA game.

In each of his next three seasons, Bryant's statistics improved—15.4 points a game in 1998, 19.9 in 1999, and 22.5 in 2000. There was some question whether Bryant and his teammate, Shaquille O'Neal, could coexist, because each is talented enough to be the main focus on offense. But when Phil Jackson was hired as head coach prior to the 1999–2000 season, he imparted his team-first philosophy on the Lakers and Bryant and O'Neal combined to lead the Lakers to the NBA championship, a six-game victory over the Indiana Pacers.

While Bryant's offensive numbers have improved, it has been his ability to defend that has demonstrated his commitment to improving his game and becoming an all-around player.

In 1998, Bryant was voted onto the All-Star team as a starter and was the youngest player in All-Star history at age 20 years old.

Bryant is the son of Joe Bryant, a forward with the Philadelphia 76ers, San Diego Clippers, and Houston

Kobe Bryant   *Diane Staskowski*

Rockets. Because his father played in Europe after his NBA career ended, Kobe spent eight years of his childhood in Italy and is fluent in Italian. His parents named him after a type of steak (kobe) seen on a menu prior to his birth.

In just four NBA seasons, Bryant has become one of the league's biggest celebrities and most marketable stars. Through the 2000 season, he had 4,240 points (15.9 average).

Carter, Vince

Born: January 26, 1977 in Daytona Beach, Florida
Vince Carter is arguably the most electrifying player in the NBA and the player most often mentioned as "the next Michael Jordan." His spectacular dunks are highlight film staples, and his charisma makes him a fan favorite throughout the league.

Carter, who was expected to attend Florida State, surprised everyone by going to the University of North Carolina, where he helped the Tar Heels reach the Final Four in 1997 and 1998. Carter, who made himself eligible for the NBA draft after his junior year, averaged 12.3 points and 4.5 rebounds a game in his three varsity seasons. He was selected by the Golden State Warriors with the fifth overall pick in the 1998 draft, then had his rights traded to the Toronto Raptors.

Carter averaged 18.3 points and 5.7 rebounds a game in 1999 and was named the Rookie of the Year. In the 2000 season, he raised his game and his profile to the next level, averaging 25.7 points and 5.8 rebounds a game. Through the 2000 season, Carter averaged 22.9 points and 5.8 rebounds a game.

Chamberlain, Wilt
Born: August 21, 1936 in Philadelphia, Pennsylvania
Died: October 12, 1999

Wilt Chamberlain was the most physically dominant player in the history of the NBA. At just a shade over 7 feet and weighing 275 pounds, he was virtually unstoppable on offense and an imposing, shot-blocking force on defense.

Chamberlain could score and rebound, almost at will, in spite of defenses that double- and triple-teamed him. He was famous for his thundering dunks, his fall-away jump shots, and his "finger roll," where the ball rolled off his fingers and into the hoop. Any discussion about the greatest player ever must include Chamberlain. He holds numerous NBA records, but his critics point to his lack of playing on championship teams as a shortfall, especially when compared to Bill Russell of the Boston Celtics.

Chamberlain and Russell developed one of the great individual rivalries of all time in any sport. It's impossible to mention one without mentioning the other, so closely were their careers intertwined. Chamberlain was, by far, the much more accomplished player individually, but Russell was the leader of the Boston Celtics dynasty that won 11 NBA championships in 13 years. Chamberlain played for only two NBA championship teams.

Chamberlain, nicknamed "Wilt the Stilt" (which he hated) and the "Big Dipper," learned the game in Philadelphia. He led Overbrook High School to records of 19–2, 19–0, and 18–1 in his three varsity seasons, starting in 1952–53. He scored 2,206 points, averaged 44.5 points a game as a senior, and had games of 90, 74, and 71 points.

Chamberlain played his college ball at the University of Kansas, leading the Jayhawks to the 1957 NCAA championship game, where they lost by one point to North Carolina in triple overtime. He was named the most outstanding player of the NCAA Tournament.

In two varsity seasons, Chamberlain averaged 29.9 points and 18.3 rebounds a game. He left school after his junior season, but couldn't play in the NBA until his class graduated. He spent the 1958–59 season playing for the Harlem Globetrotters, earning $50,000, at that time a large sum.

Chamberlain was drafted by the Philadelphia Warriors in 1959 with a territorial draft pick. The NBA created the territorial draft pick to allow teams to draft college stars who had developed local followings. In exchange for picking a local player, teams gave up a first-round draft choice. Eddie Gottlieb, the Warriors' owner, claimed Chamberlain as a territorial pick, not because of his college career at Kansas, but because of his high school career in Philadelphia.

Chamberlain's illustrious career got off to a spectacular start. In the 1960 season, he averaged a league-leading 37.6 points and 27 rebounds a game. He was named Rookie of the Year and Most Valuable Player, a feat accomplished by one other player—Wes Unseld of the Baltimore Bullets in 1969.

Chamberlain led the league in scoring for the next six seasons (1961–66), averaging 38.4, 50.4, 44.8, 36.9, 34.7, and 33.5 points a game, respectively. He also led the league in rebounding 10 more times—27.2, 1961; 25.7, 1963; 24.3, 1964; 24.6, 1966; 24.2, 1967; 23.8, 1968; 21.1, 1969; 18.2, 1971; 19.2, 1972; and 18.6, 1973.

In 1962, Chamberlain set an NBA record by scoring 100 points in a single game. The game was played against the New York Knicks in Hershey, Pa., won by the Warriors 169–147. He hit 36 of 63 shots from the floor, and despite being a notoriously poor foul shooter (54 percent for his career), Chamberlain made 28 of 32 that night against the Knicks. He shares the NBA record for most free throws made in one game with Adrian Dantley of the Utah Jazz.

The Warriors moved from Philadelphia to San Francisco in 1962. He came back to Philadelphia in January 1965, when he was traded to the 76ers. In 1966, he led the 76ers to the best record in the league, but they lost to Boston in the Eastern Division semifinals. Chamberlain won his second Most Valuable Player Award.

In 1967, the 76ers won 45 of their first 49 games and finished 68–13, best in league history at the time. They defeated the Celtics in the Eastern Division finals and defeated the Warriors in six games in the NBA Finals. One of the reasons for the 76ers' success in 1967 was coach Alex Hannum asking Chamberlain to shoot less, pass more, and play more aggressive defense. It was the first season he failed to win the league scoring title, but he led the league in shooting percentage (.683) and was third in assists (7.8). He was named Most Valuable Player.

In 1968, he won his final Most Valuable Player Award, averaging 24.3 points, 23.8 rebounds, and 8.6 assists. His 702 assists topped the league. The 76ers won the Eastern Division title in 1968, but were eliminated in the playoffs by the Celtics for the third time in four seasons.

Chamberlain was traded to the Los Angeles Lakers after the 1968 season. He spent the last five seasons of his career with the Lakers, and he averaged more than 21 points a game only once, largely because of his talented supporting cast that included Jerry West and Gail Goodrich, both future Hall of Famers. In 1972, Chamberlain helped the Lakers to an NBA-record 33-game winning streak and an NBA-record 69–13 regular season mark. He averaged 14.8 points and a league-leading 19.2 rebounds. The Lakers won the NBA championship, defeating the Knicks in five games. Chamberlain was the Most Valuable Player of the finals.

He retired after the 1972–73 season with his name prominently featured in the NBA record book. In 14 seasons, he had 31,419 points (30.1 average), 23,924 rebounds (22.9), and 4,463 assists (4.4). Through the 2000 season, he ranked second in points, second in scoring average, first in rebounds, and first in rebounds per game.

He held NBA records for most games with 50 or more points (118), most games in one season with 50 or more points (45, 1962), most minutes in one season (3,882, 1962), and most points in one season (4,029, 1962).

In the postseason, he averaged 22 points, 24.5 rebounds, and 4.2 assists a game. He ranked second all-time in rebounds (3,913).

Chamberlain also holds the distinction of never having fouled out of a game in his career—a total of 1,045 regular season games and 160 playoff games.

Chamberlain made the All-NBA first team seven times and the All-Defensive first team twice. He was selected to play in 13 All-Star Games and was Most Valuable Player in 1960. He was inducted into the Naismith Memorial Basketball Hall of Fame in 1978 and was named one of the NBA's 50 greatest players in 1996.

Chamberlain coached the San Diego Conquistadors of the American Basketball Association for one season, going 37–47 in 1974. He was an avid volleyball player who also played tennis and polo. He appeared in the 1984 film *Conan the Barbarian* and once thought about challenging Muhammad Ali to a bout.

He died of congestive heart failure at age 63.

Cooper, Cynthia
Born: April 14, 1963 in Los Angeles, California

Cynthia Cooper didn't start playing basketball until she was 16 years old, but by the time she was a senior in high school, she was one of the best players in California. She played college ball at the University of Southern California. She helped the Trojans win the national championship in 1983 and 1984. They also reached a third Final Four in 1986. During her four years, the Trojans went 114–15.

With no professional league in the United States, Cooper went to Europe, playing for Segovia in Spain (1986–87) and Parma (1987–94, 1996–97) and Alcamo (1994–96) in Italy. She led her league in scoring eight times in 10 seasons.

Cooper averaged 37.5 points a game to lead all scorers in the 1996 European Cup tournament. She played for the United States in the Goodwill Games (1986, '90), the World Championships (1986, '90), and the Pan Am Games (1987). Cooper was a member of two U.S. Olympic teams—the 1988 team, which won the gold medal, and the 1992 team, which won the bronze.

The Women's National Basketball Association (WNBA) was formed in 1997, and Cooper has been its biggest star. Playing for the Houston Comets, Cooper led them to the WNBA championship in each of the league's first four seasons. She was named Most Valuable Player of the playoffs in each season.

Cooper averaged 22 points a game in 1997, 22.7 points a game in 1998, and 22.1 points a game in 1998. She led the league in scoring all three years and was named Most Valuable Player in 1997 and 1998. She made the All-WNBA first team in each of her three seasons.

Through the 2000 season, Cooper had 2,537 points (21.1 average). She was the WNBA's all-time leading scorer.

Cousy, Bob
Born: August 9, 1928 in New York, New York

Bob Cousy was the first point guard to be known for spectacular playmaking—behind-the-back dribbles, no-look passes. He was known as "Houdini of the Hardwood," and he was the offensive catalyst for the Boston Celtics run of NBA championships.

Cousy was blessed with uncanny instincts and the ability to see the entire floor. He made split-second decisions that always seemed to get the ball to the right person in the right place.

Cousy, the son of French-born parents, didn't learn to speak English until he was seven years old. He began playing basketball when he was 11 and was an All-City player in New York when he was a senior. He played his college ball at Holy Cross, where he was an All-American as a senior in 1950.

Despite Cousy's talent and his popularity in New England, he was bypassed by the Boston Celtics and their new coach, Red Auerbach, in the 1950 NBA draft.

"Little men are a dime a dozen," said Auerbach. "I'm supposed to win, not go after local yokels."

So Cousy was drafted by the Tri-Cities Blackhawks and traded to the Chicago Stags, which folded. He ended up in Boston, because the Celtics lost a three-team coin toss.

It wasn't long before Auerbach realized Cousy would be the engine that powered a dynasty. He led the NBA in assists for eight straight seasons (1953–60), getting the ball to such standouts as Bill Russell, Tom Heinsohn, Bill Sharman, Tom "Satch" Sanders, Sam Jones, K.C. Jones, Frank Ramsey, and John Havlicek.

Cousy was also an effective scorer. Four times he averaged 20 or more points a game and six times he averaged 18 or more points a game.

From 1957 through 1963, he led them to six NBA championships. In 1957, Cousy averaged 20.6 points and led the league in assists. He was named the NBA's Most Valuable Player.

Cousy retired in 1963 and became the Boston College coach. In six seasons, he compiled a 117–38 record and led the Eagles to appearances in five National Invitation Tournaments.

In 1969, Cousy became the coach of the Cincinnati Royals. He played in seven games, before retiring as a player. He coached for five years, compiling a 141–209 record.

Cousy played 13 full seasons. He had 16,960 points (18.4 average) and 6,955 assists (7.5) in the regular season. Through the 2000 season, he ranked eighth all-time in assists. In the postseason, he had 2,018 points (18.5 average) and 937 assists (8.6).

Cousy was All-NBA 10 times and an All-Star 13 times. He was inducted into the Naismith Memorial Basketball Hall of Fame in 1970 and was named one of the NBA's 50 greatest players in 1996.

Cowens, Dave

Born: October 25, 1948 in Newport, Kentucky

At 6-9, 230 pounds, Dave Cowens was an undersized NBA center who used intensity, aggressiveness, and an unfailing will to win to hold his own against opponents such as Wilt Chamberlain, Kareem Abdul-Jabbar, and Bob Lanier, who were bigger and more powerful.

Cowens was a blue-collar player who thrived on defense, rebounding, and hard work. It wasn't unusual to see him diving onto the floor or into the stands to corral a loose ball. He was the ultimate team player, and the leadership he provided was crucial.

Cowens played his college ball at Florida State, where he was an All-American as a senior. He was selected by the Boston Celtics in the first round of the 1970 NBA draft. He averaged 17 points and 15 rebounds and shared the NBA Rookie of the Year Award with Geoff Petrie of the Portland Trail Blazers.

In 1973, Cowens averaged 20.5 points and 16.2 rebounds a game and was named Most Valuable Player. He led the Celtics to the NBA championship in 1974 (20.5 points, 13.3 rebounds) and 1976 (21 points, 16.4 rebounds).

The Celtics were 34–48 in 1970, the year before Cowens joined the team, but advanced to the playoffs seven times between 1972 and 1980.

In November 1978, Cowens replaced Tom Sanders and became player-coach of the Celtics. After finishing the season with a 27–41 record, he stepped down as

coach and remained with the team as a player. Cowens retired after the 1980 season, sat out two years, and returned in 1982 to play with the Milwaukee Bucks. He retired for good in 1983.

Cowens had 13,516 points (17.6 average) and 10,444 rebounds (13.6) in the regular season. He averaged 18.9 points and 14.4 rebounds a game in the postseason. He was inducted into the Naismith Memorial Basketball Hall of Fame in 1990 and was named one of the NBA's 50 greatest players in 1996.

Cowens spent two-plus seasons as the head coach of the Charlotte Hornets, resigning in 1999. He was named the head coach of the Golden State Warriors for the 2000 season.

Cunningham, Billy

Born: June 3, 1943 in Brooklyn, New York

Billy Cunningham learned the game in gyms and on the playgrounds of New York City. He was a tireless worker whose passion for the game was ignited when he received a basketball as a present for his fifth birthday.

Cunningham, nicknamed the "Kangaroo Kid," was known for his outstanding leaping ability. In addition to being a consummate offensive player, he was a fine passer and rebounder.

Cunningham played his college ball at the University of North Carolina, where he averaged 24.8 points and 15.4 rebounds in three seasons. He was selected by the Philadelphia 76ers in the first round of the 1965 NBA draft.

In 1967–68, Cunningham was the sixth man on one of the best teams in NBA history. The 76ers finished 68–13 during the regular season and went on to defeat the San Francisco Warriors in six games for the NBA title.

From 1969 through 1972, Cunningham averaged at least 23 points and 11 rebounds a game. After the 1972 season, Cunningham jumped to the Carolina Cougars of the rival American Basketball Association. He averaged 24.1 points, 12 rebounds, and 6.3 assists a game and was named the league's Most Valuable Player.

Cunningham played one more season in the ABA, then returned to the 76ers for the 1974–75 season. Twenty games into the 1975–76 season, he suffered a serious knee injury that forced him to retire.

Cunningham had 13,626 points (20.8 average) and 6,638 rebounds (10.1) in his NBA regular season career. Through the 2000 season, he ranked 30th all-time in scoring average. In the postseason, he averaged 19.4 points and 9.1 rebounds a game. He was All-NBA three times and an All-Star four times. He was inducted into the Naismith Memorial Basketball Hall of Fame in 1985 and was named one of the NBA's 50 greatest players in 1996.

In 1977, he was named the head coach of the 76ers. He led the team to the NBA Finals in 1980 and 1982. They lost to the Los Angeles Lakers each time. In 1983, the 76ers won the NBA title, beating the Lakers in four games and losing only one game in the entire postseason.

Cunningham spent eight years as the 76ers coach. His record was 454–196 in the regular season and 66–39 in the postseason.

After coaching, Cunningham became a broadcaster and later became a part owner of the Miami Heat.

Davies, Bob

Born: January 15, 1920 in Harrisburg, Pennsylvania
Died: April 22, 1970

Bob Davies was one of the game's first showmen and earliest superstars. He is credited with being the first to dribble the ball behind his back.

Davies went to Seton Hall University on a baseball scholarship, but was convinced to switch to basketball after the Seton Hall coach, John "Honey" Russell, saw him play just once.

Davies, nicknamed the "Harrisburg Houdini," didn't score much, averaging 11.2 points a game in three seasons, but his worth was in playmaking, passing, and leadership. He led the Pirates to 43 straight wins from 1939 to 1941 and was a two-time All-American.

After three years in the service, Davies signed with the Rochester Royals of the National Basketball League in 1945 and led them to the league title. The franchise transferred to the Basketball Association of America in 1948 and then joined the NBA in 1949. Davies led the NBA in assists in 1949, averaging 5.4 a game. In 1951, he led the Royals to the NBA championship.

In 10 seasons with the Royals, Davies had 7,770 points (13.7 average) and 2,250 assists. He was a four-time All-Star and a member of the NBA's silver anniversary team in 1970. He was inducted into the Naismith Memorial Basketball Hall of Fame in 1969.

Davies coached at Seton Hall for the 1946–47 season, while playing with the Royals, and led the Pirates to a 24–3 record. After his retirement, he coached at Gettysburg College, where he was 18–35.

DeBusschere, Dave

Born: October 16, 1940 in Detroit, Michigan

Dave DeBusschere was an outstanding all-around player who was an important cog on the great New York Knicks teams of the early 1970s.

DeBusschere played his college ball at the University of Detroit, where he averaged 24.8 points and 19.4 rebounds a game during his three seasons.

After graduating in 1962, DeBusschere was selected by the Detroit Pistons in the 1962 NBA draft. He also

was a starting pitcher in college, and he signed a contract with the Chicago White Sox in April 1961.

From 1962 through 1965, DeBusschere played basketball and baseball. He spent parts of two of those four seasons with the White Sox, compiling a 3–4 record with a 2.91 earned run average.

In November of 1964, at age 24, DeBusschere was named player-coach of the Pistons, making him the youngest head coach in NBA history. He lasted as coach until March 1967. In December 1968, DeBusschere was traded to the Knicks. He started at power forward, which allowed Willis Reed to move to his natural position, center, and the Knicks developed into a great team.

New York coach Red Holzman called DeBusschere "our Holy Grail." DeBusschere played strong defense and rebounded effectively. He could handle the ball like a guard, and he could score from inside or out.

In 1970, DeBusschere helped the Knicks beat the Los Angeles Lakers in seven games to win the NBA championship. The Knicks also beat the Lakers in 1973 in five games to win the title.

DeBusschere played 12 seasons and had 14,063 points (16.1 average) and 9,618 rebounds (11.0). In the postseason, he averaged 16 points and 12 rebounds a game.

DeBusschere played in seven All-Star Games. He was inducted into the Naismith Memorial Basketball Hall of Fame in 1982 and was named one of the NBA's 50 greatest players in 1996.

After his retirement, DeBusschere was the general manager for the Knicks and the New Jersey Nets. He also served as commissioner of the American Basketball Association.

Donovan, Anne

Born: November 1, 1961 in Ridgewood, New Jersey

Anne Donovan was the first big player in women's basketball. Standing 6-8 (and wearing a size 13 1/2 shoe), she had an effective hook shot, and changed the women's game.

Donovan played her college ball at Old Dominion University. She and Nancy Lieberman-Cline formed an outstanding 1-2 combination in 1980, leading the Lady Monarchs to a 37–1 record and the Association of Intercollegiate Athletics for Women (AIAW) national championship.

Donovan was selected for the U.S. Olympic team, but didn't participate because of the United States boycott of the Games, held in Moscow.

In her four seasons at Old Dominion, the team went 116–20. She averaged 20 points and 14.5 rebounds a game. She was a consensus All-American from 1981 through 1983. After her senior year, she won the Wade

Trophy and the Naismith Award as the national player of the year.

Donovan spent five years playing professionally in Shizuoka, Japan, and one season in Modena, Italy. In 1984, she was a member of the U.S. Olympic team that defeated South Korea for the gold medal.

Donovan spent six years as an assistant coach at her alma mater, two seasons as the head coach at East Carolina University, and one season as the head coach of the Philadelphia Rage of the American Basketball League.

Through the 2000 WNBA season, Donovan was the interim head coach of the Indiana Fever, while coach Nell Fortner coached the U.S. Olympic team for the 2000 Games in Sydney, Australia. Donovan was inducted into the Naismith Memorial Basketball Hall of Fame in 1995.

In March 2001, she was named coach of the Charlotte Sting.

Drexler, Clyde
Born: June 22, 1962 in New Orleans, Louisiana

Clyde Drexler was a consistent point producer throughout his 15-year career. He was an excellent jump shooter who had the ability to drive to the basket.

Drexler played his college ball at the University of Houston, where he was a member of a team known as "Phi Slamma Jamma." The Cougars reached the NCAA final in 1983, Drexler's junior year, but lost to North Carolina State.

Drexler, nicknamed "Clyde the Glide," left Houston after his junior year and was selected in the first round of the NBA draft by the Portland Trail Blazers. He came off the bench during his rookie season, but became a starter in his second year. He averaged 20 points or more a game seven times, including 27 points a game in 1988 and 1989.

The Trail Blazers reached the NBA Finals twice during Drexler's career. They lost to the Detroit Pistons in 1990 and the Chicago Bulls in 1992.

In February 1995, Drexler was traded to the Houston Rockets and reunited with his college teammate, Hakeem Olajuwon. The Rockets won the NBA title, beating the Orlando Magic in four straight games.

Drexler retired after the 1997–98 season, with 22,195 points (20.4 average) and 6,667 rebounds (6.1). Through the 2000 season he ranked 18th all-time in points scored. In the postseason, he had 2,963 points (20.4) and 1,002 rebounds (6.9). He ranked 16th all-time in points scored.

Drexler was All-NBA first team once and an All-Star 10 times. He was named one of the NBA's 50 greatest players in 1996.

In 1998, Drexler took over as head coach of his alma mater, hoping to lead the program back to prominence, but he retired after just two seasons.

Dumars, Joe
Born: May 24, 1963 in Shreveport, Louisiana

Joe Dumars was a complete guard who helped the Detroit Pistons win two NBA championships. He was an outstanding defensive player who developed into a solid scorer. He could play point guard or shooting guard.

Dumars played his college ball at McNeese State, where he averaged 22.5 points a game in his four seasons. The Detroit Pistons selected him in the first round of the 1985 NBA draft. The Pistons won 46 games in Dumars' rookie season, then won 50 or more over the next five seasons, making it to the NBA Finals in 1988 and winning the NBA title in 1989 and 1990. Dumars was chosen Most Valuable Player in the 1989 Finals.

Dumars spent his entire career with Detroit. He averaged in double figures in every year but his first. Three times he averaged 20 or more points a game, including a career-high 23.5 in 1993.

In addition to his production on the court, Dumars provided invaluable leadership and was widely regarded as one of the game's great sportsmen.

Dumars, who retired after the 1999 season, had 16,401 points (16.1 average) and 4,612 assists (4.5). In the postseason, he averaged 15.6 points and 4.6 assists. He was a four-time All-Defensive Team selection and a six-time All-Star.

In 1994, Dumars won the J. Walter Kennedy Citizenship Award for his community work, and in 1996, he won the NBA Sportsmanship Award. Starting in 1999, he became the vice president of player personnel for the Pistons.

Duncan, Tim
Born: April 25, 1976 in St. Croix, Virgin Islands

Tim Duncan was a rarity—a college player who stayed all four years, instead of leaving early to cash in on the big money paid by the NBA. At 7-0, 255 pounds, he was the dominant player in the country during his junior year at Wake Forest University. Had he opted for the NBA, he likely would have been among the top players selected in the 1996 NBA draft. But he enjoyed college, the lifestyle, and the basketball, so he returned for his senior season.

Duncan, a two-time All-American and Atlantic Coast Conference player of the year, was the consensus national player of the year in 1997. He averaged 16.5 points and 12.5 rebounds a game in his four seasons. He led Division I players in 1997 with 14.7 rebounds a game. He is the leading shot-blocker in ACC history (481) and no. 2 all-time in the NCAA. He was the 10th player in NCAA history to score 2,000 and grab 1,500 rebounds.

Duncan, an outstanding swimmer who didn't play organized basketball until he was in ninth grade—and only because a storm closed the pool—was selected by the San Antonio Spurs with the first overall pick in the

1997 NBA draft. He averaged 21.1 points and 11.9 rebounds a game and was named Rookie of the Year. Duncan is athletic, quick for his size, and a tenacious defender and rebounder. Along with David Robinson, who stands 7-1, the Spurs had a "twin towers" combination that was overpowering.

In Duncan's second season, which was shortened to 50 games because of a labor dispute, he posted numbers nearly identical to his first—21.7 points, 11.4 rebounds. Duncan and Robinson rallied the Spurs from a struggling start, 6–8, to victories in 31 of the final 36 regular season games. The Spurs rolled through the playoffs, losing just one game on their way to the NBA Finals. They won the NBA championship in five games over the New York Knicks. Duncan led the team against the Knicks, averaging 27.4 points and 14 rebounds a game. Twice he scored 30 or more points and was named Most Valuable Player in the finals.

In the 2000 season, Duncan averaged 23.2 points and 12.4 rebounds a game, but a knee injury hampered him late in the season and kept him from the playoffs. The Spurs were ousted in the first round by the Phoenix Suns.

In three seasons, Duncan scored 4,531 points (22.0 average) and collected 2,466 rebounds (12.0). In the postseason, he averaged 22.3 points and 10.6 rebounds a game. He made the All-NBA first team three times (only the ninth rookie to be so honored), the All-Defensive first team three times, and played in the All-Star game twice.

Edwards, Teresa
Born: July 19, 1964 in Cairo, Georgia

Teresa Edwards had a long and distinguished career that has spanned nearly 20 years. She developed a passion for the game, growing up in Cairo, Ga., despite her mother's feelings that girls shouldn't play sports. When she tried out for the basketball team as a seventh grader, she kept her participation a secret from her mother as long as she could.

Edwards played her college ball at the University of Georgia. During her four seasons (1983–86), the Lady Bulldogs were 116–17 overall. They played in four NCAA Tournaments and reached the Final Four twice (1983, '85). She was a two-time All-American, a three-time member of the All-Southeastern Conference first team, and one of only three Georgia women's basketball players to have her number retired.

Edwards, who played professionally for nine seasons in Italy, Japan, France, and Spain, was a member of four U.S. Olympic teams, three of which won gold medals (1984, '88, '96) and the fourth a bronze. She is the most decorated Olympic basketball player in history.

Through the 1996 Olympics, she held U.S. Olympic records for most games (24), most assists (116), and most

steals (56). She was second in scoring (216) and third in rebounds (53).

Edwards played three seasons in the American Basketball League (ABL), averaging 20.7 points and 6.5 rebounds a game. The ABL folded after the 1998 season.

English, Alex
Born: January 5, 1954 in Columbia, South Carolina

Alex English was one of the best players of the 1980s, but gets very little recognition. He wasn't a particularly flashy player, but he was an outstanding jump shooter and a prolific scorer.

English played his college ball at the University of South Carolina. He was chosen in the second round of the 1976 NBA draft by the Milwaukee Bucks. After two seasons in Milwaukee, he signed as a free agent with the Indiana Pacers, who traded him to the Denver Nuggets in 1980. It was in Denver that English blossomed.

From 1981 through 1989, English averaged at least 23.8 points a game. In 1983, he led the NBA in scoring, averaging 28.4 points a game, and started a string of five straight seasons in which he averaged between 26 and 29 points a game. He was the first player to have eight straight seasons of 2,000 points or more (1982–89).

What kept English from getting the acclaim he deserved was not playing on an NBA championship team.

The Nuggets made it to the playoffs nine consecutive seasons (1982–90), but never reached the NBA Finals.

In 1990, English signed with the Dallas Mavericks as a free agent, and the following season he played in Italy, before he retired.

In 15 NBA seasons, English had 25,613 points (21.5 average). Through the 2000 season, he ranked 11th all-time in points scored and 27th all-time in scoring average. In the postseason, he had 1,661 points (24.5 average), which ranked 12th all-time.

English, an eight-time All-Star, was inducted into the Naismith Memorial Basketball Hall of Fame in 1997.

Erving, Julius
Born: February 22, 1950 in Roosevelt, New York

Julius Erving, known as "Doctor J" and the "Doctor," because of the way he operated on the court, did with a basketball what no one had done before him. Erving's athleticism, grace, leaping ability, and midair creativity turned the dunk into fodder for highlight films.

Erving seemed to be able to soar through the air and hang there for impossible periods of time, always finishing his move with a spectacular slam. He changed the game, adding flamboyance and a playground mentality to a sport that was much more conservative at the time. He expanded the possibilities for the generation that followed, chief among that generation being Michael Jordan.

Julius Erving   *Reading Eagle/Times*

"I would have never had the visions I had if I hadn't seen Dr. J in his prime," said Jordan.

Erving played his college ball at the University of Massachusetts. He averaged 26.3 points and 20.2 rebounds a game in his sophomore and junior seasons (1970–71). He left for the pros before his senior season, signing a $500,000, four-year deal with the Virginia Squires of the American Basketball Association.

He spent five seasons in the ABA—the first two with Virginia, the last three with the New York Nets—and led the league in scoring three times (31.9, 1973; 27.4, 1974; 29.3, 1976). He was named the ABA Most Valuable Player in 1974 and 1976, and he shared the award with George McGinnis in 1975. The Nets won the ABA championship in 1974 and 1976, and Erving was chosen Most Valuable Player in the playoffs each time.

ABA commissioner Dave DeBusschere credited Erving with carrying the league. Erving is also the main reason the NBA agreed to absorb four teams from the ABA in 1976.

After the ABA teams were accepted into the NBA, the Nets sold Erving's contract to the Philadelphia 76ers for $3 million. Erving signed for another $3.5 million. His legend expanded, now that the NBA was his showcase.

He spent his entire career, 11 seasons, in Philadelphia and averaged 20 or more points a game in his first nine. Four times he averaged 23 or more.

In 1981, Erving was named the league's Most Valuable Player. He averaged 24.6 points, eight rebounds, and four assists a game.

The 76ers reached the playoffs in each of Erving's 11 seasons and made it to the NBA Finals in 1977, 1980, and 1982, losing to the Portland Trail Blazers and to the Los Angeles Lakers twice.

In 1983, the 76ers finally made it to the NBA Finals and won. They swept the Lakers and lost only one game throughout the postseason. Erving averaged 18.2 points and 6.4 rebounds a game during the playoffs.

Erving played four more years after the title, and only in his last two did his scoring average dip below 20 points a game (18.1, 1986; 16.8, 1987). He retired as one of the icons of the game.

In 16 seasons, ABA and NBA, Erving scored 30,026 points and had 10,525 rebounds. Through the 2000 season, he ranked fourth all-time and was one of only four players to surpass 30,000 career points.

In 11 NBA seasons, he had 18,394 points (22-point average) and 5,601 rebounds (6.7). He ranked 26th all-time in scoring average.

In the postseason, he had 3,088 points (21.9 average) and 994 rebounds (7.0). He ranked 14th all-time in points scored.

Erving was an All-NBA first-teamer five times and an All-Star 11 times. He was Most Valuable Player in the All-Star Game in 1977 and 1983.

He was inducted into the Naismith Memorial Basketball Hall of Fame in 1993 and was named one of the NBA's 50 greatest players in 1996.

Erving worked as a broadcaster for NBC Sports for several years, before leaving that position to become the executive vice president of the Orlando Magic in 1997.

Ewing, Patrick
Born: August 5, 1962 in Kingston, Jamaica

Through the 2000 season, Patrick Ewing was the bedrock of the New York Knicks franchise. One of the most dominant centers of his time, Ewing was a complete player, a warrior, a fierce competitor who played hard every night. He lived up to the considerable hype that surrounded his being drafted in 1985.

In addition to being an outstanding shot-blocker and defender, Ewing could score from inside and was accurate with his jump shot from 20 feet, making him one of the most effective outside-shooting big men in NBA history.

Ewing got a relatively late start playing basketball. It wasn't until his family moved from Kingston, Jamaica, to Cambridge, Mass., that he took up the game at age 13.

Patrick Ewing   *Diane Staskowski*

He attended Rindge & Latin High School. By the time he was a senior, he stood seven feet tall and weighed 240 pounds. The focus of an intense recruiting war, Ewing chose Georgetown University.

He spent four years playing for the Hoyas (1982–85) and was a consensus All-American three times. He won the Naismith Award and the Rupp Award as the outstanding player in the nation in 1985. In 1984, when Georgetown won the NCAA championship, he was named the outstanding player of the tournament.

Ewing also led the Hoyas to the championship game in 1982, when they were beaten on a shot by Michael Jordan, and in 1985, when they lost to Villanova in one of the biggest upsets in college basketball history.

In 1984, Ewing was a member of the Olympic gold-medal-winning U.S. basketball team, which beat Spain in the final game.

In 1985, Ewing was the major prize in the NBA draft, and the Knicks were the big winners, getting the top pick, via the lottery. He was named NBA Rookie of the Year in 1986, averaging 20 points and nine rebounds a game.

For the first 13 seasons of his career, Ewing averaged more than 20 points a game, including a career-high 28.6 points in 1990. He averaged 10 or more rebounds a game nine straight years (1990–98). Only in 1999 and 2000 did he fail to average 20 points a game. Injuries limited Ewing to 26 games in 1998, 38 games in 1999, and 62 games in 2000.

Through the 2000 season, Ewing led the Knicks to the NBA playoffs 13 times. Only in his first two seasons did the team fail to qualify. The Knicks made it to the NBA Finals in 1994, losing to the Houston Rockets in seven games, and in 1999, losing to the San Antonio Spurs in five games.

On September 20, 2000, Ewing was traded to the Seattle SuperSonics.

Ewing was a member of the original Dream Team, the U.S. men's Olympic basketball team, in 1992. The U.S. won the gold medal.

Through the 2000 season, Ewing had 23,665 points (22.8 average) and 10,759 rebounds (10.4). He ranked 14th all-time in points and 19th all-time in scoring average. In the postseason, he averaged 20.6 points and 10.5 rebounds a game.

Ewing was All-NBA once and an All-Star nine times. He was named one of the 50 greatest players in NBA history in 1996.

Frazier, Walt
Born: March 29, 1945 in Atlanta, Georgia

Walt Frazier was an outstanding guard at both ends of the floor. He was a consummate playmaker and scorer, as well as a tenacious defender, who often overplayed his man, not allowing him to get the ball, let alone score.

Frazier was nicknamed "Clyde" for his taste in clothes, which resembled those worn in the film *Bonnie and Clyde*. He wore mutton-chop sideburns and wide-brimmed hats. He was the epitome of 70s cool. But for all his flamboyance off the court, he was a fundamentally sound player on the court.

Frazier played his college ball at Southern Illinois University and was a first-round pick of the New York Knicks in the 1967 NBA draft.

From 1970 through 1975, Frazier averaged more than 20 points a game. He helped the Knicks reach the NBA Finals three times (1970, '72, '73) and win the championship twice (1970, '73).

Frazier was sent to the Cleveland Cavaliers in October 1977. He spent three seasons with the Cavaliers, retiring after playing only three games in the 1979–80 season.

Frazier had 15,581 points (18.9 average) and 5,040 assists (6.1). In the postseason, he averaged 20.7 points and 6.4 assists a game.

Frazier was All-NBA four times and a member of the NBA All-Defensive first team seven times. He was a seven-time All-Star, inducted into the Naismith Memorial Basketball Hall of Fame in 1986, and was named one of the NBA's 50 greatest players in 1996.

Through the 2000 season, Frazier was a member of the New York Knicks broadcast team.

Fulks, Joe

Born: October 26, 1921 in Birmingham, Kentucky
Died: March 21, 1976

Joe Fulks was the game's first great jump shooter, and his proficiency revolutionized the sport. Unlike today's shooters, who square their shoulders to the hoop prior to shooting, Fulks would jump and spin in either direction before shooting, launching the ball with either hand. He is credited with being the first superstar of the modern game and one of the sport's pioneers.

Fulks, nicknamed "Jumpin Joe," played his college ball at Murray State. He was signed by the Philadelphia Warriors of the Basketball Association of America in 1946. He led the BAA in scoring in 1947 (23.2 points a game) and 1948 (22.1). In 1947, he led the Warriors to the BAA title, averaging 22.2 points a game in the postseason.

In 1949, Fulks turned in one of the great performances of all time, scoring 63 points on 27 of 56 shots from the field and 9 of 14 foul shots. He broke the single-game scoring record set by George Mikan 11 days earlier. Fulks' mark stood for 10 years.

In 1949, the BAA became the National Basketball Association. Fulks continued to be a star and one of the league's drawing cards.

He played in the first two NBA All-Star Games in 1951 and 1952 and was inducted into the Naismith

Memorial Basketball Hall of Fame in 1977. In seven seasons, he averaged 16.4 points a game. In the postseason, he averaged 19 points a game.

Gallatin, Harry

Born: April 26, 1927 in Roxana, Illinois

Harry "The Horse" Gallatin was a durable, physical, and aggressive player who was one of the game's best rebounders. He wasn't a big scorer, but he was a solid defender and was able to rebound, despite standing only 6 feet, 6 inches and weighing 215 pounds.

Gallatin played in the NBA before the introduction of the 24-second clock, which required offenses to shoot within that time. As a result, there was much more of a premium on the physical play that Gallatin excelled at.

Gallatin, who played his college ball at Northeast Missouri State, joined the New York Knicks in 1948. In his 10 seasons, he finished in the top 10 in the league in rebounding six times, including 1955, when he led the league with an average of 15.3 a game.

Gallatin helped the Knicks reach the NBA Finals three consecutive years (1951–53), losing to Rochester once and the Minneapolis Lakers twice.

Gallatin spent the final season of his career with the Detroit Pistons. He retired in 1958. He went on to coach basketball at Southern Illinois-Carbondale (1959–62) and Southern Illinois-Edwardsville (1968–70), compiling a 96–66 record overall. From 1963 to 1966, he coached the St. Louis Hawks and the New York Knicks. His record with both teams was 136–120.

Gallatin, who never missed a regular season or a playoff game in his 10 years, was inducted into the Naismith Memorial Basketball Hall of Fame in 1990.

Garnett, Kevin

Born: May 19, 1976 in Mauldin, South Carolina

Kevin Garnett went from high school to the NBA and established himself as one of the best players in the league. At 6-11, 220 pounds, he is a power forward blessed with athleticism, agility, and the ability to run the floor.

Garnett spent his first three years of high school at Mauldin High in Mauldin, S.C. He was named the state's Mr. Basketball as a junior. He graduated in 1995 from Farragut Academy in Chicago. He led Farragut to a 28–2 record and was named Mr. Basketball of Illinois and was the consensus choice as national player of the year. As a senior, he averaged 25.2 points, 17.9 rebounds, 6.7 assists, and 6.5 blocks a game. He also shot 66.6 percent from the field.

In his four high school seasons, he had 2,533 points, 1,807 rebounds, and 739 blocked shots.

The Minnesota Timberwolves selected him with the fifth overall pick of the first round of the 1995 NBA draft. Garnett had a solid rookie season, averaging 10.4 points and 6.3 rebounds a game. At 19 years, 235 days, he was the third-youngest player ever to start an NBA game (January 9, 1996).

Over the next four seasons, Garnett's numbers steadily improved—from 17 points and 8 rebounds a game in 1997 to 22.9 points and 11.8 rebounds a game in 2000.

Through the 2000 season, Garnett had 6,496 points (17.7 average) and 3,350 rebounds (9.1). He made the All-NBA first team once and the All-Defensive first team once. He played in the All-Star Game three times.

Gervin, George
Born: April 27, 1952 in Detroit, Michigan
George Gervin was a point-producing machine. Whether it was by the jump shot or by a drive down the lane, he could virtually score at will.

Gervin, who grew up in a ghetto in Detroit, was cut from his high school team as a sophomore. An assistant coach, Willie Meriweather, looked out for Gervin, who played on the junior varsity team. Gervin worked out a deal with the school janitor, giving him the keys to the gym if he swept it in return, and spent hours practicing and working on his game.

He earned a scholarship to Long Beach State University, but left after the first semester in 1969. He attended Eastern Michigan University, where he averaged 17.6 points a game as a freshman. During his sophomore year, when he was averaging 29.5 points a game, Gervin hit an opponent during a brawl and was expelled from school. He began playing for a minor league team, the Pontiac (Mich.) Chaparrals, earning $500 a game.

Gervin, who was averaging 40 points a game for Pontiac, came to the attention of John Kerr, a former NBA player, who was scouting for the Virginia Squires of the American Basketball Association. After Gervin scored 50 points while Kerr was watching, Kerr signed him the same night.

Gervin, 6-7, 185 pounds, spent four seasons in the ABA, his last two full seasons with the San Antonio Spurs, who became part of the NBA in 1976.

In four ABA seasons, Gervin averaged 21.9 points a game and was an All-Star twice. When the Spurs joined the NBA, Gervin led the league in scoring in 1978 (27.2), 1979 (29.6), 1980 (33.1), and 1982 (32.3).

Nicknamed the "Iceman" for his cool, unflappable demeanor, Gervin was traded to the Chicago Bulls in 1985. He spent one season with the Bulls, then played in Italy for Banco Roma for the 1986–87 season, after which he retired.

But coping with retirement was difficult for Gervin. He became addicted to cocaine, and it took trips to three rehabilitation centers to overcome his dependence on the drug.

In 10 NBA seasons, Gervin had 20,708 points (26.2 average). Through the 2000 season, he ranked 23rd all-time in points scored and seventh all-time in scoring average. In combined points (ABA and NBA), Gervin had 26,595, which ranked 11th all-time.

Gervin was on the All-NBA first team five times and was an All-Star nine times. He was inducted into the Naismith Memorial Basketball Hall of Fame in 1996, when he was also named one of the 50 greatest players in NBA history.

Gervin spent two seasons as an assistant coach with the Spurs (1993–94) and then was named the team's Community Relations representative, a position he held through the 2000 season.

Gola, Tom
Born: January 13, 1933 in Philadelphia, Pennsylvania
Tom Gola had one of the greatest careers in college basketball history. He was an all-around player who, at 6-6, combined the passing and shooting skills of a guard and the strength and rebounding skills of a forward. He was one of the tallest players ever to play guard, in college and in the NBA.

Gola led La Salle High School in Philadelphia to the city championship as a junior in 1950. He scored 2,222 points in his career and was named All-State and All-American as a senior. He received offers from such high-profile programs as North Carolina and Kentucky, but chose to stay home and attend La Salle University, which was on the same campus as his high school.

Ordinarily, freshmen weren't eligible to play, but because La Salle's enrollment was less than 1,000, he was granted an exemption. He averaged 17.4 points and 17.1 rebounds a game in his freshman season and helped the Explorers win the 1952 National Invitation Tournament, scoring 30 points in the title game and being named Most Valuable Player in the tournament.

For the next three seasons, Gola was a consensus All-American. In 1954, he averaged 23 points and 21.7 rebounds a game and led the Explorers over Bradley to win the NCAA championship. He was named Most Valuable Player of the Final Four.

Gola, who averaged 24.2 points and 19.9 rebounds, led the Explorers back to the NCAA championship game in 1955, but they lost to the University of San Francisco, which featured Bill Russell and K.C. Jones. He was named National Player of the Year.

In his four seasons, Gola scored 2,462 points (20.3 average) and had 2,201 rebounds (18.1). He had the highest combined total of points and rebounds in NCAA history and was the NCAA's all-time leading rebounder through the 2000 season. The Explorers were 102–19 in his career.

Gola was selected by the Philadelphia Warriors in the 1955 NBA draft. The Warriors were coming off a 33–39 season and, with the introduction of the 24-second clock, needed someone to run the faster-paced offense. Gola was that person. He averaged 10.8 points and 5.9 assists a game as a rookie as the Warriors finished first in the Eastern Division and went on to win the NBA championship over the Fort Wayne Pistons in five games.

Gola remained a solid contributor with the Warriors until 1962, when he was traded to the New York Knicks. He retired after the 1965–66 season. He had 7,871 points (11.3 average), 5,617 rebounds (8.0), and 2,962 assists (4.2). In the postseason, he averaged 11.1 points, 10.0 rebounds, and 4.6 assists. He made four All-Star Game appearances.

After he retired, Gola was elected to two terms in the Pennsylvania General Assembly. He returned to La Salle as head coach for two seasons (1969–70), after which he became a successful businessman. He served one term as Philadelphia city controller and failed in a bid for the Republican mayoral nomination in 1983.

Gola was inducted into the Naismith Memorial Basketball Hall of Fame in 1975.

Goodrich, Gail

Born: April 23, 1943 in Los Angeles, California

Gail Goodrich, at 6-1, considered too small by many to excel in college or professional basketball, proved all the doubters wrong by having a Hall of Fame career.

Legendary UCLA basketball coach John Wooden called Goodrich "the greatest all-around basketball player" he's ever coached. Goodrich was an outstanding shooter and playmaker who made his mark on two of the greatest teams of all time—UCLA's unbeaten team (30–0) in 1964 and the Los Angeles Lakers' championship team in 1972.

At UCLA, Goodrich teamed with Walt Hazzard to form a spectacular backcourt. The Bruins finished 30–0 in 1964, beating Duke in the championship game. Goodrich scored 27 points against the Blue Devils. In 1965, Goodrich scored 42 points in the final against the University of Michigan. The Bruins won their second straight title and finished 28–2. Goodrich was a first-team All-American.

Goodrich was picked by the Lakers in the 1965 NBA draft. He spent three seasons with Los Angeles as a reserve, before he was left unprotected for the 1968 NBA expansion draft, used to fill the roster of new teams.

The Phoenix Suns selected Goodrich, and he became a star. He spent two seasons in Phoenix and aver-

aged 23.8 points and 6.4 assists a game in 1969 and 20 points and 7.5 assists in 1970.

Goodrich was traded back to the Lakers in 1970. He averaged 17.5 points in 1971, 25.9 points in 1972, and 23.9 points in 1973. The Lakers made the playoffs in each of those three seasons. Goodrich averaged 20 points a game or more in that three-year postseason stretch, including 23.8 points in 1972, when the Lakers beat the New York Knicks in five games to win the NBA championship. The Lakers finished 69–13 in 1972, winning an NBA-record 33 straight games.

Goodrich left the Lakers in 1976 over a contract dispute. He signed with the New Orleans Jazz as a free agent and spent three seasons with the Jazz. He strained an Achilles tendon in his first game with the team. He played only 27 games in 1977. He spent two more seasons in New Orleans, averaging 16.1 and 12.7 points a game, respectively, before retiring.

In 14 seasons, Goodrich had 19,181 points (18.6 average) and 4,805 assists (4.7). He was a member of the All-NBA first team in 1974 and was inducted into the Naismith Memorial Basketball Hall of Fame in 1996.

Greer, Hal

Born: June 26, 1936 in Huntington, West Virginia

Hal Greer was one of the most effective jump shooters of his time. So reliable was his jump shot that he used the same technique while shooting fouls, which is very unusual.

Greer was blessed with great speed, leaping ability, and a quick release. He also was a solid ballhandler and playmaker, and a tireless worker. He was fundamentally sound and consistent.

Greer was the first African American ever to play at Marshall University in Huntington, W.Va. He averaged 23.6 points and 11.7 rebounds a game as a senior (1958) and was named an All-American.

He was drafted by the Syracuse Nationals in the second round of the 1958 NBA draft. Greer arrived at the Nationals training camp uncertain about his future, but he spent his entire career with the franchise, which moved to Philadelphia and became the 76ers in 1963.

For seven straight seasons, beginning in 1964, Greer averaged 20 or more points a game, including a career-high 24.1 in 1969.

In 1967, Greer was a mainstay on one of the greatest teams in NBA history. The 76ers, who also had Wilt Chamberlain, Chet Walker, Luscious Jackson, and Billy Cunningham, finished 68–13 that season and went on to win the NBA championship, beating the San Francisco Warriors in six games. Greer averaged 27.1 points a game during the 1967 postseason.

In addition to being on one of the best teams of all time, Greer had the dubious distinction of being on the worst. The 1973 76ers finished 9–73, the worst record in

NBA history. Greer played only 38 games and averaged 5.6 points in what was his final season.

In 14 seasons, Greer had 21,586 points (19.2). Through the 2000 season, he ranked 20th all-time in points scored.

In the postseason, he averaged 20.4 points a game in 92 playoff games.

Greer was a 10-time All-Star, including 1968, when he scored 21 points and was named the game's Most Valuable Player. He was inducted into the Naismith Memorial Basketball Hall of Fame in 1981 and was named one of the NBA's 50 greatest players in 1996.

Hagan, Cliff

Born: December 9, 1931 in Owensboro, Kentucky

Cliff Hagan, a 6-4, 215-pound forward, had a spectacular college career and a solid pro career. He played his college ball at the University of Kentucky.

Hagan was a two-time All-American and helped the Wildcats to an 86–5 record in his three years, including the 1951 NCAA championship. He was suspended for the 1952–53 season because of a recruiting violation. He returned for the 1953–54 season and led the team to a 25–0 record, averaging 24 points and 13.5 rebounds a game. But when the NCAA refused to allow Hagan and two of his teammates, Frank Ramsey and Lou Tsioropoulos, to compete in the postseason, the Wildcats declined to enter the tournament.

Hagan was drafted by the Boston Celtics in 1953, but his rights were traded to the St. Louis Hawks for the rights to Bill Russell, who went on to become one of the legendary figures in the game.

Hagan, whose signature sweeping hook shot was an effective weapon, spent 10 seasons with the Hawks. He averaged 18 points and 6.9 rebounds a game. He helped them reach the NBA Finals in 1957 and win the championship in 1958, when they defeated the Celtics in six games.

Hagan announced his retirement in 1966, but a year later returned as a player-coach of the Dallas Chaparrals of the American Basketball Association. He served in that role for three seasons, averaging 11 points and 3.8 rebounds a game, and guiding Dallas to 109 wins and 90 losses.

In 10 NBA seasons, Hagan had 13,447 points (18.0 average) and 5,116 rebounds (6.9). In the postseason, he averaged 20.4 points and 8.3 rebounds.

Hagan played in five All-Star Games and was inducted into the Naismith Memorial Basketball Hall of Fame in 1977.

Havlicek, John

Born: April 8, 1940 in Martins Ferry, Ohio

John Havlicek was one of the most complete, team-oriented players in NBA history. Effective on offense and defense, he would never stop moving during a game, thereby wearing out his opponents.

Said Red Holzman, former New York Knicks coach: "It would have been fair to those who had to play him or those who had to coach against him if he had been blessed only with his inhuman endurance. God had to compound it by making him a good scorer, smart ball-handler, and intelligent defensive player, with quickness of mind, hands, and feet."

Havlicek, 6-5 and 205 pounds, played his college ball at Ohio State, where he teamed with Jerry Lucas, Larry Siegfried, and Bob Knight to win the 1960 NCAA championship. He also helped the 1961 and 1962 teams reach the NCAA title game, losing each time to the University of Cincinnati.

Havlicek was overshadowed by Lucas at Ohio State, but he still averaged 14. 6 points and 8.6 rebounds in his varsity career.

Upon graduating from Ohio State, Havlicek was drafted in the seventh round in 1962 by the Cleveland Browns of the National Football League, even though he never played college football. The Browns envisioned him as a wide receiver, but he was cut in training camp.

The Boston Celtics selected Havlicek in the first round of the 1962 NBA draft, and he took over as the team's sixth man (first reserve off the bench), replacing Frank Ramsey, who perfected the role for the Celtics. Havlicek, nicknamed "Hondo," was versatile enough to play guard or forward, and he was able to score inside or outside.

In 1966, Havlicek moved into the starting lineup and had his best season to that point, averaging 21.4 points a game. Over the next seven seasons, he averaged at least 20 points a game, including 28.9 in 1971 and 27.5 in 1972.

Havlicek played on NBA championship teams in each of his first four seasons and in six of his first seven. In the 1965 Eastern Division finals against the Philadelphia 76ers, Havlicek made one of the most memorable plays in NBA postseason history. He stole the ball from 76ers guard Hal Greer in the waning seconds to send the Celtics to the NBA Finals, which they won by beating the Los Angeles Lakers in five games.

The call—"Havlicek stole the ball"—by Celtics' radio voice Johnny Most is as famous as the steal itself.

Havlicek provided the leadership necessary to help the Celtics win two more NBA championships—in 1974, in six games over the Milwaukee Bucks, and in 1976 in six over the Phoenix Suns.

In the 1974 postseason, Havlicek averaged 27.1 points, 6.4 rebounds, and 6 assists. He was named Most Valuable Player of the NBA Finals.

In Havlicek's final season, 1977–78, he played in all 82 regular season games and averaged 16.1 points a game. He never averaged less than 14 points a game throughout his 16-year career, and only four times averaged less than 18 points a game.

In 16 seasons, all with the Celtics, Havlicek had 26,395 points (20.8 average) and 8,007 rebounds (6.3). Through the 2000 season, he ranked ninth all-time in points scored and tied for 30th in scoring average.

In the postseason, he had 3,776 points (22.0) and 1,186 rebounds (6.9). He ranked sixth all-time in points scored.

Havlicek was a member of the All-NBA first team four times, the All-NBA Defensive first team five times, and the All-Star team 13 times. The Celtics' all-time leading scorer, he was inducted into the Naismith Memorial Basketball Hall of Fame in 1983 and was named one of the NBA's 50 greatest players in 1996.

Hawkins, Connie (Cornelius)
Born: July 17, 1942 in Brooklyn, New York

Connie Hawkins' NBA résumé is brief—only seven seasons, with three teams. But there is no doubt that he was one of the most talented players ever to play the game. He had a huge wing span, long strides, and the ability to hang in midair for what seemed like an eternity.

He grew up in the Bedford-Stuyvesant section of Brooklyn and was a legendary playground player with moves that were said to predate those of Julius Erving by 15 years. He led Brooklyn Boys High to two city championships (1959–60), after which he earned a scholarship to the University of Iowa. During his freshman season at Iowa, a gambling scandal broke out in New York City and Hawkins was alleged to have introduced other players to a man later convicted of fixing games.

Hawkins was never arrested, indicted, or directly implicated in fixing games, but he was expelled from Iowa and banned from the NBA for life.

Hawkins played for two seasons (1962–63) in the American Basketball League, leading the league in scoring with an average of 27.5 points a game in 1962. He was named the league's Most Valuable Player. When the ABL folded, Hawkins spent four years touring with the Harlem Globetrotters.

In 1967, he joined the American Basketball Association, where he played for two seasons. In 1968, he was the league's Most Valuable Player, averaging a league-leading 26.8 points and 13.5 rebounds a game for the Pittsburgh Pipers, who won the ABA title.

In 1969, NBA commissioner Walter Kennedy lifted the ban against Hawkins, who brought an antitrust suit against the league. Hawkins signed with the Phoenix Suns in June 1969. He spent four seasons with the Suns (1970–73). In October 1973, he was traded to the Los Angeles Lakers, and in August 1975, he was traded to the Atlanta Hawks, who waived him in 1976, ending his career.

In his seven NBA seasons, Hawkins averaged 20 or more points a game three times, including a career-high 24.6 in 1970. He had 8,233 points (16.5 average) in his NBA career, 2,592 points (27.6) in his ABL career, and 3,295 (28.2) in his ABA career.

Hawkins was an All-NBA first teamer in 1970 and a four-time All-Star. He was inducted into the Naismith Memorial Basketball Hall of Fame in 1992. Since 1992 and through the 2000 season, he was the community relations representative for the Suns.

Hayes, Elvin
Born: November 17, 1945 in Rayville, Louisiana

Elvin Hayes was one of the most prolific-scoring big men ever to play in the NBA. Blessed with athleticism and great leaping ability, Hayes was also durable. He missed only nine games in his 16-year NBA career.

Hayes played his college ball at the University of Houston, where he participated in one of the greatest games in NCAA history.

The game against UCLA in the Houston Astrodome was billed as a matchup between Hayes, 6-9 and 235 pounds, and the Bruins' Lew Alcindor, 7-2, and 267 pounds. (Alcindor later changed his name to Kareem Abdul-Jabbar.) It drew a record crowd of 52,693 and a national television audience.

Hayes scored 39 points and hit two free throws with 28 seconds left that provided Houston's margin in a 71–69 victory that ended UCLA's winning streak at 47 games. He was a three-time All-American and a two-time National Player of the Year. During his senior year, he averaged 36.8 points and 18.9 rebounds a game. His career averages at Houston were 31 points and 17.2 rebounds a game.

In 1968, he was the first pick overall in the NBA draft by the San Diego Rockets. Hayes led the NBA in scoring, averaging 28.4 points a game. He also averaged 17.1 rebounds a game and set the single-season record for minutes played by a rookie (3,695).

In his second season, he led the league with 1,386 rebounds (16.9 average). Hayes averaged 20 or more points a game in 10 of his 15 NBA seasons. He spent four seasons with the San Diego franchise (1969–72), which moved to Houston in 1971, and he was traded to the Baltimore Bullets in June 1972.

Hayes played for the Bullets for nine seasons (1972–81) and led the team to the NBA championship in 1978, in seven games over the heavily favored Seattle SuperSonics.

Hayes was traded back to Houston in June 1981. He played for the Rockets for three seasons before retiring.

In 16 NBA seasons, Hayes had 27,313 points (21.0 average) and 16,279 rebounds (12.5). Through the 2000 season, he ranked sixth all-time in points scored, 28th all-time in scoring average, and fourth all-time in rebounds. In the postseason, Hayes averaged 22.9 points and 13 rebounds a game.

Hayes was a first-team All-NBA selection three times and an All-Star 11 times. He was inducted into the Naismith Memorial Basketball Hall of Fame in 1989 and named one of the NBA's 50 greatest players in 1996.

Heinsohn, Tom
Born: August 26, 1934 in Jersey City, New Jersey

Tom Heinsohn's role on the great Boston Celtics team, coached by Red Auerbach, was to score. As a result, he shot often, so often that he earned the nickname "Tommy Gun." But his shots usually found the mark, and his offense was a major reason the Celtics won seven NBA championships during his career.

Heinsohn had a deadly jump shot from the corners or the top of the key, and he also was effective shooting a running hook shot. In addition to providing offense, he also served as the team's practical joker, lightening things up in the locker room when necessary.

Heinsohn played his college ball at Holy Cross, where he was an All-American as a senior (1956), averaging 27.4 points and 21.1 rebounds a game. Overall, he averaged 22.1 points and 15.5 rebounds a game in three seasons.

Heinsohn was selected by the Celtics in the 1956 NBA draft and was named Rookie of the Year, averaging 16.2 points and 9.8 rebounds in the 1956–57 season. Heinsohn beat out teammate Bill Russell for the award, because Russell missed 24 games of the season to participate in the Olympic Games.

In Heinsohn's nine-year career, each spent with Boston, he averaged 16 or more points in a game eight times, including a career-high 22.1 average in 1961.

He retired after the 1965 season with 12,194 points (18.6 average) and 5,749 rebounds (8.8). In the postseason, he averaged 19.8 points and 9.2 rebounds a game. Heinsohn, a six-time All-Star, was inducted into the Naismith Memorial Basketball Hall of Fame in 1985.

Heinsohn became the head coach of the Celtics in 1969. He coached for nine seasons, had a 427–263 record (.619 winning percentage), and was named Coach of the Year in 1973. He led the team to the playoffs six times. Boston won five Atlantic Division titles under Heinsohn and two NBA championships—1974, in seven games over the Milwaukee Bucks, and 1976, in six games over the Phoenix Suns.

After he was replaced as head coach in January 1978, he worked as the analyst for CBS Sports broadcasts of NBA games and then became a member of the Boston Celtics broadcast team.

Hill, Grant
Born: October 5, 1972 in Dallas, Texas

Grant Hill followed an outstanding college career at Duke University with his almost immediate emergence as an NBA superstar. He is one of the most complete, fundamentally sound players in the game, at both ends of the floor. He is also one of the most popular players in the league.

At Duke, Hill helped the Blue Devils to the Final Four three times in his four seasons (1991–92, '94). The 1991 and 1992 teams won the national championship. The Blue Devils were the runner-up to Arkansas in 1994. He was a consensus All-American as a senior. In his four seasons, he averaged 14.9 points and 6.0 rebounds a game. He was the first player in the history of the Atlantic Coast Conference to record 1,900 points, 700 rebounds, 400 assists, 200 steals, and 100 blocked shots.

The Detroit Pistons selected Hill in the first round of the 1994 NBA draft. He averaged 19.9 points and 8.1 rebounds and was named the co-Rookie of the Year, along with Jason Kidd of the Dallas Mavericks. Hill became the first rookie in league history to lead in the voting for the All-Star Game.

Hill has been a model of consistency in his six seasons. In his first five seasons, he averaged between 19 and 21 points a game. In 2000, his average improved to 25.8 points. In his second season, he became only the 15th player in NBA history to lead his team in scoring (20.2), rebounding (9.8), and assists (6.9) in the same season.

Unfortunately for Hill, his excellence has not been enough to get the Pistons deep into the playoffs. Through the 2000 season, they qualified four times in Hill's six seasons, but never made it out of the first round. In the 2000 playoffs, Hill suffered a broken left ankle in game 2 of the Pistons first-round series against the Miami Heat. The injury, which required surgery, forced Hill to withdraw from playing on the U.S. Olympic team.

Through the 2000 season, Hill had 9,393 points (21.6 average) and 3,417 rebounds (7.9). In the postseason, he averaged 20.9 points and 7.1 rebounds a game. He made the All-NBA first team once and played in the All-Star Game five times. In 1996, he was a member of the gold-medal-winning Olympic team.

Hill's class, intelligence, and wholesome image have landed him numerous endorsements and made him a centerpiece of the NBA's marketing campaign.

The son of former Dallas Cowboys running back Calvin Hill, Grant signed with the Orlando Magic in August 2000 as a free agent.

Holdsclaw, Chamique
Born: August 9, 1977 in Flushing, New York

Chamique Holdsclaw is one of the most electrifying players in women's basketball. She is blessed with great speed, athleticism, a variety of moves, and charisma that has prompted comparisons with Michael Jordan in terms of the impact each has had on their game.

Holdsclaw led Christ the King High to a record of 106–4, four New York State titles, and one national championship in her four seasons. She scored 2,223 points and as a senior averaged 25 points, 15 rebounds, five blocked shots, three assists, and four steals a game. She was a high school All-American three times and the consensus National Player of the Year in 1995.

Holdsclaw played her college ball at the University of Tennessee, where she became the only freshman ever to start every game in her first season. She led the Lady Vols to three straight national titles (1996–98) and was twice Most Outstanding Player in the Final Four (1997–98). In four seasons, the Lady Vols had an overall record of 131–17, including 39–0 in 1998.

Holdsclaw was a two-time Player of the Year, the winner of the 1998 Sullivan Award as the nation's outstanding amateur athlete, a Sullivan finalist in 1997, and a four-time All-American.

In four seasons at Tennessee, Holdsclaw had 3,025 points (20.4 average) and 1,295 rebounds (8.8). In 1999, she was selected by the Washington Mystics as the first overall pick in the WNBA draft. She averaged 16.9 points and 7.9 rebounds a game and was named Rookie of the Year.

Through the 2000 season, she averaged 17.2 points and 7.7 rebounds.

Issel, Dan
Born: October 25, 1948 in Batavia, Illinois

To watch Dan Issel play, you would have never guessed he was a prolific-scoring forward. At 6-9, 240 pounds, he was rather awkward, without much speed or leaping ability. But what he lacked in physical talent, he made up for with hustle and hard work at both ends of the court.

He was an effective shooter from 20 feet, and he used a head fake that opponents knew was coming, but went for nonetheless. The fake allowed Issel to drive to the basket.

He played his college ball at the University of Kentucky, where he averaged 16.4 points as a sophomore and improved to 33.9 points as a senior, when he was an All-American. Overall, he averaged 25.8 points and 13 rebounds a game for the Wildcats from 1968 to 1970.

Issel was a first-round draft choice of the Detroit Pistons (NBA) and the Kentucky Colonels (ABA) in 1970. He signed with the Colonels; led the ABA in scoring his rookie season, averaging 29.9 points a game; and was named co-ABA Rookie of the Year. In 1975, he led the Colonels to the ABA championship. He spent six years in the ABA, the last with the Denver Nuggets in 1976.

Issel averaged 23 points or higher in five of those six seasons.

In 1976, the Nuggets became part of the NBA. Issel continued to be a solid scorer, averaging 21 points or more a game in six of nine seasons. He retired after the 1985 season.

Issel had 14,659 points (20.4 average) and 5,707 rebounds (7.9) in nine NBA seasons. He had 12,823 points (25.6) and 5,426 rebounds (10.9) in the ABA. Through the 2000 season, he ranked seventh all-time in combined points (27,482) and 14th all-time in scoring average (22.6).

Issel was a six-time ABA All-Star and was once an All-Star in the NBA. He was inducted into the Naismith Memorial Basketball Hall of Fame in 1993.

After he retired in 1985, Issel ran a horse farm in Kentucky before returning to the Nuggets, first as a member of the broadcast team and then as head coach, 1993–95. He became vice president and general manager of the Nuggets in 1998, then returned as head coach during the 2000 season.

Johnson, Magic (Earvin)
Born: August 14, 1959 in Lansing, Michigan

There are few players in NBA history who had the impact on the game that Earvin "Magic" Johnson did. He was blessed with all-around skills, remarkable talent, a tireless work ethic, and an unsurpassed passion for basketball. At 6-9, 255 pounds, he revolutionized the point guard position, which had never been played by anyone so tall.

Johnson, not a particularly good shooter coming out of college, developed into a great shooter through hard work. His playmaking skills and his ability to find the open man with a dazzling variety of passes were second to none. And if his ability on the court wasn't enough, his charisma, his childlike enthusiasm for the game, and his trademark smile helped save the NBA in the early 1980s, when the league suffered from empty arenas and low television ratings.

Johnson played his college ball at Michigan State University. In 1979, his sophomore season, he led the Spartans to the NCAA championship and was named Most Outstanding Player of the Final Four.

In the title game, Michigan State faced Indiana State, which entered the game undefeated. The Sycamores were led by Larry Bird, consensus Player of the Year in 1979. The matchup of Johnson against Bird for the national championship proved irresistible to fans. Through the 2000 season, the game was the highest-rated championship game of all time.

Johnson led the Spartans to a 75–64 victory, but he and Bird would continue to be rivals in the NBA. It was that personal rivalry and the team-play mentality they provided that helped the league emerge from the doldrums.

Johnson left Michigan State after his sophomore season, having averaged 17.1 points, 7.6 rebounds, and 7.1 assists in his two years. He was selected by the Los Angeles Lakers first overall in the 1979 NBA draft. He averaged 18 points, 7.7 rebounds, and 7.3 assists a game as a rookie. He made the All-Rookie Team, but lost the Rookie of the Year Award to Bird, who was drafted by the Boston Celtics.

Johnson, famous for his end-to-end rushes, amazed fans with his no-look passes, his midair spins, and his drives to the basket. His forte was razzle-dazzle, but it was all within the team concept. He chose to involve everyone.

So varied were Johnson's skills that he made the term "triple-double" part of basketball lingo. Johnson registered 136 triple-doubles—double figures in points, rebounds, and assists—during his career.

The Lakers made it to the NBA Finals in 1980. They faced the Philadelphia 76ers, and it was in game 6 of the series that Johnson had one of the most memorable games of his career. The Lakers, needing one win for the title, were without Kareem Abdul-Jabbar, who was injured. Johnson filled in at center, had 42 points, 15 rebounds, and seven assists and led the Lakers to the championship. He was named Most Valuable Player of the finals.

Johnson led the Lakers to four more NBA titles (1982, '85, '87, '88) and four finals appearances (1983–84, '89, '91). He was named Most Valuable Player of the finals in 1982 and 1987.

The rivalry between Johnson and Bird intensified in the postseason. The Lakers beat the Celtics for the title in 1985 and 1987, and lost to the Celtics for the title in 1984.

Johnson was named the league's Most Valuable Player three times. In 1987, he averaged 23.9 points and a league-leading 12.2 assists per game. In 1989, he averaged 22.5 points and 12.8 assists. In 1990, he averaged 22.3 points and 11.5 assists.

From 1983 through 1987, Johnson led the league in assists per game, including a career-high 13.1 in 1988. He twice led the NBA in steals per game (3.4 in 1981, 2.7 in 1982).

In November 1991, Johnson made a stunning announcement, telling the world he was retiring from basketball because he tested positive for HIV, the virus that causes AIDS. Johnson admitted to a promiscuous lifestyle, but worked hard as a spokesman for the disease, helping to foster acceptance and understanding for those who are stricken with it.

Johnson returned to play in the 1992 NBA All-Star Game and in a script worthy of Hollywood, he scored 25 points and was named the game's Most Valuable Player.

He also played in the 1992 Olympic Games as a member of the first Dream Team.

In 1996, Johnson made a brief comeback. He joined the Lakers for 32 games, averaging 14.6 points and 6.9 assists. He also coached the Lakers at the end of the 1994 season, compiling a 5–11 record.

Johnson retired with 17,707 points (19.5 average) and 10,141 assists (11.2 average). Through the 2000 season, he ranked second all-time in assists. In the postseason, he averaged 19.5 points and 12.3 assists. He ranked eighth all-time in points (3,701), first in assists (2,346), and fourth in games played (190).

Johnson was a member of the All-NBA first team nine times and an All-Star 12 times. He was named one of the NBA's 50 greatest players in 1996.

Johnson spent two years as a broadcaster for NBC Sports. He was named vice president of the Lakers in 1993, a position he held through the 2000 season. He was also one of the leading minority businessmen in the United States.

Jones, K.C.
Born: May 25, 1932 in Taylor, Texas

K.C. Jones was a role-player, a consummate defender, and a winner—at every level. He played his college ball at the University of San Francisco, where he teamed with Bill Russell, who would become his teammate with the Boston Celtics—to win the NCAA championship in 1955 and 1956. The Dons won 55 consecutive games during those two seasons.

Jones played in only one game during his junior season (1954), because of an emergency appendectomy. But the NCAA granted him another year of eligibility. USF lost only one game over the next two years. Jones was largely responsible for the Dons' victory in the 1955 NCAA title game. He held La Salle's All-American Tom Gola scoreless for the first 21 minutes, even though Gola was five inches taller. However, Jones was ineligible for the 1956 NCAA Tournament, because he played five seasons of college basketball.

Jones played for the gold-medal-winning U.S. Olympic team in 1956, served two years in the Army, and tried out as a defensive back with the Los Angeles Rams, before joining the Celtics, who selected him in the second round of the 1956 NBA draft.

Jones came off the bench for Boston for his five seasons, providing a solid backup playmaker to Bob Cousy and an intense defensive presence. He took over for Cousy as the starter in the 1963–64 season and led the team in assists for three straight seasons.

Jones retired after the 1967 season, having been a part of eight NBA championship teams. In nine seasons, he had 4,999 points (7.4 average) and 2,904 assists (4.3). In the postseason, he averaged 6.4 points and 3.8 assists a game.

He was inducted into the Naismith Memorial Basketball Hall of Fame in 1988. Jones went into coaching after he retired. He was the head coach at Brandeis University (1968–70), the San Diego Conquistadors of the American Basketball Association (1973), the Capital/Washington Bullets (1974–76), the Boston Celtics (1984–88), and the Seattle Supersonics (1991–92).

Jones won the NBA championship with the Celtics in 1984 and 1986. After returning to the Celtics as an assistant in 1996, he took a job coaching the New England Blizzard in the American Basketball League woman's league. He coached two seasons (1997–98), after which the league folded.

Jones, Sam
Born: June 24, 1933 in Wilmington,
North Carolina

Sam Jones was an unknown quantity when he was selected by the Boston Celtics in the first round of the 1957 NBA draft. He played his college ball at North Carolina Central College, where he never averaged more than 19 points a game.

Jones was surprised by being drafted so high, and he was unsure whether he could make it in the pros. At the same time, he was considering an offer to teach high school, which was much more of a sure thing. To help make up his mind, he asked the high school to increase his salary by $500. Had the school agreed, he would have become a teacher. The school turned him down, and he joined the Celtics.

After three years as a reserve, Jones moved into the starting lineup in the 1960–61 season and was a fixture in the backcourt for the rest of his career.

Jones was blessed with great speed and was a deadly shooter, known for his bank shot from 15 to 20 feet from the basket.

Jones averaged 21 or more points for four straight years, beginning in 1965, when he averaged a career-high 25.9 points a game. He was an integral part of the great Celtics dynasty. Boston won 10 NBA championships in Jones' 12-year career.

In his last season, the Celtics played the Los Angeles Lakers in the NBA Finals. The Lakers won the first two games of the series and were winning by a point with one second to go in game 3. Jones hit an off-balance 18-foot jump shot to win the game for Boston, which went on to win the title.

Jones had 15,411 points (17.7 average) in the regular season and 2,909 points (18.9) in the postseason. A five-time All-Star, he was inducted into the Naismith Memorial Basketball Hall of Fame in 1983 and named one of the NBA's 50 greatest players in 1996.

Jordan, Michael
Born: February 17, 1963 in Brooklyn, New York

Through his immense talent, hard work, intensity, and competitiveness, as well as the sheer force and charisma of his personality, Michael Jordan raised basketball to a new level. He redefined the game and staked a strong claim as the greatest player of all time.

He excelled individually, setting numerous NBA records; he was the consummate team player, in that he made everyone around him better; and he was the most well-known sports celebrity of his time. His impact on the game, its popularity, its marketing efforts, and its appeal to the masses cannot be overstated.

Jordan also made his mark in the business world. He is the spokesman for a variety of products, from Nike shoes and apparel to batteries to sports drinks to a long distance phone company.

Jordan was a spectacular offensive player, whose creative and acrobatic dunks were the staple of highlight films. He was an outstanding jump shooter who was at his best in the most pressure-filled situations—something he proved over and over, in college and in the NBA.

While his offense got most of the attention, Jordan was also a tenacious defensive player. He was such a complete player, there was nothing he couldn't do.

However, it wasn't always that way. Jordan was cut from his high school team when he tried out as a sophomore. That failure to make the team is said to be largely responsible for his unyielding determination to achieve success. He made the team the next year and accepted a scholarship to the University of North Carolina, where he became part of Dean Smith's disciplined, structured system. Smith was criticized by many who thought he kept Jordan reined in, but Jordan credits Smith and the Tar Heels' system for making him the team-oriented, fundamentally sound player that he was.

In his freshman year, Jordan averaged 13.5 points and 4.4 rebounds a game. The Tar Heels reached the 1982 NCAA championship against Georgetown, and Jordan made the first of many clutch shots. With 17 seconds left and North Carolina trailing by one, Jordan hit a 17-foot jump shot for the winning points.

Jordan, who had a dream about hitting the game-winning shot, said: "After we beat Georgetown for the championship, I told my father about the dream. He paused for a moment and said: 'Your life will never be the same after that shot. Your life is going to change, son.' I thought: 'Well, that's just my father talking. Of course he's going to think that about his son. And besides, no one really knows one way or the other.' I never paid that much attention to what my father said that day—until now."

Jordan averaged 20 points and 5.5 rebounds as a sophomore and 19.6 points and 5.3 rebounds as a junior. He was the consensus national Player of the Year in 1984 and an All-American.

Michael Jordan *Diane Staskowski*

After Jordan's junior season, he decided to forgo his senior year and declare his eligibility for the NBA draft. He was selected by the Chicago Bulls with the third overall pick in the 1984 NBA draft. Before joining the Bulls, Jordan was a member of the U.S. Olympic team, which won the gold medal.

In his rookie season, Jordan averaged 28.2 points a game and was named the Rookie of the Year. A foot injury limited him to 18 games in the 1986 season, but he returned in 1987 to average a league-leading 37.1 points a game.

Jordan led the league in scoring in 1988 (35.0), 1989 (32.5), 1990 (33.6), 1991 (31.5), 1992 (30.1), and 1993 (32.6). He also led the league in steals in 1988 (259), 1990 (227), and 1993 (221). He was named Most Valuable Player in 1988, 1991, and 1992. In 1988, he was also named Defensive Player of the Year, making him the only player in NBA history to win both awards in the same year.

There were plenty of highlights along the way, including one of his most famous game-winning shots (a jumper at the buzzer to lift the Bulls to a first-round playoff victory against Cleveland in 1989) and a playoff-record 63 points in a 1986 playoff game against the Boston Celtics.

But while Jordan excelled individually, he also became synonymous with winning championships, which heightened his stature even more. With the addition of Scottie Pippen in 1987–88 and several other role players such as Horace Grant and John Paxson, Jordan finally had a supporting cast and the Bulls had a 1–2 punch, with Jordan and Pippen, that would lead them to glory.

The Bulls won three straight NBA championships, starting in 1991, defeating the Los Angeles Lakers in five games, the Portland Trail Blazers in six games, and the Phoenix Suns in six games, respectively. Jordan averaged 31.1, 34.5, and 35.1 in each of the three postseasons and was named Most Valuable Player of the NBA Finals for each series.

In 1992, Jordan was also the featured member of the Dream Team, the U.S. Olympic basketball team that was made up of professionals for the first time.

Several weeks after the Bulls won their third straight NBA title, Jordan's father, James, was murdered and his body dumped into a nearby river. Jordan had lost the person he called his best friend. Prior to the start of the 1993–94 season, Jordan shocked the world. He announced he was retiring from the NBA and would pursue a career in Major League Baseball. He signed with the Chicago White Sox organization as a nondrafted free agent and joined Birmingham of the Class AA Southern League. He played 127 games and hit .202 with 17 doubles, one triple, three home runs, and 51 runs batted in. Despite doubts about his ability to play at the major league level, Jordan said the baseball players strike in 1994 is what led him to return to the NBA.

His first game back was played March 18, 1995. He wore no. 45 instead of his familiar no. 23, because he did not want to play with the last number his father saw him wear. It didn't take him long to return to form. In his third game back, against the New York Knicks at Madison Square Garden, Jordan scored 55 points.

The Bulls lost in the second round of the playoffs to the Orlando Magic. In the offseason, Jordan starred in a hugely successful film, *Space Jam*.

He entered the 1995–96 season eager to show people he was still a force. Jordan led the league in scoring (30.4 average) and led the Bulls to a 72–10 record in the regular season, the best in NBA history. Chicago won the championship, beating the Seattle SuperSonics in six games.

Two more scoring titles followed (29.6, 1997; 28.7, 1998), as did two more championships. The Bulls beat the Utah Jazz in six games in 1997 and 1998. Jordan was Most Valuable Player in 1996 and 1998, and he was Most Valuable Player in the NBA Finals in 1996, 1997, and 1998.

In game 5 of the 1997 NBA Finals against the Jazz, Jordan was ill, suffering from flulike symptoms. By the fourth quarter he was almost completely dehydrated, but he scored 38 points, rallied his team from a first-half deficit, and hit the game-winning 3-pointer.

In game 6 of the 1998 NBA Finals, Jordan topped his performance in game 5 the previous year. He scored 45 points, made a crucial defensive play by stealing the ball from Karl Malone in the final seconds, and then hit the winning jump shot for an 87–86 victory. Jordan held his follow-through after the winning basket, which happened to be the last of his career. He announced his retirement January 13, 1999.

In 13 NBA seasons, Jordan had 29,277 points (31.5 average), 5,836 rebounds (6.3), and 5,102 assists (5.4). Through the 2000 season, he was fourth all-time in points and first all-time in scoring average. He held the record for most seasons leading the league in scoring (10).

In the postseason, he averaged 33.4 points, 6.4 rebounds, and 5.7 assists a game. He was first all-time in points (5,987), scoring average, free throws (1,766), and steals (376).

He was a member of the All-NBA first team 10 times and the All-Defensive first team nine times. He was selected to play in the All-Star Game 12 times and was Most Valuable Player three times.

Jordan was named one of the NBA's 50 greatest players in 1996. During the 1999–2000 season, he was named director of basketball operations for the Washington Wizards.

Lanier, Bob

Born: September 10, 1948 in Buffalo, New York

Bob Lanier was one of the NBA's best players who accomplished much individually, but never won a championship. He stood 6-11, weighed 265 pounds, and was a dominating presence in an era that also included centers Wilt Chamberlain, Kareem Abdul-Jabbar, Willis Reed, Dave Cowens, and Bill Walton.

Lanier was a hard worker, a warrior, who made an impact at both ends of the court. He was a consistent scorer and a dominant rebounder and defender.

After failing to make his high school team until his junior year, Lanier went on to have a standout college career at St. Bonaventure. He averaged 27.6 points and 15.7 rebounds a game for his three seasons and was a consensus All-American as a senior in 1970. He led the Bonnies to the Final Four in 1970, but he suffered torn knee ligaments in the East Regional final and missed the Final Four. The Bonnies lost in the semifinals.

In 1970, he was selected as the first overall pick in the NBA draft by the Detroit Pistons. From 1974 through 1979, his first six seasons, he averaged 21 or more points a game. In five of those six seasons, he averaged double figures in rebounds a game.

The Pistons made the playoffs four times in Lanier's first four seasons, but after the team experienced a downturn, he asked to be traded. He was dealt to the Milwaukee Bucks in February 1980. The Bucks made playoffs in each of Lanier's five seasons with the team, but never advanced to the NBA Finals. He retired after the 1984 season.

In 11 seasons, Lanier had 19,248 points (20.1 average) and 9,698 rebounds (10.1). Through the 2000 season, he ranked 30th all-time in points scored. In the postseason, he averaged 18.6 points and 9.6 rebounds a game.

An eight-time All-Star, Lanier was inducted into the Naismith Memorial Basketball Hall of Fame in 1991.

Lanier spent a brief time as a head coach, taking over the Golden State Warriors in February 1995 and compiling a 12–25 record. He also served as head of the NBA Players Association and national chairman of the league's Stay in School youth program.

Leslie, Lisa

Born: July 7, 1972 in Inglewood, California

Lisa Leslie had to be talked into going out for basketball in junior high, because, at six-feet tall, she was embarrassed by her height. But she tried out for the team and became one of the greatest women players of all time.

At Morningside High in Los Angeles, she once scored 101 points in the first half. The game was called when the opposition refused to play the second half.

Leslie played her college ball at the University of Southern California, where she was a three-time All-American, the national Player of the Year in 1994, and the only player to make the All-Pacific-10 first team four straight years.

In four seasons at USC, she averaged 20.1 points and 10.1 rebounds a game. The Trojans were 89–31, made four NCAA Tournament appearances, advanced to the final eight twice, and won one Pacific-10 Conference championship.

After graduating in 1994, Leslie played for a professional team in Italy for one season, averaging 22.6 points and 11.7 rebounds a game for Sicilgesso. She then returned home to play for the U.S. women's national team and the 1996 U.S. Olympic team, which won the gold medal. The two teams had a combined record of 60–0.

Leslie led the U.S. team in scoring, averaging 19.5 points a game, and in the gold medal game against Brazil, she had 29 points and six rebounds.

Leslie joined the Los Angeles Sparks in 1997, the inaugural season for the Women's National Basketball Association (WNBA). In four WNBA seasons, she averaged 17 points and 9.1 rebounds a game.

Lieberman-Cline, Nancy

Born: July 1, 1958 in Brooklyn, New York

Nancy Lieberman-Cline is widely regarded as the women's basketball player who had the greatest impact on the game. She was an outstanding all-around player whose style, flash, and fancy passes earned her great acclaim. She was a pioneer for the advancement of the women's game.

She learned the game and developed her trademark toughness and tenacity on the playgrounds of Queens, N.Y., where she played against boys and men.

When Lieberman-Cline was a junior in high school, she was a member of the U.S. team for the 1975 Pan-Am Games. The following year, she was, at age 17, the youngest player ever to make a U.S. Olympic basketball team, male or female.

Lieberman-Cline, nicknamed "Lady Magic," played her college ball at Old Dominion University, where she was a three-time All-American. In 1979 and 1980, she led the Lady Monarchs to the Association of Intercollegiate Athletics for Women (AIAW) national championship in 1979 and 1980 and won the Wade Trophy as the national Player of the Year. She averaged 18.1 points and 9 rebounds a game in her college career.

Lieberman-Cline played in two short-lived professional leagues. In 1980, she played for the Dallas Diamonds of the Women's Basketball League (WBL), which folded after one season. In 1984, she played with Dallas in the new Women's American Basketball League (WABL), which also folded after one season.

In between playing for the WBL and WABL, Lieberman-Cline became the personal trainer for Martina Navratilova, the tennis star. Lieberman-Cline is credited with helping Navratilova turn her career around.

In 1986, Lieberman-Cline made history when she became the first female to play in a men's professional league, the United States Basketball League. She was drafted by the Springfield Fame and played two seasons, after which she became the first woman to play for the Washington Generals, the longtime foil of the Harlem Globetrotters.

Lieberman-Cline finally saw her dream of a successful women's professional league come true in 1997 with the Women's National Basketball Association (WNBA). She played for the Phoenix Mercury in 1997, then retired and became the coach and general manager of the Detroit Shock, a position she held through the 2000 WNBA season. Lieberman was inducted into the Naismith Memorial Basketball Hall of Fame in 1996.

Lobo, Rebecca

Born: October 6, 1973 in Southwick, Massachusetts

Rebecca Lobo was a key member of the University of Connecticut's undefeated (35–0) national championship team in 1995. Because of the publicity that team received and the integral role she played in its success, she became one of the best-known women basketball players in the United States.

As a youth, Lobo played for a junior high school team when she was in fourth grade and for an all-boys team when she was in fifth grade. She scored 2,596 points in high school and led her team to a 76–11 overall record.

After being recruited by every major women's basketball program in the country, Lobo accepted a scholarship from Connecticut. She led the Lady Huskies to two Big East championships and four NCAA Tournament berths. She averaged 16.9 points a game in four seasons and is Connecticut's all-time leader in rebounding (1,286) and blocked shots (396). In 1995, her senior year, she was an All-American and the winner of the Wade Trophy as the national Player of the Year.

Lobo was a member of the U.S. women's national team that won 52 straight games in 1997 in preparation for the Olympics. She was the youngest member of the U.S. Olympic team, which won the gold medal.

Lobo joined the New York Liberty of the Women's National Basketball Association (WNBA) in 1996–97. She averaged 12.4 points and 7.3 rebounds a game as a rookie and 11.7 points and 6.9 rebounds a game in her second year. In the first game of the 1999 season, Lobo suffered a torn anterior cruciate ligament. She missed the entire season. Her recovery continued through the 2000 season.

Lovellette, Clyde

Born: September 7, 1929 in Terre Haute, Indiana

Clyde Lovellette was the first player to win an NCAA championship, an Olympic basketball gold medal, and an NBA championship.

He played his college ball at the University of Kansas, where he was a two-time All-American and led the nation in scoring in 1952, averaging 28.4 points a game. Lovellette was named College Player of the Year in 1952, when the Jayhawks also won the NCAA championship. He averaged 35 points a game and was named Most Outstanding Player of the tournament.

In the 1952 Olympic Games, Lovellette was a member of the U.S. Olympic basketball team that beat the Soviet Union for the gold medal.

In 1953, Lovellette joined the Minneapolis Lakers, who won the NBA championship in his rookie season. He took over for George Mikan at center in 1954 and spent two more seasons with the Lakers. He then went from the Cincinnati Royals (1958) to the St. Louis Hawks (1959–62) and the Boston Celtics. While with the Celtics, he backed up Bill Russell and was on two NBA championship teams (1963–64).

Lovellette retired after the 1964 season with 11,947 points (17.0 average) and 7,230 rebounds (10.2). He was inducted into the Naismith Memorial Basketball Hall of Fame in 1988.

Lucas, Jerry

Born: March 30, 1940 in Middletown, Ohio

Jerry Lucas followed an outstanding college career with a Hall of Fame professional career. He wasn't particularly big or fast, but he was intelligent and analytical, characteristics that compensated for his lack of physical skills. He also developed a rather odd-looking but effective jump shot. He pushed the ball as much as he shot it, but he became deadly accurate.

Lucas earned his first acclaim as a high school player in Middletown, Ohio. He broke Wilt Chamberlain's national high school scoring record with 2,466 points. He played his college ball at Ohio State and was one of the most dominant players of all time.

Lucas led the Buckeyes to the 1960 NCAA championship as a sophomore and to the NCAA finals in his junior and senior seasons, losing each time to the University of Cincinnati. He also was a member of the 1960 U.S. Olympic team, which won the gold medal.

Lucas was a three-time All-American and a two-time college Player of the Year (1961–62). He averaged 24.3 points and 17.2 rebounds a game over his three seasons with the Buckeyes.

In 1962, the Cincinnati Royals selected Lucas in the NBA draft, but he signed with the Cleveland Pipers of the American Basketball League. The ABL folded before the start of the 1962 season, which Lucas sat out. He joined the Royals in 1963.

Lucas was named the NBA's Rookie of the Year, averaging 17.7 points and 17.4 rebounds. He spent six full seasons with the Royals and averaged 20 or more points three times and 17 or more rebounds six times. He was traded to the San Francisco Warriors in October 1969. The Warriors traded him to the New York Knicks in May 1971.

Lucas' frustration over not being on a championship team admittedly caused him to develop some bad habits. But the trade to the Knicks, which relied on a team concept, rejuvenated him. He helped the Knicks reach the NBA Finals in 1972 and win the championship in 1973. Knee problems forced him to retire after the 1974 season.

In 11 seasons, Lucas had 14,053 points (17.0 average) and 12,942 rebounds (15.6). In the postseason, he averaged 12 points and 10 rebounds a game. He was a three-time member of the All-NBA first team and a seven-time All-Star, including Most Valuable Player in the 1965 game. He was inducted into the Naismith Memorial Basketball Hall of Fame in 1979 and was named one of the NBA's 50 greatest players in 1996.

Lucas was fascinated by memory and coauthored *The Memory Book*, on the subject. He started a company that produced memory and learning materials for children.

Luisetti, Hank (Angelo)
Born: June 16, 1916 in San Francisco, California

Hank Luisetti revolutionized basketball by introducing the one-handed shot, usually released while he was running. Luisetti grew up in the Telegraph Hill section of San Francisco and counted among his friends future New York Yankee stars Frank Crosetti, Tony Lazzeri, and Joe DiMaggio. He learned to play basketball against boys who were bigger than him, and as a result, developed the one-handed shot.

Luisetti's shot was the forerunner to today's jump shot, and he helped lift the profile of the game significantly.

Luisetti played his college ball at Stanford University. During his sophomore year, the Cardinals played Long Island University at Madison Square Garden in December 1936. It was the first time the East Coast had seen Luisetti's one-handed shot. He scored 15 points against LIU, a high number in those days, and Stanford ended LIU's 43-game winning streak.

"Some of his shots would have been foolhardy if attempted by another player," wrote the *New York Times* the next day, "but with Luisetti doing the heaving, these were accepted by the crowd as a matter of course."

Over the next several years, the one-handed shot was used by players throughout the United States.

Luisetti, 6-3, 184 pounds, was a two-time national Player of the Year, a three-time All-American (1936–38), and leading scorer in the nation in 1937 (17.1 points) and 1938 (17.2). In three seasons, he averaged 16.5 points a game.

Unfortunately, Luisetti's career occurred too early. There was no postseason college tournament, nor were there any pro leagues in which he could showcase his talent. Instead, he had to play for AAU teams.

In 1944, Luisetti developed a case of spinal meningitis. He made a full recovery, but doctors made him give up basketball.

In the early 1950s, Luisetti finished second to George Mikan in voting for the greatest basketball player in the first half of the century. He was inducted into the Naismith Memorial Basketball Hall of Fame in 1959.

Macauley, Ed
Born: March 22, 1928 in St. Louis, Missouri

"Easy" Ed Macauley was undersized for a center—6-8, 190 pounds—but made up for his lack of size with enough quickness and agility to have an outstanding career.

He played his college ball at St. Louis University, where he was a two-time All-American (1948–49) and the national Player of the Year in 1949. He began his professional career with the St. Louis Bombers of the Basketball Association of America (BAA). When the BAA folded in 1950, he joined the Boston Celtics.

Macauley spent six seasons with the Celtics and averaged 17 points or more in each season. He had smooth moves and an effective hook shot that helped him compete against opponents who were bigger and stronger.

In 1956, the Celtics wanted to draft Bill Russell, who would become the centerpiece of their franchise. But to make the trade, a deal with the St. Louis Hawks had to be worked out. Macauley was to go to St. Louis, but Celtics' owner Walter Brown resisted the trade, because he "couldn't imagine the Celtics" without Macauley.

Macauley, though, had a son in St. Louis who was seriously ill, and the trade to his hometown was the best thing for him.

In his first season with the Hawks, Macauley helped them reach the NBA Finals, where they lost to the Celtics in seven games. But teaming with Bob Pettit and Cliff Hagan, Macauley experienced a championship season in 1958, when the Hawks beat the Celtics in six games.

Macauley retired after playing 14 games in the 1958–59 season. He had 11,234 points (17.5 average). In the postseason, he averaged 13.8 points a game. He was a member of the All-NBA first team three times and an All-Star seven times, including 1951, when he was named the game's Most Valuable Player. He was inducted into the Naismith Memorial Basketball Hall of Fame in

1960. At 32 years old, he was the youngest player ever inducted.

Macauley became the head coach of the Hawks in 1958 and in two seasons compiled an 89-48 record.

Malone, Karl
Born: July 24, 1963 in Summerfield, Louisiana

Karl Malone, who completed his 15th NBA season in June 2000, is one of the greatest power forwards ever. At 6-9 and 259 pounds, he is strong, muscular, and able to run the floor.

Malone, a tireless worker and a marvelously conditioned athlete, is virtually impossible to stop. He can score off the drive or the jump shot. He is a combination of finesse and power. He is also one of the best rebounders in the game and a solid defender.

Malone played his college ball at Louisiana Tech, where he averaged 18.7 points and 9.3 rebounds a game. The Utah Jazz selected him in the first round of the 1985 NBA draft.

Nicknamed "The Mailman," because he always delivers, Malone has been, along with point guard John Stockton, the centerpiece of the Utah franchise.

He has averaged 25 or more points a game in 12 of his 15 seasons, including a career-high 31.0 in 1990. He has averaged 10 or more rebounds a game 10 times. Malone has led the NBA in defensive rebounds twice.

Twice, Malone has been named the NBA's Most Valuable Player. In 1997, he averaged 27.4 points and 9.9 rebounds a game. In 1999, he averaged 23.8 points and 9.4 rebounds a game.

Malone has helped the Jazz reach the playoffs in each of his 15 seasons. The Jazz made it to the NBA Finals in 1997 and 1998, but lost both times to the Chicago Bulls in six games.

Malone is also one of the most durable players in the league. Through the 2000 season, he had missed only six games in his career.

Through the 2000 season, Malone had 31,041 points (26.0 average) and 12,618 rebounds (10.6). He ranked third all-time in points scored and eighth all-time in scoring average. He also held the record for most seasons with 2,000 points (12).

In the postseason, Malone averaged 26.6 points and 11.2 rebounds a game. He ranked fourth all-time in points scored (4,203) and seventh all-time in scoring average.

Malone was an 11-time member of the All-NBA first team, a three-time member of the All-Defensive first team, and a 12-time All-Star. He was Most Valuable Player in the All-Star game in 1989 and co-Most Valuable Player in 1993.

Malone was a member of the original Dream Team, which won the gold medal at the 1992 Olympic Games.

He also was a member of the 1996 gold-medal-winning team. In 1996, he was named one of the NBA's 50 greatest players.

Malone, Moses
Born: March 23, 1955 in Petersburg, Virginia

While in the late 1990s it wasn't unusual for high school players to jump right to the NBA, Moses Malone did it in 1974. He was the first to make such a leap since the 1940s.

Malone was a solid scorer, but he was best known for his rebounding ability. He was strong, quick, athletic, and a tireless worker, allowing him to be a dominant force on the boards, especially the offensive boards. Through the 2000 season, he was the all-time leader in offensive rebounds with 6,731.

Malone led Petersburg High to 50 straight wins and two state championships. After he declared his intention to go from high school to the pros, he was selected by the Utah Jazz of the American Basketball Association in the third round of the 1974 draft.

Malone spent two years in the ABA, until the league folded in 1976. He was chosen by the Portland Trail Blazers in the ABA dispersal draft, but was traded to the Buffalo Braves before the start of the 1976 season. The Braves then traded him to the Houston Rockets just after the start of the 1976 season.

Malone spent five seasons with the Rockets and averaged 24 or more points a game four times and 14 or more rebounds a game five times. In 1979, he averaged 24.8 points and a league-leading 17.6 rebounds a game. He also led the league in minutes played (3,390) and was named Most Valuable Player. In 1982, he won his second Most Valuable Player Award, averaging 31.1 points and a league-leading 14.7 rebounds a game.

In 1981, Malone led the Rockets to the NBA Finals, where they were beaten by the Boston Celtics in six games.

Malone became a free agent after the 1982 season and signed with the Philadelphia 76ers, who had been to the NBA Finals twice in the previous three years and were searching for the piece of the puzzle to put them over the top. Malone proved to be the missing ingredient. He averaged 24.5 points and a league-leading 15.3 rebounds.

The 76ers had the best record in the NBA and won the NBA championship in a four-game sweep over the Los Angeles Lakers. Malone was named Most Valuable Player in the NBA Finals.

Malone spent three more seasons with the 76ers and twice led the league in rebounding (13.4 in 1984, 13.1 in 1985).

In June 1986, the 76ers traded Malone to the Washington Bullets. Over the next eight years, Malone was

Moses Malone   *Diane Staskowski*

with five different teams (Atlanta, 1989–91; Milwaukee 1992–93; Philadelphia, 1994; San Antonio, 1995). He played 17 games with the San Antonio Spurs in 1994, then retired.

Malone had 27,409 points (20.6 average) and 16,212 rebounds (12.2). Through the 2000 season, he ranked fifth all-time in points scored, fifth all-time in rebounds, third all-time in games played (1,329), and first all-time in free throws attempted (11,090). He held the single-season record for most offensive rebounds (587,1979) and the single-game record for most offensive rebounds (21,982 vs. Seattle). In the postseason, he averaged 22.1 points and 13.8 rebounds a game.

In combined points (ABA, NBA), Malone is fifth all-time with 29,580.

Malone was a four-time member of the All-NBA first team and a 12-time All-Star. He was named one of the NBA's 50 greatest players in 1996.

Maravich, Pete
Born: June 22, 1947 in Aliquippa, Pennsylvania
Died: January 5, 1988
Pete Maravich was a spectacular scoring machine and one of the game's great showmen. He was the master of

creativity, firing up an array of shots, dribbling behind his back, throwing pinpoint passes, and spinning like a midair acrobat. He considered basketball to be "entertainment," and he was at center stage every time he took the court. He added to his appeal by wearing socks that drooped down to his shoetops and a floppy hairstyle that was more rock and roll than basketball.

Maravich played his college ball at Louisiana State University, where his father, Press, was the head coach. In his three varsity seasons at LSU (1968–70), he averaged 43.8, 44.2, and 44.5 points a game, respectively. Through the 2000 season, he was ranked first all-time in points scored (3,667) and scoring average. He also ranked first in single-season points (1,381, 1970) and scoring average.

He also held records for most games over 50 points (28) and most games in one season over 50 points (10, 1970). Maravich was a three-time All-American and Player of the Year in 1970. All his scoring records were accomplished without the 3-point basket, which didn't become part of the college game until the mid-1980s.

The Atlanta Hawks selected Maravich in the first round of the 1970 NBA draft. He spent four seasons with the Hawks, averaging 23 or more points a game three times. In 1974, he was traded to the New Orleans Jazz, with whom he had his greatest success in the NBA.

Maravich averaged 25.9 points a game in 1976 and led the league in scoring in 1977, averaging 31.1 points a game. The Jazz waived Maravich in January 1980, and he finished his career with the Boston Celtics, retiring after the 1980 season.

For all his individual success and the way in which he redefined the game, the knock on Maravich was that he never played on a championship team. The combined record of LSU in his three years there was 49–35, and the Tigers never reached the Final Four. Likewise, his teams never reached the NBA Finals, but in fairness, he did spend the bulk of his career with the Jazz, which was an expansion franchise.

In 10 seasons, Maravich scored 15,948 points and averaged 24.2 points a game. He was a three-time member of the All-NBA first team and five-time All-Star. He was inducted into the Naismith Memorial Basketball Hall of Fame in 1986 and was named one of the NBA's 50 greatest players in 1996.

Maravich died of a heart attack in 1988 while playing in a pickup basketball game.

McAdoo, Bob
Born: September 25, 1951 in Greensboro, North Carolina
Despite being undersized for the position at 6-9, 225 pounds, Bob McAdoo played center for most of his NBA career. He prospered because of his quickness and his

ability to shoot from the outside. McAdoo is regarded as the best-shooting center in NBA history.

McAdoo spent two years at Vincennes University, a junior college in Indiana, then transferred to the University of North Carolina. He was one of the few junior college transfers ever to play for coach Dean Smith. McAdoo played just one season for the Tar Heels (1972) and was a consensus All-American, averaging 19.5 points and 10.1 rebounds a game. North Carolina finished third in the nation that season.

He left school after his junior season and was selected by the Buffalo Braves in the first round of the 1972 NBA draft. McAdoo was named Rookie of the Year in 1973. He averaged 18 points and 9.1 rebounds a game.

McAdoo led the league in scoring for three straight years, starting in 1974, averaging 30.6, 34.5, and 31.1 points a game, respectively. In 1975, he was named Most Valuable Player. Besides the 34.5-points-per-game average, he also averaged 14.1 rebounds a game, and led the league in total rebounds with 1,155.

Bill Russell, the great center for the Celtics, said about McAdoo: "He's the greatest shooter of all-time, period. Forget that bit about the 'greatest shooting big man.'"

The Braves traded McAdoo to the New York Knicks in December 1976. The trade started a series of address changes for McAdoo, who was often criticized for his lack of defense. He went from the Knicks to the Boston Celtics to the Detroit Pistons to the New Jersey Nets to the Los Angeles Lakers.

After being the focus of his teams' offenses throughout his career, McAdoo became a role player for the Lakers, who had such superstars as Kareem Adbul-Jabbar and Magic Johnson. He did well as a supporting player, helping the Lakers reach four straight NBA Finals (1982–85) and win the championship in 1982 and 1985.

McAdoo finished his NBA career with the Philadelphia 76ers, playing 29 games in the 1986 season. He then went to Italy and spent seven seasons in the Italian League, averaging 26 or more points five times. Overall, he averaged 26.6 points and 8.7 rebounds. He retired in 1992, at age 41.

In 14 NBA seasons, McAdoo had 18,787 points (22.1 average) and 8,048 rebounds (9.4). In the postseason, he averaged 18.3 points and 7.6 rebounds. He was a member of the All-NBA first team once and an All-Star five times.

Through the 2000 season, he was an assistant coach for the Miami Heat.

McCray, Nikki

Born: December 17, 1971 in Collierville, Tennessee

Nikki McCray is among the most complete players in the women's game. She is a solid offensive player and playmaker and an outstanding defender.

McCray played her college ball at the University of Tennessee. During her four seasons (1992–95), she led the Lady Volunteers to a 122–11 record, four NCAA Tournament appearances, three Southeastern Conference titles, and one Final Four. She averaged 12.3 points and 2.3 steals a game in her four seasons, twice being named the Southeastern Conference Player of the Year (1994–95).

McCray played for the U.S. women's national team and for the U.S. Olympic team in 1996. She averaged 9.4 points in helping the U.S. team win the gold medal.

In 1997, she helped the Columbus Quest of the American Basketball League win the championship. She averaged 19.9 points and 5.0 rebounds in the regular season and 24 points a game in the playoffs. She was named the league's Most Valuable Player. McCray was one of the ABL's featured players, but after her first season, she jumped to the rival Women's National Basketball Association (WNBA). The ABL folded in 1998.

McCray averaged just over 17 points a game in the 1998 and 1999 seasons while playing for the Washington Mystics of the WNBA.

McGuire, Dick

Born: January 25, 1926 in Huntington, New York

Dick McGuire was one of the most unselfish players ever. He was an outstanding playmaker and a terrific passer. He played his college ball at St. John's University, his time there interrupted by two years of military service (1945–46). He returned in 1947 and completed his college career in 1949.

McGuire, nicknamed "Tricky Dick," joined the New York Knicks, who selected him in the first round of the 1950 draft. He led the league in assists as a rookie with 386 (5.7 per-game average) and helped the Knicks reach the NBA Finals three times (1951–53).

McGuire was traded to the Detroit Pistons in April 1957 and became the Pistons' player-coach in December 1959, his last season as a player. He coached the Pistons through the 1963 season and then was hired as the Knicks' coach in November 1965. He was replaced by Red Holzman after the 1968 season.

In 11 NBA seasons, McGuire averaged 8.0 points and 5.7 assists per game. His coaching record was 197–260 (.431 winning percentage) in seven seasons.

He was inducted into the Naismith Memorial Basketball Hall of Fame in 1993. He and his brother, Al, a former NBA player, college coach, and television commentator, are the only brothers to be enshrined in the Hall of Fame.

McHale, Kevin

Born: December 19, 1957 in Hibbing, Minnesota

Kevin McHale was tall and gangly, with long legs, broad shoulders, and a large wing span. The combination made him one of the best forwards ever. He had a variety of inside moves and was a solid rebounder and a tenacious defender. Along with forward Larry Bird and center Robert Parish—arguably the most effective front line in NBA history—he was one of the main reasons the Boston Celtics enjoyed such success in the 1980s.

McHale (6-10, 225 pounds) played his college ball at the University of Minnesota, where he averaged 15.2 points and 8.5 rebounds a game in four varsity seasons. He was selected by the Celtics in the first round of the 1980 NBA draft and made the all-rookie team in 1981, averaging 10 points and 4.4 rebounds a game.

In four of McHale's first six seasons, he came off the bench. The Celtics developed the "sixth man" concept, using a quality player off the bench to provide a lift. McHale excelled at the role, because he was difficult to stop on offense and able to play strong defense. He won the NBA's Sixth Man Award in 1984 (18.4 points, 7.4 rebounds) and 1985 (19.8, 9.0).

In 1986, McHale moved into the starting lineup and averaged 20 or more points and 8 or more rebounds a game for five consecutive years. In 1987, he averaged a career-high 26.1 points a game. Twice, he led the league in field goal percentage—.604 in 1987 and .604 in 1988.

McHale helped the Celtics reach the NBA Finals five times. Three times the Celtics won the championship—1981, 1984, and 1986.

McHale broke his foot in 1987, and the injury bothered him for the rest of his career. He retired after the 1993 season as one of the most popular players in the Celtics' storied history.

In 13 seasons, McHale had 17,335 points (17.9 average) and 7,122 rebounds (7.3 average). In the postseason, he averaged 18.8 points and 7.4 rebounds a game. He is 10th all-time in postseason games played (169).

McHale was All-NBA first team once and an All-Star seven times. He was named to the All-Defensive first team three times. He was inducted into the Naismith Memorial Basketball Hall of Fame in 1999 and named one of the NBA's 50 greatest players in 1996.

McHale returned to Minnesota after he retired to become a broadcaster for the Minnesota Timberwolves. He then was named the team's assistant general manager in 1994 and vice president of basketball operations in 1995, a job he held through the 2000 season.

Meyers, Ann

Born: March 26, 1955 in San Diego, California

Ann Meyers was the first women's basketball player to attract national attention. An all-around athlete, she earned varsity letters in seven sports in high school—field hockey, badminton, tennis, softball, volleyball, track and field, and basketball.

Meyers was named to the U.S. National basketball team in 1974, while she was still in high school, and was a member of the first U.S. women's Olympic basketball team in 1976.

After the Olympics in 1976, she went to UCLA as the first woman ever to receive a full athletic scholarship. In her four seasons, she led the team in rebounding, assists, steals, and blocked shots. She is the only player in school history, male or female, to record a quadruple-double (double figures in four statistical categories)—20 points, 14 rebounds, 10 assists, 10 steals. In 1978, Meyers led the Bruins to the national championship. She was the first player, male or female, to be named to four All-American teams. In 1978, she won the Broderick Award as Player of the Year.

After she graduated from UCLA, she recorded another first—the first woman to sign a contract with an NBA team. The Indiana Pacers gave her a three-day tryout.

Meyers played with the New Jersey Gems of the Women's Basketball League (WBL) in 1979–80. She was named the league's Most Valuable Player, but the WBL folded after one season.

With her basketball career over, because there were no professional leagues for women in the United States, Meyers turned to broadcasting, doing announcing for men's and women's games on CBS, a position which she continued to hold through the 2000 season.

In 1986, she married Don Drysdale, the Hall of Fame pitcher for the Los Angeles Dodgers. The couple had three children. In 1993, Meyers was the first woman inducted into the Naismith Memorial Basketball Hall of Fame. Two months after her induction, Drysdale died of a sudden heart attack.

Mikan, George

Born: June 18, 1924 in Joliet, Illinois

George Mikan was the person most responsible for making professional basketball a major sport. He was the game's first dominant big man, the first player to force changes in the game, the league's biggest gate attraction, and the game's first superstar.

Mikan's impact on the game we know today cannot be underestimated.

Because of Mikan, the NBA instituted rule changes that banned goaltending, doubled the width of the lane from 6 to 12 feet, and instituted the 24-second clock, forcing teams to shoot within 24 seconds and putting an end to the stalling the Lakers employed, waiting to get the ball to Mikan.

At 6-10 and 245 pounds, Mikan was double- and triple-teamed, but if he couldn't get off his patented hook shot, he could pass the ball from the pivot to another player. More often than not, though, he set up several feet from the basket and once he made his move toward the hoop, he was virtually unstoppable by one defender.

Mikan, who wore wire rim glasses and looked almost professorial, played his college ball at DePaul University, where he dominated the college game like no one else before him. He didn't play basketball in high school, because of his awkwardness and because of a broken leg that required 18 months of healing.

But at DePaul he developed into an outstanding player, thanks to the exercises and drills that coach Ray Meyer put him through. Mikan was a three-time All-American and college Player of the Year in 1945 and 1946. He led the nation in scoring both years, averaging 23.3 and 23.1 points a game, respectively.

In 1945, DePaul won the National Invitation Tournament (NIT), which was then more prestigious than the NCAA Tournament. Mikan was named the NIT's Most Valuable Player. He scored 120 points in three games, including 53 in a victory over Rhode Island.

After graduating from DePaul, Mikan was signed by the Chicago Gears of the National Basketball League (NBL) in 1946 for a record salary of $12,000. He led the NBL in scoring, averaging 16.5 points a game, and the Gears to the 1947 league championship.

When the Gears dropped out of the NBL, Mikan signed with the Minneapolis Lakers. He led the league in scoring (21.3 average) and the Lakers to the NBL title. He was also named the league's Most Valuable Player.

In 1948, the Lakers became part of the Basketball Association of America (BAA). Once again, Mikan led the league in scoring (28.3) and the Lakers to the BAA title.

In 1949, the BAA and the NBL merged to form the National Basketball Association (NBA), which has existed ever since. It didn't matter what the name of the league was, Mikan dominated it. He led the NBA in scoring for three straight years, starting in 1950 (27.4, 1950; 28.4, 1951; 23.8, 1952), and the Lakers won the league championship in 1950 and 1952.

After averaging 20.6 points in 1953 and 18.1 points in 1954, Mikan decided to retire. The injuries he had suffered over the years—broken left leg, right leg, right foot, arch on his left foot, right wrist, nose, thumb, and three fingers—began to take their toll. He returned to the Lakers for the 1955–56 season, played 37 games, and then retired for good.

Mikan coached the Lakers during the 1957–58 season, compiling a 9–30 record. He resigned in January 1958.

In nine pro seasons, Mikan had 11,764 points for a 22.6-point average. In the postseason, he averaged 23.5 points a game. He made the All-NBA first team five times, the All-NBL first team twice, and the All-BAA first team once. He was the NBL's Most Valuable Player in 1948. Mikan played in the first four NBA All-Star

Games and was Most Valuable Player in the 1953 game, when he had 22 points and 16 rebounds.

Mikan was inducted into the Naismith Memorial Basketball Hall of Fame in 1959. He was named one of the NBA's 50 greatest players in 1996, and the best basketball player of the first half of the century by the Associated Press.

In 1967, Mikan was named the first commissioner of the American Basketball Association. It was his idea for the ABA to use a red, white, and blue ball. He also helped the drive to bring the NBA back to Minnesota. The Minnesota Timberwolves franchise joined the NBA in 1989.

Miller, Cheryl
Born: January 3, 1964 in Riverside, California

Cheryl Miller is one of the best female basketball players of all time. She learned the game playing against her brothers in the backyard. One of her brothers is Reggie Miller of the Indiana Pacers, one of the best shooting guards in NBA history.

Cheryl Miller was denied a chance to play on the boys' team in high school, and she didn't want to play on the girls' team because she was so much better than everybody else. She threatened to quit the game entirely, but reconsidered when her father encouraged her to try to be the very best player she could be.

In high school, Miller scored 3,026 points in four years of varsity play—an average of 32.8 points a game. She once scored 105 points in a game, and from 1979 through 1982, she was a *Parade* All-American. Her team had a 132–4 record over four years.

After being heavily recruited, Miller accepted a scholarship to the University of Southern California, where she continued to dominate. She led the Lady Trojans to a record of 112–20 in four seasons, during which she averaged 23.6 points and 12 rebounds a game. She led Southern Cal to NCAA championships in 1983 and 1984 and was named Most Outstanding Player at each tournament; she was a four-time All-American and a three-time national Player of the Year; and she was the first basketball player at the school—male or female—to have a jersey number retired. In 1984, she and swimmer Tracy Caulkins shared the Honda Broderick Award as the outstanding female college athlete, and in 1986, she was the first female basketball player to be nominated for the Sullivan Award, emblematic of the nation's best amateur athlete.

Miller led the U.S. Olympic team to the gold medal in the 1984 Games in Los Angeles. She also won gold medals as a member of the 1983 Pan-American Games team and the 1986 Goodwill Games team.

In 1987, she suffered a serious knee injury that ended her playing career. Miller stayed in the game, working for ABC Sports as a commentator and serving as an assistant coach at her alma mater.

Miller was named the head coach in 1993. In her two seasons, she guided the Lady Trojans to a 44–14 record and the 1994 Pacific-10 Conference championship.

Miller joined Turner Sports as an analyst and reporter for NBA games on TNT and TBS. In November 1996, she became the first female to work on a nationally televised NBA game.

In 1997, Miller was named the head coach and general manager of the Phoenix Mercury of the Women's National Basketball Association (WNBA), a job she held through the 2000 season.

Miller was inducted into the Naismith Memorial Basketball Hall of Fame in 1995. She is one of only 11 women to be so honored.

Miller, Reggie

Born: August 24, 1965 in Riverside, California

With the exception of Michael Jordan, Reggie Miller is widely regarded as the best pure shooting guard of his time. His ability and his willingness to shoot, especially in pressure situations, make him one of the great clutch players in the game.

Miller played his college ball at UCLA, where he averaged 17.2 points a game in four varsity seasons, including 25.9 points in 1986 as a junior and 22.3 points as a senior. The Indiana Pacers selected him in the first round of the 1987 NBA draft, and Miller has spent his entire career with the Pacers.

Besides his reputation as an outstanding shooter, Miller is also known for his constant trash-talking and his showboating style. His verbal sparring battles with film director Spike Lee, a New York Knicks fan who sits courtside at Madison Square Garden, have been well documented.

Miller has averaged 20 or more points a game six times, including a stretch of four straight seasons, beginning in 1990. He has never failed to average double figures during his 13-year career.

Miller has led the Pacers to the playoffs 10 times. In 2000, Indiana made its first trip the NBA Finals, losing to the Los Angeles Lakers in six games. Miller's reputation as a big-game player is well deserved, because he has been at his best in the postseason. He has averaged 20 or more points eight times and 25 or more points four times.

Through the 2000 season, Miller has scored 19,792 points (19.5 average), which ranked 25th all-time. He held the record for most 3-point field goals made (1,867) and most 3-point field goals attempted (4,629). In the postseason, he averaged 23.2 points. He has played in the All-Star Game five times.

Miller is the brother of Cheryl Miller, a standout at the University of Southern California and a member of the Naismith Memorial Basketball Hall of Fame.

Reggie Miller   *Diane Staskowski*

Monroe, Earl

Born: November 21, 1944 in Philadelphia, Pennsylvania

Earl Monroe was blessed with a deadly jump shot and a variety of spinning, twisting midair moves that made him virtually impossible to guard.

Monroe learned the game on the playgrounds of South Philadelphia, where he developed the "shake and bake" style that served him so well in college and the NBA. He wasn't a great leaper, but his ability to fake and feint and juke left defenders stymied.

He played his college ball at Winston-Salem State University, under the legendary Clarence "Big House" Gaines. He averaged an NCAA Division II–leading 41.5 points a game during his senior year, when his team went 31–1 and won the NCAA Division II national championship. He was named the NCAA Division II Player of the Year.

Through the 2000 season, Monroe was the all-time leading Division II single-season scorer with 1,329 points (1967).

Monroe, nicknamed "The Pearl," was selected by the Baltimore Bullets in the first round (second pick overall) of the 1967 NBA draft. He averaged 24.3 points a game in 1968 and was named Rookie of the Year.

After four solid seasons with the Bullets in which he averaged 20 or more points a game, Monroe was traded to the New York Knicks in November 1971. At first, Monroe had difficulties acclimating himself to the Knicks. Injuries were partly responsible, as was learning to play with the Knicks' other marquee guard, Walt Frazier, who was a star in his own right. Monroe averaged just 11.9 points a game in 1972. His individual style of play didn't mesh well with the Knicks, who were much more team oriented.

But by the following season, their combined talents resulted in one of the best backcourts ever. Monroe averaged 15.5 points a game in 1973, when the Knicks won the NBA championship, beating the Los Angeles Lakers in five games.

Monroe spent seven more seasons with the Knicks, before he retired after the 1980 season because of knee problems.

In 13 seasons, Monroe scored 17,454 points (18.4 average). In the postseason, he averaged 17.9 points a game. He made the All-NBA first team once and was a four-time All-Star. He was inducted into the Naismith Memorial Basketball Hall of Fame in 1989 and was named one of the NBA's 50 greatest players in 1996.

Murphy, Calvin

Born: May 9, 1948 in Norwalk, Connecticut

Calvin Murphy was proof that good things come in small packages. He stood only 5-9, but was a pure shooter and a scoring machine who was also a deft playmaker. He could throw an array of passes or pull up and bomb away from long distance. He was blessed with great quickness.

But his biggest attribute might have been his determination. His will to succeed, even though he was undersized, made him a hero to all who were considered underdogs.

Murphy was named a high school All-American in 1966 at Norwalk High, where he was also a high school baton twirling champion. Murphy's mother, herself a basketball player, schooled him in his shooting.

Murphy played his college ball at Niagara University, where he averaged 33.1 points a game in three varsity seasons, fourth-best all-time, through the 2000 season. In 1968, he averaged 38.2 points a game, eighth-highest single-season average in NCAA history, through the 2000 season. He was a two-time All-American who once scored 68 points in a game against Syracuse in 1969, the third-highest single-game total.

The San Diego Rockets selected Murphy in the second round of the 1970 NBA draft, and he spent his entire career with the franchise, which moved to Houston in 1971.

Murphy averaged 15 or more points a game 10 times and 20 or more points a game five times. He was one of the best free throw shooters in the history of the NBA. He shot 90 percent or better six times, and he led the league twice (.958, 1981; .920, 1983). The .958 percentage was the highest single-season percentage in NBA history, through the 2000 season. He once sank 78 consecutive foul shots, a record that stood from 1981 to 1993.

Murphy, who retired after the 1983 season, had 17,949 points (17.9 average). In the postseason, he averaged 18.5 points a game. He made the All-Rookie team and was an All-Star once. He was inducted into the Naismith Memorial Basketball Hall of Fame in 1992.

Olajuwon, Hakeem

Born: January 21, 1963 in Lagos, Nigeria

Hakeem Olajuwon grew up in Nigeria playing soccer. He was a goalie. He didn't begin playing basketball until he was 15. But once he started, he worked tirelessly to learn the game, not just the fundamentals, but the finer points as well.

He graduated from Muslim Teachers College, which was actually a high school in Nigeria, in 1980, and earned a scholarship to the University of Houston. Olajuwon didn't play his freshman year, choosing instead to work out with the team and continue the learning process.

In his sophomore season (1982), Olajuwon, 7-0, 255 pounds, averaged just 8.3 points and 6.2 rebounds a game. He improved to 13.9 points and 11.4 rebounds as a junior, and 16.8 points and 13.5 rebounds as a senior. He led the nation in rebounding, field goal percentage (.675), and blocked shots (5.6 a game) as a senior.

The Cougars, known as "Phi Slamma Jamma," reached the Final Four in each of Olajuwon's three seasons, twice finishing as the runner-up (1983–84). He was named Most Outstanding Player in the NCAA Tournament in 1983 and a consensus All-American in 1984.

The Houston Rockets selected Olajuwon with the first overall pick in the 1984 NBA draft, two spots ahead of Michael Jordan, who went third to the Chicago Bulls.

Olajuwon had a fine rookie season, averaging 20.6 points and 11.9 rebounds a game, finishing second to Jordan in Rookie of the Year balloting. He was blessed with outstanding footwork, the result of his soccer-playing youth, as well as quickness, finesse, agility, strength, and power. He had a variety of inside moves around the basket and a reliable jump shot that made him a difficult player to defend. He was also a fierce rebounder and defender.

Olajuwon averaged 20 or more points a game for his first 13 seasons (1985–97), including a four-year stretch (1993–96) in which he averaged 26 or more points. He also averaged 10 or more rebounds a year and shot better than

50 percent from the field during the same span. Twice he led the NBA in rebounding (13.5, 1989; 14.0 1990) and twice he led in blocked shots (376, 1990; 342, 1993).

In 1994, Olajuwon averaged 27.3 points, 11.6 rebounds a game, and 3.7 blocked shots a game. He led the Rockets to the Midwest Division title, the second-best record in the league and the first of Houston's two straight NBA titles.

Olajuwon led the Rockets to the NBA Finals three times (1986, '94–95). They beat the New York Knicks in seven games in 1994 and the Orlando Magic in four games in 1995, when they began the playoffs as the sixth seed in the Western Conference. He was named Most Valuable Player of the finals in 1994 and 1995.

In 1989, Olajuwon became the first player in NBA history with 200 steals and 200 blocked shots in the same season. In 1990, he was the first player to record 1,000 rebounds and 300 blocked shots in the same season. He is one of only three players to have 10,000 points, 5,000 rebounds, 1,000 steals, 1,000 assists, and 1,000 blocked shots in a career.

Through the 2000 season, Olajuwon had 25,822 points (23.1 average), 12,951 rebounds (11.6), and 3,652 blocked shots (3.26). He ranked 10th all-time in points scored, 17th in scoring average, and first in blocked shots.

In the postseason, he averaged 26.6 points, 11.4 rebounds, and 3.3 blocked shots a game. He ranked seventh all-time in points scored and sixth all-time in scoring average.

Olajuwon, who was a member of the 1996 gold-medal-winning U.S. Olympic team, made the All-NBA first team six times, the All-Defensive first team five times, and the All-Star team 13 times. He was the defensive Player of the Year twice. In 1996, he was named one of the NBA's 50 greatest players.

O'Neal, Shaquille
Born: March 6, 1972 in Newark, New Jersey

With the retirement of Michael Jordan following the 1998 season, Shaquille O'Neal became the most dominant presence in the game in terms of his impact on the court and his off-the-court celebrity. At 7-1, 315 pounds, O'Neal is a powerful force at both ends of the court. He is virtually impossible to defend once he gets the ball down low.

O'Neal played his college ball at Louisiana State University, where he was a two-time All-American (1991–92). In 1991, he led NCAA Division I in rebounding, averaging 14.7 a game; and in 1992, he led NCAA Division I in blocked shots, averaging 5.2 a game. In three varsity seasons at LSU, he averaged 21.6 points and 13.5 rebounds a game.

The Orlando Magic used the first overall pick in the 1992 NBA draft to select O'Neal, who won the Rookie of the Year Award. He averaged 23.4 points and 13.9

rebounds a game. In his second season, he led the league in field goal percentage (.599), and in his third he led the league in scoring (29.3 average). In 1995, O'Neal also led the Magic to the NBA Finals, where they were swept by the Houston Rockets.

The Magic were expected to reach many more NBA Finals, with O'Neal as the centerpiece of the franchise and Anfernee Hardaway, a guard, as another emerging star. But after the 1996 season, O'Neal left Orlando and signed with the Los Angeles Lakers as a free agent. He signed a contract worth $120 million.

In his first three seasons with the Lakers, O'Neal continued to put up outstanding numbers. He averaged between 26 and 28 points and 10 and 12 rebounds a game from 1997 through 1999. But the Lakers fizzled in the playoffs each year. They were eliminated in the Western Conference semifinals three straight times.

O'Neal was criticized for not being able to lead his team to a title. That he was involved in many

Shaquille O'Neal   *Diane Staskowski*

nonbasketball ventures didn't help his cause. O'Neal starred in a movie, *Kazaam*; released five rap albums; owned a record label and a clothing company; and did television commercials and magazine ads. He became one of the most sought-after celebrities in all of sports. It was widely thought that too many outside interests had adversely affected his performance.

That all changed when Phil Jackson, who won six NBA titles with the Chicago Bulls, was named the Lakers head coach before the start of the 1999–2000 season. Jackson's influence on O'Neal, and O'Neal's acceptance of Jackson's philosophy of the game, quieted the critics. O'Neal had the best season of his career, because it ended with the Lakers winning the title.

O'Neal led the league in scoring, averaging 29.7 points a game, and was second in rebounding, averaging 13.6 a game. In the playoffs he averaged 30.7 points and 15.4 rebounds a game.

He registered a rare triple, being named Most Valuable Player of the regular season, the All-Star Game, and the NBA Finals.

About the only weakness in O'Neal's game is his free throw shooting. He has made just 53 percent throughout his career in the regular season, and 50 percent in the postseason. Often, O'Neal would have to be removed from games in the fourth quarter because the opposition would foul him, rebound the misses, and use that strategy as a way to catch up.

Through the 2000 season, O'Neal had 14,687 points (27.5 average) and 6,615 rebounds (12.4). In the postseason, he averaged 27.7 points and 12.2 rebounds. He made the All-NBA first team twice and was named as one of the NBA's 50 greatest players in 1996.

Parish, Robert

Born: August 30, 1953 in Shreveport, Louisiana

Robert Parish was a durable, dependable center who spent most of his career with the Boston Celtics. He could run the floor and shoot the turnaround jumper effectively. He was an outstanding shot blocker and a tenacious defender who was known for his even temperament and stern "game face." Along with Larry Bird and Kevin McHale, Parish completed arguably the greatest front line in NBA history.

Parish played his college ball at Centenary (La.), where he was an All-American as a senior (1976). In four varsity seasons, he averaged 21.6 points and 16.4 rebounds. He was selected by the Golden State Warriors in the first round of the 1976 NBA draft. He spent four solid seasons with the Warriors, who were not a very successful team, which frustrated Parish.

His frustration ended when he was traded in June 1980 to the Boston Celtics, who won the NBA championship in Parish's first season. Over the next six seasons,

the Celtics won two more NBA titles (1984, '86) and reached the finals twice more (1985, '87).

Parish, 7-1, 244 pounds, spent 14 seasons with the Celtics (1981–94) and averaged 15 or more points a game 11 times and 10 or more rebounds a game 10 times.

In 1994, Parish, nicknamed "The Chief," signed with the Charlotte Hornets as a free agent. He spent two seasons with the Hornets, then signed with the Chicago Bulls for the 1996–97 season, when he was a member of another NBA title team.

Parish announced his retirement in August 1997 after 21 seasons, an NBA record, through the 2000 season. He also held the record for games played (1,611).

Parish had 23,334 points (14.5 average) and 14,715 rebounds (9.1). He ranked 14th all-time in points scored, sixth all-time in rebounds, and first all-time in defensive rebounds (10,117). In the postseason, he averaged 15.3 points and 9.6 rebounds a game. He ranked 19th all-time in points scored (2,820) and fifth all-time in rebounds (1,765). He ranked sixth all-time in games played (184) and tied for second all-time in playoff appearances (16).

A nine-time All-Star, Parish was named one of the NBA's 50 greatest players in 1996.

Payton, Gary

Born: July 23, 1968 in Oakland, California

Gary Payton is one of the best all-around point guards in the NBA. He is a solid scorer and playmaker, as well as an outstanding defensive player, with quick hands and good speed. His nickname, "The Glove," comes from the way he plays tight, stifling defense. Adding to his intimidation factor is his reputation as one of the league's most outspoken trash-talkers.

Payton is also one of the most durable players in the NBA; in his 10 seasons, he has missed just two regular season games.

Payton played his college ball at Oregon State, where he was an All-American as a senior, as well as *Sports Illustrated*'s Player of the Year. In four seasons, he averaged 18.1 points and 7.8 assists a game. He is the school all-time leader in points (2,172) and assists (938).

The Seattle SuperSonics selected Payton with the second overall pick in the 1990 NBA draft. By his third season, he was recognized as one of the elite point guards in the league. He averaged 13.5 points, 4.9 assists, and 2.2 steals a game in leading the SuperSonics to the Western Conference finals. Over the next seven seasons (1994–2000), Payton never averaged fewer than 16.5 points a game. Four times in that span he averaged 20 or more points, including a career high 24.2 in 2000.

In 1996, Payton led the SuperSonics to the NBA Finals, where they lost in six games to the Chicago Bulls. The Sonics have missed the playoffs only once in Payton's career. Also in 1996, Payton was a member of the U.S. Olympic basketball team, which won the gold medal.

Through the 2000 season, Payton had 13,485 points (17.2 average), 5,548 assists (7.1), and 1,756 steals (2.23). In the postseason, he averaged 17.5 points, 6.1 assists, and 1.7 steals a game.

Payton made the All-NBA first team twice and the All-Defensive first team seven times. He is only the sixth player in NBA history to make the All-Defensive first team seven times. He was named Defensive Player of the Year in 1996, and he played in the All-Star game six times.

Pettit, Bob

Born: December 12, 1932 in Baton Rouge, Louisiana
Bob Pettit was tall, rail thin, and not expected to be able to endure the pounding of the NBA. But what he lacked in girth, he made up for with perseverance and dogged determination. He was the best forward of his era.

Pettit's basketball career got off to a rocky start as he was cut twice from his high school basketball team. But through hard work, practicing at a basket in his backyard, Pettit made the team as a junior, and as a senior, led the team to the Louisiana state title.

Pettit played his college ball at Louisiana State University, where he was a two-time All-American (1953–54). In three varsity seasons at LSU, he averaged 27.4 points and 14.6 rebounds a game. During his senior year, he averaged 31.4 points and 17.3 rebounds a game.

The Milwaukee Hawks selected Pettit in the first round of the 1954 NBA draft, and he was named the league's Rookie of the Year in 1955, averaging 20.4 points and 13.8 rebounds a game.

In his second season, the Hawks moved to St. Louis. Pettit won the first of his two league scoring titles, averaging 25.7 a game. He also led the league in scoring in 1959, averaging 29.2 points a game. Pettit was named the NBA's Most Valuable Player in each season.

Pettit led the Hawks to the NBA Finals four times (1957–58, '60–61). The Hawks beat the Celtics in six games in 1958. Pettit scored 50 points in game 6 and had 19 of the Hawks' final 21 points to clinch the victory. In their other three finals appearances, the Hawks lost to the Celtics.

Pettit averaged 20 or more points a game in each of his 11 seasons, including seven seasons of averaging 25 or more points. He also averaged 12 or more rebounds a game for 11 seasons, including nine seasons of 15 or more rebounds a game. An outstanding shooter, he never finished lower than seventh in the league in scoring.

"Bob made 'second effort' part of the sports vocabulary," said Bill Russell, the great center for the Boston Celtics. "He kept coming at you more than any other

man in the game. He was always battling for position, fighting you off the boards."

Pettit retired after the 1965 season as the first player in NBA history to score more than 20,000 career points and as the game's all-time leading rebounder.

Pettit had 20,880 points (26.4 average) and 12,851 rebounds (16.2). Through the 2000 season, he ranked 22nd all-time in points scored and sixth all-time in scoring average. In the postseason, he averaged 25.5 points and 14.8 rebounds a game. He ranked ninth in playoff scoring average.

Pettit made the All-NBA first team 10 times and the All-Star team 11 times. He was inducted into the Naismith Memorial Basketball Hall of Fame in 1970 and was named one of the NBA's 50 greatest players in 1996.

Pippen, Scottie

Born: September 25, 1965 in Hamburg, Arkansas
Scottie Pippen, best known for playing second banana to Michael Jordan on six Chicago Bulls championship teams in the 1990s, is an outstanding player in his own right. He is one of the most complete and versatile players of his time. He can shoot the jump shot, drive to the basket, handle the ball, rebound, pass, and defend

Scottie Pippen   *Diane Staskowski*

115

with the very best of them. He is athletic, explosive, and able to run the floor.

Pippen played his college ball at Central Arkansas State, where he originally made the team because he agreed also to serve as the manager. His production improved each season, from averaging 4.3 points and 3 rebounds a game as a freshman to 23.6 points and 10 rebounds a game as a senior.

Pippen was selected by the Seattle SuperSonics in the first round of the 1987 NBA draft, then was traded to the Chicago Bulls the same night.

Pippen had a solid rookie season, coming off the bench (7.9 points, 3.8 rebounds), and in his second year, he became a starter. In 1989 and 1990, the Bulls made it to the Eastern Conference finals, only to lose to the Detroit Pistons each time.

In 1991, the Bulls began their championship run that was interrupted only when Jordan left the game for nearly two seasons to pursue his dream of playing baseball. They won the NBA championship in 1991, 1992, and 1993, then registered another "threepeat," starting in 1996.

Jordan and Pippen formed a 1-2 punch that was as effective as any in the history of the game. Pippen spent 11 seasons with the Bulls and averaged 18 or more points a game eight times, six or more rebounds 10 times, and five or more assists 10 times. In 1995, he led the NBA with 232 steals. He had 150 or more steals seven seasons.

Pippen left the Bulls following the 1998 season because of a contract dispute. He was traded to the Houston Rockets, joining Hakeem Olajuwon and Charles Barkley. The combination of Pippen, Olajuwon, and Barkley didn't work. Pippen, accustomed to playing an all-court game, was stifled in the Rockets offense, which was geared to go inside to Olajuwon. After one season, he left the Rockets and joined the Portland Trail Blazers.

Pippen was a steadying, veteran influence on a young team on the rise. He helped the Trail Blazers reach the 2000 Western Conference finals. After falling behind in the series 3–1 to the Los Angeles Lakers, Pippen helped rally the Blazers to two straight wins. They eventually lost the series in seven games.

Pippen averaged 12.5 points, 6.3 rebounds, and 5 assists per game with the Trail Blazers.

Through the 2000 season, Pippen had 16,735 points (17.3 average), 6,494 rebounds (6.7), and 5,143 assists (5.3) in 13 NBA seasons. In the postseason, he averaged 17.8 points, 7.7 rebounds, and 5.3 assists per game. He ranked second all-time in playoff games played, with 198.

Pippen made the All-NBA first team three times and the All-Defensive first team eight times. A seven-time All-Star, he was named one of the NBA's 50 greatest players in 1996.

Reed, Willis
Born: June 25, 1942 in Hico, Louisiana

Willis Reed was a tough, hard-working center for the New York Knicks. He was a solid offensive player, with a dependable short-range jump shot; a tenacious rebounder and shot blocker; and the Knicks' team leader.

He played his college ball at Grambling State University, which won the National Association of Intercollegiate Athletics (NAIA) national championship during his freshman year in 1961. In four varsity seasons at Grambling, Reed averaged 18.7 points and 15.2 rebounds a game. As a senior, he averaged 26.6 points and 21.3 rebounds a game.

The New York Knicks selected him in the second round of the 1964 NBA draft. Reed was named the NBA Rookie of the Year in 1965, averaging 19.5 points and 14.7 rebounds a game.

In 1970, Reed had the best season of his career. He averaged 21.7 points and 13.9 rebounds a game. He led the Knicks to the best record in the league and was named Most Valuable Player.

The Knicks advanced to the NBA Finals in 1970 against the Los Angeles Lakers, during which Reed enjoyed the signature moment of his career. He went down with a deep thigh bruise in the fifth game of the series, and he sat out all of game 6, which the Lakers won by 22 points to tie the series.

In the seventh and deciding game at Madison Square Garden, May 8, 1970, Reed failed to join the team on the court for pregame warmups. But just minutes before tipoff, he hobbled through the tunnel and onto the court, greeted by a thunderous ovation. He started, scored the team's first two baskets, and with his courage provided an emotional lift so intense that the Knicks defeated the Lakers and won their first-ever NBA championship. Reed was named Most Valuable Player of the NBA Finals.

Reed played only 11 games in the 1972 season because of a knee injury, but he returned to play 69 games in 1973, when the Knicks won their second NBA championship, beating the Lakers in five games.

The knee injury continued to hamper Reed, and he played one more year, retiring after the 1974 season.

In 10 seasons, all with the Knicks, he had 12,183 points (18.7 average) and 8,414 rebounds (12.9). In the postseason, he averaged 17.4 points and 10.3 rebounds a game. He made the All-NBA first team once, the All-Defensive first team once, and the All-Star team seven times. He was inducted into the Naismith Memorial Basketball Hall of Fame in 1981 and named one of the NBA's 50 greatest players in 1996.

Reed coached the Knicks for two years (1978–79) and the New Jersey Nets for two years (1988–89), compiling an overall record of 82–124. He also coached Creighton University from 1982 to 1985 (52–64).

In 1989 he was named general manager of the Nets, and in 1996 he was named senior vice president of the Nets, a position he held through the 2000 season.

Robertson, Oscar

Born: November 24, 1938 in Charlotte, Tennessee

Oscar Robertson was arguably the most complete basketball player in NBA history. Along with Michael Jordan, he is widely regarded as the game's greatest all-around performer.

Robertson was an outstanding scorer, passer, and playmaker who could rebound like a forward and defend with bulldog intensity. At 6-5, 220 pounds, he was bigger and stronger than other point guards of his time, and he revolutionized the position, setting the stage for Magic Johnson and Anfernee Hardaway.

Said legendary former Boston Celtics coach Red Auerbach: "He is so great it scares me. No one came close to him."

Robertson's legend began to take shape in high school. He led Crispus Attucks High in Indianapolis to 45 straight wins, the first undefeated season in the history of Indiana high school basketball, and two consecutive state championships in 1955 and 1956. As a senior, he was named Indiana's "Mr. Basketball."

Although he was recruited by every major basketball school in the country, Robertson chose to stay at home and play his college ball at the University of Cincinnati, mainly because it was close to home. Despite a full schedule—going to school, working part time for Cincinnati Gas & Electric Co., and playing basketball—Robertson put the Bearcats on the basketball map.

He was the first sophomore to lead the nation in scoring, averaging 35.1 points a game in 1958. Robertson had one of his most memorable games in his sophomore year, when he scored 56 points in a 118–54 victory over Seton Hall at Madison Square Garden. It was one of four times he scored 50 or more points that season.

Robertson also was the country's top scorer in 1959 (32.6) and 1960 (33.7). In his three varsity seasons, Robertson, nicknamed the "Big O," for offense, averaged 33.8 points and 15.2 rebounds a game. He was named college Player of the Year in each of his three seasons.

Following his senior season, Robertson was made a co-captain, along with Jerry West, of the 1960 U.S. Olympic basketball team, which defeated the Soviet Union for the gold medal.

In 1960, Robertson was drafted by the Cincinnati Royals, and he made an immediate impact for a franchise that had been struggling. He averaged 30.5 points, 10.1 rebounds, and a league-leading 9.7 assists a game and was named Rookie of the Year.

The following season, Robertson averaged a triple-double—double figures in three statistical categories—before the phrase became part of basketball lingo. The only player to do so, through the 2000 season, he averaged 30.8 points, 12.5 assists, and a league-leading 11.4 assists in what was one of the greatest single-season performances ever. In four other seasons, Robertson missed averaging triple-doubles by either one assist or one rebound.

Robertson led the league in assists six straight years, beginning in 1964—11.0, 11.5, 11.1, 10.7, 9.7, 9.8, respectively. In his first 10 seasons, he averaged 25 or more points nine times and 30 or more points six times.

In 1964, Robertson was named the league's Most Valuable Player. He averaged 31.4 points, 9.9 rebounds, and a league-leading 11 assists a game.

Despite his consistent excellence, Robertson was unable to do it alone, and the Royals never seriously contended for an NBA championship.

In 1969, the Royals hired a new coach, Bob Cousy, the player to whom Robertson was often compared. What was expected to be a perfect blend of coach and player turned out to be anything but. Cousy changed the Royals' style of play, and Robertson didn't fit in. He was traded to the Milwaukee Bucks in April 1970. The Bucks, an expansion team, were in just their second year of existence, but they drafted 7' 2" Lew Alcindor, who later changed his name to Kareem Abdul-Jabbar in 1969.

With Alcindor as a dominant presence in the middle, Robertson provided outside shooting, ballhandling, and veteran leadership. The combination helped the Bucks win the 1971 NBA championship, the only title of Robertson's career. Robertson averaged 19.4 points, 5.7 rebounds, and 8.2 assists a game in his first season with the Bucks.

Robertson played three more seasons in Milwaukee before announcing his retirement. In 14 NBA seasons, he had 26,710 points (25.7 average), 7,804 rebounds (7.5), and 9,887 assists (9.5). Through the 2000 season, he ranked seventh all-time in points scored, ninth all-time in scoring average, and third all-time in assists. In the postseason, he averaged 22.2 points, 6.7 rebounds, and 8.9 assists a game.

Robertson made the All-NBA first team nine times and the All-Star game 12 times. He was named Most Valuable Player in the All-Star Game three times (1961, '64, '69). He was inducted into the Naismith Memorial Basketball Hall of Fame in 1979 and named one of the NBA's 50 greatest players in 1996.

Robinson, David

Born: August 6, 1965 in Key West, Florida

David Robinson isn't a center in the traditional style. He doesn't use his bulk and strength to succeed on offense or defense. Instead, Robinson is a more mobile center who often sets up away from the basket because of his ability to hit from the outside. He has a soft touch on the jump shot, as well as a hook shot and a fadeaway that are effective.

Robinson, 7-1, 250 pounds, is also an outstanding rebounder and defender who is blessed with strength, mobility, agility, and quickness.

Robinson played his college ball at the U.S. Naval Academy. When he entered the Navy, he stood only 6-4, but he grew to 7-1 and became the dominant big man in the country by the time he was a senior.

In four seasons at Navy, he averaged 21 points and 10.3 rebounds a game. During his senior year, he averaged 28.2 points and 11.8 rebounds and was the consensus choice as Player of the Year. He was a two-time All-American. He led NCAA Division I in rebounds in 1986 (13.0 a game) and blocked shots in 1986 (5.91) and 1987 (4.50).

Robinson, nicknamed "The Admiral," was selected by the San Antonio Spurs as the first pick overall in the 1987 NBA draft. Because of his military commitment with the Navy, the Spurs had to wait for two years before Robinson could join the team.

The wait was worth it. Robinson was named the 1990 Rookie of the Year. He averaged 24.3 points and 12 rebounds a game. Over the next six seasons, he averaged at least 23 points and 10 rebounds a game. In 1991, he led the league in rebounds, averaging 13 a game, and in 1994, he led the league in scoring, averaging 29.8 points a game.

In 1995, Robinson led the Spurs to the Midwest Division title and the best record in the NBA. He averaged 27.6 points and 10.8 rebounds a game and was named the league's Most Valuable Player.

In 1998, the Spurs selected Tim Duncan, a 7-0 center/forward from Wake Forest, as the first overall pick in the draft. Duncan teamed with Robinson to form a "twin towers" combination that was one of the league's best tandems.

For the good of the team, Robinson became more of a role player, deferring to Duncan's talent. Because of Robinson's unselfishness, the Spurs won the NBA championship in 1999, a season shortened to 50 games because of a labor dispute. The Spurs beat the New York Knicks in five games to win the title, and Robinson averaged 16.6 points and 11.8 rebounds a game in the NBA Finals.

Through the 2000 season, Robinson had 18,142 points (23.7 average) and 8,651 rebounds (11.3). In the postseason, he averaged 21.8 points and 11.7 rebounds a game. A member of three U.S. Olympic basketball teams (1988, '92, '96), he was Defensive Player of the Year in 1992. Robinson made the All-NBA first team four times and the All-Defensive first team four times. He was a

nine-time All-Star in 1996 and was named as one of the 50 greatest players in NBA history.

Rodman, Dennis
Born: May 13, 1961 in Trenton, New Jersey

Dennis Rodman was the bad boy of basketball. His behavior on and off the court was atrocious, leading to numerous fines and suspensions. He was known for his outlandish outfits, his ever-changing hair color, and his myriad tattoos. He went out of his way, it seemed, to cause trouble in any way he could.

But in spite of his egotism and disregard for team harmony, he is widely regarded as one of the greatest rebounding forwards in NBA history. He was able to have a major impact on the game, even though his offensive contributions were virtually nonexistent.

Rodman didn't play basketball in high school because he stood only 5-11. For three years after high school, he worked at a variety of jobs—at a car dealership, at Southwestern Bell, at the Dallas-Fort Worth airport as a janitor on the graveyard shift.

But having grown to 6-8, Rodman started playing basketball. He enrolled in a junior college and then at Southeastern Oklahoma State. In four seasons, he averaged 25.7 points and 15.7 rebounds a game. The Detroit Pistons selected him in the second round of the 1986 NBA draft.

Rodman was a reserve during his first three seasons. In 1989, he led the league in field goal percentage (.595) and helped the Pistons win their first NBA championship, beating the Los Angeles Lakers in four games. In 1990, he became a starter, averaged 8.8 points and 9.7 rebounds and won the first of his two straight Defensive Player of the Year Awards as the Pistons successfully defended their title, beating the Portland Trail Blazers in five games.

Starting in 1992, Rodman's rebounding totals jumped dramatically, and he won the NBA rebounding title for seven straight years. He averaged 16 or more rebounds in four of those seasons, including a career-high 18.7 in 1992. It was the highest average since Wilt Chamberlain's 19.2 in 1972.

The Pistons traded Rodman to the San Antonio Spurs in 1993, and after two tumultuous seasons, he was traded to the Chicago Bulls in 1995. He spent three seasons with the Bulls and was a key contributor to the team, winning three consecutive NBA titles (1996–98).

He signed as a free agent with the Los Angeles Lakers in February 1999 and was waived by the team in April 1999.

In 13 seasons, Rodman had 11,783 rebounds (13.1 average). He made the NBA All-Defensive first team seven times and was an All-Star twice.

Russell, Bill

Born: February 12, 1934 in Monroe, Louisiana

Bill Russell was the centerpiece of the greatest dynasty in all of sports, the Boston Celtics, who won 11 NBA championships in a 13-year span (1957–69).

He was a 6-10, 220-pound center who emphasized defense and rebounding, and redefined the NBA as it had been known. Russell epitomized the team concept and downplayed individual statistics and awards. He wasn't concerned with scoring points; he was concerned with winning. Nothing else mattered. He made a singular and lasting impact on the game and was one of its most dominant figures.

Russell's career began without a hint that stardom would follow. He was a third-string center on his junior varsity team. Actually, he was worse than third string. The team had 15 uniforms and 16 players, so Russell and a teammate alternated wearing the 15th uniform.

Russell made the varsity team his senior year. He was a solid but not spectacular player, at least on offense. His ability to block shots and the way he kept the opposition from penetrating the lane got the attention of a scout from the University of San Francisco. Russell was offered a scholarship, and it wasn't long before he changed the college game.

"No one had ever played basketball the way I played it," said Russell. "They had never seen anyone block shots before. I like to think I originated a whole new style of play."

In his last two years at San Francisco, Russell led the Dons to 55 straight victories, an undefeated season in 1956 (29–0), and consecutive NCAA championships. He was named the NCAA Tournament's Most Outstanding Player in 1955.

Russell averaged 20.7 points and 20.3 rebounds a game in three varsity seasons at San Francisco. Following the 1955 season, the NCAA changed several rules in an effort to level the playing field and neutralize Russell's dominance. The free throw lane was widened to 12 feet, and it became illegal for a player to touch a shot on its downward arc to the basket.

The Celtics traded Ed Macauley and Cliff Hagan, each a future Hall of Famer, to the St. Louis Hawks for the rights to Russell, who was selected third overall in the 1956 NBA draft. But because the Olympics were not held until November, Russell put off his professional career until the games were over. He helped the United States win the gold medal.

Russell, a cerebral and analytical player, joined the Celtics for 48 games of the 1956–57 season and led them to their first championship, a four-game sweep over the Minneapolis Lakers. The Celtics lost to the Hawks in the finals in 1958 and then won eight straight titles.

The Philadelphia 76ers won the championship in 1967, but the Celtics came back to win two more, with Russell serving as player-coach (1968–69).

Russell was a consistent scorer, averaging 12 or more points 12 times in 13 seasons. But he was a ferocious rebounder, averaging 20 or more rebounds a game 10 times, including five times leading the league (19.6, 1957; 22.7, 1958; 23.0, 1959; 24.7, 1964; 24.1, 1965).

Russell was always compared with the other dominant big man at the time, Wilt Chamberlain, who won numerous scoring titles, but only two NBA championships (1976, '72).

Despite Russell's lack of gaudy offensive numbers, his immense contributions did not go unnoticed. He was named the league's Most Valuable Player in 1958, 1961, 1962, 1963, and 1965.

Russell retired as a player following the 1969 season, when he also stepped down as the Celtics head coach (162–81 record in three seasons). In 13 seasons, he had 14,522 points (15.1 average) and 21,620 rebounds (22.5). Through the 2000 season, he ranked second all-time in rebounds. The NBA didn't keep statistics on blocked shots until 1973.

In the postseason, he averaged 16.2 points and 24.9 rebounds a game. Through the 2000 season, he ranked first all-time in rebounds (4,104), 21st all-time in points scored (2,673), and 11th all-time in games played (165).

Russell made the All-NBA first team three times; the All-Defensive first team once (1969), the first year of its existence; and the All-Star team 12 times. He was Most Valuable Player of the 1963 All-Star Game.

Russell returned to coaching in 1973 with the Seattle SuperSonics. He spent four seasons in Seattle, also serving as general manager, compiling a 162–166 record and resigning after the 1977 season. Ten years later, he was hired as the head coach of the Sacramento Kings, but didn't last the season before he was replaced and made a vice president. His overall record as a head coach was 341–290.

Russell was inducted into the Naismith Memorial Basketball Hall of Fame in 1974 and was named one of the NBA's 50 greatest players in 1996.

Schayes, Dolph

Born: May 19, 1928 in New York, New York

Dolph Schayes was an all-around player who was one of the most prolific scorers in the early years of the NBA. A 6-8, 220-pound forward, he was known for his drives to the basket and his ability to hit the outside shot. He was also an accurate free throw shooter (.843 percentage) who perfected his shot on a hoop four inches smaller in diameter than a regulation hoop.

Ironically, Schayes credited two broken wrists with helping improve his shooting. When he broke his right wrist, he developed his left-handed shot; when he broke his left wrist, he developed his trademark two-handed set shot.

Schayes played his college ball at New York University, where he averaged 10.2 points a game in four varsity seasons. He played his first season for the Syracuse Nationals of the National Basketball League in 1949. He averaged 12.8 points a game (rebounding statistics weren't kept) and was named NBL Rookie of the Year.

In 1950, the Nationals became part of the NBA, and Schayes spent his entire career with the same franchise, which moved to Philadelphia and became the 76ers in 1963–64, his final season.

Schayes averaged double figures in scoring and rebounding in 11 of his 16 seasons. He led the NBA in rebounding in 1951 (16.4 average). He averaged 20 or more points a game six times, including a career-high 24.9 in 1958.

Schayes also was a durable player, who once played in 706 consecutive games. When he retired, he held NBA records for games played (1,059), points (19,249), and free throws (6,979). His teams made the playoffs in every season of his career, and in 1955 won the NBA championship, defeating the Fort Wayne Pistons in seven games.

Schayes made the All-NBA first team six times and the All-Star Game 12 times. He was inducted into the Naismith Memorial Basketball Hall of Fame in 1972 and was named one of the NBA's 50 greatest players in 1996.

Schayes was the player-coach of the 76ers in 1963–64 and continued to coach them through the 1966 season, when he led the 76ers to a 55–25 record and was named Coach of the Year. He coached the Buffalo Braves for two seasons (1971–72). His overall record as a head coach was 151–172.

Sharman, Bill

Born: May 25, 1926 in Abilene, Texas

Bill Sharman is widely regarded as one of the best pure shooters in the history of the NBA. He and Bob Cousy formed one the great backcourts of all time. Cousy was the consummate playmaker, Sharman the deadly shooter who had near-perfect technique.

Sharman was an all-around athlete at the University of Southern California, playing baseball, basketball, and tennis, as well as participating in boxing, track and field, and weightlifting.

Sharman was an All-American in basketball as a senior (1950) and was drafted by the Washington Capitols in the second round of the NBA draft. He played one season with the Capitols, who disbanded. He was taken by the Fort Wayne Pistons in a dispersal draft, but refused to report. He was then traded to the Boston Celtics, where he became a fixture and a star for a decade.

In addition to being an outstanding basketball player, Sharman played five seasons of minor league baseball as an outfielder. He never appeared in a major league game, but he was called up by the Brooklyn Dodgers in 1951 and was in the dugout when Bobby Thomson of the New York Giants hit the pennant-winning home run.

Sharman averaged in double figures in every year of his career, including three seasons of 20 or more points a game. He led the NBA in foul-shooting percentage seven times (1953–57, '59, '61), including three seasons with 90 percent or better.

The Celtics won four NBA championships during Sharman's career (1957, '59–61).

Sharman retired after the 1961 season with 12,665 points (17.8 average) and an .883 foul shooting percentage. In the postseason, he averaged 18.5 points a game and hit 91 percent from the foul line.

Sharman made the All-NBA first team four times and played in the All-Star Game eight times. He was inducted into the Naismith Memorial Basketball Hall of Fame in 1975 and was named one of the NBA's 50 greatest players in 1996.

After his retirement, Sharman continued his winning ways as a coach and an executive. He spent one season (1962) as the player-coach of the Los Angeles Jets of the American Basketball League. The franchise folded after 19 games, and he became the coach of the Cleveland Pipers, leading them to the 1962 championship.

After two seasons coaching at Cal State-Los Angeles (1963–64), Sharman spent two seasons coaching the San Francisco Warriors of the NBA (1967–68) and then coached the Los Angeles franchise in the American Basketball Association for three seasons (1969–71), the latter moving to Utah. Sharman was named the ABA Coach of the Year in 1970 and led Utah to the ABA championship in 1971.

A year later, Sharman was named the coach of the Los Angeles Lakers. In his first season, he led the Lakers, with Jerry West and Wilt Chamberlain, to the best record in NBA history at the time (69–13) and the NBA championship in five games over the Los Angeles Lakers.

Sharman is the only coach to win championships in three modern-day professional leagues. He retired in 1976 after four seasons with the Lakers. His overall NBA coaching record was 333–240. He served as general manager of the Lakers from 1976 through 1982, was president of the Lakers from 1983 through 1990, and through the 2000 season, was a consultant to the Lakers.

Stockton, John

Born: March 26, 1962 in Spokane, Washington

John Stockton is substance over style and fundamentals over flash. He is a solid, consistent point guard whose only concern is his team playing well. Night in, night out,

Stockton does whatever it takes to ensure that happening.

Stockton played his college ball at Gonzaga, which is not known for turning out all-time great basketball players. He led the West Coast Conference in assists and steals in his last three seasons, and led the league in scoring as a senior.

The Utah Jazz selected Stockton in the first round of the 1984 draft. He took over as a starter in the 1987–88 season and has been a fixture ever since. A durable player, he missed only four games in his first 13 seasons.

A double-figure scorer in every season since 1988, Stockton's main contribution to the Jazz offense has been making sure everyone else got the ball. The biggest beneficiary of Stockton's accurate passes has been Karl Malone. Stockton and Malone formed one of the most effective tandems ever.

Stockton led the NBA in assists nine straight years, beginning in 1988, including an NBA-record 14.5 assists a game in 1990.

Through the 2000 season, Stockton held the all-time record for most seasons leading the league in assists and most consecutive seasons. He held the single-season record for assists (1,164, 1991).

The Jazz have been to the playoffs in every season of Stockton's career. Twice they reached the NBA Finals, losing each time to the Chicago Bulls—in six games in 1997 and 1998.

In 16 seasons, Stockton had 16,781 points (13.3 average) and 13,790 assists (11.0). He ranked first all-time in assists and second all-time in assists per game. In the postseason, he averaged 13.6 points and 10.2 assists a game. He ranked second all-time in assists (1,716) and assists per game. He also ranked first in steals (2,844).

Stockton, a member of the gold-medal-winning U.S. Olympic teams in 1992 and 1996, made the All-NBA first team twice and played in the All-Star Game nine times. In 1993, he and Malone were co–Most Valuable Players. He was named one of the NBA's 50 greatest players in 1996.

Swoopes, Sheryl
Born: March 3, 1971 in Brownfield, Texas

Sheryl Swoopes is one of the most dynamic and talented players in the history of women's basketball. In addition to her talent on the court, she is blessed with charisma and an engaging personality, which make her one of the most popular players in the game. She is the first woman to have a basketball shoe named after her: the Nike "Air Swoopes."

Swoopes grew up in Brownfield, Texas, playing basketball with her two older brothers and the rest of the boys in the neighborhood. She credits that competition with the rapid development of her game. She accepted a scholarship to the University of Texas, but left after four days, because she was homesick. She attended South Plains Junior College, located in Brownfield, and was the Junior College Player of the Year in 1991, when she averaged 25.6 points and 11.5 rebounds a game. Swoopes then played for Texas Tech University, located less than 40 miles from her home.

In 1993, her senior year, she led the Lady Raiders to the national title. In the semifinal against Vanderbilt, she had 31 points and 11 rebounds; in the final against Ohio State, Swoopes scored 47 points, the most ever scored in a championship game by a man or a woman.

Texas Tech was 58–8 in Swoopes' two seasons and won two Southwest Conference titles. She was twice named the Southwest Conference Player of the Year and was the consensus national Player of the Year in 1993, when she also was named the Sportswoman of the Year by the Women's Sports Foundation.

Swoopes was a member of the 1996 U.S. Olympic team that won the gold medal. She averaged 13 points a game and scored in double figures in seven of the eight games.

Swoopes joined the Houston Comets of the Women's National Basketball Association (WNBA) in 1997 and helped them win the league championship in each of her first three seasons. She missed the beginning of the 1997 season because of the birth of her first child, Jordan.

Through the 2000 season, Swoopes averaged 17.3 points and 5.6 rebounds a game. In the postseason, she averaged 12.4 points and 5.8 rebounds. She made the All-WNBA first team twice and was a two-time All-Star.

In 2000, she was named Most Valuable Player and Defensive Player of the Year.

Thomas, Isiah
Born: April 30, 1961 in Chicago, Illinois

Isiah Thomas was a classic point guard: an outstanding playmaker who could handle the ball and pass effectively. He could hit the jump shot from long range, but the most dangerous aspect of his arsenal was his ability to penetrate.

Thomas, who grew up in a ghetto in Chicago, was a high school All-American in 1979. He played his college ball at Indiana University, where he spent two seasons and led the Hoosiers to the 1981 NCAA championship. He was Most Outstanding Player of the NCAA Tournament, as well as a consensus All-American. Thomas left Indiana after his sophomore season.

Thomas was named a member of the U.S. Olympic basketball team in 1980, the year the United States boycotted the games, held in the Soviet Union.

He was selected by the Detroit Pistons with the second overall pick in the 1981 NBA draft. The Pistons were a moribund franchise that had won 16 and 21 games, respectively, in the previous two seasons. In Thomas' rookie year, they improved by 18 games and became a championship contender. They reached the NBA Finals in 1988, losing in seven games to the Los Angeles Lakers. In game 6, Thomas scored 43 points, including a record 25 in one quarter, while playing on a severely sprained ankle.

In 1989 and 1990, the Pistons won consecutive NBA championships, sweeping the Lakers and beating the Portland Trail Blazers in five games. Thomas was named Most Valuable Player of the 1990 finals.

Thomas was the heart of the team, known as the "Bad Boys." He averaged 20 or more points a game for five straight years (1983–87) and 10 or more assists a game for four straight years (1984–87), including a league-high 13.9 a game in 1985.

As the Chicago Bulls dominated the NBA in the 1990s and the Pistons declined, Thomas remained a consistent performer, averaging fewer than 17 points a game only twice in his last seven seasons. He retired following the 1994 season.

In 13 seasons, all with the Pistons, Thomas had 18,822 points (19.2 average) and 9,061 assists (9.3). Through the 2000 season, he ranked fourth all-time in assists. In the postseason, he averaged 20.4 points and 8.9 assists per game.

Thomas made the All-NBA first team three times and played in the All-Star Game 12 times. He was named one of the NBA's 50 greatest players in 1996.

Thomas moved into the front office after his retirement, becoming a vice president and part owner of the Toronto Raptors, a position he left in 1997, when he joined NBC Sports as a commentator on NBA telecasts. He also became the majority owner of the Continental Basketball Association in 1999. In August 2000, he was named head coach of the Indiana Pacers.

Thompson, David

Born: July 13, 1954 in Shelby, North Carolina

David Thompson jumped so high and could hang in the air so long, it seemed he defied gravity. Thompson had a 44-inch vertical leap and a variety of moves to perform before he returned to the ground. He was blessed with speed, athleticism, and a dependable outside shot.

Thompson played his college ball at North Carolina State University, where he was a three-time All-American (1973–75) and a two-time national Player of the Year (1974–75). He led the Wolfpack to the national championship in 1974—he was named Most Outstanding Player in the Final Four—and a 79–7 overall record in three varsity seasons.

In 1975, he signed with the Denver Nuggets of the American Basketball Association, averaged 26 points a game, and was named Rookie of the Year. In 1976, when the Nuggets became part of the NBA, Thompson averaged 27.1 points a game and finished second in the league in scoring to George Gervin of the San Antonio Spurs in what was the closest race ever.

Thompson averaged at least 24 points a game over the next three seasons. In 1980, a heel injury limited him to 39 games, but he came back in 1981 to average 25.5 points a game.

Despite his excellence on the court, Thompson was a troubled person off the court. He was addicted to drugs, which caused him to be late for practice or not show up at all. His erratic behavior led the Nuggets to trade him to the Seattle SuperSonics in 1982. He played two seasons with the Sonics, before injuries suffered in a fall at New York's Studio 54 ended his career.

In eight NBA seasons, Thompson scored 11,264 points. Through the 2000 season, his 22.1-point-a-game average ranked 24th all-time. Thompson made the All-NBA first team twice and played in the All-Star Game four times. He was inducted into the Naismith Memorial Basketball Hall of Fame in 1996.

Thurmond, Nate

Born: July 25, 1941 in Akron, Ohio

Nate Thurmond was as talented as any center ever to play the game. At 6-11, 235 pounds, he was a strong, powerful presence in the post. He could shoot from the outside, block shots, and rebound. He was also a tenacious defender.

Thurmond had the misfortune of playing at the same time as Wilt Chamberlain, Bill Russell, and Kareem Abdul-Jabbar, each a future Hall of Fame center, and his achievements were often overlooked. But there was no denying his greatness.

Thurmond played his college ball at Bowling Green University, where he averaged 19.9 points and 16.7 rebounds as a senior and was an All-American in 1963. The San Francisco Warriors selected him in the first round of the 1963 draft, and he made the all-rookie team, averaging 7 points and 10.4 rebounds a game. Thurmond played behind Chamberlain as a rookie, and his strong play allowed the Warriors to trade Chamberlain to the Philadelphia 76ers in 1965.

Thurmond averaged in double figures in points and rebounds for the next 10 seasons. He averaged 20 or more points five times and 18 or more rebounds five times. Twice he helped the Warriors reach the NBA Finals. They lost to the Boston Celtics in 1964 and the Philadelphia 76ers in 1967.

Thurmond spent 11 years with the Warriors, who traded him to the Chicago Bulls in September 1974. On

October 18, 1974, Thurmond became the first player ever to record a quadruple-double (double figures in four statistical categories) with 22 points, 14 rebounds, 13 assists, and 12 blocked shots.

Early in the 1975–76 season, the Bulls dealt him to the Cleveland Cavaliers, where he finished his career. In 1975, Thurmond helped lead the Cavaliers to their first playoff berth in franchise history. He retired in 1977.

In 14 seasons, Thurmond had 14,437 points (15.0 average) and 14,464 rebounds (15.0). Through the 2000 season, he ranked seventh all-time in rebounds. In the postseason, he averaged 11.9 points and 13.6 rebounds a game.

Thurmond made the All-Defensive first team twice and the All-Star Game seven times. He was inducted into the Naismith Memorial Basketball Hall of Fame in 1984 and was named one of the NBA's 50 greatest players in 1996.

Unseld, Wes

Born: March 14, 1946 in Louisville, Kentucky

Wes Unseld was undersized for a center—he was listed as 6-7, but was actually a bit smaller. His powerful build and determination allowed him to more than hold his own with the best centers of his time, including Wilt Chamberlain, Kareem Abdul-Jabbar, and Nate Thurmond. He was a ferocious rebounder and defender, a tireless worker, and his ability to throw precise outlet passes was a key to running the fast break.

Unseld, who led his high school team to two Kentucky state titles in the mid-60s, played his college ball at the University of Louisville. He averaged 20.6 points and 18.9 rebounds in three varsity seasons. The Baltimore Bullets selected him in the first round of the 1968 NBA draft as the second overall pick.

Unseld transformed the Bullets into a contender, helping them improve by 21 games and make their first of 12 straight playoff appearances. They finished 57–25, the best record in the NBA. Unseld averaged 13.8 points and 18.2 rebounds a game. He was named Rookie of the Year and Most Valuable Player. Only Chamberlain has managed to be so honored.

Unseld averaged in double figures in rebounding in all but one of his 13 seasons. He averaged 14 or more rebounds a game six times, including a league-leading 14.8 in 1975.

Unseld led the Bullets to four NBA Finals. They lost in 1971, 1975, and 1979. In 1978, the Bullets won the championship, beating the Seattle SuperSonics in seven games. He was named the Most Valuable Player in the NBA Finals.

In 13 seasons, Unseld had 10,624 points (10.8 average) and 13,769 rebounds (14.0). Through the 2000 sea-son, he ranked ninth all-time in rebounds. In the postseason, he averaged 10.8 points and 14.9 rebounds a game.

Unseld made the All-NBA first team once and the All-Star Game five times. He was inducted into the Naismith Memorial Basketball Hall of Fame in 1987 and was named one of the NBA's 50 greatest players in 1996.

Unseld coached the Bullets for seven seasons (1988–94) and compiled a 202–345 record, after which he moved into the front office.

Walton, Bill

Born: November 5, 1962 in La Mesa, California

Bill Walton had a spectacular college career, followed by an NBA career that was plagued by injuries. Had he remained healthy, there's no telling what he could have accomplished. He was an outstanding center who could do everything—score, rebound, defend, block shots, and pass.

Walton played his college ball at UCLA, under the legendary John Wooden. The Bruins won 86 of 90 games during Walton's three years, including 88 in a row, and two NCAA championships (1972–73). He was Most Outstanding Player in the Final Four in 1972 and 1973, and in the 1973 final against Memphis State, he had one of the greatest games in NCAA championship history, scoring 44 points on 21 of 22 shooting from the floor. But it was his all-around team play that impressed Wooden, who said, "He's one of those who makes all the players around him better."

Walton was named national Player of the Year three times (1972–74), an All-American three times, and the 1973 Sullivan Award winner as the nation's outstanding amateur athlete.

In 1974, the Portland Trail Blazers selected Walton with the first overall pick in the draft. But the foot injuries that would plague him throughout his career limited him to just 35 games. He averaged 12.8 points and 12.6 rebounds.

In 1977, he led the league in rebounding (14.4 a game) and averaged 18.6 points a game. He also led the Trail Blazers to the NBA championship, in six games over the Philadelphia 76ers, who won the first two games of the series. Walton was named Most Valuable Player in the NBA Finals.

Walton played 58 games in 1978. He averaged 18.9 points and 13.2 rebounds a game. He was named Most Valuable Player. He missed all of the 1979 season with foot problems. He signed with the San Diego Clippers in 1979, but played in only 14 games. He missed the next two seasons entirely, and played only 33 games in the 1982–83 season.

Walton was traded to the Boston Celtics in September 1985. He was a backup center who provided valuable minutes for the Celtics, who won the NBA championship that season. Walton played in 80 games and averaged 7.6 points and 6.8 rebounds. He won the NBA's Sixth Man Award.

Walton played in 10 games in the 1986–87 season, then sat out all of the following season before announcing his retirement.

Walton had 6,215 points (13.3 average) and 4,923 rebounds (10.5) in 468 games. In the postseason, he averaged 10.8 points and 9.1 rebounds. He made the All-NBA first team once, the All-Defensive first team twice, and was a two-time All-Star. He was inducted into the Naismith Memorial Basketball Hall of Fame in 1993 and was named one of the NBA's 50 greatest players in 1996. Through the 2000 season, he was a broadcaster for NBC Sports.

West, Jerry
Born: May 28, 1938 in Chelyan, West Virginia

Jerry West was one of the greatest pure jump shooters in the history of the NBA. So accurate was West that when the ball didn't go in, you were surprised. But his game was far from one-dimensional. He was also a fine playmaker and passer, and a dogged defender. West became such a basketball icon that it's his silhouette that makes up the NBA's official logo.

West got his start when someone in his hometown nailed a hoop to a storage shed. He became fascinated by the game and worked tirelessly, regardless of the weather, to develop his game. The same drive and determination he demonstrated as a child carried through for the rest of his basketball career.

After leading his East Bank High team to the 1956 West Virginia state championship, West had to sift through a mountain of college scholarship offers. He decided to stay at home and play for West Virginia University. He averaged 24.8 points and 13.3 rebounds a game during his three varsity seasons (1958–60), including 29.3 as a senior. He was a two-time All-American and Most Outstanding Player in the 1959 Final Four. The Mountaineers lost to California in the championship game.

The Minneapolis Lakers selected West in the first round of the 1960 NBA draft with the second overall pick. Before West joined the Lakers, who moved to Los Angeles for the 1960–61 season, he helped the United States win the gold medal in the 1960 Summer Games.

West had a solid but unspectacular rookie season, averaging 17.6 points, 7.7 rebounds, and 4.2 assists a game. But in his second season, he averaged 30.8 points and began a string of 11 straight seasons in which he averaged 25 or more points a game. Three times he averaged 30 or more points a game, including 1970, when he led the league in scoring (31.2). West shot 45 percent or higher from the field 11 times.

The Lakers made the playoffs in all but one of West's 14 seasons. They advanced to the NBA Finals nine times, but it wasn't until their penultimate visit in 1972 that they won their only NBA championship, although their failure to win in their other eight opportunities wasn't West's fault. He averaged 30 or more points a game seven times, including 40.6 points in 1965. During the Baltimore–Los Angeles playoff series in 1965, West averaged 46.5 points a game, which, through the 2000 season, was a single-series record.

In 1969, even though the Lakers lost to the Boston Celtics in seven games, West was named Most Valuable Player of the NBA Finals. Through the 2000 season, he was the only MVP not to play on the winning team.

In 1970, West hit one of his most famous playoff shots—a half-court bomb at the buzzer that sent game 3 against the New York Knicks into overtime.

West finally was part of an NBA champion in 1972. The Lakers went 69–13, including a 33-game win streak. The record was the best in NBA history until the Chicago Bulls surpassed it in 1995–96, going 72–10. West averaged 25.8 points and a league-leading 9.7 assists a game. In the NBA Finals, the Lakers beat the Knicks in five games.

West, nicknamed "Mr. Clutch," played two more seasons after the championship, retiring in 1974. Still a productive player, he averaged 20.8 points a game in his final season.

For all his greatness, West was motivated, in part, by a fear of failure. He was a fierce competitor who took every loss to heart.

"I really played out of fear that I was going to fail," West said. "If we lost, it was always my fault, and that's a terrible burden to carry around with you."

In 14 seasons, all with the Lakers, West had 25,192 points (27.0 average) and 6,238 assists (6.7). Through the 2000 season, he ranked 12th all-time in points scored and fifth all-time in scoring average. In the postseason, he averaged 29.1 points and 6.3 assists per game. He ranked second all-time in scoring average, third in points (4,457), third in field goals (1,622), and second in free throws (1,213).

West made the All-NBA first team 10 times, the All-Defensive first team four times, and was selected for the All-Star Game in each of his 14 seasons. He was inducted into the Naismith Memorial Hall of Fame in 1979 and was named one of the NBA's 50 greatest players in 1996.

West coached the Lakers for three seasons, starting in 1977, compiling a 145–101 record, and then became the team's general manager in 1982. An astute judge of talent, he is credited with putting together teams that won five NBA championships in the 1980s. In 1994, he was named executive vice president, basketball operations, a position he held until he retired in August 2000. The Lakers won the 2000 NBA championship.

Wilkens, Lenny

Born: October 28, 1937 in Brooklyn, New York

Lenny Wilkens, perhaps best known for being the winningest coach in NBA history, was also an outstanding player in college and the pros. Wilkins could score, handle the ball, and play solid defense. He was a classic all-around guard.

He played his college ball at Providence College, where he was Most Valuable Player at the National Invitation Tournament and an All-American as a senior in 1960. In three varsity seasons for the Friars, Wilkens averaged 14.9 points a game. He was selected by the St. Louis Hawks in the first round of the 1960 NBA draft.

In his rookie season, Wilkens averaged 11.7 as a starter and helped the Hawks reach the NBA Finals, where they lost to the Boston Celtics in five games.

Wilkens spent nine seasons with the Hawks, averaging double figures in points every season. In 1968, he was traded to the Seattle SuperSonics. He served as player-coach for three seasons (1970–72). In 1972, he was traded to the Cleveland Cavaliers. After two seasons in Cleveland, he spent his final season (1974–75) with the Portland Trail Blazers, also serving as player-coach.

Wilkens led the NBA in assists twice—683 in 1970 and 766 in 1972. In 15 seasons, Wilkens had 17,772 points (16.5 average) and 7,211 assists (6.7), second-highest total in league history when he retired. In the postseason, he averaged 16.1 points and 5.8 assists a game.

In 1978, Wilkens became the coach of the SuperSonics, leading them to the NBA Finals in his first season. They lost to the Baltimore Bullets. In 1979, the SuperSonics defeated the Bullets in five games to win the title.

Wilkens spent eight seasons in Seattle (1978–85), then coached Cleveland (1987–93) and the Atlanta Hawks (1994–2000). He was named Coach of the Year in 1994, leading Atlanta to a 57–25 record. In 1996, he was the coach of the U.S. Olympic team—Dream Team II—that won the gold medal.

Following the 2000 season, Wilkens left the Hawks. Several weeks later, he was named head coach of the Toronto Raptors. In 27 seasons as a head coach, his record was 1,179–981 in the regular season and 72–85 in the playoffs, through the 2000 season. He is the all-time winningest coach in NBA history, and his 72 playoff wins rank him sixth-best.

Wilkens was inducted into the Naismith Memorial Basketball Hall of Fame as a player in 1988 and as a coach in 1998. He was named one of the NBA's 50 greatest players in 1996.

Wilkins, Dominique

Born: January 12, 1960 in Paris, France

Dominique Wilkins, known as the "Human Highlight Film," was best known for his spectacular dunks and acrobatic moves. He was a great scorer who developed into a more well-rounded player later in his career.

Wilkins played his college ball at the University of Georgia, where he averaged 21.6 points and 7.5 rebounds a game in three seasons. He left school after his junior year, opting for the NBA. He was chosen by the Utah Jazz in the first round of the 1982 NBA draft, and his rights were traded to the Atlanta Hawks in September 1982.

Wilkins was a consistent scorer throughout his career. He averaged 25 or more points a game for 10 straight seasons, beginning in 1985. In 1986, he led the NBA in scoring, averaging 30.3 points a game.

Wilkins spent the first 11 seasons of his career with the Hawks (1983–93). Midway through his 12th season, he was traded to the Los Angeles Clippers. He finished out the 1994 season with the Clippers, then signed with the Boston Celtics as a free agent. After one season in Boston, he accepted a lucrative offer to play for Panatinaikos Athens of the Greek League. He averaged 20.9 points and seven rebounds a game and led the team to the European Championships for Men's Clubs. He was named Most Valuable Player of the European Final Four in Paris.

Wilkins returned to the NBA for the 1996–97 season, signing with the San Antonio Spurs. He played in Italy in 1998 and signed with the Orlando Magic in February 1999. He played 27 games with the Magic in the 1999–2000 season, before being waived.

Wilkins scored 26,668 points (24.8 average) and 7,169 rebounds (6.7). Through the 2000 season, he ranked eighth all-time in scoring. In the postseason, he averaged 25.4 points and 6.7 rebounds. Wilkins made the All-NBA team once and the All-Star team nine times.

Woodard, Lynette

Born: August 11, 1959 in Wichita, Kansas

Even though her name does not appear in the NCAA record books, Lynette Woodard has scored more points than anyone in the history of women's basketball (3,649). She played at Kansas University from 1978 through 1981, but the NCAA didn't start keeping official statistics for women's basketball until 1982.

Woodard, though, was more than just a scorer. She led the nation in rebounding as a freshman in 1978 and in steals in each of her last three seasons. She averaged 26.3 points a game, also a women's record. She was a four-time All-American and the winner of the 1981 Wade Trophy as Player of the Year.

In 1980, Woodard was named to the U.S. Olympic team, but didn't get to compete because of the U.S. boycott of the games, held in Moscow.

Woodard played professionally in Italy in 1981–82, then returned to Kansas, where she served as an academic adviser and a volunteer coach. She also prepared for the 1984 Olympics as a member of the U.S. national team, which traveled throughout the world. Woodard was named captain of the Olympic team and led it to a gold medal.

With no professional leagues available to Woodard, she tried out for the Harlem Globetrotters, and in October 1985, became the first woman to play for the team. She spent two seasons with the Globetrotters, before playing professionally in Italy and Japan.

In 1997, the Women's National Basketball Association (WNBA) was formed, and Woodard was drafted ninth overall by the Cleveland Rockers. She spent one season with Cleveland and one with the Detroit Shock, before retiring in 1998.

Worthy, James

Born: February 27, 1961 in Gastonia, North Carolina

James Worthy was one of the most effective small forwards in NBA history. Blessed with speed, athleticism, and the ability to thrive inside or outside, he was an outstanding offensive player who was at his best in big games. Magic Johnson, a Lakers teammate, called Worthy "one of the top 5 players in playoff history."

Worthy played his college ball at the University of North Carolina, where he averaged 14.5 points and 7.4 rebounds a game for the Tar Heels. As a junior in 1982, he and Michael Jordan led North Carolina to the NCAA championship. Worthy had 28 points in the final against Georgetown and was named Most Outstanding Player of the Final Four. A consensus All-American, he left school after his junior season.

The Los Angeles Lakers selected Worthy with the first overall pick in the 1982 draft, even though they had a productive small forward in Jamaal Wilkes. Worthy, the team concept having been instilled in him by coach Dean Smith at North Carolina, never complained about not starting. Instead, he tried to learn all he could from Wilkes and bided his time.

Worthy moved into the starting lineup in the 1984–85 season and became ideally suited to the Lakers' high-speed, "Showtime" attack. He averaged 17.6 points and 6.4 rebounds a game in helping the Lakers beat the Boston Celtics in six games to win the NBA championship.

The Lakers also won NBA championships in 1987 and 1988, when Worthy was named Most Valuable Player of the NBA Finals. In game 7 of the 1988 finals against the Detroit Pistons, Worthy registered a triple-double (double figures in three statistical categories)—36 points, 16 rebounds, and 10 assists—in the Lakers' 108–105 victory.

Worthy averaged 17 points or more a game eight times in his 12 seasons, including a three-year stretch when he averaged 20.5, 21.1, and 21.4, respectively.

A knee injury limited Worthy to 54 games in 1992, and in 1994, he played the fewest minutes of his career. He retired following that season.

In 12 seasons, Worthy had 16,320 points (17.6 average) and 4,708 rebounds (5.1 average). In the postseason, he averaged 21.1 points and 5.2 rebounds a game. He was named one of the NBA's 50 greatest players in 1996. Through the 2000 season, he worked as an analyst for CBS Sports and Fox Sports.

Ali, Muhammad

Born: January 17, 1942 in Louisville, Kentucky

Muhammad Ali proclaimed himself "The Greatest" and lived up to the claim. In addition to a remarkable career in the ring, he was also one of the most colorful, charismatic, and controversial athletes of our time.

Born Cassius Marcellus Clay, he began taking boxing lessons at age 12, after his new Schwinn bicycle was stolen. Joe Martin, the policeman Clay talked to about his bike, also ran a gym. When Clay vowed to get revenge, Martin suggested he come to the gym to take boxing lessons.

Clay spent six weeks learning the basics of boxing, and then had his first fight, a three-rounder that he won by split decision. When the announcement was made, Clay boasted that one day he would be "the greatest of all time."

Over the next several years, Clay continued to train diligently and began developing the style that would be unique to the heavyweight division, infuriating to boxing purists, and frustrating to opponents.

Clay carried his hands low and circled the ring on his toes, flicking his jab as he danced. But his greatest defense, as David Remnick wrote in *King of the World*, was his "quickness, his uncanny ability to gauge an opponent's punch and lean back just far enough away from it to avoid getting hit—and then strike back."

That style, even in its infancy, helped Clay win AAU and Golden Gloves titles in 1959 and 1960, and he also won the gold medal in the light heavyweight division at the 1960 Summer Olympics in Rome.

After the Olympics, Clay turned pro. He was 18 years old. Over the next three years, he moved up the ranks, finally becoming the top heavyweight contender in 1964, when he earned a title shot against Sonny Liston, a big, burly, powerful champ, who also happened to be an ex-con.

Clay was given little or no chance against Liston by the boxing media, which were put off by his bravado and braggadoccio. Clay would speak in rhymes and predict the round in which he would knock out his opponents. The press also was unimpressed with Clay's style.

The fight was held February 25, 1964, in Miami. From the beginning, Clay dominated, forcing Liston to chase him and literally beating him to the punch. After three rounds, Liston trudged to his corner, having spent himself from all the missed punches.

But when Clay went to his corner after the fourth, he began screaming because of searing pain in both eyes. Apparently, Liston's corner had doctored his gloves with a substance that caused the pain. Clay wanted to quit, but his trainer, Angelo Dundee, got plenty of water flowing in Clay's eyes and pushed him back into the ring.

Boxing

Clay spent the fifth round running, trying to elude Liston, who finally began landing punches, although not a decisive blow.

In the sixth, with his eyes clear, Clay stopped dancing and started hitting, at one point landing eight straight punches. He ended the round with two left hooks to the head. Liston returned to his corner and stayed there. He didn't answer the bell for the seventh round, and Cassius Clay was the new heavyweight champion of the world.

"I am the king," he bellowed. "I am the king. King of the world! Eat your words! Eat your words!"

Soon after he became champion, Clay announced that he had become a member of the Nation of Islam and was given the name Muhammad Ali. The reaction to his choice of religions was met with outrage and controversy. Many of the nation's leading columnists publicly criticized Ali's decision.

His next bout was a rematch with Liston, originally scheduled for November 16, 1964, at Boston Garden, but postponed until May 25, 1965, in Lewiston, Me., because Ali was hospitalized for a hernia.

The rematch lasted one round. Ali decked Liston with the so-called phantom punch or anchor punch—a blow that Liston didn't see, nor did anyone else. Ali did not move to a neutral corner right away, and Liston eventually got up, but it was ruled that he had been down for at least a count of 10 and the fight was stopped.

Ali successfully defended his title eight times, beating Floyd Patterson, George Chuvalo, Karl Mildenburger, and Ernie Terrell, among others. But in 1967, in the prime of his career, he was stripped of his title because of his refusal on religious grounds to be inducted into the armed services. He faced five years in prison and was inactive while the case was being litigated. In June 1971, the U.S. Supreme Court ruled in his favor. Ali had returned to the ring in October 1970 and defeated Jerry Quarry.

Ali's first attempt to regain the title came on March 8, 1971, in the "Fight of the Century," against Joe Frazier. In a brutally hard-fought battle, Frazier handed Ali his first loss, winning a 15-round decision.

Ali and Frazier would fight twice more. Both were classics and both were won by Ali—a 12-round decision in January 1974 and a 14th-round technical knockout in October 1975 in the "Thrilla in Manila," thought by many to be the greatest fight ever.

Ali had regained the heavyweight title in October 1974 in Kinshasa, Zaire. He beat George Foreman in a fight dubbed the "Rumble in the Jungle," in which he used his rope-a-dope strategy. He leaned against the ropes and allowed Foreman to punch himself out. Ali eventually won by knockout in the eighth round.

Ali retained the title until February 1978, when he lost a 15-round decision to Leon Spinks. Eight months later, the title was his again after a 15-round decision over Spinks in a rematch.

Shortly after the second Spinks fight, Ali announced his retirement, which didn't last. He fought Larry Holmes, the heavyweight champ, in October 1980, losing on an 11th-round technical knockout, and then fought Trevor Berbick, in December 1981, losing a 10-

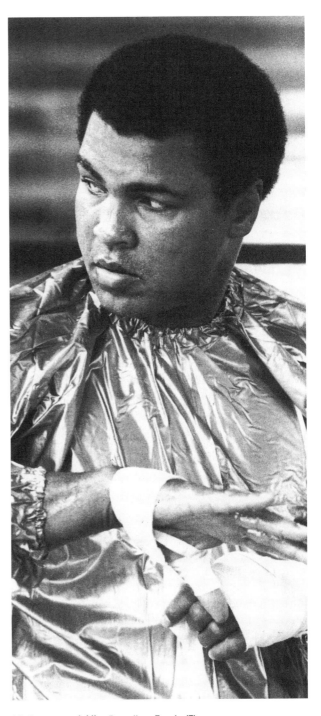

Muhammad Ali   *Reading Eagle/Times*

round decision. He retired for good after the Berbick fight.

Ali's career record was 56–5–0, with 37 wins coming by knockout. He is a member of the International Boxing Hall of Fame and the Olympic Hall of Fame. Parkinson's disease has made Ali a shadow of his former self physically, but he remains one of the most revered and accomplished athletes ever.

Arguello, Alexis

Born: April 19, 1952 in Managua, Nicaragua

Alexis Arguello overcame poverty to become a champion in three different weight classes. Forced to leave school at age 14 to go work on a dairy farm, Arguello turned pro by two years later. His first 36 fights, 34 of which were victories, took place in Nicaragua.

His first fight in the United States was in November 1974 in Los Angeles, where he won the World Boxing Association featherweight title from Ruben Olivares. He held the title until 1977, when he moved up to the super featherweight division. He took that title in January 1978, defeating Alfredo Escalera, and held it for two years, before seeking the lightweight championship.

In June 1981, Arguello won a decision against Jim Watt to win his third belt. He knocked out four challengers over the next year, before setting his sights on a fourth title—the junior welterweight title.

Arguello fought Aaron Pryor for the championship in November 1982, but lost on a 14th-round technical knockout. Ten months later, he fought Pryor again, this time losing on a 10th-round TKO.

After twice retiring, then returning, Arguello finally called it quits in 1995, with a career record of 80–8–0, with 64 wins coming by knockout.

Armstrong, Henry

Born: December 12, 1912 in Columbus, Missouri
Died: October 24, 1988

Henry Armstrong, who began fighting under the name of Melody Jackson, was the first to hold three titles simultaneously, which is especially impressive because during his era boxing had only eight weight classes.

Armstrong, nicknamed "Homicide Hank," fought often as a featherweight. Sometimes his bouts were only days apart. In 1934, *The Ring* magazine ranked him as the no. 6 contender; in 1936, he won the California–Mexico version of the world heavyweight title; and in 1937, won all 27 bouts (26 by knockout) and beat Petey Sarron for the undisputed featherweight championship.

In 1938, Armstrong defeated Barney Ross for the welterweight title, and then won a split decision in a brutal battle with Lou Ambers for the lightweight title. Armstrong gave up the featherweight title in 1938 be-

cause he couldn't make weight. He lost the lightweight title in 1939 in a rematch with Ambers. He lost the welterweight title to Fritzie Zivic in 1940.

Armstrong, a member of the International Boxing Hall of Fame, retired in 1945 with a career record of 151–21–9. He became an ordained Baptist minister.

Basilio, Carmen

Born: April 2, 1927 in Canastota, New York

Carmen Basilio, one of the toughest boxers of his time, took as many punches as he delivered, because of his aggressive style.

He began fighting in the Marine Corps and turned pro after his discharge in 1948. His first championship came in 1953 when he defeated Billy Graham for the New York State welterweight title.

After he fought Graham to a draw to retain the title, Basilio faced Kid Gavilan for the world welterweight championship. He nearly knocked out Gavilan in the second round, but eventually lost a 15-round decision.

In 1955, Basilio won the welterweight title from Tony DeMarco, when the referee stopped the fight in the 12th round. Basilio lost the title in 1956 to Johnny Sexton, losing a 15-round decision, but won a rematch six months later on a ninth-round technical knockout. Basilio moved up to the middleweight division in 1957, fought for the title and dethroned Sugar Ray Robinson on a split decision in a bloody brawl that *The Ring* magazine ranked as the 12th greatest fight of all time.

Robinson regained the title in March 1958, winning the rematch by a 15-round decision. Basilio fought three more times for the middleweight championship—twice against Gene Fullmer and once against Paul Pender—but was unsuccessful each time. He retired in August 1958 with a career record of 56–16–7, with 27 knockouts. He was inducted into the International Boxing Hall of Fame in 1990.

Benitez, Wilfred

Born: September 12, 1958 in The Bronx, New York

At age 17, Wilfred Benitez was the youngest fighter ever to win a world title when he won a 15-round decision over Antonio Cervantes for the junior welterweight championship in March 1976.

He defended the title three times, but was stripped of his belt when he didn't fight quickly enough after a car crash.

In 1979, Benitez moved up to welterweight and beat Carlos Palomino for the world title, winning a split decision. He lost the belt in November 1979 to Sugar Ray Leonard by technical knockout in the 15th round.

In 1981, Benitez again moved up in class and fought for the junior middleweight title. He beat Maurice Hope by a technical knockout in the 12th round. It was the third different title he held, and he was only 22 years old.

Benitez defended his junior middleweight title twice, the second time against Roberto Duran. But in his next fight, against Thomas Hearns, Benitez lost a 15-round decision. He tried to move up to middleweight, but never contended for a title again. Benitez, who in spite of his success was plagued throughout his career by shoddy preparation, retired in 1990. His career record was 53–8–1, with 31 knockouts. He was inducted into the International Boxing Hall of Fame in 1996.

Benvenuti, Nino (Giovanni)
Born: April 26, 1938 in Trieste, Italy

Nino Benvenuti won all 120 fights in his amateur career, concluding with the 1960 Olympic gold medal in the welterweight division. He turned pro in 1961 and won his first 65 fights, including the Italian and European middleweight titles.

Benvenuti won the junior middleweight world title, defeating Sandro Mazzinghi in a 15-round decision in December 1965. But a year later, he lost the title—and suffered his first loss as a pro—to Ki-Soo Kim.

In 1967, Benvenuti fought the first of three classic bouts with Emile Griffith for the world middleweight championship. Benvenuti won the first by decision, lost the rematch by decision, and then regained the title with a decision in March 1968.

Benvenuti retained his title until Carlos Monzon knocked him out in the 12th round in November 1970. After a second loss to Monzon, by a technical knockout in the third round in May 1971, Benvenuti retired. His career record was 82–7–1, with 35 knockouts. He was inducted into the International Boxing Hall of Fame in 1992.

Canzoneri, Tony
Born: November 6, 1908 in Slidell, Louisiana
Died: December 9, 1959

In an era of accomplished fighters, Tony Canzoneri was regarded as one of the best. He was an aggressive and powerful puncher who was knocked out only once in 175 professional fights, and that came in the final fight of his career against Al "Bummy" Davis in November 1939.

Canzoneri was a world champion in three divisions—featherweight (1927–28), lightweight (1930–33, '35–36), junior welterweight (1931–32, '33). During his 10 peak years, 1927–37, he fought in 22 title fights.

He finished with a career record of 137–24–10, with 44 knockouts. He was inducted into the International Boxing Hall of Fame in 1990.

Charles, Ezzard
Born: July 7, 1921 in Lawrenceville, Georgia
Died: May 27, 1975

Ezzard Charles turned pro in 1940 after winning 42 straight amateur bouts, a Golden Gloves championship, and the 1939 National Amateur Athletic Union middleweight title.

He began his pro career fighting as a middleweight. He moved to light heavyweight and eventually heavyweight. Charles, always a clever fighter, also was known as a hard puncher. But a 1948 bout against Sam Baroudi changed Charles' attitude about fighting.

Charles, nicknamed "The Cincinnati Cobra," knocked out Baroudi in the 10th round, doing so with a vicious flurry of punches. Baroudi never recovered from the beating and died several days later.

The death of Baroudi made Charles a less aggressive fighter who was reluctant to finish off his opponents.

Still, it didn't keep Charles from becoming the heavyweight champion. He beat Jersey Joe Walcott by decision in 1949 to win the National Boxing Association title, left vacant by the retirement of Joe Louis. Charles defended the title three times, the last of which was a victory over Louis, who came out of retirement. Charles defended the title four more times, before losing it to Walcott in July 1951. He lost again to Walcott in a 1952 title bout.

Twice more in 1954, Charles fought for the title against Walcott's successor, Rocky Marciano, but lost both times.

Charles fought four more years, retiring in 1959 with a record of 96–25–1, with 58 knockouts. He was inducted into the International Boxing Hall of Fame in 1990. Charles died, penniless, in 1975 of lateral sclerosis of the spine.

Chocolate, Kid (Eligio Sardinias-Montalbo)
Born: January 6, 1910 in Cerro, Cuba
Died: August 8, 1988

Kid Chocolate was quick, powerful, and one of the most popular fighters in the late 1920s to the late 1930s. He was undefeated as an amateur in more than 100 bouts. He turned pro in 1928 and won his first 21 fights by knockout.

Chocolate, nicknamed the "Cuban Bon Bon," was the junior lightweight champ 1931–33 and the New York world featherweight champ 1932–34. He retired in 1938 with a career record of 131–9–6, with 50 knockouts. He was inducted into the International Boxing Hall of Fame in 1991.

Conn, Billy
Born: October 8, 1917 in Pittsburgh, Pennsylvania
Died: May 29, 1993

Billy Conn was best known for one fight: his 1941 heavyweight title bout in New York's Polo Grounds against Joe Louis. Conn, who won the light heavy-weight championship by beating Melio Bettina in 1939 and held it for nearly two years, gave up the best to fight Louis.

Conn, nicknamed "The Pittsburgh Kid," weighed in at 169, 30 pounds lighter than the champ, but held his own, because of his speed and quickness. Through the 12th round, Conn was ahead on two cards and even on a third. But rather than continue the style that had been successful, Conn tried to knock out Louis in the 13th. In the process, he left himself more open than he had been throughout the fight. Louis took advantage and knocked out Conn in the 13th.

Family problems for Conn, and an injury, postponed the rematch until after World War II. But in June 1946, Louis won by an eighth-round knockout.

Conn, who turned pro at 16, never having been an amateur, retired in 1948. He had a career record of 63–12–1, with 14 knockouts. He was inducted into the International Boxing Hall of Fame in 1990.

De La Hoya, Oscar

Born: February 4, 1973 in East Los Angeles, California

Oscar De La Hoya was introduced to boxing when he was five years old. His father, Joel De La Hoya, a former professional boxer from Mexico, took him to the gym to teach the youngster how to fight his own battles. It was the same thing Joel's father had done for him as a young boy.

Those early lessons paid off, because Oscar De La Hoya has become an outstanding fighter. He has excellent boxing skills and has the ability to land punches in combinations. He has an effective jab and left hook. He has been successful against boxers and punchers.

After winning gold medals in the Goodwill Games, the U.S. National Championships, and the World Challenge, De La Hoya culminated his amateur career by winning the gold medal at the 1992 Summer Olympics, the only American to do so. He turned pro in November 1992 and won his first 17 fights. His 18th fight was against Rafael Ruelas for the International Boxing Federation lightweight title. De La Hoya won by a second-round technical knockout (TKO). After three successful title defenses, De La Hoya beat Julio Cesar Chavez in June 1996 by a fourth-round TKO to win the World Boxing Council (WBC) super lightweight title.

In April of 1997, in one of the most anticipated fights of the year, De La Hoya added the WBC welterweight title, winning a 12-round unanimous decision over Pernell Whitaker. That victory made De La Hoya one of 21 fighters to win titles in three different divisions and the youngest ever to accomplish the feat.

De La Hoya successfully defended his welterweight title eight times, before losing the first fight of his career, to Felix Trinidad, who won a majority decision in September 1999.

De La Hoya, nicknamed the "Golden Boy," is one of the sport's most popular attractions and its no. 1 box office draw outside the heavyweight division.

Dempsey, Jack (William Harrison)

Born: June 24, 1895 in Manassa, Colorado
Died: May 31, 1983

Jack Dempsey, born into a large, poor family, left school after the eighth grade and went from town to town, looking for work. He supplemented his income by challenging patrons in saloons and bars to fights. Legend has it that he never lost one of these fights.

In 1914, he turned pro, fighting mostly in the western United States. In February 1917, Dempsey was knocked out for the only time in his career, by Jim Flynn in the first round. But after that loss, he hired Jack Kearns as his manager and scored 14 first-round knockouts over the next 23 months.

Dempsey, nicknamed the "Manassa Mauler," became the world heavyweight champion in July 1919, when he defeated Jess Willard by a third-round technical knockout, after knocking him down seven times in the first round. Willard outweighed Dempsey by 58 pounds.

Dempsey successfully defended his title five times from 1920 to 1923. He should have fought Harry Wills, a top contender for the title, but Tex Rickard, a promoter, refused to arrange a mixed race bout. As a result, the New York State Athletic Commission canceled Dempsey's license to fight.

It wasn't until September 1926 that Dempsey met Gene Tunney, losing the title in a 10-round decision. It was the first time the heavyweight title had been transferred by decision. A year later, Dempsey and Tunney met in a rematch in what remains one of the most famous bouts of all time—the famous "long count."

In this rematch, held in Chicago's Soldier Field, Dempsey knocked Tunney down in the seventh round, but the count didn't start right away, because Dempsey didn't move to a neutral corner, as Illinois boxing rules dictated.

Tunney got to his feet at the count of nine, but he really had been down for 14 seconds. He recovered to win a 10-round decision.

Dempsey retired a few months later. He boxed exhibitions, managed and promoted fighters, and officiated at boxing and wrestling matches.

One of the most powerful fighters ever, Dempsey retired with a career record of 60–6–8, with 50 knockouts. He was inducted into the International Boxing Hall of Fame in 1990.

Foreman, George

Born: January 10, 1949 in Marshall, Texas

After a difficult childhood, during which he stole purses and committed other petty larcenies, George Foreman got involved with the Job Corps and turned his life around. One of seven children, Foreman began boxing in the Job Corps, then worked his way up the amateur ranks, winning 22 of his 25 amateur fights. In 1968, he won the gold medal at the Olympics.

He turned pro in 1969 and won his first 36 fights against mostly pedestrian opponents. But on January 22, 1973, he fought Joe Frazier in Kingston, Jamaica, for the undisputed heavyweight championship of the world. Foreman knocked down Frazier six times—one punch literally lifted Frazier off his feet—before winning a second-round technical knockout (TKO).

Foreman successfully defended his title twice, including a second-round TKO over Ken Norton in March 1974. That opened the door for a matchup against Muhammad Ali in Kinshasa, Zaire. It was the first ever title bout held in Africa. Foreman was a 3–1 favorite, largely because of his dominance of Frazier, but Ali utilized what was called the rope-a-dope strategy. He lay against the ropes, covered up, and allowed Foreman to punch himself out. The strategy worked. Foreman was spent by the seventh round, and Ali knocked him out in the eighth round.

After two more fights, the second a loss to Jimmy Young, Foreman retired and returned to Marshall, Texas, where he became a preacher for the Church of the Lord Jesus Christ.

But Foreman was far from finished. He unretired in 1987, more because he needed the money than any great desire to return to the limelight. Besides his age, 38, the other notable thing about Foreman's return to the ring was his personality. Where he used to be uncooperative with the press, the new Foreman was smiling and jolly. The public was taken with Foreman's metamorphosis.

Over the next four years, Foreman became a top contender and fought Evander Holyfield in April 1991 for the heavyweight title, losing a unanimous 12-round decision. He also fought for and lost the World Boxing Organization title to Tommy Morrison in June 1993.

In November 1994, after 17 months of inactivity, Foreman returned to fight Michael Moorer for the World Boxing Association and International Boxing Federation heavyweight titles. Foreman took a beating for nine rounds, but knocked out Moorer in the 10th, becoming, at 45 years, 10 months, the oldest world champion ever.

Foreman was stripped of the WBA title in March 1995 for failing to fight Tony Tucker, the no. 1 contender. He successfully defended his IBF title, beating Axel Schulz by a unanimous 12-round decision in April 1995, but was stripped of that title in June 1995 for failing to grant Schulz a rematch.

Through 1999, Foreman fought three more times, winning twice. He is presumably retired. A fight between Foreman and Larry Holmes, scheduled for January 1999 was rumored, but never took place.

Foreman's professional record was 76–5, with 68 knockouts. He went on to endorse products and work as a boxing commentator for HBO Sports.

Foster, Bob

Born: December 15, 1938 in Albuquerque, New Mexico

Bob Foster, undefeated in more than 100 amateur fights, turned pro in 1961. He won his first nine fights before losing to three top heavyweight contenders—Doug Jones, Ernie Terrell, and Zora Folley. He left the sport for a short time in 1966, when he fought only once, but he returned in 1967.

The following year, Foster won seven straight fights and earned a shot at the light heavyweight title held by Dick Tiger. Held in May 1968 at Madison Square Garden, the fight lasted just four rounds, Foster winning by a knockout, which was the first of Tiger's career.

Over the next six years, Foster successfully defended his title 14 times, winning 11 by knockout. He announced his retirement in 1974, after a draw with Jorge Ahumada. He came back in 1975, but retired for good after being knocked out twice in 1978.

Twice Foster fought for the heavyweight title, hoping to become the first light heavyweight champ to win the heavyweight title. But each time—in 1970 against Joe Frazier and in 1972 against Muhammad Ali—he was knocked out.

Foster finished his career with a 56–8–1 record, with 46 knockouts. He was inducted into the International Boxing Hall of Fame in 1990.

Frazier, Joe

Born: January 12, 1944 in Beaufort, South Carolina

Joe Frazier lost only one amateur fight—to Buster Mathis in the 1964 Olympic trials. But when Mathis couldn't participate in the Olympics because of an injury, Frazier replaced him and won the gold medal in the heavyweight division.

Frazier turned pro in 1965 and won his first 19 fights, 17 by knockout. When Muhammad Ali was stripped of his heavyweight title in 1967 for refusing draft induction, the New York State Athletic Commission pitted Frazier against Mathis for the world title, Frazier winning by an 11th-round knockout.

Frazier defended his title four times and then beat Jimmy Ellis in February 1970 to unify the heavyweight championship.

That set the stage for the "Fight of the Century," between Frazier and Ali, which took place March 8, 1971, at Madison Square Garden. The fight, seen by approximately 300 million fans, lived up to the hype. Frazier won a grueling battle with a 15th-round knockout.

Frazier successfully defended his title twice, before losing in January 1973 to George Foreman, who knocked him down six times in two rounds.

Almost a year to the day later, Frazier and Ali met in a rematch at Madison Square Garden, won by Ali in a 12-round decision.

The third fight in their trilogy, dubbed the "Thrilla in Manila," took place in September 1975 in the Philippines and is one of the greatest of all time. Ali won the early rounds, Frazier took the middle rounds, and through the 10th round, the bout was considered even. But Ali cut Frazier in the 12th, and after the 14th round Eddie Futch, Frazier's trainer, stopped the fight.

Frazier's style of constantly boring in and relying on powerful body punches to wear down his opponents was a direct contrast to that of Ali, who relied on speed, quickness, and his ability to slip punches.

Frazier retired in 1976, after another loss to Foreman (fifth-round knockout); made a one-fight comeback five years later; then retired for good. He finished his career with a 32–4–1 record, with 27 knockouts. He is a member of the International Boxing Hall of Fame and the Olympic Hall of Fame.

Fullmer, Gene

Born: July 7, 1921 in West Jordan, Utah

What Gene Fullmer lacked in polish, he made up for with punching power. He turned pro in 1951 after a stellar amateur career (70–4) and worked his way up, finally earning a title shot in 1957, when he fought Sugar Ray Robinson for the world middleweight title and won a 15-round decision. Robinson regained the title in May 1957, winning by a fifth-round knockout. There were those who thought Fullmer was finished, but that was hardly the case.

In August 1959, he defeated Carmen Basilio for the vacant National Boxing Association title and successfully defended it seven times, including wins over Joey Giardello and Robinson.

Fullmer lost his title to Dick Tiger in October 1962 on a 15-round decision. They fought to a draw in February 1963, and Tiger knocked out Fullmer in the seventh round of the bout in August 1963, after which Fullmer retired.

Overall, Fullmer fought in 13 title fights. During the last four years of his career, he fought in nothing but title fights. His career record was 55–6–3, with 24 knockouts. He was inducted into the International Boxing Hall of Fame in 1991.

Gavilan, Kid (Gerardo)

Born: January 1, 1926 in Camaguey, Cuba

Kid Gavilan began boxing at age 12 in Cuba, where he learned his famous "bolo" punch, a looping right uppercut that could lift an opponent off his feet. He turned pro in 1943 at age 16, and by 1947 he was considered a top welterweight contender. He got a world welterweight title shot in 1949 against Sugar Ray Robinson, but lost a 15-round decision.

Gavilan won the world welterweight title by beating Johnny Bratton in May 1951. He successfully defended his title six times. In April 1954, he fought Carl "Bobo" Olson for the world middleweight title, but lost a 15-round decision. In October of the same year, he lost the welterweight title to Johnny Sexton.

Gavilan retired in 1958 with a record of 107–30–6, with 28 knockouts. In 143 bouts, he was never knocked out. He was inducted into the International Boxing Hall of Fame in 1990.

Giardello, Joey

Born: July 16, 1930 in Brooklyn, New York

Despite lacking any organized amateur experience, Joey Giardello enjoyed a long career that started in 1948 and didn't end until 1967. He didn't get his first title shot until 1960, when he and Gene Fullmer fought to a draw for the National Boxing Association middleweight championship.

It wasn't until December 1963 that Giardello won his first title—at age 33—with a 15-round decision over Dick Tiger. He retained the title by beating Ruben "Hurricane" Carter in a 15-round decision, but lost the belt to Tiger in October 1965 (15-round decision).

Giardello retired in November 1965 with a career record of 96–25–1 with 58 knockouts. He was inducted into the International Boxing Hall of Fame in 1990.

Gomez, Wilfredo

Born: October 29, 1956 in Las Monjas, Puerto Rico

Wilfredo Gomez turned pro in 1974, fought to a draw in his first fight, and then won his next 32 fights by knockout. He won the World Boxing Council junior featherweight title in May 1977, knocking out Dong-Kyun Kim in the 12th round, and retained the title until December 1982, when he moved up to the featherweight division. His only loss to that point came in August 1981, when he was knocked out by Salvador Sanchez in an attempt to add the World Boxing Council featherweight title.

Once Gomez became a featherweight for good, he won the World Boxing Association title in March 1984, beating Juan LaPorte in a 12-round decision. In his first title defense, he was knocked out in the 11th round by Azumah Nelson.

Gomez won the junior lightweight title in May 1985, a decision to Rocky Lockridge, and lost it a year later to Alfredo Layne, who knocked him out in the ninth round.

In 1989, he retired with a 44–3–1 record, with 42 knockouts. He was inducted into the International Boxing Hall of Fame in 1995.

Graziano, Rocky (Thomas Barbella)
Born: January 1, 1922 in New York City
Died: May 22, 1990

Rocky Graziano grew up poor and a delinquent in New York City. He spent time in a reform school and in prison on Riker's Island. While in the Army, he was in military prison for striking an officer. But he eventually became one of the most popular fighters of his time, and after his career, he parlayed that popularity into appearing on television shows and in commercials. He also wrote a best-selling book, *Somebody Up There Likes Me*, which was made into a movie starring Paul Newman.

Graziano turned pro in 1942, but it wasn't until 1946 that he fought for a championship. He was knocked out by Tony Zale in the sixth round for the world middleweight title. It was the first of their three memorable fights.

Fight no. 2 came in July 1947, when Graziano won the title from Zale by a sixth-round knockout. The last fight came in June 1948, when Zale took the title back by knocking out Graziano in the third round.

Graziano was suspended from boxing in New York for nine months when his prison record was made public.

His next—and last—title fight came in April 1952, when he was knocked out in the third round by Sugar Ray Robinson for the world middleweight championship. Graziano fought once more and then retired in September 1952 with a career record of 67–10–6, with 52 knockouts. He was inducted into the International Boxing Hall of Fame in 1991.

Greb, Harry
Born: June 6, 1894 in Pittsburgh, Pennsylvania
Died: October 22, 1926

Harry Greb, known as the "Pittsburgh Windmill," was best known for frequent and ferocious fights. He was difficult to hit and almost impossible to avoid. His nonstop flurries came from all angles.

Greb turned pro in 1913 at age 18. Between 1913 and 1922, he fought more than 200 times, including 44 times in 1919, but lost only twice—in 1913 to Joe Chip, and in 1915 to Kid Graves when he broke his arm in the second round.

In May 1922, Greb defeated Gene Tunney in a 15-round decision for the U.S. light heavyweight title. It was the only loss of Tunney's career. Greb lost a rematch to Tunney in February 1923. In August 1923, he won the world middleweight title, beating Johnny Wilson in a 15-round decision. Greb held the title until February 1926, when he lost a 15-round decision to Tiger Flowers. In August of that year, he also lost a rematch with Flowers.

Greb died in October 1926 while undergoing surgery to repair a bone fracture at the top of his nose that resulted from an auto accident. Only then did the public realize that since 1921 Greb had fought with sight in only one eye.

Greb's record was 105–8–3, with 48 knockouts and 183 no-decisions. Many of those no-decisions were called newspaper decisions. If both fighters were still on their feet at the end of the bout, the bout was declared a no-decision. But newspaper reporters often declared a winner in these bouts. Including newspaper decisions, Greb won 264 of his 299 fights. He was inducted into the Boxing Hall of Fame in 1990.

Griffith, Emile
Born: February 3, 1938 in St. Thomas, Virgin Islands

Emile Griffith was discovered by Howard Albert, while working as a stock boy at a New York City millinery. Albert, the co-owner of the millinery, was impressed by Griffith's physique and encouraged him to try boxing.

Griffith won the New York Golden Gloves and the Inter-City tournament in 1957 and turned pro in 1958. Griffith won 21 of his first 23 fights and got his first title shot in April 1961 against Benny "Kid" Paret. Griffith knocked out Paret in the 13th round to become the world welterweight champion. In September 1961, Griffith lost a rematch with Paret on a split decision, but regained the title in March 1962, beating Paret by a 12th-round technical knockout. The referee stopped the fight because of the beating Paret had taken. He died several days later, after lapsing into a coma.

Griffith continued to fight, albeit without quite as much zeal when it came to finishing off his opponents. He added the junior middleweight title in October 1962 with a 15-round decision over Teddy Wright. In March 1963, Griffith lost the welterweight title to Luis Rodriguez, but won it back in a rematch three months later.

Griffith moved up a class in 1966, to middleweight, beating Dick Tiger for the title in a 10-round decision. Nino Benvenuti beat Griffith for the title in April 1967, only to lose the rematch in September of the same year. In their third fight, Benvenuti won a 15-round decision in March 1968.

Over the next nine years, Griffith fought five times for titles, but lost all five. He retired in 1977 with a career record of 85–24–2, with 23 knockouts. He was inducted into the International Boxing Hall of Fame in 1990.

Hagler, Marvelous Marvin

Born: May 23, 1954 in Newark, New Jersey

Marvelous Marvin Hagler (he legally had his name changed) was one of the great all-round fighters of his time. He was a powerful puncher who also had the ability to box. That combination helped him retain his world middleweight championship from 1980 to 1987.

After winning the 1973 Amateur Athletic Union middleweight championship, Hagler turned pro in May of the same year. He won 25 of his first 26 fights—the other fight was a draw—before losing two of his next three. In January 1976, he lost to Bobby "Boogaloo" Watts. Two months later, he was beaten by Willie "The Worm" Monroe. Both fighters were ranked contenders from Philadelphia.

In February 1977, Hagler won the National Boxing Federation middleweight title, beating Monroe by a 12th-round technical knockout. It wasn't until November 1979 that Hagler got his first shot at the world middleweight title, against Vito Antuofermo. That fight was declared a draw, but in September of 1978, Hagler won the title, beating Alan Minter by a third-round technical knockout.

Hagler fought 13 more times in his career, and each one was a title fight. He made 12 successful defenses, including wins over Antuofermo, Roberto Duran, and Thomas Hearns.

In April 1987, Hagler lost a 12-round split decision to Sugar Ray Leonard, who made a comeback after five years. Years after the fact, Hagler still claimed he had won the fight, which was one of the most anticipated in history.

Hagler retired after the Leonard fight. His career record was 62–3–2, with 52 knockouts. He was inducted into the International Boxing Hall of Fame in 1993.

Hearns, Thomas

Born: October 18, 1958 in Memphis, Tennessee

Thomas Hearns won 155 of 163 amateur fights, including a Golden Gloves title (1977) and two National AAU titles (1976–77). He turned pro in November 1977 and won his first 28 fights, before beating Jose "Pipino" Cuevas with a second-round knockout in August 1980 for the World Boxing Association (WBA) welterweight championship and was named Fighter of the Year by *The Ring* magazine.

After three successful title defenses, Hearns met World Boxing Council champ Sugar Ray Leonard in June 1981 in a bout to unify the title. Hearns had the lead through 12 rounds, but was knocked down in the 13th and lost by a technical knockout (TKO) in the 13th.

In December 1982, Hearns scored a 15-round decision over Wilfred Benitez to win the WBC junior middleweight title. He moved up a division in April 1985, but lost the world middleweight title to Marvin Hagler by a third-round knockout.

But Hearns knocked out Dennis Andries in the 10th round in March 1986 to win the WBC light heavyweight title, and added the WBC middleweight title in October 1986, by knocking out Juan Domingo Roldan in the fourth round.

In June 1989, Hearns and Leonard fought for the WBC super middleweight title, but the result was a draw.

Hearns became the third fighter to win world titles in four different divisions in June 1991, when he scored a 12-round decision over Virgil Hill for the WBA light heavyweight title. Only Leonard, with titles in five different divisions, has more. Over the next nine years, Hearns fought infrequently. His record through 2000 was 59–4–1, with 26 knockouts.

Holmes, Larry

Born: November 3, 1949 in Cuthbert, Georgia

Larry Holmes was the heavyweight champion of the world from June 1978 to September 1985. Only Joe Louis held the heavyweight title longer. In late 1999, in a poll by the Associated Press, Holmes tied with Jack Dempsey and Jack Johnson as the fifth-best heavyweight of all time.

Holmes grew up in the projects of Easton, Pa., the seventh of 11 children who were raised by their mother, Flossie Holmes. Holmes admitted to selling marijuana on the street corners, but later worked in a factory, shined shoes, and worked in construction as ways to earn money.

He won 19 of his 22 amateur fights and turned pro in 1973. That same year, Holmes had become a regular sparring partner for Muhammad Ali at his training camp in Deer Lake, Pa. Holmes, who traveled with Ali all over the world, credits the experience of working out with Ali as a boost to his career.

In 1978, Holmes faced Ken Norton for the World Boxing Council (WBC) heavyweight title. He won a 15-round split decision. He successfully defended his championship 21 times and came within one victory of equaling Rocky Marciano's 49-bout unbeaten streak.

He lost the title by a unanimous 15-round decision to Michael Spinks. Holmes tried four times to regain his crown, but was unsuccessful each time. He lost a rematch to Spinks, a 15-round split decision, in April 1986; lost by a fourth-round technical knockout to Mike Tyson in January 1988 (the only time he was knocked out in his career); lost a unanimous 12-round decision to Evander Holyfield in June 1992; and lost a unanimous 12-round decision to Oliver McCall in April 1995.

Holmes' status as a heavyweight champ was somewhat diminished because of the lack of top-flight opponents. He fought and defeated Norton, Earnie Shavers, and Ali, but each was past his prime. That Holmes defeated Ali, who had become an icon, was no help to his reputation, either. Public opinion was not in his favor for helping to end Ali's career.

Another factor that kept Holmes from getting more credit for his accomplishments was that he fought at the same time as Sugar Ray Leonard and Marvin Hagler, who were in lower divisions, but who commanded considerable media attention, some of which came at Holmes' expense.

Holmes also had the reputation of being a champ who couldn't hit.

Holmes retired and unretired five times. In early 1999, he was scheduled to fight former heavyweight champ George Foreman, who would have been 51 years old at the time. But the fight never came off.

He retired permanently in October 1999. His career record was 67–6, with 43 knockouts.

Holyfield, Evander

Born: October 16, 1962 in Atmore, Alabama

Evander Holyfield began boxing when he was eight years old, winning titles in the Boys Club Boxing Tournament in Southeast Atlanta. His amateur career, which should have culminated with a gold medal at the 1984 Summer Olympics in Los Angeles, ended in disappointment. After knocking out his first three opponents, Holyfield reached the semifinals, where he also knocked out that opponent, Kevin Barry of New Zealand. But the referee ruled that the punch came as he was ordering the fighters to break. Holyfield was eventually disqualified. He won the bronze medal.

Holyfield turned pro in 1984 and won his first 11 fights before getting his first title shot. In July 1986, he defeated Dwight Qawi in a split 15-round decision to win the World Boxing Association (WBA) cruiserweight championship (176–190 pounds). The bout was cited as the "Fight of the Year" by many boxing publications.

In May 1987, Holyfield won the International Boxing Federation (IBF) cruiserweight title, beating Rickey Parkey by a third-round technical knockout (TKO). In April 1988, he unified the cruiserweight title by winning the World Boxing Council (WBC) version with an eighth-round knockout of Carlos DeLeon.

Holyfield then began bodybuilding, added 25 pounds of muscle, and moved up to the heavyweight division. He won his first six fights as a heavyweight, all by knockout, and then knocked out Buster Douglas in October 1990 to win the undisputed heavyweight championship of the world. Douglas was making the first defense of the title he won by upsetting Mike Tyson in February 1990.

After three successful title defenses, against George Foreman, Bert Cooper, and Larry Holmes, Holyfield lost the championship to Riddick Bowe, who scored a unanimous 12-round decision in November 1992.

Holyfield won the rematch and the title against Bowe in November 1993, but lost a majority 12-round decision to Michael Moorer in April 1994.

After the Moorer fight, Holyfield underwent medical tests because he hadn't been feeling well. The results showed that Holyfield had a problem with the left ventricle of his heart, and he announced his retirement. But he returned more than a year later, after having received a clean bill of health, and in his second bout, he fought Bowe in November 1995 and won by an eighth-round TKO. There was no title at stake. In November 1996, Holyfield fought Tyson for the WBC heavyweight title. The fight was set because Tyson management considered Holyfield easy pickings. But Holyfield fought a brilliant fight, outdoing Tyson in every facet, and won by an 11th-round knockout. Holyfield joined Muhammad Ali as the only three-time heavyweight champion.

In a rematch with Tyson, held in June 1997, Holyfield won when Tyson was disqualified for twice biting him on the ear in the third round. Holyfield lost part of his right ear from the incident. Tyson was suspended for one year.

In November 1997, with the IBF and WBA titles at stake, Holyfield defeated Moorer by an eighth-round TKO.

Holyfield fought Lennox Lewis in March 1999 in a unification fight—Lewis was the WBC champ—and fought to a controversial draw. In the opinion of most boxing experts, Lewis won the fight, but one judge scored it in Holyfield's favor, setting up a rematch in November 1999, which Lewis won.

Through 1999, Holyfield's record was 36–4–1, with 25 knockouts. He was named Fighter of the Year by the Boxing Writers Association in 1990, 1996, and 1997, joining Ali as the only three-time winner.

Jeffries, James J.

Born: April 15, 1875 in Carroll, Ohio
Died: March 3, 1953

James J. Jeffries didn't fight as a full-time professional until he was 21, keeping a promise he made to his parents. He won his first 11 fights, before fighting Bob Fitzsimmons in June 1899 for the world heavyweight championship. A decided underdog, Jeffries won by an 11th-round knockout. He successfully defended his title seven times, retiring in 1904. But six years later, Jeffries returned to the ring to fight Jack Johnson. Touted as the "Great White Hope," Jeffries got knocked out in the 15th round. It was the only loss of his career.

Inducted into the International Boxing Hall of Fame in 1990, Jeffries finished his career with a record of 18–1–2.

Johnson, Jack

Born: March 31, 1878 in Galveston, Texas
Died: June 10, 1946

Jack Johnson became the first black heavyweight champion of the world in December 1908. He had been a top contender for the title for several years, but was denied a title shot because of his race. But Hugh D. McIntosh put up $30,000 for Johnson to fight Tommy Burns in Sydney, Australia, for the championship. Johnson won on a 14th-round technical knockout.

When Johnson returned to the United States, the search for a "Great White Hope" had already begun. In October 1909, Stanley Ketchel tried and failed, losing on a 12th-round knockout. James Jeffries was next. He came out of retirement, but Johnson dominated the fight, which ended with a knockout in the 15th round.

After the fight, a celebration by blacks across the country sparked race riots that killed 19 people. Johnson, known for his flamboyant lifestyle, heightened tensions when he married a white woman, a teenager. He was convicted of violating the Mann Act, transporting a minor across state lines for immoral purposes. While his conviction was being appealed, he fled to Canada and Europe.

In 1915, Johnson went to Havana, Cuba, to fight Jess Willard for the title. Johnson was knocked out in the 26th round.

Johnson eventually returned to the United States in 1920 and served eight months in Leavenworth Prison in Kansas. Upon his release, he fought until 1928, when he retired at age 50. In June 1946, on his way to see the Joe Louis–Billy Conn heavyweight title fight in New York, Johnson died in a car crash in North Carolina.

Johnson, whom tennis player and sports historian Arthur Ashe called the most significant black athlete in history, finished with a career record of 68–10–10, with 40 knockouts. He was inducted into the International Boxing Hall of Fame in 1990.

Jones, Roy, Jr.

Born: January 16, 1969 in Pensacola, Florida

Roy Jones, Jr., the son of a former "journeyman middleweight boxer," began fighting at age six in the garage of his family's home.

He worked his way up the amateur ranks and made the U.S. Olympic boxing team for the 1988 Olympics in Seoul, South Korea. He dominated the light middleweight division, advancing to the final against Park Si-Hun of South Korea. Jones controlled the fight, but lost a 3–2 decision that was widely criticized. Despite winning only the silver medal, Jones was voted the Outstanding Boxer of the Games.

Jones was devastated by the defeat and returned home to take up basketball. But he eventually went back

to boxing, turning pro and winning his first pro fight, a second-round knockout of Ricky Randall in May 1989.

Jones won his first 21 fights, 20 by knockout, 14 in four rounds or less. In May 1993, he beat Bernhard Hopkins by a unanimous 12-round decision to win the International Boxing Federation (IBF) middleweight title. After four successful defenses, Jones beat previously undefeated James Toney by a unanimous 12-round decision to win the IBF super middleweight title.

Jones ran his record to 33–0 before beating Mike McCallum by a unanimous 12-round decision to win the World Boxing Council (WBC) light heavyweight title in November 1996.

In Jones' next fight, in March 1997 against no. 1 contender Montel Griffin, he didn't take Griffin seriously and paid the price. Jones suffered the first loss of his career when he was disqualified for hitting Griffin, who had dropped to one knee.

In the rematch, Jones knocked out Griffin in the first round of their bout in August 1997 to regain the WBC light heavyweight title.

In 1998, Jones beat Lou Del Valle by a unanimous 12-round decision to win the World Boxing Association (WBA) light heavyweight title. During the eighth round, Del Valle knocked down Jones for the first time in his career.

In 1999, Jones fought twice, the second of which was a 12-round unanimous decision over Reggie Johnson in June for the IBF light heavyweight title.

Jones, whose record through 1999 was 40–1, with 33 knockouts, is recognized as one of the best fighters, pound-for-pound, of his time. Because he hasn't had a rival to help define his career, such as Muhammad Ali had Joe Frazier, Jones considered moving up to the heavyweight division, but at the end of 1999, that hadn't yet materialized. Jones is one of 21 fighters to hold widely accepted world titles in three divisions.

LaMotta, Jake (Giacobe)

Born: July 10, 1921 in The Bronx, New York

Jake LaMotta learned to fight at the Coxsackie Correctional Institute as a teenager. He fought as an amateur for two years and turned pro in 1941 at age 18. By 1942, LaMotta was a top-10 middleweight contender. In October of that year, he fought the first of six bouts against Sugar Ray Robinson, five of which he lost. LaMotta's only victory over Robinson came in February 1943, when he won a 10-round decision and handed Robinson the first defeat of his professional career.

Despite having a good record over the next several years, LaMotta was denied a title shot. He testified before a U.S. Senate Anti-Monopoly Subcommittee that the reason he was denied was because he refused to get involved with mobsters. He also admitted at the hearing that he took a dive in a 1947 fight against Billy Fox in return for a title shot. Finally, in June 1949, LaMotta, nicknamed the "Bronx Bull," got his first chance at a championship and beat Marcel Cerdan by a 10th-round technical knockout (TKO) to win the world middleweight title, which he retained until February 1951, when he lost to Robinson by a 13th-round TKO in the sixth meeting between the two. LaMotta, who retired in 1954 with a career record of 83–19–4 (30 knockouts), was inducted into the International Boxing Hall of Fame in 1990.

After he stopped fighting, he became an actor and wrote his autobiography, *Raging Bull,* which was made into a movie starring Robert De Niro, who won an Academy Award for his portrayal of LaMotta.

Leonard, Sugar Ray (Ray)
Born: May 17, 1956 in Palmer Park, Maryland

Sugar Ray Leonard was one of the most charismatic, stylish, and talented boxers in the history of the sport. He began boxing when he was 13 years old. His list of amateur accomplishments presaged those that would come

as a professional. Leonard won three Golden Gloves titles, two Amateur Athletic Union titles, two North American junior welterweight titles, and a Pan American Games title.

Leonard's amateur career culminated with his light welterweight gold medal in the 1976 Olympics. Initially, his plan was to land some endorsements, earn enough money to go to college, and help care for his parents. But when endorsements failed to materialize, Leonard turned pro in February 1977.

He won his first 25 fights and worked his way up the welterweight rankings, getting a shot at Wilfred Benitez and the World Boxing Council welterweight championship in November 1979. Leonard won the title with a technical knockout (TKO) in the 15th round.

Leonard made one successful title defense before facing former lightweight champion Roberto Duran, who won a closely contested 15-round decision in June 1980. In a rematch five months later, and with Leonard firmly in control, Duran quit with 16 seconds to go in the eighth round. He threw up his hands and told the referee, "*No mas,*" Spanish for "No more."

Sugar Ray Leonard   *Mike Powell/Allsport Photography*

Leonard added the World Boxing Association junior middleweight title in June 1981, knocking out Ayub Kalule in the ninth round. In September 1981, he became the undisputed welterweight champion with a 14th-round TKO of Thomas Hearns in a unification bout. Leonard was the WBC champ, Hearns the WBA champ. And then it seemed that Leonard's career was over. In November 1982, he announced his retirement, following surgery for a detached retina in June. But his retirement didn't last. He returned to the ring in May 1984 against Kevin Howard, who knocked Leonard down but eventually lost by a ninth-round TKO.

Leonard next fought in April 1987 against WBC middleweight champion Marvelous Marvin Hagler, who lost the belt by split decision.

Another 18 months passed before Leonard fought again, this time for two titles simultaneously. He faced WBC light heavyweight champion Don Lalonde at the super middleweight limit of 168, meaning two titles would be at stake. Despite suffering an early knockdown, Leonard ended the fight with a ninth-round knockout.

He retained his super middleweight title with a draw against Hearns in June 1989 and a 12-round decision over Duran in December 1989.

Leonard fought only twice more. He dropped down to fight for the WBC junior middleweight title in February 1991, but lost a 12-round decision to Terry Norris. More than six years later, in March 1997, Leonard, at 40 years of age, was knocked out by Hector "Macho" Camacho in the fifth round.

Since his retirement, Leonard has been a commercial spokesman and a boxing commentator. He was named *Sports Illustrated* Sportsman of the Year in 1984.

Leonard's career record was 36–3–1, with 25 knockouts. He was inducted into the International Boxing Hall of Fame in 1997.

Liston, Sonny (Charles)

Born: May 8, 1932 in St. Francis County, Arkansas
Died: December 12, 1970

Sonny Liston had a powerful punch, a cold stare, and a surly personality. He learned to box while serving a prison sentence for armed robbery. When he was paroled in 1952, he began his amateur career and won the 1953 National Golden Gloves championship.

He turned pro later in 1953, won 14 of his first 15 fights, but then saw his career put on hold for another prison term, this time a nine-month sentence for assaulting a police officer. After his release, he continued to move up in the rankings of the heavyweight division. In 1960, *The Ring* magazine ranked him as the no. 1 contender. Floyd Patterson, the champion, delayed giving Liston a title shot because of Liston's strength and power, and because of his alleged connections with organized

crime. But in 1962, at Comiskey Park in Chicago, Patterson met Liston with the heavyweight championship of the world on the line. The fight lasted less than one round. Liston knocked out Patterson in two minutes, six seconds, the third-fastest KO in history, at the time.

In a rematch in July 1963, Patterson didn't fare much better. He was again knocked out in the first round, the second fight lasting four seconds longer than the first. Liston's next defense came against Cassius Clay in February 1964. The contrast in styles couldn't have been more pronounced. Clay's forte was speed and quickness and constant movement. Liston was blessed with power in every punch. At the time, Clay was considered nothing more than a big-talking loudmouth who wouldn't be able to back up his boasts.

As a result, Liston was a heavy favorite, but he was dominated by Clay. Clay danced during the early rounds, forcing Liston to chase him and tiring him out. When Liston did throw a punch, more often than not, Clay was able to elude it.

The best chance Liston had came during the fifth round, when his cornermen apparently doctored his gloves with a substance that got into Clay's eyes, blinding him and causing great pain. Clay wanted to quit, but his corner convinced him to continue. Liston was unable to take advantage of Clay's temporary handicap and found himself being dominated again, after Clay's eyes cleared. When the bell rang for the seventh round, Liston didn't answer it, claiming an injured shoulder.

Liston's next fight was a rematch with Muhammad Ali, the former Clay, who had changed his name after converting to the Muslim religion. Originally, the fight was scheduled to be held in November 1964 in Boston, but was delayed because Clay required hernia surgery.

The fight took place in May 1965 in Lewiston, Me., but Liston never made it out of the first round. Ali hit him with what has been called the "phantom" punch or "anchor" punch. Liston didn't see it, and neither did anyone else.

Ali refused to retreat to a neutral corner while Liston was on the canvas. He finally got to his feet, and the referee, Jersey Joe Walcott, instructed the fighters to continue, but was overruled by Nat Fleischer, the editor of *The Ring* magazine. Fleischer said the fight should be stopped, because Liston was down longer than a 10-count. Although the rumors could never be substantiated, suspicions of a fix—that Liston took a dive—have persisted ever since.

Liston fought 16 more times after the Ali fight, but he never again fought for a championship. His last fight came in June 1970, a 10th-round technical knockout of Chuck Wepner. Six months later, Liston was found dead in his home in Las Vegas. The official cause of death was lung congestion and heart failure, but unofficially it appeared to be caused by a heroin overdose. There were also reports that he was murdered. Liston's career record was 50–4–0, with 39 knockouts. He was inducted into the International Boxing Hall of Fame in 1991.

Louis, Joe

Born: May 13, 1914 in Lafayette, Alabama
Died: April 12, 1981

During a time when segregation ruled and blacks were regarded as second-class citizens, Joe Louis was a heavyweight champion who was beloved by all people, regardless of race.

He was introduced to boxing at Brewster's Gym in Detroit, where his family had moved when he was a child. Louis learned that fighters got paid in food, and in his first fight, he won $7 worth of food, but was knocked down seven times in two rounds. He said he'd never fight again.

In 1931, when Louis was 17, he went to work at Briggs Automobile Factory, working for $1 a day. He also began taking violin lessons. But when a friend, Thurston McKinney, suggested he give boxing another try, Louis took the 50 cents his mother gave him for violin lessons and used it to rent a locker at Brewster's.

But it wasn't too much later that Holman Williams, a professional fighter, gave him some lessons and encouraged to him to get involved in the Golden Gloves competition. Louis won all but four of his 54 amateur fights, including the AAU light heavyweight national championship in 1934.

Louis turned pro later in 1934, and in less than a year was ranked the no. 9 contender for the heavyweight championship. After knocking out former champs Max Baer and Primo Carnera in 1935, he was the no. 1 contender.

In June 1936, Louis suffered his first loss. Max Schmeling knocked him out in the 12th round, before 60,000 fans at Yankee Stadium.

After six more victories, five by knockout, Louis, nicknamed the "Brown Bomber," knocked out James J. Braddock in the eight round to win the world heavyweight championship in June 1937. He was the first black heavyweight champ since Jack Johnson in the early 1900s. But unlike Johnson, who was loud and boisterous, Louis was respectful and modest. Counseled by his managers, Julian Black and John Roxborough, he was instructed to behave in such a way that would allow him to appeal to white America. It's why he was schooled to look for a knockout, because it was safer than relying on white judges for a decision.

Louis conducted himself with grace and dignity, prompting Jimmy Cannon, a popular columnist of the time, to write that Louis was a "credit to his race—the human race."

In June 1938, Louis got a rematch with Schmeling, which carried implications beyond boxing. Schmeling was held by German leaders to be an Aryan symbol. Louis met with President Franklin D. Roosevelt the night before the fight, a get-together that underlined the fight's significance. The bout was held before a crowd of 75,000 at Yankee Stadium. It lasted one round, Louis winning by knockout.

Louis defended his title successfully 17 times, mostly against challengers referred to as members of the "Bum of the Month Club." Only once, against Billy Conn in June 1941, was Louis put to the test.

Conn, a former light heavyweight champ, was leading through 12 rounds. Told by his cornermen that he needed a knockout, Louis did just that, knocking out Conn in the 13th.

In 1942, after fighting only twice, Louis enlisted in the Army and fought exhibitions for about 2 million GI's in the United States, North Africa, and Europe. In his first fight after the war, in June 1946, Louis had a rematch with Conn and knocked him out in the eighth round.

Louis' next two fights were against Jersey Joe Walcott. In the first, in December 1947, Walcott knocked Louis down twice in the first four rounds, but Louis won a controversial split decision. In the rematch in June 1948, Louis won with an 11th-round knockout, after which he announced his retirement.

But the retirement didn't last. In September 1950, Louis lost a 15-round decision to Ezzard Charles for the heavyweight championship. Louis then won eight more fights, before facing Rocky Marciano, who knocked him out in the eighth round. He retired for good after that fight.

Louis spent time in a psychiatric hospital, battled a cocaine addiction, and fought the Internal Revenue Service. He eventually became an official greeter at Caesar's Palace in Las Vegas.

Inducted into the International Boxing Hall of Fame in 1990, Louis' career record was 68–3–0, with 54 knockouts.

Marciano, Rocky (Rocco)

Born: September 1, 1923 in Brockton, Massachusetts
Died: August 31, 1969

Rocky Marciano's childhood dream was to become a major league baseball player, a catcher. Instead, he became the heavyweight champion of the world, never losing a professional fight.

He began boxing in the Army when he won a camp boxing tournament. He did have a tryout with a minor league baseball team after World War II ended, but a sore arm ended his career.

Marciano was a successful amateur fighter in New England, winning the New England Golden Gloves tournament. He packed a powerful punch, but lacked the control a top-flight heavyweight needs. But Marciano's trainer, Charlie Goldman, taught him to fight from a crouch, making him a difficult target.

Marciano turned pro in March 1947 and won his first 25 fights, 23 by knockouts, nine of those in the first round.

By 1950, he was a top-10 contender for the heavyweight championship. In October 1951, Marciano knocked out former heavyweight champ Louis, who had come out of retirement, in the eighth round.

Marciano, nicknamed the "Brockton Blockbuster," won four more bouts, all by knockout, before getting his first shot at the title. He fought Jersey Joe Walcott in September 1952 in Philadelphia. Marciano was knocked down in the first round, but recovered to take part in a brutal fight. After the 12th round, Walcott was leading on all three cards, but in the 13th, Marciano delivered a blow to Walcott's right jaw, knocking him out and earning the title.

The two fighters had a rematch in May 1953, but that ended when Marciano scored a first-round knockout.

Marciano twice defended his title against Ezzard Charles, winning both fights, but going the distance in the first. Only six times in Marciano's career did an opponent escape a knockout.

In June 1954, Marciano defended his title against Archie Moore, who was as sly as Marciano was powerful. Moore knocked the champ down in the second round, but Marciano won the fight with a ninth-round knockout. After the fight, Marciano retired, the only fighter to do so undefeated. His record was 49–0, with 43 knockouts.

Marciano, inducted into the International Boxing Hall of Fame in 1990, was killed in a plane crash in 1969 en route to Des Moines, Iowa.

Monzon, Carlos
Born: August 8, 1942 in Santa Fe, Argentina
Died: January 8, 1995
Carlos Monzon turned pro in 1963, and over the first four years of his career fought 44 times. By 1968, he was ranked eighth by *The Ring* magazine among middleweights. His first shot at the world middleweight title came in November 1970 against Nino Benvenuti, whom he knocked out in the 12th round.

The rematch between the two fighters went much quicker, Monzon winning by a third-round knockout. Over the next seven years, Monzon defended his title a record 14 times, beating such challengers as Emile Griffith, Jose Napoles, and Rodrigo Valdez. Monzon was one of the best middleweights of all time. But his personal life was not as successful. In 1988, he was convicted of mur-

dering his estranged lover. He was sentenced to 11 years in jail. In 1995, while returning to prison after a furlough for good behavior, Monzon ran his car off a road and was killed.

His last fight was in June 1977. He retired as the world middleweight champion. His career record was 87–3–9, with 59 knockouts.

Moore, Archie
Born: December 13, 1915 in Benoit, Mississippi
Archie Moore, nicknamed "The Mongoose," learned to box in a reform school in St. Louis, where he spent two years after being convicted for stealing money. Upon his release, he joined the Civilian Conservation Corps and boxed in amateur tournaments.

In 1936, he turned pro and worked his way up in the rankings. By 1940, *The Ring* magazine ranked him as the no. 4 middleweight contender.

In 1945, Moore moved up a division, to light heavyweight. He was ranked as a top contender through 1951, but never got a title shot. But finally in December 1952, at the age of 39, Moore met Joey Maxim for the world light heavyweight championship and won a 15-round decision. For the next six years, Moore held on to the title.

In 1955, Moore fought Rocky Marciano for the world heavyweight championship. He knocked the champ down in the second round, but then Marciano knocked him down in the sixth, eighth, and ninth rounds. The fight ended in the ninth.

Moore made one more attempt at the heavyweight title, fighting Floyd Patterson for the belt left vacant following Marciano's retirement, but he was knocked out in the fifth.

Moore finally lost the light heavyweight title in 1961, when the National Boxing Association took it from him for failing to defend it.

In Moore's penultimate fight, he was beaten by then Cassius Clay in November 1962 by a fourth-round technical knockout.

Moore retired in 1963, after 27 years, with a career record of 183–24–10, with 141 knockouts, more than any other fighter in boxing history. He was inducted into the International Boxing Hall of Fame in 1990.

Norton, Ken
Born: August 9, 1943 in Jacksonville, Illinois
Ken Norton didn't grow up boxing; he grew up playing football and basketball, and running track in high school. He received a scholarship to Northeast Missouri State, which he attended for two years.

Norton didn't begin his boxing career until he joined the Marines. He was 24–2 as an amateur, winning the All-Marine heavyweight title three times. He didn't turn pro until 1967, at the age of 24. Early in his career, Norton fought mostly in Southern California, where he won his first 16 fights, 15 by knockout. After he was knocked out by Jose Luis Garcia in July 1970, Norton won his next 13 bouts, before fighting Muhammad Ali for the North American Boxing Federation (NABF) heavyweight title. The fights with Ali would define Norton's career.

The first fight was held in March 1973. Ali didn't take it all that seriously, failing to train sufficiently, and paid the price. Norton broke Ali's jaw in the first round. The fight went the distance with Norton winning a split decision.

Norton didn't fare as well in the rematch in September 1973, when Ali won a split decision. Norton's next fight was in March 1974 against George Foreman for the world heavyweight title. Foreman won with a second-round knockout.

Norton claimed the NABF title from Jerry Quarry in March 1975, then in September 1976, tried to wrest the world title from Ali, who had beaten Foreman. But after leading early in the fight, Norton was unable to close it out, and lost a unanimous decision.

Norton was awarded the World Boxing Council heavyweight title when Leon Spinks refused to defend his title against Norton. But in Norton's first defense of his WBC title, against Larry Holmes in June 1978, he lost a 15-round decision.

Norton fought just five more times, twice suffering first-round knockouts, by Earnie Shavers and Gerry Cooney, before retiring in 1981.

His career record was 42–7–1, with 33 knockouts. He was inducted into the International Boxing Hall of Fame in 1992.

Patterson, Floyd

Born: January 4, 1935 in Waco, North Carolina

Along with Muhammad Ali and Sonny Liston, Floyd Patterson was one of the trio of heavyweights who defined boxing from the mid-1950s to the mid-1960s. Like so many fighters, Patterson got in trouble as a youth and spent some time in reform school, where he learned how to box. His amateur career culminated with his gold medal in the 165-pound division at the 1952 Olympic Games in Helsinki.

Patterson turned pro in 1952 as a light heavyweight, and won 30 of his first 31 fights, losing only to Joey Maxim in June 1954.

In November 1956, Patterson was given a shot at the heavyweight title, left vacant by the retirement of Rocky Marciano. He fought Archie Moore, knocked him out in the fifth round, and became the youngest ever to win the world heavyweight championship. Patterson held the title until June 1959, when he was knocked out in the third round by Ingemar Johansson. But almost a year to the day later, Patterson won the rematch, knocking out Johansson in the fifth round, and became the first fighter to regain the heavyweight title.

After knocking out Tom McNeeley in the fourth round in December 1961, Patterson faced Sonny Liston, a powerful, fearsome fighter whom many accused Patterson of avoiding.

Given the racial tensions of the 1960s, the fight between Patterson and Liston was cast as a battle of the "Good Negro," Patterson, against the "Threatening Negro," Liston, according to David Remnick's book *The King of the World*. Patterson was a much more acceptable champion to white America than Liston would be. That support was reflected by many of the leading sports columnists of the time.

The bout lasted less than one round, Liston knocking out Patterson in two minutes, six seconds.

The rematch, held in July 1963, lasted just four seconds longer, Liston winning again with a first-round knockout.

Patterson got two more chances to win the heavyweight championship—in May 1965 against Ali and in September 1968 against Jimmy Ellis—and he lost both. Patterson continued to fight, winning his next eight fights. In September 1972, he fought Ali for a second time, for the North American Boxing Federation championship, but Ali won by a seventh-round technical knockout, after which Patterson retired.

Patterson, inducted into the International Boxing Hall of Fame in 1991, had a career record of 55–8–1, with 40 knockouts.

Pep, Willie (Guiglermo Papaleo)

Born: September 19, 1922 in Middletown, Connecticut

Willie Pep began fighting as an amateur in Connecticut. He won the state flyweight title in 1938 and the bantamweight title a year later. He turned pro in 1940 and won his first 54 fights, before getting his first title shot.

In November 1943, Pep defeated Albert "Chalky" White for the world featherweight championship, winning a 15-round decision. At 20 years of age, he was the youngest to win a world title in 40 years.

Pep, nicknamed "Will 'O the Wisp," retained the world featherweight title for the next six years. Not even a 1947 plane crash, in which he suffered serious injuries, could stop Pep, who many thought would never fight again. But five months after the accident, he beat Victor Flores in a 10-round decision.

Pep lost the world featherweight title in October 1948, when Sandy Saddler knocked him out in the fourth round. Pep and Sandler would fight three more times. In February 1949, Pep regained the title, winning a 15-round decision. Saddler won the third fight, in

September 1950, on an eighth-round technical knockout (TKO), and he also won the fourth fight, in September 1951, on a ninth-round TKO.

Pep continued to fight until 1959, when he retired. Six years later, at age 42, he made a comeback, won nine nontitle fights, then retired for good after losing to Calvin Woodland in March 1966.

Pep crafted a boxing style built on speed and quickness. He was known to win rounds without having thrown a punch. His career record was 230–11–1, with 65 knockouts. He was inducted into the International Boxing Hall of Fame in 1990.

Pryor, Aaron

Born: October 20, 1955 in Cincinnati, Ohio

After a stellar amateur career in which he won 204 of 220 bouts, including two national Golden Gloves titles, Aaron Pryor turned pro in November 1976. He won his first 24 fights, 22 by knockout, before getting his first title shot, against Antonio Cervantes for the World Boxing Association junior welterweight title. Pryor won by a fourth-round knockout.

Pryor, nicknamed "The Hawk," defended his title seven times, before facing Alexis Arguello in November 1982. Arguello was trying to become the first fighter in history to win four titles in four different weight classes.

The fight was a closely contested battle. Through 13 rounds, Pryor was ahead on two cards, Arguello on one. But in the 14th round, Pryor scored a knockout that left Arguello on the canvas for four minutes.

Pryor defended his title twice more, the second defense a 10th-round knockout of Arguello in September 1983, before announcing his retirement.

He returned to the ring in June 1984, reportedly to sustain a serious drug problem. He fought once in 1984 and once in 1985. Pryor came back one more time, in August 1987, when he suffered the only loss in his career, to Bobby Joe Young on a seventh-round knockout. He fought three more times before retiring for good in 1990. Pryor did time in prison on a drug charge, lived on the streets after his release, and eventually turned his life around. He works with fighters in Cincinnati and with his local church.

Inducted into the International Boxing Hall of Fame in 1996, Pryor finished with a career record of 39–1–0.

Robinson, Sugar Ray (Walker Smith, Jr.)

Born: May 3, 1921 in Detroit, Michigan
Died: May 12, 1989

Walker Smith, Jr., took up boxing at age 11, training at Brewster's Gym, where Joe Louis trained. He and his mother moved to Harlem. When he was 15, he wanted to enter a tournament, but he needed an AAU member-ship card, which he couldn't get until he was 16. So a boxing coach, George Gainford, arranged for Smith to use the card of a recently retired fighter, Ray Robinson. Smith/Robinson won the bout.

The name stuck, and he picked up his nickname, "Sugar," from a reporter in Watertown, N.Y., who said after watching him work out, "That's a real sweet fighter you've got there. As sweet as sugar."

After winning all 89 of his recorded amateur bouts, including the 1939 and 1940 Golden Gloves title, Robinson turned pro in 1940, and by 1941 *The Ring* magazine ranked him a top welterweight contender. But his first title shot didn't come until December 1946, when he won a 15-round decision over Tommy Bell for the vacant world welterweight championship.

In Robinson's first title defense, in June 1947, he defeated Jimmy Doyle by an eighth-round technical knockout (TKO). Doyle died shortly after the fight, and Robinson donated most of his share of the purse to the Doyle family.

In all, Robinson successfully defended his title five times, before moving up a class and fighting Jake LaMotta for the world middleweight title. In the sixth meeting between the two fighters, called the "St. Valentine's Day Massacre," Robinson won a bloody battle by a 13th-round TKO.

Robinson lost his first title defense, a 15-round decision to Randy Turpin, in July 1951. But in September 1951, Robinson regained the crown from Turpin with a 10th-round TKO.

After two successful defenses, against Carl "Bobo" Olson in March 1952 and Rocky Marciano in April 1952, Robinson moved up a division and challenged Joey Maxim for the world light heavyweight championship. Maxim won on a 14th-round TKO, the first and only knockout of his career.

Robinson retired after the Maxim fight, but returned in January 1955 and regained the world middleweight title with a second-round knockout of Olson in December 1955. Robinson defeated Olson in a rematch in May 1956, then lost a 15-round decision to Gene Fullmer in January 1957. Robinson regained the championship in May 1957, knocking out Fullmer, only to lose the title to Carmen Basilio by split decision in September 1957.

In the rematch with Basilio in May 1958, Robinson overcame a virus, won a 15-round decision, and reclaimed the championship for the fifth time, a record that still stands.

Robinson lost his title to Paul Pender in January 1960 by a 15-round decision. Six months later, he lost the rematch as well. Twice he was unsuccessful in trying to win the National Boxing Association middleweight title from Fullmer. But he continued to fight for four more years, although never again for a championship. He retired in 1965 at age 44 and went on to do some acting and open a nightclub in Harlem.

Known for living the good life, Robinson's entourage included a voice coach, a drama instructor, a barber, a golf pro, a masseur, a secretary, trainers, and a dwarf mascot. Inducted into the International Boxing Hall of Fame in 1990, Robinson finished with a career record of 175–19–6, with 109 knockouts, and was widely recognized as being one of the best boxers, pound-for-pound, of all time.

Saad Muhammad, Matthew
Born: June 16, 1954 in Jenkintown, Pennsylvania

Matthew Saad Muhammad, born Maxwell Loach, was orphaned and left, along with his older brother, in the care of his aunt, who couldn't afford to provide for two children. So she told Saad Muhammad's older brother to lose him. The brother took Saad Muhammad to the Benjamin Franklin Parkway in Philadelphia and fled.

Saad Muhammad was taken to a Catholic shelter. The nuns named him Matthew, after the saint, and Franklin, after the place he was found.

Years later, after being in reform school, Saad Muhammad watched Muhammad Ali in a sparring session at a Philadelphia gym, and he decided to become a fighter. Matthew Franklin turned pro in 1974.

He won his first title in July 1977, when he knocked out Marvin Johnson in the 12th round for the vacant North American Boxing Federation light heavyweight championship. In April 1979, he defeated Johnson again, by an eighth-round technical knockout (TKO), to win the World Boxing Council light heavyweight title. It was after he won the WBC title that Saad Muhammad adopted a Muslim name.

Saad Muhammad successfully defended his title eight times, before losing it in December 1981 to Dwight Braxton (later Dwight Muhammad Qawi) by a TKO in the sixth round. A rematch with Braxton in August 1982 ended with the same result: a sixth-round knockout.

Saad Muhammad fought, with mixed results, for the next 10 years, retiring in 1992 with a record of 39–16–3, with 29 knockouts. He was inducted into the International Boxing Hall of Fame in 1998. He trains fighters in Atlantic City, N.J., and New Orleans.

Saddler, Sandy
Born: June 23, 1926 in Boston, Massachusetts

Sandy Saddler turned pro in 1944 at age 17, and fought his first bout when a substitute was needed at the last minute. He won that fight, beating Earl Roys, but lost his next, when Jock Leslie knocked him out in the third round. That was the only time in a career that lasted 12 years and 162 fights that he was knocked out.

Saddler got his first title shot in October 1948, beating Willie Pep by a fourth-round knockout. Pep won the title back in February 1949, taking a 15-round decision. In December 1949, Saddler beat Orlando Zulueta in a 10-round decision to win the vacant world junior lightweight title. In September 1950, Saddler defeated Pep by a ninth-round technical knockout (TKO) to regain the featherweight crown.

Saddler and Pep fought a fourth time, in September 1951. Saddler retained his featherweight crown with a ninth-round TKO, but both fighters were briefly suspended by the New York State Athletic Commission because of the tactics used in the bout, including gouging, wrestling, and tripping.

Following two years in the Army, Saddler defended his title two more times, winning both fights. He won a 15-round decision over Teddy Davis in February 1955 and scored a 13th-round TKO over Flash Elorde in January 1956.

He retired, as champion, in 1957 after suffering a serious eye injury in a car accident. Saddler, one of the best featherweights of all time, had a career record of 144–16–2, with 103 knockouts. He was inducted into the International Boxing Hall of Fame in 1990.

Schmeling, Max
Born: September 28, 1905 in Brandenburg, Germany

Max Schmeling turned pro in 1924 in Germany, began fighting in the United States in 1928, and by 1929 was ranked as the no. 2 heavyweight contender by *The Ring* magazine. His first title shot came in June 1930 against Jack Sharkey for the title relinquished by Gene Tunney two years earlier. Schmeling won the title on a foul, when it was determined Sharkey hit him with a low blow. It is the only time a heavyweight title was awarded because of a foul.

Schmeling retained his title in July 1931, scoring a 15th-round technical knockout over Young Stribling. But he lost the title in June 1932 in a rematch with Sharkey, who won a 15-round decision.

In 1936, Schmeling fought a young Joe Louis, knocking him down in the fourth round and knocking him out in the 12th.

Schmeling was in line for a title shot against the champ, James J. Braddock, but the bout was never sanctioned because U.S. boxing officials didn't want to risk losing the title to Europe.

Schmeling was being held up as an example of Aryan supremacy and a standard-bearer for Adolf Hitler. So all of his fights took on a social and political significance that went beyond boxing.

In 1938, after Louis became champion, a rematch was allowed. Louis knocked Schmeling out in the first round.

Schmeling retired in 1948 with a career record of 56–10–4, with 39 knockouts. He was inducted into the International Boxing Hall of Fame in 1992.

Sharkey, Jack (Joseph Cukoschay)
Born: October 26, 1902 in Binghamton, New York
Died: August 18, 1994

Jack Sharkey learned to box in the Navy and turned pro in 1924. He chose his name as a tribute to Jack Dempsey and a sailor, Tom Sharkey.

In July 1927, Sharkey fought Dempsey, and the $1.8 million gate was the largest ever for a nontitle fight. Dempsey knocked Sharkey out in the seventh round.

Sharkey fought Max Schmeling in June 1930 for the vacant world heavyweight title. Schmeling was awarded the belt because Sharkey hit him with a low blow. In the rematch in June 1932, Sharkey won the title by a 15-round decision, but he didn't hold it long. In his first defense, in June 1933 against Primo Carnera, Sharkey was knocked out in the sixth round. There was talk that because Carnera was controlled by mobsters, Sharkey had been paid to take a fall, a charge he denied.

Sharkey's last fight came in August 1936 against Joe Louis, who won by a third-round knockout.

Known for his ring skills and a variety of effective punches, Sharkey's career record was 38–13–3. He was inducted into the International Boxing Hall of Fame in 1994.

Spinks, Michael
Born: July 7, 1956 in St. Louis, Missouri

Michael Spinks first came to prominence in 1976 when he won the middleweight gold medal at the 1976 Olympic Games. He turned pro a year later and won his first 16 fights, before getting a shot at the World Boxing Association light heavyweight championship in July 1981. He won a 15-round decision over Mustafa Muhammad. Spinks successfully defended his title five times, and then unified the title in March 1983, winning a 15-round decision over Dwight Braxton. After four more successful defenses, Spinks did what no other light heavyweight has ever done: moved up a division and won the heavyweight championship of the world.

In September 1985, Spinks won a 15-round decision from Larry Holmes. Seven months later in a rematch, he won a decision from Holmes again.

Because Spinks granted Holmes a rematch, when the rules dictated otherwise, he was stripped of his championship. He knocked out Gerry Cooney in the fifth round of a nontitle fight in June 1987.

In June 1988, Spinks fought Mike Tyson for the world heavyweight title and was knocked out in the first round. That was his last fight.

Spinks, inducted into the International Boxing Hall of Fame in 1994, finished his career with a record of 31–1–0, with 21 knockouts.

Tiger, Dick
Born: August 14, 1929 in Amaigbo, Orlu, Nigeria
Died: December 14, 1971

Besides being a great champion who held titles in two weight classes, Dick Tiger was also known for his gentle demeanor and his care and concern for the people of Biafra in his native Nigeria.

Tiger turned pro in 1952, moved to England in 1955, and won the British Empire middleweight title in March 1958. He held the title until June 1960, when he lost a 15-round decision to Will Greaves. In a rematch held in November 1960, Tiger regained the title with a ninth-round technical knockout.

Tiger got his first title shot in the United States in October 1962, when he fought Gene Fullmer to a decision for the World Boxing Association middleweight championship. He beat Fullmer twice more and was recognized as the world middleweight champ.

Tiger lost a 15-round decision and the title to Joey Giardello in December 1963, but won it back by decision in October 1961, then lost it to Emile Griffith in April 1965. In December 1966, Tiger won a 15-round decision over Jose Torres for the world light heavyweight title. After a successful defense against Roger Rouse in November 1967, he lost the title to Bob Foster, who knocked him out in the fourth round in May 1968. Tiger fought for two more years, retiring in 1970 with a career record of 61–17–3, with 26 knockouts. He returned to Nigeria, where he died six months later from liver cancer.

Tunney, Gene
Born: May 25, 1897 in New York, New York
Died: November 7, 1978

Unlike many fighters who grew up in poverty and in trouble, Gene Tunney was the son of relatively well-to-do parents. After receiving a pair of boxing gloves for his 10th birthday and learning about the sport as a teenager, he joined the Marines and in 1918 won the American Expeditionary Forces light heavyweight title.

In January 1922, he won a 12-round decision from Battling Levinsky for the American light heavyweight championship. He lost the title in May 1922 to Harry Greb by a 15-round decision, then regained it in February 1923 in a 15-round decision over Greb. He also defended against Greb in December 1923, winning a 15-round decision. In September 1926, Tunney finally achieved his goal of fighting for the world heavyweight championship.

His opponent was Jack Dempsey, who lost a 10-round decision.

Almost a year to the day later, Tunney and Dempsey met in a rematch in what remains one of the most famous fights in boxing history. Held at Soldier Field in Chicago before more than 100,000 fans, Tunney was ahead through six rounds, but in the seventh Dempsey landed a right cross, followed by six more punches. Tunney was knocked down. Under Illinois boxing rules, Dempsey had to go to a neutral corner before the count could begin. Instead, Dempsey went to Tunney's corner. By the time the referee moved Dempsey to the proper corner, Tunney had been down for at least a count of four. By the time the official 10-count was concluded, Tunney was able to continue fighting.

Tunney won a 10-round decision, but the infamous long count tainted the result in the minds of many fans.

In July 1928, Tunney successfully defended his title with an 11th-round technical knockout of Tom Heeney, after which he retired and stayed retired. He was the first heavyweight champ to retire as champ.

Tunney married a steel heiress and enjoyed a successful business career. One of his sons, John, was elected to the U.S. Senate from California.

Tunney, who was inducted into the International Boxing Hall of Fame in 1990, finished with a career record of 61–1–1.

Tyson, Mike

Born: June 30, 1966 in Brooklyn, New York

Mike Tyson was one of the most dominant fighters and controversial athletes in history. He grew up in the Bedford-Stuyvesant area of Brooklyn, a tough neighborhood, where he got into trouble as a child. He was the youngest of three children, but his mother, Lorna Tyson, and father, James Kirkpatrick, never married.

Money problems forced the family to move to Brownsville, a Brooklyn neighborhood even tougher than Bedford-Stuyvesant. It was in Brownsville that Tyson joined a gang, the Jolly Stompers. By the time he was 11, he had been arrested 30 times.

When he was 12, Tyson was sent to a juvenile detention center, where he discovered boxing. His natural talent was obvious. So a counselor at the school, Bobby Stewart, a former boxer, introduced Tyson to Cus D'Amato, a professional trainer who had worked with Floyd Patterson, a former heavyweight champion.

D'Amato predicted that Tyson could become the youngest heavyweight champion of the world if he was prepared to work for it.

The bond between Tyson and D'Amato strengthened, D'Amato becoming a positive influence on a teenager who needed the guidance—in the ring and in life.

As an amateur, Tyson fought opponents with a variety of styles. He won the Golden Gloves championship in 1984 and turned pro the following year. In his first eight months as a pro, he fought 11 times, none going more than four rounds.

Tyson suffered one of the most significant losses of his career in 1985 when D'Amato died of pneumonia at age 77. Tyson was devastated.

But a little more than a year later, Tyson made D'Amato's prediction come true. In November 1986, he knocked out Trevor Berbick in the second round to win the World Boxing Council (WBC) heavyweight title, and at age 20 years, four months became the youngest heavyweight champ in history.

In March 1987, Tyson won the World Boxing Association (WBA) title, scoring a unanimous 12-round decision over James "Bonecrusher" Smith. In August 1987, he won the International Boxing Federation (IBF) title with a unanimous 12-round decision over Tony Tucker.

Tyson made six successful title defenses over the next two years, all by knockout and only one going more than five rounds. But as his professional life was going well, his personal life was beginning to fall apart. His marriage to actress Robin Givens lasted slightly more than a year, breaking up soon after an interview on ABC's 20/20 with Barbara Walters, in which Givens accused Tyson of hitting her.

In the weeks leading up to the interview, Tyson crashed his BMW into a tree in what was rumored to be a failed suicide attempt, a charge Tyson denied.

In February 1990, Tyson fought James "Buster" Douglas, a 40-to-1 underdog, in Tokyo in what was supposed to be an easy victory. But in what has been called the biggest upset in boxing history, Douglas beat Tyson, knocking him out in the 10th round.

Over the next 18 months, Tyson fought four times—all victories—before his abusive history with women landed him in more trouble. In February 1992, he was convicted of raping Desiree Washington, a contestant in the Miss Black America pageant, and sentenced to six years in prison in the Indiana state penitentiary.

His sentence was reduced to three years, and he was released in March 1995. Five days later, it was announced that he would return to the ring in August 1995 against unheralded Peter McNeeley. The fight lasted only 89 seconds.

Tyson beat Buster Mathis, Jr., in December 1995, then won the WBC heavyweight title by a third-round technical knockout (TKO) over Frank Bruno in March 1996. In September 1996, Tyson added the WBA crown with a first-round TKO over Bruce Seldon.

Tyson's next bout was against Evander Holyfield for the WBA title in November 1996. Heavily favored because of his size, strength, and power, Tyson was stunned by Holyfield, who fought a tactically brilliant fight and won on an 11th-round TKO. In the rematch in June 1997, Tyson lost all control when he was disqualified in the third round of the bout after biting off a piece of Holyfield's ear. He was suspended by the Nevada State Athletic Commission and didn't fight for 19 months.

Another altercation, in which Tyson assaulted two older men following a traffic accident in Maryland, landed him in jail again. After his release, he fought Orlin Norris. The bout was declared "no contest" when Tyson hit Norris after the bell and Norris fell and injured his knee. In January 2000, Tyson knocked out Julius Francis in the second round. His record through March 2000 was 46–3–1.

Walcott, Jersey Joe (Arnold Cream)
Born: January 31, 1914 in Merchantville, New Jersey
Died: February 25, 1994

Jersey Joe Walcott turned pro in 1930 at the age of 16, but because it was difficult for black fighters to get fights in those days, his career took a long time to take shape. During his first three years as a pro, he fought only seven times.

Even though Walcott began to fight more over the next several years, the paydays were so small he couldn't afford to support his mother and siblings. So he left boxing, got married, and eventually had six children, and then in 1944 was lured out of retirement by a promoter who gave him a $500 advance and promised him six fights over the next two years.

By 1945, perhaps because of the scarcity of fighters during World War II, Walcott began fighting more often, working his way up to a top-10 contender for the heavyweight title. He got his first title shot in December 1947. He fought gamely against the champion, Joe Louis, knocking him down twice and lasting 15 rounds. But Louis won a split decision.

In a rematch six months later, Louis knocked out Walcott in the 11th round. Louis retired shortly thereafter, and in June 1949, Walcott and Ezzard Charles fought for the vacant title, Charles winning a 15-round decision.

Walcott lost a rematch to Charles in March 1951 by a 15-round decision. But in their third fight, in July 1951, Walcott knocked out Charles in the seventh round, making him the oldest fighter to win the title. He then successfully defended his championship in June 1952, winning a 15-round decision.

Walcott fought twice more for the title, losing both times to Rocky Marciano—a 13th-round knockout in September 1952 and a first-round knockout in May 1953. Walcott became a boxing referee (he was in the ring for the second Muhammad Ali–Sonny Liston fight), a sheriff in New Jersey, and the chairman of the New Jersey State Athletic Commission. Regarded as one of the sport's finest technicians, Walcott finished with a career record of 53–18–1. He was inducted into the International Boxing Hall of Fame in 1990.

Zale, Tony
Born: May 29, 1913 in Gary, Indiana
Died: March 21, 1997

Tony Zale didn't plan on boxing as a career until he was about to graduate from high school and realized the steel mills of Gary, Ind., were his most likely place of employment. After winning 87 of 95 fights as an amateur, he turned pro in 1934. By 1939, he had worked his way up the rankings and was recognized as a top-10 middleweight contender by *The Ring* magazine.

In July 1940, Zale beat Al Hostak for the National Boxing Association middleweight title. He successfully defended it twice, and in November 1941, won the vacant world middleweight championship, beating Georgie Abrams by a 15-round decision.

After losing a 12-round decision to Billy Conn in February 1942, Zale joined the Navy and didn't fight again until 1946, when he was still considered the champ.

His three fights—all title fights against Rocky Graziano—defined his career. Zale won the first, knocking out Graziano in the sixth round in September 1946, lost the second on a sixth-round technical knockout in July 1947, and won the third on a third-round knockout in June 1948. All three fights were brutal battles that left both fighters bloodied.

Zale, nicknamed "The Man of Steel," fought once more, in September 1948 against Marcel Cerdan, who knocked him out in the 12th round. Known for his ability to take severe punishment and fight back when the bout seemed lost, Zale finished with a career record of 67–18–2. He was inducted into the International Boxing Hall of Fame in 1991.

Football

Adderley, Herb

Born: June 8, 1939 in Philadelphia, Pennsylvania

Herb Adderley was one of the best defensive backs in the history of the National Football League. He was tough against the run and virtually impenetrable against the pass.

He was the no. 1 pick of the Green Bay Packers in 1961, after a stellar career at the University of Michigan, where he was the leading rusher in 1959 and the leading receiver in 1959 and 1960.

As a rookie with the Packers, he was a running back, but soon it was determined that his preference was to play defensive back. He became a cornerstone of the Packers defense for the next nine seasons.

Adderley usually drew the opponent's best receiver. He played off the ball and used his speed to make the play. He was rarely beaten and was blessed with sure hands.

Adderley helped the Packers win five NFL championships, including the first two Super Bowls. In Super Bowl II against the Oakland Raiders, he had the first interception return for a touchdown in Super Bowl history.

After the 1969 season, he was traded to the Dallas Cowboys, who reached two Super Bowls (V, VI), winning the second 24–3 over the Miami Dolphins. Overall, Adderley played in seven NFL title games and was on the winning side six times.

Adderley retired in 1972 after 12 seasons. He had 48 career interceptions, which he returned for 1,046 yards (21.8-yard average) and seven touchdowns. A five-time Pro Bowl choice, he was inducted into the Pro Football Hall of Fame in 1980.

Aikman, Troy

Born: November 21, 1966 in West Covina, California

Troy Aikman is known as one of the most efficient and effective quarterbacks of his time. Because his team, the Dallas Cowboys, relied heavily on the running of Emmitt Smith, Aikman didn't put up big numbers. But he was an accurate passer who could throw long or short; he possessed outstanding leadership qualities; and he was a winner. Through the 2000 season, he was one of only three quarterbacks to lead his team to three Super Bowl victories.

Aikman played his first two years of college ball at the University of Oklahoma, then transferred to UCLA. In 1988, he was the winner of the Davey O'Brien Award as the nation's best quarterback and finished third in voting for the Heisman Trophy, emblematic of the best player in the country. He completed 64.8 percent of his passes at UCLA for 5,298 yards and 41 touchdowns. He threw only 17 interceptions in two seasons.

The Cowboys selected Aikman as the first pick overall in the 1989 NFL draft. The Cowboys went 1–15 in his rookie season, but three years later, won their first Super Bowl.

Troy Aikman *Diane Staskowski*

In 1992, Aikman threw for 3,445 yards and 23 touchdowns. He led the Cowboys to Super Bowl XXVII, where they defeated the Buffalo Bills 52–17. He completed 22 of 30 passes for 273 yards and four touchdowns and was named the game's Most Valuable Player.

The Cowboys repeated as NFL champs, beating Buffalo 30–13. After losing to the San Francisco 49ers in the 1994 NFC championship game, Dallas won its third Super Bowl in three years, beating the Pittsburgh Steelers 27–17 in Super Bowl XXX.

Through the 2000 season, Aikman, a six-time Pro Bowl selection, threw for 3,000 or more yards five times and completed 60 percent or more of his passes six times. He was sixth all-time in Super Bowl passing yards (689). Aikman retired in April 2001.

Allen, Marcus

Born: March 26, 1960 in San Diego, California

Marcus Allen was not a physically imposing running back (6-2, 210 pounds). Neither was he particularly fast or overpowering. But his ability to find an opening and make the most of it made him one of the best ever.

Allen was intelligent, blessed with great instincts, and a student of the game. He knew his job and the jobs of every other player on his team. He was able to elude would-be tacklers, and he was a versatile offensive threat. He had the ability to get the tough yards, especially near the end zone, and catch passes out of the backfield.

Allen, a quarterback and defensive back in high school, was switched to tailback at the University of Southern California. As a sophomore, he was moved to fullback, where his principal job was to block for tailback Charles White, the 1979 Heisman Trophy winner. But when White graduated, Allen was moved back to tailback for his junior and senior seasons. In 1980, he led the nation in all-purpose yards, averaging 179.4 yards a game. In 1981, he set NCAA records for rushing yards (2,432 yards), most 200-yard games (8), highest average rushing per game (212.9), and all-purpose yards (2,550). He was a consensus All-American and the winner of the Heisman Trophy and the Maxwell Award as the nation's outstanding college football player.

In 1982, Allen was the first-round draft choice of the Los Angeles Raiders. In the strike-shortened 1982 season, he rushed for 697 yards and led the NFL with 14 touchdowns. He was named the league's Rookie of the Year.

In 1985, Allen led the NFL in rushing with a career-high 1,759 yards and 2,314 total yards, a record through the 1999 season. He was named Most Valuable Player and Offensive Player of the Year by the Associated Press.

Allen helped the Raiders reach Super Bowl XVIII, following the 1983 season. He was named the game's Most Valuable Player, gaining 191 yards and scoring two touchdowns on 20 carries in a 38–9 victory over the Washington Redskins.

Over the next three seasons, Allen did not perform as well. In 1989, a knee injury caused him to miss most of the season. Following the 1992 season, Allen left the Raiders to sign with the Kansas City Chiefs as a free agent. He spent five solid seasons with the Chiefs, gaining 700 or more yards four times and averaging 4 yards a carry three times. In 1993, he led the NFL with 15 touchdowns.

Allen retired after the 1997 season. He was the NFL's first player to gain 10,000 rushing (12,243) and 5,000 yards receiving (5,411). Through the 2000 season, he ranked seventh all-time in rushing, eighth in all-purpose yards (17,648), and third in touchdowns (145). No running back has played more games (222) or caught more passes (587).

Allen, a six-time Pro Bowl player, works for CBS Sports as an NFL analyst.

Alworth, Lance

Born: August 3, 1940 in Houston, Texas

Lance Alworth was a graceful wide receiver with a long, loping stride and fluid gait. He had great hands, great speed, and the mentality to believe he could catch anything thrown his way.

Alworth, a running back at the University of Arkansas, was shifted to wide receiver by the San Diego Chargers, who drafted him in the second round in

1962. He spent nine seasons with the Chargers and led the American Football League in receiving in 1966 (73 catches, 1,383 yards), 1968 (68, 1,312 yards), and 1969 (64, 1,003 yards). It helped that Alworth, nicknamed "Bambi," played for head coach Sid Gillman, considered an offensive genius. Gillman's emphasis on the passing game helped make Alworth the first superstar in the AFL.

During his nine seasons with the Chargers, he caught at least one pass in every game he played, a string of 96 straight, a record when he retired.

Alworth spent the last two years of his career playing for the Dallas Cowboys and caught a touchdown pass in the Cowboys' victory over the Miami Dolphins in Super Bowl VI.

Alworth, who retired after the 1971 season, caught 542 passes for 10,266 yards and 85 touchdowns. He averaged 18.9 yards a catch; had five games of 200 yards or more, a record; 41 games of 100 yards or more; and seven straight 1,000-yard seasons. In 1965, he caught 69 passes for 1,602 yards and averaged 23.2 yards a catch.

Alworth was an All-AFL pick seven straight seasons, starting in 1963. He played in seven Pro Bowls and in 1978 was the first AFL player to be inducted into the Pro Football Hall of Fame. He was named to the NFL's 75th Anniversary All-Time Team in 1994.

Barney, Lem (Lemuel)
Born: September 8, 1945 in Gulfport, Mississippi

Lem Barney played his college ball at Jackson State University, where he had 26 interceptions in three seasons. In 1967, he joined the Detroit Lions and was named the NFL's Defensive Rookie of the Year, intercepting 10 passes and returning three for touchdowns. His first interception was of a pass thrown by Green Bay Packers quarterback Bart Starr. Barney made a diving catch, complete with a somersault, and took the ball 24 yards for a touchdown. It was a sign of things to come.

Barney was blessed with blinding speed and great quickness. It allowed him to play receivers one-on-one, which meant the Lions were free to blitz the quarterback.

He also used his speed and elusiveness to become a dangerous punt and kickoff returner. He averaged 9.2 yards on punt returns and 25.5 yards on kickoff returns.

Barney played 11 seasons, all for the Lions, and had 56 career interceptions, eight of which were returned for touchdowns. He retired after the 1977 season as one of the most popular players in franchise history.

Barney was a three-time All-Pro and a seven-time Pro Bowl player. He was inducted into the Pro Football Hall of Fame in 1992.

Baugh, Sammy
Born: March 17, 1914 in Temple, Texas

Sammy Baugh, the most prolific passer of his era, changed the way football was played. He pioneered the ball-control passing game at a time when teams relied almost exclusively on the run.

Baugh was a three-sport star in high school and was recruited as a baseball player by Texas Christian University. But when baseball coach Leo "Dutch" Meyer became the football coach, Meyer made Baugh his starting tailback. From 1934 to 1936, Baugh led TCU to 29 victories, running Meyer's "Aerial Circus" offense. At a time when most teams threw no more than 10 passes a game, Baugh threw 599 over his three seasons.

After he graduated from TCU, Baugh signed as a third baseman with the St. Louis Cardinals. When he was sent to the minor leagues, he decided to try professional football instead. Even though most observers thought Baugh was too tall (6-3) and skinny (180 pounds) to play in the NFL—legendary sportswriter Grantland Rice proclaimed him "too reedy"—Baugh made an immediate impact in his rookie season with the Washington Redskins. He led the Redskins to the 1937 NFL championship game against the Chicago Bears. Baugh passed for 354 yards, throwing touchdown passes of 55, 78, and 33 yards and rallying the Redskins to a 28–21 victory.

Baugh also led the Redskins to the NFL championship in 1942 and to the NFL title game in 1940, 1943, and 1945. In the 1943 game against the Bears and the 1945 game against the Cleveland Rams, Baugh suffered a concussion in the former and played with separated ribs in the latter.

In 1944, after spending the first seven seasons as a single-wing tailback, Baugh was switched to a T-formation quarterback. Regardless of what position he played, he revolutionized the game with his powerful right arm.

Baugh wasn't just a tailback/quarterback. For the first seven years of his career, he also played defensive back, once intercepting four passes in one game. Throughout his career, Baugh was an outstanding punter. Through the 1999 season, he still held records for career average (45.1 yards per punt) and season average (51.4 yards per punt).

In 1943, Baugh became the only player in NFL history to lead the league in passing, punting, and interceptions. He also led the league in passing five other times (1937, '40, '45, '47, '49).

Baugh retired in 1952 and held 16 major records, including yards passing (21,886), completion percentage (56.5), and touchdowns (187). His 70.1 completion percentage stood until 1982.

Baugh, a six-time All-Pro, was inducted into the Pro Football Hall of Fame as a charter member in 1963 and was a member of the NFL's 75th Anniversary All-Time Team in 1994.

After his retirement, he coached at Hardin-Simmons University for five years (1955–59), and then coached the New York Titans of the American Football League for two seasons (1960–61).

Bednarik, Chuck (Charles)
Born: May 1, 1925 in Bethlehem, Pennsylvania

His nickname was "Concrete Charlie," which tells you all you need to know about Chuck Bednarik, a tough, powerfully built (6-3, 233 pound) center/linebacker known for his punishing blocks and ferocious tackles.

Bednarik played his college ball at the University of Pennsylvania, where he was a consensus All-American in 1947 and 1948 and the winner of the Maxwell Award in 1948 as the Outstanding Player of the Year.

He joined the Philadelphia Eagles in 1949 and was an All-Pro center in his first two years in the league. In the 1951 season, Bednarik was moved to linebacker, where he excelled, making the All-Pro team for each of the next six seasons.

Bednarik was blessed with size and good speed that allowed him to defend against short passes. His ability to stop the run was legendary, because of his instincts and the reckless abandon with which he played. In 1960, when injuries took their toll on the linebacking corps, Bednarik was switched back to center and played both positions, as he did in college. He became the National Football League's last 60-minute man. Appropriately, he wore No. 60 throughout his career with the Eagles.

Bednarik was 35 years old in 1960 when the Eagles reached the NFL championship game against the Green Bay Packers. The Eagles won 17–13, when Bednarik saved a touchdown by bringing down fullback Jim Taylor at the 10-yard line. Bednarik played 58 minutes in the title game.

Earlier in the 1960 season, Bednarik made one of the most famous and most vicious tackles in NFL history. In a game against the New York Giants, Bednarik leveled Frank Gifford, who had caught a pass in Eagles' territory and was trying to get out of bounds to stop the clock. Bednarik's jarring hit caused Gifford to fumble. The Eagles recovered, and Bednarik did what was perceived to be a celebratory dance over Gifford, who lay on the field, having suffered a concussion. According to Bednarik, he wasn't aware that Gifford was hurt; he was celebrating because the Eagles recovered the fumble and virtually secured the Eastern Division championship.

Bednarik played two more seasons, then retired in 1962, missing only three games during his 14-year career. He intercepted 20 passes and returned them for 268 yards and one touchdown. He played in eight Pro Bowls and was inducted into the Pro Football Hall of Fame as a center and a linebacker in 1967.

Bell, Bobby
Born: June 17, 1940 in Shelby, North Carolina

Few pro football stars have had the versatile career that Bobby Bell had. In high school, he was a halfback and an all-state quarterback. At the University of Minnesota, he began his career as a quarterback, and also played linebacker and center, before becoming a consensus All-American as a defensive tackle. He also won the Outland Trophy in 1962 as the best lineman in the nation.

He was drafted by the Kansas City Chiefs in 1963, and one year later was an All-American Football League selection as defensive end. In 1966, Bell was moved to outside linebacker, where he excelled at stopping the run or defending against the pass.

At 6-4, 228 pounds, Bell was blessed with size, strength, speed, and quickness. He was a punishing tackler and could cover receivers. His coach in Kansas City, Hank Stram, called Bell the "most versatile athlete" he ever coached.

Bell helped the Chiefs win two AFL championships (1966, '69) and reach the Super Bowl each time. The Chiefs lost to the Green Bay Packers in Super Bowl I and upset the Minnesota Vikings in Super Bowl IV.

Bell was either All-AFL or All-NFL for six straight years, starting in 1966. He played in six straight AFL All-Star Games and the first four Pro Bowls, following the merger of the two leagues in 1970. He retired after the 1974 season with 26 career interceptions, which he returned for 479 yards and six touchdowns.

In 1983, he became the first outside linebacker to be inducted into the Pro Football Hall of Fame.

Berry, Raymond
Born: February 27, 1933 in Corpus Christi, Texas

Raymond Berry certainly didn't look like a wide receiver. He wasn't blessed with great size or speed, nor was he particularly athletic. But through an unyielding work ethic and exemplary practice habits, Berry developed into one of pro football's best players. When his teammates had long left the practice field, Berry was still there, catching passes.

What he lacked in physical attributes he made up for with good hands, outstanding leaping ability, and moves to help him elude defenders. He rarely dropped a pass.

Berry went to college at Southern Methodist University, where he caught 33 passes—only one for a touchdown—in his three seasons. He joined the Baltimore Colts in 1955, but was a long shot to make the team. Coach Weeb Ewbank was impressed with Berry's hands and his work habits at practice, so he was kept on the team as a reserve.

Berry became a starter in his third season, 1957, and led the National Football League with 800 yards receiving on 47 catches. Over the next three seasons (1958–60),

Berry led the league in receptions with 56, 66, and 74, respectively. In 1958 and 1959, the Colts won the NFL championship. In the 1958 game against the New York Giants, often called the greatest ever played, Berry caught 12 passes for 178 yards and one touchdown. In the last two minutes, he caught three passes for 62 yards from quarterback Johnny Unitas to help move the Colts into range for Steve Myhra's tying field goal. Berry and Unitas formed one of the greatest tandems in pro football history.

When Berry retired in 1967, he held records for catches (631) and yards (9,275), each of which has been broken. He caught 68 touchdown passes.

A five-time Pro Bowl player, Berry was inducted into the Pro Football Hall of Fame in 1973.

In 1984, Berry was named head coach of the New England Patriots. In 1985, the Patriots earned the wild card spot, won three road games in the playoffs, and advanced to the Super Bowl, where they lost to the Chicago Bears 46–10.

In 1986, the Patriots won the AFC East title, but lost in the first round of the playoffs to the Denver Broncos. Berry stepped down during the 1989 season. His record was 51–41.

Biletnikoff, Fred

Born: February 23, 1943 in Erie, Pennsylvania

Fred Biletnikoff was one of the most reliable, dependable receivers in NFL history. He wasn't big (6-1, 190 pounds) or fast, but he ran precise routes, had great hands, and was a student of the game, with a tireless work ethic. He always found a way to get open, and once thrown to him, the ball was caught virtually every time. The combination propelled him to an excellent career.

Biletnikoff played his college ball at Florida State University, where he was an All-American in 1964. He joined the Oakland Raiders in 1965, and for his first two seasons in the American Football League he was a part-time player. He became a starter in 1967, when he caught 40 passes, and he never caught fewer than 42 passes for the next nine seasons. He had 100 or more yards in receptions 21 times in his career. He led the AFL in 1971 with 61 catches for 929 yards and nine touchdowns, and again in 1972 with 58 catches for 802 yards and seven touchdowns.

Biletnikoff was a worrywart who developed an ulcer while at Florida State. Before each game with the Raiders, he paced and threw up. After the game, it took hours for him to calm down.

Biletnikoff also was known for using "stickum," a sticky substance that he spread on his socks and then applied to his fingers before each play.

During his 14 seasons in Oakland, the Raiders never had a losing season. They played in three AFL championship games, six AFC title games, and two Super Bowls

(II, XI). In Super Bowl XI, a 32–14 victory over the Minnesota Vikings, Biletnikoff was the game's Most Valuable Player. He caught four passes for 79 yards, three of the catches helping set up touchdowns.

Biletnikoff caught 589 passes in his career for 8,974 yards and 76 touchdowns. Through the 2000 season, he ranked 26th all-time in receptions. A six-time Pro Bowl player, he was inducted into the Pro Football Hall of Fame in 1988. Since 1994, the Biletnikoff Award has been presented to the outstanding college receiver in the country.

Blanchard, Doc (Felix)

Born: December 11, 1924 in Bishopville, South Carolina

Doc Blanchard and Glenn Davis formed one of the most effective running back tandems in college football history. Blanchard supplied the power and was known as "Mr. Inside." Davis provided the speed and was known as "Mr. Outside." Together, they helped Army win the national championship in 1944 and 1945.

Blanchard started his college career at the University of North Carolina in 1942, but left after his freshman year. He tried to enlist in the Navy's V-12 program unit, but was turned down because he was overweight and had a vision problem. Blanchard then enlisted in the Army and was assigned to the Army Air Force's ground school in Clovis, New Mexico. He was appointed to the U.S. Military Academy in 1944.

Blanchard was an All-American for three years and became the first junior ever to win the Heisman Trophy (1945) as the nation's outstanding college football player. In that same year, Blanchard became the first football player to win the Sullivan Award, given to the outstanding amateur athlete of the year. He completed his career at Army with 1,666 yards rushing and 38 touchdowns (26 rushing, seven receiving, four interception returns, one kickoff return).

In the first game of his Army career, Blanchard averaged 58 yards on kickoff returns, carried the ball four times for a 4.5-yard average, all in 17 minutes of playing time.

After graduating from West Point, he remained with the Army Air Force, retiring with the rank of colonel. While stationed in England in 1959, Blanchard's plane caught fire near London. Instead of abandoning the plane in a heavily populated area, he landed it safely at an airfield. He received a citation for bravery.

Blanda, George

Born: September 17, 1927 in Youngwood, Pennsylvania

George Blanda had one of the most remarkable careers in the history of pro football. He broke into the NFL in

1949 with the Chicago Bears and retired in 1975 at age 48. His career spanned four decades, and he became a folk hero over time as a quarterback and placekicker.

He played his college ball at the University of Kentucky and then spent 10 years with the Chicago Bears. He earned the starting quarterback's job in 1953, but after an injury sidelined him in 1954, he was relegated to a backup. He also was the placekicker. Blanda actually retired after the 1959 season because he was unhappy with his role, and entered the trucking business. But when the American Football League had its inaugural season in 1960, he joined the Houston Oilers as their starting quarterback.

Blanda wasn't blessed with great arm strength or speed, but he used his instincts and intelligence to become an effective quarterback.

In 1960, Blanda passed for 24 touchdowns and kicked for 115 points as the Oilers won the first AFL championship.

In 1961, Blanda led the AFL in passing, completing 52 percent of his throws for 3,330 yards and 36 touchdowns, including seven in one game. He kicked for 112 points in leading the Oilers to their second straight AFL championship. He was named the league's Player of the Year.

In 1965 and 1966, Blanda's performance tailed off and he became a part-time starter for the Oilers, but as a placekicker, he led the AFL in scoring with 116 points. After the 1966 season, he was released and picked up by the Oakland Raiders, which is when his legend began to take shape. Although he was primarily a kicker with the Raiders, his heroics as a backup quarterback were noteworthy. During one five-week stretch in 1970, Blanda, then 43, rode to the rescue and led the Raiders to five victories. He replaced injured starting quarterback Daryle Lamonica and threw three touchdown passes to beat the Pittsburgh Steelers; he kicked a 48-yard field goal with three seconds left to forge a tie with the Kansas City Chiefs; he threw a game-tying touchdown pass in the final two minutes and then kicked the game-winning 52-yard field goal to beat the Cleveland Browns; he threw a touchdown pass in the final four minutes to edge the Denver Broncos; and he kicked a 16-yard field goal with four seconds left to beat the San Diego Chargers.

The Raiders won the AFC Western Division title, and Blanda was named the AFC Player of the Year and the Associated Press Male Athlete of the Year.

Blanda continued as a backup quarterback and placekicker through the 1975 season. He retired just short of his 49th birthday. He holds the record as having the longest career in pro football history. Blanda played in a record 340 games, spanning 26 seasons.

Blanda completed 47 percent of his passes for 26,920 yards and 236 touchdowns. He ran for nine touchdowns, kicked 943 extra points and 335 field goals, and scored 2,002 points, an NFL record.

He was inducted into the Pro Football Hall of Fame in 1981.

Blount, Mel
Born: April 10, 1948 in Vidalia, Georgia

Mel Blount was arguably the most effective cornerback of his time. He was tough, aggressive, and a master at bump-and-run coverage, which the NFL eventually outlawed.

After starring at Southern University, Blount joined the Pittsburgh Steelers in 1970. His intimidating style and his belief that no one could beat him made him one of the keys of the Steelers' famed "Steel Curtain" defense that was a main reason the team won four Super Bowls in six seasons (1974–75, '78–79).

Blount led the NFL in interceptions with 11 in 1975 and had 57 for his career. He was a five-time Pro Bowl player.

Blount, who retired after the 1983 season, was inducted into the Pro Football Hall of Fame in 1989. He was also voted onto the NFL's 75th Anniversary All-Time Team in 1994.

Bradshaw, Terry
Born: September 2, 1948 in Shreveport, Louisiana

Terry Bradshaw of Louisiana Tech was the first player picked in the 1970 National Football League draft, by the Pittsburgh Steelers. At 6-3, 215 pounds, he was a prototype quarterback who was expected to make an immediate impact. But the combination of the pro game's sophistication and Bradshaw's small-town country boy background made his transition a difficult one. He became the starting quarterback for the Steelers in 1971, but during his first several seasons, Bradshaw had the reputation of being unintelligent and a buffoon. He was the butt of jokes and was dismissed by many as a bust.

But Bradshaw proved everyone wrong by being the only quarterback to lead his team to wins in four Super Bowls (IX, X, XIII, XIV). He was named the Most Valuable Player in Super Bowl XII (17-for-30, 318 yards, four touchdowns, one interception) and Super Bowl XIV (14-for-21, 309 yards, two touchdowns, three interceptions). In Super Bowl X, Bradshaw's 64-yard touchdown pass to Lynn Swann with about three minutes to play lifted the Steelers to a 21–17 victory over the Dallas Cowboys.

Bradshaw, blessed with a quick release, a strong arm, and the ability to throw long and short passes effectively, had his best season in 1978, when he was named the winner of the Bert Bell Trophy as the league's Most Valuable Player. He completed 56 percent of his passes and threw for 2,915 yards and a league-leading 28 touchdown passes.

Bradshaw retired after the 1983 season as one of the best quarterbacks of his era and one of the best in the postseason ever. He completed 54 percent of his passes for 27,989 yards and 212 touchdowns. Through the 2000 season, he ranked 19th all-time in touchdown passes. In the postseason, he completed 56 percent of his passes for 3,508 yards and 58 touchdowns.

Bradshaw, who was inducted into the Pro Football Hall of Fame in 1989, was an Emmy Award–winning football analyst for Fox Sports through the 2000 season.

Brown, Jim

Born: February 17, 1936 in St. Simon Island, Georgia

Jim Brown is widely regarded as the best running back and one of the greatest football players of all time. He was powerfully built (6-2, 230 pounds) and delivered more punishment than he endured, lowering his shoulder and wielding a lethal stiff arm. He was fast, explosive, and elusive. Frequently brought down by gang-tackling, Brown was always the last one up from the turf. He purposely remained on the ground a moment longer in order to conserve energy.

Brown was an all-around athlete in high school, playing baseball, basketball, and lacrosse, in addition to football. After averaging 38 points a game in basketball and 14.9 yards per carry in football for Manhasset High in Manhasset, N.Y., Brown went to Syracuse University, where he became an All-American in football and lacrosse and started on the basketball team.

Brown's most famous game at Syracuse might have been his last regular season game, against Colgate. He scored six touchdowns and kicked seven extra points in the Orangemen's 67–6 victory.

Brown was drafted by the Cleveland Browns with the fourth pick of the 1957 NFL draft. He was named Rookie of the Year, rushing for a league-leading 942 yards and scoring nine touchdowns.

Brown, whose career lasted only nine seasons, led the league in rushing eight times, which was a record through the 2000 season. He gained 1,527 yards in 1958; 1,329 yards in 1959; 1,257 yards in 1960; 1,408 yards in 1961; 1,863 yards in 1963; 1,446 yards in 1964; and 1,544 yards in 1965.

In 1962, the only year Brown failed to lead the league in rushing, he finished fourth, with 996 yards, a wrist injury suffered early in the season contributing to his performance.

The 1962 season was significant for a reason other than Brown's failure to lead the league in rushing. He was instrumental in getting head coach Paul Brown removed. Paul Brown was succeeded by Blanton Collier, who in-

stalled an offense that played to Jim Brown's strengths. He responded by rushing for 12 touchdowns and 1,863 yards, the seventh-highest single-season total through the 2000 season.

Brown led the NFL in touchdowns five times (9 in 1957, 17 in 1958, 14 in 1959, 12 in 1963, 17 in 1965), and was a four-time winner of the Most Valuable Player Award (1957–58, '63, '65). In 1964, he led the Browns to the NFL championship.

Just before the start of training camp for the 1966 season, Brown, in London filming *The Dirty Dozen*, announced his retirement. He was 30 years old and in good health. The news stunned the sports world, but Brown insisted he wanted to go out on top.

"I got out before I ever had to be like so many guys I've seen—hunched over on the bench, all scarred and banged up, watching some hot young kid out there in their place," said Brown.

Once retired, Brown continued acting, and he formed two organizations, the Black Economic Union and the Amer-I-Can Program, both of which helped to further progress of minorities in American cities. He also was charged on numerous occasions with sexual abuse. He was found guilty of a charge brought by his wife, Monique, in 1999.

Through the 2000 season, Brown, a nine-time Pro Bowl choice and a nine-time All-Pro, ranked sixth all-time in rushing yards (12,312), first in yards per carry (5.2), and fourth all-time in touchdowns (126). He was inducted into the Pro Football Hall of Fame in 1971 and was named a member of the NFL's 75th Anniversary All-Time Team in 1994.

Brown, Roosevelt

Born: October 20, 1932 in Charlottesville, Virginia

After playing college ball at Morgan State College, where he was a Little All-American selection in 1952, Roosevelt Brown joined the New York Giants as a 27th-round draft choice. Not much was expected of him, but 13 years later, he was on his way to the Pro Football Hall of Fame.

Brown was 6-3, 255 pounds with broad shoulders and a strong upper body. He was blessed with the size of an offensive tackle and the speed of a guard. The combination made him one of the premier offensive tackles of his era. He was one of the first tackles to pull and lead interference because of his speed.

The Giants also used him on defense occasionally, putting him in on goal line stands, a move that would give the rest of the defense a psychological lift.

From 1954 to 1963, Brown helped the Giants to an 86–35–5 record, six conference titles, and the 1956 NFL championship.

Brown was an eight-time All-Pro (1956–63) and a 10-time Pro Bowl player. He retired after the 1965 season because of phlebitis. He was inducted into the Pro Football Hall of Fame in 1975.

Brown, Willie

Born: June 22, 1966 in Dallas, Texas

Willie Brown was the consummate defensive back. He was blessed with toughness, mobility, quickness, and instincts that always seemed to allow him to know where the receiver was going.

When he came out of Grambling College in 1963, he wasn't highly regarded. He was cut by the Houston Oilers, then spent four years with the Denver Broncos. In 1967, he was traded to the Oakland Raiders, for whom he became the anchor of their secondary.

Brown perfected a technique called "bump-and-run coverage," where he played the receiver right off the line of scrimmage. He bumped the receiver as he came off the line and then ran with him for the rest of his pattern.

Brown had 54 career interceptions in the regular season and seven more in postseason play, including one for 75 yards and a touchdown that clinched the Raiders' Super Bowl XI victory over the Minnesota Vikings.

Brown was a big reason why the Raiders were so successful, going 128–35–7 during his 12 seasons and appearing in nine American Football League or American Football Conference title games and two Super Bowls.

Brown, a nine-time Pro Bowl player, was inducted into the Pro Football Hall of Fame in 1984. He became an assistant coach and through the 2000 season was the defensive coordinator for the Raiders.

Buchanan, Buck (Junious)

Born: September 10, 1940 in Gainesville, Alabama
Died: July 16, 1992

Buck Buchanan was an unusual combination of size (6-7, 270 pounds), strength, athleticism, and explosive speed. He was the first defensive lineman to embody so many physical talents. He changed the way defensive linemen played. He was an outstanding pass rusher, thanks to his great speed and long arms that allowed him to deflect passes, and he was a powerful run-stopper.

Buchanan played his college ball at Grambling State University, where he played offense and defense and was a Little All-American tackle in 1962. He also played basketball and ran track. He was the first player chosen in the 1963 American Football League draft by the Dallas Texans, which became the Kansas City Chiefs before the 1963 season.

Buchanan was such an imposing force that Al Davis, the general manager/coach of the Oakland Raiders, drafted Gene Upshaw, a 6-5, 255-pound guard, specifically to counteract Buchanan.

Said Upshaw: "I was big, but Buck was bigger and stronger. You don't imagine that a guy that big can be so quick. Other guys I enjoyed playing against, but when you faced Buchanan, you couldn't sleep the night before the game."

Buchanan helped the Chiefs to two American Football League championships and two Super Bowl appearances. The Chiefs lost to the Green Bay Packers in Super Bowl I, in which he was credited with the first Super Bowl quarterback sack, and upset the Minnesota Vikings in Super Bowl IV.

Buchanan retired in 1975 after a 13-year career, during which he missed just one game. He was All-AFL five times, and played in six AFL All-Star Games and the first two Pro Bowls after the AFL and NFL merged in 1970. He was inducted into the Pro Football Hall of Fame in 1990.

Butkus, Dick

Born: December 9, 1942 in Chicago, Illinois

Dick Butkus was one of the most feared defensive players in the history of the National Football League. A 6-3, 245-pound middle linebacker who spent his entire career with the Chicago Bears, Butkus played his position with intensity, relentlessness, and ferocity that set him apart. He didn't tackle ball carriers, he punished them.

Said Green Bay Packers quarterback Bart Starr, "Dick rattles your brains when he tackles you."

Butkus grew up on Chicago's South Side and went to college at the University of Illinois, where he was a consensus All-American in 1963 and 1964. In 1965, the Bears made him their first-round draft choice.

Butkus became the starter as a rookie and for nine seasons was the player that symbolized the Bears with his bruising style of play.

Butkus was hampered by a knee injury in 1970, and then, in 1973, when he reinjured the knee, he was forced to retire after nine seasons.

Butkus, who had an uncanny knack of being able to strip ball carriers with one arm while tackling them with the other, recovered 25 fumbles and recorded 22 interceptions during his career. He was an eight-time Pro Bowl player and a seven-time All-Pro. He was inducted into the Pro Football Hall of Fame in 1979 and was named a member of the NFL's 75th Anniversary All-Time Team in 1994.

Following his retirement, Butkus became an actor, broadcaster, and did television commercials. In June 2000, Butkus was named director of competition in the new XFL.

Campbell, Earl

Born: March 29, 1955 in Tyler, Texas

Earl Campbell, one of the great running backs in National Football League history, combined strength, size, and speed. He was powerfully built (5-11, 232 pounds), with thighs that were only two inches smaller in circumference than his 38-inch waist. Campbell either ran over would-be tacklers or sped by them.

He had a terrific career at the University of Texas, where he was the first player to be named All-Southwest Conference four years in a row. He rushed for 4,444 yards in his career at Texas, including 1,744 yards in 1977, when he led the nation and won the Heisman Trophy as the best player in the country.

Campbell was the first-round draft choice of the Houston Oilers in 1978, when he was named AFC Rookie of the Year and AFC Player of the Year. He led the NFL with 1,450 yards and also scored 13 touchdowns.

He led the league in rushing in each of the next two years, gaining 1,697 yards in 1979, when he won the Bert Bell Award as the NFL's Most Valuable Player, and 1,934 yards in 1980. In 1981, he led the AFC in rushing with 1,376 yards. Campbell averaged nearly 1,400 yards a season during his first six seasons and helped the Oilers reach the AFC title game twice.

By 1982, knee injuries began to take their toll. He gained just 538 yards and carried the ball 157 times in 1982. But in 1983, he rebounded to have a Campbell-like season, gaining 1,301 yards and averaging 4 yards a carry. Following the 1983 season, he was traded to New Orleans, where injuries hampered him in 1984 and forced his retirement in 1985.

Through the 2000 season, Campbell ranked 15th all-time in rushing with 9,407 yards. He scored 74 touchdowns and averaged 1,176 yards over his seven seasons.

Campbell, a three-time All-Pro and a five-time Pro Bowl player, was inducted into the Pro Football Hall of Fame in 1991.

Carter, Cris

Born: November 25, 1965 in Troy, Ohio

After a fine college career and a slow start to his professional career, Cris Carter developed into one of the finest and most prolific receivers in the history of the NFL.

Carter played his college ball at Ohio State, where he was a first-team All-American in 1986. He finished as the Buckeyes' all-time leader in receptions (168) and touchdown receptions (27). In 1987, he was selected in the fourth round of the supplemental draft by the Philadelphia Eagles. Despite starting all but one game in 1988 and 1989, and totaling 84 receptions over the two seasons, he was released by Eagles coach Buddy Ryan in September 1990 and claimed by the Minnesota Vikings, where he became a fixture.

Carter led the NFL in receptions in 1994 with 122 for 1,256 yards and seven touchdowns. In 1995, he caught 122 for 1,371 yards and 17 touchdowns. No player in the history of the NFL caught more passes over a two-year span; only one other player, Sterling Sharpe, ever had consecutive 100-catch seasons.

From 1990 through 1999, Carter averaged 97 catches, 1,169 yards, and 9.5 touchdowns.

Through the 2000 season, Carter had 1,020 receptions for 12,962 yards and 123 touchdowns. He ranked second all-time in receptions, fifth all-time in yardage, and second all-time in touchdowns. He played in eight Pro Bowls, and in 1999 was the recipient of the Byron "Whizzer" White Award, given by the NFL Players Association for community service.

Christiansen, Jack

Born: December 20, 1928 in Sublette, Kansas
Died: June 29, 1986

In his senior year in high school, Jack Christiansen's left arm was injured, the result of a shooting accident. So when he went to Colorado State University, he decided to concentrate on track and field, instead of football. But a year later, he joined the football team and became a three-year starter at safety.

Despite his lack of size (6-1, 185 pounds), Detroit Lions coach Buddy Parker made Christiansen one of the first players drafted exclusively to play defense, drafting him in 1951.

Parker practically invented the free safety position for Christiansen, allowing him to roam throughout the secondary and use his quickness, speed, and athleticism to become one of the finest defenders of his time.

Christiansen also proved to be an outstanding kick returner. In his rookie season, he returned four punts for touchdowns.

Christiansen helped the Lions to three NFL championships (1952–53, '57). He retired after the 1958 season.

Christiansen intercepted 46 passes during his eight-year career and twice led the NFL—12 in 1953, 10 in 1957. He averaged 12.8 yards per punt return and 22.5 yards per kickoff return.

A six-time All-Pro, he was inducted into the Pro Football Hall of Fame in 1970.

Csonka, Larry

Born: December 25, 1946 in Stow, Ohio

Larry Csonka was a powerful inside runner and an effective blocker, enjoying most of his success with the Miami Dolphins. He was a first-round draft choice in 1968 out of Syracuse, where he was an All-American in 1967.

Along with Jim Kiick and Eugene "Mercury" Morris, Csonka was part of a ball-control offense that helped the Dolphins reach Super Bowls VI, VII, and VIII and win VII and VIII. Their victory in Super Bowl VII over the Washington Redskins capped a 17–0 season, during which Kiick, Morris, and Csonka each surpassed 1,000 yards rushing, the only time that's happened in NFL history.

In Super Bowl VIII, a 24–7 victory over the Minnesota Vikings, Csonka rushed for 145 yards on 33 carries and scored two touchdowns. He was named the game's Most Valuable Player.

In 1975, Csonka, Kiick, and wide receiver Paul Warfield left the Dolphins to play for the Memphis Southmen of the World Football League. But the league folded after a year, and Csonka joined the New York Giants. But foot injuries limited his effectiveness. It appeared his career was over after the 1978 season, when he carried the ball only 91 times. But he rejoined the Dolphins for the 1979 season, his last, and gained 837 yards on 220 carries and scored 12 touchdowns.

Csonka rushed for 8,081 yards, averaged 4.3 yards a carry, and scored 64 touchdowns. He was a five-time Pro Bowl selection and was inducted into the Pro Football Hall of Fame in 1987.

Davis, Glenn

Born: December 25, 1925 in Claremont, California

Glenn Davis and Doc Blanchard formed one of the most effective running back tandems in college football history. Blanchard supplied the power and was known as "Mr. Inside." Davis provided the speed and was known as "Mr. Outside." Together they helped Army win the national championship in 1944 and 1945.

Davis was an all-around athlete in high school, winning 13 letters in four sports. He entered the U.S. Military Academy in 1943, but was dismissed for failing a plebe mathematics course. He was readmitted in 1944.

In 1944, his first season as a regular, Davis led the nation in scoring with 120 points and averaged 11.1 yards a carry. He won the Maxwell Award as the nation's outstanding college football player.

Davis was an All-American for three seasons at Army and in 1946 won the Heisman Trophy as the most outstanding college football player in the nation and the Associated Press Athlete of the Year Award.

Davis finished his Army career with 2,957 yards rushing, 855 yards passing, and 59 touchdowns (43 rushing, 14 receiving, two punt returns). His 8.26-yard-per-carry average is an NCAA record.

Davis served in Korea until 1950, then resigned his commission to join the Los Angeles Rams. He played with the Rams for two seasons, both of which resulted in NFL championships. He retired after the 1951 season.

Davis, Terrell

Born: October 28, 1972 in San Diego, California

Terrell Davis developed into one of the best running backs in the NFL in his first four seasons in the league. He had the speed and quickness to get outside and the strength and power to get the tough yards inside.

Davis, who played his college ball at the University of Georgia, wasn't chosen until the sixth round of the 1995 NFL draft by the Denver Broncos. Rarely has such a low-round draft choice made such an impact.

He is the lowest-drafted player ever to rush for 1,000 yards in his rookie season, running for 1,117 yards and seven touchdowns in 1995.

Davis went on to rush for 1,000 or more yards in the next three seasons—1,538 yards in 1996, 1,750 yards in 1997, and 2,008 yards in 1998, the third-highest single-season total of all time. Davis scored 23 touchdowns in 1998, also the third-highest single-season of total all-time.

Davis was named the NFL's Most Valuable Player in 1998, as well as the Offensive Player of the Year.

In 1997, Davis helped the Broncos reach Super Bowl XXXII, a 31–24 victory over the Green Bay Packers. He rushed for 157 yards and three touchdowns on 30 carries and was named the game's Most Valuable Player.

Davis' 1999 season ended prematurely when he injured his right knee, tearing his right anterior cruciate ligament and partially tearing his medial collateral ligament. He missed the final 12 games of the season.

Through the 2000 season, Davis had rushed for 6,906 yards and scored 60 touchdowns. He also caught five passes for touchdowns. He was fourth all-time in Super Bowl rushing yards (259) and ninth all-time in all-purpose yards (317).

Davis, Willie (William)

Born: July 24, 1934 in Lisbon, Louisiana

Willie Davis played his college ball at Grambling State and began his pro career with the Cleveland Browns, who drafted him in the 15th round in 1958. The Browns used Davis at a variety of positions—defensive end, defensive tackle, linebacker—but he never became a starter. He was traded to the Green Bay Packers in 1960 because coach Vince Lombardi was in need of a defensive end. Davis became the starter and went on to become one of the best at his position.

Davis had a knack for making the big play. He was blessed with great speed for a man of his size (6-3, 243 pounds). He was a talented pass rusher and a strong run-stopper. Lombardi praised him for his consistency and his intelligence.

Davis, who recovered a team-record 21 fumbles, helped the Packers win five NFL championships, including the first two Super Bowls. He was a four-time All-Pro and a five-time Pro Bowl selection. He retired after the 1969 season and was inducted into the Pro Football Hall of Fame in 1981.

Dawson, Len

Born: June 20, 1935 in Alliance, Ohio

After an outstanding college career at Purdue University, where he passed for 3,325 yards in three seasons, Len Dawson was picked in the first round by the Pittsburgh Steelers in the 1957 NFL draft. His first five seasons—three with Pittsburgh, two with the Cleveland Browns—were uneventful. He threw a total of 45 passes.

When the Browns released him after the 1961 season, he joined the Dallas Texans of the rival American Football League. Under the tutelage of head coach Hank Stram, who ran an innovative passing game, Dawson blossomed into a star.

In his first season with Dallas, Dawson led the AFL in passing, completing 61 percent of his throws for 2,759 yards and 29 touchdowns. He led the Texans to the AFL championship and was named the AFL's Player of the Year.

In 1963, the Texans moved and became the Kansas City Chiefs. Dawson led the AFL in passing in 1964 (56 percent completion rate, 2,879 yards, 30 touchdowns), in 1966 (61.6, 2,527, 26) and 1968 (58.4, 2,109, 17).

He led the Chiefs to the AFL title in 1966 and a spot in Super Bowl I against the Green Bay Packers, who won 35–10. Three years later, Dawson led the Chiefs back to the Super Bowl, where they upset the Minnesota Vikings, who were 12-point favorites, 23–7. Dawson completed 12 of 17 passes for 142 yards, one touchdown, and one interception. He was named the game's Most Valuable Player.

Dawson, who retired after the 1975 season, completed 57 percent of his passes for 28,711 yards and 252 touchdowns. Through the 2000 season, he ranked 13th all-time in touchdown passes. He played five AFL All-Star Games and one Pro Bowl. He was inducted into the Pro Football Hall of Fame in 1987.

Dawson worked as a television commentator, spending most of his broadcast career working for HBO as a host of *Inside the NFL*.

Dickerson, Eric

Born: September 2, 1960 in Sealy, Texas

Eric Dickerson was one of the most prolific running backs in NFL history. He combined speed, power, and elusiveness.

He was a consensus All-American in 1982 at Southern Methodist University, where he gained 4,450 yards and scored 48 touchdowns.

In 1983, the Los Angeles Rams made him their first-round draft pick, and he made an immediate impact as a rookie, rushing for a league-leading 1,808 yards and 18 touchdowns. He was named Offensive Rookie of the Year by the Associated Press and NFC Player of the Year.

In 1984, Dickerson broke O.J. Simpson's single-season rushing record. He ran for 2,105 yards, averaging 5.6 yards a carry, and was named the NFC Player of the Year. He also led the league in rushing in 1986, rushing for 1,821 yards and averaging 4.5 yards a carry.

While Dickerson was having no problems on the field, he and the Rams were having contract difficulties. He missed the first two games of the 1985 season due to a holdout, and three games into the 1987 season he was traded to the Indianapolis Colts in a blockbuster 10-player, three-team deal. He picked right up where he left off. Dickerson led the AFC in rushing in 1987 (1,011 yards) and in 1988 led the NFL in rushing (1,659 yards).

In 1989, Dickerson had his seventh straight season of rushing for 1,000 yards or more, an NFL record. He remained with the Colts through the 1991 season. He finished his career with one-year stays with the Los Angeles Raiders and the Atlanta Falcons, retiring in 1993.

Dickerson, a five-time All-Pro and six-time Pro Bowl player, rushed for 13,259 yards and 90 touchdowns in his career. He also caught 275 passes for 2,079 yards and six touchdowns. Through the 2000 season, he ranked fourth all-time in rushing and 13th all-time in touchdowns. He was inducted into the Pro Football Hall of Fame in 1999.

In July 2000, Dickerson, a neophyte broadcaster, was added to the broadcast team for ABC's *Monday Night Football* as a sideline reporter.

Ditka, Mike

Born: October 18, 1939 in Carnegie, Pennsylvania

Mike Ditka changed the way tight ends were used. Before Ditka, they were primarily used as blockers, but when the Chicago Bears drafted him in the first round out of the University of Pittsburgh in 1961, coach George Halas also used Ditka as a pass receiver. He became a major weapon in the Chicago offense.

Ditka was big (6-3, 228 pounds) and elusive enough to be a force over the middle or down the field.

Once Ditka caught the ball, he was difficult to bring down, not only because of his size and strength, but also because of his intensity and intimidating attitude.

Ditka's blue-collar mentality and style of play made him one of the most popular members of the Bears.

In 1961, Ditka caught 56 passes for 1,076 yards and 12 touchdowns, earning him the NFL Rookie of the Year award. In 1964, he caught 74 passes, which was a record for tight ends at the time.

Ditka helped the Bears win the 1963 NFL championship, a 14–0 victory over the New York Giants.

Ditka, who started 84 straight games for the Bears, was hampered by a foot injury in 1965, and the following year he was traded to the Philadelphia Eagles. He spent three seasons in Philadelphia and was traded again, this time to the Dallas Cowboys, where he finished his career, retiring in 1972. In 1971, Ditka caught 30 passes, in a backup role, and helped the Cowboys to a Super Bowl VI victory over the Miami Dolphins, in which he caught a touchdown pass.

Ditka returned to Chicago in 1982 as the head coach of the Bears, a post he held for 11 seasons. In 1985, he was the consensus NFL Coach of the Year, leading the Bears to a 17–1 record, including a 46–10 victory over the New England Patriots in Super Bowl XX.

Ditka, known for his temper and his feuds with the media, his assistants, and his players, resigned as the Bears' head coach in 1992, after a 5–11 record. His overall record was 112–68. He worked as a commentator for NBC Sports before becoming the head coach of the New Orleans Saints in 1997. He lasted three seasons, compiling a 15–33 record, before being fired and going back to television. Beginning in the 2000 season, he will be a commentator for NBC Sports.

Ditka, a four-time All-Pro and a five-time Pro Bowl player, caught 427 passes for 5,812 yards and 43 touchdowns. He was the first tight end inducted into the Pro Football Hall of Fame, in 1998.

Donovan, Art
Born: June 5, 1925 in The Bronx, New York

In addition to being one of the great defensive tackles of his time, Art Donovan also was known as one of the great morale builders. He was a constant source of jokes and pranks, and long after he retired he made numerous appearances on *Late Show with David Letterman*.

Donovan received a football scholarship to Notre Dame, but enlisted in the Marines instead. When he completed his three-year hitch, he returned to Notre Dame, which refused to renew his scholarship. He attended Boston College instead and became a starter.

The Baltimore Colts selected Donovan in the third round of the 1950 NFL draft. The Colts disbanded after a year, and he was picked by the Cleveland Browns, but traded to the New York Yanks, prior to the start of the 1951 season. The Yanks became the Dallas Texans in 1952, but the franchise reorganized in 1953 as the Baltimore Colts. Donovan was one of only 13 Texans to play for the Colts.

Donovan's tenure with the Colts mirrored the team's rise to prominence. The Colts won back-to-back NFL championships in 1958 and 1959. He was big (6-3, 265), but quick enough to handle the run and rush the passer equally well.

Donovan, who retired two weeks before the 1962 season began, was a four-time All-Pro and a five-time Pro Bowl player. He was inducted into the Pro Football Hall of Fame, the first Colt to be so honored, in 1968.

Dorsett, Tony
Born: April 7, 1954 in Rochester, Pennsylvania

Tony Dorsett was one of the most elusive runners of his era. At 5-11, 192 pounds, he wasn't very big, but his ability to accelerate through cracks in the line made him virtually impossible to stop. He could change directions instantaneously, and once he broke beyond the line of scrimmage, his blazing speed made him uncatchable.

Dorsett had a stellar career at the University of Pittsburgh that culminated in the Panthers winning the national championship in 1976.

Dorsett was the first player in NCAA history to rush for 1,000 yards in each of four seasons. In his senior year, he rushed for 1,948 yards, bringing his career total to a then-record 6,082 yards, which was third all-time through the 1999 season. He was the first college player to break the 6,000-yard career mark. He won the Heisman Trophy in 1976 as the nation's outstanding collegiate player.

In 1977, Dorsett was the first player chosen in the NFL draft, by the Dallas Cowboys. He was named NFL Rookie of the Year, rushing for 1,007 yards. He helped lead the Cowboys to the Super Bowl that year. He led all rushers, with 66 yards on 15 carries in Dallas' 27–10 victory over the Denver Broncos.

Dorsett rushed for 1,000 yards or more in eight of his first nine seasons in the league. The only time he failed to reach the 1,000-yard mark was in the strike-shortened season of 1982, when he ran for 745 yards and led the National Football Conference in rushing.

Dorsett helped the Cowboys reach the NFC title game five times and the Super Bowl twice. He rushed for 1,383 yards in the postseason, which was fourth all-time through the 2000 season. In a 1983 playoff game against the Minnesota Vikings, Dorsett set an NFL record for the longest run from scrimmage, 99 yards.

In 1987, Dorsett was relegated to a backup role when Herschel Walker became the starter. In 1988, he was traded to Denver, where he rushed for 703 yards. In training camp in 1989, he suffered torn knee ligaments and was forced to retire.

Dorsett played 12 seasons and rushed for 12,739 yards, which ranked fifth all-time through the 1999 seasons. He averaged 4.4 yards a carry and scored 77 touchdowns. Dorsett was also a capable receiver. He caught 382 passes in his career for 3,432 yards and 14 touchdowns.

Dorsett was an All-Pro in 1981, when he was also named NFC Player of the Year, and a four-time Pro Bowl player. He was inducted into the Pro Football Hall of Fame in 1994.

Elway, John
Born: June 28, 1960 in Port Los Angeles, Washington

John Elway had size (6-3, 215 pounds), toughness, agility, mobility, a strong arm, and the ability to throw on the run. He was smart, he was a warrior, and he possessed leadership skills second to none. He was the consummate quarterback, known for his fourth-quarter heroics and the storybook ending to a distinguished career.

Elway played his college ball at Stanford, where he set five NCAA Division I-A records and nine Pac-10 Conference records. He completed 62 percent of his passes for 9,349 yards and 77 touchdowns. He was a consensus All-American as a senior in 1982 and finished second in the voting for the Heisman Trophy, which honors the most outstanding college football player in the nation.

Elway also was an accomplished baseball player. In 1981, he was the New York Yankees' first pick in the 1981 summer draft. He played for the Yankees Class A farm club in 1982, hitting .318.

But football was his first love, and in the NFL draft he was the first pick overall by the Baltimore Colts. Elway refused to play for the Colts and forced a trade to the Denver Broncos, where he became a fixture.

In his rookie season, Elway started 10 games, completed 47.5 percent of his passes for 1,663 yards, seven touchdowns, and 14 interceptions. He helped the Broncos qualify for the AFC playoffs.

Throughout the rest of his career, which ended in 1998, Elway never threw for fewer than 2,242 yards or completed less than 53 percent of his passes. Eleven times he surpassed 3,000 yards, and in 1993, when he led the AFC in passing, he threw for 4,030 yards and 25 touchdowns.

In 1987, Elway was named the NFL's Most Valuable Player by the Associated Press. He completed 54.6 percent of his passes for 3,198 yards and 19 touchdowns.

Elway was most famous for his fourth-quarter drives. Forty times he rallied the Broncos to victory in the final period, and seven times he led them on game-tying fourth-quarter drives. The most famous comeback came on Jan. 11, 1986, against the Cleveland Browns in the AFC championship game. It is known simply as "The Drive."

With the Broncos trailing 20–13, Elway moved them 98 yards in the final minutes. A 5-yard touchdown pass to Mark Jackson with seven seconds left in regulation capped the 15-play march. The Broncos went on to win the game in overtime on Rich Karlis' 43-yard field goal.

Elway led the Broncos to the playoffs 10 times, including six AFC championship games and five Super Bowls (XXI, XXII, XXIV, XXXII, XXXIII).

In the Broncos' first three Super Bowl appearances, they were soundly defeated—39–20 by the New York Giants, 42–10 by the Washington Redskins, and 55–10 by the San Francisco 49ers. Many thought Elway would end his career without winning the game that defines a quarterback's greatness and his place in history.

The Broncos failed to make the playoffs in 1990, '92, '94, and '95, and they failed to reach the AFC championship until the 1997 postseason.

The Broncos hosted a wild card game against the Jacksonville Jaguars and then went on the road to defeat the Kansas City Chiefs and the Pittsburgh Steelers in the AFC championship to advance to Super Bowl XXXII against the favored Green Bay Packers, the defending champions. Elway led the Broncos 49 yards in five plays for the winning touchdown. He completed 12 of 22 passes for 123 yards and rushed for 17 yards and scored one touchdown.

In Super Bowl XXXIII against the Atlanta Falcons, Elway completed 18 of 29 passes for 336 yards and one touchdown. He was named the game's Most Valuable Player.

Elway debated whether to continue his career, but retired in April 1999. In 16 seasons, he completed 56.9 percent of his passes for 51,475 yards and 300 touchdowns. Through the 2000 season, he ranked second all-time in passing yardage and third all-time in touchdown passes.

He is one of only two quarterbacks in NFL history to throw for 40,000 and rush for 3,000 yards. Fran Tarkenton is the other. Elway is the only player to pass for 3,000 yards and rush for 200 yards in the same season. He did it nine times. Three times (1985, '93, '95), he accounted for more than 4,000 yards total offense. Elway rushed for 3,407 yards in the regular season and another 495 in the postseason.

Elway is second all-time in Super Bowl passing yardage (1,228) and tied for third all-time in touchdowns (4).

In the postseason, Elway is second all-time in passing yardage (4,964), third in attempts (651), and third in completions (355).

Elway was a nine-time Pro Bowl selection.

Favre, Brett
Born: October 10, 1969 in Gulfport, Mississippi

Brett Favre was a quarterback with the mentality of a linebacker. He was tough, fearless, and played with a swagger and confidence that allowed him to be one of the best of his time.

Favre was blessed with a strong arm and the ability to throw from the pocket or on the run. He gambles sometimes, but often his risks result in rewards.

Favre played his college ball at Southern Mississippi University (1987–90), where he set school records for passing yards, attempts, completions, completion percentage, and touchdowns. During the summer before his senior year, he was in a serious car accident, resulting in 30 inches of his intestines being removed. He returned to lead Southern Mississippi to an 8–3 record and a berth in the All-American Bowl. He was the game's Most Valuable Player.

Favre was a second-round pick of the Atlanta Falcons in the 1991 NFL draft. After one season, he was traded to the Green Bay Packers. In the first quarter of the third game of the year, he replaced Don Majkowski, who was injured. Favre never relinquished the starting job. He set a team single-season mark for completion percentage (64.1) and was named to the Pro Bowl team.

In 1995, Favre won the first of his three consecutive Most Valuable Player Awards. He led the league in passing with 4,413 yards and 38 touchdowns. In 1996, he led the NFC in passing with 3,899 yards and 38 touchdowns. In 1997, he threw for 3,867 yards and 35 touchdowns. He shared the 1997 Most Valuable Player award with Barry Sanders of the Detroit Lions.

Favre deserves much of the credit for restoring the Green Bay franchise to the elite level in the NFL. The Packers made the playoffs in 1993 for the first time since 1982 and for the second time since 1972. They reached the NFC championship game in 1995, losing to the Dallas Cowboys. In 1996, they reached Super Bowl XXXI, where they defeated the New England Patriots 35–21. It was the Packers' first league championship since 1967.

In 1998, Favre led the NFL in passing yards (4,212) and completion percentage (62.9). He threw 31 touchdown passes and led the Packers to Super Bowl XXXII, where they lost to the Denver Broncos 31–24.

The Packers failed to make the playoffs in 1999. Favre was hampered for much of the season by a thumb injury. He threw for 4,091 yards and 22 touchdowns. But he was sacked 35 times and threw 23 interceptions.

Through the 2000 season, Favre, a five-time Pro Bowl player, completed 61.1 percent of his passes for 34,706 yards, 258 touchdowns, and 141 interceptions. He ranked 13th all-time in yardage and eighth all-time in touchdown passes. His five straight seasons (1994–98) with 30 or more touchdown passes is an NFL record.

Fears, Tom

Born: December 3, 1922 in Guadalajara, Mexico
Died: January 4, 2000

Tom Fears began his NFL career as a defensive back for the Los Angeles Rams in 1948, even though he was a wide receiver at Santa Clara and UCLA, where he played his college ball. But he was soon switched back to wide receiver, and he made an impact throughout his career.

Fears wasn't fast, but he had good hands, used his size (6-2, 216) to advantage, and ran precise routes.

Fears led the NFL in receiving for three consecutive seasons, starting in 1948, his rookie year. He caught 51 for 698 yards and four touchdowns in 1948; 77 for 1,013 yards and nine touchdowns in 1949; and 84 for 1,116 yards and seven touchdowns in 1950. The 84 catches were a single-season high. His 18 catches against the Green Bay Packers in 1950 was a single-game high through the 1999 season.

Fears helped the Rams reach the NFL championship game in 1949 and 1950. In 1951, his 73-yard touchdown catch lifted the Rams over the Cleveland Browns for the title.

Fears retired early in the 1956 season. He had 400 catches for 5,397 yards and 38 touchdowns. He was a two-time All-Pro and was inducted into the Pro Football Hall of Fame in 1970.

Fouts, Dan

Born: June 10, 1951 in San Francisco, California

Dan Fouts was chosen in the third round of the 1973 NFL draft by the San Diego Chargers, after a solid career at the University of Oregon. At 6-3, 204 pounds, he wasn't particularly athletic, nor was he blessed with great arm strength. He became the Chargers quarterback during his rookie season, but it wasn't until Don Coryell took over as head coach in 1978 that Fouts blossomed into one of the NFL's great quarterbacks.

Coryell instituted an offense that relied on the pass. "Air Coryell," as it was called, proved to be the perfect fit for Fouts' talents.

Because of Fouts' quick release, the touch he put on the ball, and his ability to thread the ball between seams in the zone, the Chargers offense flourished.

In 1979, Fouts led the AFC in passing, completing 63 percent of his throws for 4,082 yards (single-season record at the time) and 24 touchdowns. He was named AFC Player of the Year.

In 1980, he threw for 4,715 yards and in 1981, 4,802 yards (second all-time through the 1999 season). Until he retired after the 1987 season, Fouts never threw for fewer than 2,500 yards.

Twice Fouts led the Chargers to the brink of the Super Bowl. They lost to the Oakland Raiders in the 1980 AFC title game, and to the Cincinnati Bengals the following year.

Fouts, a six-time Pro Bowl player, completed 59 percent of his passes for 43,040 yards and 254 touchdowns. Through the 2000 season, he ranked fifth all-time in yardage and 10th all-time in touchdown passes. He was ranked ninth all-time in passes intercepted (242).

Fouts, who was inducted into the Pro Football Hall of Fame in 1993, worked as a pro football analyst for NBC

Sports and then moved to ABC Sports, where he was the lead analyst on college football games. In July 2000, he was named to the broadcast team for ABC's *Monday Night Football*.

George, Bill

Born: October 27, 1930 in Waynesburg, Pennsylvania

Died: September 30, 1982

Bill George was a pioneer who invented the middle linebacker position and changed the game in the process.

He joined the Chicago Bears in 1952 after a college career at Wake Forest. George, a tackle at Wake Forest, was switched to middle guard by the Bears. During his rookie year, in a game against the Philadelphia Eagles, George got up out of his three-point stance, moved a step or two back off the line of scrimmage, and played as a third linebacker. He was able to defend against the run because of his size (6-2, 237 pounds) and strength, and stop short passes because of his speed and quickness.

George, a highly intelligent player and a student of the game, was expert in calling the Bears' defensive signals. Many a quarterback was rattled by George's ability to find just the right scheme.

George, who was known for his crewcut, spent from 1952 through 1965 with the Bears. In 1966, he joined the Los Angeles Rams and retired after that season. He had 18 career interceptions.

He was an All-Pro eight straight years, starting in 1955, and appeared in eight Pro Bowls. George was inducted into the Pro Football Hall of Fame in 1974.

Gifford, Frank

Born: August 16, 1930 in Santa Monica, California

Frank Gifford was a versatile performer and one of the most popular players of his time. After an All-American career at the University of Southern California, he was a first-round draft choice of the New York Giants in 1952.

He was primarily a defensive back during his rookie season, but in 1953, he played offense, defense, and returned punts. When Vince Lombardi took over as offensive coordinator in 1954, Gifford was moved to offense.

In 1956, Gifford rushed for 819 yards, caught 51 passes for 603 yards, and scored nine touchdowns. He was named the NFL's Player of the Year.

After he suffered a concussion, caused by a violent tackle by Philadelphia Eagles linebacker Chuck Bednarik, Gifford announced his retirement following the 1961 season. But he returned to the Giants a year later and played three more seasons, all at flanker, before retiring for good in 1964.

Gifford rushed for 3,609 yards, caught 367 passes for 6,144 yards, and scored 43 touchdowns. He was a four-time All-Pro and a seven-time Pro Bowl player. He was inducted into the Pro Football Hall of Fame in 1977.

Gifford, who worked as an announcer while he was still a player, became an analyst for CBS Sports before moving to ABC Sports in 1971, where he worked on *Monday Night Football* until 1999.

Graham, Otto

Born: December 6, 1921 in Waukegan, Illinois

If it's true that quarterbacks are judged by the number of championships they win, then Otto Graham ranks among the best ever.

Graham went to Northwestern, where he was an All-American in football and basketball in 1943–44. After spending two years in the Navy, he joined the Cleveland Browns, a charter member of the All-American Football Conference (AAFC), which began play in 1946.

Graham played for legendary coach Paul Brown, who installed the T-formation offense that relied on motion and misdirection and maximized Graham's ability to scramble and make quick decisions.

Graham, nicknamed "Automatic Otto," didn't have the strongest arm, nor was he a physical specimen, but the accuracy and leadership he displayed more than compensated. He led the Browns to four straight AAFC titles, and from 1946 through 1949 compiled a 52–4–3 record.

In 1950, the Browns joined the National Football League, and Graham picked up right where he had left off in the AAFC, despite those who doubted the Browns could match up with the stronger competition in the NFL

He led the Browns to the 1950 NFL title, a 30–28 thriller over the Los Angeles Rams in which he threw four touchdown passes. The Browns lost the 1951 and 1952 title games to Los Angeles and the Detroit Lions, respectively, but returned in 1954 to rout the Lions 56–10. After Brown convinced Graham not to retire after the 1954 season, Graham threw for two touchdowns and ran for two more in the 1955 championship game, a 38–14 victory over the Rams.

Overall, Graham led his teams to seven league championships and 10 title-game appearances in his 10 seasons. During that time, he led his team to 105 wins, 17 losses, and four ties.

Graham was all-AAFC in each of his four years in the league, and he was an NFL All-Pro in 1951, 1953, 1954, and 1955, including the league's Most Valuable Player in 1953 and 1955. He led the NFL in completion percentage three times (1953–55), in yards twice (1952–53), and in touchdown passes once (1952).

In his 10 pro seasons (AAFC, NFL combined), Graham completed 56 percent of his passes for 23,584 yards and 174 touchdowns. He also scored 44 touchdowns rushing.

Graham went on to coach at the Coast Guard Academy and the Washington Redskins, where he was 17–22–3 in four seasons. He returned to the Coast Guard Academy as athletic director in 1970 and retired in 1984.

Graham, one of the fiercest competitors of his day, was inducted into the Pro Football Hall of Fame in 1965 and was named a member of the NFL's 75th Anniversary All-Time Team in 1994.

Grange, Red (Harold)

Born: June 13, 1903 in Forksville, Pennsylvania
Died: January 28, 1991

Harold "Red" Grange was a star athlete at Wheaton High School in Wheaton, Ill., where the family moved after Grange's mother died when he was five years old. Grange earned 16 letters in football, baseball, basketball, and track. He spent his summers working on an ice truck, which increased his physique and earned him the nickname of the "Wheaton Iceman."

Grange completed his high school football career in 1921 with 75 touchdowns and 532 points in three years of varsity play. He went to the University of Illinois in 1922, where, at first, he thought about skipping football in favor of basketball and track, but some of his fraternity brothers helped convince him otherwise.

In his first varsity game against Nebraska in 1923, Grange, a sophomore, scored three touchdowns, one of which was a 66-yard punt return. In seven games that season, he rushed for 723 yards, averaged 5.6 yards a carry, and scored 12 touchdowns. The Illini won the national championship.

On October 18, 1924, Illinois and Michigan, both undefeated, met in a game that would be among Grange's most memorable. Each team was undefeated, and Grange led the Illini to a 39–14 victory. He returned the opening kickoff 95 yards for a touchdown and then scored on runs of 67, 56, and 44 yards—all in the first 12 minutes. Michigan had allowed four touchdowns in each of the previous two seasons.

Grange wasn't finished. He scored on an 11-yard run and threw a 20-yard touchdown pass. He amassed 402 yards total offense (212 rushing, 64 passing, 126 kickoff returns), almost single-handedly ending Michigan's 20-game unbeaten streak.

During his senior year, in a game against the University of Pennsylvania, Grange rushed for a career-high 237 yards, including touchdown runs of 56 and 13 yards in a 24–2 upset of the Quakers.

Grange played 20 games at Illinois. He rushed for 2,071 yards, averaged 5.3 yards a carry, caught 14 passes for 253 yards, and completed 40 of 82 passes for 575 yards. He scored 31 touchdowns, 16 from at least 20 yards out and nine from at least 50 yards out.

Grange, christened the "Galloping Ghost" by legendary sportswriter Grantland Rice, turned pro the day after his final college game. Grange's agent, C.C. "Cash and Carry" Pyle, a Champaign, Ill., theater owner, worked out a deal with George Halas, owner of the Chicago Bears, to pay Grange $3,500 a game, plus a percentage of the gate receipts.

The Bears arranged a schedule that included regular season games and exhibitions—19 games in 67 days, the first 10 of which were played in 18 days. Large crowds came to see Grange wherever he played—65,000 in New York, 75,000 in Los Angeles. His participation brought credibility to the pro game.

But the intense schedule took its toll on Grange, who was beginning to wear down.

Grange and Pyle formed the American Football League in 1926, but it lasted only one year. In the third game of the 1927 season, Grange, back in the National Football League with the New York Yankees, injured his knee and was never the same runner. He missed the entire 1928 season, and in 1929 returned to the Bears as a defensive back. His tackle of New York Giants halfback Dale Burnett at the end of the 1933 NFL championship game helped the Bears win the title, preserving a 23–21 victory. He retired after the 1934 season, and after a career in the insurance business, he became the analyst for Chicago Bears games. Grange was a charter member of the Pro Football Hall of Fame in 1963.

Green, Darrell

Born: February 15, 1960 in Houston, Texas

Darrell Green made a mark on the game the first time he touched the ball, as a rookie in 1983 with the Washington Redskins. In a preseason game against the Atlanta Falcons, Green returned a punt 61 yards for a touchdown. Ever since, he has been, if not the fastest man in the National Football League, then near the top of a very short list.

He played his college ball at Texas A&M–Kingsville where he was first-team Little All-America and the Lone Star Conference Player of the Year as a senior in 1982. He was also a track star, running a 10.08 in the 100 meters, second behind Olympic star Carl Lewis that year.

Green, a cornerback, finished second in the voting for the NFL Defensive Rookie of the Year in 1983, with 109 tackles, including a team-high 79 solo tackles.

Green, whose technique and instincts have complemented his speed, has been a mainstay in the Redskins secondary for 17 seasons through 1999. In May 2000, at age 40, he signed a new five-year contract.

Usually, cornerbacks at the relatively advanced age of 40 have long since been moved to safety, assuming they're still in the game at all. But Green continued to excel at cornerback and is one of the league's best at covering receivers. He helped the Redskins to three Super Bowls (XVI, XVIII, XXII), two of which were victories (XVI, XXII).

Green is the Redskins' all-time interception leader with 52. Through the 2000 season, he has played in seven Pro Bowls.

In addition to making an impact on the field, Green has been honored for his impact off the field, as well. In 1996, he was named the NFL's Man of the Year, an award given in recognition of his commitment to the community. He also won the Bart Starr and Ken Houston humanitarian awards.

Greene, Joe

Born: September 24, 1946 in Temple, Texas
"Mean Joe" Greene, a 6-4, 275-pound defensive tackle, was the anchor of the Pittsburgh Steelers' "Steel Curtain" defenses of the 1970s.

Greene played his college football at North Texas State and was the Steelers' first-round draft choice (fourth overall) in 1969. He was blessed with brute strength and quickness. He often was accused of being offside because of his speed off the ball.

Greene helped the Steelers to six American Football Conference championship appearances in eight years and four Super Bowl titles in six years. His role in the Steelers' first AFC Central title (1970) was typical of the impact he could have on a game. Greene had five sacks, he blocked a field goal, and he recovered a fumble in a 9-3 victory over the Houston Oilers.

Greene was named the NFL Defensive Rookie of the Year in 1969, and in 1972 and 1974 he was named the Defensive Player of the Year. He was an All-Pro eight times and played in the Pro Bowl 10 times. He was inducted into the Pro Football Hall of Fame in 1987 and was a member of the NFL's 75th Anniversary All-Time Team in 1994.

In addition to his memorable performances on the field, Greene is also famous for making one of the most memorable television commercials ever made. His ad for Coca-Cola, in which he tosses his jersey to a wide-eyed child, was a big favorite.

Gregg, Forrest

Born: October 18, 1933 in Birthright, Texas
At 6-4, 250 pounds, Forrest Gregg was considered small for an offensive tackle, but what he lacked in size, he more than compensated for with agility, intelligence, quickness, and technique.

Gregg played offensive and defensive tackle at Southern Methodist University, and when he joined the Green Bay Packers in 1956, he was expected to play defense. But he became an offensive tackle who also played guard when injuries dictated.

Gregg became a student of the game, studying films of great players such as Jim Parker and Roosevelt Brown, so that he might improve his technique. Vince Lombardi, the legendary coach of the Packers, called Gregg "the finest player I ever coached."

Gregg helped the Packers win five NFL championships, including the first two Super Bowls. He retired after the 1970 season, but was lured back to the game by the Dallas Cowboys, who suffered a rash of injuries to offensive linemen. Gregg played one season for the Cowboys (1971), who won the Super Bowl after that season.

Gregg was an eight-time All-Pro who played in nine Pro Bowls. He was inducted into the Pro Football Hall of Fame in 1977. In 1994, he was named to the NFL's 75th Anniversary All-Time Team.

Gregg became a head coach of the Cleveland Browns in 1975, then was fired with one game left in the 1977 season. In 1980, he was named head coach of the Cincinnati Bengals. One year later, he was named AFC Coach of the Year as he guided the Bengals to the Super Bowl. After four seasons, he returned to Green Bay to become head coach of the Packers in 1984.

Gregg spent four seasons in Green Bay, then took the head coaching job at Southern Methodist, which had to rebuild its program because of recruiting violations. Gregg coached for two seasons, then became the athletic director at Southern Methodist.

Griese, Bob

Born: February 3, 1945 in Evansville, Indiana
Bob Griese was the perfect quarterback to run the Miami Dolphins' ball control offense in the 1970s. He was an accurate passer and an intelligent field general.

Griese was an All-American at Purdue University in 1965 and 1966. He passed for 4,402 yards and 28 touchdowns in three seasons. In 1967, the Miami Dolphins drafted him in the first round, fourth overall, and he became the starting quarterback during his rookie year.

When Don Shula became the team's head coach in 1970, he installed a ball-control offense and Griese flourished. He led the Dolphins to three straight Super Bowl appearances (VI, VII, VIII), including victories in VII and VIII.

In 1972, the 14–7 Super Bowl victory over the Washington Redskins capped a 17–0 season.

Griese twice led the AFC in passing. In 1971, he completed 55 percent of his passes for 2,089 yards and 19 touchdowns; in 1977, he completed 59 percent of his passes for 2,252 yards and 22 touchdowns. He was named the winner of the Bert Bell Award in 1977 as the NFL's Player of the Year.

Griese retired after the 1980 season. He completed 56 percent of his passes for 25,092 yards and 192 touchdowns. Through the 2000 season, he was 32nd all-time in touchdown passes.

A two-time All-Pro and a six-time Pro Bowl player, Griese was inducted into the Pro Football Hall of Fame in 1990. Through the 2000 season, he worked for ABC Sports as a college football analyst.

Griffin, Archie
Born: August 21, 1954 in Columbus, Ohio

Archie Griffin is the only player to twice win the Heisman Trophy as the nation's outstanding college football player. The Ohio State running back topped the voting in 1974, as a junior, and in 1975. Buckeyes coach Woody Hayes called Griffin "the greatest football player I've ever coached."

Griffin combined power, speed, and the ability to break numerous tackles on a single play.

In three seasons at Ohio State, Griffin rushed for a then record 5,177 yards, a 6.1-yard-per-carry average. He was the first player in college football history to eclipse the 5,000-yard mark.

Griffin set an NCAA record for consecutive 100-yard games with 31.

Griffin did not enjoy similar success in the NFL. He joined the Cincinnati Bengals, for whom he played eight seasons. He rushed for a 4.1-yard average and seven touchdowns. He retired after the 1982 season, made a comeback in 1985 with the Jacksonville Bulls of the United States Football League, then retired for good after carrying the ball only 10 times for Jacksonville.

Through the 1999 season, Griffin was an associate director of athletics at Ohio State.

Groza, Lou
Born: January 25, 1924 in Martins Ferry, Ohio
Died: November 29, 2000

Lou Groza was the first great kicker in pro football history, and in an unusual combination of positions, he also had a solid career as a starting offensive tackle for the Cleveland Browns.

Groza, who played his college ball at Ohio State, spent three years with the Browns in the All-American Football Conference, leading the league in scoring with 84 points during his rookie year.

When the AAFC folded in 1950, the Browns joined the NFL, and Groza became a placekicking mainstay.

In 1950, the Browns won the NFL championship when he kicked a 16-yard field goal with 28 seconds left in the title game to beat the Los Angeles Rams.

Groza was an All-Pro at tackle six times from 1951 to 1957, and he led the league in field goals five times in the same stretch. At 6-3, 240 pounds, he looked much more the part of a tackle than a placekicker, but he excelled at both. He approached kicking as if it were a science, working on his technique tirelessly. He was accurate from as far away as midfield and was an effective weapon for head coach Paul Brown in a time when field goals were not regularly attempted.

Groza, nicknamed "The Toe," wore trademark high-top black shoes. He concentrated on kicking from 1959 on. He continued to be productive until his retirement in 1967.

He played 21 seasons, all with the Browns, and converted on 97 percent of his extra-point tries and 55 percent of his field goal attempts. He totaled 1,608 points, which was seventh all-time through the 1999 season. Groza was inducted into the Pro Football Hall of Fame in 1974.

Ham, Jack
Born: December 23, 1948 in Johnstown, Pennsylvania

Jack Ham, who favored brains over brawn, was one of the most intelligent and effective linebackers of his era. He was blessed with speed, quickness, and the knack for making the big play.

Jack Ham

Ham played his college ball at Penn State, dubbed "Linebacker U." Ham helped continue the tradition. He was a consensus All-American in 1970 and was the second-round draft choice of the Pittsburgh Steelers in 1971.

He was an outside linebacker on the famed "Steel Curtain" defense, one of the best in National Football League history. He was tough enough to stop the run and fast enough to cover running backs and tight ends on pass patterns. He recovered 19 fumbles and had 32 career interceptions.

Ham, whose personality was low-key, did not seek the limelight, preferring instead to let others claim the credit. Because of his blue-collar mentality, he was a crowd favorite in Pittsburgh.

Ham helped the Steelers to victories in four Super Bowls (IX, X, XIII, XIV) in a six-season span (1974–79). He was a seven-time All-Pro and an eight-time Pro Bowl selection. He was inducted into the Pro Football Hall of Fame in 1988 and was named to the NFL's 75th Anniversary All-Time Team in 1994. Through the 2000 season, he was a pro football analyst on CBS Radio, and in June 2000 he was named the analyst for Penn State football radio broadcasts.

Hannah, John

Born: April 4, 1951 in Canton, Georgia

John Hannah was big (6-2, 265 pounds), agile, powerful, and intense. That combination made him a dominating offensive lineman. He was a consensus All-American in 1972 at Alabama, where he also lettered in track and wrestling.

In 1973, he was the first-round draft choice of the New England Patriots, and he became a starter as a rookie. Hannah spent his entire career with the Patriots. He retired after the 1985 season, when the team made it to the Super Bowl, losing to the Chicago Bears 46–10.

Hannah was a four-time All-Pro and a nine-time Pro Bowl player. He was inducted into the Pro Football Hall of Fame in 1991. In 1994, he was named to the NFL's 75th Anniversary All-Time Team.

Harris, Franco

Born: March 7, 1950 in Fort Dix, New Jersey

While at Penn State, Franco Harris was the less-heralded half of a backfield that also included Lydell Mitchell. Harris rushed for 2,002 yards and scored 24 touchdowns in three seasons for the Nittany Lions, which was enough to get the attention of the Pittsburgh Steelers, who selected Harris in the first round of the 1972 NFL draft.

Once with the Steelers, Harris became one of the most acclaimed backs of his era. At 6-2, 230 pounds, Harris was big enough to get the tough yards, but it was his

Franco Harris *Diane Staskowski*

speed and agility that set him apart. He was blessed with great balance and the ability to change directions. The combination made him a much more dangerous runner than his physique suggested.

Harris gained 1,055 yards, averaged 5.6 yards a carry, and scored 10 touchdowns in 1972, and was named the NFL's Rookie of the Year. He gained 1,000 yards or more in a season eight times and 100 yards or more in a game 47 times.

Harris was part of the Pittsburgh Steelers dynasty that won four Super Bowls in six seasons (1974–75, '78–79). In the Steelers' Super Bowl IX victory over the Minnesota Vikings, Harris was named the game's Most Valuable Player. He rushed for 158 yards on 34 carries and scored one touchdown.

Harris was responsible for one of the most famous plays in NFL history—the "Immaculate Reception" in a first-round AFC playoff game in 1972. With the Oakland Raiders leading Pittsburgh 7–6 with five seconds to play, Steelers quarterback Terry Bradshaw threw a pass that bounced off the shoulder of defensive back Jack Tatum. Harris snared the ball just before it hit the ground and returned for a game-winning touchdown. The win was the first ever in the postseason for Pittsburgh.

Harris spent 12 of his 13 seasons with the Steelers. His final season, 1984, was spent with the Seattle Seahawks.

Harris rushed for 12,120 yards, averaged 4.1 yards a carry, and scored 91 touchdowns rushing. Through the 2000 season, he ranked eighth all-time in rushing and 12th all-time in touchdowns (100).

Through Super Bowl XXXII (2001), he was the all-time leader in career Super Bowl rushing with 354 yards and tied for third all-time in touchdowns (4). He is also first all-time in postseason rushing with 1,556 yards.

Harris, once an All-Pro and a nine-time Pro Bowl player, was inducted into the Pro Football Hall of Fame in 1990.

Hart, Leon

Born: November 2, 1928 in Turtle Creek, Pennsylvania

Leon Hart was the second—and last—lineman to win the Heisman Trophy as the nation's outstanding college football player while at Notre Dame. Hart, who went from 245 pounds as a freshman to 265 as a senior, was a punishing blocker, an effective receiver, and a solid defender. He was so tough to bring down that he often lined up as a fullback or ran the end-around.

Hart was an All-American during each of his three seasons (1947–49). In addition to winning the Heisman in 1949, he also was named the Associated Press Athlete of the Year and won the Maxwell Award as the best college football player in the country.

The Fighting Irish went 36–0–2 during Hart's three seasons. He caught 49 passes for 742 yards and 13 touchdowns in his college career. He also rushed for two touchdowns.

In 1950, Hart joined the Detroit Lions and played offense and defense. He helped the Lions with the NFL championship in 1952, 1953, and 1957. He retired after the 1957 season. He caught 174 passes for 2,499 yards and 26 touchdowns.

Haynes, Mike

Born: July 1, 1953 in Denison, Texas

Mike Haynes was the quintessential defensive back. He was blessed with size (6-2, 192), speed, athleticism, and intelligence. He spent hours watching film and was a tireless worker in practice. The result was, come Sunday afternoons, there was nothing he wasn't ready for.

Haynes began his career with the New England Patriots in 1976, when he intercepted eight passes and returned two for touchdowns. He also led the AFC in punt return yardage with 608 and was named the NFL's Defensive Rookie of the Year.

Haynes' reputation was such that most quarterbacks avoided throwing his way entirely. That reputation was enhanced when he joined the Los Angeles Raiders in 1983, and with Lester Hayes formed one of the most intimidating cornerback tandems in NFL history.

Haynes helped the Raiders reach Super Bowl XXVIII, a 38–9 rout of the Washington Redskins. He retired after the 1989 season with 46 career interceptions for 1,168 yards and two touchdowns. He was a four-time All-Pro and a nine-time Pro Bowl selection, who was inducted into the Pro Football Hall of Fame in 1997 and named to the NFL's 75th Anniversary All-Time Team in 1994.

Hein, Mel

Born: August 22, 1909 in Redding, California
Died: January 31, 1992

Mel Hein was the ironman of the National Football League. A center for the New York Giants, he played in every minute of every game for 15 seasons.

Hein played his college ball at Washington State, where he was a consensus All-American in 1930 as a senior. Because there was no draft at the time, Hein agreed to play for the Providence Steamrollers for $135. But when the New York Giants offered $150, he requested of the postmaster in Providence that the letter be returned to him.

Hein, who played center, guard, and tackle in college, was a center with the Giants, and he became the prototype for the position as it's played today. He played linebacker on defense and was known for his ability to defend against the pass and his jarring tackles.

Hein helped the Giants reach the NFL championship game seven times, including victories in 1934 and 1938.

He was an All-Pro for eight straight years, starting in 1933. In 1938, he was named the league's Most Valuable Player. He also played in four Pro Bowls, a game that didn't begin until late in his career.

Hein was inducted into the Pro Football Hall of Fame in 1963 and was named to the NFL's 75th Anniversary All-Time Team in 1994.

Hendricks, Ted

Born: November 1, 1947 in Guatemala City, Guatemala

Ted Hendricks wasn't built like the prototype linebacker. At 6-7, 220 pounds, he was thought to be too tall and too light to make an impact in the National Football League, but he was one of the most talented outside linebackers ever.

Hendricks, nicknamed "The Mad Stork" because of his size, played his college ball at the University of Miami, where he was a consensus All-American at defensive end as a junior and senior in 1967 and 1968. The Baltimore Colts drafted him in the second round in 1969 and shifted him to outside linebacker, where he excelled, knocking down passes, blitzing the quarterback, and stopping the run. He made 26 career interceptions and was adept at blocking kicks.

Hendricks helped the Colts reach Super Bowl V, which they won 16–13 over the Dallas Cowboys.

In 1974, Hendricks signed with the rival World Football League; as a result the Colts traded him to the Green Bay Packers for the 1974 season. The World Football League had financial problems, and Hendricks never played in the league. He signed with the Oakland Raiders in 1975 as a free agent.

He spent nine seasons with the Raiders, helping them to victories in three Super Bowls (XI, XV, XVIII).

Hendricks was a six-time All-Pro and an eight-time Pro Bowl selection. He was inducted into the Pro Football Hall of Fame in 1990 and was named to the NFL's 75th Anniversary All-Time Team in 1994.

Hirsch, Elroy

Born: June 17, 1923 in Wausau, Wisconsin

Elroy "Crazy Legs" Hirsch was a halfback at the University of Wisconsin in 1942. He finished ninth in the nation in rushing that year, averaging 5.5 yards a carry. In 1943, military training meant that he had to be transferred to the University of Michigan, where he played for one year.

He spent three years in the service, then signed with the Chicago Rockets of the All-American Football Conference, but in 1948 a fractured skull suggested his career was in jeopardy.

In 1949, he joined the Los Angeles Rams of the NFL and, thanks to protective head gear, developed into one of the best receivers of his era. Hirsch was a running back in 1949, but in 1950 he was switched to wide receiver. He became one of the first ends to split wide and operate as a flanker.

Hirsch caught 42 passes for 687 yards and seven touchdowns in 1950. In 1951, Hirsch led the NFL in receiving with 66 catches for 1,495 yards and 17 touchdowns, nine of which were 44 yards or longer. His 22.7-yard-per-catch average is the second-highest in NFL history.

Hirsch helped the Rams win the 1951 NFL championship, the last in franchise history.

Hirsch retired after the 1954 season, but made a comeback in 1955, when the Rams were hit with a rash of injuries. He played three more seasons, retiring in 1957. He caught 387 passes for 7,029 yards, an 18.4-yard average, and 60 touchdowns.

Hirsch, who was Wisconsin's athletic director from 1969 to 1987, was inducted into the Pro Football Hall of Fame in 1968.

Hornung, Paul

Born: December 23, 1935 in Louisville, Kentucky

Paul Hornung, known as the "Golden Boy," played his college football at Notre Dame, where he started his career as a fullback and ended it as a quarterback. He was a consensus All-American in 1955, and in 1956, he won the Heisman Trophy as the nation's most outstanding player. He was also the only Heisman winner to play on a losing team, as the Fighting Irish were 2–8.

Hornung was a bonus draft pick of the Green Bay Packers in 1957, and for his first several years with the Packers, he played quarterback, halfback, fullback, and tight end.

It wasn't until Vince Lombardi became the team's head coach that Hornung was limited to one position—starting halfback. He also was the placekicker.

Hornung led the NFL in scoring for three consecutive years, beginning in 1959 (94 points). In 1960, he totaled 176 points on 15 touchdowns, 15 field goals, and 41 extra points. In 1961, he totaled 146 points on 10 touchdowns, 15 field goals, and 41 extra points. Through the 2000 season, the 176 points was a single-season NFL record. The 146 points was the eighth-highest all-time total. In 1961, he helped the Packers win the NFL championship. In the title game against the New York Giants, he scored a record 19 points in a 37–0 victory. He was named the NFL's Most Valuable Player.

Injuries hampered Hornung for most of the 1962 season, and in 1963, he sat out for another reason: gambling. He and Alex Karras, a defensive lineman for the Detroit Lions, were suspended indefinitely because they bet on games and associated with undesirables.

The suspension was lifted in 1964, and Hornung returned to score 104 points. He played two more seasons, both of which were injury-plagued, before retiring in 1966.

Hornung, who played nine seasons, rushed for 3,711 yards and 50 touchdowns, and caught 130 passes for 12 touchdowns. He scored 62 touchdowns and kicked 66 field goals and 190 extra points for a total of 760 points.

A two-time Pro Bowl selection, Hornung was inducted into the Pro Football Hall of Fame in 1986. He worked as a football analyst for CBS Sports and for Notre Dame broadcasts.

Houston, Ken

Born: November 12, 1944 in Lufkin, Texas

Ken Houston, a linebacker at Prairie View A&M, was a ninth-round draft choice by the Houston Oilers in 1967. At 6-3, 198 pounds, he had the size and speed necessary to play strong safety, so he was switched and went on to become one of the best ever to play the position. He was strong enough to stop the run and quick enough to be an excellent pass defender. He was also blessed with great instincts.

With the Oilers in a rebuilding phase, Houston was traded to the Washington Redskins after the 1972 season. He became the Redskins captain and their defensive signal caller.

Houston had 49 career interceptions and returned them for 898 yards. His nine interception returns for touchdowns was an NFL record through the 2000 season.

Houston was a five-time All-Pro and a 12-time Pro Bowl player. He was inducted into the Pro Football Hall of Fame in 1986, and he was named to the NFL's 75th Anniversary All-Time Team in 1994.

Huff, Sam

Born: October 4, 1934 in Morgantown,
West Virginia

What Sam Huff lacked in size (6-1, 230 pounds) and strength, he more than made up for with toughness, determination, and keen instincts. He was always around the ball, usually finishing off plays with punishing tackles.

Huff played his college ball at the University of West Virginia, where he played tackle. He joined the New York Giants in 1956 and was moved to middle linebacker. He was best against the run, but he defended the pass well enough to intercept 30 passes during his 13-year career.

Huff became one of the most recognizable players in the game and one of the first defensive players to earn national acclaim. He appeared on the cover of *Time* magazine and was the subject of a CBS documentary, *The Violent World of Sam Huff*.

His encounters with Jim Brown of the Cleveland Browns and Jim Taylor of the Green Bay Packers helped heighten his profile.

Huff, a favorite with Giants fans, was traded to the Washington Redskins in 1964. He spent five seasons with the Redskins. After the 1967 season he retired, but he returned in 1969 as a player-coach for Vince Lombardi. Huff retired for good in 1969.

Huff was a two-time All-Pro and played in five Pro Bowls. He was inducted into the Pro Football Hall of Fame in 1982.

Hutson, Don

Born: January 31, 1913 in Pine Bluff, Arkansas
Died: June 26, 1997

Don Hutson, a tall, skinny wide receiver, helped change professional football by making the forward pass an offensive staple. Hutson was blessed with elusiveness, great speed, big hands, a long reach, and superior jumping ability.

After graduating from the University of Alabama in 1935, where he was an All-American as a senior, as well as the star of the Crimson Tide's 29–13 Rose Bowl victory over Stanford, Hutson, nicknamed the "Alabama Antelope," joined the Green Bay Packers. There was no player draft in those days, and only two teams—the Packers and the Brooklyn Dodgers—expressed interest in Hutson. He signed contracts with both. NFL president Joe Carr decided that whichever team's contract reached the NFL office first would be the team to get Hutson. Green Bay's postmark was 17 minutes earlier.

Hutson joined the NFL at a most opportune time: one year after the league decreased the circumference of the football, making it easier to throw. He made an impact on the first play of his career, when he caught an 83-yard touchdown pass in a 7–0 win over the Chicago Bears.

Hutson led the league in catches eight times, touchdowns nine times, receiving yardage seven times, and scoring five times. Hutson was also an accomplished placekicker, scoring 193 points in his career.

In 1941 and 1942, Hutson was named the league's Most Valuable Player. He caught 58 and 74 passes, respectively. The runner-up in receptions each season didn't exceed 30. He was the first receiver to gain more than 1,000 yards (1,211 in 1942). Hutson was dominant receiver, despite being double- and triple-teamed.

He is the first receiver credited with running precise, defined routes, and his ability to change directions and fake defenders made him almost impossible to cover.

Hutson played for 11 seasons. When he retired in 1945, he held virtually every NFL receiving record—catches in a game (14), in a season (74, 1942), in a career (488); touchdown catches in a game (4), in a season (17, 1942), in a career (99); most yards receiving in a game (237), in a season (1,211, 1942), in a career (8,010); most touchdown catches in playoff games (9); and yards per catch (16.4).

He had a consecutive streak of 95 games with at least one catch. Through the 1999 season, his 24.9-yards-per-catch average was the highest single-season mark in NFL history.

Hutson also caught balls on defense. As a defensive back, he had 30 interceptions.

Hutson, a nine-time All-Pro, was a member of three championship teams in Green Bay. He was inducted into the Pro Football Hall of Fame as a charter member in 1963 and was named a member of the NFL's 75th Anniversary All-Time Team in 1994.

Joiner, Charlie
Born: October 14, 1947 in Many, Louisiana

Charlie Joiner was a technician, a wide receiver who excelled in the NFL, thanks to intelligence, precise routes, and unfailing instincts. Joiner, thought by many to be too small (5-11, 188 pounds) to make a contribution in the NFL, was called "the most intelligent and perceptive receiver the game has ever seen," by legendary coach Bill Walsh.

Joiner played his college ball at Grambling State, where he was a defensive back. The Houston Oilers drafted him in 1969 and switched him to wide receiver. He was traded to the Cincinnati Bengals in 1972, then to the San Diego Chargers in 1976, when he joined an offense that could take advantage of his skills.

The Chargers, coached by Don Coryell, employed a pass-happy offense known as "Air Coryell." With quarterback Dan Fouts at the helm, Joiner prospered. He had a knack for finding the open spots in a defense, and he rarely dropped anything thrown his way. He was also durable, playing in 180 games over his 17-year career.

Joiner retired after the 1986 season as the all-time leader in receptions with 750, a record that has since been broken. He had 12,162 receiving yards, 65 touchdowns, and averaged 16.2 yards a catch. Through the 2000 season, Joiner ranked 10th all-time in catches and eighth all-time in yardage.

A three-time Pro Bowl player, Joiner was inducted into the Pro Football Hall of Fame in 1996.

Jones, Deacon (David)
Born: December 9, 1938 in Eatonville, Florida

As a 14th-round draft choice out of Mississippi Valley State in 1961 by the Los Angeles Rams, not much was expected of David Jones, but it didn't take long for him to prove otherwise.

Jones, 6-5, 272 pounds, developed into one of the most feared defensive ends in the history of the National Football League. He was blessed with explosive speed and strength, a combination that terrorized quarterbacks and running backs throughout his 14-year career.

Jones, who gave himself the nickname "Deacon" for no other reason than he considered David "too common," was the leader of the Rams' defensive line dubbed the "Fearsome Foursome." It also included Merlin Olsen, Lamar Lundy, and Roosevelt Grier. When teams tried to double- or triple-team Jones, it freed up one of the other members of the "Fearsome Foursome" to make the play.

Jones is responsible for coining the term "sack," as it relates to tackling a quarterback, and he also invented the head slap, a pass-rushing maneuver that was eventually outlawed by the NFL. Although sacks were not kept as an official statistic until 1982, Jones was credited with 26 sacks in 1967.

Jones left the Rams in 1972 and spent two seasons with the San Diego Chargers. He finished his career with the Washington Redskins, retiring after the 1974 season. In 14 years, he missed only three games.

Jones was an All-Pro six times and a Pro Bowl player eight times. He was inducted into the Pro Football Hall of Fame in 1980 and was named a member of the NFL's 75th Anniversary All-Time Team in 1994.

Jurgensen, Sonny (Christian)
Born: August 23, 1934 in Wilmington, North Carolina

Sonny Jurgensen played his college ball at Duke University, where he was a star quarterback. He was drafted by the Philadelphia Eagles in the fourth round of the 1957 NFL draft. He was a backup for four seasons with the Eagles and took over as the starter in 1961, after the retirement of Norm Van Brocklin.

Jurgensen threw for a record 3,723 yards and a record-tying 32 touchdowns in 1961. In 1964, the Eagles traded him to the Washington Redskins. He led the league in passing in 1967 (3,747 yards, 31 touchdowns), 1969 (3,102, 22), and 1974 (1,185, 11).

Jurgensen spent his last two seasons as a backup to Billy Kilmer. He retired after the 1974 season.

In 18 seasons, Jurgensen completed 57 percent of his passes for 32,224 yards and 255 touchdowns. Through the 2000 season, Jurgensen, who was a member of the Redskins broadcast team, ranked 20th all-time in yardage and eighth all-time in touchdown passes. He was a two-time All-Pro, a five-time Pro Bowl selection, and was inducted into the Pro Football Hall of Fame in 1983.

Kelly, Leroy
Born: May 20, 1942 in Philadelphia, Pennsylvania

After playing his college ball at Morgan State University, Leroy Kelly was drafted in the eighth round by the Cleveland Browns in 1964. He became the starter at running back in 1966 and rushed for 1,000 yards or more in each of his first three years as a starter. He led the NFL in rushing in 1967 (1,205 yards) and 1968 (1,239 yards, 16 touchdowns). In 1967, he also led the league in average yards per carry (5.1) and touchdowns (11), and in 1968 he won the Bert Bell Award as the league's Most Valuable Player.

Kelly played 10 seasons with the Browns, retiring in 1974. He rushed for 7,274 yards and 74 touchdowns. In 1965 and 1971, he led the NFL in punt returns.

Kelly was a five-time All-Pro and a six-time Pro Bowl player. He was inducted into the Pro Football Hall of Fame in 1994.

Krause, Paul

Born: February 19, 1942 in Flint, Michigan

Paul Krause, who played his college ball at the University of Iowa, was drafted in the second round by the Washington Redskins in 1964. He led the NFL in interceptions in his rookie year with 12. In 1968, he was traded to the Minnesota Vikings.

Krause was an integral part of the defense that helped Minnesota reach the Super Bowl four times (1969, '73–74, '76).

Krause retired after the 1979 season with 81 interceptions. Through the 2000 season, he was the all-time leader.

Krause was a four-time All-Pro and an eight-time Pro Bowl selection. He was inducted into the Pro Football Hall of Fame in 1998.

Lambert, Jack

Born: July 8, 1952 in Mantua, Ohio

From his middle linebacker position, Jack Lambert was one of the leaders of the Pittsburgh Steelers' famed "Steel Curtain" defense of the 1970s. He was a ferocious tackler whose intensity and intelligence made him an intimidating force.

Lambert was the Steelers' second-round draft choice in 1974 out of Kent State. He was taller (6-4) and lighter (220) than most middle linebackers, but he was also faster and quicker. He was solid against the run, but what set him apart was his ability to defend against the pass. His speed allowed him to cover tight ends and running backs. He had 28 career interceptions.

In 1974, Lambert was the only rookie to start for the Steelers, who won the Super Bowl, beating the Minnesota Vikings. He was named Defensive Rookie of the Year.

Lambert, a key player on one of the great defenses in NFL history, helped the Steelers to three more Super Bowl championships—1975 season, 1978 season, 1979 season. In 1976, when he recovered seven fumbles, he was named Defensive Player of the Year.

Lambert, a six-time All-Pro who played in nine Pro Bowls, was inducted into the Pro Football Hall of Fame in 1990. In 1994, he was named to the NFL's 75th Anniversary All-Time Team.

Lane, Dick

Born: April 16, 1928 in Austin, Texas

When the Los Angeles Rams gave Dick "Night Train" Lane a tryout in 1952, the team had no idea he would become one of the toughest and most accomplished cornerbacks in National Football League history.

After playing at Scottsbluff Junior College in Nebraska and then spending two years in the Army, Lane was given a tryout and, because of his size (6-1, 194 pounds), the Rams first used him as a wide receiver. But it wasn't long before he was moved to defensive back, and he made an impact immediately.

Lane, who got his nickname from the popular song of the same name, had 14 interceptions in his rookie season, which is an NFL all-time single-season record.

After the 1953 season, Lane was traded to the Chicago Cardinals, and he led the league in 1954 with 10 interceptions. He finished his career with the Detroit Lions (1959–65).

Lane was blessed with athleticism and keen instincts. He also had a mean streak and a reputation as a headhunter. He often made tackles by using the face mask or by clotheslining (forearm to ball carrier's neck) players, moves that were soon outlawed by the NFL.

Lane had 68 interceptions in his career, which ranked third all-time through the 2000 season. He returned them for 1,207 yards (second all-time) and scored five touchdowns. He was a five-time All-Pro and was inducted into the Pro Football Hall of Fame in 1974. In 1994, he was named to the NFL's 75th Anniversary All-Time Team.

Lanier, Willie

Born: August 21, 1945 in Clover, Virginia

Willie Lanier was a powerfully built middle linebacker who was blessed with speed, quickness, and the ability to inflict punishing hits.

Lanier, nicknamed "Honey Bear," was a Little All-American linebacker at Morgan State University and joined the Kansas City Chiefs in 1967. He soon became the best defensive player in the American Football League and one of the best in football after the two leagues merged in 1970.

He was a ferocious run-stopper, and also quick enough to cover tight ends and running backs on pass patterns. He had 27 career interceptions.

Lanier helped the Chiefs reach Super Bowl IV in 1970, when they upset the Minnesota Vikings 23–7.

He retired following the 1977 season. Lanier was named All-AFL or All-American Football Conference seven times, and he appeared in eight Pro Bowls. He was inducted into the Pro Football Hall of Fame in 1986 and was named to the NFL's 75th Anniversary All-Time Team in 1994.

Largent, Steve

Born: September 28, 1954 in Tulsa, Oklahoma

Steve Largent wasn't particularly big (5-11, 187 pounds); he wasn't blessed with great speed; nor was he athletic.

But he was one of the most productive receivers in the history of the National Football League.

Largent was a three-year starter at the University of Tulsa, where he led the nation in touchdown receptions in 1974 and 1975 (14 each year).

He was a fourth-round draft choice of the Houston Oilers in 1976 and was traded to the Seattle Seahawks before the season started. He spent his entire career, 14 years, with the Seahawks.

What Largent lacked in size and speed, he made up for with great hands, deceptive moves, and total concentration. There was no shortage of ways Largent used to elude defensive backs.

Largent caught at least 66 passes in each season from 1977 through 1986, except for 1982, which was shortened by a strike.

In 1989, an elbow injury caused him to miss six games, and he retired after the season as the NFL's all-time leader in receptions (819), touchdown reception (100), and yards (13,089). Through the 2000 season, he ranked seventh all-time in receptions, fourth in touchdown receptions, and fifth in yards. His eight 1,000-yard seasons ranked second to Jerry Rice (12).

Largent was twice named an All-Pro and was a seven-time Pro Bowl selection. He was inducted into the Pro Football Hall of Fame in 1995. Since 1994, he has represented Oklahoma as a Republican member of the House of Representatives.

Lary, Yale

Born: November 24, 1930 in Forth Worth, Texas

Yale Lary was a valuable member of the Detroit Lions, who won three NFL championships during his career (1952–53, '57).

Lary, who played his college ball at Texas A&M University, was drafted by the Lions in the third round of the 1952 NFL draft. He was an outstanding defensive back and punter. He was blessed with great speed and instincts that allowed him to anticipate what the quarterback and receiver would do.

As a punter, he led the NFL three times (47.1-yard average, 1959; 48.4, 1961; 48.9, 1963). His career with the Lions was interrupted by the Korean War. He missed the 1954 and 1955 seasons. He retired after the 1964 season.

In 11 seasons with the Lions, Lary had 50 interceptions, two of which he returned for touchdowns, and a 44.3-yard punting average. Through the 2000 season, he ranked fourth all-time in punting.

Lary was a four-time All-Pro and a nine-time Pro Bowl selection. He was inducted into the Pro Football Hall of Fame in 1979.

Lavelli, Dante

Born: February 23, 1923 in Hudson, Ohio

Dante Lavelli's college career at Ohio State was cut short when he was drafted after having played only three games during his freshman season. After serving in the U.S. Infantry, Lavelli was invited by coach Paul Brown to try out for the Cleveland Browns in the new All-American Football Conference (AAFC) in 1946. Brown had been Lavelli's coach at Ohio State.

In his rookie season with the Browns, Lavelli, who had great hands and ran precise routes, led the AAFC with 40 catches for 843 yards. He caught the winning touchdown pass from quarterback Otto Graham that lifted the Browns to a 14–9 victory over the New York Yanks for the AAFC championship.

Lavelli, nicknamed "Glue Fingers," was All-AAFC in 1946 and 1947.

When the AAFC folded after the 1949 season, the Browns joined the NFL, and Lavelli picked up right where he left off in the AAFC. He was an NFL All-Pro twice, and he played in three Pro Bowls.

Lavelli, who retired after the 1956 season, caught 386 passes for 6,488 yards and 62 touchdowns in his 11 seasons. He was inducted into the Pro Football Hall of Fame in 1975.

Layne, Bobby

Born: December 19, 1926 in Santa Ana, Texas
Died: December 1, 1986

Bobby Layne was as renowned for his carousing as he was for his quarterbacking. His leadership skills were in a class by themselves, and his penchant for living on the edge made him one of the game's great personalities.

Layne, who played college ball at the University of Texas, was moved from tailback to quarterback in 1947, when he led the Longhorns to a 10–1 record and a victory over Alabama in the Cotton Bowl. Overall at Texas, he completed 52 percent of his passes for 3,145 yards and 25 touchdowns. He was also an accomplished baseball pitcher for the Longhorns with a 39–7 record.

In 1948, Layne joined the Chicago Bears, and one year later he moved to the New York Bulldogs. He made his mark, though, with the Detroit Lions. From 1950 through 1958, Layne quarterbacked the Lions to three straight division titles (1952–54) and to the NFL championships in 1952 and 1953.

In the 1953 title game, the Lions trailed the Cleveland Browns 16–10 when Layne drove them 80 yards and capped the drive with a 33-yard game-winning touchdown pass to Jim Doran for a 17–16 victory.

The Lions also won the NFL championship game in 1957, but Layne missed the title game because of an ankle injury suffered late in the season.

Layne was a tough taskmaster who thought nothing of criticizing teammates and exhorting them to give extra effort. The term "field general" fit him perfectly.

He is the first quarterback to master the two-minute drill, the ability to move the team downfield quickly with time running out and the game on the line. Layne wasn't a pure passer, but his athleticism and intensity made up for it.

Layne was traded to the Pittsburgh Steelers midway through the 1958 season, but he failed to bring them a championship as he promised. He retired after the 1962 season.

In 15 seasons, Layne completed 50 percent of his passes for 26,768 yards and 196 touchdowns. Through the 2000 season, he was tied for 27th all-time in touchdown passes.

Layne also ran for 25 touchdowns and kicked 34 field goals and 120 extra points. He was a two-time All-Pro and was inducted into the Pro Football Hall of Fame in 1967.

Lilly, Bob

Born: July 26, 1939 in Olney, Texas

Bob Lilly is widely regarded as one of the greatest defensive tackles in the history of the National Football League, and as much as any player symbolizes the Dallas Cowboys.

Lilly, an All-American defensive tackle at Texas Christian University in 1960, was the first player drafted by the expansion Cowboys when they began play in the NFL in 1961. He also went on to become their first All-Pro, first Pro Bowl player, first inductee into the Ring of Honor at Texas Stadium, and first member of the Pro Football Hall of Fame.

Lilly, 6-5, 260 pounds, began his career with the Cowboys as a defensive end, but was moved to tackle. He became the cornerstone of coach Tom Landry's flex defense, which required the tackle to play a bit off the line of scrimmage, enabling him to use his size, speed, strength, and reflexes to read the play and many times make the tackle. Lilly was the key to the unit that became known as the "Doomsday Defense."

Lilly helped the Cowboys to six NFL or National Football Conference title game appearances, two Super Bowl appearances, and one Super Bowl title (1971). From 1961 to 1974, he played in 292 consecutive games, including playoffs. He missed only one game in his career, in 1974, the year he retired.

Lilly was an eight-time All-Pro and an 11-time Pro Bowl player. He was inducted into the Pro Football Hall of Fame in 1980 and was named a member of the NFL's 75th Anniversary All-Time Team in 1994.

Little, Larry

Born: November 2, 1945 in Georgetown, Georgia

Larry Little, who played his college ball at Bethune Cookman College in Florida, went undrafted by the American Football League and the National Football League. He accepted a $750 bonus to sign with the San Diego Chargers as a free agent in 1969. Chargers head coach Sid Gillman tried Little, who weighed 285 pounds at the time, at several positions, including fullback, but when it didn't work out, Little was traded to the Miami Dolphins. He became one of the best guards in NFL history and the centerpiece of one of the great running games of all time.

Once in Miami, head coach Don Shula got Little to reduce his weight to 265 pounds. The result was a guard with good speed and quickness who was also a punishing blocker.

Little opened holes for fullback Larry Csonka and halfbacks Jim Kiick and Mercury Morris, and the Dolphins rushing attack gained at least 2,000 yards a season from 1970 to 1979. In 1972, when the Dolphins won the Super Bowl and completed a 17–0 season, they rushed for 2,960 yards.

Little, who retired after the 1980 season, played in five Pro Bowls and was inducted into the Pro Football Hall of Fame in 1993.

Long, Howie (Howard)

Born: January 6, 1960 in Somerville, Massachusetts

Howie Long used his strength, explosiveness, and athleticism to become one of the best defensive ends of his time.

Long (6-5, 268 pounds) played his college ball at Villanova, where he lettered for four years. He was Most Valuable Player of the 1980 Blue-Gray Game, a postseason all-star game.

The Oakland Raiders selected Long in the second round of the 1981 draft. He became a starter in the fifth game of his second season and was a fixture for the rest of his career. He helped the Raiders reach two AFC championship games (1983, '90) and one Super Bowl (XVIII, 1983 season), in which the Raiders defeated the Washington Redskins 38–9.

Long played for 13 years with the Raiders, retiring after the 1993 season. He recorded 84 career sacks, not including 7 1/2 sacks he had in 1981, before the sack became an official NFL statistic.

Long, a three-time All-Pro and an eight-time Pro Bowl selection, was inducted into the Pro Football Hall of Fame in 2000.

Long works as an analyst on Fox Sports NFL pregame show, appears in movies, and does commercials.

Lott, Ronnie

Born: May 8, 1959 in Albuquerque, New Mexico

Ronnie Lott was a defensive back who played the position with the characteristics of a linebacker. He was a hard hitter who intimidated quarterbacks and punished wide receivers. To go along with his toughness was a sixth sense that gave him a further advantage.

Lott was an All-American defensive back at the University of Southern California. In 1981, the San Francisco 49ers made him their first-round draft pick. For the first six seasons of his career, Lott was the starter for the 49ers at cornerback. In 1985, he was moved to free safety. In 1986, he led the National Football League in interceptions with 10. He also was a key cog in the 49ers' postseason success. San Francisco won four Super Bowl championships (XVI, XIX, XXII, XXIV) during Lott's time there.

In 1991, Lott signed with the Oakland Raiders as a free agent. He not only changed teams, he also changed positions, moving to strong safety. In 1991, he led the league in interceptions with eight.

After two seasons with the Raiders, he signed as a free agent with the New York Jets, for whom he provided much needed leadership in addition to his physical presence.

Lott retired following the 1994 season. He was an All-Pro at three positions—cornerback in 1981; free safety in 1987, '90; and strong safety in 1991—and played in 10 Pro Bowls. In 1994, he was named to the NFL's 75th Anniversary All-Time Team.

Through the 2000 season, Lott had 63 career interceptions and ranked fifth all-time. He worked as a football commentator for Fox Sports. He was inducted into the Pro Football Hall of Fame in 2000.

Luckman, Sid

Born: November 21, 1916 in Brooklyn, New York
Died: July 5, 1998

Sid Luckman helped revolutionize the quarterback position while playing for coach George Halas and the Chicago Bears. Along with Sammy Baugh, Luckman made the forward pass a staple of pro offenses, which previously had relied almost exclusively on the run.

Luckman was an All-American single-wing tailback at Columbia University. Halas chose him to be the Bears quarterback, largely because of his intelligence and his all-around athletic skills. He could run, throw, handle the ball, and scramble away from would-be tacklers.

Luckman didn't play much during his rookie year, 1939, but in 1940, he became the starter and led the Bears to the National Football League championship, capped by a 73–0 victory over the Washington Redskins in the title game.

The Bears won four NFL championships (1940–41, '43, '46) with Luckman at quarterback. In 1943, he was named the NFL's Most Valuable Player. In the '43 title game, he threw for 276 yards and five touchdowns in a 41–21 victory over the Redskins. In the 1946 title game, he scored the winning touchdown on a 19-yard run in a 21–14 victory over the New York Giants.

Luckman retired after the 1950 season. He passed for 14,683 yards and 137 touchdowns during his 12-year career. He was a six-time All-Pro and was inducted into the Pro Football Hall of Fame in 1965.

Mackey, John

Born: September 24, 1941 in New York, New York

John Mackey was the first tight end to be used consistently as an offensive weapon. He was physically imposing (6-2, 224 pounds), with the speed and elusiveness to go deep.

He played his college ball at Syracuse University, and when he was drafted in the second round by the Baltimore Colts in 1963, head coach Don Shula wasn't sure whether to play him at fullback or tight end. He chose tight end, and Mackey changed the way the position was played. In addition to his offensive skills, he was a powerful blocker.

Six of his 38 career touchdowns were more than 50 yards, and twice he averaged more than 20 yards a catch for a season. His career average of 15.8 yards was comparable to a wide receiver.

Mackey spent nine seasons with the Colts, helping them to two Super Bowl appearances (III, V). He spent his final season, 1972, with the San Diego Chargers. He had 331 career receptions for 5,236 yards. A three time All-Pro and a five-time Pro Bowl selection, Mackey was inducted into the Pro Football Hall of Fame in 1992. He was the second tight end to be enshrined.

Marchetti, Gino

Born: January 2, 1927 in Smithers, West Virginia

Gino Marchetti changed the way the defensive end position was played. At 6-4, 244 pounds, he combined strength, agility, and quickness. He could stop the run and rush the passer, despite often being double- and triple-teamed.

After taking part in the Battle of the Bulge in World War II and then attending the University of San Francisco, Marchetti was drafted by the New York Yanks in the second round of the 1952 NFL draft. The Yanks moved to Dallas and became the Texans prior to Marchetti's rookie season. One year later, the team folded and Marchetti joined the Baltimore Colts.

Marchetti began his career at the same time coaches were phasing out players who played offense and defense.

He became a defensive end specialist and was the first to rush the quarterback from his position.

Marchetti was an All-Pro six times and a Pro Bowl player 10 times during his 13-year career. In 1958, when the Colts won the NFL championship, beating the New York Giants in overtime in what has been called the greatest game ever played, Marchetti was named NFL Player of the Year by the Associated Press. He was also voted the best defensive end of the NFL's first 50 years in a 1969 poll. Marchetti was inducted into the Pro Football Hall of Fame in 1972 and was named a member of the NFL's 75th Anniversary All-Time Team in 1994.

Marino, Dan

Born: September 15, 1961 in Pittsburgh, Pennsylvania

Dan Marino is arguably the greatest quarterback never to win a Super Bowl, although that void on his résumé doesn't detract from his stellar career with the Miami Dolphins.

He was one of the best pure passers in the history of the National Football League. Marino had size (6-4, 228 pounds), a strong arm, and one of the quickest releases of

Dan Marino   *Diane Staskowski*

all time. Never a mobile quarterback, Marino's ability to elude tacklers was lessened over the years by knee surgeries and a ruptured Achilles tendon in 1993. But his quick release kept him from getting sacked. His poise and confidence, especially under pressure, made him an effective leader. He was a fiery, emotional player who routinely yelled at his teammates and screamed out instructions. But he demanded that they give their best on every play, just as he did.

Marino played his college ball at the University of Pittsburgh, where he excelled as a junior. He was named to several All-America teams, and he finished fourth in voting for the Heisman Trophy, signifying the best college player in the nation. But as a senior, he tailed off somewhat. Expected to be a Heisman candidate, he failed to finish in the top five.

Marino completed 57.5 percent of his passes at Pitt for 8,597 yards and 78 touchdowns.

The Dolphins made him their first-round pick in the 1983 NFL draft. He was the 27th player taken overall and the last of six quarterbacks to be drafted in the first round.

Marino moved into the starting lineup five games into the season and earned Rookie of the Year honors. He led the AFC in passing, completing 58 percent of his throws for 2,210 yards and 20 touchdowns. He was the first rookie ever to start in the Pro Bowl at quarterback.

In 1984, Marino had the most prolific season of any quarterback in NFL history. He completed 64.2 percent of his passes for single-season records of 5,084 yards and 48 touchdown passes. His quarterback efficiency rating was 108.9, the fifth-highest ever recorded. He was named the league's Most Valuable Player.

Marino led the Dolphins to Super Bowl XIX, where they were beaten by the San Francisco 49ers 38–16. Getting to the ultimate goal in only his second season, Marino assumed there would many more trips and at least one win. But Miami made it to only two more AFC championship games (1985, '92) and lost each time.

The Dolphins were often plagued by lack of a running game, poor defenses, or both. But even though defenses could gear themselves to stopping Marino, without having to worry about stopping the run, he proved to be unstoppable, in large part because of his ability to read defenses and make the right decisions.

He threw for 4,000 or more yards six times and 3,000 or more yards seven times. His 13 seasons of 3,000 or more yards is an NFL record.

He led the NFL in passing in 1986 (4,746 yards, 44 touchdowns) and 1994 (4,453 yards, 30 touchdowns). In 1989, he led the AFC in passing (3,997 yards, 24 touchdowns). Through his first nine full seasons (1984–92), he threw for at least 3,245 yards and 21 touchdowns. During that stretch, he missed only four games.

But in the fifth game of the 1993 season, he ruptured his Achilles tendon and missed the rest of the year. His mobility was limited even further.

In 1996, Jimmy Johnson took over as head coach, succeeding Don Shula. Johnson's offensive philosophy was based on a strong running game, which, he reasoned, would lengthen Marino's career, because not so much of the offensive burden would be on the quarterback's shoulders. But the lack of effective running backs rendered the strategy ineffective.

Marino had three solid seasons under Johnson, averaging 3,357 yards and 19 touchdowns a year. In 1999, Marino suffered a nerve root injury to his throwing shoulder. He couldn't throw long anymore, nor could he get his usual pace on shorter passes. He missed five games, came back against Dallas in a Thanksgiving Day game, and threw five interceptions. He finished the season completing 55 percent of his passes for 2,450 yards, 12 touchdowns, and 17 interceptions, the only time in his career he threw more interceptions than touchdowns.

The Dolphins qualified for the playoffs and faced the Seattle Seahawks on the road in a wild card game. Marino rallied the Dolphins to victory, mounting a long drive that resulted in the winning touchdown in the final minute.

In the next round against the Jacksonville Jaguars, the Dolphins were routed 62–7. It turned out to be his last game.

In the offseason, after it was made clear by the Dolphins he was no longer in their plans, Marino entertained an offer from Minnesota coach Dennis Green to become the Vikings starting quarterback. After much deliberation, during which time he nearly accepted the offer, Marino decided to retire as a member of the Miami Dolphins after 17 seasons. He made it official in March 2000.

Through the 2000 season, Marino held NFL records for attempts (7,989), completions (4,967), yards (61,361, the equivalent of 34.9 miles), touchdown passes (420), 400-yard-plus career games (13), 300-yard-plus career games (63), and most games with four or more touchdown passes (21). He was selected for nine Pro Bowl games, tied with John Elway and Warren Moon for most appearances by a quarterback. Marino became an analyst for HBO's *Inside the NFL*.

Matson, Ollie

Born: May 1, 1930 in Trinity, Texas

Ollie Matson was an All-American running back at the University of San Francisco, setting an NCAA record by rushing for 3,166 yards in three years. He led the country

in rushing (1,566) and touchdowns (21) in 1951, his senior season.

Matson's running wasn't confined to the football field. In the 1952 Olympics he won a silver medal as part of the U.S. 4 x 400-meter relay team, and he won a bronze medal in the 400 meters. When the Olympics ended, Matson joined the Chicago Cardinals, who drafted him in the first round of the 1952 NFL draft.

Despite his speed and his offensive success in college, Matson began his pro career as a defensive back. He was named to the all-rookie team.

Matson spent the 1953 season in the Army, then came back to the Cardinals in 1954. From that point on, he was used mostly as a running back.

In 1958, Matson led the NFL in kickoff returns, averaging 35.5 yards and scoring two touchdowns. After the 1958 season, Matson was traded to the Los Angeles Rams for nine players. He spent four seasons with the Rams, the 1963 season with the Detroit Lions, and the last two years of his career with the Philadelphia Eagles.

Matson, who played 14 seasons, rushed for 5,173 yards, averaging 4.4 yards a carry, and 40 touchdowns. He caught 222 passes for 3,285 yards and 23 touchdowns. He averaged 26.2 yards and scored six touchdowns on kickoff returns, and averaged 9.2 yards and scored three touchdowns on punt returns.

Matson, a four-time All-Pro and a five-time Pro Bowl selection, was inducted into the Pro Football Hall of Fame in 1972.

Maynard, Don

Born: January 25, 1937 in Crosbyton, Texas

It took awhile before Don Maynard caught on, but once he did, he became one of the greatest receivers of his time. He played his college ball at Texas Western and was drafted in the ninth round of the 1958 NFL draft by the New York Giants, who released him after one season.

Maynard spent the 1959 season with the Hamilton Tiger-Cats of the Canadian Football League. In 1960, the American Football League had its inaugural season and Maynard was the first signee of the New York Titans. He moved into the starting lineup and caught 171 passes during his first three seasons.

In his fourth season, 1963, the Titans changed their name to the New York Jets and signed Joe Namath to a lucrative contract. Maynard became half of one of the great passing combinations of the 1960s.

Maynard led the AFL in touchdown catches in 1965 with 14, in yardage in 1967 with 1,434, and in average per catch in 1967 with 20.2 and in 1968 with 22.8.

In 1968, the Jets reached the AFL championship game against the Oakland Raiders. Maynard caught six passes for 118 yards and two touchdowns. The Jets beat the Raiders 27–23 and went on to upset the Baltimore Colts in Super Bowl III.

Maynard caught 50 or more passes for 1,000 or more yards five times in his career. Four times he averaged more than 20 yards a catch.

Maynard left the Jets after the 1972 season and finished his career by playing one season with the St. Louis Cardinals. In 15 seasons, he had 633 receptions for 11,834 yards (18.7-yard average) and 88 touchdowns.

In 1969, he was named to the All-Time AFL team, and he was inducted into the Pro Football Hall of Fame in 1987.

Mitchell, Bobby
Born: June 6, 1935 in Hot Springs, Arkansas
Bobby Mitchell, a running back at the University of Illinois, was drafted by the Cleveland Brown in the seventh round of the 1958 NFL draft. His first three years as a pro were spent as running back and as a return man.

In 1962, the Browns traded Mitchell to the Washington Redskins. He was the team's first African American star. The Redskins were the last NFL team to be integrated.

Mitchell was switched to wide receiver, and in his first year at the position, he led the NFL in receiving with 72 catches for 1,384 yards and 11 touchdowns. He caught 50 or more passes six times in his career, which ended after the 1968 season.

Mitchell, known for his great speed and long scoring plays, had 521 receptions for 7,954 yards and 65 touchdowns. He gained 14,078 combined yards and scored 91 touchdowns overall.

Mitchell was a two-time All-Pro and a four-time Pro Bowl selection. He was inducted into the Pro Football Hall of Fame in 1983.

Monk, Art
Born: December 5, 1957 in White Plains, New York
For all his success, Art Monk never received the acclaim many thought he was entitled to. Even though he ranks as one of the most accomplished wide receivers of all time, he is rarely mentioned as one of the greats, perhaps because Monk went about his business in a low-key manner and with little fanfare.

He was drafted out of Syracuse University in the first round of the 1980 NFL draft by the Washington Redskins. A running back in college, Monk was moved to wide receiver. At 6-3, 210 pounds, he was a big target. He wasn't blessed with great speed, but his precise routes, long strides, and good moves made him difficult to defend.

Monk spent many hours watching film and refining his techniques on the practice field. His hard work and dedication paid off. In 1984, he led the NFL in receiving with 106 catches (then a single-season record) for 1,372 yards and seven touchdowns. He had five straight 1,000 yard seasons and had a then record 183 straight games with at least one catch.

Monk helped the Redskins reach three Super Bowls (XVI, XVII, XXII), two of which were victories (XVI, XXII).

Monk left the Redskins after the 1992 season and joined the New York Jets. After two-plus seasons with the Jets, he ended his career with the Philadelphia Eagles in 1995.

In 14 seasons, Monk caught 940 passes for 12,721 yards and 68 touchdowns. Through the 2000 season, he ranked fourth all-time in receptions and seventh all-time in yardage. He was a two-time All-Pro and a three-time Pro Bowl player.

Montana, Joe
Born: June 11, 1956 in Monongahela, Pennsylvania
Joe Montana didn't look the part physically. He wasn't the prototype quarterback—big and strong with a cannon for an arm. But he could lay claim to being the best quarterback of all time. The more pressure-packed the situation, the better Montana seemed to play. His calm, cool demeanor came to be known as "Montana Magic." His leadership qualities were unparalleled.

Montana was an all-around athlete in high school. He was a baseball pitcher of some renown and received a basketball scholarship offer from North Carolina State. But instead, he went to Notre Dame, where he began his career as the seventh-string quarterback. But by the time he was a senior, he was noted for his ability to come off the bench and rally the Fighting Irish to miraculous comebacks, none more memorable than in the 1977 Cotton Bowl.

In Montana's final game, the Irish trailed Houston 34–12 in the third quarter. Despite suffering from the flu, he led Notre Dame to a 35–34 victory and the national championship. He threw the tying touchdown pass on the last play of the game. The extra point was kicked with no time showing on the clock.

Montana was drafted by the San Francisco 49ers in the third round of the NFL draft. Head coach Bill Walsh, one of the game's most innovative offensive minds, was installing an offense that would come to be known as the "West Coast" offense, which relied on a short, controlled passing game. No one ran it better than Montana, whose ability to throw effectively while on the move was a key to his success.

He became a starter late in 1980, his second season, when the 49ers finished 6–10. In 1981, Montana led the

49ers to a most improbable Super Bowl championship. But it was in the NFC Championship that Montana made the play that was one of his most spectacular. With 58 seconds left and San Francisco trailing the Dallas Cowboys 27–21, Montana found Dwight Clark along the back of the end zone. Clark made a leaping grab and the 49ers qualified for the Super Bowl. The play became known as "The Catch."

San Francisco faced the Cincinnati Bengals in Super Bowl XVI. Montana completed 14 of 22 passes for 157 yards and a touchdown in a 26–21 victory.

Montana was named the game's Most Valuable Player, an award he also won for Super Bowl XIX (24-for-35, 331 yards, two touchdowns), a 38–16 win over the Miami Dolphins, and Super Bowl XXIV (22-for-29, 297 yards, five touchdown passes), a 55–10 win over the Denver Broncos. He is the only player to be named Super Bowl Most Valuable Player three times.

In Super Bowl XXIII, Montana wasn't named Most Valuable Player—wide receiver Jerry Rice was. But it was Montana who rallied the 49ers to a 20–16 victory. He engineered a 92-yard drive, hitting John Taylor with the winning touchdown pass with just 34 seconds to play.

Montana left the 49ers after the 1993 season and spent his final two seasons with the Kansas City Chiefs. In 1993, he led the Chiefs to the AFC Championship game.

During his 15-year career, Montana completed 63.2 percent of his passes for 40,551 yards, 273 touchdowns, and 139 interceptions. Through the 2000 season, he ranked second all-time in passing efficiency (92.3), sixth in touchdowns, and sixth in passing yards.

In postseason play, Montana ranked second in passing efficiency (95.6), first in passing yards (5,772), first in touchdowns (45), first in completions (460), and first in games played (23) by a quarterback. He is first in Super Bowl passing yardage (1,142) and fourth in passing efficiency (127.8).

An eight-time Pro Bowl player, Montana was responsible for 31 fourth-quarter comebacks. He was named the NFL's Most Valuable Player in 1989 and 1990. He was named Associated Press Offensive Player of the Year in 1989. He was inducted into the Pro Football Hall of Fame in 2000 and was named a member of the NFL's 75th Anniversary All-Time Team in 1994.

Moon, Warren
Born: November 18, 1956 in Los Angeles, California

Warren Moon led the University of Washington to a 27–20 upset victory over Michigan in the 1978 Rose Bowl. He was named the Pacific-10 Conference Player of the Year and the Rose Bowl's Most Valuable Player. Despite a solid career, Moon was not drafted by an NFL

team, and instead signed with Edmonton Eskimos of the Canadian Football League. He took the Eskimos to five straight Grey Cup championships (1978–82).

In 1984, he signed as a free agent with the Houston Oilers. He retired after the 2000 season.

Moon spent 10 seasons with the Oilers (1984–93), three seasons with the Minnesota Vikings (1994–96), and the 1999 season with the Kansas City Chiefs.

Five times he threw for 3,000 yards or more, and four times he threw for 4,000 yards or more. Only Dan Marino of the Miami Dolphins had more 4,000-yard seasons. Moon led the NFL in passing in 1990, throwing for 4,689 yards and 33 touchdowns, and he led the AFC in 1992, throwing for 2,521 yards and 18 touchdowns.

Through the 2000 season, Moon completed 58.5 percent of his passes for 49,325 yards and 291 touchdowns. He ranked third all-time in yardage and fourth all-time in touchdown passes.

Moore, Lenny (Leonard)
Born: November 25, 1933 in Reading, Pennsylvania

Lenny Moore was one of pro football's most elusive offensive weapons. Although he was slightly built (6-1, 191 pounds), with legs so spindly they looked as if they would snap on contact, Moore was able to use his athleticism, speed, and quick feet to avoid would-be tacklers.

In his senior year at Reading High School in Reading, Pennsylvania, Moore scored 22 touchdowns. He went on to Penn State and led the Nittany Lions in all-purpose yardage for three straight years (1953–55). He was the first Penn Stater to rush for 1,000 yards in a season, and his 6.2-yard-average per carry was second all-time at Penn State through the 2000 season.

In addition to being an offensive force, Moore also made an impact as a defensive back with 10 career interceptions. According to coach Joe Paterno, Moore was one of the best all-around players in Penn State history.

In 1956, the Baltimore Colts selected him in the first round of the NFL draft, and he was named the league's Rookie of the Year, playing running back and flanker. He rushed for 649 yards, averaged 7.5 yards a carry, and scored eight touchdowns.

In 1958, Moore had his best season. He gained 1,536 yards rushing and receiving and scored 14 touchdowns in helping the Colts with the NFL championship. In the title game against the New York Giants, a 23–17 victory in overtime for Baltimore called one of the greatest games ever played, Moore caught six passes for 101 yards.

Injuries slowed Moore in 1963 and also caused some unrest with him and the organization, which accused him of malingering. Angered by what he considered unfair treatment, Moore set out to prove everyone wrong in 1964, and he had one of the best seasons of his career, scoring 20 touchdowns (an NFL single-season record at the time) and being named the Comeback Player of the Year.

Moore, nicknamed "Spats" for the way he taped his high-top shoes, played three more seasons and retired in 1967. He finished his career with 12,393 combined yards (rushing, receiving, returns) and 113 touchdowns. Through the 1999 season, he ranked seventh all-time in touchdowns.

Moore was a five-time All-Pro and a seven-time Pro Bowl player. He was inducted into the Pro Football Hall of Fame in 1975.

Motley, Marion

Born: June 5, 1920 in Leesburg, Virginia
Died: June 27, 1999

Marion Motley made an impact on the football field and off. He was a powerfully built (6-1, 232 pounds), punishing runner and blocker who was, along with teammate Bill Willis, the first African American to play pro football since 1933. While they suffered many of the same indignities as Jackie Robinson did when he broke the color line in Major League Baseball, Motley and Willis didn't get nearly as much credit.

Lenny Moore

Motley's family moved to Canton, Ohio, and he played high school ball against Massillon, coached at the time by Paul Brown, who would go on to achieve legendary status.

Motley attended South Carolina State and the University of Nevada, Reno, before entering the Navy. He played for Brown, who coached the Great Lakes Naval Training Station team.

When Brown left to coach the Cleveland Browns in the All-America Football Conference (AAFC), which had its inaugural season in 1946, Motley joined the Browns as a fullback.

The AAFC lasted only four years, and Motley was the league's all-time rushing leader with 3,024 yards, averaging 6.2 yards a carry. He also served as quarterback Otto Graham's principal blocker and protector, and played linebacker during his first two seasons in the AAFC.

In 1950, the Browns joined the National Football League, and Motley led the NFL in rushing, gaining 810 yards and averaging 5.8 yards a carry.

Over the next three years, Motley was slowed by knee injuries. He missed the entire 1954 season, retired, made a brief comeback with the Pittsburgh Steelers in 1955, but retired for good after carrying the ball two times.

Motley's combined totals from the AAFC and NFL: 4,712 yards, 39 touchdowns, and a 5.7 yard-per-carry average. He was inducted into the Pro Football Hall of Fame in 1968. In 1994, he was named to the NFL's 75th Anniversary All-Time Team.

Munoz, Anthony

Born: August 19, 1958 in Ontario, California

Anthony Munoz is widely regarded as the best offensive tackle in National Football League history. He played collegiate ball at the University of Southern California, where he blocked for Charles White, who won the 1979 Heisman Trophy. The Cincinnati Bengals made Munoz their first-round pick (third overall) in the 1980 NFL draft. His impact was almost immediate.

He was a starter as a rookie and an All-Pro in his second season. Munoz was 6-6, 278 pounds, but in spite of his size, he possessed quickness and agility. He had powerfully built legs that allowed him to take on any defensive end, no matter his size. He was equally good blocking for running backs or protecting the quarterback.

Munoz was named All-Pro seven times and a Pro Bowl player 11 times in his 13-year career. Following the 1992 season, Munoz, a free agent, signed with the Tampa Bay Buccaneers. He spent one season with the Bucs, then retired to become a television commentator.

Munoz was also involved in community affairs, and in 1991, he was named the NFL's Man of the Year for his charitable works. He was inducted into the Pro Football Hall of Fame in 1998 and was named a member of the NFL's 75th Anniversary All-Time Team in 1994.

Nagurski, Bronko (Bronislaw)
Born: November 3, 1908 in Rainy River, Ontario, Canada
Died: January 7, 1990

Bronko Nagurski was a powerfully built, hulking two-way football player who was a punishing force on offense and defense. At 6-2, 226 pounds, he outsized many linemen of his day.

He went to the University of Minnesota and was an All-American at fullback and defensive tackle, the only player ever to be so honored.

After leaving Minnesota, Nagurski signed with the Chicago Bears for $5,000. He continued to play offense and defense. In addition to running the ball, he also had some success passing it. With defenders converging on him, Nagurski would take a step back and throw it. His 2-yard touchdown pass to Red Grange allowed the Bears to beat the Portsmouth Spartans and win the 1932 NFL championship. In the 1933 NFL championship, Nagurski threw two touchdown passes in a 23–21 victory over the New York Giants.

In 1934, he added another attribute to his arsenal: He became a blocking back for Beattie Feathers, who became the first player ever to rush for 1,000 yards in a season. Feathers credited Nagurski for helping him achieve the milestone.

In 1937, Nagurski became a professional wrestler. During one three-week span, he wrestled eight times and played five games with the Bears. He retired before the 1938 season when the Bears refused to meet his salary demands of an additional $1,000. Six years later, with the league depleted by the war, Nagurski returned to the Bears. He played most of the season at tackle, but was inserted at fullback for the final regular season game. He scored one touchdown and had a key run to set up another, rallying the Bears to a 28–24 victory. Nagurski also scored a touchdown in the Bears' victory over the Washington Redskins in the NFL title game.

Because Nagurski played so many positions and because he was such an effective blocker on offense, he gained only 2,278 yards in his career. But his ability to dominate a game from every position he played made him one of the greatest players ever. In 1963, Nagurski became a charter member of the Pro Football Hall of Fame. In 1994, he was named to the NFL's 75th Anniversary All-Time Team.

Namath, Joe
Born: May 31, 1943 in Beaver Falls, Pennsylvania

Joe Namath was a football player who transcended his sport. He was flamboyant, controversial, brash, and talented. As the quarterback for the New York Jets, he engineered one of the most stunning upsets in the history of pro football and grabbed headlines with his playboy lifestyle, earning him the nickname "Broadway Joe." He had an aura about him, a sense of style that was different from any player before him. Dan Jenkins, an acclaimed sportswriter, called him "pro football's very own Beatle."

Namath played his college ball at the University of Alabama and led the Crimson Tide to the 1964 national title. Legendary coach Paul "Bear" Bryant called him "the greatest athlete I ever coached."

Namath, drafted by the New York Jets of the American Football League, signed a three-year contract for a reported $400,000, double any pro football contract at the time. In 1965, he completed 48.2 percent of his passes and threw for 2,220 yards and 18 touchdowns. He was named the league's Rookie of the Year.

He led the league in passing yardage in 1966 (3,379) and in 1967 (4,007), a professional record at the time.

It was during the 1967 season that Namath led the Jets to the AFL championship, throwing three touchdown passes in a 27–23 victory over the Oakland Raiders. The victory put them in Super Bowl III against the Baltimore Colts, who were installed as 18-point favorites.

On the Thursday before the game, Namath made a bold prediction: "We're gonna win. I personally guarantee it." At the time it seemed ludicrous. In the first two Super Bowls, the AFL representative hadn't come within 19 points of the champion Green Bay Packers.

But he made his prediction come true. The Jets used a short, controlled passing game, the running of fullback Matt Snell, the effective play-calling of Namath, and a strong defense to upset the Colts 16–7. Namath completed 17 of 28 passes for 206 yards. He was named Most Valuable Player.

The victory by the Jets was one of the most significant in pro football history because it gave the AFL the credibility it didn't have. The two leagues merged in 1970.

Namath never again reached such heights. His career was hampered by numerous injuries—he underwent five knee operations—and non-football-related problems, such as his ownership in a restaurant, Bachelors III, which he was forced to give up by NFL Commissioner Pete Rozelle. The lack of a potent running game hampered Namath's and the Jets' success, as well.

But when he was healthy, there was no one better. Namath had a quick release, which helped overcome his lack of mobility, and a sixth sense about calling plays. He could throw the ball long or short and thread it into seemingly impossible situations.

In 1972, Namath led the NFL with 2,816 yards and 19 touchdown passes. He was a consensus All-Pro selection.

Namath spent four more seasons with the Jets. They finished below .500 each year. In 1977, he joined the Los Angeles Rams, but appeared in only six games and retired after one season, which was plagued by injuries.

In 13 seasons, Namath completed 50 percent of his passes for 27,663 yards, 173 touchdowns, and 220 interceptions. Through the 2000 season, he ranked tied for 38th all-time in touchdown passes and tied for 15th all-time in interceptions.

Namath, a five-time Pro Bowl selection, was inducted into the Pro Football Hall of Fame in 1985. After his retirement, he worked as a television commentator, including a stint on *Monday Night Football*.

Nevers, Ernie

Born: June 11, 1903 in Willow Grove, Minnesota
Died: May 3, 1976

Ernie Nevers was one of the most versatile athletes of the 20th century. At Stanford University in the 1920s, Nevers earned 11 varsity letters in four sports—football, basketball, baseball, and track and field.

As legend has it, Nevers once pitched in a baseball game and threw the discus in a track meet on the same day. He struck out the side in the first inning and raced to the track stadium, wearing his baseball uniform and spikes. He showed up just in time for the discus. He let fly with his throw and headed back to the baseball game before the discus hit the ground. Supposedly, he made it back to the game in time to take his turn at bat.

Nevers gave up track at the urging of his baseball coach and earned a spot on Stanford's all-time baseball team, hitting .400 over his three years. He captained the basketball team and is credited with developing the overhead hook shot.

But it was football in which Nevers earned his greatest acclaim. He was a powerful runner, blessed with speed and acceleration. In the 1925 Rose Bowl against Notre Dame and the fabled Four Horseman, Nevers had the game of his life.

He rushed for 114 yards, punted for a 42-yard average, and, according to one report, made three-quarters of the tackles for the Cardinals. He played all 60 minutes—on two broken ankles.

In 1926, Nevers joined the Duluth Eskimos of the National Football League. He earned $15,000, the highest salary at the time. Duluth played 29 games in 1926, 28 on the road, and Nevers played all but 27 minutes. The Eskimos folded after the 1927 season.

In 1928, Nevers suffered a broken neck and didn't play at all. He returned for the 1929 season as the player-coach of the Chicago Cardinals. On November 28, 1929, Nevers scored all the Cardinals' points in a 40–6 victory over the Chicago Bears. He ran for six touchdowns and kicked four extra-points. Through the 2000 season, it is still the single-game record for most points scored and most touchdowns scored in one game.

In the Cardinals' next game, against Dayton, Nevers again scored all his team's points in a 19–0 victory.

Nevers retired after the 1931 season. His final appearance was in a charity all-star game. He scored all his team's points in a 26–14 win.

In addition to playing football, Nevers also pitched for the St. Louis Browns and gave up two of Babe Ruth's 60 home runs in 1927. He played three years (1926–28) and had a 6–12 record with a 4.64 earned run average.

Nevers was inducted into the Pro Football Hall of Fame in 1963.

Newsome, Ozzie

Born: March 16, 1956 in Muscle Shoals, Alabama

Ozzie Newsome was a consummate tight end and a respected team leader throughout his 13-year career, spent entirely with the Cleveland Browns. He had size (6-2, 232 pounds), good speed that allowed him to get deep, and was a solid blocker.

Newsome played his college ball at the University of Alabama, where he was an All-American, and was one of two first-round draft picks by the Browns in 1978.

Newsome, nicknamed the "Wizard of Oz," had 89 catches in 1983 and 1984, when he led the AFC with 1,001 yards. Six times he caught 50 or more passes in a season, and he had a 150-game streak in which he caught at least one pass.

Newsome was an important ingredient for the Browns, who reached three AFC championship games in a four-year stretch (1986–90).

Newsome retired after the 1990 season with 662 receptions for 7,980 yards and 47 touchdowns. Through the 2000 season, he was the all-time leading tight end receiver and ranked 14th all-time among all receivers.

A two-time All-Pro and a three-time Pro Bowl selection, Newsome was inducted into the Pro Football Hall of Fame in 1999. He was also a solid citizen, winning the NFL Players Association Byron "Whizzer" White Award for community service in 1990 and the Ed Block Courage Award for playing despite injuries in 1986.

Through the 2000 season, he was the vice president of football operations for the Baltimore Ravens.

Nitschke, Ray

Born: December 29, 1936 in Elmwood Park, Illinois
Died: March 8, 1998

Ray Nitschke was the heart and soul of the Green Bay Packers defenses. A 6-3, 235-pound middle linebacker, he was a ferocious tackler who was blessed with strength, speed, and toughness. But more than his physical attributes was his desire and unwavering will to excel, a trait that rubbed off on his teammates.

Nitschke lost both his parents by the time he was 10 years old, and he was cared for by an older brother. Nitschke got into trouble on the streets, and he credits football with keeping him out of prison. He went to the University of Illinois, where he played fullback and linebacker. In 1958, his rookie season with the Packers, he became the starter and was a fixture until he retired after the 1972 season.

Nitschke helped the Packers win five National Football League championships during a seven-year span in the 1960s, including Super Bowl I and Super Bowl II. In the Packers' 16–7 victory over the New York Giants in the 1962 title game, he was named the game's Most Valuable Player.

Nitschke played in one Pro Bowl and was a three-time All-Pro. He was inducted into the Pro Football Hall of Fame in 1978 and was named a member of the NFL's 75th Anniversary All-Time Team in 1994.

Nomellini, Leo

Born: June 19, 1924 in Lucca Italy

Leo Nomellini was big (6-3, 264 pounds), strong, powerful, and versatile. He was also very successful, especially considering he didn't play football until he was in the Marines in 1942.

Nomellini was given a scholarship to the University of Minnesota in 1946. After spending his sophomore season as a guard, he was shifted to tackle as a junior and senior and was an All-American each year.

The San Francisco 49ers chose him in the first round of the 1950 NFL draft. He spent his first three seasons as an offensive tackle, then was switched to defensive tackle.

Nomellini, who retired after the 1963 season, spent his entire career with the 49ers. He was a six-time All-Pro (twice on offense, four times on defense) and a 10-time Pro Bowl selection. In his 14-year career he never missed a game—174 in the regular season, 266 overall. He was inducted into the Pro Football Hall of Fame in 1969.

Olsen, Merlin

Born: September 15, 1940 in Logan, Utah

Off the field, Merlin Olsen was quiet and soft-spoken; on the field, he was a technically precise, powerfully built defensive tackle for the Los Angeles Rams, and a force for 15 years.

Olsen was a consensus All-American and Outland Trophy winner, as the nation's outstanding lineman, at Utah State in 1961. The Los Angeles Rams made him their first-round draft pick in 1962.

Olsen became a starter in the third game of his rookie season and played in 208 regular season games, including the last 198 consecutively.

Olsen, 6-5, 270 pounds, became a charter member of the "Fearsome Foursome," the Rams defensive line that also included Deacon Jones, Lamar Lundy, and Roosevelt Grier. Olsen and Jones were the left side of the line and they worked together, pioneering stunts and looping paths to the quarterback that made them a perfect tandem.

In addition to his physical skills, Olsen was a Phi Beta Kappa. His ability to study the game and his opponents added to his effectiveness.

Olsen was a six-time All-Pro and played in 14 consecutive Pro Bowls, an NFL record. He retired in 1976 and was inducted into the Pro Football Hall of Fame in 1982. In 1994, he was named to the NFL's 75th Anniversary All-Time Team.

After he left the game, he became the no. 1 analyst on NBC's coverage of the National Football League. He also went on to an acting career, which included a starring role in *Little House on the Prairie*.

Otto, Jim

Born: January 5, 1938 in Wausau, Wisconsin

Jim Otto, who played his college ball at the University of Miami, joined the Oakland Raiders in 1960, the inaugural season of the American Football League, when he went undrafted by teams in the National Football League.

He came to the Raiders as an undersized center (6-2, 205 pounds), but in the next year he added 50 pounds, which enabled him to dominate defenders who, in many cases, were bigger and faster. Otto relied on speed, technique, and toughness.

Otto became the starting center for Oakland in his rookie season and was the only All-AFL center in the 10-year existence of the league. Otto never missed a game for the Raiders, starting 210 regular season games and all 13 postseason games in his 15 years. He suffered a broken nose 10 times and a variety of knee injuries, but he always was able to answer the bell.

Otto, who wore "00" as his uniform number, helped the Raiders win seven AFL Western Division titles and one AFL championship, after which they lost to the Green Bay Packers in Super Bowl II.

Otto, who retired in 1974, was a 12-time Pro Bowl player. He was inducted into the Pro Football Hall of Fame in 1980.

Page, Alan

Born: August 7, 1945 in Canton, Ohio

Alan Page was not a typical defensive tackle in that he relied mostly on brains, not brawn. He was slimmer than most defensive tackles (6-4, 245 pounds), and he depended on his quickness off the ball, his speed, and his intelligence to wreak havoc on opposing offenses.

Page was a consensus All-American at Notre Dame in 1966. He played defensive end for the Fighting Irish, but was moved to tackle by the Minnesota Vikings, who drafted him in 1967. Along with Jim Marshall and Carl Eller, Page was the anchor for the Vikings' "Purple People Eaters" defense.

In 1971, Page became the first defensive player to be named Player of the Year by the Associated Press. He had 109 tackles, 35 assists, 10 sacks, and three safeties.

Page helped the Vikings win four NFC championships (1969, '73, '74, '76), but they failed four times to win the Super Bowl. Despite their failure to win the big game, the Vikings were consistently excellent from 1968 through 1977, going 104–35–1.

The Vikings released Page during the 1978 season because his weight dropped to 220 pounds, the result of a running program he used. The Chicago Bears signed Page, and he started in Chicago for four seasons. He retired after the 1981 season.

Page's career lasted 15 seasons, during which time he never missed a game, starting 238 games. He recovered 24 fumbles, blocked 28 kicks, registered 164 sacks, and made 1,431 tackles. A nine-time All-Pro and Pro Bowl player, Page was inducted into the Pro Football Hall of Fame in 1988.

Page, who earned a law degree while playing for the Vikings, serves as an associate justice in the Minnesota Supreme Court.

Parker, Jim

Born: April 3, 1934 in Macon, Georgia

Jim Parker was considered one of the greatest offensive tackles ever to play in the National Football League—and also one of the greatest guards. He was a massive lineman (6-3, 273 pounds) who was especially large for his time.

Parker was a consensus All-American guard and the Outland Trophy winner, the nation's outstanding lineman as a senior at Ohio State in 1956. He was drafted by the Baltimore Colts in 1957 and became the starting offensive tackle. He was named an All-Pro from 1958 through 1961, when he was moved to guard. Parker was an All-Pro at guard from 1962 through 1965.

Parker played on the left side of the line and protected quarterback Johnny Unitas' blind side. He was a powerful straight-ahead blocker for the run, but he excelled at pass blocking because of his size, balance, quickness, and technique. He was often referred to as Unitas' "bodyguard."

Parker joined the Colts and was a big reason for their postseason success, including NFL titles in 1958 and 1959.

Parker, who played in eight Pro Bowls, retired after the 1967 season, during which he was slowed by injuries. He was the first pure offensive lineman to be inducted into the Pro Football Hall of Fame, in 1973. In 1994, he was named to the NFL's 75th Anniversary All-Time Team.

Payton, Walter

Born: July 25, 1954 in Columbia, Mississippi
Died: November 1, 1999

Walter Payton, blessed with elusive moves and an explosive first step, was also one of the most punishing runners in the history of the National Football League. He loved contact. Given a choice between running out of bounds or taking on a would-be tackler, Payton always chose the latter. He was 5-10 and 200 pounds with a body that was perfectly sculpted and expertly conditioned. In spite of his willingness to take a hit, he missed only one game in his 13-year career, when he was a rookie suffering from a sprained ankle. He insists he could have played.

He was a Little All-American at Jackson State University, where he scored 66 career touchdowns and got his degree in 3 1/2 years. Payton was drafted in the first round, the fourth player overall, by the Chicago Bears in 1975. His rookie season was solid (679 yards); the rest of his career was spectacular.

Payton led the National Football Conference (NFC) in rushing five times (1976–80), including a career-high 1,872 yards in 1977.

Payton, nicknamed "Sweetness," was also an excellent receiver who could do just as much damage after catching a pass. Mike Ditka, his coach with the Bears, called Payton "the most complete football player I ever saw."

Payton was named the league's Most Valuable Player in 1977 and in 1985, when the Bears won the Super Bowl, routing the New England Patriots 46–10. Payton gained only 61 yards in Super Bowl XX, and he wasn't given the ball either time the Bears were on the New England 1-yard line. Some people suspected friction between Payton and Ditka, but both players denied it.

Through the 2000 season, Payton held NFL records for most yards in a career (16,726) and most 100-yard games (77). He scored 110 rushing touchdowns and 15 by reception. His 125 total touchdowns ranked him fifth all-time. He gained 4,537 yards on 492 catches.

Payton, a nine-time Pro Bowl player, retired after the 1987 season. He was inducted into the Pro Football Hall of Fame in 1993 and was named a member of the NFL's 75th Anniversary All-Time Team in 1994.

In February 1999, Payton was diagnosed with a rare liver disease. He was put on a list to receive a transplant, but developed bile duct cancer and died November 1, 1999.

Reed, Andre

Born: January 29, 1964 in Allentown, Pennsylvania

Andre Reed proved that great football players don't need to play their college ball at perennial football factories. He played at Kutztown State College, now Kutztown University, a Division II school located about two hours from Philadelphia. He caught 142 passes for 2,020 yards and 14 touchdowns for Kutztown. The Buffalo Bills drafted him in the fifth round in 1985.

Reed wasn't particularly big or fast, but he ran precise routes, had good hands, and was fearless going across the middle.

In 1988, Reed led the AFC in receptions with 88 for 1,312 yards and nine touchdowns. In 15 seasons with the Bills he caught 70 or more passes in a season five times and had 1,000 or more yards four times.

He helped the Bills reach the Super Bowl four straight times (1990–93) and through the 2000 season was second all-time in Super Bowl receptions with 27 for 323 yards. He was third all-time in postseason receptions with 85 for 1,229 yards.

Reed caught 951 passes for 13,198 yards and 87 touchdowns. He ranked third all-time in receptions and third all-time in yardage.

Reed, a seven-time Pro Bowl selection, was released by the Bills after the 1999 season and signed by the Denver Broncos for the 2000 season.

Rice, Jerry

Born: October 13, 1962 in Starkville, Mississippi

Jerry Rice is considered the greatest wide receiver in the history of the National Football League. Blessed with size (6-2, 196 pounds), speed, agility, and soft hands, Rice has been virtually impossible to stop. He can go deep, he can be a possession receiver, he can go across the middle, and he can block with the best of them.

Rice is also known for his tireless work ethic, his obsession about running precise patterns, and a workout regimen that made him one of the most durable players in the league.

Rice played his college ball at Mississippi Valley State, a Division I-AA school. During his four years, he was a consensus All-American as a junior and senior and set 18 Division I-AA records. Many pro scouts doubted

Rice's ability because of the system he played in. The perception was that the Delta Devils just threw the deep pass, and that Rice was undisciplined.

But San Francisco 49ers coach Bill Walsh thought otherwise, and when draft day came in 1985, he traded up to select Rice with the 16th pick in the first round. Two other wide receivers—Al Toon (10th) and Eddie Brown (13th)—were chosen before Rice.

Rice was named the NFL's Most Valuable Player in 1987, when he caught 65 passes for 1,078 yards and 23 touchdowns. He led the league in scoring with 138 points, the first wide receiver to do so since Elroy "Crazy Legs" Hirsch in 1951.

In 1990, he led the NFL in receiving with 100 catches for 1,502 yards and 13 touchdowns, and in 1993, he was named the NFC Offensive Player of the Year with 98 catches for 1,503 yards and 16 touchdowns. In 1995, he set a single-season record with 1,848 yards and caught a career-high 122 passes. In 1996, Rice led the NFL with 108 catches for 1,254 yards and eight touchdowns.

In 1997, Rice missed 13 games with a torn anterior cruciate ligament. It was the first time he had missed a game at any level. He was expected to miss between four and six months, but he returned to the lineup in just under three months. But in his first game back, he caught a touchdown pass and suffered a fractured patella on the play.

He came back in 1998 to start all 16 games, catching 82 passes for 1,157 yards and nine touchdowns. He was the first receiver over age 35 to record a 1,000-yard season. He recorded his 12th straight 1,000-yard season, an NFL record, and increased his streak of consecutive games catching at least one pass to 193, also an NFL record.

In 1999, the 49ers slumped to their worst record since 1980. Quarterback Steve Young missed much of the season with a concussion, and as a result Rice's numbers declined. He caught 61 passes for 687 yards and five touchdowns.

Rice helped the 49ers to victories in Super Bowls XXIII, XXIV and XXIX. In Super Bowl XXIII, a 20–16 win over the Cincinnati Bengals, Rice caught 11 passes for 215 yards and one touchdown and was named the game's Most Valuable Player.

Through the 2000 season, Rice owned Super Bowl records for catches (28), yards (512), touchdowns (7), and points (42). He held postseason records for catches (124) and yardage (1,811).

Rice holds virtually every NFL record for receiving. Through the 2000 season, he ranked first all-time in receptions (1,275), receiving yards (19,104), total touchdowns (182), receiving touchdowns (176), most 100-yard games (64), most 1,000-yard seasons (12), most 100-catch seasons (4), most single-season receiving yards

(1,848), most receiving touchdowns in a single season (22), most consecutive 100-catch seasons (3), and most seasons with 50 or more receptions (13).

Rice, a 10-time All-Pro and a 12-time Pro Bowl selection through the 1999 season, signed a two-year contract with the 49ers in June 2000.

Riggins, John
Born: August 4, 1949 in Seneca, Kansas

John Riggins was a hard-running, powerfully built fullback (6-2, 240 pounds) who seemed to get better as he got older.

Riggins played his college ball at Kansas University, where he rushed for 1,131 yards as a senior and 2,706 yards in his career. He was a first-round draft choice of the New York Jets in the 1971 NFL draft. He spent the first five years of his career with the Jets, then signed as a free agent with the Washington Redskins.

Riggins rushed for 1,000 yards or more five times in his career; four times came with the Redskins.

In 1982, a season shortened by a strike, Riggins helped the Redskins reach Super Bowl XVII, a 27–17 victory over the Miami Dolphins. Riggins rushed for 166 yards and one touchdown—a 43-yard game-winner—on 38 carries and was named the game's Most Valuable Player.

In 1983, Riggins rushed for 1,347 yards and 24 touchdowns and was named the winner of the Bert Bell Award as the NFL's Most Valuable Player.

Riggins retired after the 1985 season with 11,352 yards and 104 rushing touchdowns. He also caught 250 passes for 2,090 yards and 12 touchdowns. Through the 2000 season, he ranked 10th all-time in rushing yardage and seventh all-time in touchdowns (116). He was inducted into the Pro Football Hall of Fame in 1992.

Robustelli, Andy
Born: December 6, 1925 in Stamford, Connecticut

Andy Robustelli, who played his college ball at Arnold College, was a 19th-round draft choice of the Los Angeles Rams in 1951. Despite long odds, he developed into one of the best defensive ends of his time. He was an intelligent player, blessed with quickness and speed.

Robustelli played five seasons with the Rams before being traded to the New York Giants in 1956. In nine seasons with the Giants, he played in six NFL championship games and was on one winner (1956). He also played in two NFL title games with the Rams, who won in 1951.

Robustelli won the Bert Bell Award in 1962 as the NFL's Most Valuable Player. He retired after the 1964 season, having missed only one game in 14 years.

Robustelli was a seven-time All-Pro and an eight-time Pro Bowl selection. He was inducted into the Pro Football Hall of Fame in 1971.

Sanders, Barry
Born: July 16, 1968 in Wichita, Kansas

Throughout a college career that saw him win the 1988 Heisman Trophy, and a pro career with the Detroit Lions, Barry Sanders redefined elusiveness and excitement.

Despite his small stature (5-8, 200 pounds) and fears that his body wouldn't be able to take the constant pounding in the NFL, Sanders was a potential highlight film every time he touched the ball. Give him a crack and he was gone; assume he was corralled and he would escape from the situations that were seemingly inescapable.

Jim Brown called him a "little genius"; Gale Sayers said he would "pay to watch him play." In addition to his dazzling array of moves and jukes and stops and starts, Barry Sanders was strong enough to get tough yards inside.

During his career at Oklahoma State, Sanders set 13 NCAA records, including single-season marks in 1988 for rushing yards (2,628), rushing touchdowns (37), yards per game (238.9), all-purpose yardage (3,250), and points (234). He won the Heisman Trophy as the nation's outstanding college football player.

Sanders passed up his senior season at Oklahoma State and entered the NFL draft after his junior year. He was chosen in the first round (third pick overall) of the 1989 draft by the Detroit Lions. He gained 1,470 yards, scored 14 touchdowns, and led the NFC in rushing. He was named the NFL's Offensive Rookie of the Year.

In 1990, Sanders, soft-spoken and deeply religious, won the first of his four NFL rushing titles. He gained 1,304 yards, averaged 5.1 yards a carry, and scored 13 touchdowns. He also was the league's leading rusher in 1994 (1,883 yards, 5.7 average, seven touchdowns), 1996 (1,553, 5.1, 11), and 1997 (2,053, 6.1, 11). He was named Offensive Player of the Year in 1994 and 1997, and Most Valuable Player in 1997, when he shared the award with Brett Favre.

His 2,000-yard season in 1997 was only the third ever recorded and the second-highest total, behind Eric Dickerson's 2,105 yards (1984).

Sanders was the only player in NFL history to rush for 1,000 yards in 10 consecutive seasons and his first 10 seasons in the league. He averaged 1,527 yards over those 10 years. He is the only player in NFL history to record five seasons of 1,500 or more yards and the only player to surpass 1,500 yards in four straight seasons (1994–97). His 14 straight games of 100 yards or more is also an NFL record.

Barry Sanders   *Diane Staskowski*

Sanders ended the 1998 season with the all-time NFL rushing record in sight. He trailed the leader, Walter Payton, by 1,458 yards, well within his reach during the 1999 season. But Sanders became embroiled in a contract dispute with the Lions, made good on his threat to sit out the entire season, then effectively retired.

Through the 2000 season, his career rushing total of 15,269 yards ranked second all-time. He averaged 5.0 yards a carry and scored 99 rushing touchdowns. He caught 352 passes for 2,921 yards and 10 touchdowns. His 18,308 all-purpose yards ranked third all-time, and his 109 touchdowns ranked eighth all-time.

Sanders is a five-time All-Pro and a 10-time Pro Bowl player.

Sanders, Deion (also baseball)
Born: August 9, 1967 in Fort Myers, Florida

Deion Sanders was one of the most electrifying and controversial athletes of his time. He had athleticism and blazing speed—he once ran the 40 in 4.2 seconds while wearing shoulder pads—which allowed him to single-handedly change the course of a football game. His versatility allowed him to play football and baseball simultaneously for part of his career. His glitzy lifestyle, his penchant for jewelry, and his brash personality, which bordered on arrogance, made him a lightning rod for controversy.

Sanders played his college ball at Florida State, where he was a two-time All-American defensive back and winner of the Jim Thorpe Award as the nation's outstanding defensive back. On the day of his final regular season game, he arrived at the stadium in a limo and wearing a top hat and tails. His nicknames, "Prime Time" and "Neon Deion," were well earned.

Sanders was also a center fielder on the baseball team and a sprinter on the track team. He once played in the first game of a baseball tournament, ran a leg on the 4 x 100 relay team, then returned to the baseball team and got the game-winning hit in the second game of the day. His multisport versatility would follow him throughout his career.

In 1989, the Atlanta Falcons drafted him in the first round. In his first regular season game with the Falcons he returned an interception 68 yards for a touchdown. He was also playing with the New York Yankees at the time, and the touchdown came five days after he had hit a home run, making him the first player to homer in the major leagues and score an NFL touchdown the same week.

Sanders was released by the Yankees in 1990 and signed with the Atlanta Braves. Playing for a baseball and a football team in the same city made life much easier.

In 1992, Sanders hit .304, stole 28 bases, and led the National League with 14 triples. In the World Series, a seven-game loss to the Toronto Blue Jays, he hit .533 and stole five bases, although his football commitment to the Falcons allowed him to play in only four games. He is the only athlete to play in a Super Bowl and a World Series.

In 1993, Sanders hit .276 and stole 19 bases in 95 games. He remained with the team through the postseason, which ended with a loss to the Philadelphia Phillies in the National League Championship Series. Despite arriving late to the Falcons, he led the NFC with seven interceptions.

Sanders spent 1994 and part of 1995 with the Cincinnati Reds. He also played for the San Francisco

Deion Sanders *Diane Staskowski*

Giants in 1995. He didn't play at all in 1996 and returned to the Reds in 1997, his last year as a major league player.

In 1994, Sanders signed with the San Francisco 49ers and was named the NFL Defensive Player of the Year with six interceptions, 37 tackles, and 15 passes defensed. He also tied Ronnie Lott's team record of three interceptions returned for touchdowns. He helped the 49ers to Super Bowl XXIX, which they won 49–26 over the San Diego Chargers.

Sanders' brilliance wasn't just in the numbers he put up. It was the impact he had on a game. Defensively, he was an outstanding cover cornerback who effectively took away half the field from the quarterback. His tackling skills were questionable, but because of his speed, few quarterbacks bothered to throw his way. He was also a fine punt and kickoff returner, as well as a wide receiver, which was added to his job description.

In 1995, he joined the Dallas Cowboys as a free agent and helped the Cowboys win Super Bowl XXX, 27–17 over the Pittsburgh Steelers.

For the first 11 games of the 1996 season, he was a regular at cornerback and wide receiver, making him the first two-way player since Chuck Bednarik of the Philadelphia Eagles, who retired in 1962.

Sanders had 45 tackles and two interceptions on defense and 36 catches for 475 yards on offense.

In 1997 and 1998, Sanders continued to be a defensive presence and an offensive weapon for the Cowboys, although injuries began to take their toll. He missed the final three games in 1997 with a fractured rib, and in 1998, a toe injury suffered in the 10th game bothered him for the rest of that season and into the 1999 season.

Following the 1999 season, the Cowboys released Sanders, who signed a seven-year, $55 million contract with the Washington Redskins, where he was expected to be a starter.

Through the 2000 season, Sanders had 48 career interceptions and returned them for 1,187 yards and eight touchdowns. He was a seven-time Pro Bowl player.

Sayers, Gale
Born: May 30, 1943 in Wichita, Kansas

Gale Sayers played only 68 games over his seven injury-plagued seasons, but during that time, short as it was, he made his mark as perhaps the most breathtaking open-field runner in the history of the National Football League.

Sayers was an electrifying offensive force. He was quick to hit the hole, blessed with great speed and acceleration, and able to change directions and elude would-be tacklers when it seemed there was no escape.

Sayers was a two-time All-American at the University of Kansas in 1963 and 1964. In three years at Kansas, he gained 2,675 yards and averaged 6.5 yards a carry, including 7.1 yards as a junior.

In 1965, the Chicago Bears made Sayers their first-round choice in the NFL draft, and he was named Rookie of the Year and an All-Pro. He set an NFL single-season record for touchdowns (22) and gained 2,272 combined yards. The touchdown record stood for 10 years and remains a record for rookies.

Against the San Francisco 49ers in the next-to-last game of the 1965 season, Sayers tied an NFL record by scoring six touchdowns—four rushing, one on a pass reception, and one on a punt return.

Sayers led the league in rushing twice—1,231 yards in 1966 and 1,032 yards in 1969. The second rushing title was a miracle, of sorts. It came after a severe knee injury during the 1968 season. Kermit Alexander, a defensive back for the San Francisco 49ers, used a submarine tackle to try to stop Sayers. The hit tore Sayers' medial collateral ligament in three places. Many assumed his career to be over, but Sayers defied conventional medical wisdom.

In 1970, he suffered another serious knee injury. Two knee surgeries couldn't repair the damage. Sayers attempted to come back in 1971, but played in only two games and was forced to retire.

Sayers gained only 4,956 yards in his career, but he averaged 5 yards per carry. He also averaged 11.7 yards per catch, an NFL-record 30.6 yards per kickoff return, and 14.5 yards per punt return.

Sayers, a four-time Pro Bowl player, was inducted into the Pro Football Hall of Fame in 1977.

Schmidt, Joe

Born: January 18, 1932 in Pittsburgh, Pennsylvania

One of the most intimidating linebackers of his era, Joe Schmidt's career blossomed from humble beginnings. After playing his college ball at the University of Pittsburgh, where he was hampered by injuries, he was drafted in the seventh round by the Detroit Lions in 1953. He started his career as an outside linebacker and was moved to middle linebacker in 1953. He had the ability to stop the run—he was a ferocious tackler—and drop into pass coverage. He was blessed with strength, mobility, and leadership skills that made him the anchor of the Lions' defense.

Schmidt, who made 24 career interceptions, helped the Lions win two NFL championships (1953, '57). He was an eight-time All-Pro; he shared the 1960 Associated Press Athlete of the Year Award with Philadelphia quarterback Norm Van Brocklin; and he played in nine Pro Bowls. He was inducted into the Pro Football Hall of Fame in 1973.

From 1967 to 1972, Schmidt was the head coach of the Lions. He had a 43–34–7 record. He went on to become a front office executive for the team.

Selmon, Lee Roy

Born: October 20, 1954 in Eufaula, Oklahoma

Lee Roy Selmon was one of the elite defensive ends of his time. Blessed with size (6-3, 250 pounds), speed, and athleticism, he often was moved to outside linebacker so he could roam with a bit more freedom.

Selmon played his college ball at the University of Oklahoma, where he was a consensus All-American and the winner of the 1975 Outland Trophy (best interior lineman) and the Lombardi Award (best lineman).

In 1976, Selmon was the first player chosen in the NFL draft by the expansion Tampa Bay Buccaneers. He helped the Bucs win the NFC Central title in 1979 and 1981. In 1979, he was named the NFL's Defensive Player of the Year.

Selmon spent his entire career, nine seasons, with Tampa Bay. He retired after the 1984 season with 78 1/2 sacks. He was a three-time All-Pro and a five-time Pro Bowl selection. He was inducted into the Pro Football Hall of Fame in 1995.

Shell, Art

Born: November 26, 1946 in Charleston, South Carolina

Art Shell was quiet and soft-spoken off the field and powerful and intimidating on it. He was one of the finest offensive tackles of his era, a punishing blocker who was as intelligent (he knew the offensive assignments of each of his teammates) as he was talented.

Shell joined the Oakland Raiders in 1968 after a Little All-American career at Maryland State-Eastern Shore College. He broke into the starting lineup immediately and played in 142 consecutive games from 1968 to 1978, until a knee injury, suffered prior to the 1979 season, caused him to miss five games.

Shell helped the Raiders to 11 playoff appearances, nine AFL or AFC championship appearances, and two Super Bowl victories (XI, XV). In Super Bowl XI, a 32–14 victory over the Minnesota Vikings, Shell and guard Gene Upshaw were instrumental in the Raiders rushing for 266 yards, most of it coming against the Vikings' pair of Alan Page and Jim Marshall, perennial All-Pros.

Shell retired midway through the 1982 season. He played in eight Pro Bowls and was inducted into the Pro Football Hall of Fame in 1989.

After his retirement, he joined the Raiders as an assistant coach, and four games into the 1989 season was named head coach. He was the second African American head coach in NFL history. He was fired as the Raiders head coach in 1994. Through the 2000 season, Shell was an offensive line coach with the Atlanta Falcons.

Simpson, O.J. (Orenthal James)
Born: July 9, 1947 in San Francisco, California

O.J. Simpson was one of the most productive and most elusive running backs in National Football League history. He was blessed with great instincts, acceleration, and moves.

Simpson began playing football without any hint of success. At Galileo High in San Francisco, Simpson's legs were so thin because he had rickets as a child, they were called "pencil pins." Yet as a senior, he was an All-City running back, but not an honor student. As a result, he enrolled at City College of San Francisco, where he scored 26 touchdowns and averaged 9.9 yards a carry in his first season. In his second season, he scored 28 touchdowns, but more important, he earned enough transferable credits to gain admission to the University of Southern California in 1967.

Simpson, who played only 18 games for the Trojans, gained 3,187 yards and scored 34 touchdowns. In 1967, his 64-yard touchdown run, which was a self-contained highlight film, lifted USC to a 21–20 victory over crosstown rival UCLA. The Trojans earned the Rose Bowl bid and went on to win the national championship with a victory over Ohio State.

As a senior, Simpson rushed for 1,654 yards, then an NCAA record, and also carried the ball a then record 334 times. He won the 1968 Heisman Trophy as the nation's most outstanding player.

In 1969 he was the first player chosen in the NFL draft, by the Buffalo Bills. His first three years in Buffalo were as a supporting player. The Bills head coach, John Rauch, featured a passing attack, but it led to only eight wins in three seasons. Rauch was fired, and Lou Saban was named his successor. Saban implemented an offense that could take advantage of Simpson's talents. The result was impressive: Simpson led the NFL in rushing with 1,251 yards.

In 1973, Simpson, nicknamed "Juice," ran behind a line dubbed the "Electric Company," because it was said to "turn on the Juice." He broke Jim Brown's single-season rushing record by gaining 2,003 yards in 14 games. He averaged 6.0 yards a carry and broke the record with 200 yards in the season finale in the snow against the New York Jets at Shea Stadium. Simpson was named the NFL's Most Valuable Player, the Offensive Player of the Year, and the Associated Press Athlete of the Year.

In 1975, Simpson led the league in rushing with 1,817 yards, gained a combined 2,243 yards (426 receiving), and scored 23 touchdowns, and in 1976, he led the

league with 1,503 yards. In all, he rushed for 1,000 yards or more five times.

In 1977, his last season with the Bills, a knee injury limited him to 557 yards. He spent two seasons with the San Francisco 49ers, retiring after the 1979 season.

Through the 2000 season, Simpson ranked 11th all-time in rushing yardage (11,236) and 18th in all-purpose yards (14,368). He averaged 4.7 yards a carry and scored 61 career touchdowns rushing and 14 by reception.

Simpson has two of the top four single-game rushing performances. He gained 273 yards in November 1976 against the Detroit Lions, and he gained 250 yards against the New England Patriots in September 1973. Walter Payton has the top single-game performance—275 yards against the Minnesota Vikings in November 1977.

Simpson, a five-time All-Pro and a six-time Pro Bowl player, was inducted into the Pro Football Hall of Fame in 1985. In 1994, he was named to the NFL's 75th Anniversary All-Time Team.

After he retired, Simpson enjoyed a successful career as a television commentator, and he also became an actor. He also was the first African American athlete to be featured in a national television ad campaign. Simpson was famous for running through airports in Hertz rental car commercials.

In June 1994, he was accused of murdering his ex-wife, Nicole Brown Simpson, and her friend, Ronald Goldman. The nation became obsessed with the case. Simpson was found not guilty in the criminal trial and found guilty in the civil trial.

Singletary, Mike
Born: October 9, 1958 in Houston, Texas

Mike Singletary didn't have the size of a prototype middle linebacker. He stood just 6-0 and weighed only 230 pounds. But he was blessed with determination and dedication that helped him overcome his physical deficiencies to become one of the best middle linebackers of his era.

Singletary was an All-American in 1979 and 1980 and the Southwest Conference Player of the Year in 1980 at Baylor University.

Singletary was drafted by the Chicago Bears in 1980 and developed into a complete player. At first, he was used primarily against the run and taken out of the game on third-down passing situations. This frustrated him because he hated to leave the field. So to ensure that he was an every-down linebacker, he worked on pass coverages after practices and eventually mastered the techniques.

Singletary was an intense player who became the leader of the Chicago Bears defense. He helped lead them to a 15–1 record in 1985. The Bears reached Super Bowl XX, where they defeated the New England Patriots 46–10.

Singletary, who retired after the 1992 season, played for 12 years. He had 44 interceptions, 12 fumble recoveries, and 12 quarterback sacks. He was a four-time All-Pro and the NFL Defensive Player of the Year in 1985. A 10-time Pro Bowl player, Singletary was inducted into the Pro Football Hall of Fame in 1998.

Smith, Bruce

Born: June 18, 1963 in Norfolk, Virginia

Bruce Smith, who played his college ball at Virginia Tech, was a consensus All-American and the Outland Trophy winner as the best college lineman in the United States in 1984. The Buffalo Bills made him the first overall pick in the 1985 NFL draft, and he has gone on to become one of the best defensive ends in the history of the game.

At 6-4, 275 pounds, he is powerfully built and blessed with the speed and quickness usually associated with linebackers. Smith, an excellent run stopper, is best known for his ability to rush the quarterback, either by a speed rush around his blocker or by knifing through holes between blockers. He is a student of the game in that he watches films on his opponents to try to get any edge available.

Smith, the anchor of the Bills' defense, has helped lead them into the playoffs 10 times, including four consecutive appearances in the Super Bowl (XXV, XXVI, XXVII, XXVIII), all losses.

Through the 2000 season, Smith had 181 sacks, which ranked second all-time to Reggie White. Smith was an eight-time All-Pro and an 11-time Pro Bowl player.

Smith signed with the Washington Redskins prior to the 2000 season.

Smith, Emmitt

Born: May 15, 1969 in Pensacola, Florida

Emmitt Smith is proof positive that successful NFL running backs don't need to be especially big or fast. Smith is neither, but he is one of the best running backs of all time. At 5-9, 203 pounds, Smith used his powerful legs and hips to wear out tacklers with his straight-ahead style of running. He was a grinder who always seemed to get the tough yards, particularly near the goal line.

Smith played his college ball at the University of Florida, where he set 58 school records in three seasons and was a consensus All-American in 1989. The Dallas Cowboys selected him in the first round of the 1990 NFL draft, and he was the offensive foundation of their three Super Bowl championship seasons.

Emmitt Smith   *Diane Staskowski*

After a solid rookie season, in which he gained 937 yards and scored 11 touchdowns, Smith led the NFL in rushing for three straight seasons (1,563 yards, 12 touchdowns in 1991; 1,713, 18 in 1992; 1,486, 9 in 1993). He was only the fourth player in NFL history to lead the league in rushing three consecutive seasons. In 1993, he was named the NFL's Most Valuable Player.

In 1994, he led the league in touchdowns with 22, while rushing for 1,484 yards. In 449 carries, he didn't fumble once.

In 1995, he led the league for a fourth time, rushing for 1,773 yards and 25 touchdowns, an NFL single-season record.

Smith helped the Cowboys win three Super Bowls in a four-year stretch (1992–93, '95). In Super Bowl XXVIII, he was named the game's Most Valuable Player. He rushed for 132 yards and two touchdowns on 30 carries, and also caught four passes for 26 yards in a 30–13 victory over the Buffalo Bills.

Through the 2000 season, Smith was one of only two running backs in NFL history—Barry Sanders was the other—to rush for 1,000 yards or more in 10 consecutive seasons. One of the reasons for his success has been his durability. He started 180 of 185 possible games, including the postseason.

Through the 2000 season, Smith rushed for 15,106 yards and 145 touchdowns. He ranked first all-time in rushing touchdowns and third all-time in rushing. He needed 1,307 yards to overtake Sanders for second place and 1,561 yards to surpass Walter Payton as the all-time leading rusher.

Smith, a nine-time Pro Bowl player, was second all-time in touchdowns with 156 (145 rushing, 11 receiving) and the only player to rush for 1,400 or more yards in five straight seasons (1992–95).

Smith, Jackie

Born: February 2, 1940 in Columbia, Mississippi

Jackie Smith, who played his college ball at Northwestern Louisiana, was a 10th-round draft choice of the St. Louis Cardinals in 1963. He went on to have an outstanding career and is recognized as one of the best tight ends of all time.

Smith was a fine receiver and a punishing blocker. Seven times he caught 40 or more passes in a season. His best season came in 1971, when he caught 56 passes for 1,205 yards and nine touchdowns.

Smith spent 15 seasons with the Cardinals before joining the Dallas Cowboys in 1978, his final season. He helped the Cowboys reach Super Bowl XIII against the Pittsburgh Steelers. Despite his fine career, Smith is probably most remembered for dropping what would have been a sure touchdown pass in the end zone of the Steelers' 35–31 victory.

When Smith retired, he was the all-time leading tight end receiver with 480 catches for 7,918 yards and 40 touchdowns. He was an All-Pro once and a five-time Pro Bowl selection. He was inducted into the Pro Football Hall of Fame in 1994.

Starr, Bart (Bryan Bartlett)

Born: January 9, 1934 in Montgomery, Alabama

Bart Starr was the 17th-round draft choice of the Green Bay Packers in 1956, after an unspectacular career at the University of Alabama as a quarterback. The first three years of his pro career were similarly unspectacular. But in 1960, when Vince Lombardi was named head coach of the Packers, Starr took over as the starter and began a career that would be an unqualified success.

Starr ran the Packers' ball-control offense to perfection. He was intelligent, played within himself, and was a master tactician who always seemed to make the right decisions.

If the mark of a great quarterback is his ability to win championships, then Starr ranks as one of the best ever. From 1960 through 1967, the Packers appeared in six NFL championship games and won five, including the first two Super Bowls. Starr was named Most Valuable Player in both games. In Super Bowl I, a 35–10 victory over the Kansas City Chiefs, he completed 16 of 23 for

250 yards, two touchdowns, and one interception. In Super Bowl II, a 33–14 victory over the Oakland Raiders, he completed 13 of 24 for 202 yards and one touchdown.

Starr's most famous playoff game was the 1967 NFL championship against the Dallas Cowboys in the famous "Ice Bowl." The temperature in Green Bay was minus 13 and the wind chill was 48 below. The field was the equivalent of concrete because the below-ground heating system didn't work.

The Packers took a 14–0 lead, but Dallas went ahead 17–14 with 4:50 left. Green Bay took over at its 32. Two key completions by Starr helped move the ball to the 11. Two more plays moved the ball to the 1 with 30 seconds left. The Packers, facing third and goal at the 1, called their final timeout.

Green Bay could have attempted a pass that could've been thrown away and then gone for a tying field goal. But Starr suggested running a quarterback sneak. Said Lombardi: "Then do it, and let's get the hell out of here."

Starr, knifing into a crack created by guard Jerry Kramer and center Ken Bowman, scored the winning touchdown in what has become one of the most famous plays in NFL history.

Starr led the NFL in passing in 1962 (2,438 yards, 12 touchdowns), 1964 (2,144 yards, 15 touchdowns), and 1966 (2,257 yards, 14 touchdowns). He once went 294 passes without throwing an interception (1964–65).

Starr's passing numbers are not as prolific as they might be, because Green Bay relied on a punishing running game as the focus of its offense. But when Starr did throw, he was uncannily accurate. His career completion percentage was 57.4 percent.

Starr, who retired after the 1971 season, threw for 24,718 yards and 52 touchdowns. He was inducted into the Pro Football Hall of Fame in 1977.

In 1975, Starr returned to Green Bay as head coach. He coached through the 1983 season and had a record of 53–77–2.

Staubach, Roger

Born: February 5, 1942 in Cincinnati, Ohio

Roger Staubach was a resourceful quarterback and one of the toughest competitors to play the game. He was best known for his scrambling ability and his performance under pressure.

Staubach attended the U.S. Naval Academy, and in 1963 won the Heisman Trophy as the nation's outstanding college football player.

The Dallas Cowboys drafted Staubach in 1965, even though he still had to fulfill his commitment to the Navy for four years. He joined the team in 1969 and two years later was named the starting quarterback. He was 29 years old.

During the 1971 season, Staubach, known as "Roger the Dodger," led the NFC in passing, throwing for 1,882 yards and 15 touchdowns. He led the Cowboys to Super Bowl VI and a victory over the Miami Dolphins in which he completed 12 of 19 passes for 119 yards and two touchdowns. He was named the game's Most Valuable Player. He also was named Most Valuable Player in the league.

Staubach missed much of the 1972 season with a shoulder injury, but in a first-round playoff game against the San Francisco 49ers he engineered one of the comebacks for which he was famous. He threw two touchdown passes in the final 70 seconds to rally the Cowboys to a 30–28 victory.

Staubach's most famous comeback victory came in the 1975 divisional playoffs against the Minnesota Vikings. With the Cowboys trailing 14–10 with time running out, Staubach threw a 50-yard "Hail Mary" pass that Drew Pearson caught in the end zone for a 17–10 victory. Dallas went on to the Super Bowl, where they lost to the Pittsburgh Steelers.

Those comebacks were Staubach's signature. He always seemed to find a way to win. His ability to elude would-be tacklers, throw on the run, excel on third-down situations, and communicate his never-say-die attitude to his teammates set him apart. Twenty-three times during his career, he led the Cowboys to come-from-behind victories, including 14 in the last two minutes.

He also was one of the most consistent players in the league. From 1973 through 1979, Staubach was the NFC's leading passer four times, including 1979, when he threw for 3,586 yards and 27 touchdowns.

Staubach led the Cowboys to two more Super Bowl appearances—a victory over the Denver Broncos in Super Bowl XII and a loss to Pittsburgh in Super Bowl XIII.

Staubach helped the Cowboys win 73 percent of their games during the nine seasons he started. They made the playoffs eight times, won the NFC Championship four times, and won two of four Super Bowls.

Staubach, a three-time All-Pro and a four-time Pro Bowl selection, threw for 22,700 yards and 153 touchdowns. He ran for 2,264 yards and 20 touchdowns. He was inducted into the Pro Football Hall of Fame in 1985.

Stenerud, Jan
Born: November 26, 1942 in Festund, Norway
Jan Stenerud attended the University of Montana on a skiing scholarship, and joined the football team as a junior. He joined the Kansas City Chiefs in 1967, when he led the AFL with 21 field goals. In 1970, he led the AFL in scoring with 116 points on 30 field goals and 26 extra points.

Stenerud spent 13 seasons with the Chiefs (1967–79), four seasons with the Green Bay Packers (1980–83), and two seasons with the Minnesota Vikings (1984–85). In 1981, he made 22 of 24 field goal attempts, which was a record at the time.

Stenerud, who played for 19 seasons, totaled 1,699 points on 373 field goals and 580 extra points. He converted on 67 percent of his field goals and 97.6 percent of his extra points.

Stenerud scored 100 or more points in seven seasons. He was a four-time All-Pro and a six-time Pro Bowl player. He was the first pure kicker inducted into the Pro Football Hall of Fame, in 1991.

Stephenson, Dwight
Born: November 11, 1957 in Murfreesboro, North Carolina
Dwight Stephenson played his college ball at the University of Alabama, where legendary coach Paul "Bear" Bryant called him "the greatest center I've ever coached." Don Shula, Stephenson's coach with the Miami Dolphins, agreed. Stephenson had it all—size, strength, speed, quickness, and agility. He could pass block and run block equally well. He was regarded as the best center of his era.

Stephenson was chosen by the Dolphins in the second round of the 1980 NFL draft and for eight seasons was the anchor of the offensive line. The Dolphins developed all their blocking schemes around Stephenson, who was able to handle nose tackles and middle linebackers one-on-one, thanks to his ability to explode off the ball after he snapped it.

Stephenson's career was cut short due to a devastating knee injury in 1987. A five-time Pro Bowl player, he was inducted into the Pro Football Hall of Fame in 1998.

Tarkenton, Fran
Born: February 3, 1940 in Richmond, Virginia
Unlike other quarterbacks, who stayed in the pocket and ran only when necessary, Fran Tarkenton made scrambling a habit. His willingness to try to elude defensive linemen in pursuit and take off and run when the opportunity presented itself was a revolutionary strategy. He wasn't noted for his arm strength, but he had great touch and obviously had the ability to throw on the run.

Tarkenton, who played his college ball at the University of Georgia, joined the expansion Minnesota Vikings in 1961. He entered the Vikings' first regular-season game in relief, threw four touchdown passes and ran for another, and engineered a 37–13 upset of the Chicago Bears. He was the starter from then on.

Tarkenton remained with the Vikings until 1967, when he was traded to the New York Giants, where he played for five seasons before being traded back to Minnesota.

By this time in his career, Tarkenton had become less of a scrambler and more of a conventional pocket passer. His skills as a leader also were outstanding. From 1973 through 1978, he led the Vikings to six straight NFC Central Division titles and three Super Bowls (VIII, IX, XI), all losses.

Tarkenton was named the NFL Player of the Year in 1975, when he led the NFC in passing with 2,994 yards and 25 touchdowns.

Tarkenton retired after the 1978 season. In 18 seasons, he completed 57 percent of his passes for 47,003 yards and 342 touchdowns. He also ran for 3,674 yards and 32 touchdowns.

Through the 2000 season, he ranked second all-time in touchdown passes, third all-time in passes intercepted (266), and fourth all-time in passing yardage.

A two-time All-Pro and a nine-time Pro Bowl player, Tarkenton was inducted into the Pro Football Hall of Fame in 1986.

Taylor, Charley
Born: September 28, 1941 in Grand Prairie, Texas

Charley Taylor played his college ball at Arizona State University, where he was an acclaimed running back. He joined the Washington Redskins in 1964 and spent his first two years at the same position. He rushed for 755 yards and caught 53 passes for 814 yards and was named the NFL's Rookie of the Year.

But in 1966, Redskins head coach Otto Graham switched Taylor to wide receiver, much to Taylor's displeasure. At 6-3, 210 pounds, Graham knew the mismatch problems Taylor would cause for smaller defensive backs. The move worked. Taylor led the NFL in receiving in 1966 (72 catches, 1,119 yards, 12 touchdowns) and 1967 (70, 990, 12).

In addition to having the size, speed, and quick moves to be a big-play wide receiver, Taylor also took pride in his ability to block downfield. He was a complete wide receiver.

Taylor was plagued by injuries during the 1970 and 1971 seasons, and he missed the 1976 season entirely with a shoulder injury. He returned in 1977, but caught only 14 passes and announced his retirement.

Taylor, who played 13 seasons, all with the Redskins, caught 649 passes for 9,110 yards (14.1-yard average) and 79 touchdown receptions. When he retired, his 649 catches was an NFL record. Through the 2000 season, he ranked 17th all-time. His 90 touchdowns overall ranked him 17th all-time.

Taylor, a seven-time Pro Bowl player, was inducted into the Pro Football Hall of Fame in 1984.

Taylor, Jim
Born: September 20, 1935 in Baton Rouge, Louisiana

Jim Taylor was the prototype fullback—big (6-0, 214 pounds), strong, and powerful. He was a bruising runner and a punishing blocker. He was an All-American at Louisiana State University in 1957 and a second-round draft choice of the Green Bay Packers in 1958.

Taylor became a starter in his second season, which was the first year for head coach Vince Lombardi. From 1960 through 1964, Taylor rushed for 1,000 or more yards each season, including a career-high 1,472 yards and 19 touchdowns in 1962. He was named the league's Most Valuable Player by the Associated Press.

Taylor never led the NFL in rushing, but four times he finished second to Jim Brown of the Cleveland Browns.

Taylor helped the Packers win four NFL championship games (1961–62, '65–67). He left Green Bay after the 1966 season to play for the New Orleans Saints. He retired in 1967 after one season.

Taylor rushed for 8,597 yards and 83 touchdowns. He caught 225 passes for 1,756 yards and 10 touchdowns. A two-time All-Pro and a five-time Pro Bowl selection, he was inducted into the Pro Football Hall of Fame in 1976.

Taylor, Lawrence
Born: February 4, 1959 in Williamsburg, Virginia

Lawrence Taylor redefined playing linebacker, in particular, and redefined playing defense, in general. He was strong, explosive, and virtually unstoppable. He was a fierce pass rusher who was a dominant force. He changed the game by making pass rushing part of a linebacker's job description.

Taylor, the son of a shipyard worker, was not a highly regarded player coming out of high school. He received two scholarship offers—one from the University of Richmond, and the other from the University of North Carolina, which he accepted.

Taylor, nicknamed "L.T.," was moved to linebacker during his junior year at North Carolina, and he was a consensus All-American as a senior. The New York Giants made him their first-round draft pick in 1981, when he was named NFL Defensive Player of the Year and Rookie of the Year, the only rookie to be so honored.

He was also named Defensive Player of the Year in 1982 and 1986, when he had 20 1/2 sacks, led the Giants to the Super Bowl championship, and became the only defensive player to win the NFL Player of the Year Award.

Taylor also helped the Giants win Super Bowl XXI. The Giants made the playoffs in seven of Taylor's 13 seasons.

Lawrence Taylor   *Diane Staskowski*

He retired in 1993 with 132 1/2 sacks and 10 consecutive Pro Bowl appearances, an NFL record.

Taylor's life had a dark side, as well. He entered a drug rehabilitation center in 1986 and was suspended for drug abuse in 1988. Twice since his retirement Taylor was arrested for trying to buy crack cocaine from an undercover cop.

There was some sentiment that Taylor's off-the-field troubles might keep him from being inducted into the Pro Football Hall of Fame, but those thoughts were unfounded. He was inducted in 1999, and is widely regarded as the greatest linebacker in pro football history. He was also named a member of the NFL's 75th Anniversary All-Time Team in 1994.

Thorpe, Jim (also track and field)
Born: May 28, 1888 in Prague, Oklahoma
Died: March 28, 1953

Jim Thorpe was one of the most accomplished, versatile, and storied athletes of all time. His exploits in several sports—football, track and field, Major League Baseball—have made him a figure of almost mythic proportions.

Thorpe was born in Indian Territory, now known as Oklahoma. His father was part Irish, part Native American; his mother was a member of the Sac and Fox tribes. His Indian name was "Wa-Tho-Huk" and meant "Bright Path."

As legend has it, Thorpe spent much of his youth battling his father, Hiram, who sent him away to a boarding school 300 miles from their home. After Thorpe escaped, was enrolled in public school, and then ran away, his father sent him to the Carlisle Indian Industrial School in Pennsylvania, where Thorpe was trained to become a tailor.

One night in the spring of 1907, Thorpe, dressed in overalls and engaged in a work detail, happened by the field where the track team was practicing. He asked if he could try to clear the high bar, which was set at 5-9. The jumpers snickered at the notion, but the snickering stopped when Thorpe cleared the bar easily.

The football and track coach at the school was the legendary Glenn "Pop" Warner, who found an instant track star.

Thorpe, a strong and hulking physical specimen, also wanted to try football, but Warner, fearing an injury that might ruin his track career, refused. But he finally relented, and Thorpe helped Carlisle to a 10–2 record in 1908 and was named a third team All-American.

Thorpe left Carlisle for North Carolina after the 1909 spring track season to play minor league baseball in the Carolina League. He played for two years and earned $125 a month, but the cost would be much greater.

When Thorpe returned to Oklahoma in 1911, he received a letter from Warner, urging him to return to Carlisle to complete his education. Thorpe was back in Pennsylvania for the start of the 1911–12 school year. Carlisle went 11–1 that season, including an 18–15 upset of Harvard, in which Thorpe started the game on the sideline, his legs heavily bandaged because of an injury. After his team fell behind, Thorpe removed the bandages, entered the game, and scored 13 points in the victory.

In 1912, Thorpe traveled to Sweden to participate in the 1912 Summer Olympics, where he won the pentathlon and decathlon, in which he scored 841.2 of a possible 1,000 points.

But several months after the Olympics were completed it was discovered that Thorpe had played for pay in the Carolina League and therefore was not an amateur. The Olympic Committee demanded he return his Olympic medals.

Thorpe played Major League Baseball from 1913 through 1919, and from 1915 through 1920, he played football for the Canton Bulldogs, who drew crowds from between 8,000 and 10,000. He was the first big-name athlete to play pro football.

Thorpe, his baseball career over in 1919, became the first president of the American Professional Football Association, which later became the National Football League.

Thorpe played for the Cleveland Indians (1921), the Oorang Indians (1922–23), the Rock Island Independents (1924), the New York Giants (1925), Canton (1926), and the Chicago Cardinals (1928).

After his athletic career ended at 38, Thorpe drifted from job to job, the instability in his life due in large part to alcoholism.

Thorpe suffered the first of three heart attacks in 1943. In 1951, he entered the hospital to have a cancerous growth removed from his lip. The newspapers reported that he was a charity patient, and donations poured in from across the country. He suffered his second heart attack in August 1952, and eight months later his third heart attack was fatal.

Thorpe's widow tried unsuccessfully to have the state of Oklahoma erect a monument in her late husband's honor. When that failed, the coal-mining town of Mauch Chunk, Pennsylvania, looking for a tourist attraction, agreed to change its name to Jim Thorpe if Thorpe's body could be buried there. The body was transported to Mauch Chunk, and a monument costing $15,000 stands in his honor.

Thorpe was voted the outstanding male athlete of the half century (1900–50) by the Associated Press. In 1982, the International Olympic Committee restored Thorpe's medals from 1912 and presented them to his family. A movie of Thorpe's life, *Jim Thorpe—All-American*, starring Burt Lancaster, premiered in 1951.

Thorpe was a charter member of the Pro Football Hall of Fame, inducted in 1963.

Tittle, Y. A. (Yelberton Abraham)
Born: October 24, 1926 in Marshall, Texas

Y.A. Tittle began his career with the Baltimore Colts in the All-American Football Conference (AAFC) in 1948. When the AAFC folded in 1950, the Colts became part of the National Football League, but went out of business after one season.

Tittle joined the San Francisco 49ers in 1951. In 1957, he led the NFL in completion percentage (63.1) and touchdown passes (17). He was named the league's Player of the Year by United Press International.

Unhappy sharing time with two other quarterbacks, Tittle was traded to the New York Giants in 1961.

For a short time, he shared time with Charlie Conerly, but by the end of the 1961 season, Tittle earned the starting job. He led the Giants to division championships in 1961, 1962, and 1963. In 1962, he threw for 3,224 yards and a league-leading 33 touchdown passes. In 1963, he led the NFL in passing, completing 60.2 percent of his throws for 3,145 yards and 36 touchdowns. He won his second UPI Player of the Year Award.

Tittle retired after the 1964 season, having completed 55 percent of his passes for 33,070 yards and 242 touchdowns. A three-time All-Pro and a six-time Pro Bowl player, Tittle was inducted into the Pro Football Hall of Fame in 1971.

Trippi, Charley
Born: December 14, 1922 in Pittston, Pennsylvania

Charley Trippi was best known for his versatility. He was a halfback, quarterback, kicker, and defensive back at the University of Georgia, and a halfback, quarterback, and defensive back in the pros.

In 1946, his senior year at Georgia, he rushed for 1,315 yards and was named the Maxwell Award winner as the best player in college football.

In 1947, he signed a $100,000 contract to play for the Chicago Cardinals of the NFL. He led the Cardinals to the 1947 NFL championship, rushing for 203 yards and returning a punt 75 yards for a touchdown in the title game.

Trippi spent five years at halfback, two years at quarterback, and his last two years at defensive back. He retired after the 1955 season. He rushed for 3,506 yards and 51 touchdowns, and he caught 130 passes for 1,321 yards and 11 touchdowns.

Trippi, an All-Pro in 1948, was inducted into the Pro Football Hall of Fame in 1968.

Tunnell, Emlen
Born: March 25, 1925 in Bryn Mawr, Pennsylvania
Died: July 22, 1975

Emlen Tunnell was a pioneer in the National Football League. He was the first defensive star, the first African American to become an NFL assistant coach, and the first African American to be inducted into the Pro Football Hall of Fame.

Tunnell broke a vertebra during his freshman year at the University of Toledo and was told by doctors that his football career was over. He was rejected by the Army and the Navy during World War II. He eventually was accepted into the Coast Guard and then enrolled at the University of Iowa, where he played defensive back. Despite having a year of eligibility remaining with Iowa, Tunnell left in 1948 and signed with the New York Giants. It wasn't long before he became one of the most accomplished defensive backs in the game.

Known as "Emlen the Gremlin," Tunnell was a key to the Giants' "Umbrella Defense," which changed the way defensive was played because it dropped linebackers into pass coverage. Tunnell had quick reactions and the ability to strike at the last instant and turn sure completions into interceptions.

Tunnell was also known for ability to return punts. He is regarded as the first great punt returner in NFL history.

Tunnell, who played on NFL championship teams in New York (1956) and Green Bay (1961), retired after the 1961 season. Through the 2000 season, his 79 career interceptions ranked second all-time. He was inducted into the Pro Football Hall of Fame in 1967.

Unitas, John

Born: May 7, 1933 in Pittsburgh, Pennsylvania

From humble beginnings, Johnny Unitas become one of the greatest quarterbacks in National Football League history. He was stoop-shouldered, skinny, and lightly regarded. After being rejected by Notre Dame because he was too small, Unitas went to play for the University of Louisville, where he had a solid career that included not only playing quarterback, but also punting, returning kickoffs and punts, and playing safety on defense.

He was a ninth-round draft choice of the Pittsburgh Steelers in 1955, but he never made it out of training camp. Unitas, one of four quarterbacks on the Steelers roster, was cut before the start of the regular season.

With no other offers, Unitas went to play for the Bloomfield Rams, a semipro team in the Greater Pittsburgh League. His salary was $6 a game.

Following the season with Bloomfield, Unitas received a call from Don Kellett, general manager of the Baltimore Colts, who were looking to add depth at the quarterback position. Unitas joined the Colts as their third-string quarterback.

When the no. 2 quarterback, Gary Kerkorian, quit football, Unitas moved up a spot and was second behind George Shaw. In the fourth game of the 1956 season, Shaw broke his leg. Unitas played the final eight games as the starter and led the Colts to four victories.

The Colts finished 5–7 in 1956. Over the next 15 years, the Colts, with Unitas entrenched as the starting quarterback, never suffered a losing season. The one-time castoff developed into a fearless player. He stood in the pocket against the rush and seemed to have a sixth sense that told him when to deliver the ball. He was at his best when the game was on the line and the clock was ticking down. He always made the right call at the right time, and his ability to dissect defenses was legendary.

Unitas, known for his crew cut and trademark high-top black shoes, is responsible for two streaks, both of which were unbroken through the 2000 season. He led the league in touchdown passes for four straight seasons (1957–60), and starting with the final game of the 1956 season, he threw a touchdown pass in 47 consecutive regular season games. If the playoffs were counted, the streak would be 49 straight. The second-longest streak is Dan Marino's 30.

In 1958, Unitas led the Colts to the NFL championship, beating the New York Giants for the title in what has been called "The Greatest Game Ever Played."

The game is responsible for making football a television staple.

The Colts took a 14–3 lead at the half, but the Giants rallied to go ahead 17–14. With 1:56 left, Baltimore got the ball on its 14, and Unitas drove them downfield with three passes to Raymond Berry for 62 yards. Steve Myhra kicked a game-tying field goal with seven seconds to play.

In the first sudden death overtime in NFL history, the Giants won the toss, but were unable to move the ball and had to punt. Unitas took over and drove the Colts to the winning touchdown, defining his career in the process. He moved the Colts 80 yards in 13 plays, fullback Alan Ameche scoring the game-winning touchdown from 1 yard out.

One play spoke volumes about Unitas' ability. With the ball at the 7 and within chip-shot field goal range for Myhra, Unitas opted for a pass to Jim Mutscheller that took the ball to the 1.

Asked afterward why he risked a pass when another run or two would've resulted in victory, Unitas said, "When you know what you're doing, you're not going to be intercepted."

Obviously, Unitas knew what he was doing. He won the Most Valuable Player Award in 1959, 1964, and 1967. He led the league in passing yardage four times (1957, '59–60, '63), completion percentage once (1967), and completions three times (1959–60, '63).

Unitas was troubled by injuries in the later years of his career. He missed most of the 1968 season with a torn muscle in his right elbow and had arm problems in 1971 and 1972, his last year with the Colts. He was traded to the San Diego Chargers in 1973, his final season.

In 18 seasons, Unitas completed 55 percent of his passes for 40,239 yards and 290 touchdowns. Through the 2000 season, he ranked fifth all-time in touchdown passes and seventh all-time in yards passing. A 10-time Pro Bowl player and five-time All-Pro, Unitas played on three NFL championship teams (1968–69, '71), was inducted into the Pro Football Hall of Fame in 1979, and was named a member of the NFL's 75th Anniversary All-Time Team in 1994.

Upshaw, Gene

Born: August 15, 1945 in Robstown, Texas

Gene Upshaw's football career got a late start. He didn't play until he was a senior in high school. But he walked on at Texas A&I College, where he eventually earned a scholarship, and he was drafted by the Oakland Raiders in the first round of the 1967 American Football League draft.

Upshaw, 6-5, 255 pounds, had the size to play tackle, but Raiders owner Al Davis slotted him at guard because of his speed and his ability to block 6-7, 270-pound Buck Buchanan of the Kansas City Chiefs, Oakland's main rival. The Upshaw-Buchanan battles were classics.

Upshaw's combination of size and speed was complemented by intensity and intelligence. For 14 years, Upshaw played left guard, and future Hall of Famer Art Shell played left tackle for the Raiders. They formed one of the most effective tandems in NFL history.

Upshaw helped the Raiders reach the AFL/AFC championship game 10 times and the Super Bowl three times (II, XI, XV). The Raiders won Super Bowl XI and Super Bowl XV. He was a three-time All-Pro and a seven-time Pro Bowl selection.

He retired after the 1981 season. He was inducted into the Pro Football Hall of Fame in 1987 and was named to the NFL's 75th Anniversary All-Time Team in 1994.

Upshaw has been the executive director of the NFL Players Association since 1987. In 1994, he accepted the application of a salary cap, which limited how much teams could pay in salary.

Van Brocklin, Norm

Born: March 15, 1926 in Eagle Butte, South Dakota
Died: May 2, 1983

Norm Van Brocklin played his college ball at the University of Oregon, where he was an All-American as a senior in 1948. He was a fourth-round draft choice of the Los Angeles Rams in 1949, and he spent most of his first several seasons in Los Angeles as the backup to Bob Waterfield.

In 1950, Van Brocklin, as the backup, led the NFL in passing, completing 54.5 percent of his passes for 2,061 yards and 18 touchdowns. He also was the backup in 1951, when the Rams won the NFL title, but it was his 73-yard touchdown pass to Tom Fears that lifted the Rams to a 24–17 victory over the Cleveland Browns. Also in 1951, he passed for 554 yards against the New York Yanks, and that, through the 2000 season, stood as a single-game record.

Van Brocklin also led the league in passing in 1952 (1,736 yards, 14 touchdowns) and 1954 (2,637 yards, 13 touchdowns).

In 1958, he was traded to the Philadelphia Eagles, where he was the starter and the team leader. Known for his fiery attitude—hence the nickname "Stormin' Norman"—he led the Eagles to the 1960 NFL championship, a 17–13 upset over the Green Bay Packers. Van Brocklin threw for 2,471 yards and 24 touchdowns in 1960 and was named the league's Most Valuable Player. He retired after that season.

In 12 seasons, Van Brocklin completed 53.6 percent of his passes for 23,611 yards and 173 touchdowns.

Through the 2000 season, he tied for 38th all-time in touchdown passes.

Van Brocklin, an eight-time Pro Bowl player, was inducted into the Pro Football Hall of Fame in 1971.

Van Buren, Steve

Born: December 20, 1920 in La Ceiba, Honduras

Steve Van Buren was a speedy, powerful runner who was difficult to bring down and who could make a legitimate claim to being the best running back in the 1940s. His strength was running up the middle, but he was quick enough to be able to elude tacklers.

Van Buren played his college ball at Louisiana State University. As a senior, he led the nation in scoring with 110 points and was second in rushing with 847 yards.

Van Buren, nicknamed "Movin Van," joined the Philadelphia Eagles in 1944 and became the centerpiece of their offense. He led the National Football League in rushing four times in a five-year stretch (832 yards, 1945; 1,008 yards, 1947; 945 yards, 1948; 1,146 yards, 1949). He set an NFL record in 1947, then broke his own record two years later. He led the NFL in scoring in 1945 with 110 points on 18 touchdowns and two points-after touchdowns.

Van Buren helped the Eagles reach the NFL championship game three straight years, starting in 1947. The Eagles lost to the Chicago Cardinals in their first appearance, but beat the Cardinals 7–0 in 1948, with Van Buren scoring the only touchdown, and beat the Los Angeles Rams 14–0 in 1949. Van Buren gained a record 196 yards against the Rams.

Steve Van Buren   *Reading Eagle/Times*

Injuries limited his effectiveness in 1950 and 1951, and after he suffered a knee injury in training camp in 1952, he retired.

Van Buren played eight seasons, all with the Eagles, and gained 5,860 yards, an NFL record at the time. He also held records for rushing attempts (1,320), rushing touchdowns (69), most touchdowns in a season (18, 1945), most years leading the league in rushing (4), and most yards in an NFL title game.

Van Buren, a three-time All-Pro, was inducted into the Pro Football Hall of Fame in 1965 and was named to the NFL's 75th Anniversary All-Time Team in 1994.

Walker, Doak
Born: January 1, 1927 in Dallas, Texas
Died: September 27, 1998

Doak Walker had an outstanding career at Southern Methodist University, where he was an All-American running back for three seasons (1947–49) and the Heisman Trophy winner as the nation's outstanding college football player in 1948. He finished third in Heisman voting in 1947 and third in 1949.

In addition to running back, he also played quarterback, receiver, punt and kick returner, and defensive back. He was such a fan favorite that SMU switched its home games from Ownby Stadium to the 47,000-seat Cotton Bowl, which was expanded to 75,000 seats by his senior year.

At 5-11, 173 pounds, Walker was somewhat undersized for the NFL, and when he joined the Detroit Lions in 1950, some observers wondered if he would be able to withstand the rigors of the pro game. He answered those questions quickly by leading the league in scoring in his rookie season with 128 points on 11 touchdowns, eight field goals, and 38 points-after touchdowns. He also led the league in scoring in 1955 (seven touchdowns, nine field goals, 27 points-after touchdowns for 96 points).

Walker helped the Lions win the NFL championship in 1952 and 1953. In the 1952 game, he ran 67 yards for the winning touchdown.

Walker, despite the lure of a big contract offer from the Lions, abruptly retired from the game after the 1955 season to enter private business.

In six seasons, Walker rushed for 1,520 yards and scored 12 touchdowns. He caught 152 passes for 2,539 yards and 21 touchdowns. He kicked 183 points-after touchdowns and 49 field goals. He scored 534 points.

A four-time All-Pro and a five-time Pro Bowl player, Walker was inducted into the Pro Football Hall of Fame in 1986. Since 1989, the Doak Walker Award is given annually to the best college running back in the nation.

Walker was involved in a skiing accident in early 1998 that left him paralyzed. He died from complications from paralysis.

Warfield, Paul
Born: November 28, 1942 in Warren, Ohio

Unfortunately, Paul Warfield played his entire career for teams that emphasized the run. Had he played in a passing offense, there is no telling what statistics he could have accumulated. Regardless, Warfield was one of the most feared receivers of his era, even though he never caught more than 52 passes in any one season.

He played his college ball at Ohio State, where he was a running back. When he joined the Cleveland Browns in 1964, he was shifted to wide receiver. Warfield ran precise patterns and had excellent speed and soft hands. He was a big-play threat who was almost always double-teamed.

Warfield spent six seasons in Cleveland. The Browns went 59–23–2, qualified for the postseason five times, and won the NFL championship in 1964.

In 1970, he was traded to the Miami Dolphins, which relied primarily on the running of Larry Csonka and Jim Kiick.

In 1971, Warfield led the league with 11 touchdown catches, and in 1972, he led the league in average per catch (20.9 yards). He helped the Dolphins reach three consecutive Super Bowls (VI, VII, VIII). They won Super Bowl VII and Super Bowl VIII, the culmination of a perfect season (17–0).

Warfield, along with Csonka and Kiick, left the Dolphins in 1975 to play for the Memphis Southmen in the rival World Football League. After the WFL folded, Warfield returned to play two more seasons for the Cleveland Browns. He retired after the 1977 season.

Warfield was a five-time All-Pro and an eight-time Pro Bowl player. In 13 NFL seasons, he caught 427 passes for 8,565 yards. Through the 2000 season, his 20.1 yard-per-catch average was a record. He was inducted into the Pro Football Hall of Fame in 1983.

Webster, Mike
Born: March 18, 1952 in Tomahawk, Wisconsin

Mike Webster is generally considered the best center in the history of the National Football League. He played his college ball at the University of Wisconsin and was a fifth-round draft pick of the Pittsburgh Steelers in 1974.

Webster (6-1, 255 pounds) worked out tirelessly lifting weights. He also was a student of the game, perfecting the blocking techniques that were his trademark. In addition to his strength, Webster also was known for his toughness and durability. He missed only four games in his first 16 seasons and once played in 177 consecutive games over a 10-year span (1976–85).

Webster, the anchor of the Steelers' offensive line, helped the team win four Super Bowls (IX, X, XIII, XIV). He spent 15 seasons with the Steelers and his last two seasons with the Kansas City Chiefs. He retired after the 1990 season.

Webster was a five-time All-Pro and a nine-time Pro Bowl player. No member of the Steelers played more seasons (15) or more games (220) with the team. He was inducted into the Pro Football Hall of Fame in 1997 and was named to the NFL's 75th Anniversary All-Time Team in 1994.

White, Randy

Born: January 15, 1953 in Wilmington, Delaware

At 6-4, 257 pounds, Randy White was considered undersized to play defensive tackle. But his strength, quickness, intensity, and toughness made him one of the best ever to play the position.

In 1975, White was an All-American defensive end at the University of Maryland. He won the Lombardi Award and the Outland Trophy as the best lineman in the nation. The Dallas Cowboys made him their first-round draft choice in 1975, and in his rookie season he was used as a defensive end and outside linebacker.

In 1976, the Cowboys moved White to right defensive tackle in their famous "Flex Defense," meaning he played slightly off the line of scrimmage, between the center and the guard, allowing him a split second longer to read the play.

If teams ran at White, he was strong enough to fight off multiple blockers to make the play. If teams chose to run away from White, he was often able to chase down ball carriers with his speed. He also was an effective pass rusher.

White's strength came from his obsession with weightlifting. The strongest player on the Cowboys roster, White was nicknamed "Manster," for half man, half monster.

From 1975 through 1982, White, who anchored Dallas' Doomsday Defense, helped the Cowboys to six National Football Conference championship games and three Super Bowls (X, XII, XIII). In Super Bowl XII, a 27–10 victory over the Denver Broncos, White and defensive end Harvey Martin were named co–Most Valuable Players, a rarity for defensive players.

White was a five-time All-Pro and a Pro Bowl player for nine straight years (1977–85). He retired following the 1988 season and was inducted into the Pro Football Hall of Fame in 1994.

White, Reggie

Born: December 19, 1961 in Chattanooga, Tennessee

Reggie White combined size (6-5, 290 pounds), strength, quickness, and speed to become one of the most dominant defensive ends in the history of the National Football League.

White was a consensus All-American at the University of Tennessee in 1983. In 1984, he joined the Memphis Showboats of the now-defunct United States Football League (USFL). After two seasons in Memphis, White signed with the Philadelphia Eagles in 1985, meaning he played an 18-game schedule with Memphis in the spring and 13 games with the Eagles that fall.

White, playing for head coach Buddy Ryan, a defensive genius, developed into a ferocious defender who could rush the quarterback and stop the run.

That White was such a feared defender was in direct contrast to his other mission in life: He was an ordained Baptist minister who was known for his humanitarianism and altruism.

White, nicknamed the "Minister of Defense," left the Eagles after the 1992 season and signed as a free agent with the Green Bay Packers. The Packers, who had fallen on hard times, began their rise to prominence with White's arrival. They made the playoffs in each of

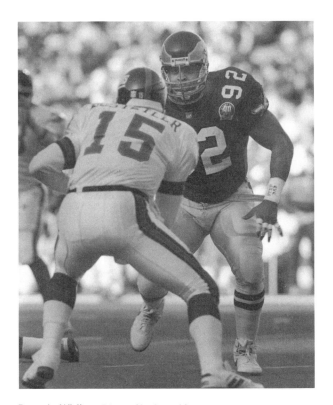

Reggie White *Diane Staskowski*

White's six seasons there and won the Super Bowl following the 1996 season, their first in 29 years.

White, a 13-time Pro Bowl player, retired after the 1998 season as the NFL's all-time sack leader with 198. In 1987, he had a league-leading 21 sacks, one short of the single-season record set by Mark Gastineau of the New York Jets. White, however, managed his total in only 12 games. The season was shortened by a strike. White was named the NFL's Defensive Player of the Year in 1987. In 1994, he was named to the NFL's 75th Anniversary All-Time Team.

After one year out of football, White came out of retirement and signed with the Carolina Panthers for the 2000 season. He retired after the season.

Wilson, Larry

Born: March 24, 1938 in Rugby, Idaho

Larry Wilson was one of the toughest players of his era. He was a punishing tackler with a nose for the ball.

Wilson played offense and defense at the University of Idaho. He joined the St. Louis Cardinals in 1960 and was tried at halfback, before he was eventually moved to free safety.

Wilson could stop the run, and he was equally adept in pass coverage. It was as if he had a sixth sense that allowed him get to the ball. At 6-0, 190 pounds, he wasn't an imposing physical specimen, but he took on bigger linemen, backs, and receivers willingly.

Wilson is credited with being the first free safety to blitz the quarterback. He did it against the New York Giants in September 1961, tackling quarterback Charlie Conerly for an 11-yard loss. Wilson used the tactic repeatedly, and other teams soon followed suit.

Wilson, who retired following the 1972 season, had 52 career interceptions, including a league-leading 10 in 1966. He was a four-time All-Pro and an eight-time Pro Bowl selection. He was inducted into the Pro Football Hall of Fame in 1978 and named to the National Football League's 75th Anniversary All-Time Team in 1994.

Winslow, Kellen

Born: November 5, 1957 in St. Louis, Missouri

Kellen Winslow was a tight end by trade, but because of his size, speed, and athleticism, he made the impact of a wide receiver. He was considered one of the best tight ends ever to play the game, and the way he played it changed the way tight ends were utilized.

Winslow played his college ball at the University of Missouri, where he was a consensus All-American as a senior. He was the first-round draft choice of the San Diego Chargers in 1979.

Winslow led the NFL in receiving in 1980 (89 catches, 1,290 yards, nine touchdowns) and 1981 (88, 1,075, 10). In 1982, a strike-shortened season, Winslow led the AFC with 54 catches for 754 yards and six touchdowns.

Winslow was most famous for his performance in San Diego's 41–38 overtime victory in a 1981 AFC divisional playoff game. He caught 13 passes for 166 yards and blocked a potential game-winning field goal as time expired in regulation. The Chargers were one game short of making it to the Super Bowl, losing to the Cincinnati Bengals in the AFC championship game.

Winslow, whose career was cut short by a knee injury, played nine seasons, all with the Chargers. He retired after the 1987 season. He caught 541 passes for 6,741 yards and 45 touchdowns. A five-time Pro Bowl player, Winslow was inducted into the Pro Football Hall of Fame in 1995 and was named to the NFL's 75th Anniversary All-Time Team in 1994.

Wood, Willie

Born: December 23, 1936 in Washington, D.C.

Willie Wood played his college ball at the University of Southern California, but was not drafted. He joined the Green Bay Packers in 1960 as a free agent and developed into one of the premier safeties of his time.

Wood was a key cog on the Packers' five NFL championship teams (1961–62, '65–67), including the first two Super Bowls.

Wood retired after the 1971 season with 48 interceptions for 699 yards and two touchdowns. In 1961, he led the NFL in punt returns, and in 1962, he led the league in interceptions.

Wood, a seven-time All-Pro and an eight-time Pro Bowl player, was inducted into the Pro Football Hall of Fame in 1989.

Woodson, Rod

Born: March 10, 1965 in Ft. Wayne, Indiana

Rod Woodson's speed, athleticism, and fearlessness made him one of the great cover cornerbacks of all time. At 6-0, 200 pounds, he was a punishing tackler who was also strong against the run. Woodson was so effective that quarterbacks became reluctant to throw his way.

Woodson played his college ball at Purdue University, where he was an All-American in 1986 as a kick returner and a defensive back. The Pittsburgh Steelers chose him in the first round of the 1987 NFL draft, but he held out for more money until midseason and was used mostly as a returner.

In 1988, Woodson started all 16 games and returned a kickoff 92 yards for a touchdown, the first by a Steeler since 1978.

In 1993, Woodson had eight interceptions, 95 tackles, two sacks, 28 passes defensed, two forced fumbles, and one blocked field goal. He was named NFL Defensive Player of the Year.

After another outstanding season in 1994, Woodson suffered a torn anterior cruciate ligament in the season opener against the Detroit Lions. Thanks to a remarkable recovery, he returned to play in Super Bowl XXX against the Dallas Cowboys. He was the first NFL player to suffer such a knee injury and come back to play in the same season.

In 1996, Woodson started all 16 games, had six interceptions, and received the Ed Block Courage Award from his teammates.

Woodson left the Steelers and joined the San Francisco 49ers for the 1997 season. In 1998, he signed with the Baltimore Ravens. He was switched from cornerback to safety in 1999, and he responded with seven interceptions, two of which he returned for touchdowns.

Through the 2000 season, Woodson had 58 interceptions and nine touchdowns. A seven-time Pro Bowl selection and a five-time All-Pro, he was named to the NFL's 75th Anniversary All-Time Team in 1994.

Young, Steve

Born: October 11, 1961 in Salt Lake City, Utah

Steve Young was one of the most complete and versatile quarterbacks in NFL history. He could throw accurately, long or short; he could scramble and throw on the run; he could take off out of the pocket; and he had leadership skills and toughness that were second to none.

Young played his college ball at Brigham Young University, which was founded and named for his great-great-great-grandfather. In 1983, he led all Division I-A quarterbacks with 3,902 yards, 33 touchdown passes, and 395.1 yards of total offense per game. He finished second in the 1983 Heisman Trophy voting.

Young, a consensus All-American in 1983, joined the Los Angeles Express of the United States Football League. When the franchise folded in 1985, he became a member of the Tampa Bay Buccaneers.

Tampa Bay traded him to the San Francisco 49ers in 1987, and he was Joe Montana's backup for four seasons.

He took over as the 49ers starting quarterback in the 1991 season and prospered in the West Coast offense, developed by 49ers coach Bill Walsh. The West Coast offense relied mostly on short- to medium-range passes.

Steve Young *Diane Staskowski*

Young led them to the NFC championship game in each of his first two seasons, but they were beaten by the Dallas Cowboys both times.

In 1994, Young guided the 49ers to Super Bowl XXIX. They had beaten the Cowboys in the NFC title game, then routed the San Diego Chargers 49–26 in the Super Bowl. Young was named the game's Most Valuable Player. He completed 24 for 36 passes for 325 yards and a record six touchdowns. The Super Bowl victory was a relief for Young, who failed in his first two attempts to win a title and for years played in the shadow of Montana.

Young led the NFC in passing six times from 1991 to 1997, tying Sammy Baugh. He was named the NFL's Most Valuable Player in 1992 (66 percent completion, 3,465 yards, 25 touchdown passes) and 1994 (70 percent completion, 3,969 yards, 35 touchdown passes). Twice he has thrown for more than 4,000 yards in a season (4,023 in 1993, 4,170 in 1998).

Young missed virtually all of the 1999 season with a concussion suffered in the third game of the season. After much deliberation, including discussions with Denver coach Mike Shanahan about joining the Broncos, Young announced his retirement in June 2000.

Through the 2000 season, Young ranked first all-time in passing efficiency (a quarterback rating system based on completion percentage, average gain, touchdown percentage, and interception percentage). He completed 64.3 percent of his passes for 33,124 yards, 232 touchdowns, and 107 interceptions. He ranked first in completion percentage, average gain (7.98), and touchdown-to-interception ratio (2.16).

His 1994 season was the best ever by a quarterback, based on the passing efficiency rating (112.8). His 1992 season ranked as the seventh-best all-time (107). His 36 touchdown passes in 1998 tied for fifth all-time for a single season, and his 232 career touchdown passes ranked 16th all-time.

He also held the record for most touchdown passes in a Super Bowl game (6, 1995) and most career touchdowns rushing by a quarterback (43).

Young was a seven-time Pro Bowl choice.

Golf

Alcott, Amy

Born: February 22, 1956 in Kansas City, Missouri

Amy Alcott joined the LPGA Tour in 1975, just six months after finishing high school, won the third tournament she entered, and was named Rookie of the Year. She went on to win 28 more tour events, including five major championships—Peter Jackson Classic (1979, now the du Maurier Classic), U.S. Women's Open (1980), and Nabisco Dinah Shore Invitational (1983, '88, '91). Her 1998 Dinah Shore title, coming after her first winless season since joining the tour, was celebrated by a jump in the lake off the 18th green.

Alcott won the 1980 Vare Trophy for low scoring average and finished in the top 10 on the money list in nine consecutive years (1978–86).

In 1999, after the LPGA Tour changed its Hall of Fame requirements, Alcott was inducted into the LPGA Hall of Fame. She had been one tournament victory short of qualifying since 1991. Through the 1999 season, Alcott earned $3,346,139 and ranked 16th all-time.

Anderson, Willie

Born: May 1880 in North Berwick, Scotland
Died: October 25, 1910

Willie Anderson is regarded as the first great American golfer. The son of a Scottish greenkeeper, Anderson immigrated to America in 1895, and two years later finished second in the U.S. Open at the age of 17. He won the U.S. Open in 1901, and then won three more consecutively, beginning in 1903. Only three other golfers—Ben Hogan, Bobby Jones, and Jack Nicklaus—have won four Open titles, and no one has won it three consecutive times. Anderson finished in the top five in 11 Opens, a record shared by Nicklaus.

Anderson, a member of the World Golf Hall of Fame, was also a four-time winner of the Western Open, which was considered the second most important tournament in the United States.

Anderson died suddenly at age 30. His death has been officially attributed to arteriosclerosis, but it has been speculated that heavy drinking might have been a contributing factor.

Armour, Tommy

Born: September 24, 1895 in Edinburgh, Scotland
Died: September 11, 1968

Tommy Armour's career as a world-class golfer was an improbable one. He was blinded by a head injury suffered in World War I and regained sight in his right eye after six months. Armour, who had been a good golfer as a youth, decided to make the game his career.

He turned professional in 1924, then made his reputation as a teacher, helping Bobby Jones with his swing. In 1927, Armour, known as the "Silver Scot," claimed his first major victory in the 1927 U.S. Open, where he beat Henry Cooper in a playoff.

Armour won the 1931 British Open and reached the PGA Championship final twice, beating Gene Sarazen in 1930 and losing to Johnny Revolta in 1935. He retired as a player in 1935, but continued to teach. His pupils included Babe Didrikson Zaharias. In 1952, he and Herb Graffis wrote *How to Play Your Best Golf All the Time*, one of the best-selling instructional books ever.

Armour won 24 titles in his career and is a member of the World Golf Hall of Fame.

Ballesteros, Seve

Born: April 9, 1957 in Pedrena, Spain

One of the most imaginative and stylish players in the history of golf, Seve Ballesteros won two Masters (1980, '83) and three British Opens (1979, '84, '88). His 1979 victory at Royal Lytham made him the youngest winner since Tom Morris, Jr., in 1868.

Ballesteros taught himself to play golf while he was a caddie in his native Spain. He used one club—a 3-iron—that had been given to him and learned to play a variety of shots. He would sneak on the course after dusk, because caddies were not supposed to use the course. He turned pro in March 1974 at age 17, and two years later finished in a tie for second at the 1976 British Open with Jack Nicklaus and won the Order of Merit, the European Tour's equivalent of the money list. He also won the Order of Merit in 1977. He has had a reputation for being wild off the tee, but his imagination and ability to create shots helped him recover from trouble. For instance, in his 1979 British Open victory at Royal Lytham and St. Annes, Ballesteros hit only eight fairways in four rounds, using his driver. That was not the way to negotiate Royal Lytham, renowned for its narrow fairways and difficult rough, but he always found a way.

He is an eight-time member of the European Ryder Cup team, and in the 1997 Ryder Cup at Valderrama, Spain, Ballesteros captained the Europeans to a 14 1/2–13 1/2 victory over the United States, allowing them to retain the Cup.

Through the 2000 season, Ballesteros won a dozen different national opens and more than 70 tournaments in 17 countries worldwide. He earned more than $1.5 million, and in 1999 was inducted into the World Golf Hall of Fame.

Berg, Patty

Born: February 13, 1918 in Minneapolis, Minnesota

Patty Berg is a charter member of the LPGA Hall of Fame (1951) and one of the game's foremost goodwill ambassadors. She began playing golf at 14, when her parents thought football to be too rough. She quarterbacked an otherwise all-boys team in her neighborhood—the 50th Street Tigers, featuring legendary University of Oklahoma coach Bud Wilkinson at tackle.

After a stellar amateur career, in which she won 29 titles in seven years, the 1938 U.S. Amateur among them, and played on two Curtis Cup teams, Berg turned pro, even though there was no ladies professional tour at the time. She made her livelihood by giving clinics and exhibitions.

In 1939, she underwent surgery for an emergency appendectomy and was hospitalized for a month. In 1941, she was sidelined for 18 months following a serious auto accident in which she suffered a badly broken leg.

After serving as a lieutenant in the Marines (1942–45), Berg won the 1946 U.S. Women's Open and helped found the Ladies Professional Golf Association in 1948. She was the tour's first president.

Between 1948 and 1962, she won 44 titles. She led the LPGA in earnings three times (1954, '55, '57) and won the Vare Trophy for low scoring average three times (1953, '55, '56).

In 1980, Berg had hip replacement surgery, which ended her playing career, although she continued to give clinics and exhibitions until she was into her 70s. She is a three-time winner of the Associated Press Female Athlete of the Year Award (1938, '43, '55) and a member of the Women's Sports Hall of Fame and the LPGA Hall of Fame. Overall, Berg won 57 LPGA titles and earned $190,760.

Boros, Julius

Born: March 3, 1920 in Fairfield, Connecticut
Died: May 28, 1994

Julius Boros was a short-hitter, but deadly accurate. That style served him well and helped him become one of the most consistent players on the PGA Tour. An accountant by trade, he decided to take a shot at pro golf after he turned 30.

Boros, a member of the World Golf Hall of Fame, won the U.S. Open in 1952 and again in 1963, when he birdied two of the final three holes and then won a three-way playoff with Jackie Cupit and Arnold Palmer. From 1950 through 1963, he finished in the top 10 in the Open nine times. Only Ben Hogan had a better record since World War II.

Boros was the leading money winner on the PGA Tour in 1952 and 1955 and the PGA Tour Player of the Year in 1952 and 1963.

In 1968, at age 48, he won the PGA Championship and became the oldest player ever to win a major championship. Boros played on four U.S. Ryder Cup teams and in 1967 was the second-oldest player ever chosen.

Boros won 18 PGA Tour events and earned $1,004,861.

Bradley, Pat
Born: March 24, 1951 in Westford, Massachusetts

One of the most consistent players in LPGA Tour history, Pat Bradley enjoyed what might be the best single season ever. In 1986, she won three of the four major championships (Nabisco Dinah Shore, LPGA Championship, du Maurier Championship) and six events overall. She set a single-season earnings record ($492,021), won the Vare Trophy for low-scoring average, and was named Rolex Player of the Year.

Her other major championship victories came in the 1980 Peter Jackson Classic (now the du Maurier Classic), the 1982 U.S. Women's Open, and the 1985 du Maurier Classic.

Bradley, one of only two women to win all four major championships, was inducted to the LPGA Hall of Fame in 1991.

Bradley joined the LPGA Tour in 1974. Through the 1995 season, she entered 582 events and finished in the top ten 302 times, 205 of those in the top five. She is a two-time Rolex Player of the Year and leading money winner (1986, '91).

In 1988, Bradley was diagnosed as having Graves disease (hyperthyroidism). She plummeted to 109th on the money list that year, but rebounded in 1989 to win a tournament and earn more than $420,000. From 1989 through 1991, Bradley won eight tournaments.

Through the 2000 season, Bradley, named captain for the 2000 U.S. Solheim Cup team, won 31 tour events and earned $5,743,605, seventh all-time.

Caponi, Donna
Born: January 29, 1945 in Detroit, Michigan

Donna Caponi's first victory came in 1969 at the U.S. Women's Open, making her one of only 13 to break through at the Open. She went on to win four more majors—U.S. Women's Open (1970), Peter Jackson Classic (1976, now du Maurier Classic), and LPGA Championship (1979, '81). Caponi was only the second player to win back-to-back Opens. Mickey Wright was the first. Since then, four others have accomplished the feat.

From 1969 through 1981, Caponi finished in the top five on the money list seven times, including second in 1976 and 1980.

In 1988, she curtailed her playing career to work as a television commentator, which she continues, announcing for NBC, TBS, and The Golf Channel. Caponi had 24 career victories on the LPGA Tour.

Carner, JoAnne
Born: April 4, 1939 in Kirkland, Washington

Nicknamed the "Great Gundy"—her maiden name was Gunderson—and later "Big Momma," JoAnne Carner followed up a fine amateur career with a Hall of Fame pro career. She won five U.S. amateur titles (1957, '60, '62, '66, '68), second all-time to Glenna Collett Vare, and competed on four Curtis Cup teams. She also won an LPGA event—the 1969 Burdine's Invitational—as an amateur. She is the last LPGA member to win a tournament as an amateur. Carner is the only player to have won the U.S. Girls' Junior, the U.S. Women's Amateur, and the U.S. Women's Open.

She joined the LPGA Tour in 1970 and over the next 15 years won 42 events, including two U.S. Women's Opens (1971, '76). Carner won three money titles (1974, '82, '83), three Rolex Player of the Year Awards (1974, '81, '82), and five Vare Trophies for low scoring average (1974–75, '81–83). Most of her success came after she turned 40. Nineteen of her 43 career victories came in her 40s. Her victory in the 1985 Safeco Classic, the last of her career, made her, at 46, the oldest player to win a tour event. Her victory in the 1982 World Championship of Women's Golf, the 35th win of her career, qualified her for the LPGA Hall of Fame.

JoAnne Carner   *Diane Staskowski*

In 1994, Carner was the victorious captain of the U.S. Solheim Cup team, which defeated the European team 13–7.

Casper, Billy

Born: June 24, 1932 in San Diego, California

Known as one of the game's deadliest putters, Billy Casper won 51 PGA Tour events, including two U.S. Opens (1959, '66) and the Masters (1970).

In the 1959 Open at Winged Foot Golf Club in Mamaroneck, N.Y., he one-putted 31 of the 72 holes. In 1966 at the Olympic Club in San Francisco, he trailed Arnold Palmer by seven shots with nine holes to play. But he rallied to force a tie and then defeated Palmer in an 18-hole playoff the following day (69–73), coming from two strokes down with eight holes to play. He used only 117 putts in 90 holes.

Because he defeated Palmer, who was king with the galleries and golf fans throughout the country, Casper never became as popular as he might have. In his Masters victory, which came in a playoff against Gene Littler, Casper one-putted six of the first seven holes and went on to win by five shots (69–74).

Casper won two PGA Tour money titles (1966, '68), two Player of the Year Awards (1966, '70), and five Vardon Trophies for low stroke average (1960, '63, '65, '66, '68). He won 51 events on the PGA Tour and eight on the Senior PGA Tour, including the 1983 U.S. Senior Open. He was a member of eight U.S. Ryder Cup teams between 1961 and 1975 and was the nonplaying captain in 1979.

Casper is a member of the World Golf Hall of Fame.

Charles, Bob

Born: March 14, 1936 in Carterton, New Zealand

Generally regarded as one of the finest left-handers ever to play the game, Bob Charles has won 75 tournaments worldwide, with wins on five continents. His most significant victory came in the 1963 British Open, which he won in a 36-hole playoff over Phil Rodgers at Royal Lytham and St. Annes.

Charles has five PGA Tour wins and 23 on the Senior PGA Tour, ranking him fourth all-time through the 2000 season.

Cooper, Harry

Born: August 6, 1904 in Leatherhead, England

Harry Cooper was one of the prominent PGA Tour players in the 1920s and 1930s. A perennial contender in the U.S. Open, he finished in the top 10 of the U.S. Open seven times, including runner-up finishes in 1927 and 1936. The closest he came to winning was in 1926. He

was changing his clothes for the award ceremony, but Tommy Armour birdied two of the final holes to tie, and then defeated Cooper in an 18-hole playoff.

In all, Cooper won 31 PGA Tour events, tied for 13th all-time. He also won the inaugural Vardon Trophy for low stroke average in 1937.

Couples, Fred

Born: October 3, 1959 in Seattle, Washington

One of the most popular players in golf, Fred Couples is known for his laid-back attitude and a fluid, seemingly effortless, but powerful swing.

Couples, who was introduced to the game by his late father, was an All-American at the University of Houston, but in 1980 at age 21, he left school early to join the PGA Tour. He got his first tour win in 1983, the Kemper Open, and won three more times through the 1990 season.

In 1991, Couples began to emerge as one of the best players on tour. He won twice and was named PGA Tour Player of the Year. In 1992, Couples repeated as Player of the Year, winning three times, including the Masters; leading the tour in earnings with more than $1.3 million; and winning the Vardon Trophy for low stroke average for the second straight year. With his victory in the Masters, Couples capped a streak in which he won three tournaments and finished second twice in six events.

Couples has been a member of five Ryder Cup teams and three President's Cup teams, and he is a four-time winner of the World Cup with Davis Love III.

Through the 2000 season, Couples had 14 PGA Tour victories and had earned more than $12.2 million, which ranked seventh all-time. Couples, who has been bothered by chronic back problems, was forced to curtail his schedule in 1999.

Crenshaw, Ben

Born: January 11, 1952 in Austin, Texas

Ben Crenshaw, known for his smooth and accurate putting stroke, has won 19 PGA Tour events through the 1999 season, including two Masters championships (1984, '95). His victory in the 1995 Masters came just days after he served as a pallbearer for his longtime friend and teacher, Harvey Penick.

He won three consecutive NCAA championships (1971–73), joined the PGA Tour in 1973, and won his first start as a pro—the San Antonio–Texas Open.

Crenshaw, who was not an accurate driver, didn't win again until 1976, when he had three victories and finished second on the money list.

Crenshaw, a noted golf historian, was a member of four Ryder Cup teams and was the nonplaying captain for the 1999 competition at the Country Club in Brookline, Mass., won by the United States.

Daniel, Beth

Born: October 14, 1956 in Charleston, South Carolina

Beth Daniel joined the LPGA Tour in 1979 following a stellar amateur career in which she won two U.S. amateur titles (1975, '77) and was a member of two U.S. Curtis Cup teams (1976, '78).

She was named the LPGA Rookie of the Year in 1979, when she won one tournament and finished 10th on the money list. Over the next six seasons, Daniel won 13 times and twice finished no. 1 on the money list (1980, '81). In 1980, Daniel won four times, had 22 top 10 finishes in 27 events, led the money list with $231,000, and was named Player of the Year.

After a 4 1/2-year victory drought, Daniel returned to form with four wins in 1989, when she won the first of three Vare Trophies for low scoring average. In 1990, she had the best season of her career. She won seven events, including her only major title, the Mazda LPGA Championship; finished in the top ten 20 times in 25 tournaments; earned a then record $863,578; and was named Player of the Year.

In 1994, she won four tournaments, had 11 top 10 finishes in 25 events, was second on the money list with $659,426, and won her third Player of the Year Award. Daniel, plagued by back problems throughout her career, missed most of the 1997 season with a shoulder injury and thoracic muscle spasms. She was a member of five Solheim Cup teams and was inducted into the LPGA Hall of Fame in 2000. Through 2000, she had 32 LPGA Tour victories.

Davies, Laura

Born: October 5, 1963 in West Byfleet, England

Laura Davies, the longest hitter in the history of women's golf, first made a name for herself in the United States by winning the U.S. Women's Open in 1987 as a non-member of the LPGA Tour, which doesn't count the victory as official. She defeated JoAnne Carner and Ayako Okamoto in an 18-hole playoff.

Davies has won three other major championships: McDonald's LPGA Championship (1994, '96) and the du Maurier Classic (1996).

Through 2000, Davies won 19 LPGA Tour events since joining the tour in 1987. She was the leading money winner in 1994 ($687,201) and the Rolex Player of the Year in 1996, when she won four times and earned $927,302, good for second on the money list.

In 1997, Davies won the Standard Register Ping tournament for the fourth consecutive year. She joins Gene Sarazen and Walter Hagen as the only players to win the same event four years in a row.

Davies, who plays all over the world on a regular basis, led the women Professional Golfers European Tour Order of Merit (money list) in 1985, 1986, and 1996. She is a six-time member of the European Solheim Cup team, and in 1988 was named a Member of the British Empire by Queen Elizabeth II. The honor is one of the highest bestowed upon British citizens.

Demaret, Jimmy

Born: May 10, 1910 in Houston, Texas
Died: December 28, 1983

Jimmy Demaret was a fashion plate and one of the most charismatic characters the game has ever known. He changed the way golfers dressed by introducing color to his outfits, which were made from lighter, cooler materials originally intended for ladies' clothing.

Demaret had his best season in 1947, when he topped the money list, with $27,936, and won the Vardon Trophy for low stroke average. He won 31 PGA Tour events, tying him for 13th place all-time.

He led the tour in 1940 with six victories, one of which was his first Masters championship. Demaret became the first player to win the Masters three times. In 1947, he beat Byron Nelson and Frank Stranahan by two shots, and in 1950, he overcame a four-shot deficit to defeat Jim Ferrier by two.

Because of his glib nature and sense of humor, Demaret got involved in golf on television in its infancy. He was the host of the Emmy Award–winning *Shell's Wonderful World of Golf*, with Gene Sarazen. Demaret's association with the producer of the Shell show led to *Legends of Golf*, which aired in 1978 and is considered the stimulus for the Senior PGA Tour.

Demeret is a member of the World Golf Hall of Fame.

De Vincenzo, Roberto

Born: April 14, 1923 in Buenos Aires, Argentina

Roberto de Vincenzo is best known for the tournament he should have won, but lost. In the 1968 Masters, de Vincenzo signed his scorecard for a score higher than he actually recorded. Tommy Aaron, his playing partner, marked a par 4 on his card for the 17th hole, when de Vincenzo made a 3. Under the Rules of Golf, the higher score stands, meaning instead of being tied with Bob Goalby, he finished second.

De Vincenzo won approximately 230 tournaments worldwide, including the 1967 British Open and eight in the United States. At 44, he was the oldest winner of the British Open in the 20th century. He also won the inaugural U.S. Senior Open in 1980. He represented

Argentina 17 times in the Canada and World Cups, leading Argentina to victory in 1953. He is a member of the World Golf Hall of Fame.

Diegel, Leo

Born: April 27, 1899 in Detroit, Michigan
Died: May 8, 1951
Leo Diegel, a prominent PGA Tour player in the 1920s and 1930s, won 11 times on tour. His best year was 1928, when he won the Canadian Open and the PGA Championship, stopping the four-year winning streak of Walter Hagen by beating him in the quarterfinals. He successfully defended his PGA title in 1929, beating Johnny Farrell in the final. Diegel won the Canadian Open four times (1924–25, '28–'29).

Duval, David

Born: November 9, 1971 in Jacksonville, Florida
It took awhile, but after seven seconds and four thirds, David Duval broke through in spectacular fashion. He won his last three starts to conclude the 1997 season and followed that with four more wins in 1998. The seven wins in a 12-month period were the most since Tom Watson won eight in 1979–80. Duval finished a close second to Mark O'Meara for 1998 PGA Player of the Year, but he did top the money list, with nearly $2.6 million, and win the Vardon Trophy for low scoring average.

In 1999, Duval was considered the no. 1 player in the world. He was the first player since Johnny Miller in 1974 to win four tournaments before the Masters and the first player since Nick Price in 1993–94 to win four events in consecutive years. One of those victories came in the Bob Hope Chrysler Classic, where he closed with a final-round 13-under 59, the lowest closing round in PGA Tour history.

Duval, who in March 1999 snapped Tiger Woods' streak of 41 straight weeks as the no. 1 player in the world, fell back to no. 2 in August.

A standout player at Georgia Tech, Duval is one of only three players to be named a Division I first-team All-American four times, joining Gary Hallberg and Phil Mickelson. Duval was the 1993 College Player of the Year.

Through the 2000 season, Duval had 12 PGA Tour victories and played on three President's Cup teams and the 1999 U.S. Ryder Cup team.

Elder, Lee

Born: July 14, 1934 in Dallas, Texas
Lee Elder was the first African American to qualify for the Masters. His win in the 1974 Monsanto Open, in which he birdied three of the final four holes and then beat Peter Oosterhuis on the fourth playoff hole, qualified him to play at Augusta National. In all he won four times on the PGA Tour, eight times on the Senior PGA Tour, and was a member of the 1979 U.S. Ryder Cup team.

In 1972, he became the first African American to go to South Africa and compete in a multiracial tournament, and he did so on the condition that the gallery be integrated and that he and his wife be allowed to stay in the hotel of their choice.

Elder taught himself the game by sneaking onto all-white courses at night. He didn't play his first round of golf until he was 16 years old. Although he never attended college, he was inducted into the NCAA Hall of Fame for his contributions to blacks and colleges.

Els, Ernie

Born: October 17, 1969 in Johannesburg, South Africa
Ernie Els began playing golf when he was nine years old. He was also an accomplished tennis player, but by 14 had concentrated fully on golf. He turned pro in 1989 and joined the PGA Tour in 1994.

Els became the first foreign player since Alex Smith (1906, '10) to win the U.S. Open more than once. He won the 1994 Open at Oakmont Country Club in a playoff over Loren Roberts and Colin Montgomerie. Els entered the final round with a two-stroke lead, but shot 73 to fall into a tie. In the 18-hole playoff, Montgomerie shot 78 and was eliminated. Els and Roberts each shot 74. Els won with a par on the second hole of sudden death. In 1997, he won at Congressional Country Club by one over Montgomerie, after making a birdie on the 71st hole.

In 1992, Els joined Gary Player as the only players to have won the South African Open, the South African PGA, and the South African Masters in the same year.

Through the 2000 season, Els won eight PGA Tour events and had more than 20 victories worldwide. He was member of nine Dunhill Cup teams, four World Cup teams, and three President's Cup teams, including 1998, when he was 3–1–1 in a victory over the United States.

Faldo, Nick

Born: July 18, 1957 in Welwyn Garden City, England
Known as Nick "Fold-o" by the European press for his tendency to collapse in major championships, Faldo revamped his swing in 1985 and the hard work paid off. He has won three British Opens (1987, '90, '92) and three Masters (1989, '90, '96). The 1996 Masters was one of the most memorable in major championship history.

Entering the final round, he trailed Greg Norman by six shots, but shot 5-under 67 to Norman's 78 and won by five.

Faldo lost an 18-hole playoff to Curtis Strange for the 1988 U.S. Open title. He was ranked no. 1 in the World Golf Ranking for 81 weeks in 1993–94.

Faldo, who took up the game after seeing Jack Nicklaus on television, had a fine amateur record in England and earned a scholarship to the University of Houston. But he stayed on campus for only 10 weeks before dropping out and returning home. In 1976, he turned pro.

From 1977 through 1984, Faldo had a solid career, mainly on the European PGA Tour. He won 11 tournaments and also won one tournament on the PGA Tour. But he realized to take his game to the next level he needed to make major changes, which he did, working with David Leadbetter.

Faldo went winless for nearly two years while refining the swing changes, but in 1987, he won the British Open by making 18 pars in the final round. He enjoyed great success into the late 1990s, when his game and his personal life encountered difficulties. Through the 2000 season, he had six PGA Tour victories, 34 victories worldwide, and has been a member of 11 European Ryder Cup teams.

Floyd, Raymond

Born: September 4, 1942 in Fort Bragg, North Carolina

Raymond Floyd is one of golf's fiercest competitors. He has won 22 times on the PGA Tour and 13 times on the Senior PGA Tour. In 1992, he became the first person to win an event on both tours. He won the Doral-Ryder Open, and then 16 days later, won the GTE Classic, which was his first Senior Tour victory. He donated the $67,500 first prize to the Hurricane Andrew relief fund.

Floyd, who joined the tour in 1963, and Sam Snead are the only players in PGA Tour history to win tournaments in four decades. The first 12 years of Floyd's career were, in his words, "just a means to an end." Floyd enjoyed living the good life, and his winnings allowed him to live it. As a result, he never realized his full potential. But in 1975, Floyd met Maria, who would become his wife. The marriage and Maria's influence helped him to become more focused on golf. From 1977 through 1992, he won 15 PGA Tour events.

Floyd, who won the 1983 Vardon Trophy for low stroke average, has four major titles: PGA Championship (1969, '82); the Masters (1976), by eight strokes; U.S. Open (1986), at age 43. He also has four Senior Tour majors: The Tradition (1994), PGA Seniors Championship (1995), and Senior Players Championship (1996, '00).

A member of eight Ryder Cup teams, Floyd was the nonplaying captain in 1989. He was inducted into the World Golf Hall of Fame in 1989.

Guldahl, Ralph

Born: November 22, 1911 in Dallas, Texas
Died: June 11, 1987

Ralph Guldahl's career was curious, in that when he was good, he was very good, and when he was bad, he was terrible. He first made headlines at age 21 by finishing second in the 1933 U.S. Open. Soon afterward, he began to struggle, and in 1935 gave up golf. In 1936, he returned after considerable practice and changing his grip. He led the tour in scoring average. Over the next three years, Guldahl became one of only six players to win back-to-back U.S. Open Championships (1937–38), and he also won a Masters Championship (1939).

He and Sam Snead won the Inverness Four-Ball in 1940, but that was his last victory. Guldahl struggled mightily to regain his touch, but he was unable to do so. He left the tour in 1942, made sporadic appearances during World War II, then quit entirely. Guldahl won 16 PGA Tour events and is a member of the World Golf Hall of Fame.

Hagen, Walter

Born: December 21, 1892 in Rochester, New York
Died: October 6, 1969

Walter Hagen was golf's first great character. He was a happy-go-lucky swashbuckler who is credited with injecting color and personality into the sport. He was known to stay out until the wee hours of the morning, living the good life, often showing up for his morning tee times in a limousine. He dressed in silk shirts and garish clothing that contrasted with the staid fashions worn by the rest of the players.

It has been said that Hagen did for golf what Babe Ruth did for baseball. He had style and panache, not to mention talent and the ability to produce a great shot when a pressure situation demanded it. He often hit errant shots during a round, but almost always managed to extricate himself from the trouble.

Said Hagen: "I expect to make at least seven mistakes each round. Therefore, when I make a bad shot, I don't worry about it."

Hagen first burst onto the golf scene at the 1913 U.S. Open. He was 21 years old and finished fourth, behind Francis Ouimet, Harry Vardon, and Ted Ray.

The next year, Hagen registered a wire-to-wire victory in the U.S. Open, beating Chick Evans and serving notice that he would make a lasting impact on the sport. Hagen's other U.S. Open title came in 1919. He entered the final round trailing the leader, Mike Brady, by five shots. But he forced a tie and beat Brady by a shot in an 18-hole playoff.

In addition to the two U.S. Open titles, Hagen won the British Open four times (1922, '24, '28, '29) and the PGA Championship five times (1921, '24–27), the last four consecutively. He didn't play in 1922 and lost the 1923 final to Gene Sarazen. That's the only match he lost during those six years.

In the 1926 PGA final against Leo Diegel, Hagen proved himself the master of gamesmanship, failing to concede a 20-inch putt on the 18th hole, after conceding six- and eight-foot putts earlier in the match. Diegel, thinking the putt was tougher than it was, missed it and lost the match.

Hagen's 11 major championship victories rank him third all-time behind Jack Nicklaus and Bobby Jones. He wasn't able to play the Masters, which didn't start until 1934.

Hagen won more than 75 tournaments in all, 40 on the PGA Tour, which ties him for seventh all-time.

One of his most famous victories came against Jones, then regarded as the greatest golfer in the world, in 1926 in a special 72-hole challenge match in Florida. Hagen won the match 11-and-10 and with it the $7,600 first prize, the richest in golf history up to that time. Afterward, he went out and bought Jones an $800 set of diamond and platinum cufflinks.

But one of Hagen's most important contributions to the game, and one that won't be found in the record books, is the fight he waged to improve the way professional golfers were treated. In Hagen's day, professional golfers were looked upon as second-class citizens. They weren't allowed to use the locker rooms, and they were treated much like servants, especially in England.

That began to change in 1920, when Hagen, competing in his first British Open, was shown his "dressing quarters," which happened to be a peg on the wall in the pro shop. Incensed, he had his chauffeur drive the limousine to the front of the clubhouse and he changed each day of the tournament in the car. It wasn't long afterward that professionals were allowed in the clubhouse.

Hagen, known as the "Haig" and "Sir Walter," is a member of the World Golf Hall of Fame.

Haynie, Sandra
Born: June 4, 1943 in Fort Worth, Texas

After winning the 1958 and '59 Texas Amateur championships, Sandra Haynie joined the LPGA Tour in 1961 and won her first LPGA Tour event in 1962 at age 18. Over the next 15 years she won 39 tournaments, including the LPGA Championship (1965, '74) and the U.S.

Women's Open (1974). In 1970, Haynie won twice, finished second on the money list, and was named the LPGA Player of the Year.

Haynie curtailed her 1977–80 schedule, due to injuries and business interests, but returned as a full-time player in 1981. The following year, she enjoyed her best season, winning twice, including a major championship (Peter Jackson Classic, now the du Maurier Classic), and earning $245,432.

Haynie finished in the top five on the money list 11 times and was the runner-up five times.

Her last full season on tour was 1989. Haynie has 42 career victories, which ranked eighth all-time through the 1999 season. She was inducted into the LPGA Hall of Fame in 1977.

Hogan, Ben
Born: August 13, 1912 in Dublin, Texas
Died: July 25, 1997

Ben Hogan's story is one of the most remarkable in sports history. He was born in Dublin, Texas, a town of 2,500 people and no golf courses. When his father died, the family moved to Fort Worth, where Ben delivered newspapers. When he was 12, he found out that caddying paid more, so he went to work at Glen Garden Country Club.

It was at that time that the game began to fascinate him. He took to practicing his swing on the front lawn of his house, going so far as to turn himself from his natural left-handed stance to right-handed. In the annual Christmas Day caddie tournament, Hogan shared first place with Byron Nelson, who went on to great fame himself.

In 1931, at age 19, Hogan turned pro, even though he was plagued with a hook that took him years to cure. His first victory as a pro didn't come until 1940, the result of hours and hours of practice, finally ridding his swing of that hook. Hogan's drive and determination are as legendary as his ball-striking and shot-making ability.

His powers of concentration and focus also were unmatched. He was nicknamed the "Iceman" for his no-nonsense approach to the game.

Said Bobby Jones: "I thought I was a hard fighter. I thought [Walter] Hagen and [Gene] Sarazen both were. We're not in a class with this fellow Hogan. He's fighting for every inch, every foot, every yard on a golf course."

After Hogan broke through, winning the 1940 North and South Open, he followed that with five more victories in 1941. He never finished lower than fifth place in 26 events. From 1940 to 1942, he was the tour's leading money winner and the winner of the Vardon Trophy for low stroke average.

Hogan served in the Army Air Corps during World War II and returned to the tour in 1945. Over the next 4 1/2 years, he won 35 tournaments, including two PGA Championships (1946, '48) and the U.S. Open (1948).

But his career appeared to be over after a serious car accident in 1949. Hogan and his wife, Valerie, were returning home from a tournament when their car collided head-on with a Greyhound bus. Hogan suffered devastating injuries: a double fracture of the pelvis, a broken collarbone, and a broken left ankle. He probably saved his own life by throwing himself in front of Valerie to save her life: the impact of the crash drove the steering column into the driver's seat.

There was justifiable concern whether Hogan would ever walk again, let alone play golf. But the drive and determination that served him so well on the golf course was the main reason he was able to return to the golf course.

Hogan, known for his ever-present white cap, had to relearn how to walk and swing a golf club, but he managed it. Eleven months after the accident, he lost to Sam Snead in a playoff for the Los Angeles Open title.

In the 1950 U.S. Open at Merion Golf Club in suburban Philadelphia, Hogan, battling pain and fatigue, lost his lead on the final day, on which 36 holes were played. But he won the championship the following day, beating Tom Fazio and Lloyd Mangrum in an 18-hole playoff.

Because of his injuries, Hogan was forced to curtail his playing schedule, but he continued to excel, particularly in the major championships.

In 1951, Hogan successfully defended his U.S. Open title and also won the Masters. After taking the year off in 1952, he came back with his best season ever. He entered six tournaments and won five in 1953, including the U.S. Open, the Masters, and the British Open in his only appearance in the event. This gave him the Grand Slam of the majors. He was unable to win the PGA Championship because it was scheduled at the same time as the British Open.

Hogan finished in the top 10 of every U.S. Open he entered from 1940 through 1960 and never finished lower than seventh in the Masters from 1941 through 1956. He retired in 1960, having won 63 PGA Tour events, third all-time, and three Vardon Trophies for low stroke average. He is a member of the World Golf Hall of Fame.

Inkster, Juli
Born: June 24, 1960 in Santa Cruz, California

Juli Inkster is one of only three women to have won the U.S. Women's Amateur three years in a row (1980–82),

joining Glenna Collett Vare and Virginia Van Wie. She is also one of only two women, along with Pat Bradley, to have won each of the four modern major championships.

In 1983, Inkster became the first LPGA rookie to win two major championships in one year. She won the Nabisco Dinah Shore and the du Maurier Classic and was named Rookie of the Year. Inkster also won the Nabisco Dinah Shore in 1989.

In 1999, Inkster completed her personal Grand Slam by winning the U.S. Women's Open and the McDonald's LPGA Championship. Her victory in the Open, by five shots, was particularly satisfying. In 1994, she had a two-stroke lead over Patty Sheehan with two holes to play, but Sheehan forced a tie by making birdies on her final two holes and went on to win an 18-hole playoff the next day.

Overall in 1999, Inkster won five times, finished in the top ten 18 times in 24 events, missed only one cut, placed in the top 10 of each of the four major championships, and ranked in the top 10 of seven statistical categories, including second in the Vare Trophy for low scoring average and second in the Rolex Player of the Year balloting.

What made Inkster's 1999 season even more impressive is that her accomplishments on the golf course didn't interfere with her being a wife and mother. She has two daughters.

Through the 2000 season, Inkster had 25 LPGA Tour victories. Her last victory of 1999, in the Safeway LPGA Golf Championship, earned her a spot in the LPGA Hall of Fame, under a new point system adopted in 1998.

Irwin, Hale
Born: June 3, 1945 in Joplin, Missouri

Hale Irwin, a two-sport athlete at the University of Colorado, made a wise career move in choosing golf over football. He was twice an all-Big Eight defensive back for the Buffaloes. He also won the 1967 NCAA golf championship.

Irwin joined the PGA Tour in 1968 and won 20 tournaments, including three U.S. Opens (1974, '79, '90). His third Open title was the most dramatic. He sunk a 45-putt for a birdie on the 72nd hole to force a tie with Mike Donald, and then made a 10-footer for birdie on the 19th playoff hole for the victory. At 45, he became the oldest U.S. Open champion.

Irwin's streak of 86 consecutive cuts made (1975–78) is the third longest in tour history, behind Jack Nicklaus and Byron Nelson. He played on five Ryder Cup teams and was the captain of the inaugural President's Cup team in 1994.

Irwin joined the Senior PGA Tour in 1995 and has been the dominant force. He won nine times in 1997 and seven times in 1998. Among his victories are five senior major championships—1996 PGA Seniors, 1997 PGA Seniors, 1998 PGA Seniors and U.S. Senior Open, and 1999 Senior Players.

Through 2000, he won 29 events and finished in the top three in 63 of the 130 events he entered. His combined earnings were more than $17.7 million.

Jameson, Betty

Born: May 19, 1919 in Norman, Oklahoma

Betty Jameson made her mark early, winning the Texas Publinx title at age 13 and the Southern Championship at age 15. In 1939, she won the first of her two straight U.S. Women's Amateur titles.

She turned professional in 1945 and was a founding member of the LPGA in 1948.

Jameson, inducted into the LPGA Hall of Fame in 1951 as a founding member, won 10 tournaments, including the 1947 U.S. Women's Open, where she was the first woman to post a score lower than 300 in a 72-hole event.

In 1952, Jameson conceived the idea of honoring the player with the lowest stroke average, donating a trophy in the name of Glenna Collett Vare.

Jones, Bobby

Born: March 17, 1902 in Atlanta, Georgia
Died: December 18, 1971

As a boy, Bobby Jones lived just off the 13th fairway at Atlanta's East Lake course. He learned the game by using an old ball and cut-down club, and by the time he was nine years old, he was the club's junior champion. In 1916, he won the Georgia Amateur at age 14, when he qualified for the U.S. Amateur for the first time.

But Jones' development as a player was stunted by his temper, which always seemed to get the best of him. Many people thought it would keep him from becoming a great player.

The 1921 British Open provides a case in point: After taking 58 shots over the first 11 holes, Jones picked up and never finished his round. According to golf etiquette, it was an unjustifiable act.

But that episode appeared to teach Jones a lesson. He worked hard to control his emotions, his efforts finally paying off at the 1923 U.S. Open, where he beat Bobby Cruickshank in an 18-hole playoff.

With that breakthrough victory, the floodgates opened for Jones. From 1923 through 1930, he finished lower than second in the Open only once and won at least one major American title each year. He also won Open titles in 1926, 1929, and 1930; he won British Open titles in 1926, 1927, and 1930; and he won the U.S. Amateur in 1924, 1925, 1927, 1928, and 1930.

In 1930, Jones won his only British Amateur championship, but that gave him a sweep of all four major championships in the same year and allowed him to complete the only Grand Slam ever accomplished.

Jones retired from competition following the 1930 season. He was a graduate of Georgia Tech and Harvard Law School, but never practiced law.

He spent his retirement filming instructional movie shorts and working for Spalding Sporting Goods. Perhaps his most enduring legacy is the golf course he designed—Augusta National, site of the Masters, which Jones also started in 1934. Jones played in the Masters each year until 1947, when he withdrew with a sore shoulder. At first, it was thought he had bursitis, but instead, the injury was the first symptom of a spinal ailment that confined him to a wheelchair.

Ironically, Jones overcame the temper tantrums of his youth and was renowned as a great sportsman. The United States Golf Association bestows the Bob Jones Award annually to recognize distinguished sportsmanship.

King, Betsy

Born: August 13, 1955 in Reading, Pennsylvania

Betsy King's career is proof that patience is a virtue. She joined the LPGA Tour in 1977, after a successful career at Furman University, where she was named Athlete of the Year and Scholar Athlete of the Year as a senior.

Her first tour victory, however, didn't take place for seven years. But in 1984, after a number of near-misses and considerable frustration, King won the Women's Kemper Open, ending a string of 195 events without a trip to the winner's circle.

King went on to win twice more that year, propelling her to the money title ($266,771) and her first of three Rolex Player of the Year Awards (1984, '89, '93).

From 1984 through 1989, King won 20 events, making her the winningest pro, male or female, during that time period.

She won the money title in 1989, when she set a single-season earnings record ($654,132), and again in 1993. Her 1989 season was a model of consistent excellence. She shot 33 rounds in the 60s, won six events, and finished in the top 10 in 20 of 25 events.

Among her most significant victories are the U.S. Women's Open (1989, '90), the Nabisco Dinah Shore Invitational (1987, '90, '97), and the Mazda LPGA Championship (1992), which she won with a record score of 17-under 267 at Bethesda Country Club and became the

Betsy King   *Diane Staskowski*

first LPGA player to score in the 60s in all four rounds of a major championship (68-66-67-66).

In 1995, her victory in the ShopRite LPGA Classic was the 30th of her career, securing her a place in the LPGA Hall of Fame.

She is a five-time member of the Solheim Cup team, and the LPGA's all-time leading money winner with more than $6.5 million through 2000. After struggling in 1999, King won the Hawaiian Ladies Open in March 2000. It was the 32nd win of her career and her first since 1997.

In 1996, a tournament bearing her name—the Betsy King Classic—was added to the LPGA schedule and held at Berkleigh Country Club near Reading, Pa., where she was born in 1955.

King has won numerous awards for her humanitarianism. She has organized Habitat for Humanity home-building projects; raised money for a variety of charities, such as the Easter Seal Society; visited orphans in Romania as part of a relief effort; and served as a board member for the Fellowship of Christian Athletes.

Through 2000, King had 33 LPGA Tour victories, which tied her for 12th all-time.

Kite, Tom
Born: December 9, 1945 in Austin, Texas

Tom Kite was one of the most consistent players on the PGA Tour, although it took him a while to reach the winner's circle. Kite joined the PGA Tour in 1972 after sharing the NCAA title with Ben Crenshaw in 1971. He went winless until 1980, when he won his first two PGA Tour events. In 1981, Kite won once and finished in the top 10 21 times in 26 events. He topped the money list and won the first of two consecutive Vardon Trophies for low stroke average.

In 1989, Kite again was the leading money winner, with nearly $1.4 million, and was the PGA Player of the Year.

Through the 2000 season, he had 19 tour victories. From 1981 through 1993, he won at least one tournament each year, except for 1988.

Kite shed the title of "best player never to win a major" at the 1992 U.S. Open at Pebble Beach. He withstood high winds and brutal conditions to fire an even-par 72 in the final round.

Kite was a seven-time member of the U.S. Ryder Cup team. In 1997, he was the nonplaying captain in a loss to Europe.

He joined the Senior PGA Tour in 2000, winning twice.

Little, Lawson
Born: June 23, 1910 in Newport, Rhode Island
Died: February 1, 1968

Lawson Little accomplished something that Bobby Jones never did: He won the U.S. and British Amateur championships two years in a row (1934–35). During that span, he won 34 consecutive matches. He won the 1935 Sullivan Award as the outstanding U.S. amateur athlete.

Little turned pro in 1936. His most significant victory was the 1940 U.S. Open championship, in which he defeated Gene Sarazen in an 18-hole playoff.

Little won eight PGA Tour titles and is a member of the World Golf Hall of Fame.

Littler, Gene
Born: July 21, 1930 in San Diego, California

After winning the 1953 U.S. Amateur championship, Gene Littler won the 1954 San Diego Open, a PGA Tour event, as an amateur, meaning he never had to qualify for a tour event. He won 29 tournaments on the PGA Tour and eight on the Senior PGA Tour. His most significant victory was the 1961 U.S. Open at Oakland Hills Country Club. He also lost a playoff to Billy Casper for the 1970 Masters title and to Lanny Wadkins for the 1977 PGA Championship.

Nicknamed "The Machine" for his fluid swing, Littler was a seven-time member of the U.S. Ryder Cup team. In 1972, he underwent surgery for cancer of the lymphatic system, but he returned that fall. He capped his comeback by winning the 1973 St. Louis Children's Hospital Classic. He is member of the World Golf Hall of Fame.

Locke, Bobby (Arthur)

Born: November 20, 1917 in Germiston, Transvaal, South Africa
Died: March 9, 1987

Bobby Locke began making a name for himself after World War II, when he finished second in the 1946 British Open, third in the 1947 U.S. Open, and first in the 1949 British Open. He also won the British Open in 1950, 1952, and 1957.

Locke's success was the result of a number of unorthodox methods, including compensating for a lack of distance off the tee by hitting a pronounced hook. He didn't practice much, preferring to play by feel, and he was a fine putter, despite a stroke that also used a hook.

Locke, who was renowned for his fashionable outfits, demanded and received appearance fees, which annoyed American players, and he angered the press by requesting $100 for those questions that were of an instructional nature. The PGA eventually banned him in 1949, claiming he failed to honor commitments. He was reinstated in 1951, but played infrequently in the United States thereafter.

He was the first player to win golf tournaments internationally, presaging the careers of Gary Player and Greg Norman. Locke won 10 PGA Tour victories and is a member of the World Golf Hall of Fame.

Lopez, Nancy

Born: January 6, 1957 in Torrance, California

Nancy Lopez won her first important championship—the New Mexico Women's Amateur—at age 12. She followed that with two USGA Junior Girls Championships

Nancy Lopez *Diane Staskowski*

(1972, '74) and three Western Junior Championships. In 1975, while a senior in high school, she entered the U.S. Women's Open as an amateur and tied for second. The next year, Lopez won the Association of Intercollegiate Athletics for Women (AIAW) national championship while at the University of Tulsa and played on the U.S. Curtis Cup and World Amateur teams.

When Lopez turned pro, she had one of the greatest rookie seasons in golf history. In 1978, she won nine LPGA tournaments, including a record five straight—Greater Baltimore Classic, Coca-Cola Classic, Golden Lights Championship, LPGA Championship, and Bankers Trust Classic. She was the LPGA Rookie of the Year and the Rolex Player of the Year. She won the Vare Trophy for low stroke average (71.76), breaking Carol Mann's record that had stood since 1968, and was the leading money winner. In addition to her accomplishments, Lopez focused considerable attention on the LPGA Tour, not only with her play, but with her engaging personality and her winning smile. She would do for the LPGA what Arnold Palmer did for the PGA Tour.

Lopez went on to win three more Rolex Player of the Year Awards (1979, '85, '88), two more Vare Trophies (1979, '85), and one more money title (1985).

In 1979, she won eight tournaments, and in 1985, she won five, including the LPGA Championship, which she also won in 1978 and 1989. Lopez entered 25 events in 1985 and finished in the top ten 21 times.

Lopez scored her 35th career victory at the 1987 Sarasota Classic, which happened to be the site of her first tour victory. That win qualified her for the LPGA Hall of Fame. She was inducted July 20, 1987, as the 11th member.

Lopez's best season financially came in 1989, when she earned $487,153, good for third on the money list.

About the only thing missing from Lopez's otherwise stellar résumé is a U.S. Women's Open championship. She has registered seven top-10 finishes in the Open, but has never been able to break through.

In 1997, she fired four rounds in the 60s, the first woman to do so, but finished one shot behind Alison Nicholas. Lopez just missed a birdie putt on the 72nd hole that would've forced a playoff.

Lopez married Ray Knight, a former Major League Baseball player and manager, in October 1982. They have three daughters.

Through the 2000 season, Lopez had 48 tour victories, which ranked sixth all-time. She earned more than $5.2 million, which ranked 10th all-time. She was named "Golfer of the Decade" by Golf magazine as part of the Centennial of Golf in America celebration in 1988. She also has been given the 1992 Flo Hyman Award by the Women's Sports Foundation and the 1998 Bob Jones Award by the United States Golf Association.

Love, Davis III
Born: April 13, 1964 in Charlotte, North Carolina

Davis Love III is the son of Davis Love, Jr., a highly regarded golf instructor who was killed in a plane crash in 1988. Love was born shortly after his father had contended in the 1964 Masters.

A graduate of the University of North Carolina, Love won the Atlantic Coast Conference Championship and the prestigious North-South Championship in 1984. He turned pro in 1985 and got his first PGA Tour victory in 1987.

In 1997, Love won his first major championship, the PGA Championship at Winged Foot Country Club. Love shot rounds of 66-71-66-66 for a five-stroke victory over Justin Leonard.

In 1998, Love won the MCI Classic at Harbour Town Golf Links for the fourth time in his career. He went winless in 1999.

Through the 2000 season, Love won 13 PGA Tour events and earned more than $14.8 million. He and Fred Couples teamed for a record four straight World Cup titles. Love is a four-time member of the U.S. Ryder Cup team and a four-time member of the President's Cup team.

Love, who is a devoted family man (he and his wife have two children), wrote a book entitled Every Shot I Take as a tribute to his father.

Mangrum, Lloyd
Born: August 1, 1914 in Trenton, Texas
Died: November 17, 1973

Lloyd Mangrum turned pro at age 15, but didn't win his first tournament until 1938, when he was 24. He won 36 tournaments in his PGA Tour career, good for 10th all time. Mangrum won two Purple Hearts in World War II. He returned to the tour in 1946 to score his most significant victory: the 1946 U.S. Open in a playoff. After the first 18 extra holes, Mangrum, Byron Nelson, and Vic Ghizzi each shot 72, requiring another 18 holes. Mangrum shot 72, Nelson and Ghizzi 73s.

In 1949, Mangrum earned another distinction: He was part of the longest playoff in tour history. He and Cary Middlecoff went 11 holes at the Motor City Open. Darkness intervened and co-winners were declared.

He won seven times in 1948, four times in 1949, five times in 1950, and four times in 1951, when he led the money list and won the Vardon Trophy for low stroke average. He also won the Vardon in 1953.

In the 1950 U.S. Open, Mangrum lost in an 18-hole playoff to Ben Hogan. In 1999, Mangrum was inducted into the World Golf Hall of Fame.

Mann, Carol

Born: February 3, 1941 in Buffalo, New York

It took four years before Carol Mann won her first LPGA tournament. She joined the tour in 1960, with her first victory coming in the 1964 Western Open, a major championship at the time. In 1965, she won her second major, the U.S. Women's Open. Mann's best season came in 1968, when she won 10 tournaments and the Vare Trophy for low scoring average. Mann was one of four players to win 10 or more events in one year. Betsy Rawls, Kathy Whitworth, and Mickey Wright were the others. Mann's 72.04 stroke average in 1968 was a record that stood until Nancy Lopez broke it in 1978.

In 1969, Mann won eight times and was the tour's leading money winner with $49,152.

In all, Mann won 38 LPGA events. She was inducted into the LPGA Hall of Fame in 1977 and retired from competition in 1981.

Mann was a key figure in the formation of the modern LPGA and is a former president of the organization. She has been a trustee of the Women's Sports Foundation since 1979, serving as president 1985–90.

Martin, Casey

Born: June 2, 1972 in Eugene, Oregon

Casey Martin became a household name in 1998, when he sued the PGA Tour for the right to use a cart during tournaments. Martin was born with a birth defect, Klippel-Trenaunay-Webber syndrome, a circulatory problem that made Martin's leg brittle and walking difficult. He had to wear a strong support stocking to keep the swelling down. Martin sued under the Americans with Disabilities Act; the PGA Tour maintained that walking was an integral part of the game. A federal court in Oregon ruled in Martin's favor, and he was allowed a cart. Right after the trial, Martin won the Lakeland Classic on the then Nike Tour.

In 1999, Martin finished in the top 15 on the Nike Tour money list to gain playing privileges on the PGA Tour in 2000.

In March 2000, the 9th U.S. Circuit Court of Appeals upheld the lower court ruling, and Martin could continue to ride. The Supreme Court will rule on the case. Martin was a second-team All-American at Stanford in 1994. His teammates at Stanford included Tiger Woods.

Middlecoff, Cary

Born: January 6, 1921 in Halls, Tennessee

Cary Middlecoff's promising career as a dentist never materialized. A doctor of dental surgery, Middlecoff served in the U.S. Army Dental Corps. He won the 1945 North and South Open and earned an invitation to participate on the Walker Cup team. But he declined, deciding instead to try the PGA Tour.

It proved to be a wise decision.

Middlecoff, known as a very slow player, won 40 tour events, tied for seventh all-time with Walter Hagen. Middlecoff was also consistent. He finished second 30 times, third 23 times, and in the top ten 181 times.

Middlecoff won seven times in 1949, six times in 1951, and six times in 1955. He won three major championships: the U.S. Open in 1949 and 1956 and the Masters, by seven shots, in 1955. In 1956, he also won the Vardon Trophy for low stroke average.

Middlecoff, a member of three U.S. Ryder Cup teams, never received the acclaim he might have because his contemporaries included Ben Hogan and Sam Snead. Back troubles in the early 1960s forced him to retire from the game. Middlecoff worked as a television commentator and also wrote several books on golf, including *Advanced Golf* and *The Golf Swing*.

Miller, Johnny

Born: April 29, 1947 in San Francisco, California

Johnny Miller joined the PGA Tour in 1969 and won 24 tournaments, tying him for 20th place all-time. But he will be most remembered for his victory in the 1973 U.S. Open at Oakmont Country Club in suburban Pittsburgh.

Miller closed with a final-round 7-under 63 to beat John Schlee by five shots. The 63 is still the lowest 18-hole score in major championship history. His other major championship win, the 1976 British Open, also came by a comfortable margin: by six strokes over Jack Nicklaus and Seve Ballesteros.

His best season was 1974, when he won eight times, led the tour in earnings with $352,021, and was named PGA Tour Player of the Year.

His last tour victory came at the AT&T Pebble Beach Pro-Am in 1994, more than 22 years after his first tour win at the 1971 Southern Open.

Miller played on two U.S. Ryder Cup teams (1973, '75). He was the first player elected to the new World Golf Hall of Fame in 1996. As the lead analyst for NBC Sports golf coverage, Miller has been popular with the fans, but his candor has drawn criticism from the players.

Nelson, Byron

Born: February 4, 1912 in Fort Worth, Texas

Byron Nelson grew up next to the Glen Garden Country Club, where he learned the game and caddied, along with Ben Hogan, who also went on to greatness. Nelson had success as an amateur, but couldn't afford to play too often because of the Depression. He turned pro in 1932, tried the pro tour in 1934 and 1935, then took a job as a club pro in New Jersey in 1936.

In 1936, steel shafts began replacing hickory, and Nelson made some adjustments to his swing to account for the different equipment. He was the first player to do so. Nelson won five major championships: two Masters (1937, '42), two PGA Championships (1940, '45), and one U.S. Open (1939). He also won the 1939 Vardon Trophy for low stroke average. His 52 PGA Tour victories rank him fifth all-time.

In 1945, Byron Nelson put together a streak that will be virtually impossible to break. He won 11 consecutive PGA Tour events, starting with the Miami Four-Ball March 11 and continuing through the Canadian Open August 4. He actually won a 12th event in Spring Lake, N.J., but it wasn't counted as official because the purse was below the PGA minimum. His earnings for those 11 tournaments was only $63,335 in war bonds, or 14.5 percent of the total prize money available, a staggering amount.

Nelson, who entered 30 events in 1945, won 18 tournaments, finished second in seven others, and never finished lower than ninth. He averaged 68.33 strokes per round. The previous year, he won eight times and averaged 69.67 strokes a round for 85 rounds. By the end of 1945, Nelson's streak of consecutive events without missing a cut ended at 113, a record that still stands today.

Ironically, Nelson was able to compete in 1945 only because he was exempted from joining the service due to hemophilia. The stress and strain of the streak took its toll on Nelson, who played one more full season in 1946, winning six times. He also won the last tournament he played, in 1949.

Nelson was named the Associated Press Male Athlete of the Year in 1944 and 1945 and served as an analyst for ABC Sports golf coverage. He is a member of the World Golf Hall of Fame.

Nicklaus, Jack

Born: January 21, 1940 in Columbus, Ohio

Arguably the greatest golfer of all time, Jack Nicklaus, with victories in 20 major championships (18 professional and the U.S. Amateur twice), has set the standard to which others are compared. His powerful swing, his precise and efficient course management, and his ability to succeed under pressure have resulted in an incomparable record.

Born in Columbus, Ohio, Nicklaus, the son of a pharmacist, was 10 years old when he played his first nine holes and shot 51. He won the first of five straight Ohio State Junior Championships in 1952 at age 12. Four years later, he won the Ohio State Open, a 72-hole stroke-play event, shooting 64 and 72 in the final two rounds.

Jack Nicklaus   *Diane Staskowski*

Nicklaus, nicknamed the Golden Bear, won his first national title, the U.S. National Jaycees Championship, in 1957, the same year he qualified for his first U.S. Open, where he missed the cut. That appearance in the U.S. Open, held at the Inverness Club in Toledo, Ohio, began a remarkable streak of 43 consecutive Open appearances (through 1999). His streak of consecutive major championships ended at 154 in 1998, when he failed to enter the British Open because of a hip problem.

His first major championship victory came in the 1959 U.S. Amateur at the Broadmoor in Colorado Springs, Colo., where he defeated defending champion Charlie Coe 1-up. The following year he was runner-up to Arnold Palmer in the U.S. Open at Cherry Hills in Denver.

Nicklaus ended his amateur career in 1961 by winning his second U.S. Amateur, easily beating Dudley Wysong 8-and-6 at Pebble Beach Golf Links in Pebble Beach, Calif. He also won the NCAA championship and tied for fourth at the U.S. Open.

In 1962, Nicklaus joined the PGA Tour and claimed his first victory as a professional at the U.S. Open, beating Palmer in an 18-hole playoff at Oakmont Country Club. He won three more times in his debut season, finished third on the money list ($61,868), and was named PGA Tour Rookie of the Year.

From that year forward, Nicklaus compiled a list of accomplishments that earned him the distinction of being named "Golfer of the Century" by *Golf* magazine,

219

in conjunction with the Centennial of Golf in America Celebration.

He won 71 PGA Tour events, including at least one tournament a year for 17 straight seasons (1962–78), and was named PGA Tour Player of the Year five times (1967, '72, '73, '75, '76). Eight times he was no. 1 in scoring average (1964, '65, '71, '72, '73, '74, '75, '76), and eight times he was the tour's leading money winner (1964, '65, '67, '71, '72, '73, '75, '76). He also participated in the Ryder Cup matches as a player and twice as captain (1983, '87).

But it was in the major championships where Nicklaus separated himself from his peers and ensured his place in history. He won six Masters (1963, '65, '66, '72, '75, '86), five PGA Championships (1963, '71, '73, '75, '80), four U.S. Opens (1962, '67, '72, '80), and three British Opens (1966, '70, '78). He is a multiple Grand Slam winner—the only player to accomplish this.

By comparison, Walter Hagen, second to Nicklaus in professional major championship victories, has 11. Ben Hogan and Gary Player have nine each; Tom Watson has eight.

And when Nicklaus didn't win major championships, he usually contended. He has 48 top three finishes, including 19 seconds, and 56 top five finishes.

Nicklaus' most stirring and most improbable victory came in the 1986 Masters at age 46, making him the oldest player ever to win at Augusta National. With his son, Jackie, as his caddie, Nicklaus shot 7-under 65 in the final round.

In 1990, Nicklaus joined the Senior PGA Tour, where he continued to win major championships. His first two senior victories came in majors—the Tradition, which he has won four times (1990, '91, '95, '96), and the Senior Players Championship. He also won the U.S. Senior Open in 1991 and 1993 and the PGA Seniors Championship in 1991.

In addition to excelling on the course, Nicklaus also is one of the world's most respected golf course architects. More than 150 courses internationally have been designed, codesigned, or redesigned by Nicklaus, with more than 50 under construction. Twenty-four of his courses have regularly appeared in the top 100 lists of various publications.

In January 1999, Nicklaus underwent surgery to have his right hip replaced. He returned to the Senior PGA Tour in mid-May, more than two months ahead of schedule.

Although he retired in 2000, he played in all four major championships, which will mark the last time that happens.

Norman, Greg

Born: February 10, 1955 in Queensland, Australia

Greg Norman grew up as a "skinny, scrawny youth," to use his description. So to prove himself tougher than his physique, he took part in contact sports—rugby, Australian rules football, and cricket, to name a few.

It wasn't until Norman was 16 that he took up golf. It took him two years to go from a 27 handicap to a scratch golfer. He turned pro in 1976, and through 1982 won at least one tournament a year, including the Australian Open, the Australian Masters, and the Dunlop Masters.

In 1983, he joined the PGA Tour and had 18 PGA Tour victories through 2000 and 56 victories worldwide. He was the first player to surpass $10 million in earnings on the PGA Tour, and the first player to earn $1 million (1990–93, '94–95) four years in a row. He won three money titles (1986, '90, '95), three Vardon Trophies for low stroke average (1988, '89, '94), and was named PGA Player of the Year in 1995.

But for all his accomplishments, Norman, nicknamed "The Great White Shark," is most famous for the ones that got away. In the 1986 PGA Championship at Inverness Club, Bob Tway holed a bunker shot on the 72nd hole to beat Norman by one shot. The following year at the Masters, Larry Mize holed a 140-foot pitch shot from off the 10th green on the first hole of sudden death to make Norman a runner-up again. Norman also lost playoffs at the 1984 U.S. Open to Fuzzy Zoeller and the 1993 PGA Championship to Paul Azinger.

His most spectacular collapse came at the 1996 Masters. Norman was the class of the field during the first three rounds and entered the final round with a six-shot lead over Nick Faldo. But Norman ballooned to a 6-over 78, while Faldo closed with a 5-under 67. Norman has won two major championships, both British Open titles. In 1986 at Turnberry, he opened with a 74, but came back with a tournament-record-tying 63 to lead by two. He closed with rounds of 74–69 to beat Gordon Brand by two shots.

At Royal St. Georges in 1993, Norman trailed Faldo and Corey Pavin by one stroke after 54 holes, but finished with a 64 to beat Faldo by two.

Norman underwent shoulder surgery in April 1998 that reduced his schedule to only three events. He returned to the PGA Tour in 1999 and played in 12 events.

In addition to golf, Norman is a golf course designer and architect; he developed a popular strain of turf grass that bears his name; he operates a vineyard; and he has numerous endorsements, including a line of clothing.

Olazabal, Jose Maria

Born: February 5, 1966 in Fuenterrabia, Spain

Jose Maria Olazabal, who lived on a golf course, the son of a greenskeeper, began playing golf at age four. He would sneak onto the course at dusk and chip and putt. He won a number of youth titles and then went on to have great success as an amateur, winning the Spanish and Italian amateurs in 1983. As an 18-year-old he beat Colin Montgomerie 5-and-4 in the final of the 1984 British Amateur Championship.

He turned pro in 1985 and had a remarkable rookie season in 1986, winning two tournaments (European Masters and Sanyo Open) and finishing second in the European Order of Merit—the highest ever finish by a rookie.

In the 1990 World Series of Golf, Olazabal won by 12 shots, the biggest winning margin on the PGA Tour since 1975. He opened with a 61 and finished with three consecutive 67s.

In 1994, Olazabal, a master of the short game, won his first major championship, the Masters, by two strokes. In 1995, he developed a serious foot problem that threatened his career. The pain was so severe he could barely walk, and for a time it looked as if he would have to retire. But a German doctor diagnosed his condition, and after an 18-month absence from competitive golf, Olazabal returned.

In 1999, he won his second Masters championship. Through the 2000 season, Olazabal had 23 victories. He was a six-time member of the European Ryder Cup team.

O'Meara, Mark
Born: January 13, 1957 in Goldsboro, North Carolina

In 1998, at age 41, Mark O'Meara became the oldest player to win two major championships—the Masters and the British Open—in the same year, joining Nick Price and Nick Faldo as the only players in the '90s to do so.

At the Masters, O'Meara birdied the final two holes to edge Fred Couples and David Duval. He joined Arnold Palmer and Art Wall as the only players to birdie the final two holes to win. The victory came in O'Meara's 15th start at Augusta National, the most for any first-time champion. O'Meara was only the fifth player in Masters history to win after not leading in the first three rounds.

At the British Open, O'Meara entered the final round trailing by two, but shot 68 to force a playoff with Brian Watts. O'Meara won the four-hole playoff by two shots (17–19).

At the PGA Championship, where he tied for fourth, O'Meara made a strong run at becoming the first player to win three majors in one year since Ben Hogan in 1953.

O'Meara was chosen by his peers as the winner of 1998 PGA Tour Player of the Year.

Through the 2000 season, O'Meara had 16 victories on the PGA Tour and seven victories worldwide. He was

the 1981 PGA Tour Rookie of the Year and the 1979 U.S. Amateur champion.

Ouimet, Francis
Born: May 8, 1893 in Brookline, Massachusetts
Died: September 2, 1967

Francis Ouimet is known as "the father of American golf." His victory in the 1913 U.S. Open over Englishmen Ted Ray and Harry Vardon brought golf to the front pages of newspapers and helped change the public's perception of a sport it thought was only for the wealthy.

Ouimet had taken time off from his job at a sporting goods manufacturer to compete in the 1913 U.S. Amateur, where he lost in the second round. He entered the U.S. Open, because Robert Watson, the president of the United Golf Association, asked him to, even though he had no intention of taking more time off from work to play.

But Ouimet did play when his supervisor noticed his name on the entry list. The tournament was held at the Country Club in Brookline, Mass., where he had caddied since he was 11. He had never played the entire course, because the greenskeeper would chase him off the course.

Ouimet, Ray, and Vardon were tied after 72 holes, forcing an 18-hole playoff. With two holes to play, Ouimet led Vardon by one and Ray by two. Ouimet birdied the 17th hole, where Vardon bogeyed, and went on to become the first amateur ever to win the Open.

Herbert Warren Wind, the great golf writer, wrote: "Here was a person all of America, not just golfing America, could understand—The boy from the 'wrong side of the street, the caddie, the kid who worked during his summer vacations from high school—America's idea of an American hero.'"

Ouimet also won the 1914 and 1931 U.S. Amateur, the 1914 French Amateur, and the 1917 Western Amateur.

In 1951, he became the first non-Briton ever elected captain of the Royal and Ancient Golf Club of St. Andrews.

Ouimet is a member of the World Golf Hall of Fame and had a stamp dedicated to him by the U.S. Postal Service.

Palmer, Arnold
Born: September 10, 1929 in Latrobe, Pennsylvania

To many people, Arnold Palmer *is* golf. He is the reason they play it and watch it; he is the reason the game has become so popular.

Palmer's impact on the game, especially as it relates to television, cannot be minimized. He came along at the time golf was becoming a television staple. His charisma, combined with his go-for-broke style and famous charges, was perfect for a sport trying to get a foothold with the masses.

Palmer, nicknamed "The King," grew up in Latrobe, Pa., a small town in the western half of the state. His father, Milfred, was the golf professional and course superintendent at Latrobe Country Club, where Palmer learned the game.

The family house was just off the sixth hole at Latrobe Country Club, and Palmer would sit by that hole for hours, watching golfers tee off.

He began caddying at age 11, and it wasn't long before he could beat most of the older caddies at the club. Palmer dominated golf in high school and in western Pennsylvania. He won his first of five West Penn Amateur championships when he was 17.

He went to college at Wake Forest University, where he was the no. 1 player on the golf team and one of the best players in the country. Palmer left Wake Forest during his senior year, devastated by the death of his friend and teammate Ben Worsham in an auto accident. He joined the U.S. Coast Guard for three years, and after his discharge returned to Wake Forest to continue his education.

But prior to graduation, he left for good and began working in sales near Cleveland. In 1954, he won the U.S. Amateur championship, before turning pro in the fall of 1954.

His first professional victory came in the 1955 Canadian Open. His first major championship came in the 1958 Masters, which he also won in 1960, 1962, and 1964. Palmer won the British Open in 1961 and 1962. But perhaps his most famous victory—the one that endeared him to the public and was largely responsible for the formation of "Arnie's Army"—was his win in the 1960 U.S. Open at Cherry Hills in Denver, Colo. Palmer entered the final round in 15th place and seven shots behind the leader, Mike Souchak. Spurred on by clubhouse talk that he was too far behind to win, he set out to prove the doubters wrong.

He started quickly by driving the first green and two-putting for birdie. At the second, he chipped in for a birdie; and at the third he tapped in for birdie after barely missing an eagle putt.

Palmer completed the front nine in 5-under 30 and added another birdie on the back to finish at 4-under 280, beating Jack Nicklaus, an amateur, by two shots.

In all, Palmer won 60 PGA Tour events, which ranks him fourth all-time. He was the first tour player to surpass the $1 million mark in career earnings, and he is tied with Nicklaus for the most consecutive years winning at least one tournament (17).

Palmer won the money title four times (1958, '60, '62, '63) and the Vardon Trophy for low stroke average four times (1961, '62, '64, '67). He was twice named PGA Player of the Year (1960, '62), and his 22 victories in Ryder Cup matches is a record. He was Ryder Cup captain in 1963 and 1975. He also has 10 victories on the Senior PGA Tour.

Palmer is the first athlete to parlay his success in the arena into a lucrative corporate empire. That empire began to take off in 1964, under the guidance of Mark McCormack and his company, known today as International Management Group.

No sports figure has been more marketed, licensed, exhibited, and promoted. He remains one of the most recognizable and highest-paid athlete endorsers.

Palmer has won just about every major award given, including Associated Press Athlete of the Decade for the 1960s, the Hickock Award (1960), and *Sports Illustrated*'s Sportsman of the Year (1960).

Pepper, Dottie

Born: August 17, 1965 in Saratoga Springs, New York

Dottie Pepper is one of the most fiery competitors on the LPGA Tour as her 12–4–1 record in five Solheim Cup matches proves. In the 1998 Cup, she was 4–0 and helped lead the United States to a 16–12 victory over Europe.

Through the 2000 season, Pepper had 17 LPGA tour victories, including two major championships—the 1992 and 1999 Nabisco Dinah Shore. Her best season was 1992, when she won four times, topped the money list with nearly $700,000, won the Vare Trophy for low stroke average, and was named Rolex Player of the Year.

Picard, Henry

Born: November 28, 1907 in Plymouth, Massachusetts
Died: April 30, 1997

Henry Picard was a prominent PGA Tour player of the late 1930s. His breakthrough year came in 1938, when he won the Masters and reached the semifinals of the PGA Championship. He was even better in 1939. He won the PGA, beating Byron Nelson. Picard, 1-down going to the final hole, birdied after Nelson parred. On the first extra hole, Picard's drive came to rest under a truck. He got relief, hit his approach to seven feet, and birdied to win the title. He also won seven other tournaments in 1939. Picard had 26 PGA Tour wins, the last coming in 1941. Through the 1999 season, he ranked 19th all-time.

He was a member of eight U.S. Ryder Cup teams.

Player, Gary

Born: November 1, 1935 in Johannesburg,
South Africa

Gary Player is probably the most well-traveled player in golf history—not to mention one of the best. It is estimated that he has traveled more than 10 million miles since he turned pro in 1953.

Through 2000, Player won more than 160 titles worldwide. Twenty-one of those victories came on the PGA Tour.

He is one of only five players—Gene Sarazen, Ben Hogan, Jack Nicklaus, and Tiger Woods are the others—to win each of the four Grand Slam championships. He won three Masters (1961, '74, '78), three British Opens (1959, '68, '74), two PGA Championships (1962, '72), and one U.S. Open (1965). He completed his Grand Slam with the 1965 Open at age 29.

In his 1978 Masters win, Player entered the final round trailing the leader, Hubert Green, by seven shots. He fired an 8-under 64, making birdies on seven of the final 10 holes to win by a shot. The next week, at the Tournament of Champions, he also won after trailing by seven in the final round.

Player, the leading money winner on the PGA Tour in 1961, won three consecutive tournaments—he won the Houston Open, following his Masters and Tournament of Champions victories—and the only player in the 20th century to win the British Open in three different decades. He won PGA Tour events in five different decades.

Player joined the Senior PGA Tour in 1985. Through 2000, he won 19 events, including the 1998 Northville Long Island Classic at age 62, making him the second-oldest winner on the Senior Tour. He also won six Senior Tour major championships—PGA Seniors Championship (1986, '88, '90), U.S. Senior Open (1987–88), and Senior Players Championship (1987).

Player, just 5-9, 155 pounds, is known for his devotion to physical fitness. He is a renowned golf course architect, with more than 100 courses worldwide. He also has received great acclaim for his horse-breeding business.

Player is a member of the World Golf Hall of Fame.

Price, Nick

Born: January 28, 1957 in Durban, South Africa

In Nick Price's first season on the PGA Tour, 1983, he won the World Series of Golf. His next tour victory did not come for eight years. He won twice in 1991 and from 1992 through 1994 dominated the tour as no one since Tom Watson had a decade earlier. Price won 11 times in three seasons, including three major championships: 1992 PGA Championship, 1994 British Open, and 1994 PGA Championship.

Price became one of only six players since 1945 to win consecutive majors (Ben Hogan, Jack Nicklaus, Arnold Palmer, Lee Trevino, Tom Watson). He, Nick Faldo, and Mark O'Meara were the only players in the '90s to win two majors in the same season. Price finished eagle-birdie-par to make up a two-stroke deficit to Jesper Parnevik and win the British Open.

Overall in 1994, Price won five times and topped the money list for the second straight year. He also was named the PGA Player of the Year for the second straight year. Price won the Vardon Trophy for low stroke average in 1993 and 1997.

Through the 2000 season, Price, a four-time member of the International President's Cup team, had 16 victories on the PGA Tour and 24 victories worldwide.

Rawls, Betsy

Born: May 4, 1928 in Spartanburg, South Carolina

Betsy Rawls won the 1949 Texas Amateur at age 21, just four years after taking up the game. She joined the LPGA Tour in 1951 and went on to win 53 tournaments, ranking her fourth all-time.

Rawls won four U.S. Women's Opens (1951, '53, '57, '60), two LPGA Championships (1959, '69), and two Western Opens (1952, '59). She won the money title and the Vare Trophy for low stroke average in 1959, when she won 10 tournaments. Inducted into the LPGA Hall of

Gary Player *Diane Staskowski*

Fame in 1960, Rawls retired in 1975 and served for six years as the LPGA Tour's Tournament Director. In 1981, she took over as executive director for the McDonald's Championship, which became the McDonald's LPGA Championship in 1994, one of the LPGA's four majors.

Rawls was not a long hitter, but what she lacked in distance she made up for around the greens with her great touch and shot-making ability.

Rawls, who graduated from the University of Texas with degrees in physics and mathematics, is also an expert at the Rules of Golf. She was the first woman to serve on the Rules Committee for the men's U.S. Open.

Rodriguez, Chi Chi (Juan)
Born: October 23, 1935 in Bayamon, Puerto Rico

Chi Chi Rodriguez is one of golf's great showmen and goodwill ambassadors. His routine after making a birdie—wielding his putter like a sword and then putting it back into an imaginary sheath—has been a favorite of fans for years.

Rodriguez grew up in poverty and gravitated to the game by hitting tin cans with a guava tree stick. He worked as a caddie and a shoeshine boy at a local course, developing his game at the same time. He caddied until he joined the U.S. Army at age 19.

Rodriguez turned pro in 1960, won eight PGA Tour events, and was a member of the 1973 U.S. Ryder Cup team.

It wasn't until he joined the Senior PGA Tour that he made his mark. From 1986 through 1993, he won 22 times on the Senior Tour. He was the leading money winner in 1987, when he won seven events, including the PGA Seniors Championship. His other senior major came in the 1986 Senior Players Championship. Through 1999, he won more than $6 million on the Senior Tour.

Rodriguez has raised more than $5 million for charity through his Chi Chi Rodriguez Foundation in Clearwater, Fla. He was inducted into the World Golf Hall of Fame in 1992 and the World Humanitarian Sports Hall of Fame in 1994.

Sarazen, Gene
Born: February 27, 1902 in Harrison, New York
Died: May 13, 1999

Gene Sarazen, nicknamed "The Squire," was the first player to win all four professional major championships. He won the U.S. Open in 1922 at age 20, when he birdied the 72nd hole for a 68. He became the first winner to break 70 in the final round. He also won his first of two consecutive PGA Championships in 1922. His second PGA Championship victory came on the second playoff hole against Walter Hagen.

Then Sarazen's career hit a lull. He won 20 tournaments between 1927 and 1932, but none was a major championship. In reviewing some slow-motion film, he noticed he was holding the club too loosely. So he developed an unusually heavy club to strengthen his hands during practice. His resurgence was also helped by his invention of the sand wedge, which he accomplished by soldering an extra piece of metal onto his niblick, which made the sole heavier and broader.

Sarazen won the U.S. Open and the British Open in 1932 and took his third PGA Championship in 1933. He completed his personal Grand Slam (one of only five players to do so) with his victory in the 1934 Masters, in which he recorded one of the most famous shots in golf history. Trailing Craig Wood by three shots with four holes to play, Sarazen, using a 4-wood from 220 yards into the 15th green, holed the shot for a double eagle. He tied Wood and won a 36-hole playoff the next day.

"That double eagle wouldn't have meant a thing if I hadn't won the playoff the next day," said Sarazen. "The aspect I cherish most is that both Walter Hagen and Bobby Jones witnessed the shot."

Sarazen, christened Eugenio Saraceni, was the son of a New York carpenter. He started playing golf and caddying at age 10. When he was 14, he contracted empyema, a lung ailment that nearly killed him. Four years later, he was still weak from the disease and could barely break 80. But two years later, Sarazen won his first pro tournament, the New Orleans Open, and he was on his way to a great career.

At 5-4, he was the shortest of any great golfer. In all he won 38 U.S. tour events and was a six-time member of the Ryder Cup team.

After World War II, Sarazen became one of the first golf commentators on television, and for years hosted *Shell's Wonderful World of Golf*.

Always clad in his trademark knickers, Sarazen was one of the sport's most effective goodwill ambassadors. He, Byron Nelson, and Sam Snead shared the honor of "starting" the Masters. They were the first players to tee off on the first day of the tournament.

Sheehan, Patty
Born: October 27, 1956 in Middlebury, Vermont

After winning the 1980 Association of Intercollegiate Athletics for Women national championship and winning all four matches for the U.S. Curtis Cup team, Patty Sheehan joined the LPGA Tour and made an immediate impact by winning the 1981 Rookie of the Year Award.

From 1981, Sheehan won at least one tournament a year for 15 of the next 16 years. Through 2000, she won three LPGA Championships (1983, '84, '93), two U.S. Women's Opens (1992, '94), one Nabisco Dinah Shore

Patty Sheehan *Diane Staskowski*

(1996), one Vare Trophy for low stroke average (1984), and one Rolex Player of the Year (1983).

Through the 2000 season, Sheehan had never led the money list, but she had finished second five times and finished in the top ten 12 straight years, starting in 1982. Her victory in the 1992 Open at Oakmont Country Club came in an 18-hole playoff over Juli Inkster. Sheehan birdied the final two holes of regulation to force the tie. In all, Sheehan has 35 LPGA Tour victories. She was inducted into the LPGA Hall of Fame in 1993.

Sheehan, a highly rated snow skier, is the daughter of BoBo Sheehan, the 1956 U.S. Olympic ski team coach. She has received many honors for her charitable work, which includes a house in northern California for troubled teenage girls. She was one of eight athletes chosen in 1987 as the *Sports Illustrated* Sportsmen of the Year, and she also won the 1994 Flo Hyman Award.

Sigel, Jay
Born: November 13, 1943 in Narberth, Pennsylvania

Jay Sigel was one of the nation's finest amateur golfers of all time. He won consecutive U.S. Amateur championships in 1982–83, three U.S. Mid-Amateur titles, and the 1979 British Amateur. He was a member of seven U.S. Walker Cup teams and twice served as nonplaying captain. He holds the record for most appearances and most points won in Walker Cup history.

Sigel was the low amateur at the Masters three times (1981, '82, '88) as well as at the 1980 British Open and the 1984 U.S. Open.

In 1993, Sigel turned pro and joined the Senior PGA Tour. Through 2000, he won six Senior Tour events.

Singh, Vijay
Born: February 22, 1963 in Lautoka, Fiji

Vijay Singh is the only world-class golfer from the island of Fiji. He learned the game from his father, an airplane technician who also taught golf. He grew up admiring the swing of Tom Weiskopf and used it as a model for his own.

Singh, whose first name means "victory" in Hindi, joined the PGA Tour in 1993 and was named Rookie of the Year, winning once and earning more than $650,000. Through the 2000 season, he won nine tour events, including the 1998 PGA Championship and the 2000 Masters. He has 18 victories worldwide.

Snead, Sam
Born: May 27, 1912 in Hot Springs, Virginia

Sam Snead is known for all the tournaments he won—a record 81 on the PGA Tour—and the one tournament he failed to win—the U.S. Open.

Snead, who had one of the game's smoothest, most fluid, and graceful swings, won seven major championships—the Masters (1949, '52, '54), the PGA Championship (1942, '49, '51), and the British Open (1946).

He came close to winning the U.S. Open on several occasions. In 1937, his first Open, he finished second. In 1939 at Philadelphia Country Club, he came to the final hole needing only a par 5 to win, but he thought he needed a birdie. He ended up three-putting for a triple-bogey 8 and lost by two shots.

In 1947, Snead made a putt at the final hole to force an 18-hole playoff with Lew Worsham. After 17 holes of the playoff, they were still tied, but Snead missed a 2 1/2 footer and Worsham made a putt from the same distance.

Snead's best year on tour came in 1950, when he won 11 events, the third-highest total ever. He was the PGA Player of the Year in 1949; the winner of the Vardon Trophy for low stroke average in 1938, '49, '50, and '55; and the money leader in 1938, '49, and '50.

Snead, nicknamed "Slammin' Sammy," was the first to break 60 in a significant competition in 1959, when he shot 59 at The Greenbrier, his home course.

In 1965, Snead became the oldest winner of a tour event when he won the Greater Greensboro Open at age 52 years, 10 months. It was his eighth win at the Greater Greensboro, a tour record for wins in a single event.

Snead was the first player in tour history to shoot his age or better when he fired rounds of 67 and 66 at the age of 67 in the 1979 Quad Cities Classic.

A seven-time member of the Ryder Cup team, Snead also served as captain three times.

The latter part of Snead's career was hurt by a case of the "yips," a putting "disease." It caused Snead to develop a sidesaddle style of putting.

He is credited with being one of the founders of the Senior PGA Tour in 1980, but played in only 37 events before retiring in 1987. He is a member of the World Golf Hall of Fame.

Sorenstam, Annika
Born: October 9, 1970 in Stockholm, Sweden

Annika Sorenstam developed into one of the most consistently outstanding players on the LPGA Tour. Sorentstam began playing golf at age 12. She was a member of the Swedish National Team from 1978 to 1992 and was the World Amateur champion in 1992. She attended the University of Arizona, where she was the co–College Player of the Year and the NCAA champion in 1991, the NCAA runner-up in 1992, and an All-American in 1991 and 1992.

She joined the LPGA Tour in 1994 and was named Rookie of the Year. Known for her consistency and accurate putting stroke, Sorenstam was the leading money winner in 1995, '97, and '98, when she was also Rolex

Player of the Year. She won the Vare Trophy for low stroke average in 1995, '96, and '98, when she set a record of 69.99.

Sorenstam won the 1995 and '96 U.S. Women's Open titles and became the 13th player in LPGA history to make the Open her first victory and only the sixth player to win consecutive Opens.

She won seven times in 1997, surpassed the $1 million mark in earnings in '97 and '98, and finished out of the top 10 only four times in 21 starts in 1998. In 1999, Sorenstam won twice and finished fourth on the money list with $863,186. In March 2000, Sorenstam's victory in the Welch's/Circle K Championship qualified her for the LPGA Hall of Fame, under a new system adopted in 1998. Sorenstam can't be inducted into the Hall until 2004, when she will fulfill the requirement of being an LPGA member for 10 years.

Through 2000, Sorenstam has 23 LPGA Tour victories and more than $6.2 million in career earnings.

Stacy, Hollis

Born: March 16, 1954 in Savannah, Georgia

Hollis Stacy is one of only two players to have won the USGA Junior Girls Championship three straight years (1969–71), and by winning the 1969 event at 15 years, four months, she is the youngest winner of the event.

She turned pro in 1974 and through 2000 had won 18 times on the LPGA Tour. Stacy won three U.S. Women's Opens—1977, '78, and '84. She is one of only four women to have won the title three or more times. Her other major championship win came in the 1983 Peter Jackson Classic, now the du Maurier Classic.

Stephenson, Jan

Born: December 22, 1951 in Sydney, Australia

Jan Stephenson, blonde and blue-eyed, was at the center of the LPGA Tour's marketing campaign when she joined the tour in 1974. But there was more to her than cheesecake poses on calendars.

Stephenson proved herself on the course. Through the 2000 season, she had 16 tour victories, including three major championships—1981 Peter Jackson Classic (now the du Maurier Classic), the 1982 LPGA Championship, and the 1984 U.S. Women's Open.

Through the 2000 season, Stephenson had gone winless since 1987. In 1990, she was mugged while attending a basketball game in Miami. The ring finger on her left hand was broken in two places, and the injury has hampered her ever since.

From 1990 through 1998, Stephenson finished 50th or lower on the money list five times. But prior to the 1999 season, she revamped her putting style, and the result was her best season in 11 years. Stephenson earned

nearly $300,000, finished 29th on the money list, lowered her scoring average by nearly 1.5 strokes to 71.95, and registered four top-10 finishes, including two seconds.

She became the first woman pro to design golf courses and works extensively with a variety of charities.

Stewart, Payne

Born: January 30, 1957 in Springfield, Missouri
Died: October 25, 1999

Payne Stewart, known for his trademark knickers, has three major championships among his 10 PGA Tour titles—two U.S. Opens (1991, '99) and a PGA Championship (1989). He won his first Open in an 18-hole playoff over Scott Simpson. His 1999 Open victory at Pinehurst No. 2 was ensured with a 15-foot birdie putt on the 72nd hole, the longest putt ever to win a U.S. Open on the final hole.

In the 1989 PGA Championship, Stewart entered the final round trailing the leader, Mike Reid, by six shots, but rallied with a 67 to win by one.

Stewart also has seven victories worldwide and was a four-time member of the U.S. Ryder Cup team.

Stewart, along with five other people, was killed in a Learjet crash. The plane took off from Orlando, Fla., and flew uncontrolled for four hours before crashing into a field in Mina, S.D. He was on his way to the season-ending Tour Championship in Houston, and his death stunned the golf world. The PGA Tour did not play on Friday of the Tour Championship so that the players could attend a memorial service in Orlando.

Stockton, Dave, Sr.

Born: November 2, 1941 in San Bernardino, California

Dave Stockton is renowned as one of golf's finest putters. He won 11 PGA Tour events, including two PGA Championships (1970, '76). He is a two-time member of the U.S. Ryder Cup team and in 1991 served as nonplaying captain.

He joined the Senior PGA Tour in 1991 and through 2000 had won 14 times. Among those 14 wins are three major championships—1996 U.S. Senior Open, 1992 and 1994 Senior Players Championships. Stockton was the Senior Tour's leading money winner in 1993 and '94.

Strange, Curtis

Born: January 30, 1955 in Norfolk, Virginia

Curtis Strange became the first player since Ben Hogan (1950–51) to successfully defend his U.S. Open title. Strange won in 1988 at The Country Club, defeating

Nick Faldo in an 18-hole playoff. Strange forced the play-off with one of the finest bunker shots of all time. He blasted to within 12 inches on the 72nd hole and tapped in for par.

The following year at Oak Hill Country Club he won by a stroke, thanks to a crucial birdie on the 16th hole. He began the final round three shots out of the lead. Strange made a run at a third straight U.S. Open, but fell out of contention in the final round.

In 1997, he reduced his playing schedule to become the lead golf analyst for ABC Sports. He will serve as captain of the U.S. Ryder Cup team in 2001. Through the 2000 season, Strange won 17 PGA Tour events.

Suggs, Louise

Born: September 9, 1923 in Atlanta, Georgia

Louise Suggs was a founder and a charter member of the LPGA Tour in 1951 and the first woman elected to the LPGA Hall of Fame, also in 1951.

Suggs had an accomplished amateur career, high-lighted by wins in the Southern Amateur (1941–47), the North-South Amateur (1942, '46, '48), and the U.S. Amateur (1947).

She turned professional in July 1948 and won three major championships before the LPGA Tour was formed: Titleholders (1946) and Western Open (1946, '47).

Suggs won 50 tour events, including eight major championships—LPGA Championship (1957), U.S. Women's Open (1949, '52), Titleholders (1954, '56, '59), and Western Open (1949, '53). Her 14-stroke victory in the 1949 Open is still a record.

Suggs was the tour's leading money winner in 1953 and 1960 and the Vare Trophy winner for low stroke average in 1957. She ranks fifth all-time in career victories.

Thomson, Peter

Born: August 23, 1929 in Melbourne, Australia

Peter Thomson, a native of Australia, made his name in the British Open. He made his British Open debut in 1951 and over the next seven years won four championships and finished second three times. He won three straight, starting in 1954, was the runner-up to Bobby Locke in 1957, then won again in 1958 in a playoff.

He is the only man in the 20th century to win three successive Opens.

Thomson won his fifth Open in 1965, when he out-dueled Christy O'Connor and Brian Huggett and as a result, got the respect he deserved from the American contingent as a master of links golf. Only Harry Vardon won more British Opens.

In 1984, Thomson joined the Senior PGA Tour. He won 11 tournaments, 10 coming in 1985, when he led the tour in earnings with nearly $400,000. He also won the 1984 PGA Seniors Championship, a Senior Tour major.

In 1998 and 2000, he was captain of the International President's Cup team. Thomson, whose interests range from politics to music to golf course architecture, is a member of the World Golf Hall of Fame.

Trevino, Lee

Born: December 1, 1939 in Dallas, Texas

Lee Trevino's first introduction to golf came as a boy growing up in a ramshackle house near a country club in Dallas. He found balls and sold them back to the members. He dropped out of school at age 13 and began working on the ground crew and on his game.

He was good enough to make the Marines' golf team when he was stationed in Japan. Upon his discharge in 1961, after two years spent mostly in Asia, Trevino made a living as a golf hustler, using a taped-up soda bottle as a club and not losing a match. Trevino joined the PGA Tour in 1967 and won Rookie of the Year honors. The following year, he won the U.S. Open at Oak Hill Country Club, becoming the first player in Open history to shoot all four rounds under par and in the 60s.

In 1971, Trevino, known for his wit and fun-loving personality, won his second Open title, defeating Jack Nicklaus in an 18-hole playoff at Merion Golf Club, which began with Trevino playfully tossing a rubber snake at Nicklaus to ease the tension.

Trevino, nicknamed "Super Mex," won back-to-back British Open titles in 1971–72. He also won two PGA Championships (1971, '84). His second PGA title, at age 44, ended a 3 1/2-year victory drought.

The only hole in Trevino's résumé is his failure to win the Masters. His left-to-right ball flight was directly opposite of what Augusta National requires.

Trevino was a five-time winner of the Vardon Trophy for low stroke average (1970–72, '74, '80), the leading money winner in 1970, and the PGA Player of the Year in 1971. Through the 2000 season, his 27 PGA Tour wins ranked him 18th all-time. He was a member of six U.S. Ryder Cup teams and was captain of the 1985 team.

That total might have been greater, but Trevino, along with Bobby Nichols and Jerry Heard, was struck by lightning at the 1975 Western Open. He has been hampered by back problems ever since.

He joined the Senior PGA Tour in 1989 and through 2000 was the tour's all-time leader in career victories with 29. Trevino led the tour in earnings in 1990 and 1992 and was named Senior Tour Player of the Year in 1990, 1992, and 1994.

Trevino was the Associated Press Male Athlete of the Year and the *Sports Illustrated* Sportsman of the Year in 1971. He was elected to the World Golf Hall of Fame in 1981.

Vardon, Harry

Born: May 9, 1870 in Isle of Jersey, England
Died: March 20, 1937

For nearly 30 years, starting in 1890, Harry Vardon was the leading British professional golfer. He won a record six British Open titles (1896, '98–99, 1903, '11, '14) and one U.S. Open title (1900).

Vardon was the first golfer to be able to sustain himself from prize winnings and exhibition fees. His globe-trotting was a forerunner to Walter Hagen, and later to Bobby Locke, Peter Thomson, and Gary Player.

Vardon popularized the overlapping grip, which bears his name, and the modern golf swing, which took full advantage of the rubber-cored ball. He seldom took a divot when he swung, a method that became widely imitated.

After finishing second in the 1902 British Open, Vardon was stricken by tuberculosis. He also came down with the putting "yips," which got so bad he once whiffed a putt in a tournament.

His second-place finish in the 1920 U.S. Open was the last time he contended in a major championship.

Vare, Glenna Collett

Born: June 20, 1903 in New Haven, Connecticut
Died: February 10, 1989

Glenna Collett Vare was a contemporary of Bobby Jones, and like Jones, dominated amateur golf and conducted herself with class and dignity. She grew up playing baseball, but at age 13, she was introduced to golf by her mother, who thought it more ladylike.

Collett Vare won a record six U.S. Women's Amateur championships (1922, '25, '28–30). She also won the Canadian Women's Amateur (1923–24) and was a finalist in the British Women's Amateur (1929–30).

In 1933 and 1934, she took time off to raise her two children, but returned in 1936 to beat 17-year-old Patty Berg 3-and-2 to win the amateur for the sixth time, in front of some 15,000 people.

Vare stopped playing competitively after her sixth amateur title, although she continued to play recreationally into her mid-80s.

Since 1952, the LPGA Tour has awarded the Vare Trophy in her honor to signify the player with the lowest stroke average.

She is a member of the International Women's Sports Hall of Fame and the World Golf Hall of Fame.

Venturi, Ken

Born: May 15, 1931 in San Francisco, California

Ken Venturi has spent more than 30 years as a television golf analyst for CBS Sports. But before his TV career, he was a fine player, winning 14 PGA Tour events, including the 1964 U.S. Open at Congressional Country Club.

Through three rounds of the Open, Venturi trailed by two strokes. With the temperature near 100 degrees and the humidity stifling, it was unclear whether Venturi, who suffered from a circulatory problem in his hands, would be able to survive the final round. The third and fourth rounds were played on the same day. But with a doctor following him, Venturi shot a final-round 70 and won the Open in what remains one of the most courageous and inspiring performances ever.

Venturi won three more events in 1964, and in 1966 won the final tournament of his career—the Lucky International in his hometown.

Venturi is also remembered for a tournament he lost. As an amateur, he led the 1956 Masters by four strokes entering the final round. But he ballooned to an 80 on a windy day and was the runner-up to Jack Burke, Jr., by one stroke.

Watson, Tom

Born: September 4, 1949 in Kansas City, Missouri

After a slow start and two near-misses at the U.S. Open in 1974 and 1975, Tom Watson broke through to become the best player in the game from the mid-'70s through the early '80s.

After a solid but unspectacular amateur career, Watson joined the tour in 1971. It wasn't until 1974 that he won his first PGA Tour event, the Western Open.

Watson had chances to win the Open in 1974, when he took a one-shot lead into the final round, only to shoot 79 and tie for fifth place. In 1975, he led by three shots through the first two rounds, but he closed with rounds of 78 and 77 and tied for ninth. But later in 1975, Watson finally broke through in a major, winning the British Open in a playoff with Jack Newton. From 1975 through 1977, Watson won at least three events each year.

Watson has eight major championship titles—the Masters (1977, '81), the U.S. Open (1982), and the British Open (1975, '77, '80, '82, '83). In 1982, he became one of only five players to win the U.S. and British Opens the same year (Bobby Jones, Gene Sarazen, Ben Hogan, Lee Trevino).

Two of Watson's major championship victories will be remembered, more than the others, for their compelling drama. In the 1977 British Open at Turnberry, Watson and Jack Nicklaus dueled over the final two rounds, Watson shooting 65–65 to Nicklaus' 65–66 to win by a shot.

Then in the 1982 Open at Pebble Beach, Watson, tied for the lead with Nicklaus, holed a virtually impossible chip from the deep rough on the 17th hole of the final round to turn a potential bogey—or worse—into a birdie. He then birdied the 18th to win by two strokes.

Tom Watson   *Reading Eagle/Times*

Webb, Karrie

Born: December 21, 1974 in Ayr, Queensland, Australia

In just three full seasons on the LPGA Tour, Karrie Webb became the best female player in the world, dominating the LPGA Tour the way Tiger Woods dominated the PGA Tour.

Webb turned pro in 1994 and competed on the Futures Tour and the Women's Professional Golfers European Tour (WPGET). In 1995, she won the Women's British Open and was named WPGET Rookie of the Year.

Webb qualified for the LPGA Tour in 1996 and was named LPGA Rookie of the Year. She won four times, finished in the top ten 15 times in 25 events, and led the money list with $1,002,000. She was the first woman to reach the $1 million mark in single-season earnings.

Over the next two seasons, Webb won five times and finished out of the top 20 just five times in 48 events. In 1997, she won the Vare Trophy for low scoring average. In 1999, Webb dominated. In 25 events, she had six wins, six seconds, four thirds, and finished 22 times in the top 10. She led the money list with a record $1,591,959, won the Vare Trophy for low scoring average (record 69.43), and was named the Rolex Player of the Year.

Among Webb's victories in 1999 was her first major championship. She shot a final-round 6-under 66 to win the du Maurier Championship by two strokes over Laura Davies.

Webb's fine play continued in 2000. She won her first three LPGA starts and the Australian Ladies Open, a nontour event. In her bid to win four straight, she finished second to Charlotta Sorenstam.

Through 2000, Webb had 23 LPGA Tour victories, including the Nabisco Championship and the U.S. Women's Open. She earned $1,876,853, a single-season record.

Watson led the PGA Tour in earnings five times, (1977–80, '84), won the Vardon Trophy for low stroke average three times (1977–79), and was named PGA Player of the Year six times (1977–80, '82, '84).

Following the 1984 season, Watson went winless until the final event of the 1987 season. Then came another long winless drought—9 1/2 years—before Watson won the 1996 Memorial Tournament. His last PGA Tour victory came at the 1998 MasterCard Colonial.

Watson was a four-time member of the U.S. Ryder Cup team and was the nonplaying captain in 1993. He joined the Senior Tour in September 1999 and won the second event he entered.

Whitworth, Kathy

Born: September 27, 1939 in Monahans, Texas

Kathy Whitworth didn't take to golf when she first began learning the game in 1954 at age 15. She was a natural athlete, but golf wasn't coming to her naturally. So she talked her parents into getting her private lessons. Eventually, she became a pupil of Harvey Penick, the legendary instructor who taught Betsy Rawls, Ben Crenshaw, and Tom Kite. It wasn't long before Whitworth took off.

She won the 1957 New Mexico Women's Amateur and received a golf scholarship to Odessa Junior College in Odessa, Texas. But she quit after a year to turn pro.

Whitworth joined the LPGA Tour in 1958, and after a few slow seasons won her first tour event in 1962.

Eighty-seven more followed, making Whitworth the all-time leader in career victories on the men's and women's tours.

Whitworth was the LPGA Tour's leading money winner seven times (1965–68, '70–73), Player of the Year seven times (1966–69, '70–72), and the Vare Trophy winner for low stroke average seven times (1965–67, '69–72).

In 1981, she became the first LPGA player to surpass $1 million in career earnings.

She won six major championships—Titleholders (1965–66), LPGA Championship (1967, '71, '75), Western Open (1967)—and was the Associated Press Female Athlete of the Year in 1965 and 1967. But like Sam Snead, who holds the record for wins on the PGA Tour, Whitworth never won a U.S. Women's Open.

Whitworth's last official victory came in the 1985 United Virginia Bank Classic. In 1990 and '92, Whitworth was the captain of the U.S. Solheim Cup team. She is a member of the LPGA Hall of Fame.

Woods, Tiger (Eldrick)
Born: December 30, 1975 in Cypress, California

Ever since he appeared on *The Mike Douglas Show* at age two, hitting golf balls with Bob Hope and James Stewart looking on, Eldrick "Tiger" Woods seemed certain to achieve stardom. He hasn't disappointed.

Woods has followed a record-setting amateur career with a pro career that has the potential to become one of the greatest of all time.

Nicknamed "Tiger" after a Vietnamese soldier and friend of his father, Vuong Dang Phong, to whom his father had also given that nickname, Woods' interest in the game began early, when he was six months old. He watched his father, Earl, hitting golf balls, and started imitating his swing. Woods shot 48 for nine holes at age three, was featured in *Golf Digest* at age five, and won his first Optimist International Junior tournament at age eight. At 14, he was the youngest ever to win the Insurance Youth Golf Classic, and the following year, he won the first of his three straight U.S. Junior Amateur titles. Woods played in his first professional event in 1992, at age 16, and in 1993, entered three more PGA Tour events.

But he really began making a name for himself starting in 1994, when he won his first U.S. Amateur championship and became the youngest person to do so, at age 18. Woods, trailing by as many as six holes in the 36-hole final and by three holes with nine remaining, rallied to beat Trip Kuehne 1-up.

He repeated in 1995, beating Buddy Marucci 2-up, and won his third straight in 1996 with another rally. Woods trailed Steve Scott by five holes after the first round of the 36-hole final and was two down with three

holes to play. But he birdied 16 and 17 to get even, then clinched it on the 38th hole.

With his "threepeat," Woods did what Jerome Travers and Bob Jones failed to do. He became the only golfer to win three consecutive U.S. Amateur titles.

Woods played in his first major championships in 1995. He made the cut in the Masters and the British Open, but was forced to withdraw from the U.S. Open with an injured wrist.

Woods also made an impact on NCAA golf. In his sophomore year at Stanford, he won eight tournaments and finished lower than third only twice in 14 events. He won the Fred Haskins and the Jack Nicklaus College Player of the Year Awards.

Woods turned pro August 27, 1996, and in only eight starts won twice (Las Vegas Invitational, Walt Disney World/Oldsmobile Classic), finished in the top 10 five times, and earned nearly $800,000. He was named PGA Tour Rookie of the Year, and he also was named the *Sports Illustrated* Sportsman of the Year.

Woods began 1997 as he ended '96: appearing to be invincible. He won the season-opening Mercedes Championship in a playoff over Tom Lehman. Then in April at the Masters, he won his first professional major championship with a remarkable performance.

He shot rounds of 70–66–65–69 for a record-setting, 18-under 270 total, one better than the previous mark held by Jack Nicklaus and Raymond Floyd. At 21 years, three months, and 14 days, Woods was the youngest Masters champion ever and the first major championship winner of African or Asian heritage.

Woods won by 12 strokes, the widest margin in Masters history and the widest margin of victory in the 20th century. Only Tom Morris' 13-stroke win in the 1862 British Open exceeded it.

For the year, Woods won four times and led the money list. The Associated Press chose Woods as the 1997 Male Athlete of the Year, and the PGA Tour, the PGA of America, and the Golf Writers Association of America chose him as Player of the Year.

In 1998, Woods won three tour events and finished fourth on the money list. Because of his "falloff," there were murmurs that perhaps he would fail to live up to the standards he had set in 1997. But Woods was in the midst of making several swing changes that paid dividends in 1999.

Woods had one of the best seasons in PGA Tour history in 1999. He won eight times, including the PGA Championship; finished in the top ten 16 times in 21 events; made all 21 cuts; won the Vardon Trophy for low stroke average (a record 68.43); and led the money list with more than $6.6 million. He was named PGA Player of the Year and the Associated Press Male Athlete of the Year.

He became the first player since Johnny Miller in 1974 to win eight times in one season and the first since

Ben Hogan to win four consecutive starts. Woods won his last four starts in 1999 and his first two starts in 2000. Woods' streak of six straight wins was tied for second with Ben Hogan (1948). Byron Nelson won 11 straight in 1945. To win his sixth in a row, the AT&T Pebble Beach National Pro-Am, Woods came from seven shots down with seven holes to play.

Woods' awesome 2000 season included wins in the U.S. and British Opens and the PGA Championship, making him only the second player in history to win three majors in one year. (The other is Ben Hogan [1953].) These wins made Woods the fifth man to complete the Grand Slam.

But to focus on Woods' impact only in terms of wins, statistics, and earnings is to overlook the sociological ramifications of his success. Woods, who is to golf what Michael Jordan was to basketball, signed lucrative endorsement contracts, and he made the game appealing and more accessible to people of color.

Through 2000, Woods had 24 victories, including four majors, on the PGA Tour and three victories worldwide. He was a two-time member of the U.S. Ryder Cup team and a member of the 1998 and 2000 President's Cup teams. Woods continued his winning career with a victory at the Masters in April 2001.

Wright, Mickey

Born: February 14, 1935 in San Diego, California

Mickey Wright did for the LPGA Tour what Arnold Palmer did for the PGA Tour. She helped increase the tour's stature and popularity because she drew large galleries at tournaments and large audiences on television.

Wright, a tireless worker who practiced long hours, had a swing that was considered technically perfect. Said Betsy Rawls, one of Wright's peers: "Mickey's swing was as flawless as a golf swing can be—smooth, efficient, powerful, rhythmical, and beautiful."

Wright joined the LPGA Tour in 1955 and won 82 events, second to Kathy Whitworth. Seventy-one of those victories came during a 10-year span (1959–68). In 1963, she won 13 events of the 32 tour events (40.6%), a feat that will probably never be duplicated.

Wright won a record-tying four U.S. Women's Opens (1958, '59, '61, '64), a record four LPGA Championships (1958, '60, '61, '63), three Western Opens (1962, '63, '66), and two Titleholders (1961, '62).

She led the tour in earnings four times (1962–64) and won the Vare Trophy for low stroke average five times (1960–64).

Wright's popularity placed her under pressure, not only to perform, but also to help market the tour. Her schedule began to take a toll on her game. When she injured her wrist right before the 1965 U.S. Women's Open, she announced her retirement. But it didn't last. Wright returned to the tour in 1966 and over the next three years won 17 tournaments, before retiring again in 1969 because of an adverse reaction to sunlight, an aversion to flying, and foot problems.

Wright didn't stay away completely, though. From 1972 to 1980, she averaged six events a year and won the 1972 Colgate Dinah Shore Winner's Circle. Her last paycheck on tour came Feb. 4, 1980.

In 1985, Wright and Kathy Whitworth teamed up to play in the Legends of Golf, a Senior PGA Tour event.

Wright was named the Associated Press Female Athlete of the Year in 1963 and 1964. She was inducted into the LPGA Hall of Fame in 1964. She is also a member of the International Women's Sports Hall of Fame and the World Golf Hall of Fame.

Zaharias, Babe (Mildred)

(also track and field)

Born: June 26, 1914 in Port Arthur, Texas
Died: September 27, 1956

Babe Didrikson Zaharias is one of the greatest female athletes of all time, and certainly the greatest female athlete of the first half of the 20th century.

Wrote Grantland Rice, the legendary sportswriter: "She is beyond all belief until you see her perform. Then you finally understand that you are looking at the most flawless section of muscle harmony, of complete mental and physical coordination, that the world of sport has ever seen."

One of seven children, Zaharias got her nickname for hitting five home runs in one game as a teenager.

At Beaumont High, she averaged 30 points a game for the basketball team. She then joined a team sponsored by the Dallas-based Employers Casualty Co. She led the team to the AAU national finals three straight years, leading her team to the championship in 1931, when she scored 195 points in six tournament games.

Zaharias then convinced the insurance company to start a track team. She won AAU national titles in the long jump, low hurdles, javelin throw, and baseball throw in 1930 and 1931. At the 1932 AAU national championships, she entered eight of 10 events and won five of them, including the shot put, which she attempted for the first time, and tied for first in another. She set four world records and won the team championship—all by herself—with 30 points. She was a one-woman team. The Illinois Women's Athletic Club finished second with 22 points. It had 22 members.

The AAU championships were also the tryouts for the 1932 Olympics. Zaharias, who was not without self-confidence, brazenly predicted that she was going to "beat everybody in sight."

She entered five of the six women's events, but then the Olympic Committee ruled women could enter only three events. She chose the javelin, the 80-meter hurdles, and the high jump.

Zaharias won the gold in the javelin, setting an Olympic record of 133–4 on her first throw, despite the javelin slipping out of her hand. She also set a record in winning the gold in the hurdles.

That left the high jump, in which Zaharias jumped 5-5 1/2 to tie Jean Shiley. But because Zaharias used a style of jumping that caused her head to clear the bar before her body, she was awarded the silver medal.

Following the Olympics, Zaharias went on a barnstorming tour with her own basketball team; she toured with the House of David baseball team; and she played exhibition billiards matches. At the same time, she was honing her golf game. It was Rice who suggested she take up the game, and she took lessons from Gene Sarazen, Walter Hagen, and Tommy Armour. Zaharias won the second tournament she entered—the 1935 Texas Women's Amateur. But two weeks later, the United States Golf Association declared her a professional, because of her earnings from her barnstorming tour.

So she and Sarazen went on an exhibition tour, in part to promote Babe Didrikson golf clubs, and on that tour she met George Zaharias, a professional wrestler. They developed an immediate rapport and were married in December 1938. George Zaharias quit wrestling to manage his wife's career, which was about to take off on the golf course.

In 1943, Zaharias was reinstated as an amateur after fulfilling the USGA's requirement that she not make paid appearances for three years. Over the next four years, she won 40 tournaments, including 17 in a row in 1946 and 1947. She won the 1946 U.S. Women's Amateur, and in 1947 became the first American to win the British Amateur. Zaharias turned pro in 1947 and was just as dominant. Along with Patty Berg, Zaharias helped found the LPGA Tour and was its biggest star. Her career lasted only eight years, but during that time she won 31 of the 128 events she entered.

She led the tour in earnings for four straight years (1948–51) and won the Vare Trophy for low stroke average (1954). Of her 41 LPGA Tour wins, 10 were major championships—U.S. Women's Open (1948, '50, '54), Titleholders (1947, '50, '52), and Western Open (1940, '44, '45, '50).

In 1953, Zaharias was diagnosed with rectal cancer. She underwent surgery, but vowed to return, largely to "show people not to be afraid of cancer."

In 1954, Zaharias won five tournaments, including the Open. Two years later, the cancer was detected in her spine and another operation was required. She died at age 43.

Zaharias is a member of the International Women's Sports Hall of Fame, the LPGA Hall of Fame, the National Track and Field Hall of Fame, and the World Golf Hall of Fame. The Associated Press named her Female Athlete of the Year in 1931, 1945–47, 1950, and 1954. She was also voted the Woman Athlete of the First Half of the 20th Century in a poll conducted by the Associated Press.

Hockey

Abel, Sid

Born: February 22, 1918 in Melville, Saskatchewan, Canada
Died: February 8, 2000

Sid Abel was the center on the Detroit Red Wings' famed "Production Line," which had Gordie Howe at right wing and Ted Lindsay at left wing. Coach Jack Adams put the line together during the 1947–48 season. During the 1949–50 season, the "Production Line" combined for 215 points, including 92 goals. Abel's uncanny ability to distribute the puck was the key to the line's success.

The "Production Line" was broken up after the 1951–52 season, when Abel asked to be traded to the Chicago Blackhawks, where he could be player-coach.

Abel was a two-time NHL All-Star and the 1949 winner of the Hart Trophy as the league's Most Valuable Player. He also was a member of three Stanley Cup–winning teams with Detroit (1943, '50, '52).

In 14 National Hockey League seasons, he scored 189 goals and had 283 assists for 472 points in the regular season, and 28 goals and 30 assists in 97 playoff games.

He retired as a player following the 1953–54 season. He returned to coach the Red Wings during the 1957–58 season and remained in the position for 10 1/2 seasons. His overall coaching record was 382-426-155.

Abel was inducted into the Hockey Hall of Fame in 1969 and voted No. 85 on the list of the NHL's Top 100 Players of All Time by *The Hockey News*.

Barber, Bill

Born: July 11, 1952 in Callender, Ontario, Canada

Bill Barber played a key role in the Philadelphia Flyers' Stanley Cup–winning teams in 1974 and 1975.

He joined the Flyers 11 games into the 1973 season and scored 65 points on 30 goals and 35 assists as a rookie.

He retired in 1984 after undergoing knee surgery. After coaching the Hershey Bears in the American Hockey League and serving as the Flyers' director of pro scouting, Barber became the coach of the Philadelphia Phantoms, the Flyers' affiliate in the AHL, a post he held through the 1999–2000 season.

A three-time All-Star, Barber scored 883 points on 420 goals and 463 assists in 11 seasons. In 129 playoff games, he scored 88 points on 53 goals and 55 assists. He was inducted into the Hockey Hall of Fame in 1990.

Barber took over as coach of the Flyers in the 2000–01 season.

Bathgate, Andy

Born: August 28, 1932 in Winnipeg, Manitoba, Canada

Andy Bathgate joined the New York Rangers for 18 games during the 1952–53 season and became a fixture in the Big Apple for the next 10 seasons, during which he established himself as an all-around player.

In 1959, he won the Hart Trophy as the league's Most Valuable Player, scoring 88 points on 40 goals and 48 assists. The following year, he tied Bobby Hull for the scoring title with 84 points (28 goals, 56 assists). He also twice led the league in assists (1962, '64).

Midway through the 1963–64 season, Bathgate was traded to the Toronto Maple Leafs, which he helped lead to the 1964 Stanley Cup. Bathgate was traded to Detroit a year later. He finished his career with the Pittsburgh Penguins, retiring in 1971.

In 17 NHL seasons, Bathgate had 973 points (349 goals, 624 assists) and was a four-time All-Star. In 54 playoff games he had 35 points (21 goals, 14 assists). In addition to his statistics, Bathgate indirectly made a significant contribution to the game on Nov. 1, 1959, when one of his shots hit goalie Jacques Plante in the face. The injury prompted Plante to return to the ice wearing a face mask, a move that other goalies followed.

Bathgate was inducted into the Hockey Hall of Fame in 1978 and voted No. 58 on the list of the NHL's Top 100 Players of All Time by *The Hockey News*.

Belfour, Ed
Born: April 21, 1965 in Carman, Manitoba, Canada

Ed Belfour has been one of the best goaltenders of his time. A calm, quiet leader, he prefers to use his body more than his stick or his glove, but his unorthodox style has proven quite successful.

He led the University of North Dakota to the NCAA Division I hockey championship in 1986 and signed with the Chicago Blackhawks in 1987. After two seasons in the minors, he was promoted to the Blackhawks. He became the starting goaltender in the 1990–91 season. He had a 43-19-7 record with a league-low 2.47 goals-against average. He was named the winner of the Calder Trophy for Rookie of the Year and the Vezina Trophy for allowing the fewest goals during the season.

In 1993, Belfour won his second Vezina Trophy. He was 41-18-11 with a 2.59 goals-against average.

Near the end of the 1997 season, Belfour was traded to the San Jose Sharks. He signed as a free agent with the Dallas Stars prior to the 1997–98 season.

Belfour continued his outstanding play with Dallas. In 1998 he won 37 games with a league-best 1.88 goals-against average, in 1999 he won 35 with a 1.99 goals-against average, and in 2000 he won 32 with a 2.10 goals-against average. He is the first goalie in NHL history to win 30 or more games in six separate seasons. In 1999, he helped the Stars win the Stanley Cup.

Belfour's record was 308-195-82 with a 2.62 goals-against average and 49 shutouts. Through the 2000

season, he ranked 14th all-time in victories. His 75 playoff victories ranked sixth all-time.

Beliveau, Jean
Born: August 31, 1931 in Trois-Rivieres, Quebec, Canada

Jean Beliveau spent his entire 18-year career with the Montreal Canadiens and helped the organization win 10 Stanley Cups, five with him as captain. He was blessed with size (6-3, 205 pounds) deceptive speed, toughness, and instinct that served him like a sixth sense.

In his third NHL season (1955–56), he won the scoring title (88 points) and the Hart Trophy as the league's Most Valuable Player. He also won the Hart in 1964. Beliveau worked for the Canadiens' owner, Molson Brewery, on off-days and during the summer, but his position with the team never affected his relationship with the players as captain. He carried extra money on the road for rookies who might be short on cash, and he was a commanding presence in the locker room.

In 18 NHL seasons, Beliveau scored 1,219 points (507 goals, 712 assists) in 1,125 games. In 162 playoff games, he scored 176 points (79 goals, 97 assists).

Beliveau was a 10-time All-Star and winner of the Ross Trophy in 1956 for most points scored and the Conn Smythe Award in 1965 as the Most Valuable Player in the playoffs. He was inducted into the Hockey Hall of Fame in 1972 and was voted No. 7 on the list of the NHL's Top 100 Players of All Time by *The Hockey News*.

Benedict, Clint
Born: September 26, 1894 in Ottawa, Ontario, Canada
Died: November 12, 1976

Clint Benedict was the first goalie ever to wear a face mask, starting in 1929 after a shot by Howie Morenz that broke his nose. But he wore the mask for only a few days because the nosepiece interfered with his vision on low shots. Later in the same season, he suffered another broken nose and retired.

It wasn't until Jacques Plante began wearing a mask during the 1959 season that it reappeared.

Benedict played 13 seasons with the Ottawa Maroons. His record was 191-142-28 with a 2.31 goals-against average. He led the league in goals-against average for five straight years (1919–23). His playoff record was 25-18-4 with a 1.80 goals-against average in 48 games. His teams won four Stanley Cups.

He was inducted into the Hockey Hall of Fame in 1965 and was voted No. 77 on the list of the NHL's Top 100 Players of All Time by *The Hockey News*.

Bentley, Doug

Born: September 13, 1916 in Delisle, Saskatchewan, Canada

Died: November 24, 1972

Doug Bentley was the left wing on the famous "Pony Line," which also featured Max Bentley (Doug's brother) and Bill Mosienko. After failing to score more than 12 goals in each of his first three seasons, Bentley exploded in 1942–43, scoring 73 points (33 goals, 40 assists) to win the scoring title.

In 13 seasons, he scored 543 points (219 goals, 324 assists) in 566 games. In 23 playoff games, he scored 17 points (9 goals, 8 assists).

Bentley, a four-time All-Star, was named the Blackhawks' best player of the half-century in 1950, inducted into the Hockey Hall of Fame in 1964, and voted No. 73 on the list of the NHL's Top Players of All Time by *The Hockey News*.

Bentley, Max

Born: March 1, 1920 in Delisle, Saskatchewan, Canada

Died: January 19, 1984

Max Bentley was the player nobody wanted. The Boston Bruins thought he wasn't big enough, and the Montreal Canadiens' team doctor diagnosed him with a bad heart. But he eventually earned a tryout with the Chicago Blackhawks, largely based on the recommendation of his brother, Doug, and in his third season had 26 goals and 70 points.

Bentley, a center on the "Pony Line" along with Doug and Bill Mosienko, won two scoring titles with the Blackhawks (1945–46), the Lady Byng Trophy for sportsmanship (1943), and the Hart Trophy as the league's Most Valuable Player (1946). Bentley is one of only four players—along with Wayne Gretzky, Red Berenson, and Harvey Jackson—to have scored four goals in one period. When Gretzky first broke into the league, many old-timers compared him to Bentley.

In November 1947, Chicago traded him to Toronto, and the deal still stands as one of the worst in franchise history. The Blackhawks finished last in eight of the next 10 seasons, and Bentley helped the Maple Leafs to three Stanley Cups (1948, '49, '51). In 12 NHL seasons, Bentley scored 544 points (245 goals, 299 assists) in 646 games. In 51 playoff games, he scored 45 points (18 goals, 27 assists).

Bentley was a two-time All-Star. He was inducted into the Hockey Hall of Fame in 1966 and voted No. 48 on the list of the NHL's Top 100 Players of All Time by *The Hockey News*.

Bossy, Mike

Born: January 22, 1957 in Montreal, Quebec, Canada

Mike Bossy was the driving force for the New York Islanders teams that won four consecutive Stanley Cups (1980–83). He was a smooth skater blessed with an accurate shot. As his coach, Al Arbour, once said, "When he shoots, it doesn't even look like he touches the puck."

In 1977, Bossy became the first rookie to score 50 goals. He reached 60 goals five times. His nine straight 50-goal seasons is a record, and he became the first player to tie Maurice Richard's record of 50 goals in 50 games. He averaged the most goals per season (57.3) in league history.

Bossy, a right wing, was an eight-time All-Star. He won the Conn Smythe Trophy as the Most Valuable Player in the 1982 Stanley Cup, scoring seven goals in a four-game sweep of Vancouver. He also won the Calder Trophy for Rookie of the Year in 1978 and the Lady Byng Trophy for sportsmanship in 1983, '84, and '86.

Bossy spent his entire career with the Islanders, playing 10 seasons and retiring in 1987. In 752 games, he scored 1,126 points on 573 goals and 553 assists. His 85 playoff goals rank him sixth all-time, and his 160 points tie him for 12th all-time, through the 2000 season.

He was inducted into the Hockey Hall of Fame in 1991 and was voted No. 20 on the list of the NHL's Top 100 Players of All Time by *The Hockey News*.

Boucher, Frank

Born: October 7, 1901 in Ottawa, Ontario, Canada

Died: December 12, 1977

Frank Boucher was the center on one of the most dominant lines of the late '20s to mid '30s. His linemates, brothers Bill and Bun Cook, helped the New York Rangers win two Stanley Cups (1928, '33).

In 14 seasons, Boucher scored 423 goals on 161 goals and 262 assists. He was a four-time All-Star and won the Lady Byng Trophy for sportsmanship times in eight seasons. The NHL gave him the trophy to keep in 1935, then had a new one made. After retiring in 1938, Boucher became the Rangers' coach. He is credited with several innovations, including pulling the goaltender for an extra skater late in the game, developing the box defense for defending penalties, and adding the red line to speed up play.

Boucher was inducted into the Hockey Hall of Fame in 1958 and was voted No. 61 on the list of the NHL's Top 100 Players of All Time by *The Hockey News*.

Ray Bourque   *National Hockey League*

Bourque, Ray
Born: December 28, 1960 in Montreal, Quebec, Canada

Ray Bourque has been regarded as the best defenseman of his era and one of the most well-rounded defensemen ever. He was solid on both ends of the ice—tough in the corners and in front of the net, a terrific passer, and a strong skater.

Bourque was a first-round draft choice of the Boston Bruins in 1979, when he scored 65 points on 17 goals and 48 assists. He became the first nongoaltender to win the Calder Trophy as Rookie of the Year and secure a first-team All-Star spot. His 19 straight All-Star selections is an NHL record, and only Gordie Howe had more overall All-Star appearances with 21. He and Howe are tied with 12 first-team selections.

Bourque won the Norris Trophy as the league's outstanding defenseman five times (1987, '88, '90, '91, '94), and he is one of only two defensemen—Paul Coffey is the other—to record more than 1,000 assists.

Bourque entered the 2000–01 season with most career goals by a defenseman (403). Bourque was second in career assists for a defenseman (1,117) and second in career points by a defenseman (1,520). Bourque was one of only five players in NHL history (Wayne Gretzky, Howe, Marcel Dionne, Coffey) to reach 1,000 career assists. Bourque had 10 or more goals in each of his

22 seasons and 30 or more assists in 21 of his 22 seasons.

He was voted No. 14 on the list of the NHL's Top 100 Players of All Time by *The Hockey News*. In March 2000, Bourque, wanting to play with a Stanley Cup contender, was traded by Boston to the Colorado Avalanche.

Bower, Johnny
Born: November 8, 1924 in Prince Albert, Saskatchewan, Canada

Johnny Bower helped the Toronto Maple Leafs win four Stanley Cups (1962–64, '67) as one of the NHL's best goaltenders.

Bower was a first-team All-Star in 1961 at age 37, when he also won the Vezina Trophy as the league's best goaltender. In 1965, Bower shared the Vezina Trophy with his teammate Terry Sawchuk.

In 15 seasons, Bower had a .551 winning percentage, 37 shutouts, and a 2.52 goals-against average. In 74 playoff games, he had a .507 winning percentage, a 2.52 goals-against average, and five shutouts.

He was inducted into the Hockey Hall of Fame in 1976 and was voted No. 87 on the list of the NHL's Top 100 Players of All Time by *The Hockey News*.

Brimsek, Frank
Born: September 26, 1913 in Eveleth, Minnesota

Early in the 1938–39 season, Frank Brimsek replaced Tiny Thompson at goal for the Boston Bruins, much to the dismay of the fans. But it didn't take Brimsek long to win them over. He won 12 of his first 15 games, six by shutout, and had a string of 231 minutes, 54 seconds of scoreless play. After that was broken, he went 220 minutes, 24 seconds without allowing a goal. Overall, he had 10 shutouts as a rookie.

Brimsek acquired the nickname "Mr. Zero" and led the Bruins to the Stanley Cup with a 1.25 goals-against average during the playoffs. He won the Calder Trophy as Rookie of the Year and the Vezina Trophy as best goaltender.

Brimsek helped the Bruins to another Stanley Cup in 1941, and he won a second Vezina Trophy in 1942. An eight-time All-Star, he played 10 seasons, had a .568 winning percentage and a 2.70 goals-against average.

In 1943, Brimsek joined the U.S. Coast Guard, returned to the Bruins two years later, and retired in 1950 after spending his final season with the Chicago Blackhawks. Brimsek, who had 40 career shutouts, was inducted into the Hockey Hall of Fame in 1966 and was voted No. 67 on the list of the NHL's Top 100 Players of All Time by *The Hockey News*.

Broda, Turk (Walter)
Born: May 15, 1914 in Brandon, Manitoba, Canada
Died: October 17, 1972

Turk Broda became a goaltender because he was too chubby to play another position. But his athletic style and his unflappable demeanor made him one of the best of all time. Said his coach, Jack Adams, "He could tend goal in a tornado and never blink an eye."

Broda joined the Toronto Maple Leafs in 1936, when he was purchased from the Detroit Olympics of the International League for the record price of $8,000. Except for a two-year stint in the military, he spent each of his 14 seasons with the Leafs. He had a winning percentage of .562, 62 shutouts, and a 2.53 goals-against average.

Broda helped the Maple Leafs to five Stanley Cups (1942, '45, '47, '48, '51). He had a 2.15 goals-against average in the playoffs and also recorded 13 shutouts. He was a three-time All-Star and a two-time winner of the Vezina Trophy as the league's best goaltender (1941, '48).

He was inducted into the Hockey Hall of Fame in 1967 and was voted No. 60 on the list of the NHL's Top 100 Players of All Time by *The Hockey News*.

Bucyk, John
Born: May 12, 1935 in Edmonton, Alberta, Canada

John Bucyk was never the most stylish player in the National Hockey League, nor the most graceful. But the 6-0, 215-pound left wing for the Boston Bruins was an effective player for more than 20 years.

He was traded to Boston from Detroit in 1956 for goaltender Terry Sawchuk, and during his first 10 years, the Bruins made the playoffs only twice.

But in 1967, Phil Esposito and Bobby Orr joined the team, and the Bruins enjoyed consistent success. Bucyk, nicknamed "The Chief," helped lead Boston to the Stanley Cup in 1970 and 1972. He was the oldest player to have a 50-goal season, at age 36, and he recorded seven 30-goal seasons after he turned 32.

In 23 seasons, Bucyk scored 1,369 points on 556 goals and 813 assists. In 124 playoff games, he had 103 points on 41 goals and 62 assists.

Through the 2000 season, Bucyk ranked 15th all-time in points, 15th in goals, 21st in assists, and fourth in games played (1,540). He was a two-time All-Star and a two-time winner of the Lady Byng Trophy for sportsmanship (1971, '74).

Bucyk was inducted into the Hockey Hall of Fame in 1981 and was voted No. 45 on the list of the NHL's Top 100 Players of All Time by *The Hockey News*.

Cheevers, Gerry
Born: December 7, 1940 in St. Catharines, Ontario, Canada

Gerry Cheevers became the starting goaltender for the Boston Bruins in 1967 and helped lead them to two Stanley Cups (1970, '72). Nicknamed "Cheesy," he was particularly effective in the clutch.

Cheevers left the Bruins after the 1971–72 season and joined Cleveland of the World Hockey Association. In 418 regular season NHL games, he had a 2.89 goals-against average. In 88 playoff games, he had eight shutouts and a 3.30 goals-against average. He was inducted into the Hockey Hall of Fame in 1985.

Chelios, Chris
Born: January 25, 1962 in Chicago, Illinois

Chris Chelios, blessed with instinct, strong skating skills, and toughness, was one of the league's most rugged defensemen and one of its most emotional players. Twice he was cut by his junior team when he was a teenager, but he persevered, eventually landing a spot in the U.S. Olympic program. He joined the Montreal Canadiens in 1984, and two years later helped them win the Stanley Cup. Chelios, a six-time All-Star, won the Norris Trophy as the league's best defenseman in 1989, 1993, and 1996. His 1989 Norris Trophy made him the first with a right-handed shot ever to win the award.

Chelios spent seven seasons with Montreal (1984–90) and became the first American-born player to be named captain of the Canadiens. He was traded to the Chicago Blackhawks in 1990. In nine seasons with the Blackhawks, Chelios led the team's defensemen in scoring seven times. He led the Blackhawks into the Stanley Cup final in 1992, scoring 21 points in the playoffs, a team record.

In March 1999, Chelios was traded to the Detroit Red Wings.

Through the 2000 season, Chelios had 832 points on 168 goals and 664 assists. He was a 10-time All-Star, including four times on the first team.

He was voted No. 40 on the list of the NHL's Top 100 Players of All Time by *The Hockey News*.

Clancy, King
Born: February 25, 1903 in Ottawa, Ontario, Canada
Died: November 10, 1986

King Clancy was one of the first puck-carrying defensemen when he played for the Ottawa Senators in the early 1920s. He joined the Toronto Maple Leafs in 1930, when coach Conn Smythe acquired him for two players and $35,000, money won at the track. The following season, Clancy helped the Maple Leafs to the Stanley Cup. Clancy retired as a player in 1937, then coached the Montreal Maroons for half the 1937–38 season before becoming an NHL referee. In 1953, he returned to coach the Maple Leafs, and after three seasons behind the bench, he became assistant general manager.

In 16 seasons, Clancy, a four-time All-Star, scored 280 points on 137 goals and 143 assists. He was inducted into the Hockey Hall of Fame in 1958 and was voted No. 52 on the list of the NHL's Top 100 Players of All Time by *The Hockey News*.

Clapper, Dit (Aubrey)

Born: February 9, 1907 in Newmarket, Ontario, Canada

Died: January 21, 1978

Dit Clapper was an All-Star at two positions—defenseman and right wing. He was big (6-2, 200 pounds), powerful, and renowned for the precision of his play. He made few mistakes.

Clapper spent his first 11 seasons as a defenseman, then switched to right wing. A six-time All-Star, he earned recognition at both positions.

He joined the Boston Bruins in 1927 and became the first player to spend 20 seasons with the same team. He helped Boston to three Stanley Cups (1929, '39, '41). Clapper became the Bruins' player-coach in 1945 and continued coaching through the 1948–49 season. He retired from playing in 1947, and his number was the first ever retired by the Bruins.

Clapper scored 474 points on 228 goals and 246 assists. He was voted No. 41 on the list of the NHL's Top 100 Players of All Time by *The Hockey News*.

Clarke, Bob

Born: August 13, 1949 in Flin Flon, Manitoba, Canada

Bob Clarke was the heart and soul of the Philadelphia Flyers, which won Stanley Cups in 1974 and 1975 and reached the finals twice more before he retired in 1984. His determination, discipline, and spirit typified those Flyers teams, known as the "Broad Street Bullies."

Clarke, a diabetic who disliked talking about the disease, wasn't big, strong, or fast, nor was he blessed with a hard shot, but his work ethic set him apart. In a poll of NHL coaches, he was judged to be the best penalty killer, checker, faceoff man, and leader.

His overtime goal in the second game of the 1974 Stanley Cup finals against Boston propelled the Flyers to their first Cup, which was also the first Cup won by an expansion team.

Clarke, a four-time All-Star, won the Hart Trophy as the league's Most Valuable Player (1973, '75, '76), the

Selke Trophy for the best defensive forward (1983), and the Masterson Trophy for exemplifying "perseverance, sportsmanship and dedication" to hockey.

In 15 NHL seasons, Clarke scored 1,210 points on 358 goals and 852 assists. Twice he led the league in assists (1975, '76). In 135 playoff games, he had 119 points on 42 goals and 77 assists.

After he retired in 1984, Clarke became the general manager of the Flyers. Later, he joined the Florida Panthers in a similar role and put together a team that reached the Stanley Cup finals in 1996. He returned to the Flyers as president and general manager in June 1994.

Clarke was inducted into the Hockey Hall of Fame in 1987 and was voted No. 23 on the list of the NHL's Top 100 Players of All Time by *The Hockey News*.

Coffey, Paul

Born: June 1, 1961 in Weston, Ontario, Canada

Paul Coffey is regarded as the finest offensive defenseman in National Hockey League history. His speed and deft passing skills, especially the long pass, have helped Coffey become the highest-scoring defenseman in league history.

Coffey has been well traveled in his 20 seasons, spending time with nine teams, but it's his first team—the Edmonton Oilers—with which he is most identified. He joined the Oilers as a rookie in 1980 and helped them to three Stanley Cups (1984, '85, '87). He was also on a Stanley Cup–winning Pittsburgh team in 1991.

He spent seven seasons with the Oilers (1981–87) and was traded to the Pittsburgh Penguins in 1987. He played with the Penguins until February 1992, when he was traded to the Los Angeles Kings. From there, he played for the Detroit Red Wings (1993–96), Hartford Whalers (1996), Philadelphia Flyers (1997–98), Chicago Blackhawks (1999), Carolina Hurricanes (1999–2000), and Boston Bruins (2000–).

Through the 2000 season, he was second all-time in goals (396), first in assists (1,135), and first in points (1,531). He had the most goals in one season (48, 1985–86), most assists in one game (6, March 14, 1986), and most points in one game (8, March 14, 1986). He was second all-time in assists among all players and seventh all-time in points.

Coffey was third all-time with 131 playoff assists and fifth all-time with 196 playoff points.

Coffey, a 14-time All-Star, including four times on the first team, won the Norris Trophy as the league's best defenseman in 1985, '86, '89.

Coffey was voted No. 28 on the list of the NHL's Top 100 Players of All Time by *The Hockey News*.

Conacher, Charlie

Born: December 10, 1909 in Toronto, Ontario, Canada

Died: December 30, 1967

Charlie Conacher was the right wing on the Toronto Maple Leafs' famous "Kid Line" near the end of the 1928–29 season with Harvey Jackson and Joe Primeau. The line would total more than 850 points over seven seasons.

Conacher, who had the hardest shot in the league, won the Ross Trophy as the league's top scorer in 1934 and 1935. In 12 seasons, he scored 30 or more goals four times and 20 or more goals six times, despite an injury-filled career.

In 12 seasons, he scored 398 points on 225 goals and 173 assists. Conacher, a five-time All-Star, was inducted into the Hockey Hall of Fame in 1961 and was voted No. 36 on the list of the NHL's Top 100 Players of All Time by *The Hockey News*.

Cook, Bill

Born: October 9, 1895 in Brantford, Ontario, Canada

Died: May 5, 1986

Bill Cook was the preeminent right wing of his era. He was the right wing on the New York Rangers' famous "A Line," along with his brother, Bun, and Frank Boucher. He was the catalyst for the Rangers' Stanley Cup championships in 1928 and 1933. He won the Ross Trophy as the league's leading scorer in 1927 and 1933.

Cook, a rough player who didn't hesitate to fight, retired after the 1936–37 season and coached the Cleveland Barons in the American Hockey League and later the Rangers in the early 1950s.

In 11 seasons, Cook scored 367 points on 229 goals and 138 assists. He was inducted into the Hockey Hall of Fame in 1952 and was voted No. 44 on the list of the NHL's Top 100 Players of All Time by *The Hockey News*.

Cournoyer, Yvan

Born: November 22, 1943 in Drummondville, Quebec, Canada

Yvan Cournoyer, nicknamed the "Roadrunner," was known for his blazing speed and acceleration. He joined the Montreal Canadiens in 1963 after just five games in the minor leagues.

Cournoyer, who spent his entire career with the Canadiens, scored 25 or more goals in 12 consecutive seasons. He reached the 40-goal plateau four times. He was particularly dangerous on the power play.

Cournoyer, a right wing, helped lead the Canadiens to 10 Stanley Cup championships (1965, '66, '68, '69, '71, '73, '76–79). In 1973, he won the Conn Smythe Trophy as Most Valuable Player in the playoffs. He scored a playoff record 15 goals.

In 16 seasons, Cournoyer scored 863 points on 428 goals and 435 assists. In 147 playoff games, he scored 127 points on 64 goals and 63 assists. A four-time All-Star, Cournoyer was inducted into the Hockey Hall of Fame 1982 and was voted No. 98 on the list of the NHL's Top 100 Players of All Time by *The Hockey News*.

Cowley, Bill

Born: June 12, 1912 in Bristol, Quebec, Canada

Died: December 31, 1993

Bill Cowley was one of the best passers in the history of the National Hockey League. He was a center who made his wings better. He led the league in assists three time (1939, '41, '43); he won the Ross Trophy as the league's leading scorer and the Hart Trophy as the league's Most Valuable Player in 1941. He also won the Hart Trophy in 1943.

Cowley, a five-time All-Star, led the Boston Bruins to two Stanley Cups (1939, '41). In 13 seasons, he scored 548 points on 195 goals and 353 assists. He retired in 1947. He was inducted into the Hockey Hall of Fame in 1968 and was voted No. 53 on the list of the NHL's Top 100 Players of All Time by *The Hockey News*.

Delvecchio, Alex

Born: December 4, 1931 in Fort William, Ontario, Canada

Alex Delvecchio spent his entire career with the Detroit Red Wings (1951–74), making him the third National Hockey League player—Dit Clapper and Gordie Howe were the others—to spend 20 years with the same team.

Delvecchio, a center, was known for his clean play. He never had more than 37 penalty minutes in a season, and he was a three-time winner of the Lady Byng Award for sportsmanship (1959, '66, '69). He finished in the top 10 in scoring 11 times.

In 24 seasons, Delvecchio scored 1,281 points on 456 goals and 825 assists. In helping the Red Wings to three Stanley Cup championships (1952, '54, '55), he scored 104 points in the playoffs on 35 goals and 69 assists. He was inducted into the Hockey Hall of Fame in 1977 and was voted No. 82 on the list of the NHL's Top 100 Players of All Time by *The Hockey News*.

Denneny, Cy

Born: December 23, 1891 in Farran's Point, Ontario, Canada

Died: September 10, 1970

Cy Denneny was one of the most prolific goal scorers of his time. In 13 seasons, from 1917 to 1929, the left winger

241

had four seasons in which he averaged better than a goal a game and scored 20 or more goals seven times. He never finished lower than fourth in scoring.

Denneny's .755 goals-per-game percentage ranks third behind Mario Lemieux (.823) and Mike Bossy (.762) among players with at least 200 career goals.

He won four Stanley Cups with the Ottawa Senators (1920, '21, '23, '27) and one with the Boston Bruins (1929), when he served as player-coach.

In 13 seasons, Denneny, who pioneered the curved stick, scored 315 points on 246 goals and 69 assists. He won the Ross Trophy as the league's leading scorer in 1924. He was inducted into the Hockey Hall of Fame in 1959 and was voted No. 62 on the list of the NHL's Top 100 Players of All Time by *The Hockey News*.

Dionne, Marcel

Born: August 3, 1951 in Drummondville, Quebec, Canada

Marcel Dionne was one of the best small men ever to play in the National Hockey League. At 5-8, he was a solid skater, a deft puck handler, and a good passer.

Dionne was the second pick in the 1971 amateur draft, behind Guy Lafleur. He spent the first four years of his career with the Detroit Red Wings, and then jumped to the Los Angeles Kings as a free agent for a five-year $1.5 million contract.

In Los Angeles, he was the center of the famous "Triple Crown Line," along with Dave Taylor and Charlie Simmer. Dionne reached the 50-goal mark six times in seven seasons with the Kings and scored 100 points in a season eight times. In 1980, he won the Ross Trophy as the league's leading scorer. He also won the Lady Byng Trophy for sportsmanship in 1975 and 1977.

Dionne was never on a Stanley Cup–winning team. In fact, the Kings had only four winning seasons in the 12 Dionne spent there. He was traded to the New York Rangers in 1987 and retired in 1989.

Through the 2000 season, Dionne, a three-time All-Star, scored 1,771 points on 731 goals and 1,040 assists. He ranked third all-time in points and goals, and seventh all-time in assists.

He was inducted into the Hockey Hall of Fame in 1992 and was voted No. 38 on the list of the NHL's Top 100 Players of All Time by *The Hockey News*.

Dryden, Ken

Born: August 8, 1947 in Hamilton, Ontario, Canada

Montreal Canadiens fans were introduced to Ken Dryden in 1971, when he was called up from the minors.

The goaltender helped the Canadiens beat the Boston Bruins, Minnesota North Stars, and Chicago Blackhawks and win a most improbable Stanley Cup

championship. Dryden won the Conn Smythe Trophy as Most Valuable Player in the playoffs.

The following year, Dryden won the Calder Trophy as the league's Rookie of the Year.

Dryden and the Canadiens won five more Cups (1973, '76–79), and Dryden won five Vezina Trophies as the league's best goaltender (1973, '76–79).

He was tall (6-4), athletic, and cat-quick. He also was unique among hockey players, in that he graduated from Cornell University with a pre-law degree, and when he sat out the 1974–75 season, due to a contract dispute, he got his law degree at McGill University.

Dryden, a six-time All-Star, had a .758 winning percentage, a 2.24 goals-against average, and 46 shutouts in seven seasons. In 112 playoff games, his winning percentage was .714, and his goals-against average was 2.40. He had 10 shutouts.

He retired in 1979 to practice law, and in May 1997, he became the president and general manager of the Toronto Maple Leafs.

Dryden was inducted into the Hockey Hall of Fame in 1983 and was voted No. 25 on the list of the NHL's Top 100 Players of All Time by *The Hockey News*.

Durnan, Bill

Born: January 22, 1915 in Toronto, Ontario, Canada
Died: October 31, 1972

Bill Durnan used his athleticism to his advantage in goal tending. He frustrated shooters with his ability to switch his stick from one hand to the other, meaning the shooters were always facing his glove hand.

Durnan was so good, he won the Vezina Trophy as the league's best goalie in six of his seven seasons with the Montreal Canadiens (1944–47, '49–50). He was also a six-time All-Star and the last NHL goalie to record shutouts in four consecutive games.

In 1950, Durnan retired when his nerves and the strain of playing the position got the best of him.

In his seven seasons, he had a winning percentage of .626 and a goals-against average of 2.36. He recorded 34 shutouts. He helped the Canadiens win two Stanley Cup championships (1944, '46). In 45 playoff games, he had a .600 winning percentage and a 2.07 goals-against average.

Durnan was inducted into the Hockey Hall of Fame in 1964 and was voted No. 34 on the list of the NHL's Top 100 Players of All Time by *The Hockey News*.

Esposito, Phil

Born: February 20, 1942 in Sault Ste. Marie, Ontario, Canada

Phil Esposito was sent from the Chicago Blackhawks to the Boston Bruins after the 1966–67 season. It proved to be a good deal for everyone but the Blackhawks.

Esposito became one of the most prolific scorers in league history. He had a big body (6-1, 205 pounds) that could take up space in the crease, and indeed, he got a lot of "garbage goals." But he also was a deft passer who could dictate the speed of the game. In 1969, his second year with the Bruins, Esposito became the first NHL player to eclipse the 100-point mark, with 49 goals and 77 assists. He also won the scoring title from 1971 through 1974, scoring at least 130 points each year, including 152 points in 1971, when he recorded 76 goals and 76 assists. The 76 goals were the most ever scored in one season, outdistancing the previous mark, set by Bobby Hull, by 18. Esposito also took 550 shots in 1976, which was 124 more than the second-highest total, which Esposito recorded in 1977.

He helped lead the Bruins to the Stanley Cup title in 1970 and 1972, and he won the Hart Trophy as the league's Most Valuable Player in 1969 and 1974.

Esposito was traded to the New York Rangers in 1975, largely because his forceful personality took its toll on the organization. He retired in 1981.

In 18 seasons, Esposito, an eight-time All-Star, scored 1,590 points on 717 goals and 873 assists. In 130 playoff games, he scored 137 points on 61 goals and 76 assists. Through the 2000 season, he ranked fifth all-time in points, 16th in assists, and fourth in goals.

Esposito became the general manager of the Rangers in 1986, twice taking over as coach. In 1992, he became the general manager of the Tampa Bay Lightning. Esposito was a driving force in bringing an NHL franchise to Florida.

He was inducted into the Hockey Hall of Fame in 1984 and was voted No. 18 on the list of the NHL's Top 100 Players of All Time by *The Hockey News*.

Esposito, Tony

Born: April 23, 1943 in Sault Ste. Marie, Ontario, Canada

Tony Esposito had one of the most remarkable rookie seasons in NHL history. In 1970, he won 38 games, posted 15 shutouts (two more than the modern record), and had a 2.17 goals-against average. He won the Calder Trophy as Rookie of the Year and the Vezina Trophy as the league's best goaltender.

Esposito also won the Vezina in 1972, and shared it with Philadelphia's Bernie Parent in 1974.

One of the first goalies to use the butterfly style, meaning he flopped to his knees to make saves, Esposito was a five-time All-Star. He twice made it to the Stanley Cup finals (1971, '73).

In 16 seasons, Esposito had a .566 winning percentage and a 2.92 goals-against average. He had 76 career shutouts. Through the 2000 season, he ranked fourth all-time in wins (886) and seventh all-time in shutouts.

In 99 playoff games, he had a .459 winning percentage and a 3.07 goals-against average, with six shutouts.

He was inducted into the Hockey Hall of Fame in 1988, and he was voted No. 79 on the list of the NHL's Top 100 Players of All Time by *The Hockey News*.

Federov, Sergei

Born: December 13, 1969 in Pskov, Russia

Sergei Federov is a strong two-way player who has been a mainstay with the Detroit Red Wings since 1990, when he joined the team after leaving the Russian team prior to the Goodwill Games. He made the all-rookie team, with 31 goals and 48 assists for 79 points, and was second in voting for the Calder Trophy, given to the Rookie of the Year.

In his 10 seasons, all with the Red Wings, Federov has scored 30 or more goals six times and 100 or more points twice. His best season was 1994, when he had 56 goals and 64 assists for a career-high 120 points. He won the Hart Trophy as the league's Most Valuable Player. Federov is the only European to be named Most Valuable Player.

Federov also won the Frank J. Selke Trophy as the league's best defensive foward in 1994 and 1996.

Through the 2000 season, Federov had 301 goals and 433 assists in the regular season. In the playoffs, he had 42 goals and 92 assists for 134 points.

Fuhr, Grant

Born: September 28, 1952 in Spruce Grove, Alberta, Canada

When you think about the Edmonton Oilers teams that won the Stanley Cup in 1984, 1985, 1987, and 1988, you probably think of Wayne Gretzky, Mark Messier, and a prolific offense. But Grant Fuhr, the goaltender for the Oilers, also deserved much of the credit. He was tenacious, unflappable, and at his best in the clutch.

He was durable, too. Fuhr, arguably the most prominent African American to play in the NHL, won the Vezina Trophy in 1988 as the league's best goaltender, playing a record 75 games. His record was 40-24-9 with a goals-against average of 3.43 and four shutouts.

Fuhr was suspended for six months in 1990 for using cocaine. In 1991, he was traded to Toronto. He also played for Buffalo and Los Angeles before signing with St. Louis in 1995. There he set a record of 79 games in 1995–96, including 76 starts. During the 1998–99 season, Fuhr was plagued by knee and groin injuries. He was limited to 39 games and was 16–11–8 with a 2.44 goals-against average. After the season, he announced that the 1999–2000 would be his last. The Calgary Flames, looking for a backup goaltender, acquired Fuhr from the Blues for a third-round draft pick.

Through 2000, Fuhr's career record was 403-295-114 with a 3.38 goals-against average and 25 shutouts. Among active goaltenders, Fuhr trailed only Patrick Roy of the Colorado Avalanche in victories. Fuhr ranked sixth all-time in career wins.

In 150 playoff games, he has a winning percentage of .647 and a goals-against average of 2.92, with six shutouts.

A six-time All-Star, Fuhr was voted No. 70 on the list of the NHL's Top 100 Players of All Time by *The Hockey News*.

Gainey, Bob

Born: December 13, 1953 in Peterborough, Ontario, Canada

Bob Gainey is recognized as one of the best defensive forwards ever to play the game. His specialty was neutralizing the opposition's top scorer. He won the Frank Selke Trophy for defensive excellence by a forward from 1978 to 1981.

Gainey helped the Canadiens to five Stanley Cup championships (1976–79, '86) and was the winner of the Conn Smythe Trophy as Most Valuable Player in the playoffs in 1979, when he scored 16 points in 16 games.

In 1989, Gainey retired from the Canadiens, then became the head coach of the Minnesota North Stars in 1990. In 1991, he led the North Stars to the Stanley Cup final. Through the 2000–01 season, he was the general manager of the Dallas Stars, who won the 1999 Stanley Cup.

In 16 seasons with Montreal, Gainey scored 501 points on 239 goals and 262 assists. In 182 playoff games, he scored 73 points on 25 goals and 48 assists.

Gainey was inducted into the Hockey Hall of Fame in 1992 and was voted No. 86 on the list of the NHL's Top 100 Players of All Time by *The Hockey News*.

Gartner, Mike

Born: October 29, 1959 in Ottawa, Ontario, Canada

Mike Gartner, blessed with a hard, accurate shot, was the fifth-leading goal-scorer in National Hockey League history through the 1999 season. He reached the 40-goal mark seven times in his career, during which he played for Washington, Minnesota, the New York Rangers, Toronto, and Phoenix.

In 19 seasons, Gartner had 1,335 points on 708 goals and 627 assists. He ranked 18th all-time in points. In 122 playoff games, he has 93 points on 43 goals and 50 assists. He was voted No. 89 on the list of the NHL's Top 100 Players of All Time by *The Hockey News*.

Geoffrion, Bernie

Born: February 16, 1931 in Montreal, Quebec, Canada

Bernie "Boom Boom" Geoffrion was so nicknamed because of the sound his shot made when it clanged off the boards at the Montreal Forum. He pioneered the slap shot as a principle offensive weapon.

Geoffrion joined the Canadiens in 1950 for 18 games, and the following season he won the Calder Trophy as Rookie of the Year. He won the Hart Trophy as the league's Most Valuable Player in 1961, when he became the second player ever to score 50 goals in a season. To accomplish the feat, Geoffrion scored 23 goals in his last 26 games, and played in only 64 of the 70 games that season. Geoffrion also won two Ross Trophies as the league's leading scorer in 1955 and 1961.

Besides being a prolific scorer, Geoffrion was tough. In 1958, he collapsed at a practice with a ruptured bowel. He was administered the last rites of the Catholic Church, and after life-saving emergency surgery, was told his season was over. Six weeks later, he returned to help the Canadiens win their third straight Stanley Cup. In 1961, he made teammate Doug Harvey cut the cast off his leg so that he could play in the Stanley Cup semifinals against Chicago.

Geoffrion, who in addition to his on-ice talent was blessed with a beautiful singing voice, retired in 1964, but came out of retirement in 1966 and spent two seasons with the New York Rangers. He became coach of the Rangers in 1968, but stomach problems forced him to resign before the season ended. He also coached the expansion Atlanta Flames in 1972, but again, quit abruptly.

In 16 seasons, Geoffrion scored 822 points on 393 goals and 429 assists. In 132 playoff games, he scored 118 points on 58 goals and 60 assists.

Geoffrion, a three-time All-Star, helped the Canadiens win six Stanley Cup championships (1953, '56–60). He was inducted into the Hockey Hall of Fame in 1972 and was voted No. 42 on the list of the NHL's Top 100 Players of All Time by *The Hockey News*.

Gretzky, Wayne

Born: January 26, 1961 in Brantford, Ontario, Canada

Wayne Gretzky was to the National Hockey League what Michael Jordan was to the National Basketball League: the greatest player in the history of his sport, and a cultural icon whose impact went far beyond the arena.

To many people, Wayne Gretzky *was* hockey because of the way he dominated the game. He started early, learning to skate not long after he learned to walk. His first instructor was his father, Walter, who built a rink in the backyard. It was Walter Gretzky who helped develop

Wayne Gretzky *National Hockey League*

his son's instincts. "Don't go where the puck is," Walter would say, "go where it's going to be."

By the time Gretzky was six, he was playing in a league with 10-year-olds, and when he was 10, he was playing against teenagers and doing rather well. He finished the 1971–72 season with 378 goals and 120 assists in 69 games in the Brantford atom league.

After scoring 182 points in 64 games for Sault Ste. Marie, Gretzky attracted the attention of the Indianapolis Racers of the fledgling World Hockey Association. He signed a four-year, $875,000 contract. He was 18 years old.

After only eight games, the Racers, having financial difficulties, sold Gretzky's contract to the Edmonton Oilers, for whom he scored 104 points on 43 goals and 61 assists.

When the WHA folded, Edmonton joined the National Hockey League in 1979, and Gretzky began creating his legend against the best in the world. His nickname, "The Great One," was a perfect fit.

Gretzky, blessed with speed, moves, and uncanny peripheral vision, led the Oilers to four Stanley Cup championships (1984, '85, '87, '88), twice winning the Conn Smythe Trophy as Most Valuable Player in the playoffs (1985, '88).

During his stay in Edmonton, Gretzky averaged nearly 192 points a year. He scored 50 goals in the first 39 games of the 1981–82 season; he scored a point in 51

straight games to start the 1983–84 season; and he played an integral role for Team Canada in two Canada Cup victories (1984, '87).

But after the Oilers' fourth Stanley Cup championship, he was the key figure in one of the most noteworthy trades in sports history. He was dealt to the Los Angeles Kings, where he spent the next 7 1/2 seasons. The Kings never won a Stanley Cup, but they did reach the finals in 1993, losing to Montreal in five games.

Gretzky's impact on Los Angeles and on hockey in the western United States was significant. Because of his talent, charisma, and character, the sport gained a foothold in places such as California (three franchises) and Arizona.

In February 1996, he was traded to the St. Louis Blues, and in July 1996, he signed as a free agent with the New York Rangers.

In 1998, Gretzky enjoyed two milestones: He played for Canada in the Winter Olympic Games in Nagano, Japan, and he led the NHL in assists for the 16th time. Among his 67 assists that year was the 1,851st of his career, which gave him more assists than any other player had points.

Gretzky ended his career with the Rangers, retiring after the 1998–99 season and 20 years in the NHL.

He owns 61 National Hockey League records. The highlights:

Career: goals, 894; assists, 1,963; points, 2,857; hat tricks, 50; 40-goal seasons, 12; 50-goal seasons, 9; 60-goal seasons, 5; consecutive 40-goal seasons, 12; consecutive 60-goal seasons, 4; 100-point seasons, 15; consecutive 100-point seasons, 13. *Season:* goals, 20, 1981–82; assists, 163, 1985–86; points, 215, 1985–86; hat tricks, 10, 1981–82, 1983–84. *Career playoffs:* points, 382; goals, 122; assists, 260; game-winning goals, 22.

Gretzky won the Hart Trophy as the league's Most Valuable Player nine times (1980–87, '89); the Ross Trophy as the league's scoring champion 10 times (1981–87, '90–91, '93); the Conn Smythe Trophy as playoff Most Valuable Player twice (1985, '88); and the Lady Byng Trophy for sportsmanship four times (1980, '91–93). He was also a 12-time All-Star.

Instead of waiting the usual three years for induction into the Hockey Hall of Fame, Gretzky was inducted in 2000. He was voted the No. 1 player of all time by *The Hockey News*.

Hainsworth, George
Born: June 26, 1895 in Toronto, Ontario, Canada
Died: October 9, 1950

George Hainsworth stood just 5-5, but because of his mechanics and precision, he was one of the dominant goaltenders of his era. He took over for Georges Vezina as the Montreal Canadiens' goalie in 1926 as a 31-year-old rookie. He won the first three Vezina Trophies as the league's outstanding goaltender.

In 1928–29, Hainsworth allowed just 43 goals in 44 games, registering 22 shutouts. He helped lead Montreal to the Stanley Cup in 1930 and 1931.

In 11 seasons, Hainsworth had a .609 winning percentage and a 1.91 goals-against average, with 94 shutouts. He was inducted into the Hockey Hall of Fame in 1961 and was voted No. 46 on the list of the NHL's Top 100 Players of All Time by *The Hockey News*.

Hall, Glenn

Born: October 8, 1931 in Humboldt, Saskatchewan, Canada

Glenn Hall pioneered the butterfly style of goaltending, meaning he flopped to his knees to make saves. That style, along with his quick hands, earned him the nickname "Mr. Goalie."

After eight years in junior and minor league hockey, Hall, a member of the Detroit Red Wings, won the Calder Trophy as the NHL Rookie of the Year in 1956.

Hall played in 906 regular season games, including a streak of 502 straight, which started in 1955 and ended 13 games into the 1962–63 season with Chicago, where he was traded in 1957. He helped the Blackhawks to the 1961 Stanley Cup championship. Hall was selected by the St. Louis Blues in the 1967 expansion draft. He won the Conn Smythe Trophy as Most Valuable Player in the playoffs in 1968. He also won three Vezina Trophies as the league's best goaltender (1963, '67, '69).

In 16 seasons, Hall had a winning percentage of .545 and a goals-against average of 2.51, with 84 shutouts. Through the 2000 season, he ranked fifth all-time in wins (407) and third all-time in shutouts (84).

In 115 playoff games, his winning percentage was .430 and his goals-against 2.79, with six shutouts. He was inducted into the Hockey Hall of Fame in 1975 and was voted No. 16 on the list of the NHL's Top 100 Players of All Time by *The Hockey News*.

Harvey, Doug

Born: December 19, 1924 in Montreal, Quebec, Canada
Died: December 26, 1989

Doug Harvey played defense in a different way. Instead of carrying the puck up ice and passing to a forward, Harvey would float by his own net, enticing the opposition toward him, and then deliver a perfect pass to a teammate to start the attack.

Harvey's style and ability helped the Montreal Canadiens to six Stanley Cup championships (1953, '56–60).

He won the Norris Trophy as the league's best defenseman seven times (1955–58, '60–62), and he was an 11-time All-Star.

Harvey was traded to the New York Rangers in 1961, when he became active in the players' union. He spent the 1961–62 season as player-coach, but quit after one year, saying he "couldn't be one of the boys." He played two more seasons with the Rangers and spent five years in the minors before returning for one season with the St. Louis Blues. He retired in 1969. Harvey had several jobs in hockey after his retirement, but a drinking problem dominated his life. He spent his final years doing odd jobs and living in an old railway touring car at an Ottawa racetrack. He died of cirrhosis.

In 20 seasons, Harvey scored 540 points on 88 goals and 452 assists. In 137 playoff games, he had 72 points on eight goals and 64 assists. He was inducted into the Hockey Hall of Fame in 1973 and was voted No. 6 on the list of the NHL's Top 100 Players of All Time by *The Hockey News*.

Hasek, Dominik

Born: January 29, 1965 in Pardubice, Czechoslovakia (now the Czech Republic)

Dominik Hasek, nicknamed "The Dominator," was just that—the dominant goaltender of his era. After playing

Dominik Hasek *National Hockey League*

only 25 games with the Chicago Blackhawks, he was traded to Buffalo in 1992, where he has been a fixture ever since. Hasek, a six-time All-Star, won the Vezina Trophy as the league's best goaltender four times (1994–95, '97–99). He also won the Hart Trophy as the league's Most Valuable Player in 1997 and 1998, becoming the first goalie since Jacques Plante (1962) to do so and the first goalie ever to win it twice.

In 1997–98, Hasek recorded 13 shutouts, the most since Tony Esposito's 15 in 1969–70. Hasek also was a key to the Czech Republic's winning the gold medal at the 1998 Winter Olympic Games in Nagano, Japan.

Through the 2000 season, Hasek had a career record of 210-150-68 with a 2.26 goals-against average and 45 shutouts. In 56 playoff games, his winning percentage was 29–22 with a 2.06 goals-against average and five shutouts.

Hasek announced plans to retire after the 1999–2000 season, but a groin injury caused him to miss most of that season, and so he decided to play the 2000–01 season.

He was voted No. 95 on the list of the NHL's Top 100 Players of All Time by *The Hockey News*.

Horton, Tim

Born: January 12, 1930 in Cochrane, Ontario, Canada

Died: February 20, 1974

Tim Horton, a defenseman who played from 1952 to 1974, was one of the strongest players of his time and also one of the best.

He played the body, not the puck, but he exceeded 100 penalty minutes only once in his career. According to his coach, Punch Imlach of the Toronto Maple Leafs, Horton didn't have a "mean bone in his body. If he had, they would have had to make a rule against him."

In addition to his defensive skills, Horton had a powerful slap shot. He helped the Leafs to four Stanley Cup championships (1962–64, '67) and was a six-time All-Star. Horton died in a car crash en route to his home in Fort Erie, Ontario.

In 22 seasons, he scored 518 points on 115 goals and 403 assists. He was inducted into the Hockey Hall of Fame in 1977 and was voted No. 43 on the list of the NHL's Top 100 Players of All Time by *The Hockey News*.

Howe, Gordie

Born: March 31, 1928 in Floral, Saskatchewan, Canada

Gordie Howe, known as "Mr. Hockey," enjoyed one of the most remarkable careers in all of sport. He played 33 pro seasons, before he finally retired in 1980 at age 52.

Howe spent one season with Omaha in the United States Hockey League; 33 seasons with the Detroit Red Wings of the National Hockey League; six seasons with the Houston Aeros of the World Hockey Association, after a two-year retirement; and his final season with the Hartford Whalers of the NHL.

Howe joined the Red Wings in 1946–47 as an 18-year-old rookie. He became part of the famed "Production Line," as the right wing, with Sid Abel and Ted Lindsay, each of whom had versatile skills. Howe was an accurate passer, a skilled scorer, a solid defender, and a player who wasn't afraid to go into the corners.

In the late '40s through the mid '50s, Howe led the Red Wings to two Stanley Cup finals (1949–50) and four Stanley Cup championships (1950, '52, '54–55). In 1949–50, Lindsay, Abel, and Howe finished 1-2-3 in the league in scoring.

During the 1950 playoffs against Toronto, Howe suffered a devastating injury, although no one is quite sure how it happened. Howe skated toward Maple Leafs captain Ted Kennedy, who said Howe missed trying to check him and crashed into the boards. Howe claims Kennedy accidentally high-sticked him. The result was a fractured skull. Emergency surgery was performed to relieve pressure on Howe's brain.

But he was back the following season to play in all 70 games and win the Ross Trophy as the league's leading scorer by 20 points over Montreal's Maurice Richard. Howe won five more Ross Trophies (1952–54, '57, '63) and at age 40, he scored a career-high 103 points.

For 20 straight seasons, 1949–50 through 1968–69, Howe was among the top five scorers in the NHL, and for 22 straight seasons, starting in 1949–50, he never scored fewer than 23 goals. No athlete has been so effective and so durable for so long.

By 1969, Howe continued to play at a high level, but his disgust with the Red Wings organization grew. When he realized he was only the third-highest-paid player on the team, the owner, Bruce Norris, increased his salary from $45,000 to $100,000. But for Howe, it still wasn't enough, and in 1971, tired of losing, he retired from hockey.

But two years later, in 1973, the World Hockey Association began play. Mark and Marty Howe, Gordie's sons, had signed with the Houston Aeros. Intrigued by the prospect of playing with his sons, Gordie Howe also joined the Aeros, and is the only father to play professional hockey with his sons.

Howe was the league's Most Valuable Player in 1974. In six WHA seasons, he averaged 29 goals and 84 points.

Howe returned to the NHL for one season, 1979–80, with the Hartford Whalers. He retired at age 52 with 801 goals in the NHL and another 174 in the WHA.

In 26 NHL seasons, Howe scored 1,850 points on 801 goals and 1,049 assists. Through the 2000 season, he ranked second all-time in goals behind Wayne Gretzky and sixth all-time in assists. In 157 playoff games, he scored 160 points on 68 goals and 92 assists.

Howe, a 21-time All-Star, was inducted into the Hockey Hall of Fame in 1972 and was voted No. 3 on the list of the NHL's Top 100 Players of All Time by *The Hockey News*.

Hull, Bobby
Born: January 3, 1939 in Pointe Anne, Ontario, Canada

Bobby Hull was known as the "Golden Jet," for obvious reasons. He was a lightning-fast skater—timed at 28.3 mph with the puck, 29.7 mph without it—and his slap shot was, as one player described it, like a "small town coming at you."

His slap shot was timed at 118 mph, more than 30 mph faster than average. The combination of speed, power, and physical strength (5-10, 195 pounds) made Hull a scoring machine.

He joined the Chicago Blackhawks in 1957 and scored just 31 goals during his first two years. But he won the Ross Trophy as the league's leading scorer in his third season, and won it twice more, in 1962 and 1966.

In 1965–66, he broke the NHL's single-season record for goals with 54, and three years later, he broke it again with 58.

Hull, a 12-time All-Star at left wing, won the Hart Trophy as the league's Most Valuable Player in 1965 and 1966.

In addition to being a prolific scorer, Hull was not afraid to voice his opinion or stand up for what he thought was right. A salary dispute in 1968 resulted in a long training camp holdout. The following year, he missed Chicago's first 11 games in a controversy over deferred income.

In 1971, the NHL considered banning curved sticks. Hull threatened to boycott the playoffs. A compromise was reached, allowing a half-inch of curvature.

So, given his outspokenness and his dissatisfaction with management, perhaps it wasn't a surprise when Hull signed a 10-year, $2.75 million contract with the Winnipeg Jets of the World Hockey Association.

Hull's signing gave the league instant credibility. He was the WHA's Most Valuable Player in 1973 and 1975.

In 1979, the Jets joined the National Hockey League. Hull remained with the team for part of the season, until moving to the Hartford Whalers. He retired in 1980.

In 16 NHL seasons, Hull scored 1,170 points on 610 goals and 560 assists. Through the 2000 season, he ranked 31st all-time in points and tied for ninth all-time in goals.

In 119 playoff games, he scored 129 points on 62 goals and 67 assists. He was inducted into the Hockey Hall of Fame in 1983 and was voted No. 8 on the list of the NHL's Top 100 Players of All Time by *The Hockey News*.

Hull, Brett
Born: August 9, 1964 in Belleville, Ontario, Canada

Brett Hull, the son of hockey legend Bobby Hull, has been a productive scorer and a feared shooter throughout his career. He began his NHL career in 1986 with the Calgary Flames, and near the end of his second season in Calgary was traded to the St. Louis Blues.

Hull led the league in goals in 1990 (72), 1991 (86), and 1992 (70). In 1991, he was named the Hart Trophy winner as Most Valuable Player in the league. In addition to his 86 goals, a record for right wings and the third-highest single-season total of all time, he had 45 assists for 131 points. In 1990, he won the Lady Byng Trophy for sportsmanship.

Hull remained with the Blues through the 1998 season. In his 10 full seasons with the team, he scored 40 or more goals eight times and 100 or more points four times.

In July 1998, Hull signed as a free agent with the Dallas Stars. In his first season in Dallas, he had 32 goals and 26 assists for 58 points and helped lead the Stars to the Stanley Cup championship, scoring the Cup-winning goal in game 6 against the Buffalo Sabres.

Hull has 610 goals and 494 assists for 1,104 career points in the regular season. Through the 2000 season, he was tied for ninth all-time in goals with his father.

Jackson, Harvey
Born: January 19, 1911 in Toronto, Ontario, Canada
Died: June 25, 1966

Eighteen-year-old left wing Harvey "Busher" Jackson became the youngest member of the Toronto Maple Leafs' famous "Kid Line," joining Charlie Conacher and Joe Primeau. They combined for 836 points during their seven seasons together. Jackson was among the league's top 10 scorers five times and won the Ross Trophy as the league's leading scorer in 1932. In 1932, he helped Toronto to the Stanley Cup championship, and in 1934, he was the first player to score four goals in one period. In 15 seasons, Jackson scored 475 points on 241 goals and 234 assists. A 12-time All-Star, he was inducted into the Hockey Hall of Fame in 1971 and was voted No. 55 on the list of the NHL's Top 100 Players of All Time by *The Hockey News*.

Jagr, Jaromir

Born: February 15, 1972 in Kladno, Czechoslovakia (now the Czech Republic)

Jaromir Jagr is one of the most dynamic and talented players of his era. Blessed with blazing speed, athleticism, grace, and the ability to handle the puck, Jagr has been instant offense during his career, which has all been spent with the Pittsburgh Penguins.

Jagr, the fifth player selected overall in the NHL entry draft, joined the Penguins for the 1990–91 season and has made an impact ever since. He has scored 30 or more goals in nine of his 10 seasons with the Penguins. He has topped the 100-point mark three times.

Through the 2000 season, Jagr won the Art Ross Trophy, given to the player who leads the league in scoring, four times—1995 (32 goals, 38 assists, 70 points), 1998 (35-67-102), 1999 (44-83-127), and 2000 (42-54-96). He shared the league lead for assists in 1998 and 1999. In 1999, Jagr won the Hart Trophy as the league's Most Valuable Player. He finished second in the voting in 2000.

In 1991 and 1992, Jagr teamed with the legendary Mario Lemieux and helped lead the Penguins to consecutive Stanley Cup championships.

In his 10 seasons with the Penguins, Jagr has 387 goals and 571 assists for 958 points. In the playoffs, he has 63 goals and 72 assists for 135 points.

In 1998, he led the Czech Republic to a gold medal at the Winter Olympics in Nagano, Japan.

Kelly, Red (Leonard)

Born: July 9, 1927 in Simcoe, Ontario, Canada

Red Kelly was an outstanding defenseman blessed with the skills of a forward. He led NHL defensemen in goals eight times, in assists three times, and in points five times. He was the first defenseman to score 10 or more goals in nine straight seasons. Kelly helped the Detroit Red Wings to four Stanley Cup championships (1950, '52, '54–55) and the Toronto Maple Leafs to four titles (1962–64, '67). In 1954, he won the first Norris Trophy awarded for being the league's best defenseman. He also won the Lady Byng Trophy for sportsmanship in 1951, 1953, 1954, and 1961. He and Bill Quackenbush are the only defensemen to win the award.

In 20 seasons, Kelly scored 823 points on 281 goals and 542 assists. He was inducted into the Hockey Hall of Fame in 1969 and was voted No. 22 on the list of the NHL's Top 100 Players of All Time by *The Hockey News*.

Kennedy, Ted

Born: December 12, 1925 in Humbertsone, Ontario, Canada

Ted Kennedy, a center for the Toronto Maple Leafs, was involved in one of the sport's ugliest incidents in the 1950 Stanley Cup semifinals against the Detroit Red Wings. He avoided a check from Gordie Howe, who crashed into the boards and fractured his skull. The Red Wings, who thought Kennedy high-sticked Howe, exacted their revenge in the next game. Kennedy was deliberately cross-checked and attacked by players and a fan. He wasn't seriously hurt and came back to score a goal in the Cup-clinching fifth game.

Kennedy, a fierce competitor, won the 1955 Hart Trophy as the league's Most Valuable Player even though he scored only 10 goals. He led Toronto to five Stanley Cup titles (1945, '47–49, '51) and was a three-time All-Star.

In 14 seasons, he scored 560 points on 231 goals and 329 assists. In 78 playoff games, he scored 60 points on 29 goals and 31 assists. He was inducted into the Hockey Hall of Fame in 1966 and was voted No. 57 on the list of the NHL's Top 100 Players of All Time by *The Hockey News*.

Keon, Dave

Born: March 2, 1940 in Noranda, Quebec, Canada

Dave Keon was a solid, two-way center who spent most of his career with the Toronto Maple Leafs. He excelled on faceoffs, penalty killing, and defending against the opposition's no. 1 center.

Keon, a two-time All-Star, won the Lady Byng Trophy for sportsmanship (1962–63), the Calder Trophy as Rookie of the Year (1961), and the Conn Smythe Trophy as Most Valuable Player in the playoffs (1967). He helped lead the Maple Leafs to four Stanley Cup championships (1962–64, '67).

Keon left the Maple Leafs in 1975 for the World Hockey Association. He turned in four 20-goal seasons, before ending his career with the Hartford Whalers of the NHL in 1982.

In 18 NHL seasons, he scored 989 points on 396 goals and 590 assists. He was inducted into the Hockey Hall of Fame in 1986, and he was voted No. 69 on the list of the NHL's Top 100 Players of All Time by *The Hockey News*.

Kurri, Jari

Born: May 18, 1960 in Helsinki, Finland

Perhaps best known for being Wayne Gretzky's linemate, first with the Edmonton Oilers and then with the Los Angeles Kings, Jari Kurri was the consummate two-way player. He could score and he added a defensive presence.

He and Gretzky teamed up during Kurri's rookie season in 1980. Kurri scored 50 or more goals in four of the eight seasons he and Gretzky were linemates. In 1984–85, Kurri set a record for goals by a right winger with 71. That same year, he scored 19 goals in 18 playoff games as the Oilers won their second straight Stanley Cup championship. For those who thought Kurri's point totals were dependent upon Gretzky, Kurri proved them wrong. In the two seasons after Gretzky was traded to Los Angeles in 1988, Kurri scored 102 and 93 points, respectively.

After salary dispute with Edmonton, Kurri played in Italy before returning to the NHL and rejoining Gretzky in Los Angeles. He also played for the New York Rangers, the Anaheim Mighty Ducks, and the Colorado Avalanche. He retired in 1998.

Through the 2000 season, Kurri ranked 14th all-time in points (1,398) and 12th in goals (601). In the playoffs, he ranked fifth all-time in points (233), third in goals (106), and third in assists (127).

Kurri, a five-time All-Star, won the 1985 Lady Byng Trophy for sportsmanship and helped the Oilers to five Stanley Cup championships (1984–85, '87–88, '90). He was voted No. 50 on the list of the NHL's Top 100 Players of All Time by *The Hockey News*.

Lafleur, Guy

Born: September 20, 1951 in Thurso, Quebec, Canada

Guy Lafleur loved hockey so much that as a child he often slept in his equipment so that he could spend less time getting to the rink. That passion for the game continued during his 17 seasons in the National Hockey League.

Lafleur's speed, playmaking ability, and goal-scoring talent made him one of the most complete players in NHL history.

He was drafted by the Montreal Canadiens after scoring 209 points in 62 games with the Quebec Ramparts junior team in 1970–71. During his first three pro seasons, he surpassed the 50-point mark, but starting with the 1974–75 season and continuing through 1979–80, he averaged 54 goals and 128 points.

Lafleur won the first of his three Ross Trophies as the league's leading scorer in 1975–76 with 125 points on 56 goals and 69 assists. He also won it in 1976–77 (56 goals, 80 assists) and in 1977–78 (60 goals, 72 assists).

In 1976–77, Lafleur won the first of two consecutive Hart Trophies as the league's Most Valuable Player, and he also won the Conn Smythe Trophy as Most Valuable Player in the playoffs, scoring 10 goals and 11 assists in 15 games.

Lafleur, a right wing, scored 125 points in 1978–79, but then saw his production decline, largely because of the defense-oriented system installed by Montreal coach Jacques Lemaire. Nineteen games into the 1984–85 season, Lafleur announced his retirement. He was elected to the Hockey Hall of Fame in 1988, and days later, returned to the rink with the New York

Rangers, where he spent two seasons. His career finally ended after the 1990–91 season with the Quebec Nordiques.

Lafleur scored 1,353 points on 560 goals and 793 assists. Through the 2000 season, he ranked 16th all-time in points and 14th in goals. In 128 playoff games, he scored 134 points on 58 goals and 76 assists. He was a six-time All-Star who helped lead the Canadiens to five Stanley Cup championships. He was voted No. 11 on the list of the NHL's Top 100 Players of All Time by *The Hockey News*.

Lalonde, Newsy (Edouard)

Born: October 31, 1887 in Cornwall, Ontario, Canada
Died: November 21, 1970

Edouard Lalonde acquired his nickname because he worked as a newspaper reporter and printer at the *Cornwall Freeholder* as a youth. His favorite sport was lacrosse—he was named Canada's best lacrosse player of the half-century—and he didn't take up hockey until he was 16.

He played in several hockey leagues and joined the Montreal Canadiens of the National Hockey League when it was organized in 1917. His best NHL season came in 1919–20, when he scored 36 goals and 42 points. A year later, he became the first player to lead the league in goals (33), assists (8), and points (41).

Lalonde, a center, was a feisty player, competing when "hockey was genuinely a mug's racket," according to one sportswriter.

Lalonde retired after the 1927 season, went on to coach the Canadiens from 1932 to 1935, and was elected to the Hockey Hall of Fame in 1950. He was voted No. 32 on the list of the NHL's Top 100 Players of All Time by *The Hockey News*.

Leetch, Brian

Born: March 3, 1968 in Corpus Christi, Texas

Brian Leetch made an almost immediate impact in the National Hockey League. He joined the New York Rangers at the end of the 1987–88 season after a successful career in college and with the U.S. National team.

In 1979, he won the Calder Trophy as the league's Rookie of the Year, scoring 23 goals (a record for a rookie defenseman) and 71 points.

Leetch won the Norris Trophy as the league's best defenseman in 1992 (22 goals, 80 assists) and 1997 (20 goals, 58 assists) and the Conn Smythe Trophy as Most Valuable Player in the playoffs in 1994, when the Rangers won the Stanley Cup. He was the first American player to win the Conn Smythe.

Leetch, an eight-time All-Star, was voted No. 71 on the list of the NHL's Top 100 Players of All Time by *The Hockey News*.

Lemieux, Mario

Born: October 5, 1965 in Montreal, Quebec, Canada

At 6-4, 210 pounds, Mario Lemieux had size, speed, and an instinct for the game that couldn't be taught. Bobby Orr, the Hall of Fame defenseman from the Boston Bruins, proclaimed Lemieux the most talented player in NHL history.

"He can do more things than any player I've seen," said Orr. "When he wants to play, it's scary."

It certainly was for the opposition. Lemieux was drafted first overall by the Pittsburgh Penguins in 1984 after averaging more than four points a game during his final season in junior hockey.

Mario Lemieux *National Hockey League*

He picked up right where he left off, scoring 100 points and winning the Calder Trophy as the league's Rookie of the Year.

During his next two seasons, Lemieux, a center, scored 141 and 107 points, respectively. But in spite of his statistics and his obvious talent, there were questions about whether Lemieux pushed himself hard enough or could lead a team to the championship. It wouldn't be too much longer before he answered his critics.

In 1991 and 1992, Lemieux led the Penguins to consecutive Stanley Cup championships, despite coping with serious injuries each year.

During the first Cup year in 1991, he missed the first 50 games of the season after disc surgery on his back. But he returned to score 45 points in 26 regular season games and 44 points in 23 playoff games. The following year, back spasms and a broken hand kept him out of action several times, but in the playoffs he scored 34 points in 15 games. He won the Conn Smythe Trophy as Most Valuable Player in the playoffs in both years.

Lemieux won the Ross Trophy as the league's leading scorer in 1988 (168 points), 1989 (199), 1992 (131), 1993 (160), 1996 (161), and 1997 (122). He also won the Hart Trophy as the league's Most Valuable Player in 1988, 1993, and 1996, and the Masterson Trophy for perseverance and sportsmanship in 1993.

He had overcome a lot—injuries, the early misgivings of players and the media about his willingness to work hard, and a town, Pittsburgh, that took a while to catch on to hockey. But Lemieux's most critical obstacle was discovered in January 1993. He was being treated for the back problems that had plagued him throughout his career when doctors found a lump in his neck. Further examination revealed it to be Hodgkin's disease. He underwent two months of radiation, missed 20 games, but still managed to win the Ross Trophy.

He missed most of the 1994–95 season with back problems, but came back again to win scoring titles in 1996 and 1997.

Lemieux announced his retirement following the 1997 season and was inducted into the Hockey Hall of Fame without the customary three-year wait. He finished his 12-year career with 1,494 points on 613 goals and 881 assists. Through the 2000 season, he ranked 10th all-time in points, eighth all-time in goals, and 15th all-time in assists. He averaged 2.005 points per game.

In 89 playoff games, he scored 155 points on 70 goals and 85 assists. He ranked 17th all-time in points and 13th all-time in goals. He was voted No. 4 on the list of the NHL's Top 100 Players of All Time by *The Hockey News*.

But Lemieux's contribution to the game, especially to the game in Pittsburgh, didn't end with his retirement. When the Penguins' ownership wanted to move the team, Lemieux put together a group that ended up buying the team and keeping it in the Steel City, with him as the owner.

In December 2000, Lemieux came out of retirement and resumed his career with the Penguins.

Lindros, Eric

Born: February 28, 1973 in London, Ontario, Canada

At 6-4, 236 pounds, Eric Lindros developed into one of the most dominant players in the game. Blessed with size, speed, and strength, he provided an imposing presence for the Philadelphia Flyers at both ends of the ice.

After an outstanding minor league career, Lindros was chosen by the Quebec Nordiques with the first pick overall in the 1991 National Hockey League entry draft. He was acquired by the Flyers in a major trade that sent six players, two future draft picks, and $15 million to the Nordiques. When the Nordiques tried to alter the terms of the deal, an arbitrator got involved and awarded Lindros to the Flyers.

Lindros has had a star-crossed career with the Flyers. In the strike-shortened season of 1995, he had 29 goals and 41 assists for 70 points in 46 games and was named the Hart Trophy winner as the league's Most Valuable Player. The following year, he was a finalist for the Hart Trophy, with 47 goals and 68 assists for 115 points.

Lindros has scored 40 or more goals and 90 or more points in four of his eight seasons with the team. In 1997, he led the Flyers to the Stanley Cup finals, where they lost to the Detroit Red Wings in four games.

Injuries, though, have limited Lindros' effectiveness. Excluding the strike season of 1995, he has played in 70 or more games just twice, and three times he has played in 55 or fewer. A series of concussions kept Lindros out of 27 games and most of the playoffs in the 2000 season. He returned during the Stanley Cup playoffs, but suffered another concussion.

As of September 2000, his health and his future with the Flyers was uncertain.

Through the 2000 season, Lindros had 290 goals and 369 assists in the regular season and 24 goals and 33 assists in 120 playoff games.

Lindsay, Ted

Born: July 29, 1925 in Renfrew, Ontario, Canada

That his nicknames included "Terrible Ted" and "Scarface" tells you all you need to know about Ted Lindsay, who helped spearhead the Detroit Red Wings dynasty in the early to mid '50s. But in addition to his ability to brawl and wield his stick, Lindsay was also a proficient scorer.

Lindsay, a left wing, played on the famed "Production Line," along with Gordie Howe and Sid Abel. He helped lead the Red Wings to Stanley Cup championships in 1950, 1952, 1954, and 1955. In 1950, he won the Ross Trophy as the league's scoring leader with 78 points on 23 goals and 55 assists.

In 1957, the Red Wings traded Lindsay to the Chicago Blackhawks because of his involvement in the NHL Players' Association. He played three seasons with Chicago, retired for four years, then came back to Detroit for one more season at the age of 39. He finally retired in 1965.

In 17 seasons, Lindsay scored 851 points on 379 goals, including 57 game-winners and 472 assists. In 133 playoff games, he scored 96 points on 47 goals and 49 assists.

A nine-time All-Star, Lindsay was inducted into the Hockey Hall of Fame in 1966 and was voted No. 21 on the list of the NHL's Top 100 Players of All Time by *The Hockey News*.

Mahovlich, Frank

Born: January 10, 1938 in Timmins, Ontario, Canada

Had Frank Mahovlich gotten along with his coach, Punch Imlach, during his years in Toronto, there's no telling the heights he might have reached. But Mahovlich, a gentle man, couldn't cope with the stress inflicted by his demanding coach.

Nicknamed the "Big M," Mahovlich, a left wing, joined the Maple Leafs in 1957 and won the Calder Trophy as the league's Rookie of the Year, outdistancing Bobby Hull of the Chicago Blackhawks. In 1961, he was driving for a 50-goal season, but as his scoring pace tailed off, he scored 43 and never scored more than 36 for Toronto, partly because he was stuck in a defense-oriented system.

After Mahovlich left the Maple Leafs to receive treatment for depression, he was traded to Detroit in 1968. Three years later, the rebuilding Red Wings traded him to Montreal, where he helped the Canadiens to two Stanley Cups (1971, '73). He also won four Cups with the Maple Leafs (1962–64, '67).

In 17 NHL seasons, he scored 1,103 points on 533 goals and 570 assists. In 137 playoff games, he scored 118 points on 51 goals and 67 assists. A nine-time All-Star, he was inducted into the Hockey Hall of Fame in 1981 and was voted No. 26 on the list of the NHL's Top 100 Players of All Time by *The Hockey News*.

Malone, Joe

Born: February 28, 1890 in Sillery, Quebec, Canada
Died: May 15, 1969

Joe Malone, nicknamed "Phantom Joe," was one of the great early scorers in the National Hockey League. When he joined the Montreal Canadiens in the league's first season in 1917–18, he scored five goals in the first game and finished the season with 44 goals in 20 games. Playing for Quebec in 1919, Malone recorded the only seven-goal game in league history. He won the Ross Trophy as the league's leading scorer in 1918 and 1920.

In seven seasons, Malone, a center, scored 167 points on 146 goals and 21 assists. He was inducted into the Hockey Hall of Fame in 1950 and was voted No. 39 on the list of the NHL's Top 100 Players of All Time by *The Hockey News*.

Messier, Mark

Born: January 18, 1961 in Edmonton, Alberta, Canada

Although Wayne Gretzky was responsible for most of the scoring, Mark Messier provided much of the heart for the Edmonton Oilers' dynasty in the mid to late '80s that resulted in their winning five Stanley Cup championships in seven seasons (1984–85, '87–88, '90). Messier's last Cup with the Oilers came after Gretzky had been traded to the Los Angeles Kings.

Mark Messier   *National Hockey League*

Messier, a center, joined the Oilers early in the 1979–80 season. When Edmonton won its first Stanley Cup, he was the Conn Smythe Trophy winner as Most Valuable Player in the playoffs, scoring eight goals and 19 assists in 19 games.

In 1990, he won the Hart Trophy as the league's Most Valuable Player, scoring 129 points on 45 goals and 84 assists. The following season, Messier insisted that the Oilers double his $1 million salary. When they refused, he was traded to the New York Rangers, for whom he filled a much-needed leadership void. He scored the Stanley Cup–clinching goal in the seventh game against Vancouver.

In 1992, Messier won his second Hart Trophy, scoring 107 points on 35 goals and 72 assists, and in 1994, he led the Rangers to their first Stanley Cup championship in 54 years. He became the first player to captain two different title teams.

Messier left New York in the summer of 1997, joining the Vancouver Canucks as an unrestricted free agent.

Through the 2000 season, Messier ranked fourth all-time in career points (1,714), sixth in 100-point seasons (6), fourth in assists (1,087), sixth in goals (627), and seventh in games played (1,479). He was ranked first in playoff games played (236), second in playoff career points (295), second in playoff career goals (109), and second in playoff career assists (186).

Messier, a 15-time All-Star, including four times as a first-teamer, was voted No. 12 on the list of the NHL's Top 100 Players of All Time by *The Hockey News*.

Messier returned to the Rangers for the 2000–01 season.

Mikita, Stan

Born: May 20, 1940 in Sokolov, Czechoslovakia (now the Czech Republic)

Stan Mikita was one of the best all-round players in National Hockey League history. He could pass, stick-handle, and score. Early in his career, he could also fight, amassing nearly 100 penalty minutes in each of his first seven seasons. But one night his two-year-old daughter, Meg, who had watched that night's game on television, asked why he spent so much of the game sitting down (in the penalty box), while the other players were on the ice skating.

Mikita got the message. The next season, 1964–65, he cut his penalty minutes to 58 from 154. The season after that, he had only 12 penalty minutes.

Mikita, a center, spent his entire 21-year career with the Chicago Blackhawks, beginning with the 1958–59 season. He won the Ross Trophy as the league's scoring champion (1964–65, '67–68), and he twice won the Hart Trophy as the league's Most Valuable Player (1967–68).

In 1966–67, Mikita became the first Triple Crown winner in NHL history, winning the Ross, the Hart, and the Lady Byng Trophy for sportsmanship. He repeated the feat the following season.

Starting in 1969, injuries kept Mikita from scoring at his customary pace. He suffered a serious head injury, chronic back problems, and a broken heel. He retired in 1980 as the Blackhawks' all-time leader in games, assists and points.

In 22 seasons, Mikita, an eight-time All-Star, scored 1,467 points on 541 goals and 926 assists. Through the 2000 season, he ranked 11th all-time in points, 20th in goals, and ninth in assists.

In 155 playoff games, he scored 59 goals and 91 assists. He was inducted into the Hockey Hall of Fame in 1983 and was voted No. 17 on the list of the NHL's Top 100 Players of All Time by *The Hockey News*.

Moore, Dickie

Born: January 6, 1931 in Montreal, Quebec, Canada

Dickie Moore's career was plagued with injuries, some of which were suffered before he turned pro in 1951. As a boy, he was hit by a car and broke both knees. While with the Montreal Canadiens, he broke his collarbone twice, tore cartilage in both knees, and underwent several shoulder operations. He also played with a broken wrist for the last three months of the 1957–58 season. No matter, he went on to win the first of two consecutive Ross Trophies as the league's leading scorer.

Moore, a left winger, scored 84 points in 1958 and a then record 96 the following year. He was known as a hard worker and the ultimate team player, helping Montreal to six Stanley Cup titles (1953, '56–60).

In 1964, he was traded to the Toronto Maple Leafs. Moore ended his career in 1968, playing one season with the expansion St. Louis Blues.

A three-time All-Star, Moore scored 608 points on 261 goals and 347 assists in 14 seasons. In 135 playoff games, he had 110 points on 46 goals and 64 assists. He was inducted into the Hockey Hall of Fame in 1974 and was voted No. 31 on the list of the NHL's Top 100 Players of All Time by *The Hockey News*.

Morenz, Howie

Born: June 21, 1902 in Mitchell, Ontario, Canada
Died: March 8, 1937

The story of Howie Morenz's career and tragic death is almost as compelling as his career was remarkable. Blessed with great speed and terrific skating ability, he was said to have talent that transcended any era.

Morenz, a center, joined the Montreal Canadiens in 1923–24, after a successful amateur career in Stratford.

He won three Hart Trophies as the league's Most Valuable Player (1928, '31, '32) and two Ross Trophies as the league's leading scorer (1928, '31). In 1934, Morenz was traded to Chicago, and then to New York the following season. In 1936, he was back with Montreal.

It was during a game against the Blackhawks that Morenz suffered the injury that ended his career. He was checked into the boards by defenseman Earl Seibert and fell feet first, his skate digging into the wood. A bone snapped in his left leg.

Morenz became so depressed that he might not be able to play again that he suffered a nervous breakdown and required a strait jacket at one point. A month after the injury, he died of an embolism, although some theorized that he really died of a broken heart.

His body lay in state at the Montreal Forum, and as many as 40,000 people filed by to pay their respects in what was among the most well-attended funerals in Canadian history. In 14 seasons, Morenz scored 467 points on 270 goals and 197 assists. In 47 playoff games, he scored 32 points on 21 goals and 11 assists. A three-time All-Star, Morenz was voted the player of the half-century by the Canadian press. He was inducted into the Hockey Hall of Fame in 1945, and he was voted No. 15 on the list of the NHL's Top 100 Players of All Time by *The Hockey News*.

Orr, Bobby

Born: March 20, 1948 in Parry Sound, Ontario, Canada

All Bobby Orr did, according to his Boston Bruins teammate Phil Esposito, was "change the face of hockey all by himself."

Blessed with the skills of a center, Orr redefined the way defensemen played the game, and he routinely made the impossible seem routine, at least for him.

Orr joined the Bruins in 1966 at the age of 18, signing a contract for $25,000, more than triple the usual rookie salary. He won the 1967 Calder Trophy as the league's Rookie of the Year, and continued to win awards for the rest of his career. He dominated the game with speed, acceleration, skating ability, and power that other players could only dream about. Said teammate Johnny Bucyk, "Bobby has 16 levels of fast."

Orr failed to win the Norris Trophy as the league's best defenseman during his rookie year, prompting the player who did win it, New York's Harry Howell, to say, "I'm glad I won it now, because it's going to belong to Orr from now on."

Howell was right. For the next eight seasons (1968–75), Orr won the Norris Trophy, more than any other player in NHL history.

Orr is the only defenseman to win the Ross Trophy as the league's leading scorer. He won it in 1970, scoring

120 points on 33 goals and 87 assists, and again in 1975, scoring 135 points on 46 goals and 89 assists. In 1971, he registered 139 points on 37 goals and a record 102 assists.

Orr had six straight seasons of 100 or more points and won the Hart Trophy as the league's Most Valuable Player three consecutive years, starting in 1970, when he became the only player to win four major awards—Hart, Norris, Ross, Smythe—in the same year. The Bruins won the Stanley Cup twice during Orr's career, 1970 and 1972, and he was the Conn Smythe Trophy winner as Most Valuable Player in the playoffs each time. In the first Cup victory, over St. Louis, Orr scored the winning goal in overtime in the fourth and final game. Two years later, he had 19 assists to break the record held by Montreal's Jean Beliveau.

During the 1974–75 season, Orr scored a career-high 46 goals, but after that, knee injuries impacted his play.

He left the Bruins in 1976, following a salary dispute, and joined the Chicago Blackhawks as a free agent. He played in 20 games that season, missed the next season with injuries, and retired after six games into the 1978–79 season.

In 657 regular season games, Orr scored 915 points on 270 goals and 645 assists. In 74 playoff games, he scored 92 points on 26 goals and 66 assists. A nine-time All-Star, Orr was inducted into the Hockey Hall of Fame in 1979. He was voted No. 2 on the list of the NHL's Top 100 Players of All Time by *The Hockey News*.

Parent, Bernie

Born: April 3, 1945 in Montreal, Quebec, Canada

Bernie Parent broke in with the Boston Bruins, joined the Philadelphia Flyers in the 1967 expansion draft, was traded to Toronto in 1971, and then left the National Hockey League for the rival World Hockey Association. But when the Philadelphia Blazers moved to Vancouver, Parent refused to go. The Flyers reacquired him, and he led the franchise to two Stanley Cup championships (1974–75).

Each year he was named the winner of the Conn Smythe Trophy as Most Valuable Player in the playoffs. He also won the Vezina Trophy as the league's best goaltender both years.

A two-time All-Star, Parent was inducted into the Hockey Hall of Fame in 1984, and he was voted No. 63 on the list of the NHL's Top 100 Players of All Time by *The Hockey News*.

Park, Brad

Born: July 6, 1945 in Toronto, Ontario, Canada

Brad Park was a hard-nosed defenseman who had the acceleration of a forward. The New York Rangers drafted him no. 1 overall in 1966, and he joined the team two years later. He broke into the league as the no. 1 draft choice of the New York Rangers in 1968.

Thirteen games into the 1975–76 season, Park, who had undergone five knee surgeries by the time he was 28, was traded to Boston. Despite playing on what amounted to one leg, he hit double figures in goals five times in seven seasons with the Bruins. He finished his career in Detroit, where he played two seasons.

A seven-time All-Star and winner of the 1984 Masterson Trophy, honoring perseverance, sportsmanship, and dedication, Park was inducted into the Hockey Hall of Fame in 1988 and was voted No. 49 on the list of the NHL's Top 100 Players of All Time by *The Hockey News*.

Perreault, Gilbert

Born: November 13, 1950 in Victoriaville, Quebec, Canada

Gilbert Perreault was the total package. A center, he was blessed with strong skating and stick-handling ability, power, and finesse. He spent his entire 17-year career with the Buffalo Sabres, and in a poll of Buffalo fans, he was voted the greatest athlete ever to perform in the city, outpointing O.J. Simpson of the Bills.

Best known for centering the "French Connection" line, with Rene Robert and Rick Martin, Perreault scored 30 or more goals in a season 10 times, and he holds all the Sabres' offensive records.

Perreault won the 1971 Calder Trophy as Rookie of the Year (38 goals, 34 assists) and the 1973 Lady Byng Trophy for sportsmanship.

A two-time All-Star, Perreault scored 1,326 points (512 goals, 814 assists) in his career. Through the 2000 season, he ranked 21st all-time in points, 24th in goals, and 20th in assists. In 90 playoff games, he scored 103 points on 33 goals and 70 assists. He was voted No. 47 on the list of the NHL's Top 100 Players of All Time by *The Hockey News*.

Pilote, Pierre

Born: December 11, 1931 in Kenogami, Quebec, Canada

Despite not taking up the game until he was age 16, Pierre Pilote developed into a solid, all-round defenseman for the Chicago Blackhawks and the Toronto Maple Leafs. He won the Norris Trophy as the league's best defenseman three consecutive years (1963–65) and was runner-up two other times. In 1964–65, he scored 59 points, which was a record for defensemen at the time.

An eight-time All-Star, Pilote scored 498 points on 80 goals and 418 assists in 14 seasons. In 86 playoff games, he scored 61 points on eight goals and 53 assists. He was inducted into the Hockey Hall of Fame in 1975 and was voted No. 59 on the list of the NHL's Top 100 Players of All Time by *The Hockey News.*

Plante, Jacques

Born: January 17, 1929 in Shawinigan Falls, Quebec, Canada
Died: February 26, 1986

Jacques Plante was the first to make the goalie mask a permanent part of his equipment—even though the Montreal Canadiens management was not pleased with his decision. In 1959, after a shot by the New York Rangers' Andy Bathgate hit Plante in the face, Plante, who wore a mask in practice, insisted upon wearing it in games.

Plante also was one of the first goalies to leave the net to retrieve a puck and pass it to a teammate to start a rush up ice.

The innovations helped Plante become one of the game's most effective goaltenders. He won five consecutive Vezina Trophies as the league's best goalie, and seven in all (1956–60, '62, '69). In 1962, he also won the Hart Trophy as the league's Most Valuable Player, posting a 42-14-14 record with a 2.37 goals-against average. He had three seasons with at least 40 wins. Through the 1999 season, his 434 career wins ranked third all-time.

Plante was traded from Montreal to the New York Rangers in 1963. He joined the expansion St. Louis Blues in 1967 and also played with Toronto and Boston, before retiring in 1973.

In 17 seasons, Plante had a .614 winning percentage and a 2.38 goals-against average. Through the 1999 season, he ranked fourth all-time in shutouts (82).

In 112 playoff games, he had a .657 winning percentage and a 2.17 goals-against average. He recorded 14 shutouts. Through the 2000 season, he ranked seventh all-time in wins (71), tied for first in shutouts (15), and was seventh in goals-against average (2.16).

A seven-time All-Star, Plante was inducted into the Hockey Hall of Fame in 1978 and was voted No. 13 on the list of the NHL's Top 100 Players of All Time by *The Hockey News.*

Potvin, Denis

Born: October 29, 1953 in Ottawa, Ontario, Canada

Drafted first overall by the New York Islanders in 1973, Denis Potvin was the cornerstone of the team that won four consecutive Stanley Cups (1980–83), only the third team in NHL history to do so.

He was a defenseman who possessed offensive skills, along with a rugged approach to the game. He was the triggerman on the Islanders power play and a devastating checker.

Potvin scored at least 20 goals nine times—tying Boston's Ray Bourque—and scored at least 30 three times, something only seven defensemen have accomplished. In his rookie year (1973–74), Potvin scored 54 points and won the Calder Trophy as the league's Rookie of the Year. He won the Norris Trophy as the league's best defenseman in 1976, '78, and '79.

Potvin had his best season in 1978–79, scoring 101 points. He retired in 1988 as the NHL's all-time leader among defensemen in goals, assists, and points, records since broken by Bourque and Paul Coffey.

A seven-time All-Star, Potvin scored 1,052 points on 310 goals and 742 assists in 15 seasons, all with the Islanders. In 185 playoff games, he scored 164 points on 56 goals and 108 assists. Through the 2000 season, he ranked 11th all-time in points and 12th in assists. He was inducted into the Hockey Hall of Fame in 1991 and was voted No. 19 on the list of the NHL's Top 100 Players of All Time by *The Hockey News.*

Primeau, Joe

Born: January 24, 1906 in Lindsay, Ontario, Canada
Died: May 14, 1989

Joe Primeau was the center on the famous "Kid Line" of the Toronto Maple Leafs, along with Harvey "Busher" Jackson and Charlie Conacher.

In 1932, Primeau recorded 37 assists, a record that would stand for eight years. In 1932, he won the Lady Byng Trophy for sportsmanship and helped the Maple Leafs to the Stanley Cup.

In nine seasons, Primeau scored 243 points on 66 goals and 177 assists. In 38 playoff games, he scored 23 points on five goals and 18 assists. He was inducted into the Hockey Hall of Fame in 1963 and was voted No. 92 on the list of the NHL's Top 100 Players of All Time by *The Hockey News.*

Ratelle, Jean

Born: October 3, 1940 in Lac St. Jean, Quebec, Canada

Jean Ratelle was a prolific scorer and one of the cleanest players of his era. He spent 13 of his 20 NHL seasons with the New York Rangers, where he centered the "Gag Line" of Rod Gilbert and Vic Hadfield. He also played for the Boston Bruins.

Ratelle, who played in 1,300 games, collected only 276 penalty minutes. He twice won the Lady Byng Trophy for sportsmanship (1972, '76), and he also won the Masterson Trophy (1971) for exemplifying the qualities of perseverance, sportsmanship, and dedication to hockey.

Ratelle scored 1,267 points on 491 goals and 776 assists. Through the 1999 season, he ranked 21st all-time in points and 29th in goals. In 123 playoff games, he had 98 points on 32 goals and 66 assists. He was inducted into the Hockey Hall of Fame in 1985.

Richard, Henri
Born: February 29, 1936 in Montreal, Quebec, Canada

Henri Richard, nicknamed the "Pocket Rocket" because at 5-7, 160 pounds he was smaller than his more famous brother, Maurice "The Rocket" Richard, was a fine all-around player. He was blessed with stamina, toughness, speed, cleverness, and superb stick-handling and passing skills.

He also was a winner: In 11 of Richard's 20 seasons, all spent with Montreal, the Canadiens won the Stanley Cup.

Richard, a center, joined the Canadiens in 1955 and scored 1,046 points on 358 goals and 688 assists. In 180 playoff games, he scored 129 points on 49 goals and 80 assists. He won the Masterson Trophy in 1974 for exemplifying the qualities of perseverance, sportsmanship, and dedication to hockey.

A three-time All-Star, Richard was inducted into the Hockey Hall of Fame in 1979 and was voted No. 29 on the list of the NHL's Top 100 Players of All Time by *The Hockey News*.

Richard, Maurice
Born: August 4, 1921 in Montreal, Quebec, Canada
Died: May 27, 2000

Maurice "The Rocket" Richard was one of the fastest skaters and most accomplished goal scorers in the history of the National Hockey League. He was blessed with strength, a quick first step, and an effective backhand shot. He was a rarity in that he was a left-handed-shooting right winger, which allowed him to cut into the middle from the right side and shoot at a better angle.

Richard, prone to injuries as a junior, joined the Canadiens for the 1942–43 season, but played in only 16 games before being sidelined with a broken ankle. When he returned the following season, he joined Elmer Lach and Toe Blake to form the famous "Punch Line." Richard scored 32 goals that season, which was a prelude to the future. During the 1944–45 season, Richard scored 50 goals in a 50-game season. He played 18 seasons, all for the Canadiens, and finished among the top five goal-scorers 15 times. Richard was also famous for his feistiness. In 1955, NHL president Clarence Campbell suspended Richard for the rest of the regular season and the playoffs for hitting an official. The punishment caused the "Richard Riot" at the Montreal Forum. Fans caused more than $100,000 in damage in downtown Montreal.

Richard helped the Canadiens to eight Stanley Cup championships (1944, '46, '53, '56–60). He was known as a player who came through in the clutch, scoring 83 game-winning goals and 28 game-tying goals during his career. In the playoffs, he had 18 game-winners.

A nine-time All-Star and winner of the 1947 Hart Trophy as the league's Most Valuable Player, Richard scored 965 points on 544 goals and 421 assists. In 133 playoff games, he had 126 points on 82 goals and 44 assists. He retired in 1960, was inducted into the Hockey Hall of Fame in 1961, and was voted No. 5 on the list of the NHL's Top 100 Players of All Time by *The Hockey News*.

Said Campbell: "We all have a lesson to learn from this man. . . what he has accomplished through complete and utter dedication to his work. Never. . . have I met a man with such singleness of purpose and so completely devoted to his profession."

Robinson, Larry
Born: June 2, 1951 in Winchester, Ontario, Canada

Larry Robinson, a rugged defenseman who spent the bulk of his career with the Montreal Canadiens, provided a physical presence and the ability to take control of almost any situation.

He joined the Canadiens in the 1972–73 season and was on the first of six Stanley Cup–winning teams (1973, '76–79, '86). Robinson's streak of 20 consecutive playoff appearances is an NHL record.

Robinson won the Norris Trophy as the league's best defenseman twice (1977, '80), and he was the Conn Smythe Trophy winner as Most Valuable Player in the playoffs in 1978.

In 1991–92, Robinson finished his career with the Los Angeles Kings. He was an assistant coach with the New Jersey Devils and became the head coach of the Kings in 1995. He joined the New Jersey Devils as an assistant coach and was elevated to head coach in March 2000, leading them to the Stanley Cup.

In 20 seasons, Robinson, a six-time All-Star, scored 958 points on 208 goals and 750 assists. In 227 playoff games, he scored 144 points on 28 goals and 116 assists. Through the 2000 season, he ranked 22nd all-time in playoff points and eighth all-time in assists.

He was inducted into the Hockey Hall of Fame in 1995 and was voted No. 24 on the list of the NHL's Top 100 Players of All Time by *The Hockey News*.

Roy, Patrick
Born: October 5, 1965 in Quebec City, Quebec, Canada

Patrick Roy, one of most talented goalies of all time, is at his best when the stakes are the highest. Known for his competitiveness on the ice and his engaging personality off it, Roy has been a favorite of fans and the media.

He spent the first 11-plus seasons of his career with the Montreal Canadiens. He led the league in goals-against average in 1989 (2.47) and 1992 (2.36). He won the Vezina Trophy for allowing the fewest goals in 1989, 1990, and 1992.

Roy (pronounced Wah) helped the Canadiens win the Stanley Cup in 1986 and 1993. He won the Conn Smythe Trophy each time as Most Valuable Player in the playoffs. In 1986, he posted a 1.92 goals-against average in the playoffs, and in 1993, he won 10 consecutive overtime playoff games, recording more than 90 minutes of scoreless play in sudden death.

In December 1995, he was traded to the Colorado Avalanche, where he continued to excel. His goals-against average was less than 2.35 in each of his four full seasons (1997–2000), and in 1996 he helped the Avalanche to the Stanley Cup championship.

Roy entered the 2001 season with 444 wins, second all-time and just four shy of surpassing Terry Sawchuk as the all-time winningest goalie in the NHL. His regular season record, through the 2000 season, was 444-264-103 with 48 shutouts and a 2.63 goals-against average.

In Stanley Cup play, Roy's record was 121-73 with 15 shutouts and a 2.47 goals-against average.

Salming, Borje

Born: April 17, 1951 in Kiruna, Sweden

Borje Salming was the first European player to star in the NHL. He endured the actions of goons and racist comments to become one of the finest defensemen of his era. His success paved the way for other European players to join the NHL.

Salming, who had an outstanding junior career, made a name for himself at the 1972 and 1973 World Championships. Following the 1972–73 season, he was named the outstanding player in Sweden. It was about this time that Salming was noticed by a Toronto scout, who signed him before the start of the 1973–74 season.

Salming was a fine skater and passer, and had a hard shot. He played 16 years for the Maple Leafs and topped the 70-point mark four times. Twice he was runner-up for the Norris Trophy, which goes to the league's best defenseman.

A six-time All-Star, Salming scored 787 points on 150 goals and 637 assists in 17 seasons, the last of which was spent with Detroit. His 768 points with the Leafs are third on the team's all-time list. In 81 playoff games, he scored 49 points on 12 goals and 37 assists. He was inducted into the Hockey Hall of Fame in 1996 and was voted No. 74 on the list of the NHL's Top 100 Players of All Time by *The Hockey News*.

Savard, Serge

Born: January 22, 1946 in Montreal, Quebec, Canada

Serge Savard was a stalwart defenseman who spent 15 seasons with the Montreal Canadiens and one with the Winnipeg Jets. He was the first defenseman ever to win the Conn Smythe Trophy as Most Valuable Player in the playoffs (1969).

Savard helped the Canadiens to eight Stanley Cup championships (1966, '68–69, '71, '73, '76–79). His career nearly ended when he broke his leg during the 1969–70 season and then rebroke it the following year.

He retired in 1981, but was convinced to join the Jets, which had failed to make the playoffs in their first two NHL seasons. Savard led the Jets to an 80-point season, 48 more than the previous year, and a berth in the playoffs.

In 17 seasons, he scored 439 points on 106 goals and 333 assists. In 130 playoff games, he scored 68 points on 19 goals and 49 assists. He won the Masterson Trophy for sportsmanship in 1979 and was voted No. 81 on the list of the NHL's Top 100 Players of All Time by *The Hockey News*.

Sawchuk, Terry

Born: December 28, 1929 in Winnipeg, Manitoba, Canada

Died: May 31, 1970

Terry Sawchuk is the standard by which National Hockey League goaltenders are measured. He played more seasons, more games, and had more shutouts than any other goalie in league history.

He began playing goalie at age 10, after his brother, Mike, also a goalie, died at age 17 of a heart ailment. Sawchuk joined the Detroit Red Wings in 1950 and won the Calder Trophy as Rookie of the Year in 1951. He was the first player to be named Rookie of the Year in three leagues—the U.S. Hockey League, the American Hockey League, and the NHL.

Sawchuk, who crouched low in the goal in order to better see the puck, had a goals-against average of less than 2.00 during his first five seasons. In 1952, when the Red Wings won the Stanley Cup, he had four playoff shutouts and gave up only five goals in eight games.

Sawchuk played for three other Stanley Cup championship teams—Detroit (1952, '54) and Toronto ('64). He won the Vezina Trophy as the league's outstanding goalie four times (1952–53, '55, '65).

Sawchuk, who suffered numerous injuries throughout his career, was despondent following the 1969–70 season with the New York Rangers, largely because of his inability to repair his marriage. At his home in Mineola, N.Y., Sawchuk picked a fight with teammate Ron Stewart. The two fell over a barbecue pit, and Sawchuk suffered internal injuries. He appeared to be on the road to recovery, but his liver had been damaged during surgery, and a blood clot eventually killed him at age 40.

In 20 seasons, Sawchuk had a .562 winning percentage, a 2.52 goals-against average, and a record 103 shutouts. Through the 2000 season, he was ranked first in wins (447) and shutouts (103).

In 106 playoff games, he had a .529 winning percentage, a 2.54 goals-against average, and 12 shutouts. He was ranked 11th in playoff wins (54) and fifth in shutouts (12).

A seven-time All-Star, he was inducted into the Hockey Hall of Fame in 1971 and was voted No. 9 on the list of the NHL's Top 100 Players of All Time by *The Hockey News*.

Schmidt, Milt

Born: March 5, 1918 in Kitchener, Ontario, Canada

Milt Schmidt, a center for the Boston Bruins, was considered the best two-way player in the National Hockey League in the late 1940s. He was fast, a strong skater, and a clever stick-handler who never gave up the puck without a fight.

Schmidt, a center, joined the Boston Bruins in 1936. In 1940, he helped the Bruins to the Stanley Cup championship, the same year he won the Ross Trophy as the league's leading scorer (52 points on 20 goals, 32 assists).

In 1942, Schmidt and his linemates on the famous "Kraut Line," Woody Dumart and Bobby Bauer, enlisted in the Royal Canadian Air Force. They returned to the team three years later.

Schmidt had his best offensive seasons after the war—62 points in 1946–47, 61 points in 1950–51, when he also won the Hart Trophy as the league's Most Valuable Player.

Schmidt retired in 1955 and coached the Bruins for the next seven years. From 1967 through 1972, he was the team's general manager.

In 16 seasons, all with Boston, Schmidt scored 575 points on 229 goals and 346 assists. In 86 playoff games, he scored 49 points on 24 goals and 25 assists. A four-time All-Star, he was inducted into the Hockey Hall of Fame in 1961 and was voted No. 27 on the list of the NHL's Top 100 Players of All Time by *The Hockey News*.

Schriner, Sweeney (David)

Born: November 30, 1911 in Saratov, Russia

Died: July 4, 1990

Sweeney Schriner was the first Russian-born player to play in the National Hockey League. He won the 1935 Calder Trophy as Rookie of the Year. He also won the Ross Trophy twice—in 1936 and 1937—as the league's leading scorer.

Schriner, a left wing, helped the Toronto Maple Leafs to two Stanley Cup championships (1942, '45). A three-time All-Star, he scored 405 points on 201 goals and 204 assists in 11 seasons. In 59 playoff games, he scored 29 points on 18 goals and 11 assists. He was inducted into the Hockey Hall of Fame in 1962 and was voted No. 91 on the list of the NHL's Top 100 Players of All Time by *The Hockey News*.

Shore, Eddie

Born: November 25, 1902 in Ft. Qu'Appelle, Saskatchewan, Canada

Died: March 16, 1985

It was once said of Eddie Shore that every time he had the puck, one of three things would happen—a goal, an assist, or a fight. He was one of the NHL's all-time great defensemen, a combination of offensive skill and defensive toughness.

Shore, who joined the Boston Bruins in 1929, skated in an unusual crouch that made it almost impossible to knock him down. But *he* had no problem knocking players down. He was a frequent fighter, who collected 1,047 penalty minutes in his 14-year career and a long list of injuries. He had 978 stitches, 80 cuts, a fractured back, a fractured hip, and a broken collarbone. His nose was broken 14 times, and his jaw was fractured five times. His left ear was almost torn off in a fight and both eyeballs were split.

Shore's most infamous incident came in 1933, when he flipped Toronto's Ace Bailey into the air. Bailey landed on his head, suffered a fractured skull, and nearly died.

Shore won the Hart Trophy as the league's Most Valuable Player four times (1933, '35, '36, '38). Only Gordie Howe and Wayne Gretzky have won it more times.

Shore retired in 1940 with 284 points on 105 goals and 179 assists. In 55 playoff games, he scored 19 points on six goals and 13 assists. Shore was inducted into the Hockey Hall of Fame in 1947 and was voted No. 10 on the list of the NHL's Top 100 Players of All Time by *The Hockey News*.

Sittler, Darryl

Born: September 18, 1950 in Kitchener, Ontario, Canada

Darryl Sittler, a center, led the Toronto Maple Leafs in scoring from 1973 through 1980. He scored the game-winning goal in the 1976 Canada Cup. He also scored 10 points in one game against the Boston Bruins during the 1975–76 season and five goals in a playoff game against the Philadelphia Flyers.

Sittler was traded to Philadelphia in 1981 and ended his career in Detroit in 1985. In 15 seasons, Sittler scored

1,121 points on 484 goals and 637 assists. In 76 playoff games, he scored 74 points on 29 goals and 45 assists. He was inducted into the Hockey Hall of Fame in 1989 and was voted No. 93 on the list of the NHL's Top 100 Players of All Time by *The Hockey News*.

Smith, Billy

Born: December 12, 1950 in Perth, Ontario, Canada

Billy Smith was one of the greatest playoff goalies in National Hockey League history. He joined the New York Islanders in the 1972 expansion draft and became a force in goal when the team won four straight Stanley Cup championships (1980–83). Smith won the 1982 Vezina Trophy as the league's best goaltender and the 1983 Conn Smythe Trophy as Most Valuable Player in the playoffs.

In 18 seasons, Smith had a winning percentage of .556 and a goals-against average of 3.17. Through the 2000 season, he ranked 15th all-time in wins (305). He had 22 shutouts. In 132 playoff games, he had a winning percentage of .710 and a goals-against average of 2.73, with five shutouts. He ranked third all-time in playoff wins (88) and tied for fourth in games played (132).

Smith was inducted into the Hockey Hall of Fame in 1993 and was voted No. 80 on the list of the NHL's Top 100 Players of All Time by *The Hockey News*.

Stasny, Peter

Born: September 18, 1956 in Bratislava, Czechoslovakia (now the Czech Republic)

Peter Stasny joined the Quebec Nordiques in 1980 and became the cornerstone of the franchise. He topped the 100-point mark in each of his first six seasons, and only Wayne Gretzky scored more points in the 1980s.

A five-time All-Star center, Stasny scored 1,239 points on 450 goals and 789 assists in 15 seasons. Through the 2000 season, he ranked 23rd all-time in points. In 93 playoff games, he scored 105 points on 33 goals and 72 assists. He retired in 1995, was inducted into the Hockey Hall of Fame in 1998, and was voted No. 56 on the list of the NHL's Top 100 Players of All Time by *The Hockey News*.

Stewart, Nels

Born: December 29, 1902 in Montreal, Quebec, Canada

Died: August 21, 1952

Nels Stewart, nicknamed "Old Poison," was the first NHL player to score more than 300 career goals. He joined the Montreal Maroons in 1926 and helped the team to the Stanley Cup championship in his rookie season, winning the Hart Trophy as Most Valuable Player

and the Ross Trophy as the scoring leader. He scored 34 goals in 36 games. He also won the Hart Trophy in 1930.

Stewart, a center, retired in 1940. In 15 seasons, he scored 515 points on 324 goals and 191 assists. In 54 playoff games, he scored 28 points on 15 goals and 13 assists. He was inducted into the Hockey Hall of Fame in 1962 and was voted No. 51 on the list of the NHL's Top 100 Players of All Time by *The Hockey News*.

Trottier, Bryan

Born: July 17, 1956 in Val Marie, Saskatchewan, Canada

Bryan Trottier was one of the most accomplished centers of his era, combining offensive skill with superior defense and leadership.

Said Gordie Howe: "Bryan could play with any man on any team in any era. When there's a loose puck, he's always there to get it."

He joined the New York Islanders for the 1975–76 season and won the Calder Trophy as the league's Rookie of the Year, scoring 95 points on 32 goals and 63 assists. In 1977–78, he led the league with 77 assists. The following year, Trottier scored 134 points on 47 goals and 87 assists. He won the Ross Trophy as the league's leading scorer and the Hart Trophy as Most Valuable Player.

In 1980, the Islanders won the first of their four straight Stanley Cup championships. During that stretch, Trottier topped the 100-point mark three times. He won the 1980 Conn Smythe Trophy as Most Valuable Player in the playoffs, scoring 29 points, a record at the time. He also scored 29 points in each of the next two playoffs.

In July 1990, the Pittsburgh Penguins signed Trottier, and he helped them win the Stanley Cup in 1991 and 1992. He retired in 1994.

In 18 seasons, he scored 1,425 points on 524 goals and 901 assists. Through the 2000 season, he ranked 12th all-time in points, 22nd in goals, and 11th in assists.

In 221 playoff games, he scored 184 points on 71 goals and 113 assists. He ranked sixth all-time in points, 12th in goals, 10th in assists, and fourth in games played. A four-time All-Star, he was inducted into the Hockey Hall of Fame in 1997 and was voted No. 30 on the list of the NHL's Top 100 Players of All Time by *The Hockey News*.

Ullman, Norm

Born: December 26, 1935 in Provost, Alberta, Canada

Norm Ullman was one of the highest-scoring centers of his time, as well as one of the game's best forecheckers. He joined the Detroit Red Wings in 1955 and scored at least 20 or more goals for 12 straight seasons. In 1967, he was traded to the Toronto Maple Leafs. He spent two seasons in the World Hockey Association, before retiring in 1977.

In 20 NHL seasons, he scored 1,229 points on 490 goals and 739 assists. In 106 playoff games, he scored 83 points on 30 goals and 53 assists. A two-time All-Star, Ullman was inducted into the Hockey Hall of Fame in 1982 and was voted No. 90 on the list of the NHL's Top 100 Players of All Time by *The Hockey News*.

Vezina, Georges

Born: January 7, 1888 in Chicoutimi, Quebec, Canada

Died: March 26, 1926

Georges Vezina, cool under pressure, was nicknamed the "Chicoutimi Cucumber." He played during a time when National Hockey League rules prohibited goalies dropping to their knees to stop the puck, but he still allowed just over three goals a game.

Vezina was also durable, never missing a game. He played in 328 straight regular season games and 39 playoff games. He led the Montreal Canadiens to two Stanley Cup championships (1916, '24).

In 1925, he started the opener against Pittsburgh, despite severe chest pains. He left the ice after the first period and never returned. Vezina died four months later of tuberculosis at age 38.

A year later, the league honored his memory with the creation of the Vezina Trophy, presented to the goaltender(s) on the team that allowed the fewest goals.

In nine seasons, Vezina had a .561 winning percentage and a 3.28 goals-against average. In 26 playoff games, he had a .680 winning percentage and a 2.78 goals-against average. He was inducted into the Hockey Hall of Fame in 1945 and was voted No. 75 on the list of the NHL's Top 100 Players of All Time by *The Hockey News*.

Yzerman, Steve

Born: May 9, 1965 in Cranbrook, British Columbia, Canada

At just 5-11 and 185 pounds, Steve Yzerman isn't an imposing figure, but the impact he has made on the National Hockey League during his career has been major.

Yzerman joined the Detroit Red Wings in 1983 and finished second in voting for the Calder Trophy, awarded to the Rookie of the Year. He had 30 goals and 59 assists for 80 points.

Yzerman, a center, scored 40 or more goals in a season six times and 100 or more points six times. He has led the Red Wings in points 12 times and goals and assists 10 times.

In 1989, he had 62 goals and 65 assists for 127 points. He was named the winner of the Lester B. Pearson Award, voted on by the NHL Players' Association, as the outstanding player of the year. His best year came in 1993, when he had 58 goals and 79 assists for 137 points. Yzerman has led the Red Wings to Stanley Cup championships in 1997 and 1998. He won the Conn Smythe Trophy as Most Valuable Player in the 1998 playoffs.

Through the 2000 season, Yzerman had 627 goals and 935 assists for 1,562 points. In the playoffs, he has 61 goals and 91 assists for 152 points. He ranked seventh all-time in points, eighth in assists, and sixth in goals in the regular season. In the playoffs, he ranked 16th all-time in points.

Olympians

Albright, Tenley

figure skating

Born: July 18, 1935 in Newton Center, Massachusetts

Tenley Albright was a success on and off the ice. She realized both of her childhood dreams—to become a surgeon and to win an Olympic gold medal.

Albright got her first pair of skates when she was seven years old, and she persuaded her father to flood their backyard. She joined a skating club the next year.

When Albright was 11, she was stricken with poliomyelitis, also known as infantile paralysis. One day she could walk, the next day she could not. She made a rapid recovery, winning the Eastern U.S. Junior Ladies championship four months later.

Albright won the first of her five straight U.S. championships in 1952, the same year she won a silver medal at the Olympic Games. In 1953, she became the first American woman to win the world championship. She also won the world title in 1955.

Albright entered Radcliffe College as a pre-med student in 1953 and still managed to skate full time, practicing from 4 to 6 A.M. She left school in 1956 in order to train for the Olympics and to fend off a challenge from Carol Heiss, another U.S. skater. During a practice session less than two weeks before the Olympics, Albright fell, her left skate cutting into her right ankle. She slashed a vein and scraped a bone. Despite the injury, Albright won the gold medal, becoming the first American woman ever to do so. Two weeks later, the ankle still bothering her, Albright finished second to Heiss at the world championships. Albright won the U.S. championship in 1956, then retired. She returned to Radcliffe, graduating in just three years, and graduated from Harvard Medical School, one of only six women in a class of 130.

Ashford, Evelyn

track and field

Born: April 15, 1957 in Shreveport, Louisiana

Evelyn Ashford was one of the great female sprinters of all time. Her excellence spanned five Olympic Games and three different decades.

Ashford began running in high school after the football coach at her Roseville, Calif., high school challenged her to race some of his players. The coach had seen her run in phys. ed. class. She beat the fastest player on the team and won the rest of the races she ran.

In 1975, Ashford was one of the first women to be awarded an athletic scholarship to UCLA. At the 1976 Olympics, she finished fifth in the 100-meter dash. In 1977 and 1978, Ashford won four Association of Intercollegiate Athletics for Women (AIAW) national championships. She left school in 1978 to train full time for the 1980 Olympics, held in Moscow, which never materialized for U.S. athletes because of the boycott of the Games.

Ashford had to wait until the 1984 Olympics in Los Angeles to realize her dream of a gold medal. Because of a nagging hamstring injury, she withdrew from the 200 meters and concentrated on the 100 meters. She won the gold in the 100, running an Olympic record 10.97 and beating Heike Drechsler of East Germany. Ashford was also a member of the gold medal–winning 4 x 100-meter relay team.

In 1986, Ashford gave birth to a daughter, but returned to competition shortly thereafter. She earned a spot on the 1988 U.S. Olympic team and despite running against younger women, won a silver medal in the 100 meters and ran the anchor leg for the gold medal–winning 4 x 100-meter relay.

Ashford was 35 years old by the time the 1992 Olympics were held, but she qualified as a sprinter and a member of the relay team. She won her fourth gold medal in the 4 x 100-meter relay. She was the oldest American woman ever to win an Olympic medal.

Ashford was inducted into the International Women's Sports Hall of Fame and the National Track and Field Hall Fame in 1997.

Babashoff, Shirley

swimming

Born: January 31, 1957 in Whittier, California

Shirley Babashoff won more Olympic medals (eight) than any other U.S. woman in history, but it's what she failed to win—an individual gold medal—that is also remembered. However, that shortcoming should be accompanied by an asterisk, because in the 1976 Olympics she finished behind East German swimmers, who later admitted they had taken anabolic steroids.

At the 1972 Olympics, Babashoff lowered her world record in the 200-meter freestyle by nearly a second, but finished second to Australia's Shane Gould. She also won a silver medal in the 100-meter freestyle and a gold medal in the 400-meter freestyle relay.

At the 1976 Olympic Trials, Babashoff won the 100-, 200-, 400-, and 800-meter freestyle events and the 400-meter individual medley, breaking six U.S. records and one world record in the process. She entered the Olympics as the favorite in four freestyle events, but won silver medals, each time losing to an East German. Again, she won a gold as a member of the 400-meter freestyle relay.

Babashoff won 27 national championships, set six individual world records, and was on five world-record-setting relay teams.

Of Babashoff's 13 Olympic and world championship silver medals, 10 came behind East Germans. When Babashoff went public with her accusations about the East Germans' drug use, she was labeled a sore loser and nicknamed "Surly Shirley." When her suspicions were proven true, she asked, "What is the statute of limitations on cheating?"

Babashoff was inducted into the International Swimming Hall of Fame in 1982 and the U.S. Olympic Hall of Fame in 1987.

Bannister, Roger

track and field

Born: March 23, 1929 in Harrow, Middlesex, England

Roger Bannister was the first man to run the mile in less than four minutes (3:59.4), on May 4, 1954. Prior to Bannister's breaking the barrier, a sub-four-minute mile was considered physically impossible.

Bannister, a 25-year-old medical student at Oxford University, was not running in an actual race, but rather, was paced by two rabbits (fast runners used to set a fast pace). His quarter-mile splits were 57.5 seconds, 60.7 seconds, 62.3 seconds, and 58.9 seconds. Complicating Bannister's attempt was a 15 mph crosswind encountered during the race with gusts as high as 25 mph.

In 1954, Bannister was named *Sports Illustrated* first Sportsman of the Year, and *Runner's World* magazine selected his accomplishment as the single greatest running moment of the 20th century.

In addition to the record in the mile, he was also the British mile champion in 1951, 1953, and 1954. He was a finalist in the 1,500 meters in the 1952 Olympics.

Bannister retired from competition after he completed medical school in December 1954. He practiced neurological medicine. He was knighted in 1975.

Beamon, Bob

track and field

Born: August 29, 1946 in Jamaica, New York

It took Bob Beamon just one jump to make history and ensure his legend forever. He entered the 1968 Olympics as a favorite to win a medal, but also with the reputation for lacking discipline. He didn't even have a coach because he was suspended from Texas-El Paso University for refusing to compete against Brigham Young University, because of the racial policies of the Mormon church.

Beamon was being helped by Ralph Boston, who won long jump medals at three consecutive Olympics. After Beamon fouled on his first two attempts in the preliminaries, Boston reminded him that he could take off well before the board and still qualify for the finals, which he did.

As he prepared for his first jump in the finals, Beamon told himself, "Don't foul." He hit the mark perfectly, soared through the air, and landed with such momentum that he ended up out of the back of the pit.

The world record was 27 feet, 4 3/4 inches. Beamon jumped 29 feet, 2 1/2 inches. The previous world record had been improved upon by only 8 1/2 inches in 33 years. Beamon extended it by nearly two feet in one jump.

"Compared to this jump, we are as children," said Igor Ter-Ovanesyan, a long jumper from the Soviet Union.

Beamon never came close to approaching his record jump again. In fact, he failed to surpass 27 feet for the rest of his career. He won his second straight Amateur Athletic Union (AAU) championship in 1969, but competed sporadically thereafter. He tried a comeback in 1972, but he failed to make the Olympic team.

Beamon's record stood until 1991, when it was broken by Mike Powell, who jumped 29 feet, 4 1/2 inches.

Beamon was inducted into the U.S. Olympic Hall of Fame in 1983.

Benoit Samuelson, Joan
marathon
Born: May 16, 1957 in Cape Elizabeth, Maine

Joan Benoit Samuelson was one of the great women's marathoners. As a child growing up in Maine, she enjoyed skiing, but when she suffered a broken leg during a slalom race in high school and began running as part of her rehabilitation, she fell in love with running.

In high school, she was an outstanding middle- and long-distance runner, even though at the time, women were not encouraged to be athletes. Benoit Samuelson has said that at times she was so embarrassed to be a runner that when cars passed, she would stop and pretend she was looking at flowers.

She continued to excel at Bowdoin College in Maine. In 1979, she decided to enter the Boston Marathon. Caught in traffic on the way to her first marathon, Benoit Samuelson hopped out of the car and ran about two miles through the woods to get to the race. She entered as an unknown, but finished as the winner, and in record time (2 hours, 35 minutes, 15 seconds).

Benoit Samuelson, the shy, retiring type, was suddenly in demand as a celebrity. She was invited to make appearances and endorse products. She disliked the publicity, almost enough to give up running.

In 1981, she nearly gave up running for health reasons. She suffered from chronic heel pain and underwent surgery on both Achilles tendons. In Benoit Samuelson's first marathon after surgery, in 1982, she broke the women's American record (2:26:11). In the 1983 Boston Marathon, she finished in 2:22:42, eclipsing the world record by nearly three minutes. She also set American records in 1983 in the 10-kilometer, half-marathon, 10-mile, and 25-kilometer runs.

Benoit Samuelson's greatest fame came at the 1984 Olympic Games in Los Angeles. It was the first time the women's marathon was a sanctioned Olympic event, and she trained diligently for the race. But in March 1984, she suffered a knee injury that required two surgeries, the second of which was completed April 25, 17 days before the Olympic Trials.

Benoit Samuelson not only competed at the trials, she won. At the Olympic marathon, Benoit Samuelson, bothered by the slow pace at the start, took the lead at the three-mile mark. The other competitors, most notably the favorite, Grete Waitz, assumed Benoit Samuelson went out too fast and would soon be forced to slow down because of her injured knee. But Benoit Samuelson kept increasing her lead. Halfway through the race, she led by 90 seconds, and deeper into the race she led by as much as two minutes. She won in 2:24.52.

In the 1985 Chicago Marathon, she set an American record (2:21.21) and was named the winner of the Sullivan Award as the nation's outstanding amateur athlete. In 1987, she ran the Boston Marathon while three months pregnant.

Biondi, Matt
swimming
Born: October 8, 1965 in Moraga, California

Matt Biondi was one of the most accomplished Olympic athletes ever, in any sport. His 11 Olympic medals tie him with Mark Spitz for the most career medals by an American athlete.

Biondi, 6 feet, 6 inches, and 200 pounds, was considered big for a swimmer, but his size and powerful strokes were a boost to his stamina. He won his first gold medal swimming the 400-meter freestyle relay team at age 18 at the 1984 Olympics. In 1987, he won the NCAA 100- and 200-yard freestyle championships, and in 1988, six weeks before the Olympics, he set a world record in the 100-meter freestyle (48.42) that stood for nine years. He has held the American record in the 100- and 200-meter freestyle since 1985.

At the 1988 Games, Biondi became a household name. He won a record-tying seven medals, including five golds. He took gold in the 50- and 100-meter freestyle and as a member of the 400- and 800-meter freestyle and the 400-meter medley relay teams. He won a silver in the 100-meter butterfly and a bronze in the 200-meter freestyle.

At the 1992 Olympics, Biondi won his eighth career gold medal as a member of the 400-meter freestyle relay team. He also won a silver in the 50-meter freestyle. Biondi joined Tom Jager as the only U.S. swimmer to win gold medals at three different Olympics.

Biondi, who retired after the 1992 Games, set 12 world records, won 17 U.S. championships, and won 13 NCAA championships. He was named World Swimmer of the Year in 1986 and 1988, and was inducted into the International Swimming Hall of Fame in 1997.

Blair, Bonnie
speed skating
Born: March 18, 1964 in Cornwall, New York

Bonnie Blair is one of the most decorated Olympic athletes of all time, with five gold medals and one bronze medal.

Blair was born into a skating family. She began entering races when she was four years old and won her first major speed skating race, the Illinois state championship, when she was seven.

Blair got her first taste of the Olympics in 1980, when she competed in a qualifying race for the Olympic Trials. She failed to make the team, but she set her sights on the 1984 Games in Sarajevo, Yugoslavia.

Blair made the U.S. Olympic team and finished eighth in the 500 meters. It was a respectable first effort, but Blair returned to the United States determined to improve. So she embarked on a training program that included skating, weight training, running, biking, and roller skating. The hard work paid off. From 1985 through 1990, she was the U.S. sprint champion. In 1986, she set her first world record, in the 500 meters.

At the 1988 Olympics, Blair won a gold medal in the 500 meters and a bronze in the 1,000 meters. At the next two Olympics, in 1992 and 1994, she dominated like few athletes ever have. She won gold medals in the 500 meters and the 1,000 meters at each venue. In 1992, she won the Sullivan Award as the nation's outstanding amateur athlete.

In addition to her talent, Blair was tremendously popular with the fans and the media. She was viewed as an American hero because of her work ethic and her engaging personality.

Blair finished off her career by winning the 500 meters and the 1,000 meters in 1994 and 1995 at the World Cup and the world sprint championships.

The Women's Sports Foundation honored Blair as the Sportswoman of the Year in 1994 and 1995, and *Sports Illustrated* named her and Norwegian speed skater Johann Olav Koss as Sportsmen of the Year.

Blankers-Koen, Fanny (Francina)
track and field
Born: April 26, 1918 in Baarn, The Netherlands

Fanny Blankers-Koen was the first woman to win four gold medals at one Olympics, the 1948 Games in London. Her first Olympics came at age 18 in 1936 in Berlin, where she failed to medal, but she did come away with an autograph from the star of the 1936 Games, Jesse Owens.

The 1940 and 1944 Games were canceled due to World War II, which cost Blankers-Koen her prime years. Nevertheless, in 1948, at age 30, she made history. She won the 100-meter dash and the 80-meter hurdles, then considered returning home because the European tabloids criticized her for not being a model housewife and mother. But her coach, who was also her husband, Jack Blankers, convinced her to stay. She won gold medals in the 200 meters and the 4 x 100-meter relay.

Blankers-Koen might have won more medals in 1948—she held world records in the long jump and high jump and was the Dutch champion javelin thrower—but Olympic rules limited participants to three individual events.

Blankers-Koen was named the Associated Press Female Athlete of the Year in 1948, and the Dutch government named a rose, a gladiolus, and a candy bar after her. She was inducted into the International Women's Sports Hall of Fame in 1982.

Boitano, Brian
figure skating
Born: October 27, 1963 in Mountainview, California

Brian Boitano won four straight U.S. championships (1985–88), two world championships (1986, '88), and an Olympic gold medal (1988). Overall, he won 50 championships, including 23 international gold medals.

Boitano was one of the most powerful skaters of his time and one of the best jumpers. His 1988 Olympic gold medal came as a result of a head-to-head battle with Brian Orser of Canada. Boitano skated a flawless long program to win the gold medal.

Boitano turned professional in 1989 and won 16 professional titles. He starred in two television specials with Katerina Witt, two-time Olympic gold medalist. In 1994, Boitano was reinstated as an amateur and finished second to Scott Davis in the U.S. championships. At the 1994 Olympics, he finished sixth.

Boitano was inducted into the U.S. Figure Skating Hall of Fame in 1996.

Boston, Ralph
track and field
Born: May 9, 1939 in Laurel, Mississippi

Ralph Boston was the first track and field athlete to medal in the long jump in three consecutive Olympics (1960, '64, '68).

At the 1960 Games, Boston jumped 26 feet, 7 3/4 inches to win the gold and break Jesse Owens' Olympic record, set in 1936. Two weeks prior to the Olympics, Boston jumped 26-11 1/4 inches to break Owens' world record by three inches.

Boston set and broke his own world record several times in 1961, going as far as 27-2. After Igor Ter-Ovanesyan of the Soviet Union set the world record in 1962 at 27-3 1/2 inches, Boston tied it in August 1964 and broke it in September (27-4 3/4).

At the 1964 Olympic Games, Boston jumped into a strong headwind. He later advised Lynn Davies of Great Britain how to deal with the wind and the advice allowed Davies to upset Boston and win the gold. Boston took the silver.

Once again, at the 1968 Games, Boston gave a tip to Bob Beamon of the United States, suggesting he move his approach back a few inches. Beamon listened, jumped a world-record 29-2 1/2 inches, and won the gold. Boston won the bronze.

In addition to his Olympic record, Boston won the NCAA long jump title in 1960, the Amateur Athletic Union (AAU) outdoor championship from 1961 through 1966, and the AAU indoor championship in 1961.

He was inducted into the U.S. Track and Field Hall of Fame in 1975 and the U.S. Olympic Hall of Fame in 1985.

Bricso-Hooks, Valerie
track and field
Born: July 6, 1960 in Greenwood, Mississippi

Valerie Brisco-Hooks made history at the 1984 Olympics by becoming the first person to win the 200 meters and 400 meters in the same Games.

Brisco-Hooks, who grew up in the South Central section of Los Angeles, began running as a tribute to her brother, Robert, who was killed by a stray bullet. Valerie was determined to become a champion to honor her brother.

After an outstanding high school career, in which she was the top-ranked sprinter in California, Brisco-Hooks went to college at California State University at Northridge, coached by Bob Kersee. Kersee developed Brisco-Hooks to her full potential. She won the Association of Intercollegiate Athletics for Women (AIAW) 200-meter championship in 1979 and was a member of the gold medal-winning 4 x 100-meter relay team at the Pan-American Games.

In 1981 she married Alvin Hooks, a former college teammate who was a wide receiver with the Philadelphia Eagles at the time. Alvin Jr., their son, was born the following year.

Brisco-Hooks returned to the track in 1983, but needed to lose 40 pounds of postpregnancy weight. She followed a strict diet and a rigorous workout regimen to get herself back in shape. She lifted weights three times a week and did 250 pushups and 1,000 situps a day.

At the 1984 Games, Brisco-Hooks won the 200 and 400 meters, setting an American record in each event, and was a member of the 4 x 100-meter relay team that won the gold medal. She became the first female to win three gold medals at a single Olympics in a quarter-century.

At the 1988 Olympics, Brisco-Hooks won a silver medal as part of the 4 x 100-meter relay team. She was inducted into the U.S. Track and Field Hall of Fame in 1995.

Bubka, Sergei
track and field
Born: December 4, 1963 in Voroshilovgrad, Ukraine

In 1991, Sergei Bubka was the first pole-vaulter to clear 20 feet indoors and outdoors. He set the world indoor record of 20-2 on February 21, 1993, and the world outdoor record of 20-1 on September 20, 1992. Through September 2000, he held the world record in both events.

Bubka was a six-time world champion (1983, '87, '91, '93, '95, and '97) and the only athlete to win a gold medal in each of the six world championships held between 1983 and 1997. He won the gold medal at the 1988 Olympics in Seoul, South Korea, vaulting an Olympic-record 19-4 1/4, which has since been broken.

He failed to clear a height at the 1992 Games, and he withdrew from the 1996 Games with a partially torn Achilles tendon in his right foot.

Button, Dick
figure skating
Born: July 18, 1929 in Englewood, New Jersey

Dick Button has been a figure skating fixture for nearly a half-century—first as an outstanding skating champion and then as the voice of figure skating on ABC Sports.

Button began skating when he was 11 years old. He wanted a pair of figure skates for Christmas, but was disappointed when his father purchased hockey skates instead. The exchange was made and one of the great careers in the sport was born, although not immediately.

Because Button stood only 5 feet, 2 inches tall and weighed 160 pounds, his first teacher predicted he would never be a good skater. His parents took him to another teacher and Button blossomed. Five years later, in 1956, he won the first of his seven consecutive U.S. championships. He won five straight world championships (1948–52), and was the first American ever to win the world title.

In 1948, he became the first North American man to win an Olympic gold medal, and through the 1998 Winter Games he remained the youngest ever to win Olympic gold in figure skating (age 18). Button won the 1949 Sullivan Award as the nation's outstanding amateur athlete. Through 2000, he was the only figure skater to have won the Sullivan.

In 1952, Button, a senior at Harvard University, won his second Olympic gold medal as he became the first skater ever to perform a triple loop (three revolutions) in competition. Through the 1998 Games he was the only American to win two Olympic gold medals in figure skating.

Button was inducted into the U.S. Olympic Hall of Fame in 1983 and the U.S and World Figure Skating Halls of Fame in 1976.

Caulkins, Tracy

swimming

Born: January 11, 1963 in Winona, Minnesota

Tracy Caulkins made her mark on swimming, in the United States and internationally, as few others ever have. She won championships and set records in every stroke and then retired at age 21.

She began her career when she was eight years old, agreeing to join the neighborhood swim club and swim only backstroke so she wouldn't get her face wet.

Caulkins won five gold medals and one silver medal at the 1978 world championships in Berlin and became the youngest person ever to win the Sullivan Award as the nation's outstanding amateur athlete.

In 1980, Caulkins should have represented the United States in the Olympic Games, but the boycott of the Moscow Games kept her home.

Not being able to participate in the 1980 Olympics proved to be an incentive for Caulkins, who worked tirelessly over the next four years to realize her dream. She entered the University of Florida in 1981 and dominated college swimming. She was named the winner of the Broderick Cup in 1983 and 1984 as the nation's outstanding collegiate female athlete. In 1984, she set NCAA records in all of her individual events—200-meter individual medley (IM), 400 IM, 100-meter breaststroke, and 200-meter butterfly. She also helped her team set NCAA records in the 800-meter freestyle relay and the 400-meter freestyle relay.

Overall, Caulkins won 12 NCAA championships at Florida from 1982 through 1984.

To prepare for the 1984 Olympic Trials, Caulkins swam five hours a day, six days a week. At the Olympic Games in Los Angeles, she won the gold medal in the 200-meter IM (Olympic record 2:12.64) and the 400 IM. She also swam the breaststroke leg of the gold medal–winning 4 x 100 medley relay.

Caulkins set 63 U.S. records and five world records and won a record 48 individual national titles. She is the only swimmer, man or woman, to set American records in every stroke (freestyle, breaststroke, butterfly, backstroke). She was inducted into the International Swimming Hall of Fame in 1990.

Coe, Sebastian

track and field

Born: September 29, 1956 in London, England

Sebastian Coe, an outstanding middle distance runner, set eight outdoor and three indoor world records between 1979 and 1981.

In 1979, in the space of 41 days, he set world records in the 800 meters, the mile, and the 1,500 meters, making him the first man in more than 50 years to own the world record in the 800 and 1,500 meters. In July 1980, Coe added the world record in the 1,000 meters, meaning that for a brief time, he held world records at four distances.

At the 1980 Olympics in Moscow, Coe won the 1,500 meters and finished second in the 800 meters, each race a duel between Coe and Steve Ovett, his countryman.

Coe broke four more world records in 1981—the 800 meters, the 1,000 meters, and the mile twice. His time of 1:41.73 in the 800 meters stood for 16 years, before being broken by Wilson Kipketer of Denmark in 1997.

At the 1984 Olympics in Los Angeles, Coe won the 1,500 in an Olympic-record time of 3:32.53. He took a silver in the 800 meters.

Coe failed to make the British Olympic team in 1988, then retired from competition in 1989. In 1992, he was elected a Conservative member of Parliament.

Comaneci, Nadia

gymnastics

Born: November 12, 1961 in Onesti, Romania

Nadia Comaneci's performance at the 1976 Olympic Games in Montreal set a new standard for excellence. She won five medals and scored seven perfect 10s. She was the first gymnast ever to receive a perfect score in the Olympics. Comaneci won gold medals in the all-around competition, the balance beam, and the uneven bars. She won a bronze in floor exercise and a silver in the team competition.

She continued her mastery four years later at the 1980 Olympics in Moscow. Comaneci won gold medals on the balance beam and in floor exercise, and a silver in the team competition. She failed to win the all-around gold, although that decision has been widely regarded to have been politically motivated. Comaneci lost to Elena Davidova of the Soviet Union by less than .1 of a point.

Judges took 28 minutes to award Comaneci a 9.85 for what appeared to be a perfect routine on the balance beam.

In two Olympics, she won five gold medals, three silver, and one bronze. She was a hero in her homeland. Comaneci announced her retirement at age 19.

She worked as a coach in Romania, but was not happy living in a socialist country. So in 1989, she walked six hours to the Hungarian border and defected to the United States. Comaneci settled in Norman, Okla., where she began working with coach Paul Ziert. She began training and performed exhibitions with Bart Conner, a member of the U.S. gymnastics team and a pupil of Ziert's. Conner and Comaneci were engaged in 1994 and married two years later.

Conner, Bart
gymnastics
Born: March 28, 1958 in Chicago, Illinois
Bart Conner is the most decorated American male gymnast ever and counts among his numerous championships and honors two Olympic gold medals.

He was introduced to gymnastics when he was 10 years old because his parents thought it would be a good outlet for his abundance of energy.

In 1974, he won the U.S. Gymnastics Federation all-around championship, and in 1976, he enrolled at the University of Oklahoma and helped elevate the program to one of the best in the nation. In 1978, he won the NCAA all-around championship, and the Sooners won the team championship. In 1979, he tied for the title in floor exercise.

Conner became only the second American to win a gold medal in an international event when he won the pommel horse at the 1979 world championships. At the 1980 Olympic Trials, he was the high scorer, but didn't compete because of the United States boycott of the Games, held in Moscow.

Conner suffered a potentially career-threatening injury in 1983, when he tore his right biceps muscle. He missed the 1984 U.S nationals because of it. Forty percent of the score from that meet were to be used to select the Olympic team. Conner was granted a waiver and allowed to compete at the Olympic Trials and earned a place on the team.

Conner won the gold medal on the parallel bars at the 1984 Olympics and finished fifth in floor exercise, the highest finish ever for an American male. He helped the U.S. win the gold medal in the team competition.

After the Olympics, Conner retired from competition and became a television commentator. He married Nadia Comaneci, an Olympic gold medal gymnast, in 1996.

Daehlie, Bjorn
cross-country skiing
Born: June 19, 1967 in Elverum, Norway
Bjorn Daehlie established himself as the best cross-country skier in the world by winning 12 medals in three Olympics, including a record eight gold medals. His 12 medals are also a record for the Winter Games.

At the 1992 Olympics, he won gold in the 15-kilometer pursuit, 50-kilometer freestyle, and 4 x 10-kilometer relay. He also won a silver in the 30-kilometer classical. At the 1994 Games, he won a gold in the 10-kilometer classical and the 15-kilometer pursuit, and a silver in the 30-kilometer freestyle and the 4 x 10-kilometer relay. At the 1998 Games, he won gold in the 10-kilometer classical, the 50-kilometer freestyle, and the 4 x 10-kilometer relay.

Decker Slaney, Mary
track and field
Born: August 4, 1958 in Bunnvale, New Jersey
Mary Decker Slaney was one of the greatest runners in the history of the sport, in the United States and internationally, but she is probably best known for the misfortune that befell her in the Olympic Games.

Decker Slaney began running at age 11, then two years later ran a 4:55 mile and set an age-group record in the 800 meters. She was a tireless worker who thrived on the competition, but her intense training regimen actually worked against her. In 1974, X rays revealed that she suffered from stress fractures in her lower legs, a condition that caused her to miss the 1976 Olympics in Montreal.

In 1977, she underwent surgery to correct compartment syndrome, the result of her calf muscles growing too large for the sheaf that contained them.

Finally recovered from the surgery and her physical problems, Decker Slaney set four records at the Olympic Trials. But her dream to win an Olympic medal was thwarted by the United States' boycott of the Moscow Games.

After another setback, a torn Achilles tendon that required two surgeries, Decker Slaney returned to form in 1982, when she was the fastest woman at every distance between 800 and 10,000 meters. She set indoor world records in the mile, the 2,000 meters, and the 3,000 meters. She set an outdoor world record in the 5,000 meters. In her first attempt at 10,000 meters, she set a world record and broke the U.S. record by 42 seconds. She was named the Associated Press Female Athlete of the Year, the winner of the Sullivan Award as the nation's outstanding amateur athlete, and the Women's Sports Foundation Amateur Sportswoman of the Year.

In 1983, Decker Slaney won the gold medal in the 1,500 meters and the 3,000 meters in the first World

269

Track and Field Championships. She repeated as the Women's Sports Foundation Amateur Sportswoman of the Year and was named the *Sports Illustrated* Sportsman of the Year.

Decker Slaney entered the 1984 Olympic Trials with seven world records and qualified for the 1,500 and 3,000 meters. She decided to concentrate on the 3,000. She was considered a lock to win a medal, but midway through the race, she was accidentally tripped by Zola Budd, a South African who ran barefooted. Decker Slaney fell hard, rolled onto the infield, and writhed in pain. Her dream of an Olympic medal was once again dashed.

Decker Slaney persevered and qualified in the 1,500 and the 3,000 meters for the 1988 Olympics, but failed to medal in either event. At the 1992 Games, following more surgery on her Achilles tendon and her heel, she failed to make the U.S. team. Three more years of inactivity followed, recovering from still other heel injuries and stress fractures, after which Decker Slaney made one last attempt at the Olympics, at age 38. She made the U.S. team, but finished seventh in her 5,000-meter heat and didn't advance.

Through July 2000, Decker Slaney held American records in 1,500 meters (3:57.12), the mile (4:17.71), the 2,000 meters (5:32.7), and the 3,000 meters (8:25.83).

De Varona, Donna

swimming

Born: April 26, 1947 in San Diego, California

Donna de Varona was an outstanding swimmer, a television pioneer, and a crusader for women's sports. She began swimming when she was three years old and entered her first race at nine.

In 1960, at age 13, she became the youngest member of the U.S. Olympic team. She qualified for the 400-meter individual medley, considered one of the more difficult events because it requires four different strokes (backstroke, butterfly, breaststroke, and freestyle).

De Varona didn't medal at the 1960 Games. Over the next four years, she won 13 Amateur Athletic Union (AAU) national championships.

At the 1964 Olympics in Rome, de Varona won two gold medals. She set an Olympic record in the 400 individual medley and a world record as part of the 400-meter freestyle relay team.

De Varona retired after the 1964 Olympics, having set 18 world records and winning 37 national titles. She was hired by ABC Sports as a commentator, the first female sports broadcaster at one of the three major networks.

De Varona also worked for the passage of Title IX of the Equal Education Amendment that guaranteed women equal athletic opportunities in school. She was a cofounder of the Women's Sports Foundation in 1974 and served as the organization's president from 1979 through 1984.

Devers, Gail

track and field

Born: November 19, 1966 in Seattle, Washington

Gail Devers, one of the best sprinters and hurdlers of all time, very nearly saw her career end because of a serious disease.

Devers started running in high school, first as a distance runner, then as a sprinter. As a senior at Sweetwater High School in National City, Calif., she won the 100 meters, the 100-meter hurdles, and finished second in the long jump to take fourth place in the team standings all by herself at the California state meet. She accepted a scholarship to UCLA and won nine Pacific-10 Conference titles in two years, and in 1988 she was the NCAA champion in the 100 meters.

Devers qualified for the 1988 U.S. Olympic team in the 100-meter hurdles, but finished eighth in her heat at the Games. Her showing was uncharacteristically substandard. When she returned home, she began to experience weight fluctuations, memory loss, migraine headaches, and temporary vision loss in one eye. Periodically, she would menstruate without stopping, and the slightest cut or scratch would make her bleed profusely. She was diagnosed as suffering from Graves' disease, a severe type of hyperthyroidism. Doctors discovered a cyst on her thyroid and tried to treat it with radiation. The radiation caused her feet to swell, and she had to be carried around. She came close to having both feet amputated, but a change in her diet and thyroid medication helped her make a miraculous recovery.

A year later, she won the silver medal in the 100-meter hurdles at the 1991 world championships. At the 1992 Olympics, Devers won the 100 meters, and was leading in the 100-meter hurdles when she tripped over the final hurdle and finished fifth.

Devers doubled at the 1993 world championships, winning the 100 meters and the 100-meter hurdles. In 1994, a hamstring problem kept her from entering the hurdles, but in 1995, she came back and won the 100-meter hurdles at the world championships.

At the 1996 Olympics, Devers won two gold medals—in the 100 meters and the 4 x 100-meter relay. She became the second woman to win the gold in the 100 meters in consecutive Olympics—the other is Wyomia Tyus. She won her third gold medal in the 100-meter hurdles at the 1999 world championships, and in July 2000, she qualified for the 2000 Olympics by winning the 100-meter hurdles at the Olympic Trials.

Evans, Janet

swimming

Born: August 28, 1971 in Placentia, California

Janet Evans is one of the most successful American female Olympic athletes in history and one of the best swimmers of all time. Her talent, combined with a down-to-earth, cheery personality made her a fan favorite.

Evans learned to swim as a toddler and entered her first race at age five. In high school, she set national records in the 200-yard individual medley and the 500-yard freestyle.

At the 1988 Olympics in Seoul, South Korea, Evans, who was 17 and stood only 5 feet, 5 inches tall and was dwarfed by the muscular swimmers from East Germany, won three gold medals—400-meter freestyle (world-record 4:03.85), 800-meter freestyle (Olympic-record 8:20.20), and 400-meter individual medley (4:37.76). She was the only American woman to win a gold medal at the Seoul Games.

In 1989, Evans continued to dominate, winning seven national championships. She received the Sullivan Award as the nation's outstanding amateur athlete and the Sportsman of the Year Award from the U.S. Olympic Committee.

Evans entered Stanford University in 1990 and won consecutive NCAA titles in 500- and 1,650-yard freestyle. She also won the 400-yard individual medley in 1990. She left school in 1991 when the NCAA limited practice time to 20 hours a week.

At the 1992 Olympics, Evans wasn't quite the dominant force she had been four years earlier. Still, she won a gold medal in the 800 freestyle and a silver in the 400 freestyle. With five medals (four gold, one silver), she is second to speed skater Bonnie Blair for most medals won by an American woman. Evans qualified for the 1996 Games in Atlanta, but failed to win a medal.

Evans was the first swimmer ever to win back-to-back Olympics and world championships in one event—800-meter freestyle (1988, '92 Olympics; 1991, '94 worlds). She also won the 1991 world championship in the 400 freestyle. She and Mark Spitz are the only two Americans to win four individual Olympic medals.

Evans, who did not lose an 800- or 1,500-meter freestyle race for more than eight years, has 45 U.S. titles (second all-time), and through July 2000, held world records in the 400- (4:03.85, 1988), 800- (8:16.22, 1989), and 1,500-meter freestyle (15:52.10, 1988).

Ewry, Ray

track and field

Born: October 14, 1873 in Lafayette, Indiana

Died: September 29, 1937

Ray Ewry has won more Olympic gold medals, 10, than anyone else in history. He suffered from polio as a child and was confined to a wheelchair for a time. He exercised his legs until he could walk, then began jumping to strengthen them.

Ewry played football and was the captain of the track team at Purdue University. After graduating, he joined the New York Athletic Club and went on to make Olympic history.

Ewry won the standing high jump and the standing long jump in 1900, 1904, 1906, and 1908, and the standing triple jump in 1900 and 1904, after which the event was discontinued. All the standing events were discontinued in 1912. Ewry was also a 15-time national champion in the standing events (1898–1910). He was inducted into the National Track and Field Hall of Fame in 1974 and the U.S. Olympic Hall of Fame in 1983.

Fleming, Peggy

figure skating

Born: July 27, 1948 in San Jose, California

Like Sonja Henie before her, Peggy Fleming changed figure skating, introducing an athletic element and combining it with artistic elegance that made her one of the most popular figure skaters of all time.

Fleming didn't begin skating until she was nine years old, after her family moved from California to Cleveland. Her father, a press operator at a newspaper, worked a part-time job to help pay for the coaching, rink fees, and travel expenses.

The family moved back to California in 1960, and Fleming began to rise through the ranks. Tragedy struck in 1961 when her coach was among those U.S. team members killed in a plane crash in Belgium. Fleming struggled with the loss, but continued to skate.

In 1964, she finished sixth at the Olympic Games, and in 1965, she won the first of five consecutive U.S. championships. At age 15, she was, at the time, the youngest ever to win a U.S. title. She was second in the 1965 North American championships and third in the 1965 world championships.

In June 1965, the family moved to Colorado Springs, Colo., so that Fleming could train with coach Carlo Fassi and acclimate herself for the impending World Championships that would be held in Davos, Switzerland. Fleming won the World Championships for three consecutive years, beginning in 1968.

At the 1968 Olympics in Grenoble, France, Fleming, wearing outfits her mother made for her, turned in a spectacular performance. She won the only gold medal for the United States at the 1968 Games and helped turn the sport into the popular attraction it is today. She was named the Associated Press Female Athlete of the Year.

Fleming turned pro after the Olympics and was the star of ice shows and television specials. She also worked as a commentator for ABC Sports and was a spokesperson for a number of products.

Fleming returned to prominence in 1999 as a breast cancer survivor. She appeared on television and radio programs, telling her story and serving as an inspiration to women throughout the world.

Fosbury, Dick
track and field
Born: March 6, 1947 in Portland, Oregon

Dick Fosbury revolutionized the high jump with his "Fosbury Flop." Instead of going over the bar horizontally, Fosbury developed a technique in which he propelled his shoulders over the bar first and then allowed his back, rear, calves, and feet to follow. Arching his back after his shoulders cleared the bar gave him more clearance and a greater margin for error. The "Fosbury Flop" also allowed jumpers to build up more speed on their approach to the bar.

Fosbury began tinkering with the technique when he was 16 years old. He improved from 5 feet, 3 3/4 inches to 6 feet, 6 3/4 inches within two years. At Oregon State University in 1968, Fosbury became the first ever to clear 7 feet at an indoor NCAA meet.

At the 1968 Olympics in Mexico City, Fosbury missed on his first two attempts, but cleared 7 feet, 4 1/4 inches on his third attempt to set an Olympic record and win the gold medal.

There were dire predictions that competitors using the "Fosbury Flop" would suffer broken necks, but those predictions proved unfounded. Fosbury's new technique was used by all three medalists at the 1976 Olympics and by 13 of the 16 finalists at the 1980 Games. Ever since, the "Fosbury Flop" has been used by virtually all high jumpers. The last time the world record was held by a straddle jumper was 1978, when Volodomir Yashchenko of the Soviet Union jumped 7 feet, 8 inches.

Fosbury was inducted into the National Track and Field Hall of Fame in 1981 and the U.S. Olympic Hall of Fame in 1992.

Fraser, Dawn
swimming
Born: September 4, 1937 in Sydney, Australia

Dawn Fraser was one of the greatest swimmers in Olympic history. Her longevity and her determination to battle back from a near-tragedy are a testament to her outstanding career.

Fraser was the daughter of a soccer player who knew little about swimming and didn't encourage his daughter to get involved. When she did discover the sport, it was because she suffered from asthma and swimming helped strengthen her lungs.

Fraser, who was naturally athletic, was 14 years old when Harry Gallagher, an acclaimed swim coach in Australia, suggested to her parents that lessons would be a good thing. She worked hard for five years, and at the 1956 Olympics in Melbourne, Australia, she won the gold medal in the 100-meter freestyle in 1:02, a world record, and a gold in the 4 x 100-meter free relay. She repeated her victory in the 100 freestyle at the 1960 Games in Rome (1:01.2, Olympic record) and at the 1964 Games in Tokyo (59.5, Olympic record). Fraser became the first woman to win four gold medals, the first swimmer to win an event in three straight Olympics, and the first woman to break one minute in the 100 freestyle.

When Fraser competed at the 1964 Olympics, she was given the nickname "Granny," because at 27, she was older than most of the rest of the competitors. She also was coming back from a serious injury. Seven months before the 1964 Games, she was involved in a car accident. Her mother was killed, and Fraser suffered a chipped vertebra in her back. Although doctors predicted her career was over, Fraser persevered and won the gold in the 100 free and a silver as part of the 4 x 100-meter relay.

Fraser took part in three Olympics and won four gold and four silver medals. She also set 39 world records during her career. She was inducted into the International Women's Sports Hall of Fame in 1985.

Gable, Dan
wrestling
Born: October 25, 1948 in Waterloo, Iowa

Dan Gable is a renowned wrestler and wrestling coach whose success is unsurpassed. He was undefeated during his high school career (64–0) and lost one match during his college career at Iowa State University, where he was 118–1.

Gable won the NCAA title at 130 pounds in 1968 and at 137 pounds in 1969. His only loss came in the 142-pound final in 1970, his senior year.

At the 1972 Summer Olympics, Gable won the gold medal at 149 pounds without yielding a point in any of his six matches. He trained for seven hours a day, every day, for three years to prepare himself for the Games.

Gable retired in 1973, then was named wrestling coach at the University of Iowa in 1977. He led the Hawkeyes to 21 Big Ten championships in 21 years. They won nine straight NCAA titles, equaling the longest streak of national titles by any school in any sport, and 15 NCAA titles in 21 years (1978–86, '91–93, '95–97). His career record at Iowa was 355–21–5. The Hawkeyes averaged 17 wins and one loss a season, losing more than one dual meet only five times in 21 seasons. He coached

152 All-Americans, 45 national champions, 106 Big Ten champions, and 10 Olympians, including four gold medalists.

Gable retired in 1997 and became assistant to the athletic director at Iowa, focusing on fund-raising and promoting wrestling worldwide.

Gable was the U.S. Olympic coach in 1980, 1984, and 2000. His 1984 team, which featured four Hawkeyes, won seven gold medals.

Gable was inducted into the USA Wrestling Hall of Fame in 1980 and the U.S. Olympic Hall of Fame in 1985. He was named the nation's outstanding wrestler by the Amateur Athletic Union (AAU) in 1970 and the U.S. Wrestling Federation in 1971. He was *Amateur Wrestling News'* Man of the Year in 1970.

Gebrselassi, Haile
track and field
Born: April 18, 1973 in Assela, Ethiopia

Haile Gebrselassi is the preeminent distance runner of his time. The son of a poor farmer, Gebrselassi had to run six miles a day each way to get to school. He entered his first marathon at age 16, and with no formal training finished in a respectable 2 hours, 42 minutes.

In 1992, he won the world junior championships in the 5,000 and 10,000 meters. The following year, he won the world championship in the 10,000 meters and finished second in the 5,000. He won the world championship in the 10,000 meters again in 1995, and in 1996 he won the world indoor championship in the 3,000 and 5,000 meters.

Gebrselassi set world records in the 10,000 meters in June 1998 (26:22.75) and the 5,000 meters later the same month (12:39.36).

Gebrselassi won the gold medal in the 10,000 meters at the 1996 Olympics in an Olympic record 27:07.34. At the 1999 world championships, he won the 10,000 meters.

Gebrselassi is the first man since 1978 to hold world records in the 5,000 and 10,000 meters simultaneously, and the first man to break 13 minutes and 27 minutes, respectively.

Greene, Maurice
track and field
Born: July 23, 1974 in Kansas City, Kansas

Maurice Greene set the world record in the 100 meters (9.79) in Athens, Greece, in June 1999, earning him the title of world's fastest man.

Greene was a triple gold medalist at the 1999 world championships, winning the 100 and 200 meters and running the anchor leg for the 4 x 100-meter relay. He is the first ever to win the 100 and 200 at the world championships and only the fourth athlete ever to win three gold medals in a single world championship.

Greene qualified for the 2000 Olympics in the 100 meters and attempted to qualify in the 200 meters. But in a much-anticipated showdown against Michael Johnson, Greene and Johnson pulled up lame in the 200-meter final and neither made the Olympic team in that event.

Griffith Joyner, Florence
track and field
Born: December 21, 1959 in Los Angeles, California
Died: September 21, 1998

Florence Griffith Joyner, known as "FloJo," was one of the greatest female sprinters ever. She also had a sense of style and charisma that made her one of the most popular athletes in America.

Griffith Joyner, one of 11 children, learned early on that nothing was accomplished without hard work. Her parents were divorced when she was four, and her mother worked as a seamstress, trying to make ends meet.

Griffith Joyner was seven years old when she began running in races at the Sugar Ray Robinson Youth Foundation. She won almost every race, even when she ran against boys. In 1973 and 1974, she won the annual Jesse Owens Youth Games, and when she graduated from Jordan High School in 1978, she held school records in sprints and the long jump.

Griffith Joyner entered California State University at Northridge, but had to leave school because she ran out of money. While working as a bank teller, her college track coach, Bob Kersee, helped her return to college. When Kersee began working at UCLA, where he would coach and later marry Jackie Joyner, Griffith Joyner enrolled at UCLA. She failed to qualify for the 1980 Olympic team, which didn't go to the Games in Moscow, because of the United States' boycott, but she won the NCAA 200-meter title in 1982 and the 400-meter title in 1983.

Griffith Joyner won the silver medal in the 200 meters at the 1984 Games, but afterward, her enthusiasm for running track waned. She began working two jobs and neglected her training. She met Al Joyner, Jackie Joyner's brother and an Olympic athlete himself, and he convinced her to resume training. They were married in October 1987. Joyner's advice and his wife's return to serious workouts paid off.

At the 1988 Olympic Trials, Griffith Joyner set a world record in the 100 meters (10.49). At the Olympic Games in Seoul, South Korea, she won gold medals in the 100 (10.54) and 200 (world record 21.34). She also won a gold medal in the 4 x 100-meter relay and a silver medal in the 4 x 400-meter relay.

It wasn't just Griffith Joyner's speed that made her a fan favorite, it was her style. She wore colorful, one-legged unitards and painted her long fingernails with the Olympic rings.

Griffith Joyner was named the Associated Press Female Athlete of the Year and the Sullivan Award winner as the nation's outstanding amateur athlete.

Because Griffith Joyner's development from a solid sprinter in the 1984 Games to the fastest woman in the world four years later seemed to happen so suddenly, there were accusations that she was using illegal steroids to enhance her performance. But she steadfastly denied such claims, and none were ever proved.

Griffith Joyner, who retired in 1989, capitalized on her Olympic performance by landing numerous endorsement deals. She also served on the President's Council on Physical Fitness and Sports.

In 1996, she was hospitalized for one day after suffering a seizure during a flight. She died of heart seizure in 1998.

Griffith Joyner was inducted into the Track and Field Hall of Fame in 1995 and the International Women's Sports Hall of Fame in 1998.

Hamill, Dorothy
figure skating
Born: July 26, 1956 in Chicago, Illinois

Dorothy Hamill began skating at age eight on a pond near her home in Greenwich, Conn. Once she saw her friends skating backward, she convinced her parents to allow her to take skating lessons. From those ordinary beginnings, a champion was born.

After she finished seventh at the 1971 world championships, Hamill's parents took her out of public school so that she could devote all her time—seven hours a day, six days a week—to practice. She began taking lessons with Carlo Fassi, the coach who helped mold Peggy Fleming into an Olympic gold medalist. Stronger and more athletic than Fleming, Hamill and Fassi took advantage of her style and created routines that emphasized her jumping ability. They also created a new move, the "Hamill Camel," which was a camel spin into a sit spin.

In 1974, she won the first of three consecutive U.S. championships and earned a silver medal in the world championships.

At the 1976 Olympics at Innsbruck, Austria, Hamill won the gold medal with a spectacular performance. She also won a gold medal at the world championships in 1976.

Hamill's sense of style, her All-American good looks, and her famous "wedge" hairstyle made her a favorite of fans of all ages.

She turned pro in 1977, signing a seven-figure contract to headline for the Ice Capades, in which she performed until 1984. Hamill won four consecutive World Professional Figure Skating Championships, starting in 1984. She also appeared in television specials and skated exhibitions.

In 1994, with the Ice Capades on the brink of bankruptcy, Hamill purchased the troupe and resurrected the Ice Capades.

She was inducted into the U.S. Olympic Hall of Fame in 1991.

Hamilton, Scott
figure skating
Born: August 28, 1958 in Toledo, Ohio

Scott Hamilton overcame a serious childhood illness to become a figure skating champion. When he was two years old, he was diagnosed with Schwachman's syndrome, a rare intestinal disease that prevents the body from absorbing nutrients. Hamilton stopped growing and had to be kept alive by feeding tubes and other treatments.

At age nine, Hamilton began skating after watching his sister, and practicing actually helped the disease improve. He was free of symptoms by the time he reached the junior level.

Hamilton, still thought to be too small and frail by many experts, practiced hard, but when his mother died in 1978, he was so distraught he considered giving up the sport. He continued, although he never rose higher than third in the U.S. rankings.

In 1980, Hamilton changed coaches, going from the legendary Carlo Fassi to Don Laws, who intensified his training. At the 1981 U.S. championships, he received his first perfect score and won the gold medal. Hamilton won the next three U.S. titles and four straight world titles (1981–84). At the 1984 Olympics in Sarajevo, Yugoslavia, Hamilton won the gold medal.

Hamilton turned pro after the 1984 Games. He founded and coproduced *Stars on Ice*. In 1997, he was diagnosed with testicular cancer. But again, he overcame the disease and was back on the ice in less than a year.

Hayes, Bob
track and field (also football)
Born: December 20, 1942 in Jacksonville, Florida

Bob Hayes enjoyed outstanding careers in two sports—track and field and football. In the early 1960s, Hayes was the first person to run the 60-yard dash in less than six seconds and the first to run the 100-yard dash in 9.1 seconds.

Hayes, known as the "World's Fastest Human" in his prime, went to college at Florida A&M University, where he won the NCAA 200-meter dash championship. He also was the Amateur Athletic Union (AAU) 100-yard champ from 1962 through 1964.

At the 1964 Olympics, Hayes won the 100 meters in world-record time (10.0) and ran the anchor leg on the victorious 4 x 100-meter relay team (world-record 39.0). Hayes turned a two-meter deficit into a three-meter victory.

Hayes joined the Dallas Cowboys after the Olympics and had a fine career as a wide receiver. In 12 seasons, he caught 371 passes for 7,414 yards (20-yard average) and 71 touchdowns. He was an All-Pro in 1966.

Hayes was inducted into the National Track and Field Hall of Fame in 1976. In 1979, he was convicted of drug trafficking and served 18 months of a five-year sentence.

Heiden, Eric
speed skating
Born: June 14, 1958 in Madison, Wisconsin

Eric Heiden turned in one of the most dominant performances in Olympic history at the 1980 Games in Lake Placid, N.Y., winning gold medals in five individual speed skating events.

Heiden first competed in the Olympics in 1976 and failed to medal. But in 1977, he won the overall title at the world championships and successfully defended it in 1978 and 1979. He entered the 1980 Olympics as the favorite at every distance. He won his first four races—the 500, 1,000, 1,500, and 5,000 meters.

The night before the 10,000 meters, in which a victory would make him the first Olympic athlete to win five individual gold medals in one Olympics, Heiden had trouble sleeping. He ended up oversleeping and had little time for breakfast or his usual warm-up. No matter, he won the 10,000 meters and broke the world record by six seconds. He won the 1980 Sullivan Award as the nation's outstanding amateur athlete.

Marathoner Bill Rodgers compared Heiden's feat to a runner winning gold medals in every distance from 400 meters to 10,000 meters. "Eric has done the impossible," said Rodgers.

Heiden, who could have cashed in on his Olympic fame on a much bigger scale, endorsed only a few products, preferring not to sell himself the way Bruce Jenner and Mark Spitz did in capitalizing on their Olympic success.

Heiden retired from speed skating soon after the 1980 Games and took up cycling. He won the 1985 U.S. Pro Cycling Championship. But he quit cycling after a crash in the 1986 Tour de France. He entered Stanford Medical School and is now an orthopedist practicing in California.

Heiss, Carol
figure skating
Born: January 20, 1940 in New York, New York

Carol Heiss dominated women's figure skating from 1956 through 1960. Her rivalry with Tenley Albright was one of the best the sport has ever seen.

Heiss began skating when she was six years old and showed promise right away. After winning the U.S. Novice title at age 11 and U.S. Junior title at age 12, she moved up to the championship level and finished fourth at the 1953 world championships.

When Heiss was 14, she collided on the ice with her younger sister, Nancy, and suffered a severed tendon below the calf. The injury was career-threatening, but Heiss made a full recovery.

From 1953 through 1956, she finished second to Albright at the U.S. championships, the 1953 and 1955 world championships, and at the 1956 Olympics.

Heiss finally defeated Albright at the 1956 world championships. It was the first of her five straight titles in the event. Heiss won the U.S. championship from 1957 through 1960 and the North American championship in 1957 and 1959.

At the 1960 Olympic Games in Squaw Valley, Idaho, Heiss won the gold medal. She retired shortly thereafter. A brief professional career followed, but Heiss left the ice completely to devote all her time to raising her four children. Heiss married Hayes Alan Jenkins, the 1956 Olympic gold medalist, in 1961.

Eighteen years after her retirement, Heiss returned to the ice as a coach. She also served on the U.S. Olympic Committee and the U.S. Figure Skating Association's board of directors. She was inducted into the U.S. Figure Skating Hall of Fame in 1976 and the International Women's Sports Hall of Fame in 1992.

Henie, Sonja
figure skating
Born: April 8, 1912 in Oslo, Norway
Died: October 12, 1969

Sonja Henie changed the course of figure skating in the 1920s to the sport we know today. The sport used to be boring to watch. Competitors would do compulsory figures, followed by a long program of technical movements, done while music played randomly in the background.

Henie, who was born into affluence, had the luxury of learning on private skating rinks and taking skating and ballet lessons. She choreographed her routines, incorporating sits, spins, and leaps into her program. She was graceful and athletic, timing her moves to the music, and she helped figure skating's popularity increase dramatically. She changed from the long skirts and black skates, the fashion of the day, into shorter skirts, often fur-trimmed, and skating boots.

Henie entered her first Olympics in 1924 at age 11. Some of her movements were so revolutionary, the judges were shocked. She finished third in the freestyle skate, but because of a poor performance in the compulsories, she finished last.

Henie continued to work hard, and in 1926, she finished second in the world championships. The following year, she won the first of her 10 consecutive world championships, a feat that has never been duplicated.

Just after she won her first world championship, Henie watched a performance by Anna Pavlova, the acclaimed Russian ballerina. Henie was so impressed by Pavlova's artistry, she began to add touches of ballet to her skating.

Henie won three consecutive Olympic gold medals, in 1928, 1932, and 1936, a record that still stands. She turned pro in 1936 and became a Hollywood star. She made 13 films, virtually all about figure skating. In 1940, she began the Sonja Henie Hollywood Ice Revue, which toured the country and made her a millionaire.

Henie retired in 1960. She was diagnosed with leukemia a short time later. In 1969, she died while riding on a plane that was taking her from Paris to Oslo for medical treatment. She was inducted into the International Women's Sports Hall of Fame in 1982.

Hyman, Flo (Flora)

volleyball

Born: July 29, 1954 in Inglewood, California
Died: January 24, 1986

Flo Hyman is regarded as the best U.S. women's volleyball player of all time. Best known for her spiking ability and her defensive skills, the 6-5 Hyman was a three-time All-American at the University of Houston (1974–76). She left school after her junior year to join the national team, based in Colorado. The U.S. team played without a coach for three months in 1975 and failed to qualify for the 1976 Olympics. Still, Hyman stuck by the team.

The U.S. finished fifth at the 1978 World Championships and qualified for the 1980 Olympic Games. But Hyman and the team couldn't participate because of the United States boycott of the Games. In 1981, she was the first U.S. woman to be named to the All-World Cup team.

Hyman and the U.S. team finally made it to the Olympics in 1984 and won a silver medal, the highest finish ever for the U.S women's team.

After the Olympics, Hyman went to Japan to play professionally. In 1986, during a match in Japan, Hyman collapsed and died of heart failure. An autopsy revealed that she suffered from Marfan's syndrome, a congenital disorder that affects tall, thin people. Her condition had gone undetected.

As a tribute to Hyman, the Women's Sports Foundation gives an award annually to the female athlete who embodies Hyman's "dignity, spirit and commitment to excellence." Hyman was inducted into the International Women's Sports Hall of Fame in 1986 and the Volleyball Hall of Fame in 1988.

Indurain, Miguel

cycling

Born: July 16, 1964 in Villava, Spain

Miguel Indurain is one of only four cyclists to win the Tour de France five times and the only person to do it in consecutive years. The other five-time winners were Bernard Hinault and Jacques Anquetil of France and Eddy Merckx of Belgium.

Indurain started his string in 1991. In 1996, his bid for a sixth straight Tour de France failed, as he finished 11th. Later in 1996, he won the Olympic gold medal in the time trial at the Atlanta Games.

Indurain, one of the most popular athletes ever in Spain, announced his retirement in February 1997, when he couldn't find a cycling team willing to pay him the $8 million salary he required.

Jansen, Dan

speed skating

Born: June 17, 1965 in West Allis, Wisconsin

Dan Jansen realized the agony and ecstasy of the Olympics with his heartbreaking failures at the 1988 and 1992 Games and his inspiring victory at the 1994 Games.

He entered the 1988 Games as the favorite in the 500- and 1,000-meter races. But just before the 500 meters, he learned his sister, Jane, died after a lengthy battle against leukemia. After a fast start, Jansen fell in the first turn and failed to medal. In the 1,000 meters four days later, Jansen fell again and left without a medal.

Jansen vowed he would be back, but at the 1992 Games at Albertville, France, he failed to win a bronze medal in the 500 meters by .16 of a second.

Because the International Olympic Committee changed the Olympic schedule so that the Winter and Summer Games did not take place in the same year, Jansen had to wait only two years for another chance at a medal.

He entered the 1994 Games as the world-record holder in the 500 meters. At 35.76 seconds, he was the only skater ever to break 36 seconds. But in the Olympic 500, Jansen slipped and placed eighth. In his last chance for a medal, Jansen came through. He won the 1,000 meters in world-record time and celebrated with a victory lap, holding his infant daughter, Jane.

Jansen retired after the Olympics and established the Dan Jansen Foundation, which contributes to amateur speed skating and the National Leukemia Society. He also works as a commentator for CBS Sports.

Jenner, Bruce
track and field
Born: October 28, 1949 in Mt. Kisco, New York

Bruce Jenner won the gold medal in the decathlon at the 1976 Olympics with a world-record 8,617 points. He began his athletic career with little fanfare. He attended Graceland College in Iowa on a football scholarship, but he injured his knee and didn't play after his freshman year.

In 1971, he began training for the decathlon and made the U.S. Olympic team in 1972. He finished 10th in the Games, held at Munich, Germany, but in 1974, he won the Amateur Athletic Union (AAU) national championship. In 1975, he won the Pan-American Games, and prior to the 1976 Olympics, he successfully defended his AAU title.

Jenner was the favorite to win the gold medal entering the Games in Montreal. Through eight events, he had a lead that was insurmountable. In the final event, the 1,500 meters, Jenner ran his best time ever and set the world record.

Jenner was named the winner of the 1976 Sullivan Award as the nation's outstanding amateur athlete and Associated Press Male Athlete of the Year.

Jenner parlayed his gold medal into a lucrative career that included television and movies. He was inducted into the National Track and Field Hall of Fame in 1980 and the U.S. Olympic Hall of Fame in 1986.

Johnson, Michael
track and field
Born: September 13, 1967 in Dallas, Texas

Michael Johnson accomplished one of the greatest feats in Olympic history by becoming the first man to win the 200 and 400 meters at the same Games.

Clyde Hart, Johnson's coach at Baylor University, never expected Johnson to become a world-class sprinter. But Johnson's hard work and determination helped him achieve greatness. His work ethic was unsurpassed, and his meticulous attention to detail kept him from overlooking virtually anything. He recorded his workouts daily in a journal and measured the position of his blocks to the sixteenth of an inch.

Johnson had several disappointments at the Olympics. In 1988, he was hampered by leg injuries, and in 1992, he suffered food poisoning that kept him from running in the 200-meter final.

At the 1996 Olympics in Atlanta, the schedule was rearranged so that Johnson would be able to attempt his unprecedented 200/400 double. He won the 400 in 43.49 (Olympic record) and then stunned the world with his victory in the 200, setting a world record (19.32) and winning by the largest margin since Jesse Owens won at the 1936 Games. The picture of Johnson seeing his time and reacting in disbelief has become a freeze frame of the Atlanta Games.

Johnson was named the winner of the 1996 Sullivan Award as the nation's outstanding amateur athlete and the Associated Press Male Athlete of the Year.

At the 2000 Olympic Trials, Johnson qualified for the 400 meters and attempted to qualify for the 200, in a much-anticipated showdown with Maurice Greene, the world record holder in the 100 meters. Johnson pulled up lame in the final, followed closely by Greene, who also was injured. Neither runner made the team in that event.

Johnson is a two-time world champion in the 200 meters (1991, '95) and a four-time champion in the 400 meters (1993, '95, '97, '99). He is a three-time world champion as a member of the 4 x 400-meter relay team (1993, '95, '99), and at the 1993 world championships he ran the anchor leg in a world-record 42.94 and helped the team to a world record 2:54.29. At the 1999 world championships, he set a world record in the 400 meters (43.18).

Johnson wrote an autobiography, *Slaying the Dragon*, released in 1996, and has done numerous television commercials.

Johnson, Rafer
track and field
Born: August 18, 1934 in Hillsboro, Texas

Rafer Johnson was one of the best decathletes of all time. Not surprisingly, he was an excellent all-around athlete at Kingburg High School in Kingburg, Calif. He averaged nine yards a carry for the three-time state champion football team, he batted over .400 for the baseball team, he averaged 17 points a game for the basketball team, and he was an outstanding sprinter and long jumper on the track team. He accepted a track scholarship to UCLA.

When he was a junior in high school, Johnson observed Bob Mathias, the reigning Olympic decathlon champion. Johnson decided he wanted to become a decathlete, and less than a month later he won the state junior decathlon championship.

He won the decathlon at the 1955 Pan-American Games and qualified for the 1956 Olympics in the long jump and decathlon. But a knee injury and an abdominal tear forced him to withdraw from the long jump and led to his silver medal in the decathlon.

In 1958, Johnson set a world record with 8,302 points. He was involved in an automobile accident in 1959 and was unable to train for more than 18 months. He resumed training just seven months before the 1960 Olympic Games in Rome.

He set a world record of 8,683 points at the 1960 Olympic Trials, and then was in a closely contested battle for the gold medal with his UCLA teammate and training partner C.K. Yang.

Entering the final event, the 1,500-meter run, Johnson had to finish within 10 seconds of Yang to win the gold medal. Yang's best time in the 1,500 was 4:36; Johnson's was 4:54.2. Johnson's strategy was never to allow Yang to get too far away. He followed it perfectly, refusing to let Yang pull away. Johnson finished one second behind Yang, his time six seconds faster than his personal best. Johnson was named Associated Press Male Athlete of the Year.

After his retirement, Johnson starred in several movies. In 1984, he was chosen to light the Olympic Torch at the Games in Los Angeles.

Jones, Marion
track and field
Born: October 12, 1975 in Los Angeles, California

Marion Jones attempted to make history at the 2000 Olympics in Sydney, Australia, by becoming the first track athlete, male or female, to win five gold medals at one Olympics. Jones won the 100 meters, 200 meters, and long jump at the U.S Olympic Trials in July 2000. She also would be a member of the 4 x 100- and 4 x 400-meter relay teams. She wound up with three gold and two bronze, becoming the first woman to win five track and field medals in one Olympics.

Jones was a high school track star, winning the California state championship in the 100 and 200 meters in each of her four years. She was unbeaten in both races after her freshman year. As a senior, she also won the state long jump title.

Jones, who was named California Division I high school basketball player of the year as a senior, played basketball at the University of North Carolina. She hit the title-winning shot at the buzzer of the championship game. She passed up her senior year of eligibility, but during her three seasons, the Tar Heels went 92–10 and never lost a game in the Atlantic Coast Conference.

Jones did not compete at all in 1996, and missed a chance to qualify for the 1996 Olympics because of a broken foot suffered while she was practicing for the World University Games with the U.S. basketball team.

In 1997, Jones won the 100 meters at the world championship and was a member of the gold medal–winning 4 x 100-meter relay team. In 1998, she was undefeated in every competition until her final event of the year, when she was beaten by Heike Drechsler of Germany in the long jump. Jones was the unanimous choice as *Track & Field News'* Athlete of the Year.

Jones won the gold medal in the 100 meters at the 1999 world championships. She injured her back in the 200-meter semifinals and didn't compete for the rest of the season. Still, she managed to run the second-fastest 100 meters of all time (10.65, behind Florence Griffith Joyner's 10.49) and the second-fastest 200 meters (21.62, behind Griffith Joyner's 21.34).

Jones is married to C.J. Hunter, a shot putter who was a member of the 2000 Olympic team, although he did not compete because of injury and revocation of his credential by the International Olympic Committee.

Joyner-Kersee, Jackie
track and field
Born: March 3, 1962 in East St. Louis, Illinois

Jackie Joyner-Kersee is widely regarded as one of the greatest athletes ever. Her class, style, charisma, and personality also combine to make her one of the most popular athletes ever.

Joyner-Kersee began showing an interest in track and field at age nine. She and her friends would put sand in potato chip bags spread in front of the Joyner's front porch and make a long jump pit. When she watched the 1976 Summer Olympics on television, she vowed that she would do her best someday to make the team.

An all-around athlete who also played volleyball and basketball, Joyner-Kersee won four straight national junior pentathlon championships. The movie *Babe*, about Babe Didrikson, helped convince her to compete in multiple events.

Her best sport in high school was basketball. She led her Lincoln High team to the Illinois state championship and accepted a basketball scholarship to UCLA, where she was a four-year starter and an All-American (1980–84).

In 1980, she met Bob Kersee, who encouraged her to work on multiple events. She chose to concentrate on the heptathlon in 1982. The heptathlon, virtually unknown at the time, consists of the 200-meter dash, high jump, long jump, javelin, shot put, 100-meter hurdles, and 800-meter run. Joyner-Kersee's outstanding performances in the heptathlon helped increase the event's popularity.

In 1984, she scored 6,659 points to break the American record at the U.S. Olympic Trials. She won the silver medal at the Summer Games, missing out on gold by .06 seconds in the final event, the 800 meters, because of a strained hamstring.

Jackie Joyner-Kersee   *Andy Lyons/Allsport Photography*

"When I lost the gold medal by five points," she said, "I knew it was because of my poor mental approach. I vowed right then I would never again allow myself to be weak mentally."

In 1986, at the Goodwill Games in Moscow, Joyner-Kersee set a world record in the heptathlon with 7,148 points. She was the first woman to eclipse 7,000 points. Several weeks later at the U.S. Olympic Sports Festival, she set another record, compiling 7,158 points. She won the 1986 Sullivan Award as the nation's outstanding amateur athlete. She also married Kersee.

In 1987, she tied the world record in the long jump (24 feet, 5 1/2 inches), won the heptathlon and the long jump at the world championships, and became the first woman ever to win an individual event and a multievent at an Olympic-level competition since Harold Osborne did in 1924. She was named the Associated Press Female Athlete of the Year.

At the 1988 Olympics in Seoul, South Korea, she won another gold medal in the heptathlon, breaking her own record with 7,291 points, a mark that stood through July 2000. She hurt her knee in the high jump, and many thought she might not be able to compete, let alone win

gold and set a record. She also won the gold medal in the long jump, setting an Olympic record of 24 feet, 3 1/4 inches.

Joyner-Kersee again won two medals at the 1992 Olympics in Barcelona, Spain. She scored 7,044 points to win a gold medal in the heptathlon and jumped 23 feet, 2 1/2 inches to win the bronze in the long jump.

After the 1992 Olympics, many wondered if she would retire, but she vowed to remain competitive until the 1996 Games in Atlanta so she could end her career on American soil.

Joyner-Kersee failed to win at the Olympic Trials. She finished second by three points to Kim Blair. Suffering from an injured right hamstring, Joyner-Kersee was forced to withdraw from the Olympic heptathlon. Six days after withdrawing, she proclaimed herself healthy enough to enter the long jump. Entering her final jump, she was in sixth place out of eight competitors. On her last jump, she went 22 feet, 11 3/4 inches to win the bronze medal by one inch.

Joyner-Kersee's final heptathlon was at the 1998 Goodwill Games. She won by 23 points and announced her retirement. In July 2000, she came out of retirement to try and qualify for the Olympics in the long jump, but her bid fell short.

Keino, Kip

track and field

Born: January 17, 1940 in Nandi Hills, Kenya

Kip Keino—real name Hezekiah Kipchoge Keino—learned to run as a child by herding goats and training in Kenya's hill country. In the mid 1960s, Keino set world records in the 3,000-meter run (7:39.6) and the 5,000-meter run (13:24.2).

At the 1968 Olympics, Keino won a gold medal in the 1,500 meters, upsetting favored American Jim Ryan, and a silver in the 5,000 meters. On his way to the stadium for the 1,500 meters, his cab was stuck in traffic. Rather than risk missing the race, Keino jogged the final mile to the stadium.

Keino also competed, but didn't medal, in the 10,000 meters. He was leading the 10,000 meters with two laps to go, but collapsed due to the effects of a gall bladder infection he suffered leading up to the Games.

At the 1972 Olympics, Keino won silver in the 1,500 meters and gold in the 3,000-meter steeplechase.

Kidd, Billy

skiing

Born: April 13, 1943 in Burlington, Vermont

Billy Kidd was the first American man to win an Olympic skiing medal, taking a silver in the slalom and a bronze in the alpine combined at the 1964 Games.

In 1968, he beat Frenchman Jean Claude Killy to win the World Cup slalom and repeated his victory the following year. In 1970, Kidd won the world alpine combined event, the first world championship ever won by an American skier.

Kidd turned pro, joining the International Ski Racing Association (ISRA). He won the giant slalom and the alpine combined events at the ISRA world championships.

Kidd retired in 1972 because of nagging injuries. He became the ski director at Steamboat Springs, Colo., helped coach the U.S. ski team, and did some television commentary.

Killy, Jean Claude

skiing

Born: August 30, 1943 in St. Cloud Alsace, France

Jean Claude Killy is one of the most accomplished skiers in the history of the Winter Olympics, although his first appearance at the Games, in 1964, provided no hints to his future greatness.

Killy failed to finish in the downhill or the slalom at Innsbruck, Austria. But after the Olympics, he became the dominant figure in the sport. In the 1966–67 season, he won every downhill race he entered and won the first World Cup, awarded for consistency in a series of international races. He repeated his World Cup victory in the 1967–68 season and led France to the world team championship.

At the 1968 Olympics, Killy won gold medals in the downhill, the slalom, and the giant slalom, making him only the second in Olympic history to accomplish the triple. Austria's Anton Sailer was the other in 1956.

Killy's gold medal in the slalom was not without controversy. Austria's Karl Schranz, Killy's closest competitor, claimed an unidentified man came onto the course during his second run. He was awarded another run and defeated Killy. But Killy was awarded the gold medal when Schranz was disqualified for missing two gates on his first run. Schranz contended the reason he missed the gates was because of the unidentified man. The case went before the Jury of Appeal, which declared Killy the winner.

King, Micki (Maxine)

diving

Born: July 26, 1944 in Pontiac, Michigan

Micki King, who started diving when she was 10 years old, became an All-American water polo player at the University of Michigan. She was encouraged to resume diving by Dick Kimball, Michigan's water sports coach.

King won the 3-meter national outdoor champ four times (1965 '67, '69, '70), the l-meter champion in 1967, and the platform champion in 1969. She was the 3-meter indoor champ in 1971 and 1972 and the platform champ in 1965 and 1971.

King entered the 1968 Olympics as the favorite in the springboard competition, and through eight dives she was the leader. On her ninth dive, she hit her forearm on the board. She performed her 10th dive, but fell to fourth place.

At the 1972 Games, King took the lead on her eighth dive and finished with the same dive, a 1 1/2 somersault on which she broke her arm four years earlier. King won the gold medal and retired from competition shortly after the Olympics.

King, a colonel in the Air Force, became diving coach at the Air Force Academy. In 1978, she was transferred to Tacoma, Wash., where she continued to coach diving. She was inducted into the International Women's Sports Hall of Fame in 1983.

Kiraly, Karch

volleyball

Born: November 3, 1960 in Jackson, Michigan

Karch Kiraly is widely recognized as one of the best volleyball players ever. He was Most Valuable Player in California as a high school senior. He led UCLA to national championships in 1979, 1981, and 1982, and a second-place finish in 1980. During his four years, UCLA won 123 of 128 matches.

Kiraly, a member of the U.S. national team from 1981 to 1989, led the United States to gold medals at the 1984 and 1988 Olympics, at the 1982 and 1986 world championships, and at the 1987 Pan-American Games.

At the 1996 Olympics, Kiraly teamed with Kent Steffes to win the gold medal in the inaugural beach volleyball competition. Kiraly attempted to qualify for the 2000 Games, but a shoulder injury ended his bid.

Klammer, Franz

skiing

Born: December 3, 1954 in Mooswald, Austria

Franz Klammer is widely regarded as one of the greatest downhill skiers ever. He won four consecutive World Cup downhill titles, starting in 1975, and also won in 1983.

At the 1976 Olympics, Klammer was the favorite in the downhill, but entering his final run, he trailed Bernhard Russi of Switzerland by a fraction of a second. In one of the most famous and most replayed runs in Olympic history, Klammer skied with reckless abandon, charging the course and risking a fall at every turn. But when he crossed the finish line he had overtaken Russi by one-third of a second and won the gold medal.

Korbut, Olga

gymnastics

Born: May 16, 1955 in Grodno, Belarussia (now Belarus)

Olga Korbut took the 1972 Summer Olympics by storm and revolutionized women's gymnastics. Standing 4 feet, 11 inches, and weighing only 80 pounds, she served as a substitute for an injured teammate. Korbut introduced flash and style into gymnastics, where it had never existed before. Her bright eyes and her genuine smile made her a fan favorite around the world. The joy she exuded when she performed also was something new to the sport.

She performed moves on the uneven bars and the balance beams that were daring and exciting. She set the tone and opened the door for the acrobatic gymnasts who followed her.

Korbut qualified for a sports school in the Soviet Union when she was 11 years old. There she was urged to become more innovative and stylish. In 1969, she was fifth at the Soviet national championships, and in 1970, she won her first national title, on the vault horse.

Korbut placed third in the Soviet national championships in 1972 and qualified for the Olympic team. At the Games in Munich, Germany, she won individual gold medals in floor exercise and balance beam, a silver in uneven bars, and helped the Soviets win the team gold medal.

In 1976, Korbut had to yield center stage to Nadia Comaneci of Romania, but she still won a silver medal in the balance beam.

Korbut retired after the 1976 Games and became a coach in Minsk. After returning home after a tour of America, Korbut developed thyroid problems, which came from radiation poisoning. Minsk is located near Chernobyl, site of a nuclear reactor explosion in 1987. She used her celebrity status to solicit funds for the victims. She moved to Atlanta in 1991, where she has taught gymnastics.

Korbut was inducted into the International Women's Sports Hall of Fame in 1982.

Koss, Johann Olav

speed skating

Born: October 29, 1968 in Drammen, Norway

Johann Olav Koss won two medals at the 1992 Winter Olympics—gold in the 1,500 meters and silver in the 10,000 meters. Just one week before the Olympics, Koss was hospitalized for stomach pains, which turned out to be caused by a blockage in his pancreatic tract. Nine days after leaving the hospital, he won the 1,500 meters.

After the 1992 Games, Koss focused on his medical school studies and on the technical aspects of skating. He experimented with high-altitude training on a trip to Nepal in 1993, but discovered it had no beneficial effects.

At the 1994 Olympics in Lillehammer, Norway, Koss won gold medals in the 1,500, 5,000, and 10,000 meters and set world records in each event. He retired shortly after the 1994 Olympics to enter medical school.

In 1994, he and Bonnie Blair, a U.S. speed skater, shared the *Sports Illustrated* Sportsman of the Year Award.

Kwan, Michelle

figure skating

Born: July 7, 1980 in Torrance, California

Michelle Kwan is one of the most accomplished and popular figure skaters of her time. In a survey of 1,000 advertising agency creative marketing directors and marketing executives done by Burns Sports Celebrity Services, Kwan ranked as the ninth most appealing athletic endorser. She was the only female to make the list.

Kwan finished second at the U.S. championships in 1994, 1995, and 1997, and second at the world championships in 1997. In 1996 and 1998, she won the U.S. and world championships.

At the 1998 U.S. championship, Kwan was not expected to do well. She had suffered a stress fracture that cost her two months of training prior to the competition in January. Right before the short program, there was some question whether she would be able to compete. But her performance in the short program was called one of the best ever by many experts. Her free skate two days later also was excellent. She earned seven perfect 6.0s for artistic merit on the short program and eight on the free skate.

Kwan entered the 1998 Olympic Games as the favorite, but a conservatively skated free skate cost her the gold medal, won by Tara Lipinski. Two months after the Olympics, Kwan won the world championship.

Kwan finished second in the 1999 U.S. championship. She won the 1999 world championship and the 2000 U.S. and world championships. From 1995 through September 2000, Kwan has never finished lower than second. The graceful way with which she dealt with the disappointment of a silver medal at the 1998 Games earned her more popularity and numerous endorsement deals.

Kwan enrolled at UCLA in the summer of 1999 and allowed schoolwork to take precedence over her skating. But during the 2000 winter quarter she scaled back her classes to just one and returned to a three-practice-a-day schedule. She took off the 2000 spring quarter to concentrate on her skating. Her goal is to qualify for the 2002 Olympics.

Lewis, Carl
track and field
Born: July 1, 1961 in Birmingham, Alabama
Carl Lewis is one of the greatest all-around athletes of all time. He medaled in four Olympics, and had the United States not boycotted the 1980 Games, held in Moscow, he most certainly would have medaled in five.

Lewis grew up in Willingboro, N.J., just across the Delaware River from Philadelphia. He was undersized until he experienced a growth spurt at age 15. The spurt was so severe he wore crutches for one month while his body adjusted to the change in size.

He attended the University of Houston in 1979 and won NCAA championships in the long jump (1980–81) and the 100 meters (1981). In 1980, he qualified for the U.S. Olympic team in the long jump and as a member of the 4 x 100-meter relay team, but the U.S. boycott postponed his dream.

By 1981, Lewis was ranked no. 1 in the United States in the long jump and the 100 meters. At the 1983 U.S. championships, he managed a rare triple, winning the 100 meters, 200 meters, and long jump. That feat hadn't been accomplished since 1936. At the world championships two months later, he also tripled.

Lewis made history at the 1984 Olympics in Los Angeles, winning four gold medals and equaling the performance of Jesse Owens at the 1936 Games. Lewis won gold in the 100 meters, 200 meters, long jump, and as a member of the 4 x 100-meter relay team.

At the 1988 Olympics, Lewis took gold in the 100 meters and the long jump and a silver in the 200 meters, and at the 1992 Games, he added two more gold medals (long jump, 4 x 100-meter relay).

His gold medal in the 1988 100 meters was not without controversy. Lewis finished second to Ben Johnson of Canada, but Johnson was disqualified, having tested positive for steroids. Lewis was awarded the gold medal. He ran a 9.92, a world record.

Lewis boycotted the 1989 world championships, protesting the Athletics Congress, one of the sport's governing bodies, for not doing more to cut down drug use. Lewis also cut back on his sprint schedule, in hopes of breaking Bob Beamon's long jump record, set in 1968.

Lewis didn't break Beamon's record of 29 feet, 2 1/2 inches. Mike Powell did at the 1991 world championships, jumping 29 feet 4 1/2 inches.

At the 1992 Olympics, Lewis appeared to have lost his invincibility. He didn't qualify for the 100 meters or 200 meters, but got a spot on the 4 x 100-meter relay. Lewis rose to the occasion, outjumping Powell to win gold in the long jump and anchoring the relay team to a gold medal in world-record time.

Lewis' last hurrah came at the 1996 Olympics in Atlanta, where, at age 35, he won a gold medal in the long jump. The gold medal was his ninth; only Ray Ewry has more (10).

Because Lewis was outspoken, opinionated, and did not hesitate to blow his own horn, he was not popular with other athletes, nor was he embraced by the public, as people would expect for someone of his stature. But there was no denying his greatness.

Lewis was named winner of the 1981 Sullivan Award as the nation's outstanding amateur athlete, and in 1983 and 1984 he was voted the Associated Press Male Athlete of the Year. He was inducted into the U.S. Olympic Hall of Fame in 1985.

Lipinski, Tara
figure skating
Born: June 10, 1982 in Philadelphia, Pennsylvania
Tara Lipinski is the youngest skater ever to win the world championship and the youngest ever to win an Olympic gold medal.

Lipinski's first skates were roller skates. She won a regional championship in New Jersey at age five, and when she was six, she traded in her wheels for blades. She progressed rapidly, going from her first lesson to her first medal in a national competition in less than six years—a silver medal at the 1994 national novice meet.

In 1991, Lipinski's father, Jack, was transferred to a new job in Sugar Land, Texas. For Tara to continue her training, she had to practice at 3 A.M. She returned to the rink after school. After one school year in Texas, the family made a decision: Jack would remain in Texas, but Tara and her mother, Patricia, would return to the Delaware skating rink where she trained while living in Philadelphia.

The sacrifice paid off. Lipinski won the gold medal at the 1994 U.S. Sports Festival. She was 12 years and one month old, the youngest ever to win a medal at the sports festival.

In 1995, Lipinski and her mother moved again, to Bloomfield Hills, Mich., where she could work with acclaimed coach Richard Callaghan.

In 1996, she was third at the world championship, and in 1997 she won the U.S. national championship and the world championship. She was the youngest ever to win the U.S. and world titles.

In 1998, Lipinski, defending her U.S. national title, was in fourth place entering the long program. Only the top three would make the Olympic team. Needing a strong performance, Lipinski delivered and won the silver medal.

At the 1998 Olympic Games in Nagano, Japan, Lipinski defeated Michelle Kwan, who was heavily favored, to win the gold medal. In the long program, Kwan skated conservatively, and Lipinski, sensing an opening, skated virtually flawlessly to win the gold medal. She became the youngest figure skating gold medalist in history at 15 years, seven months. She and Kwan gave the United States its first 1-2 finish since 1956. After the Olympics, in April 1998, Lipinski decided to turn pro.

Louganis, Greg

diving

Born: January 29, 1960 in San Diego, California

Greg Louganis is the greatest diver in history. Blessed with athleticism, strength, and grace, he was often compared to Rudolf Nureyev, the acclaimed Russian ballet dancer.

But Louganis' personal story and what he overcame is just as compelling as his accomplishments. Louganis' parents were 15 years old and unwed when he was born. His father was Samoan, his mother Swedish. He was adopted at nine months old. His adoptive father was very demanding. He grew up being teased by classmates because of the color of his skin (he was called "nigger") and because he suffered from dyslexia. Louganis said the taunts were so hurtful he considered committing suicide on three different occasions.

Louganis, also teased because of his athletic pursuits, went from dancing lessons to gymnastics, before he took to diving. Coached by Sammy Lee, himself a two-time Olympic diving gold medalist, Louganis won a silver medal in the platform event at the 1976 Olympics. It was also during the 1976 Olympics that Louganis confronted the reality of his homosexuality.

In 1978, Louganis won the world platform championship and the Amateur Athletic Union (AAU) 1- and 3-meter titles. In 1979, he won gold medals in the springboard and platform events at the Pan-American Games. Because of the U. S.'s boycott, he was unable to participate in the 1980 Moscow Olympics. At the 1982 world championships, he was the first diver ever to record a perfect 10 score from all seven judges in a major international meet.

At the 1984 Olympics in Los Angeles, Louganis became the first male diver to win the platform and springboard events since 1928. He also became the first diver ever to surpass the 700-point barrier in the platform (710.91). He was named the winner of the Sullivan Award as the nation's outstanding amateur athlete.

Louganis continued to dominate, winning the springboard and platform events at the 1986 world championships and the 1987 Pan-American Games. At the 1988 Olympics in Seoul, South Korea, he won two more gold medals, but not without a close call.

During the springboard qualifying, Louganis hit his head on the board while doing a 2 1/2 somersault from a pike position. The gash on Louganis' head required five stitches. But what most concerned Louganis about the cut was his medical condition: He was HIV-positive, something only a small circle of friends knew and something he wouldn't disclose publicly until years later. Louganis steeled himself and returned to the pool some 20 hours later to win the springboard. He won the platform later in the week.

Louganis retired after the 1988 Games and later went public with his homosexuality at the 1994 Gay Games. His autobiography, *Breaking the Surface*, was published in 1995, when he revealed he was HIV-positive.

Louganis won 47 national AAU titles, six world championships, three NCAA championships, and five Olympic medals during his career. He was inducted into the U.S. Olympic Hall of Fame in 1985.

Lynn, Janet (Janet Lynn Nowicki)

figure skating

Born: April 6, 1953 in Chicago, Illinois

Janet Lynn began skating when she was three years old, and when she was in first grade, her parents drove her more than 100 miles twice a week to train.

In 1966, at age 13, Lynn won the U.S. junior ladies championship. Three years later, she finished third at the U.S. championship. In 1969, she won the first of her five straight U.S. titles. She was third at the 1972 world championships and second at the 1973 world championship. Lynn didn't fare as well in international competition because she wasn't as strong in the compulsory figures. A graceful, elegant performer, her strength was free skating.

At the 1972 Olympics in Sapporo, Japan, Lynn fell during her long program, but she got up smiling. She won the bronze medal and endeared herself to fans everywhere.

Lynn turned pro after the 1972 Olympics. She signed a $1.45 million contract with Ice Follies. She was the highest-paid female skater in the world. She skated professionally for two years before exercise-induced asthma forced her to retire. She returned to the ice in 1980, won the first U.S. professional skating championship, then retired for good.

Mahre, Phil

skiing

Born: May 10, 1957 in Yakima, Washington

Phil Mahre was one of the best American male skiers ever. He won U.S. championships in the giant slalom in 1975, 1977, 1978, and 1979.

In 1979, during a race in Lake Placid, N.Y., Mahre suffered a severely broken left ankle. A metal plate and seven screws were inserted. Mahre returned to the slopes in less than six months. At the 1980 Olympics at Lake Placid, he won a silver medal in the slalom.

In 1981, Mahre defeated Ingemar Stenmark, the top skier in the world, to win the World Cup overall title, the first American to do so. He successfully defended his title in 1982 and 1983.

At the 1984 Olympics, Mahre won the gold medal in the slalom. His twin brother, Steve, won the silver. No other brother combination has ever won a gold and silver in the same alpine race in Olympic history.

Both brothers retired shortly after the 1984 Games. They turned pro and also raced sports cars.

Mathias, Bob

track and field

Born: November 27, 1930 in Tulare, California

Bob Mathias began training for the decathlon three months before the 1948 Olympic Games. He was an outstanding all-around athlete in high school, averaging about nine yards a carry in football and 18 points a game in basketball. He could high jump five feet by the time he was 11 years old and long jump 15. He set 21 California state high school records.

Still, he had no experience in the decathlon and had never performed four of the 10 events that make up this grueling test of endurance.

But Mathias, who overcame acute anemia, chicken pox, measles, and whooping cough as a child, won the first marathon he ever participated in—at the Pacific Coast Games—and then finished first at the Olympic Trials, defeating three-time national champion Irving Mondschein. Mathias was the youngest member ever of a U.S. Olympic track team.

At the 1948 Games in London, Mathias won the decathlon with 7,139 points. He was the youngest male Olympic champion in history and was named the winner of the Sullivan Award as the nation's outstanding amateur athlete.

Mathias attended Stanford University and played fullback for the football team. He played in the 1952 Rose Bowl, making him the only person to compete in the Rose Bowl and the Olympics in the same year. He won the 1952 Olympic Trials and won his second gold medal in the 1952 Games in Helsinki, Finland. He set a world record with 7,887 points and won by 912 points, the largest margin in Olympic history. He became the only two-time winner of the Olympic decathlon.

Mathias won each of the 11 decathlons he entered, including the Amateur Athletic Union (AAU) championships from 1948 through 1950 and 1952.

Mathias retired after the 1952 Games. He later appeared in four movies, including *The Bob Mathias Story*, and he served four terms as a U.S. congressman, after which he played a leading role in the development of the U.S. Olympic Training Center.

Mathias was inducted into the National Track and Field Hall of Fame in 1974 and the U.S. Olympic Hall of Fame in 1983.

Matson, Randy

track and field

Born: March 5, 1945 in Kilgore, Texas

Randy Matson put on 30 pounds on the advice of his coach, Emil Mamaliga, at Texas A&M University. He went from 215 pounds to 245 pounds in seven months. He threw the shot put six feet farther than he ever had.

Matson won the 1964 Amateur Athletic Union (AAU) national championship as a freshman at Texas A&M. He also won five straight AAU titles, starting in 1966.

Matson won the silver medal at the 1964 Olympics, and in 1965 became the first man to throw the shot 70 feet (70 feet, 7 1/4 inches). No one else reached the 70-foot barrier until 1972. In 1971, Matson broke his world record with a throw of 71-5 1/4.

At the 1968 Olympics, Matson won the gold medal. He attempted to qualify for the 1972 Olympic team, but finished fourth at the trials.

Matson won the NCAA championship in the shot put and the discus in 1966 and 1967. He was named the winner of the 1967 Sullivan Award as the nation's outstanding amateur athlete and was inducted into the National Track and Field Hall of Fame in 1984.

McCormick, Pat

diving

Born: May 12, 1930 in Seal Beach, California

Pat McCormick, an outstanding diver, was best known for doing dives usually attempted by men and considered too dangerous for women. A natural athlete and a self-taught diver, McCormick nearly made the U.S. Olympic team in 1948 while in high school.

At the 1952 Olympics and again at the 1956 Games, McCormick won gold medals in the springboard and the platform events, a double equaled only by Greg Louganis in 1984 and 1988. In 1956, she was named the winner of the Sullivan Award as the nation's outstanding amateur athlete.

McCormick's signature dives were a back dive and a one-and-a-half twist with a somersault that was particularly daring for the time.

McCormick won 27 national and international titles in her career. She was inducted into the U.S. Olympic Hall of Fame in 1984 and the International Women's Sports Hall of Fame in 1985. She is the mother of Kelly McCormick, who won a silver medal in the springboard at the 1984 Olympics and a bronze in the springboard at the 1988 Games.

Meagher, Mary T.

swimming

Born: October 27, 1964 in Louisville, Kentucky

Mary T. Meagher set her first world record at the 1979 Pan-American Games when she was 14 years old, winning the 200-meter butterfly. She continued to have a significant impact on her sport for the rest of her career.

She qualified for the 1980 U.S. Olympic team in three individual events and two relays, but the United States' boycott of the Games, held in Moscow, kept her from competing. She briefly considered retirement, but pressed on with her sights set on the 1984 Games.

In the meantime, she lowered her own world records in the 100-meter butterfly (57.93) and the 200-meter butterfly (2:05.96). At the University of California, she won the NCAA 200-yard butterfly in 1983.

At the 1984 Olympics in Los Angeles, Meagher's decision not to retire proved to be the right one. She won gold medals in the 100- and 200-meter butterfly and the 4 x 100-meter medley relay team.

Back in college after the Olympics, Meagher won the 200-yard butterfly three straight years (1985–87) and the 100-yard butterfly in 1985 and 1987. In 1987, she won the Broderick Cup as the outstanding female college athlete in the nation.

In 1985, Meagher won both butterfly events in the short-course (yards) and long-course (meters) championships, and in 1986, she won the world championship in the 200-meter butterfly.

Meagher capped her career with a bronze medal in the 200 butterfly at the 1988 Olympic Games in Seoul, South Korea.

She was inducted into the International Women's Sports Hall of Fame and the International Swimming Hall of Fame in 1993.

Meyer, Debbie

swimming

Born: August 14, 1952 in Annapolis, Maryland

Debbie Meyer suffered from asthma as a child, so her family moved to California to take advantage of better weather conditions. She began to swim competitively in 1965 and was one of the best in the world within two years.

Meyer won 19 Amateur Athletic Union (AAU) titles from 1967 through 1971. She set world records in the 400- and 800-meter freestyle at the 1967 Pan-American Games.

At the 1968 Olympic Trials, Meyer set world records in the 200-, 400-, and 800-meter freestyle events. At the Games in Mexico City, she won gold medals in each of the three events and became the first swimmer to win three gold medals at one Olympics.

Meyer, named World Swimmer of the Year three times (1967–69), won the Sullivan Award in 1968 as the nation's outstanding amateur athlete. She was inducted into the International Swimming Hall of Fame in 1977, the U.S. Olympic Hall of Fame in 1986, and the International Women's Sports Hall of Fame in 1987.

Miller, Shannon

gymnastics

Born: March 10, 1977 in Rolla, Missouri

Shannon Miller is the most decorated American gymnast, male or female, in history. She has won more Olympic (7) and world championship (9) medals than anyone.

Miller began in gymnastics in 1982 at age five, after receiving a trampoline for Christmas. Although she showed great promise, her development was hindered somewhat by her shyness. Judges grade not only on technical merit, but also on a gymnast's ability to entertain and connect with the crowd. In addition, Miller was a perfectionist, and her frustration over not performing a routine as well as she could often left her in tears.

When Miller was nine, she met coach Steve Nunno, who began working on channeling Miller's frustration into a more positive emotion.

By the time Miller was 13, she qualified for the U.S. national team, and in 1992, she helped the U.S. team win a silver medal at the world championships. With her sights set on the 1992 Olympics, Miller fell during a workout and dislocated her elbow. Given a choice of wearing a cast for six weeks, which would force her to miss the Olympics, or having surgery, she chose surgery. She competed in the U.S. championship one month after the operation and won a gold medal on the balance beam and a bronze in the vault.

At the 1992 Olympics, Miller won five medals, the most of any U.S. athlete at the '92 Games. She won silver in the all-around and balance beam, and bronze in the uneven bars, floor exercise, and team competition. Her second-place finish in the all-around was the highest ever by an American gymnast at a nonboycotted Games.

Miller won world championships in 1993 and 1994, the only American gymnast to win consecutive world all-around titles.

At the 1996 Olympics in Atlanta, Miller won the gold medal on the balance beam and also helped the U.S. team to the first team gold medal ever.

Miller, a three-time nominee for the Sullivan Award, given to the nation's outstanding amateur athlete, was training to make her third Olympic team for the 2000 Olympics in Sydney, Australia, but failed to qualify.

Mills, Billy
track and field
Born: June 30, 1938 in Pine Ridge, South Dakota

Billy Mills registered one of the biggest upsets in Olympic history with his victory in the 10,000 meters at the 1964 Games in Tokyo.

Mills, who grew up on the Oglala Sioux Reservation, was orphaned at age 12, after which he went to live at the Haskell Institute in Kansas. He started running to get in shape for boxing, but after losing several fights, he gave up boxing and focused on running.

Mills attended the University of Kansas, where he ran distance events and was All-Big Eight in the 10,000 meters and in cross-country.

In the Olympic 10,000 meters, Mills fell to third place behind Mohamed Gamoudi of Tunisia, and Ron Clarke, the world-record holder from Australia. Just when it seemed Mills had no chance of winning, he sprinted past the leaders with 50 yards to go and won by three yards in an Olympic record 28:24.4 He was the first American ever to win the event.

Mills, who also finished 14th in the Olympic marathon in 1964, set a world record (27:11.6) in the six-mile run at the Amateur Athletic Union (AAU) championship. When injuries kept him out of the 1968 Olympics, Mills announced his retirement. He was inducted into the National Track and Field Hall of Fame in 1976 and the U.S. Olympic Hall of Fame in 1984.

Moses, Edwin
track and field
Born: August 31, 1955 in Dayton, Ohio

Edwin Moses owns one of the most remarkable streaks in all of sports. He dominated the 400-meter hurdles for nearly 10 years, during which time he never lost a race.

Moses was a sophomore on an academic scholarship at Morehouse College in Atlanta. He concentrated mainly on the 400 meters and the 110-meter hurdles. When he entered the 1976 Olympic Trials, he had never run the 400-meter hurdles in an international meet, but he qualified for the team, and at the Games in Montreal, he won the gold medal in 47.64 seconds, a world record. Moses also won by eight meters, the greatest margin of victory in Olympic history.

Moses was a perfect physical specimen for the hurdles, and he also was a cerebral athlete who focused on the technical aspects of the event. Because he was blessed with a stride that measured 9 feet, 9 inches, Moses was able to take just 13 strides between hurdles, as compared to between 14 and 17 strides taken by other runners.

On August 26, 1977, Moses lost to Harald Schmid of Germany. Two weeks later, he defeated Schmid and went on to win 122 straight races, 107 of them finals. He missed a chance to win a gold medal in the 1980 Games because of the United States' decision to boycott the Moscow Olympics. At the 1984 Olympics, Moses won his second gold medal.

Moses' streak ended on June 4, 1987, in Madrid, Spain. He lost to Danny Harris, who finished second at the 1984 Olympics. Three months later, Moses came back to win the world championship, his second (1983, '87).

At the 1988 Olympics, Moses won the bronze medal in the 400-meter hurdles. He retired shortly thereafter.

Moses won the 1983 Sullivan Award as the nation's outstanding amateur athlete. In 1984, he was named the *Sports Illustrated* Sportsman of the Year, an award he shared with gymnast Mary Lou Retton, and the U.S. Olympic Committee's Sportsman of the Year.

He was inducted into the U.S. Olympic Hall of Fame in 1985 and the National Track and Field Hall of Fame in 1994.

Naber, John

swimming

Born: January 20, 1956 in Evanston, Illinois

John Naber predicted Olympic greatness for himself when he was nine years old. While on a family vacation to Greece, he visited Olympia and told his parents he would someday be an Olympic champion.

Naber didn't start swimming competitively until he was 13 years old, but he made his dream come true at the 1976 Olympics. He won four gold medals and one silver medal, and each of the four golds were won in world-record time.

Naber won the 100- and 200-meter backstroke and was a member of the 800-meter freestyle relay and the 400-meter medley relay. His silver medal came in the 200-meter freestyle.

Naber was the first man to break two minutes in the 200-meter backstroke and the first under 56 seconds in the 100-meter backstroke. Both world records stood seven years, until 1983.

Prior to the 1976 Games, Naber had won 15 NCAA championships swimming for the University of Southern California.

Naber won 17 U.S. national championships in backstroke, set 12 American backstroke records, and was a member of seven U.S. national champion relay teams. He also set six world records.

Naber was named the World Male Swimmer of the Year in 1976 and won the Sullivan Award in 1977 as the nation's outstanding amateur athlete. He was inducted into the International Swimming Hall of Fame in 1982 and the U.S. Olympic Hall of Fame in 1984.

Nurmi, Paavo

track and field

Born: June 13, 1897 in Turku, Finland

Died: October 2, 1973

Paavo Nurmi, one of the great middle- and long-distance runners of his time, won 12 Olympic medals, nine of them gold.

He made his Olympic debut at the 1920 Games in Antwerp, Belgium, and won gold medals in the 10,000-meter run, the 8,000-meter cross-country run, and the team cross-country competition. He also won a silver in the 5,000 meters.

At the 1924 Olympics in Paris, Nurmi made most of the headlines as he outdid his performance of four years earlier. He took gold medals in the 1,500 meters (3:53.6) and 5,000 meters (14:31.2), running the races within an hour of each other and setting Olympic records in both. With one lap to go in the 1,500 meters and Nurmi comfortably ahead, he checked the stopwatch he wore, then tossed it into the infield.

Two days later, he won the 10,000-meter cross-country run, surviving high heat and a difficult course. Only 15 of the 38 starters made it to the finish. He also won gold medals in the 3,000-meter team cross-country and the 10,000-meter team cross-country.

At the 1928 Games in Amsterdam, Nurmi won the gold in the 10,000 meters in an Olympic-record time of 30:18.8. He also took silvers in the 5,000 meters and the 3,000-meter steeplechase.

O'Brien, Dan

track and field

Born: July 18, 1966 in Portland, Oregon

Dan O'Brien, an Olympic gold medalist and three-time world champion in the decathlon, is probably best known for the Olympics he failed to participate in.

O'Brien, an all-around athlete, was an all-state football and basketball player and a four-time state track champion during his senior year at Henley High School in Klamath Falls, Ore.

After being a "party animal" for several years at the University of Idaho, O'Brien failed to qualify for the 1988 Olympics after injuring his leg in the Olympic Trials. He won the world championship in 1991, 1993, and 1995.

Heavily favored to make the 1992 U.S. Olympic team, O'Brien no-heighted in the pole vault, finished 11th, and failed to qualify, which ruined an elaborate marketing campaign staged by Reebok. Later in 1992, he scored 8,891 points to set a world record that stood for seven years.

In 1994, O'Brien admitted that he battled a drinking problem and that he was under medication for attention deficit disorder.

O'Brien made the U.S. Olympic team in 1996 and won the gold medal, scoring 8,824 points. A stress fracture suffered in 1997 kept him out of action the entire year. He won the decathlon at the 1998 Goodwill Games, his only competition of the year, and he was ranked no. 1 in the world by *Track and Field News* for a record sixth year.

O'Brien failed in his bid to qualify for the 2000 Olympics.

Oerter, Al

track and field

Born: August 19, 1936 in Astoria, New York

Al Oerter's outstanding career as a discus thrower stretched through four different decades and four Olympic Games.

Oerter didn't have the look of an Olympic champion growing up. He was skinny and had no championship aspirations. He expected he'd join his father's plumbing business. But he began throwing the discus for fun and earned a track scholarship to the University of Kansas.

Oerter was a trend-setter when it came to training habits. He preferred wheat bread over white and broiled meat over fried. He was also blessed with a muscular frame, but was quite lithe.

He came to the 1956 Olympics as a virtual unknown and defeated world-record holder Fortune Gordien of the United States. Oerter's first throw was a personal-best 184 feet, 11 inches. Gordien couldn't beat it.

In 1957, Oerter survived a near-fatal car accident. He finished second to Rink Babka at the U.S. Olympic Trials and wasn't favored to win the gold medal at the 1960 Games. He trailed Babka after the first four throws, but on his fifth throw, thanks to a tip from Babka about changing his style, Oerter threw 194 feet, 2 inches to win his second gold.

In 1962, Oerter became the first person to exceed a throw of 200 feet, and after holding and losing the world record a number of times, he eventually held it at 206 feet, 6 inches in April 1964. He surrendered the world record prior to the 1964 Olympics and entered the Games with a slipped disk in his neck and torn rib cartilage. Oerter was wrapped in bandages and given a shot of Novacain. He proclaimed that if he didn't make the winning throw on his first attempt, he would have no chance. But after four throws, he was in third place. On his fifth throw, Oerter threw 200 feet, 1 inch, which was enough to win the gold.

Oerter won his fourth and final Olympic gold medal at the 1968 Games, despite a torn thigh muscle and a disc problem that required him to wear a surgical collar. After a poor throw and a foul, Oerter discarded the collar and threw 212 feet, 6 inches, five feet farther than his personal best.

Oerter retired after the 1968 Games, but returned to attempt to qualify for the 1980 Games. At age 43, he threw 33 feet farther than his first gold-medal winning toss in 1956. He finished fourth and missed making the U.S. team by one spot.

In addition to the Olympic medals, Oerter also was the Amateur Athletic Union (AAU) national champion in 1957, 1959, 1960, 1962, 1964, and 1966. He won a gold medal at the Pan-American Games in 1959.

Oerter was inducted into the National Track and Field Hall of Fame in 1974 and the U.S. Olympic Hall of Fame in 1983.

Owens, Jesse (James)

track and field
Born: September 12, 1913 in Danville, Alabama
Died: March 31, 1980

Jesse Owens made his mark in Olympic competition as one of the great track stars of all time. But what he accomplished socially and politically in the 1936 Games resonated as much or more.

James Cleveland Owens was the son of an Alabama sharecropper, and by the time he was seven years old, he was expected to pick 100 pounds of cotton a day.

The family moved to Cleveland when Owens was nine, and it was then and there that he picked up his nickname. Asked by a teacher what his first name was, Owens said, "J.C." The teacher thought he said Jesse, and the name stuck.

Because the family couldn't afford any athletic equipment, Owens took to running. By the time he was a senior at Cleveland East Technical High School, Owens ran the 100 in 9.4, tying a scholastic world record; ran the 220 in 20.7 seconds; and long-jumped 24-9 5/8.

Owens attended Ohio State University, where, in 1935 as a sophomore, he broke four world records and tied another within 70 minutes in the same afternoon at the Big Ten meet in Ann Arbor, Mich.

Owens tied the record in the 100 (9.4) and set records in the long jump (26-8 1/4), the 220 (20.3), and the 220-yard low hurdles (22.6). The record in the 220 was also accepted as the world record for the 200 meters.

Owens accomplished his feats while suffering from a back injury, caused by a fall while horsing around with his buddies.

Owens, by now a household name in the United States, became a worldwide figure in the 1936 Olympic Games in Berlin. The Games were often referred to as the "Nazi Olympics," because of Adolf Hitler's prediction of Aryan supremacy over the U.S. and its "African auxiliaries," which he called Owens and other African Americans on the team.

Jesse Owens

The first event in which Owens competed was the 100-meter dash. With Hitler watching on August 3, 1936, Owens burst from lane 1 and, thanks to a late surge, won the race in an Olympic-record 10.3 seconds. He followed that with gold medals in the long jump (26-5 1/2, Olympic record), the 200 meters (20.7, Olympic record), and the 4 x 100-meter relay (39.8, world record). His four gold medals were unequaled until Carl Lewis won four at the 1984 Games in Los Angeles.

Owens was named the Associated Press Male Athlete of the Year, but he was disappointed that he didn't win the Sullivan Award, given to the year's outstanding amateur athlete. The Sullivan went to Glenn Morris, the Olympic decathlon champion, who was white. Owens was not allowed to enter the Waldorf-Astoria by the front door for a reception in his honor, nor was he ever invited to the White House to meet the president.

Owens did not return home a hero, at least not in the eyes of the Amateur Athletic Union (AAU), which suspended him for refusing to participate in an exhibition tour in Europe. As a result, his career was effectively over.

For a while, Owens earned money by racing against dogs, horses, and motorcycles during a barnstorming tour. He went into public relations and later worked for the U.S. Olympic Committee. His efforts helped avoid a walkout of African-American athletes at the 1968 Games in Mexico City, Mexico. But because of his antimilitancy stance, Owens was criticized for being an "Uncle Tom."

Owens wrote two books—*Blackthink*, 1970, which criticized militancy, and *I Have Changed*, 1972, which retracted many of his earlier opinions.

Owens, who smoked a pack of cigarettes a day, died of lung cancer in March 1980. He is a member of the National Track and Field Hall of Fame and the Olympic Hall of Fame.

Powell, Mike

track and field

Born: November 10, 1968 in Philadelphia, Pennsylvania

Mike Powell had the misfortune of competing at the same time as Carl Lewis, also a long jumper. Powell often found himself in Lewis' considerable shadow. So it was somewhat surprising when, in August 1991, Powell broke Bob Beamon's long jump record that had been set at the 1968 Olympics. Many experts considered the record unbreakable, and if it were broken, Lewis would be the one to do it.

Lewis won the gold medal, to Powell's silver, at the 1988 Olympics and would do so again in the 1992 Olympics.

But at the 1991 world championships in Tokyo, Powell jumped 29 feet, 4 1/2 inches and broke Beamon's record by 2 inches. Through 2000, Powell's record still stood. He was named the winner of the 1991 Sullivan Award as the nation's outstanding amateur athlete.

Powell said after the record that he wasn't as concerned with Beamon's mark as he was with beating Lewis.

In 1993, Powell won the U.S. national championship and the world championship in the long jump.

Prefontaine, Steve

track and field

Born: January 25, 1951 in Coos Bay, Oregon
Died: May 30, 1975

Steve Prefontaine was one of the greatest distance runners in U.S. history. In high school, he set an interscholastic record in the two-mile (8:46.6) that eclipsed the previous record by almost seven seconds.

He went to college at the University of Oregon and was the first athlete ever to win the same event, 5,000 meters, four years in a row (1970–73). Prefontaine, known as "Pre," won the NCAA cross-country championship in 1970, 1971, and 1973 and the Amateur Athletic Union (AAU) 5,000-meter title in 1971 and 1973.

Prefontaine wasn't blessed with great finishing speed, so his style was to set a fast, early pace and wear out his competition. That didn't work at the 1972 Olympics, where he wore out too quickly and finished fourth.

In 1974, Prefontaine was offered $200,000 to turn pro and join the International Track Association, but he declined the offer, preferring instead to compete in the 1976 Olympics. But in 1975, just hours after winning the 5,000 meters at an invitational meet in Eugene, Ore., he was killed in a one-car accident.

When he died, he held the American records in the two-mile, 3,000 meters, three-mile, and 5,000 meters. He was inducted into the National Track and Field Hall of Fame in 1991.

Retton, Mary Lou

gymnastics

Born: January 24, 1968 in Fairview, West Virginia

Mary Lou Retton became an American hero with one vault in the 1984 Olympics in Los Angeles. But her emergence as a national celebrity began years earlier.

Retton, who took acrobatic and ballet lessons, eventually got involved in sports as an outlet for her energy. She took up gymnastics at age seven and imagined herself as an Olympic champion while watching Nadia Comaneci in the 1976 Games.

In 1983, realizing that Retton couldn't progress in Fairview, W. Va., her parents allowed her to move in with a family in Houston so she could be coached by the legendary Bela Karolyi, who had developed Comaneci.

Retton did not have the classic build of a gymnast. At 4 feet, 9 inches, and 92 pounds, she was boxier and more compact than most gymnasts. But she proved the skeptics wrong. It all came together at the 1984 Games.

Two months before the Games, Retton underwent arthroscopic surgery to remove torn cartilage from her right knee. By the time the Olympics began, she was completely recovered.

In the all-around competition, Retton trailed Ekaterina Szabo, the reigning world champion and Olympic favorite, by .05 point. In the final event, the vault, Retton earned perfect 10s from every judge. She became the first American woman to win a medal of any kind in gymnastics. She also won silver medals in the individual vault and team competition and a bronze in the floor exercise and uneven bars.

The effect of Retton's spectacular performance under pressure was enhanced by her charming personality and smiling face. She was named the Associated Press Female Athlete of the Year in 1984. She also shared the *Sports Illustrated* Sportsman of the Year Award with hurdler Edwin Moses.

Retton gained even more fame with her face on a Wheaties box and appearances on numerous television shows. Nine years after her gold medal–winning performance, a national poll ranked her and Dorothy Hamill as the two most popular female athletes in the country.

Reynolds, Butch (Henry)

track and field

Born: June 8, 1964 in Akron, Ohio

Butch Reynolds set the world record in the 400 meters (43.29) on August 16, 1988. The record stood until 1999, when it was broken by Michael Johnson.

Reynolds won a silver medal in the 400 meters at the 1988 Olympics. He also anchored the gold medal–winning 4 x 400-meter relay team to a world record (2:56.16).

In 1990, Reynolds was banned by the International Amateur Athletics Federation (IAAF) for allegedly testing positive for steroids. Reynolds sued the IAAF, and in 1992, the U.S. Supreme Court ordered the U.S. Olympic Committee to allow Reynolds to compete in the 1992 Olympic Trials. The IAAF threatened to suspend any runners who ran against Reynolds. The 400-meter trials were put off for four days, when the IAAF backed down. By the time Reynolds reached the final, he was exhausted and finished fifth.

Reynolds sued the IAAF in 1992 and won a $27.4 million judgment. In May 1994, a court of appeals voided the judgment, and the Supreme Court refused to hear the case.

In 1993, he won a gold medal in the 400 meters at the world indoor championships, a silver medal in the 400 at the world championships, and a gold in the 4 x 400-meter relay. At the 1995 world championships, he won a silver in the 400 and a gold in the 4 x 400-meter relay.

Richards, Bob

track and field

Born: February 20, 1926 in Champaign, Texas

Bob Richards dominated the pole vault for 10 years, beginning in 1947. He tied for the 1947 NCAA championship while a student at the University of Illinois, and in 1948 won the first of his Amateur Athletic Union (AAU) outdoor titles and eight AAU indoor titles.

Richards, who became a fully ordained minister in 1948 and was dubbed the "Vaulting Vicar" by sportswriters, won a bronze medal in the 1948 Olympics.

At the 1952 Games, Richards won the gold medal with an Olympic-record vault of 14-11. In the 1956 Olympics, he repeated as gold medalist, vaulting an Olympic-record 14-11 1/2. He is the only pole vaulter to win gold medals at consecutive Olympics.

Richards, who won gold medals at the Pan-American Games in 1951 and 1955, competed in the decathlon, winning the AAU championship in 1951, 1954, and 1956. He qualified for the 1956 Olympics, but finished 12th because of an injury.

Richards retired in 1957 and went on to great fame as the athlete pictured on the Wheaties box. He also did television commercials for Wheaties and some television and radio commentary.

Richards, winner of the 1951 Sullivan Award as the nation's outstanding amateur athlete, was inducted into the National Track and Field Hall of Fame in 1975 and the U.S. Olympic Hall of Fame in 1983.

Rodgers, Bill

track and field

Born: December 23, 1947 in Hartford, Connecticut

Bill Rodgers was one of the best distance runners in the United States during the mid-1970s and early 1980s. Rodgers was a distance runner at Wesleyan University, but stopped running during his senior year.

Then, watching Frank Shorter win the marathon at the 1972 Olympics, Rodgers' interest was rekindled.

He finished third in the 1975 international cross-country championships, the highest finish ever for an American man.

Rodgers won the Boston Marathon four times (1975, '78–80) and the New York Marathon four times (1976–79). He qualified for the 1976 Olympics, but failed to medal. He was inducted into the National Track and Field Hall of Fame in 1999.

Rudolph, Wilma
track and field
Born: June 23, 1940 in Bethlehem, Tennessee
Died: November 12, 1994

Wilma Rudolph was the first American woman to win three Olympic gold medals in track and field. That she reached such heights was a tribute to her determination and will to succeed.

Rudolph, the 17th of 21 children, weighed only 4 1/2 pounds at birth. She was diagnosed with polio when she was four years old, and she also suffered from pneumonia and scarlet fever. As a result of the polio, she grew up needing to wear a brace on her right leg. After five years of wearing the brace, the nine-year-old Rudolph suddenly removed it one day and began to walk without help. With the help of her brothers and sisters, Rudolf had been practicing for some time.

It wasn't long before Rudolph began racing—and beating—all the children in her neighborhood. She became a fine high school basketball player and also ran track. In four seasons of high school track, she was undefeated.

In 1956, at age 16, Rudolph qualified for the Olympics in Melbourne, Australia, and won a bronze medal in the 4 x 100-meter relay.

Rudolph made history four years later at the 1960 Olympic Games in Rome. She won gold medals in the 100 meters, 200 meters, and the 4 x 100-meter relay. She set the world record in the 200 meters at the Olympic Trials (22.9) and a world record in the 100 meters in a preliminary heat at the Games (10.3).

Rudolph became an international star, was introduced to President John F. Kennedy, given a ticker tape parade, and showered with a variety of awards. The Associated Press named her the Female Athlete of the Year in 1960 and 1961, and she won the Sullivan Award as the nation's outstanding amateur athlete.

Rudolph retired in 1963, earned her college degree, and raised four children. She wrote her autobiography, *Wilma*, in 1977 and began the Wilma Rudolph Foundation to promote amateur athletics.

Rudolph was inducted into the International Women's Sports Hall of Fame, the National Track and Field Hall of Fame, and the Olympic Hall of Fame. She died in 1994 of brain cancer.

Ryun, Jim
track and field
Born: April 29, 1947 in Wichita, Kansas

Jim Ryun still holds the record as the youngest person ever to run a sub-four-minute mile. At 17 years, 37 days,

he ran a 3:59.0. He still holds the high school record for the mile at 3:55, set in 1963.

Ryun qualified for the 1964 U.S. Olympic team, reaching the semifinals of the 1,500 meters. In 1965, Ryun won the first of his three Amateur Athletic Union (AAU) national titles in the mile.

Ryun set three world records in 1966, one each in the 880-yard run (1:44.9), the 1,500 meters (3:33.1), and the mile (3:51.3). He was named the winner of the Sullivan Award as the nation's outstanding amateur athlete.

In 1967, he ran a 3:51.1 mile, a record that stood for five years. He also won the 1967 NCAA title in the mile.

Ryun came down with mononucleosis in 1968 and missed much of the season, although he did qualify for the 1968 Olympic team in the 1,500 meters. He had gone more than three years without losing in the mile or the 1,500 meters, and he entered the Olympics as a favorite. But Kip Keino of Kenya set a fast pace in the 1,500 meters and Ryun never caught up and took the silver.

Ryun retired in 1969, but made a comeback in 1972, making the Olympic team in the 1,500 meters. He fell during a preliminary at the Games, ending his hopes for a medal.

Ryun was inducted into the National Track and Field Hall of Fame in 1980. He is a member of the U.S. House of Representatives from Kansas.

Salazar, Alberto
track and field
Born: August 7, 1958 in Havana, Cuba

Alberto Salazar was one of the outstanding marathoners of his time. He set one world record and six U.S. records in the marathon, the 5,000 meters, and the 10,000 in his career.

His debut was the New York City Marathon, and he won in 2:09.41, a course record and the fastest marathon debut ever. In 1982, he successfully defended his title, winning in a world-record time of 2:03.13. He won his third straight New York Marathon in 1982, finishing in 2:09.29.

Salazar won the 1982 Boston Marathon in a course-record 2:08.51.

Salazar qualified for the 1980 and 1984 Olympic teams, but failed to medal.

Scherbo, Vitaly
gymnastics
Born: January 13, 1972 in Minsk, Russia

Vitaly Scherbo made history at the 1992 Olympics by winning an unprecedented six gold medals. He was first in all-around, pommel horse, parallel bars, rings, vault, and team all-around. At the 1996 Olympics in Atlanta, Ga., he won four bronze medals—all-around, vault, parallel bars, and horizontal bars.

Scherbo also won 12 gold, seven silver, and four bronze medals at the world championships from 1991 to 1996.

Schollander, Don
swimming
Born: April 30, 1946 in Charlotte, North Carolina
Don Schollander made history at the 1964 Summer Games by becoming the first swimmer to win four gold medals at one Olympics and the first American since Jesse Owens in 1936 to win that many gold medals.

Schollander, who grew up in Lake Oswego, Ore., got off to a strong start. He was the top swimmer in his age group for two years, then came down with pneumonia when he was 11 years old and spent a month in bed. When he returned to the pool, he had moved up to a higher age group and was no longer as successful. He wanted to quit, but his father advised against it, saying he could quit when he was at the top of his age group, but not the bottom.

Schollander persevered and became a dominant swimmer, specializing in freestyle. He won the Amateur Athletic Union (AAU) national outdoor 200-meter freestyle from 1962 through 1967. He won the AAU outdoor 100-meter freestyle in 1964, 1966, and 1967; the 400-meter in 1966; the indoor 200-yard from 1963 through 1967; and the 500-yard indoor in 1964.

At the 1964 Olympics, Schollander won gold medals in the 100- and 400-meter freestyle and as a member of the 400- and 800-meter freestyle relay teams. He won the Sullivan Award in 1964 as the nation's outstanding amateur athlete and was named the Associated Press Male Athlete of the Year.

At the 1968 Games, he took a silver medal in the 200-meter freestyle and a gold as a member of the 800-meter freestyle relay. He retired after the 1968 Olympics. He was inducted into the International Swimming Hall of Fame in 1965 and the U.S. Olympic Hall of Fame in 1983.

Seagren, Bob
track and field
Born: October 17, 1946 in Pomona, California
Bob Seagren was one of the best pole vaulters in the world during the late 1960s and early 1970s. A student at the University of Southern California, Seagren won the NCAA outdoor championship in 1967 and 1969 and the Amateur Athletic Union (AAU) outdoor championship in 1966, 1969, and 1970. He also won a gold medal at the Pan-American Games in 1967.

Seagren won the gold medal at the 1968 Olympics (Olympic-record 17-8 1/2) and might have duplicated his feat at the 1972 Games. But a controversy over the style of pole he used likely cost him a second gold medal. Seagren was one of many vaulters who used a carbon pole. He used it to set a world record of 18-5 3/4 inches at the 1972 Olympic Trials; earlier in 1972, he became the first American to vault over 18 feet. Shortly before the Olympics began, the International Amateur Athletic Federation (IAAF) banned the pole. Seagren and other vaulters protested, and the IAAF lifted the ban, only to reinstitute it the night before qualifying. Seagren, forced to use an unfamiliar pole, won a silver. The gold medal winner, Wolfgang Nordwig of East Germany, didn't use a carbon pole and therefore didn't have to change.

Seagren, who gained fame on a different stage by winning the inaugural *Superstars* competition on ABC, was inducted into the National Track and Field Hall of Fame in 1986.

Shorter, Frank
track and field
Born: October 31, 1947 in Munich, Germany
Frank Shorter was one of the United States' greatest marathoners. Born in Germany, the son of an American doctor, he attended Yale University, where he was the NCAA 10,000-meter champion in 1969. He also won the Amateur Athletic Union (AAU) cross-country championship 1970–73, the three-mile championship in 1970, and the six-mile championship in 1970 and 1971.

Shorter first ran the marathon in 1971 and won a gold medal at the Pan-American Games that year. He won the 1972 Olympic Trials and won the gold medal at the Games in Munich, Germany, running the second-fastest time in Olympic history (2:12.19.8).

When Shorter entered the stadium in Munich for the final lap of the marathon, he was greeted with boos from the crowd. The displeasure wasn't directed at Shorter. An imposter had entered the stadium before Shorter, posing as the race leader. Shorter entered as security was getting the imposter off the track. When the fans realized the winner was Shorter, they cheered enthusiastically.

Shorter also finished fifth in the 10,000 meters at the 1972 Olympics, the third-highest finish by an American in that event. He was named the winner of the Sullivan Award as the nation's outstanding amateur athlete.

At the 1976 Games in Montreal, Shorter missed by 50 seconds becoming only the second marathoner ever to successfully defend his gold medal. He finished second, but still ran the second-fastest time ever (2:10.45.8).

Shorter, forced to retire in 1979 because of a foot injury, founded Frank Shorter Sportswear, a company that sells running apparel. He also served as a television commentator.

Shorter was inducted into the U.S. Olympic Hall of Fame in 1984 and the National Track and Field Hall of Fame in 1989.

Spitz, Mark

swimming

Born: February 10, 1950 in Modesto, California

Mark Spitz was one of the greatest swimmers of all time, but despite his success, he was never embraced by the public for his accomplishments.

Spitz's demanding father, Arnold, an executive for a steel company, had a motto: "Swimming isn't important; winning is."

Said Arnold Spitz to his son before a race, "There are eight guys in that pool for the race, but only one is a winner. The others are bums." A tireless worker, Mark Spitz became obsessed with winning and satisfying his father.

After winning a variety of Amateur Athletic Union (AAU) championships while swimming for legendary coach George Haines in high school in Santa Clara, Calif., Spitz entered the 1968 Olympics, predicting that he would win six gold medals. He won two, as a member of the 400- and 800-meter freestyle relays. He won a silver in the 100 butterfly and a bronze in the 100-meter freestyle.

After his Olympic disappointment, Spitz went to Indiana University and led the Hoosiers to four straight NCAA championships and won the 100-yard butterfly from 1969 through 1972. He also won the NCAA 200- and 500-yard freestyle in 1969 and the 200-yard butterfly in 1971 and 1972. In 1971, Spitz won the Sullivan Award as the nation's outstanding amateur athlete.

At the 1972 Olympics, he made up for his disappointing showing at the previous Games by winning gold medals and setting world records in each of the seven events he entered—100- and 200-meter butterfly, 100- and 200-meter freestyle, 400- and 800-meter freestyle relay, and 400-meter medley relay. No one ever won more gold medals in a single Olympics. His ranks as one of the greatest performances in Olympic history. He was named the Associated Press Male Athlete of the Year in 1972.

Spitz, who made an ill-fated comeback attempt in 1989 at age 39, set 23 world and 35 American records. He won 26 U.S. national championships.

Spitz was inducted into the International Swimming Hall of Fame in 1977 and the U.S. Olympic Hall of Fame in 1983.

Stenmark, Ingemar

skiing

Born: March 18, 1956 in Tarnaby, Sweden

Ingemar Stenmark won more World Cup races than any skier in history—86 in the slalom and giant slalom over a 16-year period. He won three World Cup overall championships (1976–78), and at the 1980 Olympics, he won gold medals in the slalom and giant slalom.

Stenmark won eight World Cup slalom titles (1975–81, '83) and six giant slalom titles (1977–81, '84).

Stevenson, Teofilo

boxing

Born: March 29, 1952 in Las Tunas, Oriente, Cuba

Teofilo Stevenson was one of the greatest boxers in Olympic history. He won gold medals in the heavyweight division in three Olympics (1972, '76, '80), the only boxer ever to accomplish the feat.

He won his first gold medal in a walkover against Ion Alexe, a Romanian, who withdrew because of a broken thumb.

In 1972, he took a total of just 7 minutes, 22 seconds to defeat his first three opponents. In the final, after his opponent, Mircea Simon of Romania, was knocked down, Simon's corner threw in the towel.

In the semifinals of the 1980 Games, Istvan Levai ran about for three rounds and became the first of Stevenson's opponents to go the distance. In the final, Stevenson defeated Pyotr Zayev for his third gold medal.

Stevenson, who never turned professional, could have participated in the 1984 Games in Los Angeles, but Cuba was one of the countries that boycotted the Olympics. Still, he remained an effective boxer for several more years, winning the world amateur championship in 1986 at age 34.

Stones, Dwight

track and field

Born: December 6, 1953 in Los Angeles, California

Dwight Stones was America's premier high jumper in the 1970s. He won the Amateur Athletic Union (AAU) championship in 1973, 1974, 1976, 1977, 1978, and 1983.

In 1972, he won the U.S. Olympic Trials, jumping 7-3. At the Olympics in Munich, Germany, he jumped 7-3 again and won a bronze medal. Stones set the world record of 7 feet, 6 5/8 inches in 1973 and broke his own mark in winning the 1976 NCAA outdoor championship, jumping 7 feet, 7 inches.

Stones was one of the favorites heading into the 1976 Olympics in Montreal, but because the retractable domed stadium in Montreal didn't close completely, leaving the high jump area wet, he could never get used to the conditions. He jumped 7-4 and won a silver medal.

Stones set his third and final world record four days after the Olympics, jumping 7 feet, 7 1/4 inches. He competed until 1979, when he was suspended for accepting money for competing on *Superstars,* a made-for-television competition. Stones attempted a comeback in 1983, but retired after not making the 1984 U.S. Olympic team.

Stones, who does television commentary work, was inducted into the National Track and Field Hall of Fame in 1998.

Street, Picabo
skiing
Born: April 3, 1971 in Triumph, Idaho

Picabo Street was the best female alpine skier of the 1990s, but her unusual first name attracted nearly as much attention as her skiing. The child of Stubby and Dee Street, self-described "classic flower children," Picabo didn't have a first name for the first three years of her life. Her birth certificate listed her as "Baby Girl." The family traveled extensively, and one of their trips took them to Mexico. When a name was needed on "Baby Girl's" passport, Stubby and Dee came up with Picabo (pronounced peek-a-boo), the name of a town in Idaho that is a Native American word for "shining waters."

As a child, Street played a variety of sports with boys, and was every bit as good as they were. She got involved in skiing when her elementary school began a weekly program. By age 16, in 1988, she was a member of the U.S. Ski Team. She won the junior downhill and Super G titles.

Despite her ability, Street was a free spirit who lacked discipline and the willingness to work hard. In July 1990, she was dismissed from the team when she showed up out of shape. When her parents, who had moved to Hawaii, found out what happened, they challenged her to join them and get herself in shape. She rejoined the team in 1991. In 1993, her rededication paid off with a silver medal in the downhill combined event at the world alpine ski championships. At the 1994 Olympic Games in Lillehammer, Norway, Street won the silver medal in the downhill. The combination of performance and personality made Street a celebrity beyond skiing. She appeared on *Sesame Street,* did talk shows, and became the first woman to sign with Nike Sports Management Group, an agency with a client list that included Ken Griffey, Jr., Scottie Pippen, and Deion Sanders.

Street won six of nine races and became the first American ever to win the downhill season World Cup championship.

In 1996, Street tore the anterior cruciate and the medial collateral ligaments in her left knee and did not ski for six months. She came back to win the gold medal in the Super G at the 1998 Olympics at Nagano, Japan. But in March 1998, she had a terrible fall while competing in the World Cup Finals. She broke her leg and severely injured her knee. Street plans to return to racing in 2001 with her sights set on the 2002 Games in Salt Lake City.

Thompson, Daley
track and field
Born: July 30, 1958 in London, England

Daley Thompson won gold medals in the decathalon in two consecutive Olympic Games (1980, 1984). As a child, he was sent off to a state-supported boarding school because he was hyperactive and prone to street fighting. At the boarding school, he discovered sports. He was best at running and jumping.

Thompson enrolled in a small London college and set his sights on becoming a world-class sprinter, but his coach convinced him that the decathlon would be his best hope for worldwide acclaim.

Thompson's first decathlon came in 1975 at the Welsh Open. Because he was only 16, he needed a special waiver to compete, but he won, exceeding the previous record by 2,000 points.

Thompson qualified for the 1976 Olympics and finished 18th, behind Bruce Jenner, the winner. Thompson was determined to break Jenner's world record of 8,617 points, which he accomplished in 1980 in Austria. Later that year, he won the gold medal at the Olympic Games.

At the 1984 Games, Thompson repeated his gold medal performance, scoring a world-record 8,798 points.

Thompson, Jenny
swimming
Born: February 26, 1973 in Georgetown, Massachusetts

Jenny Thompson is the all-time leader in career Olympic gold medals for a U.S. female, with seven. She is first in total swimming medals, with eight.

Thompson's parents divorced when she was two years old, and her mother had to pinch pennies in order to be able to afford lessons. But the money and Thompson's hard work paid off. In 1987, she became the youngest U.S. swimmer to win a gold medal when she won the 50-meter freestyle at the Pan-American Games. She accepted a scholarship to Stanford University in 1991 and had one of the greatest college careers ever. In four years, she won 19 NCAA titles (individual and relay) and led the Cardinal to four straight NCAA team championships. She was named U.S. Swimming's Swimmer of the Year in 1993, when she won six gold medals at the Pan Pacific meet, five NCAA titles, and five national titles.

Just as impressive as her performances in the pool was getting her degree, in human biology, on time.

Thompson set a world record in the 100-meter freestyle at the 1992 Olympic Trials, becoming the first American woman in nearly 60 years to do so, and she was favored to win five gold medals at the Games in Barcelona, Spain. She won gold medals as part of the 400-meter freestyle and 400-meter medley relay teams, and a silver medal in the 100 freestyle. She was disappointed with her performance, but used it as an incentive to improve. She responded with her Swimmer of the Year season in 1993, but more disappointment followed. She failed to medal at the 1994 world championships, and she failed to qualify for an individual event at the 1996 Olympics in Atlanta, although she did win three gold medals as part of the 400-meter freestyle, the 800-meter freestyle, and 400-meter medley relay teams.

In 1998, Thompson finally won individual titles in the 100 freestyle and 100 butterfly, and added gold medals in the 400-meter freestyle relay and 400-meter medley relay. In 1999, among the records Thompson broke was that for the 100-meter butterfly (57.88), which had been held for 18 years by Mary T. Meagher.

Thompson, who owns 23 national titles, qualified for the 2000 Games in Sydney, Australia. She won two gold and one bronze medal.

Tomba, Alberto

skiing

Born: December 19, 1966 in Bologna, Italy

Alberto Tomba has won more Olympic medals in alpine skiing than anyone. Known for his flamboyant personality and his aggressive skiing style, Tomba won gold medals in the slalom and giant slalom at the 1988 Olympics, a gold medal in the giant slalom in the 1992 Olympics, and silver medals in the slalom in 1992 and 1994.

Tomba, whose nickname "La Bomba" means the bomb, was the first alpine skier to win gold medals in consecutive Olympics and the first alpine skier to win medals in three different Olympics.

In 1995, Tomba won the World Cup title (based on points earned in all five alpine disciplines—slalom, giant slalom, downhill, combined, super giant slalom) while only racing in the slalom and giant slalom.

Tomba won World Cup season titles in slalom in 1988, 1992, 1994, and 1995. He won the World Cup giant slalom in 1988, 1991, 1992, and 1995.

Toomey, Bill

track and field

Born: January 10, 1939 in Philadelphia, Pennsylvania

Bill Toomey won the Amateur Athletic Union (AAU) national pentathlon championship in 1960, 1961, 1963,

and 1964. But because the pentathlon wasn't an Olympic event, he began competing in the decathlon.

In his first attempt to make the U.S. Olympic team, he finished fourth at the 1964 Olympic Trials.

Toomey went on to win five AAU national decathlon championships (1965–69). At the 1968 Olympics, Toomey won the gold medal with an Olympic-record 8,193 points. Through the 1996 Games, his time in the 400 meters, 45.6, was still a world record.

In 1969, Toomey set a world record with 8,417 points. It was the 12th time he scored 8,000 or more points in the event. He was named the winner of the Sullivan Award as the nation's outstanding athlete.

Torrence, Gwen

track and field

Born: June 12, 1965 in Atlanta, Georgia

Gwen Torrence was one of the most versatile sprinters of her time. She was a world-class competitor in distances from 60 meters to 400 meters.

Torrence was a reluctant runner at first. During high school, she would practice only after the other girls had gone home, and she preferred street shoes to spikes because she considered spikes "too flashy."

At the University of Georgia, Torrence was the 1987 NCAA champion in the 100 and 200 meters. In 1991, she won silver medals in the 100 and 200 at the world championships.

Torrence won the 1992 U.S. Olympic Trials in the 100 and 200, and at the 1992 Games, she won gold in the 200 and as a member of the 4 x 100-meter relay. She finished fourth in the 100.

Torrence won another gold medal at the 1996 Games as a member of the 4 x 100-meter relay team, and she also took bronze in the 100 meters.

Torrence, who has had a difficult relationship with the media, also has been involved in her share of controversy. During the 1992 Olympics, she accused some of the competitors in the 100-meter final of taking drugs.

She suffered an injury to her left leg and missed most of the 1998 season. Torrence didn't compete at all in 1999.

Torvill, Jayne/Dean, Christopher

figure skating

Born (Torvill): October 7, 1957 in Nottingham, England

Born (Dean): July 27, 1958 in Nottingham, England

Jayne Torvill and Christopher Dean were the most accomplished ice dancers ever. Under the guidance of legendary coach Betty Callaway, they created programs that told stories and were performances, not just routines.

They won four straight ice dancing world championships, beginning in 1981. At the 1984 Olympic Games in Sarajevo, Yugoslavia, they are credited with one of the greatest performances in figure skating history. Their interpretation of Ravel's "Bolero" earned them nine perfect scores for artistic impression and three more perfect scores for technical merit. They won the gold medal.

Torvill and Dean turned professional and won the world professional ice dancing championship in 1985. In 1994, their request for Olympic reinstatement was granted, and they won the bronze medal at the Games in Lillehammer, Norway.

Tyus, Wyomia
track and field
Born: August 29, 1945 in Griffin, Georgia

Wyomia Tyus was the first woman to win Olympic gold medals in the 100-meter dash in consecutive Olympics, a feat later matched by Gail Devers. She got involved in sports to be able to play with her brothers. Although she liked basketball best, she was the Georgia high school sprint champion and in 1962 won the 50-, 75-, and 100-yard dashes at the Amateur Athletic Union (AAU) girls national championships.

Tyus won eight AAU championships, including the 100 meters at the National AAU Women's Outdoor Championships in 1964, which qualified her for the U.S. Olympic team. She won the Olympic gold medal in the 100 meters and was also a member of the 4 x 100-meter relay, which won a silver medal.

Tyus won the AAU 100-yard dash in 1965 and 1966, the 220-yard dash in 1966, and the 60-meter dash for three straight years, beginning in 1965.

Tyus qualified for her second Olympics in 1968 at Mexico City. The racial climate in the United States presented a dilemma for Tyus. She had to decide whether to compete or stay home because it was difficult to represent a country that she felt was unfair to African Americans.

Tyus decided to compete, and she won the gold medal in the 100 meters, setting a world record (11.0). She also ran the anchor leg for the 4 x 100-meter relay team, which also won the gold medal in a world-record time (42.8). Although Tyus didn't protest as did U.S. athletes John Carlos and Tommie Smith—raising their black-gloved hands in a "black power" salute on the medals podium—she did wear dark shorts after winning her medal and dedicated her victory to Carlos and Smith for the cause they espoused.

Tyus retired after the 1968 Olympics, but when the International Track Association was formed in 1973, she returned to competition, winning all 22 races in 1974. She was inducted into the U.S. Olympic Hall of Fame in 1985, the International Women's Sports Hall of Fame in 1981, and the National Track and Field Hall of Fame in 1980.

Van Dyken, Amy
swimming
Born: February 15, 1973 in Englewood, Colorado

Amy Van Dyken overcame a severe case of asthma to become an Olympic champion. She was diagnosed with asthma when she was 10 months old. One doctor called it the worst case he had ever seen. She was the butt of jokes among kids in her neighborhood because she always wore an inhaler around her neck. Van Dyken's activities were limited, but doctors suggested she take up swimming to improve her lung capacity.

She started slowly, unable to swim the length of the pool until she was 13, often finishing last in events against much younger children, but through hard work she developed into an outstanding swimmer. Van Dyken was a two-time high school state champion, in the 50- and 100-meter butterfly, and was named Colorado Swimmer of the Year.

At the University of Arizona in 1993, Van Dyken won the silver medal in the 50-yard freestyle at the NCAA championships. Van Dyken left Arizona after two years and transferred to Colorado State University, where she won the 50-yard freestyle at the 1994 NCAA championships, setting an American record in the process. She also won a bronze medal in the same event at the 1994 world championships.

The NCAA named her the Swimmer of the Year. Van Dyken left school after the 1993–94 school year to train full time with the U.S. national team. Van Dyken had a problem in that some of the medication she took for her asthma was banned by the International Olympic Committee. As a result, she had to make do with less effective medication, which didn't keep her from achieving greatness.

At the 1996 Olympics in Atlanta, Van Dyken became the first American woman to win four gold medals at one Olympics. She won the 50-meter freestyle and the 100-meter butterfly and was on the winning 400-meter free and 400-meter medley relays.

After the Olympics, Van Dyken returned to Colorado State to get her degree. She graduated in 1997. In 1998, she won three gold medals at the world championships (50-meter freestyle, 400-meter free relay, 400-meter medley relay.)

Van Dyken qualified for the 2000 Games in Sydney, Australia, and won a bronze medal as a member of the 4 x 100 freestyle relay team.

Viren, Lasse
track and field
Born: July 22, 1949 in Myrskyla, Finland

Lasse Viren was the fourth runner in Olympic history to win the 5,000- and 10,000-meter runs in the same Olympics. He is the only runner in Olympic history to do it in consecutive Olympics (1972, 1976). In the 1976 Games, he also finished fifth in the marathon.

Waitz, Grete
distance running
Born: October 1, 1953 in Oslo, Norway

Grete Waitz, one of the great distance runners of all time, is most identified with the New York City Marathon, which she won a record nine times.

Waitz began running with her brothers, and by the time she was age 16, she won the Norway junior championships in the 400 and 800 meters. The following year she won Norway's national championship in the 800 and 1,500 meters. In 1975, she set a world record in the 3,000 meters.

By the late 1970s, her husband, Jack Waitz, got her to run longer distances, and in 1978 he convinced her to enter the New York City Marathon. Grete, who had never run a marathon and was a bit intimidated by the distance of 26 miles, 385 yards, decided to run because she thought it was a good way to see America.

Despite suffering from muscle cramps and dehydration, Waitz finished first, her world record (2:32:30) eclipsing the previous mark by two minutes.

In 1979, Waitz successfully defended her title and became the first woman ever to complete a marathon in less than 2:30 (2:27:33). In 1980, she set another world record (2:25:41). Waitz went on to win in 1982 through 1986 and also in 1988.

Waitz also won world cross-country championships in 1978, 1979, 1981, and 1983. At the first world marathon championships in 1983, she was three minutes faster than the field.

At the 1984 Olympic Games in Los Angeles, Waitz won the silver medal in the first Olympic marathon ever contested as a sanctioned event. She retired in 1990 after battling a variety of injuries.

Waitz was named the female runner of the quarter century by *Runner's World* magazine in 1991, and she was inducted into the International Women's Sports Hall of Fame in 1995.

Weissmuller, Johnny
swimming
Born: June 2, 1904 in Windber, Pennsylvania
Died: January 20, 1984

Johnny Weissmuller is perhaps best known as the star of Tarzan movies, but his career as an Olympic swimmer was one of the best ever.

Weissmuller began swimming on the advice of his doctor to increase his strength. At age 15 he joined the Illinois Athletic Club, where coach Bill Bachrach saw him work out. Bachrach promised that if Weissmuller

worked with him for a year and would follow his every instruction and "be a slave," he "might break every record there is." It was about a year later that Weissmuller entered his first serious competitive event. He won the 1921 Amateur Athletic Union (AAU) 200-yard freestyle. He went on to set world records in the 300-meter freestyle and 150-yard backstroke in 1922. In 1923, he set another record in the 150-yard backstroke, breaking the old mark by 6.8 seconds.

At the 1924 Olympics, Weissmuller won gold medals in the 100- and 400-meter freestyle, setting an Olympic record in the 100 and a world record in the 400. He was also a member of the gold medal–winning 800-meter freestyle relay team and the bronze medal-winning U.S. water polo team.

Fifteen more national championships followed over the next three years, and at the 1928 Olympics, Weissmuller won two more gold medals, in the 400-meter freestyle and as a member of the 800-meter freestyle relay team.

Weissmuller won more national titles (38) than any other U.S. male swimmer and is third all-time behind Tracy Caulkins (48) and Janet Evans (45). He was named the Associated Press Swimmer of the First Half-Century.

Weissmuller was the first person to swim the 100 meters in less than one minute (1922), and his record in the 100-yard freestyle, set in 1927, stood until 1944.

Weissmuller swam professional exhibitions after the 1928 Olympics. In 1932, he was chosen to star in Tarzan movies, appearing in 12.

Weissmuller was inducted into the International Swimming Hall of Fame in 1965 and the U.S Olympic Hall of Fame in 1983.

Wilkins, Mac
track and field
Born: October 15, 1950 in Eugene, Oregon

Mac Wilkins was one of the greatest all-around throwers ever. He competed in the discus, javelin, and hammer throw and was nationally ranked in all three. He was the 1973 NCAA champion in the discus and the U.S champion six times (1973, '76–80).

At the 1976 Olympics, Wilkins set an Olympic record of 224 feet in one of the qualifying rounds. He won the gold medal with a throw of 221-5.

Wilkins made the 1980 Olympic team, which didn't compete because of the United States' boycott of the Moscow Games. He won a silver medal at the 1984 Games and qualified for but didn't medal at the 1988 Games.

Wilkins was a two-time silver medalist at the world championships (1977, '79) and ranked no. 1 in the world in 1976 and 1980. He was ranked no. 1 in the United

States from 1976 through 1982. He was inducted into the National Track and Field Hall of Fame in 1993.

Witt, Katerina
figure skating
Born: December 3, 1965 in Karl-Marx-Stadt, East Germany (now Chemnitz, Germany)

Katerina Witt was the dominant women's figure skater of the 1980s. She skated with grace and style and was one of the most beautiful and captivating performers of all time.

Witt, whose parents couldn't afford to pay for her lessons and travel, had her expenses paid by the East German government. Under the tutelege of coach Jutta Miller, starting at age 10, Witt developed into a champion. She trained six hours a day, 11 months of the year. In 1982, at age 16, she won the first of her six straight European championships, and finished second to Elaine Zayak at the world championships.

Witt, who had never won a world championship entering the 1984 Olympics, won the Olympic gold medal, beating Rosalind Sumners by one-tenth of a point.

In the 1988 Olympics, Witt became the first skater to win consecutive gold medals since Sonja Henie won three straight (1928, '32, '36). Witt's prime competitor was Debi Thomas of the United States. Thomas was the more athletic skater; Witt excelled in style and artistry. Both skaters chose music from the opera *Carmen*, but Witt won the gold.

Witt, who won world championships in 1984, 1985, and 1987, won her final world title in 1988. She turned pro, teaming up with Brian Boitano, the 1988 male gold medalist, for several television specials, one of which, *Carmen on Ice*, resulted in an Emmy Award in the category of classical music/dance.

After working as a commentator for the 1992 Olympics, rules changes allowed professional figure skaters to compete in the Olympics. Witt qualified for the 1994 Olympics and finished seventh.

Yamaguchi, Kristi
figure skating
Born: July 12, 1971 in Hayward, California

Kristi Yamaguchi's dream of a career in figure skating took shape in 1976, when she watched Dorothy Hamill win the gold medal.

Yamaguchi was born with a deformity in that both feet were turned inward. To correct the problem, she had to wear plaster casts reinforced with metal bars to force her feet into the correct position. After the casts were removed, she had to wear corrective shoes.

She began taking skating lessons when she was 6 years old to help strengthen her legs and improve her co-

ordination. Yamaguchi got serious about the sport when she was eight, getting up each morning at 4 A.M. so that she could practice before school started.

Her first success came in the pairs competition with Rudy Galindo. They won a bronze medal at the 1986 world junior championships, the gold medal at the world juniors in 1988, and the gold medal at the U.S. nationals in 1989 and 1990.

Yamaguchi was also developing as a singles skater. She won silver medals at the U.S. nationals for three straight years, starting in 1989. In 1988, she won gold medals in the individual and pairs competition at the 1988 world juniors.

Yamaguchi and Galindo split in 1991 so that she could concentrate on singles competition. She won the gold medal at the world championships in 1991 and the U.S. nationals in 1992.

At the 1992 Olympics, Yamaguchi battled Midori Ito of Japan and Tonya Harding of the United States for the gold medal. Ito and Harding were athletic skaters; Yamaguchi was more artistic. Artistry won out as Yamaguchi won the gold medal. She was the first American to do so since Hamill in 1976. Yamaguchi capped her 1992 season by winning her second straight world championship. She is only the second U.S. woman—Peggy Fleming is the other—to successfully defend her world title.

Following the 1992 Olympics, Yamaguchi turned pro and skated for *Stars on Ice*. She was inducted into the U.S. Figure Skating Hall of Fame in 1998.

Young, Sheila
cycling, speed skating
Born: October 14, 1950 in Detroit, Michigan

Sheila Young was a two-sport athlete who became a world and Olympic champion in both. Although she wasn't fond of winter sports and her father had to bribe her to go to the skating rink, Young finally began to enjoy skating.

She worked hard, began to improve dramatically, and became a junior national champion. Coach Peter Schotting predicted Young could be a world champion if she worked with him for a year. She did just that, following a rigorous training program. Because Young did not have a rink to skate on in the summer, she took up cycling and realized that she could be successful in both sports.

In 1970 and 1971, she won national speed skating championships, and in 1972, she qualified for the Olympics and missed winning a bronze medal in the 500 meters by .08 of a second.

In 1973, Young did the unthinkable. She won the gold medal in the 500-meter sprint at the World Speedskating Championships and also won the women's sprint at the World Cycling Championships. The cycling title came despite suffering a nasty gash on her head because of a fall.

At the 1976 Olympics, Young became the first American athlete, male or female, to win three medals. She won the gold in the 500 meters, silver in the 1,500 meters, and bronze in the 1,000 meters. She also doubled at the speed skating/cycling world championships for the second time.

Young retired from competition, married cyclist Jim Ochowicz, and gave birth to their first child. After five years, she returned to competition and won the 1981 World Cycling Championships. She finished second in the 1982 world championships, after which she retired for good.

Young was inducted into the International Women's Sports Hall of Fame in 1981.

Zatopek, Emil

track and field
Born: September 19, 1922 in Koprivnice, Czechoslovakia
Died: November 23, 2000

Emil Zatopek accomplished one of the rarest feats in Olympic history. At the 1952 Games in Helsinki, Finland, he won the 5,000 and 10,000 meters and the marathon. He is the only runner ever to complete the demanding triple.

Zatopek didn't make his Olympic debut until he was 26 years old, World War II depriving him of some of his prime years. At the 1948 Olympics in London, Zatopek won the gold medal in the 10,000 meters, just two months after he ran it for the first time, and took a silver in the 5,000 meters.

At the 1952 Olympics, Zatopek started by winning the 10,000 meters in an Olympic-record time of 29:17. He set another Olympic record in winning the 5,000 meters (14.06.6). No one had won the 5,000 and 10,000 in the same Games since 1912, and only four runners have ever managed the double.

Zatopek then ran the marathon for the first time ever. He stayed close to the favorites until the 16-mile mark, then decided the pace was too slow and surged ahead. He won in an Olympic-record time of 2:23.04.

Zatopek set 20 world records at distances ranging from 5,000 to 30,000 meters.

Agassi, Andre

Born: April 29, 1970 in Las Vegas, Nevada

Andre Agassi is one of the most charismatic players in tennis history. He is flamboyant, daring, and supremely talented, although at times throughout his career, his work ethic has been lacking. He is as renowned for his garish clothes, his numerous endorsements, and his "image is everything" personality as for his tennis game.

Agassi turned pro in 1987 at age 17, won his first tournament, and earned a spot in the U.S. top 10. He was ranked in the world top 10 for the next five years, rising as high as third in 1988.

A player most comfortable at the baseline because of his powerful and accurate groundstrokes, Agassi won his first Grand Slam championship in 1992 at a most unlikely venue—Wimbledon, which is played on grass, a surface not conducive to baseline play. But Agassi, seeded 12th, defeated Goran Ivanisevic in a five-set final.

Agassi's ranking fell to 20th in 1994, but he became only the third nonseeded player to win the U.S. Open when he defeated Michael Stich in three sets. Agassi underwent wrist surgery in 1994, and there was a chance his career was over. But under the tutelage of Brad Gilbert, a former tour player, he rebounded.

In 1995, Agassi won his third major championship, the Australian Open, and ended the year ranked second behind Pete Sampras, his chief rival and tormentor. Sampras beat Agassi in the final of the 1995 U.S. Open, a defeat that had a lingering effect. Other than winning the gold medal at the 1996 Summer Olympics, the year was a washout. His ranking fell to eighth, and the following year he fell all the way to 141st. Many thought he was finished, that his lackadaisical approach to training had finally caught up to him.

But Agassi decided to rededicate himself to the game. He improved his serve and got into the best shape of his career. His return of serve, already one of his strengths, became even stronger.

In 1998, Agassi won four tournaments and vaulted to sixth in the world rankings. But 1999 validated his comeback and produced a remarkable transformation. He won the French Open, a Grand Slam event, rallying from two sets down to beat Andrei Medvedev, and made history in the process.

Agassi became only the fifth player to win each of the four Grand Slams, joining Don Budge, Roy Emerson, Rod Laver, and Fred Perry.

In the summer of 1999, Agassi made it all the way to the Wimbledon final, losing to Sampras, and then won his second U.S. Open, beating Todd Martin in five sets. He ended the year with the no. 1 ranking, which Sampras had held since 1993.

Agassi also distinguished himself in Davis Cup play, helping the United States to victories in 1990, 1992, and 1995. A disagreement with the U.S. Tennis Association limited his participation, but he returned to play in 2000 for newly appointed captain John McEnroe.

In 2000, Agassi won his second Autralian Open.

Ashe, Arthur

Born: July 10, 1943 in Richmond, Virginia
Died: February 6, 1993

Arthur Ashe was one of the most important athletes not only in tennis but in all of sports. He was an activist, a crusader, and a symbol for racial equality. Ashe grew up in Richmond, Va., and displayed an affinity for tennis at an early age, improving through high school and earning a scholarship to UCLA. He helped the Bruins to the NCAA championship in 1965, when he also won the NCAA individual championship.

Ashe joined the Army after graduating from UCLA with a degree in business administration. In 1968, playing as an amateur, Ashe, a first lieutenant, won the U.S. Amateur and the U.S. Open.

In 1970, he won his second major championship, the Australian Open. He is the only African American to win a major tennis singles title, and because he became a superstar in a historically white sport, Ashe became a trailblazer as well.

He was one of the most popular players of his time, and he conducted himself with grace and dignity, regardless of the outcome. He was not afraid to stand up for what he believed was right. He was especially outspoken about apartheid in South Africa. In 1973, Ashe was granted a visa to visit the country and became the first African American male to win a title there.

In 1975, Ashe had the best season of his career, winning the World Championship Tennis title and the Wimbledon singles title. He was ranked fourth in the world. His Wimbledon victory over heavily favored and top-seeded Jimmy Connors was one of the most intelligent matches ever played. Ashe, renowned as a big-hitting, big-serving slasher, changed his tactics. He took the pace off his serve and his groundstrokes. Connors couldn't cope and lost in four sets.

Ashe's career was cut short in 1979 when he suffered a heart attack. He officially retired in 1980, with 33 career victories.

Ashe, who was a stalwart for U.S. Davis Cup teams as a player (10 years, 27 singles match wins), began a five-year stint as captain in 1981, leading the team to Davis Cup championships in 1981 and 1982.

Even though his tennis career was over, Ashe immersed himself in a variety of endeavors and causes. He worked as a commentator for HBO Sports and ABC Sports; he wrote for the *Washington Post* and *Tennis* magazine; and he published a three-volume history of the African American athlete, entitled *A Hard Road to Glory*.

Ashe continued to fight for equality, returning to South Africa and also protesting against U.S. policy toward Haiti. He also founded charitable organizations such as the National Junior Tennis League, the ABC Cities Tennis Program, the Athlete-Career Connection, and the Safe Passage Foundation, which helped further the education of needy children.

Through a blood transfusion in 1988, Ashe contracted AIDS. He kept the disease a secret, in hopes of raising his daughter, Camera, in as normal an environment as possible. But when *USA Today* was about to go public with the story, Ashe, his wife, Jeanne, by his side, held a press conference in April 1992 to announce it himself. He contracted pneumonia, a complication of AIDS, and died February 6, 1993.

Ashe, who was inducted into the International Tennis Hall of Fame in 1985, distinguished himself as a tennis player and a humanitarian.

Austin, Tracy

Born: December 12, 1962 in Rolling Hills, California

Tracy Austin was a tennis prodigy who became a member of the International Tennis Hall of Fame in 1992. Austin won 25 U.S. Tennis Association junior titles. In 1977, she became the youngest winner of a professional tournament, when she won an Avon Futures event in Portland, Ore., as an unseeded amateur. That same year, she became the youngest quarterfinalist in U.S. Open history.

Austin turned pro in 1978 and in 1979 had a breakthrough season. She won the Italian Open, ending Chris Evert's 125-match winning streak on clay in the process, and also won the U.S. Open, again defeating Evert, to become the youngest winner in Open history. In 1981, Austin won her second Open title, outlasting Martina Navratilova in three sets. In both years, the Associated Press named her the Female Athlete of the Year. Austin's other major title came in 1980, when she won the Wimbledon mixed doubles championship with her brother, John. They are the only siblings to have won the title. Back problems eventually took their toll and ended Austin's career. Her last victory came in 1982.

Austin was renowned for her powerful, accurate groundstrokes and unwavering mental toughness. She won 29 career titles and earned nearly $2 million. She was ranked in the world's top 10 from 1979 to 1981.

After her retirement, Austin worked as a television commentator.

Becker, Boris

Born: November 22, 1967 in Leiman, Germany

Boris Becker burst onto the professional tennis scene in 1985 at age 17 at Wimbledon. With his big serve, powerful volleys, and willingness to dive all over the court,

Becker beat Kevin Curran in four sets to become the youngest player ever to win Wimbledon. He was also the first German and the first unseeded player to claim the world's most prestigious title.

A year later, Becker successfully defended his title with a straight-sets victory over Ivan Lendl. Becker lost in the 1988 final to Stefan Edberg, but beat Edberg for the championship in 1989, which was one of the best seasons of his career. He compiled a 64–8 record and won six of the 13 tournaments, including the U.S. Open, in five sets over Lendl.

Becker reached the Wimbledon final three more times. He lost to Edberg in 1990, to countryman Michael Stich in 1991, and to Pete Sampras in 1995.

Becker won the Australian Open in 1991, beating Lendl for the third time in a major, and at age 28, when it seemed as if his best tennis was a thing of the past, he won his second Australian Open, beating Michael Chang.

He helped Germany to two Davis Cup titles (1988–89) and at one point had won 21 straight Davis Cup matches. He retired following the 1999 season, with 49 career victories.

Betz, Pauline

Born: August 6, 1919 in Dayton, Ohio

Pauline Betz, a tomboy as a child, began playing tennis because her mother thought it more ladylike than other sports. She didn't take formal lessons until she was 15 years old, but became proficient enough to earn a scholarship to Rollins College. Betz, renowned for her athleticism, quickness, and competitiveness, won four U.S. women's championships in five years (1942–44, '46). She also reached the final in 1941 and 1945.

In 1946, in her only appearance at the All-England Club, she won the Wimbledon singles title without losing a set, beating Louise Brough in the final.

Betz's amateur career was cut short in 1947, when the U.S. Tennis Association declared her a professional because she looked into the possibility of starting a pro tour for women. She toured professionally in 1947, playing exhibitions against Sarah Palfrey Cooke and Gertrude "Gussy" Moran, winning against each player easily. Betz later toured with Jack Kramer and Pancho Segura.

Betz became a teaching professional after her retirement from competition. Betz was inducted into the International Tennis Hall of Fame in 1965.

Borg, Bjorn

Born: June 6, 1956 in Soldertaljie, Sweden

Bjorn Borg was one of the most dominant players in the game during the mid-'70s and early '80s. He was strong, athletic, quick, and able to retrieve shots that were seemingly irretrievable. His stamina was unsurpassed. He hit the ball with heavy topspin off both wings, but his two-fisted backhand was his most potent weapon.

Borg first made his mark in 1974 at age 18 as the youngest winner of the Italian Open. That same spring, he also became the youngest winner of the French Open, winning the first of his record six French championships (1974–75, '78–81).

But it was at Wimbledon where Borg secured his place in history. His natural style of play was from the baseline, hardly the tactic to succeed on the grass courts at the All-England Club. But prior to the 1976 championships, Borg turned himself into a grass-court player by working tirelessly on improving his serve and volley.

He won the 1976 Wimbledon singles title without losing a set, beating Ilie Nastase in the final. That began a streak for Borg at Wimbledon that wouldn't end until 1981.

Borg beat Jimmy Connors in 1977 and again in 1978, when he won in a five-set final. In 1979, Borg defeated Roscoe Tanner in five sets. He became the first player since Fred Perry (1934–36) to win three straight and the first player since Tony Wilding (1910–13) to win four straight.

In 1980, Borg made history by winning his fifth straight Wimbledon singles title in one of the most memorable matches ever played. He defeated John McEnroe 1–6, 7–5, 6–3, 6–7 (16–18), 8–6. The fourth-set tiebreaker saw Borg fail to convert five match points. That he came back to win in the fifth set is testament to his mental toughness. Borg increased his winning streak at Wimbledon to 41 straight matches in reaching the 1981 final against McEnroe, who won in four sets.

Because Borg was stoic and Connors and McEnroe were fiery and demonstrative, the rivalries between Borg and Connors and especially between Borg and McEnroe helped the sport reach unmatched popularity.

The only thing missing on Borg's résumé was a U.S. Open title. (He never played the Australian Open.) Borg reached the U.S. Open final four times, but failed to win. In the 1980 Open final, Borg lost in four sets to McEnroe in a match that, for all intents and purposes, ended his career. A dispute with the Association of Tennis Professionals, which wanted Borg to play more events, helped hasten his retirement in 1982.

Borg made numerous comebacks, in 1991, 1992, and 1993, but never won a match. He has been playing senior events, renewing his rivalries with Connors and McEnroe.

Inducted into the International Tennis Hall of Fame in 1987, Borg won 62 titles, including 11 Grand Slam events, which ties him for third with Rod Laver. Roy Emerson is second, and Pete Sampras leads with 13.

Borotra, Jean

Born: August 13, 1898 in Arbonne, France
Died: July 17, 1994

Jean Borotra was best known for his speed and his ability to retrieve shots from all over the court. Nicknamed the "Bounding Basque from Biarritz," Borotra's greatest fame came from his Davis Cup play.

Borotra, Rene Lacoste, Henri Cochet, and Jacques Brugnon formed the Four Musketeers. They led France to its first Davis Cup in 1927 and held it for five more years.

Borotra won the Australian singles (1928), the French singles (1931), and the Wimbledon singles (1924, '26). He also won nine Grand Slam doubles titles. Beginning in 1924, he spent nine straight years ranked in the top 10 in the world, rising as high as no. 2 in 1926. He was inducted into the International Tennis Hall of Fame in 1976.

Brough, Louise

Born: March 11, 1923 in Oklahoma City, Oklahoma

Louise Brough, regarded as one of the best volleyers in women's tennis, won five Wimbledon singles titles (1948–50, '55). She also won five Wimbledon doubles titles, all paired with Margaret Osborne duPont (1946, '48–50, '54) and four Wimbledon mixed doubles titles (1946–48, '50). From 1946 through 1955, Brough appeared in 21 of the 30 finals.

Her U.S. Open record wasn't so impressive. She reached the singles final six times, winning only in 1947. But her doubles record was extraordinary. Paired with duPont, Brough won 12 titles (1942–49, '50, '55–57).

They also won the French women's doubles three times (1946–47, '49) and the Australian doubles once (1950).

Brough was ranked in the U.S. top 10 for 16 years and was in the world top ten 12 times, including no. 1 in 1955. She was inducted into the International Tennis Hall of Fame in 1967.

Budge, Don

Born: June 13, 1915 in Oakland, California
Died: January 26, 2000

Don Budge was an all-around player with a big serve and one of the finest backhands in tennis history.

Budge, who began playing on the hardcourts of California, was named to the Davis Cup team in 1935 at age 19. Two years later, he won Wimbledon (singles, doubles, and mixed doubles) and the U.S. National singles and mixed doubles. He also led the U.S. to its first Davis Cup in 11 years. But the 4–1 victory over Britain was preceded by one of the most famous matches of Budge's career.

In order to reach the Challenge Round against Britain, the U.S. had to defeat Germany. With the score

tied at two matches each, Budge faced Baron Gottfried van Cramm in the deciding match. After trailing 4–1 in the fifth set, Budge rallied for an 8–6 win. That year, he was the first tennis player to win the Sullivan Award as the nation's top amateur athlete.

In 1938, Budge rejected a $50,000 offer to turn professional. The result of that decision was, to this day, one of the best seasons in tennis history. He became the first player to win the Grand Slam: the championships of Australia, France, Wimbledon, and the United States. He beat John Bromwich to win the Australian, Roderich Menzel to win the French, Bunny Austin to win Wimbledon, and Gene Mako to win the U.S. title.

The term "Grand Slam" was not part of the tennis vocabulary until Alison Danzig of the *New York Times* coined the phrase and used it to describe Budge's accomplishment.

Also in 1938, Budge helped the United States to the Davis Cup with a win over Australia in the final. He went 43–2 for the year and won six of the eight tournaments he entered. Budge turned pro in 1939, touring with Ellsworth Vines, Fred Perry, Bill Tilden, and Bobby Riggs. He won the U.S. Pro in 1940 and 1942.

In 1942, Budge joined the Air Force. A shoulder injury suffered in training limited his effectiveness. He made it to the U.S. Pro final in 1946–47, 1949, and 1953, but lost each time.

He was inducted into the International Tennis Hall of Fame in 1964 and was selected by *Tennis* magazine as one of the greatest players of the 20th century.

Bueno, Maria

Born: October 11, 1939 in São Paulo, Brazil

Maria Bueno was known for her grace, style, and fluidity on the court. She was a power player who was blessed with touch.

She had no formal training as a youth, but improved by playing against boys and men when she was five years old. She won the Brazilian women's championship at 14 and joined the world tour three years later.

Bueno, whose best surface was grass, won three Wimbledon singles titles (1959–60, '64). She also won four U.S. National singles titles (1959, '63–64, '66).

Bueno's best years were 1959, 1960, 1964, and 1966, when she was ranked no. 1 in the world. She was ranked in the top 10 1958–68. Unfortunately, her best tennis was behind her when open tennis and prize money started in 1968.

In addition to her singles success, Bueno was an accomplished doubles player as well. She won 12 Grand Slam doubles titles, with six different partners.

After a variety of injuries to her arm and leg, Bueno attempted a comeback in 1975. She finally retired in

1977 and was inducted into the International Tennis Hall of Fame in 1978.

Casals, Rosemary

Born: September 16, 1948 in San Francisco, California

Rosie Casals was one of the best doubles players of all time. Of her 112 career doubles titles, 56 came with Billie Jean King as her partner. Only Martina Navratilova won more doubles titles (162).

Casals won 12 Grand Slam titles. She won doubles titles at Wimbledon (1967–68, '70–71, '73) and the U.S. Open (1967, '71, '74, '82), and mixed doubles titles at Wimbledon (1970, '72) and the U.S. Open (1975).

Casals and King also were partners in helping the women's pro tour get off the ground in 1971.

Cochet, Henri

Born: December 14, 1901 in Lyon, France
Died: April 1, 1987

Henri Cochet, one of the heralded Four Musketeers along with Jean Borotra, Rene Lacoste, and Jacques Brugnon, was a magician with a racket. There seemed to be nothing he couldn't accomplish on the court because of his speed and his incredible touch.

Cochet, a diminutive 5-6, 145 pounds, won the French Open four times (1926, '28, '30, '32), Wimbledon twice (1927, '29), and the U.S. Nationals once (1928) when he ended Bill Tilden's six-year run as champion.

He also was instrumental in France's run of six straight Davis Cup championships (1927–32).

Cochet, who was inducted into the International Tennis Hall of Fame in 1976, was the no. 1 player in the world from 1928 to 1931 and was ranked in the top 10 in the world 10 times 1922–33.

Connolly Brinker, Maureen

Born: September 17, 1934 in San Diego, California
Died: June 21, 1969

Maureen Connolly Brinker began playing tennis at age nine. Her first love was horses, but because her mother couldn't afford a horse or lessons, Maureen turned her attention to tennis.

Even though her career ended prematurely, before she turned 20 Brinker made a case for being one of the best female players of all time.

When she was 14, she became the youngest ever to win the national junior girls championship, winning 56 straight matches in the process.

Brinker, nicknamed "Little Mo," played from the baseline, using powerful and accurate groundstrokes. Two years after winning the national junior girls title, she won

the U.S. championship, becoming, at 16 years, 11 months, the second youngest ever to win the title. (Tracy Austin won at 16 years, 9 months in 1979).

In 1952, Brinker won her first Wimbledon singles title and her second straight U.S. title. In 1953, she became the first female to win the Grand Slam within a calendar year, taking the Australian, French, Wimbledon, and U.S. titles. She won 10 of 12 tournaments that year and registered a 61–2 match record.

In 1954, Brinker won her third straight Wimbledon and her second straight French championship. That brought her total to nine Grand Slam tournaments won, all consecutively, and a 50-match winning streak.

Brinker was named the Associated Press Female Athlete of the Year for three straight years, beginning in 1951.

But just after winning the U.S. clay singles and doubles titles in 1954, Brinker's career was cut short by a traffic accident. While riding horseback, a cement truck grazed her right leg and threw her to the ground. The leg was seriously damaged, and her tennis career was over.

"I knew immediately I'd never play again," said Brinker, who married Norman Brinker, an equestrian, in 1952.

Brinker recovered enough to give tennis lessons, but tragedy struck again when, at age 34 in 1969, she died of cancer.

She was inducted into the International Tennis Hall of Fame in 1968 and the International Women's Sports Hall of Fame in 1987.

Connors, Jimmy

Born: September 2, 1952 in Belleville, Illinois

Jimmy Connors, one of the most enduring personalities in the game, began playing tennis at age three, taught by his mother, Gloria, and grandmother, Bertha Thompson, also known as "Two Mom." He developed into one of the most accomplished players in the game.

Connors, a left-hander, played with reckless abandon, giving everything on every point. He threw himself into his trademark two-fisted backhand and owned one of the best returns of serve in the history of the game.

After spending one year at UCLA in 1971, when he won the NCAA singles title and was named an All-American, Connors turned pro in 1972 and won the first of his record 109 singles titles.

In 1973, he won his first major title, the U.S. Pro Championship, beating Arthur Ashe in a five-set final. He shared the no. 1 ranking in the United States with Stan Smith. Connors had one of his best seasons ever in 1974. He won the Australian Open, Wimbledon, and the U.S. Open. His chance for a Grand Slam was ruined by politics. Because Connors had signed a contract to play World Team Tennis, he was banned from playing in the

French Open by the Association of Tennis Professionals (ATP) and the French tennis administration.

Connors and his agent, Bill Riordan, sued the ATP and its president, Arthur Ashe, for $10 million, alleging that his freedom had been restricted.

Though he was unable to win the Grand Slam, Connors nevertheless enjoyed a remarkable season in 1974. His match record was 99–4 in 20 tournaments, 14 of which he won. He took over the no. 1 ranking in the world in July 1974 and held it for 159 straight weeks. He spent a total of 263 weeks ranked first, which is third behind Pete Sampras and Ivan Lendl.

In the Wimbledon and U.S. Open finals in 1974, Connors destroyed Ken Rosewall in each final, winning 6–1, 6–1, 6–4 at Wimbledon and 6–1, 6–0, 6–1 at the Open.

Connors played in the next four U.S. Open finals, winning in 1976 and 1978. He became the first player to appear in five straight Open finals since Bill Tilden played in eight straight (1918–25).

Connors also has the distinction of winning the U.S. Open on three different surfaces. He won his 1974 title on grass at Forest Hills; his 1976 title on clay at Forest Hills; and his 1978, 1982, and 1983 titles on hardcourts at the U.S. National Tennis Center.

Connors reached the Wimbledon final five more times (1975, '77–78, '82, '84), but won only in 1982, when he defeated John McEnroe in five sets. In 1975, he lost to Ashe, whom he was suing. He also lost twice to Bjorn Borg (1977–78) during Borg's run of five straight championships, and to McEnroe in 1984.

Early in Connors' career he was a controversial figure—boorish, petulant, antiestablishment. He was a lightning rod for controversy and criticism. But as he got older, he mellowed and became one of the most popular players in tennis history, largely because the fans appreciated his total effort on the court. Connors always put on a good show.

No show was more memorable than his performance in the 1991 U.S. Open. Coming off a wrist injury that kept him sidelined and dropped his ranking to 936th in the world the previous year, Connors climaxed his comeback at the Open, held in New York City, where he was extremely popular.

In the first round, Connors rallied from two sets down to beat Patrick McEnroe in a match that lasted four hours, 20 minutes. After easy wins over Michael Schapers and 10th-seeded Karol Novacek, Connors faced Aaron Krickstein in the fourth round and again mounted a memorable comeback. Trailing 2–5 in the fifth and final set, Connors won the set in a tiebreaker. The match ended in just under five hours, the 20,000 in attendance loving every minute of it, and it all took place on his 39th birthday. Connors defeated Paul Haarhuis in the quarterfinals and became the second-oldest semifinalist, behind Rosewall, in U.S. Open

history. But his run ended in the semis; he was beaten by Jim Courier in straight sets.

After Connors' retirement in 1993, he became the prime mover behind the senior tour for players 35 and over, where he renewed his rivalries with Bjorn Borg and John McEnroe. He was inducted into the International Tennis Hall of Fame in 1998.

Court, Margaret Smith
Born: July 16, 1942 in Alsbury, Australia

Margaret Smith Court is one of the most accomplished players in the history of women's tennis. Her 62 Grand Slam championships in singles, doubles, and mixed doubles are more than any man or woman has ever won.

Court, nearly six feet tall, was called "The Arm" by Billie Jean King, one of her major rivals, because of her reach at the net. Court relied on a serve-and-volley style and had solid groundstrokes.

Court's first major success came in the 1960 Australian Open when she was only 18 years old. It was the first of seven straight Australian titles. She won 11 in all, also winning in 1969, 1970, 1971, and 1973.

In 1970, Court became only the second woman to win the Grand Slam, taking the Australian, French, Wimbledon, and U.S. titles within the same calendar year. She won 21 of 27 tournaments that year and had a match record of 104–6.

Court's victory over King in the 1970 Wimbledon final was memorable. Suffering from a sprained ankle, she managed to defeat King 14–12, 11–9.

Court also won Wimbledon in 1963 and 1965. She won the French title five times (1962, '64, '69–70, '73) and the U.S. title five times (1962, '65, '69, '70, '73).

In 1971, Court retired to have her second child, but returned in 1973 to win the Australian, French, and U.S. titles. But 1973 was also the year of one of her most unfortunate experiences. She accepted the challenge to play 55-year-old Bobby Riggs in a nationally televised match on Mother's Day and was beaten soundly, 6–1, 6–2, in what became known as the "Mother's Day Massacre." Court's loss enticed Billie Jean King to face Riggs—and beat him—in the "Battle of the Sexes" in September 1973.

Court, who won 92 singles titles in her career, was ranked in the top 10 in the world 13 times between 1961 and 1975, including seven times at no. 1 (1962–65, '69–70, '73). She was inducted into the International Tennis Hall of Fame in 1979 and the International Women's Sports Hall of Fame in 1986.

Davenport, Lindsay
Born: June 8, 1976 in Palos Verdes, California

Lindsay Davenport did not begin her pro tennis career as a junior prodigy. Unlike many of her opponents who dedicated their lives to the sport at an early age by attending intense tennis camps, Davenport went to high school and lived what could be termed a normal life.

She made her debut on the Women's Tennis Association (WTA) Tour in 1993, when she won her first professional tournament.

In 1994, she became the first American woman to be ranked in the top 10 in the world since Jennifer Capriati in 1990. Davenport won a gold medal in the 1996 Summer Olympics in Atlanta and also helped the United States team win the Federation Cup, a team competition between countries.

Davenport had her breakthrough season in 1998. She led the tour with 69 singles match victories and won six titles, including the U.S. Open, her first Grand Slam title. She defeated Martina Hingis in straight sets.

Davenport rose to no. 1 in the world rankings. She was the third American to be ranked first since the WTA Tour rankings were introduced in 1975, and the first since Chris Evert in 1985.

Davenport won her second Grand Slam title at Wimbledon in 1999. She defeated Steffi Graf in straight sets and also won the Wimbledon doubles title with Corina Morariu.

In 2000, Davenport won her third Grand Slam title, the Australian Open. She also was the runner-up at Wimbledon, falling to Venus Williams.

Through 2000, Davenport had won 29 career singles titles and more than $11 million in prize money.

DuPont, Margaret Osborne
Born: March 4, 1918 in Joesph, Oregon

Margaret Osborne duPont was one of the most successful doubles players in tennis history. Teamed with Louise Brough, she won 12 U.S., five Wimbledon, and three French titles. From 1942 through 1957, they lost only eight matches. In the U.S. championships alone, they won 12 of the 14 times they entered and 58 of 60 matches. DuPont also enjoyed success in singles. She won the French title twice (1946, '49), Wimbledon once (1947), and the U.S. title three times (1948–50).

DuPont spent 14 years ranked in the top 10 in the world between 1946 and 1957, including first from 1947 to 1950. She was inducted into the International Tennis Hall of Fame in 1967.

Edberg, Stefan
Born: January 19, 1966 in Vastervik, Sweden

Whereas most Swedish tennis players were backcourt players, with two-handed backhands, who relied almost exclusively on their groundstrokes, Stefan Edberg was a serve-and-volley player, with a one-handed backhand who attacked at every opportunity. Edberg won his first

major at the 1985 Australian Open, where he beat countryman Mats Wilander. He also won the Australian in 1987.

He won the first of his two Wimbledon titles in 1988, rallying from two sets down in the semifinals to beat Miloslav Mecir and from one set down to beat Boris Becker in the final. After losing to Becker in the 1989 final, Edberg won his second Wimbledon title, beating Becker in a five-set final in 1990.

Edberg won the U.S. Open twice. In 1991, he routed Jim Courier 6–2, 6–4, 6–0, and in 1992 he beat Pete Sampras in four sets. To reach the 1992 Open final, Edberg outlasted Michael Chang in a five-set semifinal that lasted nearly 5 1/2 hours. Edberg, one of the gentlemen of the sport, was ranked in the top 10 in the world 10 times, including no. 1 twice, in 1990 and 1991.

He retired after the 1996 season, ending his string of consecutive appearances in Grand Slam events at 54. Edberg won 41 singles titles and led Sweden to three Davis Cup championships (1984–85, '87).

Emerson, Roy
Born: November 3, 1936 in Black Butt, Australia

Roy Emerson was one of the best of a talented group of Australian players. Known for his fitness and athleticism, he was successful in singles and doubles.

He won 12 Grand Slam singles titles, more than anyone in history until Pete Sampras surpassed him in 2000. Emerson also owns 16 Grand Slam doubles titles—won with five different partners.

Emerson, known as "Emmo," won the Australian singles title six times (1961, '63–67), the French singles twice (1963, '67), Wimbledon twice (1964, '65), and the U.S. Nationals twice (1961, '64).

Roy Emerson   *Diane Staskowski*

He helped Australia to eight Davis Cup titles (1959–62, '64–67), compiling a 22–2 record in singles and 13–2 in doubles.

Emerson was ranked in the top 10 in the world nine times, including first in 1964 and 1965. He had one of his most successful seasons in 1964, winning 17 tournaments and all but six of 115 matches.

He was inducted into the International Tennis Hall of Fame in 1982.

Evert, Chris

Born: December 21, 1954 in Fort Lauderdale, Florida
Chris Evert was best known for her unerring play at the baseline—she was a human backboard—and her unshakeable focus, a combination that helped her become one of the greatest champions in tennis history.

The daughter of a teaching pro, Jimmy Evert, Chris began playing when she was five. Too weak to hold the racket with one hand, she developed a two-handed backhand that would become her trademark, not to mention a lethal weapon.

Evert succeeded by rooting herself to the baseline and getting everything back. Her groundstrokes were powerful and accurate; her patience level was astounding. So was her breakthrough.

In the 1971 U.S. Open at Forest Hills, her first, Evert reached the semifinals at age 16 years, eight months, and 20 days. She lost to Billie Jean King in straight sets that day, but it was a sign of things to come.

Writer Grace Lichtenstein wrote of Evert's coming-out party: "Men thought her adorable, little girls worshipped her, middle-aged mothers came up to her at tournaments and told her she had restored their faith in youth. She was Miss American Pie." She was also a fierce competitor, known as the "Ice Maiden" and "Little Miss Icicle."

Evert enjoyed her greatest success at the French and U.S. Opens. She won the French a record seven times (1974–75, '79–80, '83, '85, '86) and the U.S. Open six times (1975–78, '80, '82), second only to Molla Mallory (8) and Helen Wills Moody (7). Evert also won Wimbledon in 1974, 1976, and 1981 and the Australian Open in 1982 and 1984. She won at least one Grand Slam title in a record 13 consecutive years (1974–86). Evert also put together some remarkable winning streaks. In 1974, she won 54 straight matches. From August 1973 to May 1979, she won 125 straight matches on clay. The string was broken by Tracy Austin at the Italian Open.

The early part of her career featured a rivalry with Evonne Goolagong, an Australian who was athletic and graceful. Evert held a 21–12 edge.

But the rivalry that people remember most was with Martina Navratilova, whose attacking, serve-and-volley style was a direct contrast to Evert. They brought out the best in each other, each raising the other's game to a new level, each respecting the other as an athlete and a person.

Navratilova won 43 of their 80 matches, but Evert managed to upset Navratilova to win the French Open in 1985 and 1986.

In 1989, Evert retired. She played her final match at the U.S. Open, losing in the quarterfinals to Zina Garrison. Evert left the court with a simple wave to a wildly cheering crowd. Garrison left in tears, having ended the career of such a beloved figure. Evert won 154 singles titles, second to Navratilova, and had a win-loss record of 1,309–146 for a winning percentage of .899, also a record. She was named the Associated Press Female Athlete of the Year in 1974, 1975, 1977, and 1980. She was ranked in the top 10 in the world 17 times, including first in 1975, 1976, 1977, 1980, and 1981.

Of the 57 Grand Slam events she entered, Evert made it at least to the semifinals 53 times and won 18.

Evert, who had a much-publicized relationship with Jimmy Connors in the mid-'70s, married John Lloyd, a British tennis player, but divorced him after eight years. She and former Olympic skier Andy Mill are married and have three sons.

Evert, who works as a commentator for NBC Sports, was inducted into the International Tennis Hall of Fame 1995 and the International Women's Sports Hall of Fame in 1982. She was No. 49 on ESPN's list of the top 50 North American Athletes of the Century.

Gibson, Althea

Born: August 25, 1927 in Silver, South Carolina
Althea Gibson was a trailblazer and a pioneer, the first African American to win Wimbledon and U.S. titles.

Gibson was tall (5-11) and athletic with a powerful serve and solid groundstrokes. She began playing in American Tennis Association (ATA) events and won the women's singles title for 10 straight years, beginning in 1947. The ATA, an all-black organization, convinced the U.S. Tennis Association to let her play in the U.S. Nationals at Forest Hills. Her first appearance in the tournament came in 1950 at age 23. She defeated Barbara Knapp in straight sets and had Louise Brough, the reigning Wimbledon champ, in trouble. Gibson led 1–6, 6–3, 7–6, but a thunderstorm suspended play, and when the match resumed, Brough closed it out by winning three straight games.

Gibson won the U.S. title in 1957 and 1958, when she also won Wimbledon titles. She was named the Associated Press Female Athlete of the Year in both years. Her other major singles title came in 1956 at the French championships.

Gibson was the first black to win a Wimbledon title in 1956, when she won the doubles with Angela Buxton.

Gibson turned pro in 1959, touring with Karol Fageros and playing prior to Harlem Globetrotters games. Gibson won 114 of 118 matches.

Gibson turned to golf and played for several years on the LPGA Tour. She returned to tennis for a few events in 1968, but her age proved too much of an obstacle. She was inducted into the International Tennis Hall of Fame in 1971 and the International Women's Sports Hall of Fame in 1980.

Gonzalez, Pancho

Born: May 9, 1928 in Los Angeles, California
Died: July 3, 1995

Pancho Gonzalez was a fiery competitor with a booming serve and great athletic ability. He had confrontations with his opponents, officials, and the media, but they only served to make him play harder.

Because he quit school, he wasn't allowed to play in southern California junior tournaments, but when he got out of the Navy in 1946, he demonstrated his considerable talents.

He won the U.S. Nationals at age 20 in 1948 and successfully defended his title the following year. In 1949, he helped the United States win the Davis Cup.

But that was it for his amateur career. He turned pro and went on tour with Jack Kramer, who won 96 of their 123 matches. Gonzalez was replaced on the tour by Pancho Segura, but resurfaced in 1954 along with Segura, Don Budge, Lew Hoad, Tony Trabert, and Frank Sedgman. From then on, Gonzalez was the main attraction, beating the competition and drawing the fans.

One of Gonzalez's most famous matches occurred at Wimbledon in 1969, when, at age 41, he defeated Charlie Pasarell in a five-set match that lasted five hours, 12 minutes. Gonzalez won 22–24, 1–6, 16–14, 6–3, 11–9, saving seven match points in the fifth set.

Gonzalez became the oldest player to win a pro tournament in 1972, when, three months before his 44th birthday, he won an event in Des Moines, Iowa.

Gonzalez, inducted into the International Tennis Hall of Fame in 1968, played on the over-45 Grand Masters circuit, captained the U.S. Davis Cup team, and became an instructor and television announcer. He died of cancer in Las Vegas, where he was the longtime teaching pro at Caesars.

Goolagong, Evonne

Born: July 31, 1951 in Griffith, New South Wales, Australia

Evonne Goolagong was one of the most graceful tennis players ever. Known for her carefree attitude, Goolagong seemed to float across the court rather than run. An Aborigine, Goolagong was first noticed by Vic Edwards, who

ran a tennis school in Sydney, Australia. Edwards convinced her parents to move to Sydney, which they did in 1967.

Goolagong won her first major singles title in 1971 at the French Open. That same year, she upset Margaret Court to win the Wimbledon championship. The Associated Press named her Female Athlete of the Year.

She reached the Wimbledon final three more times, but lost to Billie Jean King in 1972 and 1975 and to Chris Evert in 1976. Goolagong beat Evert to win the 1980 Wimbledon title, which equaled Bill Tilden's record for the longest time between titles.

Goolagong also won four Australian Opens (1974–77) and reached the U.S. Open final four straight years, beginning in 1973.

Her rivalry with Evert was particularly memorable because their playing styles were so different. Goolagong was an aggressive serve-and-volleyer; Evert stayed on the baseline. Evert led 21–12, but only 5–4 in the majors.

Goolagong retired after the 1983 season and was inducted into the International Tennis Hall of Fame in 1988 and the International Women's Sports Hall of Fame in 1989. Goolagong won 43 singles and nine doubles titles and was ranked in the top 10 in the world nine times.

Graf, Steffi

Born: June 14, 1969 in Neckerau, Germany

Steffi Graf is one of the most athletic and most accomplished players in the history of women's tennis. Blessed with speed, determination, and an indomitable work ethic, Graf can make a claim as the greatest female player ever.

She first came to prominence in 1986 as a 16-year-old when she defeated Chris Evert in the final of the Family Circle Cup in Hilton Head, S.C. A year later, Graf won her first Grand Slam singles title with a victory over Martina Navratilova at the French Open. In 1988, Graf became the third woman—Maureen Connolly Brinker and Margaret Court were the others—to win the Grand Slam (Australian, French, Wimbledon, U.S. titles in the same calendar year). Then she went the Grand Slam one better by making it a Golden Slam, winning the gold medal at the 1998 Summer Olympics in Seoul, South Korea. Graf won 11 titles overall in 1988, out of the 14 events she entered, and had a match record of 73–3. Her performance in 1989 was nearly as impressive. She won the Australian, Wimbledon, and U.S. titles. Of the 16 tournaments she entered, she won 14, amassing an 86–2 match record.

Graf won the Australian four times (1988–89, '90, '94), the French six times (1987–88, '93, '95–96, '99), Wimbledon seven times (1988–89, '91–93, '95–96), and the U.S. Open five times (1988–89, '93, '95, '96).

Her 22 Grand Slam singles titles rank second all-time to Court, who has 24. Since advancing to the U.S. Open semifinals in 1985 until the Australian Open in 1997, Graf has made the quarterfinals in every Grand Slam she entered except one. She was defeated in the first round at Wimbledon in 1994 by Lori McNeil.

Between 1987 and 1990, Graf reached the final of every Grand Slam (12) and won 10.

What makes Graf's résumé even more remarkable are the injuries and personal problems that plagued her. She suffered from calf, knee, back, leg, foot, and wrist injuries throughout her career, as well as severe sinus problems.

Her father, Peter, who introduced her to tennis as a child, was jailed in 1995 and convicted in 1997 of income tax evasion. But during those two years, she remained focused, winning the French, Wimbledon, and U.S. Open titles each year.

The tragic stabbing of Monica Seles, her chief rival, in 1993 also caused her emotional difficulty. Gunther Parche, Seles' attacker at the German Open, was a Graf fan. He attacked Seles so that Graf could return to the top, a situation that caused her considerable anguish. But through it all, she persevered.

Her victory in the 1999 French Open over top-seeded Martina Hingis was a testament to her will. She had spent most of 1998 injured, and she was using the French to get her game in shape for Wimbledon. But Graf won in three sets to the delight of the highly partisan crowd.

Soon after the French Open, Graf talked about retiring, then recanted, but after losing the Wimbledon final to Lindsay Davenport, she made it official. Her career was over. Graf spent eight years as the no. 1 ranked player in the world (1987–90, '93–96), including a record run of 186 consecutive weeks. She won 106 events, third all-time behind Navratilova (167) and Evert (154). She was also the all-time leading money winner with more than $21 million.

Hart, Doris
Born: June 20, 1925 in St. Louis, Missouri

When Doris Hart was a young girl, she developed a serious knee infection, not polio as was widely reported at the time. One doctor recommended amputation, but her leg eventually was saved.

As therapy, Hart began playing tennis with her brother. Her legs, despite being bowed, improved, and she became one of the best players of her time.

Hart moved well on the court, despite having suffered the infection, and she was blessed with solid groundstrokes and was an all-around player.

She won the Australian singles once (1949), the French twice (1950, '52), Wimbledon once (1951), and

the U.S. twice (1954–55). Hart was also an accomplished doubles player. She won 30 doubles and mixed doubles Grand Slam titles. Hart and partner Shirley Fry won four straight French titles (1950–53) and three straight Wimbledon titles (1951–53).

Hart also excelled in Wightman Cup play (team competition between the U.S. and Britain), losing only one match in 10 years (1946–55).

Hart, who was ranked in the top 10 in the world for 10 straight years, beginning in 1946, including first in 1951, was inducted into the International Tennis Hall of Fame in 1969.

Hoad, Lew
Born: November 23, 1934 in Sydney, Australia
Died: July 3, 1994

Lew Hoad was a strong and chance-taking player, one of the best in the world when he was on his game. He lacked the patience and consistency of his countryman Ken Rosewall, with whom he is so often linked, since they grew up in the same town, but he was a formidable competitor nonetheless.

Hoad won four Grand Slam singles titles: Australian, 1956; French 1956; Wimbledon, 1956–57. In 1956, his best year, he won 15 singles titles and 17 doubles titles, and nearly captured the Grand Slam (the Australian, French, Wimbledon, and U.S. titles in a calendar year). But Rosewall stopped him in the U.S. championship, which is the only Grand Slam title to elude him.

Hoad helped the Australians to two Davis Cup championships, in 1953, when he defeated Tony Trabert of the United States to even the match at 2–2, and in 1955, when he and Rosewall teamed to win all five points.

Hoad, who was ranked in the top 10 in the world for five straight years, beginning in 1952, including no. 1 in 1956, was inducted into the International Tennis Hall of Fame in 1980.

Jacobs, Helen
Born: August 8, 1908 in Berkeley, California
Died: June 2, 1997

Helen Jacobs had the misfortune of being a contemporary of Helen Wills Moody, who proved to be a career-long nemesis.

Four times Jacobs lost to Moody in Wimbledon finals and once each in the U.S. and French finals.

Jacobs finally defeated Moody—for the first and only time—in the U.S. final in 1933, although that victory was tainted. With Jacobs leading 3–0 in the third set, Moody told the umpire she couldn't continue because of back pain.

Jacobs' victory over Moody was part of a run of four straight U.S. Nationals victories (1932–35). In 1932, in addition to winning the title, Jacobs also made fashion history. She was the first woman to wear shorts.

Jacobs reached the U.S. final eight times from 1928 to 1940. She also won a Wimbledon title in 1936.

Jacobs' biggest strengths were her determination and her effective net game. She was ranked in the top 10 in the world 12 straight times, beginning in 1928, including no. 1 in 1936. She was inducted into the International Tennis Hall of Fame in 1962.

King, Billie Jean
Born: November 22, 1943 in Long Beach, California

Few people have had as much impact on sports and society as Billie Jean King. Besides being one of the best tennis players of all time, she was also a crusader and an activist for change, especially in the area of equality for women and women athletes. King, who played softball as a young girl, was encouraged to play tennis by her father, who thought it more ladylike. She took to tennis immediately, her progress helped along by the coaching of former great Alice Marble.

King's first taste of fame came at Wimbledon in 1961 at age 17, when she won the doubles with Karen Hantzke. That was the first of 10 doubles titles and four mixed doubles titles at Wimbledon.

King also won the singles at Wimbledon six times (1966–68, '72–73, '75). Her 20 titles at the All-England Club is an all-time record, exceeding Elizabeth Ryan by one. All of Ryan's titles were in doubles and mixed doubles. King's 20th title came in 1980 in the doubles with Martina Navratilova.

King also won the Australian singles in 1968, the French in 1972, and the U.S. singles in 1967, 1971, 1972, and 1974.

Three times—at Wimbledon in 1967 and 1973 and at the U.S. Nationals in 1967—King won the singles, the doubles, and the mixed doubles.

Overall, King won 39 Grand Slam titles in singles, doubles, and mixed doubles, third behind Margaret Court (62) and Navratilova (55). Many of her major doubles titles were won with Rosemary Casals.

King was the first female player to turn pro, in 1968. In 1971, playing in the Pacific Southwest Championships, she was outraged that Hall of Fame player Jack Kramer, the event's promoter, offered less than one-eighth of the total purse to the women. King protested, but Kramer stood firm, so the women boycotted the tournament and staged one of their own in Houston.

Sponsored by Phillip Morris and Virginia Slims cigarettes, the tournament was more successful than anyone expected. It paved the way for the Virginia Slims tour, which debuted in 1971. King also led the fight that resulted in the U.S. Open awarding equal prize money to the women, starting in 1973.

King was the first female athlete to exceed $100,000 in prize money in a year (1971), when she won $117,000, and she also was the first female coach of a pro team with men, serving as player-coach for the Philadelphia Freedoms of the World Team Tennis League, which she founded and which remains one of her pet projects.

But perhaps King's most significant contribution—to tennis and to society—was her participation in the "Battle of the Sexes" match against Bobby Riggs on Sept. 30, 1973, in the Houston Astrodome.

Riggs, a hustler and a showman, had tried repeatedly to entice King to play him. He wanted to prove that a 55-year-old man could beat a top woman player. King refused, until Riggs defeated Margaret Court on Mother's Day. After the "Mother's Day Massacre," King felt she had no choice but to take on Riggs.

The match, with its circus atmosphere and excessive hype, was held before a record crowd of 30,472 and broadcast live on ABC. King won easily 6–4, 6–3, 6–3, and in the process helped raise the awareness of women in sports and also helped create a tennis boom. The sport was never more popular than in the 10 years after that match.

"She changed the nature of sport in America," said Richard Lapchick, founder and director of the Study of Sport and Society in Boston. "There were a lot of women desiring to participate in sports, a lot of men resisting them, and very few men embracing them. She, through the greatness of her game, but even more because of who she is, stood in the face of those men and wiped away the stereotypes and cobwebs." King's crusading helped the passage of Title IX, the federal law that guarantees equal funding for women's collegiate sports and increased the awareness and the opportunities for women in sports. King was named the *Sports Illustrated* Sportswoman of the Year in 1972 and the Associated Press Female Athlete of the Year in 1973.

King retired in 1983 at age 39, but that year, before calling it quits, she became the oldest female to win a pro tournament, and she made an inspirational run to the Wimbledon semifinals, where she lost to 18-year-old Andrea Jaeger.

Despite numerous knee surgeries, she won 67 singles titles, which ranks her fifth all-time, and was ranked in the top 10 in the world 18 times, including five times at no. 1 (1966–68, '71, '74). She was inducted into the International Tennis Hall of Fame in 1987 and the International Women's Sports Hall of Fame in 1980.

Kramer, Jack
Born: August 1, 1921 in Las Vegas, Nevada

Jack Kramer had an impact on tennis as a player, a promoter, and a television commentator. He earned his first acclaim in 1939 at age 18, when he was selected to represent the United States in the Davis Cup final against

Australia. Along with Joe Hunt, who grew up with Kramer in southern California, they played doubles in a losing effort. After serving time in the U.S. Coast Guard, Kramer won the U.S. National, his first Grand Slam singles title. He repeated in 1947, when he also won the Wimbledon singles, beating Tom Brown in 48 minutes. He lost only six games in the straight-sets final and 37 games in seven matches.

Kramer lost two matches in 1946 and one in 1947, when he won eight of the nine tournaments he entered and 48 of 49 matches. His success came from what was termed "the big game," Kramer's attacking after his serve and often on return of serve. He turned pro after rallying from two sets down to win the U.S. singles title over Frank Parker.

Kramer toured with Bobby Riggs, the reigning U.S. Pro champion, and won 69 of 89 matches. After Riggs took over as promoter, Kramer beat Pancho Gonzalez 96–27. It wasn't long before Kramer became not only a promoter, but the leader of pro tennis. He signed several of the top Australians—Ken Rosewall, Lew Hoad, Ashley Cooper, and Mal Anderson—who were dominating the game. He also signed Gonzalez, who was one of the game's marquee attractions.

Kramer devised the Grand Prix of men's tennis, which led to a season-ending championship for the top eight players, and helped form the Association of Tennis Professionals, the union for men's players. He also worked as a commentator for ABC, CBS, and NBC.

Kramer was the no. 1 ranked player in the world in 1946 and 1947. He was inducted into the International Tennis Hall of Fame in 1968.

Lacoste, Rene
Born: July 2, 1904 in Paris, France
Died: October 12, 1996

One of the famed Four Musketeers, along with Jean Borotra, Henri Cochet, and Jacques Brugnon, Rene Lacoste, nicknamed "The Crocodile," excelled from the backcourt, both with the effectiveness of his shots and his strategy.

He helped France win the Davis Cup in 1927 and 1928. A year later, after winning the French Open, he retired from competition. He was the captain of the victorious French Davis Cup teams in 1931 and 1932.

He also won the French Open in 1925 and 1927, the U.S. National in 1926 and 1927, and Wimbledon in 1925 and 1928. One of his most famous matches came against Bill Tilden in the 1927 U.S. National. Tilden pressured Lacoste consistently, but Lacoste was up to every challenge, prevailing 11–9, 6–3, 11–9.

Lacoste's other contributions to the game included designing the first cotton short-sleeved shirt specifically for tennis—the shirt bore a crocodile on the breast—and

developing the steel racket (Wilson T-2000) that Jimmy Connors used for years.

Lacoste was inducted into the International Tennis Hall of Fame in 1976.

Laver, Rod
Born: August 9, 1938 in Rockhampton, Australia

He started out as a small child who was frequently sick. He blossomed into one of the greatest players of all time. Nicknamed "The Rocket," Laver was short (5-8 1/2), but solidly built at 145 pounds. He practically invented topspin, produced by hitting the ball from low to high, resulting in a shot that clears the net comfortably, then dives rapidly and takes a skidding bounce.

A left-hander, Laver's topspin was made all the more effective because of the strength of his left arm, which looked as if it should hang from Popeye.

He reached the first of six straight Wimbledon finals in 1959. He lost the first two—to Alex Olmedo and Neale Fraser, respectively—then won the next four. He beat Chuck McKinley in 1961 and Marty Mulligan in 1962. He turned pro after the 1962 season and didn't play Wimbledon again until 1968, when pros and amateurs were eligible. He beat countrymen Tony Roche in 1968 and John Newcombe the following year.

His Wimbledon titles in 1962 and 1969 were jewels in a pair of historic seasons: Laver won the Grand Slam in both. In 1962, he became only the second man—Don Budge was the other—to win the Australian, French, Wimbledon, and U.S. championships in the same calendar year.

As impressive as his 1962 Slam season was, his repeat in 1969 was even more impressive because he was playing against the best in the world—pros and amateurs. He won 17 singles titles that year and had a match record of 106–6.

In addition to the major titles won during the Grand Slam years, Laver also won the 1960 Australian championship and nine major doubles championships. He owns 20 Grand Slam titles in singles, doubles, and mixed doubles, and ranks fifth all-time. His 11 Grand Slam singles titles tie him for third with Bjorn Borg, one behind Roy Emerson and two behind Pete Sampras.

Laver also helped Australia win the Davis Cup four straight years beginning in 1959. He returned in 1971, when pros were permitted, to add a fifth Cup for Australia. He never played in a losing Davis Cup series.

As a professional, Laver won the U.S. Pro Championship five times, including four straight, beginning in 1966.

Laver, who was the first tennis player to surpass the $1 million mark in earnings, was ranked in the top 10 in the world 13 times, including four times at no. 1 (1961–62, '68–69). He won 47 pro singles titles, reached the final in 21 others, and was inducted into the International Tennis Hall of Fame in 1981.

On July 27, 1998, 13 days before his 60th birthday, Laver suffered a "moderate" stroke according to doctors. He was in Los Angeles, taping a television interview with ESPN. He spent about a month at UCLA Medical Center and eventually enjoyed an almost complete recovery.

Lendl, Ivan
Born: March 7, 1960 in Ostrava, Czechoslovakia (now the Czech Republic)

Ivan Lendl had his first big breakthrough in 1984, after several years of solid but unspectacular results. He had gained the reputation of a player who failed to win in pressure situations, having lost twice in the U.S. Open finals (1982–83) and once each in the French Open (1981) and the Australian Open (1983) finals.

In 1984 in the French Open final, it looked as if the pattern would continue. Lendl trailed John McEnroe two sets to none and was twice down a break in the fourth set. But instead of folding, Lendl rallied and defeated McEnroe 3–6, 2–6, 6–4, 7–5, 7–5. Lendl lost to McEnroe in the U.S. Open final in 1984, but wouldn't lose again for four years. Lendl won three straight U.S. Opens, beginning in 1985, beating McEnroe, Miloslav Mecir, and Mats Wilander, respectively.

He also reached the final in 1988 and 1989, but lost to Wilander and Boris Becker. His loss to Wilander in 1988 ended his winning streak at the Open at 27 matches, second to Bill Tilden, who was unbeaten in 42 straight (1920–26).

Lendl also won the Australian Open (1989–90) and two more French titles (1986–87). His eight Grand Slam titles tie him for sixth all-time, four behind the coleaders Roy Emerson and Pete Sampras.

Lendl played from the baseline, using heavy topspin off his forehand and backhand. He did not have an overly powerful serve, nor was he a natural volleyer–two reasons he never won a Wimbledon singles title, despite all his hard work to become a grass court player. Lendl reached the final twice, but lost in straight sets each time—to Boris Becker in 1986 and to Pat Cash in 1987.

Lendl spent 13 years (1980–92) ranked in the top 10 in the world, including four times at no. 1 (1985–87, '89). In all, he was ranked first for 270 weeks, second all-time to Pete Sampras, who surpassed him in 1999.

Overall, Lendl won 94 singles titles, second to Jimmy Connors (109). His match record of 1,279–274 (.805) also was second to Connors.

Back problems forced him to retire in 1993. He lives in Connecticut with his wife, Samantha, and their six children. He plays tennis exhibitions occasionally and is an avid golfer, who plays on the Celebrity Golf Tour.

Lenglen, Suzanne
Born: May 24, 1899 in Paris, France
Died: July 4, 1938

Suzanne Lenglen made her mark in 1919 at age 20, when she won her first Wimbledon singles title, beating seven-time champion Dorothea Douglass Chambers. The match itself was memorable, Lenglen winning 10–8, 4–6, 9–7, but so were her dress and her choice of beverages between games.

In a day when women played tennis in long, flowing dresses, Lenglen showed up at Wimbledon wearing a dress cut just above her ankles. It caused quite the stir, as did the brandy Lenglen sipped to calm her nerves.

After that victory, Lenglen's popularity soared worldwide. Her game was one of graceful movements and deadly accurate groundstrokes.

Lenglen went on to win five more Wimbledon titles (1920–23, '25) and two French titles (1925–26). She never won a U.S. National title. But in 1921, she reached the final, only to default to Molla Mallory because of an asthma condition that left her weeping and coughing.

In 1926, Lenglen turned pro and, for $50,000, played a series of matches against Mary K. Browne, winning all 38. Four male pros eventually joined the tour, but Lenglen retained top billing. The tour was so successful that she received a $25,000 bonus; Browne received $25,000 and the men split $77,000.

Lenglen, who died in 1938 of pernicious anemia, won 81 singles titles and 73 doubles titles during her career. She was inducted into the International Tennis Hall of Fame in 1978.

Mallory, Molla Bjurstedt
Born: March 6, 1884 in Oslo, Norway
Died: November 22, 1959

Molla Mallory was an unusually hard hitter who had effective groundstrokes. She was a determined and tireless competitor.

Mallory won a record eight U.S. championships (1915–18, '20–22, '26). She also reached the final in 1923 and 1924, losing each time to Helen Wills. Her victory in 1926, over Elizabeth Ryan, made her the oldest winner of a major title at age 42.

The most famous of Mallory's matches occurred in the second round of the 1921 U.S. championship against Suzanne Lenglen. After Mallory won the first set, Lenglen approached the umpire's stand out of breath, coughing, and crying. She told the umpire she was too ill to continue. It was Lenglen's only defeat as an amateur.

Mallory was ranked in the top 10 in the world for three years, beginning in 1925, the first year of the rankings. She was inducted into the International Tennis Hall of Fame in 1958.

Mandlikova, Hana

Born: February 19, 1962 in Prague,
Czechoslovakia (now the Czech Republic)

Hana Mandlikova won four Grand Slam singles titles—Australian (1980, '87), French (1981), U.S. Open (1985). Her U.S. Open victory over Martina Navratilova was her biggest prize. She defeated Chris Evert in the semis, before conquering Navratilova in three sets.

Mandlikova helped Czechoslovakia win the Federation Cup three straight years, beginning in 1983. She retired at 28 with 27 singles titles and 15 doubles titles. She was ranked in the top 10 in the world seven times, rising as high as third in 1984 and 1985.

Mandlikova was inducted into the International Tennis Hall of Fame in 1994.

Marble, Alice

Born: September 28, 1913 in Beckworth, California
Died: December 13, 1990

Alice Marble was the first woman to play a serve-and-volley game. Her strong serve and aggressive, attacking style was a stark contrast to the baseline strategy that most women employed.

She learned the game on the public courts of Golden Gate Park in San Francisco, where she was a mascot and ballgirl for the San Francisco Seals, a minor league baseball team that featured Joe DiMaggio.

Her career ended almost before it started. In 1933, while playing a tournament in East Hampton, N.Y., Marble was forced to play the singles and doubles semifinals and finals in one day. The heat was oppressive, the temperature reaching 100 degrees. She passed out from sunstroke. The following spring, she collapsed again. She was misdiagnosed with tuberculosis and committed to a sanatarium.

Her coach, Eleanor Tennant, got her released from the sanatarium after several months and, through a diet and exercise program, got her back to good health. Marble's career then took off.

She beat Helen Jacobs for the U.S. National title in 1936. Marble also won the U.S. title for three straight years, beginning in 1940, and the 1939 Wimbledon title.

Marble was named the Associated Press Female Athlete of the Year in 1939 and 1940. She was ranked in the top 10 in the world in 1933, 1936, 1937, 1938, and 1939, including first in 1939.

Marble turned pro in 1941, touring with Mary Hardwick and winning 72 of 75 matches. She was inducted into the International Tennis Hall of Fame in 1964.

McEnroe, John

Born: February 16, 1959 in Wiesbaden, Germany

Known as much for his fiery temperament as for his remarkable skill, John McEnroe was a racket-carrying lightning rod for the game.

His talent was unsurpassed, and his touch and artistry at the net were in a class by themselves. But so was his temper. He was outspoken, controversial, boorish, and arrogant. He was penalized, fined, and even disqualified from the 1990 Australian Open for his language.

Were it not for allowing himself to be distracted by noise coming from the headset of a television cameraman at courtside, he might have won the 1984 French Open title. Instead, his outbursts cost him. He squandered a two-sets-to-none lead and lost to Ivan Lendl.

McEnroe made his mark early, winning his first Grand Slam title—the French Open mixed doubles with Mary Carillo—when he was a 17-year-old amateur. That same year, he advanced to the Wimbledon semifinals, losing to Jimmy Connors.

His first Grand Slam title came in 1980 at age 20, when he won the first of his four U.S. Open titles. He also won the Open in 1980, 1981, and 1984. The 1980 and 1981 victories were against his chief rival, Bjorn Borg.

And it was against Borg that McEnroe played what was his most memorable match, and one of the most exciting finals in Wimbledon history, even though it was a loss.

In 1980, Borg beat McEnroe for his fifth straight Wimbledon title, but it didn't come easily. McEnroe won the fourth-set tiebreaker 18–16, turning back five match points in the process, before Borg prevailed 8–6 in the fifth.

But the following year, McEnroe won the rematch, beating Borg in four sets. After reaching the 1982 final, but losing to Connors, McEnroe won in 1983 and 1984, beating Chris Lewis and Connors, respectively. His left-handed serve and flawless volleying skills were perfect for the grass courts at the All-England Club.

McEnroe also was one of the best doubles players in history. He won five titles at Wimbledon and four at the U.S. Open, all but two with Peter Fleming.

In 1999, McEnroe was named captain of the U.S. Davis Cup team. His loyalty to the team as a player surely figured in the decision. He helped the U.S. win the Cup five times (1978–79, '81–82, '92) and played one of the most memorable matches when, in a 1982 quarterfinal against Sweden, he outlasted Mats Wilander in a five-set marathon that lasted more than 6 1/2 hours.

He holds U.S. Davis Cup records for years played (12), singles wins (41), and singles and doubles wins combined (59).

McEnroe spent 10 years ranked in the top 10 in the world, including four years at no. 1 (1981–84). He won

77 singles tournaments, third all-time behind Connors and Ivan Lendl, and 77 doubles titles. His total of 154 victories is a record.

He retired after the 1992 season, but returned to Wimbledon in 1999 to play mixed doubles with Steffi Graf. They reached the final, but Graf withdrew in order to conserve her energy for the women's final, which she lost to Lindsay Davenport. McEnroe does television commentary for CBS, NBC, and USA Network.

Moody, Helen Wills

Born: October 6, 1905 in Centerville, California
Died: January 1, 1998

Helen Wills Moody was known as "Little Miss Poker Face" for her undemonstrative nature, which was misunderstood by fans and the media, who accused her of not enjoying the game.

Said Moody: "When I play, I become entirely absorbed in the game. I love the feel of hitting a ball hard, the pleasure of a rally. Anyone who really loves the game can hardly be blamed for becoming completely absorbed by it while in the fun of play." That focus, along with her powerful groundstrokes from both sides, were responsible for a career that ranks her as one of the best ever.

Moody enjoyed her greatest success at Wimbledon, which she won eight times (1927–30, '32–33, '35, '38) in nine tries. She suffered her only loss in 1924, in her first appearance. She also won the U.S. national championship seven times (1923–25, '27–29, '31) and the French Open four times (1928–30, '32). From 1927 through 1932, she didn't lose one set in singles, and between 1919 and 1938, she won 91 percent of her matches and had a 158-match winning streak.

Moody's 19 Grand Slam titles rank third behind Margaret Court (24) and Steffi Graf (22). In 1928, she became the first player to win three majors—French, Wimbledon, U.S.—in the same year.

While Moody and Suzanne Lenglen were contemporaries, they met only once, in 1926, Lenglen winning 6–3, 8–6. After that match, Wills was sidelined with appendicitis and Lenglen turned pro.

Moody's other chief rival was Helen Jacobs, who lost all but one match. Jacobs' only win came in the 1933 U.S. National final. Moody trailed in the third set, when she retired from the match due to back pain.

Moody was named the Associated Press Female Athlete of the Year in 1935 and was inducted into the International Tennis Hall of Fame in 1959.

Nastase, Ilie

Born: July 19, 1946 in Bucharest, Romania

Ilie Nastase was regarded as the bad boy of tennis—often referred to as "Nasty." His behavior could range from outlandish to arrogant. He was fined, disqualified, and suspended, but it did no good. Yet in spite of being frequently out of control on the court, his talent was undeniable. Nastase was athletic and played an all-around game. He was as comfortable at the net as at the baseline.

He won two Grand Slam singles titles—the 1972 U.S. Open and the 1973 French Open—and reached the Wimbledon final twice, losing to Stan Smith in five sets in 1972 and to Bjorn Borg in straight sets in 1976.

Nastase helped make Romania a major factor in Davis Cup competition. Three times he led his team into the final against the U.S., only to lose each time (1969, '71–72).

Nastase was ranked in the top 10 in the world eight times from 1970 to 1977, including No. 1 in 1973, when he won 15 tournaments and had a match record of 118–17. Through the 2000 season, his 57 tournament titles rank seventh all-time. He was inducted into the International Tennis Hall of Fame in 1991.

Nastase got involved in politics in 1996, running for mayor of Bucharest, but was defeated.

Navratilova, Martina

Born: October 8, 1956 in Prague, Czechoslovakia (now the Czech Republic)

When Martina Navratilova first attracted the attention of the tennis world, reaching the quarterfinals at the 1973 French Open at 16 years of age, she was overweight and out of shape. She had talent, but lacked discipline.

But following a disappointing 1976 season, Navratilova lost weight and began a rigorous training regimen that helped her become one of the finest women athletes in the world and one of the elite players in the history of women's tennis.

Navratilova, who learned the game from her mother and stepfather and defected to the United States after the 1975 U.S. Open (she became a U.S. citizen in 1981), is the winningest player in tennis history—male or female. She has 167 singles titles, 162 doubles titles, and eight mixed doubles titles. She won 87 percent of her singles matches, 89 percent of her doubles matches, 83 percent of her mixed doubles matches, and 48 percent of all the tournaments she entered.

Navratilova played an attacking, serve-and-volley style, but was solid enough from the baseline to win the French Open, held on slow red clay, in 1982 and 1984. She also reached the French final three other times.

Navratilova won three Australian Open titles (1981, '83, '85) and four U.S. Open titles (1983–84, '86–87). But her greatest success came at Wimbledon, where she won a record nine singles titles (1978–79, '82–87, '90). She broke Helen Wills Moody's record, established 50 years earlier, by beating Zina Garrison in 1990, and her six consecutive victories broke Suzanne Lenglen's record of five (1919–23).

Navratilova reached the final in her last Wimbledon (1994), losing to Conchita Martinez. She closed the book on her career at the All-England Club with records for the most consecutive finals (9), most matches (279), singles wins (119), doubles wins (80), and overall wins (243).

Starting in 1985 and continuing through 1987, Navratilova reached the final of all 11 Grand Slam events. (The Australian wasn't played in 1986.) She won six.

Like John McEnroe, Navratilova was an outstanding singles player who was just as talented in doubles. She won 31 Grand Slam doubles titles—eight Australian, seven French, seven Wimbledon, and nine U.S. Open. She also won seven Grand Slam mixed doubles titles—two French, three Wimbledon, and two U.S. Open.

Navratilova and her partner, Pam Shriver, were one of the great teams in tennis history. They won 20 major titles together, tying Louise Brough and Margaret Osborne duPont, and a doubles Grand Slam in 1984. Their record 109-match winning streak, started in 1983, was snapped in the 1985 Wimbledon doubles final by Liz Smylie and Kathy Jordan. At the 1987 U.S. Open, Navratilova won all three events, only the third time that's been accomplished in the Open era (since 1968).

Navratilova's rivalry with Chris Evert was one of the most memorable in all of sports. Their contrasting styles—Navratilova was the aggressor, Evert the baseline counterpuncher—made for some epic confrontations.

Evert won 21 of the first 25 matches played—the first in Akron, Ohio, in 1973—but 15 years later Navratilova finished with a 43–37 edge. They brought out the best in each other, each raising the other's game to a new level, each respecting the other as an athlete and a person.

Navratilova was a fixture in the ranking of the top 10 players in the world. From 1975 through 1982, she never dropped below fourth. She ascended to first in 1978 and 1979, fell to third in 1980, then owned the no. 1 spot from 1982 through 1987, a string of 150 consecutive weeks.

Newcombe, John

Born: May 23, 1944 in Sydney, Australia

John Newcombe was one of only two players—countryman Rod Laver was the other—to win the Wimbledon and U.S. singles titles as an amateur and as a pro. Newcombe was the last amateur champion at Wimbledon in 1967. He won as a pro in 1970 and 1971. He won the U.S. championship in 1967 and again in 1973. Newcombe's other Grand Slam titles came in the Australian championships in 1973 and 1975.

He was also an excellent doubles player, especially when partnered with Tony Roche. Newcombe and Roche won five Wimbledon doubles titles, a modern record. They also won one U.S., two French, and four Australian doubles titles.

Newcombe's 25 Grand Slam titles—seven in singles, 17 in doubles, and one in mixed doubles—rank second all-time behind Roy Emerson (28).

At 19 years old in 1963, Newcombe was one of the youngest Australians ever to play in the Davis Cup. He helped the Aussies win five Cups, including four straight from 1964 to 1967.

Newcombe was ranked in the top 10 in the world for seven straight years, starting in 1968. He was no. 1 in 1970 and 1971 and No. 2 in 1973 and 1974. He won 32 singles titles and 41 doubles titles in his career.

He was appointed Australia's Davis Cup captain in 1995 and led the team to the Davis Cup title in 1999.

Perry, Fred

Born: May 18, 1909 in Stockport, England
Died: February 2, 1995

Fred Perry didn't begin playing tennis until he was 18 years old, but he made up for lost time by taking to the game quickly.

His first success came in Davis Cup competition. He led Britain to the 1933 Cup, ending France's six-year hold. The Brits held the Cup through 1936 as Perry won every singles match he played in the four Challenge Rounds (final rounds).

Perry won the Australian singles in 1934; the French singles in 1935; the Wimbledon singles in 1934, 1935, and 1936; and the U.S. Nationals in 1933, 1934, and 1936. His Wimbledon titles came without the loss of a set in the finals, where he beat Jack Crawford in 1934 and Baron Gottfried von Cramm in 1935 and 1936. Perry is the last British male to win a Wimbledon title.

He became the first player to win all four Grand Slam events. His eight Grand Slam titles tie him for sixth all-time.

Perry turned pro and won the U.S. Pro Championship in 1938 and 1941. He was inducted into the International Tennis Hall of Fame in 1975.

Riggs, Bobby

Born: February 25, 1918 in Los Angeles, California
Died: October 10, 1995

Bobby Riggs, who had a fine career in the late '30s and early '40s, is best remembered for his role in the "Battle of the Sexes" much ballyhooed matches against Margaret Court and Billie Jean King in 1973.

Riggs was a hustler and a master of gamesmanship who would take on any comers and make any bet.

In 1973, he met Court for no other reason than to prove that a 55-year-old man could beat a woman at the peak of her career. The match, which took place on Mother's Day, was later dubbed the "Mother's Day Massacre" because Riggs won in straight sets. Court's loss proved to be tennis' gain, as King agreed to meet Riggs. The match was held in the Houston Astrodome before a record tennis crowd of 30,472 and broadcast live on ABC. King beat Riggs convincingly 6–4, 6–4, 6–3 and tennis received a huge surge in popularity. Ironically, Riggs, a self-proclaimed "male chauvinist pig," helped give women's sports their most significant boost ever.

During his prime, Riggs, only 5-8, played with touch, finesse, and intelligence. He used the drop shot and the lob to full advantage.

At Wimbledon in 1939, Riggs' only appearance there, he won the singles, doubles, and mixed doubles titles, and bet on himself with a London bookmaker and took home $108,000.

Riggs also won the U.S. Nationals in 1939 and 1941. He was ranked in the top 10 in the world in 1937, 1938, and 1939, when he rose to no. 1.

He turned pro in 1942 and won the U.S. Professional Championship in 1946, 1947, and 1949. He went on tour with Don Budge and Jack Kramer, among others, and drew huge crowds.

Riggs was inducted into the International Tennis Hall of Fame in 1967.

Roche, Tony

Born: May 17, 1945 in Tarcutta, New South Wales, Australia

Tony Roche won only one Grand Slam singles title (1966 French), but was one of the best doubles players ever. He and countryman John Newcombe won 12 Grand Slam doubles titles, including five at Wimbledon. They were one of four male teams to win each of the four Grand Slam doubles titles.

Roche was ranked in the top 10 in the world six consecutive years, beginning in 1965, rising to no. 2 in 1969. He won 12 pro singles titles and 27 pro doubles titles. He was inducted into the International Tennis Hall of Fame in 1986 and has coached several prominent professionals, including Ivan Lendl.

Rosewall, Ken

Born: November 2, 1934 in Sydney, Australia

Ken Rosewall, who had one of the most effective backhands in tennis history, was one of the game's most enduring stars. Despite standing only 5-7 and weighing 135 pounds, Rosewall, nicknamed "Muscles," was never hampered by his lack of size. He was an all-around player who was successful on all surfaces.

Rosewall's fitness and his good fortune to avoid serious injury contributed to his longevity. He was first

Ken Rosewall *Diane Staskowski*

ranked in the top 10 in the world in 1952; he fell out of the top 10 in 1975.

In between, Rosewall won eight Grand Slam singles titles—Australian (1953, '55, '71–72), French (1953, '68), and U.S. (1956, '70). He also won nine Grand Slam doubles titles and one mixed doubles title. His 18 major titles tie him for seventh all-time. The only thing missing from his résumé is a Wimbledon singles title. Rosewall is one of the best players never to win that title. He reached the final four times (1954, '56, '70, '74).

Rosewall helped Australia win the Davis Cup three times (1953, '55, '56). He turned pro in 1956 and went on to win three U.S. Pro Championships (1963, '65, '71). In 1972, Rosewall faced Rod Laver in the World Championship of Tennis (WCT) final in what was a riveting match that lasted 3 1/2 hours, Rosewall winning 4–6, 6–0, 6–3, 6–7, 7–6. Rosewall won 32 professional titles, was the second player to surpass $1 million in earnings, and retired in 1977. His victory over Tom Gorman in a Hong Kong tournament, just after he turned 43, made him the second-oldest ever to win a tournament in the Open era (since 1968). Pancho Gonzalez was the oldest.

Rosewall was inducted into the International Tennis Hall of Fame in 1980.

Sampras, Pete

Born: August 12, 1971 in Washington, D.C.

In 1990, Pete Sampras surprised the tennis world—and himself—by winning the U.S. Open. He was one month past his 19th birthday and seeded 12th. Before beating Andre Agassi in the final, he had to defeat former Open champs Ivan Lendl and John McEnroe along the way.

But that was probably the last time Pete Sampras surprised anyone by winning a tournament because in the intervening years he has become one of the best players of all time.

Athletic, determined, and blessed with a powerful serve, Sampras has won 12 more Grand Slam tournaments since that breakthrough victory in 1990 and has the most career Grand Slam singles titles with 13.

Sampras, who grew up idolizing Rod Laver, the two-time Grand Slam winner from Australia, started out as a baseline player with a two-handed backhand. But at 14 years old, Sampras' style changed. He began hitting a one-handed backhand and developed a serve-and-volley game.

Sampras has had his greatest success at Wimbledon, where he has won seven times (1993–95, '97–99, 2000) and holds the modern record for victories. Willie Renshaw won seven titles (1881–86, '89), but from 1877 through 1921, the defending champion qualified for the following year's final.

Sampras won four of his Wimbledon titles in straight sets and was taken to five sets only once, in 1998 by Goran Ivanisevic. Sampras made it to the quarterfinals in 1996, but was defeated by Richard Krajicek, the eventual champion. Sampras' 25-match winning streak from 1993 through 1996 is the third-longest in history, trailing Bjorn Borg (41) and Rod Laver (31).

In addition to his 1990 U.S. Open title, Sampras also won it in 1993, 1995, and 1996. Sampras' other Grand Slam titles came in the Australian Open in 1994 and 1997. The only void on his résumé is a French Open title. The slow red clay on which the French is played is not suited to Sampras' attacking style of play. His best showing in the French came in 1996, when he reached the semifinals and lost to Yevgeny Kafelnikov, the eventual champ.

Sampras was clearly the best player of the 1990s. He was, in fact, rarely challenged by anyone on a consistent basis. The rivalry that many tennis fans anticipated between Sampras and Andre Agassi failed to materialize for any length of time, primarily because Agassi's career had so many peaks and valleys during the decade. Sampras and Agassi did meet in the 1999 Wimbledon final, Sampras winning in straight sets, but another encounter in the 1999 U.S. Open didn't take place because Sampras was forced to withdraw with a back injury.

Sampras' Davis Cup career through 1999 was a mixed bag. He was beaten twice in the 1991 final against France, but helped the U.S. to victories in 1992, over Switzerland, and 1995, over Russia.

Sampras, whose career has been plagued by injuries, was the no. 1 player in the world for six straight seasons (1993–98), breaking the record of five straight held by Jimmy Connors (1974–78). Sampras ended the 2000 season ranked third.

Sanchez Vicario, Arantxa
Born: December 18, 1971 in Barcelona, Spain

Through 2000, Arantxa Sanchez Vicario won 11 Grand Slam titles in singles, doubles, and mixed doubles, including the French Open twice (1989, '94) and the U.S. Open once (1994). Her 1989 win at the French made her the first Spanish woman to win a major singles title.

Sanchez Vicario helped Spain to five Federation Cup titles (1991, '93–95, '98). She also competed in two Olympics, winning a bronze (singles) and silver (doubles) in 1992 and a silver (singles) and bronze (doubles) in 1996.

She was ranked in the top 10 in the world every year since 1989, including second in 1993 and 1994.

Santana, Manuel
Born: May 10, 1938 in Madrid, Spain

Manuel Santana, blessed with remarkable racket control, was called a "magician" by Rod Laver. He won the French championships twice (1961, '64), Wimbledon once (1966), and the U.S. Nationals once (1965).

He was a stalwart for Spain in Davis Cup play, participating in 120 singles and doubles matches between 1958 and 1973.

Santana's career is credited for helping Spain develop tennis players. He spent seven years ranked in the top 10 in the world, including first in 1966. He was inducted into the International Tennis Hall of Fame in 1984.

Sedgman, Frank
Born: October 29, 1927 in Mount Albert, Victoria, Australia

Frank Sedgman helped Australia regain its supremacy in Davis Cup competition, leading the Aussies to three consecutive victories, beginning in 1950.

Sedgman won the Australian singles in 1949 and 1950, the Wimbledon singles in 1952, and the U.S. singles in 1951 and 1952. He also won 17 doubles and mixed doubles Grand Slam titles, including the only men's doubles Grand Slam in history, with Ken McGregor in 1951.

Sedgman and McGregor won seven straight major doubles titles, and Sedgman ran his streak to eight, partnering with John Bromwich. In 1952, his final season as an amateur, he won the singles, doubles, and mixed doubles (Doris Hart) at Wimbledon. Sedgman turned pro in 1953 and went on tour with Jack Kramer and later with Pancho Gonzalez.

Sedgman was ranked in the top 10 in the world in each of his three years as an amateur, including first in 1951 and 1952.

He was inducted into the International Tennis Hall of Fame in 1979.

Segura, Pancho

Born: June 20, 1921 in Guayaquil, Ecuador

Pancho Segura was the first player to use a two-handed forehand, a stroke he developed out of necessity. He was weak as a child, suffering from rickets. But his unorthodox style didn't keep him from being successful. He was a master strategist, with an effective forehand and lob.

Segura, who earned a tennis scholarship to the University of Miami, won the U.S. Intercollegiate singles title three straight years (1943–45). He turned pro in 1947 and won the U.S. Pro Championships three straight years (1950–52) and made the final four other times.

Segura, who was inducted into the International Tennis Hall of Fame in 1984, was a coach and adviser to Jimmy Connors and was key to Connors' development as an all-time champion.

Seles, Monica

Born: December 2, 1973 in Novi Sad, Yugoslavia

Monica Seles was on her way to becoming one of the greatest of all time when she was stabbed in the back by Gunther Parche on April 30, 1993. During a changeover of a quarterfinal match at the German Open in Hamburg, Germany, Parche came onto the court and stabbed Seles. He was a Steffi Graf fan who thought hurting Seles would return Graf to the top ranking in the world.

Seles was never the same player after the attack. She returned to competition in August 1995 in an exhibition match against Martina Navratilova in Atlantic City, N.J. She won only one Grand Slam singles title since—the 1996 Australian Open.

Prior to the incident, Seles was dominant. She won eight Grand Slam titles in three seasons—Australian (1991–92), French (1990–92), and U.S. Open (1991–92). Her three consecutive victories in the French Open made her the first player to accomplish that feat since Margaret Court did in 1970.

Seles also was ranked as the no. 1 player in the world in 1991 and 1992, taking it away from Graf, who held it from 1987 through 1990.

Seles was known for her two-handed forehand and backhand and a loud, high-pitched grunt that, at times, annoyed her opponents.

Through 2000, Seles had won 44 tournaments and was ranked eighth in the world.

Shriver, Pam

Born: July 4, 1962 in Baltimore, Maryland

Pam Shriver and Martina Navratilova formed one of the best doubles teams in tennis history. Together they won a record-tying 20 Grand Slam titles, including a Grand Slam in 1984 and a record 109-match winning streak that ended in 1985.

Shriver and Navratilova won 79 titles overall. Shriver also won an Olympic gold medal in 1988, when she and Zina Garrison won the doubles.

In 1978, Shriver was the youngest finalist in U.S. Open history at 16 years, two months. She lost in straight sets to Chris Evert.

Shriver won 21 singles titles and 93 doubles titles. She was ranked in the top 10 in the world nine times (1980–88), rising as high as no. 4 four times.

Smith, Stan

Born: December 14, 1946 in Pasadena, California

Stan Smith, one of the most popular players in tennis, won two Grand Slam singles titles—Wimbledon (1972) and the U.S. Open (1971). He and his partner, Bob Lutz, also won the U.S. Open doubles four times and the Australian Open once.

Perhaps Smith's most significant accomplishments came in the Davis Cup. For 11 years, beginning in 1968, Smith played in 24 matches, was on the winning team 22 times, and won the decisive point 16 times. He helped the United States to the Davis Cup title five consecutive years (1968–72) and seven overall (1978–79).

Smith was an All-American at the University of Southern California and the NCAA singles champion in 1968. He and Lutz won the NCAA doubles title in 1967 and 1968.

Smith won 39 singles titles and 61 doubles titles during his career. He was ranked in the top 10 in the world six times (1970–75), including first in 1972. He was inducted into the International Tennis Hall of Fame in 1987.

Stolle, Fred

Born: October 8, 1938 in Hornsbury, New South Wales, Australia

Fred Stolle is one of just 11 players to win all four Grand Slam doubles titles—Australian (1963–64, '66), French (1965, '68), Wimbledon (1962, '64), U.S. (1965–66, '69). He also won six Grand Slam mixed doubles titles.

Stolle's most significant singles championships came at the 1965 French and 1966 U.S. championships. Three times he was the runner-up at Wimbledon (1963–65). He helped Australia win the Davis Cup three times (1964–66).

Stolle was ranked in the top 10 in the world four times, rising as high as second in 1964 and 1966. He continues his involvement in tennis by playing exhibitions and working as a television commentator for ESPN. He was inducted into the International Tennis Hall of Fame in 1985.

Tilden, Bill

Born: February 10, 1893 in Germantown, Pennsylvania
Died: June 5, 1953

Bill Tilden was one of the greatest players in tennis history. Blessed with a powerful serve, he nevertheless played from the baseline, where he was equally effective from the forehand or backhand side. He was a masterful tactician from the backcourt, with the ability to utilize the lob and the drop shot.

Wrote Will Grimsley of the Associated Press: "He was more than a mere striker of the ball. He was a tactician, an artist. The racket was like a violin in his hands."

Tilden, nicknamed "Big Bill," was virtually unbeatable from 1920 through 1926, when he won Wimbledon the only two times he entered (1920–21) and dominated in the United States. He won the U.S. Nationals six straight times, beginning in 1920. He lost the 1926 U.S. final to Rene Lacoste, but won his seventh title in 1929. He also won a third Wimbledon championship in 1930, at the age of 37.

In the Davis Cup, Tilden led the United States to seven consecutive championships (1920–26), and at one point, won 13 singles matches in a row.

Tennis wasn't Tilden's only love. He also was involved in writing (a novel, short stories, tennis instruction books) and acting. He was suspended by the U.S. Tennis Association in 1928 for writing about the Wimbledon championships while he was competing, in violation of the organization's amateur rule. As a result he was removed from the Davis Cup team of which he was star and captain. But the French protested—such was Tilden's star power—and the American ambassador, Myron T. Herrick, intervened. Tilden was allowed to compete.

But when he returned home, he was found guilty of violating the amateur rule and was suspended from playing in the U.S. Nationals that year. Eligible in 1929, Tilden won his seventh title.

He disqualified himself as an amateur when he decided to make a series of motion pictures for profit. But in 1931, after the stock market crash left him nearly broke, Tilden turned pro and revived the tour.

He was such a big name that he toured until close to his 50th birthday.

Tilden's life ended in tragedy, though. He was convicted on a morals charge and was imprisoned in 1947. A parole violation sent him back to prison in 1949.

He died in Los Angeles of a heart attack, with his bags packed to play in the U.S. Pro Championship in Cleveland.

From 1919 through 1930, Tilden was ranked in the top 10 in the world, including six straight years at no. 1 (1920–25). He was inducted into the International Tennis Hall of Fame in 1959.

Trabert, Tony

Born: August 16, 1930 in Cincinnati, Ohio

Tony Trabert won five Grand Slam singles titles, including three in 1955. He won the French Open in 1954 and 1955, Wimbledon in 1955, and the U.S. championship in 1953 and 1955. His victory in the 1955 French Open was the last by an American male until Michael Chang won in 1989.

He won 18 singles titles and 12 doubles titles (all with Vic Seixas) in 1955. His match record in singles was 106–7 and included a 36-match winning streak.

Trabert helped the U.S. to the Davis Cup final five times (1951–55). The U.S. won the Davis Cup in 1954, beating Australia 3–2.

Trabert was ranked in the top 10 in the world in 1951, 1953, 1954, and 1955, including first in 1953 and 1955. He spent five years as U.S. Davis Cup captain (1976–80), winning the Cup in 1978 and 1979.

Trabert also became a respected instructor and a television commentator for CBS Sports.

Vilas, Guillermo

Born: August 17, 1952 in Mar del Plata, Argentina

Guillermo Vilas was a classic baseliner with powerful groundstrokes hit with severe topspin. He won four Grand Slam singles titles—Australian (1978–79), French (1977), U.S. Open (1977).

His best season was 1977, when he won 17 tournaments, tying Rod Laver's single-season record, and won 50 consecutive matches.

His U.S. Open victory that year came against Jimmy Connors in the last Open match played at Forest Hills Stadium.

Vilas won 62 singles titles and nearly $5 million during his career. He was ranked in the top 10 in the world nine straight years, beginning in 1974, including second in 1977. He was inducted into the International Tennis Hall of Fame in 1991. He is the only Argentine to be enshrined.

Vines, Ellsworth

Born: September 28, 1911 in Los Angeles, California
Died: March 17, 1994

Ellsworth Vines was tall (6-2) and thin (143 pounds), but he had a powerful serve. He played amateur tennis for just four years (1930–33), but he was ranked in the top 10 in the world for the last three and was first in the United States for the last two.

Vines' best year was 1932, when he won Wimbledon and successfully defended his U.S. Nationals title. But the following year, Vines lost in the Wimbledon final and lost two matches in the Davis Cup semifinal against Britain. He turned professional in 1934 and toured with Bill Tilden, winning 47 matches to 26.

Vines also toured with Fred Perry, considered the best amateur in the world before he turned pro, but Vines won 32 matches to Perry's 29 in 1937 and 49 to 35 in 1938. He retired after losing 21 of 39 matches to Don Budge in 1939.

Vines went on to become a professional golfer who won five tour events in 1944 and 1945, and later served as a teaching pro at La Quinta Country Club in Palm Springs, Calif.

Vines was inducted into the International Tennis Hall of Fame in 1962.

Wade, Virginia

Born: July 10, 1945 in Bournemouth, England

Virginia Wade, one of the game's most graceful and dignified players, won her only Wimbledon singles title in 1977, during the tournament's centenary. To mark the occasion, it was the first time Queen Elizabeth attended the tournament in 25 years. Wade beat Chris Evert in the semifinals and Betty Stove in the final. Wade also won the Australian Open in 1972 and the U.S. championship in 1967. She was also an accomplished doubles player, winning four Grand Slam titles.

Wade, inducted into the International Tennis Hall of Fame in 1989, won 55 singles titles and more than $1.5 million in her career. She was ranked in the top 10 in the world 13 straight years, beginning in 1967, including second in 1968. She played at Wimbledon for a record 26 straight years.

Wilander, Mats

Born: August 22, 1964 in Vaxjo, Sweden

Mats Wilander was a classic baseliner in the mold of countryman Bjorn Borg. Wilander won seven Grand Slam singles championships—Australian (1983–84, '88), French (1982, '85, '88), U.S. Open (1988).

His best season was 1988, when he won three of the four majors, the first person to do so since Jimmy Connors in 1974.

Wilander led Sweden to three Davis Cup championships (1984–85, '87) and seven straight finals (1983–89). He also played in two of the longest Davis Cup matches ever. In 1982, his five-set victory over John McEnroe of the U.S. lasted six hours, 32 minutes. In 1989, his five-set victory over Horst Skoff of Austria lasted six hours, four minutes.

Wilander won 33 titles and nearly $8 million in his career. He was ranked in the top 10 in the world for seven straight years, beginning in 1982, including first in 1988.

Williams, Serena

Born: September 26, 1981 in Saginaw, Michigan

Serena Williams and her older sister, Venus, have become two of the most successful and popular players in tennis.

Coached by their father, Richard, Serena and Venus grew up in Compton, Calif., where they learned the game. Compton is a city plagued by poverty and crime, and the Williams sisters played on the public courts, despite the danger that surrounded them.

Richard was criticized for not allowing his daughters to play U.S. Tennis Association junior tournaments, but he insisted his way was best. The results have proved him right.

Serena, powerfully built and athletic, made her Women's Tennis Association (WTA) tour debut in 1997, and she defeated two top-10 players, Mary Pierce and Monica Seles, in just her second WTA event. Her world ranking rose from 102nd in 1997 to 40th in 1998 to fifth in August 2000.

Serena won her first Grand Slam title at the U.S. Open in 1999, beating Martina Hingis. She became the first African American woman since Althea Gibson in 1958 to win the U.S. Open.

In July 2000, she reached the semifinals of Wimbledon, where she lost to Venus, who went on to win the championship. Through August 2000, she had won eight career singles titles and eight doubles titles, all with Venus.

Along with sister Venus, she won the Olympic gold medal in doubles in 2000.

Williams, Venus

Born: June 17, 1980 in Lynwood, California

Venus Williams and her younger sister, Serena, have become two of the most successful and popular players in the game.

Coached by their father, Richard, Serena and Venus grew up in Compton, Calif., where they learned to play tennis. Compton is a city plagued by poverty and crime, and the Williams sisters played on the public courts, despite the danger that surrounded them.

Richard was criticized for not allowing his daughters to play U.S. Tennis Association junior tournaments, but he insisted his way was best. The results have proved him right.

Venus made her professional debut in 1994, at age 14, at a Women's Tennis Association (WTA) tour event in Oakland. She led the no. 2 player in the world, Arantxa Sanchez Vicario 6–3, 3–0, but couldn't hold on.

Venus didn't play any pro tournaments in 1995 and played sparingly in 1996 and 1997. The highlight of 1997 was reaching the final of the U.S. Open. Venus became the first unseeded woman to reach the final in the Open era (since 1968). She lost in straight sets to Martina Hingis.

Venus won her first WTA event in March 1998, when she reached the quarterfinals of the Australian Open, the French Open, and Wimbledon, and the semifinals of the U.S. Open.

Venus and Serena reached the final of the 1999 Lipton Championship. Venus beat Serena in the first all-sister final in 115 years.

In July 2000, Venus won her first Grand Slam championship, beating Lindsay Davenport in the Wimbledon singles final. She became the first African American woman to win Wimbledon since Althea Gibson in 1958.

Through August 2000, Venus had won 15 career singles titles and eight doubles titles, all with Serena.

Along with sister Serena, she won the Olympic gold medal in doubles in 2000.

Motorsports

Allison, Bobby
Born: December 3, 1937 in Miami, Florida

Bobby Allison began his career in 1961, starting in the sportsman class and moving onto modifieds, before joining the Winston Cup circuit.

Allison was at his best on the superspeedways, winning 47 of his 84 races, including the Daytona 500, NASCAR's biggest race, three times.

Allison had his best year in 1972, when he won 10 races and finished second 12 times in 31 races. Twice, in 1971 and in 1982, Allison won eight races.

After four runner-up finishes, Allison won his only Winston Cup season points championship in 1983, at age 46. His last race came at the Miller High Life 500 at Pocono International Raceway in Long Pond, Pa. He survived a nearly fatal crash on the first lap of the race.

Two of Allison's sons weren't so fortunate. Clifford died from injuries suffered while practicing at Michigan International Speedway in Brooklyn, Mich., and Davey was killed in a helicopter crash in 1993.

In 717 career races, Allison won 84 times (tied for third all-time through 2000) and registered 86 seconds and 71 thirds. He won 57 poles and earned $7.1 million. He was named Driver of the Year in 1971, 1972, and 1983, and the Most Popular Driver of the Year in 1971, 1972, 1973, 1981, 1982, and 1983. He was inducted into the Motorsports Hall of Fame of America in 1992 and the International Motorsports Hall of Fame in 1993.

Amato, Joe
Born: June 13, 1944 in Exeter, Pennsylvania

Joe Amato is the only driver to win the National Hot Rod Association (NHRA) Top Fuel season championship five times (1984, '88, '90–92). Since beginning his career in 1982, he has finished in the top 10 of the Top Fuel season point standings in each of his 19 seasons.

Amato, who began racing go-karts at age 11, was the first NHRA driver to exceed 260 mph and 280 mph. His six victories in 1990 tied the NHRA record for most victories in one season.

Amato has 52 Top Fuel career victories. Through 2000, he ranked first all-time in Top Fuel victories and fifth all-time in overall victories.

Andretti, Mario
Born: February 28, 1940 in Montona, Italy

Mario Andretti is one of the most versatile, most successful, and most popular race car drivers of all time. He has won the most significant races on all three major circuits—Indy car, NASCAR, and Formula One.

Said legendary race-team owner Roger Penske, for whom Andretti drove for a time: "Mario is the best all-around driver I've ever had. He's a racer's racer—completely dedicated, single-minded, and passionately competitive."

Andretti came to the United States at age 15, after having grown up in Montona, Italy, where his father, Alvise, was a prosperous farm administrator. But Alvise lost his land in World War II, and the family ended up in a displaced persons camp from 1948 to 1955. It was during this time that Andretti developed a fascination with auto racing, idolizing Italian driver and Grand Prix champion Alberto Ascari.

In June 1955, the Andretti family came to the United States and settled in Nazareth, Pa., a small town near Allentown. Andretti and his twin, Aldo, worked in an uncle's garage. In 1959, they began racing a Hudson Hornet sportsman's stock car, taking turns behind the wheel. In their first four races, they each won twice.

While Aldo's career was slowed by a crash in 1959 in which he suffered a fractured skull, Mario's career took off. After racing modified stock cars for two seasons, Andretti got his first Indy car ride in Trenton, N.J., in April 1964. He finished 11th. He won his first Indy car race in 1965, the Hoosier Grand Prix; he was named Rookie of the Year at the Indianapolis 500; and he won the Indy car championship, finishing in the top four in 10 of 17 starts.

Andretti won the Indy car title again in 1967, when he also won the Daytona 500, the most significant race on the NASCAR circuit.

After second-place finishes in the Indy car championship in 1967 and 1968, Andretti won the title in 1969, when he won nine races and posted his only victory in the Indianapolis 500.

From 1975 through 1981, Andretti spent most of his time on the Formula One circuit. He won 16 pole positions and 12 races, and in 1978, won the world championship, only the second American to do so.

In 1981, Andretti spent four months as the Indianapolis 500 champion. In an unusual turn of events, Andretti lost the race to Bobby Unser, but Unser was later penalized for passing under a caution flag. Andretti was declared the winner of the race. Unser and his car owner, Roger Penske, appealed the decision, and four months later, Unser was awarded the victory.

Andretti won his fourth Indy car championship in 1984, when he won six races and sat on the pole nine times.

Andretti retired in September 1994 with 52 Indy car wins and 67 pole positions in 407 races. Through 2000, he ranked first all-time in races and pole positions and second all-time in victories. His Indy car earnings were more than $11.5 million. He also earned more than $1 million on other racing circuits.

Andretti, whose career lasted 36 years, was the only person to be named Driver of the Year in three dif-

Mario Andretti   *Reading Eagle/Times*

ferent decades (1967, 1978, 1984) and the only driver to win the Daytona 500, the Indianapolis 500, and Formula One world championship. He is one of only three drivers to win races on paved ovals, road courses, and dirt tracks in the same season, and with his 52nd victory in April 1993, he became the first driver to win Indy car races in four decades and races of all types in five decades.

Andretti and his son, Michael, became Indy car's first father-son team. Andretti's nephew, John, also is a driver, running on the NASCAR circuit.

Andretti was inducted into the Motorsports Hall of Fame of America in 1990 and the International Motorsports Hall of Fame in 2000.

Andretti, Michael

Born: October 5, 1962 in Bethlehem, Pennsylvania

Michael Andretti, the son of racing legend Mario Andretti, is one of the most successful Indy car drivers of all time. He began racing go-karts at age 10, and from 1972 through 1979, he won 50 of the 75 races he entered.

Andretti made his Indy car debut in 1983 and had his first victory in 1984. He won his only Indy car season points championship in 1991, when he had nine victories and earned a then record $2.4 million. At one point in 1991, he was so dominant, he won three straight races and four of five.

Andretti has been the runner-up in the season points championship five times (1986–87, '90, '92, '96).

Through 2000, Andretti had 40 career Indy car victories, ranking him third all-time, behind A.J. Foyt (67) and his father (52).

Bernstein, Kenny

Born: September 6, 1944 in Lake Forest, California

Kenny Bernstein is one of the most successful and popular drivers on the National Hot Rod Association (NHRA) circuit. His fan-friendly nature and accessibility have helped raise the profile of drag racing and attract new fans to the sport.

Bernstein began his drag racing career in the late 1960s. He primarily raced Funny Cars until switching to the Top Fuel division in 1990. In 1992, he was the first driver to break the 300 mph barrier, going 301.70 at Gainesville Raceway in Gainesville, Fla.

Bernstein won the NHRA Funny Car season points championship for five straight years, beginning in 1985. In 1996, he won the NHRA Top Fuel season points championship. He is the only driver to win a season title in both divisions in NHRA history.

Bernstein has 30 Funny Car victories in his career and 23 Top Fuel victories. Through 2000, he ranked third all-time in Funny Car wins, tied for fourth all-time in Top Fuel wins, and fourth all-time in overall wins.

Clark, Jim

Born: March 4, 1936 in Kilmany, Scotland
Died: April 7, 1968

Jim Clark was a two-time winner of the Formula One world championship (1963, '65). He nearly won the 1962 world championship, but lost it to Graham Hill. In 1963, Clark won four straight races and seven of 10 on his way to the title.

Clark received just as much notoriety in 1963 for a race he didn't win. He entered the Indianapolis 500 in a Formula One car, which was sleeker than the Indy cars and had the engine in the rear. Clark and his car were the butt of jokes until the competitors realized it was a contender.

Clark and Parnelli Jones battled for the Indy 500, with Jones winning and Clark earning Rookie of the Year honors. Two years later, Clark won the Indy 500, outdistancing Jones by more than a lap. He was the first driver to exceed 160 mph in the race.

In winning his second world championship in 1965, Clark won five straight races. In April 1968, Clark was killed in a crash during a Formula 2 race in Heidelberg, Germany.

Clark won 25 races and 33 pole positions in just 77 starts. Through 2000, he was tied for sixth all-time in victories and tied for second all-time in pole positions. He

was inducted into the International Motorsports Hall of Fame and the Motorsports Hall of Fame of America in 1990.

Earnhardt, Dale

Born: April 29, 1951 in Kannapolis, North Carolina
Died: February 18, 2001

Dale Earnhardt was either one of the most popular or least-liked drivers on the NASCAR circuit. His hard-charging, never-give-an-inch style made him either a hero or a villain, depending upon your point of view.

Earnhardt, nicknamed "The Intimidator," was an aggressive driver who routinely bumped and taped other cars who stood between him and better track position or him and the finish line.

Earnhardt joined the NASCAR circuit in 1975 and began racing full time in 1979, when he won one race, had 11 top-5 finishes, and was named Rookie of the Year. In 1980, he won his first Winston Cup season points championship, becoming the first driver to win the Rookie of the Year Award and the Winston Cup title in consecutive years.

Dale Earnhardt   *NASCAR*

Earnhardt, who drove his trademark black No. 3 Chevrolet, also won the Winston Cup season points championship in 1986, 1987, 1990, 1991, 1993, and 1994. He was runner-up in 1989 and 1995.

Earnhardt's most significant victory came in NASCAR's most important race, the Daytona 500. In 1998, in his 20th start, he won the Daytona 500 and broke a 59-race winless streak in the process. Later in 1998, he saw his record streak of 53 consecutive races running at the finish ended.

Earnhardt had 76 victories, 281 top-five finishes, 428 top-10 finishes, and more than $41.4 million in earnings in 661 races. He ranked sixth all-time in victories and first in earnings.

In addition to driving, Earnhardt also owned a race team featuring two NASCAR Winston Cup cars, one driven by his son, Dale, Jr., and one Busch Series car.

Earnhardt was killed in a last-lap crash at the Daytona 500 on February 8, 2001.

Elliott, Bill

Born: October 8, 1955 in Dawsonville, Georgia

Bill Elliott had one of the great seasons in modern NASCAR history in 1985, claiming 11 pole positions, winning 11 races, and earning more than $2.4 million in prize money. He won the 1985 Daytona 500, NASCAR's biggest race, from the pole position.

In 1987, Elliott won the Daytona 500 again, and in 1988, he won six races, finishing in the top ten 22 times in 22 races to win the Winston Cup season point championship.

Elliott switched race teams in 1992, joining legendary car owner Junior Johnson, and had another banner season. He won five times, including four races consecutively; earned nearly $1.7 million; and finished second in the Winston Cup season point championship by 10 points, the narrowest margin ever.

From 1983 through 1992, Elliott won at least one race each year. His last win came in 1994. From 1995 through 2000, Elliott has gone winless.

Through 2000, Elliott had 40 victories, 155 top-five finishes, and 285 top-10 finishes. He won 49 pole positions and earned more than $23 million. Elliott was the Driver of the Year in 1985 and 1988, and he was named the Most Popular Driver 14 times between 1984 and 1999.

Fangio, Juan-Manuel

Born: June 24, 1911 in Balcarce, Argentina
Died: July 17, 1995

Juan-Manuel Fangio began his racing career by running in a converted Ford taxi. The races were long and took place over two weeks with stages held each day. No mechanics were allowed and drivers had to complete all repairs.

Just before the start of World War II, Fangio won the Gran Premio International del Norte, a race from Buenos Aires to Peru and back, a distance of 6,000 miles.

It wasn't until Fangio was 36 years old that he began racing on the Formula One circuit in Europe. He won his first world championship in 1951, then missed most of the 1952 season after he broke his neck in an accident at Monza, Italy.

In 1954, Fangio won the first of four straight world championships. He retired in 1958 with 24 victories, 10 seconds, and 28 pole positions. Through 2000, he ranked eighth all-time in victories, fifth in poles, and first in five world championships.

He was inducted into the International Motorsports Hall of Fame in 1990.

Fittipaldi, Emerson

Born: December 12, 1946 in São Paolo, Brazil

Emerson Fittipaldi won championships on the Formula One and the Indy car circuit, making him one of only three drivers to accomplish the feat. He began racing motor bikes and karts, eventually moving from Brazil to England, where he was tutored by Jim Russell, owner of a legendary driving school.

Fittipaldi joined the Formula One circuit in 1970. In 1971, his season was cut short by an accident, not on the track, but on the road on his way home. The injuries weren't life-threatening, but just serious enough to make his 1971 season lackluster.

Fittipaldi rebounded in 1972 to win the world championship, the youngest winner in history. He won his second world championship in 1974. In 1976, Fittipaldi formed his own race team, but with little success. He went back to Brazil in debt. He rebuilt his wealth and made a comeback on the Indy car circuit, driving for renowned team owner Roger Penske.

Fittipaldi won the Indianapolis 500 in 1989 and 1993. He also won the Indy car season points championship in 1989. He retired in 1996 after suffering neck injuries in the U.S. 500.

Fittipaldi won 14 Formula One races and recorded 13 seconds and eight thirds in 144 starts. Through 2000, he was tied for 12th all-time in victories.

In Indy car competition, he won 22 races, claimed 17 pole positions, and earned $14,293,625. Through the 2000 season, he was tied for 14th all-time in victories, 12th in pole positions, and fourth in earnings.

Force, John

Born: May 4, 1949 in Yorba Linda, California

John Force is the winningest driver in the history of the National Hot Rod Association (NHRA) and one of the circuit's most popular figures. His charisma, engaging

John Force   *Reading Eagle/Times*

personality, and availability to the fans and the media have made him one of the most effective ambassadors for his sport.

Force began his career in 1978 and reached nine final rounds before getting his first victory, in 1987. Since then, he has been a dominant force in the Funny Car division.

Force has won more NHRA Funny Car season championships than anyone (ten: 1990–91, '93–2000). He has 92 NHRA national event victories, which is also first all-time, in Funny Car and overall.

Force won 13 races, a single-season record, in 1996, and in 1998 he became the first Funny Car driver to run faster than 4.80 seconds (4.787). He has won at least one NHRA national event in each season since 1987.

In 1996, Force was named the Driver of the Year in balloting by the national motor sports media. He was the first drag racer ever accorded that honor.

Foyt, A.J. (Anthony Joseph)

Born: January 16, 1935 in Houston, Texas

A.J. Foyt is an icon among race car drivers. He was a talented, hard-nosed, no-nonsense person whose full-out, always-charging driving style made him one of the most successful drivers of all time.

In addition to his outstanding record, Foyt is also known for his brash personality and volatile temperament. Said Foyt's father: "Talking to A.J. when he's angry is like dancing with a chainsaw." Foyt was frequently involved in shouting matches and shoving matches—with his competitors and even with members of his own crew.

He began racing as a teenager in Houston, Texas, where he ran roadsters, motorcycles, and midget cars. His first victory came at age 18 in a midget race at Playland Park, a quarter-mile dirt track in Houston.

Foyt dropped out of school to pursue racing full time, and in 1957 joined the U.S. Auto Club (USAC) circuit. He ran in his first Indianapolis 500 in 1958 and two years later won his first Indy car race and his first Indy car season championship.

In 1961, Foyt won his first Indianapolis 500, at a record speed of 139.13 mph, and also became the first driver to successfully defend his Indy car season championship.

Foyt took the season championship again in 1953, winning three races and finishing no lower than eighth in any race. In 1964, he had one of the great seasons in Indy car history. He won 10 of the 13 races he entered, including his second Indianapolis 500, and won the Indy car season championship.

Foyt, the first driver to win the Indianapolis 500 four times, also won in 1967 and 1977. He also won Indy car season championships in 1975 and 1978.

Foyt's expertise wasn't limited to Indy cars. He is the only driver to have won the Indianapolis 500, the Daytona 500 (1972), and the 24 Hours of Le Mans (with Dan Gurney in 1967). Foyt is also the only driver to have at least 20 victories in USAC's four major categories—Indy cars (67), stock cars (41), sprint cars (28), and midgets (20).

Foyt's last Indy car victory came in 1981 at Pocono International Speedway in Long Pond, Pa. His last Indianapolis 500 appearance was in 1992, when he finished ninth. He entered the 1993 Indy 500, but retired on the first day of qualifying. Foyt has been an Indy car race team owner ever since. Through the 2000 season, he fielded two teams in the Indy Racing League.

For all his accomplishments, Foyt is most linked with the Indianapolis 500. In addition to winning four times, he is the only person to have driven in the race for 35 consecutive years. He completed 4,909 laps around Indianapolis Motor Speedway for a total of 12,272.5 miles, the equivalent of five trips from New York to San Francisco. He earned more than $2.6 million in the Indy 500.

Through 2000, Foyt ranked first all-time in career Indy car victories (67) and second in Indy car pole positions (53). He earned $5,357,789.

A.J. Foyt *Reading Eagle/Times*

Foyt was inducted into the Motorsports Hall of Fame of America in 1989 as a charter member and the International Motorsports Hall of Fame in 2000.

Garlits, Don
Born: January 14, 1932 in Tampa, Florida

Don Garlits, known as "Big Daddy," is considered the father of drag racing. He was an accomplished driver, and continued to be an innovator and a technological pioneer after his retirement from the track.

He is credited with developing the Top Fuel dragster, with its engine in the rear, and the fire resistant suit. The rear-engine dragster revolutionized the sport, because it protected the driver from flying debris and fire.

Garlits won 35 National Hot Rod Association (NHRA) Top Fuel event championships. He was the first driver ever to accelerate from a standing start to 200 mph in a quarter-mile. He was also the first to exceed 170 mph (1957), 180 mph (1958), 200 mph (1964), 240 mph (1968), 250 mph (1975), and 270 mph (1986).

Garlits was the NHRA Top Fuel season champion in 1975, 1985, and 1986, the latter coming when he was 52 years old. Through 2000, his 35 NHRA national wins ranked eighth all-time. In 1989, he was inducted into the Motorsports Hall of Fame of America as a charter member.

Glidden Bob
Born: August 18, 1944 in Whiteland, Indiana

Bob Glidden is the second-winningest driver in the history of the National Hot Rod Association (NHRA). He had 85 NHRA Pro Stock victories and won the Pro Stock season championship nine times (1975, '78–80, '85–89).

Through 2000, Glidden was ranked second all-time in Pro Stock victories and second all-time in overall victories. He was inducted into the Motorsports Hall of Fame of America in 1994.

Gordon, Jeff
Born: August 4, 1971 in Vallejo, California

Jeff Gordon was the most successful NASCAR driver of the 1990s. Because of his success and the ease with which he appeared to dominate, he was not all that popular with those fans whose favorite drivers weren't winning. But his performance helped make the sport more attractive to the masses and make casual fans much more interested.

Gordon, who grew up in Indiana, began racing go-karts at age five. During the 1970s and early 1980s, he won three national quarter-midget championships and four national go-kart class championships. In 1986, on his 16th birthday, he became the youngest driver ever granted a license to participate in U.S. Auto Club (USAC) races. Over the next four years he won 22 races

Jeff Gordon *NASCAR*

and recorded 55 top-five finishes in 93 starts. In 1990, at age 19, he won the USAC midget series national championship, the youngest ever to win that title.

In 1991, Gordon joined the NASCAR Busch Series, one step below the NASCAR Winston Cup series, and was named Rookie of the Year. He had three seconds, one third, and 10 top-10 finishes. In 1992, Gordon won his first Busch Series race and set a series record for capturing 11 pole positions in a single season.

Gordon moved up to the Winston Cup series in 1993, recording one pole position, two seconds, seven top-fives, and 14 top-10 finishes. He was named Winston Cup Rookie of the Year.

Gordon got his first NASCAR Winston Cup victory at Charlotte in 1994, and he also won the inaugural Brickyard 400, held at the famed Indianapolis Motor Speedway. He finished eighth in the Winston Cup season points standings.

Over the next four years, Gordon, driving his distinctive, rainbow-colored No. 24 Chevrolet, dominated. He won 40 races from 1995 through 1998, including 13 in 1998, when he also won four consecutive races. He won the Winston Cup season series

points championship in 1995, the youngest ever to do so; 1997, when he won the Daytona 500; and 1998. In 1996, he finished second. In addition to the victories, he also demonstrated consistency, registering 90 top-five finishes in 158 starts.

In 1999, Gordon's race team underwent radical changes. His longtime crew chief, Ray Evernham, left to form his own race team and the absence took its toll. Gordon won seven races, including his second Daytona 500, but finished sixth in the Winston Cup season points standings, his lowest finish since 1994.

Another change of crew chiefs prior to the 2000 season, plus the loss of many members of his renowned "Rainbow Warriors" pit crew, continued his struggles.

Through 2000, Gordon had 52 victories and 129 top-five finishes in 257 races. He ranked seventh all-time in victories, and only two drivers—Richard Petty and Dale Earnhardt with seven apiece—have won more Winston Cup season points titles. He held the record for most money won in a season ($9,306,584 in 1988) and most consecutive years leading the circuit in victories (five: 1995–99).

Gurney, Dan

Born: April 13, 1931 in Port Jefferson, New York

Dan Gurney was one of the most versatile drivers of all time, as well as one of the sport's great innovators. He is widely regarded as the man who shaped the modern era of rear-engine Indy Cars.

Gurney began as an amateur drag racer and as a high school student built a car that went 138 mph on the Bonneville Salt Flats in Utah.

Gurney raced Formula One cars, won seven races, and finished in the top five in the world championship standings four times in five years. His victory in the 1967 Belgium Grand Prix is the only Formula One victory by an American driver in a car he built.

Gurney also drove Indy cars, winning seven races; sports cars, 18 race wins; and stock cars, five race wins. He retired after the 1970 season and was inducted into the International Motorsports Hall of Fame in 1990 and the Motorsports Hall of Fame of America in 1991.

Hakkinen, Mika

Born: September 28, 1968 in Vantaa, Finland

Mika Hakkinen is one of the best Formula One drivers of his time. He began his racing career, like many drivers, in go-karting, at age five. He won his first race when he was seven and was a five-time champion in Finland.

After rising through the ranks, Hakkinen moved to Formula One competition in 1991. In 1995, he was involved in a serious crash that nearly took his life. He suffered head injuries and was in a coma, but he recovered and went on to finish fifth in the Formula One world championship in 1996. In 1997, he registered his first victory, in the European Grand Prix.

Hakkinen won the world championship in 1998 and 1999. Through 2000, he had 18 career victories, tying him for 11th all-time.

Hill, Graham
Born: February 15, 1929 in London, England
Died: November 29, 1975

Graham Hill didn't begin racing until he was 24 years old. His first experience in a race car came about as a result of an ad in the newspaper for the Universal Racing Club, which allowed customers to drive a race car for five shillings a lap. Hill drove four laps.

He entered into a deal with the owner of another race school, whereby Hill would exchange labor for the chance to race one of the owner's cars. Hill began competing in races and teaching at the school.

Hill joined the Formula One circuit in 1958 as a full-time driver, a scenario that would be impossible to imagine today. He won the world championship in 1962 and 1968. In 1969, he was injured in a serious accident at Watkins Glen. He resumed racing after he recovered, but without any of his previous success.

In 1975, Hill was killed when the plane he was piloting became lost in fog and crashed.

During Hill's Formula One career, he had 14 wins, 15 seconds, and seven thirds in 1,976 starts. Through 2000, he was tied for 12th all-time in victories and eighth all-time in starts. He was inducted into the International Motorsports Hall of Fame in 1990.

Jarrett, Dale
Born: November 26, 1956 in Newton, North Carolina

Dale Jarrett, son of NASCAR legend Ned Jarrett, began racing full time on the NASCAR Winston Cup circuit in 1987. He got his first victory in 1991, went winless in 1992, then won one race a year from 1993 through 1995. In 1993, his one victory came in the Daytona 500, the circuit's most prestigious race.

Jarrett began to emerge as a force in 1996, when he won four times, had 14 other top-five finishes, and ranked third in the Winston Cup season points standings.

Over the next three seasons, Jarrett won 14 times and finished third twice and second once in the Winston Cup points race. In 1996, he won his second Daytona 500. He finally won the season points championship in 1999. He had four victories and 20 other top-five finishes.

Through 2000, Jarrett had 24 victories, 139 top-five finishes, and earnings of more than $27.8 million.

Jarrett, Ned
Born: October 12, 1932 in Newton, North Carolina

Ned Jarrett began racing under an assumed name because his parents weren't happy with his choice of sports. But before long he raced under his own name because he couldn't keep his victories a secret.

Jarrett made his Winston Cup debut in 1953 and won his first race in 1959. In 1961, he won only once, but his consistency—33 top 10s in 40 starts—resulted in his winning the season points championship. He won six races in 1962 and eight in 1963, when he finished in the top ten 38 times in 50 races.

In 1964, he had 15 victories and seven runner-up finishes, and in 1965, he won 13 times, finished second 13 times, and third 10 times. His remarkable consistency was enough to win his second season points title.

During 1966, Jarrett lost his sponsorship when Ford pulled out of stock car racing. He retired and promoted races at tracks in North Carolina.

Jarrett, the father of Dale Jarrett, also an accomplished stock car driver, became a television commentator in the early 1980s, a role he continued through August 2000.

In 351 races, Jarrett had 50 wins, 37 seconds, and 38 thirds. He won 35 poles and earned $289,146. He was inducted into the International Motorsports Hall of Fame in 1991 and the Motorsports Hall of Fame of America in 1997.

Johnson, Junior
Born: June 29, 1930 in Wilkes, North Carolina

Junior Johnson was an outstanding driver, a highly successful car owner, and one of the great characters in the history of NASCAR.

Johnson, called the "last American hero" by author Tom Wolfe, grew up on a farm in North Carolina and was said to have raced cars with souped-up engines at high speeds and ran moonshine, which eventually caught up with him. He served some jail time in the 1950s.

In 1953, he turned to stock car racing and won 50 races and 47 pole positions in 313 starts. Through the 2000 season, Johnson was tied for 10th all-time in career victories. Johnson's biggest victory came at the 1960 Daytona 500. His best season came in 1965, when he won 13 races and 10 pole positions in 36 starts.

He retired in 1966 at age 35 and became a car owner. Among those who drove for Johnson were Bobby Allison, LeeRoy Yarbrough, Cale Yarborough, Gordon Johncock, Darrell Waltrip, Terry Labonte, Geoff Bodine, and Bill Elliott.

As an owner, Johnson has won six Winston Cup season series championships (1976–78, Yarborough; 1981–82, '85, Waltrip) and two Daytona 500s (1969, Yarbrough; 1977, Yarborough).

Johnson, who retired as an owner following the 1995 season, won 139 races and 128 poles in his 31 years as an owner, earning $22.1 million. He was inducted into the International Motorsports Hall of Fame in 1990 and the Motorsports Hall of Fame of America in 1991.

Jones, Parnelli (Rufus Parnell)
Born: August 12, 1933 in Texarkana, Arkansas

Parnelli Jones was an accomplished race car driver who succeeded on a number of different circuits. He moved to California as a child, where he began as a jalopy racer. He moved on to dirt and sprint car racing by the time he was 17. He won the Midwest Sprint Car title in 1960.

Jones entered the Indianapolis 500 in 1961. He qualified fifth, finished 12th, and was named Rookie of the Year. In 1962, he finished fifth, and in 1963, he was the winner, despite a mechanical problem. With less than 100 miles to go, Jones' car began spraying oil on the track. The chief steward, Harlen Fengler, considered black-flagging Jones, but decided against it when the oil spray stopped.

In 1967, driving in a revolutionary turbine-powered car that ran on kerosene, Jones led A.J. Foyt by 52 seconds with three laps to go in the Indy 500 when the bearings froze in his gearbox, robbing him of what looked like a sure victory.

Jones retired from Indy car racing that day, although he continued to compete in Off-Road and Trans-Am races, and went on to become a car owner. He won the Indy 500 as an owner twice—in 1970 and 1971 with Al Unser behind the wheel.

Jones won six Indy car races, 25 sprint car races, 25 midget races, and 13 stock car races. He was inducted into the International Motorsports Hall of Fame in 1990 and the Motorsports Hall of Fame of America 1990.

Lauda, Niki (Andreas Nikolaus)
Born: February 22, 1949 in Vienna, Austria

Niki Lauda joined the Formula One circuit in 1972 and in 1975 won the first of his three world championships.

In 1976, Lauda led the world championship standings again. In a race at Nurburgring, Germany, he crashed and suffered severe burns to his head, and toxic gases damaged his lungs and his blood. He lapsed into a coma and was given last rites. But he rallied and six weeks later was back behind the wheel.

In 1977, Lauda won his second world championship, despite winning only three races. Midway through the 1979 season, Lauda suddenly retired and went to do television commentary and devote time to his airline business.

By 1982, Lauda returned to Formula One racing, largely for financial reasons. He went winless in 1983, but in 1984, won his third world championship, by just one-half point. Lauda retired for good in 1985.

In 171 career starts, Lauda had 25 firsts, 20 seconds, nine thirds, and 24 poles. Through August 2000, he was tied for sixth all-time in victories. He was inducted into the International Motorsports Hall of Fame in 1993.

Mansell, Nigel
Born: August 8, 1953 in Upton-on-Severn, England

Nigel Mansell was one of the most popular drivers of all time, especially on the Formula One circuit, where fans appreciated his talent, his competitiveness, and his passion for the sport.

Like so many other Formula One drivers, Mansell, whose boyhood idol was Jim Clark, began by karting. As he rose through the different levels of racing on his way to the Formula One circuit, he also made sure he had an education, earning a degree in engineering at Birmingham Polytechnic in England.

He made his Formula One debut in 1980 and had his first victory in 1985. He finished second in the world championship standings in 1986, 1987, and 1991, before winning the world championship in 1992, when he won a season-record nine races, including the first five consecutively.

In 1993, Mansell left Formula One to run Indy cars and won the season point championship, becoming the first rookie to do so and the first to hold the Indy car and Formula One titles at the same time. He returned to Formula One in 1994 and retired in 1995.

Mansell won 31 Formula One races, finished second 17 times, and third 11 times. He won 32 pole positions. Through 2000, he ranked fourth all-time in victories and fourth all-time in poles. He had five Indy car wins and 10 pole positions.

Mears, Rick
Born: December 3, 1951 in Wichita, Kansas

Rick Mears is one of the most accomplished Indy car drivers of all time. He began his competitive career as a teenager, racing desert motorcycles. To ease the fears of his mother, he switched to a dune buggy built by his father, Bill, a former race car driver.

In 1976, Mears made his Indy car debut, finishing eighth, in the California 500. In the final two events of the season he finished ninth, and he was named U.S. Auto Club (USAC) Rookie of the Year. He also won the Pikes Peak Hill Climb.

In 1977, Mears competed in eight USAC races and registered four top-10 finishes. Roger Penske, one of the most successful Indy car team owners of all time, hired Mears as the substitute for Mario Andretti, who was pursuing the Formula One championship in Europe. Mears

Rick Mears   *Reading Eagle/Times*

joined Team Penske full time in 1978, when he won three races and was named co–Rookie of the Year at the Indianapolis 500.

Mears won his first Indy 500 in 1979, becoming only the 10th driver to win from the pole position. He finished in the top 10 in all 14 of his starts and won the Championship Auto Racing Teams (CART) series championship.

Mears won two more CART series championships in 1981 and 1982, amassing 10 wins, eight pole positions, and 18 top-five finishes over the two years.

In 1984, Mears won his second Indy 500, but his season ended early because of a crash during practice at Sanair, Quebec. He severely injured both feet and ankles, and it was feared he would never walk again, let alone return to racing. It took several operations and months of rehabilitation before Mears returned in 1985.

He won his third Indy 500 in 1988 and his fourth in 1991, making him one of only three drivers (Al Unser, Sr., A.J. Foyt) to win the Indy 500 four times.

Another accident, in May 1992 at Indianapolis Motor Speedway, resulted in Mears' breaking his wrist. He missed most of the rest of the season. He announced his retirement at the annual Penske Christmas party in 1992.

Mears, known for his low-key personality and his team-player mentality, had 29 Indy car victories and won 40 pole positions during his career. Through 2000, he ranked seventh all-time in wins. In addition to his four Indy 500 wins were four other 500-mile race wins.

Mears held records for most poles at the Indy 500 (6), most wins from the pole (3), and most 500-mile race poles (16). He was tied for second with Al Unser, Sr., and Bobby Unser for most 500-mile race victories. He was the first driver to earn more than $10 million in Indy car racing.

Since his retirement, Mears has served as an adviser to the Penske Racing Team. He was inducted into the International Motorsports Hall of Fame in 1997.

Moss, Stirling

Born: September 17, 1929 in London, England
Stirling Moss never won the Formula One world driving championship, but he was, nevertheless, one of the great drivers of all time. He was born into a racing family, as his father, a dentist, had previously been a race car driver, running in the Indianapolis 500 in 1924 and 1925.

Moss began his racing career in 1946, much to the dismay of his parents. He moved up through the ranks and joined the Formula One circuit in 1950. His career lasted until 1962, when he was seriously injured in a crash. He suffered a partially paralyzed left side and was in a coma.

Moss did return in May 1963, rode around a track for 30 minutes, got out of his car, and said, "I'm retiring."

Moss had 16 victories, five seconds, and 16 poles in 66 starts on the Formula One circuit. Through 2000, he ranked 11th all-time in victories. He was inducted into the International Motorsports Hall of Fame in 1990.

Muldowney, Shirley

Born: January 19, 1940 in Schenectady, New York
Shirley Muldowney was a pioneer who changed drag racing. She broke the gender barrier and by doing so overcame discrimination and hostility from men in the sport who didn't think women belonged. Muldowney proved otherwise by her performance.

She won her first National Hot Rod Association (NHRA) national event title in 1976 in the Top Fuel division. In 1977, she became the first woman to win an NHRA season points championship, in Top Fuel. She also won NHRA season Top Fuel titles in 1980 and 1982.

Muldowney survived a near-fatal crash in 1984. In a race in Montreal, Muldowney suffered broken bones in all 10 fingers, a broken pelvis, and serious injuries to her legs. The bones in her left leg had to be fused, which resulted in her left leg being an inch shorter than her right. She underwent major surgery five times and needed 18 months to recover.

Muldowney returned to racing in 1986 and was voted Comeback Driver of the Year by the American Auto

Racing Writers and Broadcasters of America. In 1989, she joined the elite four-second club with a run of 4.974 seconds (quarter-mile track) at the Keystone Nationals in Reading, Pa., and went on to become the first driver to post sub-five-second runs in three consecutive national events. She finished in the top 10 in points through the 1990 season, when she cut back her schedule.

Muldowney raced sporadically throughout the 1990s, but in 2000, returned to the U.S. Nationals, the sport's most prestigious race, for the first time in 10 years. She qualified for the 16-driver elimination finals, but was defeated in the first round. She was considering returning to the NHRA circuit, at least on a part-time basis, in 2001.

Muldowney had 18 victories in NHRA national events. Through 2000, she was tied for eighth all-time in Top Fuel victories and tied for 24th all-time in overall career victories.

In 1983, a movie about Muldowney's life and career, *Heart Like a Wheel*, was released. She was inducted into the Motorsports Hall of Fame of America in 1990.

Pearson, David

Born: December 22, 1934 in Whitney, South Carolina
David Pearson was one of the greatest drivers in the history of the NASCAR. He followed up his Rookie of the Year season in 1960 with victories in the Winston Cup season point series championship in 1966, 1968, and 1969.

In 1966, he won 14 races and finished in the top 10 18 other times in 42 starts. In 1968, he was even more dominant, winning 16 times and finishing in the top ten 22 times in 48 races.

Pearson won the Daytona 500 in 1976; the Winston 500 in 1972, 1973, and 1974; the Coca Cola 600 in 1961, 1974, and 1976; and the Southern 500 in 1976, 1977, and 1979.

Pearson and Richard Petty waged one of the most spirited rivalries in NASCAR history. From 1963 through June 1977, they finished first and second to each other 63 times. Pearson won 33, Petty 30.

Pearson was on the pole in one of every five races he started and had a winning percentage of 18.29, both records through 2000. He ranked second all-time to Petty with 105 victories and second all-time to Petty in pole positions with 113. He earned $2.48 million. In 574 career starts, he finished in the top five 295 times.

Pearson, a television commentator, was inducted into the International Motorsports Hall of Fame and the Motorsports Hall of Fame of America in 1993.

Petty, Lee

Born: March 14, 1914 in Randleman, North Carolina
Died: April 5, 2000
Lee Petty was the patriarch of one of NASCAR racing's premier families. Petty's son, Richard, is the all-time winningest driver. Richard's son, Kyle, is a veteran NASCAR driver. Kyle's son, Adam, was an up-and-coming star who was killed in a crash at New Hampshire Speedway in June 2000.

Lee Petty began racing in 1949 at age 35. In 12 seasons of Grand National racing, he never finished lower than sixth, and three times he was the Grand National champion (1954, '58, '59). In 1959, he was dominant, finishing 41 of 49 events and winning 12. He earned an unprecedented $46,000.

Petty won the first Daytona 500 in 1959. His career ended in 1961 after a violent crash during a qualifying race for the Daytona 500.

Petty became the overseer of the family racing business after he stopped driving. He had 55 victories during his career, which ranked seventh all-time, through the 1999 season. He was inducted into the International Motorsports Hall of Fame in 1990 and the Motorsports Hall of Fame of America in 1996.

Petty died several weeks after surgery for a stomach aneurysm.

Petty, Richard

Born: July 2, 1937 in Randleman, North Carolina
Richard Petty, known as "The King," is widely regarded as the greatest NASCAR driver of all time, as well as one of the most popular. Nine times he was voted most popular driver on the circuit (1962, '64, '68, '74–78).

Petty's charisma, his humility, and his remarkable talent did for stock car racing what Arnold Palmer did for golf.

The son of Lee Petty, an outstanding driver himself, Richard was in his father's pit crew at the age of 12, but his father refused to let him compete until he turned 21. Just 10 days after his 21st birthday, on July 10, 1958, Richard raced for the first time and finished sixth.

Petty learned early on that success depended on being smooth, not flashy. So he drove aggressively, but also under control. That philosophy paid off. In 1959, Petty was the NASCAR Rookie of the Year. He went on to set virtually every record of consequence in the sport during a career that spanned five decades (1958–92).

Petty won his first Winston Cup season points championship in 1964. He won nine races, including his first of a record seven Daytona 500s. With his success, though, came jealousy on the part of his competitors, who claimed that his engines were too big. Disappointed by the pettiness, Petty spent much of 1965 as a drag racer—he ran in only 14 NASCAR races. But he returned to NASCAR full time in 1966, after a 1965 crash in Georgia in a drag racer killed an eight-year-old boy.

Petty won his second Daytona 500 in 1966 and finished in the top five in 20 of 39 races. He won the

Winston Cup championship in 1967, 1971, 1972, 1974, 1975, and 1979, and was runner-up in 1976 and 1977.

In 1967, Petty, driving his familiar No. 43 as he did throughout his career, had one of the great seasons of all time. In 48 starts, he won 27 races, including 10 straight, both of which were records through the 2000 season. From 1967 through 1971, Petty won 92 races.

Petty's other Daytona 500 victories came in 1971, 1973, 1974, 1979, and 1981. Through the 2000 race, no other driver had won more than four Daytona 500s.

While Petty was having success, he also developed a rivalry with David Pearson, the other dominant driver of that era. Between 1963 and 1967, Petty and Pearson finished first or second to each other 63 times, with Pearson winning 33.

Petty's 1979 victory in the Daytona 500 came after he had 40 percent of his stomach removed in 1978 because of ulcers.

Petty, known for his trademark cowboy hat and wraparound sunglasses, got his last victory in 1984, at the Firecracker 400. He retired in 1992 with 200 career victories, 95 more than Pearson, who is in second place. In 1,177 races, Petty also has 155 seconds, 102 thirds, and a total of 356 top-five finishes. He won 127 pole positions and earned $7,755,409.

Through 2000, he held the record for most consecutive years with at least one victory (13, 1960–72), most wins from the pole (61), and most wins from the pole in one season (15, 1967).

After he retired as a driver, Petty followed in the footsteps of his father and oversaw the family's race

Bobby Allison (left) and Richard Petty   *Reading Eagle/Times*

teams, which included Richard Petty's son, Kyle, and Kyle's son, Adam, who was killed in a crash at New Hampshire Motor Speedway in July 2000.

Petty was inducted into the Motorsports Hall of Fame of America in 1989.

Piquet, Nelson
Born: August 17, 1952 in Rio de Janeiro, Brazil

Nelson Piquet began his racing career by racing under an assumed name—"Piket"—because his family didn't approve of his racing. But he was so successful, the secret could not be kept for long. He was the Brazilian kart champion in 1971 and 1972. Piquet rose through the ranks and joined the Formula One circuit in 1978.

Piquet won three world championships (1981, '83, '87). In winning his 1983 championship, Piquet was the first driver to use a turbo engine.

After his third and final world championship, Piquet switched teams twice before retiring in early 1991.

During his Formula One career, Piquet won 23 times, had 20 seconds, and had 17 thirds. He also claimed 24 pole positions. Through 2000, he ranked ninth all-time in victories and first all-time in starts (204). He was inducted into the International Motorsports Hall of Fame in 2000.

Prost, Alain
Born: February 24, 1955 in St. Chamond, France

Alain Prost was one of the greatest Formula One drivers in history. His career could have started in 1979, when he was offered a ride by Team McLaren, but he turned it down because he felt he wasn't properly prepared for the Formula One circuit.

He joined the circuit in 1980 and won his first title in 1985, when he also won the world championship. He also won the world championship in 1986 and 1989. Then came a drought as Prost was overshadowed by Ayrton Senna. They had an intense rivalry that went beyond the track. Senna won the world championship in 1990 and 1991, and there were some who thought that Prost's time had passed.

But after sitting out the 1992 season, having been fired from the Ferrari team in 1991, Prost won his fourth world championship in 1993, then retired following the season. He had 51 victories, 35 seconds, and 20 thirds. He claimed 20 pole positions.

Through 2000, he was first all-time in victories and podium finishes (1-2-3 finishes). He also earned more championship points than anyone in history. Only Juan-Manuel Fangio won more world championship titles (5). Prost also was runner-up for the world championship in 1983, 1984, 1988, and 1990.

He was inducted into the International Motorsports Hall of Fame in 1999.

Prudomme, Don
Born: May 6, 1941 in Granada Hills, California

Don "The Snake" Prudomme, one of the most accomplished drag racers of all time, earned his nickname because he was so quick at the starting line. His talent, charisma, and the appeal of his rivalry with Tom "The Mongoose" McEwen helped bring much-needed attention to the sport from new fans and the media.

Prudomme started as a Top Fuel driver in 1965, but by 1973 had switched to Funny Cars (a dragster that looks like a street car). Starting in 1975, Prudomme won four straight National Hot Rod Association (NHRA) Funny Car season championships. He had six national event victories in 1975 and seven in 1976.

Prudomme had 14 NHRA victories in Top Fuel and 35 in Funny Car. Through 2000, he ranked third all-time in Funny Car and seventh all-time overall. He was inducted into the Motorsports Hall of Fame of America in 1991 and the International Motorsports Hall of Fame in 2000.

Rahal, Bobby
Born: January 10, 1953 in New Albany, Ohio

Bobby Rahal was one of the most accomplished Indy car drivers of his time. He began his Indy car career in 1982 and was named Rookie of the Year, winning twice and finishing second in the season points championship.

He won twice in 1984 and 1985, then won consecutive season points championships. In 1986, he won nine races, including the Indianapolis 500, and in 1987 he won three times.

Rahal had one win each in 1988 and 1989. He went winless in 1990 for the first time in his Indy car career, although he did finish second five times. He rebounded in 1991 to win four times, and in 1992 he won his third season points championship, winning three times.

Rahal retired after the 1998 season with 24 Indy car victories and 18 pole positions in 247 starts. Through 2000, he ranked 11th all-time in victories and 11th in poles.

Rahal, who owns his own race team, was appointed interim chief operating officer of Championship Auto Racing Teams (CART), one of two Indy car–governing bodies, in June 2000.

Roberts, Fireball (Glenn)
Born: January 20, 1931 in Apopka, Florida
Died: July 2, 1964

Fireball Roberts was one of NASCAR's most successful and most-loved drivers. He did for stock car racing what Arnold Palmer did for golf: attract a broader base of fans to the sport.

Roberts got his nickname because of his exploits as a pitcher. He was a hard-throwing right-hander who was tagged "Fireball" by an opposing hitter. The name stuck.

While he was in college at the University of Florida, he began racing in Daytona Beach and Jacksonville. He left school after three years and began racing full-time.

Roberts won many of NASCAR's biggest races: the 1962 Daytona 500 from the pole position; the 1958 and 1963 Southern 500; the 1959 and 1962 Firecracker 250; and the 1963 Firecracker 400.

In May 1964, Roberts was involved in a fiery crash in the World 600 at Charlotte Motor Speedway. He died less than two months later. At the time of his death, he was the all-time leader in victories with 32. He had 85 top-five finishes and earned 35 pole positions in just 204 starts.

Roberts was inducted into the International Motorsports Hall of Fame in 1990 and the Motorsports Hall of Fame of America in 1995.

Rutherford, Johnny
Born: March 12, 1938 in Coffeyville, Kansas

Johnny Rutherford, known as "Lone Star J.R.," started racing in 1959, driving modified stock cars at Devil's Bowl Speedway, near Dallas. He was the U.S. Auto Club (USAC) sprint car champion in 1965, and he made his debut in Indy car racing in 1962.

His first Indy car victory came in 1965 in a 250-mile race in Atlanta. In 1966, one week before practice began for the Indianapolis 500, Rutherford broke both arms in a crash and missed the rest of the year.

Rutherford won his first Indianapolis 500 in 1974. He also won in 1976 and 1980. Only A.J. Foyt, Rick Mears, and Al Unser won more Indy 500s. Rutherford also won the Pocono 500 in 1974, making him the first Indy car driver to win two 500-mile races in the same season.

Rutherford won his only Indy car season championship in 1980, when, in addition to winning the Indy 500, he won four other races and finished in the top five 10 times in 12 starts.

Rutherford's final victory came in the 1986 Michigan 500. He was the oldest driver ever to win a 500-mile race.

Rutherford won 27 Indy car races during his career and claimed 23 pole positions. Through 2000, he ranked eighth all-time in victories and seventh all-time in pole positions. He was inducted into the Motorsports Hall of Fame of America in 1996.

Schumacher, Michael
Born: January 3, 1969 in Huerth-Hermuelheim, Germany

Michael Schumacher is one of the best Formula One drivers of his time. His first racing experience, at age four, was in a go-kart powered by a lawn mower engine.

He is a two-time Formula One champion (1994–95). He won his first race in 1992 at the Belgium Grand Prix, and through 2000 he had 46 career victories, the most among active drivers and second-best all-time.

Since 1992, Schumacher has never finished lower than fifth in the world championship standings.

He won the World Championship in 2000.

Senna, Ayrton
Born: March 21, 1960 in São Paulo, Brazil
Died: May 1, 1994

Ayrton Senna grew up as an awkward child with a motor coordination problem. He was quite interested in cars so his father, a successful businessman and landowner, gave him a one-horsepower go-kart. The gift transformed Senna's personality. He became focused and confident, and the threat of losing his driving privileges was an incentive for him to be a better student.

At age 13, he began racing karts and won his first race. Senna moved through the ranks, finding success at every level, on his way to the Formula One circuit, which he joined in 1984. He won three world championships (1988, '90–91) and finished second in 1989.

Senna was killed in a crash at Imola, Italy, in May 1994. He won 41 Formula One races, had 23 seconds, and had 16 thirds in 161 starts. Through August 2000, he ranked second all-time in victories and first all-time in poles. He was inducted into the International Motorsports Hall of Fame in 2000.

Stewart, Jackie
Born: June 11, 1939 in Milton, Dunbartonshire, Scotland

Jackie Stewart was one of the most successful, popular, and recognizable drivers of all time. He grew up in a racing family. His father ran motorcycles, and his older brother ran sports cars. When Jackie began racing, his parents weren't in favor of it because of his older brother's crashes. But he started driving the family Jaguar, moved on to the Grand Touring class, and then Formula 3.

Stewart was offered a Formula One ride in 1964, but turned it down because he felt he wasn't ready. Later in 1964, he accepted a Formula One ride and joined the circuit full-time in 1965.

Stewart won his first world championship in 1969, when he won seven of the 14 races he entered. He also won the world championship in 1971 (five victories) and 1973 (six victories). He was honored with the Order of the British Empire for his accomplishments in 1971.

Stewart thought about retiring in 1972 because he suffered from a bleeding ulcer, but he returned in 1973 and won his third world championship and retired at the end of the season.

Stewart won 27 Formula One races in his career, had 11 seconds, five thirds, and 17 poles in just 99 starts. Through 2000, he ranked fifth all-time in victories. Only two drivers won more world championships.

After his retirement, Stewart went to work for ABC Sports as a commentator on its auto racing coverage. He was inducted into the International Motorsports Hall of Fame in 1990.

Unser, Al
Born: May 29, 1939 in Albuquerque, New Mexico

Al Unser is part of one of the great racing families of all time. The younger brother of Bobby and the father of Al Unser, Jr., Al Unser began racing modified roadsters in Albuquerque, N.Mex., at age 18. He made his Indy car debut in Milwaukee in 1964; he also won the Pikes Peak Hill Climb later in 1964, ending Bobby's six-year win streak, and again in 1965.

Unser made a name for himself on the Indy car circuit in 1968, winning five straight races. A broken leg, suffered in a motorcycle accident, forced him to miss some of the 1969 season, but he still won five races in 19 starts.

In 1970, Unser had one of the best seasons ever by an Indy car driver. He won 10 times, including the

Al Unser *Reading Eagle/Times*

Indianapolis 500, and finished first in the season points championship. His Indy 500 victory made him and Bobby the only brothers ever to win the race.

Unser successfully defended his Indy 500 title in 1971. He is one of only four back-to-back winners. In 1978, he won his third Indy 500, along with the Pocono 500 and the California 500. He was the first driver to complete a "Triple Crown" sweep.

Unser joined Penske Racing in 1983. He finished in the top five 10 times and won his second season points championship. Two years later, he won the season points championship again, finishing one point ahead of Al, Jr. At 46, Unser was the oldest Indy car season champ.

In 1987, Unser wasn't scheduled to run the Indianapolis 500, but got into the race as a substitute for Danny Ongais, who was injured. Unser won the race. He is one of three four-time winners of the race, joining Foyt and Rick Mears, who was his Penske Racing teammate.

Unser had 39 Indy car victories in his career, claimed 27 pole positions, and earned $6,740,843. Through 2000, he ranked fourth all-time in victories and sixth in poles. He was inducted into the Motorsports Hall of Fame of America in 1991 and the International Motorsports Hall of Fame in 1998.

Unser, Bobby
Born: February 20, 1934 in Albuquerque, New Mexico

Bobby Unser is part of one of the great racing families of all time. He is the oldest brother of Al, a four-time Indianapolis 500 champion, and the uncle of Al, Jr., the 1994 Indy 500 winner.

Unser, who began his racing career by driving modified stock cars, won the state title at age 15 and again at age 17. He won the first of his six straight Pikes Peak Hillclimbs in 1958. Overall, he won 13 Pikes Peak Hill Climb, the last of which came in 1986, after he retired from Indy car driving.

Unser made his Indy car debut in 1962, and he had his first victory in 1967. In 1968, Unser won the first of his three Indianapolis 500s. He won the first of his two season points championships, winning again in 1974.

Unser also won the Indianapolis 500 in 1975 and 1981. He is the only driver to win the race in three different decades.

In 1981, Unser won the Indy 500 by eight seconds over Mario Andretti, but the U.S. Auto Club (USAC), which sanctioned the race, ruled Unser passed illegally under a caution flag. USAC penalized him a lap and awarded the victory to Andretti. Unser and his car owner, Roger Penske, appealed the decision, and four months later, Unser was awarded the victory.

Unser retired from racing in 1982 as one of the most accomplished drivers of all time. Of his 31 Indy car victories, seven came in 500-mile races. He claimed 49 pole positions. Through 2000, he ranked fifth all-time in victories and third all-time in pole positions.

Unser, who worked as a television commentator, was inducted into the International Motorsports Hall of Fame in 1990 and the Motorsports Hall of Fame of America in 1994.

Vukovich, Bill

Born: December 13, 1918 in Fresno, California
Died: May 30, 1955

Bill Vukovich, known as the "Mad Russian," had a driving style that was best described as hard-charging and aggressive. During one period he was thrown through a fence in three consecutive races. He threatened to quit because the cost of crash helmets was too high.

Vukovich won the West Coast midget car title in 1946 and 1947 and the national midget car title in 1950.

In 1952, Vukovich nearly won the Indianapolis 500. He led the race for 192 laps before a quarter-inch pin on the steering arm broke and sent his car into the wall.

The following year, Vukovich won the Indy 500 in oppressive heat. He was one of only five drivers to finish the race without relief. In 1954, he repeated as Indy 500 champion, averaging a record 130.840 mph.

In 1955, Vukovich appeared to be on his way to a third straight Indy 500 victory. He was dominating the race until he became involved in an accident along the backstretch. He tried to get through the cars, but a car spun into his path. Vukovich's car flew over the wall. The crash was fatal.

Vukovich was inducted into the International Motorsports Hall of Fame in 1991 and the Motorsports Hall of Fame of America in 1992.

Waltrip, Darrell

Born: February 5, 1947 in Owensboro, Kentucky

Darrell Waltrip announced his retirement following the 1999 season and closed out his outstanding NASCAR career with a "Victory Tour" in 2000.

He began racing full-time on the NASCAR Winston Cup circuit in 1975, when he won twice and finished seventh in the Winston Cup season series points standings. From 1977 through 1980, Waltrip won 24 races and finished in the top five of the Winston Cup points standings each year. In 1979, he finished second to Richard Petty by just 11 points.

In 1981 and 1982, Waltrip won 12 races and the Winston Cup season points title each year. He was particularly dominant in 1981, winning four consecutive

Darrell Waltrip *NASCAR*

races and recording 21 top-five, 25 top-10s, and 11 pole positions in 31 starts.

Waltrip, known as "D.W.," won his third Winston Cup season points title in 1985. From 1983 through 1989, he won at least three races a year five times and finished in the top five six times. In 1989, one of Waltrip's six victories came in the Daytona 500, the circuit's most prestigious race.

Waltrip registered his last victory in 1992. Through 2000, he had 84 victories, 276 top-five finishes, 387 top-10 finishes, and more than $18.1 million in earnings. He tied for third all-time in victories and fourth all-time in pole positions with 59. In 1989 and 1990, he was voted Most Popular Driver of the Year.

Yarborough, Cale (William Caleb)

Born: March 27, 1939 in Sardis, South Carolina

Known as a hard-charging driver, Cale Yarborough was one of the all-time great drivers on the NASCAR circuit. Through the 2000 season, he was the only driver to win three consecutive Winston Cup season series point championships (1976–78).

Yarborough, who claimed he raced as hard to win the pole as he did in the race, also won the Daytona 500 four times (1968, '77, '83, '84), the Winston 500 twice (1978, '84), and the Southern 500 five times (1968, '73–74, '78, '82).

In 559 career starts, Yarborough won 83 times and finished second 59 times. He won 70 pole positions and earned just over $5 million. Through 2000, he ranked fifth all-time in victories and third all-time in pole positions.

Yarborough was inducted into the International Motorsports Hall of Fame in 1993 and the Motorsports Hall of Fame of America in 1994.

Other Sports

Akers, Michelle
soccer
Born: February 1, 1966 in Santa Clara, California
Michelle Akers has been a mainstay on the U.S. national women's soccer team since 1985. She was a three-time high school All-American at Shorecrest High in Seattle, Wash., and a four-time All-American at the University of Central Florida in Orlando.

Through 2000, Akers scored 104 goals. She is one of only four players to score 100 or more goals in international competition. Akers is the all-time leading scorer in Women's World Cup history with 12 goals, including 10 in 1991. She helped the United States win the World Cup in 1991 and 1999. She also was a member of the 1996 U.S. Olympic team, which won the gold medal.

Akers has overcome her share of injuries and physical problems. She has undergone 10 knee surgeries, and in 2000 had an operation on her shoulder that led her to announce her retirement in August 2000 from international competition. She also suffers from chronic fatigue and immune dysfunction syndrome.

Anthony, Earl
bowling
Born: April 27, 1938 in Kent, Washington
Earl Anthony's dream was to play major league baseball, but an ankle injury ended his career. He turned to bowling and became one of the best of all time.

Through the 2000 season, Anthony, who joined the Professional Bowlers Association (PBA) tour in 1970, ranked first in career victories with 41. In 1975, he was the first bowler to earn more than $100,000 in a season, and in 1982 he became the first to hit $1 million in career earnings. He led the PBA in average in 1973 (215.80), 1974 (219.34), 1975 (219.06), 1980 (218.54), and 1983 (216.65).

Anthony, a left-hander, led the tour in earnings in 1974 ($99,585), 1975 ($107,585), 1976 ($110,833), 1981 ($164,737), 1982 ($134,760), and 1983 ($135,605). He was named the PBA Player of the Year six times (1974–76, '81–83).

Anthony won the PBA National championship six times (1973–75, '81–83), the Firestone (now the Brunswick World) Tournament of Champions twice (1974, '78), and the American Bowling Congress Masters tournament twice (1977, '84).

Anthony, known for his crew cut and glasses, was inducted into the PBA Hall of Fame in 1981.

Arcaro, Eddie (George Edward)
horse racing
Born: February 19, 1916 in Cincinnati, Ohio
Died: November 14, 1997
Eddie Arcaro was one of the best jockeys ever. He quit school in 1930, at age 14, to become an exercise boy. He began riding in 1931. Over the next three

years, he developed into one of the most talented riders in the country.

Early in his career, Arcaro was known as a rough rider. Once, near the end of a race, he used his leg to hold the leg of another jockey all the way to the finish line. On another occasion, he tried to drive another jockey into the rail. He was suspended for the first incident and had his license revoked for a year for the second. As he matured, though, he became a much more intelligent and controlled rider.

Arcaro had his first victory in a Triple Crown race at the 1938 Kentucky Derby, aboard Lawrin.

Arcaro won 17 Triple Crown races in his career. He won the Derby in 1938, 1941 (Whirlaway), 1945 (Hoop Jr), 1948 (Citation), and 1952 (Hill Gail). He won the Preakness in 1941 (Whirlaway), 1948 (Citation), 1950 (Hill Prince), 1951 (Bold), 1955 (Nashua), and 1957 (Bold Ruler). He won the Belmont in 1941 (Whirlaway), 1942 (Shut Out), 1945 (Pavot), 1948 (Citation), 1952 (One Count), and 1955 (Nashua).

Arcaro is the only jockey ever to win the Triple Crown—the Derby, Preakness, and Belmont in the same year—twice (1941, '48).

Arcaro was the leading money-winner six times (1940, '42, '48, '50, '52, '55). He retired in 1962.

During his 31-year career, Arcaro had 4,779 victories in 24,092 races. He won 554 stakes races and earned more than $30 million. He was inducted into the National Horse Racing Hall of Fame in 1958.

Lance Armstrong   *Diane Staskowski*

Armstrong, Lance

cycling

Born: September 18, 1971 in Plano, Texas

Lance Armstrong is one of cycling's greatest champions and one of the most inspiring stories in all of sports. He is a two-time winner of the Tour de France, the most prestigious and grueling race in cycling, and he is a cancer survivor.

Armstrong began cycling when he was a teenager. He won the Iron Kids Triathlon (running, swimming, and cycling) when he was 13 years old. It wasn't long before cycling took precedence over running and swimming. He qualified to train with the U.S. Olympic developmental team in Colorado Springs, Colo., during his senior year in high school in 1988, and in 1989 he qualified for the junior world championships in Moscow. In 1991, he won the U.S. national amateur championship. Armstrong remained an amateur until after the 1992 Olympics, in which he finished 14th, and turned pro in 1992. In his first professional race, the 1992 Classico San Sebastian, he finished 27 minutes behind the winner. He might have given up were it not for the encouragement of his mother, who insisted he keep working.

In 1993, Armstrong won 10 titles, including the world championship and the U.S. Pro Championship. Over the next several years, he spent most of his time in Europe, where cycling is extremely popular. In 1995 he was named *Velo News* American Male Cyclist of the Year. He also won a stage in the Tour de France.

In October 1996, it appeared his career was over. He was forced off his bike in severe pain and diagnosed with advanced testicular cancer, which had spread to his stomach, lungs, and brain. He underwent three operations over the next three weeks, and his chances for recovery were no better than 50-50. Armstrong's treatment included the most aggressive form of chemotherapy available, and the effects were devastating, weakening him further.

The chemotherapy was administered in three separate five-day stretches. His hair fell out, he was often nauseated, and he lost as much as 15 pounds. But the chemotherapy began to work, and one year after his diagnosis, he was declared cancer-free. Just as important as the chemotherapy in his recovery was his incredible will and determination, his outstanding physical conditioning, and the unwavering support he received from family and friends.

Armstrong established the Lance Armstrong Foundation to benefit cancer research and promote awareness and early detection. He also became a spokesman for testicular and other forms of cancer.

He returned to competition in 1998 by winning a 56-kilometer sprint in Austin, Texas. He won three more races in 1998 and finished fourth in the Tour de Spain, one of the elite races in the world.

In 1999, Armstrong put the finishing touches on his comeback by winning the Tour de France and becoming an American hero in the process. In 2000, he successfully defended his championship.

Bailey, Jerry

horse racing

Born: August 29, 1957 in Dallas, Texas

Jerry Bailey is the only jockey to win three consecutive Eclipse Awards as the outstanding jockey of the year (1995–97). He also led all jockeys in earnings those same three years, earning a single-season record $19.4 million in 1996.

Bailey won the Kentucky Derby in 1993 (Sea Hero) and 1996 (Grindstone); the Preakness Stakes in 1991 (Hansel) and 2000 (Red Bullet); and the Belmont Stakes in 1991 (Hansel).

Through March 2000, Bailey ranked 19th all-time in victories with 26,345 races. He was inducted into the National Horse Racing Hall of Fame in 1995.

Beckenbauer, Franz

soccer

Born: September 11, 1945 in Munich, Germany

Franz Beckenbauer helped Germany win the World Cup as a player in 1974 and as manager in 1990. He also helped Germany to the European championship in 1972, the World Club Cup in 1976, the European Cup in 1974, 1975, and 1976, and the European Cup-winners Cup in 1967.

Beckenbauer made his national team debut in 1965, and a year later, helped Germany reach the World Cup final, where it lost to England. He was named European Player of the Year in 1972 and 1976.

In 1977, Beckenbauer left Germany to play for the New York Cosmos of the North American Soccer League. He led the Cosmos to three straight NASL titles and was named the league's Most Valuable Player in 1976.

Burton, Nelson, Jr.

bowling

Born: June 5, 1942 in St. Louis, Missouri

Nelson (Bo) Burton, Jr., won 17 career titles on the Professional Bowlers Association (PBA) tour. He led the

tour in average in 1970 (214.91) and was named the PBA Player of the Year. In 1976, he won the American Bowling Congress Masters tournament. In 1978, he earned $67,003, a career best, and won the Bowling Proprietors Association of America U.S. Open.

Burton was inducted into the PBA Hall of Fame in 1979. From 1986 through 1999, when network coverage ended, he was an analyst for ABC Sports.

Carter, Don

bowling

Born: July 29, 1926 in St. Louis, Missouri

Don Carter was an outstanding bowler and one of the sport's foremost ambassadors and promoters. He was known for his "bent-arm" delivery.

He played minor league baseball for one season after serving in World War II, then began managing a bowling center in St. Louis. He was named Bowler of the Year in 1953, 1954, 1957, 1958, 1960, and 1962 by a vote of the Bowling Writers Association of America (BWAA).

Carter won the BWAA All-Star Tournament (now the U.S. Open) four times (1953–54, '57–58), the PBA National championship once (1960), and the American Bowling Congress (ABC) Masters tournament once (1961).

Carter led the Professional Bowlers Association (PBA) tour, which was formed in 1959, in earnings in 1960 ($22,525) and 1962 ($49,972). He won six PBA tour titles and was inducted into the PBA Hall of Fame as a charter member in 1975. In 1970, he was voted the greatest bowler of all time, and was elected to the ABC Hall of Fame.

Cauthen, Steve

horse racing

Born: May 1, 1960 in Covington, Kentucky

Steve Cauthen is the youngest rider ever to win the Triple Crown. In 1978, at age 18, he won the Kentucky Derby, the Preakness, and the Belmont Stakes, aboard Affirmed. He was named the *Sports Illustrated* Sportsman of the Year, the only jockey to be so honored.

In 1977, he was the first jockey ever to exceed $6 million in earnings in one year, and the Associated Press named him Male Athlete of the Year.

Cauthen, known as "The Kid," became a huge celebrity, but it didn't last long. In 1979, he lost 110 consecutive races, and as if that weren't enough, he was having difficulty controlling his weight. He was tall for a jockey (5 feet, 6 inches), and to maintain his riding weight of 115 pounds, he followed a 700-calorie-a-day diet.

Eventually, he accepted an offer of more than $1 million to ride in England, where jockeys are allowed an extra two or three pounds. Cauthen was the English champion in 1984, 1985, and 1987. He retired in 1993 after winning nearly 3,000 races.

In 1985, worried that he might be drinking too much, Cauthen entered an alcohol rehabilitation program, but afterward said he wasn't an alcoholic. In 1988, he suffered a broken neck in a fall and spent seven months recovering.

Cauthen won the 1977 Eclipse Award as the outstanding jockey of the year. He was inducted into the National Horse Racing Hall of Fame in 1994.

Chastain, Brandi

soccer

Born: July 21, 1968 in San Jose, California

Brandi Chastain scored the most memorable goal in U.S. women's soccer history. In the final of the 1999 Women's World Cup on July 10, 1999, in the Rose Bowl, Chastain scored the winning goal on the United States' fifth penalty kick to beat China.

After she scored, Chastain tore off her shirt in celebration. Fortunately, she wore a sports bra underneath. The picture made the cover of *Newsweek*, *Time*, and *Sports Illustrated*, along with newspapers throughout the world.

Chastain's goal not only gave the U.S. the World Cup, but it also focused a great deal of attention on women's soccer and helped elevate the sport.

In the 1999 Women's World Cup quarterfinals against Germany, Chastain scored a goal into the U.S. goal, but then redeemed herself by scoring a goal in the second half to tie the game at 2–2.

Chastain played her college soccer at Santa Clara University. She led her team to two Final Four appearances. She was named an All-American as a senior.

Chastain was a member of the 1991 gold medal–winning Women's World Cup team and the 1996 U.S. Olympic team, which also won a gold medal.

Cordero, Angel, Jr.

horse racing

Born: November 8, 1942 in Santurce, Puerto Rico

Angel Cordero, Jr., was a two-time Eclipse Award winner as the outstanding Jockey of the Year (1982–83). He led the nation in victories in 1968 and in earnings in 1976, 1982, and 1983.

Cordero won the Kentucky Derby in 1974 (Cannonade), 1976 (Bold Forbes), and 1985 (Spend a Buck); the Preakness Stakes in 1980 (Codex) and 1984 (Gate Dancer); and the Belmont Stakes in 1976 (Bold Forbes).

Cordero, who retired in 1992, ranked sixth all-time in career victories with 7,057, through March 2000. He

was inducted into the National Horse Racing Hall of Fame in 1988.

Dancer, Stanley

harness racing

Born: July 25, 1927 in Edinburg, New York

Stanley Dancer was one of the great harness racing drivers of all time. He was the leading money winner in 1961, 1962, 1964, and 1966, and in 1968 he was named Driver of the Year.

Dancer is the only driver to win the trotting Triple Crown twice—in 1968 (Nevele Pride) and 1972 (Super Bowl). The trotting Triple Crown is made up of the Yonkers Trot, the Hambletonian, and the Kentucky Futurity. Dancer also won the pacing Triple Crown (Cane Pace, Little Brown Jug, Messenger Stakes) in 1970 (Most Happy Fella).

Dancer won the Yonkers Trot six times (1959, '65, '68, '71–72, '75), the Cane Pace four times (1964, '70—71, '76), and the Hambletonian five times (1974, '76–77, '80, '83).

Dancer was inducted into the Harness Racing Living Hall of Fame in 1970.

Day, Pat

horse racing

Born: October 13, 1953 in Brush, Colorado

Pat Day is one of the most accomplished jockeys of all time. An outstanding high school wrestler and a former rodeo rider, Day got his first victory in July 1973 at Prescott Downs in Arizona.

While he has never led in jockeys' earnings, he has led in victories in 1982, 1983, 1984, 1986, 1990, and 1991.

Day won the Kentucky Derby in 1992 (Lil E. Tee); the Preakness Stakes in 1985 (Tank's Prospect), 1990 (Summer Squall), 1994 (Tabasco Cat), 1995 (Timber Country), and 1996 (Louis Quatorze); and the Belmont Stakes in 1989 (Easy Goer), 1994 (Tabasco Cat), and 2000 (Commendable).

Day won the Eclipse Award as the outstanding Jockey of the Year in 1984, 1986, 1987, and 1991. Through March 2000, Day ranked third all-time in career victories with 7,616. He was inducted into the National Horse Racing Hall of Fame in 1991.

Fernandez, Lisa

softball

Born: February 22, 1971 in Long Beach, California

Lisa Fernandez is one of the most talented softball players of all time. At UCLA, she was a four-time All-American, a two-time member of the NCAA championship team, and a three-time winner of the Honda Broderick Award, as the nation's outstanding female college athlete. As a senior, she led the nation in batting (.510) and earned run average (0.23). Her career record at UCLA was 93–7.

Fernandez helped the United States win the gold medal at the 1996 Olympics in Atlanta. She hit .348 with eight hits and five runs batted in during the Games. On the mound, she was 1–1 with 31 strikeouts and a 0.33 earned run average.

She also was a member of gold medal–winning teams at the 1999 Pan-American Games, the International Softball Federation Women's World Championships (1995–98), and the 1998 South Pacific Classic.

Fernandez was a seven-time Amateur Softball Association All-American (ASA); the ASA Most Valuable Player in 1991, 1992, 1997, and 1998; and the ASA Sports Woman of the Year in 1991 and 1992.

Fillion, Herve

harness racing

Born: February 1, 1940 in Angers, Quebec, Canada

Herve Fillion is the all-time winningest harness racing driver. He was the first driver to win more than 400 races in one year (1968), and he went on to do it 14 more times.

Fillion was named Driver of the Year 10 times (1969–74, '76, '78, '81, '89). Through the 2000 season, he ranked first in victories with 14,783, nearly double the total of Walter Case, Jr., who ranked second. Fillion earned more than $85 million, third all-time.

The only thing missing from Fillion's résumé is a victory in any of trotting's Triple Crown races (Yonkers Trot, Hambletonian, Kentucky Futurity). Fillion was inducted into the Harness Racing Living Hall of Fame in 1976.

Hamm, Mia (Mariel)

soccer

Born: March 17, 1972 in Selma, Alabama

Mia Hamm has been to women's soccer in the United States what Michael Jordan was to basketball. She has transcended her sport, helped increase the popularity and profile of women's soccer, appeared in numerous television and print ads, and served as a role model for girls, demonstrating to them that anything's possible.

Hamm, in addition to being the most popular women's soccer player in the world, is also one of the most talented. On May 16, 1999, in a match against Brazil in Orlando, Fla., Hamm scored the 108th goal of her career, making her the all-time international scoring leader among men and women. Through the 2000 season, she had 127 goals and 108 assists.

Hamm, the daughter of a fighter pilot, grew up as an "Army brat." She spent most of her youth in Texas, where she impressed John Cossaboon, coach of an Olympic development team. During a U.S. Soccer Federation tournament in 1987, Hamm was noticed by Anson Dorrance, the coach at the University of North Carolina, where Hamm played her college soccer.

Hamm led the Tar Heels to four straight NCAA championships (1990–93) and was a three-time All-American. She completed her college career as the Atlantic Coast Conference's all-time leader in goals (103), assists (72), and points (278). Hamm had her no. 19 retired by North Carolina in 1994.

Hamm, the youngest person ever to play for the U.S. national team (15 years, 140 days, in 1987), was the first-ever three-time U.S. soccer Athlete of the Year, man or woman (1994–96). She helped the U.S. team to two Women's World Cup titles—in 1991 and 1999—and the Olympic gold medal at the 1996 Games in Atlanta and the silver medal in the 2000 Games in Sydney. She was named Most Valuable Player in the 1995 World Cup, scoring three goals, including the tying goal in a losing effort against Norway in the championship game.

Hamm was named Athlete of the Year by the Women's Sports Foundation in 1997.

Hartack, Bill

horse racing

Born: December 9, 1932 in Colver, Pennsylvania

Along with Eddie Arcaro and Willie Shoemaker, Bill Hartack formed a trio of outstanding jockeys.

Hartack and Arcaro are tied for the most victories in the Kentucky Derby with five. Hartack won in 1957 (Iron Liege), 1960 (Venetian Way), 1962 (Decidedly), 1964 (Northern Dancer), and 1969 (Majestic Prince).

He won the Preakness Stakes in 1956 (Fabius), 1964 (Northern Dancer), and 1969 (Majestic Prince). He won the Belmont Stakes only once, in 1960 aboard Celtic Ash. Twice, in 1964 and 1969, Hartack won the first two legs of the Triple Crown, but was unable to take the third at the Belmont.

Hartack was the leading money winner in 1956 and 1957. His 1957 total of $3,060,501 was a record that stood for 10 years.

Through most of the 1950s, Hartack rode for Calumet Farms, one of the most famous stables in the United States. But a disagreement over how to handle the horses—Hartack liked to go to the front right away, while the trainers preferred for him to hold back—resulted in his being dismissed.

Hartack retired in 1981 with 4,272 wins and more than $26 million in earnings. He was inducted into the National Horse Racing Hall of Fame in 1959.

Joyce, Joan
softball
Born: August 1, 1940 in Waterbury, Connecticut

Joan Joyce was an outstanding softball player who made her name with the Raybestos Brakettes of Stamford, Conn. She joined the team when she was 14 years old and helped the Brakettes win 11 national championships in 20 years. She pitched 105 no-hitters and 33 perfect games. Her career record was 509 victories and 33 losses.

When Joyce didn't pitch, she played first base. Her career batting average was .327. She was an All-American 18 straight years and was Most Valuable Player of the National Softball Association eight times. She retired in 1973.

Joyce also excelled in basketball, volleyball, and bowling. From 1975 through 1984, she played on the LPGA Tour. She was inducted into the National Softball Hall of Fame in 1983 and the International Women's Sports Hall of Fame in 1989.

Krone, Julie
horse racing
Born: July 24, 1963 in Eau Claire, Michigan

In August 2000, Julie Krone became the first woman ever inducted into the Horse Racing Hall of Fame. She is the most successful female jockey of all time, with 3,545 victories, including 119 stakes races, and more than $81 million in earnings.

Krone began taking riding lessons at age five, and when she was 15 years old, her mother drove her to Churchill Downs in Kentucky to get her a summer job at the track. Using a forged birth certificate, because 16 was the minimum age to work at the track, Krone got a job as a morning workout rider. That fall, she returned home and began racing on fairground tracks. She eventually quit high school and went to Tampa Bay Downs racetrack in Florida.

Krone got her first professional ride on January 30, 1980. It also turned out to be her first victory. She won her first riding title in 1982 at Atlantic City Racetrack, and she was the first woman to win the riding title at a major track (1987, Monmouth Park, New Jersey; 1992 and 1993, Gulfstream Park, Florida). In 1987, she became one of only six jockeys to win six races in one day (August 19, 1987, Monmouth Park).

Krone was the first woman to compete in the Breeders' Cup, in 1988, and the first to win a Triple Crown race, aboard longshot Colonial Affair at the 1993 Belmont Stakes.

Krone, who overcame considerable resistance from a sport that was almost entirely male dominated, also had to overcome several serious injuries. In 1989 at the Meadowlands, she fell and shattered her left arm. Two months after her victory in the Belmont, she broke her ankle, re-

quiring two plates and 14 screws, and suffered a cardiac contusion from being kicked in the chest after a fall at Saratoga Race Course in New York. In 1995 at Gulfstream Park, she fractured her left hand. Krone has also been treated for post-traumatic stress disorder.

The wear and tear finally took its toll, and on April 25, 1999 at Lone Star Track in Grand Prairie, Texas, she retired, winning the final three races she entered. Krone is a commentator for the Television Games Network, a 24-hour horse racing and interactive wagering network.

LeMond, Greg
cycling
Born: June 26, 1961 in Lakewood, California

Greg LeMond is responsible for raising the profile of the Tour de France in the United States. He took up cycling at age 14 after watching a road race, the course for which went right by his house. He requested and received permission to enter the Tour of Fresno, because he was only 16, and finished second.

At the junior world championships in 1979, LeMond was the first to win three medals, winning a gold in the 120-kilometer road race, a silver in the 3,000-meter pursuit, and a bronze in the 70-kilometer team time trial.

LeMond won his first major title in 1983, a 169-mile race in Switzerland, and later that year won the professional road race world championship.

LeMond finished second in the 1985 Tour de France, and in 1986, became the first American and the first non-European ever to win cycling's most prestigious and grueling event. Less than a year after his Tour de France victory, LeMond, hunting with relatives, was accidentally shot in the back. Two of the pellets lodged in the lining of his heart, his right lung collapsed, he lost three-quarters of his blood supply, and there was fear he might suffer spinal damage.

LeMond vowed he would compete in the Tour de France again, although few people expected him to realize his goal. After a long rehabilitation period, he entered the 1989 Tour de France, and entering the final stage of the 21-stage race was in second place, 50 seconds behind the leader, Laurent Fignon. Despite the huge deficit he had to overcome, LeMond won the stage and the Tour de France by eight seconds, the closest finish in the 85-year history of the event.

In 1990, LeMond won the Tour de France for the third time and was named Sportsman of the Year by *Sports Illustrated*. In 1991, he won the Jesse Owens International Award.

LeMond retired from cycling in 1994 after he was diagnosed with mitochondrial myopathy, a rare form of muscular dystrophy.

Greg LeMond   *Diane Staskowski*

Maradona, Diego

soccer

Born: October 30, 1960 in Buenos Aires, Argentina

Diego Maradona was one of the preeminent players of his time. He was the captain and Most Valuable Player of the 1986 World Cup, won by Argentina over West Germany. In 1990, he led Argentina back to the World Cup final, but this time Germany won the rematch.

Maradona led Napoli to Italian League titles in 1987 and 1990 and the Union of European Football Associations Cup in 1989.

Maradona's brilliant career has been tarnished by a number of arrests and suspensions. In 1991, he was suspended for testing positive for cocaine and marijuana. He returned as Argentina's captain for the 1994 World Cup, only to be removed from the tournament after two games because a drug test revealed five banned substances in his urine.

McCarron, Chris

horse racing

Born: March 27, 1955 in Dorchester, Massachusetts

Through the 2000 season, Chris McCarron won six Triple Crown races—Kentucky Derby (1987, Alysheba; 1994, Go for Gin), Preakness Stakes (1987, Alysheba; 1992, Pine Bluff), Belmont Stakes (1986, Danzig Connection; 1997, Touch Gold).

He led all jockeys in earnings in 1980, 1981, and 1984, and through 1999 he was the all-time leader in earnings with more than $233 million.

McCarron began his career as a groom and a horse walker. He started riding in 1974 and got his first victory in 1974, when he set a single-season record for victories with 546. He also led in victories in 1975 with 648.

Through March 2000, he ranked seventh all-time with 6,874 wins. He won the 1980 Eclipse Award as the outstanding jockey of the year and was inducted into the National Horse Racing Hall of Fame in 1989.

Pelé (Edson Arantes do Nascimento)

soccer

Born: October 21, 1940 in Tres Coracoes, Brazil

Pelé is the most famous player in the history of soccer. His talent, charisma, and international impact on the game was immeasurable.

Pelé, born Edson Arantes do Nascimento, grew up in a small Brazilian town. His family was very poor, so poor that Pelé learned how to play soccer with a grapefruit or with a stocking stuffed with rags. He got his first soccer ball as a gift when he was 10 years old and practiced with it for hours on end.

He doesn't remember how he came by his nickname, but he does remember getting into fights at school because he didn't like when classmates referred to him as Pelé.

His father, Dondinho, taught him the fundamentals of the game—how to kick with either foot, how to use his head, and how to dribble. When Pelé was 15, he was transferred from his local soccer club in Bauru to the big-city club in Santos. His first duties were as an errand boy to the players, but it wasn't long before his remarkable skills earned him a place in the lineup.

Pelé led Santos to six straight championships in his first six seasons, during which he averaged a goal a game.

His greatest achievements came in World Cup competition. In 1958, Pelé became the youngest ever to play on a World Cup champion team as he scored two goals and helped Brazil to a 5–2 victory over Sweden. In the 1962 World Cup, Pelé suffered a pulled muscle in the first round and missed the rest of the tournament. Still, Brazil successfully defended its title with a 3–1 victory over Czechoslovakia.

In 1970, Pelé scored once and led Brazil to an unprecedented third World Cup title, beating Italy 4–1.

Pelé retired from soccer in 1974, but returned to play in the United States. He signed a three-year, $4.7 million contract to play for the New York Cosmos in the North American Soccer League (NASL). Pelé put soccer on the map in the U.S. and gave the NASL instant credibility.

In the 15 games he played in 1975, six were sold out and 10 set club records. In 1977, when the Cosmos moved to Giants Stadium in East Rutherford, N.J., the team consistently outdrew the New York Mets and the New York Yankees.

In 1977, after leading the Cosmos to their third straight NASL championship, he retired for good. His final game, at Giants Stadium, attracted 78,000 fans.

In 21 seasons, he scored 1,281 goals and averaged just under one goal a game. In addition to his accomplishments on the field, Pelé also made a major contribution as a worldwide ambassador for the game.

Pincay, Laffit, Jr.

horse racing

Born: December 29, 1946 in Panama City, Panama

Laffit Pincay, Jr., is the winningest jockey of all time. He rode his 8,834th winner at Hollywood Park in Inglewood, Calif., on December 10, 1999. Willie Shoemaker had held the previous record since 1970.

Pincay began his career after his parents divorced and he moved with his father to Venezuela. He worked as a hot-walker and a groom, starting at age 15, for no pay. In his spare time, he learned to ride. He got his jockey license at age 17 and rode his first winner at the Presidente Remon Racetrack on May 16, 1964.

Pincay came to the United States in July 1966. He spoke only Spanish and taught himself English by watching the television game show *Hollywood Squares*. He won his first race in the U.S. at Arlington Park in Chicago.

Pincay won the 1984 Kentucky Derby aboard Swale. He also won the Belmont Stakes three times—1982 (Conquistador Cielo), 1983 (Caveat), and 1984 (Swale).

Throughout his career, Pincay has had difficulty controlling his weight, so he limited himself to 850 calories a day and worked out daily. He has also endured his share of difficulties—personal and professional. Pincay's first wife, Linda, committed suicide in 1985, leaving him to raise their two young children. (He remarried in 1992.)

On the track, he has broken his collarbone 11 times, suffered 10 broken ribs, had two spinal fractures, two punctured lungs, two broken thumbs, and a sprained ankle.

At the time Pincay broke Shoemaker's record, he had ridden 8,834 winners in 44,647 mounts in 35 years of racing. He had earned more than $270 million. He led all jockeys in earnings for five straight years, beginning in 1970. He also led in 1979 and 1985. Pincay won the Eclipse Award as the outstanding Jockey of the Year in 1971, 1973–74, 1979, and 1985. He was inducted into the National Horse Racing Hall of Fame in 1975.

Roth, Mark
bowling
Born: April 10, 1951 in Brooklyn, New York

Mark Roth was one of the most consistent and successful bowlers on the Professional Bowlers Association (PBA) tour. He led the tour in average in 1976 (215.97), 1977 (218.17), 1978 (219.83), 1979 (221.66), and 1981 (216.70). He was the top money winner in 1977 ($105,585), 1978 ($134,500), 1979 ($124,517), and 1984 ($158,712).

Roth won the U.S. Open in 1984. He was the PBA Player of the Year in 1977, 1978, 1979, and 1984. Through the 2000 season, he won 36 PBA tour events, second all-time to Earl Anthony, and earned more than $1.5 million. He was inducted into the PBA Hall of Fame in 1987.

Shoemaker, Willie
horse racing
Born: August 19, 1931 in Fabens, Texas

Willie Shoemaker was one of the most successful jockeys of all time. He was blessed with a sixth sense that allowed him to get the most out of his rides.

Shoemaker was born prematurely. He weighed less than two pounds and measured only 10 1/2 inches. Legend has it that his grandmother placed him in a shoebox and put the shoebox next to the oven to help keep him alive.

He moved to southern California after his parents divorced and at the age of 16 took a job cleaning stables at a thoroughbred ranch. He stood 4 feet, 11 inches and weighed 96 pounds. He soon became an exercise rider and got his first professional ride on March 19, 1949. One month later, he had his first victory. By the end of the year he totaled 219 victories, second in the nation.

Shoemaker led all jockeys in earnings 10 times between 1951 and 1964, and in 1953 he set a record for victories (485) that stood for 24 years.

Shoemaker won his first Kentucky Derby in 1955 aboard Swaps. In 1957, Shoemaker looked like a shoo-in to win his second Derby, aboard Gallant Man, but he stood up too soon before the finish line and ended up second. The embarrassment of such a faux pas might have adversely affected other jockeys, but Shoemaker took it in stride.

Said Eddie Arcaro, another all-time great jockey: "He's the only one I know who could have suffered that kind of experience in a race like the Derby without going to pieces. That little son of a gun is going to go on and on."

Shoemaker won the Derby in 1959 (Tomy Lee), 1965 (Lucky Debonair), and 1986 (Ferdinand); the Preakness Stakes in 1963 (Candy Spots) and 1967 (Damascus); and the Belmont Stakes in 1957 (Gallant Man), 1959 (Sword Dancer), 1962 (Jaipur), 1967 (Damascus), and 1975 (Avatar). His 1986 victory, at age 54, made him the oldest jockey ever to win a Kentucky Derby.

Shoemaker suffered two serious injuries—a broken leg in 1968 and a broken pelvis, ruptured bladder, and nerve damage to his leg in 1969. But he rebounded in 1970 with his 6,033rd career victory, breaking Johnny Longden's all-time record at the time.

By 1988, Shoemaker wasn't getting nearly as many rides as he was accustomed to. After a nine-month farewell tour, he rode his last winner on January 20, 1990, at Gulfstream Park in Florida. His final race came on February 3, 1990, at Santa Anita Park in California. He finished fourth. It was the 40,352nd race of his career.

Shoemaker won 8,883 races, including 1,009 stakes races, and more than $123 million in purses. He was the all-time leader in victories until 1999, when Laffit Pincay, Jr., broke his record.

Shoemaker retired to become a trainer. On April 8, 1991, on his way home from playing golf, he lost control of his Ford Bronco. It went off the road and down a 50-foot embankment. The crash left him paralyzed from the neck down. He continued to train horses until he retired in November 1997. As a trainer he won 90 races in 713 starts and nearly $3.7 million in earnings. He was inducted into the National Horse Racing Hall of Fame in 1958.

Weber, Dick
bowling
Born: December 23, 1929 in Indianapolis, Indiana
Dick Weber was one of the best bowlers of all time. The son of a bowling center manager, he started bowling when he was 10 years old.

Dick Weber *Reading Eagle/Times*

Weber won his first Professional Bowlers Association (PBA) tour title in 1959. He won the Bowling Proprietors Association of American (BPAA) All-Star Tournament (now the U.S. Open) in 1962, 1963, 1965, and 1966. He led the PBA tour in earnings in 1959 ($7,672), 1961($26,280), 1963 ($46,333), and 1965 ($47,675), and in average in 1965 (211.90).

Weber was named the PBA Player of the Year in 1965 and the Bowling Writers Association of America Bowler of the Year in 1961, 1963, and 1965.

In 1991, Weber suffered a mild stroke during a PBA Senior Tour event, but in early 1992, he came back to win the Touring Pro Senior Doubles with Justin Hromek, giving him professional wins in five consecutive decades.

Weber has 26 PBA career victories. He was inducted into the PBA Hall of Fame as a charter member in 1975, and is a member of the ABC Hall of Fame. In addition to his bowling, Weber also gained a measure of fame from his appearances on *Late Show with David Letterman*.

Williams, Walter Ray, Jr.
bowling
Born: October 6, 1959 in Stockton, California

Through the 2000 season, Walter Ray Williams, Jr. was the all-time earnings leader on the Professional Bowlers Association (PBA) tour with $2,403,763. His 30 PBA tour victories ranked him third all-time, behind Earl Anthony and Mark Roth.

Williams, who won the U.S. Open in 1998, led the tour in average in 1993 (222.98), 1996 (225.37), 1997 (222.00), and 1998 (226.13). He led in earnings in 1986 ($145,550), 1993 ($296,370), 1996 ($244,630), 1997 ($240,544), and 1998 ($238,225).

Williams was named PBA Player of the Year in 1993, 1996, 1997, and 1999. He was inducted into the PBA Hall of Fame in 1995.

Appendixes

Timeline

1900

May 11: Jim Jeffries retains his heavyweight championship by knocking out James J. (Gentleman Jim) Corbett in the 23rd round of their bout in Coney Island, N.Y.

August 10: The United States defeats the British Isles 3–0 in the first-ever Davis Cup matches at Longwood Cricket Club, near Boston.

October 28: The second modern Olympic Games are held in conjunction with the World's Fair in Paris. The United States dominates the track and field events, winning 53 medals with 55 team members.

1901

January 11: The first National Bowling Championships, sanctioned by the American Bowling Congress, are held in Chicago.

February 27: The National League Rules Committee announces that all foul balls will count as strikes, except after two strikes.

October 4: *Columbia* defeats *Shamrock II*, the British challenger, as a United States yacht successfully defends the America's Cup title for the 11th time.

1902

January 1: In the first Rose Bowl, Michigan remains unbeaten with a 49–0 defeat of Stanford. The Wolverines ended the season scoring 550 points and yielding none.

September 28: In just its second season, the American League outdraws the National League, 2.2 million to 1.68 million.

1903

August 8: The United States loses the Davis Cup for the first time, 4–1 to the British Isles.

September 2: *Reliance*, a United States yacht, successfully defends the America's Cup, defeating *Shamrock III* of Britain.

October 13: The Boston Pilgrims of the American League defeat the Pittsburgh Pirates of the National League in the first World Series.

1904

October 10: The World Series is canceled when manager John McGraw and owner John T. Brush of the National League pennant-winning New York Giants refuse to play the Boston Pilgrims of the American League, which was considered inferior by McGraw and Brush.

November 23: The third Olympic Games of the modern era are held in conjunction with the World's Fair in St. Louis. With the Europeans skipping the Games, the Americans win 244 out of 281 medals.

1905

May 13: Jim Jeffries retires as the undefeated heavyweight champion of the world.

July 3: Jeffries referees the bout between Marvin Hart and Jack Root to determine the champion. Hart knocks out Root in the 12th round.

July 8: May Sutton, an 18-year-old American, becomes the first overseas player to win a Wimbledon singles title. She beats defending champ Dorothea Douglass.

October 14: Christy Mathewson throws three shutouts, and the New York Giants win the World Series, 4–1 over the Philadelphia Athletics.

November 30: The University of Chicago ends Michigan's 56-game unbeaten streak in college football.

1906

February 23: Tommy Burns, from Canada, wins the world heavyweight title in a 20-round decision over Marvin Hart.

September: College football enacts two rule changes—legalizing the forward pass and requiring 10 yards for a first down.

October 14: The Chicago White Sox, known as the "Hitless Wonders," win the American League pennant with a team batting average of just .230. They hit only .196 in the World Series, but beat the Chicago Cubs 4–2.

1907

April 19: Tom Longboat of Canada wins the Boston Marathon (in 2:24:24) and lowers the course record by more than five minutes.

October 12: The Chicago Cubs complete the first four-game sweep of a World Series. They beat the Detroit Tigers after the first game ended in a 12-inning 3–3 tie.

October 12: Margaret Curtis defeats her sister, Harriot Curtis, to win the U.S. Women's Amateur Golf Championship.

1908

September 23: Fred Merkle's baserunning gaffe, "Merkle's Boner," with two out in the bottom of the ninth against the Chicago Cubs costs the New York Giants the National League pennant. With Merkle on first, he failed to touch second when the winning run was singled in from third. The game was ruled a tie and replayed after the season was over. The Cubs won the game and the pennant.

October 14: The Chicago Cubs beat the Detroit Tigers 4–1 to repeat as World Series champs.

December 26: Jack Johnson becomes the first black fighter to win the world heavyweight championship. He beat Tommy Burns with a 14th-round technical knockout.

1909

April 12: Philadelphia's Shibe Park is the first concrete and steel baseball stadium. The opening game attracts more than 31,000 fans, a major league record.

October 16: The Detroit Tigers lose their third straight World Series, this time to the Pittsburgh Pirates in seven games.

1910

April 14: William Howard Taft becomes the first president to throw out a ceremonial first pitch of the season.

July 4: Jim Jeffries, the former heavyweight champion and the "Great White Hope," returns to the ring after five years of retirement, but is knocked out in the 15th round by black champion Jack Johnson.

October 9: Ty Cobb, an unpopular player, sits out the final two games of the season to protect his American League–leading .383 batting average. But Cleveland's Nap Lajoie goes 8-for-8 in a doubleheader to finish with a .384 average. Among those hits were six "gift" bunt singles, allowed by a pulled-back infield. A week later Ban Johnson, the American League president, awards the batting title to Cobb.

October 23: The Philadelphia Athletics win their first World Series title.

1911

May 30: Ray Harroun wins the first Indianapolis 500, winning the race in six hours, 42 minutes, eight seconds. His average speed was 74.606 mph.

June 24: John McDermott, a 21-year-old former caddie, is the first American-born golfer to win the U.S. Open.

October 6: Cy Young loses the final game of his career and finishes as baseball's all-time winningest pitcher with a 511–316 record.

November 11: Carlisle Indian School of Pennsylvania, led by Jim Thorpe's four field goals, beats Harvard 18–15. Thorpe's fourth field goal, from 48 yards, was the game winner.

1912

March 13: Quebec beats Moncton to win the first Stanley Cup in which each team skated six-a-side and the game had three 20-minute periods.

April 20: Fenway Park opens in Boston.

July 15: Jim Thorpe wins the gold medal in the decathlon, one week after winning gold in the pentathlon. The Olympic Games, held in Stockholm, Sweden, are the first to use electronic timing and a public address system.

October 16: Smokey Joe Wood, who won 34 games during the regular season for the Boston Red Sox, wins three more in a World Series victory over the New York Giants.

1913

January 27: Jim Thorpe admits he played minor league baseball for $25 a game. He is declared a professional and stripped of his Olympic medals and records from the 1912 Games in Stockholm, Sweden.

July 28: After an 11-year absence, the Davis Cup returns to the United States, which defeats the British Isles.

September 30: Francis Ouimet, 20 years old and an amateur, defeats British pros Harry Vardon and Ted Ray in a playoff to win the U.S. Open golf championship.

1914

April 13: Baseball's third professional league, the Federal League, begins play with eight teams.

August 21: Walter Hagen wins the U.S. Open golf championship, the first major victory of his career.

October 13: The Boston Braves, in last place on July 18, complete a remarkable turnaround, win the pennant, and beat the Philadelphia Athletics in the World Series.

1915

April 5: Jess Willard knocks out 37-year-old heavyweight champion Jack Johnson in the 26th round of their fight in Havana, Cuba.

October 3: Ty Cobb sets a single-season record with his 96th stolen base. The record will stand until 1962.

December 22: The Federal League ceases operation after two seasons. The American and National League owners agree to buy back players who jumped leagues.

1916

January 1: The Rose Bowl is played after a 14-year absence. Washington State defeats Brown.

September 9: Chick Evans wins the U.S. Amateur tennis championship and becomes the first player to hold the U.S. Open and Amateur titles in the same calendar year.

October 7: Georgia Tech defeats Cumberland College of Lebanon, Tenn., 222–0 in the most one-sided college football game of the century. Cumberland brought only 15 players to the game.

October 14: Jim Barnes wins the first PGA Championship for touring golf professionals, beating Jock Hutchison 1-up.

1917

May 2: Cincinnati's Fred Toney and the Chicago Cubs' Hippo Vaughn throw gems against each other. The Reds win 1–0 in 10 innings on a single, two errors, and a swinging bunt, their only two hits off Vaughn. Toney retired the Cubs in the bottom of the 10th for a no-hit victory.

October 15: The New York Giants lose their fourth World Series of the decade, falling to the Chicago White Sox.

1918

June 22: Molla Bjurstedt becomes the first woman to win the U.S. Tennis Championship four straight times.

August 24: Newton D. Baker, the U.S. secretary of war, changes his view of baseball. At first he ruled it nonessential and ordered the major leagues to end their seasons by September 1. But he reconsidered and allowed the World Series to be played, as long as 10 percent of all proceeds went to war charities.

September 11: The Boston Red Sox win their third World Series title in four years. Boston pitcher Babe Ruth sets a record of 29.2 scoreless innings.

1919

April 1: An influenza epidemic that claimed 548,000 lives in the U.S. and 20 million worldwide, cancels the deciding game of the Stanley Cup finals between Montreal and Seattle.

June 11: Sir Barton becomes the first horse to win the Kentucky Derby, the Preakness Stakes, and the Belmont Stakes in the same year.

July 4: Jack Dempsey knocks down heavyweight champion Jess Willard seven times in the first round. He wins the title on a fourth-round technical knockout.

August 12: Man O'War is beaten, by Upset, for the only time in his 21-race career.

October 9: The Cincinnati Reds beat the Chicago White Sox in the World Series. Eight "Black Sox" will ultimately be banished from baseball for taking bribes to throw the series.

1920

January 3: The New York Yankees buy the contract of Babe Ruth for $125,000.

September 17: The American Professional Football Association, a forerunner of the National Football League, is founded in Canton, Ohio. Twelve teams pay $100 each for a franchise.

October 1: The New York Yankees are the first baseball team to surpass the 1 million mark in attendance.

November 12: Judge Kenesaw Mountain Landis is hired as the first commissioner of baseball.

1921

July 2: In the first fight to have a $1 million gate, Jack Dempsey retains his heavyweight title by knocking out

Georges Carpentier in the fourth round. The bout is also the first aired on radio.

August 5: The first major league baseball game is broadcast, Pittsburgh vs. the Philadelphia Phillies on KDKA-AM in Pittsburgh.

September 28: Walter Hagen becomes the first American-born pro golfer to win the PGA Championship.

October 13: The New York Giants beat the New York Yankees in the first World Series broadcast on radio.

1922

June 23: Walter Hagen becomes the first American-born golfer to win the British Open.

June 24: The American Professional Football Association changes its name to the National Football League.

August 18: Gene Sarazen wins the PGA Championship and becomes the first golfer to win the PGA and the U.S. Open in the same year.

1923

January 10: The American Amateur Union (AAU) registers women in all sports under its jurisdiction.

April 18: Yankee Stadium opens with a crowd of 74,200. Reportedly, 25,000 others are turned away.

July 15: Bobby Jones wins the U.S. Open, his first major golf championship.

September 14: Jack Dempsey knocks down challenger Luis Firpo seven times in the first round; Firpo rallies to knock Dempsey through the ropes and onto the press row; and Dempsey knocks out Firpo 57 seconds into the second round.

1924

July 27: Distance runner Paavo Nurmi of Finland wins five gold medals at the Summer Olympics in Paris.

September 30: Rogers Hornsby of the St. Louis Cardinals finishes the regular season with a .424 batting average, highest of the century.

October 18: Legendary sportswriter Grantland Rice dubs the Notre Dame backfield of Stuhldreher, Miller, Crowly, and Layden "The Four Horsemen."

December 1: The National Hockey League opens its seventh season with its first U.S. franchise, the Boston Bruins.

1925

May 30: Peter DePaolo is the first winner of the Indianapolis 500 to average more than 100 mph (101.13).

September 19: Bill Tilden wins the U.S. Tennis Championships for the sixth straight time.

November 15: The first professional basketball league, the American Basketball League, opens with nine teams.

1926

February 26: Suzanne Lenglen, a six-time Wimbledon champ, beats Helen Wills, a three-time U.S. champ, 6–3, 8–6 in an exhibition.

May 12: Walter Johnson, at age 38, becomes the second pitcher to win 400 games. Only Cy Young won more.

July 10: Bobby Jones becomes the first golfer to win the U.S. and British Opens in the same year.

September 16: Henri Cochet ends Bill Tilden's string of U.S. Tennis Championships at six.

September 27: Jack Dempsey loses a unanimous 10-round decision to Gene Tunney for the world heavyweight championship.

1927

January 7: The Harlem Globetrotters play their first official pro basketball game, in Hinckley, Illinois.

June 4: The United States, led by Gene Sarazen and playing captain Walter Hagen, defeats Great Britain in the first Ryder Cup matches.

July 18: Ty Cobb gets the 4,000th hit of his career.

September 22: Gene Tunney scores a unanimous 10-round decision over Jack Dempsey to retain the world heavyweight title.

September 30: Babe Ruth hits his 60th home run of the season.

November 5: Walter Hagen wins his fourth PGA Championship in a row and his fifth overall.

1928

February 18: Sonja Henie wins her first figure skating gold medal.

April 14: The New York Rangers win their first Stanley Cup.

August 12: Germany returns to the Olympics, and women are allowed to compete for the first time.

October 3: Leo Diegel snaps Walter Hagen's 22-match unbeaten streak in the quarterfinals of the PGA Championship. He goes on to win the title.

1929

January 2: California defensive lineman Roy Riegels recovers a fumble and returns it 64 yards in the wrong direction. He was stopped at the California 1 by a teammate. Georgia Tech went on to win 8–7.

August 24: Helen Wills wins her sixth U.S. Tennis Championship and sweeps the U.S., French, and Wimbledon titles for the second straight year.

November 28: Ernie Nevers, a halfback for the Chicago Cardinals, scores six touchdowns and kicks four extra points for an NFL-record 40 points.

1930

June 7: Gallant Fox becomes the second three-year-old to win the Kentucky Derby, Preakness Stakes, and Belmont Stakes in the same year. Charles Hatton, a sportswriter for the *Daily Racing Form*, dubs it the "Triple Crown."

July 4: Helen Wills Moody wins her fourth straight Wimbledon singles title, one day before Bill Tilden wins his third title, and first since 1921.

July 30: Uruguay defeats Argentina in the first World Cup soccer championship.

September 27: Bobby Jones completes the first calendar-year sweep of golf's four major championships with his victory in the U.S. Amateur.

September 28: Hack Wilson sets a major single-season record with his 189th and 190th runs batted in.

1931

March 31: Notre Dame football coach Knute Rockne is killed, along with seven others, in a plane crash in Kansas. He was 43.

August 20: Helen Wills Moody wins the U.S. Tennis Championship for the seventh time in nine years.

October 10: Pepper Martin of the St. Louis Cardinals wins the first Associated Press Male Athlete of the Year Award. He helps the Cardinals win the World Series by hitting .500 and stealing five bases.

1932

February 15: The first Winter Olympics are held in the United States, with the U.S. winning the most medals (12).

June 25: Using his new invention, and the sand wedge, Gene Sarazen wins the U.S. Open with a tournament record score of 2-under 286.

October 1: Babe Ruth hits his famous "called shot," a home run into the center field bleachers.

1933

January 13: Augusta National Golf Club officially opens.

June 10: Johnny Goodman becomes the last amateur of the century to win the U.S. Open Golf Championship.

July 6: The first major league baseball All-Star Game is held, at Comiskey Park in Chicago.

December 17: The Chicago Bears win the first official NFL championship game, defeating the New York Giants 23–21.

1934

March 25: Horton Smith beats Craig Wood to win the first Augusta National Invitational. The tournament would come to be known as the Masters.

July 10: Carl Hubbell of the New York Giants strikes out Babe Ruth, Lou Gehrig, Jimmie Foxx, Al Simmons, and Joe Cronin consecutively in the All-Star Game at the Polo Grounds.

December 29: The first college basketball doubleheader is held at Madison Square Garden. Westminster (Pa.) beats St. John's and NYU beats Notre Dame.

1935

April 8: Gene Sarazen holes his second shot on the par-5 15th for a double eagle. He goes on to win the Masters in a playoff.

May 24: Crosley Field in Cincinnati is the site of the first night game in major league baseball history, between the Reds and the Philadelphia Phillies.

May 25: Babe Ruth, playing for the Boston Braves, hits the final three home runs of his career, at Forbes Field in Pittsburgh.

June 2: Babe Ruth retires.

August 31: Glenna Collett Vare wins her record sixth U.S. Women's Amateur, beating Patty Berg.

December 10: Jay Berwanger, a halfback for the University of Chicago, wins the first Downtown Athletic Club Trophy, which is renamed the Heisman Trophy in 1936.

1936

February 2: The Baseball Hall of Fame inducts its charter class: Ty Cobb, Babe Ruth, Honus Wagner, Christy Mathewson, and Walter Johnson.

May 30: Lewis Meyer win his third Indianapolis 500 in nine years. The average speed of 109.069 is the fastest in the 25-year history of the race.

July 3: Fred Perry wins the Wimbledon singles title for the third straight year. He is the last Englishman to win the title in the 20th century.

August 3: Jesse Owens wins an unprecedented four gold medals at the Summer Olympics in Berlin.

December 1: Minnesota wins the first college football national championship, finishing atop the Associated Press top 20, which is conducted for the first time.

1937

March 8: Howie Morenz of the Montreal Canadiens, one of the top attractions in the National Hockey League, dies of a heart attack while in the hospital recovering from a leg fracture. He was 34.

March: The center jump after each score in college basketball games is eliminated. Also, each team is given 10 seconds to move the ball across the midcourt line.

June 5: War Admiral becomes the third Triple Crown winner of the decade.

July 20: Don Budge wins what is called by some the "greatest tennis match ever played." He defeats Gottfried von Cramm of Germany 6–8, 5–7, 6–4, 6–2, 8–6 in a Davis Cup semifinal.

1938

March 16: Temple wins the first National Invitation Basketball Tournament, routing Colorado.

June 15: Johnny Vander Meer becomes the first major league pitcher to throw consecutive no-hitters. He beat Brooklyn 6–0, in the first night game at Ebbets Field, and four days later beats the Boston Braves 3–0.

June 21: Heavyweight champion Joe Louis knocks out Max Schmeling in the first round to avenge the only loss of his pro career.

July 2: Helen Wills Moody wins her eighth straight Wimbledon singles title, a record.

September 24: Don Budge becomes the first player to sweep all four major tennis titles in one calendar year: Australian, French, Wimbledon, U.S.

1939

March 27: In the first national collegiate men's basketball tournament, Oregon defeats Ohio State for the championship. The tournament, started by the National Association of Basketball Coaches, will be taken over the by the NCAA in 1940.

May 2: Lou Gehrig benches himself for "the good of the team," and ends his consecutive games streak at 2,130.

1940

February: The Winter and Summer Olympic Games are canceled because of the outbreak of World War II.

July: The British Open and Wimbledon are canceled until World War II is over.

December 8: The Chicago Bears win the NFL championship by beating the Washington Redskins 73–0. The Bears rush for 381 yards, the Redskins 5.

1941

June 7: Whirlaway, ridden by Eddie Arcaro, becomes the fifth Triple Crown winner.

June 18: Joe Louis, trailing Billy Conn on points, scores a 13th-round knockout, after Conn tries and fails to knock out Louis.

July 17: Joe DiMaggio's hitting streak is ended at a record 56 games.

September 28: Ted Williams gets six hits in a doubleheader on the final day of the season to boost his average to .406.

October 5: Brooklyn Dodgers catcher Mickey Owen drops a third strike with two out in the ninth inning, costing the Dodgers a chance to even the World Series with the New York Yankees, who clinch the Series the next day.

1942

January 1: Because of the attack on Pearl Harbor three weeks earlier, the Rose Bowl is moved to Durham, N.C. Oregon State upsets Duke. The game returns to Pasadena, Calif., in 1943.

January 15: President Franklin D. Roosevelt gives baseball the "green light" to continue playing during the war.

1943

April 7: The NFL allows the Philadelphia Eagles and the Pittsburgh Steelers to merge rosters. The team is known as the "Steagles."

June 5: Count Fleet, ridden by Johnny Longden, wins the Triple Crown.

October 11: The New York Yankees beat the St. Louis Cardinals to win their 10th World Series.

December 26: The Chicago Bears win their third NFL title in four years. Quarterback Sid Luckman throws five touchdown passes to beat Washington.

1944

February: The Winter and Summer Olympics are canceled because of the continuation of World War II.

October 1: The St. Louis Browns clinch the first pennant in their history, beating the New York Yankees on the final day of the regular season.

December 18: Led by running backs Glenn Davis and Doc Blanchard, No. 1 Army defeats No. 2 Navy.

1945

March 18: Maurice Richard becomes the first NHL player to score 50 goals in a season, which is only 50 games long.

August 19: Byron Nelson's 11-tournament winning streak ends at the Memphis Invitational. He finishes fourth.

December 1: No. 1 Army beats No. 2 Navy for the second straight year.

1946

March 26: Oklahoma A&M, which beats North Carolina, becomes the first team to win consecutive NCAA men's basketball championships.

June 2: Assault, ridden by Warren Mehrtens, becomes the third Triple Crown winner of the decade.

September 1: Patty Berg wins the first U.S. Women's Open, beating Betty Jameson.

September 20: The Cleveland Browns beat the Miami Seahawks in the first game of the new All-America Football Conference.

November 9: No. 1 Army and No. 2 Notre Dame play to a scoreless tie, despite each team having an explosive offense.

1947

April 15: Jackie Robinson, the first African American to play in the major leagues, makes his debut by going 0-for-3 against the Boston Braves.

July 19: Babe Didriksen Zaharias wins a tournament in Colorado Springs for her 17th straight amateur victory.

December 5: Joe Louis retains his heavyweight championship by winning a 15-round split decision over Jersey Joe Walcott.

December 12: The National Association for Stock Car Auto Racing (NASCAR) is formed.

1948

June 12: Citation, ridden by Eddie Arcaro, becomes the fourth Triple Crown winner of the decade.

July 3: Louise Brough wins the singles, doubles, and mixed doubles titles at Wimbledon, only the third woman to win all three the same year. Suzanne Lenglen and Alice Marble are the others.

August 6: Bob Mathias wins the gold medal in the decathlon, making him the youngest gold medalist in Olympic history.

August 16: Babe Ruth dies at age 53 from throat cancer.

1949

February 2: Ben Hogan suffers serious injuries when his car collides head-on with a bus. It's feared his career is over, but he returns to the tour in 11 months.

February 7: Joe DiMaggio of the New York Yankees is the first baseball player to earn $100,000 a year.

March 1: Joe Louis relinquishes his heavyweight championship, which he held for 11 years and eight months.

June 22: Ezzard Charles beats Jersey Joe Walcott to fill the vacant heavyweight championship.

July: Gussie Moran wears lace-trimmed panties under her tennis skirt, causing an uproar at Wimbledon.

1950

June 10: Ben Hogan wins the U.S. Open, 16 months after being seriously injured in a car accident.

September 27: Joe Louis tries—and fails—to regain his heavyweight championship, losing to Ezzard Charles.

October 1: Babe Didriksen Zaharias wins the U.S. Women's Open, completing a sweep of the three major championships on the Ladies Professional Golf Association, which is in its inaugural season.

October 7: Notre Dame's 39-game unbeaten streak in college football is snapped by Purdue.

1951

July 18: Jersey Joe Walcott, at age 37, knocks out Ezzard Charles to win the heavyweight championship.

September 4: Maureen Connolly, at age 16, becomes the youngest woman to win the U.S. Nationals singles title.

October 3: Bobby Thomson's three-run homer off Brooklyn Dodgers pitcher Ralph Branca gives the New York Giants the National League pennant. The Giants trailed the Dodgers by 13 1/2 games on August 11.

October 10: The New York Yankees beat the New York Giants to win their third straight World Series.

1952

January 24: Three African Americans—Ted Rhodes, Bill Spiller, and Eural Clark—enter the Phoenix Open, under a rule that allows blacks to play if the sponsor agrees.

February 29: Dick Button wins the world figure skating championship for the fifth straight time.

March 23: Bill Mosienko of the Chicago Blackhawks scores the fastest hat trick in National Hockey League history—21 seconds.

July 27: Emil Zatopek wins the 5,000-meters, 10,000-meters, and marathon gold medals in the Helsinki Summer Olympics games. The marathon was his first.

October 7: The New York Yankees rally from a 3–2 deficit to beat the Brooklyn Dodgers and win their fourth straight World Series.

1953

March 18: The Boston Braves move to Milwaukee.

July 10: Ben Hogan wins the British Open, making him the first player to win the Masters, U.S. Open, and British Open in the same calendar year. He did not enter the PGA Championship.

September 7: Maureen Connolly wins the U.S. Nationals and completes the first Grand Slam by a woman.

October 5: The New York Yankees win their fifth straight World Series.

October 24: Notre Dame ends Georgia Tech's 31-game unbeaten streak.

1954

May 6: Roger Bannister is the first person to run the mile in less than four minutes, finishing in 3:59.4.

July 3: Babe Didriksen Zaharias wins the U.S. Women's Open by 12 strokes, 15 months after undergoing surgery for colon cancer.

September 17: Rocky Marciano retains his world heavyweight championship by knocking out Ezzard Charles in the eighth round.

October 30: The National Basketball Association institutes the 24-second clock and limits each team to six fouls per quarter.

1955

February 22: Maureen Connolly retires from tennis because of injuries suffered from a horse-riding accident.

May 30: Bill Vuckovich, the two-time defending Indianapolis 500 champion, is killed in a five-car crash while leading the race.

September 21: In his last heavyweight title defense, Rocky Marciano knocks out light heavyweight champion Archie Moore.

October 4: The Brooklyn Dodgers beat the New York Yankees in seven games to win their first World Series in eight attempts.

1956

March 25: Bill Russell leads the University of San Francisco to an undefeated season and its second straight NCAA basketball championship.

September 9: Lew Hoad's quest for a tennis Grand Slam is ended by Ken Rosewall at the U.S. Nationals.

September 27: Babe Didriksen Zaharias, the female athlete of the first half-century, dies at age 42 from colon cancer.

November 30: Floyd Patterson knocks out Archie Moore to become the youngest world heavyweight champ ever.

1957

March 23: No. 1 North Carolina beats No. 2 Kansas and Wilt Chamberlain in triple overtime to win the NCAA basketball championship.

April 13: The first National Basketball Association championship is won by the Boston Celtics, in double overtime over the St. Louis Hawks in the seventh game of the finals.

September 8: Althea Gibson becomes the first African American to win the U.S. Nationals title.

October 5: For the first time in 24 years, Great Britain wins the Ryder Cup.

November 16: Notre Dame, an 18-point underdog, beats Oklahoma and ends the Sooners' 47-game unbeaten streak.

1958

March 25: Sugar Ray Robinson wins the world middleweight championship for the fifth time, beating Carmen Basilio.

April 6: Arnold Palmer gets his first major championship victory, winning the Masters.

April 15: The first major league game takes place on the West Coast as the San Francisco Giants beat the Los Angeles Dodgers.

June 29: Pelé scores two goals, leading Brazil to its first World Cup.

October 8: The New York Yankees win their sixth World Series of the decade, rallying from a 3–1 deficit to beat the Milwaukee Braves.

December 28: In what is called the "greatest football game ever played," the Baltimore Colts beat the New York Giants 23–17 in sudden death to win the NFL title.

1959

February 22: The first Daytona 500, held at the new Daytona International Speedway, is won by Lee Petty in a photo finish.

March 21: California upsets West Virginia and Jerry West to win the NCAA basketball title.

May 26: Harvey Haddix of the Pittsburgh Pirates throws 12 perfect innings, but loses 1–0 to the Milwaukee Braves in the bottom of the 13th.

June 26: Ingemar Johansson knocks down Floyd Patterson seven times in the third round to win the world heavyweight championship.

August 14: The American Football League announces plans to challenge the NFL with an eight-team league in 1960.

1960

January 26: Pete Rozelle, 33, is elected commissioner of the NFL.

April 14: The Montreal Canadiens win their record fifth straight Stanley Cup championship.

June 20: Floyd Patterson knocks out Ingemar Johansson and becomes the first former heavyweight champ to regain the title.

October 13: Bill Mazeroski's ninth-inning home run in game 7 gives the Pittsburgh Pirates their first World Series championship.

November 16: Elgin Baylor scores a record 71 points for the Los Angeles Lakers against the New York Knicks.

1961

April 16: The Chicago Blackhawks win the Stanley Cup for the first time in 23 years.

April 29: ABC's *Wide World of Sports* is broadcast for the first time.

July 14: Arnold Palmer becomes the first American to win the British Open since Ben Hogan in 1953.

October 1: Roger Maris hits his 61st home run of the season, breaking Babe Ruth's mark.

December 6: Ernie Davis of Syracuse becomes the first African American to win the Heisman Trophy.

1962

March 2: Wilt Chamberlain of the Philadelphia Warriors sets an NBA single-game record by scoring 100 points against the New York Knicks in Hershey, Pennsylvania.

April 22: The Toronto Maple Leafs win their first Stanley Cup since 1951, beating the Chicago Blackhawks.

June 17: Jack Nicklaus wins his first major championship, beating Arnold Palmer in an 18-hole playoff for the U.S. Open title.

September 11: Rod Laver becomes the second male player to win the tennis Grand Slam.

September 25: Sonny Liston wins the world heavyweight title, knocking out Floyd Patterson in 2:06 of the first round.

1963

April 17: Paul Hornung of the Green Bay Packers and Alex Karras of the Detroit Lions are suspended for one year by NFL Commissioner Pete Rozelle for betting on their own teams to win.

June 21: Bob Hayes of Florida A&M sets a world record of 9.1 seconds in the 100-yard dash.

July 22: Sonny Liston retains his heavyweight championship with another first-round knockout of Floyd Patterson.

1964

February 25: Sonny Liston loses his heavyweight championship to Cassius Clay, a 7-1 underdog, who stuns the world.

April 26: The Boston Celtics win their sixth straight NBA title, the first team in professional sports to do so.

May 30: A.J. Foyt wins his second Indianapolis 500 in a race marred by a crash that kills Eddie Sachs and Dave McDonald.

October 15: Bob Gibson pitches three complete games and leads the St. Louis Cardinals to their first World Series title since 1946.

November 7: The Milwaukee Braves announce they'll move to Atlanta.

1965

January 13: The San Francisco Warriors trade Wilt Chamberlain to the Philadelphia 76ers.

April 4: Sam Snead, 52, becomes the oldest winner of a PGA Tour event by winning the Greater Greensboro Open.

April 9: The Astrodome opens in Houston.

May 25: Muhammad Ali, formerly Cassius Clay, retains his world heavyweight title with a controversial first-round knockout of Sonny Liston.

September 29: Sandy Koufax of the Los Angeles Dodgers becomes the first major league pitcher to throw four no-hitters with a 1–0 perfect game against the Chicago Cubs.

1966

March 19: Texas Western becomes the first team to win the NCAA basketball championship with an all-black starting lineup. The Miners beat Kentucky, which was all-white.

April 28: The Boston Celtics beat the Los Angeles Lakers to win their eighth straight NBA title.

June 8: The NFL and AFL announce plans to merge by the 1970 season.

July 9: With his victory in the British Open, Jack Nicklaus becomes just the fourth player to win all four major championships.

July 17: Jim Ryun of the University of Kansas breaks the world record in the mile, running 3:51.5.

November 19: No. 1 Notre Dame and No. 2 Michigan State play to a 10–10 tie.

1967

January 15: Green Bay defeats Kansas City in the first AFL-NFL World Championship game (Super Bowl I).

February 2: The American Basketball Association is formed and will challenge the NBA, starting in the fall.

April 28: Muhammad Ali is stripped of his heavyweight title for refusing induction into the U.S. Army on religious grounds.

August 20: Charlie Sifford becomes the first African American to win a PGA Tour event, the Greater Hartford Open.

October 1: The Boston Red Sox win their first American League pennant since 1946.

October 18: The Kansas City A's get approval to move to Oakland.

1968

January 20: The University of Houston, led by Elvin Hayes, snaps UCLA's 47-game winning streak with a 71–69 victory in the Astrodome.

March 22: UCLA avenges its loss to Houston with a 101–69 victory in the NCAA semifinals.

March 23: UCLA wins the NCAA basketball championship, beating North Carolina.

April 14: Bob Goalby is declared the winner of the Masters, when Roberto DeVincenzo signs an incorrect scorecard.

September 9: Arthur Ashe becomes the first African American male to win a national singles title with his victory in the U.S. Open.

September 14: Denny McLain of the Detroit Tigers becomes the first 30-game winner since Dizzy Dean in 1934.

1969

January 12: The New York Jets, a 19-point underdog, upset the Baltimore Colts 16–7 in Super Bowl III.

May 5: The Boston Celtics win their ninth NBA championship of the decade and 11th in 13 years.

September 8: Rod Laver wins the U.S. Open to win the Grand Slam for the second time.

October 16: The New York Mets upset the Baltimore Orioles and win the World Series in five games.

December 5: No. 1 Texas defeats No. 2 Arkansas 15–14 and President Richard Nixon declares the Longhorns national champs.

1970

January 11: The Kansas City Chiefs upset the Minnesota Vikings 23–7 to win Super Bowl IV.

March: Pete Maravich of Louisiana State ends his college career, averaging 44.2 points a game over three seasons.

May 8: The New York Knicks beat the Los Angeles Lakers to win their first NBA title.

May 10: Bobby Orr scores the clinching goal against the St. Louis Blues to give the Boston Bruins their first Stanley Cup since 1941.

September 13: Margaret Smith Court wins the U.S. Open and becomes the second female to win the Grand Slam.

September 20: The Cleveland Browns beat the New York Jets in the first *Monday Night Football* broadcast.

October 26: Muhammad Ali, out of boxing for 3 1/2 years, returns to the ring and knocks out Jerry Quarry in the third round.

1971

January 17: Jim O'Brien kicks a last-second 32-yard field goal to lift Baltimore over Dallas 16–13 in Super Bowl V.

March 8: In the first-ever matchup of undefeated heavyweight champs, Joe Frazier wins a unanimous 15-round decision over Muhammad Ali.

June 28: The U.S. Supreme Court, by an 8–0 vote, overturns Muhammad Ali's conviction for draft evasion.

October 3: Billie Jean King becomes the first female to win $100,000 in one year.

1972

January 8: The NCAA rules that freshmen will be allowed to play football and basketball.

February 20: A.J. Foyt, a three-time winner of the Indianapolis 500, wins the Daytona 500 with a record average speed of 161.550.

April 13: The first players' strike in baseball history ends after one week.

June 19: By a 5–3 vote, the U.S. Supreme Court upholds baseball's reserve clause.

June 23: President Richard Nixon signs the Higher Education Act into law. It includes Title IX, prohibiting sex bias in college athletic programs.

September 5–6: Arab terrorists kill two members of the Israeli Olympic team and kidnap nine others. Fifteen more are killed at an airport.

December 23: Franco Harris' "Immaculate Reception" helps the Pittsburgh Steelers beat the Oakland Raiders in the AFC playoffs.

1973

January 11: The American League will use the designated hitter rule on a three-year trial basis.

January 14: The Miami Dolphins beat the Washington Redskins in Super Bowl VII to complete the first undefeated season (17–0) in NFL history.

January 22: George Foreman knocks down heavyweight champion Joe Frazier six times, and the fight ends on a second-round technical knockout.

March 26: Bill Walton scores 44 points, leading UCLA to its seventh straight NCAA basketball championship and ninth in 10 years.

June 9: Secretariat wins the Belmont Stakes by 31 lengths to become the first Triple Crown winner in 25 years.

September 17: Billie Jean King beats Bobby Riggs in the "Battle of the Sexes."

December 16: O.J. Simpson of the Buffalo Bills rushes for 2,003 yards, breaking Jim Brown's record of 1,863 yards.

1974

January 19: UCLA's 88-game winning streak is snapped by Notre Dame, which rallies from 11 down with 3:32 to play.

February 17: Richard Petty wins his fifth Daytona 500, which is shortened to 450 miles because of the energy crisis.

April 8: Hank Aaron becomes baseball's all-time home run leader, hitting his 715th to break Babe Ruth's record.

June 12: Little League officials allow girls to play baseball.

August 29: Moses Malone becomes the first player to go from high school to the pros, when he signs with the Utah Stars of the ABA.

October 30: Muhammad Ali knocks out George Foreman in the eighth round to reclaim the world heavyweight title.

1975

January 12: The Pittsburgh Steelers win the first NFL championship in their 42-year history.

March 31: In John Wooden's last game, UCLA beats Kentucky for its 10th national title.

July 5: Arthur Ashe, a decided underdog, stuns Jimmy Connors in the Wimbledon final. Ashe becomes the first African American male to win the title.

October 1: Muhammad Ali beats Joe Frazier in the "Thrilla in Manila," when Frazier's corner throws in the towel after the 14th round.

October 21: Carlton Fisk of the Boston Red Sox hits one of the most memorable home runs in World Series history to win game 6 against the Cincinnati Reds.

December 6: Archie Griffin of Ohio State becomes the only player to win the Heisman Trophy twice.

1976

March 29: Indiana wins its first NCAA basketball championship since 1953, beating Michigan in the title game to finish the season unbeaten.

June 17: The American Basketball Association folds. The NBA accepts Denver, Indiana, New Jersey, and San Antonio.

October 21: The New York Yankees, in the World Series for the first time since 1964, are swept by the St. Louis Cardinals.

1977

March 28: Marquette's Al McGuire, coaching his final game, sees his team beat North Carolina to win the NCAA basketball title.

May 30: A.J. Foyt wins the Indianapolis 500 for the fourth time.

June 11: Seattle Slew becomes the second Triple Crown winner of the decade.

July 1: England's Virginia Wade wins the women's singles title at Wimbledon, which celebrates its 100th anniversary.

July 9: Tom Watson shoots 65 to outduel Jack Nicklaus, who shoots 66, to win the British Open at Turnberry.

October 18: The New York Yankees' Reggie Jackson, "Mr. October," hits three home runs in game 6 of the World Series.

1978

February 15: Leon Spinks wins the world heavyweight title by upsetting Muhammad Ali.

June 10: Affirmed wins the Triple Crown, and Alydar becomes the first horse to finish second in all three races.

June 18: Nancy Lopez wins the Rochester International, her fifth straight LPGA Tour victory.

September 15: Muhammad Ali wins the world heavyweight title for the third time, beating Leon Spinks.

October 8: Mario Andretti wins the Formula One driving championship. He is the first American to do so since Phil Hill in 1961.

1979

January 21: The Pittsburgh Steelers beat the Dallas Cowboys and become the first team to win the Super Bowl three times.

March 26: Magic Johnson leads Michigan State to the NCAA basketball title, beating Larry Bird and Indiana State.

September 9: Tracy Austin, age 16, becomes the youngest tennis player to win the U.S. Open.

November 30: Sugar Ray Leonard wins his first world title: the welterweight crown, beating Wilfred Benitez.

1980

January 20: The Pittsburgh Steelers win their fourth Super Bowl.

February 22: The U.S. hockey team defeats the Soviet Union in the semifinals and goes on to win the Olympic gold medal.

April 12: The U.S. Olympic Committee announces its support of President Jimmy Carter's boycott of the Summer Games in Moscow.

April 12: Bill Rodgers wins his third straight Boston Marathon, and Rosie Ruiz, the first woman to finish, is exposed as a fraud.

May 16: Magic Johnson, playing center in place of injured Kareem Abdul-Jabbar, leads the Los Angeles Lakers to the NBA championship against the Philadelphia 76ers.

July 2: Bjorn Borg defeats John McEnroe in five sets to win his fifth straight Wimbledon singles title.

October 2: Muhammad Ali comes out of retirement at age 38 and loses to heavyweight champion Larry Holmes by an 11th-round technical knockout.

October 21: The Philadelphia Phillies win their first World Series in the history of the franchise, beating the Kansas City Royals.

1981

January 25: The Oakland Raiders become the first wild card team to win a Super Bowl, beating the Philadelphia Eagles 27–10.

February 15: Richard Petty wins the Daytona 500 for the seventh time.

July 31: A baseball players' strike, lasting 50 days, ends. Thirty-eight percent of the schedule is lost.

1982

March 25: Wayne Gretzky becomes the first NHL player to score 200 points in one season.

March 29: Michael Jordan hits a jump shot in the final minute to lead North Carolina to the NCAA basketball title over Georgetown. It is coach Dean Smith's first national championship.

June 20: Tom Watson chips in from the deep rough on the 71st hole of the U.S. Open at Pebble Beach to beat Jack Nicklaus.

November 16: The NFL players strike ends after 57 days. The season is reduced from 16 games to nine.

1983

January 1: Penn State wins its first college football national championship, beating Georgia in the Sugar Bowl.

April 4: North Carolina State stuns heavily favored Houston to win the NCAA college basketball championship.

May 28: Martina Navratilova loses to unseeded Kathy Horvath in the fourth round of the French Open. It's her only loss of the year and keeps her from winning the Grand Slam.

May 31: The Philadelphia 76ers win their first NBA championship in 16 years, beating the Los Angeles Lakers.

1984

January 1: Miami (Fla.) wins its first college football national championship, holding off top-ranked Nebraska 31–30 in the Orange Bowl.

March 29: In the middle of the night, the Baltimore Colts move to Indianapolis.

April 5: Kareem Abdul-Jabbar moves past Wilt Chamberlain to become the NBA's all-time scoring leader.

August 3: Mary Lou Retton scores perfect 10s in the floor exercise and vault and wins the gold medal in the gymnastics all-around competition.

August 11: Carl Lewis ties Jesse Owens by winning his fourth gold medal of the Summer Games.

1985

April 1: Top-seeded Georgetown is upset by eighth-seeded Villanova in the NCAA basketball championship.

May 12: Kathy Whitworth wins the 88th LPGA tournament of her career, No. 1 all-time for men and women.

July 7: Seventeen-year-old Boris Becker becomes the youngest Wimbledon men's singles champ and the first unseeded player to win the title.

September 11: Pete Rose of the Cincinnati Reds becomes baseball's all-time hit leader with 4,192. He eclipses Ty Cobb's record.

September 15: The United States loses the Ryder Cup for the first time in 28 years.

September 21: Michael Spinks hands Larry Holmes the first loss of his career and becomes the first light heavyweight to win the heavyweight title.

1986

April 2: College basketball adopts the 3-point shot.

April 13: Jack Nicklaus, at 46, becomes the oldest winner of the Masters.

July 27: Greg LeMond is the first non-European cyclist to win the Tour de France.

October 25: The New York Mets rally past the Boston Red Sox to win the World Series.

November 22: Mike Tyson knocks out Trevor Berbick to become the youngest world heavyweight champ in history.

1987

January 25: The New York Giants win their first Super Bowl, scoring 30 points in the second half to beat the Denver Broncos.

April 6: Fighting for the first time in three years, Sugar Ray Leonard scores a 12-round split decision over Marvin Hagler.

June 4: Edwin Moses' 10-year, 122-race win streak is snapped by Danny Harris at a meet in Madrid.

September 27: The European team, led by Seve Ballesteros, wins the Ryder Cup for the second straight time.

October 25: A strike by NFL players ends after 24 days.

1988

March: Susan Butcher wins the Iditarod Trail Sled Dog Race for the third straight time.

August 8: The first night game is played at Wrigley Field. Rain postpones the game against Philadelphia after 3 1/2 innings.

August 9: Wayne Gretzky is traded by the Edmonton Oilers to the Los Angeles Kings.

September 24: Ben Johnson sets an Olympic record of 9.79 in the 100-meter dash, but is disqualified after failing a urine test.

October 1: Steffi Graf wins the gold medal at the Summer Olympics. She also wins the Grand Slam.

October 15: Injured Kirk Gibson's pinch-hit home run in the bottom of the ninth lifts the Los Angeles Dodgers to a victory over the Oakland Athletics in game 1 of the World Series.

1989

January 22: Joe Montana guides the San Francisco 49ers on an 11-play, 92-yard touchdown drive with 3:10 left to beat the Cincinnati Bengals in Super Bowl XXIII.

February 19: Darrell Waltrip wins his first Daytona 500, going the last 132.5 miles without refueling.

August 24: Baseball Commissioner A. Bartlett Giamatti bans Pete Rose from baseball for life after he finds Rose guilty of betting on major league games.

September 1: Commissioner of baseball A. Bartlett Giamatti dies of a heart attack.

October 17: Right before the start of game 3 of the World Series, an earthquake measuring 7.1 on the Richter Scale hits the Bay Area. The Series is postponed for 10 days.

1990

February 10: Buster Douglas records one of the biggest upsets in boxing history, knocking out heavyweight champion Mike Tyson in the 10th round.

April 9: The baseball season opens, a week late, after a 32-day lockout of spring training camps.

May 24: The Edmonton Oilers win their fifth Stanley Cup in seven years, beating the Boston Bruins.

July 7: Martina Navratilova wins a record ninth Wimbledon singles title, beating Zina Garrison.

October 25: Evander Holyfield knocks out heavyweight champ Buster Douglas in the third round.

1991

April 1: In its ninth trip to the Final Four, Duke wins its first NCAA basketball championship, beating Kansas.

May 1: Nolan Ryan, at age 44, becomes the oldest pitcher to throw a no-hitter. It's the seventh of his career.

June 12: The Chicago Bulls, led by Michael Jordan, win their first NBA championship.

August 30: Mike Powell leaps 29 feet 4 1/2 inches to beat Bob Beamon's long jump record.

November 7: Magic Johnson announces his retirement from the NBA because he has the HIV virus that causes AIDS.

1992

April 10: Duke beats Michigan to become the first NCAA basketball champion to repeat since UCLA won six straight titles (1967–73).

August 2: Jackie Joyner-Kersee wins her second straight heptathlon gold medal at the Summer Olympics.

August 8: The Dream Team, led by Michael Jordan and Magic Johnson, wins the Olympic gold medal.

October 24: The Toronto Blue Jays become the first Canadian team to win the World Series.

1993

March 4: Texas Tech, led by Sheryl Swoopes' record 47 points, wins the NCAA women's basketball championship, beating Ohio State.

April 14: Mario Lemieux of the Pittsburgh Penguins misses two months of the season after undergoing cancer treatment, but returns to win his fourth scoring title.

April 30: Monica Seles is stabbed in the back by a deranged Steffi Graf fan during a changeover at the German Open.

October 6: Michael Jordan announces his retirement from the NBA.

November 14: Miami Dolphins coach Don Shula wins his 325th game and surpasses the Chicago Bears' George Halas as the winningest NFL coach of all time.

1994

January 1: Florida State coach Bobby Bowden wins his first college football national championship, beating Nebraska.

March 23: Wayne Gretzky scores his 802nd goal to surpass Gordie Howe as the NHL's top goal-scorer.

June 14: The New York Rangers beat the Vancouver Canucks to win their first Stanley Cup in 44 years.

August 8: Jeff Gordon wins the Brickyard 400, the first stock car race held at the Indianapolis Motor Speedway.

August 12: Baseball players go on strike, which leads to the cancellation of the World Series.

November 5: George Foreman, 45, knocks out Michael Moorer to win the world heavyweight championship.

1995

January 11: A lockout of players by NHL owners ends after 103 days. The regular season is reduced from 84 to 48 games.

March 19: Michael Jordan returns to the NBA after a 17-month absence.

April 2: The University of Connecticut women win their first NCAA basketball championship and finish the season at 35–0.

October 3: Former Heisman Trophy winner O.J. Simpson is found not guilty of murdering his wife and her friend.

1996

January 2: Nebraska wins its second straight college football national championship, routing Florida 62–24.

June 16: Michael Jordan leads the Chicago Bulls to their fourth NBA title of the decade. The Bulls win a record 72 games in the regular season.

July 19: Muhammad Ali lights the Olympic flame to begin the Summer Games in Atlanta.

November 9: Evander Holyfield knocks out Mike Tyson in the 11th round.

1997

March 22: Tara Lipinski, 14, becomes the youngest figure skater to win a world championship.

April 13: Tiger Woods wins the Masters by 12 strokes, setting a record with a score of 18-under 270. He is the youngest ever to win the tournament and the first African American.

June 28: In a Las Vegas bout, Mike Tyson bites off part of Evander Holyfield's ear and is disqualified.

August 26: Michael Jordan commits to playing the 1997–98 season for the Chicago Bulls. He is paid $35 million.

October 26: The Florida Marlins, in the National League for only five years, win the World Series, beating the Cleveland Indians.

1998

January 25: Denver quarterback John Elway leads the Broncos to their first Super Bowl win in four tries.

February 15: Dale Earnhardt wins his first Daytona 500.

June 14: Michael Jordan hits the game-winning jumper with 5.2 seconds left to lift the Chicago Bulls over the Utah Jazz. It's their sixth NBA title of the decade.

July 12: France wins the World Cup for the first time, beating Brazil.

1999

January 6: A lockout of NBA players by owners ends after six months. The season is reduced from 82 games to 50.

January 31: John Elway leads the Denver Broncos to their second straight Super Bowl victory.

April 18: Wayne Gretzky plays his final game. He retires as a member of the New York Rangers.

June 6: With his victory in the French Open, Andre Agassi becomes one of only five players to win each of the four Grand Slam events.

July 10: The United States wins the Women's World Cup, defeating China on a penalty-kick goal by Brandi Chastain.

July 26: Lance Armstrong, a cancer survivor, becomes the second American to win the Tour de France.

2000

January 30: The St. Louis Rams cap an improbable season with a victory in the Super Bowl over the Tennessee Titans.

March 13: Miami Dolphins quarterback Dan Marino retires after 17 years.

June 18: Tiger Woods wins the U.S. Open at Pebble Beach Golf Links by a record 15 shots.

June 22: ABC Sports names comedian Dennis Miller as a commentator for *Monday Night Football*.

July 8: Venus Williams becomes the first African American woman to win the Wimbledon singles title since Althea Gibson in 1958.

July 23: Lance Armstrong wins his second consecutive Tour de France.

August 20: Tiger Woods wins the PGA Championship in a playoff over Bob May.

August 26: The Houston Comets win their fourth straight WNBA championship.

September 9: Venus Williams wins the U.S. Open tennis championship, her second straight Grand Slam title.

September 10: Indiana basketball coach Bob Knight is fired after 29 years.

September 27: Venus Williams wins the gold medal in women's singles at the Summer Olympics in Sydney. She and sister Serena win the gold medal doubles.

September: Marion Jones of the United States becomes the first female to win five track and field medals at one Olympics.

October 8: Europe defeats the United States 14 1/2–11 1/2 to wind the Solheim Cup.

October 26: The New York Yankees beat the New York Mets in five games to win their 26th World Series championship.

November 13: Boston Red Sox pitcher Pedro Martinez wins his second straight American League Cy Young Award and third award overall.

November 14: Arizona Diamondbacks Randy Johnson wins his second straight National League Cy Young Award and third award overall.

November 28: Bill France, NASCAR president since 1972, announces his retirement.

December 5: Karl Malone of the Utah Jazz passes Wilt Chamberlain for second place on the NBA's career scoring list.

December 9: Florida State quarterback Chris Weinke, at 28, becomes the oldest winner of the Heisman Trophy.

December 11: The Texas Rangers sign shortstop Alex Rodriguez to a 10-year $252 million contract.

December 27: Mario Lemieux of the Pittsburgh Penguins returns to the ice after being retired for 3 1/2 years.

Directory

AUTO RACING

CART
Championship Auto Racing
   Teams
755 W. Big Beaver Rd.
Suite 800
Troy, MI 48084
248-362-8800

IRL
Indy Racing League
4565 West 16th St.
Indianapolis, IN 46222
317-484-6526

FIA-Formula One
Federation Internationale de
   L'Automobile
2 Chemim de Blandonnet
1215 Geneva 15, Switzerland
011-41-2254-4400

NASCAR
National Assn. for Stock Car
   Auto Racing
P.O. Box 2875
Daytona Beach, FL 32120
904-253-0611

NHRA
National Hot Rod
   Association
2035 Financial Way
Glendora, CA 91741
626-914-4761

MAJOR LEAGUE BASEBALL

Office of the Commissioner
245 Park Ave.
31st Floor
New York, NY 10160
212-931-7800

Player Relations Committee
350 Park Ave.
New York, NY 10022
212-339-7400

Major League Baseball Players
   Association
12 East 49th St.
24th Floor
New York, NY 10017
212-826-0808

American League

American League Office
245 Park Ave.
28th Floor
New York, NY 10167
212-931-7600

Anaheim Angels
P.O. Box 2000
Anaheim, CA 92803
714-940-2000

Baltimore Orioles
333 West Camden St.
Baltimore, MD 2101
410-685-9800

Boston Red Sox
Fenway Park
4 Yawkey Way
Boston, MA 02215
617-267-9440

Chicago White Sox
Comiskey Park
333 W. 35th St.
Chicago, IL 60616

Cleveland Indians
Jacobs Field
2401 Ontario St.
Cleveland, OH 44114
216-420-4200

Detroit Tigers
Comerica Park
2100 Woodward Ave.
Detroit, MI 48216
313-471-4000

Kansas City Royals
P.O. Box 419969
Kansas City, MO 64141
816-921-8000

Minnesota Twins
Hubert H. Humphrey
   Metrodome
34 Kirby Puckett Place
Minneapolis, MN 55415
612-375-1366

New York Yankees
Yankee Stadium
Bronx, NY 10451
718-293-4300

Oakland Athletics
7677 Oakport, Suite 200
Oakland, CA 94621
510-638-4900

Seattle Mariners
P.O. Box 4100
Seattle, WA 98104
206-346-4000

Tampa Bay Devil Rays
Tropicana Field
One Stadium Dr.
St. Petersburg, FL 33705
727-825-3137

Texas Rangers
1000 Ballpark Way
Arlington, TX 76011
817-273-5222

Toronto Blue Jays
SkyDome
One Blue Jays Way, Suite 3200
Toronto, Ontario, Canada
    M5V 1J1
416-341-1000

National League

National League Office
245 Park Ave.
28th Floor
New York, NY 10167
212-931-7700

Arizona Diamondbacks
P.O. Box 2095
Phoenix, AZ 85001
602-462-6500

Atlanta Braves
P.O. Box 4064
Atlanta, GA 30302
404-522-7630

Chicago Cubs
1060 West Addison St.
Chicago, IL 60613
773-404-2827

Cincinnati Reds
100 Cynergy Ave.
Cincinnati, OH 45202
513-421-4510

Colorado Rockies
Coors Field
2001 Blake St.
Denver, CO 80205
303-292-0200

Florida Marlins
2267 N.W. 199th St.
Miami, FL 33056
305-626-7400

Houston Astros
Enron Field
P.O. Box 288
Houston, TX 77001
713-259-8000

Los Angeles Dodgers
1000 Elysian Park Ave.
Los Angeles, CA 90012
323-224-1500

Milwaukee Brewers
Milwaukee County Stadium
P.O. Box 3099
Milwaukee, WI 53201
414-933-4114

Montreal Expos
P.O. Box 500, Station M
Montreal, Quebec, Canada
    H1V 3N7
514-253-3434

New York Mets
12301 Roosevelt Ave.
Flushing, NY 11368
718-507-6387

Philadelphia Phillies
P.O. Box 7575
Philadelphia, PA 19101
215-463-6000

Pittsburgh Pirates
P.O. Box 7000
Pittsburgh, PA 15212
412-323-5000

St. Louis Cardinals
250 Stadium Plaza
St. Louis, MO 63102
314-421-3060

San Diego Padres
P.O. Box 2000
San Diego, CA 92112
619-881-6500

San Francisco Giants
Pacific Bell Park
24 Willie Mays Plaza
San Francisco, CA 94107
415-972-2000

PRO BASKETBALL

NBA

League Office
Olympic Tower
645 Fifth Ave.
New York, NY 10022
212-407-8000

NBA Players Association
1700 Broadway, Suite 1400
New York, NY 10019
212-655-0880

Atlanta Hawks
One CNN Center, Suite 405
South Tower
Atlanta, GA 30303
404-827-3800

Boston Celtics
151 Merrimac St., 4th Floor
Boston, MA 02114
617-523-6050

Charlotte Hornets
100 Hive Drive
Charlotte, NC 28217
704-357-0252

Chicago Bulls
United Center
1901 West Madison St.
Chicago, IL 60612
312-455-4000

Cleveland Cavaliers
Gateway Arena
One Centre Court
Cleveland, OH 44115
216-420-2000

Dallas Mavericks
Reunion Arena
777 Sports St.
Dallas, TX 75207
214-748-1808

Denver Nuggets
Pepsi Center
1000 Chopper Pl.
Denver, CO 80204
303-405-1100

Detroit Pistons
Palace of Auburn Hills
Two Championship Dr.
Auburn Hills, MI 48326
248-377-0100

Golden State Warriors
1011 Broadway, 20th floor
Oakland, CA 94607
510-986-2200

Houston Rockets
2 Greenway Plaza, Suite 400
Houston, TX 77046
713-627-3865

Indiana Pacers
125 S. Pennsylvania St.
Indianapolis, IN 46204
317-263-2100

Los Angeles Clippers
Staples Center
1111 S. Figueroa St., Suite 1000
Los Angeles, CA 90015
213-745-0400

Los Angeles Lakers
555 N. Nash St.
El Segundo, CA 90245
213-742-7100

Miami Heat
American Airlines Arena
1 SE Third Ave., Suite 2300
Miami, FL 33136
305-577-4328

Milwaukee Bucks
Bradley Center
1001 N. Fourth St.
Milwaukee, WI 53203

Minnesota Timberwolves
Target Center
600 First Ave. North
Minneapolis, MN 55403
612-673-1600

New Jersey Nets
390 Murray Hill Pkwy.
East Rutherford, NJ 07073
201-935-8888

New York Knickerbockers
Madison Square Garden
2 Penn Plaza, 14th Floor
New York, NY 10121
212-465-6000

Orlando Magic
2 Magic Place
Orlando Arena
Orlando, FL 32910
407-916-2400

Philadelphia 76ers
First Union Center
3601 S. Broad St.
Philadelphia, PA 19148
215-339-7600

Phoenix Suns
201 E. Jefferson
Phoenix, AZ 85004
602-379-7900

Portland Trail Blazers
One Center Court, Suite 200
Portland, OR 97227
503-234-9291

Sacramento Kings
One Sports Parkway
Sacramento, CA 95834
916-928-0000

San Antonio Spurs
Alamodome
100 Montana St.
San Antonio, TX 78203
210-554-7700

Seattle SuperSonics
190 Queen Anne Ave., N.,
   Suite 200
Seattle, WA 98109
206-281-5800

Toronto Raptors
40 Bay St., Suite 400
Toronto, Ontario, Canada
   M5J 2X2
416-815-5600

Utah Jazz
Delta Center
301 West South Temple
Salt Lake City, UT 84101
801-325-2500

Vancouver Grizzlies
General Motors Place
800 Griffiths Way
Vancouver, B.C., Canada V6B 6G1
604-899-7650

Washington Wizards
MCI Center
601 F Street NW
Washington, D.C. 20071
202-661-5000

WNBA

Women's National Basketball
   Association
645 5th Ave.
New York, NY 10022
212-688-9622

Charlotte Sting
3308 Oaklace Blvd., Suite 8
Charlotte, NC 28208
704-357-0252

Cleveland Rockers
Gund Arena
One Center Court
Cleveland, OH 44115

Detroit Shock
Palace of Auburn Hills
Two Championship Dr.
Auburn Hills, MI 48326
248-377-0100

373

Houston Comets
Two Gateway Plaza, Suite 400
Houston, TX 77046-3865
713-627-9622

Indiana Fever
Conseco Fieldhouse
125 S. Pennsylvania St.
Indianapolis, IN 46204
317-917-2500

Los Angeles Sparks
Great Western Forum
3900 W. Manchester Blvd.
Inglewood, CA 90306
310-330-2434

Miami Sol
American Airlines Arena
601 Biscayne Blvd.
Miami, FL 33132
305-577-4328

Minnesota Lynx
Target Center
600 First Ave. N.
Minneapolis, MN 55403
612-673-1600

New York Liberty
Two Penn Plaza
New York, NY 10121
212-564-9622

Orlando Miracle
2 Magic Place
8701 Matland Summit Blvd.
Orlando, FL 32810
407-916-2400

Phoenix Mercury
America West Arena
201 E. Jefferson St.
Phoenix, AZ 85004
602-514-8333

Portland Fire
One Center Court
Portland, OR 97227
503-234-9291

Sacramento Monarchs
ARCO Arena
One Sports Pkwy.
Sacramento, CA 95834
916-928-0000

Seattle Storm
Key Arena
190 Queen Anne Ave. N.
Seattle, WA 98109
206-374-9622

Utah Starzz
Delta Center
301 West South Temple
Salt Lake City, UT 84101
801-325-2500

Washington Mystics
MCI Center
601 F St. NW
Washington, D.C. 20004
202-661-5000

Major NCAA Conferences

Atlantic Coast Conference
P.O. Drawer ACC
Greensboro, NC 27417-6724
336-854-8787

2000–2001 members: *Basketball and Football* (9)—Clemson, Duke, Florida State, Georgia Tech, Maryland, North Carolina, North Carolina State, Virginia, and Wake Forest.

Big East Conference
56 Exchange Terrace
Providence, RI 02903
401-272-9108

2000–2001 members: *Basketball* (13)—Boston College, Connecticut, Georgetown, Miami-FL, Notre Dame, Pittsburgh, Providence, Rutgers, St. John's, Seton Hall, Syracuse, Villanova, and West Virginia. *Football* (8)—Boston College, Miami-FL, Pittsburgh, Rutgers, Syracuse, Temple, Virginia Tech, and West Virginia.

Big 12 Conference
2201 Stemmons Fwy., 28th Floor
Dallas, TX 75207
214-742-1212

2000–2001 members: *Basketball and Football* (12)—Baylor, Colorado, Iowa State, Kansas, Kansas State, Missouri, Nebraska, Oklahoma, Oklahoma State, Texas, Texas A&M, and Texas Tech.

Big Ten Conference
1500 West Higgins Road
Park Ridge, IL 60068-6300
847-696-1010

2000–2001 members: *Basketball and Football* (11)—Illinois, Indiana, Iowa, Michigan, Michigan State, Minnesota, Northwestern, Ohio State, Penn State, Purdue, and Wisconsin.

Big West Conference
Two Corporate Park, Suite 206
Irvine, CA 92606
949-261-2525

2000–2001 members: *Basketball* (12)—Boise State, CS-Fullerton, Cal Poly-SLO, Idaho, Long Beach State, Nevada, New Mexico State, North Texas, Pacific, UC-Irvine, UC-Santa Barbara, and Utah State. *Football* (7)—Arkansas State, Boise State, Idaho, Nevada, New Mexico State, North Texas, and Utah State.

Conference USA
35 East Wacker Dr., Suite 650
Chicago, IL 60601
312-553-0483

2000–2001 members: *Basketball* (12)—UAB, Cincinnati, DePaul, Houston, Louisville, Marquette, Memphis, UNC-Charlotte, Saint Louis, South Florida, Southern Miss, and Tulane. *Football* (9)—UAB, Army, Cincinnati, East Carolina, Houston, Louisville, Memphis, Southern Miss, and Tulane.

Mid-American Conference
24 Public Square, 15th Floor
Cleveland, OH 44113
216-566-4622

2000–2001 members: *Basketball and Football* (13)—Akron, Ball State, Bowling Green, Buffalo, Central Michigan, Eastern Michigan, Kent, Marshall, Miami-OH, Northern Illinois,

Ohio University, Toledo, and Western Michigan.

Mountain West Conference
P.O. Box 35670
Colorado Springs, CO 80935
719-533-9500

2000–2001 members: *Basketball and Football* (9)—Air Force, Brigham Young University, Colorado State, UNLV, New Mexico, San Diego State, Utah, and Wyoming.

Pacific-10 Conference
800 South Broadway, Suite 400
Walnut Creek, CA 94596
925-932-4411

2000–2001 members: *Basketball and Football* (10)—Arizona, Arizona State, California, Oregon, Oregon State, Stanford, UCLA, USC, Washington, and Washington State.

Southeastern Conference
2201 Civic Center Blvd.
Birmingham, AL 35203
205-458-3000

2000–2001 members: *Basketball and Football* (12)—Alabama, Arkansas, Auburn, Florida, Georgia, Kentucky, LSU, Mississippi State, Ole Miss, South Carolina, Tennessee, and Vanderbilt.

Western Athletic Conference
9250 East Costilla Ave., Suite 300
Englewood, CO 80112
303-799-9221

2000–2001 members: *Basketball and Football* (8)—Fresno State, Hawaii, Rice, San Jose State, SMU, TCU, Tulsa, and UTEP.

OTHER MAJOR DIVISION I CONFERENCES

America East
10 High St., Suite 860
Boston, MA 02110
617-695-6269

2000–2001 members: *Basketball* (10)—Boston University, Delaware, Drexel, Hartford, Hofstra, Maine, New Hampshire, Northeastern, Towson, and Vermont.

Atlantic 10 Conference
2 Penn Center Plaza
Philadelphia, PA 19102
215-751-0500

2000–2001 members: *Basketball* (12)—Dayton, Duquesne, Fordham, George Washington, La Salle, Massachusetts, Rhode Island, St. Bonaventure, St. Joseph's, Temple, and Xavier.

Big South Conference
6428 Bannington Dr., Suite A
Charlotte, NC 28226
704-341-7990

2000–2001 members: *Basketball* (8)—Charleston Southern, Coastal Carolina, Elon, High Point, Liberty, NC-Asheville, Radford, and Winthrop.

Colonial Athletic Association
8625 Patterson Ave.
Richmond, VA 23229
804-754-1616

2000–2001 members: *Basketball* (9)—American, East Carolina, George Mason, James Madison, NC-Wilmington, Old Dominion, Richmond, Virginia Commonwealth, and William and Mary.

Gateway Football Conference
1000 Union Station, Suite 105
St. Louis, MO 63103
314-421-2268

2000–2001 members: *Football* (7)—Illinois State, Indiana State, Northern Iowa, Southern Illinois, SW Missouri State, Western Illinois, and Youngstown State.

Ivy League
330 Alexander St.
Princeton, NJ 08544
609-258-6426

2000–2001 members: *Basketball and Football* (8)—Brown, Columbia, Cornell, Dartmouth, Harvard, Pennsylvania, Princeton, and Yale.

Metro Atlantic Athletic Conference
1090 Amboy Ave.
Edison, NJ 08837
732-225-0202

2000–2001 members: *Basketball* (10)—Canisius, Fairfield, Iona, Loyola-MD, Manhatten, Marist, Niagara, Rider, St. Peter's, and Siena. *Football* (9)—Canisius, Duquesne, Fairfield, Georgetown, Iona, LaSalle, Marist, St. Peter's, and Siena.

Mid-Eastern Athletic Conference
102 North Elm St., SE Building, Suite 401
Greensboro, NC 27401
336-275-9961

2000–2001 members: *Basketball* (11)—Bethune-Cookman, Coppin State, Delaware State, Florida A&M, Hampton, Howard, MD-Eastern Shore, Morgan State, Norfolk State, North Carolina A&T, and South Carolina State. *Football* (9)—Bethune-Cookman, Delaware State, Florida A&M, Hampton, Howard, Morgan State, Norfolk State, North Carolina A&T, and South Carolina State.

Midwestern Collegiate Conference
201 South Capitol Ave., Suite 500
Indianapolis, IN 46225
317-237-5622

2000–2001 members: *Basketball* (8)—Butler, Cleveland State, Detroit Mercy, Illinois-Chicago, Loyola-IL, Wisconsin-Green Bay, Wisconsin-Milwaukee, and Wright State.

Missouri Valley Conference
1000 St. Louis Union Station, Suite 105
St. Louis, MO 63103
314-421-0339

2000–2001 members: *Basketball* (10)—Bradley, Creighton, Drake, Evansville, Illinois State, Indiana State, Northern Iowa, Southern Illinois, SW Missouri State, and Wichita State.

Northeast Conference
220 Old New Brunswick Rd.
Piscataway, NJ 08854
732-562-0877

2000–2001 members: *Basketball* (12)—Central Connecticut State, Fairleigh Dickinson, LIU-Brooklyn, Maryland-Baltimore County, Monmouth, Mount St. Mary's, Quinnipiac, Robert Morris, Sacred Heart, St. Francis-NY, St. Francis-PA, and Wagner. *Football* (8)—Albany, Central Connecticut State, Monmouth, Robert Morris, Sacred Heart, St. Francis-PA, Stony Brook, and Wagner.

Ohio Valley Conference
278 Franklin Road, Suite 103
Brentwood, TN 37027
615-371-1698

2000–2001 members: *Basketball* (10)—Austin Peay State, Eastern Illinois, Eastern Kentucky, Middle Tennessee State, Morehead State, Murray State, SE Missouri State, Tennessee-Martin, Tennessee State, and Tennessee Tech. *Football* (8)—Eastern Illinois, Eastern Kentucky, Murray State, SE Missouri State, Tennessee-Martin, Tennessee State, Tennessee Tech, and Western Kentucky.

Patriot League
3897 Adler Place, Building C, Suite 310
Bethlehem, PA 18017
610-691-2414

2000–2001 members: *Basketball* (7)—Army, Bucknell, Colgate, Holy Cross, Lafayette, Lehigh, and Navy. *Football* (7)—Bucknell, Colgate, Fordham, Holy Cross, Lafayette, Lehigh, and Towson.

Pioneer Football League
1000 St. Louis Union Station, Suite 105
St. Louis, MO 63103
314-421-2268

2000–2001 members: *Football* (5)—Butler, Dayton, Drake, San Diego, and Valparaiso.

Southern Conference
1 West Pack Square, Suite 1508
Asheville, NC 28801
828-255-7872

2000–2001 members: *Basketball* (12)—Appalachian State, The Citadel, College of Charleston, Davidson, East Tennessee State, Furman, Georgia Southern, UNC-Greensboro, Tennessee-Chattanooga, VMI, Western Carolina, and Wofford. *Football* (9)—Appalachian State, The Citadel, East Tennessee State, Furman, Georgia Southern, Tennessee-Chattanooga, VMI, Western Carolina, and Wofford.

Southland Conference
8150 North Central Expressway, Suite 930
Dallas, TX 75206
214-750-7522

2000–2001 members: *Basketball* (11)—Lamar, McNeese State, Nicholls State, NE Louisiana, Northwestern State, Sam Houston State, SE Louisiana, Southwest Texas State, Stephen F. Austin State, Texas-Arlington, and Texas-San Antonio. *Football* (8)—Austin State, Jacksonville State, McNeese State, Nicholls State, Northwestern State, Sam Houston State, Southwest Texas State, and Troy State.

Southwestern Athletic Conference
1500 Sugar Bowl Drive, Superdome
New Orleans, LA 70112
504-523-7574

2000–2001 members: *Basketball and Football* (10)—Alabama A&M, Alabama State, Alcorn State, Arkansas-Pine Bluff, Grambling State, Jackson State, Mississippi Valley State, Prairie View A&M, Southern-Baton Rouge, and Texas Southern.

Sun Belt Conference
One Galleria Blvd., Suite 2115
Metairie, LA 70001
504-834-6000

2000–2001 members: *Basketball* (9)—Arkansas-Little Rock, Arkansas State, Denver, Florida International, Louisiana Tech, New Orleans, South Alabama, SW Louisiana, and Western Kentucky.

Trans America Athletic Conference
3370 Vineville Ave., Suite 108-B
Macon, GA 31204
912-474-3394

2000–2001 members: *Basketball* (10)—Campbell, Central Florida, Florida Atlantic, Georgia State, Jacksonville, Jacksonville State, Mercer, Samford, Stetson, and Troy State.

West Coast Conference
1200 Bayhill Dr.
San Bruno, CA 94066
650-873-8622

2000–2001 members: *Basketball* (8)—Gonzaga, Loyola Marymount, Pepperdine, Portland State, St. Mary's, San Diego, San Francisco, and Santa Clara.

PRO FOOTBALL

National Football League

League Office
280 Park Ave.
New York, NY 10017
212-450-2000

NFL Management Council
280 Park Ave.
New York, NY 10017
212-450-2000

NFL Players Association
2021 L Street NW, Suite 600
Washington, DC 20036
202-463-2200

AFC

Baltimore Ravens
11001 Owings Mills Blvd.
Owings Mills, MD 21117
410-654-6200

Buffalo Bills
One Bills Drive
Orchard Park, NY 14127
716-648-1800

Cincinnati Bengals
One Bengals Drive
Cincinnati, OH 45204
513-621-3550

Cleveland Browns
76 Lou Groza Blvd.
Berea, OH 44017
440-891-5000

Denver Broncos
13655 Broncos Pkwy.
Englewood, CO 80112
303-649-9000

Indianapolis Colts
7001 W. 56th St.
Indianapolis, IN 46254
317-297-2658

Jacksonville Jaguars
One Stadium Place
Jacksonville, FL 32202
904-633-6000

Kansas City Chiefs
One Arrowhead Drive
Kansas City, MO 64129
816-920-9300

Miami Dolphins
7500 SW 30th St.
David, FL 33314
954-452-7000

New England Patriots
Foxboro Stadium
Route 1
Foxboro, MA 02035
508-543-8200

New York Jets
1000 Fulton Ave.
Hempstead, NY 11550
516-560-8100

Oakland Raiders
1220 Harbor Bay Pkwy.
Alameda, CA 94502
510-864-5000

Pittsburgh Steelers
Three Rivers Stadium
300 Stadium Circle
Pittsburgh, PA 15212
412-323-0300

San Diego Chargers
4020 Murphy Canyon Rd.
San Diego, CA 92123
619-874-4500

Seattle Seahawks
11220 N.E. 53rd St.
Kirkland, WA 98033
425-827-9777

Tennessee Titans
7640 Hwy. 70 South
Nashville, TN 37228
615-656-4000

NFC

Arizona Cardinals
8701 S. Hardy Dr.
Tempe, AZ 85284
602-379-0101

Atlanta Falcons
One Falcon Place
Suwanee, GA 30174
770-945-1111

Carolina Panthers
800 South Mint St.
Charlotte, NC 28202-1502
704-358-7000

Chicago Bears
Halas Hall
1000 Football Drive
Lake Forest, IL 60045
847-295-6600

Dallas Cowboys
Cowboys Center
One Cowboys Pkwy.
Irving, TX 75063
972-556-9900

Detroit Lions
Pontiac Silverdome
1200 Featherstone Rd.
Pontiac, MI 48342
248-335-4131

Green Bay Packers
1265 Lombardi Ave.
Green Bay, WI 54304
920-496-5700

Minnesota Vikings
9520 Viking Drive
Eden Prairie, MN 55344
612-828-6500

New Orleans Saints
5800 Airline Drive
Metairie, LA 70003
504-733-0255

New York Giants
Giants Stadium
East Rutherford, NJ 07073
201-935-8111

Philadelphia Eagles
Veterans Stadium
3501 S. Broad St.
Philadelphia, PA 19148
215-463-2500

St. Louis Rams
One Rams Way
St. Louis, MO 63045
314-982-7267

San Francisco 49ers
4949 Centennial Blvd.
Santa Clara, CA 95054
408-562-4949

Tampa Bay Buccaneers
One Buccaneer Place
Tampa, FL 33607
813-870-2700

Washington Redskins
Redskin Park
21300 Redskin Park Drive
Washington, DC 20041
703-478-8900

GOLF

LPGA Tour
(Ladies Professional Golf
    Association)
100 International Golf Drive
Daytona Beach, FL 32124
904-274-6200

PGA of America
100 Avenue of the Champions
Palm Beach Gardens, FL 33410
561-624-8400

PGA European Tour
Wentworth Drive, Virginia Water
Surrey, England GU25 4LX
011-44-1344-842881

PGA Tour
112 PGA Tour Blvd.
Ponte Vedra, FL 32082
904-285-3700

Royal & Ancient Golf
    Club of St. Andrews
St. Andrews, Fife
Scotland KY16 9JD
011-44-1334-472112

USGA
(United States Golf Association)
P.O. Box 708, Liberty Corner Road
Far Hills, NJ 07931
908-234-2300

PRO HOCKEY

NHL–National Hockey League

League Offices

Montreal
1800 McGill College Ave.,
    Suite 2600
Montreal, Quebec, Canada
    H3A 3J6
514-288-9220

New York
1251 Sixth Ave., 47th Floor
New York, NY 10020
212-789-2000

Toronto
1 International Blvd.
Rexdale, Ontario, Canada
    M9W 6L9
416-981-2777

NHL Players' Association
777 Bay St.,
    Suite 2400
P.O. Box 121
Toronto, Ontario, Canada
    M5G 2C8
416-408-4040

Mighty Ducks of Anaheim
2695 E. Katella Ave.
Anaheim, CA 92806
714-940-2900

Atlanta Thrashers
1 CNN Center
13th S. Tower
Atlanta, GA 30303
404-584-7825

Boston Bruins
1 Fleet Center, Suite 250
Boston, MA 02114
617-624-1900

Buffalo Sabres
Marine Midland Arena
One Seymour H. Knox III Plaza
Buffalo, NY 14203-3096
716-855-4100

Calgary Flames
Canadian Airlines
    Saddledome
P.O. Box 1540 Station M
Calgary, Alberta, Canada
    T2P 3B9
403-777-2177

Carolina Hurricanes
The Raleigh Entertainment
    Sports Arena
1400 Edwards Mill Rd.
Raleigh, NC 27607
919-467-7825

Chicago Blackhawks
United Center
1901 West Madison St.
Chicago, IL 60612
312-455-7000

Colorado Avalanche
Pepsi Center
1000 Chopper Pl.
Denver, CO 80204
303-405-1100

Dallas Stars
211 Cowboys Pkwy.
Irving, TX 75063
972-868-2890

Detroit Red Wings
Joe Louis Sports Arena
600 Civic Center Drive
Detroit, MI 48226
313-396-7544

Edmonton Oilers
11230-110th St.
Edmonton, Alberta, Canada
    T5G 3H7
614-414-4000

Florida Panthers
National Car Rental Center
1 Panther Pkwy.
Sunrise, FL 33323
954-835-7000

Los Angeles Kings
Staples Center
555 N. Nash St.
El Segundo, CA 90245
310-419-3160

Montreal Canadiens
Molson Centre
1260 Rue de la
    Gauchetiere West
Montreal, Quebec, Canada
    H3B 5E8
514-932-2582

Nashville Predators
501 Broadway
Nashville, TN 57203
615-770-2300

New Jersey Devils
Continental Airlines Arena
P.O. Box 504
East Rutherford, NJ 07073
201-935-6050

New York Islanders
Nassau Veterans' Memorial
    Coliseum
Uniondale, NY 11553
516-794-4100

New York Rangers
Madison Square Garden
2 Penn Plaza, 14th Floor
New York, NY 10121
212-465-6486

Ottawa Senators
1000 Palladium Dr.
Kanata, Ontario, Canada K2V 1A5
613-599-0250

Philadelphia Flyers
First Union Center
3601 S. Broad St.
Philadelphia, PA 19148
215-465-4500

Phoenix Coyotes
Cellular One Ice Den
9375 E. Bell Rd.
Scottsdale, AZ 85260
602-473-5600

Pittsburgh Penguins
Civic Arena
66 Mario Lemieux Place
Pittsburgh, PA 15219
412-642-1800

St. Louis Blues
Kiel Center
1401 Clark Ave.
St. Louis, MO 63103
314-622-2500

San Jose Sharks
525 West Santa Clara St.
San Jose, CA 95113
408-287-7070

Tampa Bay Lightning
Ice Palace
401 Channelside Drive
Tampa, FL 33602
813-301-6500

Toronto Maple Leafs
Air Canada Centre
40 Bay St., Suite 500
Toronto, Ontario, Canada
    M5J 2X2
416-815-5500

Vancouver Canucks
General Motors Place
800 Griffiths Way
Vancouver, B.C., Canada
    V5K 3N7
604-899-4600

Washington Capitals
MCI Center
601 F St. NW
Washington, D.C. 20004
202-628-3200

AHL

American Hockey League
One Monarch Place
Springfield, MA 01144
413-781-2030

IHL

International Hockey League
1395 E. Twelve Mile Rd.
Madison Heights, MI 48701
248-546-3230

IIHF

International Ice Hockey
    Federation Parkring 11
CH-8002 Zurich, Switzerland
011-411-289-8600

SOCCER

FIFA

Federation Internationale de
    Football Assn.
P.O. Box 85
0830 Zurich, Switzerland
011-41-1-384-9595

MLS

Major League Soccer
110 E. 42nd St., 10th Floor
New York, NY 10017
212-450-1200

Chicago Fire
311 W. Superior St., #444
Chicago, IL 60610
312-705-7200

Colorado Rapids
555 17th St., Suite 3350
Denver, CO 80202
303-299-1570

Columbus Crew
Columbus Crew Stadium
2121 Velma Ave.
Columbus, OH 43211
614-447-2739

Dallas Burn
2602 McKinney, Suite 200
Dallas, TX 75204
214-979-0303

Kansas City Wizards
706 Broadway St., Suite 706
Kansas City, MO 64105
816-472-4625

Los Angeles Galaxy
1010 Rose Bowl Dr.
Pasadena, CA 91103
626-432-1540

Miami Fusion
2200 Commercial Blvd.,
    Suite 104
Ft. Lauderdale, FL 33309
954-717-2200

New England Revolution
Foxboro Stadium
60 Washington St.
Foxboro, MA 02035
508-543-5001

New York/New Jersey MetroStars
One Harmon Plaza,
    3rd Floor
Secaucus, NJ 07094
201-583-7000

San Jose Clash
3550 Stevens Creek Blvd.,
    Suite 200
San Jose, CA 07094
408-241-9922

Tampa Bay Mutiny
Raymond-James Stadium
4042 N. Himes
Tampa, FL 33607
813-386-2000

Washington D.C. United
13832 Redskin Dr.
Herndon, VA 20171
703-478-6600

OTHER SOCCER

CONCACAF
Confederation of North, Central
    American & Caribbean
    Association of Football
725 Fifth Ave., 17th Floor
New York, NY 10022
212-308-0044

U.S. Soccer
United States Soccer Federation
Soccer House
1801-1811 South Prairie Ave.
Chicago, IL 60616
312-808-1300

NPSL
National Professional League
115 Dewalt Ave. NW, 5th Floor
Canton, OH 44702
330-455-4625

USL
United Soccer League
14497 N. Dale Mabry Hwy.,
    Suite 201
Tampa, FL 33618
813-963-3909

SWIMMING

FINA
Federation Internationale de
    Natation Amateur
9 Ave de Beaumont
1012 Lausanne, Switzerland
011-4121-312-6602

TENNIS

ATP Tour
Association of Tennis
    Professionals
201 ATP Tour Blvd.
Ponte Vedra Beach, FL 32082
904-285-8000

ITF
International Tennis Federation
Palliser Rd., Barons Court
London, England W14 9EN
011-44-181-878-6464

World Team Tennis
445 North Wells,
    Suite 404
Chicago, IL 60610
312-245-5300

USTA
United States Tennis
    Association
70 West Red Oak Lane
White Plains, NY 10604
914-696-7000

WTA Tour
Women's Tennis
    Association
1266 East Main St., 4th Floor
Stamford, CT 06902
203-978-1740

TRACK AND FIELD

IAAF
International Amateur Athletics
    Federation
17 rue Princesse Florestine
BP 359 MC-98007
    Monaco Cedex
377-93-10-8888

USA Track and Field
P.O. Box 120
Indianapolis, IN 46206
317-261-0500

APPENDIX 3

Halls of Fame

INTERNATIONAL TENNIS HALL OF FAME NEWPORT, R.I.

Men

Adee, George   1964
Alexander, Fred   1961
Allison, Wilmer   1963
Alonso, Manuel   1977
Ashe, Arthur   1985
Behr, Karl   1969
Borg, Bjorn   1987
Borotra, Jean   1976
Bromwich, John   1984
Brookes, Norman   1977
Brugnon, Jacques   1976
Budge, Don   1964
Campbell, Oliver   1955
Chace, Malcolm   1961
Clark, Clarence   1983
Clark, Joseph   1955
Clothier, William   1956
Cochet, Henri   1976
Connors, Jimmy   1998
Cooper, Ashley   1991
Crawford, Jack   1979
David, Herman   1998
Doeg, John   1962
Doherty, Lawrence   1980
Doherty, Reginald   1980
Drobny, Jaroslav   1983
Dwight, James   1955
Emerson, Roy   1982

Etchebaster, Pierre   1978
Falkenburg, Bob   1974
Fraser, Neale   1984
Garland, Chuck   1969
Gonzales, Pancho   1968
Grant, Bryan (Bitsy)   1972
Griffin, Clarence   1970
Hackett, Harold   1961
Hewitt, Bob   1992
Hoad, Lew   1980
Hovey, Fred   1974
Hunt, Joe   1966
Hunter, Frank   1961
Johnston, Bill   1958
Jones, Perry   1970
Kodes, Jan   1990
Kramer, Jack   1968
Lacoste, Rene   1976
Larned, William   1956
Larsen, Art   1969
Laver, Rod   1981
Lott, George   1964
Mako, Gene   1973
McEnroe, John   1999
McGregor, Ken   1999
McKinley, Chuck   1986
McLoughlin, Maurice   1957
McMillan, Frew   1992
McNeill, Don   1965
Mulloy, Gardnar   1972
Murray, Lindley   1958
Myrick, Julian   1963
Nastase, Ilie   1991
Newcombe, John   1986
Nielsen, Arthur   1971

Olmedo, Alex   1987
Osuna, Rafael   1979
Parker, Frank   1966
Patterson, Gerald   1989
Patty, Budge   1977
Perry, Fred   1975
Pettitt, Tom   1982
Pietrangeli, Nicola   1986
Quist, Adrian   1984
Ralston, Dennis   1987
Renshaw, Ernest   1983
Renshaw, William   1983
Richards, Vincent   1961
Riggs, Bobby   1967
Roche, Tony   1986
Rosewall, Ken   1980
Santana, Manuel   1984
Savitt, Dick   1976
Schroeder, Ted   1966
Sears, Richard   1955
Sedgman, Frank   1979
Segura, Pancho   1984
Seixas, Vic   1971
Shields, Frank   1964
Slocum, Henry   1955
Smith, Stan   1987
Stolle, Fred   1985
Talbert, Bill   1967
Tilden, Bill   1959
Trabert, Tony   1970
Van Ryn, John   1963
Vilas, Guillermo   1991
Vines, Ellsworth   1962
von Cramm, Gottfried   1977
Ward, Holcombe   1956

Washburn, Watson   1965
Whitman, Malcolm   1955
Wilding, Anthony   1978
Williams, Richard 2nd   1957
Wood, Sidney   1964
Wrenn, Robert   1955
Wright, Beals   1956

Women

Atkinson, Juliette   1974
Austin, Bunny   1997
Austin, Tracy   1992
Barger-Wallach, Maud   1958
Betz Addie, Pauline   1965
Bjurstedt Mallory, Molla   1958
Bowrey, Lesley Turner   1997
Brough Clapp, Louise   1967
Browne, Mary   1957
Bueno, Maria   1978
Cahill, Mabel   1976
Casals, Rosie   1996
Connolly Brinker, Maureen   1968
Dod, Charlotte (Lottie)   1983
Douglass Chambers, Dorothy
   1981
Evert, Chris   1995
Fry Irvin, Shirley   1970
Gibson, Althea   1971
Goolagong Cawley, Evonne   1988
Hansell, Ellen   1965
Hard, Darlene   1973
Hart, Doris   1969
Haydon Jones, Ann   1985
Heldman, Gladys   1979
Hotchkiss Wightman, Hazel
   1957
Jacobs, Helen Hull   1962
King, Billie Jean   1987
Lenglen, Suzanne   1978
Mandlikova, Hana   1994
Marble, Alice   1964
McKane Godfree, Kitty   1978
Moore, Elisabeth   1971
Mortimer Barrett, Angela   1993
Nuthall Shoemaker, Betty   1977
Osborne duPont, Margaret   1967
Palfrey Danzig, Sarah   1963
Roosevelt, Ellen   1975
Round Little, Dorothy   1986
Ryan, Elizabeth   1972
Sears, Eleanora   1968
Smith Court, Margaret   1979
Sutton Bundy, May   1956
Townsend Toulmin, Bertha   1974

Wade, Virginia   1989
Wagner, Marie   1969
Wills Moody Roark, Helen   1959

Contributors

Baker, Lawrence Sr.   1975
Chatrier, Philippe   1992
Collins, Bud   1994
Cullman, Joseph F. 3rd   1990
Danzig, Allison   1968
Davis, Dwight   1956
Gray, David   1985
Gustaf V (King of Sweden)   1980
Hester, W.E. (Slew)   1981
Hopman, Harry   1978
Hunt, Lamar   1993
Laney, Al   1979
Martin, Alastair   1973
Martin, William M.   1982
Maskell, Dan   1996
Outerbridge, Mary   1981
Pell, Theodore   1966
Tingay, Lance   1982
Tinling, Ted   1986
Van Alen, James   1965
Wingfield, Walter Clopton   1997

NATIONAL BASEBALL HALL OF FAME & MUSEUM COOPERSTOWN, N.Y.

Catchers

Bench, Johnny   1989
Berra, Yogi   1972
Bresnahan, Roger   1945
Campanella, Roy   1969
Cochrane, Mickey   1947
Dickey, Bill   1954
Ewing, Buck   1939
Ferrell, Rick   1984
Hartnett, Gabby   1955
Lombardi, Ernie   1986
Schalk, Ray   1955

First Basemen

Anson, Cap   1939
Beckley, Jake   1971
Bottomley, Jim   1974
Brouthers, Dan   1945
Cepeda, Orlando   1999

Chance, Frank   1946
Connor, Roger   1976
Foxx, Jimmie   1951
Gehrig, Lou   1939
Greenberg, Hank   1956
Kelly, George   1973
Killebrew, Harmon   1984
McCovey, Willie   1986
Mize, Johnny   1981
Sisler, George   1939
Terry, Bill   1954

Second basemen

Carew, Rod   1991
Collins, Eddie   1939
Doerr, Bobby   1986
Evers, Johnny   1946
Fox, Nellie   1997
Frisch, Frankie   1947
Gehringer, Charlie   1949
Herman, Billy   1975
Hornsby, Rogers   1942
Lajoie, Nap   1937
Lazzeri, Tony   1991
Morgan, Joe   1990
Robinson, Jackie   1962
Schoendienst, Red   1989

Shortstops

Aparicio, Luis   1984
Appling, Luke   1964
Bancroft, Dave   1971
Banks, Ernie   1977
Boudreau, Lou   1970
Cronin, Joe   1956
Davis, George   1998
Jackson, Travis   1982
Jennings, Hugh   1945
Maranville, Rabbit   1954
Reese, Pee Wee   1984
Rizzuto, Phil   1994
Sewell, Joe   1977
Tinker, Joe   1946
Vaughan, Arky   1985
Wagner, Honus   1936
Wallace, Bobby   1953
Ward, Monte   1964
Yount, Robin   1999

Third basemen

Baker, Frank   1955
Brett, George   1999

Collins, Jimmy   1945
Kell, George   1983
Lindstrom, Fred   1976
Mathews, Eddie   1978
Robinson, Brooks   1983
Schmidt, Mike   1995
Traynor, Pie   1948

Left fielders

Brock, Lou   1985
Burkett, Jesse   1946
Clarke, Fred   1945
Delahanty, Ed   1945
Goslin, Goose   1968
Hafey, Chick   1971
Kelley, Joe   1971
Kiner, Ralph   1975
Manush, Heinie   1964
Medwick, Joe   1968
Musial, Stan   1969
O'Rourke, Jim   1945
Simmons, Al   1953
Stargell, Willie   1988
Wheat, Zack   1959
Williams, Billy   1987
Williams, Ted   1966
Yastrzemski, Carl   1989

Center fielders

Ashburn, Richie   1995
Averill, Earl   1975
Carey, Max   1961
Cobb, Ty   1936
Combs, Earle   1970
DiMaggio, Joe   1955
Doby, Larry   1998
Duffy, Hugh   1945
Hamilton, Billy   1961
Mantle, Mickey   1974
Mays, Willie   1979
Roush, Edd   1962
Snider, Duke   1980
Speaker, Tris   1937
Waner, Lloyd   1967
Wilson, Hack   1979

Right fielders

Aaron, Hank   1982
Clemente, Roberto   1973
Crawford, Sam   1957
Cuyler, Kiki   1968
Flick, Elmer   1963

Heilmann, Harry   1952
Hooper, Harry   1971
Jackson, Reggie   1993
Kaline, Al   1980
Keeler, Willie   1939
Kelly, King   1945
Klein, Chuck   1980
McCarthy, Tommy   1946
Ott, Mel   1951
Rice, Sam   1963
Robinson, Frank   1982
Ruth, Babe   1936
Slaughter, Enos   1985
Thompson, Sam   1974
Waner, Paul   1952
Youngs, Ross   1972

Pitchers

Alexander, Grover   1938
Bender, Chief   1953
Brown, Mordecai   1949
Bunning, Jim   1996
Carlton, Steve   1994
Chesbro, Jack   1946
Clarkson, John   1963
Coveleski, Stan   1969
Dean, Dizzy   1953
Drysdale, Don   1984
Faber, Red   1964
Feller, Bob   1962
Fingers, Rollie   1992
Ford, Whitey   1974
Galvin, Pud   1965
Gibson, Bob   1981
Gomez, Lefty   1972
Grimes, Burleigh   1964
Grove, Lefty   1947
Haines, Jess   1970
Hoyt, Waite   1969
Hubbell, Carl   1947
Hunter, Catfish   1987
Jenkins, Ferguson   1991
Johnson, Walter   1936
Joss, Addie   1978
Keefe, Tim   1964
Koufax, Sandy   1972
Lemon, Bob   1976
Lyons, Ted   1955
Marichal, Juan   1983
Marquard, Rube   1971
Mathewson, Christy   1936
McGinnity, Joe   1946
Niekro, Phil   1997
Newhouser, Hal   1992

Nichols, Kid   1949
Palmer, Jim   1990
Pennock, Herb   1948
Perry, Gaylord   1991
Plank, Eddie   1946
Radbourne, Old Hoss   1939
Rixey, Eppa   1963
Roberts, Robin   1976
Ruffing, Red   1967
Rusie, Amos   1977
Ryan, Nolan   1999
Seaver, Tom   1992
Spahn, Warren   1973
Sutton, Don   1998
Vance, Dazzy   1955
Waddell, Rube   1946
Walsh, Ed   1946
Welch, Mickey   1973
Wilhelm, Hoyt   1985
Willis, Vic   1995
Wynn, Early   1972
Young, Cy   1937

Managers

Alston, Walter   1983
Durocher, Leo   1994
Hanlon, Ned   1996
Harris, Bucky   1975
Huggins, Miller   1964
Lasorda, Tommy   1997
Lopez, Al   1977
Mack, Connie   1937
McCarthy, Joe   1957
McGraw, John   1937
McKechnie, Bill   1962
Robinson, Wilbert   1945
Selee, Frank   1999
Stengel, Casey   1966
Weaver, Earl   1996

Umpires

Barlick, Al   1989
Chylak, Nestor   1999
Conlan, Jocko   1974
Connolly, Tom   1953
Evans, Billy   1973
Hubbard, Cal   1976
Klem, Bill   1953
McGowan, Bill   1992

From Negro Leagues

Bell, Cool Papa (OF)   1974

Charleston, Oscar (1B-OF)   1976
Dandridge, Ray (3B)   1987
Day, Leon (P-OF-2B)   1995
Dihigo, Martin (P-OF)   1977
Foster, Rube (P-MGR)   1981
Foster, Willie (P)   1996
Gibson, Josh (C)   1972
Irvin, Monte (OF)   1973
Johnson, Judy (3B)   1975
Leonard, Buck (1B)   1972
Lloyd, Pop (SS)   1977
Paige, Satchel (P)   1971
Rogan, Wilber (P)   1998
Wells, Willie (SS)   1997
Williams, Joe (P)   1999

Pioneers and Executives

Barrow, Ed   1953
Bulkeley, Morgan   1937
Cartwright, Alexander   1938
Chadwick, Henry   1938
Chandler, Happy   1982
Comiskey, Charles   1939
Cummings, Candy   1939
Frick, Ford   1970
Giles, Warren   1979
Griffith, Clark   1946
Harridge, Will   1972
Hulbert, William   1995
Johnson, Ban   1937
Landis, Kenesaw Mountain   1944
MacPhail, Larry   1978
MacPhail, Lee   1998
Rickey, Branch   1967
Spalding, Al   1939
Veeck, Bill   1991
Weiss, George   1971
Wright, George   1937
Wright, Harry   1953
Yawkey, Tom   1980

NAISMITH MEMORIAL BASKETBALL HALL OF FAME SPRINGFIELD, MASS.

Men

Abdul-Jabbar, Kareem   1995
Archibald, Nate   1991
Arizin, Paul   1977
Barlow, Thomas (Babe)   1980
Barry, Rick   1987

Baylor, Elgin   1976
Beckman, John   1972
Bellamy, Walt   1993
Belov, Sergei   1992
Bing, Dave   1990
Bird, Larry   1998
Borgmann, Benny   1961
Bradley, Bill   1982
Brennan, Joe   1974
Cervi, Al   1984
Chamberlain, Wilt   1978
Cooper, Charles (Tarzan)   1976
Cosic, Kresimir   1996
Cousy, Bob   1970
Cowens, Dave   1991
Cunningham, Billy   1986
Davies, Bob   1969
DeBernardi, Forrest   1961
DeBusschere, Dave   1982
Dehnert, Dutch   1968
Endacott, Paul   1971
English, Alex   1997
Erving, Julius (Dr. J)   1993
Foster, Bud   1964
Frazier, Wilt   1987
Friedman, Marty   1971
Fulks, Joe   1977
Gale, Laddie   1976
Gallatin, Harry   1991
Gates, William (Pop)   1989
Gervin, George   1996
Gola, Tom   1975
Goodrich, Gail   1996
Greer, Hal   1981
Gruenig, Robert   1963
Hagan, Cliff   1977
Hanson, Victor   1960
Havlicek, John   1983
Hawkins, Connie   1992
Hayes, Elvin   1990
Haynes, Marques   1998
Heinsohn, Tom   1986
Holman, Nat   1964
Houbregs, Bob   1987
Howell, Bailey   1997
Hyatt, Chuck   1959
Issel, Dan   1993
Jeannette, Buddy   1994
Johnson, Bill (Skinny)   1976
Johnston, Neil   1990
Jones, K.C.   1989
Jones, Sam   1983
Krause, Edward (Moose)   1975
Kurland, Bob   1961
Lanier, Bob   1992

Lapchick, Joe   1966
Lovellette, Clyde   1988
Lucas, Jerry   1979
Luisetti, Hank   1959
Macauley, Ed   1960
Maravich, Pete   1987
Martin, Slater   1981
McCracken, Branch   1980
McCracken, Jack   1962
McDermott, Bobby   1988
McGuire, Dick   1993
McHale, Kevin   1999
Mikan, George   1959
Mikkelsen, Vern   1995
Monroe, Earl   1990
Murphy, Calvin   1993
Murphy, Charles (Stretch)   1960
Page, Harlan (Pat)   1962
Pettit, Bob   1970
Phillip, Andy   1961
Pollard, Jim   1977
Ramsey, Frank   1981
Reed, Willis   1981
Risen, Arnie   1998
Robertson, Oscar   1979
Roosma, John   1961
Russell, Bill   1974
Russell, John (Honey)   1964
Schayes, Dolph   1972
Schmidt, Ernest J   1973
Schommer, John   1959
Sedran, Barney   1962
Sharman, Bill   1975
Steinmetz, Christian   1961
Thompson, David   1996
Thompson, John (Cat)   1962
Thurmond, Nate   1984
Twyman, Jack   1982
Unseld, Wes   1988
Vandivier, Robert (Fuzzy)   1974
Wachter, Ed   1961
Walton, Bill   1993
Wanzer, Bobby   1987
West, Jerry   1979
Wilkens, Lenny   1989
Wooden, John   1960
Yardley, George   1996

Women

Blazejowski, Carol   1994
Crawford, Joan   1997
Curry, Denise   1997
Donovan, Anne   1995
Harris, Lucy   1992

Lieberman-Cline, Nancy   1996
Meyers, Ann   1993
Miller, Cheryl   1995
Semenova, Juliana   1993
White, Nera   1992

Teams
Buffalo Germans   1961
First Team   1959
New York Renaissance   1963
Original Celtics   1959

Referees
Enright, Jim   1978
Hepbron, George   1960
Hoyt, George   1961
Kennedy, Pat   1959
Leith, Lloyd   1982
Mihalik, Red   1986
Nucatola, John   1977
Quigley, Ernest (Quig)   1961
Shirley, J. Dallas   1979
Strom, Earl   1995
Tobey, Dave   1961
Walsh, David   1961

Coaches
Allen, Forrest (Phog)   1959
Anderson, Harold (Andy)   1984
Auerbach, Red   1968
Barry, Sam   1978
Blood, Ernest (Prof)   1960
Cann, Howard   1967
Carlson, Henry (Doc)   1959
Carnesecca, Lou   1992
Carnevale, Ben   1969
Carril, Pete   1997
Case, Everett   1981
Conradt, Judy   1998
Crum, Denny   1994
Daly, Chuck   1994
Dean, Everett   1966
Diaz-Miguel, Antonio   1997
Diddle, Ed   1971
Drake, Bruce   1972
Gaines, Clarence (Bighouse)   1981
Gardner, Jack   1983
Gill, Amory (Slats)   1967
Gomelsky, Aleksandr   1995
Hannum, Alex   1998
Harshman, Marv   1984

Haskins, Don   1997
Hickey, Eddie   1978
Hobson, Howard (Hobby)   1965
Holzman, Red   1986
Iba, Hank   1968
Julian, Alvin (Doggie)   1967
Keaney, Frank   1960
Keogan, George   1961
Knight, Bob   1991
Kundla, John   1995
Lambert, Ward (Piggy)   1960
Litwack, Harry   1975
Loeffler, Ken   1964
Lonborg, Dutch   1972
McCutchan, Arad   1980
McGuire, Al   1992
McGuire, Frank   1976
Meanwell, Walter (Doc)   1959
Meyer, Ray   1978
Miller, Ralph   1988
Moore, Billie   1999
Nikolic, Aleksandar   1998
Ramsay, Jack   1992
Rubini, Cesare   1994
Rupp, Adolph   1968
Sachs, Leonard   1961
Shelton, Everett   1979
Smith, Dean   1982
Taylor, Fred   1985
Thompson, John   1999
Wade, Margaret   1984
Watts, Stan   1985
Wilkens, Lenny   1998
Wooden, John   1972
Woolpert, Phil   1992

Contributors
Abbott, Senda Berenson   1984
Bee, Clair   1967
Brown, Walter A.   1965
Bunn, John   1964
Douglas, Bob   1971
Duer, Al   1981
Embry, Wayne   1999
Fagen, Clifford B.   1983
Fisher, Harry   1973
Fleisher, Larry   1991
Gottlieb, Eddie   1971
Gulick, Luther   1959
Harrison, Les   1979
Hepp, Ferenc   1980
Hickox, Ed   1959
Hinkle, Tony   1965
Irish, Ned   1964

Jones, R. William   1964
Kennedy, Walter   1980
Liston, Emil (Liz)   1974
McLendon, John   1978
Mokray, Bill   1965
Morgan, Ralph   1959
Morgenweck, Frank (Pop)   1962
Naismith, James   1959
Newell, Pete   1978
O'Brien, John J (Jack)   1961
O'Brien, Larry   1991
Olsen, Harold G.   1959
Podoloff, Maurice   1973
Porter, Henry (HV)   1960
Reid, William A.   1963
Ripley, Elmer   1972
St. John, Lynn W.   1962
Saperstein, Abe   1970
Schabinger, Arthur   1961
Stagg, Amos Alonzo   1959
Stankovic, Boris   1991
Steitz, Ed   1983
Taylor, Chuck   1968
Teague, Bertha   1984
Tower, Oswald   1959
Trester, Arthur (AL)   1961
Wells, Cliff   1971
Wilke, Lou   1982
Zollner, Fred   1999

INTERNATIONAL BOXING HALL OF FAME, CANASTOTA, N.Y.

Modern Era
Ali, Muhammad   1990
Angott, Sammy   1998
Arguello, Alexis   1992
Armstrong, Henry   1990
Basilio, Carmen   1990
Benitez, Wilfredo   1996
Benvenuti, Nino   1992
Berg, Jackie (Kid)   1994
Bivins, Jimmy   1999
Brown, Joe   1996
Burley, Charley   1992
Canto, Miguel   1998
Cerdan, Marcel   1991
Cervantes, Antonio   1998
Charles, Ezzard   1990
Conn, Billy   1990
Elorde, Gabriel (Flash)   1993

Foster, Bob   1990
Frazier, Joe   1990
Fullmer, Gene   1991
Galaxy, Khaosai   1999
Gavilan, Kid   1990
Giardello, Joey   1993
Gomez, Wilfredo   1995
Graham, Billy   1992
Graziano, Rocky   1991
Griffith, Emile   1990
Hagler, Marvelous
        Marvin   1993
Harada, Masahiko (Fighting)
   1995
Jack, Beau   1991
Jenkins, Lew   1999
Jofre, Edre   1992
Johnson, Harold   1993
LaMotta, Jake   1990
Leonard, Sugar Ray   1997
Liston, Sonny   1991
Louis, Joe   1990
Marciano, Rocky   1990
Maxim, Joey   1994
Montgomery, Bob   1995
Monzon, Carlos   1990
Moore, Archie   1990
Muhammad, Matthew
        Saad   1998
Napoles, Jose   1990
Norton, Ken   1992
Olivares, Ruben   1991
Oritz, Carlos   1991
Ortiz, Manuel   1996
Patterson, Floyd   1991
Pedroza, Eusebio   1999
Pep, Willie   1990
Perez, Pascual   1995
Pryor, Aaron   1996
Robinson, Sugar
        Ray   1990
Rodriguez, Luis   1997
Saddler, Sandy   1990
Saldivar, Vicente   1999
Sanchez, Salvador   1991
Schmeling, Max   1992
Spinks, Michael   1994
Tiger, Dick   1991
Torres, Jose   1997
Walcott, Jersey Joe   1990
Williams, Ike   1990
Wright, Chalky   1997
Zale, Tony   1991
Zarate, Carlos   1994
Zivic, Fritzie   1993

Old-Timers

Ambers, Lou   1992
Attell, Abe   1990
Baer, Max   1995
Britton, Jack   1990
Brown, Panama Al   1992
Burns, Tommy   1996
Canzoneri, Tony   1990
Carpentier, Georges   1991
Chocolate, Kid   1991
Choynski, Joe   1998
Corbett, James J.   1990
Coulon, Johnny   1999
Darcy, Les   1993
Delaney, Jack   1996
Dempsey, Jack   1990
Dempsey, Jack (Nonpareil)   1992
Dillon, Jack   1995
Dixon, George   1990
Driscoll, Jim   1990
Dundee, Johnny   1991
Fitzsimmons, Bob   1990
Flowers, Theodore (Tiger)   1993
Gans, Joe   1990
Genaro, Frankie   1998
Gibbons, Mike   1992
Gibbons, Tommy   1993
Greb, Harry   1990
Griffo, Young   1991
Herman, Pete   1997
Jackson, Peter   1990
Jeanette, Joe   1997
Jeffries, James J.   1990
Johnson, Jack   1990
Ketchel, Stanley   1990
Kilbane, Johnny   1995
LaBarba, Fidel   1996
Langford, Sam   1990
Lavigne, George (Kid)   1998
Leonard, Benny   1990
Lewis, John Henry   1994
Lewis, Ted (Kid)   1992
Loughran, Tommy   1991
Lynch, Benny   1998
Mandell, Sammy   1998
McAuliffe, Jack   1995
McCoy, Charles (Kid)   1991
McFarland, Packey   1992
McGovern, Terry   1990
McLarnin, Jimmy   1991
McVey, Sam   1999
Miller, Freddie   1997
Nelson, Battling   1992
O'Brien, Philadelphia Jack   1994
Rosenbloom, Maxie   1993

Ross, Barney   1990
Ryan, Tommy   1991
Sharkey, Jack   1994
Steele, Freddie   1999
Stribling, Young   1996
Tendler, Lew   1999
Tunney, Gene   1990
Villa, Pancho   1994
Walcott, Joe (Barbados)   1991
Walker, Mickey   1990
Welsh, Freddie   1997
Wilde, Jimmy   1990
Williams, Kid   1996
Wills, Harry   1992

Pioneers

Belcher, Jem   1992
Brain, Ben   1994
Broughton, Jack   1990
Burke, James (Deaf)   1992
Bribb, Tom   1991
Donovan, Prof. Mike   1998
Duffy, Paddy   1994
Figg, James   1992
Jackson, Gentleman John   1992
Johnson, Tom   1995
King, Tom   1992
Langham, Nat   1992
Mace, Jem   1990
Mendoza, Daniel   1990
Molineaux, Tom   1997
Morrissey, John   1996
Pearce, Henry   1993
Richmond, Bill   1999
Sam, Dutch   1997
Sayers, Tom   1990
Spring, Tom   1992
Sullivan, John L.   1990
Thompson, William   1991
Ward, Jem   1995

Non-Participants

Andrews, Thomas S.   1992
Arcel, Ray   1991
Arum, Bob   1999
Ballarati, Giuseppe   1999
Blackburn, Jack   1992
Brady, William A.   1998
Brenner, Teddy   1993
Chambers, John Graham   1990
Clancy, Gil   1993
Coffroth, James W.   1991
D'Amato, Cus   1995

Donovan, Arthur   1993
Duff, Mickey   1999
Dundee, Angelo   1992
Dundee, Chris   1994
Dunphy, Don   1998
Duva, Lou   1998
Egan, Pierce   1991
Fleischer, Nat   1990
Fox, Richard K.   1997
Futch, Eddie   1994
Goldman, Charley   1992
Goldstein, Ruby   1994
Goodman, Murray   1999
Humphreys, Joe   1997
Jacobs, Jimmy   1993
Jacobs, Mike   1990
Johnston, Jimmy   1999
Kearns, Jack (Doc)   1990
King, Don   1997
Liebling, A.J.   1992
Lonsdale, Lord   1990
Markson, Harry   1992
Mercante, Arthur   1995
Muldoon, William   1996
Odd, Gilbert   1995
O'Rourke, Tom   1999
Parker, Dan   1996
Parnassus, George   1991
Queensberry, Marquis of   1990
Rickard, Tex   1990
Rudd, Irving   1999
Siler, George   1995
Solomons, Jack   1995
Steward, Emanuel   1996
Taub, Herman   1998
Walker, James J. (Jimmy)   1992

PRO FOOTBALL HALL OF FAME CANTON, OHIO

Quarterbacks
Baugh, Sammy   1963
Blanda, George (also PK)   1981
Bradshaw, Terry   1989
Clark, Dutch   1963
Conzelman, Jimmy   1964
Dawson, Len   1987
Driscoll, Paddy   1965
Fouts, Dan   1993
Graham, Otto   1965
Herber, Arnie   1966

Jurgensen, Sonny   1983
Layne, Bobby   1967
Luckman, Sid   1965
Namath, Joe   1985
Parker, Clarence (Ace)   1972
Starr, Bart   1977
Staubach, Roger   1985
Tarkenton, Fran   1986
Tittle, Y.A.   1971
Unitas, Johnny   1979
Van Brocklin, Norm   1971
Waterfield, Bob   1965

Running Backs
Battles, Cliff   1968
Brown, Jim   1971
Campbell, Earl   1991
Canadeo, Tony   1974
Csonka, Larry   1987
Dickerson, Eric   1999
Dorsett, Tony   1994
Dudley, Bill   1966
Gifford, Frank   1977
Grange, Red   1963
Guyon, Joe   1966
Harris, Franco   1990
Hinkle, Clarke   1964
Hornung, Paul   1986
Johnson, John Henry   1987
Kelly, Leroy   1994
Leemans, Tuffy   1978
Matson, Ollie   1972
McAfee, George   1966
McElhenny, Hugh   1970
McNally, Johnny (Blood)   1963
Moore, Lenny   1975
Motley, Marion   1968
Nagurski, Bronko   1963
Nevers, Ernie   1963
Payton, Walter   1993
Perry, Joe   1969
Riggins, John   1992
Sayers, Gale   1977
Simpson, O.J.   1985
Strong, Ken   1967
Taylor, Jim   1976
Thorpe, Jim   1963
Trippi, Charley   1968
Van Buren, Steve   1965
Walker, Doak   1986

Ends & Wide Receivers
Alworth, Lance   1978

Badgro, Red   1981
Berry, Raymond   1973
Biletnikoff, Fred   1988
Chamberlin, Guy   1965
Ditka, Mike   1988
Fears, Tom   1970
Hewitt, Bill   1971
Hirsch, Elroy (Crazylegs)   1968
Hutson, Don   1963
Joiner, Charlie   1996
Largent, Steve   1995
Lavelli, Dante   1975
Mackey, John   1992
Maynard, Don   1987
McDonald, Tommy   1998
Millner, Wayne   1968
Mitchell, Bobby   1983
Newsome, Ozzie   1999
Pihos, Pete   1970
Smith, Jackie   1994
Taylor, Charley   1984
Warfield, Paul   1983
Winslow, Kellen   1996

Linemen (pre-World War II)
Edwards, Turk (T)   1969
Fortmann, Dan (G)   1985
Healey, Ed (T)   1964
Hein, Mel (C)   1963
Henry, Pete (T)   1963
Hubbard, Cal (T)   1963
Kiesling, Walt (G)   1966
Kinard, Bruiser (T)   1971
Lyman, Link (T)   1964
Michalske, Mike (G)   1964
Musso, George (T-G)   1982
Stydahar, Joe (T)   1967
Trafton, George (C)   1964
Turner, Bulldog (C)   1966
Wojciechowicz, Alex (C)   1968

Offensive Linemen
Bednarik, Chuck (C-LB)   1967
Brown, Roosevelt (T)   1975
Dierdorf, Dan (T)   1996
Gatski, Frank (C)   1985
Gregg, Forrestt (T-G)   1977
Groza, Lou (T-PK)   1974
Hannah, John (G)   1991
Jones, Stan (T-G-DT)   1991
Langer, Jim (C)   1987
Little, Larry (G)   1993
Mack, Tom (G)   1999

McCormack, Mike (T)   1984
Mix, Ron (T-G)   1979
Munoz, Anthony (T)   1998
Otto, Jim (C)   1980
Parker, Jim (G)   1973
Ringo, Jim (C)   1981
St. Clair, Bob (T)   1990
Shaw, Billy (G)   1999
Shell, Art (T)   1989
Stephenson, Dwight (C)   1998
Upshaw, Gene (G)   1987
Webster, Mike (C)   1997

Defensive Linemen

Atkins, Doug   1982
Buchanan, Buck   1990
Creekmur, Lou   1996
Davis, Willie   1981
Donovan, Art   1968
Ford, Len   1976
Greene, Jon   1987
Jones, Deacon   1980
Jordan, Henry   1995
Lily, Bob   1980
Marchetti, Gino   1972
Nomellini, Leo   1969
Olsen, Merlin   1982
Page, Alan   1988
Robustelli, Andy   1971
Selmon, Lee Roy   1995
Stautner, Ernie   1969
Weinmeister, Arnie   1984
White, Randy   1994
Willis, Bill   1977

Linebackers

Bell, Bobby   1983
Butkus, Dick   1979
Connor, George (DT-OT)   1975
George, Bill   1974
Ham, Jack   1988
Hendricks, Ted   1990
Huff, Sam   1982
Lambert, Jack   1990
Lanier, Willie   1986
Nitschke, Ray   1978
Schmidt, Joe   1973
Singletary, Mike   1998
Taylor, Lawrence   1999

Defensive Backs

Adderley, Herb   1980

Barney, Lem   1992
Blount, Mel   1989
Brown, Willie   1984
Christiansen, Jack   1970
Haynes, Mike   1997
Houston, Ken   1986
Johnson, Jimmy   1994
Krause, Paul   1998
Lane, Dick (Night
    Train)   1974
Lary, Yale   1979
Renfro, Mel   1996
Tunnell, Emlen   1967
Wilson, Larry   1978
Wood, Willie   1989

Placekicker

Stenerud, Jan   1991

Coaches

Brown, Paul   1967
Ewbank, Weeb   1978
Flaherty, Ray   1976
Gibbs, Joe   1996
Gillman, Sid   1983
Grant, Bud   1994
Halas, George   1963
Lambeau, Curly   1963
Landry, Tom   1990
Lombardi, Vince   1971
Neale, Earle (Greasy)   1969
Noll, Chuck   1993
Owen, Steve   1966
Shula, Don   1997
Walsh, Bill   1993

Contributors

Bell, Bert   1963
Bidwill, Charles   1967
Carr, Joe   1963
Davis, Al   1992
Finks, Jim   1995
Halas, George   1963
Hunt, Lamar   1972
Mara, Tim   1963
Mara, Wellington   1997
Marshall, George   1963
Ray, Hugh (Shorty)   1966
Reeves, Dan   1967
Rooney, Art   1964
Rozelle, Pete   1985
Schramm, Tex   1991

HOCKEY HALL OF FAME TORONTO, ONTARIO, CANADA

Forwards

Abel, Sid   1969
Adams, Jack   1959
Apps, Syl   1961
Armstrong, George   1975
Bailey, Ace   1975
Bain, Dan   1945
Baker, Hobey   1945
Barber, Bill   1990
Barry, Marty   1965
Bathgate, Andy   1978
Bauer, Bobby   1996
Beliveau, Jean   1972
Bentley, Doug   1964
Bentley, Max   1966
Blake, Toe   1966
Bossy, Mike   1991
Boucher, Frank   1958
Bowie, Dubbie   1945
Broadbent, Punch   1962
Bucyk, John (Chief)   1981
Burch, Billy   1974
Clarke, Bobby   1987
Colville, Neil   1967
Conacher, Charlie   1961
Conacher, Roy   1998
Cook, Bill   1952
Cook, Bun   1995
Cournoyer, Yvan   1982
Cowley, Bill   1968
Crawford, Rusty   1962
Darragh, Jack   1962
Davidson, Scotty   1950
Day, Hap   1961
Delvecchio, Alex   1977
Denneny, Cy   1959
Dionne, Marcel   1992
Drillon, Gordie   1975
Drinkwater, Graham   1950
Dumart, Woody   1992
Dunderdale, Tommy   1974
Dye, Babe   1970
Esposito, Phil   1984
Farrell, Arthur   1965
Foyston, Frank   1958
Frederickson, Frank   1958
Gainey, Bob   1992
Gardner, Jimmy   1962
Geoffrion, Bernie   1972

Gerard, Eddie   1945
Gilbert, Rod   1982
Gilmour, Billy   1962
Goulet, Michel   1998
Gretzky, Wayne   1999
Griffis, Si   1950
Hay, George   1958
Hextall, Bryan   1969
Hooper, Tom   1962
Howe, Gordie   1972
Howe, Syd   1965
Hull, Bobby   1983
Hyland, Harry   1962
Irvin, Dick   1958
Jackson, Busher   1971
Joliat, Aurel   1947
Keats, Duke   1958
Kennedy, Ted (Teeder)   1966
Keon, Dave   1986
Lach, Elmer   1966
Lafleur, Guy   1988
Lalonde, Newsy   1950
Laprade, Edgar   1993
Lemaire, Jacques   1984
Lemieux, Mario   1997
Lewis, Herbie   1989
Lindsay, Ted   1966
MacKay, Mickey   1952
Mahovlich, Frank   1981
Malone, Joe   1950
Marshall, Jack   1965
Maxwell, Fred   1962
McDonald, Lanny   1992
McGee, Frank   1945
McGimsie, Billy   1962
Mikita, Stan   1983
Moore, Dickie   1974
Morenz, Howie   1945
Mosienko, Bill   1965
Nighbor, Frank   1947
Noble, Reg   1962
O'Connor, Buddy   1988
Oliver, Harry   1967
Olmstead, Bert   1985
Patrick, Lynn   1980
Perreault, Gilbert   1990
Phillips, Tom   1945
Primeau, Joe   1963
Pulford, Bob   1991
Rankin, Frank   1961
Ratelle, Jean   1985
Richard, Henri   1979
Richard, Maurice (Rocket)   1961
Richardson, George   1950
Roberts, Gordie   1971

Russel, Blair   1965
Russell, Ernie   1965
Ruttan, Jack   1962
Scanlan, Fred   1965
Schmidt, Milt   1961
Schriner, Sweeney   1962
Seibert, Oliver   1961
Sittler, Darryl   1989
Smith, Alf   1962
Smith, Clint   1991
Smith, Hooley   1972
Smith, Tommy   1973
Stanley, Barney   1962
Stastny, Peter   1998
Stewart, Nels   1962
Stuart, Bruce   1961
Taylor, Fred (Cyclone)   1947
Trihey, Harry   1950
Trottier, Bryan   1997
Ullman, Norm   1982
Walker, Jack   1960
Walsh, Marty   1962
Watson, Harry   1994
Watson, Harry (Moose)   1962
Weiland, Cooney   1971
Westwick, Harry (Rat)   1962
Whitcroft, Fred   1962

Goaltenders

Benedict, Clint   1965
Bower, Johnny   1976
Brimsek, Frankie   1966
Broda, Turk   1967
Cheevers, Gerry   1985
Connell, Alex   1958
Dryden, Ken   1983
Durnan, Bill   1964
Esposito, Tony   1988
Gardiner, Chuck   1945
Giacomin, Eddie   1987
Hainsworth, George   1961
Hall, Glenn   1975
Hern, Riley   1962
Holmes, Hap   1972
Hutton, J.B. (Bouse)   1962
Lehman, Hughie   1958
LeSueur, Percy   1961
Lumley, Harry   1980
Moran, Paddy   1958
Parent, Bernie   1984
Plante, Jacques   1978
Rayner, Chuck   1973
Sawchuk, Terry   1971
Smith, Billy   1993

Thompson, Tiny   1959
Tretiak, Vladislav   1989
Vezina, Georges   1945
Worsley, Gump   1980
Worters, Roy   1969

Defensemen

Boivin, Leo   1986
Boon, Dickie   1952
Bouchard, Butch   1966
Boucher, George   1960
Cameron, Harry   1962
Clancy, King   1958
Clapper, Dit   1947
Cleghorn, Sprague   1958
Conacher, Lionel   1994
Coulter, Art   1974
Dutton, Red   1958
Flaman, Fernie   1990
Gadsby, Bill   1970
Gardiner, Herb   1958
Goheen, F.X. (Moose)   1952
Goodfellow, Ebbie   1963
Grant, Mike   1950
Green, Wilf (Shorty)   1962
Hall, Joe   1961
Harvey, Doug   1973
Horner, Red   1965
Horton, Tim   1977
Howell, Harry   1979
Johnson, Ching   1958
Johnson, Ernie   1952
Johnson, Tom   1970
Kelly, Red   1969
Laperriere, Jacques   1987
Lapointe, Guy   1993
Laviolette, Jack   1962
Mantha, Sylvio   1960
McNamara, George   1958
Orr, Bobby   1979
Park, Brad   1988
Patrick, Lester   1947
Pilote, Pierre   1975
Pitre, Didier   1962
Potvin, Denis   1991
Pratt, Babe   1966
Pronovost, Marcel   1978
Pulford, Harvey   1945
Quackenbush, Bill   1976
Reardon, Kenny   1966
Robinson, Larry   1995
Ross, Art   1945
Salming, Borje   1996
Savard, Serge   1986

Seibert, Earl   1963
Shore, Eddie   1947
Simpson, Joe   1962
Stanley, Allan   1981
Stewart, Jack   1964
Stuart, Hod   1945
Wilson, Gordon (Phat)   1962

Referees and Linesmen

Armstrong, Neil   1991
Ashley, John   1981
Chadwick, Bill   1964
D'Amico, John   1993
Elliott, Chaucer   1961
Hayes, George   1988
Hewitson, Bobby   1963
Ion, Mickey   1961
Pavelich, Matt   1987
Rodden, Mike   1962
Smeaton, J. Cooper   1961
Storey, Red   1967
Udvari, Frank   1973
van Hellemond, Andy   1999

Builders

Adams, Charles   1960
Adams, Weston W., Sr.   1972
Ahearn, Frank   1962
Ahearne, J.F. (Bunny)   1977
Allan, Sir Montagu   1945
Allen, Keith   1992
Arbour, Al   1996
Ballard, Harold   1977
Bauer, Fr. David   1989
Bickell, J.P.   1978
Bowman, Scotty   1991
Brown, George   1961
Brown, Walter   1962
Buckland, Frank   1975
Butterfield, Jack   1980
Calder, Frank   1945
Campbell, Angus   1964
Campbell, Clarence   1966
Cattarinich, Joseph   1977
Dandurand, Leo   1963
Dilio, Frank   1964
Dudley, George   1958
Dunn, James   1968
Francis, Emile   1982
Gibson, Jack   1976
Gorman, Tommy   1963
Griffiths, Frank A.   1993
Hanley, Bill   1986

Hay, Charles   1984
Hendy, Jim   1968
Hewitt, Foster   1965
Hewitt, W.A.   1945
Hume, Fred   1962
Imlach, Punch   1984
Ivan, Tommy   1964
Jennings, Bill   1975
Johnson, Bob   1992
Juckes, Gordon   1979
Kilpatrick, John   1960
Knox, Seymour III   1993
Leader, Al   1969
LeBel, Bob   1970
Lockhart, Tom   1965
Loicq, Paul   1961
Mariucci, John   1985
Mathers, Frank   1992
McLaughlin, Frederic   1963
Milford, Jake   1984
Molson, Hartland   1973
Morrison, Ian (Scotty)   1999
Murray, Athol (Pere)   1998
Nelson, Francis   1945
Norris, Bruce   1969
Norris, James D.   1962
Norris, James, Sr.   1958
Northey, William   1945
O'Brien, J.A.   1962
O'Neill, Brian   1994
Page, Fred   1993
Patrick, Frank   1958
Pickard, Allan   1958
Pilous, Rudy   1985
Poile, Bud   1990
Pollock, Sam   1978
Raymond, Donat   1958
Robertson, John Ross   1945
Robinson, Claude   1945
Ross, Philip   1976
Sather, Glen   1997
Sebetzki, Gunther   1995
Selke, Frank   1960
Sinden, Harry   1983
Smith, Frank   1962
Smythe, Conn   1958
Snider, Ed   1988
Stanley, Lord of Preston   1945
Sutherland, James   1945
Tarasov, Anatoli   1974
Torrey, Bill   1995
Turner, Lloyd   1958
Tutt, William Thayer   1978
Voss, Carl   1974
Waghorne, Fred   1961

Wirtz, Arthur   1971
Wirtz, Bill   1976
Ziegler, John   1987

MOTORSPORTS HALL OF FAME OF AMERICA NOVI, MICH.

Drivers

Allison, Bobby   1992
Andretti, Mario   1990
Arfons, Art   1991
Baker, Cannonball   1989
Bettenhausen, Tony   1997
Brabham, Jack   1998
Breedlove, Craig   1993
Bryan, Jimmy   1999
Campbell, Sir Malcolm   1994
Cantrell, Bill   1992
Chenoweth, Dean   1991
Chrisman, Art   1997
Clark, Jim   1990
Cook, Betty   1996
Cunningham, Briggs   1997
Davis, Jim   1997
DeCoster, Roger   1994
DePalma, Ralph   1992
DePaolo, Peter   1995
Donahue, Mark   1990
Follmer, George   1999
Foyt, A.J.   1989
Garlits, Don   1989
Glidden, Bob   1994
Gurney, Dan   1991
Hanauer, Chip   1995
Hart, C.J.   1999
Hill, Phil   1989
Holbert, Al   1993
Horn, Ted   1993
Jarrett, Ned   1997
Jenkins, Bill (Grumpy)   1996
Johnson, Junior   1991
Jones, Parnelli   1992
Kalitta, Connie   1992
Kurtis, Frank   1999
Leonard, Joe   1991
Lockhart, Frank   1999
McLaren, Bruce   1995
Mann, Dick   1993
Markle, Bart   1999
Mays, Rex   1995
Mears, Rick   1998
Meyer, Louis   1993

Muldowney, Shirley   1990
Muncy, Bill   1989
Musson, Ron   1993
Nordskog, Bob   1997
Oldfield, Barney   1989
Parks, Wally   1993
Pearson, David   1993
Petrali, Joe   1992
Petty, Lee   1996
Petty, Richard   1989
Prudhomme, Don   1991
Revson, Peter   1996
Roberts, Fireball   1995
Roberts, Kenny   1990
Rutherford, Johnny   1996
Seebold, Bill   1999
Shaw, Wilbur   1991
Slock, Tim   1999
Smith, Malcolm   1996
Thompson, Mickey   1990
Unser, Al   1991
Vukovich, Bill, Sr.   1992
Ward, Rodger   1995
Wood, Gar   1990
Yarborough, Cale   1994

Pilots

Cochran, Jacqueline   1993
Curtiss, Glenn   1990
Doolittle, Jimmy   1989
Earhart, Amelia   1992
Falck, Bill   1994
Greenmoyer, Darryl   1997
Shelton, Lyle   1999
Turner, Roscoe   1991

Contributors

Agajanian, J.C.   1992
Bignotti, George   1993
Black, Keith   1995
Chapman, Colin   1997
Chevrolet, Louis   1995
Duesenberg, Fred   1997
Economacki, Chris   1994
Ford, Henry   1996
France, Bill, Sr.   1990
Hall, Jim   1994
Hulman, Tony   1991
Little, Bernie   1994
Miller, Harry   1999
Penske, Roger   1995
Rickenbacker, Eddie   1994
Rose, Mauri   1996

Shelby, Carroll   1992
Watson, A.J.   1996

INTERNATIONAL MOTORSPORTS HALL OF FAME TALLADEGA, ALA.

Allison, Bobby   1993
Allison, Davey   1998
Ascari, Alberto   1992
Baker, Buck   1990
Bettenhausen, Tony   1991
Brabham, Jack   1990
Campbell, Sir Malcolm   1990
Caracciola, Rudolph   1998
Clark, Jim   1990
DePalma, Ralph   1991
Donahue, Mark   1990
Evans, Richie   1996
Fangio, Juan Manuel   1990
Flock, Tim   1991
Gregg, Peter   1992
Gurney, Dan   1990
Haley, Donald   1996
Hill, Graham   1990
Hill, Phil   1991
Holbert, Al   1993
Isaac, Bobby   1996
Jarrett, Ned   1991
Johncock, Gordon   1999
Johnson, Junior   1990
Jones, Parnelli   1990
Lauda, Niki   1993
Lorenzen, Fred   1991
Lund, Tiny   1994
Mays, Rex   1993
McLaren, Bruce   1991
Meyer, Louis   1992
Moss, Stirling   1990
Nuvolari, Tazio   1998
Oldfield, Barney   1990
Parsons, Benny   1994
Pearson, David   1993
Petty, Lee   1990
Prost, Alain   1999
Roberts, Fireball   1990
Roberts, Kenny   1992
Rose, Mauri   1994
Rutherford, Johnny   1996
Scott, Wendell   1999
Shaw, Wilbur   1991
Smith, Louise   1999

Stewart, Jackie   1990
Surtees, John   1996
Thomas, Herb   1994
Turner, Curtis   1992
Unser, Al, Sr.   1998
Vukovich, Bill   1991
Ward, Rodger   1992
Weatherly, Joe   1994
Yaborough, Cale   1993

Contributors

Bignotti, George   1993
Champman, Colin   1994
Chevrolet, Louis   1992
Ferrari, Enzo   1994
Ford, Henry   1993
France, Bill Sr.   1990
Granatelli, Andy   1992
Hulman, Tony   1990
Hyde, Harry   1999
Marcum, John   1994
Matthews, Banjo   1998
Moody, Ralph   1994
Parks, Wally   1992
Penske, Roger   1998
Porsche, Ferdinand   1996
Rickenbacker, Eddie   1992
Shelby, Carroll   1991
Thompson, Mickey   1990
Yunick, Smokey   1990

WORLD GOLF HALL OF FAME JACKSONVILLE, FLA.

Men

Anderson, Willie   1975
Armour, Tommy   1976
Ball, John, Jr.   1977
Ballesteros, Seve   1999
Barnes, Jim   1989
Boros, Julius   1982
Braid, James   1976
Casper, Billy   1978
Cooper, Lighthorse Harry   1992
Cotton, Thomas   1980
Demaret, Jimmy   1983
De Vicenzo, Roberto   1989
Evans, Chick   1975
Faldo, Nick   1998
Floyd, Ray   1989
Guldahl, Ralph   1981

Hagen, Walter   1974
Hilton, Harold   1978
Hogan, Ben   1974
Irwin, Hale   1992
Jones, Bobby   1974
Little, Lawson   1980
Littler, Gene   1990
Locke, Bobby   1977
Mangrum, Lloyd   1999
Middlecoff, Cary   1986
Miller, Johnny   1998
Morris, Tom, Jr.   1975
Morris, Tom, Sr.   1976
Nelson, Byron   1974
Nicklaus, Jack   1974
Ouimet, Francis   1974
Palmer, Arnold   1974
Player, Gary   1974
Runyan, Paul   1990
Sarazen, Gene   1974
Smith, Horton   1990
Snead, Sam   1974
Taylor, John H.   1975
Thomson, Peter   1988
Travers, Jerry   1976
Travis, Walter   1979
Trevino, Lee   1981
Vardon, Harry   1974
Watson, Tom   1988

Women
Alcott, Amy   1999
Berg, Patty   1974
Bradley, Pat   1991
Carner, JoAnne   1985
Daniel, Beth   1999
Haynie, Sandra   1977
Howe, Dorothy C.H.   1978
Jameson, Betty   1951
King, Betsy   1995
Lopez, Nancy   1989
Mann, Carol   1977
Rawls, Betsy   1987
Sheehan, Patty   1993
Suggs, Louise   1979
Vare, Glenna Collett   1975
Wethered, Joyce   1975
Whitworth, Kathy   1982
Wright, Mickey   1976
Zaharias, Babe Didrikson   1974

Contributors
Campbell, William   1990

Corcoran, Fred   1975
Crosby, Bing   1978
Dey, Joe   1975
Graffis, Herb   1977
Harlow, Robert   1988
Hope, Bob   1983
Jones, Robert Trent   1987
Roberts, Clifford   1978
Rodriguez, Chi Chi   1992
Ross, Donald   1977
Shore, Dinah   1994
Tufts, Richard   1992

AWARDS

ASSOCIATED PRESS ATHLETES OF THE YEAR

Male
1931   Pepper Martin, baseball
1932   Gene Sarazen, golf
1933   Carl Hubbell, baseball
1934   Dizzy Dean, baseball
1935   Joe Louis, boxing
1936   Jesse Owens, track
1937   Don Budge, tennis
1938   Don Budge, tennis
1939   Nile Kinnick, college football
1940   Tom Harmon, college football
1941   Joe DiMaggio, baseball
1942   Frank Sinkwich, college football
1943   Gunder Haegg, track
1944   Byron Nelson, golf
1945   Byron Nelson, golf
1946   Glenn Davis, college football
1947   Johnny Lujack, college football
1948   Lou Boudreau, baseball
1949   Leon Hart, college football
1950   Jim Konstanty, baseball
1951   Dick Kazmaier, college football
1952   Bob Mathias, track
1953   Ben Hogan, golf
1954   Willie Mays, baseball
1955   Hopalong Cassady, college football

1956   Mickey Mantle, baseball
1957   Ted Williams, baseball
1958   Herb Elliott, track
1959   Ingemar Johansson, boxing
1960   Rafer Johnson, track
1961   Roger Maris, baseball
1962   Maury Wills, baseball
1963   Sandy Koufax, baseball
1964   Don Schollander, swimming
1965   Sandy Koufax, baseball
1966   Frank Robinson, baseball
1967   Carl Yastrzemski, baseball
1968   Denny McLain, baseball
1969   Tom Seaver, baseball
1970   George Blanda, pro football
1971   Lee Trevino, golf
1972   Mark Spitz, swimming
1973   O.J. Simpson, pro football
1974   Muhammad Ali, boxing
1975   Fred Lynn, baseball
1976   Bruce Jenner, track
1977   Steve Cauthen, horse racing
1978   Ron Guidry, baseball
1979   Willie Stargell, baseball
1980   U.S. Olympic hockey team
1981   John McEnroe, tennis
1982   Wayne Gretzky, hockey
1983   Carl Lewis, track
1984   Carl Lewis, track
1985   Dwight Gooden, baseball
1986   Larry Bird, pro basketball
1987   Ben Johnson, track
1988   Orel Hershiser, baseball
1989   Joe Montana, pro football
1990   Joe Montanta, pro football
1991   Michael Jordan, pro basketball
1992   Michael Jordan, pro basketball
1993   Michael Jordan, pro basketball
1994   George Foreman, boxing
1995   Cal Ripken, Jr., baseball
1996   Michael Johnson, track
1997   Tiger Woods, golf
1998   Mark McGwire, baseball
1999   Tiger Woods, golf
2000   Tiger Woods, golf

Female
1931   Helene Madison, swimming
1932   Babe Didrikson, track

1933	Helen Jacobs, tennis
1934	Virginia Van Wie, golf
1935	Helen Wills Moody, tennis
1936	Helen Stephens, track
1937	Katherine Rawls, swimming
1938	Patty Berg, golf
1939	Alice Marble, tennis
1940	Alice Marble, tennis
1941	Betty Hicks Newell, golf
1942	Gloria Callen, swimming
1943	Patty Berg, golf
1944	Ann Curtis, swimming
1945	Babe Didrikson Zaharias, golf
1946	Babe Didrikson Zaharias, golf
1947	Babe Didrikson Zaharias, golf
1948	Fanny Blankers-Koen, track
1949	Marlene Bauer, golf
1950	Babe Didrikson Zaharias, golf
1951	Maureen Connolly, tennis
1952	Maureen Connolly, tennis
1953	Maureen Connolly, tennis
1954	Babe Didrikson Zaharias, golf
1955	Patty Berg, golf
1956	Pat McCormick, diving
1957	Althea Gibson, tennis
1958	Althea Gibson, tennis
1959	Maria Bueno, tennis
1960	Wilma Rudolph, track
1961	Wilma Rudolph, track
1962	Dawn Fraser, swimming
1963	Mickey Wright, golf
1964	Mickey Wright, golf
1965	Kathy Whitworth, golf
1966	Kathy Whitworth, golf
1967	Billie Jean King, tennis
1968	Peggy Fleming, skating
1969	Debbie Meyer, swimming
1970	Chi Cheng, track
1971	Evonne Goolagong, tennis
1972	Olga Korbut, gymnastics
1973	Billie Jean King, tennis
1974	Chris Evert, tennis
1975	Chris Evert, tennis
1976	Nadia Comaneci, gymnastics
1977	Chris Evert, tennis
1978	Nancy Lopez, golf
1979	Tracy Austin, tennis
1980	Chris Evert Lloyd, tennis
1981	Tracy Austin, tennis
1982	Mary Decker Tabb, track
1983	Martina Navratilova, tennis
1984	Mary Lou Retton, gymnastics
1985	Nancy Lopez, golf
1986	Martina Navratilova, tennis
1987	Jackie Joyner-Kersee, track
1988	Florence Griffith Joyner, track
1989	Steffi Graf, tennis
1990	Beth Daniel, golf
1991	Monica Seles, tennis
1992	Monica Seles, tennis
1993	Sheryl Swoopes, basketball
1994	Bonnie Blair, speed skating
1995	Rebecca Lobo, college basketball
1996	Amy Van Dyken, swimming
1997	Martina Hingis, tennis
1998	Se Ri Pak, golf
1999	U.S. Soccer Team
2000	Marion Jones, track

JAMES E. SULLIVAN MEMORIAL AWARD

Presented annually by the Amateur Athletic Union since 1930, the Sullivan Award is named after the former AAU president and given to the athlete, who "by his or her performance, example and influence as an amateur, has done the most during the year to advance the cause of sportsmanship." An athlete cannot win the award more than once.

1930	Bobby Jones, golf
1931	Barney Berlinger, track
1932	Jim Bausch, track
1933	Glenn Cunningham, track
1934	Bill Bonthron, track
1935	Lawson Little, golf
1936	Glenn Morris, track
1937	Don Budge, tennis
1938	Don Lash, track
1939	Joe Burk, rowing
1940	Greg Rice, track
1941	Leslie MacMitchell, track
1942	Cornelius Warmerdam, track
1943	Gilbert Dodds, track
1944	Ann Curtis, swimming
1945	Don Blanchard, football
1946	Arnold Tucker, football
1947	John B. Kelly, Jr., rowing
1948	Bob Mathias, track
1949	Dick Button, skating
1950	Fred Wilt, track
1951	Bob Richards, track
1952	Horace Ashenfelter, track
1953	Sammy Lee, diving
1954	Mal Whitfield, track
1955	Harrison Dillard, track
1956	Pat McCormick, diving
1957	Bobby Morrow, track
1958	Glenn Davis, track
1959	Parry O'Brien, track
1960	Rafer Johnson, track
1961	Wilma Rudolph, track
1963	John Pennel, track
1964	Don Schollander, swimming
1965	Bill Bradley, basketball
1966	Jim Ryun, track
1967	Randy Matson, track
1968	Debbie Meyer, swimming
1969	Bill Toomey, track
1970	John Kinsella, swimming
1971	Mark Spitz, swimming
1972	Frank Shorter, track
1973	Bill Walton, basketball
1974	Rich Wohlhuter, track
1975	Tim Shaw, swimming
1976	Bruce Jenner, track
1977	John Naber, swimming
1978	Tracy Caulkins, swimming
1979	Kurt Thomas, gymnastics
1980	Eric Heiden, speed skating
1981	Carl Lewis, track
1982	Mary Decker, track
1983	Edwin Moses, track
1984	Greg Louganis, diving
1985	Joan Benoit Samuelson, track
1986	Jackie Joyner-Kersee, track
1987	Jim Abbott, baseball
1988	Florence Griffith-Joyner, track
1989	Janet Evans, swimming
1990	John Smith, wrestling
1991	Mike Powell, track
1992	Bonnie Blair, speed skating
1993	Charlie Ward, football
1994	Dan Jansen, speed skating

1995	Bruce Baumgartner, wrestling	1998	Chamique Holdsclaw, basketball
1996	Michael Johnson, track	1999	Coco and Kelly Miller, basketball
1997	Peyton Manning, football	2000	Rulon Gardner, wrestling

Glossary

American Bowling Congress (ABC)   The official rule-making body of bowling.

Ace   In golf, a hole in one; in tennis, an outright winning serve that the receiver doesn't touch.

Assist   In hockey and basketball, the pass that immediately precedes a goal or a field goal, respectively. In hockey, a maximum of two assists are awarded per goal; in basketball, only one assist is awarded; in baseball, an assist is awarded when a fielder throws out a runner.

Backhand   In tennis, a stroke hit from the side of the body opposite the racket hand.

Backstroke   In swimming, a stroke in which the swimmer must stay on his or her back, except during turns.

Balk   In baseball, an illegal move by a pitcher with a runner on base. When a balk is committed, the runner or runners advance one base.

Ballhandler   In basketball, the player who directs the play, usually the point guard.

Bank shot   In basketball, a ball that hits the backboard before falling through the hoop.

Bantamweight   In boxing, a division with a 118-pound weight limit.

Baseline   In tennis, the back line of the court, joining the sidelines. A baseliner is a player who stays near the baseline.

Batting average   In baseball, the number of hits divided by the number of at-bats.

Birdie   In golf, completing a hole in 1-under par.

Blitz   In football, when the defensive team sends several players to try to sack the quarterback.

Bogey   In golf, completing a hole in 1-over par.

Bowling Proprietors Association of America (BPAA)   A trade organization of people who own bowling centers.

Breaststroke   In swimming, a stroke that requires simultaneous movements of the arms on the same horizontal plane. The hands are pushed forward from the breast on or under the surface of the water. The kick is a simultaneous thrust of the legs.

Bunker   In golf, a hazard filled with sand.

Butterfly   In swimming, a stroke that features the simultaneous overhead stroke of the arms, combined with a dolphin kick.

Camel spin   In figure skating, a spin done on one leg with the non-skating leg extended in the air parallel to the ice.

Center   In football, the offensive lineman who snaps the ball to the quarterback; in basketball, usually the tallest player on the team, who plays close to the basket.

Check, checking   In hockey, any defensive or guarding tactic.

Compulsory figures   In figure skating, required moves performed by all skaters. No longer a part of competitions.

Cruiserweight   In boxing, a division with a 190-pound limit.

Decathlon   In men's track and field, it consists of 10 events: 100-meter sprint, long jump, shot put, high jump, 400-meter sprint, 110-meter hurdles, discus, pole vault, javelin, and 1,500-meter run.

Decision   In boxing, a bout decided by the scoring of ringside judges.

Default   In tennis, the termination of a match other than by completing it, either by a walkover (the match is never begun, because a participant either concedes or doesn't show up) or retirement (a player is unable to continue due to illness or injury).

Defenseman   In hockey, two players who make up a team's defensive unit.

Designated hitter   In baseball, a player who bats in place of the pitcher and does not have a position in the field. The American League uses the designated hitter rule; the National League does not. Also referred to as DH.

Double bogey   In golf, completing a hole in 2-over par.

Double-double   In basketball, reaching double digits in two statistical categories.

Double eagle   In golf, completing a hole in 3-under par.

Double play   In baseball, when two players of the batting team are put out on the same play as a result of continuous action by the defense.

Draw   In boxing, a bout that results in neither fighter being declared the winner.

Drop shot   In tennis, a softly hit shot intended to barely clear the net.

Eagle   In golf, completing a hole in 2-under par.

Earned run average   In baseball, the average number of earned runs scored on a pitcher per nine innings. It is calculated by taking the number of earned runs scored on the pitcher, divided by the total number of innings pitched, and multiplied by nine.

Extra point   In football, a placekick from the 2-yard line after a touchdown, also known as a point-after touchdown (PAT).

Face off   In hockey, a the act of starting play by dropping the puck between the sticks of two players, one from each team.

Fastbreak   In basketball, after a rebound, the offense moves the ball quickly upcourt in order to score before the defense is in position.

Field goal   In basketball, a shot worth two points if it goes through the basket; in football, a placekick worth three points if it goes through the goal posts.

First down   In football, the first chance out of four that the offense has to gain 10 yards. If it gains 10 yards, it gets another first down.

Forecheck   In hockey, to closely guard an opponent, usually done by forwards trying to regain control of the puck.

Forehand   In tennis, a stroke hit from the same side of the body as the racket hand.

Forward   In basketball, players who are bigger than guards, smaller than the center, and usually play near the basket; in hockey, the center, the left wing, and the right wing; players who usually make up the attacking line.

Free agent   A player whose contract expires, allowing him to negotiate and sign a contract with another team.

Free skate   In figure skating, the free skate counts for 66.7 percent of a skater's final score. It does not have required elements. The skater chooses his or her own music and choreography.

Freestyle   In swimming, the stroke is characterized by alternate overhead motions of the arms and a flutter kick.

Funny Car   In drag racing, short-wheelbased cars with a fiberglass replica of a production car body. The engines are mounted in the front of the car.

Goals-against average   In hockey, a measure of a goaltender's effectiveness, calculated by dividing the number of goals against by the number of minutes played.

Grand Slam   In tennis and golf, the rare feat of winning each of the four major championships in the same year. The Australian, French, Wimbledon and U.S. Opens make up the tennis Grand Slam. The Masters, U.S. Open, British Open and PGA Championship make up the golf Grand Slam. In baseball, a home run with the bases loaded.

Groundstroke   In tennis, a stroke made after the ball has bounced.

Guards   In basketball, usually the smallest players on the court, who are responsible for setting up plays, scoring, and making passes; in football, the offensive linemen on either side of the center.

Hat trick   In hockey, three goals in one game scored by the same player.

Heavyweight   In boxing, the division with no weight minimum.

Heptathlon   In women's track and field, it consists of seven events: 100-meter hurdles, high jump, shot put, 200-meter sprint, long jump, javelin, and 800-meter run.

Hole in one   In golf, a ball that goes into the cup from a tee shot.

Hook   In boxing, a punch thrown from wide out, into the body or face, with the arm bent at a right angle; in basketball, a one-handed overhead shot made with the back arm when the body is turned sideways to the basket.

Individual medley   In swimming, it features all four competitive strokes: butterfly, backstroke, breaststroke, and freestyle, performed by one swimmer.

Interception   In football, a pass picked off by a defender.

Jab   In boxing, a short punch into the body or face.

Junior middleweight   In boxing, a division with a 154-pound limit. Also known as a super welterweight.

Junior welterweight   In boxing, a division with a 140-pound limit. Also known as a super lightweight.

Light heavyweight   In boxing, a division with a 175-pound limit.

Lightweight   In boxing, a division with a 135-pound limit.

Linebacker   In football, defensive players who are positioned behind the defensive linemen.

Line of scrimmage   In football, an imaginary line that no player may cross before the ball is snapped.

Long course   In swimming, a 50-meter racing pool.

Long program   In figure skating, an alternative expression for the free skate.

Majority decision   In boxing, a bout in which two judges favor one fighter and the third scores a draw.

Marathon   In track and field, a race of 26 miles, 385 yards.

Match play   In golf, a form of competition where holes are won, lost, or halved. The winner has won the most holes.

Medalist   In golf, the lowest tournament qualifying score.

Medal play   In golf, a form of competition where strokes are recorded. The winner has the fewest number of strokes. Also known as stroke play.

Medley relay   In swimming, each stroke—butterfly, backstroke, freestyle, breaststroke—by four different swimmers.

Middleweight   In boxing, a division with a 160-pound limit.

Mixed doubles   In tennis, doubles with a male and female player on each side.

No-hitter   In baseball, a game in which the pitcher does not allow a hit. Players who reach base on errors or walks do not affect a no-hitter.

Own goal   In soccer, a goal resulting from a member of the defensive team accidentally putting the ball into his or her own net.

Par   In golf, the number of shots needed to complete a hole, figuring two to reach the green, plus two putts. The pars for each individual holes are added to get the course's par.

Passing shot   In tennis, a shot that is driven beyond the reach of an opponent at the net.

Penalty killing   In hockey, the act of preventing a team with a power play from scoring.

Perfect game   In baseball, a pitcher retiring all 27 batters he faces; in bowling, 12 strikes in a row, also known as a 300 game.

Pinch-hitter   In baseball, a batter substituted for another batter. The original batter cannot return to the game.

Pinch-runner   In baseball, a player substituted for a base runner. The original runner cannot return to the game.

Pocket   In football, the area behind the offensive line, where the quarterback is protected by his blockers.

Pole   In auto racing, the best position on the starting grid, earned by the driver with the fastest qualifying time.

Power-play goal   In hockey, a goal scored with one or more members of the opposing team in the penalty box.

Pro-am   In golf, a tournament in which pros are paired with amateur partners.

Pro Stock   In drag racing, cars that most closely resemble cars one would see on the street, but featuring extensive engine modification, sophisticated chassis and suspension development, and a 500-cubic inch engine.

Qualifying   In auto racing, preliminary sessions in which cars' starting positions are determined based on their speed.

Relief pitcher   In baseball, all pitchers who enter a game subsequent to the starter.

Royal & Ancient Golf Club   Located in St. Andrews, Scotland, it is the governing body for golf worldwide, except for the United States and Mexico.

Run batted in   In baseball, the number of runners able to score, including the batter, as a result of the batter's at-bat. For example, if a batter hits a home run with two men on base, he is credited with three runs batted in. Runs batted in are not credited because of errors. Also referred to as RBI.

Rush   In hockey, moving the puck toward the opponent's goal; in football, a running attempt.

Sack   In football, tackling the quarterback behind the line of scrimmage.

Sacrifice   In baseball, a bunt on which the batter is put out, while another runner advances.

Safety   In football, being tackled in or having the ball go out of bounds from one's own end zone. The defensive team receives two points and the ball. Also, a defensive back, whose primary job is to cover pass receivers.

Save   In baseball, when a relief pitcher maintains a lead for his team until the game is over; in hockey, the act of a goalie stopping a shot.

Secondary   In football, a reference to the defensive backs.

Serve-and-volley   In tennis, a style of play where the server rushes the net after serving to get in position to volley.

Short course   In swimming, a 50-yard pool.

Short game   In golf, those techniques used on and around the green, including chipping, pitching, and putting.

Short-handed goal   In hockey, a goal scored when one or more of the opposing players are in the penalty box.

Short program   In figure skating, the two-minute, 40-second program that consists of eight required elements, set to music of the skater's choice.

Skyhook   In basketball, a hook shot released above the level of the basket; popularized by Kareem Abdul-Jabbar.

Slap shot   In hockey, a shot in which the stick is raised above the shoulder on the backswing and then driven with considerable velocity into the puck.

Slugging percentage   In baseball, a measure of a batter's ability to hit for extra bases. It is calculated by dividing the total number of bases reached safely by the total number of times at bat.

Spare   In bowling, knocking all 10 pins down in two attempts.

Special teams   In football, players who participate in kickoffs, punts, and field goals.

Split decision   In boxing, a bout in which two of the three judges favor one fighter, who is declared the winner.

Steeplechase   In track and field, a race in which runners negotiate a series of walls and water-filled trenches. The men's 3,000-meter steeplechase has 28 walls and seven water jumps.

Stolen base   In baseball, when a runner advances to the next base without a hit, putout, force out, fielder's choice, error, balk, passed ball, or wild pitch. The runner usually starts for the next base when the pitcher begins his windup, and gets a stolen base if the catcher fails to throw him out.

Strike   In baseball, a pitch that is over the plate and not swung at, or a pitch that is swung at and missed or fouled off; in bowling, knocking all 10 pins down on one attempt.

Stroke play   In golf, a tournament in which the winner has the fewest number of strokes. Also known as medal play.

Super lightweight   In boxing, a division with a 140-pound limit. Also known as a junior welterweight.

Super middleweight   In boxing, a division with a 168-pound limit.

Super welterweight   In boxing, a division with a 154-pound limit. Also known as a junior middleweight.

Swingman   In basketball, a player who can play guard and forward.

Technical knockout   In boxing, a fight stopped by the referee because one fighter is injured, unwilling to continue, or unable to continue in the referee's judgment.

Three-point shot   In basketball, a field goal made from beyond an arc 23 feet from the basket in the NBA and 19 feet, 9 inches from the basket in high school and college.

Top Fuel   In drag racing, the quickest-accelerating of all dragsters. They are powered by supercharged, custom-built 500-cubic-inch engines mounted behind the driver.

Topspin   In tennis, an overspin put on the ball by brushing the ball from low to high. Topspin allows the ball to be hit very hard and high over the net and still keep it in the court.

Touchdown   In football, when a team crosses the opponent's goal line with the ball. It is worth six points.

Triple Crown   In baseball, a batter who leads the league in batting average, home runs, and runs batted in; in horse racing, winning the Kentucky Derby, Preakness, and Belmont Stakes in the same year.

Triple-double   In basketball, when a player records double digits in three statistical categories.

Triple play   In baseball, when three players of the batting team are put out on the same play as a result of continuous action by the defense.

Turnover   Losing possession of the ball or the puck during play.

Two-minute drill   In football, several plays called in the huddle to save time near the end of a half or the end of a game.

Two-point conversion   In football, running a play from scrimmage, starting at the 2-yard line, following a touchdown.

United States Golf Association (USGA)   The governing body of golf in the United States and Mexico.

United States Tennis Association (USTA)   The governing body of tennis in the United States.

Uppercut   In boxing, a punch thrown from below or even with the waist.

Volley   In tennis, to hit the ball before it touches the ground. The stroke is usually executed at the net.

Welterweight   In boxing, a division with a 147-pound limit.

Zone defense   In basketball, a defense where players cover an area of the court, as opposed to a particular man. It is not permitted in the NBA.

Bibliography

Adams, Chuck, et al. *PGA Tour Media Guide 1999.* (Ponte Vedra, Fla.: PGA Tour Creative Services, 1999.)

Allen, Kevin. "King of the Crease." *The Hockey News 2000–01 Yearbook*, 31–34.

Association of Tennis Professionals. http://atptour. com. December 6, 1999.

Atlanta Braves. http://www.atlantabraves.com March 8, 2000.

Ashe Jr., Arthur R. *Hard Road to Glory.* (New York: Amistad Press, 1993).

Barkow, Al, and David Barrett. "*Golf Greats: 100 Legends of the Game.*" (Lincolnwood, Ill.: Publications International, Ltd., 1998.)

Baseball Online Library. www.sportsline.com March 7, 2000.

Berra, Yogi. *The Yogi Book.* (New York: Workman Publishing, 1998.)

Berretta, Bob ed. *Army Football Media Guide 2000.* (West Point, N.Y.: U.S. Military Academy, 2000).

Berry, Kevin. "Teofilo Stevenson: The greatest Olympic boxer." *Sydney Morning Herald.* May 16, 2000. http://smh.com.au August 7, 2000.

Best of a Century. http://members.tripod.com January 14, 2000.

Beyer, Andrew. "Down the stretch, Pincay still going strong." Washington Post Online. December 11, 1999. http://www.washingtonpost.com August 18, 2000.

Bill Rodgers Running Center. http://www.bill-rodgers.com August 7, 2000.

Bjarkman, Peter C. *The Biographical History of Basketball,* (Lincolnwood, Ill.: Masters Press, 1998.)

Bonavita, Mark, and Brendan Roberts eds. *The Sporting News Baseball Register, 1999 edition.* (St. Louis: *The Sporting News,* 1999).

Bonavita, Mark, and Sean Stewart eds. *The Sporting News Baseball Register, 1998 edition.* (St. Louis: *The Sporting News,* 1998).

Bonavita, Mark and Sean Stewart eds. *The Sporting News Baseball Register, 1997 edition.* (St. Louis: *The Sporting News,* 1997).

Broussard, Marc and Brendan Roberts eds. *The Sporting News Official NBA Register, 1999–2000 edition.* (St. Louis: *The Sporting News,* 1999).

Broussard, Marc and Craig Carter eds. *The Sporting News Official NBA Guide, 1999–2000 edition.* (St. Louis: *The Sporting News,* 1999).

Brown, Chris and Jerry Peters eds. *Carolina Hurricanes Media Guide 2000.*

Brown, Gerry and Michael Morrison eds. *The 2000 ESPN Information Please Sports Almanac.* (New York: Hyperion Books, 1999).

Bibliography

Brown, Gerry and Michael Morrison, eds. *The 1999 ESPN Information Please Sports Almanac.* (New York: Hyperion Books, 1998).

Bucek, Jeanine et al., ed. *The Baseball Encyclopedia: Tenth Edition.* (New York: McMillan, 1996).

Canella, Stephen. "Home Run Central." *Sports Illustrated.* March 6, 2000, 36–41.

Carlton, Chuck. "Seeking one last waltz with veteran band." *The Hockey News 2000–01 Yearbook*, 114–119.

CART. http://www.cart.com September 5, 2000.

CBS Sportsline. http://cbssportsline.com October 20, 1999.

CNN/SI—*Sports Illustrated for Women.* http://sportsillustrated.cnn.com July 19, 2000.

Collins, Bud and Zander Hollander eds. *Bud Collins' Tennis Encyclopedia.* 3d ed. (Detroit: Visible Ink Press, 1997).

Considine, Tim. *The Language of Sport.* (New York: Facts On File, Inc. 1992).

Cook, Kevin. "Tyson busters." *Sports Illustrated.* December 6, 1999, 34–36.

Coomes, Mark. "The 'Kid' rides again." The Courier Journal online. May 22, 2000. http://www.courier-journal.com August 18, 2000.

Championship Auto Racing Teams, Inc. *FedEx Championship Series Media Guide 1999.* (Troy, Mich.: Championship Auto Racing Teams, Inc., 1999).

Cycling News. http://www.cyclingnews.com July 27, 2000.

Cynthia Cooper Official Website. http://www.coophoops.com July 16, 2000.

DAC Journal, Magazine of the Downtown Athletic Club. December 1999, Volume 74, No. 1.

Darroch, Doug. "Greatest college basketball player: Tom Gola." Philly.com. nd. http://sports.philly.com July 18, 2000.

Dater, Adrian. "Anything less than Cup would spell disaster." *The Hockey News 2000–01 Yearbook*, 100–105.

Davis, Karen, John Hahn, Michael Kuta, and Kathi Reichert. *Detroit Red Wings Media Guide 2000.*

Delacourt, Christian. *Boxing.* (New York: Universe Publishing, 1997).

Deutsch, Richard, and Richard Hoffer. "Inside Boxing." *Sports Illustrated.* June 14, 1999.

Dryden, Michael, and Stephen Ulmer, eds. *The Top 100 NHL Hockey Players of All Time.* (Toronto: McClelland & Stewart 1998).

Evander Holyfield. http://ipcress.com January 16, 2000.

First Base Sports. http://firstbasesports.com September 27, 2000.

Fish, Wayne. "Flyers ready to shake 'Team Turmoil' Tag." *The Hockey News 2000–01 Yearbook*, 160–163.

Flatter, Ron. "Bo Knows stardom and disappointment." http://espn.com/sportscentury August 12, 2000.

———, "He made racing not so Petty." http://espn.com/sportscentury August 12, 2000.

———, "Louganis never lost drive to dive." http://espn.com/sportscentury August 12, 2000.

———, "Shoemaker made racing history." http://espn.com/sportscentury August 12, 2000.

———, "Three-peating wasn't enough for Oerter." http://espn.com/sportscentury August 12, 2000.

Fox Sports Net—Olbermann's Real 50. http://www.foxsports.com July 27, 2000.

Freeman, Brad ed. *Chicago Blackhawks Media Guide 2000.*

Dan Gable—Competitor Supreme. http://www.dangable.com July 27, 2000.

Detroit Lions. http://www.detroitlions.com April 21, 2000.

Gilbert, Michael ed. *Buffalo Sabres Media Guide 2000.*

Golf Europe. http://www.golfeurope.com March 23, 2000.

Golf Online. http://www.golfonline.com November 24, 1999.

Golfer Profiles. http://library.thinkquest.org November 26, 1999.

Grand Prix Hall of Fame. http://ddavid.com August 25, 2000.

Hassan, John, ed. *The 1998 ESPN Information Please Sports Almanac*. (New York: Hyperion Books, 1997).

Hassan, John, ed. *The 1997 ESPN Information Please Sports Almanac*. (Boston: Houghton Mifflin, 1996).

HBO Boxing: Greats. http://hbo.com/boxing January 14, 2000.

Helka, Mike. "Weary Stars remain in thick of things." *The Hockey News 2000–01 Yearbook*. 110–113.

Hickok, Ralph. *A Who's Who of Sports Champions. Their Stories & Records*. (Boston: Houghton Mifflin Co., 1995).

Hilton, John. "Thorpe brings world fame to Carlisle." Cumberlink, nd. http://www.cumberlink.com June 17, 2000.

Hoffer, Richard, and Franz Lidz. "Inside Boxing," *Sports Illustrated*. November 1, 1999.

Holland, Heidi ed. *Boston Bruins Media Guide 2000*.

Hunter, Don and Al Pearce. *The Illustrated History of Stock Car Racing* (Osceola, Wis.: MBI Publishing Co., Osceola, 1998).

International Amateur Athletic Association. http://iaaf.org July 23, 2000.

International Boxing Hall of Fame. http://www.ibhof.com May 17, 1999.

International Motorsports Hall of Fame. http://www.motorsportshalloffame.com August 27, 2000.

International Tennis Hall of Fame. http:www.tennisfame.com August 27, 1999.

Jack Nicklaus: Facts and Figures. (North Palm Beach, Fla.: Golden Bear International, Inc., 1998).

Jim Ryun Ministeries. http://www.anchoryourlife.com August 7, 2000.

Jockeys Guild Online. http://jockeyguild.com August 19, 2000.

Johnson, Anne Janette. *Great Women in Sports*. (Detroit: Visible Ink Press, 1996).

Johnson, Salvatore. *The Official U.S. Open Almanac*. (Dallas: Taylor Publishing Co., 1995).

Jordan, Michael. *For the Love of the Game: My Story by Michael Jordan* (New York: Crown Publishers, Inc. 1998).

Kelly, Larry ed. *Dallas Stars Media Guide 2000*

Kim, Stuart. "Kristi Yamaguchi: a biography." http://www.polaris.net July 28, 2000.

Lance Armstrong On-line! http://www.lancearmstrong.com July 25, 2000.

Lancer, Dave, Dave Senko and Phil Stambaugh eds. *Senior PGA Tour Media Guide 1999*. (Ponte Vedra, Fla.: PGA Tour Creative Services, 1999).

Latino Legends in Sports. http://www.latinosportslegends.com March 16, 2000.

Leder, Jane. *Grace & Glory: A Century of Women in the Olympics*. (Chicago: Triumph Books, 1996).

Longman, Jere. "Leap into history." *The Week Magazine*. August 24, 1997. http://www.the-week.com July 28, 2000.

Loverro, Thom. "Handlers trying to change Tyson's image." *Washington Times*. January 14, 1999. http://www.elibrary.com January 13, 2000.

LPGA Tour. *LPGA Tour Media Guide 2000*. (Daytona Beach, Fla.: LPGA Tour, 2000).

LPGA Tour. *LPGA Tour Media Guide 1999*. (Daytona Beach, Fla.: LPGA Tour, 1999).

MacCambridge, Michael, ed. *ESPN Sports Century*. (New York: Hyperion, 1999).

Major League Baseball. www.majorleaguebaseball.com February 25, 2000.

McLeod, Maurice. "Tyson: The man behind the myth." *Voice*. February 22, 1999. http://www.elibrary.com January 13, 2000.

McGhee, Khary K. "Roy Jones honored." Gannett News Service, December 13, 1999.

Meserle, Mike. *Sports Illustrated's 20th Century Sports: Images of Greatness*. (Kingston, N.Y.: Total/Sports Illustrated, 1999).

Bibliography

Middleweight Boxing Champion of the World. http://www.royjonesjr.com January 7, 2000.

Mitchard, Jacquelyn. "Tyson brings out the worst in boxing." Tribune Media Services. March 3, 1999. http://www.elibrary.com January 12, 2000.

Moore, David Leon. "Kiraly digs for another shot." *USA Today*. August 3, 2000, p. 3C.

Motorsports Hall of Fame. http://www.mshf.com August 22, 2000.

Murray, Tom, ed. *Sport Magazine: All-Time All-Stars*. New York: Atheneum Press, 1977.

Nack, William. "Hurtin.'" *Sports Illustrated*. March 13, 2000, 64–75.

Nadel, John. "Rod Laver improved a day after suffering stroke," Associated Press, July 29, 1998. http://www.elibrary.com January 5, 2000.

National Association for Stock Car Auto Racing. *NASCAR Winston Cup Series Media Guide 2000*. (Winston-Salem, N.C.: Sports Marketing Enterprises, 2000).

National Association for Stock Car Auto Racing. *The Official NASCAR Preview and Press Guide 2000*. (Charlotte, N.C.: UMI Publications, Inc., 2000).

National Baseball Hall of Fame. http://www.baseballhalloffame.org March 1, 2000.

National Basketball Association. http://www.nba.com June 26, 2000.

National Hockey League. http://nhl.com August 20, 2000.

NHRA. http://nhra.com August 27, 2000.

National Hot Rod Association. *NHRA Winston Drag Racing 1999 Media Guide*. (Winston-Salem, N.C.: Sports Marketing Enterprises, 1999).

National Thoroughbred Racing Association. http://www.ntra.com August 18, 2000.

NBC Olympics. http://www.nbcolympics.com September 27, 2000.

New York Mets. http://www.mets.com March 9, 2000.

New York Yankees. http://www.yankees.com March 8, 2000.

NFL Players Inc. http://www.sportsline.com March 8, 2000.

Official Site of the 2000 U.S. Open. http://usopen.org August 27, 2000.

Orca Bay Sports and Entertainment. http://www.canucks.com March 25, 2000.

Oscar De La Hoya. http://oscardelahoya.com December 6, 1999.

Pedulla, Tom. "Krone Blazes path for all horseowners." *USA Today*. August 7, 2000.

PGA European Tour. http://www.europetour.com October 6, 1999.

PGA Tour. http://www.pgatour.com September 27, 1999.

Phillips, John. "Jones adds WBA title to WBC lightheavy crown." Reuters, July 19, 1998. http://www.elibrary.com January 12, 2000.

Price, S.L. "Standing tall." *Sports Illustrated*. September 16, 1998. http://CNNSI.com January 12, 2000.

Professional Bowlers Association. http://pbatour.com August 24, 2000.

Pro Football Hall of Fame. http://www.profootballhof.com June 6, 2000.

Roger Maris. http://www.rogermaris.com March 1, 2000.

Radnedge, Keir. *The World Encyclopedia of Soccer: The Definitive Illustrated History*. (SevenOaks, 2000).

Remnick, David. *King of the World: Muhammad Ali and the Rise of an American Hero*. (New York: Vintage Books. 1999.)

Richards, Steve. "The victory ride that won't end." *The Boston Globe*. November 6, 1999. http://www.boston.com August 18, 2000.

Roberts, Brendan, and David Walton, ed. *The Sporting News Baseball Register, 2000 edition*. (St. Louis: The Sporting News, 2000).

Roberts, James B., and Alexander G. Skutt. *The Boxing Register: International Boxing Hall of Fame Official Record Book*. (Ithaca, N.Y.: McBooks Press 1999).

Rosasco, John ed. *New York Rangers Media Guide 2000.*

San Francisco Giants. http://www.sfgiants.com February 5, 2000.

Saturday Night Slam. "Dan Gable Biography: a great amateur wrestling story." http://saturdaynightslam.com July 27, 2000.

Schare, Alex. *The Naismith Memorial Basketball Hall of Fame's 100 Greatest Basketball Players of All Time.* (New York: Pocket Books, 1997).

Schell, Michael J. *Baseball's All-Time Best Hitters.* (Princeton, N.J.: Princeton University Press, 1999).

Schott, Tom ed. *Purdue Football Media Guide 2000.* (West Lafayette, Ind.: Purdue Athletic Public Relations Communications Office.)

Schultz, Jeff. "New-look Tyson still full of old rage." *The Atlanta Constitution,* January 14, 1999. http://www.elibrary.com January 13, 2000.

Schwartz, Larry. "Galloping Ghost scared opponents." http://espn.com/sportscentury July 6, 2000.

Schwartz, Larry. "Mario Andretti synonymous with racing." http://espn.com/sportscentury August 12, 2000.

Severiano Ballesteros. http://www.seveballesteros.com March 20, 2000.

Shirley Muldowney. http://www.shirleymuldowney.com August 27, 2000.

Shouler, Ken. *The Real 100 Best Baseball Players of All Time.* (Lenexa, Kan.: Addax Publishing Group, 1998.)

Smith, Craig, Rita Stein and Pete Kowalski eds. *2000 Championships Media Guide.* (Far Hills, N.J.: The United States Golf Association, 2000.)

Smith, Ron. *The Sporting News Selects Baseball's Greatest Players.* (St. Louis: The Sporting News, 1998).

————. *The Sporting News Selects Football's 100 Greatest Players: A Celebration of the 20th Century's Best.* (St. Louis: The Sporting News, 1999).

SoccerTimes.com. http://www.soccertimes.com August 20, 2000.

Splash. "Team of the Century." April/May 2000. Volume 8. Issue 2.

Sports Illustrated editors. *Sports Illustrated 2000 Sports Almanac.* (New York: Time, Inc., 1999).

Stallsmith, Shelly. "Carlisle Indian School student became world's greatest athlete." CumberLink nd. http://www.cumberlink.com June 17, 2000.

Starkey, Joe. "No more Czech jokes, just wins and results." *The Hockey News 2000–01 Yearbook,* 168–171.

Stewart, Sean, and Kyle Veltrop ed. *The Sporting News Baseball Register, 1996 edition.* (St. Louis: The Sporting News, 1996).

Sugar, Bert Randolph. *The 100 Greatest Athletes of All Time: A Sports Editor's Personal Ranking.* (New York: Citadel Press, 1995).

————. "The 100 greatest boxers of all-time." http://hbo.com January 14, 2000.

TaraLipinski.com. http://www.taralipinski.com July 27, 2000.

The Cyber Boxing Zone. http://cyberboxingzone.com January 14, 2000.

The Legendary Greg LeMond. http://gl.nidus.net July 27, 2000.

The New World Sports Academy. http://laureus.com August 7, 2000.

The Official Ozzie Smith Website. http://www.ozzie-smith.com February 25, 2000.

The Official Tiger Woods Website. http://www.sportsline.com February 20, 2000.

The Official Website of Eric Lindros. http://elindros.net March 23, 2000.

The Sporting News Baseball. http.//www.thesportingnews.com March 9, 2000

The Steamroller on the WTA. http://www.williamssisters.com January 12, 2000.

The Wonderful Venus Williams. http://www.williamssisters.com January 12, 2000.

Total Baseball. http://www.totalbaseball.com February 24, 2000.

Bibliography

Triplett, Mike. "Cool Davenport is making a racket only with her racket." *Sacramento Bee.* July 30, 1999 http://www.sacbee.com January 12, 2000.

USA Basketball. http://www.usabasketball.com July 17, 2000.

USA Gymnastics. http://www.usa-gymnastics.org July 27, 2000.

USA Softball. http://www.usasoftball.com August 18, 2000.

USA Track and Field. http://www.usatf.org July 23, 2000.

The U.S. Figure Skating Association. *The Official Book of Figure Skating.* (New York: Simon & Schuster, 1998).

United States Olympic Committee. http:www.usoc.org March 23, 2000.

Vecsey, George. *McGwire and Sosa: Baseball's Greatest Home Run Story.* (London: Carlton Books, 1998).

Victoria Sun. "Laver battles back from stroke," Gannett News Service. October 12, 1998. http://www.elibrary.com January 5, 2000.

Wallechinsky, David. *Sports Illustrated Presents The Complete Book of the Summer Olympics.* (Boston: Little, Brown and Company, 1996).

Wayne Gretzky Homepage. http://jetlink.net January 4, 2000.

Wertheim, Jon L. "Inside Tennis." *Sports Illustrated.* August 19, 1998. http://cnnsi.com January 12, 2000.

Williams, Andre. "A real champ," *The Morning Call,* Allentown, Pa. December 19, 1999. http://www.elibrary.com December 27, 1999.

Winter Olympics—CBS Sportsline. http://poll.sportsline.com July 27, 2000.

WNBA. http://www.wnba.com August 16, 2000.

Wojnarowski, Adrian. "A vote for two athletes who transcended sport." *The Record,* Hackensack, N.J., December 26, 1999.

Women's Soccer World Online. http://womensoccer.com July 27, 2000.

Yahoo! Sport—Mika Hakkinen. http://uk.sports.yahoo.com August 27, 2000.

———. Michael Schumacher. http://uk.sports.yahoo.com August 27, 2000.

Index

Boldface page numbers denote main entries.

A

Aaron, Hank **3–4,** 14, 42, 60, 70, 73
Aaron, Tommie 70
Aaron, Tommy 209
ABC Cities Tennis Program 302
ABC Hall of Fame 341, 349
ABC-TV 110, 146, 159, 163, 166, 219, 228, 267, 270, 272, 292, 302, 311, 312, 317, 337, 341
Abdul-Jabbar, Kareem **77–78,** 86, 96, 99, 103, 108, 117, 122, 123
Abel, Sid **235,** 247, 252
Abrams, Cal 6
Abrams, Georgie 147
Adams, Jack 235, 239
Adderley, Herb **149**
Advanced Golf (Middlecoff) 218
Agassi, Andre **301–302,** 317, 318
Ahumada, Jorge 132
Aikman, Troy **149–150**
Akers, Michelle **339**
Albert, Howard 134
Albright, Tenley **263,** 275
Alcindor, Lew. *See* Abdul-Jabbar, Kareem
Alcott, Amy **205**
Alexander, Grover Cleveland **4,** 24, 67, 74
Alexander, Kermit 189
Alexe, Ion 293
Ali, Muhammad 85, **127–129,** 132, 133, 135–136, 137, 139, 141, 142, 144, 147
All-ABA 79
All-AFL 151, 156, 172, 183
All-American
  basketball 77, 79, 80, 82, 83, 85, 86, 87, 88, 89, 91, 93, 96, 97, 98, 99, 100, 103, 104, 105, 107, 108, 109, 110, 112, 113, 114, 118, 120, 121, 122, 123, 124, 125, 126
  football 150, 152, 155, 156, 157, 158, 159, 163, 165, 166, 167, 168, 169, 170, 175, 177, 181, 182, 183, 184, 185, 187, 189,

190, 191, 194, 198, 199, 200, 201, 202
  golf 208, 210, 218, 226
  soccer 339, 342, 343
  softball 342, 343, 344
All-American Football Conference (AAFC) 163, 164, 166, 169, 172, 173, 180, 196
All-BAA 110
All-Century Team 4, 7, 8, 14, 15, 18, 24, 25, 28, 31, 35, 38, 40, 42, 43, 48, 58, 59, 60, 61, 65, 69, 72, 74
Allen, Marcus **150**
All-England Club 303, 311, 314, 316
Allison, Bobby **323,** 330, 334
Allison, Clifford 323
Allison, Davey 323
All-NBA 78, 79, 80, 81, 85, 86, 88, 90, 91, 92, 93, 96, 97, 99, 102, 105, 107, 108, 109, 110, 112, 113, 114, 115, 117, 119, 120, 121, 122, 123, 124, 125
All-NBA Defensive first team 78, 88, 89, 92, 93, 96, 102, 109, 115, 116, 118, 123, 124
All-Pro 151, 152, 155, 156, 157, 158, 159, 160, 162, 163, 165, 166, 167, 168, 169, 170, 171, 172, 173, 174, 175, 176, 177, 178, 180, 183, 184, 186, 187, 189, 190, 191, 192, 193, 194, 196, 197, 198, 199, 200, 201, 202
All-Star
  baseball 5, 6, 7, 8, 9, 10, 11, 12, 13, 14, 17, 19, 21, 22, 24, 25, 26, 28, 29, 30, 31, 32, 34, 35, 36, 39, 43, 44, 50, 51, 52, 53, 54, 55, 57, 61, 64, 65, 66, 67, 68, 71, 72, 73
  basketball 78, 79, 80, 81, 83, 85, 86, 87, 88, 89, 90, 91, 92, 93, 94, 95, 96, 97, 98, 99, 102, 103, 105, 106, 107, 109, 110,

112, 113, 114, 115, 116, 117, 118, 119, 120, 121, 122, 123, 124, 125
  football 156, 159
  hockey 235, 236, 237, 238, 239, 240, 241, 242, 243, 244, 245, 247, 248, 250, 251, 252, 253, 254, 255, 256, 257, 259, 260, 261
All-Star Tournament 341, 349. *See also* U.S. Open: bowling
All-Time AFL team 178
All-Time team, NFL 75th Anniversary 151, 154, 155, 156, 164, 165, 167, 168, 169, 170, 171, 172, 174, 175, 176, 179, 180, 181, 183, 184, 185, 190, 195, 197, 198, 199, 200, 201, 202
All-WNBA first team 85, 121
Alomar, Roberto **4–5**
Alworth, Lance **150–151**
Amateur Athletic Union (AAU)
  basketball 105
  boxing 127, 130, 135, 138, 140, 143
  diving 283
  golf 232
  swimming 270, 285, 293, 297
  track and field 265, 267, 275, 277, 284, 286, 288, 289, 290, 291, 292, 295, 296
  wrestling 273
Amateur Softball Association (ASA) 343
Amateur Wrestling News 273
Amato, Joe **323**
Ambers, Lou 129
Ameche, Alan 197
American Association 63
American Auto Racing Writers and Broadcasters of America 332–333
American Basketball Association (ABA) 73, 77, 79, 85, 86, 87, 90, 93, 95, 96, 98, 100, 106, 107, 110, 120, 122

American Basketball League (ABL) 88, 89, 96, 100, 104–105, 108, 120
American Bowling Congress (ABC) Masters 339, 341
American Football Conference (AFC) 153, 154, 156, 157, 161, 162, 165, 167, 168, 174, 176, 179, 182, 185, 189, 198, 201
American Football League (AFL) 151, 152, 153, 154, 156, 159, 164, 172, 174, 177, 178, 181, 183, 189, 193, 197
American Hockey League (AHL) 235, 241, 258
American League 3, 5, 7, 8, 9, 10, 11, 12, 13, 14, 15, 16, 17, 18, 19, 21, 22, 23, 24, 26, 27, 28, 29, 30, 31, 33, 34, 35, 36, 38, 40, 41, 43, 44, 46, 47, 49, 50, 51, 52, 53, 54, 55, 57, 58, 59, 60, 63, 64, 66, 68, 70, 71, 72, 73, 74–75
American League Championship Series (ALCS) 3, 9, 12, 14, 29, 33, 34, 36, 41, 46, 48, 51, 53
American Professional Football Association 195
Amer-I-Can Program 155
Americans with Disabilities Act (ADA) 218
American Tennis Association (ATA) 308
Anaheim Angels 29, 32, 48. *See also* California Angels
Anaheim Mighty Ducks 250
Anderson, Mal 312
Anderson, Willie **205**
Andretti, Aldo 324
Andretti, Alvise 324
Andretti, John 324
Andretti, Mario **323–324,** 325, 331, 337
Andretti, Michael **324–325**
Andries, Dennis 135
Anquetil, Jacques 276

Anthony, Earl **339,** 347, 349
Antuofermo, Vito 135
Aparicio, Luis **5**
Appling, Luke **5–6**
Arbour, Al 237
Arcaro, Eddie **339–340,** 343, 347
Archibald, Nate **78**
Arguello, Alexis **129,** 143
Arizin, Paul **78**
Arizona Diamondbacks 35
Arizona State University 194
Armour, Tommy **205–206,** 208, 233
Armstrong, Henry **129**
Armstrong, Lance **340–341**
Army, U.S. 153, 158
Arnold College 186
Art Ross Trophy 249
Ascari, Alberto 324
Ashburn, Rich **6**
Ashe, Arthur 137, **302,** 306
Ashe, Camera 302
Ashe, Jeanne 302
Ashford, Evelyn 263–264
Associated Press Athlete of the Decade 222
Associated Press Athlete of the Year
  baseball 9, 17, 18, 38, 41, 54, 66, 72
  basketball 81, 110, 135
  figure skating 271
  football 150, 154, 158, 159, 161, 168, 176, 179, 184, 189, 190, 194, 196
  golf 206, 219, 222, 228, 231, 232, 233
  gymnastics 290
  horse racing 341
  swimming 292, 293, 297
  tennis 302, 305, 308, 309, 311, 314, 315, 320
  track and field 266, 269, 274, 277, 278, 279, 282, 289, 291
Association of Intercollegiate Athletics for Women (AIAW) 87, 103, 217, 224, 263, 267
Association of Tennis Professionals (ATP) 303, 306, 312
Athlete-Career Connection 302
Athletics Congress 282
Atlanta Braves 3, 4, 13, 14, 25, 35, 39, 42, 47, 49, 50, 52, 53, 67, 70, 73, 188
Atlanta Falcons 159, 161, 162, 164, 188, 190
Atlanta Flames 244
Atlanta Hawks 73, 80, 96, 107, 125
Atlantic Coast Conference (ACC) 88, 97, 217, 278, 343
AT&T Pebble Beach National Pro-Am 218, 232
Auburn University 32, 33, 78
Auerbach, Red 85, 97, 117
Augusta National 210, 214, 220, 221, 228
Austin, Bunny 304
Austin, John 302
Austin, Tracy **302,** 305, 308
Australian Ladies Open 230
Australian Masters 220
Australian Open 220, 301, 302, 303, 305, 306, 307, 308, 309, 310, 313, 314, 315, 316, 318, 319, 321, 322
Averill, Earl 17
Avon Futures 302

Ayako Okamoto 209
Azinger, Paul 220

B
Babashoff, Shirley **264**
Babe (film) 278
Babka, Rink 288
Bacharach Giants 11
Bachrach, Bill 297
Baer, Max 140
Bailey, Ace 259
Bailey, Jerry **341**
Ballesteros, Seve **206,** 218
Baltimore Bullets 80, 84, 96, 112, 123, 124, 125
Baltimore Colts 152, 153, 160, 161, 169, 175, 176, 178, 179, 181, 184, 196, 197
Baltimore Elite Giants 11, 25
Baltimore Orioles 5, 13, 14, 23, 30, 33, 41, 47–48, 51, 54, 55, 56, 58, 61, 64, 66, 67, 70
Baltimore Ravens 182, 202
Bankers Trust Classic 217
Banks, Ernie **6,** 42, 47
Bannister, Roger **264**
Barber, Bill **235**
Barkley, Charles **78–79,** 116
Barney, Lem **151**
Baroudi, Sam 130
Barry, Kevin 136
Barry, Rick **79**
Bar Starr Award 165
baseball **3–75,** 173, 187–188, 195
Baseball Encyclopedia, The 39
Baseball Hall of Fame 4, 5, 6, 7, 8, 9, 10, 12, 13, 14, 15, 16, 17, 18, 19, 20, 21, 22, 23, 24, 25, 26, 27, 28, 29, 30, 31, 32, 33, 34, 35, 36, 37, 38, 39, 40, 41, 42, 43, 44, 45, 46, 47, 48, 49, 50, 51, 52, 53, 55, 56, 57, 58, 59, 60, 61, 62, 63, 65, 66, 67, 68, 69, 70, 71, 72, 73, 74, 75, 109
Baseball Writers Association of America 23
basketball **77–126,** 278
Basketball Association of America (BAA) 87, 92, 105, 110
Bathgate, Andy **235–236,** 256
Bauer, Bobby 259
Baugh, Sammy **151–152,** 175, 202
Baylor, Elgin **79–80**
Baylor University 190, 277
Beamon, Bob **264–265,** 267, 282, 289
Bearcats 117
Beckenbauer, Franz **341**
Becker, Boris **302–303,** 307, 313
Bednarik, Chuck **152,** 163, 188
Belfour, Ed **236**
Belgium Grand Prix 329, 336
Beliveau, Jean **236,** 255
Bell, Bobby **152**
Bell, Cool Papa **6–7,** 25
Bell, Tommy 143
Bellamy, Walt **80**
Belmont Stakes 340, 341, 342, 343, 344, 346, 347
Bench, Johnny **7,** 11, 13, 21, 47, 51, 70
Benedict, Clint **236–237**
Benitez, Wilfred **129–130,** 135, 138

Benoit Samuelson, Joan **265**
Bentley, Doug **237**
Bentley, Max **237**
Benvenuti, Nino **130,** 134, 141
Berbick, Trevor 128–129, 146
Berenson, Red 237
Berg, Patty **206,** 229, 233
Bernstein, Kenny **325**
Berra, Yogi **7–8,** 13, 21
Berry, Raymond **152–153,** 197
Bert Bell Award 154, 166, 171, 186
Bethune Cookman College 174
Betsy King Classic 215
Bettina, Melio 131
Betz, Pauline **303**
Biletnikoff, Fred **153**
Biletnikoff Award 153
Bing, Dave **80–81**
Bing Steel 81
Biondi, Matt **265–266**
Bird, Larry 78, **81–82,** 98–99, 109, 114
Birmingham Barons 43, 50
Black, Julian 140
Black Economic Union 155
Blackhawks, Tri-Cities 85
Black Sox Scandal 16, 33, 58
Blackthink (Owens) 289
Blair, Bonnie **266,** 271, 281
Blair, Kim 279
Blake, Toe 257
Blanchard, Doc **153,** 158
Blanda, George **153–154**
Blankers, Jack 266
Blankers-Koen, Fanny **266**
Blazejowski, Carol **82**
Bloomfield Rams 197
Blount, Mel **154**
Blue Devils 94, 97
Blue-Gray Game 174
Blue Ridge League 72
Bob Hope Chrysler Classic 210
Bob Jones Award 214, 217
Bob Mathias Story, The (film) 284
Bodine, Geoff 330
Boggs, Wade 8
Boitano, Brian **266,** 298
Bond, Florence Jackson 32
Bonds, Barry xi, **8–9,** 47
Bonds, Bobby 8
Bonnies 103
Borg, Bjorn **303,** 306, 312, 314, 315, 318, 321
Boros, Julius **206–207**
Borotra, Jean **304,** 305, 312
Bossy, Mike **237,** 242
Boston, Ralph 264, **266–267**
Boston Braves 3, 16, 20, 30, 39, 42, 59, 63, 65, 69, 70
Boston Bruins 237, 238, 239, 240, 241, 242, 243, 251, 254, 255, 256, 259
Boston Celtics 78, 80, 81, 84, 85, 86, 95, 96, 97, 99, 100, 102, 104, 105, 106, 107, 108, 109, 114, 115, 117, 119, 120, 122, 123, 124, 125, 126
Boston College 86, 160
Boston Marathon 265, 290, 291
Boston Red Sox 5, 8, 9, 10, 11, 12, 13, 14, 16, 17, 19, 21, 22, 23, 28, 34, 41, 47, 50, 51, 53, 58, 62, 64, 66, 71, 72, 74
Boston University 15

Bosworth, Brian 32
Boucher, Frank **237,** 241
Boudreau, Lou **9,** 39
Bourque, Ray **238,** 256
Bowdoin College 265
Bowe, Riddick 136
Bower, Johnny **238**
Bowler of the Year 341
bowling 339, 341, 347, 348–349
Bowling Green University 122
Bowling Proprietors Association of America (BPAA) U.S. Open 341, 349
Bowling Writers Association of America (BWAA) 341, 349
Bowman, Bob 45
Bowman, Ken 192
boxing **127–147,** 293
Boxing Writers Association 136
Braddock, James J. 140, 144
Bradley, Alva 9
Bradley, Bill **82–83**
Bradley, Pat **207,** 213
Bradley University 93
Bradshaw, Terry 66, **154–155,** 167–168
Brady, Mike 212
Branch Rickey Award 64
Brand, Gordon 220
Brandeis University 100
Bratton, Johnny 133
Braves. *See* Atlanta Braves; Boston Braves; Milwaukee Braves
Braxton, Dwight 144, 145. *See also* Qawi, Dwight Muhammad
Breaking the Surface (Louganis) 283
Breeders' Cup 344
Brett, George **9–10**
Brickyard 400 329
Bricso-Hooks, Robert 267
Bricso-Hooks, Valerie **267**
Brigham Young University 202, 264
Brimsek, Frank **238**
Brinker, Norman 305
British Amateur Championship 214, 215, 221, 226, 233
British Open 206, 208, 209, 210, 211, 212, 213, 214, 216, 218, 219, 220, 221, 222, 223, 224, 226, 228, 229, 231, 232
British Women's Amateur 229
Brock, Lou **10,** 16
Broda, Turk **239**
Broderick Cup 109, 268, 285
Broglio, Ernie 10
Bromwich, John 304, 318
Brooklyn Dodgers 7, 11, 19, 25, 30, 32, 37, 38, 41, 42, 45, 48, 53, 56, 57, 59, 63, 64, 65, 70, 72, 120, 170
Brotherhood Award 64
Brough, Louise 303, **304,** 307, 308, 316
Brown, Eddie 185
Brown, Jim **155,** 170, 186, 190, 194
Brown, Nicole 190
Brown, Paul 155, 163, 166, 173, 180
Brown, Roosevelt **155–156,** 165
Brown, Three Finger **10**
Brown, Tom 312
Brown, Walter 105
Brown, Willie **156**
Browne, Mary K. 313
Brugnon, Jacques 304, 305, 312

Bruins (UCLA) 77, 94, 96, 109, 123, 302
Bruno, Frank 146
Brunswick World Tournament of Champions 339
Bryant, Joe 83
Bryant, Kobe **83**
Bryant, Paul "Bear" 181, 193
Bubka, Sergei **267**
Buchanan, Buck **156,** 198
Buckeyes 104, 157, 166
Bucknell University 42
Bucyk, John **239,** 254
Budd, Zola 270
Budge, Don 301, **304,** 309, 312, 317, 321
Bueno, Maria **304–305**
Buffalo Bills 150, 185, 190, 191, 255
Buffalo Braves 106, 108, 120
Buffalo Sabres 243, 247, 248, 255
Bunning, Jim **10–11**
Burdine's Invitational 207
Burke, Jack, Jr. 229
Burnett, Dale 164
Burns, Tommy 137
Burns Sports Celebrity Services 281
Burton, Nelson, Jr. **341**
Busch Series 326, 329
Butkus, Dick **156**
Button, Dick **267–268**
Buxton, Angela 308
Byron "Whizzer" White Award 157, 182

C

Calder Trophy 236, 237, 238, 243, 244, 246, 249, 250, 251, 252, 254, 255, 256, 258, 259, 260, 261
Calgary Flames 243, 248
California 500 331, 337
California Angels 12, 19, 33–34, 56, 59, 64, 67, 70, 73. *See also* Anaheim Angels
California League 19
California State University 120, 267, 273
Callaghan, Richard 283
Callaway, Betty 295
Camacho, Hector "Macho" 139
Campanella, Roy **11,** 25, 39
Campbell, Clarence 257
Campbell, Earl **157**
Canada Cup 210, 245, 259
Canadian Football League 177, 179
Canadian Open 210, 219, 222
Canadian Women's Amateur 229
Cane Pace 342
Cannon, Jimmy 140
Canseco, Jose **11–12**
Canton Bulldogs 195
Capital/Washington Bullets 100
Caponi, Donna **207**
Capriati, Jennifer 307
Cardinals (Stanford) 105
Carew, Rod **12**
Carey, Max 6
Carillo, Mary 314
Carlos, John 296
Carlton, Steve **12,** 32, 60
Carmen on Ice (TV film) 298
Carner, JoAnne **207–208,** 209
Carnera, Primo 140, 145

Carolina Cougars 86
Carolina Hurricanes 240
Carolina League 195
Carolina Panthers 201
Carr, Joe 170
Carrasquel, Chico 5
CART (Championship Auto Racing Teams) 332, 335
Carter, Cris 157
Carter, Don 341
Carter, Gary **12–13,** 21
Carter, Joe 13
Carter, Ruben "Hurricane" 133
Carter, Vince 83–84
Casals, Rosemary **305,** 311
Case, Walter, Jr. 343
Cash, Pat 313
Casper, Billy **208,** 215
Caulkins, Tracy 110, **268,** 297
Cauthen, Steve **341–342**
CBS Radio 167
CBS-TV 97, 109, 126, 150, 163, 169, 170, 229, 277, 312, 315, 320
Celebrity Golf Tour 313
Centennial of Golf in America 217, 220
Central Arkansas State University 116
Central Division 194
Cepeda, Orlando **13,** 44
Cepeda, Perucho 13
Cerdan, Marcel 138, 147
Cervantes, Antonio 129, 143
Cesar Chavez, Julio 131
Chamberlain, Wilt xi, 80, **84–85,** 86, 94, 103, 104, 118, 119, 120, 122, 123
Chambers, Dorothea Douglass 313
Chance, Dean 41
Chang, Michael 303, 307, 320
Charles, Bob 208
Charles, Ezzard **130,** 140, 141, 147
Charleston, Oscar **13–14,** 25
Charlotte Hornets 83, 86, 114
Charlotte Motor Speedway 336
Charlotte Sting 88
Chastain, Brandi **342**
Chattanooga Black Lookouts 50
Cheevers, Gerry **239**
Chelios, Chris **239**
Chicago American Giants 6, 13
Chicago Bears 151, 153, 154, 156, 159–160, 163, 164, 170, 173, 175, 181, 182, 184, 189, 190–191, 193
Chicago Blackhawks 235, 236, 237, 238, 239, 240, 242, 244, 246, 247, 248, 252, 253, 254, 255
Chicago Bulls 79, 88, 93, 102, 106, 112, 114, 115, 116, 118, 121, 122–123, 124
Chicago Cardinals 172, 177, 182, 195, 196, 198
Chicago Cubs 4, 6, 9, 10, 13, 17, 19, 22, 23, 26, 27, 29, 30, 31, 32, 34, 37, 38, 39, 41, 42, 44, 45, 49, 55, 60, 64, 65, 66, 69, 70, 72
Chicago Gears 110
Chicago Marathon 265
Chicago Packers 80
Chicago Rockets 169
Chicago Stags 85

Chicago White Sox 5, 10, 12, 16, 19, 21, 22, 26, 27, 32, 33, 39, 58, 62, 63, 65, 67–68, 69, 70, 73, 87, 102
Chi Chi Rodriguez Foundation 224
Chip, Joe 134
Chock Full O' Nuts Corp. 57
Chocolate, Kid 130
Christiansen, Jack **157**
Chuvalo, George 128
Cincinnati Bengals 32, 162, 165, 166, 171, 179, 180, 185, 201
Cincinnati Reds 7, 11, 16, 21, 27, 29, 31, 33, 42, 46, 47, 49, 51, 55, 56, 57, 62, 63, 64, 70, 74, 188
Cincinnati Royals 78, 86, 104, 105, 117
City College of San Francisco 190
Clancy, King **239–240**
Clapper, Dit **240,** 241
Clark, Dwight 179
Clark, Jim **325,** 331
Clarke, Bob **240**
Clarke, Ron 286
Class B Interstate League 43
Classico San Sebastian 340
Clay, Cassius Marcellus. *See* Ali, Muhammad
Clemens, Doug 10
Clemens, Roger **14**
Clemente, Roberto **14,** 63
Cleveland Barons 241
Cleveland Broncos 239
Cleveland Browns 95, 154, 155, 158, 159, 160, 161, 162, 163, 165, 166, 170, 171, 173, 178, 180, 182, 194, 198, 199
Cleveland Cavaliers 92, 102, 123, 125
Cleveland Indians 5, 7, 9, 12, 13, 19, 20, 25, 27, 33, 35, 37, 38–39, 41, 43, 48, 49, 50, 52, 56, 61, 65, 66, 70, 73, 74, 195
Cleveland Pipers 104, 120
Cleveland Rams 151
Cleveland Rockers 126
Coach of the Year 120, 125, 160, 165
Coast Guard Academy 164
Cobb, Amanda 15
Cobb, Ty 8, 10, 12, 13, **14–15,** 16, 28, 29, 31, 33, 35, 57, 63, 66, 69
Cobb, W. H. 15
Coca-Cola 165
Coca-Cola 600 333
Coca-Cola Classic 217
Cochet, Henri 304, **305,** 312
Cochrane, Mickey **15–16,** 22, 24, 40
Coe, Charlie 219
Coe, Sebastian **268**
Coffey, Paul 238, **240,** 256
Colgate Dinah Shore Winner's Circle 232
Colgate University 155
College of Idaho 80
Collier, Blanton 165
Collins, Eddie **16,** 33
Collins, Jimmy 16
Colorado Avalanche 238, 244, 250, 258
Colorado Rockies 47
Colorado State University 157, 296
Columbia University 16, 175
Columbus Quest 108
Comaneci, Nadia **268–269,** 281, 289, 290

Comeback Driver of the Year 332
Comeback Player of the Year 34, 44, 180
Conacher, Charlie **241,** 248, 256
Conan the Barbarian (film) 85
Conerly, Charlie 196, 201
Conn, Billy **130–131,** 137, 140, 147
Conner, Bart **269**
Connolly Brinker, Maureen **305,** 309
Connor, Roger 59
Connors, Gloria 305
Connors, Jimmy 302, 303, **305–306,** 308, 312, 313, 314, 315, 318, 319, 320, 321
Conn Smythe Trophy 236, 237, 241, 242, 244, 245, 246, 249, 250, 251, 253, 255, 257, 258, 260, 261
Continental Basketball Association 122
Cook, Bill 237, **241**
Cook, Bun 237, 241
Cooke, Sarah Palfrey 303
Cooney, Gerry 142, 145
Cooper, Ashley 312
Cooper, Bert 136
Cooper, Cynthia **85**
Cooper, Harry 208
Cooper, Henry 206
Cordero, Angel, Jr. **342**
Cornell University 242
Coryell, Don 162, 171
Cossaboon, John 343
Costas, Bob 40
Cotton Bowl 173, 178, 199
Cougars 88, 112
Couples, Fred **208,** 217, 221
Courier, Jim 306, 307
Cournoyer, Yvan **241**
Court, Margaret Smith **306,** 309, 310, 311, 315, 316–317, 319
Cousy, Bob 85–86, 99, 117, 120
Cowens, Dave **86,** 103
Cowley, Bill **241**
Crawford, Jack 316
Crawford, Sam **16**
Cream, Arnold. *See* Walcott, Jersey Joe
Creighton University 116
Crenshaw, Ben **208–209,** 215, 230
Crimson Tide 170, 181
Cronin, Joe **16–17,** 29, 31, 71
Crosetti, Frank 105
cross-country skiing 269
Csonka, Larry **157–158,** 174, 199
Cuban Winter League 32
Cuevas, Jose "Pipino" 135
Cukoschay, Joseph. *See* Sharkey, Jack
Cunningham, Billy **86–87,** 94
Cupit, Jackie 206
Curran, Kevin 303
Curtis Cup 206, 207, 209, 217, 224
cycling 275, 276, 298–299, 340–341, 344–345
Cy Young Award 12, 14, 19, 20, 21, 24, 25, 31, 34, 35, 38, 39, 41, 49, 51, 52, 61, 62, 65, 66, 73

D

Daehlie, Bjorn **269**
Dallas Chaparrals 95
Dallas Cowboys 97, 149, 150, 151, 154, 160, 162, 165, 169, 174, 177,

Index

179, 188, 191, 192, 193, 200, 202, 275
Dallas Diamonds 103
Dallas Mavericks 89, 97
Dallas Stars 236, 244, 248
Dallas Texans 156, 159, 160, 175
D'Amato, Cus 146
Dancer, Stanley **342**
Daniel, Beth **209**
Dan Jansen Foundation 277
Dantley, Adrian 84
Danzig, Alison 304
Darcy, Pat 21
Davenport, Lindsay **306–307,** 310, 315, 322
Davey O'Brien Award 149
Davidova, Elena 268
Davies, Bob **87**
Davies, Laura **209,** 230
Davies, Lynn 267
Davis, Al 156, 197
Davis, Al "Bummy" 130
Davis, Glenn 153, **158**
Davis, Sammy 43
Davis, Scott 266
Davis, Teddy 144
Davis, Terrell **158**
Davis, Willie **158–159**
Davis Cup 301, 302, 303, 304, 305, 307, 308, 309, 310, 311–312, 314, 315, 316, 317, 318, 319, 320, 321
Dawson, Andre 8, **17**
Dawson, Len **159**
Day, Pat **342**
Daytona 500 323, 324, 326, 328, 329, 330, 333, 334, 336, 338
Dean, Christopher 295–296
Dean, Dizzy **17,** 20
Dean, Paul 17
DeBusschere, Dave **87,** 90
Decker Slaney, Mary **269–270**
Defensive Player of the Year 102, 118, 121, 188, 191, 194, 201, 202
De La Hoya, Joel 131
De La Hoya, Oscar **131**
DeLeon, Carlos 136
Delta Devils 185
Del Valle, Lou 137
Delvecchio, Alex **241**
DeMarco, Tony 129
Demaret, Jimmy **209**
Dempsey, Jack **131,** 135, 145, 146
De Niro, Robert 138
Denneny, Cy **241–242**
Denver Broncos 153, 154, 156, 158, 160, 161, 162, 179, 185, 193, 200, 202
Denver Nuggets 89, 98, 122
DePaul University 110
Detroit Lions 151, 157, 162, 163, 168, 169, 172, 173, 177, 186, 187, 189, 190, 199, 202
Detroit Olympics 239
Detroit Pistons 80, 81, 87, 88, 92, 97, 98, 103, 108, 116, 118, 122, 126
Detroit Red Wings 235, 236, 239, 240, 241, 242, 243, 246, 247, 249, 252, 255, 258, 259, 260, 261
Detroit Shock 104, 126
Detroit Tigers 10, 14, 15, 16, 19, 24, 26, 27, 29, 31, 35, 36, 39, 42, 45, 49, 50, 63, 69
De Varona, Donna **270**

Devers, Gail **270,** 296
Devil's Bowl Speedway 336
De Vincenzo, Roberto **209–210**
Dickerson, Eric **159,** 186
Dickey, Bill 7, 15, **17–18,** 25, 52
Didrikson, Babe 278. *See also* Zaharias, Mildred "Babe"
Diegel, Leo **210,** 212
DiMaggio, Joe 17, **18,** 40, 47, 50, 63, 105, 314
Dionne, Marcel 238, **242**
Dirty Dozen, The (film) 155
Ditka, Mike **159–160,** 184
diving 280, 283, 285
Division I
    basketball 77, 78, 88, 113, 118
    golf 210
    hockey 236
Division II (basketball) 111
Doak Walker Award 199
Doby, Larry **19**
Donald, Mike 213
Donovan, Anne **87–88**
Donovan, Art **160**
Dons 99, 119
Doral-Ryder Open 211
Doran, Jim 173
Dorrance, Anson 343
Dorsett, Tony **160–161**
Douglas, Buster 136, 146
Dowd, John 58
Downing, Al 3
Doyle, Jimmy 143
Dream Teams 81, 91, 99, 102, 106, 125
Drechsler, Heike 264, 278
Drexler, Clyde 79, **88**
Driver of the Year 323, 324, 326, 327
Dryden, Ken **242**
Drysdale, Don **19,** 109
Duke University 94, 97, 171
Duluth Eskimos 182
Dumars, Joe **88**
Dumart, Woody 259
du Maurier Championship 207, 230
du Maurier Classic 205, 207, 209, 212, 213, 227
Duncan, Tim **88–89,** 118
Dundee, Angelo 127
Dunhill Cup 210
Dunlop Masters 220
DuPont, Margaret Osborne 304, **307,** 316
Duran, Roberto 130, 135, 138, 139
Durnan, Bill **242**
Durocher, Leo 20, 43
Duval, David **210,** 221
Dykes, Jimmy 5

E

Eagles 86
Earnhardt, Dale **325–326,** 329
Earnhardt, Dale, Jr. 326
East Carolina University 88
Eastern Conference 116
Eastern Division 84, 94, 95, 152
Eastern Michigan University 93
Eastern U.S. Junior Ladies championship 263
Eckersley, Dennis **19–20**
Eckert, William 61
Eclipse Award 341, 342, 346, 347
Edberg, Stefan 303, **307**

Ed Block Courage Award 182, 202
Edmonton Eskimos 179
Edmonton Oilers 240, 243, 245, 249, 250, 253
Edwards, Teresa **89**
Edwards, Vic 309
Edwards, Vince 32
Elder, Lee **210**
Elizabeth II 209, 321
Eller, Carl 184
Elliott, Bill **326,** 330
Ellis, Jimmy 132, 142
Elorde, Flash 144
Els, Ernie **210**
Elway, John **161,** 177
Emerson, Roy 301, 303, **307–308,** 312, 313, 316
English, Alex **89**
Equal Education Amendment 270, 311
Erving, Julius 79, **89–91,** 96
Escalera, Alfredo 129
ESPN 59, 308, 313, 320
Esposito, Phil 239, **242–243,** 254
Esposito, Tony **243,** 247
European Championships for Men's Clubs 125
European Cup 85, 341
European Grand Prix 330
European Masters 221
European Order of Merit 206, 209, 221
European PGA Tour 206, 209, 211
Evans, Chick 211
Evans, Janet **271,** 297
Evernham, Ray 329
Evert, Chris 302, 307, **308,** 309, 310, 314, 316, 319, 321
Evert, Jimmy 308
Every Shot I Take (Love) 217
Ewbank, Weeb 152
Ewing, Patrick **91**
Ewry, Ray **271,** 282
Explorers 93, 94

F

Fageros, Karol 309
Falcons 188
Faldo, Nick **210–211,** 220, 221, 223, 228
Family Circle Cup 309
Fangio, Juan-Manuel **326,** 335
Farragut Academy 92
Farrell, Johnny 210
Fassi, Carlo 271, 274
Favre, Brett **161–162,** 186
Fazio, Tom 213
Fears, Tom **162,** 198
Feathers, Beattie 181
Federal League 52
Federation Cup 307, 314, 318
Federov, Sergei **243**
Feller, Bob 20
Fellowship of Christian Athletes 215
Fengler, Harlen 331
Fernandez, Lisa **342–343**
Ferrari team 335
Ferrier, Jim 209
Fighting Irish 184
Fignon, Laurent 344
figure skating 263, 266, 267–268, 271–272, 274, 275–276, 281–283, 284, 295–296, 298

Fillion, Herve **343**
Final Four
    basketball 77, 80, 82, 83, 85, 89, 93, 97, 98, 99, 103, 108, 112, 122, 124, 125, 126
    soccer 342
Fingers, Rollie **20**
Finley, Charles O. 31
Firecracker 250 336
Firecracker 400 334, 336
Firestone Tournament of Champions 339
Fisk, Carlton 7, 13, **21,** 47
Fittipaldi, Emerson **326**
Fitzsimmons, Bob 136
Fleischer, Nat 139
Fleming, Peggy **271–272,** 274, 298
Fleming, Peter 314
Flo Hyman Award 217, 226
Flood, Curt 21
Flores, Victor 142
Florida A&M University 274
Florida Marlins 17, 51, 52
Florida Panthers 240
Florida State League 48
Florida State University 86, 153, 187
Flowers, Tiger 134
Floyd, Maria 211
Floyd, Raymond **211,** 231
Flynn, Jim 131
Folley, Zora 132
football 32, **149–203,** 275
Force, John **326–327**
Ford 330
Ford, Whitey **21–22,** 24
Fordham University 22
Foreman, George 128, **132,** 133, 136, 142
Formula One 323, 324, 325, 326, 329, 330, 331, 332, 335, 336, 337
Formula 2 325
Formula 3 336
Fortner, Nell 88
Fort Wayne Pistons 94, 120
Fosbury, Dick **272**
Fosse, Ray 57
Foster, Bob **132,** 145
Fouts, Dan **162–163,** 171
Fox, Billy 138
Fox, Nelson 5, **22**
Fox Sports 126, 155, 174, 175
Foxx, Jimmie **22,** 27, 29, 31, 50
Foyt, A.J. 325, **327–328,** 331, 332, 336, 337
Francis, Julius 147
Franco, John 64
Frank Selke Trophy 243, 244
Frank Shorter Sportswear 293
Fraser, Dawn **272**
Fraser, Neale 312
Frazier, Joe 128, 132, **132–133,** 137
Frazier, Walt **91–92,** 112
Fred Haskins Player of the Year Award 231
Freedom National Bank 57
French Amateur 221
French Open 301, 303, 305, 306, 308, 309, 310, 312, 313, 314, 315, 316, 318, 319, 320, 321, 322
Frey, Jim 9
Friars 125
Frisch, Frankie 20, **22–23,** 30
Fry, Shirley 310

Fuhr, Grant **243–244**
Fulks, Joe **92**
Fullmer, Gene 129, **133**, 143, 145
Funny Cars 325, 327, 335
Furman University 214
Futch, Eddie 133
Futures Tour 230

G

Gable, Dan **272–273**
Gaines, Clarence 111
Gainesville Raceway 325
Gainey, Bob **244**
Gainford, George 143
Galindo, Rudy 298
Gallagher, Harry 272
Gallatin, Harry **92**
Gamoudi, Mohamed 286
Garagiola, Joe 7
Garcia, Jose Luis 142
Garciaparra, Nomar **23**
Garlits, Don **328**
Garnett, Kevin **92–93**
Garrison, Zina 308, 315, 319
Gartner, Mike **244**
Garvey, Steve **23**, 70
Gastineau, Mark 201
Gavilan, Kid 129, **133**
Gebrselassi, Haile **273**
Gehrig, Lou 8, 17, 18, **23–24**, 27, 29, 31, 36, 39, 42, 44, 47, 54, 68
Gehringer, Charlie **24**, 50
Geoffrion, Bernie **244**
George, Bill **163**
Georgetown University 91, 100, 126
Georgia Amateur 214
Georgia State League 67
Georgia Tech 210, 214
German Open 310, 319
Gervin, George **93**, 122
Gettysburg College 52, 87
Ghizzi, Vic 217
Giamatti, A. Bartlett 58
Giardello, Joey 133, **133**, 145
Gibson, Althea **308–309**, 321, 322
Gibson, Bob **24–25**, 40, 41
Gibson, Josh **25**, 39
Gifford, Frank 152, **163**
Gilbert, Brad 301
Gilbert, Rod 256
Gillman, Sid 151, 174
Givens, Robin 146
Glavine, Tom **25**
Glidden, Bob **328**
Goalby, Bob 209
Gola, Tom **93–94**, 99
Golden Gloves 127, 130, 134, 135, 138, 139, 140, 143, 146
Golden Lights Championship 217
Golden State Warriors 84, 86, 103, 114
Gold Glove 3, 7, 8, 9, 10, 14, 17, 21, 23, 28, 29, 30, 36, 39, 43, 44, 47, 48, 54, 55, 60, 64
Goldman, Charlie 141
Goldman, Ronald 190
golf **205–233**, 309, 313
Golf Channel, The 207
Golf Digest 231
Golfer of the Century 219
Golfer of the Decade 217
Golf magazine 217, 219
Golf Swing, The (Middlecoff) 218

Golf Writers Association of America 231
Gomez, Lefty **25–26**
Gomez, Wilfredo **133–134**
Gonzaga College 121
Gonzalez, Juan **26**
Gonzalez, Pancho **309**, 312, 317, 318
Goodrich, Gail 85, **94**
Goodwill Games 85, 110, 131, 243, 279, 287
Goolagong, Evonne 308, **309**
Gordien, Fortune 288
Gordon, Jeff **328–329**
Gorman, Tom 317
Goslin, Goose **26**
Gossage, Goose **26–27**
Gottlieb, Eddie 84
Gould, Shane 264
Graceland College 277
Graf, Peter 310
Graf, Steffi 307, **309–310**, 315, 319
Graffis, Herb 206
Graham, Billy 129
Graham, Otto **163–164**, 173, 180, 194
Grambling State University 70, 116, 156, 158, 171
Grand Masters circuit 309
Grand National 333
Grand Prix 324, 330
Grand Prix of Tennis 312
Grand Slam
  golf 213, 214, 220, 223, 224, 232
  tennis 301, 303, 304, 305, 306, 307, 308, 309, 310, 311, 312, 313, 314, 315, 316, 317, 318, 319, 320, 321, 322
Grange, Red **164**, 181
Gran Premio International del Norte 326
Grant, Horace 102
Graves, Kid 134
Gray, Jim 58
Graziano, Rocky **134**, 147
Greater Baltimore Classic 217
Greater Greensboro Open 226
Greater Pittsburgh League 197
Greaves, Will 145
Greb, Harry **134**, 145
Green, Darrell **164–165**
Green, Dennis 177
Green, Hubert 223
Green Bay Packers 149, 151, 152, 156, 158, 159, 161, 162, 165, 169, 170, 181, 183, 192, 193, 194, 196, 198, 200–201
Greenberg, Hank 5, 22, **27**
Greenbrier, The 226
Greene, Joe **165**
Greene, Maurice **273**, 277
Green League 125
Greer, Hal **94–95**
Gregg, Forrest **165**
Gretzky, Walter 244–245
Gretzky, Wayne 237, 238, 243, **244–245**, 248, 249, 250, 253, 259, 260
Grey Cup 179
Grier, Roosevelt 171, 183
Griese, Bob **165–166**
Griffey, Ken, Jr. xi, **27–28**, 294
Griffey, Ken, Sr. 27
Griffin, Archie **166**

Griffin, Montel 137
Griffith, Emile 130, **134**, 141, 145
Griffith Joyner, Florence **273–274**, 278
Grimsley, Will 320
Grove, Lefty **28**, 51
Groza, Lou **166**
GTE Classic 211
Guldahl, Ralph **211**
Gurney, Dan 328, **329**
Gwynn, Tony 12, **28–29**, 48
gymnastics 268–269, 281, 285–286, 289–290

H

Haarhuis, Paul 306
Hackenschmidt, George 72
Hadfield, Vic 256
Hadley, Bump 15
Hagan, Cliff **95**, 105
Hagen, Walter 209, 210, **211–212**, 218, 220, 224, 229, 233
Hagler, Marvelous Marvin **135**, 136, 139
Haines, George 293
Hainsworth, George **245–246**
Hakkinen, Mika **329–330**
Halas, George 159, 164, 175
Hall, Glenn **246**
Hallberg, Gary 210
Ham, Jack **166–167**
Hambletonian 342, 343
Hamill, Dorothy **274**, 290, 298
Hamilton, Scott **274**
Hamilton Tiger-Cats 177
Hamm, Mia **343**
Hannah, John **167**
Hannum, Alex 84
Hantzke, Karen 311
Harbour Town Golf Links 217
Hardaway, Anfernee 113, 117
Harding, Tonya 298
Hardin-Simmons University 152
Hard Road to Glory, A (Ashe) 302
Hardwick, Mary 314
Harlem Globetrotters 24, 84, 96, 104, 126, 309
Harness Racing Living Hall of Fame 342, 343
Harris, Danny 286
Harris, Franco **167–168**
Harrisburg Giants 13, 14
Hart, Clyde 277
Hart, Doris **310**, 318
Hart, Leon **168**
Hartack, Bill 343
Hartford Whalers 240, 247, 248, 249
Hart Trophy 235, 236, 237, 240, 241, 243, 244, 245, 247, 248, 249, 250, 251, 252, 253, 254, 255, 256, 257, 259, 260
Harvard University 195, 214, 263, 268
Harvey, Doug 244, **246**
Hasek, Dominik **246–247**
Havlicek, John 85, **95–96**
Hawaiian Ladies Open 215
Hawkeyes (Univ. of Iowa) 272, 273
Hawkins, Connie **96**
Hayes, Bob **274–275**
Hayes, Elvin **96–97**
Hayes, Lester 168
Hayes, Woody 166

Haynes, Mike **168**
Haynie, Sandra **212**
Hazzard, Walt 94
HBO 132, 159, 177, 302
Heard, Jerry 228
Hearns, Thomas 130, **135**, 139
Heart Like a Wheel (film) 333
Heeney, Tom 146
Heiden, Eric **275**
Heifetz, Jascha 43
Heilmann, Harry **29**
Hein, Mel **168**
Heinsohn, Tom 85, **97**
Heisman Trophy 32, 149, 150, 153, 157, 158, 160, 161, 166, 168, 169, 176, 180, 186, 190, 192, 199, 202
Heiss, Carol 263, **275**
Heiss, Nancy 275
Hemus, Solly 24
Henderson, Rickey 10, **29–30**
Hendricks, Ted **168–169**
Henie, Sonja 271, **275–276**, 298
Hernandez, Keith 66
Herrick, Myron T. 320
Hershey Bears 235
Hertz Rent-A-Car 190
Herzog, Whitey 64
Hickock Award 222
Hill, Calvin 97
Hill, Graham 325, **330**
Hill, Grant **97**
Hill, Virgil 135
Hinault, Bernard 276
Hingis, Martina 307, 310, 321, 322
Hirsch, Elroy **169**, 185
Hirschbeck, John 5
Hitler, Adolf 288–289
Hoad, Lew 309, **310**, 312
hockey **235–261**
Hockey Hall of Fame 235, 236, 237, 238, 239, 240, 241, 242, 243, 244, 245, 246, 247, 248, 249, 250, 251, 252, 253, 254, 255, 256, 257, 258, 259, 260, 261
Hockey News, The 235, 236, 237, 238, 239, 240, 241, 242, 243, 244, 245, 246, 247, 248, 249, 250, 251, 252, 253, 254, 255, 256, 257, 258, 259, 260, 261
Hodges, Gil **30**, 59
Hogan, Ben 205, 206, **212–213**, 217, 218, 220, 221, 223, 227, 229, 232
Holdsclaw, Chamique **97–98**
Hollywood Squares 347
Holmes, Flossie 135
Holmes, Larry 128, 132, **135–136**, 142, 145
Holy Cross 85, 97
Holyfield, Evander 132, 135, **136**, 146–147
Holzman, Red 87, 95, 108
Homestead Grays 6, 13, 25, 39
Honda Broderick Award 110, 343
Hooks, Alvin 267
Hooks, Alvin, Jr. 267
Hoosier Grand Prix 324
Hoosiers 121, 293
Hope, Bob 231
Hope, Maurice 129
Hopkins, Bernhard 137
Hornsby, Rogers 12, 22–23, 28, 29, **30–31**, 33, 50, 63
Hornung, Paul **169**

Index

horse racing 339–340, 341–342, 343, 344, 346–348
Horton, Tim **247**
Hostak, Al 147
House of Representatives, U.S. 11, 173, 291
Houston, Ken **170**
Houston Aeros 247
Houston Astros 8, 22, 34, 42, 46, 47, 55, 60, 67
Houston Comets 85, 121
Houston Oilers 154, 156, 157, 165, 170, 171, 173, 178, 179
Houston Open 223
Houston Rockets 79, 81, 83, 88, 91, 96, 106, 112–113, 116
Howard, Kevin 139
Howe, Gordie 235, 238, 241, **247–248,** 249, 252, 259, 260
Howe, Mark 247
Howe, Marty 247
Howell, Harry 254
Howsam, Bob 51
How to Play Your Best Golf All the Time (Armour) 206
Hoyas 91
Hromek, Justin 349
Hubbell, Carl 19, 29, **31**
Huff, Sam **170**
Huggett, Brian 228
Huggins, Miller 23, 24, 59
Hull, Bobby 236, 243, **248,** 252
Hull, Brett **248**
Hunt, Joe 312
Hunter, Catfish **31–32**
Hunter, C.J. 278
Hutson, Don **170–171**
Hyman, Flo **276**

I

IBF (International Boxing Federation) 131, 132, 136, 137, 146
Ice Capades 274
Ice Follies 284
I Have Changed (Owens) 289
Illinois Women's Athletic Club 232
Imlach, Punch 247, 252
Indiana Fever 88
Indiana Pacers 82, 83, 89, 109, 110, 111, 122
Indianapolis 500 324, 325, 326, 327, 331, 332, 335, 336, 337, 338
Indianapolis ABCs 13
Indianapolis Clowns 3
Indianapolis Colts 159
Indianapolis Motor Speedway 328, 329, 332
Indianapolis Racers 245
Indiana State University 81, 98
Indiana University 80, 81, 121, 293
Indurain, Miguel **276**
Indy 500 325
Indy car 323, 324, 325, 326–327, 329, 331, 332, 335, 336, 337
Indy Racing League 328
Inkster, Juli **213,** 226
Inside the NFL (TV program) 159, 177
Insurance Youth Golf Classic 231
Internal Revenue Service (IRS) 140
International Amateur Athletics Federation (IAAF) 290, 292
International Boxing Hall of Fame 129, 130, 131, 132, 133, 134, 135, 136, 137, 138, 139, 140, 141, 142, 143, 144, 145, 146, 147
International League 39, 56, 239
International Management Group 222
International Motorsports Hall of Fame 323, 324, 325, 326, 328, 329, 330, 331, 332, 333, 335, 336, 337, 338
International Olympic Committee 196, 276, 278, 296
International President's Cup 223, 228
International Ski Racing Association (ISRA) 280
International Softball Federation Women's World Championships 343
International Swimming Hall of Fame 264, 266, 268, 285, 287, 292, 293, 297
International Tennis Hall of Fame 302, 303, 304, 305, 306, 307, 308, 309, 310, 311, 312, 313, 314, 315, 316, 317, 318, 319, 320, 321
International Track Association 289, 296
International Women's Sports Hall of Fame 229, 232, 233, 264, 266, 272, 274, 275, 276, 280, 281, 285, 291, 296, 297, 299, 305, 306, 308, 309, 311, 344
Inverness Club 219, 220
Inverness Four-Ball 211
Iowa State University 272
Irvin, Monte 32
Irwin, Hale **213–214**
Issel, Dan **98**
Italian Amateur 221
Italian League 82, 108, 346
Italian Open 302, 303, 308
Ivanisevic, Goran 301, 318

J

J. Walter Kennedy Citizenship Award 88
Jack Nicklaus College Player of the Year Award 231
Jackson, Bo **32–33**
Jackson, Harvey 237, 241, **248,** 256
Jackson, Joe 33
Jackson, Luscious 94
Jackson, Mark 161
Jackson, Melody. *See* Armstrong, Henry
Jackson, Phil 83, 114
Jackson, Reggie **33–34**
Jackson State University 151, 184
Jacksonville Bulls 166
Jacksonville Jaguars 161, 177
Jacobs, Helen **310–311,** 314, 315
Jaeger, Andrea 311
Jager, Tom 265
Jagr, Jaromir 249
Jameson, Betty **214**
Jansen, Dan **276–277**
Jansen, Jane 276
Jarrett, Dale **330**
Jarrett, Ned **330**
Jayhawks 84, 104
Jeffries, James J. **136,** 137
Jenkins, Dan 181
Jenkins, Ferguson **34,** 62
Jenkins, Hayes, Alan 275
Jenner, Bruce 275, **277,** 294
Jesse Owens International Award 344
Jesse Owens Youth Games 273
Jeter, Derek **34**
Jim Thorpe—All-American (film) 196
Jim Thorpe Award 187
Job Corps 132
jockeys 339–340, 341–342, 343, 344, 346–348
Johansson, Ingemar 142
Johncock, Gordon 330
Johnson, Ban 38
Johnson, Ben 282
Johnson, Jack 135, **136,** 137, 140
Johnson, Jimmy 177
Johnson, Judy 25
Johnson, Junior 326, **330–331**
Johnson, Magic 81, **98–99,** 108, 117, 126
Johnson, Marvin 144
Johnson, Michael 273, **277,** 290
Johnson, Rafer **277–278**
Johnson, Randy **34–35**
Johnson, Reggie 137
Johnson, Walter 4, 19, 25, **35,** 51, 52, 69, 74
Joiner, Charlie **171**
Jones, Bobby 205–206, 212, **214,** 215, 224, 229, 231
Jones, Chipper **35**
Jones, Deacon **171,** 183
Jones, Doug 132
Jones, K.C. 85, 93, **99–100**
Jones, Marion **278**
Jones, Parnelli 325, **331**
Jones, Roy, Jr. 137
Jones, Sam 85, **100**
Jordan, James 102
Jordan, Kathy 316
Jordan, Michael xi, 79, 83, 89–90, 91, 98, **100–102,** 111, 112, 113, 115, 116, 117, 126, 232, 244, 343
Joyce, Joan 344
Joyner, Al 273
Joyner-Kersee, Jackie 273, **278–280**
Jurgensen, Sonny **171**

K

Kafelnikov, Yevgeny 318
Kaline, Al **35–36**
Kalule, Ayub 139
Kansas City Athletics 6, 9, 31, 33, 36, 39, 41, 50, 63
Kansas City Chiefs 150, 152, 154, 156, 159, 161, 172, 179, 192, 193, 198, 200
Kansas City Monarchs 6, 50, 56
Kansas City Royals 9, 13, 32, 52, 60
Kansas City Stars 7
Kansas University 125, 186
Karlis, Rich 161
Karolyi, Bela 290
Karras, Alex 169
Kazaam (film) 114
Keane, Johnny 24
Kearns, Jack 131
Keeler, Willie 8, **36**
Keino, Kip **280,** 291
Kellett, Don 197
Kelly, George 67
Kelly, Leroy **171–172**
Kelly, Red 249
Kemper Open 208
Ken Houston Award 165
Kennedy, John F. 291
Kennedy, Ted 247, **249**
Kennedy, Walter 96
Kent State University 172
Kentucky Colonels 98
Kentucky Derby 340, 341, 342, 343, 346, 347
Kentucky Futurity 342, 343
Keon, Dave **249**
Kerkorian, Gary 197
Kerr, Dickie 48
Kerr, John 93
Kersee, Bob 267, 273, 278, 279
Ketchel, Stanley 137
Keystone Nationals 333
Kidd, Billy **280**
Kidd, Jason 97
Kiick, Jim 157, 158, 174, 199
Killebrew, Harmon **36**
Killy, Jean Claude **280**
Kilmer, Billy 171
Kimball, Dick 280
Kim, Dong-kyun 133
Kim, Ki-Soo 130
Kiner, Ralph 36, **37,** 64
King, Betsy **214–215**
King, Billie Jean 305, 306, 308, 309, **311,** 316–317
King, Micki **280**
King of the World, The (Remnick) 127, 142
Kipketer, Wilson 268
Kiraly, Karch **281**
Kirkpatrick, James 146
Kite, Tom **215,** 230
Klammer, Franz **281**
Klein, Chuck **37**
Knapp, Barbara 308
Knight, Bob 95
Knight, Ray 217
Korbut, Olga **281**
Koss, Johann Olav 266, **281**
Koufax, Sandy 19, **37–38,** 40, 41, 51, 60
Krajicek, Richard 318
Kramer, Jack 303, 309, **311–312,** 317, 318
Kramer, Jerry 192
Krause, Paul **172**
Krickstein, Aaron 306
Krone, Julie **344**
Kuehne, Trip 231
Kurri, Jari **249–250**
Kutztown State College 185
Kwan, Michelle **281–282,** 283

L

Labonte, Terry 330
Lach, Elmer 257
Lacoste, Rene 304, 305, **312,** 320
Lady Bulldogs 89
Lady Byng Trophy 237, 239, 241, 242, 245, 248, 249, 250, 254, 255, 256
Lady Huskies 104
Lady Monarchs 87, 103
Lady Raiders 121
Lady Trojans 110, 111
Lady Volunteers 98, 108
Lafleur, Guy 242, **250**
Lajoie, Napoleon "Nap" 28, 33, **38**
Lakeland Classic 218
Lalonde, Don 139

Lalonde, Newsy **250**
Lambert, Jack **172**
Lamonica, Daryle 154
LaMotta, Jake 137–**138,** 143
Lancaster, Burt 196
Lance Armstrong Foundation 341
Landis, Kenesaw Mountain 15, 33, 45, 66
Landry, Tom 174
Lane, Dick **172**
Lanier, Bob 86, **103**
Lanier, Willie **172**
Lapchick, Richard 311
LaPorte, Juan 133
Largent, Steve **172–173**
Larsen, Don **38**
La Russa, Tony 21
Lary, Yale **173**
La Salle University 93, 94, 99
Lasorda, Tommy 52
Las Vegas Invitational 231
Late Show with David Letterman (TV program) 160, 349
Lau, Charley 9
Lauda, Niki **331**
Lavelli, Dante **173**
Laver, Rod 301, 303, **312–313,** 316, 317, 318, 320
Laws, Don 274
Layne, Alfredo 134
Layne, Bobby **173–174**
Lazzeri, Tony 4, 105
Leadbetter, David 211
Lee, Sammy 283
Lee, Spike 111
Leetch, Brian **250–251**
Legends of Golf (Senior PGA Tour) 232
Legends of Golf (TV documentary) 209
Lehman, Tom 231
Lemaire, Jacques 250
Le Mans 328
Lemieux, Mario 242, 249, **251–252**
Lemon, Bob **38–39**
LeMond, Greg **344–345**
Lendl, Ivan 303, 306, **313,** 314, 315, 317
Lendl, Samantha 313
Lenglen, Suzanne **313,** 315, 316
Leonard, Buck 39
Leonard, Justin 217
Leonard, Sugar Ray 129, 135, 136, **138–139**
Leslie, Jock 144
Leslie, Lisa **103**
Lester B. Pearson Award 261
Levai, Istvan 293
Levinsky, Battling 145
Lewis, Carl 164, **282,** 289
Lewis, Chris 314
Lewis, Lennox 136
Lichtenstein, Grace 308
Lieberman-Cline, Nancy 87, **103–104**
Lilly, Bob **174**
Lincoln University 32
Lindros, Eric **252**
Lindsay, Ted 235, 247, **252**
Lipinski, Jack 283
Lipinski, Tara 282, **282–283**
Lipton Championship 322

Liston, Sonny 127–128, **139–140,** 142, 147
Little, Larry **174**
Little, Lawson **215**
Little House on the Prairie (TV series) 183
Littler, Gene 208, **215–216**
Little Rock College 17
Lloyd, John 308
Loach, Maxwell. *See* Saad Muhammad, Matthew
Lobo, Rebecca **104**
Locke, Bobby **216,** 228, 229
Lockridge, Rocky 134
Lombardi, Vince 158, 163, 165, 169, 170, 192, 194
Lombardi Award 189, 200
Lone Star Conference 164
Long, Howie **174**
Long Beach State University 93
Longden, Johnny 347
Long Island University 105
Lopez, Nancy **216–217,** 218
Los Angeles Clippers 80, 125
Los Angeles Dodgers 3, 5, 11, 13, 19, 22, 23, 33, 36, 40, 41, 47, 48, 51, 52, 56, 65, 67, 70, 72, 73, 109
Los Angeles Express 202
Los Angeles Jets 120
Los Angeles Kings 25, 240, 242, 243, 245, 249, 250, 253, 257
Los Angeles Lakers 77, 80, 81, 82, 83, 84–85, 87, 90, 94, 95, 96, 99, 100, 102, 106, 108, 111, 112, 113, 114, 116, 118, 120, 122, 124, 126
Los Angeles Open 213
Los Angeles Raiders 150, 159, 168
Los Angeles Rams 99, 158, 159, 162, 163, 166, 169, 171, 172, 177, 182, 183, 186, 198
Los Angeles Sparks 103
Lott, Ronnie **175,** 188
Louganis, Greg **283,** 285
Lou Gehrig Award 54, 64
Louis, Joe 43, 130, 131, 135, 137, **140,** 141, 143, 144, 145, 147
Louisiana State University (LSU) 107, 113, 115, 194, 198
Louisiana Tech 106, 154
Louisville Cardinals 69
Love, Davis, III 208, **217**
Love, Davis, Jr. 217
Lovellette, Clyde **104**
LPGA (Ladies Professional Golf Association) Championship 207, 212, 213, 217, 223, 224, 227, 228, 231, 232
LPGA Hall of Fame 205, 206, 207, 209, 212, 213, 214, 215, 217, 218, 223–224, 226, 227, 228, 231, 232, 233
LPGA Tour 205, 206, 207, 209, 212, 213, 214, 215, 217, 218, 222, 223, 224, 226, 227, 228, 229, 230–231, 232, 233, 309, 344
Lucas, Jerry 80, 95, **104–105**
Luckman, Sid **175**
Lucky International 229
Lucky to Be Alive (Campanella) 11
Luisetti, Hank **105**
Lundy, Lamar 171, 183
Lutz, Bob 319
Lynn, Fred 53

Lynn, Janet **284**

M

Macauley, Ed **105–106**
Mack, Connie 16, 38
Mackey, John **175**
Maddux, Greg 25, **39**
Mahovlich, Frank **252**
Mahre, Phil **284**
Mahre, Steve 284
Majkowski, Don 162
Mako, Gene 304
Mallory, Molla Bjurstedt 308, 313, **313–314**
Malone, Joe **252–253**
Malone, Karl 102, **106**
Malone, Moses **106–107**
Mamaliga, Emil 284
Mandlikova, Hana **314**
Mangrum, Lloyd 213, **217**
Manley, Effie 32
Mann, Carol 217, **218**
Man of the Year Award 181
Mansell, Nigel **331**
Mantle, Elvin "Mutt" 40
Mantle, Mickey 19, 38, **40,** 41, 48, 64
Maradona, Diego **346**
marathon 265, 284, 286, 290–291, 292, 297, 299
Maravich, Pete **107**
Maravich, Press 107
Marble, Alice 311, **314**
Marchetti, Gino **175–176**
Marciano, Rocky 130, 135, **140–141,** 142, 143, 147
Marichal, Juan **40–41**
Marino, Dan xi, **176–177,** 179, 197
Maris, Roger 40, **41,** 44, 45, 65
Marshall, Jim 184, 189
Marshall University 94
Martin, Billy 33, 39
Martin, Casey **218**
Martin, George 9
Martin, Harvey 200
Martin, Joe 127
Martin, Pepper 20
Martin, Rick 255
Martin, Todd 301
Martinez, Conchita 316
Martinez, Pedro **41**
Martinsburg Blue Socks 72
Marucci, Buddy 231
Maryland State-Eastern Shore College 189
MasterCard Colonial 230
Masters 206, 208, 209, 210–211, 212, 213, 214, 215, 217, 218, 219, 220, 222, 223, 224, 226, 228, 229, 231, 232
Masterson Trophy 240, 251, 255, 256, 257, 258
Mathews, Eddie **41–42**
Mathewson, Christy 4, **42,** 69, 74
Mathias, Bob 277, **284**
Mathis, Buster 132
Mathis, Buster, Jr. 146
Matson, Ollie **177**
Matson, Randy **284–285**
Mattingly, Don **42–43**
Maxim, Joey 141, 142, 143
Maxwell Award 150, 152, 158, 168, 196
Maynard, Don **177–178**

Mays, Willie 3, 8, 14, 19, **43,** 57, 60, 64, 73
Mazda LPGA Championship 209, 214
Mazeroski, Bill **43–44**
Mazzinghi, Sandro 130
McAdoo, Bob **107–108**
McCall, Oliver 135
McCallum, Mike 137
McCarron, Chris **346**
McCormack, Mark 222
McCormick, Kelly 285
McCormick, Pat **285**
McCovey, Willie **44**
McCray, Nikki **108**
McDonald's LPGA Championship 209, 213, 224
McEnroe, John 302, 303, 306, 313, **314–315,** 316, 317, 321
McEnroe, Patrick 306
McEwen, Tom 335
McGill University 242
McGinnis, George 90
McGraw, John 13, 22, 50, 67, 69
McGregor, Ken 318
McGuire, Al 108
McGuire, Dick 108
McGwire, Mark 36, 41, **44–45,** 65
McHale, Kevin 78, **108–109,** 114
MCI Classic 217
McIntosh, Hugh D. 137
McKinley, Chuck 312
McKinney, Thurston 140
McNeeley, Peter 146
McNeeley, Tom 142
McNeese State University 88
McNeil, Lori 310
McPhee, John 82
Meagher, Mary T. **285,** 295
Mears, Bill 331
Mears, Rick **331–332,** 336, 337
Mecir, Miloslav 307, 313
Medvedev, Andrei 301
Medwick, Joe 20, **45**
Memorial Tournament 230
Memory Book, The (Lucas) 105
Memphis Showboats 200
Memphis Southmen 158, 199
Memphis State 123
Menzel, Roderich 304
Mercedes Championship 231
Merckx, Eddy 276
Merion Golf Club 213, 228
Meriweather, Willie 93
Messier, Mark 243, **253**
Mexican League 32, 50
Meyer, Debbie 285
Meyer, Leo "Dutch" 151
Meyer, Ray 110
Meyers, Ann **109**
Miami Dolphins 149, 151, 157, 158, 160, 165, 174, 176, 177, 179, 186, 193, 199
Miami Four-Ball 219
Miami Heat 87, 97, 108
Michigan 500 336
Michigan International Speedway 323
Michigan-Ontario League 24
Michigan State University 54, 81, 98, 99
Mickelson, Phil 210
Middle Atlantic League 21
Middlecoff, Cary 217, **218**
Midori Ito 298

Midwest Division 113, 118
Midwest Sprint Car 331
Mikan, George 92, 104, 105, **109–110**
Mike Douglas Show, The (TV program) 231
Mikita, Stan **253–254**
Mildenburger, Karl 128
Mill, Andy 308
Miller, Cheryl **110–111**
Miller, Hack 72
Miller, Johnny 210, **218,** 231
Miller, Jutta 298
Miller, Ray 54
Miller, Reggie 110, **111**
Miller, Shannon **285–286**
Miller High Life 500 323
Mills, Billy **286**
Milwaukee Braves 3, 42, 49, 61, 63, 65
Milwaukee Brewers 3, 20, 46, 67, 74, 75
Milwaukee Bucks 77, 78, 86, 89, 95, 97, 103, 107, 117
Milwaukee Hawks 115
Minneapolis Lakers 80, 92, 104, 109, 110, 119, 124
Minneapolis Millers 43
Minnesota North Stars 242, 244
Minnesota Timberwolves 93, 109, 110
Minnesota Twins 12, 19, 31, 36, 38, 46, 53, 73
Minnesota Vikings 73, 152, 153, 156, 157, 159, 160, 167, 172, 177, 179, 184, 189, 190, 193, 194
Minter, Alan 135
Mississippi Valley State University 171, 185
Mitchell, Bobby **178**
Mitchell, Dale 38
Mitchell, Lydell 167
Mize, Johnny **45–46**
Mize, Larry 220
Mobile Black Bears 70
Mobile Tigers 50
Molitor, Paul **46**
Molson Brewery 236
Monday Night Football (TV program) 32, 159, 163, 182
Mondschein, Irving 284
Monk, Art **178**
Monroe, Earl **111–112**
Monroe, Marilyn 18
Monroe, Willie 135
Monsanto Open 210
Montana, Joe **178–179,** 202
Montclair State College 82
Montgomery, Colin 210, 221
Montreal Canadiens 236, 237, 239, 241, 242, 244, 245, 246, 247, 250, 252–253, 254, 256, 257, 258, 261
Montreal Expos 12, 13, 17, 34, 41, 51, 57, 64, 72
Montreal Maroons 240, 260
Montreal Royals 56
Monzon, Carlos 130, **141**
Moody, Helen Wills 308, 310, **315**
Moon, Warren 177, **179**
Moore, Archie **141,** 142
Moore, Dickie 254
Moore, Lenny **179–180**
Moorer, Michael 132, 136
Moran, Gertrude "Gussy" 303

Morariu, Corina 307
Morehouse College 286
Morenz, Howie 236, **254**
Morgan, Joe **46–47,** 51
Morgan State University 155, 171, 172
Morris, Eugene "Mercury" 157, 158, 174
Morris, Glenn 289
Morris, Tom, Jr. 206, 231
Morrison, Tommy 132
Moses, Edwin **286–287,** 290
Mosienko, Bill 237
Moss, Stirling **332**
Most, Johnny 95
Most Outstanding Player 98, 110, 112, 119, 122, 123, 124, 126
Most Popular Driver of the Year 323, 326, 338
Most Valuable Player (MVP)
  baseball 3, 6, 7, 8, 11, 12, 13, 14, 15, 16, 17, 18, 19, 20, 22, 23, 24, 25, 26, 27, 28, 29, 30, 31, 33, 35, 36, 37, 38, 40, 41, 43, 45, 46, 47, 48, 49, 53, 54, 55, 56, 57, 59, 60, 63, 64, 65, 66, 68, 70, 72, 75
  basketball 78, 79, 80, 81, 82, 84, 85, 86, 88, 89, 90, 93, 95, 96, 99, 102, 105, 106, 108, 109, 110, 113, 114, 115, 116, 117, 118, 119, 121, 122, 123, 124, 125, 126
  football 150, 153, 154, 155, 157, 158, 159, 161, 162, 167, 168, 169, 170, 171, 174, 175, 179, 181, 183, 184, 185, 186, 190, 191, 192, 193, 194, 197, 198, 202
  hockey 235, 236, 237, 240, 241, 242, 243, 244, 245, 246, 247, 248, 249, 250, 251, 252, 253, 255, 256, 257, 258, 259, 260, 261
  soccer 341, 343, 346
  softball 344
Motley, Marion **180**
Motor City Open 217
Motorsports Hall of Fame of America 323, 324, 325, 328, 329, 330, 331, 333, 335, 336, 337, 338
Mountaineers 124
Muhammad, Mustafa 145
Muldowney, Shirley **332–333**
Mulligan, Marty 312
Munoz, Anthony **180–181**
Munson, Thurman **47**
Murphy, Calvin **112**
Murphy, Dale **47**
Murray, Eddie 44, **47–48**
Murray State University 92
Musial, Stan 12, **48**
Mutscheller, Jim 197
Myhra, Steve 153, 197

N

Naber, John **287**
Nabisco Dinah Shore Invitational 205, 207, 213, 214, 222, 224–225, 230
Nagurski, Bronko **181**
NAIA (National Association of Intercollegiate Athletics) 116
Naismith Memorial Basketball Hall of Fame 78, 79, 80, 81, 82, 83, 85,

86, 87, 88, 89, 91, 92, 93, 94, 95, 96, 97, 98, 100, 103, 104, 105, 107, 108, 109, 110, 111, 112, 115, 116, 117, 119, 120, 122, 123, 124, 125
Namath, Joe 177, **181–182**
Napoles, Jose 141
NASCAR (National Association for Stock Car Auto Racing) 323, 324, 325, 326, 328, 329, 330, 333, 335, 336, 338
Nashua 43
Nastase, Ilie 303, **315**
National Association for the Advancement of Colored People (NAACP) 57
National Basketball Association (NBA) 73, 77, 78, 79, 80, 81, 82, 83, 84, 85, 86, 87, 88, 89, 90, 91, 92, 93, 94, 95, 96, 97, 98–99, 100, 102, 103, 104, 105, 106, 107–108, 109, 110, 111, 112, 113, 114, 115, 116, 117, 119, 120, 121, 122, 123, 124, 125, 126
National Basketball League (NBL) 87, 110, 120, 244
National Boxing Association 130, 133, 141, 143, 147
National Boxing Federation 135
National Championships, U.S. 131
National Conference of Christians and Jews 64
National Football Conference (NFC) 150, 159, 160, 161, 162, 174, 179, 184, 185, 186, 188, 189, 193, 194, 200, 202
National Football League (NFL) 32, 33, 73, 95, 149, 150, 151, 152, 153–155, 156, 157, 158, 159, 160, 161, 162, 163, 164, 165, 166, 167, 168, 169, 170, 171, 172, 173, 174, 175, 176, 177, 178, 179, 180, 181, 182, 183, 184, 185, 186, 187, 188, 189, 190, 191, 192, 193, 194, 195, 196, 197, 198, 199, 200, 201, 202
National Hockey League (NHL) 25, 235, 236, 237, 238, 239, 240, 241, 243, 244, 245, 246, 247, 248, 249, 250, 251, 252, 253, 254, 255, 256, 257, 258, 259, 260, 261
National Horse Racing Hall of Fame 340, 341, 342, 343, 344, 346, 347, 348
National Hot Rod Association (NHRA) 323, 325, 326, 327, 328, 332, 333, 335
National Invitation Tournament (NIT) 86, 93, 110, 125
National Junior Tennis League 302
National League 3, 4, 6, 7, 8, 10, 11, 12, 13, 14, 16, 17, 19, 20, 22, 23, 25, 26, 28, 29, 30, 31, 32, 34, 35, 36, 37, 38, 39, 40, 42, 43, 44, 45, 47, 48, 49, 50, 51, 52, 53, 56, 57, 60, 61, 63, 64, 65, 66, 67, 68, 69, 70, 72, 73, 74, 188
National League Championship Series (NLCS) 23, 25, 29, 35, 39, 46, 52, 57, 66, 67, 188
National Leukemia Society 277
Nationals, Syracuse 94
National Softball Association (NSA) 344

National Softball Hall of Fame 344
National Track and Field Hall of Fame 233, 264, 271, 272, 275, 277, 284, 285, 286, 287, 288, 289, 290, 291, 292, 293, 294, 296, 298
National Youth Administration 56
Naval Academy, U.S. 118, 192
Navratilova, Martina 302, 305, 308, 309, 310, 311, 314, **315–316,** 319
Navy, U.S. 153, 180
NBA Players Association 103
NBA Sportsmanship Award 88
NBC-TV 91, 99, 122, 124, 160, 162–163, 183, 207, 218, 308, 312, 315
NCAA Hall of Fame 210
NCAA (National Collegiate Athletic Association) 56
  basketball 78, 79, 81, 82, 84, 88, 91, 93, 94, 95, 96, 98, 99, 100, 103, 104, 108, 110, 111, 112, 113, 119, 121, 123, 125, 126
  diving 283
  football 150, 158, 160, 161, 166, 177, 190
  golf 208, 213, 215, 219, 226, 231
  gymnastics 269
  hockey 236
  soccer 343
  softball 342
  swimming 265, 266, 268, 271, 287, 293, 294, 296
  tennis 302, 305, 319
  track and field 267, 270, 272, 273, 275, 282, 285, 289, 290, 291, 292, 293, 295
  wrestling 272
Negro American League 3, 6, 56
Negro League 6, 13, 32, 39, 50, 51, 56
Negro League Baseball Museum 25
Negro National League 11, 32, 43, 48
Negro Southern League 50
Nelson, Azumah 133
Nelson, Byron 209, 212, 213, 217, **218–219,** 222, 224, 232
Nevada State Athletic Commission 147
Nevers, Ernie **182**
Newark Eagles 32, 48
Newcombe, Don **48–49**
Newcombe, John 312, **316,** 317
Newell, Pete 80
New England Blizzard 100
New England Patriots 153, 160, 162, 167, 168, 184, 190, 191
New Hampshire Motor Speedway 333, 335
Newhouser, Hal **49**
New Jersey Devils 257
New Jersey Gems 82, 109
New Jersey Nets 78, 87, 108, 116, 117
New Jersey State Athletic Commission 147
Newman, Paul 134
New Mexico Women's Amateur 216, 230
New Orleans Jazz 80, 94, 107
New Orleans Open 224
New Orleans Saints 157, 160, 194
Newsome, Ozzie **182**
Newsweek 342
Newton, Jack 229
New York Athletic Club 271

New York Bulldogs 173
New York City Marathon 297
New York Cosmos 341, 346
New Yorker, The 82
New York Giants
    baseball 13, 22, 23, 29, 30, 31, 32,
       40, 41, 42, 43, 45, 50, 57, 61, 64,
       67, 70, 72, 120
    football 152, 153, 155, 158, 159,
       161, 163, 164, 168, 169, 170,
       175, 176, 177, 179, 181, 183,
       186, 193, 194, 195, 196, 197,
       201
New York Islanders 237, 256, 260
New York Jets 175, 177–178, 181,
    186, 190, 201
New York Knicks 80, 82, 83, 84, 85,
    87, 89, 91, 92, 94, 95, 102, 105,
    108, 111, 112, 113, 116, 118, 124
New York Liberty 82, 104
New York Lincoln Giants 13
New York Marathon 290, 291
New York Mets 6, 8, 10, 13, 29, 30,
    31, 32, 37, 43, 48, 52, 59, 61, 62,
    65, 346
New York Nets 90
New York Rangers 235, 237, 241, 242,
    243, 244, 245, 246, 250, 253, 254,
    255, 256, 258
New York State Athletic Commission
    131, 132, 144
New York Times 105, 304
New York Titans 152, 177
New York University (NYU) 27, 120
New York Yankees 3, 4, 7, 8, 10, 14,
    16, 17, 18, 19, 21, 23, 24, 26–27,
    29, 30, 31, 32, 33, 34, 35, 38, 39,
    40, 41, 42–43, 44, 45–46, 47, 49,
    52, 54, 55, 56, 58, 59, 63, 64, 65,
    68, 69, 70, 73, 105, 161, 188, 346
New York Yanks 160, 173, 175, 198
NFL Players Association 157, 182,
    198
NHL Players' Association 252, 261
Niagara University 112
Nicholas, Alison 217
Nichols, Bobby 228
Nicklaus, Jack 205, 206, 211, 212,
    213, 218, **219–220**, 222, 223, 228,
    229, 231
Niekro, Joe 49
Niekro, Phil **49**
Nielson, Jimmy. *See* Irvin, Monte
Nike Corporation 121
Nike Sports Management Group 294
Nike Tour 218
Nitschke, Ray **183**
Nittany Lions 167, 179
Nomellini, Leo **183**
Nordwig, Wolfgang 292
Norman, Greg 211, 216, **220**
Norris, Bruce 247
Norris, Orlin 147
Norris, Terry 139
Norris Trophy 238, 239, 240, 246,
    249, 250, 254, 255, 256, 257, 258
North American Athletes of the Cen-
    tury 308
North American Boxing Federation
    (NABF) 142, 144
North American Soccer League
    (NASL) 341, 346
North Carolina Central College 100

North Carolina State University 88,
    93, 122, 178
Northeast Missouri State University
    92, 141
North Open 212, 218
North-South Amateur 228
North-South Championship 217
North Texas State University 165
Northville Long Island Classic 223
Northwestern Louisiana University
    192
Northwestern University 163
Norton, Ken 132, 135, **141–142**
Notre Dame University 83, 160, 168,
    169, 178, 182, 184, 197
Novacek, Karol 306
Novratilova, Martina 104
Nowicki, Janet Lynn. *See* Lynn,
    Janet
Nunno, Steve 286
Nureyev, Rudolf 283
Nurmi, Paavo **287**

O
Oakland Athletics 8, 11, 12, 13, 18,
    19, 20, 23, 27, 29, 30, 31, 33, 34,
    44, 47, 61, 67, 71
Oakland Oaks 79
Oakland Raiders 32, 33, 149, 153,
    154, 156, 162, 167, 169, 174, 175,
    177–178, 181, 183, 189, 190, 192,
    197, 198
O'Brien, Dan **287**
Ochowicz, Jim 299
O'Connor, Christy 228
Odessa Junior College 230
Oerter, Al **287–288**
Offensive Player of the Year 158, 185,
    186, 190
off-road races 331
Ohio State Junior Championship 219
Ohio State Open 219
Ohio State University 95, 104, 121,
    157, 166, 173, 184, 190, 199, 288
Oklahoma State University 186
Olajuwon, Hakeem 79, 88, **112–113,**
    116
Olazabal, Jose Maria **220–221**
Old Dominion University 87–88,
    103
Olivares, Ruben 129
Olmedo, Alex 312
Olsen, Merlin 171, **183**
Olson, Carl "Bobo" 133, 143
Olympic Games **263–299**
    1900 271
    1904 271
    1906 271
    1908 271
    1912 195
    1920 287
    1924 276, 287, 297
    1928 276, 287, 297, 298
    1932 232–233, 276, 298
    1936 266, 276, 277, 282, 288–289,
       298
    1940 266
    1944 266
    1948 266, 268, 284, 285, 290, 299
    1952 104, 142, 177, 263, 264, 268,
       284, 285, 290, 299
    1956 97, 99, 119, 226, 263, 272, 275,
       277, 285, 288, 290, 291

    1960 80, 104, 117, 124, 127, 130,
       266, 267, 270, 272, 275, 278,
       288, 291
    1964 82, 132, 266, 267, 270, 271,
       272, 275, 280, 285, 286, 288,
       291, 292, 296
    1965 285
    1968 132, 264, 266, 267, 271, 272,
       280, 285, 286, 288, 289, 291,
       292, 293, 295, 296
    1972 264, 272, 277, 280, 281, 284,
       285, 289, 290–291, 291, 292,
       293, 297, 298
    1976 103, 109, 138, 145, 263, 264,
       268, 269, 272, 274, 275, 276,
       277, 278, 281, 283, 286, 287,
       289, 290–291, 292, 293–294,
       294, 297, 298, 299
    1980 82, 87, 121, 125, 263, 266,
       268–269, 269, 272, 273, 275,
       276, 282, 283, 284, 285, 286,
       288, 291, 293, 294
    1982 269
    1984 88, 89, 91, 102, 110, 126, 136,
       264, 265, 266, 267, 268, 269,
       270, 273, 274, 276, 278, 281,
       282, 283, 284, 285, 286, 289,
       290, 291, 293, 294, 296, 297,
       298
    1988 85, 89, 118, 137, 264, 265, 266,
       267, 268, 270, 271, 273, 276,
       277, 279, 281, 282, 283, 285,
       286, 287, 289, 290, 295, 298,
       319
    1992 79, 81, 85, 91, 99, 102, 106,
       118, 121, 131, 264, 265, 266,
       267, 269, 270, 271, 276, 277,
       279, 281, 282, 286, 287, 289,
       291, 295, 298, 318, 340
    1994 266, 269, 276, 281, 294, 295,
       296, 298
    1996 79, 89, 97, 103, 106, 108, 113,
       115, 118, 121, 125, 267, 270,
       271, 273, 276, 277, 278, 279,
       281, 282, 286, 287, 291, 295,
       296, 301, 307, 318, 339, 342,
       343
    1997 104
    1998 245, 247, 249, 269, 282, 283,
       294, 309
    2000 88, 97, 270, 273, 277, 278, 281,
       286, 287, 295, 296, 321, 322,
       343
    2002 282, 294
Olympic Hall of Fame 129, 133, 264,
    265, 266, 268, 271, 272, 273, 274,
    277, 282, 283, 284, 285, 286, 287,
    288, 289, 290, 291, 292, 293, 296,
    297
O'Meara, Mark 210, **221,** 223
O'Neal, Shaquille xi, 83, **113–114**
Ongais, Danny 337
Oorang Indians 195
Oosterhuis, Peter 210
Optimist International Junior tourna-
    ment 231
Orangemen 155
Order of the British Empire 336
Oregon State University 114, 272
Orlando Magic 88, 91, 97, 102, 113,
    125
Orr, Bobby 239, 251, **254–255**
Orser, Brian 266

Osborne, Harold 279
Ott, Mel **50**
Ottawa Maroons 236
Ottawa Senators 239, 242
Otto, Jim **183**
Ouimet, Francis 211, **221**
Outland Trophy 152, 183, 184, 189,
    191, 200
Outrageous (Barkley) 78
Outstanding Player of the Year 152
Ovett, Steve 268
Owen, Marv 45
Owens, Jesse 266, 267, 277, 282,
    288–289, 292
Oxford University 82, 264

P
Pacific Coast Conference 56, 111, 161
Pacific Coast Games 284
Pacific Coast League 18, 39, 70
Pacific-10 Conference 103, 161, 179,
    270
Pacific Southwest Championships 311
Page, Alan **184,** 189
Paige, Satchel 25, 39, **50–51**
Palmer, Arnold 206, 208, 217, 219,
    221–222, 223, 232, 333, 335
Palmer, Jim **51, 67**
Palmer, Milfred 222
Palomino, Carlos 129
Pan-American Games 85, 103, 110,
    138, 267, 277, 281, 283, 285, 288,
    290, 292, 294, 343
Panatinaikos Athens 125
Parade 110
Parche, Gunther 310, 319
Parent, Bernie 243, **255**
Paret, Benny "Kid" 134
Parish, Robert 78, 109, **114**
Park, Brad 255
Parker, Buddy 157
Parker, Frank 312
Parker, Jim 165, **184**
Parkey, Rickey 136
Park Si-Hun 137
Parnevik, Jesper 223
Pasarell, Charlie 309
Paterno, Joe 179
Patterson, Floyd 128, 139, 141, **142,**
    146
Pavin, Corey 220
Pavlova, Anna 276
Paxson, John 102
Payton, Gary **114–115**
Payton, Walter **184–185,** 187, 190,
    192
PBA Hall of Fame 339, 341, 347, 349
PBA National Championship 339,
    341
Pearson, David **333,** 334
Pearson, Drew 193
Pebble Beach Golf Links 215, 218,
    219, 229, 232
Pelé **346**
Pender, Paul 129, 143
Penick, Harvey 208, 230
Pennsylvania State University 167,
    179
Penske, Roger 323, 324, 326, 331, 337
Penske Racing Team 332, 337
Pep, Willie **142–143,** 144
Pepper, Dottie **222**
Perez, Tony **51**

Index

Perreault, Gilbert **255**

Perry, Fred 301, 303, 304, **316,** 321

Perry, Gaylord **52**

Peter Jackson Classic 205, 207, 212, 227

Petrie, Geoff 86

Pettit, Bob 105, **115**

Petty, Adam 333, 335

Petty, Kyle 333, 335

Petty, Lee **333**

Petty, Richard 329, **333–335,** 338

PGA Championship 206–207, 210, 211, 212, 213, 215, 217, 219, 220, 221, 222, 223, 224, 226, 227, 228, 231, 232

PGA Seniors Championship 211, 214, 220, 223, 224, 228

PGA Tour 206, 207, 208, 210, 211, 212, 213, 215, 216, 217, 218, 219, 220, 221, 222, 223, 224, 226, 227, 228, 229, 230, 231, 232

Philadelphia Athletics 15, 16, 20, 22, 28, 33, 38, 42, 52, 59, 63, 66, 68, 71–72, 74

Philadelphia Blazers 255

Philadelphia Eagles 152, 157, 160, 163, 171, 177, 178, 188, 198, 199, 200, 267

Philadelphia Flyers 235, 240, 252, 255, 259

Philadelphia Freedoms 311

Philadelphia Hillsdales 13

Philadelphia Naval Air Materials Center 78

Philadelphia Phantoms 235

Philadelphia Phillies 4, 6, 9, 10, 11, 12, 13, 21, 22, 34, 37, 38, 40, 46, 47, 51, 54, 55, 57, 60, 61, 65, 72, 188

Philadelphia Rage 88

Philadelphia 76ers 78, 79, 83, 84, 86, 87, 90, 94–95, 99, 106, 107, 108, 119, 120, 122, 123

Philadelphia Warriors 78, 84, 92, 94

Phillip Morris 311

Phoenix Coyotes 244

Phoenix Mercury 104, 111

Phoenix Suns 79, 89, 94, 95, 96, 97, 102

Piazza, Mike **52**

Picard, Henry **222**

Pierce, Mary 321

Pikes Peak Hill Climb 331, 337

Pilote, Pierre **255–256**

Pincay, Laffit, Jr. **346–347**

Pinehurst No. 2 227

Pipp, Wally 23

Pippen, Scottie 102, **115–116,** 294

Piquet, Nelson **335**

Pirates 87

Pittsburgh Crawfords 6, 13, 14, 25, 50

Pittsburgh Panthers 160

Pittsburgh Penguins 236, 240, 249, 251–252, 260, 261

Pittsburgh Pipers 96

Pittsburgh Pirates 8, 11, 14, 16, 23, 25, 26, 27, 34, 37, 43–44, 63, 66, 68, 69, 70, 72

Pittsburgh Steelers 66, 150, 154, 159, 161, 165, 167–168, 172, 174, 180, 188, 192, 193, 197, 199, 200, 201–202

Plank, Eddie **52**

Plante, Jacques 236, 247, **256**

Player, Gary 210, 216, 220, **223,** 229

Player of the Year.

  basketball 96, 98, 100, 103, 104, 105, 107, 109, 110, 111, 113, 117, 121, 123, 125

  bowling 339, 341, 347, 349

  football 154, 159, 161, 162, 163, 164, 172, 176, 179, 184, 190, 194, 196

  golf 208, 209, 210, 212, 215, 218, 220, 221, 223, 226, 228, 231

  See also specific Player of the Year awards

  soccer 341

Pocono 500 336, 337

Pocono International Speedway 323, 328

pole vaulting 267, 290, 292

Pontiac Chaparrals 93

Portland Trail Blazers 86, 88, 90, 102, 106, 116, 118, 122, 123, 125

Portsmouth Spartans 181

Postal Service, U.S. 221

Potvin, Denis **256**

Powell, Mike 265, 282, **289**

Prairie View A&M 170

Preakness Stakes 340, 341, 342, 343, 346, 347

Prefontaine, Steve **289**

Prescott Downs 342

President's Council on Physical Fitness and Sports 274

President's Cup 208, 210, 213, 217, 232

Price, Nick 210, 221, **223**

Primeau, Joe 241, 248, **256**

Princeton Tigers 82

Pro Bowl selection 149, 150, 151, 152, 153, 154, 155, 156, 157, 158, 159, 160, 161, 162, 163, 165, 166, 167, 168, 169, 170, 171, 172, 173, 174, 175, 176, 177, 178, 179, 180, 182, 183, 184, 185, 186, 187, 188, 189, 190, 191, 192, 193, 194, 195, 196, 197, 198, 199, 200, 201, 202, 203

Pro Cycling Championship 275

Professional Bowlers Association (PBA) 339, 341, 347, 349

Professional Golfers European Tour 206, 209, 211

Pro Football Hall of Fame 149, 151, 152, 153, 154, 155, 156, 157, 158, 159, 160, 161, 162, 163, 164, 165, 166, 167, 168, 169, 170, 171, 172, 173, 174, 175, 176, 177, 178, 179, 180, 181, 182, 183, 184, 185, 186, 189, 190, 191, 192, 193, 194, 195, 196, 197, 198, 199, 200, 201

Prost, Alain **335**

Pro Stock Championship 328

Providence College 125

Providence Steamrollers 168

Prudomme, Don **335**

Pryor, Aaron 129, **143**

Puckett, Kirby **53**

Purdue University 159, 165, 201, 271

Pyle, C.C. 164

Q

Qawi, Dwight Muhammad 136, 144. *See also* Braxton, Dwight

Quackenbush, Bill 249

Quad Cities Classic 226

Quakers 164

Quarry, Jerry 128, 142

Quebec Nordiques 250, 252, 253, 260

Quebec Ramparts 250

Queens College 82

R

Radcliffe College 263

Raging Bull (LaMotta) 138

Rahal, Bobby **335**

Ramsey, Frank 85, 95

Randall, Ricky 137

Ratelle, Jean **256–257**

Rauch, John 190

Rawls, Betsy 218, **223–224,** 230, 232

Ray, Ted 211, 221

Raybestos Brakettes 344

Reebok Corporation 287

Reed, Andre **185**

Reed, Willis 87, 103, **116–117**

Reese, Pee Wee **53,** 57

Reid, Mike 227

Remnick, David 127, 142

Renshaw, Willie 318

Retton, Mary Lou 286, **289–290**

Revolta, Johnny 206

Reynolds, Butch **290**

Reynolds, Carl 18

Rice, Grantland 42, 151, 164, 232, 233

Rice, Jerry 173, 179, **185–186**

Rice, Jim **53–54**

Richard, Henri **257**

Richard, Maurice 237, 247, **257**

Richards, Bob **290**

Richardson, Bobby 44

Richmond, Lee 10

Rickard, Tex 131

Rickey, Branch 11, 32, 56, 63

Riggins, John **186**

Riggs, Bobby 304, 306, 311, 312, **316–317**

Ring, Jimmy 22

Ring, The magazine 129, 135, 139, 141, 143, 144, 147

Ring of Honor 174

Riordan, Bill 306

Ripken, Cal, Jr. 23, **54**

Robert, Rene 255

Roberto Clemente Award 54, 64

Roberts, Fireball **335–336**

Roberts, Loren 210

Roberts, Robin 44, **54–55**

Robertson, Charlie 10

Robertson, Oscar 80, **117**

Robinson, Brooks **55,** 64

Robinson, David 89, **117–118**

Robinson, Frank **55–56**

Robinson, Jackie 11, 19, 25, 32, 50, 53, **56–57,** 180

Robinson, Larry **257**

Robinson, Sugar Ray 129, 133, 134, 137, 138, **143–144**

Roche, Tony 312, 316, **317**

Rochester Royals 87, 92

Rock Island Independents 195

Rodgers, Bill 275, **290–291**

Rodgers, Phil 208

Rodman, Dennis **118**

Rodriguez, Alex 23, **57**

Rodriguez, Chi Chi **224**

Rodriguez, Luis 134

Roldan, Juan Domingo 135

Rolex Player of the Year Award 207, 209, 213, 214, 217, 222, 226–227, 230

Rollins College 303

Rookie of the Year

  baseball 7, 11, 12, 21, 44, 47, 48, 52, 53, 56, 70

  basketball 77, 79, 80, 81, 84, 86, 89, 91, 97, 98, 99, 102, 105, 108, 112, 113, 117, 118, 120, 122, 123

  football 150, 151, 155, 157, 159, 160, 164, 165, 167, 172, 176, 179, 186, 189, 194

  golf 205, 209, 217, 219, 221, 224, 226, 228

  hockey 236, 237, 238, 242, 243, 244, 246, 249, 250, 251, 252, 254, 255, 256, 258, 259, 260, 261

Roosevelt, Franklin D. 140

Rose, Pete 8, 51, **57–58**

Roseboro, John 41

Rose Bowl 170, 179, 182, 190, 284, 342

Rosewall, Ken 306, 310, 312, **317**

Ross, Barney 129

Ross Trophy 236, 241, 242, 244, 245, 247, 248, 250, 251, 252, 253, 254–255, 259, 260

Roth, Mark **347,** 349

Rouse, Roger 145

Roxborough, John 140

Roy, Patrick 244, **257–258**

Royal and Ancient Golf Club of St. Andrews 221

Royal Lytham 206, 208

Royal St. Georges 220

Roys, Earl 144

Rozelle, Pete 181

Rubustelli, Andy **186**

Rudolph, Wilma **291**

Ruelas, Rafael 131

Ruffing, Red **58**

Rules of Golf 224

Runner's World magazine 264, 297

Rupp Award 91

Russell, Bill xi, 80, 84, 85, 93, 95, 97, 99, 104, 105, 108, 115, **119,** 122

Russell, Jim 326

Russell, John "Honey" 87

Russi, Bernhard 281

Ruth, Babe 3, 13, 15, 16, 17, 18, 22, 23, 24, 25, 27, 29, 31, 33, 36, 37, 39, 40, 41, 42, 45, **57–58,** 60, 63, 64, 68, 69, 182, 211–212

Rutherford, Johnny **336**

Ryan, Buddy 157, 200

Ryan, Elizabeth 311, 313

Ryan, Jim 280

Ryan, Nolan 12, 32, 47, **59–60**

Ryder Cup 206, 207, 208–209, 210, 211, 213, 215, 216, 217, 218, 220, 221, 222, 224, 226, 227, 228, 230, 232

Ryun, Jim **291**

S

Saad Muhammad, Matthew **144**

Saban, Lou 190

Sacramento Kings 119

Saddler, Sandy 142–143, **144**

Safeco Classic 207

Safe Passage Foundation 302
Safeway LPGA Golf Championship 213
Sailer, Anton 280
St. Annes 206, 208
St. Bonaventure College 103
St. John's University 108
St. Louis Blues 243, 245, 246, 248, 254, 255, 256
St. Louis Bombers 105
St. Louis Browns 7, 17, 20, 26, 30, 31, 39, 50, 52, 59, 63, 68, 182
St. Louis Cardinals 4, 8, 9, 10, 12, 13, 17, 19, 20, 21, 22–23, 24, 26, 30, 31, 36, 40, 41, 44–45, 46, 48, 53, 61, 63, 64, 65, 66, 67, 70, 74, 75, 151, 178, 192, 201
St. Louis Children's Hospital Classic 216
St. Louis Giants 13
St. Louis Hawks 92, 95, 104, 105, 106, 115, 119, 125
St. Louis Stars 6
St. Louis Terriers 52
St. Louis University 105
Salazar, Alberto 291
Salming, Borje 258
Sampras, Pete 301, 303, 306, 307, 312, 313, 317–318
San Antonio Spurs 88, 89, 91, 93, 107, 118, 122, 125
San Antonio–Texas Open 208
Sanchez, Salvador 133
Sanchez Vicario, Arantxa 318, 322
Sandberg, Ryne 60
Sanders, Barry 162, 186–187, 191, 192
Sanders, Deion 187–188, 294
Sanders, Tom "Satch" 85, 86
San Diego Chargers 150–151, 154, 162, 171, 174, 175, 188, 197, 201, 202
San Diego Clippers 83, 123
San Diego Conquistadors 85, 100
San Diego Open 215
San Diego Padres 4, 13, 20, 23, 27, 28, 29, 35, 44, 49, 52, 62, 64, 73
San Diego Rockets 96, 112
San Francisco 49ers 150, 161, 175, 176, 178–179, 183, 185, 186, 188, 189, 190, 193, 196, 202
San Francisco Giants 8, 11, 12, 13, 19, 27, 43, 44, 47, 52, 56, 65, 188
San Francisco Seals 18, 70, 314
San Francisco Warriors 79, 86, 94, 105, 120, 122
San Jose Sharks 236
Santa Clara University 162, 342
Santana, Manuel 318
Sanyo Open 221
Saraceni, Eugenio. See Sarazen, Gene
Sarasota Classic 217
Sarazen, Gene 206, 209, 212, 215, 223, 224, 229, 233
Sardinias-Montalbo, Eligio. See Chocolate, Kid
Sarron, Petey 129
Satchel Paige All-Stars 50
Savard, Serge 258
Sawchuk, Mike 258
Sawchuk, Terry 238, 239, 258–259
Sayers, Gale 186, 188–189
Schapers, Michael 306

Schayes, Dolph 119–120
Scherbo, Vitaly 291–292
Schlee, John 218
Schmeling, Max 140, 144–145
Schmid, Harald 286
Schmid, Joe 189
Schmidt, Mike 42, 47, 60–61
Schmidt, Milt 259
Schoendienst, Red 61
Schollander, Don 292
Schotting, Peter 298
Schranz, Karl 280
Schriner, Sweeney 259
Schultz, Axel 132
Schumacher, Michael 336
Schwann, Lynn 154
Scott, Steve 231
Scottsbluff Junior College 172
Seagren, Bob 292
Seattle Mariners 14, 23, 27, 29, 34, 52, 57, 72
Seattle Seahawks 32, 168, 173, 177
Seattle SuperSonics 91, 96, 100, 102, 114–115, 116, 119, 122, 123, 125
Seattle University 80
Seaver, Tom 61–62
Sedgman, Frank 309, 318–319
Segura, Pancho 309, 319
Seibert, Earl 254
Seixas, Vic 320
Seldon, Bruce 146
Seles, Monica 310, 319, 321
Selke Trophy 240
Selmon, Lee Roy 189
Senior PGA Tour 208, 209, 210, 211, 213–214, 215, 220, 222, 223, 224, 226, 227, 228, 230, 232
Senior Players Championship 211, 214, 220, 223, 224, 227
Senior Tour Player of the Year 228
Senna, Ayrton 335, 336
Sense of Where You Are, A (McPhee) 82
Sesame Street (TV program) 294
Seton Hall University 87, 117
Severance, Al 78
Sexton, Johnny 129, 133
Shanahan, Mike 202
Shantz, Bobby 10
Sharkey, Jack 144, 145
Sharkey, Tom 145
Sharman, Bill 85, 120
Sharpe, Sterling 157
Shavers, Earnie 135, 142
Shaw, George 197
Sheehan, BoBo 226
Sheehan, Patty 213, 224–226
Shell, Art 189–190, 198
Shell's Wonderful World of Golf (TV program) 209, 224
Sherry, Norm 37
Shiley, Jean 233
Shoemaker, Willie 343, 346, 347–348
ShopRite LPGA Classic 215
Shore, Eddie 259
Shorter, Frank 290–291, 292–293
Shriver, Pam 316, 319
Shula, Don 165, 174, 175, 177, 193
Siegfried, Larry 95
Sigel, Jay 226
Si-Hun, Park 137
Simmer, Charlie 242

Simmons, Al 28, 29, 31, 62–63
Simon, Mircea 293
Simpson, O.J. 159, 190, 255
Simpson, Scott 227
Singh, Vijay 226
Singletary, Mike 190–191
Sisler, Dick 6
Sisler, George 15, 29, 43–44, 63
Sittler, Darryl 259–260
Sixth Man Award 109, 124
skiing 280, 281, 284, 293, 294, 295
Skoff, Horst 321
Slaughter, Enos 63
Slaying the Dragon (Johnson) 277
Smith, Alex 210
Smith, Billy 260
Smith, Bruce 191
Smith, Dean 100, 108, 126
Smith, Emmitt 149, 191–192
Smith, Jackie 192
Smith, James 146
Smith, Lee 64
Smith, Ozzie 64
Smith, Stan 305, 315, 319
Smith, Tommie 296
Smith, Walker, Jr. See Robinson, Sugar Ray
Smoltz, John 25
Smylie, Liz 316
Smythe, Conn 239
Snead, Sam 211, 213, 218, 224, 226, 231
Snell, Matt 181
Snider, Duke 6, 57, 63, 64–65
soccer 339, 341, 342, 343, 346
softball 342–343, 344
Solheim Cup 207, 208, 209, 215, 222, 231
Somebody Up There Likes Me (Graziano) 134
Sonja Henie Hollywood Ice Revue 276
Sorenstam, Annika 226–227
Sorenstam, Charlotta 230
Sosa, Sammy 41, 44, 45, 65
Souchak, Mike 222
South African Masters 210
South African Open 210
South African PGA 210
South Carolina State University 180
Southeastern Conference 89, 108
Southeastern Oklahoma State University 118
Southern 500 333, 336, 338
Southern Amateur 228
Southern Championship 214
Southern Illinois University 92
Southern Methodist University (SMU) 152, 159, 165, 199
Southern Mississippi University 162
Southern Open 212, 218
Southern University 154
South Pacific Classic 343
South Plains Junior College 121
Southwest Conference 121, 157, 190
Soviet Union 104
Space Jam (film) 102
Spahn, Warren 43, 49, 65
Spalding Sporting Goods 214
Spanish Amateur 221
Spartans 98
Speaker, Tris 13, 15, 29, 33, 66

speed skating 266, 275, 276–277, 281, 298–299
Spinks, Leon 128, 142
Spinks, Michael 135, 145
Spira, Howard 73
Spitz, Arnold 293
Spitz, Mark 265, 271, 275, 293
Sports Illustrated 342. See also Sportsman of the Year; Sportswoman of the Year
Sportsman of the Year
  baseball 54, 66
  basketball 81, 114
  boxing 139
  cycling 344
  golf 222, 226, 228, 231
  gymnastics 290
  horse racing 341
  speed skating 266, 281
  track and field 264, 270, 286
Sportswoman of the Year
  basketball 121, 343
  gymnastics 290
  speed skating 266
  tennis 311
Springfield Fame 104
Stacy, Hollis 227
Stallard, Tracy 41
Standard Oil 67
Standard Register Ping 209
Stanford University 83, 105, 161, 170, 182, 218, 231, 271, 275, 284, 294
Stanley Cup 235, 236, 237, 238, 239, 240, 241, 242, 243, 244, 245, 246, 247, 248, 249, 250, 251, 252, 253, 254, 255, 256, 257, 258, 259, 260, 261
Stargell, Willie 34, 66
Starr, Bart 151, 156, 192
Stars on Ice 274, 298
Stasny, Peter 260
Staubach, Roger 192–193
Steffes, Kent 281
Steinbrenner, George 8, 73
Stenerud, Jan 193
Stengel, Casey 7, 18
Stenmark, Ingemar 284, 293
Stephenson, Dwight 193
Stephenson, Jan 227
Stevenson, Teofilo 293
Stewart, Bobby 146
Stewart, Jackie 336–337
Stewart, James 231
Stewart, Nels 260
Stewart, Payne 227
Stewart, Ron 258
Stich, Michael 301, 303
Stockton, Dave, Sr. 227
Stockton, John 106, 120–121
Stolle, Fred 319–320
Stones, Dwight 293–294
Stove, Betty 321
Stram, Hank 152, 159
Stranahan, Frank 209
Strange, Curtis 211, 227–228
Street, Dee 294
Street, Picabo 294
Street, Stubby 294
Stribling, Young 144
Study of Sport and Society 311
Sugar Ray Robinson Youth Foundation 273
Suggs, Louise 228

Index

Sullivan, Eddie. *See* Collins, Eddie
Sullivan Award
  basketball 82, 98, 110, 123
  diving 283
  figure skating 268
  football 153
  hockey 215
  marathon 265
  speed skating 266, 275
  swimming 271, 285, 287, 292, 293
  tennis 304
  track and field 269, 274, 277, 279, 282, 284, 286, 289, 290, 291, 295
Sumners, Rosalind 298
Super Bowl I 149, 152, 156, 158, 159, 165, 183, 188, 192, 201
Super Bowl II 149, 153, 158, 165, 183, 192, 198, 201
Super Bowl III 172, 175, 178, 181
Super Bowl IV 152, 156, 159, 172
Super Bowl V 149, 169, 174, 175
Super Bowl VI 149, 151, 158, 160, 165, 174, 193, 199
Super Bowl VII 158, 165, 172, 199
Super Bowl VIII 154, 158, 165, 172, 194, 199
Super Bowl IX 154, 167, 172, 193, 194, 200
Super Bowl X 154, 172, 200
Super Bowl XI 153, 156, 167, 169, 189, 194, 198
Super Bowl XII 154, 160, 172, 193, 200
Super Bowl XIII 154, 167, 172, 192, 193, 200
Super Bowl XIV 154, 167, 200
Super Bowl XV 165, 169, 178–179, 189, 198
Super Bowl XVI 165, 175, 178, 179
Super Bowl XVII 178, 186
Super Bowl XVIII 150, 165, 169, 174
Super Bowl XIX 153, 167, 175, 176, 179
Super Bowl XX 160, 184, 191, 194
Super Bowl XXI 161, 194
Super Bowl XXII 161, 165, 175, 178
Super Bowl XXIII 179, 185
Super Bowl XXIV 161, 175, 179, 185
Super Bowl XXV 185, 191
Super Bowl XXVI 185, 191
Super Bowl XXVII 150, 185, 191
Super Bowl XXVIII 168, 191
Super Bowl XXIX 185, 188, 191, 202
Super Bowl XXX 150, 188, 202
Super Bowl XXXI 201
Super Bowl XXXII 158, 161, 162, 168
Super Bowl XXXIII 161
Superstars (TV program) 292, 294
Supreme Court, U.S. 21, 128, 218, 290
Sutter, Bruce **66–67**
Sutton, Don 51, **67**
Swedish National Team 226
swimming 264, 265–266, 268, 270, 271, 272, 285, 287, 292, 293, 294–295, 296, 297
Swoopes, Sheryl **121**
Sycamores 81, 98
Syracuse University 80, 94, 112, 155, 157, 175, 178
Szabo, Ekaterina 290
Szymanski, Aloys. *See* Simmons, Al

T

Tampa Bay Buccaneers 32, 180, 189, 202
Tampa Bay Devil Rays 8, 12
Tampa Bay Lightning 243
Tanner, Roscoe 303
Tar Heels (Univ. of North Carolina) 83, 100, 108, 126, 278, 343
Tarkenton, Fran 161, **193–194**
Tatum, Jack 168
Taylor, Charley **194**
Taylor, Dave 242
Taylor, Jim 152, 170, **194**
Taylor, John 179
Taylor, Lawrence **194–195**
TBS 207
Team Canada 245
Team McLaren 335
Television Games Network 344
Tennant, Eleanor 314
tennis **301–322**
Tennis magazine 302, 304
Ter-Ovanesyan, Igor 265, 267
Terrell, Ernie 128, 132
Terry, Bill **67**
Terry, Ralph **44**
Texas A&I 197
Texas Amateur 212, 223
Texas A&M University 164, 173, 284
Texas Christian University (TCU) 151, 174
Texas-El Paso University 264
Texas Longhorns 173
Texas Publinx 214
Texas Rangers 11, 26, 27, 34, 52, 57, 60, 65
Texas Tech University 121
Texas Western University 177
Texas Women's Amateur 233
Thomas, Debi 298
Thomas, Frank **67–68**
Thomas, Isiah **121–122**
Thompson, Bertha 305
Thompson, Daley **294**
Thompson, David **122**
Thompson, Jenny **294–295**
Thompson, Tiny 238
Thomson, Bobby 3, 120
Thomson, Peter **228,** 229
Thorpe, Jim **195–196**
Thurmond, Nate **122–123**
Tiger, Dick 132, 133, 134, **145**
Tigers (Auburn Univ.) 32
Tigers (Louisiana State Univ.) 107
Tilden, Bill 304, 305, 306, 309, 312, 313, **320,** 321
Time 170, 342
Titleholders 228, 231, 232, 233
Title IX 311. *See also* Equal Education Amendment
Tittle, Y.A. **196**
Tomba, Alberto **295**
Toney, James 137
Toomey, Bill **295**
Toon, Al 185
Top Fuel 323, 325, 328, 332, 333, 335
Top 100 Players of All Time (NHL) 236, 237, 238, 239, 240, 241, 242, 243, 244, 245, 246, 247, 248, 249, 250, 251, 252, 253, 254, 255, 256, 257, 258, 259, 260, 261
Toronto Blue Jays 5, 12, 13, 14, **29,** 46, 49, 73, 188

Toronto Maple Leafs 236, 237, 238, 239, 240, 241, 242, 243, 244, 247, 248, 249, 252, 254, 255, 256, 258, 259, 260
Toronto Raptors 84, 122, 125
Torrence, Gwen **295**
Torres, Jose 145
Torvill, Jayne **295–296**
Tour de France 275, 276, 340, 341, 344
Tour de Spain 341
Tournament of Champions 223
Trabert, Tony 309, 310, **320**
Trachsel, Steve 45
track and field 195, 263–265, 266–267, 268, 269–270, 271, 272, 273–275, 277–280, 282, 284–285, 286–289, 290–291, 292–294, 295, 296–298, 299
Track and Field Hall of Fame 274
Track & Field News 278, 287
Tradition, The 211, 220
Trans-Am races 331
Travers, Jerome 231
Traynor, Pie **68**
Trevino, Lee 223, **228,** 229
Trinidad, Felix 131
Triple Crown
  baseball 22, 23, 26, 28, 30, 37, 38, 40, 42, 45, 56, 72, 74
  hockey 254
  horse racing 340, 341, 342, 343, 344, 346
  motorsports 337
Trippi, Charley **196**
Trojans 85, 103, 190
Trottier, Bryan **260**
Tsioropoulos, Lou 95
Tucker, Tony 132, 146
Tunnell, Emlen **196–197**
Tunney, Gene 131, 134, 144, **145–146**
Tunney, John 146
Turnberry 220, 229
Turner Sports 111
Turpin, Randy 143
Tway, Bob 220
Tyson, Lorna 146
Tyson, Mike 135, 136, 145, **146–147**
Tyus, Wyomia 270, **296**

U

UCLA (Univ. of California at Los Angeles)
  baseball 56
  basketball 77, 94, 96, 109, 111, 123
  figure skating 282
  football 149, 162, 190
  softball 342–343
  tennis 302, 305
  track and field 263, 270, 273, 277, 278
  volleyball 281
Ullman, Norm **260–261**
Union of European Football Associations Cup 346
Unitas, Johnny 153, 184, **197**
United Golf Association 221
United Press International 196
United States Auto Club (USAC) 327, 328, 329, 331, 336, 337
United States Basketball League 104

United States Football League (USFL) 166, 200, 202
United States Golf Association (USGA) 214, 216–217, 227, 233
United States Hockey League 247, 258
United Virginia Bank Classic 231
Universal Racing Club 330
University of Alabama 170, 173, 181, 182, 192, 193
University of Arizona 226, 296
University of Arkansas 97, 150
University of California 285
University of Central Florida 339
University of Cincinnati 37, 95, 104, 117
University of Colorado 213
University of Connecticut 104
University of Detroit 87
University of Florida 191, 268, 336
University of Georgia 89, 125, 158, 193, 196, 295
University of Houston 88, 96, 112, 208, 211, 276, 282
University of Idaho 201, 287
University of Illinois 9, 156, 164, 178, 183, 290
University of Iowa 96, 172, 196, 272–273
University of Kansas 84, 104, 189, 286, 288
University of Kentucky 93, 95, 98, 154
University of Louisville 123, 197
University of Maryland 83, 200
University of Massachusetts 90
University of Miami 79, 169, 183, 319
University of Michigan 24, 63, 94, 149, 164, 169, 179, 280
University of Minnesota 109, 152, 181, 183
University of Missouri 201
University of Montana 193
University of Nebraska 164
University of Nevada 180
University of North Carolina 83, 86, 100, 108, 126, 153, 194, 217, 278, 343
University of North Dakota 236
University of Oklahoma 41, 149, 189, 206, 269
University of Oregon 162, 198, 289
University of Pennsylvania 152, 164
University of Pittsburgh 159, 160, 176, 189
University of Richmond 194
University of San Francisco 93, 99, 119, 175, 177
University of South Carolina 89
University of Southern California 85, 103, 110–111, 120, 150, 163, 175, 180, 190, 201, 287, 292, 319
University of Tennessee 98, 108, 200
University of Texas 78, 121, 157, 173, 224
University of Toledo 196
University of Tulsa 173, 217
University of Washington 179
University of West Virginia 170
University of Wisconsin 169, 199
Unseld, Wes 84, **123**
Unser, Al, Jr. 337
Unser, Al, Sr. 331, 332, 336, **337**

Unser, Bobby 324, 332, **337–338**
UPI Player of the Year Award 196
Upshaw, Gene 156, 189, **197–198**
U.S. 500 326
U.S. Amateur 206, 214, 215, 219, 221, 222, 226, 228, 231, 302
U.S. Figure Skating Association 275
U.S. Figure Skating Hall of Fame 266, 268, 275, 298
U.S. Girls Junior Open 207
U.S. Gymnastics Federation 269
U.S. Junior Amateur 231
U.S. Mid-Amateur 226
U.S. National Jaycees Championship 219
U.S. Nationals 333
U.S. National Tennis Center 306
U.S. Olympic Committee 271, 275, 286, 289, 290
U.S. Olympic Sports Festival 279
U.S. Olympic Training Center 284
U.S. Open 222
   bowling 341, 347, 349
   golf 205, 206, 208, 210, 211–212, 213, 214, 215, 216, 217, 218, 219, 220, 221, 223, 224, 226, 227–228, 229, 231, 232
   tennis 301, 302, 303, 304, 305, 306, 307, 308, 309, 310, 311, 313, 314, 315, 316, 317, 318, 319, 320, 321, 322
U.S. Pro Championship 305, 312, 316, 317, 319, 320, 321, 340
U.S. Senior Open 208, 209, 214, 220, 223, 227
U.S. Soccer Federation 343
U.S. Sports Festival 283
U.S. Swimming 294
U.S. Tennis Association 301, 302, 303, 308, 320, 321
U.S. Track and Field Hall of Fame 267
U.S. Walker Cup 226
U.S. Women's Amateur Open 207, 213, 214, 229, 233
U.S. Women's Open 205, 206, 207, 209, 212, 213, 214, 217, 218, 223, 224, 226, 227, 228, 230, 231, 232, 233
U.S. Wrestling Federation 273
USA Network 315
USA Today 302
USA Wrestling Hall of Fame 273
Utah Jazz 79, 84, 102, 106, 121, 125
Utah Stars 73
Utah State University 183

V
Valdez, Rodrigo 141
Van Brocklin, Norm 171, 189, **198**
Van Buren, Steve **198–199**
Vancouver Canucks 237, 253
Vancouver Grizzlies 79
Vanderbilt University 121
Van Dyken, Amy **296**
Van Wie, Virginia 213
Vardon, Harry 211, 221, 228, **229**
Vardon Trophy 208, 209, 210, 211, 212, 213, 215, 217, 218, 219, 220, 222, 223, 226, 228, 230, 231
Vare, Glenna Collett 207, 213, 214, **229**

Vare Trophy 205, 206, 207, 209, 213, 217, 218, 222, 223, 226, 227, 228, 229, 230, 231, 232, 233
Veeck, Bill 9
Velo News 340
Venturi, Ken **229**
Vezina, Georges 245, **261**
Vezina Trophy 236, 238, 239, 242, 243, 246, 247, 255, 256, 258, 260, 261
Vilas, Guillermo **320**
Villanova University 78, 91, 174
Vincennes University 108
Vincent, Fay 73
Vines, Ellsworth 304, **320–321**
Violent World of Sam Huff, The (film) 170
Viren, Lasse **296–297**
Virginia Slims Tour 311
Virginia Squires 90, 93
Virginia Tech 191
volleyball 276, 281
Volleyball Hall of Fame 276
von Cramm, Baron Gottfried 304, 316
Vukovich, Bill **338**

W
Waddell, Rube **68**
Wade, Virginia **321**
Wade Trophy 82, 87–88, 103, 104, 125
Wadkins, Lanny 215
Wagner, Honus 12, 48, 64, **69, 75**
Waitz, Grete 265, **297**
Waitz, Jack 297
Wake Forest University 88, 118, 163, 222
Walcott, Jersey Joe 130, 139, 140, 141, **147**
Walker, Chet 94
Walker, Doak **199**
Walker, Harry 6
Walker, Herschel 160
Walker Cup 218
Wall, Art 221
Walsh, Bill 171, 178, 185, 202
Walsh, Ed **69**
Walt Disney World/Oldsmobile Classic 231
Walters, Barbara 146
Walton, Bill 103, **123–124**
Waltrip, Darrell 330, **338**
Waner, Lloyd **69–70**
Waner, Paul 7, 8, **69–70**
Wanninger, Pee Wee 23
Warfield, Paul 158, **199**
Warner, Glenn "Pop" 195
Washington, Desiree 146
Washington Bullets 79, 81, 106
Washington Capitals 244
Washington Capitols 120
Washington Generals 104
Washington Mystics 98, 108
Washington Post 302
Washington Redskins 150, 151, 158, 161, 164–165, 168, 170, 171, 172, 174, 175, 178, 181, 186, 188, 191, 194
Washington Senators 16–17, 21, 25, 26, 30, 35, 36, 63, 66, 67, 68, 72, 73
Washington State University 168
Washington Wizards 102

Waterfield, Bob 198
water polo 280
Watkins Glen 330
Watson, Robert 221
Watson, Tom 210, 220, 223, **229–230**
Watt, Jim 129
Watts, Bobby 135
Watts, Brian 221
Weaver, Earl 51
Webb, Karrie **230**
Weber, Dick **348–349**
Webster, Mike **199–200**
Weiskopf, Tom 226
Weissmuller, Johnny **297**
Welch's/Circle K Championship 227
Welsh Open 294
Wepner, Chuck 139
Wertz, Vic 43
Wesleyan University 290–291
West, Jerry 80, 85, 117, 120, **124**
Western Amateur 221
Western Conference 79, 113, 114, 116, 121
Western Division 183
Western Junior Championships 217
Western Open 205, 218, 223, 228, 229, 231, 232, 233
West Penn Amateur 222
West Point Military Academy, U.S. 153, 158
West Virginia University 124
Whitaker, Pernell 131
White, Albert "Chalky" 142
White, Charles 150, 180
White, Randy **200**
White, Reggie 191, **200–201**
Whitworth, Kathy 218, **230–231**, 232
Wichita State 82
Wightman Cup 310
Wilander, Mats 307, 313, 314, **321**
Wildcats 95, 98
Wilding, Tony 303
Wilhelm, Hoyt **70**
Wilkens, Lenny **125**
Wilkes, Jamaal 126
Wilkins, Dominique **125**
Wilkins, Mac **297–298**
Wilkinson, Bud 206
Willard, Jess 131, 137
Williams, Billy **70–71**
Williams, Hollman 140
Williams, Mitch 13
Williams, Richard 321
Williams, Serena 321
Williams, Ted 9, 44, **71–72**, 74
Williams, Venus 307, **321–322**
Williams, Walter Ray, Jr. **349**
Willis, Bill 180
Willis, Harry 131
Wills, Helen 313
Wills, Maury 10, **72**
Wilma (Rudolph) 291
Wilma Rudolph Foundation 291
Wilson, Hack 50, **72**
Wilson, Johnny 134
Wilson, Larry **201**
Wimbledon 301, 302, 303, 304, 305, 306, 307, 308, 309, 310, 311, 312, 313, 314, 315, 316, 317, 318, 319, 320, 321, 322
Wind, Herbert Warren 221

Winfield, Dave **73**
Winnipeg Jets 248, 258
Winslow, Kellen **201**
Winston 500 338
Winston Cup 323, 325, 326, 329, 330, 333, 334, 338
Winston-Salem State University 111
Witt, Katerina 266, 298
Wolfe, Tom 330
Wolfpack 122
Woman Athlete of the First Half of the 20th Century 233
Women's American Basketball League (WABL) 103–104
Women's Basketball League (WBL) 82, 103–104, 109
Women's British Open 230
Women's Kemper Open 214
Women's National Basketball Association (WNBA) 82, 85, 88, 98, 103, 104, 108, 111, 121, 126
Women's Professional Golfers European Tour (WPGET) 230
Women's Sports Foundation 121, 217, 218, 266, 269, 270, 276, 343
Women's Sports Hall of Fame 206
Women's Tennis Association (WTA) 307, 321, 322
Women's World Cup 339, 342, 343
Wood, Craig 224
Wood, Willie **201**
Woodard, Lynette **125–126**
Wooden, John 77, 94, 123
Woodland, Calvin 143
Woods, Earl 231
Woods, Tiger 210, 218, 223, 230, **231–232**
Woodson, Rod **201–202**
World 600 336
World Amateur 217, 226
World Boxing Association (WBA) 129, 132, 133, 135, 136, 137, 139, 143, 145, 146
World Boxing Council (WBC) 131, 133, 135
World Boxing Organization (WBO) 132
World Challenge 131
World Championship of Tennis (WCT) 317
World Championship of Women's Golf 207
World Championships
   basketball 85
   hockey 258
World Championship Tennis 302
World Cup 208, 210, 217, 266, 293, 294, 295, 341, 343, 346
World Figure Skating Hall of Fame 268
World Football League (WFL) 169, 199
World Golf Hall of Fame 205, 206, 208, 209, 210, 211, 213, 215, 216, 217, 218, 219, 221, 223, 224, 226, 228, 229, 232, 233
World Golf Ranking 211
World Hockey Association (WHA) 239, 245, 247, 248, 249, 255, 261
World Humanitarian Sports Hall of Fame 224
World Professional Figure Skating Championship 274

Index

World Series
1838 18
1903 74
1905 42
1906 10, 15, 69
1907 10, 15
1908 10, 15
1909 69
1910 10, 16
1911 16, 52
1913 16, 52
1914 58
1916 59
1917 16
1918 58, 59
1919 33
1920 66
1921 22
1922 22
1924 26, 35, 73
1925 68
1926 4, 30
1927 68
1929 63, 73
1930 63
1931 63
1932 29, 59
1933 23, 31, 50, 67
1934 17, 24, 26, 45
1935 15, 26, 27
1936 18, 25
1937 18

1938 18
1939 18
1941 9
1945 27, 49
1947 56
1948 9, 19, 20, 39, 50
1950 21, 54
1951 32, 40
1952 30, 64
1954 43, 70
1955 11, 53, 64, 65
1956 3, 38
1957 42, 61, 65
1959 5, 22
1960 14, 43–44
1962 43, 44
1963 38
1964 8, 10, 21, 24
1965 19, 36, 38
1966 5, 51, 55
1967 10, 13, 21, 41, 74
1968 10, 21, 24, 36, 41, 61
1969 30, 59, 61
1970 55
1971 66
1972 20, 31, 33, 57
1973 8, 20, 31, 33
1974 20, 23, 31, 33
1975 7, 21, 46, 47
1976 7, 46, 47
1977 33, 47
1978 27, 33, 39, 47

1979 48, 66
1980 12, 57, 60
1981 73
1982 54, 64, 67, 75
1983 47, 48
1985 9, 64
1986 13
1987 53, 64
1988 11, 19
1989 11, 19
1990 11, 19
1991 53
1992 13, 73, 188
1993 13, 46
1995 25, 48
2000 52
World Series of Golf 221, 223
World Swimmer of the Year 266
World Team Tennis League 305, 311
World Track and Field Championship 269–270
World University Games 82, 278
Worsham, Ben 222
Worsham, Lou 226
Worthy, James **126**
wrestling 272–273
Wright, Mickey 207, 218, **232**
Wright, Teddy 134
Wynn, Early **73–74**
Wysong, Dudley 219

X

XFL 156

Y

Yale University 292
Yamaguchi, Kristi **298**
Yang, C.K. 278
Yarborough, Cale 330, **338**
Yarbrough, LeeRoy 330
Yashchenko, Volodomir 272
Yastrzemski, Carl **74**
Yonkers Trot 342, 343
Young, Bobby Joe 143
Young, Cy 4, 35, **74**
Young, Jimmy 132
Young, Sheila **298–299**
Young, Steve 185, **202–203**
Yount, Robin **74–75**
Yzerman, Steve **261**

Z

Zaharias, George 233
Zaharias, Mildred "Babe" 206, **232–233**, 278
Zale, Tony 134, **147**
Zatopek, Emil **299**
Zayak, Elaine 298
Zayev, Pyotr 293
Ziert, Paul 269
Zivic, Fritzie 129
Zoeller, Fuzzy 220
Zulueta, Orlando 144